The BOYS™

OMNIBUS
VOLUME TWO

D1455748

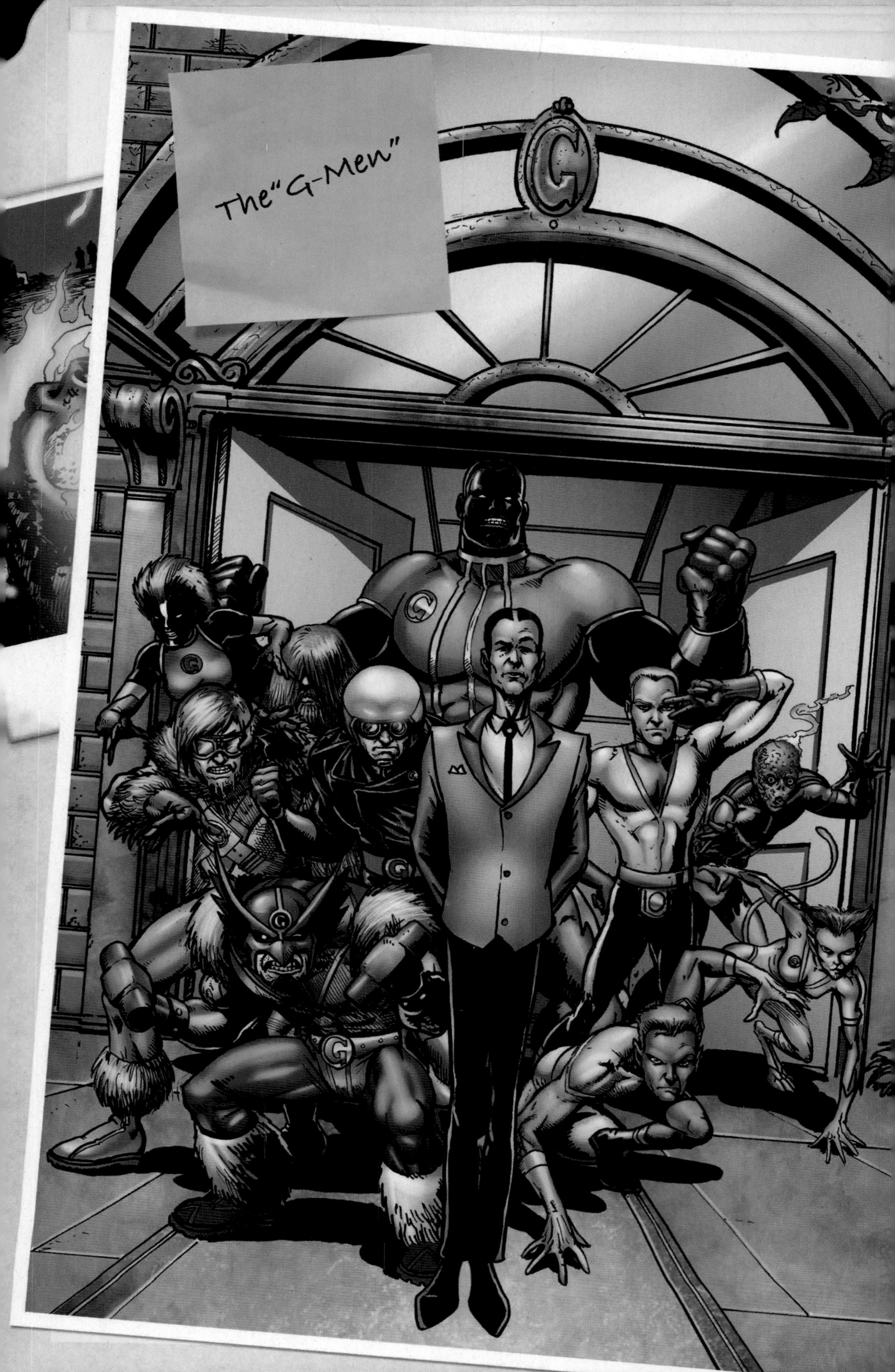
The "G-Men"

CONTENTS
The BOYS™

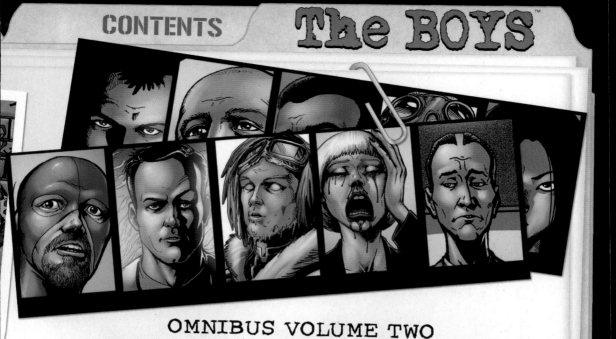

OMNIBUS VOLUME TWO

The Boys created by: GARTH ENNIS & DARICK ROBERTSON

Written by: GARTH ENNIS
Illustrated by: DARICK ROBERTSON
& JOHN HIGGINS #26, 28
Colored by: TONY AVIÑA
Lettered by: SIMON BOWLAND
Series covers by: DARICK ROBERTSON & TONY AVIÑA
Book design by: JASON ULLMEYER
Editor: JOE RYBANDT

Collects issues fifteen through thirty of The Boys, published by Dynamite.

DYNAMITE®

Nick Barrucci, CEO / Publisher
Juan Collado, President / COO
Brandon Dante Primavera, V.P. of IT and Operations

Joe Rybandt, Executive Editor
Matt Idelson, Senior Editor

Alexis Persson, Creative Director
Cathleen Heard, Senior Graphic Designer
Nick Pentz, Graphic Designer
Matthew Michalak, Graphic Designer

Alan Payne, V.P. of Sales and Marketing
Vince Letterio, Director of Direct Market Sales
Rex Wang, Director of Sales and Branding
Vincent Faust, Marketing Coordinator

Jim Kuhoric, Vice President of Product Development
Jay Spence, Director of Product Development
Mariano Nicieza, Director of Research & Development

www.DYNAMITE.com | Facebook: **/Dynamitecomics**
Instagram: **/Dynamitecomics** | Twitter: **@dynamitecomics**

Standard ISBN:978-1-524-10970-7 | Exclusive ISBN: 978-1-524-11345-2
Twelfth Printing 15 14 13 12 Printed in Canada

For information regarding press, media rights, foreign rights, licensing, promotions, and advertising e-mail: marketing@dynamite.com

For Owen and Andrew
– Darick Robertson

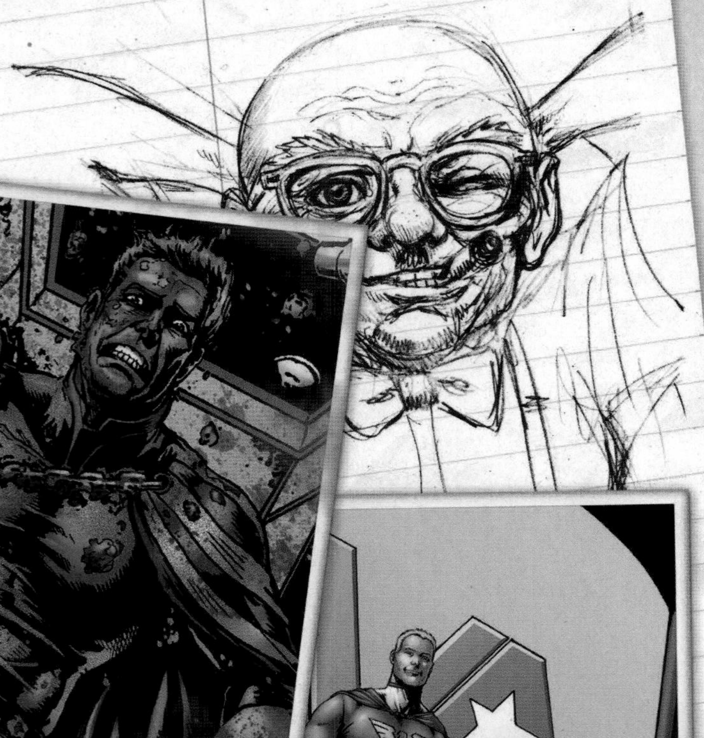

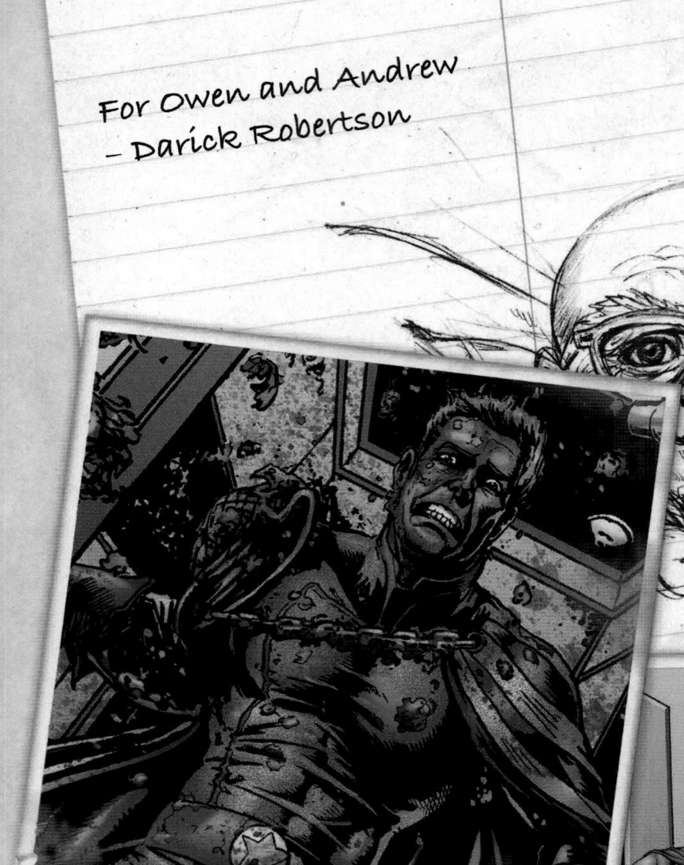

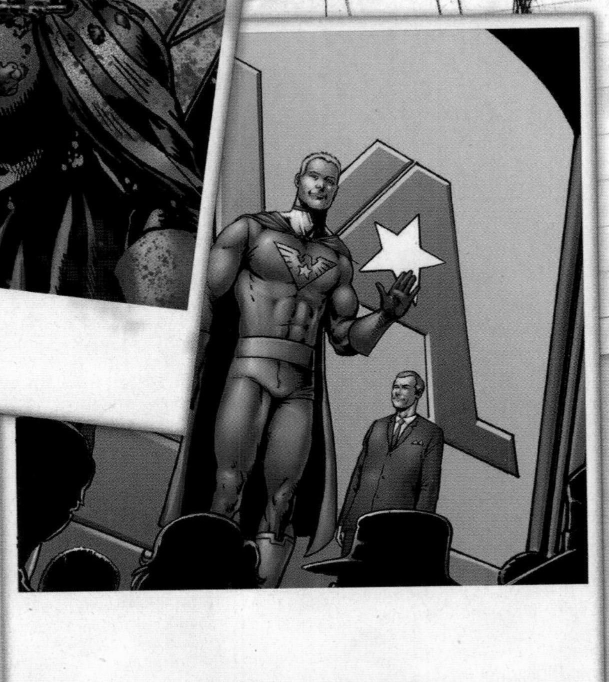

CONTENTS

BONUS MATERIALS

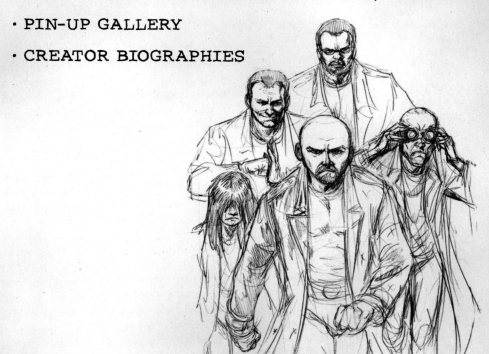

INTRODUCTION

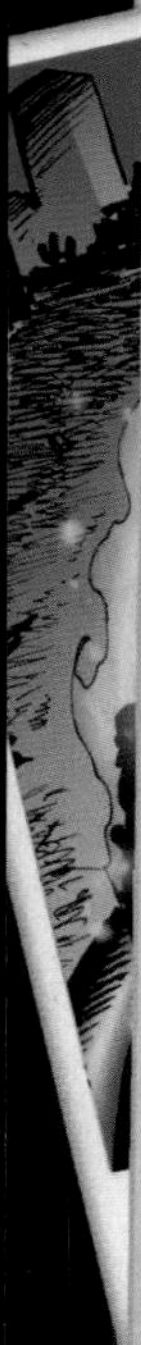

GARTH ENNIS IS A DIRTY FUCKING LIAR.

All great writers are, of course, but Garth does most of his lying to the press. Whenever I read an interview with the guy, he goes on and on about how much he absolutely hates superheroes.

Well, I call bullshit.

I mean, for someone who supposedly hates the capes-and-tights set, he sure does write about them an awful lot, doesn't he? After the success of *Preacher* (whose fans should be on the lookout for a very cool surprise hidden in plain sight somewhere in these pages), Garth could have written about pretty much anything for his next original ongoing series. No one put a gun to his head and told him he had to tell the super-powered story in your hot little hands, right?

But anyone who's ever read his *Hitman #34*—one of the best, most ass-lickingly reverential stories ever written about Superman—knows Garth's deepest, darkest secret. Sure, he may hate bad superhero comics, he may hate the way that genre has a stranglehold on the entire industry, but deep down, he loves the four-color bastards.

He might counter that *The Boys* exists primarily to demean and degrade these hoary old icons, but after a while, Garth's he-doth-protest-too-much routine starts to sound like one of those politicians who's constantly introducing anti-gay legislation, only to inevitably be caught toe-tapping into the next stall of an airport bathroom.

Besides, if *The Boys* were just about "taking the piss" out of superheroes, it would have grown stale twenty-nine issues ago. But like *Watchmen* and *Marshall Law* and many of the better comics of the last thirty years, *The Boys* isn't just a brilliant satire of the genre, but also a powerful metaphor for real-world ills.

Seriously.

Even though the big liar will claim that this is all just supposed to be a bit of subversive fun, I think Garth is really writing a damning examination of America's military-industrial complex (or "military-industrial-congressional," as Eisenhower originally wanted to call it). I've never asked him, but I imagine Garth's feelings about this institution are much like his true feelings about superheroes: begrudging respect when used wisely, virulent anger when abused.

Yeah, Ennis probably fancies himself being *The Boys'* acerbic, ass-kicking Butcher, but in reality, he's much more like Wee Hughie, the sweet kid who may have misgivings about the supes, but somehow always ends up going down on them until his face is covered in... well, you'll see.

Speaking of Hughie, this series obviously wouldn't exist without the man who keeps Garth honest, artist and co-creator Darick Robertson. Now here's a guy who genuinely ADORES superheroes, as anyone who's ever seen his embarrassing Halloween photos can attest. But Darick is also one of the geniuses behind the decidedly non-superheroic *Transmetropolitan*, and he's become a master of making even a scene with two characters talking in a dark room every bit as visually dynamic as a massive brawl between hundreds of costumed gods. I'm always humbled by his beautiful, efficient storytelling. In just one chapter in this collection, Darick and Garth manage to say more about 9/11 than artist Tony Harris and I have said in five years' worth of our likeminded series *Ex Machina* (plug plug).

These boys will try to convince you that their book is a black comedy or a political thriller or a sci-fi actioner, but let's call a spade a fucking spade. This is a superhero comic, the best one being published today.

I tell you no lie.

Brian K. Vaughan
Los Angeles
June 2009
(For *The Boys Definitive Edition Vol. 2*)

Brian K. Vaughan has worked as a writer/producer on the hit TV series *Runaways* and *Lost*, and has co-created the comic books *Y: The Last Man*, *Ex Machina*, *Pride of Baghdad*, *Paper Girls* and *Saga*. He's not ashamed to say he's also written some books with superheroes in them.

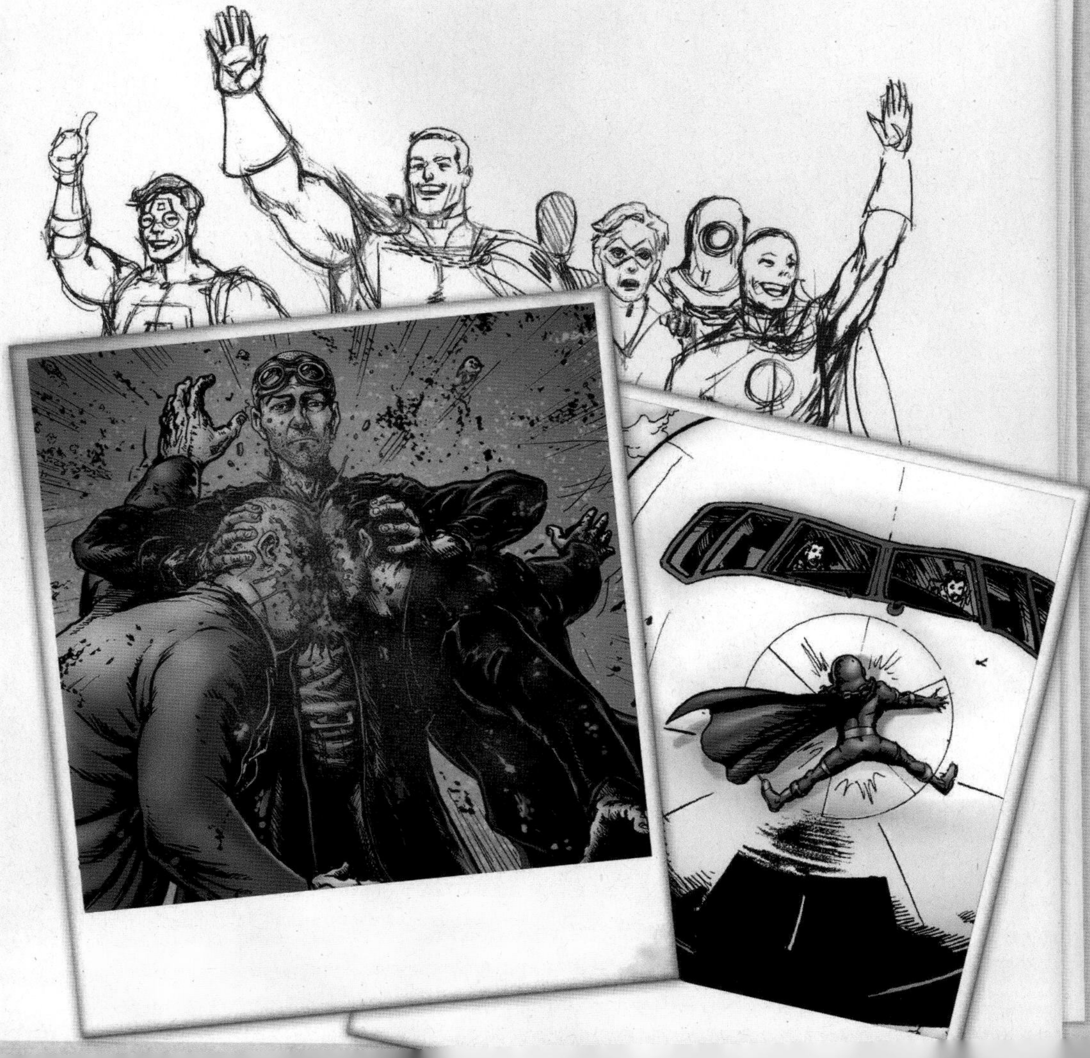

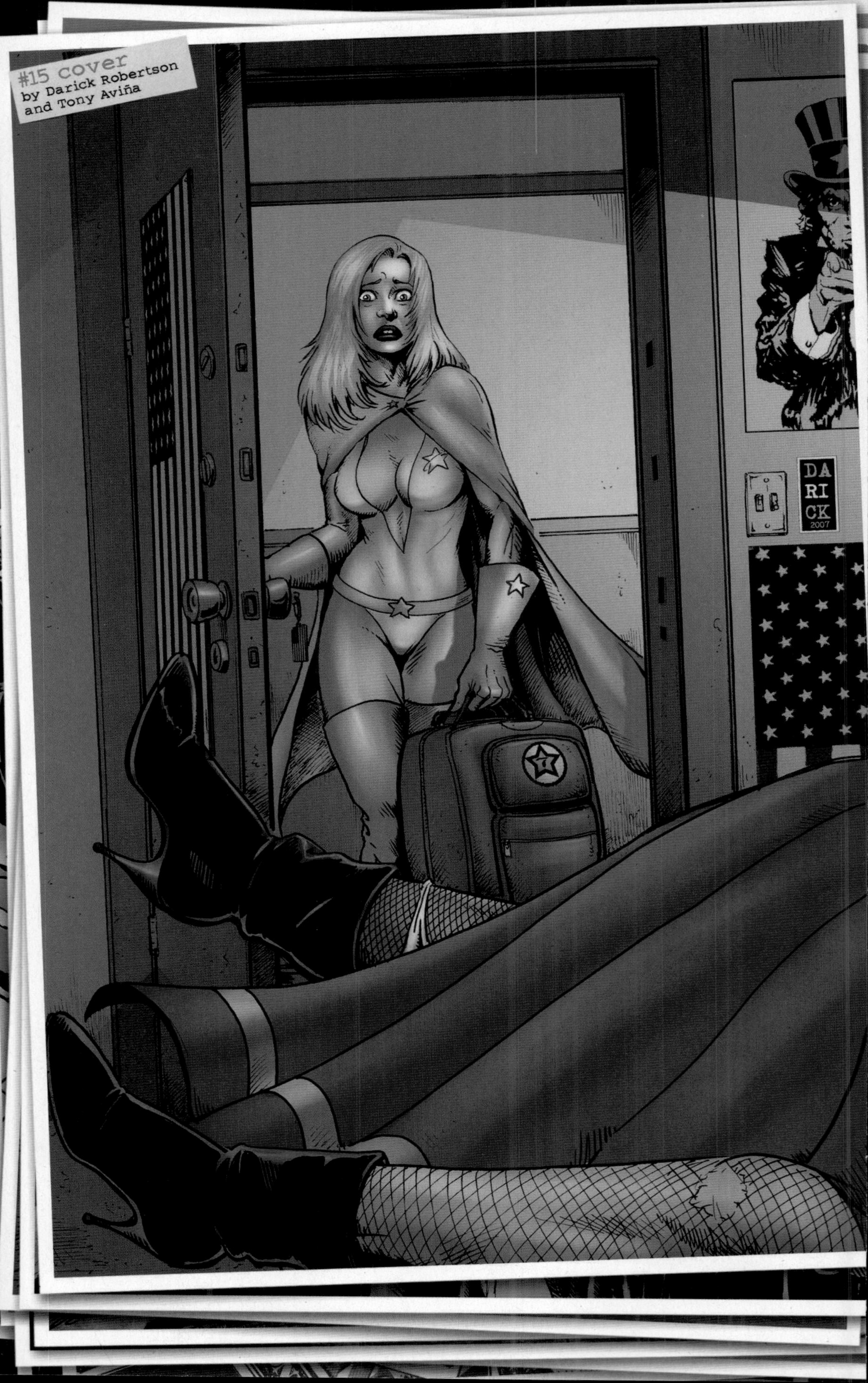

DA
RI
CK
2007

#15 cover
by Darick Robertson
and Tony Aviña

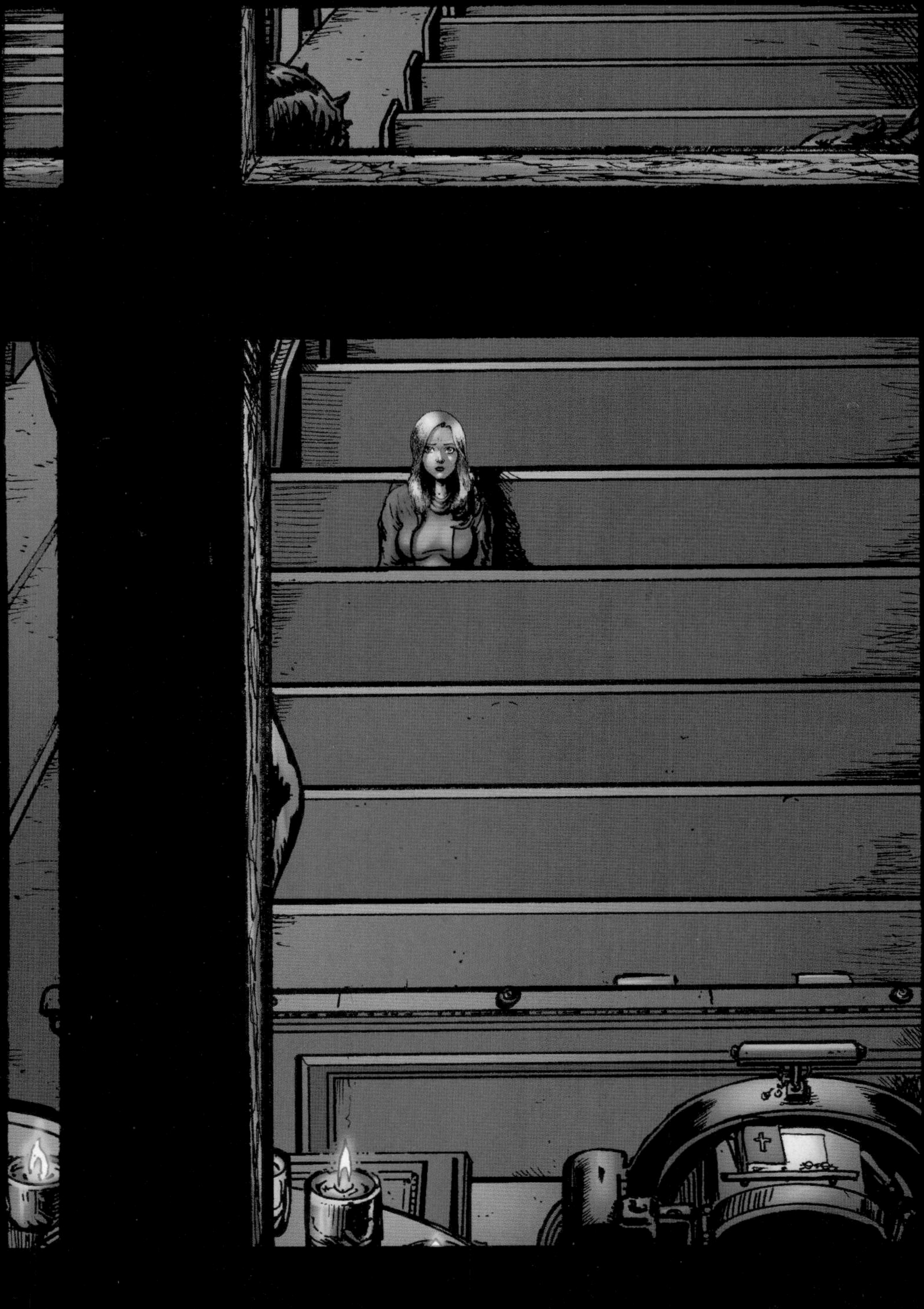

GOOD FOR THE SOUL
part one

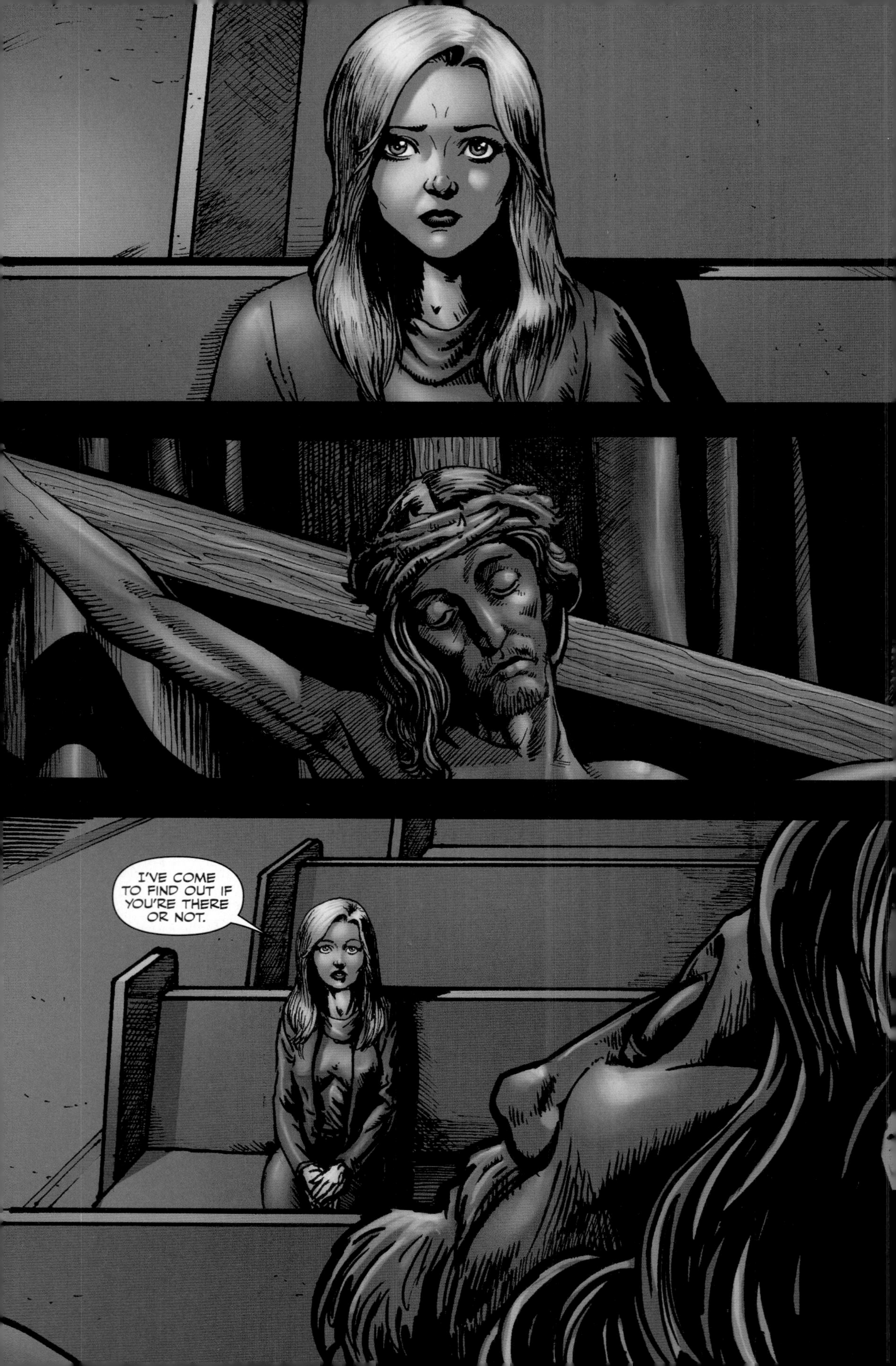
I'VE COME TO FIND OUT IF YOU'RE THERE OR NOT.

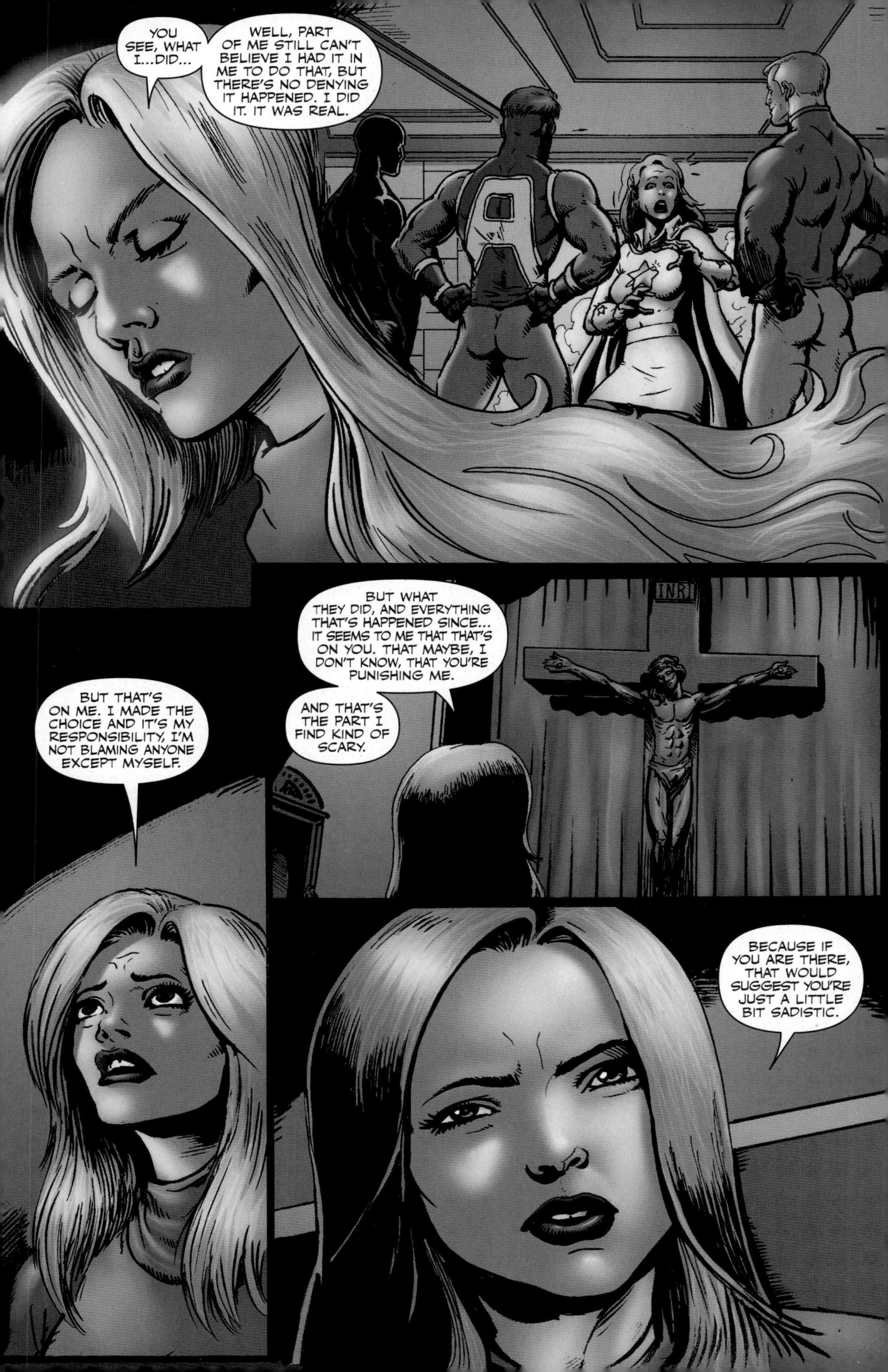

YOU SEE, WHAT I...DID...
WELL, PART OF ME STILL CAN'T BELIEVE I HAD IT IN ME TO DO THAT, BUT THERE'S NO DENYING IT HAPPENED. I DID IT. IT WAS REAL.
BUT THAT'S ON ME. I MADE THE CHOICE AND IT'S MY RESPONSIBILITY, I'M NOT BLAMING ANYONE EXCEPT MYSELF.
BUT WHAT THEY DID, AND EVERYTHING THAT'S HAPPENED SINCE... IT SEEMS TO ME THAT THAT'S ON YOU. THAT MAYBE, I DON'T KNOW, THAT YOU'RE PUNISHING ME.
AND THAT'S THE PART I FIND KIND OF SCARY.
INRI
BECAUSE IF YOU ARE THERE, THAT WOULD SUGGEST YOU'RE JUST A LITTLE BIT SADISTIC.

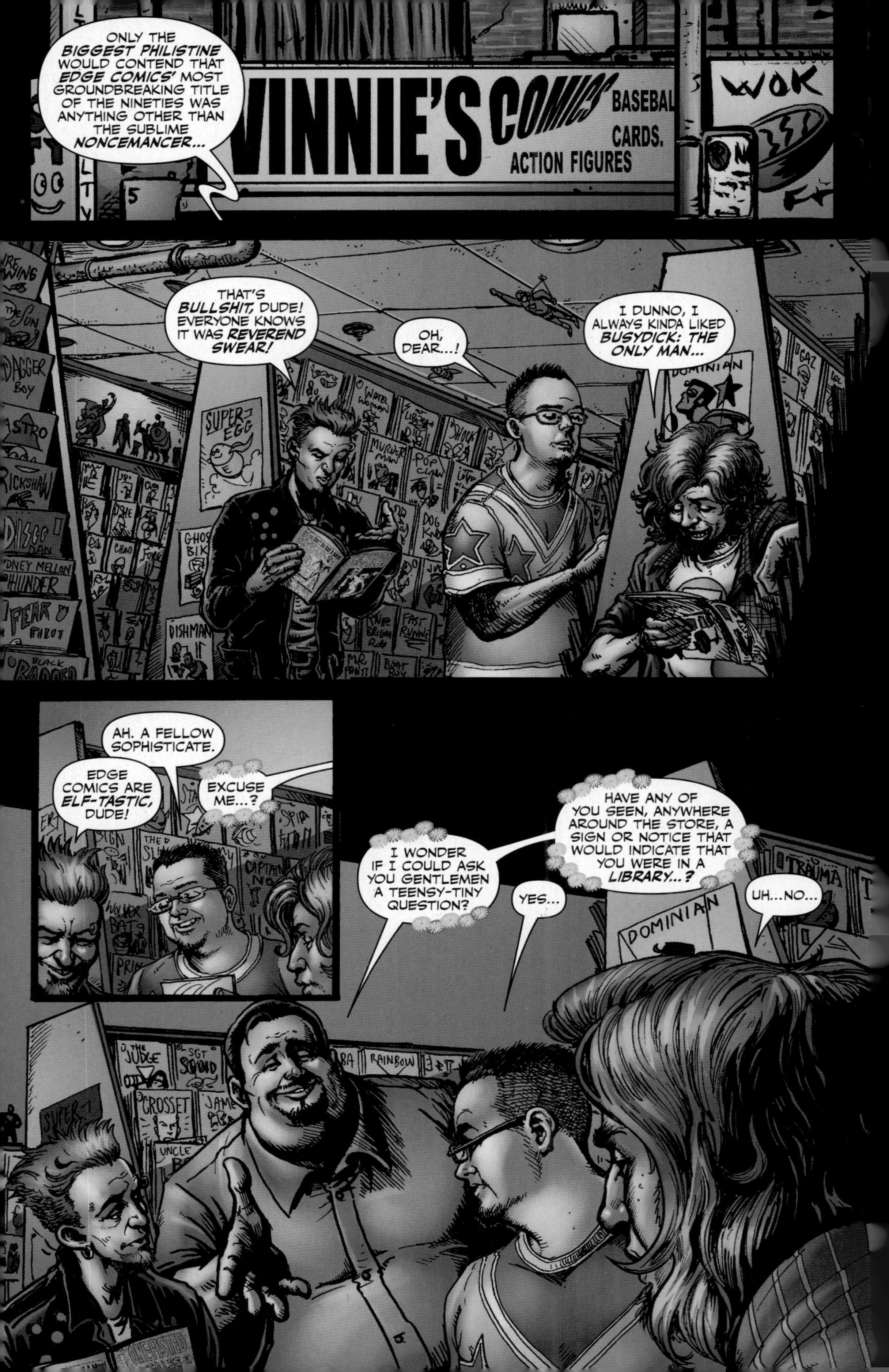
ONLY THE BIGGEST PHILISTINE WOULD CONTEND THAT EDGE COMICS' MOST GROUNDBREAKING TITLE OF THE NINETIES WAS ANYTHING OTHER THAN THE SUBLIME NONCEMANCER...
VINNIE'S COMICS
BASEBAL CARDS.
ACTION FIGURES
WOK
THAT'S BULLSHIT, DUDE! EVERYONE KNOWS IT WAS REVEREND SWEAR!
OH, DEAR...!
I DUNNO, I ALWAYS KINDA LIKED BUSYDICK: THE ONLY MAN...
AH. A FELLOW SOPHISTICATE.
EDGE COMICS ARE ELF-TASTIC, DUDE!
EXCUSE ME...?
I WONDER IF I COULD ASK YOU GENTLEMEN A TEENSY-TINY QUESTION?
YES...
HAVE ANY OF YOU SEEN, ANYWHERE AROUND THE STORE, A SIGN OR NOTICE THAT WOULD INDICATE THAT YOU WERE IN A LIBRARY...?
UH...NO...

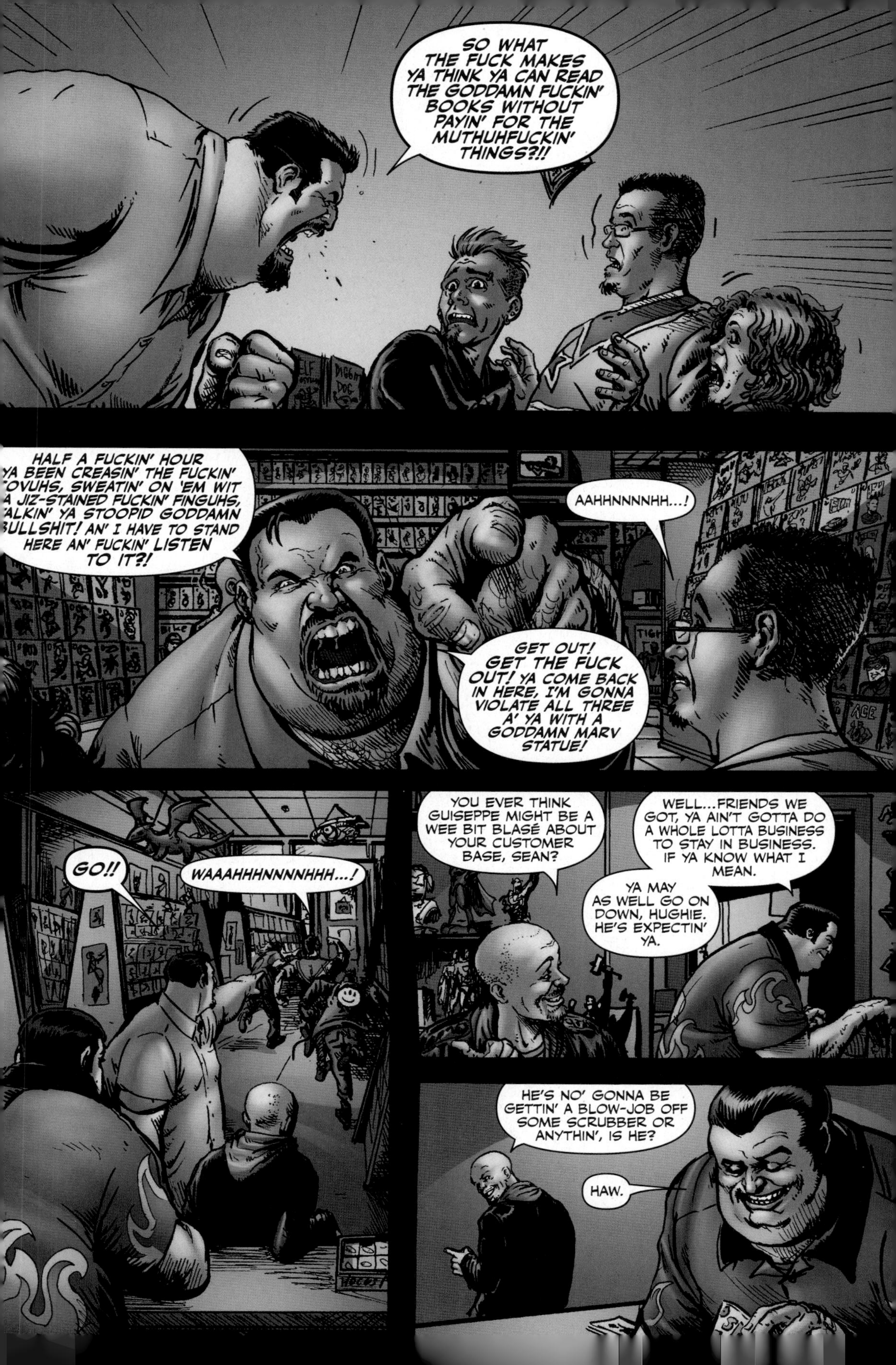
SO WHAT THE FUCK MAKES YA THINK YA CAN READ THE GODDAMN FUCKIN' BOOKS WITHOUT PAYIN' FOR THE MUTHUHFUCKIN' THINGS?!!
HALF A FUCKIN' HOUR YA BEEN CREASIN' THE FUCKIN' COVUHS, SWEATIN' ON 'EM WIT A JIZ-STAINED FUCKIN' FINGUHS, TALKIN' YA STOOPID GODDAMN BULLSHIT! AN' I HAVE TO STAND HERE AN' FUCKIN' LISTEN TO IT?!
AAHHNNNNHH...!
GET OUT! GET THE FUCK OUT! YA COME BACK IN HERE, I'M GONNA VIOLATE ALL THREE A' YA WITH A GODDAMN MARV STATUE!
GO!!
WAAAHHHNNNNHHH...!
YOU EVER THINK GUISEPPE MIGHT BE A WEE BIT BLASÉ ABOUT YOUR CUSTOMER BASE, SEAN?
WELL...FRIENDS WE GOT, YA AIN'T GOTTA DO A WHOLE LOTTA BUSINESS TO STAY IN BUSINESS. IF YA KNOW WHAT I MEAN.
YA MAY AS WELL GO ON DOWN, HUGHIE. HE'S EXPECTIN' YA.
HE'S NO' GONNA BE GETTIN' A BLOW-JOB OFF SOME SCRUBBER OR ANYTHIN', IS HE?
HAW.

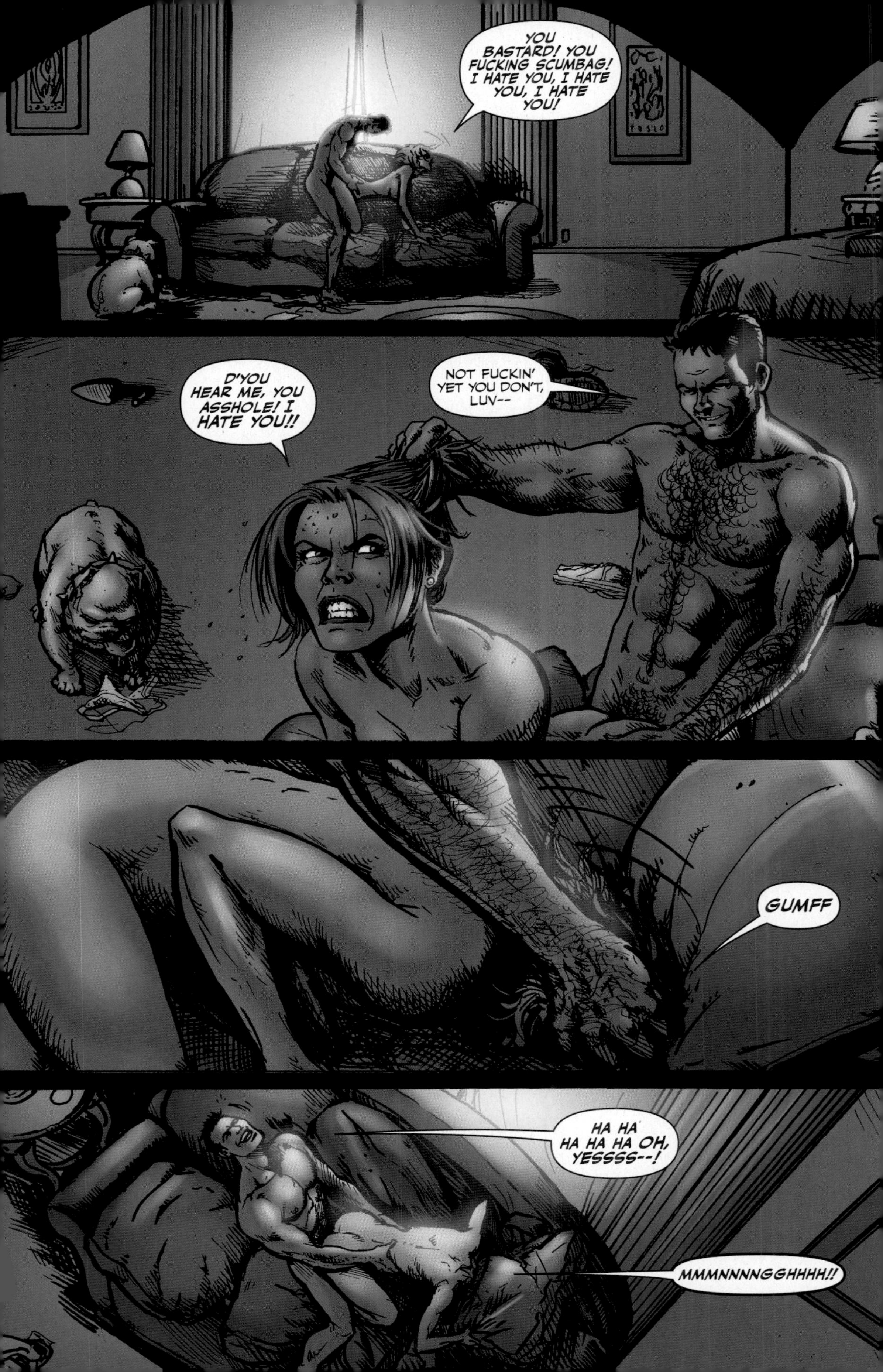
YOU BASTARD! YOU FUCKING SCUMBAG! I HATE YOU, I HATE YOU, I HATE YOU!
D'YOU HEAR ME, YOU ASSHOLE! I HATE YOU!!
NOT FUCKIN' YET YOU DON'T, LUV--
GUMFF
HA HA HA HA HA OH, YESSSS--!
MMMNNNNGGHHHH!!

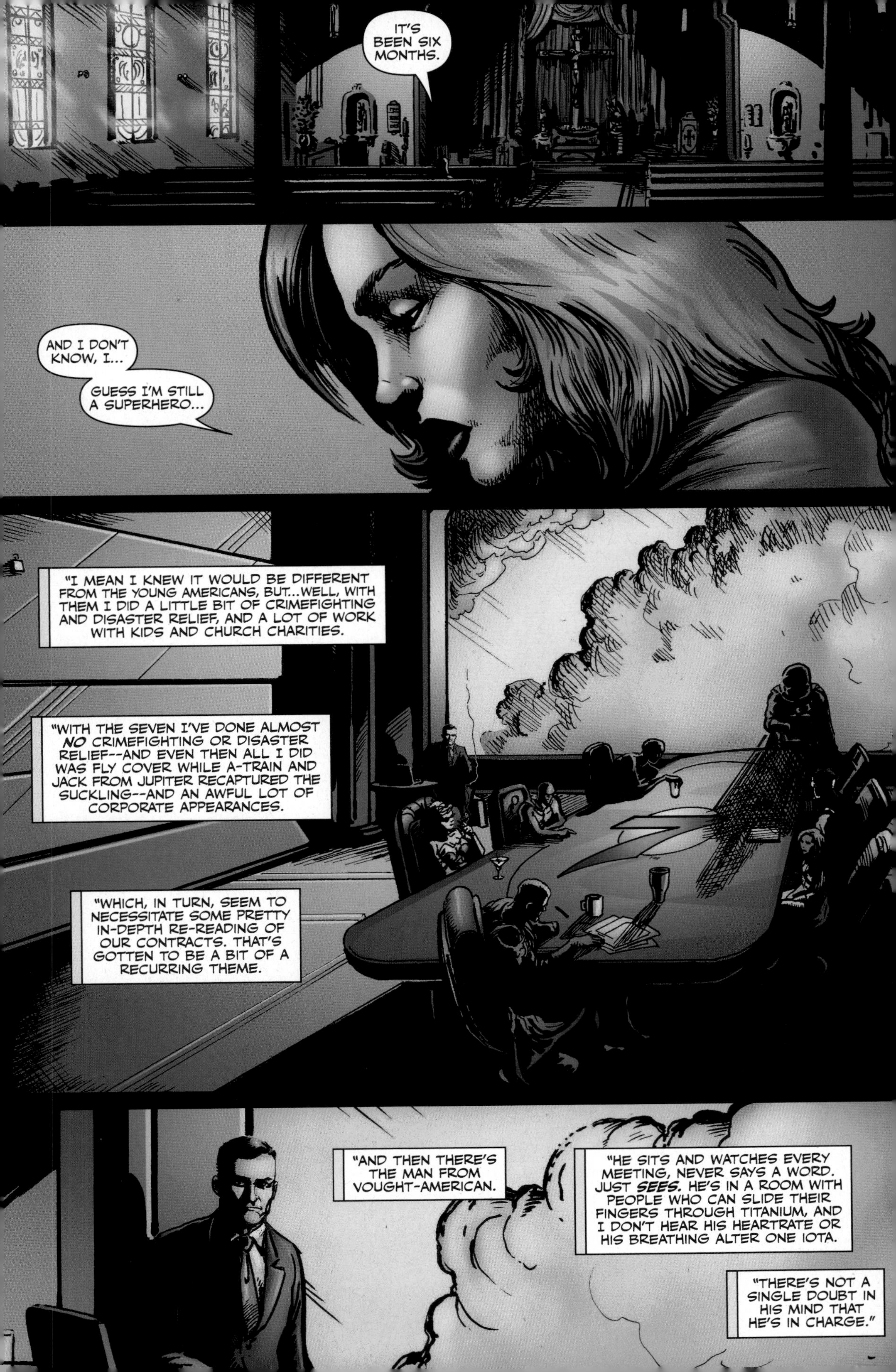
IT'S BEEN SIX MONTHS.
AND I DON'T KNOW, I...
GUESS I'M STILL A SUPERHERO...
"I MEAN I KNEW IT WOULD BE DIFFERENT FROM THE YOUNG AMERICANS, BUT...WELL, WITH THEM I DID A LITTLE BIT OF CRIMEFIGHTING AND DISASTER RELIEF, AND A LOT OF WORK WITH KIDS AND CHURCH CHARITIES.
"WITH THE SEVEN I'VE DONE ALMOST *NO* CRIMEFIGHTING OR DISASTER RELIEF--AND EVEN THEN ALL I DID WAS FLY COVER WHILE A-TRAIN AND JACK FROM JUPITER RECAPTURED THE SUCKLING--AND AN AWFUL LOT OF CORPORATE APPEARANCES.
"WHICH, IN TURN, SEEM TO NECESSITATE SOME PRETTY IN-DEPTH RE-READING OF OUR CONTRACTS. THAT'S GOTTEN TO BE A BIT OF A RECURRING THEME.
"AND THEN THERE'S THE MAN FROM VOUGHT-AMERICAN.
"HE SITS AND WATCHES EVERY MEETING, NEVER SAYS A WORD. JUST *SEES.* HE'S IN A ROOM WITH PEOPLE WHO CAN SLIDE THEIR FINGERS THROUGH TITANIUM, AND I DON'T HEAR HIS HEARTRATE OR HIS BREATHING ALTER ONE IOTA.
"THERE'S NOT A SINGLE DOUBT IN HIS MIND THAT HE'S IN CHARGE."

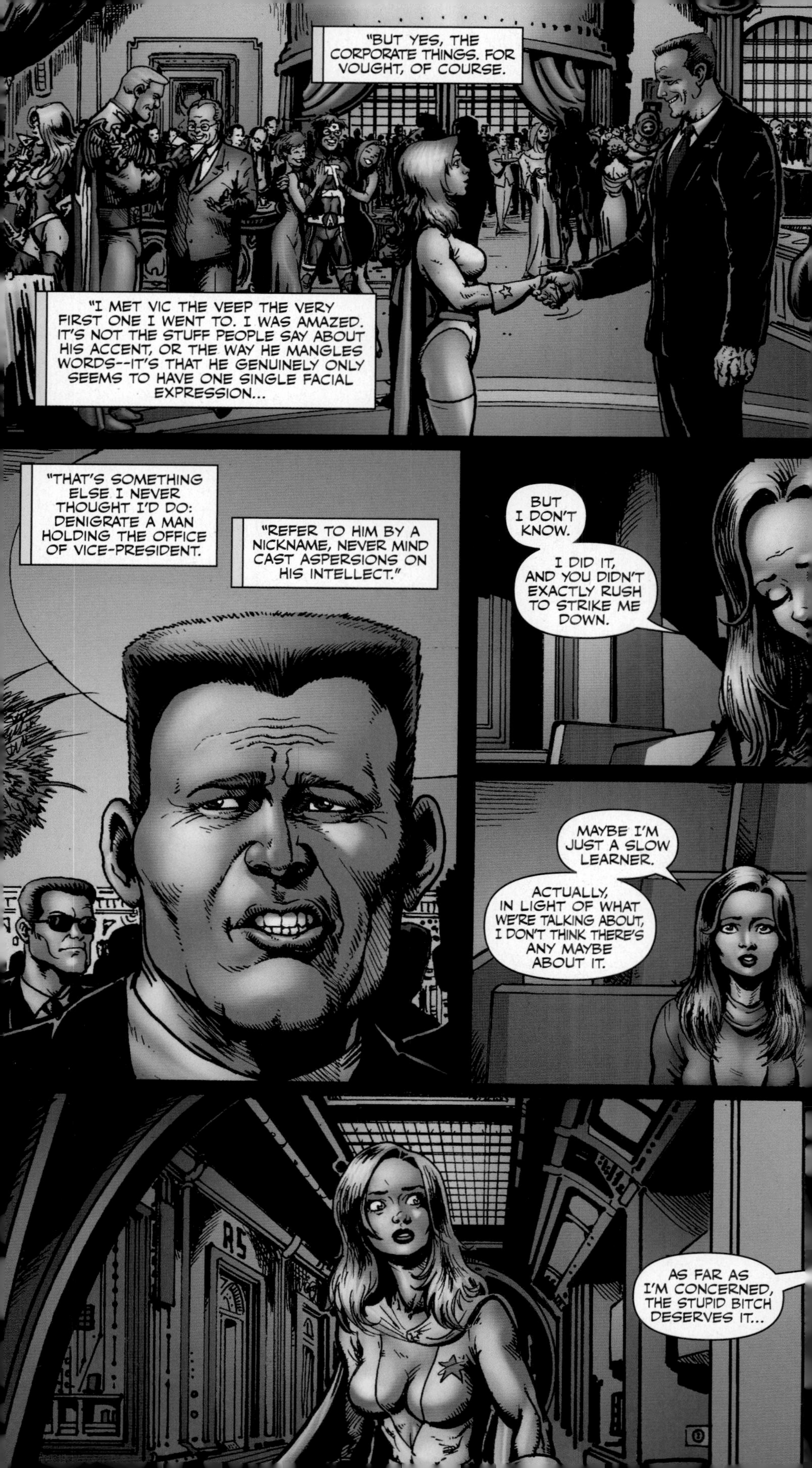
"BUT YES, THE CORPORATE THINGS. FOR VOUGHT, OF COURSE.
"I MET VIC THE VEEP THE VERY FIRST ONE I WENT TO. I WAS AMAZED. IT'S NOT THE STUFF PEOPLE SAY ABOUT HIS ACCENT, OR THE WAY HE MANGLES WORDS--IT'S THAT HE GENUINELY ONLY SEEMS TO HAVE ONE SINGLE FACIAL EXPRESSION...
"THAT'S SOMETHING ELSE I NEVER THOUGHT I'D DO: DENIGRATE A MAN HOLDING THE OFFICE OF VICE-PRESIDENT.
"REFER TO HIM BY A NICKNAME, NEVER MIND CAST ASPERSIONS ON HIS INTELLECT."
BUT I DON'T KNOW.
I DID IT, AND YOU DIDN'T EXACTLY RUSH TO STRIKE ME DOWN.
MAYBE I'M JUST A SLOW LEARNER.
ACTUALLY, IN LIGHT OF WHAT WE'RE TALKING ABOUT, I DON'T THINK THERE'S ANY MAYBE ABOUT IT.
AS FAR AS I'M CONCERNED, THE STUPID BITCH DESERVES IT...

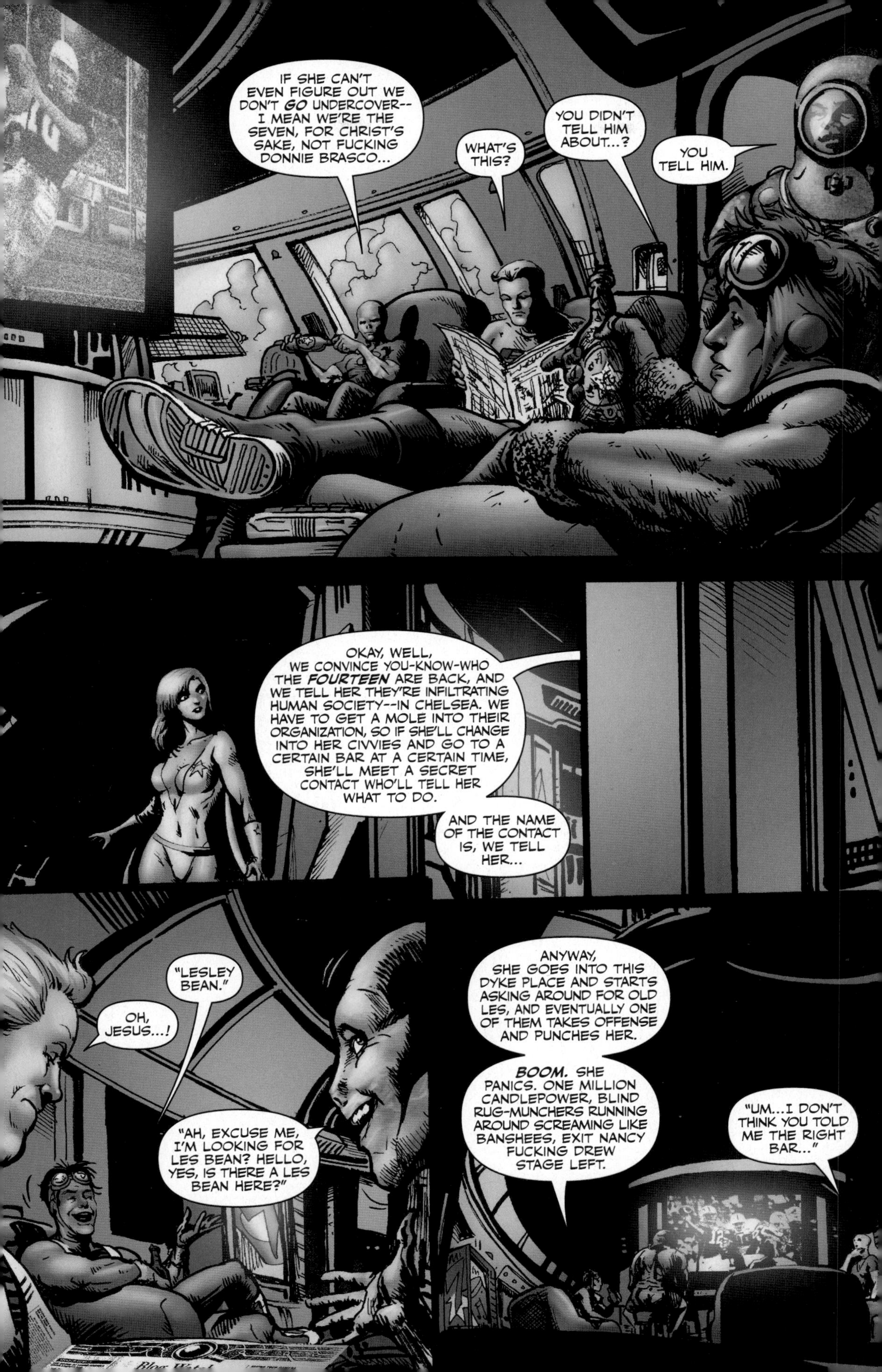
IF SHE CAN'T EVEN FIGURE OUT WE DON'T GO UNDERCOVER-- I MEAN WE'RE THE SEVEN, FOR CHRIST'S SAKE, NOT FUCKING DONNIE BRASCO...
WHAT'S THIS?
YOU DIDN'T TELL HIM ABOUT...?
YOU TELL HIM.
OKAY, WELL, WE CONVINCE YOU-KNOW-WHO THE FOURTEEN ARE BACK, AND WE TELL HER THEY'RE INFILTRATING HUMAN SOCIETY--IN CHELSEA. WE HAVE TO GET A MOLE INTO THEIR ORGANIZATION, SO IF SHE'LL CHANGE INTO HER CIVVIES AND GO TO A CERTAIN BAR AT A CERTAIN TIME, SHE'LL MEET A SECRET CONTACT WHO'LL TELL HER WHAT TO DO.
AND THE NAME OF THE CONTACT IS, WE TELL HER...
"LESLEY BEAN."
OH, JESUS...!
"AH, EXCUSE ME, I'M LOOKING FOR LES BEAN? HELLO, YES, IS THERE A LES BEAN HERE?"
ANYWAY, SHE GOES INTO THIS DYKE PLACE AND STARTS ASKING AROUND FOR OLD LES, AND EVENTUALLY ONE OF THEM TAKES OFFENSE AND PUNCHES HER.
BOOM. SHE PANICS. ONE MILLION CANDLEPOWER, BLIND RUG-MUNCHERS RUNNING AROUND SCREAMING LIKE BANSHEES, EXIT NANCY FUCKING DREW STAGE LEFT.
"UM...I DON'T THINK YOU TOLD ME THE RIGHT BAR..."

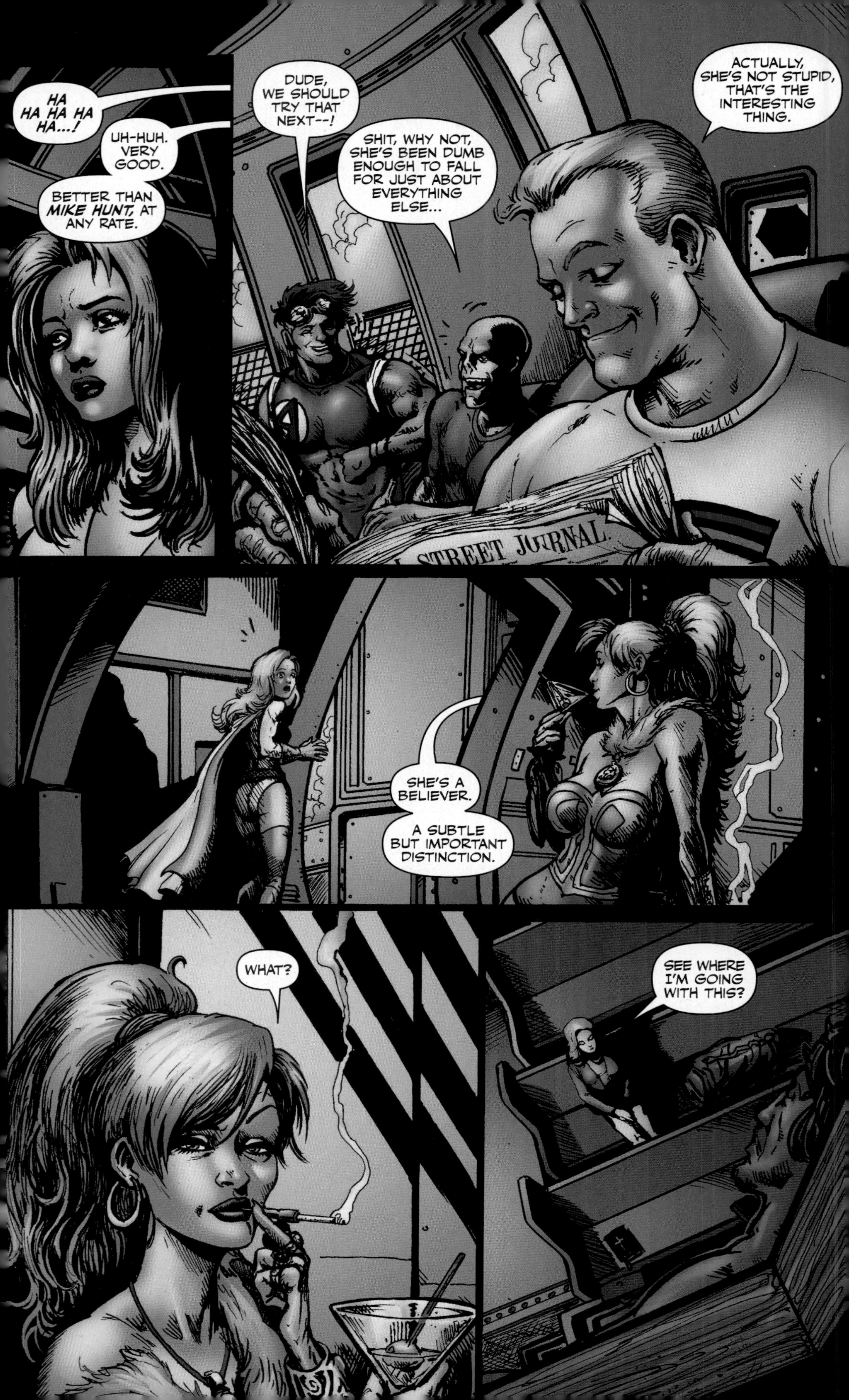
HA HA HA HA HA...!
UH-HUH. VERY GOOD.
BETTER THAN *MIKE HUNT,* AT ANY RATE.
DUDE, WE SHOULD TRY THAT NEXT--!
SHIT, WHY NOT, SHE'S BEEN DUMB ENOUGH TO FALL FOR JUST ABOUT EVERYTHING ELSE...
ACTUALLY, SHE'S NOT STUPID, THAT'S THE INTERESTING THING.
STREET JOURNAL
SHE'S A BELIEVER.
A SUBTLE BUT IMPORTANT DISTINCTION.
WHAT?
SEE WHERE I'M GOING WITH THIS?

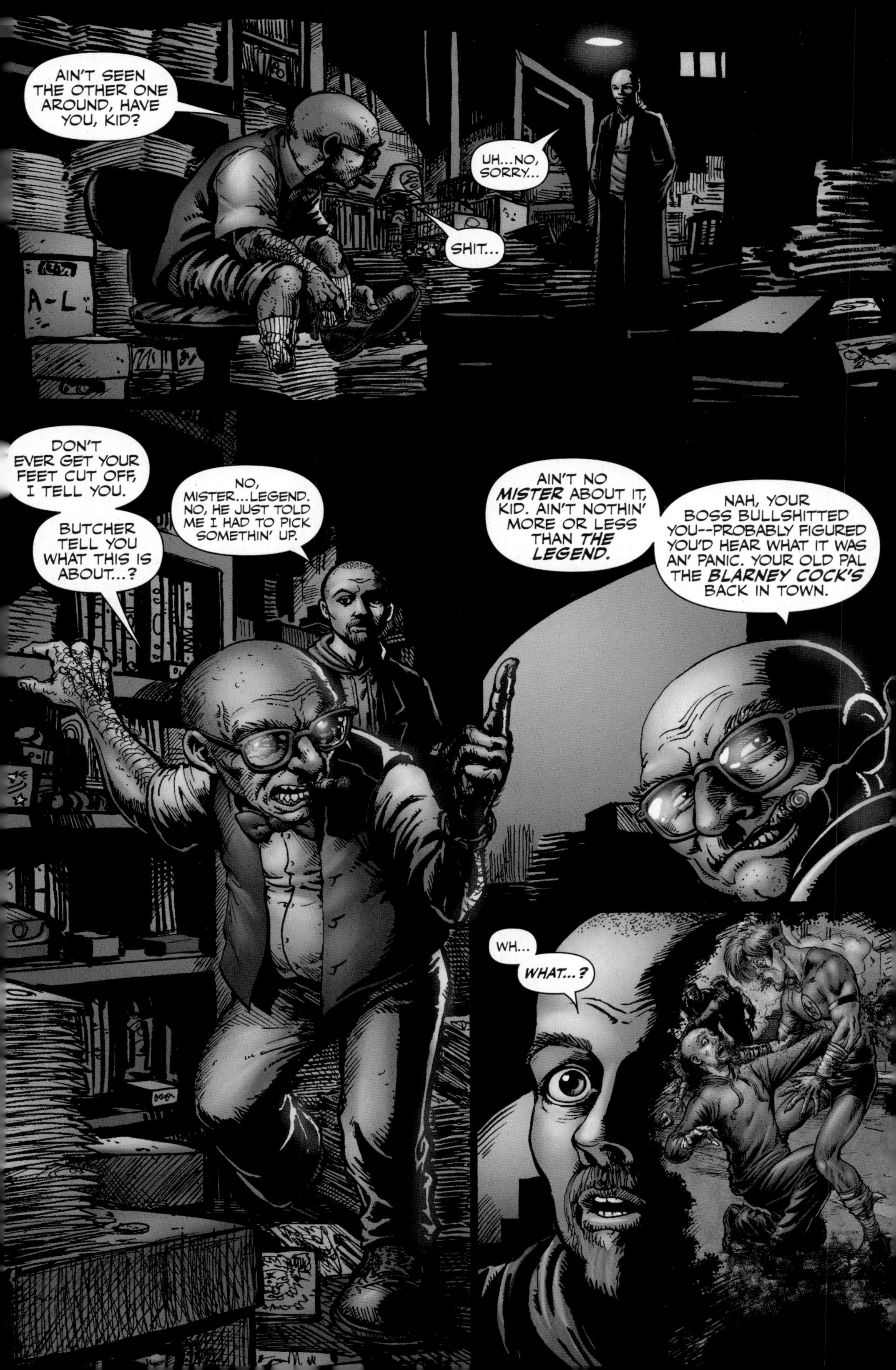
AIN'T SEEN THE OTHER ONE AROUND, HAVE YOU, KID?
UH...NO, SORRY...
SHIT...
DON'T EVER GET YOUR FEET CUT OFF, I TELL YOU.
BUTCHER TELL YOU WHAT THIS IS ABOUT...?
NO, MISTER...LEGEND. NO, HE JUST TOLD ME I HAD TO PICK SOMETHIN' UP.
AIN'T NO MISTER ABOUT IT, KID. AIN'T NOTHIN' MORE OR LESS THAN THE LEGEND.
NAH, YOUR BOSS BULLSHITTED YOU--PROBABLY FIGURED YOU'D HEAR WHAT IT WAS AN' PANIC. YOUR OLD PAL THE BLARNEY COCK'S BACK IN TOWN.
WH...
WHAT...?

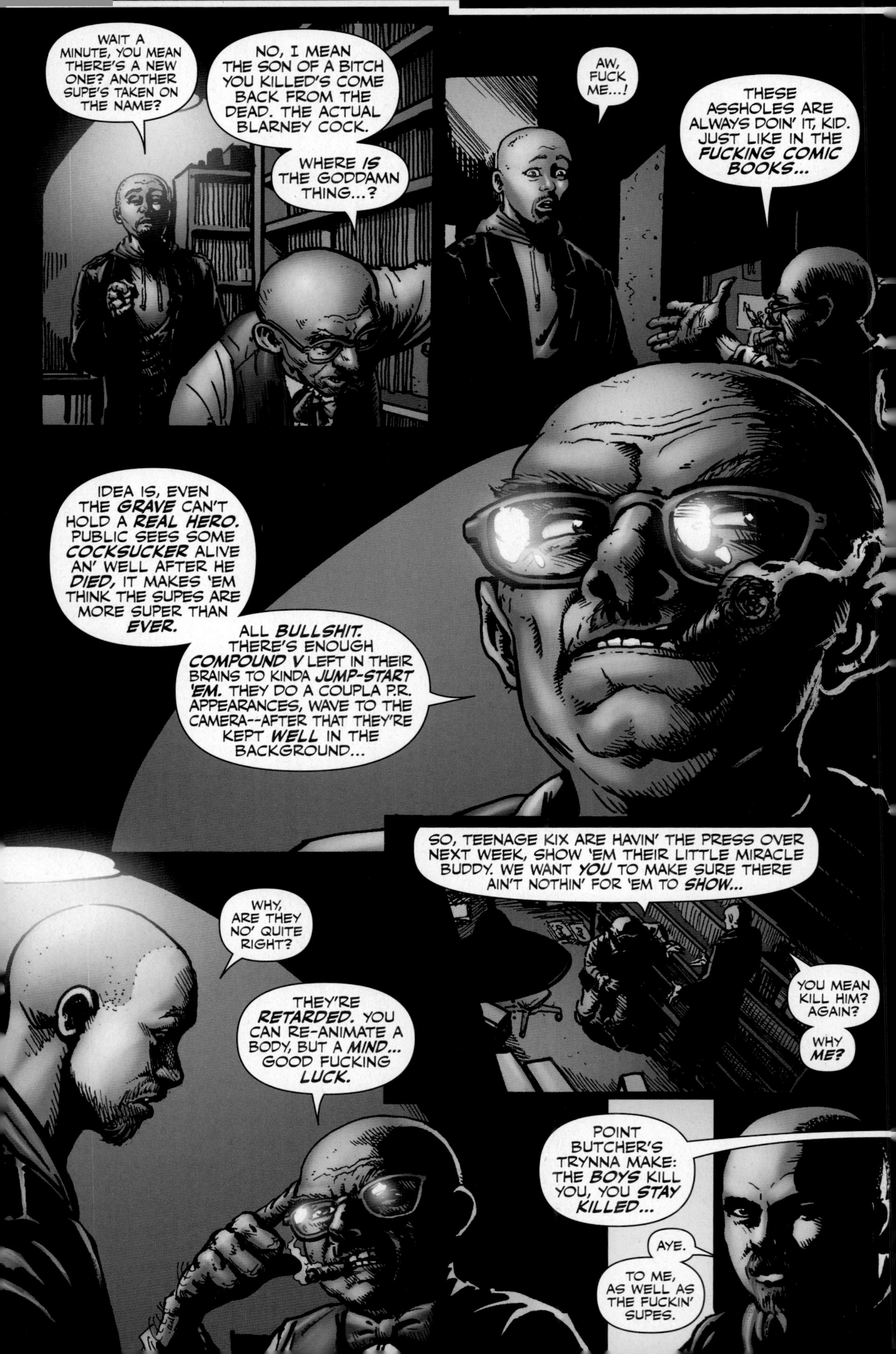
WAIT A MINUTE, YOU MEAN THERE'S A NEW ONE? ANOTHER SUPE'S TAKEN ON THE NAME?
NO, I MEAN THE SON OF A BITCH YOU KILLED'S COME BACK FROM THE DEAD. THE ACTUAL BLARNEY COCK.
WHERE *IS* THE GODDAMN THING...?
AW, FUCK ME...!
THESE ASSHOLES ARE ALWAYS DOIN' IT, KID. JUST LIKE IN THE *FUCKING COMIC BOOKS...*
IDEA IS, EVEN THE *GRAVE* CAN'T HOLD A *REAL HERO.* PUBLIC SEES SOME *COCKSUCKER* ALIVE AN' WELL AFTER HE *DIED,* IT MAKES 'EM THINK THE SUPES ARE MORE SUPER THAN *EVER.*
ALL *BULLSHIT.* THERE'S ENOUGH *COMPOUND V* LEFT IN THEIR BRAINS TO KINDA *JUMP-START 'EM.* THEY DO A COUPLA P.R. APPEARANCES, WAVE TO THE CAMERA--AFTER THAT THEY'RE KEPT *WELL* IN THE BACKGROUND...
SO, TEENAGE KIX ARE HAVIN' THE PRESS OVER NEXT WEEK, SHOW 'EM THEIR LITTLE MIRACLE BUDDY. WE WANT *YOU* TO MAKE SURE THERE AIN'T NOTHIN' FOR 'EM TO *SHOW...*
YOU MEAN KILL HIM? AGAIN?
WHY *ME?*
WHY, ARE THEY NO' QUITE RIGHT?
THEY'RE *RETARDED.* YOU CAN RE-ANIMATE A BODY, BUT A *MIND...* GOOD FUCKING *LUCK.*
POINT BUTCHER'S TRYNNA MAKE: THE *BOYS* KILL YOU, YOU *STAY KILLED...*
AYE.
TO ME, AS WELL AS THE FUCKIN' SUPES.

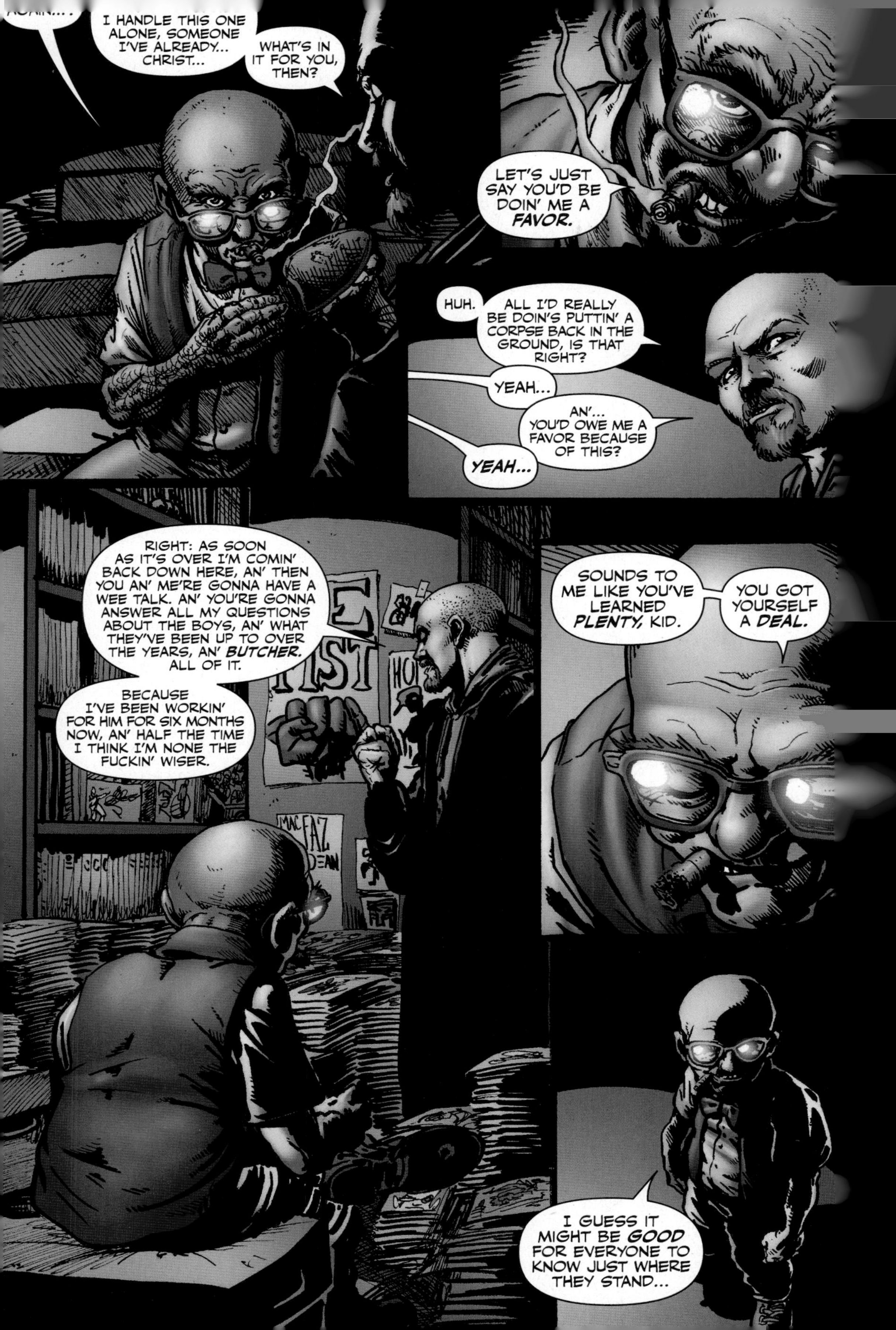
I HANDLE THIS ONE ALONE, SOMEONE I'VE ALREADY... CHRIST...
WHAT'S IN IT FOR YOU, THEN?
LET'S JUST SAY YOU'D BE DOIN' ME A *FAVOR.*
HUH.
ALL I'D REALLY BE DOIN'S PUTTIN' A CORPSE BACK IN THE GROUND, IS THAT RIGHT?
YEAH...
AN'... YOU'D OWE ME A FAVOR BECAUSE OF THIS?
YEAH...
RIGHT: AS SOON AS IT'S OVER I'M COMIN' BACK DOWN HERE, AN' THEN YOU AN' ME'RE GONNA HAVE A WEE TALK. AN' YOU'RE GONNA ANSWER ALL MY QUESTIONS ABOUT THE BOYS, AN' WHAT THEY'VE BEEN UP TO OVER THE YEARS, AN' *BUTCHER.* ALL OF IT.
BECAUSE I'VE BEEN WORKIN' FOR HIM FOR SIX MONTHS NOW, AN' HALF THE TIME I THINK I'M NONE THE FUCKIN' WISER.
SOUNDS TO ME LIKE YOU'VE LEARNED *PLENTY,* KID.
YOU GOT YOURSELF A *DEAL.*
I GUESS IT MIGHT BE *GOOD* FOR EVERYONE TO KNOW JUST WHERE THEY STAND...

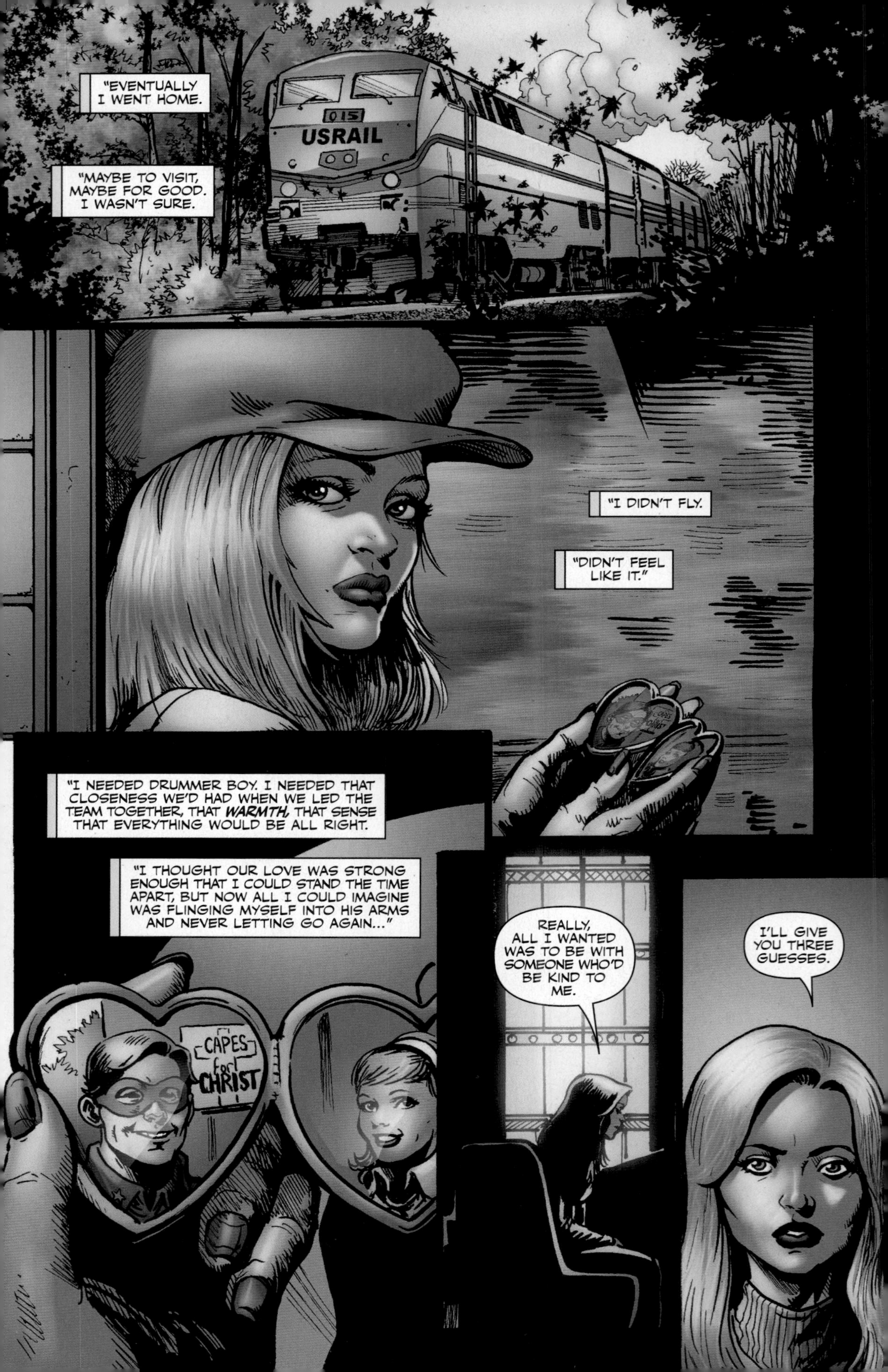

"EVENTUALLY I WENT HOME.
USRAIL
"MAYBE TO VISIT, MAYBE FOR GOOD. I WASN'T SURE.
"I DIDN'T FLY.
"DIDN'T FEEL LIKE IT."
"I NEEDED DRUMMER BOY. I NEEDED THAT CLOSENESS WE'D HAD WHEN WE LED THE TEAM TOGETHER, THAT *WARMTH,* THAT SENSE THAT EVERYTHING WOULD BE ALL RIGHT.
"I THOUGHT OUR LOVE WAS STRONG ENOUGH THAT I COULD STAND THE TIME APART, BUT NOW ALL I COULD IMAGINE WAS FLINGING MYSELF INTO HIS ARMS AND NEVER LETTING GO AGAIN..."
CAPES for CHRIST
REALLY, ALL I WANTED WAS TO BE WITH SOMEONE WHO'D BE KIND TO ME.
I'LL GIVE YOU THREE GUESSES.

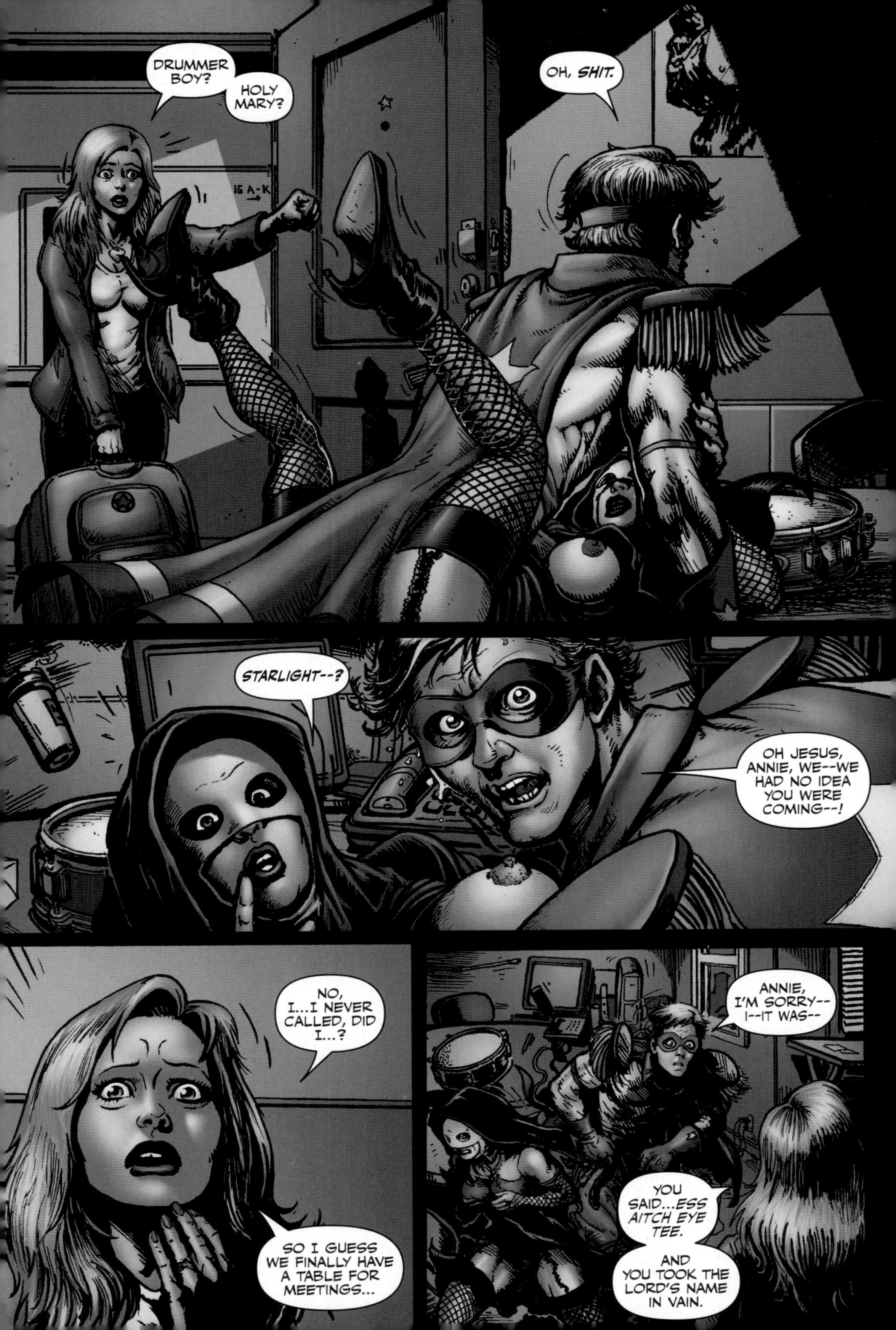
DRUMMER BOY?
HOLY MARY?
OH, SHIT.
STARLIGHT--?
OH JESUS, ANNIE, WE--WE HAD NO IDEA YOU WERE COMING--!
NO, I...I NEVER CALLED, DID I...?
SO I GUESS WE FINALLY HAVE A TABLE FOR MEETINGS...
ANNIE, I'M SORRY-- I--IT WAS--
YOU SAID...ESS AITCH EYE TEE.
AND YOU TOOK THE LORD'S NAME IN VAIN.

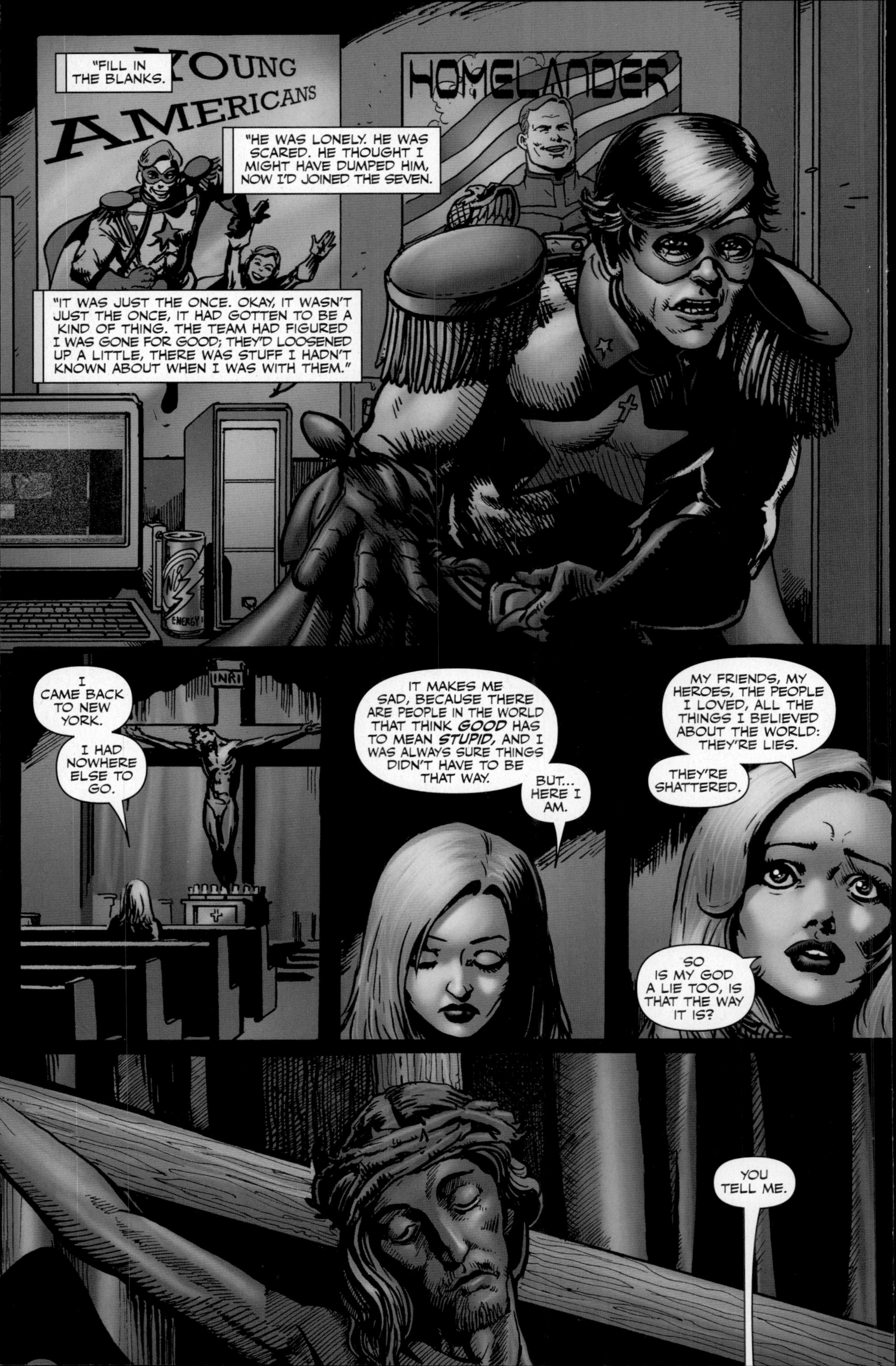
"FILL IN THE BLANKS.
YOUNG AMERICANS
HOMELANDER
"HE WAS LONELY. HE WAS SCARED. HE THOUGHT I MIGHT HAVE DUMPED HIM, NOW I'D JOINED THE SEVEN.
"IT WAS JUST THE ONCE. OKAY, IT WASN'T JUST THE ONCE, IT HAD GOTTEN TO BE A KIND OF THING. THE TEAM HAD FIGURED I WAS GONE FOR GOOD; THEY'D LOOSENED UP A LITTLE, THERE WAS STUFF I HADN'T KNOWN ABOUT WHEN I WAS WITH THEM."
INRI
I CAME BACK TO NEW YORK.
I HAD NOWHERE ELSE TO GO.
IT MAKES ME SAD, BECAUSE THERE ARE PEOPLE IN THE WORLD THAT THINK GOOD HAS TO MEAN STUPID, AND I WAS ALWAYS SURE THINGS DIDN'T HAVE TO BE THAT WAY.
BUT... HERE I AM.
MY FRIENDS, MY HEROES, THE PEOPLE I LOVED, ALL THE THINGS I BELIEVED ABOUT THE WORLD: THEY'RE LIES.
THEY'RE SHATTERED.
SO IS MY GOD A LIE TOO, IS THAT THE WAY IT IS?
YOU TELL ME.

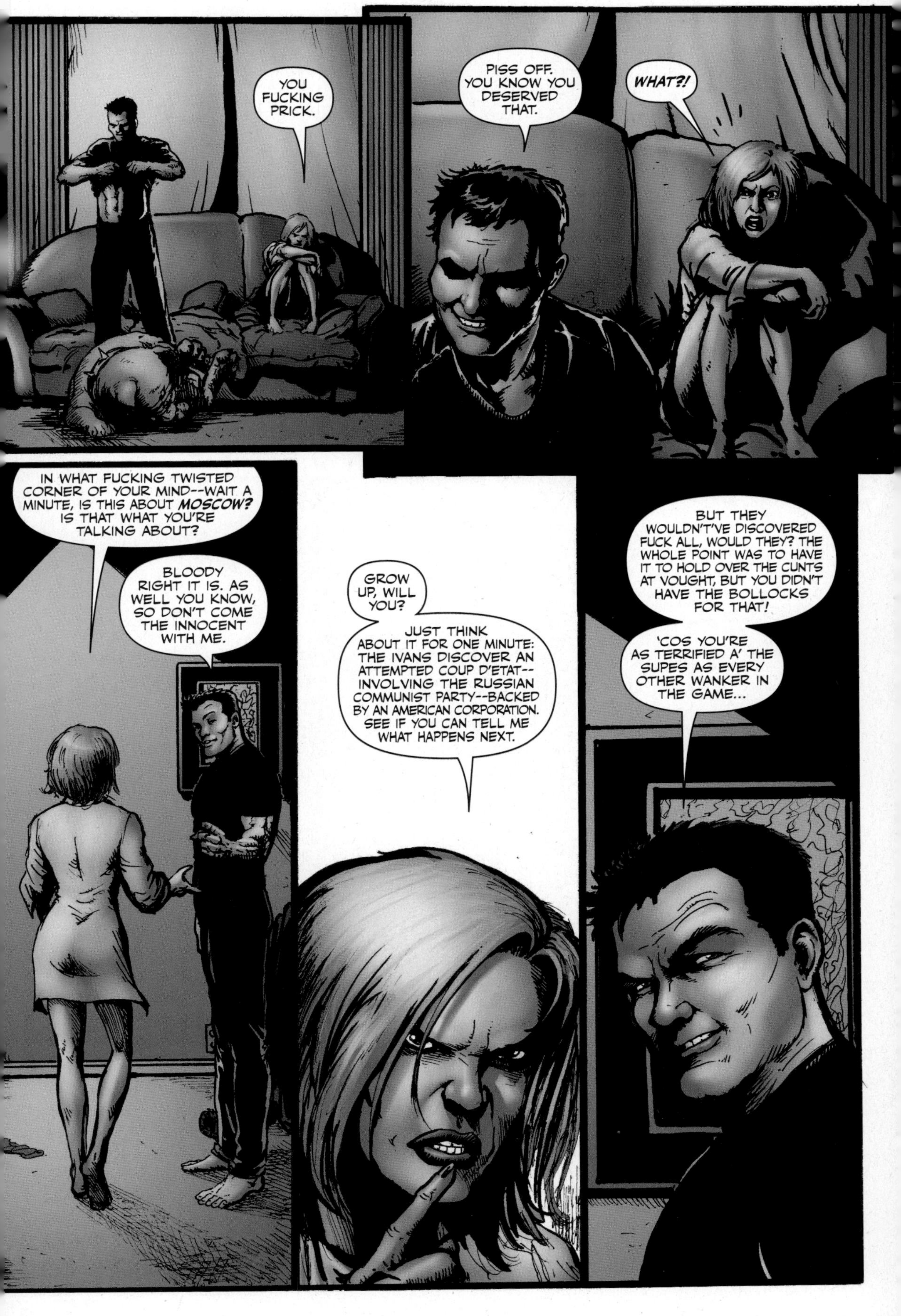
YOU FUCKING PRICK.
PISS OFF. YOU KNOW YOU DESERVED THAT.
WHAT?!
IN WHAT FUCKING TWISTED CORNER OF YOUR MIND--WAIT A MINUTE, IS THIS ABOUT MOSCOW? IS THAT WHAT YOU'RE TALKING ABOUT?
BLOODY RIGHT IT IS. AS WELL YOU KNOW, SO DON'T COME THE INNOCENT WITH ME.
GROW UP, WILL YOU?
JUST THINK ABOUT IT FOR ONE MINUTE: THE IVANS DISCOVER AN ATTEMPTED COUP D'ETAT--INVOLVING THE RUSSIAN COMMUNIST PARTY--BACKED BY AN AMERICAN CORPORATION. SEE IF YOU CAN TELL ME WHAT HAPPENS NEXT.
BUT THEY WOULDN'T'VE DISCOVERED FUCK ALL, WOULD THEY? THE WHOLE POINT WAS TO HAVE IT TO HOLD OVER THE CUNTS AT VOUGHT, BUT YOU DIDN'T HAVE THE BOLLOCKS FOR THAT!
'COS YOU'RE AS TERRIFIED A' THE SUPES AS EVERY OTHER WANKER IN THE GAME...

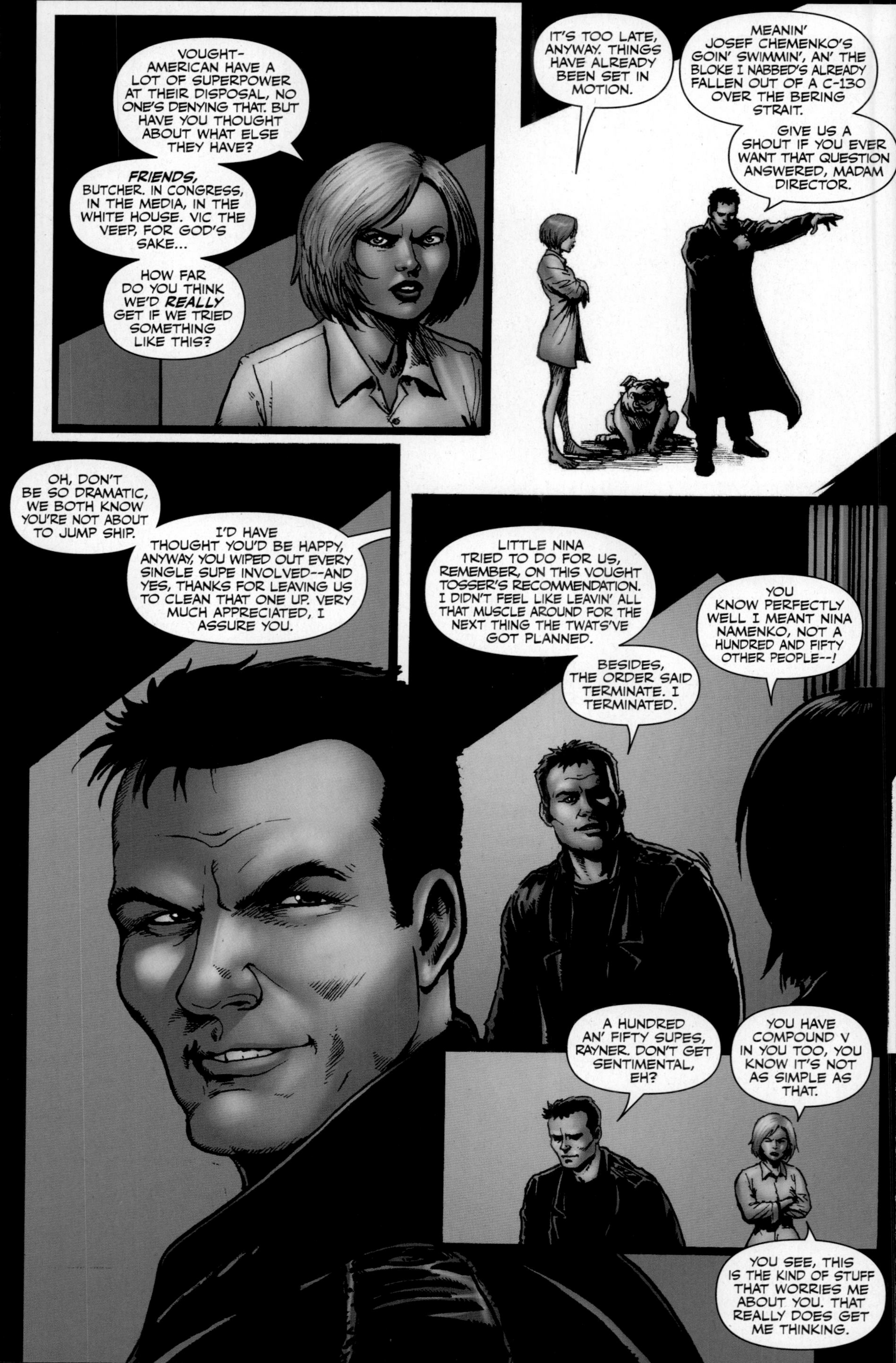
VOUGHT-AMERICAN HAVE A LOT OF SUPERPOWER AT THEIR DISPOSAL, NO ONE'S DENYING THAT. BUT HAVE YOU THOUGHT ABOUT WHAT ELSE THEY HAVE?
FRIENDS, BUTCHER. IN CONGRESS, IN THE MEDIA, IN THE WHITE HOUSE. VIC THE VEEP, FOR GOD'S SAKE...
HOW FAR DO YOU THINK WE'D REALLY GET IF WE TRIED SOMETHING LIKE THIS?
IT'S TOO LATE, ANYWAY. THINGS HAVE ALREADY BEEN SET IN MOTION.
MEANIN' JOSEF CHEMENKO'S GOIN' SWIMMIN', AN' THE BLOKE I NABBED'S ALREADY FALLEN OUT OF A C-130 OVER THE BERING STRAIT.
GIVE US A SHOUT IF YOU EVER WANT THAT QUESTION ANSWERED, MADAM DIRECTOR.
OH, DON'T BE SO DRAMATIC, WE BOTH KNOW YOU'RE NOT ABOUT TO JUMP SHIP.
I'D HAVE THOUGHT YOU'D BE HAPPY, ANYWAY. YOU WIPED OUT EVERY SINGLE SUPE INVOLVED--AND YES, THANKS FOR LEAVING US TO CLEAN THAT ONE UP. VERY MUCH APPRECIATED, I ASSURE YOU.
LITTLE NINA TRIED TO DO FOR US, REMEMBER, ON THIS VOUGHT TOSSER'S RECOMMENDATION. I DIDN'T FEEL LIKE LEAVIN' ALL THAT MUSCLE AROUND FOR THE NEXT THING THE TWATS'VE GOT PLANNED.
BESIDES, THE ORDER SAID TERMINATE. I TERMINATED.
YOU KNOW PERFECTLY WELL I MEANT NINA NAMENKO, NOT A HUNDRED AND FIFTY OTHER PEOPLE--!
A HUNDRED AN' FIFTY SUPES, RAYNER. DON'T GET SENTIMENTAL, EH?
YOU HAVE COMPOUND V IN YOU TOO, YOU KNOW IT'S NOT AS SIMPLE AS THAT.
YOU SEE, THIS IS THE KIND OF STUFF THAT WORRIES ME ABOUT YOU. THAT REALLY DOES GET ME THINKING.

WELL IF I EVER STICK A CAPE ON AN' START USIN' ORDINARY HUMAN BEIN'S TO WIPE ME ARSE WITH, YOU'LL KNOW YOU WERE RIGHT TO WORRY, WON'T YOU?

LOOK... I DIDN'T MEAN...

YOU REMEMBER THE DAY WE MET?

WHAT?

NOVEMBER OH-ONE. CHRIST, THE FUCKIN' GLEAM YOU HAD IN YOUR EYE.

BE NICE TO PUT IT DOWN TO ME WINNIN' CHARM, BUT THAT WEREN'T IT. DAKOTA BOB HAD JUST GONE INTO PAKISTAN.

B-52 STRIKES WERE SPILLIN' OVER INTO AFGHANISTAN. QUITE A LONG WAY OVER, AS A MATTERA FACT.

AN' YOU AN' THE REST WERE FUCKIN' LOVIN' IT, 'COS EVERY VILLAGE GOT HIT--FORGETTIN' THE WOMEN AN' KIDDIES FOR A MINUTE-- MEANT ANOTHER LOTTA TALIBAN GONE.

AN' EVERY *ONE* A' THEM CUNTS WENT DOWN MEANT ANOTHER EYEWITNESS DEAD AN' BURIED. TO THE SHIT THE COMPANY HAD 'EM DOIN', WHEN YOU WERE ALL SUCH GOOD MATES BACK IN THE EIGHTIES.

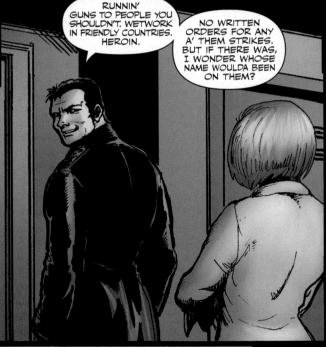

RUNNIN' GUNS TO PEOPLE YOU SHOULDN'T. WETWORK IN FRIENDLY COUNTRIES. HEROIN.

NO WRITTEN ORDERS FOR ANY A' THEM STRIKES. BUT IF THERE WAS, I WONDER WHOSE NAME WOULDA BEEN ON THEM?

WE DESERVE EACH OTHER, YOU AN' ME.

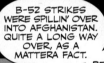

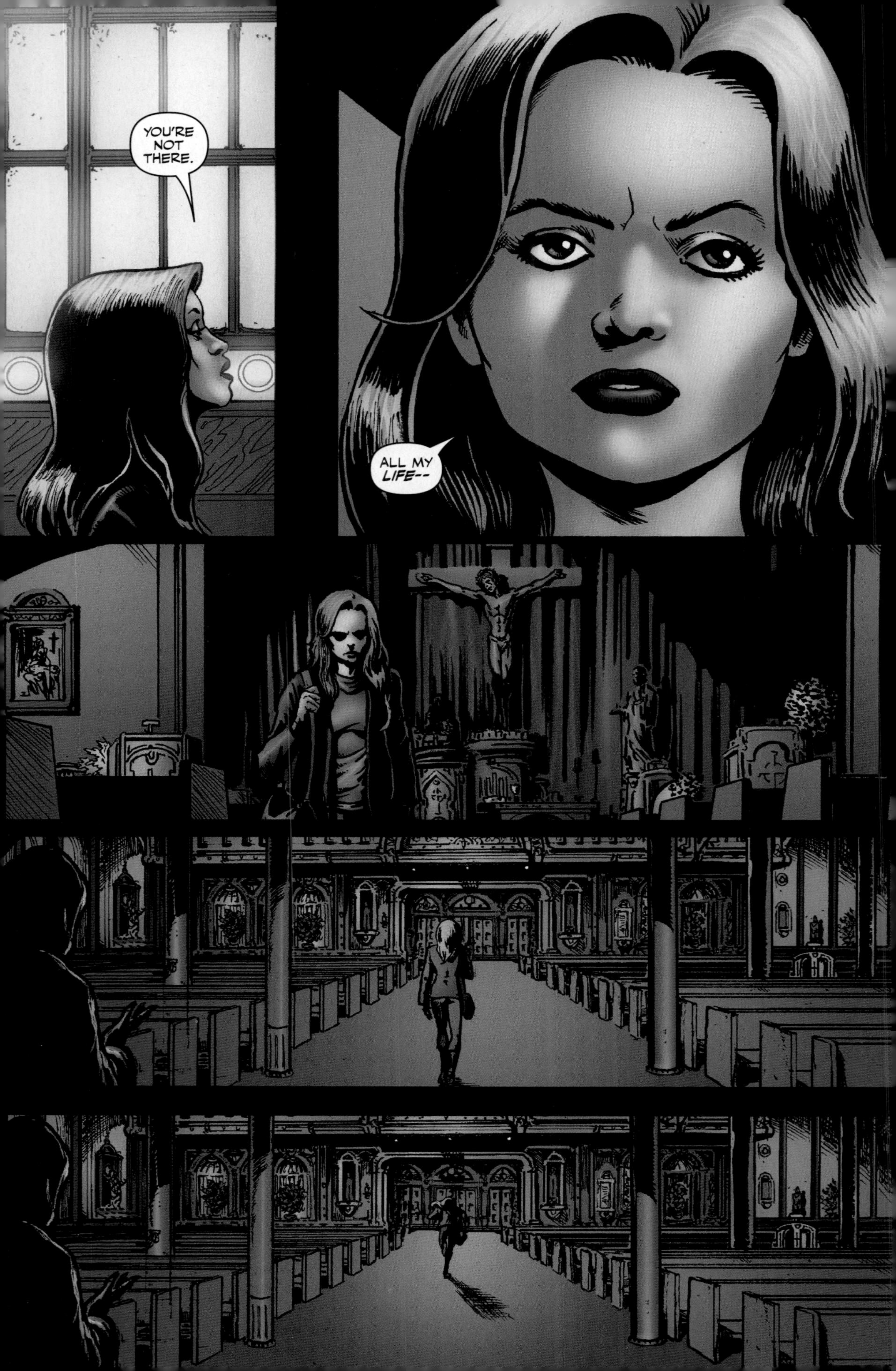
YOU'RE NOT THERE.
ALL MY *LIFE--*

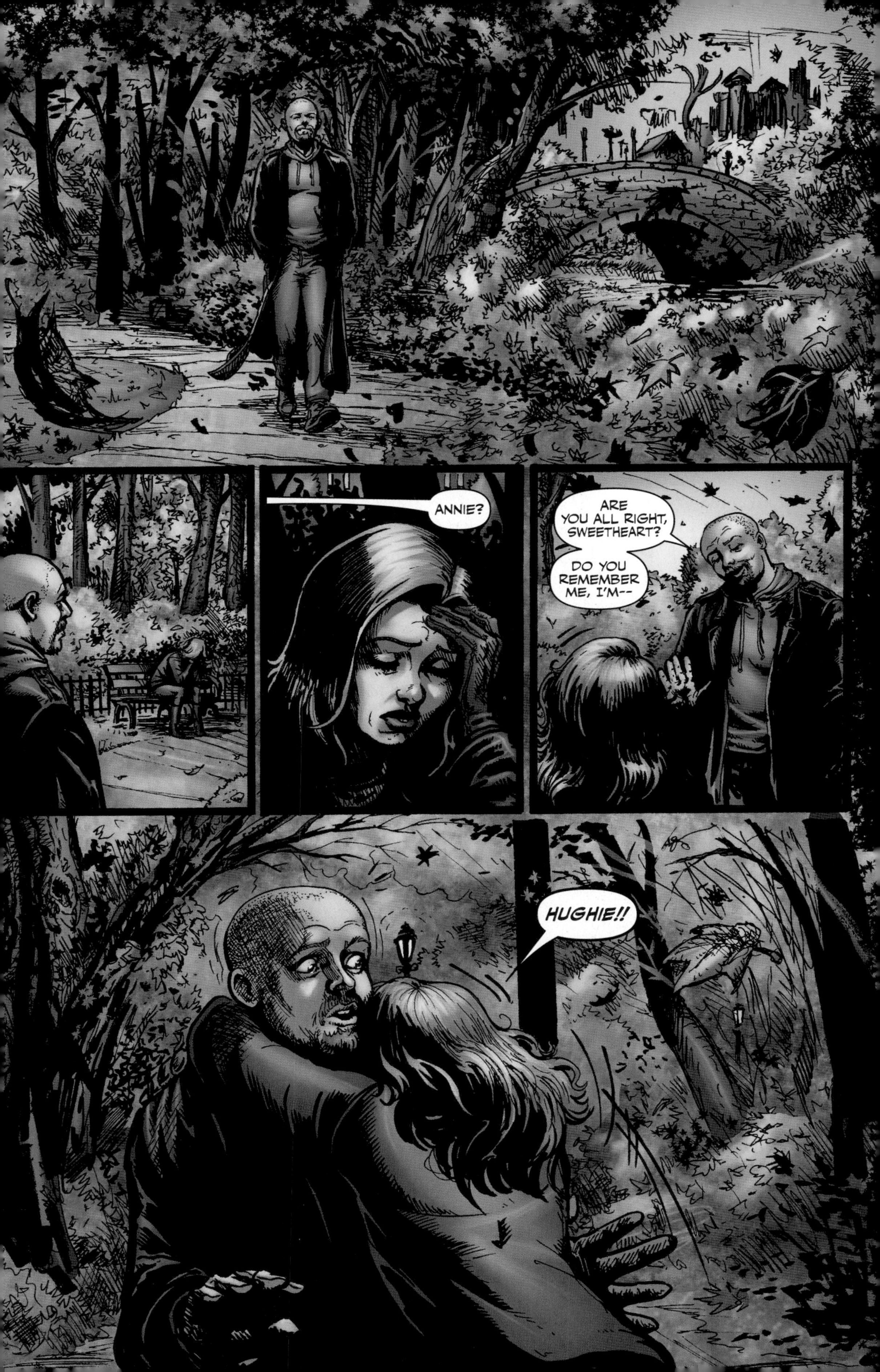
ANNIE?
ARE YOU ALL RIGHT, SWEETHEART?
DO YOU REMEMBER ME, I'M--
HUGHIE!!

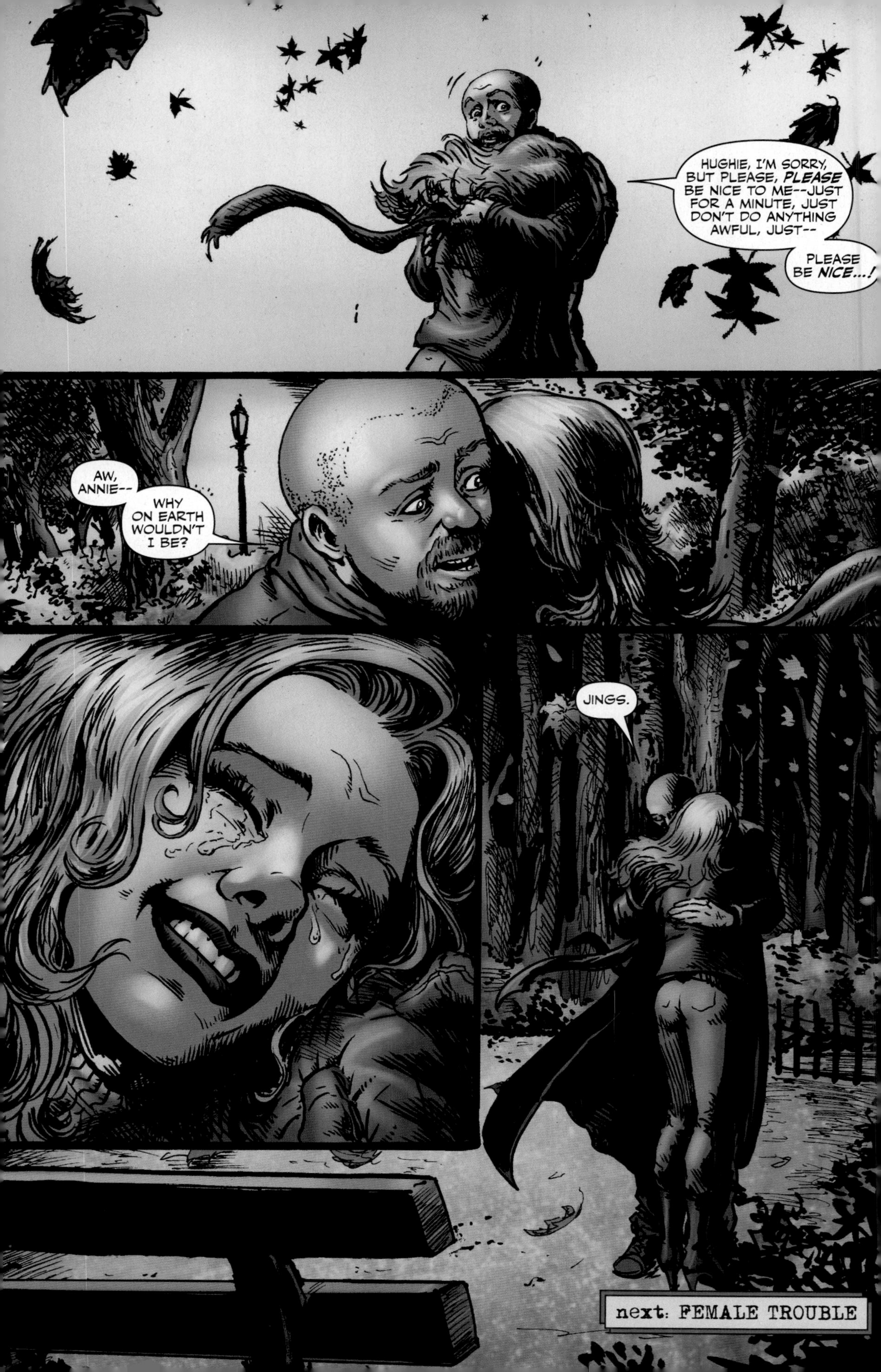
HUGHIE, I'M SORRY, BUT PLEASE, PLEASE BE NICE TO ME--JUST FOR A MINUTE, JUST DON'T DO ANYTHING AWFUL, JUST--
PLEASE BE NICE...!
AW, ANNIE--
WHY ON EARTH WOULDN'T I BE?
JINGS.
next: FEMALE TROUBLE

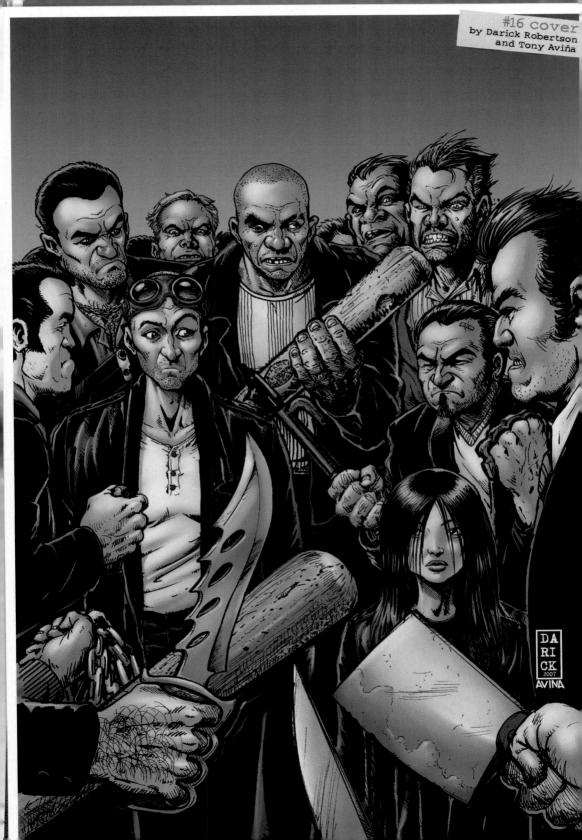

#16 cover
by Darick Robertson
and Tony Aviña

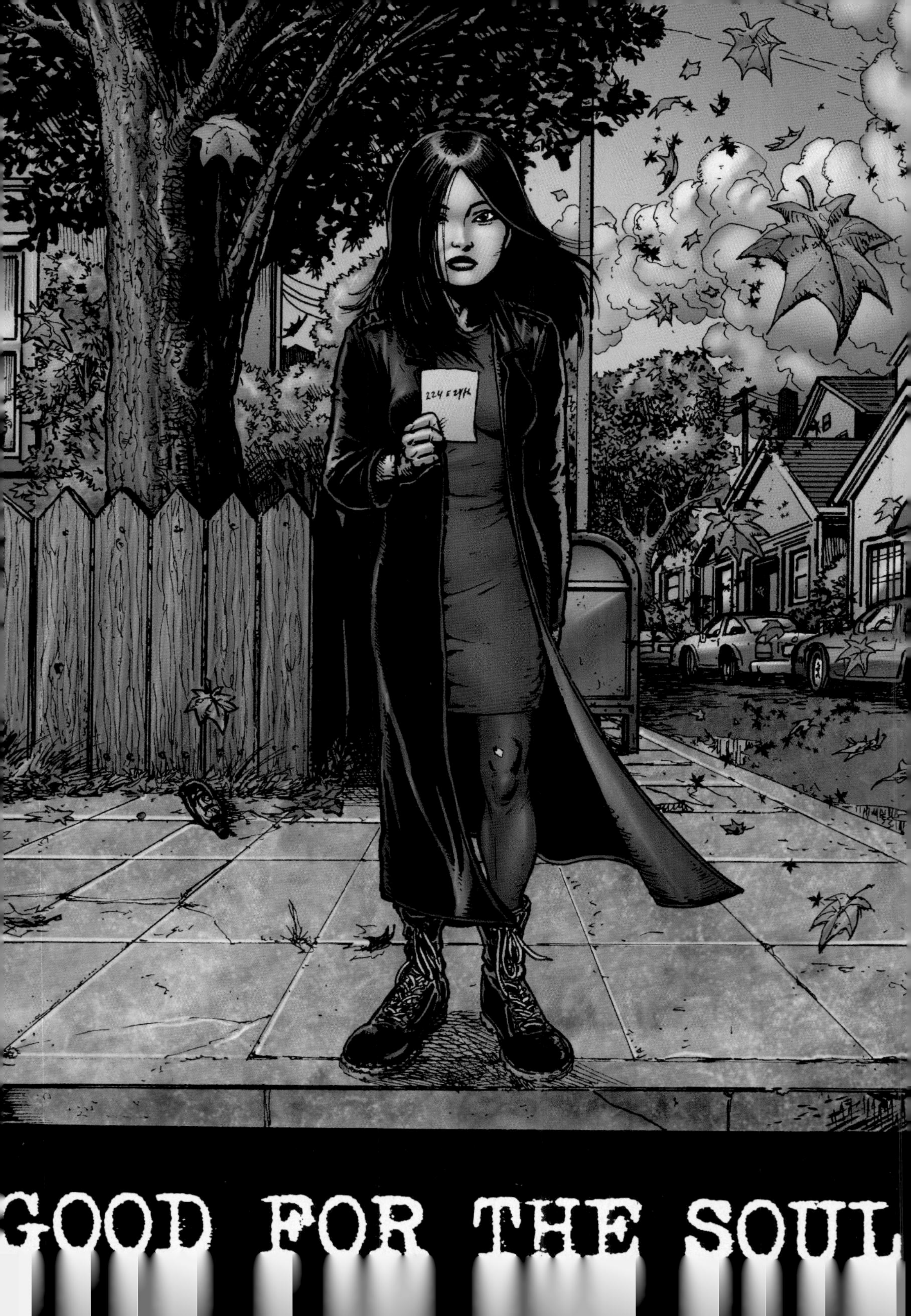

GOOD FOR THE SOUL

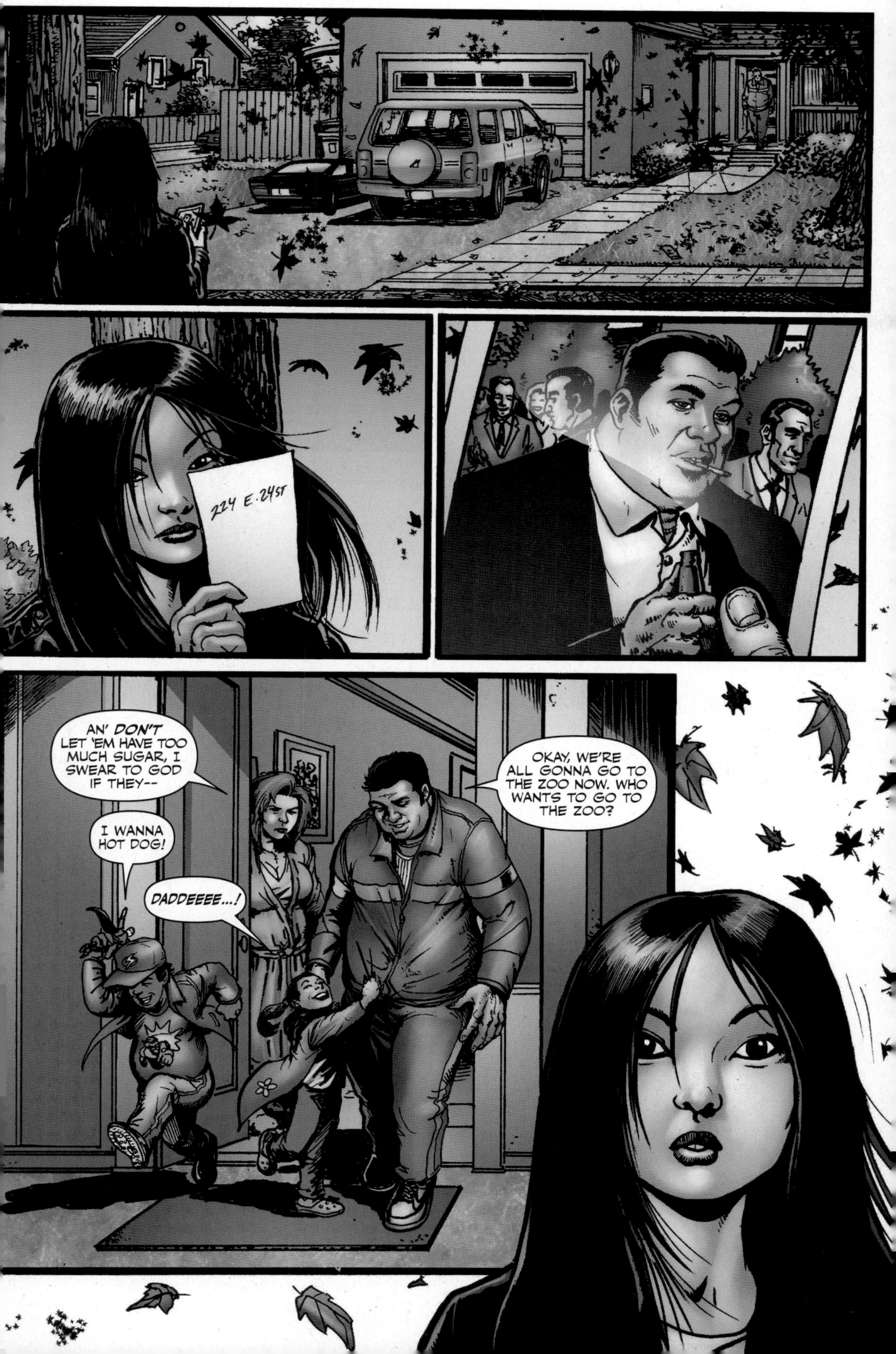
224 E. 24ST
AN' DON'T LET 'EM HAVE TOO MUCH SUGAR, I SWEAR TO GOD IF THEY--
OKAY, WE'RE ALL GONNA GO TO THE ZOO NOW. WHO WANTS TO GO TO THE ZOO?
I WANNA HOT DOG!
DADDEEEE...!

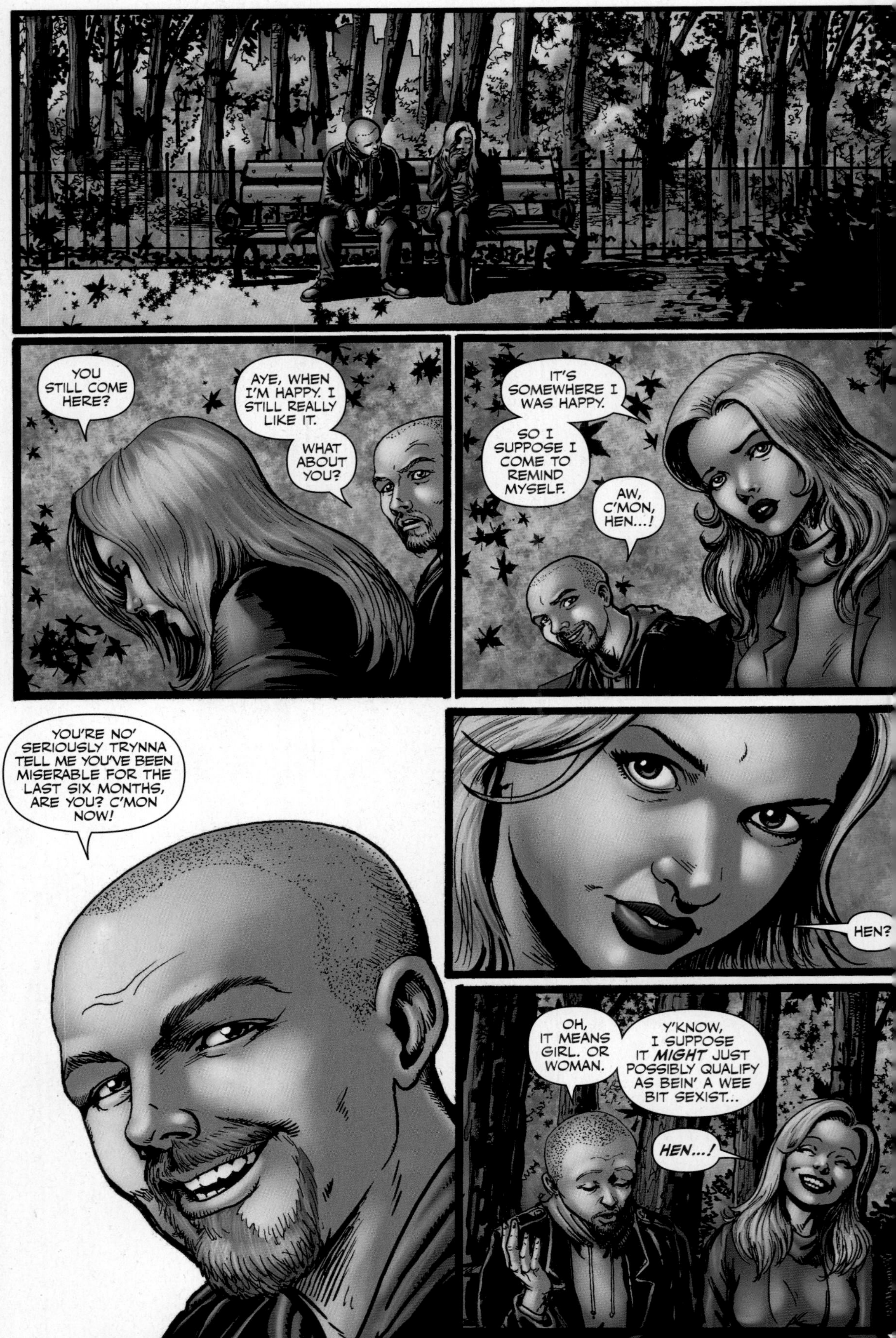
YOU STILL COME HERE?
AYE, WHEN I'M HAPPY. I STILL REALLY LIKE IT.
WHAT ABOUT YOU?
IT'S SOMEWHERE I WAS HAPPY.
SO I SUPPOSE I COME TO REMIND MYSELF.
AW, C'MON, HEN...!
YOU'RE NO' SERIOUSLY TRYNNA TELL ME YOU'VE BEEN MISERABLE FOR THE LAST SIX MONTHS, ARE YOU? C'MON NOW!
HEN?
OH, IT MEANS GIRL. OR WOMAN.
Y'KNOW, I SUPPOSE IT *MIGHT* JUST POSSIBLY QUALIFY AS BEIN' A WEE BIT SEXIST...
HEN...!

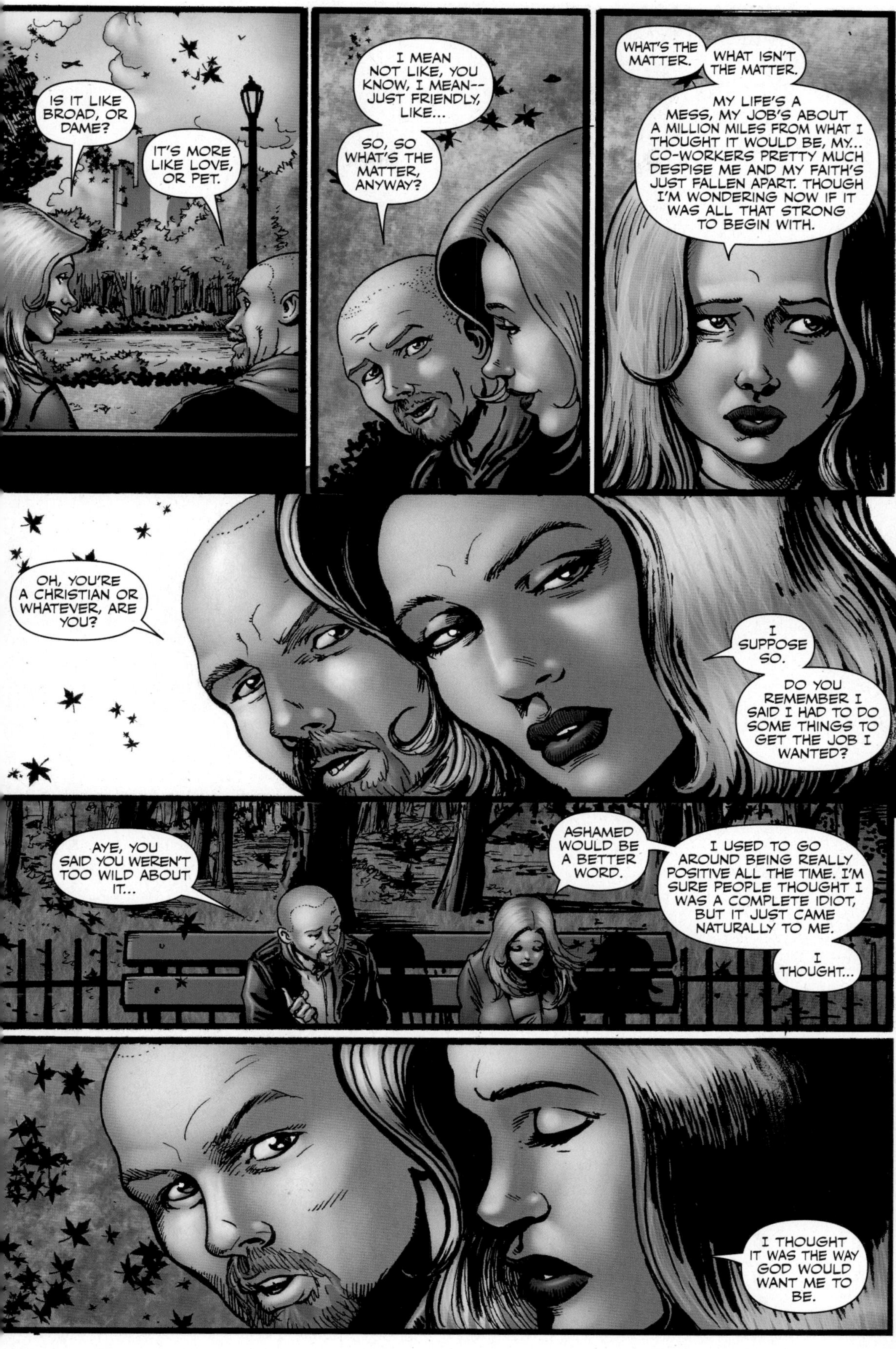
IS IT LIKE BROAD, OR DAME?
IT'S MORE LIKE LOVE, OR PET.
I MEAN NOT LIKE, YOU KNOW, I MEAN-- JUST FRIENDLY, LIKE...
SO, SO WHAT'S THE MATTER, ANYWAY?
WHAT'S THE MATTER.
WHAT ISN'T THE MATTER.
MY LIFE'S A MESS, MY JOB'S ABOUT A MILLION MILES FROM WHAT I THOUGHT IT WOULD BE, MY... CO-WORKERS PRETTY MUCH DESPISE ME AND MY FAITH'S JUST FALLEN APART. THOUGH I'M WONDERING NOW IF IT WAS ALL THAT STRONG TO BEGIN WITH.
OH, YOU'RE A CHRISTIAN OR WHATEVER, ARE YOU?
I SUPPOSE SO.
DO YOU REMEMBER I SAID I HAD TO DO SOME THINGS TO GET THE JOB I WANTED?
AYE, YOU SAID YOU WEREN'T TOO WILD ABOUT IT...
ASHAMED WOULD BE A BETTER WORD.
I USED TO GO AROUND BEING REALLY POSITIVE ALL THE TIME. I'M SURE PEOPLE THOUGHT I WAS A COMPLETE IDIOT, BUT IT JUST CAME NATURALLY TO ME.
I THOUGHT...
I THOUGHT IT WAS THE WAY GOD WOULD WANT ME TO BE.

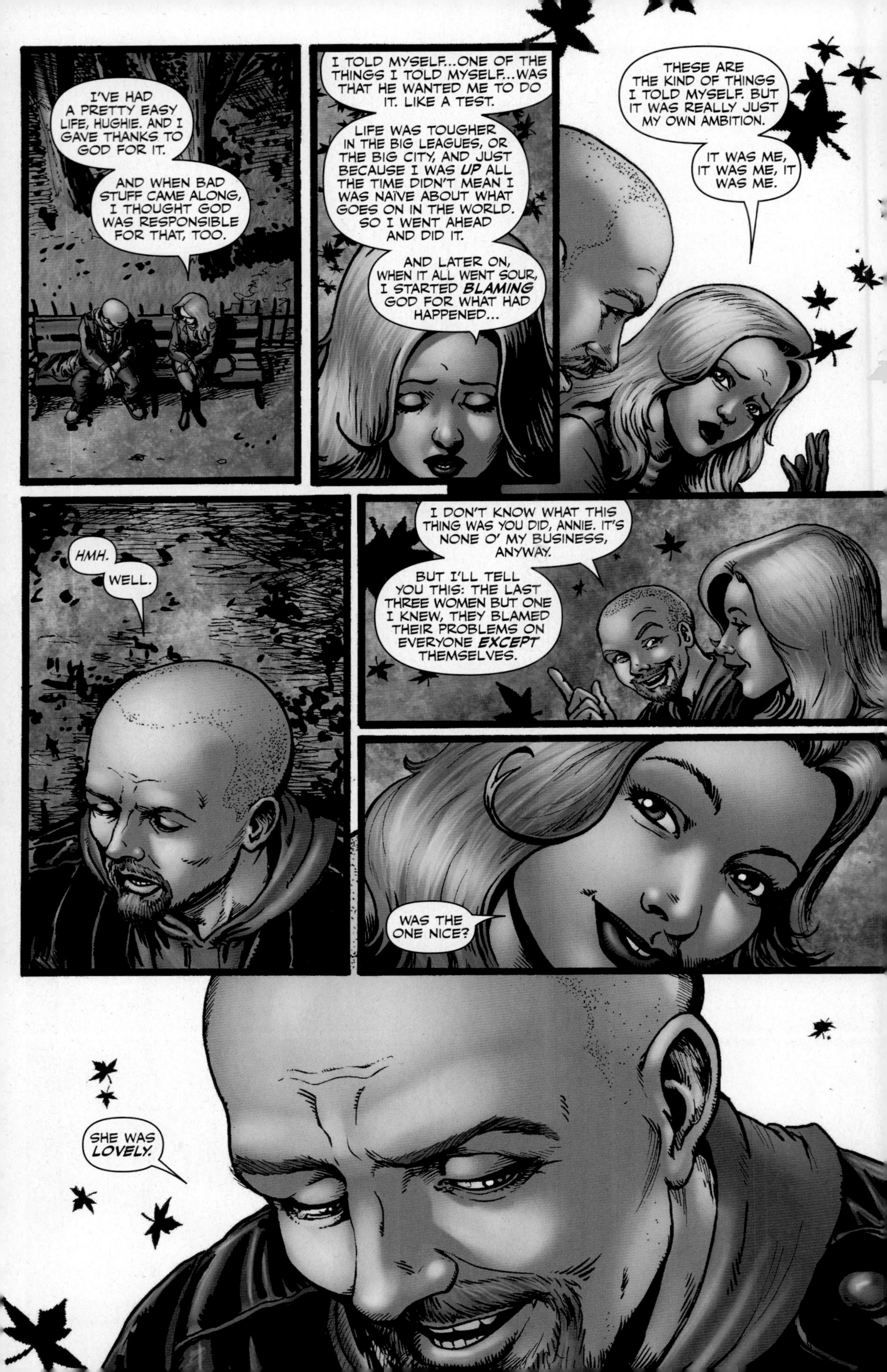
I'VE HAD A PRETTY EASY LIFE, HUGHIE. AND I GAVE THANKS TO GOD FOR IT.
AND WHEN BAD STUFF CAME ALONG, I THOUGHT GOD WAS RESPONSIBLE FOR THAT, TOO.
I TOLD MYSELF...ONE OF THE THINGS I TOLD MYSELF...WAS THAT HE WANTED ME TO DO IT. LIKE A TEST.
LIFE WAS TOUGHER IN THE BIG LEAGUES, OR THE BIG CITY, AND JUST BECAUSE I WAS UP ALL THE TIME DIDN'T MEAN I WAS NAÏVE ABOUT WHAT GOES ON IN THE WORLD. SO I WENT AHEAD AND DID IT.
AND LATER ON, WHEN IT ALL WENT SOUR, I STARTED BLAMING GOD FOR WHAT HAD HAPPENED...
THESE ARE THE KIND OF THINGS I TOLD MYSELF. BUT IT WAS REALLY JUST MY OWN AMBITION.
IT WAS ME, IT WAS ME, IT WAS ME.
HMH.
WELL.
I DON'T KNOW WHAT THIS THING WAS YOU DID, ANNIE. IT'S NONE O' MY BUSINESS, ANYWAY.
BUT I'LL TELL YOU THIS: THE LAST THREE WOMEN BUT ONE I KNEW, THEY BLAMED THEIR PROBLEMS ON EVERYONE EXCEPT THEMSELVES.
WAS THE ONE NICE?
SHE WAS LOVELY.

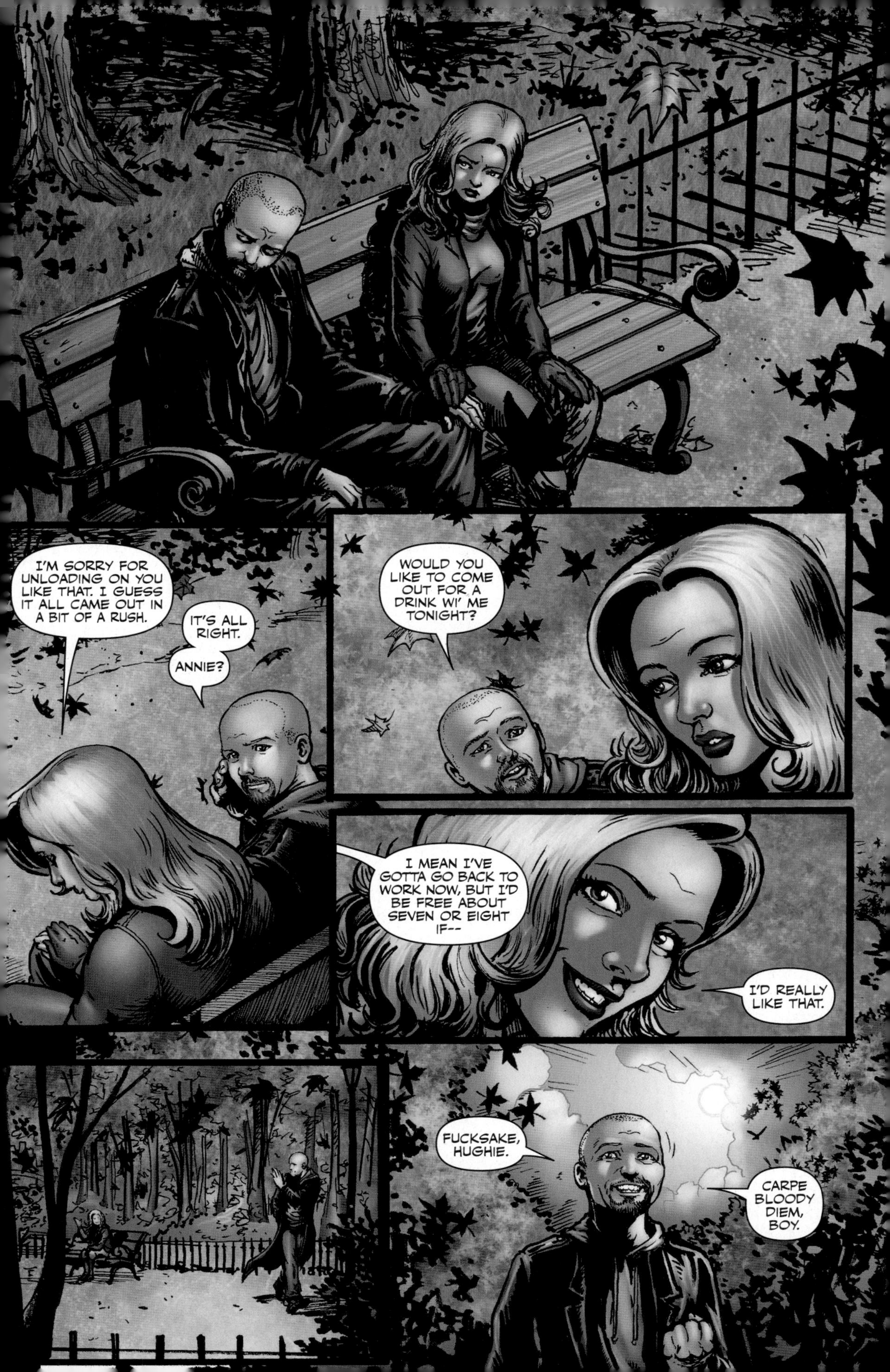
I'M SORRY FOR UNLOADING ON YOU LIKE THAT. I GUESS IT ALL CAME OUT IN A BIT OF A RUSH.
IT'S ALL RIGHT.
ANNIE?
WOULD YOU LIKE TO COME OUT FOR A DRINK WI' ME TONIGHT?
I MEAN I'VE GOTTA GO BACK TO WORK NOW, BUT I'D BE FREE ABOUT SEVEN OR EIGHT IF--
I'D REALLY LIKE THAT.
FUCKSAKE, HUGHIE.
CARPE BLOODY DIEM, BOY.

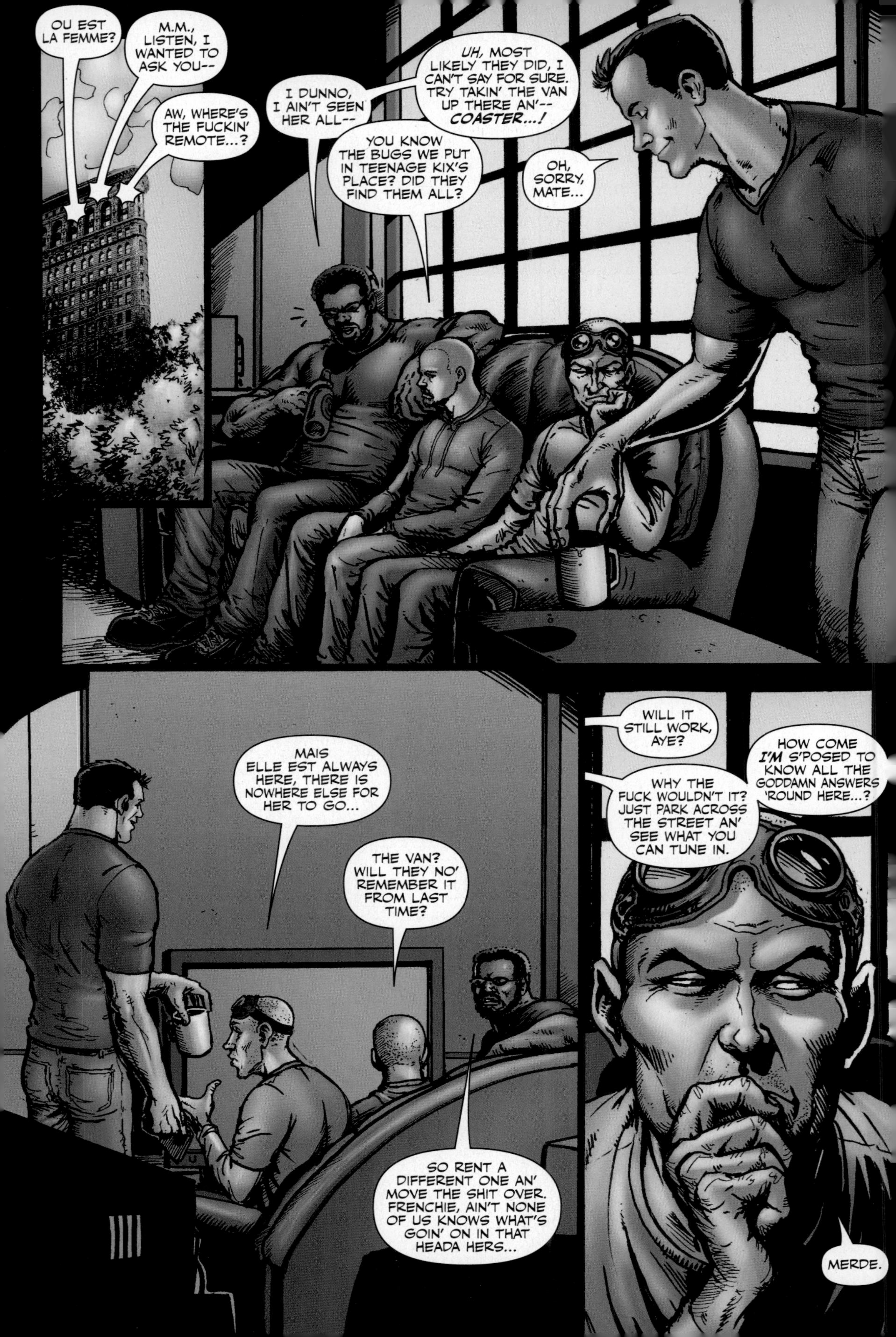
OU EST LA FEMME?
M.M., LISTEN, I WANTED TO ASK YOU--
AW, WHERE'S THE FUCKIN' REMOTE...?
I DUNNO, I AIN'T SEEN HER ALL--
YOU KNOW THE BUGS WE PUT IN TEENAGE KIX'S PLACE? DID THEY FIND THEM ALL?
UH, MOST LIKELY THEY DID, I CAN'T SAY FOR SURE. TRY TAKIN' THE VAN UP THERE AN'-- COASTER...!
OH, SORRY, MATE...
MAIS ELLE EST ALWAYS HERE, THERE IS NOWHERE ELSE FOR HER TO GO...
THE VAN? WILL THEY NO' REMEMBER IT FROM LAST TIME?
SO RENT A DIFFERENT ONE AN' MOVE THE SHIT OVER. FRENCHIE, AIN'T NONE OF US KNOWS WHAT'S GOIN' ON IN THAT HEADA HERS...
WILL IT STILL WORK, AYE?
WHY THE FUCK WOULDN'T IT? JUST PARK ACROSS THE STREET AN' SEE WHAT YOU CAN TUNE IN.
HOW COME I'M S'POSED TO KNOW ALL THE GODDAMN ANSWERS 'ROUND HERE...?
MERDE.

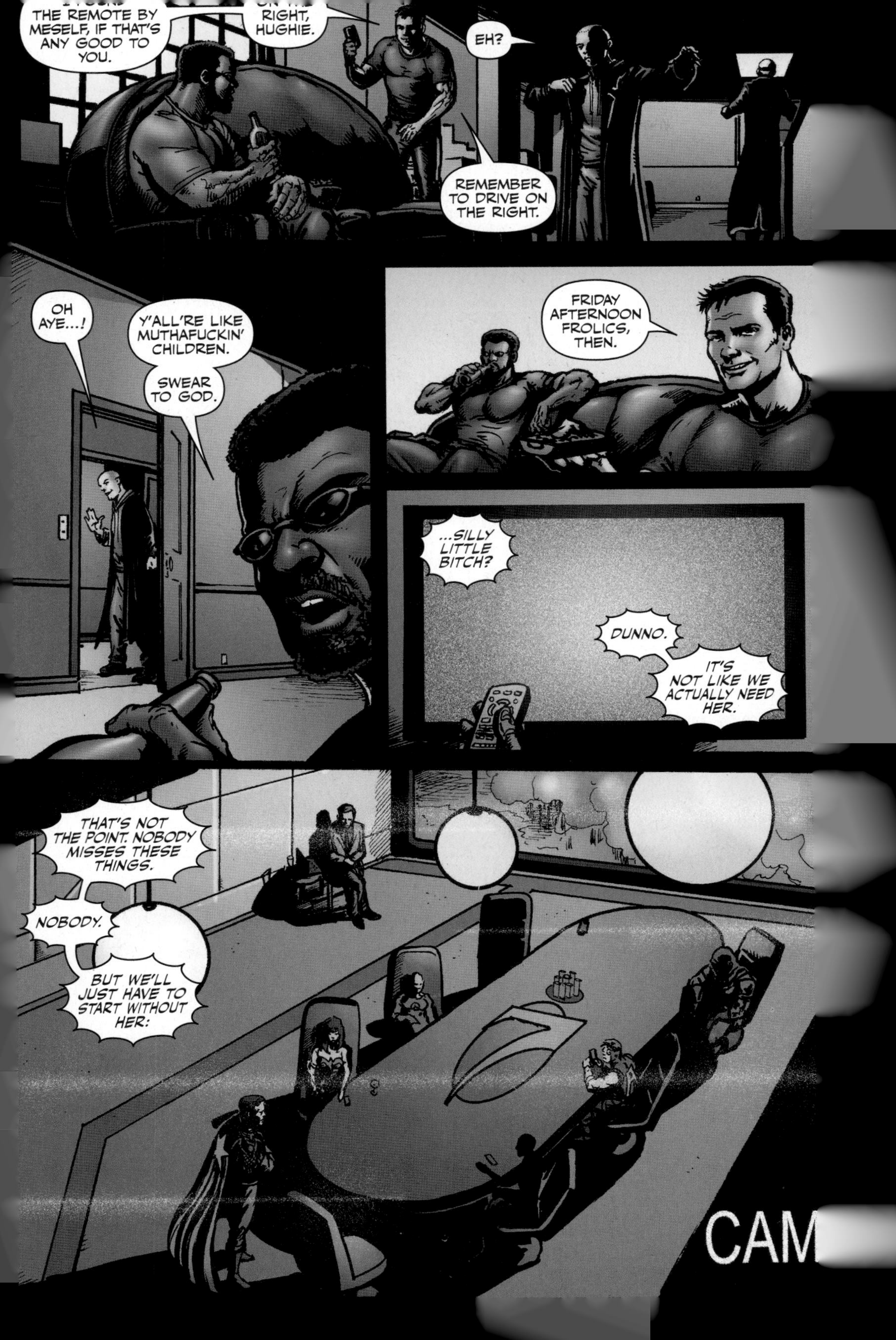
THE REMOTE BY MESELF, IF THAT'S ANY GOOD TO YOU.
RIGHT, HUGHIE.
EH?
REMEMBER TO DRIVE ON THE RIGHT.
OH AYE...!
Y'ALL'RE LIKE MUTHAFUCKIN' CHILDREN.
SWEAR TO GOD.
FRIDAY AFTERNOON FROLICS, THEN.
...SILLY LITTLE BITCH?
DUNNO.
IT'S NOT LIKE WE ACTUALLY NEED HER.
THAT'S NOT THE POINT. NOBODY MISSES THESE THINGS.
NOBODY.
BUT WE'LL JUST HAVE TO START WITHOUT HER:
CAM

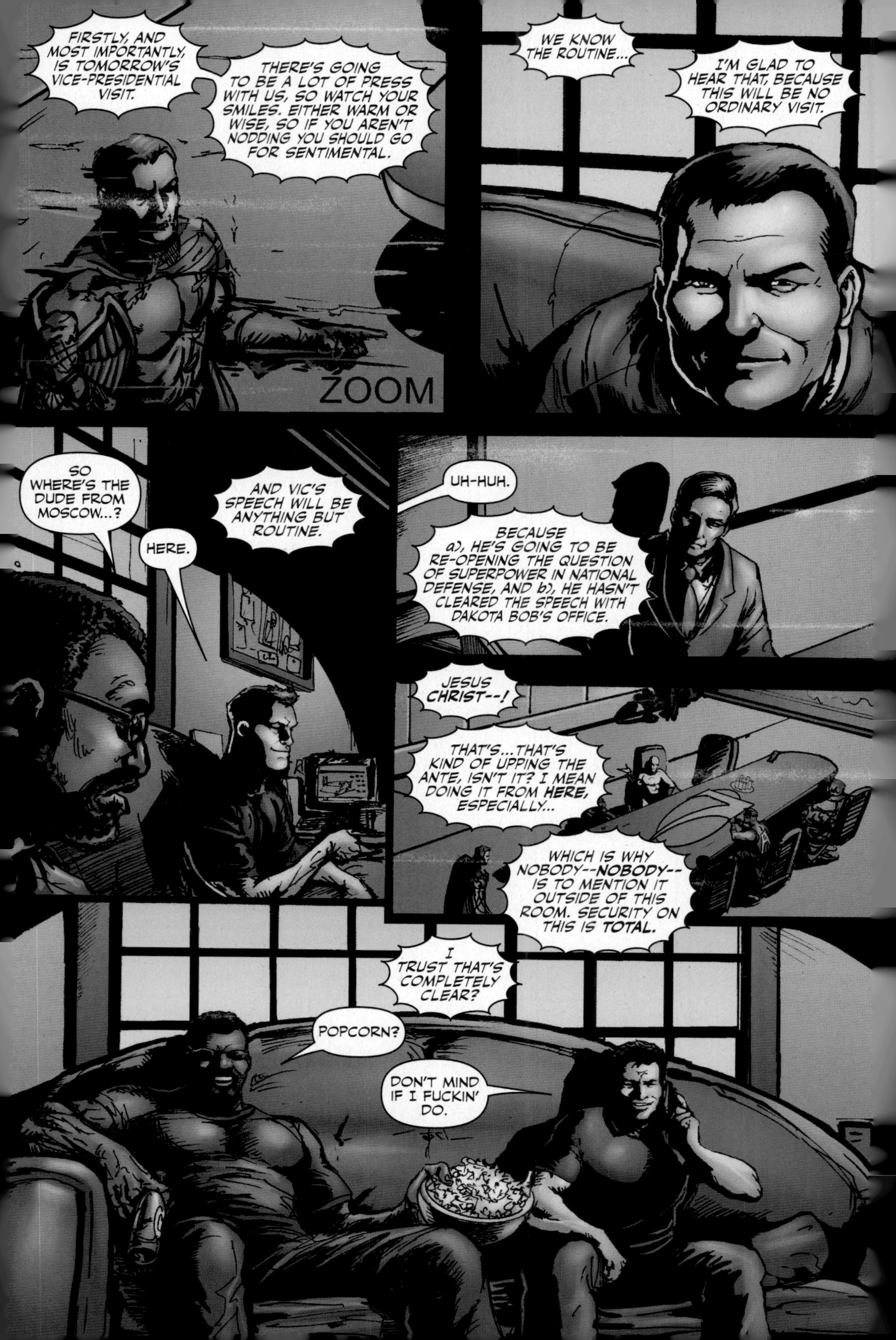
FIRSTLY, AND MOST IMPORTANTLY, IS TOMORROW'S VICE-PRESIDENTIAL VISIT.
THERE'S GOING TO BE A LOT OF PRESS WITH US, SO WATCH YOUR SMILES. EITHER WARM OR WISE, SO IF YOU AREN'T NODDING YOU SHOULD GO FOR SENTIMENTAL.
ZOOM
WE KNOW THE ROUTINE...
I'M GLAD TO HEAR THAT, BECAUSE THIS WILL BE NO ORDINARY VISIT.
SO WHERE'S THE DUDE FROM MOSCOW...?
HERE.
AND VIC'S SPEECH WILL BE ANYTHING BUT ROUTINE.
UH-HUH.
BECAUSE a), HE'S GOING TO BE RE-OPENING THE QUESTION OF SUPERPOWER IN NATIONAL DEFENSE, AND b), HE HASN'T CLEARED THE SPEECH WITH DAKOTA BOB'S OFFICE.
JESUS CHRIST--!
THAT'S...THAT'S KIND OF UPPING THE ANTE, ISN'T IT? I MEAN DOING IT FROM HERE, ESPECIALLY...
WHICH IS WHY NOBODY--NOBODY--IS TO MENTION IT OUTSIDE OF THIS ROOM. SECURITY ON THIS IS TOTAL.
I TRUST THAT'S COMPLETELY CLEAR?
POPCORN?
DON'T MIND IF I FUCKIN' DO.

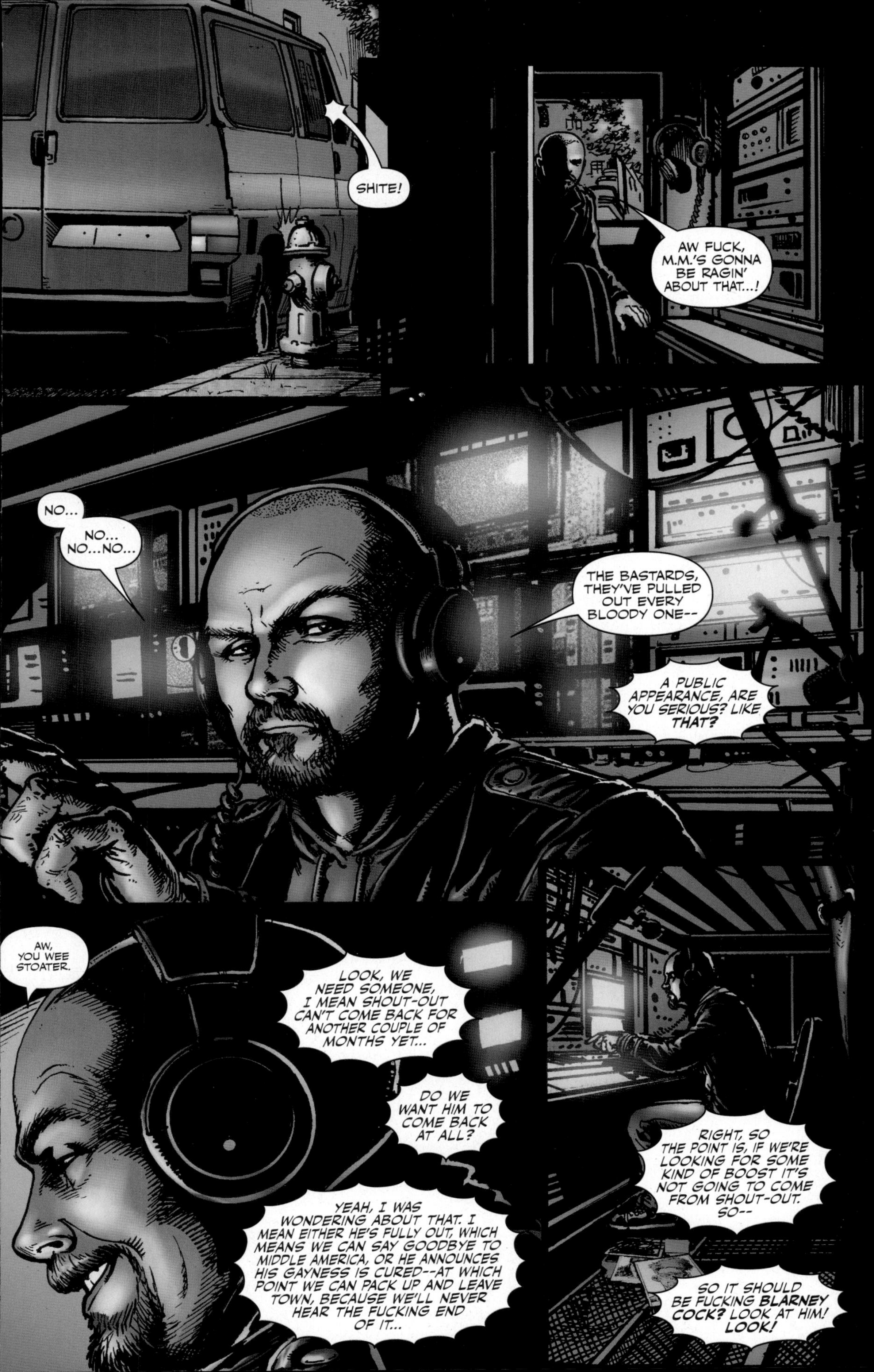
SHITE!
AW FUCK, M.M.'S GONNA BE RAGIN' ABOUT THAT...!
NO...
NO... NO...NO...
THE BASTARDS, THEY'VE PULLED OUT EVERY BLOODY ONE--
A PUBLIC APPEARANCE, ARE YOU SERIOUS? LIKE THAT?
AW, YOU WEE STOATER.
LOOK, WE NEED SOMEONE, I MEAN SHOUT-OUT CAN'T COME BACK FOR ANOTHER COUPLE OF MONTHS YET...
DO WE WANT HIM TO COME BACK AT ALL?
YEAH, I WAS WONDERING ABOUT THAT. I MEAN EITHER HE'S FULLY OUT, WHICH MEANS WE CAN SAY GOODBYE TO MIDDLE AMERICA, OR HE ANNOUNCES HIS GAYNESS IS CURED--AT WHICH POINT WE CAN PACK UP AND LEAVE TOWN, BECAUSE WE'LL NEVER HEAR THE FUCKING END OF IT...
RIGHT, SO THE POINT IS, IF WE'RE LOOKING FOR SOME KIND OF BOOST IT'S NOT GOING TO COME FROM SHOUT-OUT. SO--
SO IT SHOULD BE FUCKING BLARNEY COCK? LOOK AT HIM! LOOK!

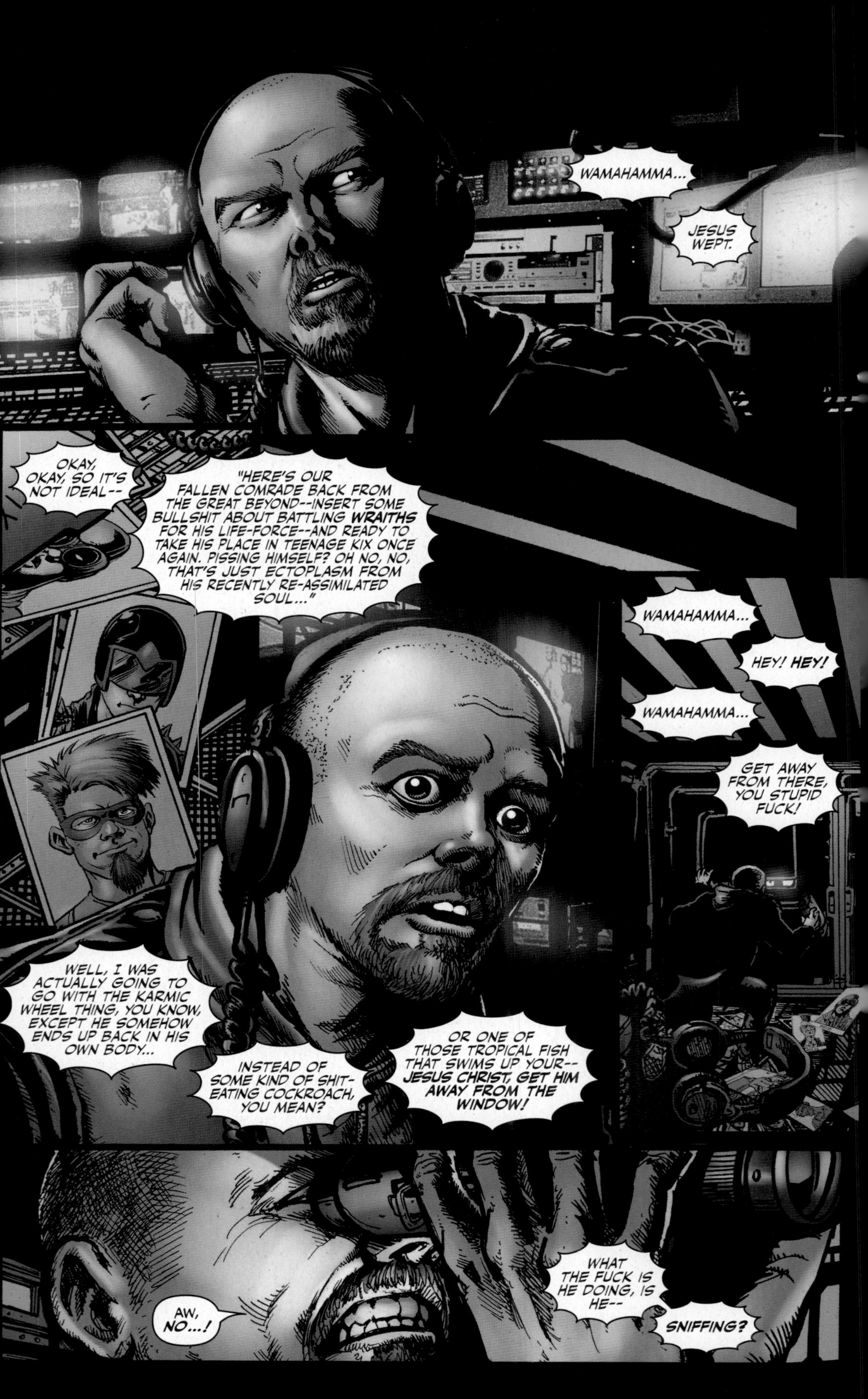
WAMAHAMMA...
JESUS WEPT.
OKAY, OKAY, SO IT'S NOT IDEAL--
"HERE'S OUR FALLEN COMRADE BACK FROM THE GREAT BEYOND--INSERT SOME BULLSHIT ABOUT BATTLING WRAITHS FOR HIS LIFE-FORCE--AND READY TO TAKE HIS PLACE IN TEENAGE KIX ONCE AGAIN. PISSING HIMSELF? OH NO, NO, THAT'S JUST ECTOPLASM FROM HIS RECENTLY RE-ASSIMILATED SOUL..."
WAMAHAMMA...
HEY! HEY!
WAMAHAMMA...
GET AWAY FROM THERE, YOU STUPID FUCK!
WELL, I WAS ACTUALLY GOING TO GO WITH THE KARMIC WHEEL THING, YOU KNOW, EXCEPT HE SOMEHOW ENDS UP BACK IN HIS OWN BODY...
INSTEAD OF SOME KIND OF SHIT-EATING COCKROACH, YOU MEAN?
OR ONE OF THOSE TROPICAL FISH THAT SWIMS UP YOUR-- JESUS CHRIST, GET HIM AWAY FROM THE WINDOW!
AW, NO...!
WHAT THE FUCK IS HE DOING, IS HE--
SNIFFING?

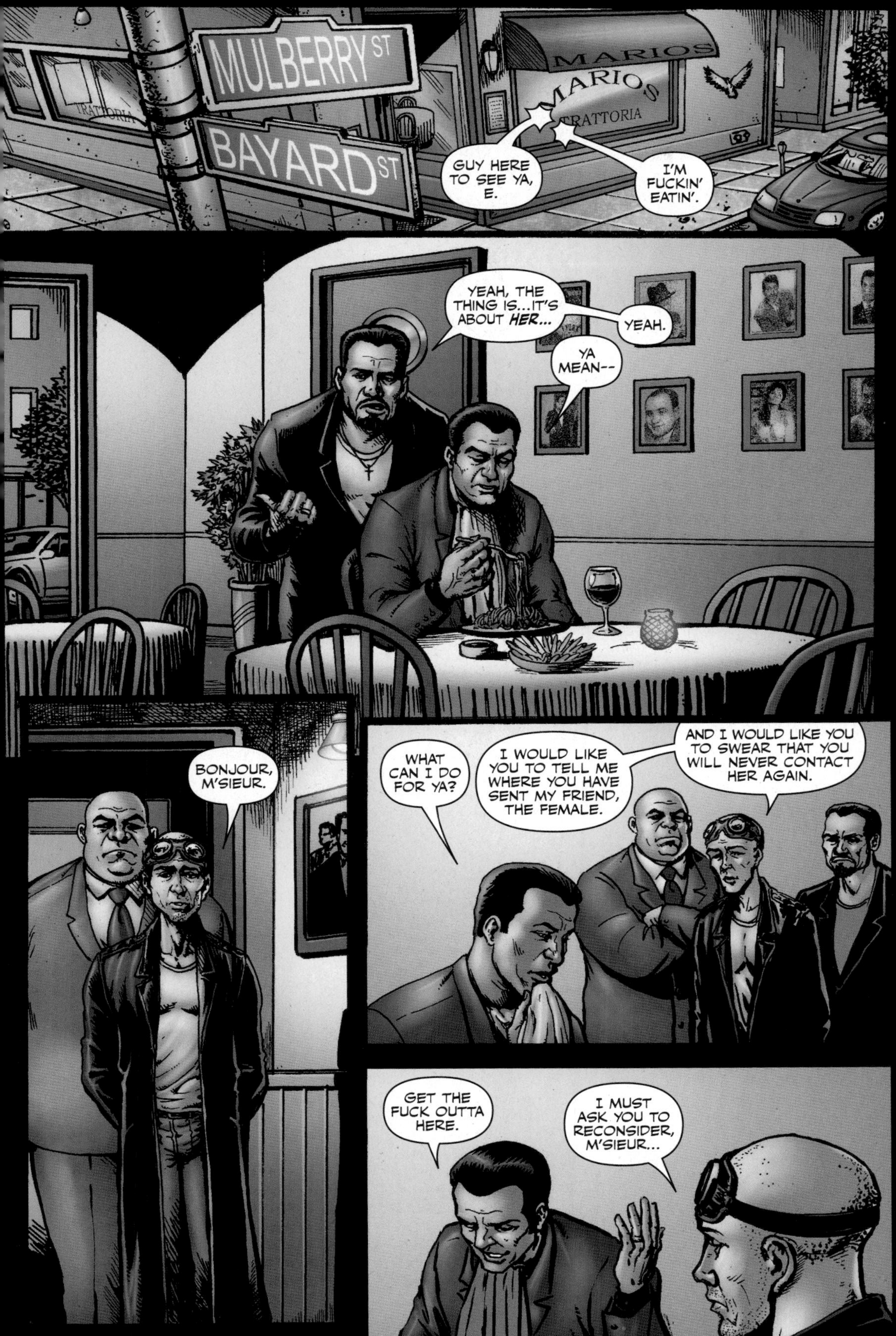
MULBERRY ST
BAYARD ST
MARIOS
MARIOS TRATTORIA
TRATTORIA
GUY HERE TO SEE YA, E.
I'M FUCKIN' EATIN'.
YEAH, THE THING IS...IT'S ABOUT *HER*...
YEAH.
YA MEAN--
BONJOUR, M'SIEUR.
WHAT CAN I DO FOR YA?
I WOULD LIKE YOU TO TELL ME WHERE YOU HAVE SENT MY FRIEND, THE FEMALE.
AND I WOULD LIKE YOU TO SWEAR THAT YOU WILL NEVER CONTACT HER AGAIN.
GET THE FUCK OUTTA HERE.
I MUST ASK YOU TO RECONSIDER, M'SIEUR...

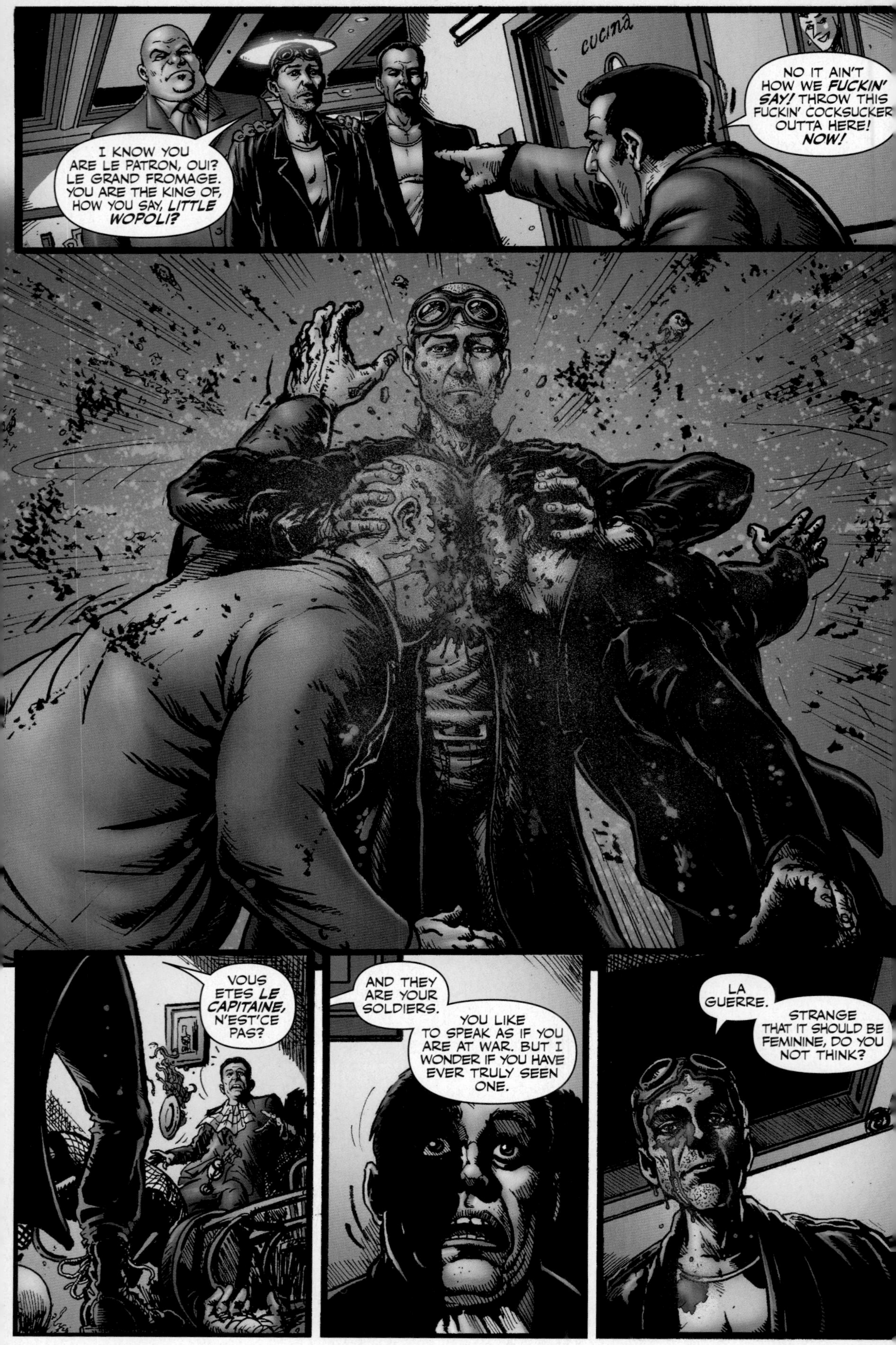
I KNOW YOU ARE LE PATRON, OUI? LE GRAND FROMAGE. YOU ARE THE KING OF, HOW YOU SAY, LITTLE WOPOLI?
NO IT AIN'T HOW WE FUCKIN' SAY! THROW THIS FUCKIN' COCKSUCKER OUTTA HERE! NOW!
cucina
VOUS ETES LE CAPITAINE, N'EST'CE PAS?
AND THEY ARE YOUR SOLDIERS.
YOU LIKE TO SPEAK AS IF YOU ARE AT WAR. BUT I WONDER IF YOU HAVE EVER TRULY SEEN ONE.
LA GUERRE.
STRANGE THAT IT SHOULD BE FEMININE, DO YOU NOT THINK?

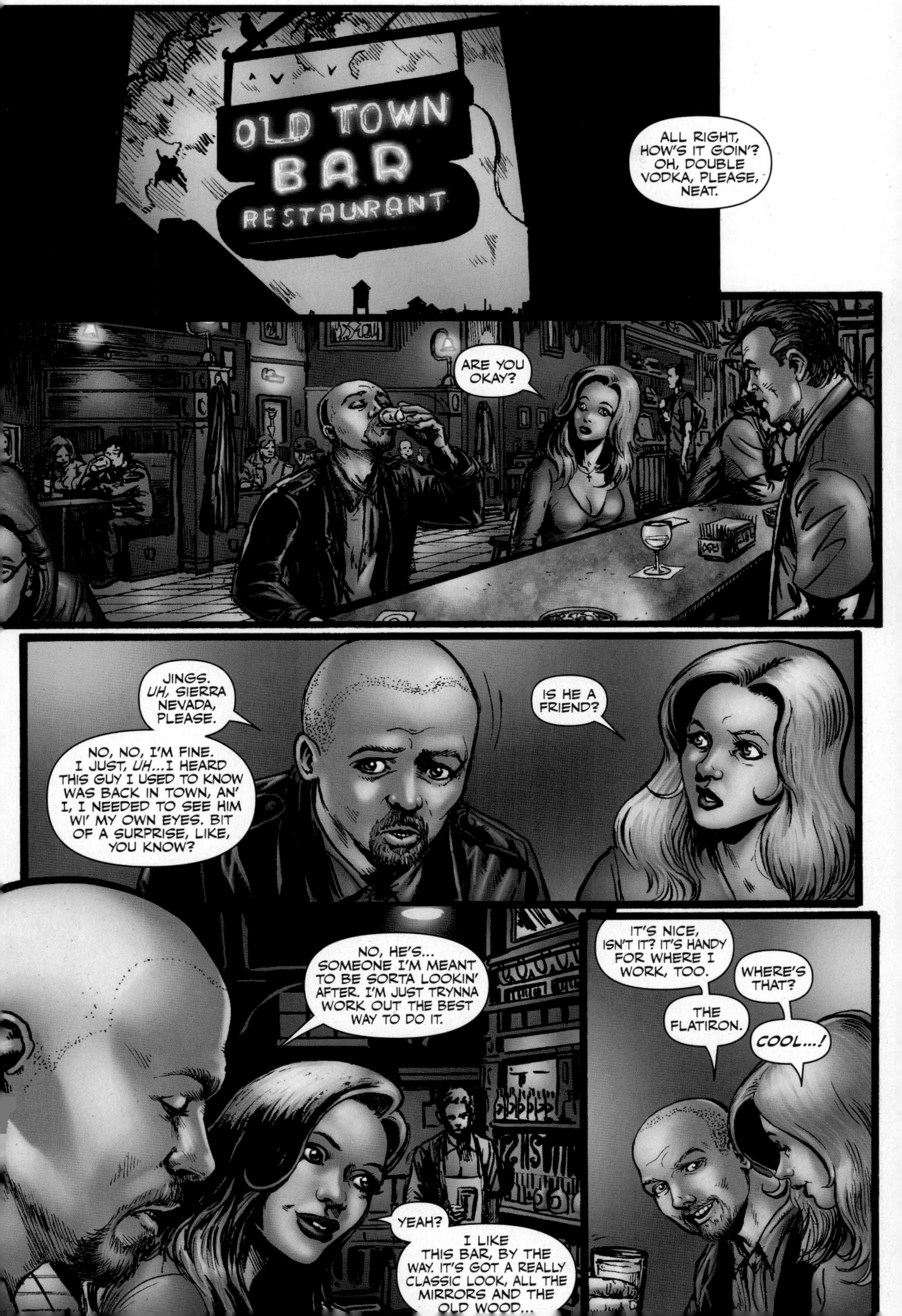
OLD TOWN BAR RESTAURANT
ALL RIGHT, HOW'S IT GOIN'? OH, DOUBLE VODKA, PLEASE, NEAT.
ARE YOU OKAY?
JINGS. UH, SIERRA NEVADA, PLEASE.
NO, NO, I'M FINE. I JUST, UH... I HEARD THIS GUY I USED TO KNOW WAS BACK IN TOWN, AN' I, I NEEDED TO SEE HIM WI' MY OWN EYES. BIT OF A SURPRISE, LIKE, YOU KNOW?
IS HE A FRIEND?
NO, HE'S... SOMEONE I'M MEANT TO BE SORTA LOOKIN' AFTER. I'M JUST TRYNNA WORK OUT THE BEST WAY TO DO IT.
YEAH?
I LIKE THIS BAR, BY THE WAY. IT'S GOT A REALLY CLASSIC LOOK, ALL THE MIRRORS AND THE OLD WOOD...
IT'S NICE, ISN'T IT? IT'S HANDY FOR WHERE I WORK, TOO.
WHERE'S THAT?
THE FLATIRON.
COOL...!

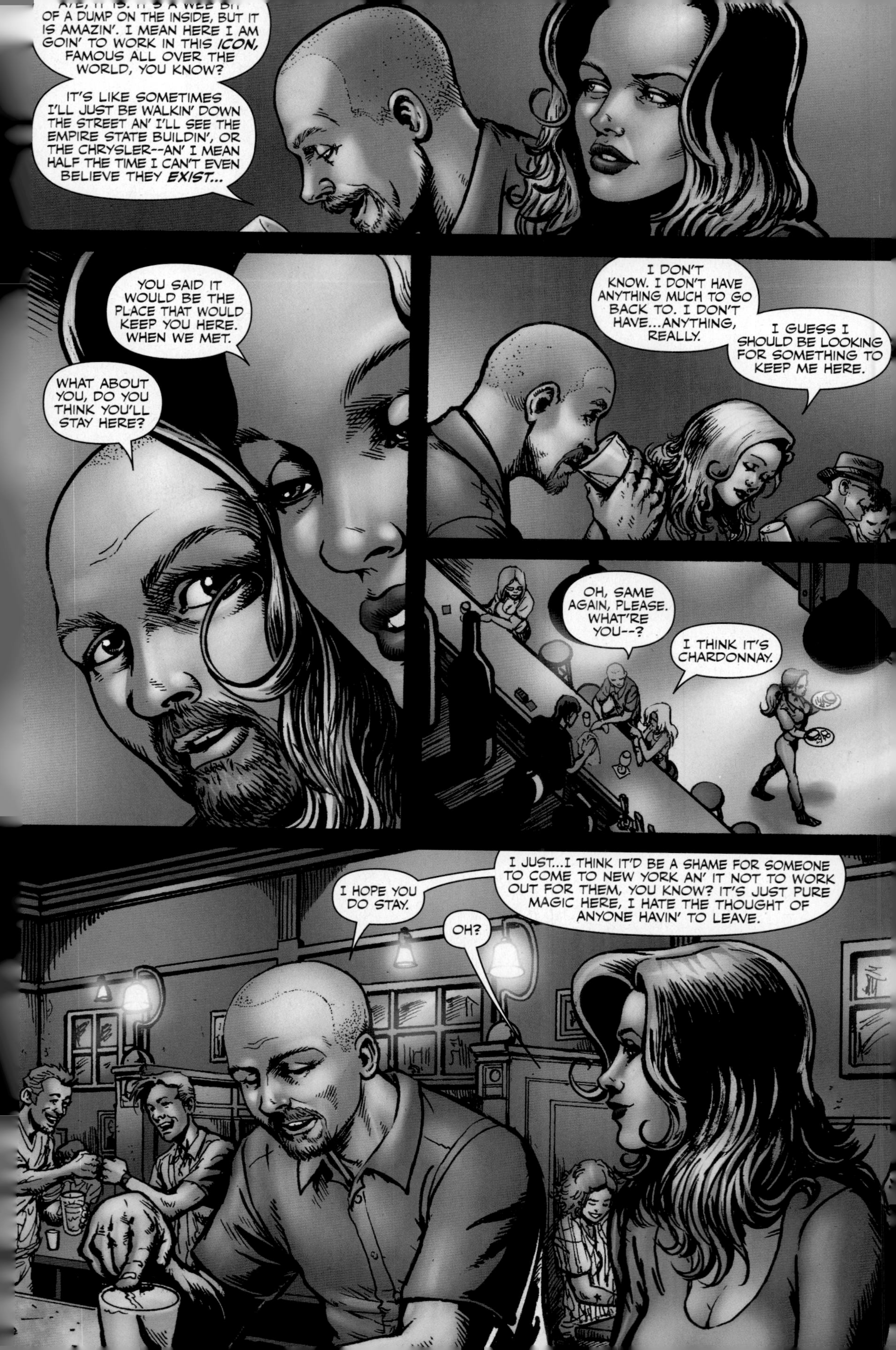
OF A DUMP ON THE INSIDE, BUT IT IS AMAZIN'. I MEAN HERE I AM GOIN' TO WORK IN THIS *ICON*, FAMOUS ALL OVER THE WORLD, YOU KNOW?
IT'S LIKE SOMETIMES I'LL JUST BE WALKIN' DOWN THE STREET AN' I'LL SEE THE EMPIRE STATE BUILDIN', OR THE CHRYSLER--AN' I MEAN HALF THE TIME I CAN'T EVEN BELIEVE THEY ***EXIST...***
YOU SAID IT WOULD BE THE PLACE THAT WOULD KEEP YOU HERE. WHEN WE MET.
WHAT ABOUT YOU, DO YOU THINK YOU'LL STAY HERE?
I DON'T KNOW. I DON'T HAVE ANYTHING MUCH TO GO BACK TO. I DON'T HAVE...ANYTHING, REALLY.
I GUESS I SHOULD BE LOOKING FOR SOMETHING TO KEEP ME HERE.
OH, SAME AGAIN, PLEASE. WHAT'RE YOU--?
I THINK IT'S CHARDONNAY.
I HOPE YOU DO STAY.
I JUST...I THINK IT'D BE A SHAME FOR SOMEONE TO COME TO NEW YORK AN' IT NOT TO WORK OUT FOR THEM, YOU KNOW? IT'S JUST PURE MAGIC HERE, I HATE THE THOUGHT OF ANYONE HAVIN' TO LEAVE.
OH?

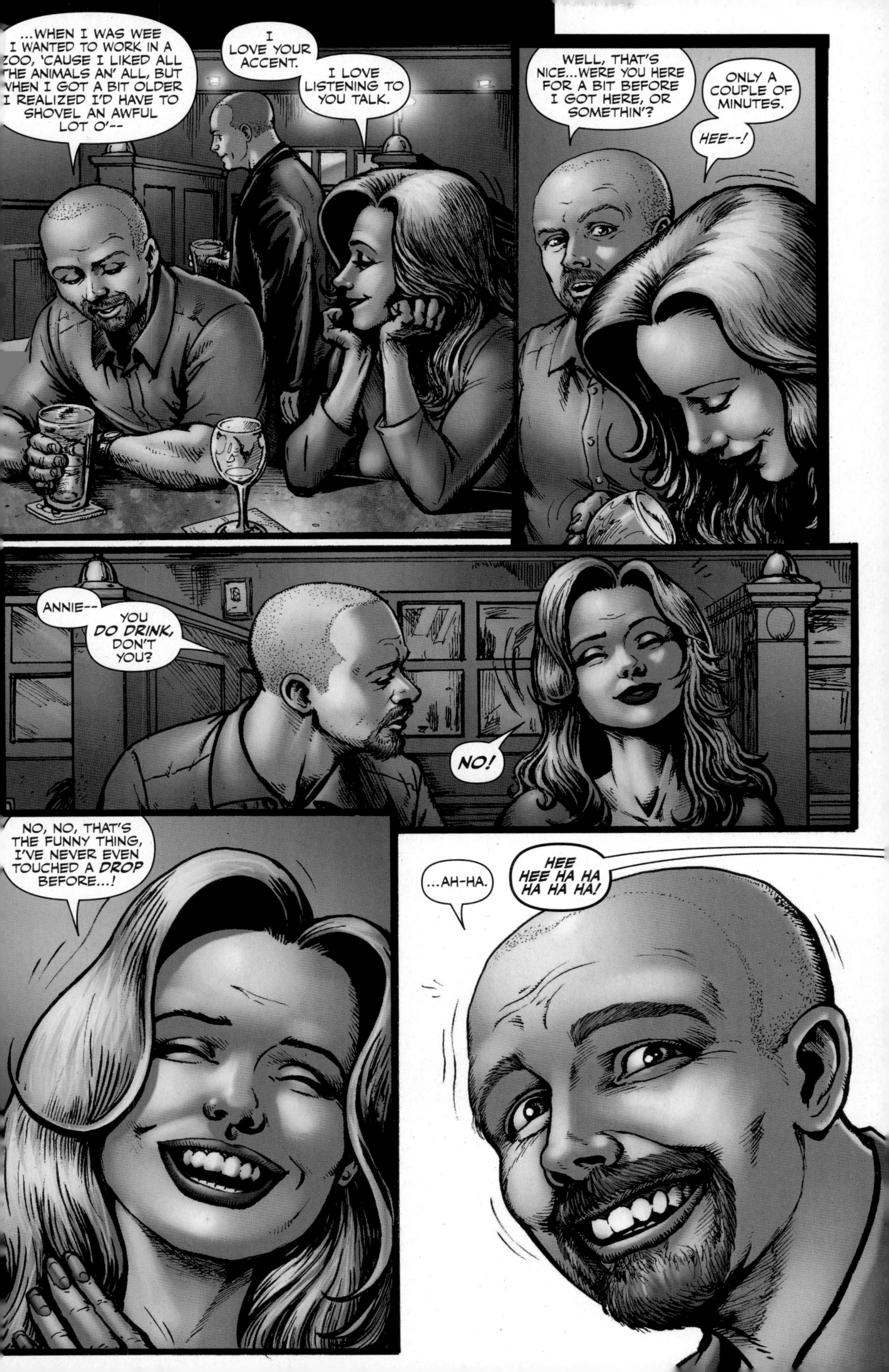
...WHEN I WAS WEE I WANTED TO WORK IN A ZOO, 'CAUSE I LIKED ALL THE ANIMALS AN' ALL, BUT WHEN I GOT A BIT OLDER I REALIZED I'D HAVE TO SHOVEL AN AWFUL LOT O'--
I LOVE YOUR ACCENT.
I LOVE LISTENING TO YOU TALK.
WELL, THAT'S NICE...WERE YOU HERE FOR A BIT BEFORE I GOT HERE, OR SOMETHIN'?
ONLY A COUPLE OF MINUTES.
HEE--!
ANNIE--
YOU DO DRINK, DON'T YOU?
NO!
NO, NO, THAT'S THE FUNNY THING, I'VE NEVER EVEN TOUCHED A DROP BEFORE...!
...AH-HA.
HEE HEE HA HA HA HA HA!

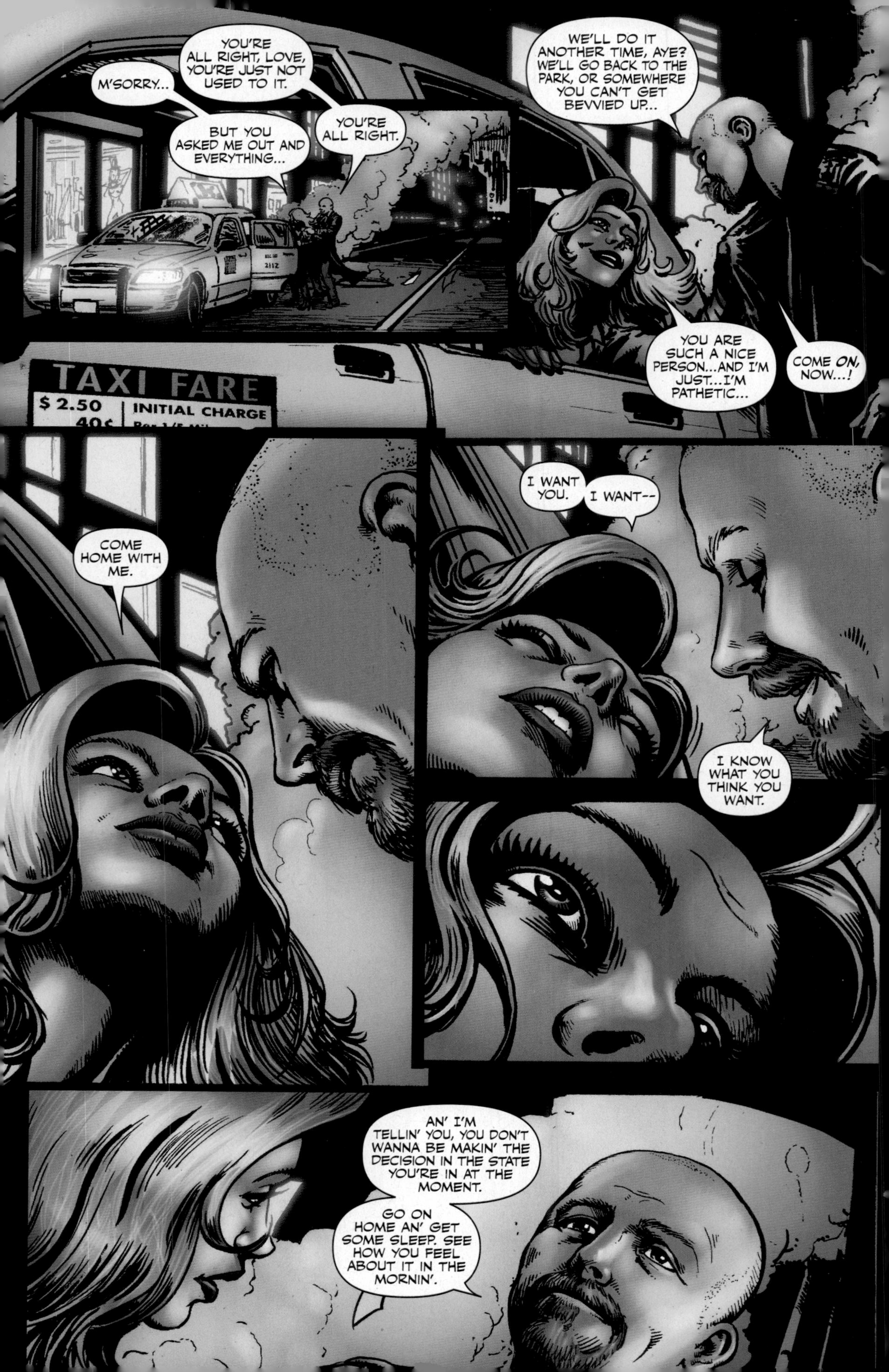
M'SORRY...
YOU'RE ALL RIGHT, LOVE, YOU'RE JUST NOT USED TO IT.
BUT YOU ASKED ME OUT AND EVERYTHING...
YOU'RE ALL RIGHT.
WE'LL DO IT ANOTHER TIME, AYE? WE'LL GO BACK TO THE PARK, OR SOMEWHERE YOU CAN'T GET BEVVIED UP...
YOU ARE SUCH A NICE PERSON...AND I'M JUST...I'M PATHETIC...
COME ON, NOW...!
TAXI FARE
$ 2.50 INITIAL CHARGE
COME HOME WITH ME.
I WANT YOU.
I WANT--
I KNOW WHAT YOU THINK YOU WANT.
AN' I'M TELLIN' YOU, YOU DON'T WANNA BE MAKIN' THE DECISION IN THE STATE YOU'RE IN AT THE MOMENT.
GO ON HOME AN' GET SOME SLEEP. SEE HOW YOU FEEL ABOUT IT IN THE MORNIN'.

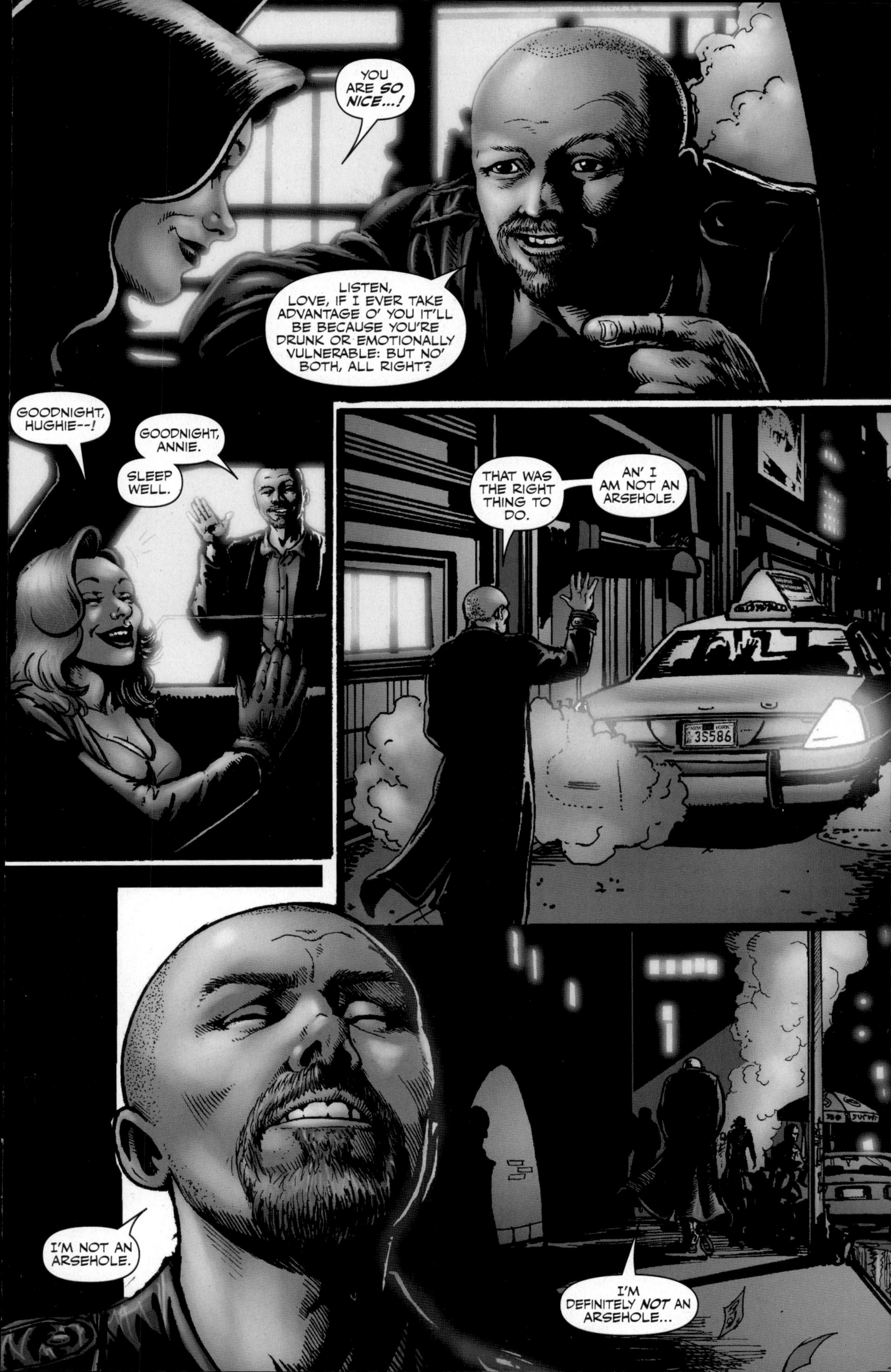
YOU ARE SO NICE...!
LISTEN, LOVE, IF I EVER TAKE ADVANTAGE O' YOU IT'LL BE BECAUSE YOU'RE DRUNK OR EMOTIONALLY VULNERABLE: BUT NO' BOTH, ALL RIGHT?
GOODNIGHT, HUGHIE--!
GOODNIGHT, ANNIE.
SLEEP WELL.
THAT WAS THE RIGHT THING TO DO.
AN' I AM NOT AN ARSEHOLE.
NEW YORK
3S586
I'M NOT AN ARSEHOLE.
I'M DEFINITELY NOT AN ARSEHOLE...

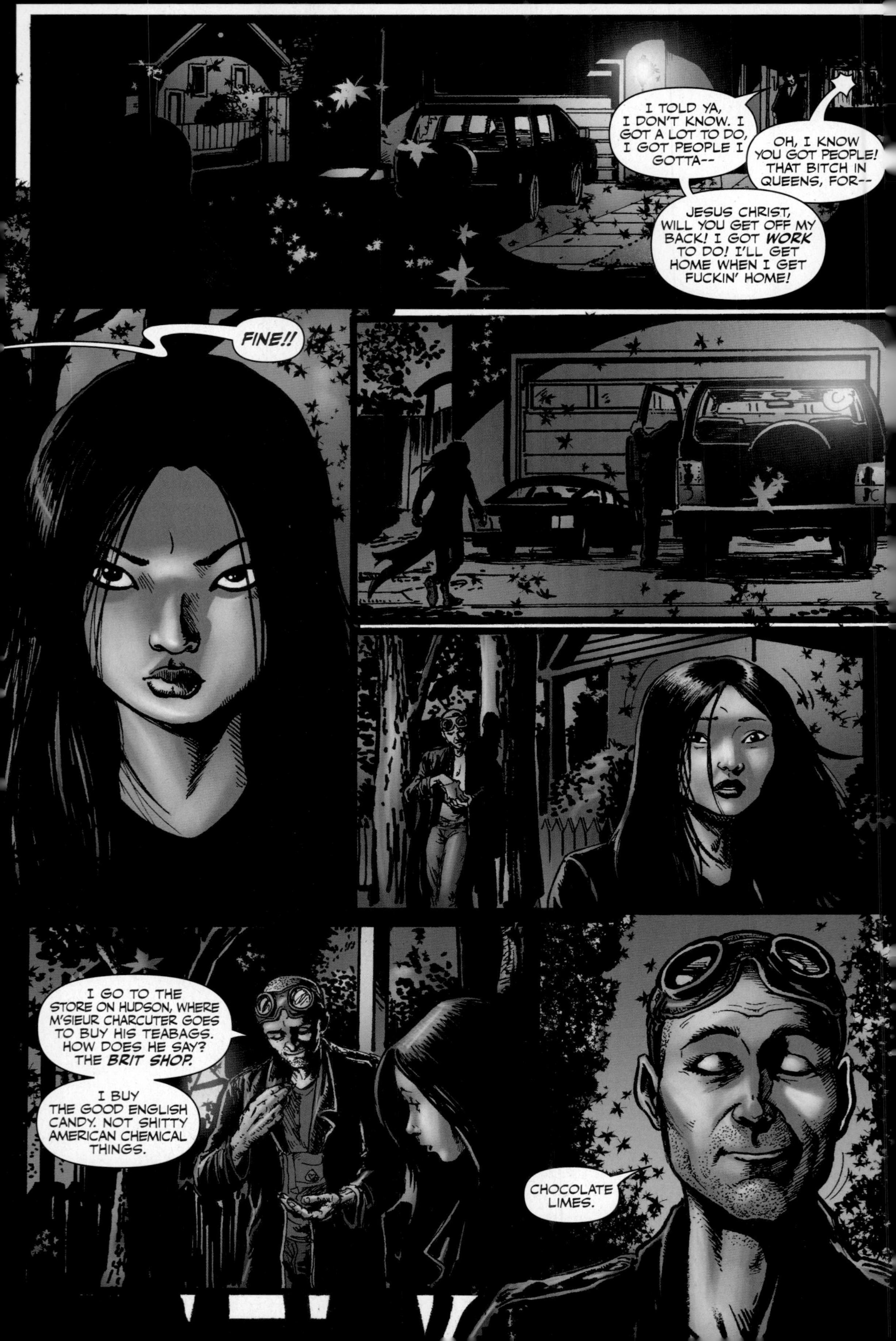
I TOLD YA, I DON'T KNOW. I GOT A LOT TO DO, I GOT PEOPLE I GOTTA--
OH, I KNOW YOU GOT PEOPLE! THAT BITCH IN QUEENS, FOR--
JESUS CHRIST, WILL YOU GET OFF MY BACK! I GOT WORK TO DO! I'LL GET HOME WHEN I GET FUCKIN' HOME!
FINE!!
I GO TO THE STORE ON HUDSON, WHERE M'SIEUR CHARCUTER GOES TO BUY HIS TEABAGS. HOW DOES HE SAY? THE BRIT SHOP.
I BUY THE GOOD ENGLISH CANDY. NOT SHITTY AMERICAN CHEMICAL THINGS.
CHOCOLATE LIMES.

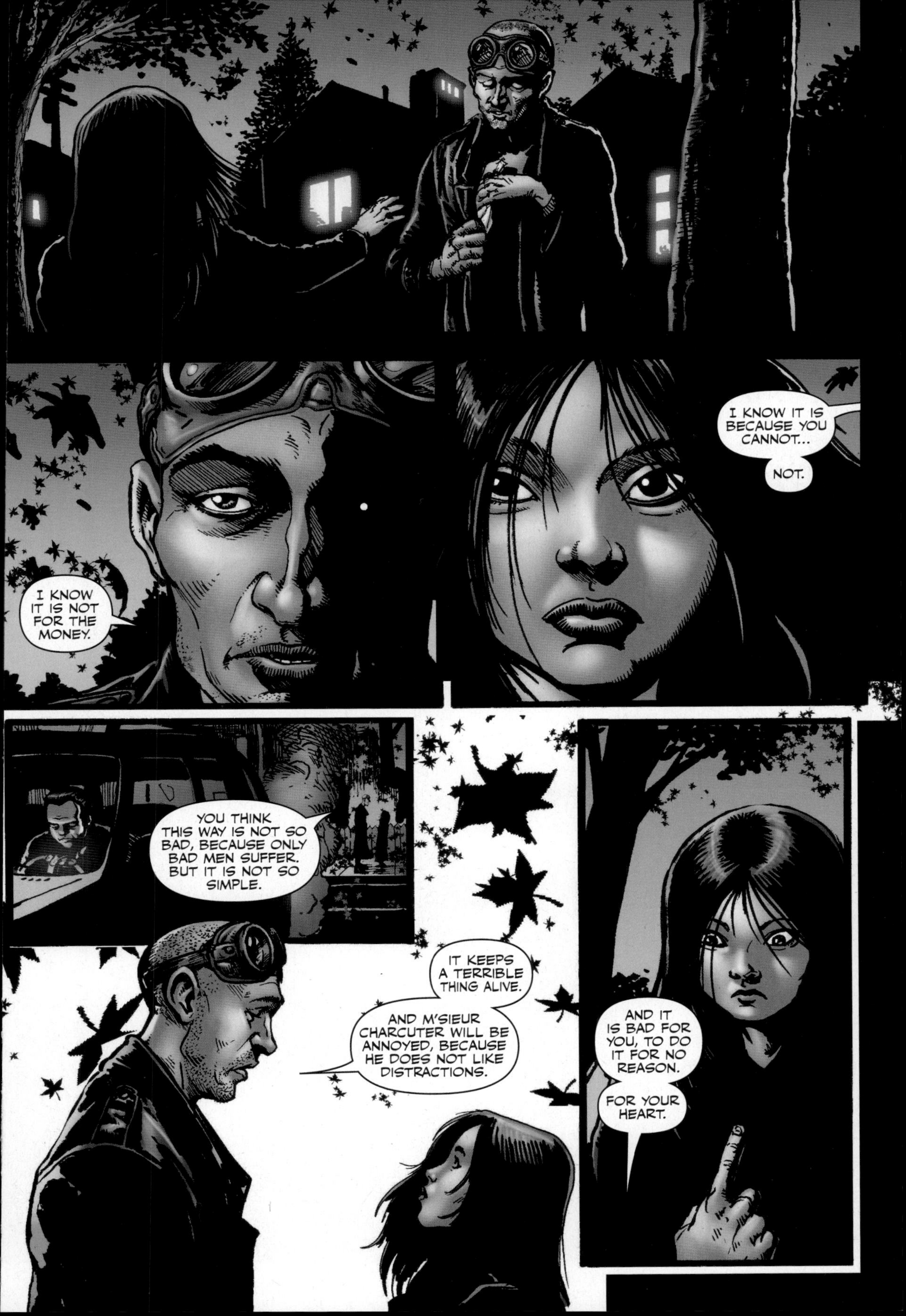
I KNOW IT IS NOT FOR THE MONEY.
I KNOW IT IS BECAUSE YOU CANNOT...
NOT.
YOU THINK THIS WAY IS NOT SO BAD, BECAUSE ONLY BAD MEN SUFFER. BUT IT IS NOT SO SIMPLE.
IT KEEPS A TERRIBLE THING ALIVE.
AND M'SIEUR CHARCUTER WILL BE ANNOYED, BECAUSE HE DOES NOT LIKE DISTRACTIONS.
AND IT IS BAD FOR YOU, TO DO IT FOR NO REASON.
FOR YOUR HEART.

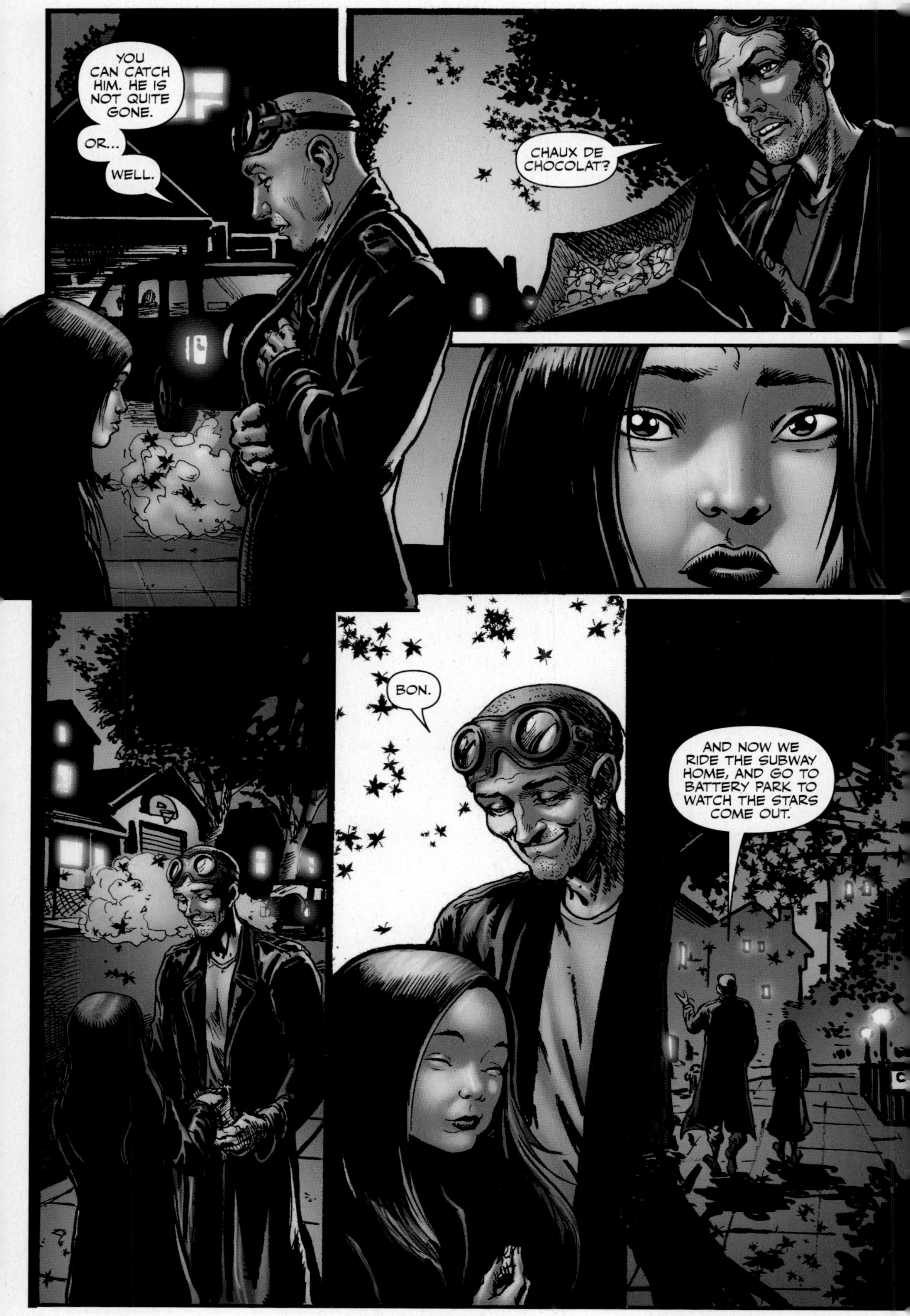
YOU CAN CATCH HIM. HE IS NOT QUITE GONE.
OR...
WELL.
CHAUX DE CHOCOLAT?
BON.
AND NOW WE RIDE THE SUBWAY HOME, AND GO TO BATTERY PARK TO WATCH THE STARS COME OUT.

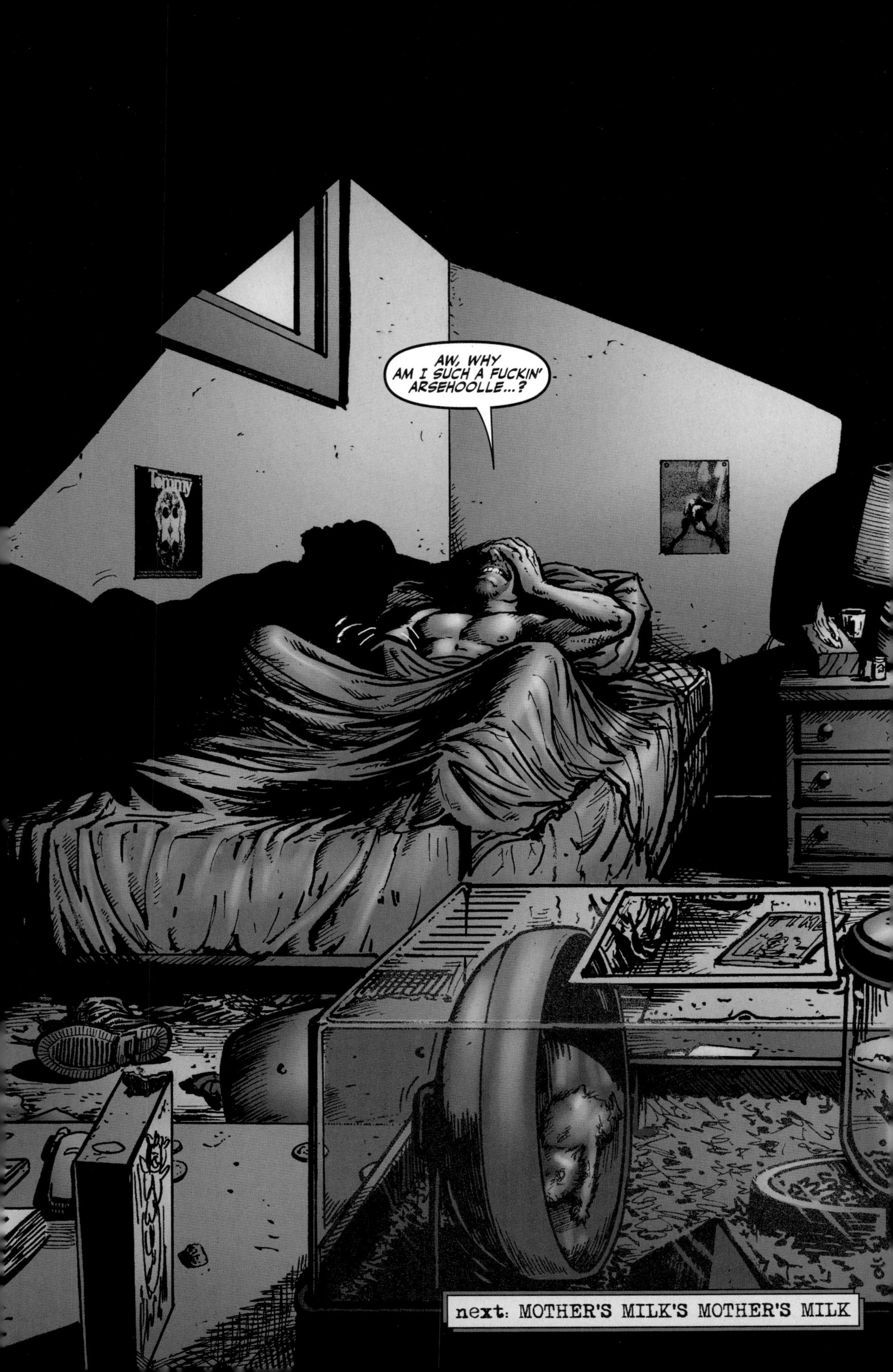
AW, WHY AM I SUCH A FUCKIN' ARSEHOOLLE...?
Tommy
next: MOTHER'S MILK'S MOTHER'S MILK

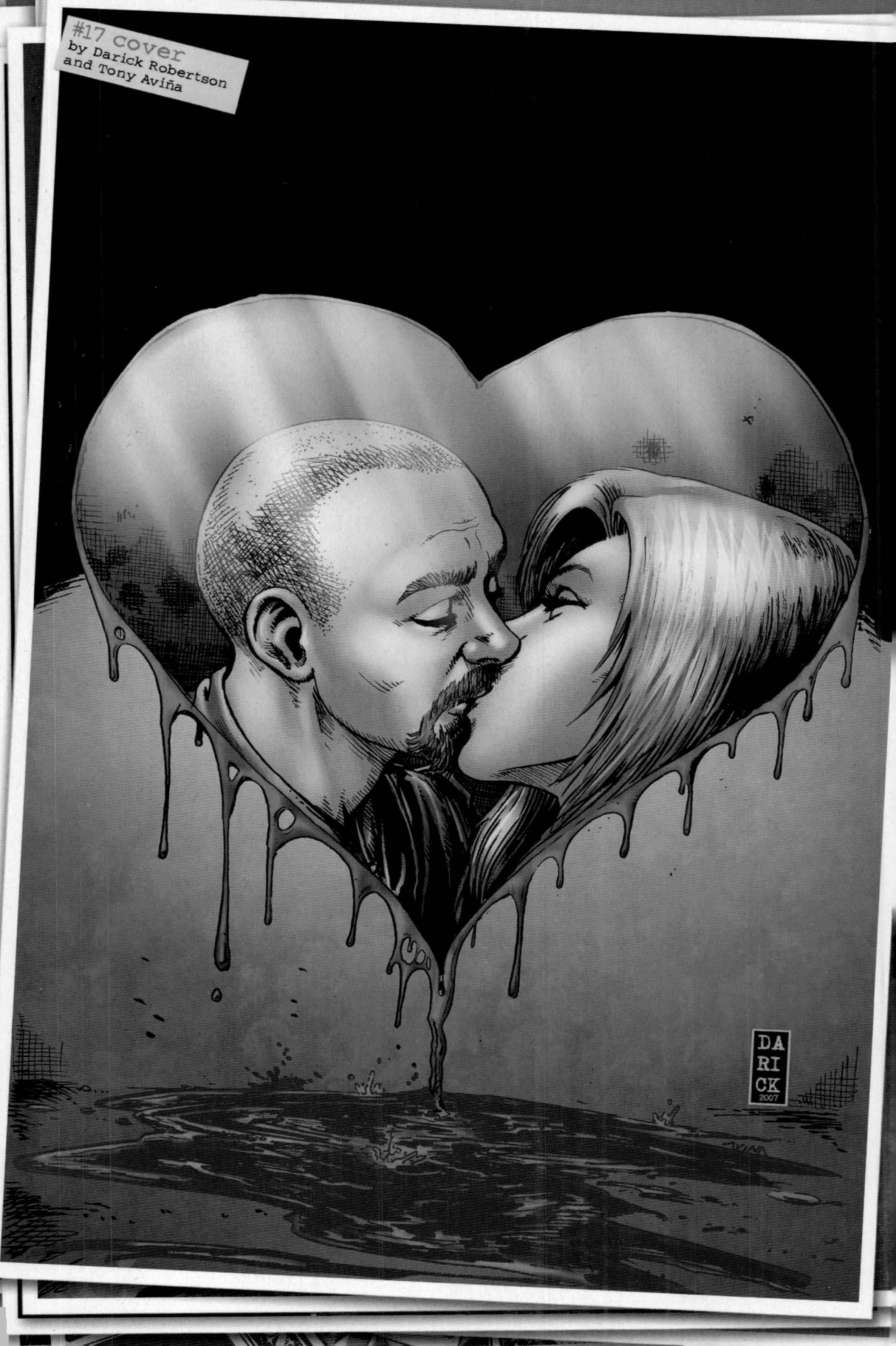

#17 cover
by Darick Robertson
and Tony Aviña

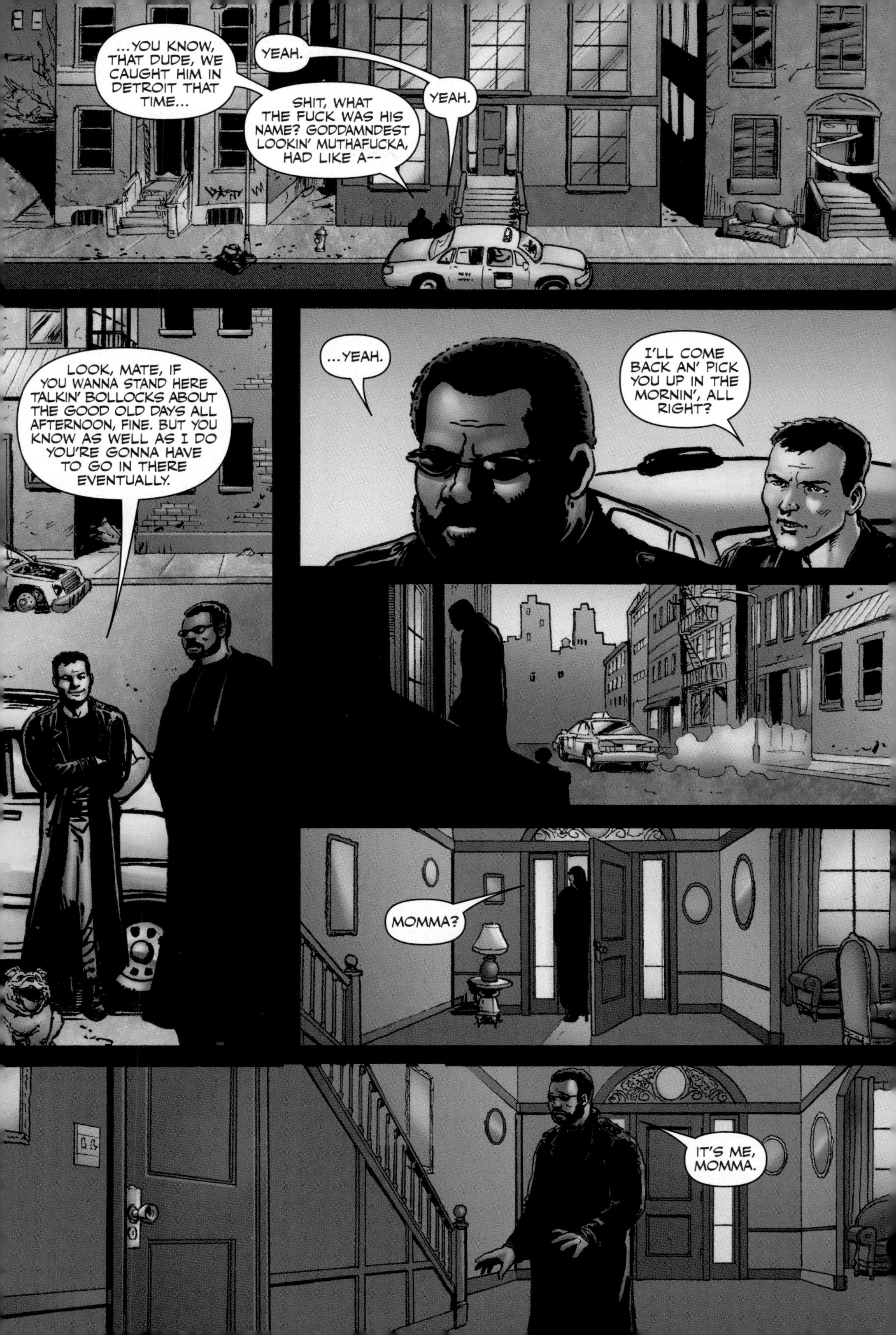
...YOU KNOW, THAT DUDE, WE CAUGHT HIM IN DETROIT THAT TIME...
YEAH.
SHIT, WHAT THE FUCK WAS HIS NAME? GODDAMNDEST LOOKIN' MUTHAFUCKA, HAD LIKE A--
YEAH.
LOOK, MATE, IF YOU WANNA STAND HERE TALKIN' BOLLOCKS ABOUT THE GOOD OLD DAYS ALL AFTERNOON, FINE. BUT YOU KNOW AS WELL AS I DO YOU'RE GONNA HAVE TO GO IN THERE EVENTUALLY.
...YEAH.
I'LL COME BACK AN' PICK YOU UP IN THE MORNIN', ALL RIGHT?
MOMMA?
IT'S ME, MOMMA.

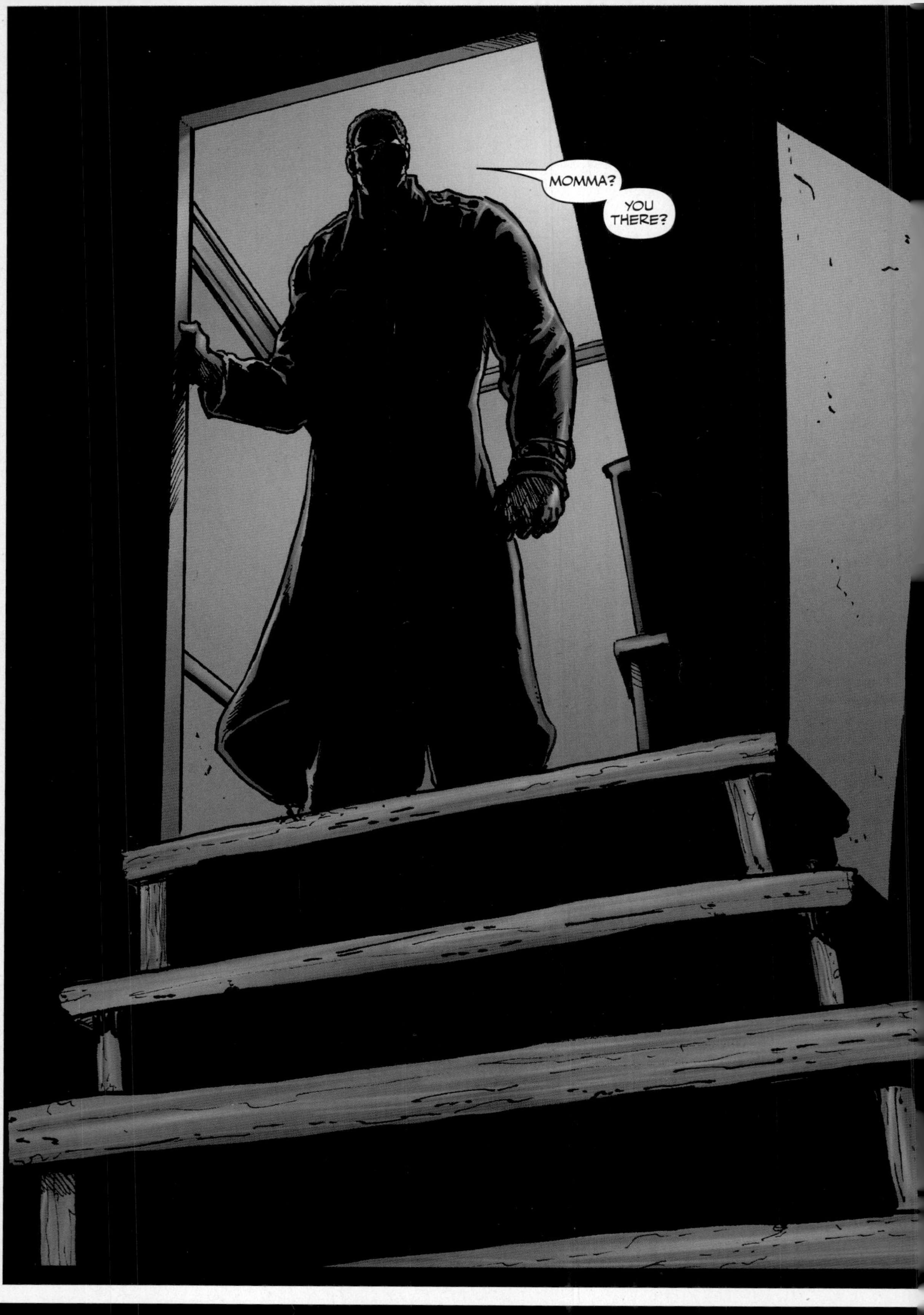
MOMMA?
YOU THERE?

GOOD FOR THE SOUL part three

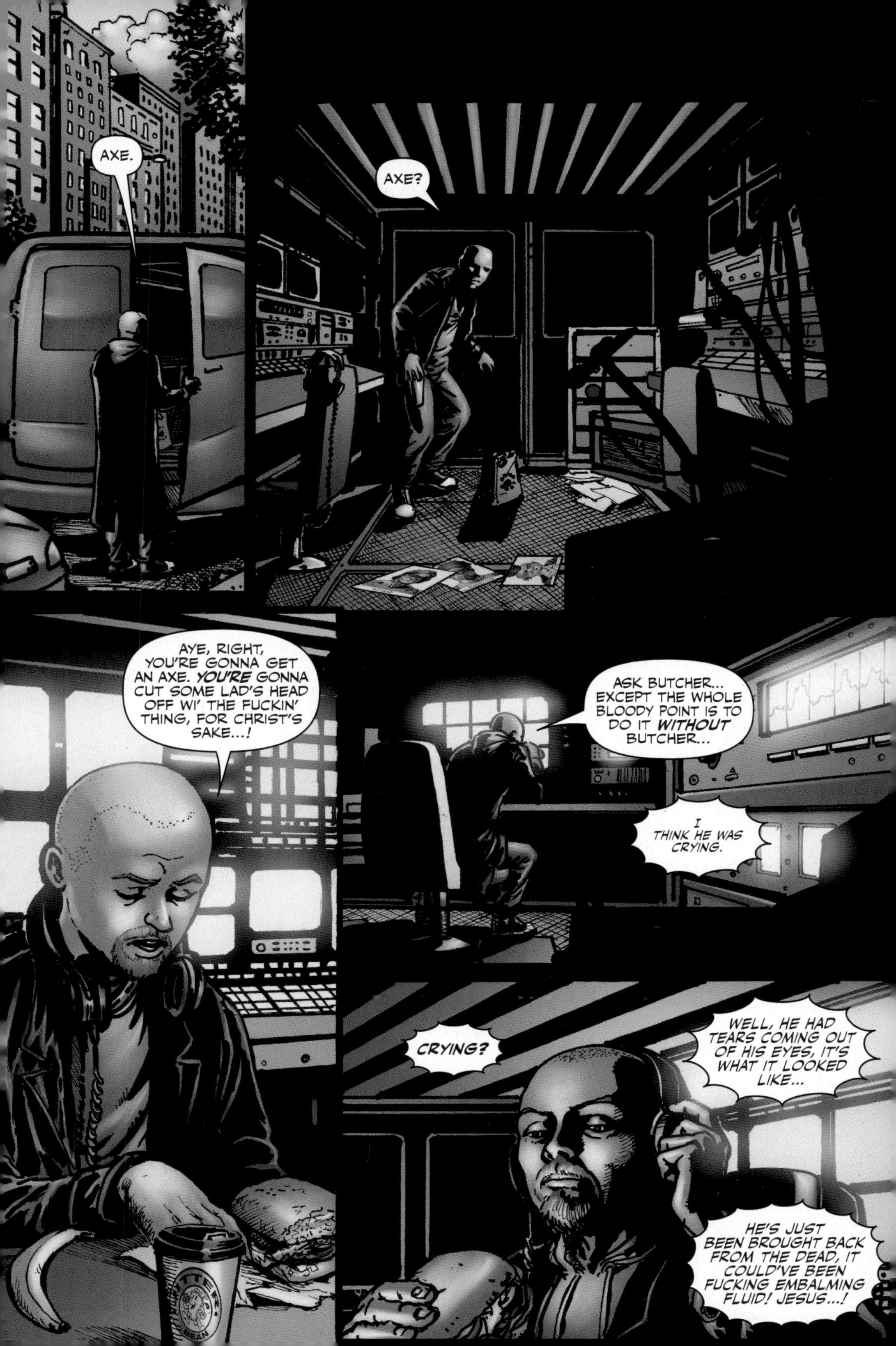
AXE.
AXE?
AYE, RIGHT, YOU'RE GONNA GET AN AXE. YOU'RE GONNA CUT SOME LAD'S HEAD OFF WI' THE FUCKIN' THING, FOR CHRIST'S SAKE...!
ASK BUTCHER... EXCEPT THE WHOLE BLOODY POINT IS TO DO IT WITHOUT BUTCHER...
I THINK HE WAS CRYING.
CRYING?
WELL, HE HAD TEARS COMING OUT OF HIS EYES, IT'S WHAT IT LOOKED LIKE...
HE'S JUST BEEN BROUGHT BACK FROM THE DEAD, IT COULD'VE BEEN FUCKING EMBALMING FLUID! JESUS...!

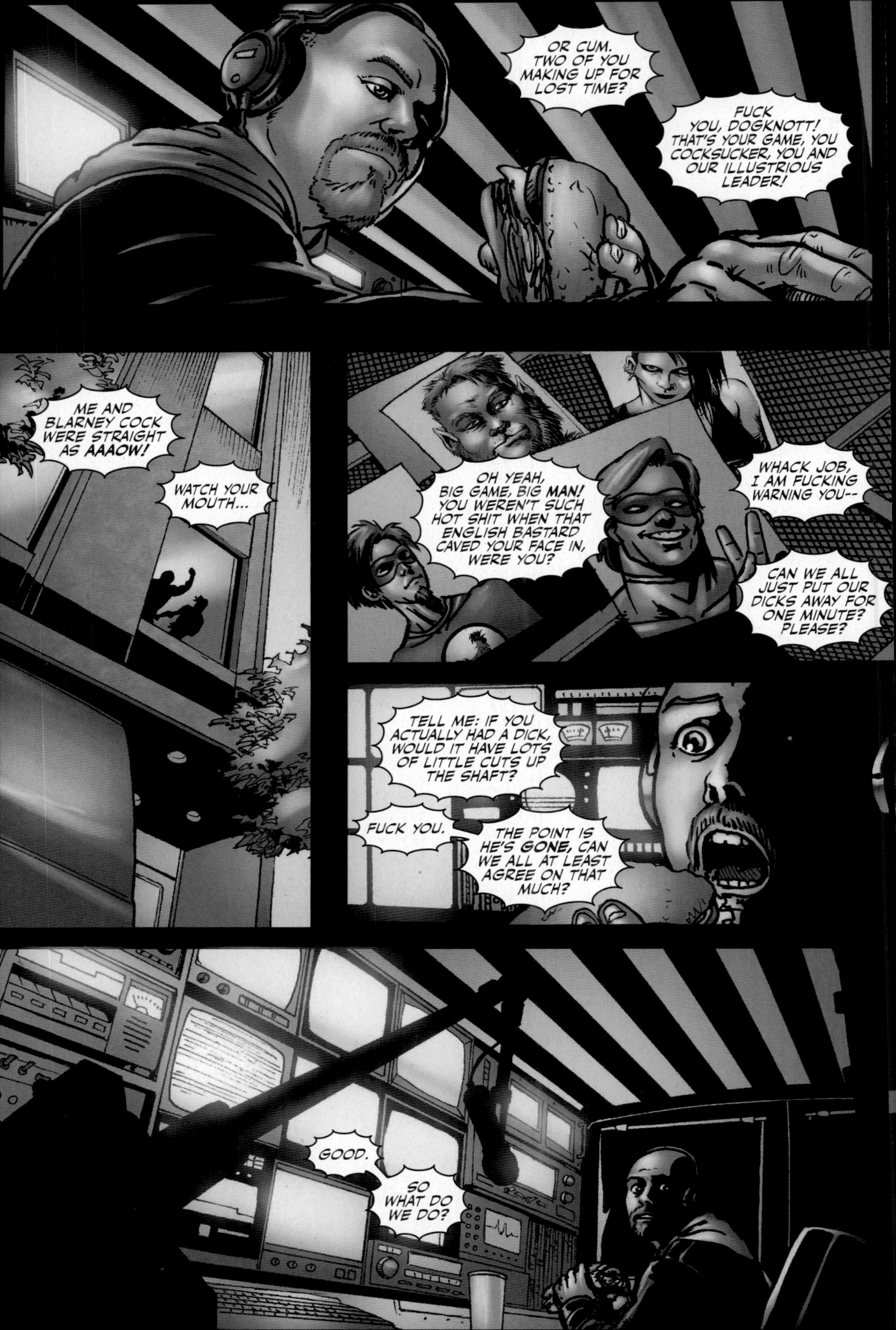
OR CUM. TWO OF YOU MAKING UP FOR LOST TIME?
FUCK YOU, DOGKNOTT! THAT'S YOUR GAME, YOU COCKSUCKER, YOU AND OUR ILLUSTRIOUS LEADER!
ME AND BLARNEY COCK WERE STRAIGHT AS AAAOW!
WATCH YOUR MOUTH...
OH YEAH, BIG GAME, BIG MAN! YOU WEREN'T SUCH HOT SHIT WHEN THAT ENGLISH BASTARD CAVED YOUR FACE IN, WERE YOU?
WHACK JOB, I AM FUCKING WARNING YOU--
CAN WE ALL JUST PUT OUR DICKS AWAY FOR ONE MINUTE? PLEASE?
TELL ME: IF YOU ACTUALLY HAD A DICK, WOULD IT HAVE LOTS OF LITTLE CUTS UP THE SHAFT?
FUCK YOU.
THE POINT IS HE'S GONE, CAN WE ALL AT LEAST AGREE ON THAT MUCH?
GOOD.
SO WHAT DO WE DO?

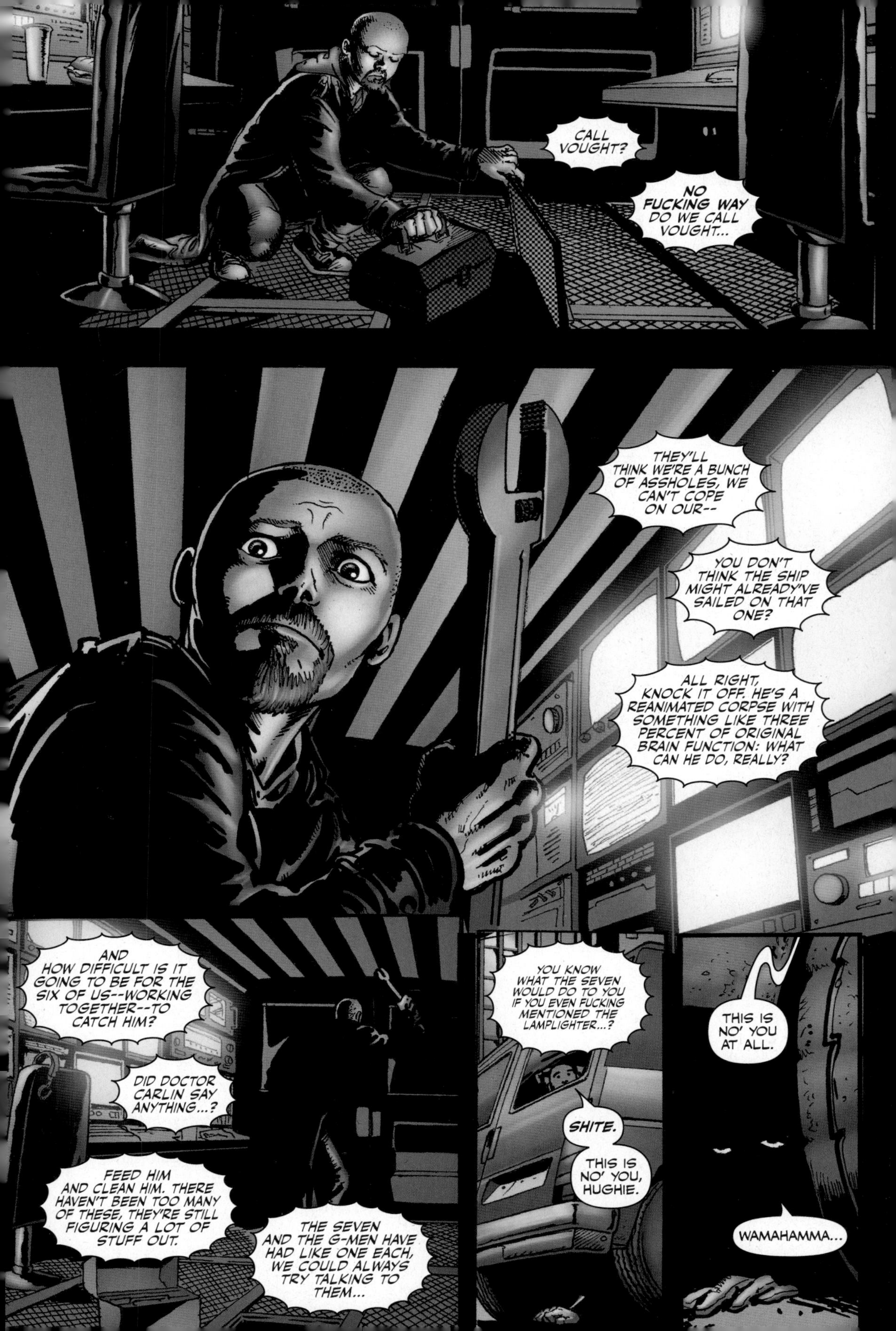
CALL VOUGHT?
NO FUCKING WAY DO WE CALL VOUGHT...
THEY'LL THINK WE'RE A BUNCH OF ASSHOLES, WE CAN'T COPE ON OUR--
YOU DON'T THINK THE SHIP MIGHT ALREADY'VE SAILED ON THAT ONE?
ALL RIGHT, KNOCK IT OFF. HE'S A REANIMATED CORPSE WITH SOMETHING LIKE THREE PERCENT OF ORIGINAL BRAIN FUNCTION: WHAT CAN HE DO, REALLY?
AND HOW DIFFICULT IS IT GOING TO BE FOR THE SIX OF US--WORKING TOGETHER--TO CATCH HIM?
DID DOCTOR CARLIN SAY ANYTHING...?
FEED HIM AND CLEAN HIM. THERE HAVEN'T BEEN TOO MANY OF THESE, THEY'RE STILL FIGURING A LOT OF STUFF OUT.
THE SEVEN AND THE G-MEN HAVE HAD LIKE ONE EACH, WE COULD ALWAYS TRY TALKING TO THEM...
YOU KNOW WHAT THE SEVEN WOULD DO TO YOU IF YOU EVEN FUCKING MENTIONED THE LAMPLIGHTER...?
SHITE.
THIS IS NO' YOU, HUGHIE.
THIS IS NO' YOU AT ALL.
WAMAHAMMA...

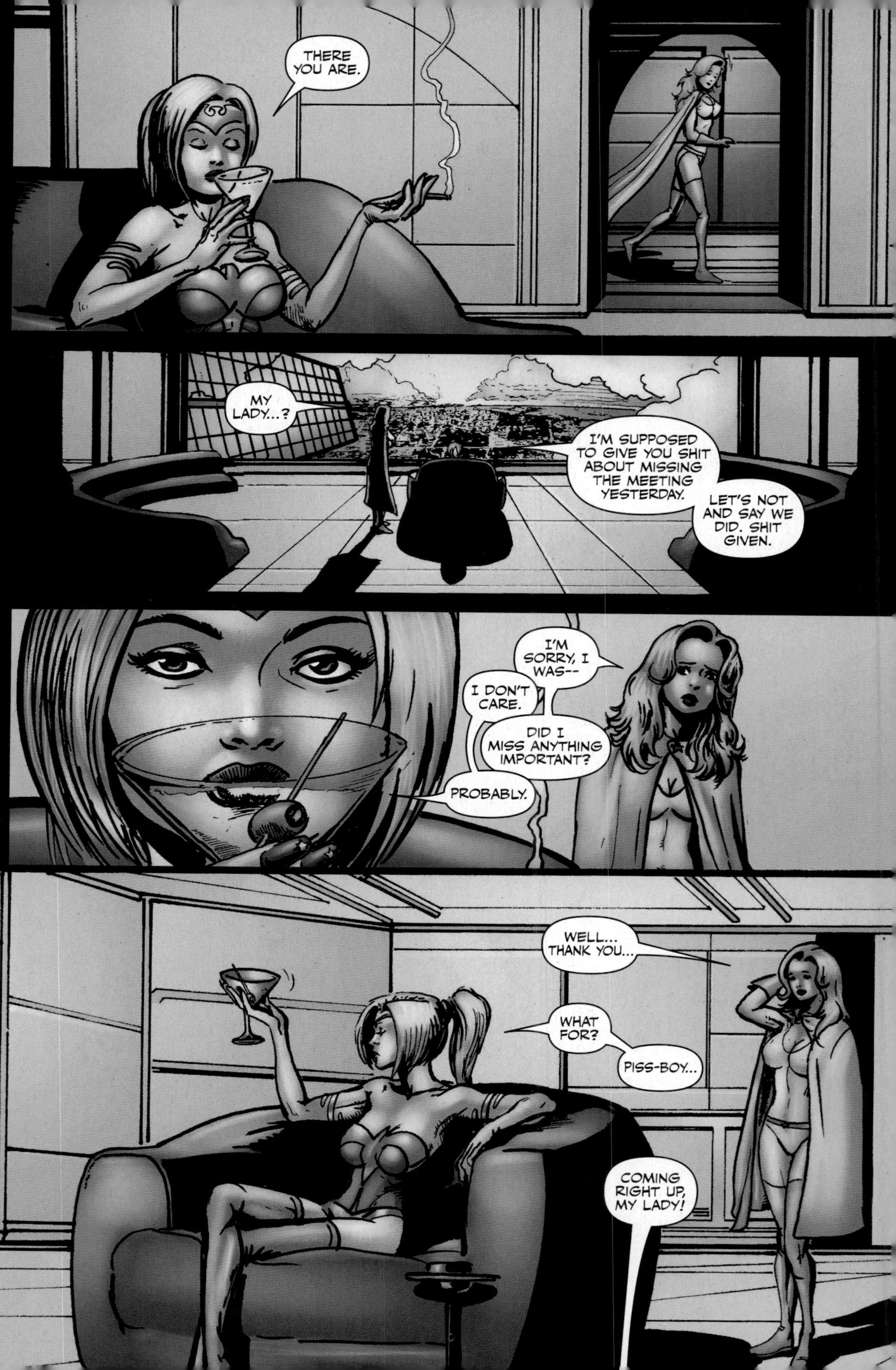
THERE YOU ARE.
MY LADY...?
I'M SUPPOSED TO GIVE YOU SHIT ABOUT MISSING THE MEETING YESTERDAY.
LET'S NOT AND SAY WE DID. SHIT GIVEN.
I'M SORRY, I WAS--
I DON'T CARE.
DID I MISS ANYTHING IMPORTANT?
PROBABLY.
WELL... THANK YOU...
WHAT FOR?
PISS-BOY...
COMING RIGHT UP, MY LADY!

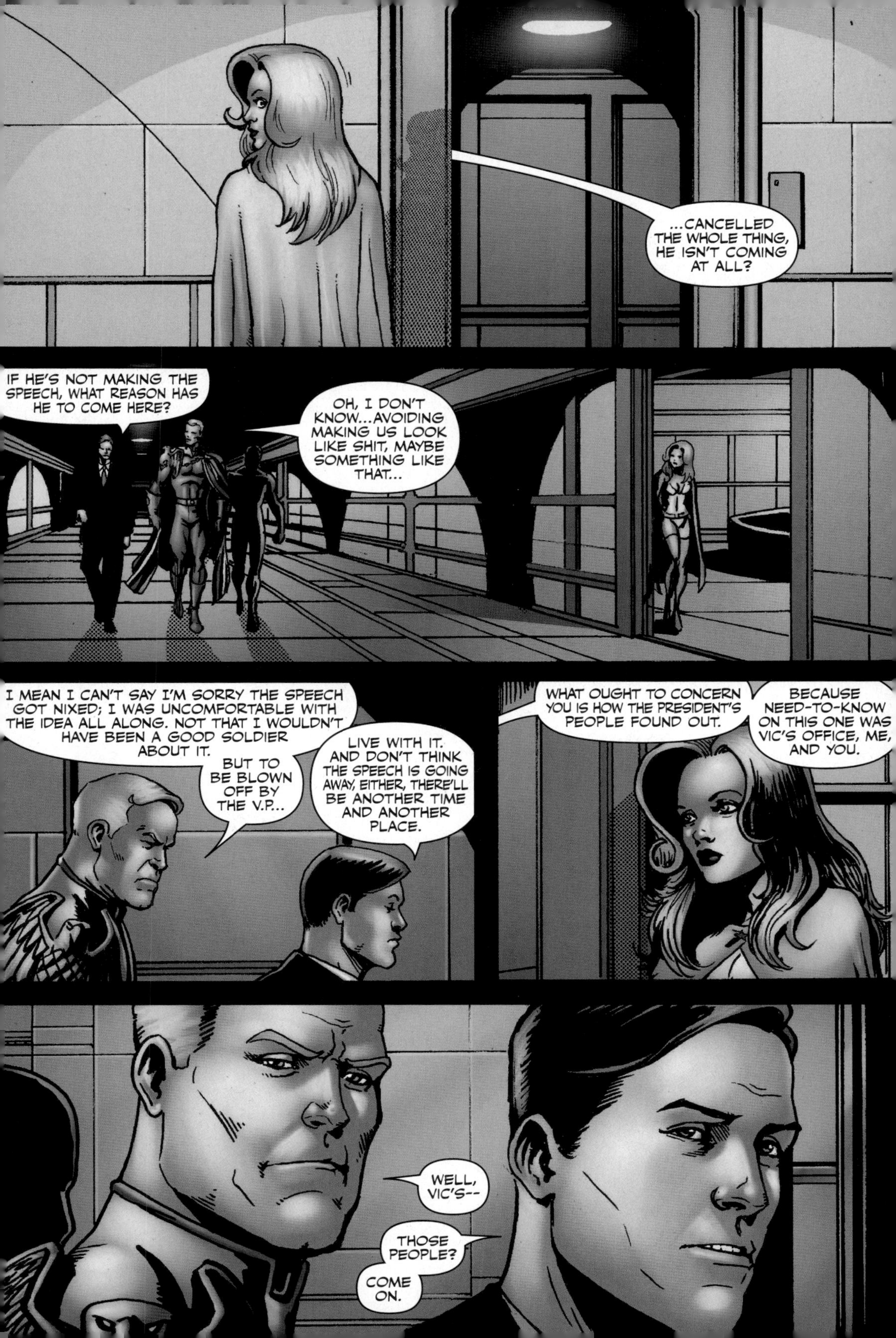
...CANCELLED THE WHOLE THING, HE ISN'T COMING AT ALL?
IF HE'S NOT MAKING THE SPEECH, WHAT REASON HAS HE TO COME HERE?
OH, I DON'T KNOW...AVOIDING MAKING US LOOK LIKE SHIT, MAYBE SOMETHING LIKE THAT...
I MEAN I CAN'T SAY I'M SORRY THE SPEECH GOT NIXED; I WAS UNCOMFORTABLE WITH THE IDEA ALL ALONG. NOT THAT I WOULDN'T HAVE BEEN A GOOD SOLDIER ABOUT IT.
BUT TO BE BLOWN OFF BY THE V.P...
LIVE WITH IT. AND DON'T THINK THE SPEECH IS GOING AWAY, EITHER. THERE'LL BE ANOTHER TIME AND ANOTHER PLACE.
WHAT OUGHT TO CONCERN YOU IS HOW THE PRESIDENT'S PEOPLE FOUND OUT.
BECAUSE NEED-TO-KNOW ON THIS ONE WAS VIC'S OFFICE, ME, AND YOU.
WELL, VIC'S--
THOSE PEOPLE?
COME ON.

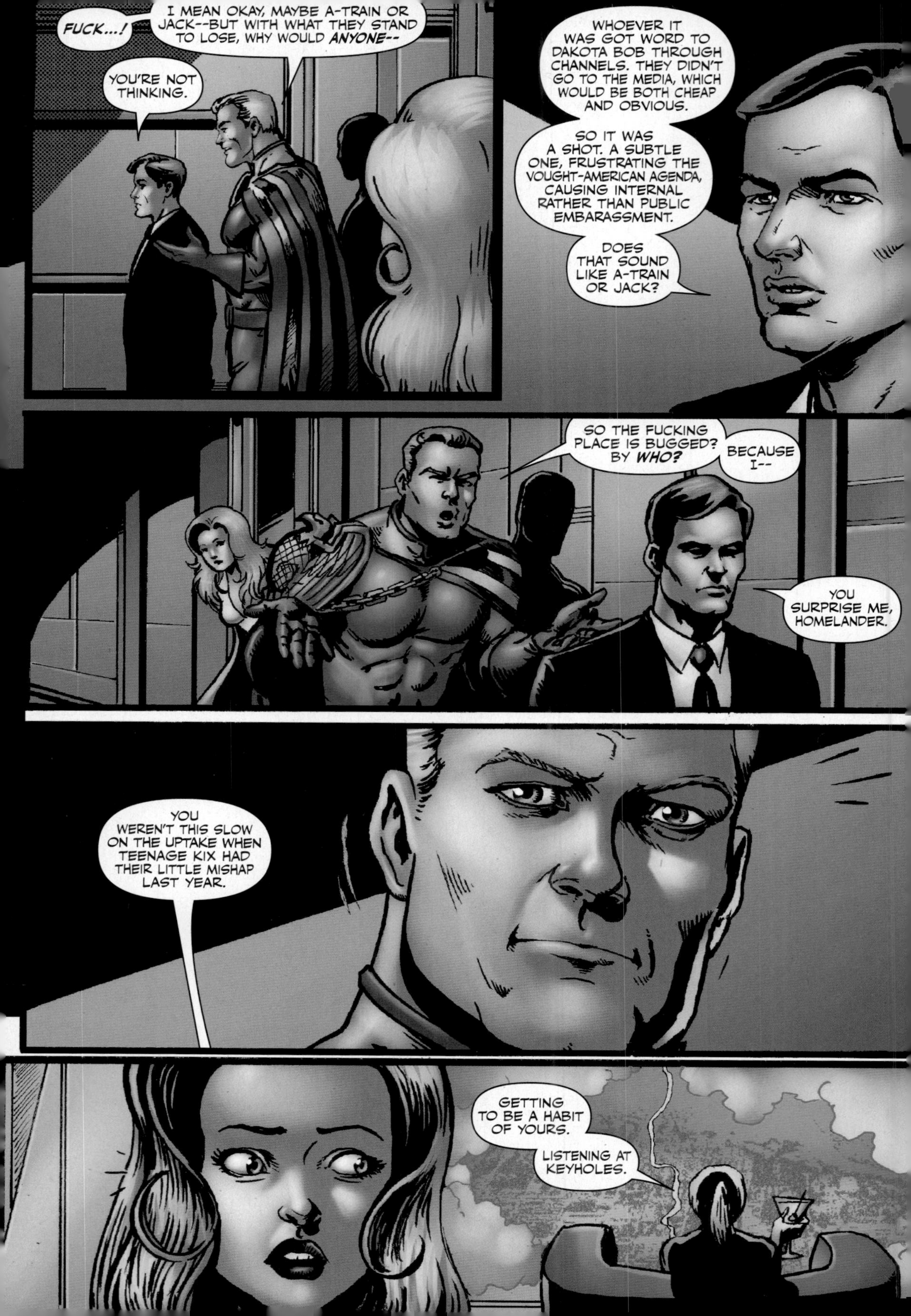
FUCK...!
I MEAN OKAY, MAYBE A-TRAIN OR JACK--BUT WITH WHAT THEY STAND TO LOSE, WHY WOULD ANYONE--
YOU'RE NOT THINKING.
WHOEVER IT WAS GOT WORD TO DAKOTA BOB THROUGH CHANNELS. THEY DIDN'T GO TO THE MEDIA, WHICH WOULD BE BOTH CHEAP AND OBVIOUS.
SO IT WAS A SHOT. A SUBTLE ONE, FRUSTRATING THE VOUGHT-AMERICAN AGENDA, CAUSING INTERNAL RATHER THAN PUBLIC EMBARASSMENT.
DOES THAT SOUND LIKE A-TRAIN OR JACK?
SO THE FUCKING PLACE IS BUGGED? BY WHO?
BECAUSE I--
YOU SURPRISE ME, HOMELANDER.
YOU WEREN'T THIS SLOW ON THE UPTAKE WHEN TEENAGE KIX HAD THEIR LITTLE MISHAP LAST YEAR.
GETTING TO BE A HABIT OF YOURS.
LISTENING AT KEYHOLES.

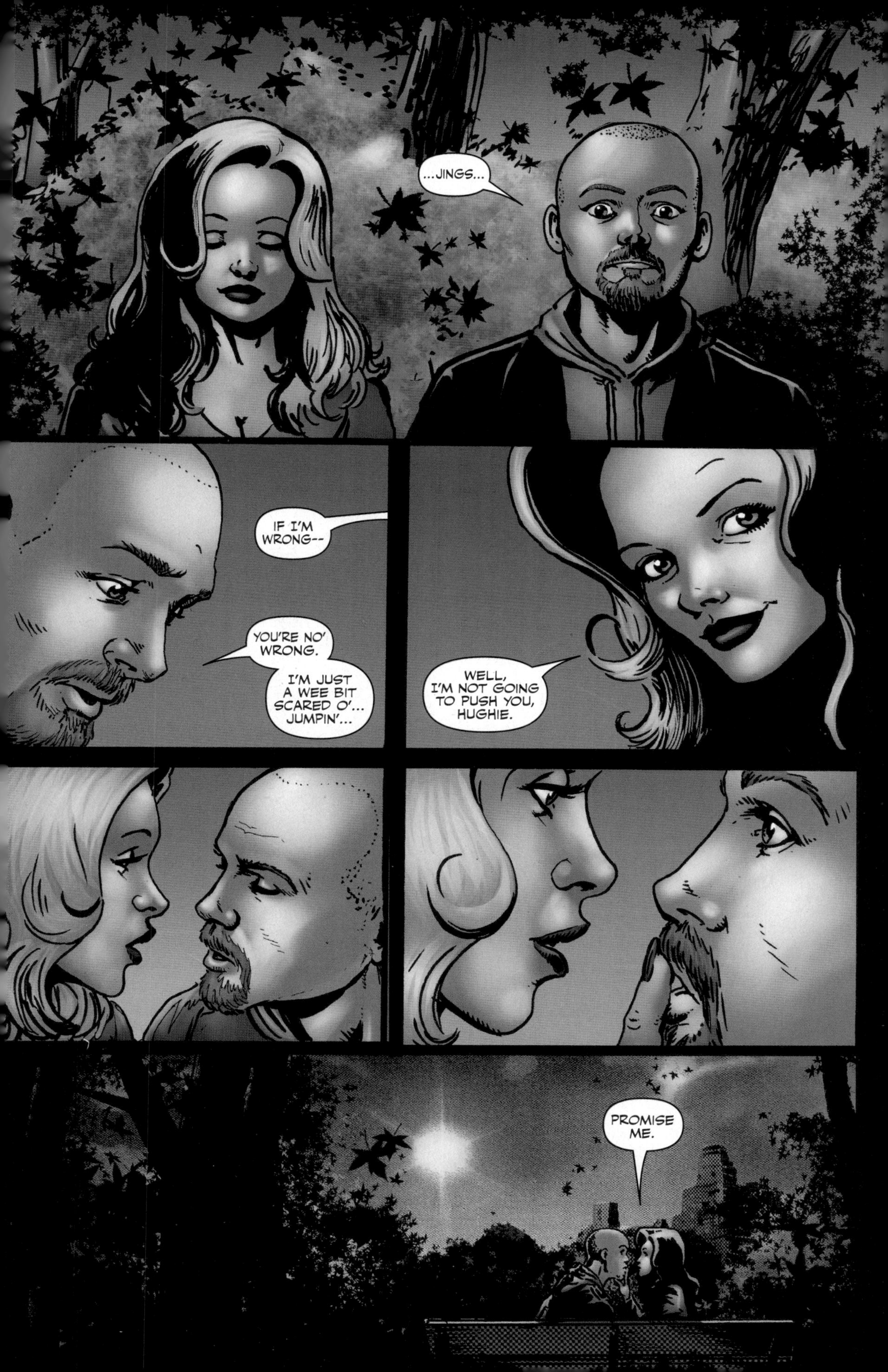

...JINGS...
IF I'M WRONG--
YOU'RE NO' WRONG.
I'M JUST A WEE BIT SCARED O'... JUMPIN'...
WELL, I'M NOT GOING TO PUSH YOU, HUGHIE.
PROMISE ME.

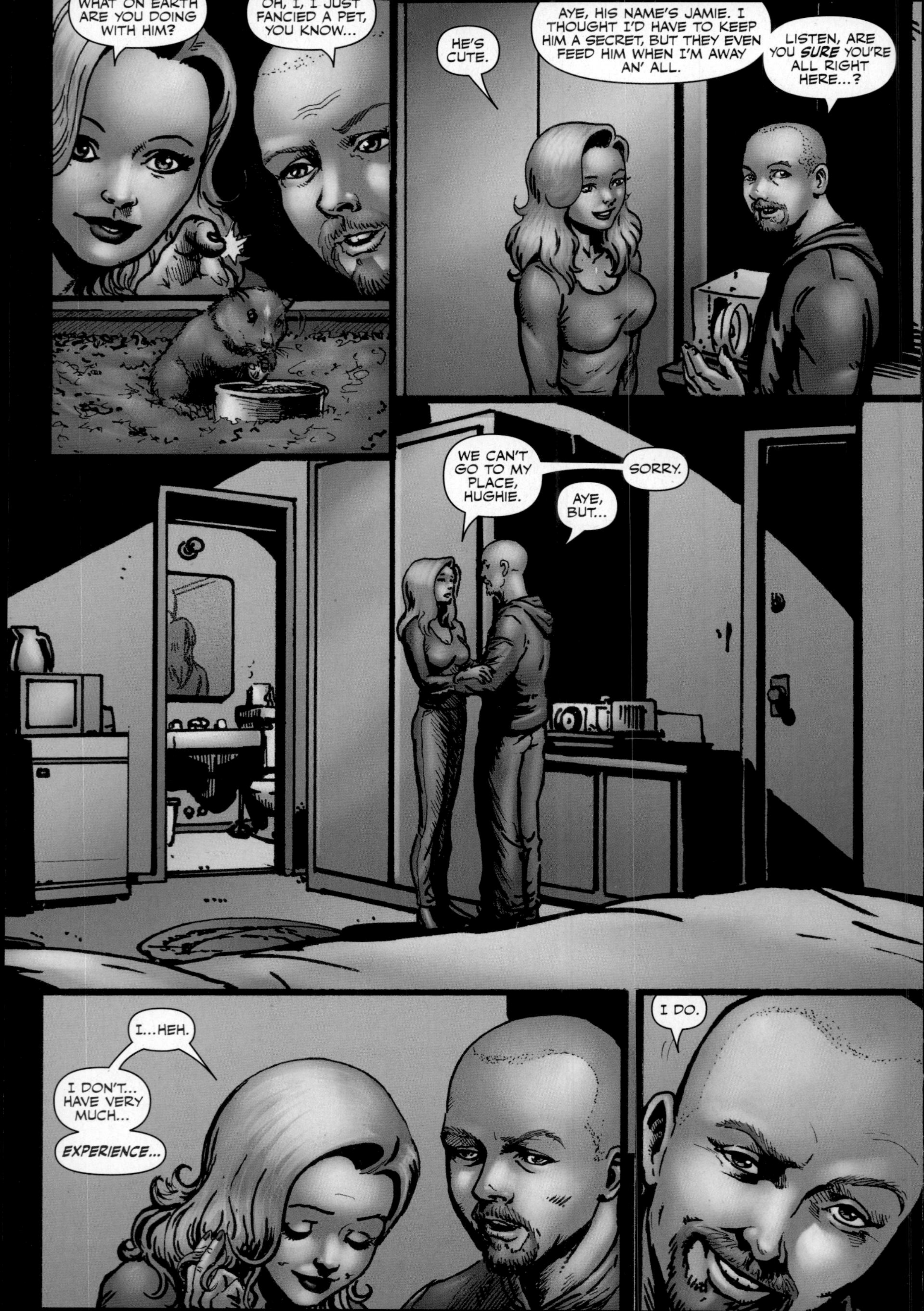
WHAT ON EARTH ARE YOU DOING WITH HIM?
OH, I, I JUST FANCIED A PET, YOU KNOW...
HE'S CUTE.
AYE, HIS NAME'S JAMIE. I THOUGHT I'D HAVE TO KEEP HIM A SECRET, BUT THEY EVEN FEED HIM WHEN I'M AWAY AN' ALL.
LISTEN, ARE YOU *SURE* YOU'RE ALL RIGHT HERE...?
WE CAN'T GO TO MY PLACE, HUGHIE.
SORRY.
AYE, BUT...
I...HEH.
I DON'T... HAVE VERY MUCH...
EXPERIENCE...
I DO.

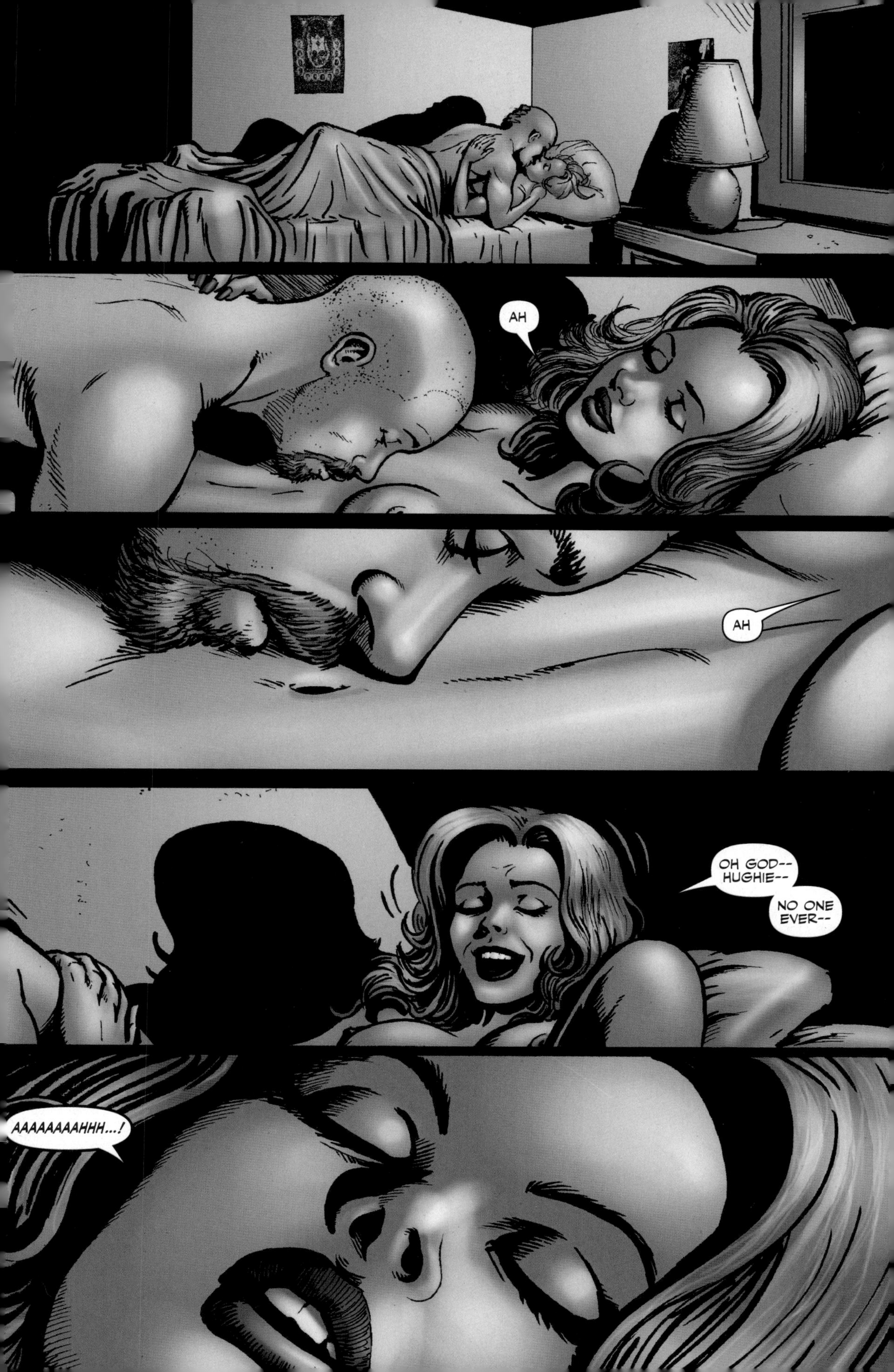
AH
AH
OH GOD--
HUGHIE--
NO ONE
EVER--
AAAAAAAAHHH...!

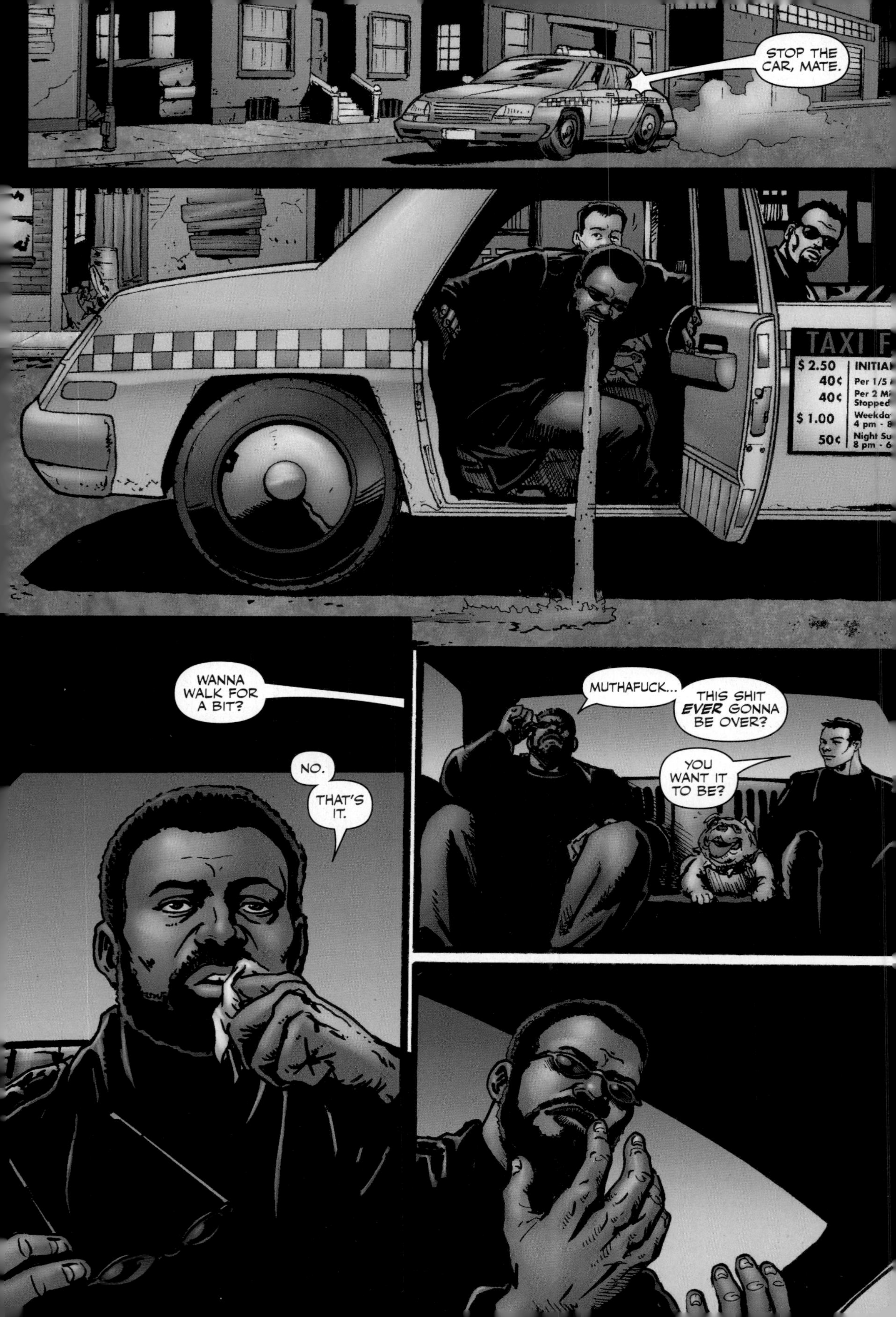
STOP THE CAR, MATE.
TAXI
$ 2.50
40¢
40¢
$ 1.00
50¢
WANNA WALK FOR A BIT?
NO.
THAT'S IT.
MUTHAFUCK...
THIS SHIT *EVER* GONNA BE OVER?
YOU WANT IT TO BE?

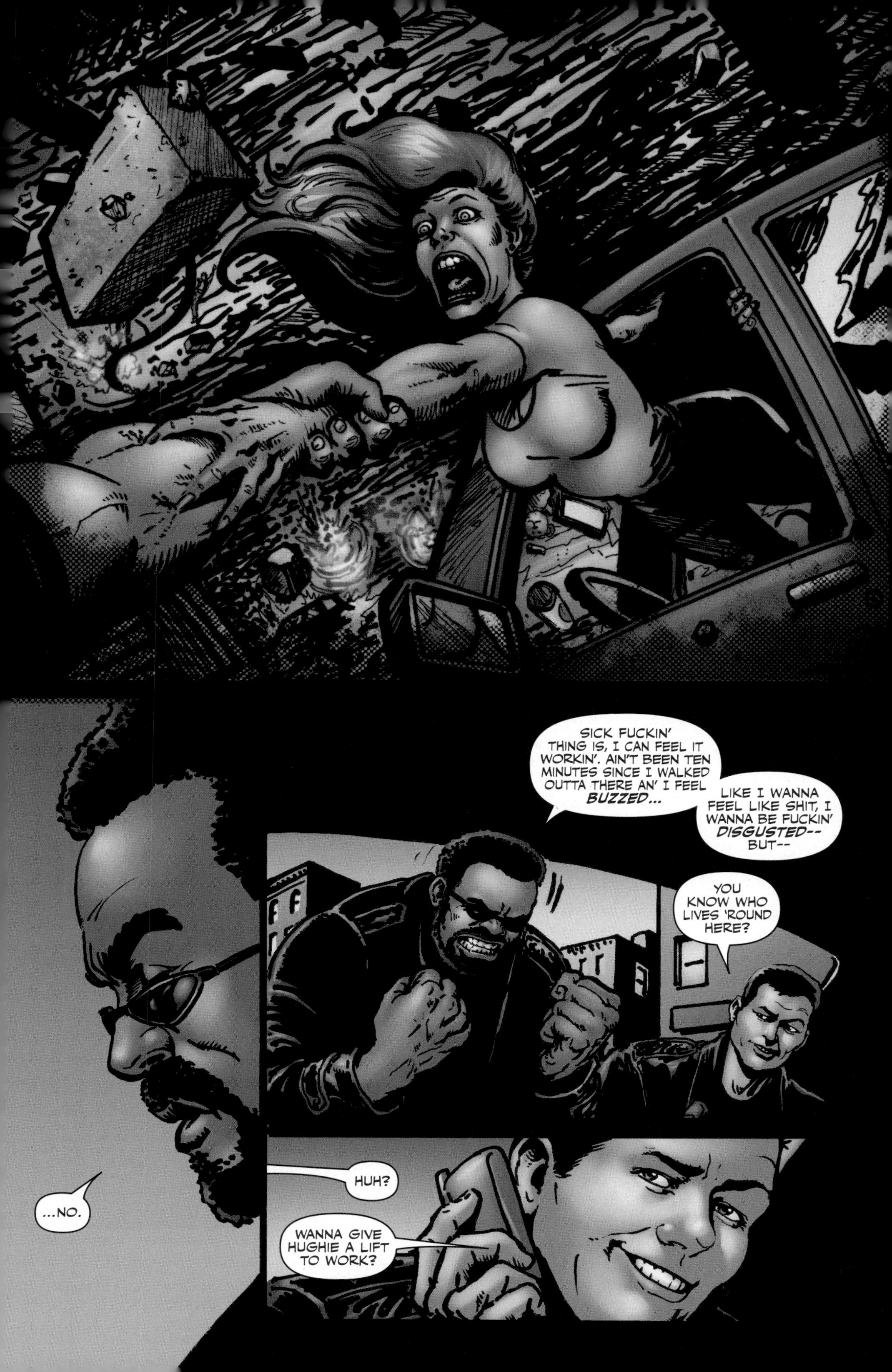
SICK FUCKIN' THING IS, I CAN FEEL IT WORKIN'. AIN'T BEEN TEN MINUTES SINCE I WALKED OUTTA THERE AN' I FEEL *BUZZED...*
LIKE I WANNA FEEL LIKE SHIT, I WANNA BE FUCKIN' *DISGUSTED--* BUT--
YOU KNOW WHO LIVES 'ROUND HERE?
...NO.
HUH?
WANNA GIVE HUGHIE A LIFT TO WORK?

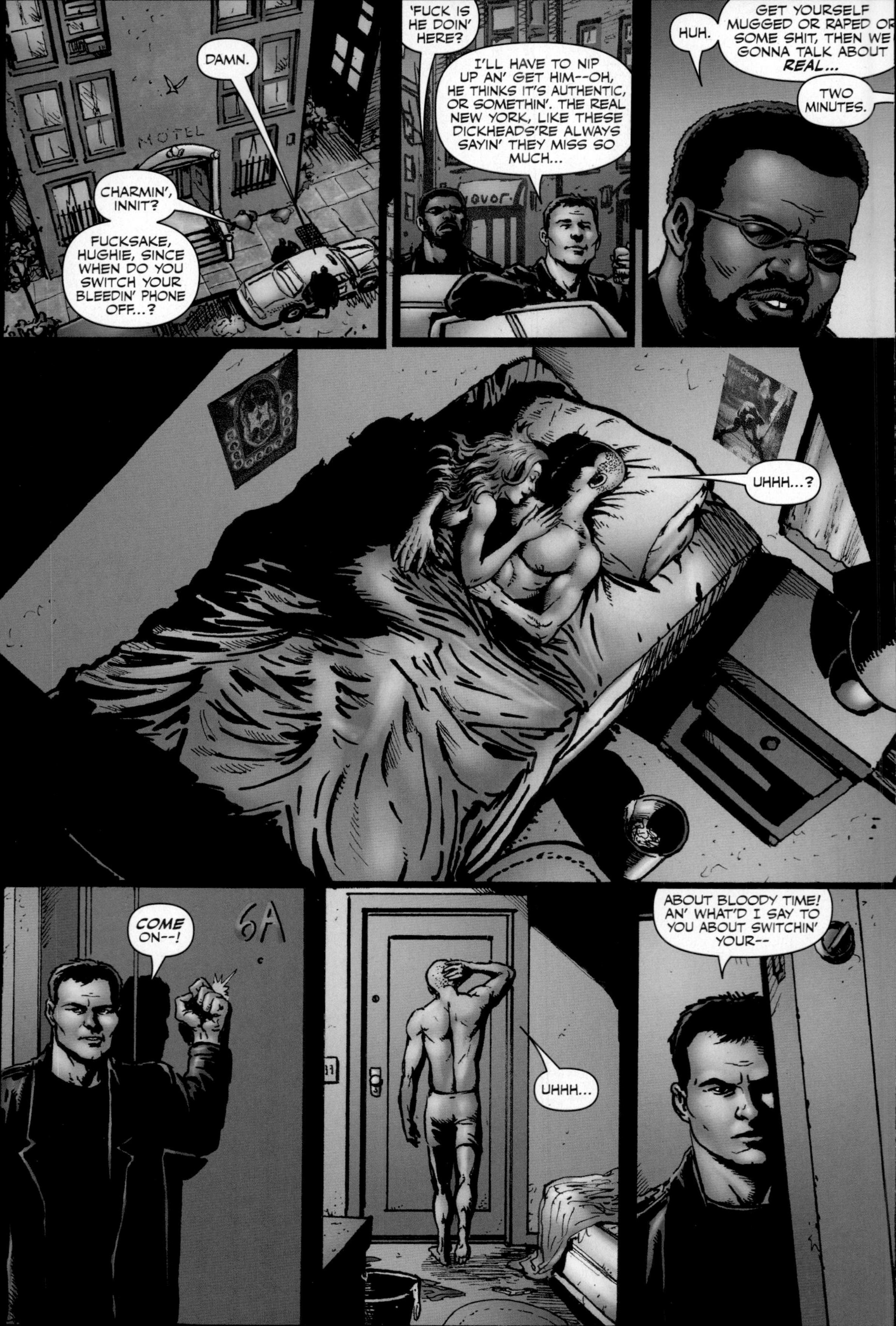
DAMN.
CHARMIN', INNIT?
FUCKSAKE, HUGHIE, SINCE WHEN DO YOU SWITCH YOUR BLEEDIN' PHONE OFF...?
MOTEL
'FUCK IS HE DOIN' HERE?
I'LL HAVE TO NIP UP AN' GET HIM--OH, HE THINKS IT'S AUTHENTIC, OR SOMETHIN'. THE REAL NEW YORK, LIKE THESE DICKHEADS'RE ALWAYS SAYIN' THEY MISS SO MUCH...
HUH.
GET YOURSELF MUGGED OR RAPED OR SOME SHIT, THEN WE GONNA TALK ABOUT *REAL*...
TWO MINUTES.
UHHH...?
COME ON--!
6A
UHHH...
ABOUT BLOODY TIME! AN' WHAT'D I SAY TO YOU ABOUT SWITCHIN' YOUR--

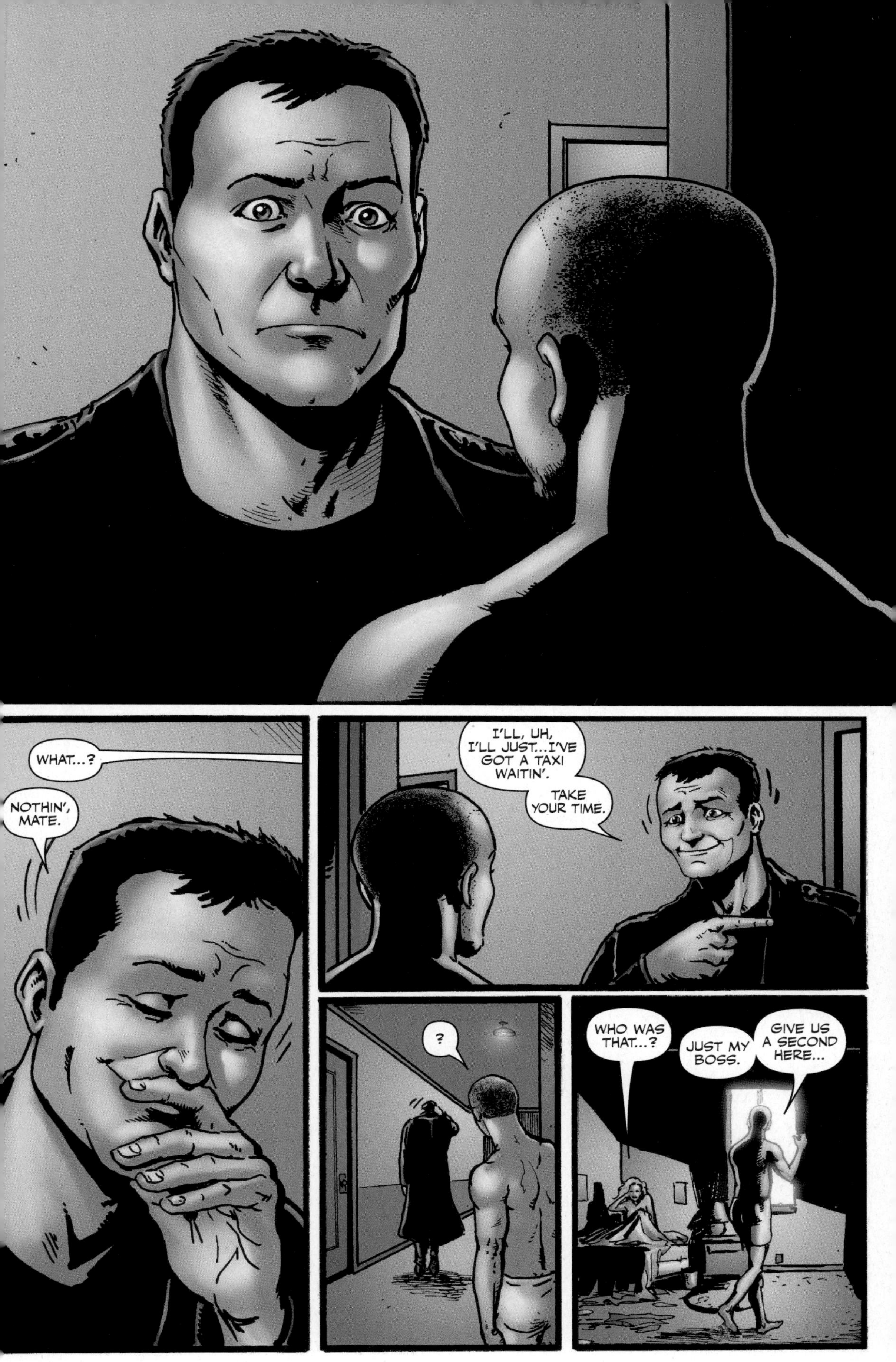
WHAT...?
NOTHIN', MATE.
I'LL, UH, I'LL JUST...I'VE GOT A TAXI WAITIN'.
TAKE YOUR TIME.
?
WHO WAS THAT...?
JUST MY BOSS.
GIVE US A SECOND HERE...

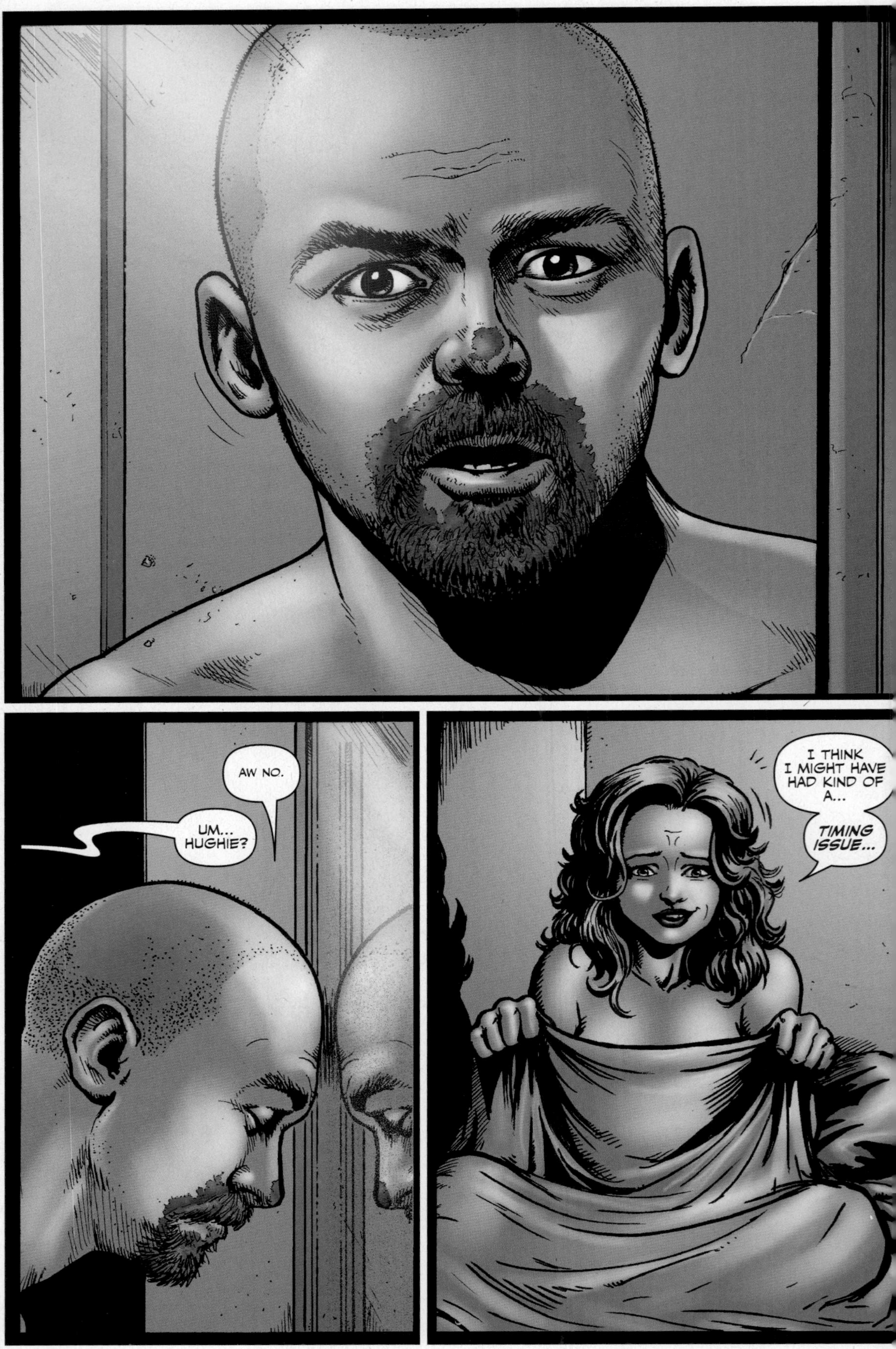
AW NO.
UM... HUGHIE?
I THINK I MIGHT HAVE HAD KIND OF A...
TIMING ISSUE...

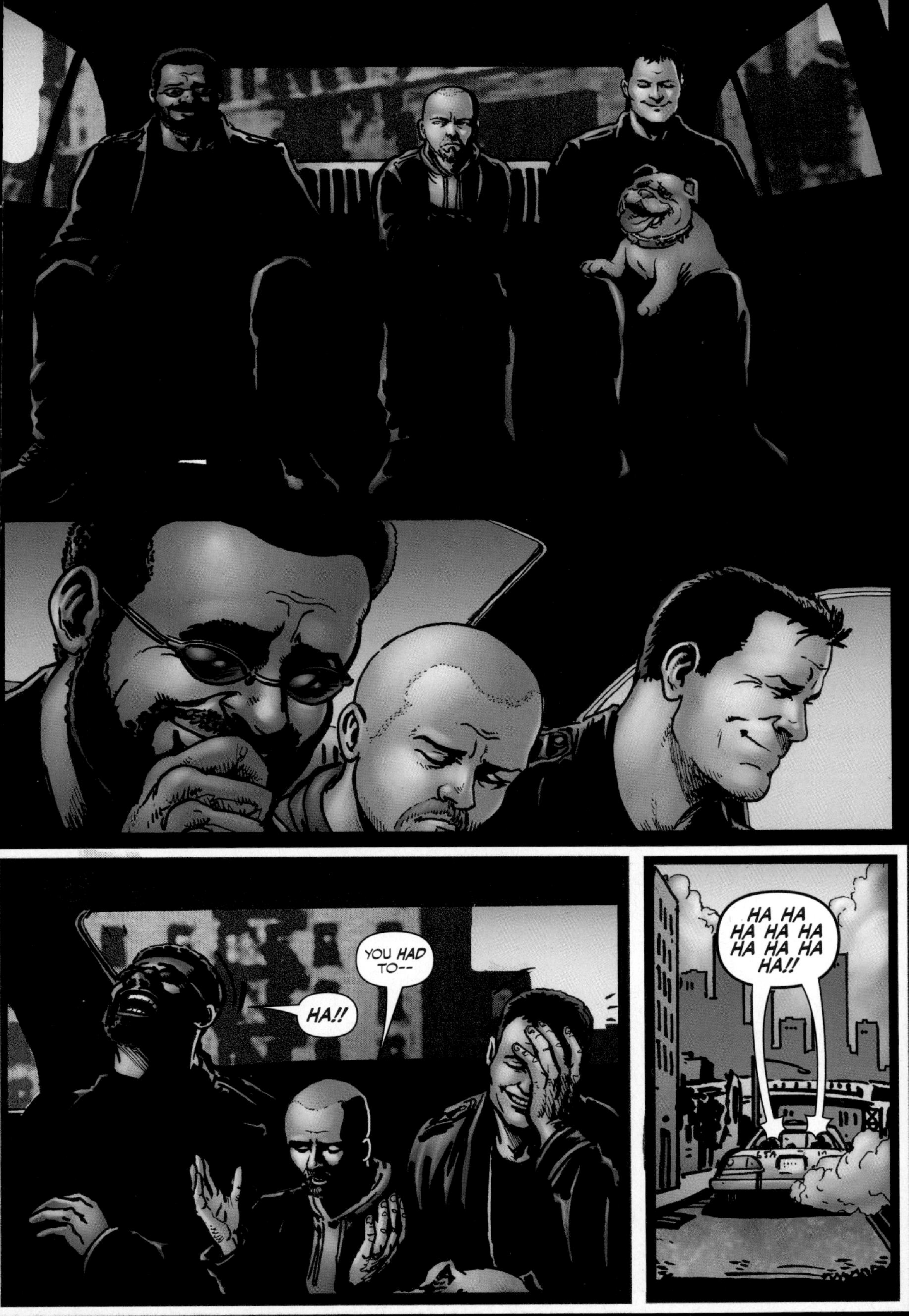
YOU HAD TO--
HA!!
HA HA HA HA HA HA HA HA HA!!

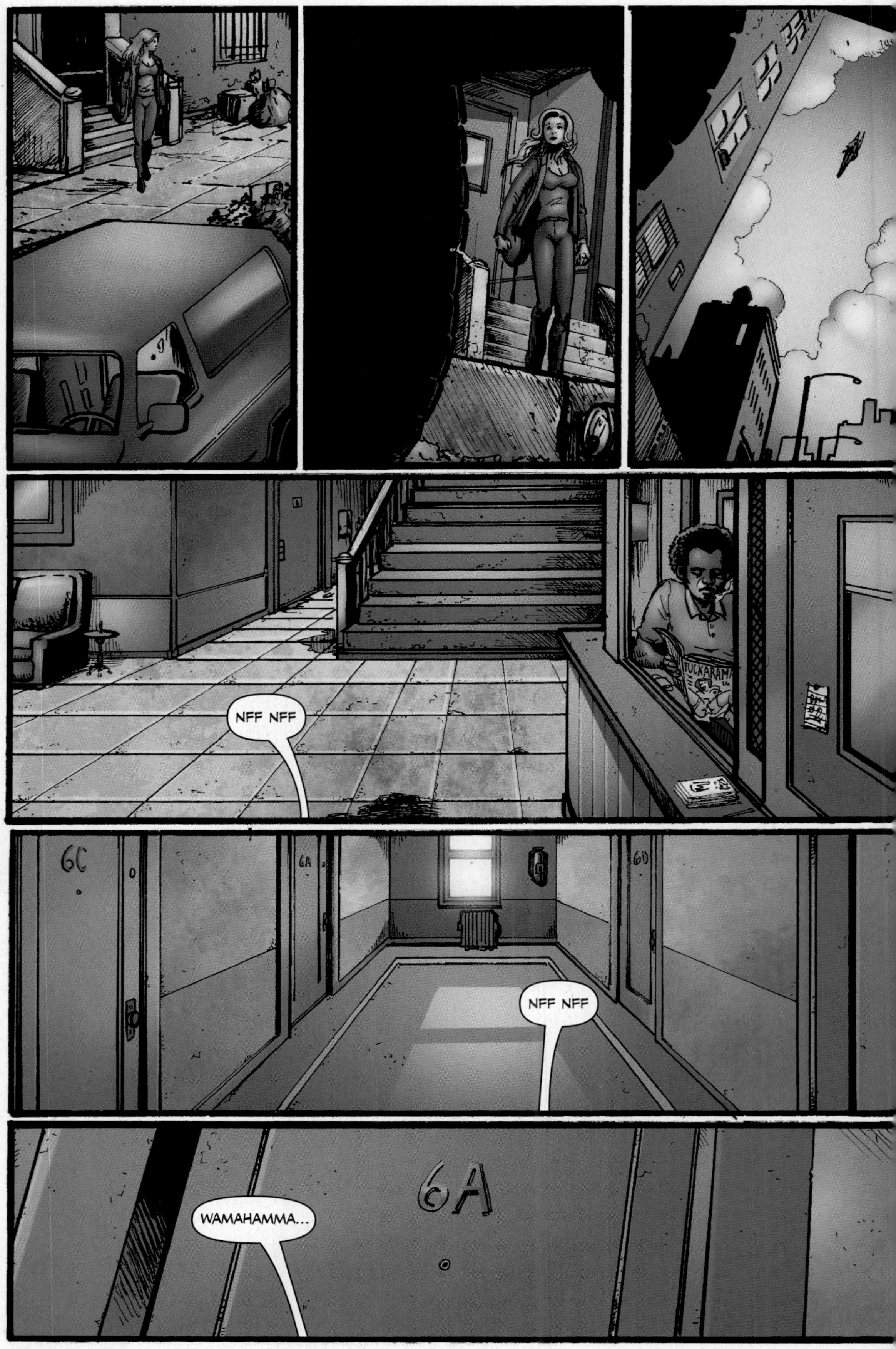
FUCKARAMA
NFF NFF
6C
6A
NFF NFF
6A
WAMAHAMMA...

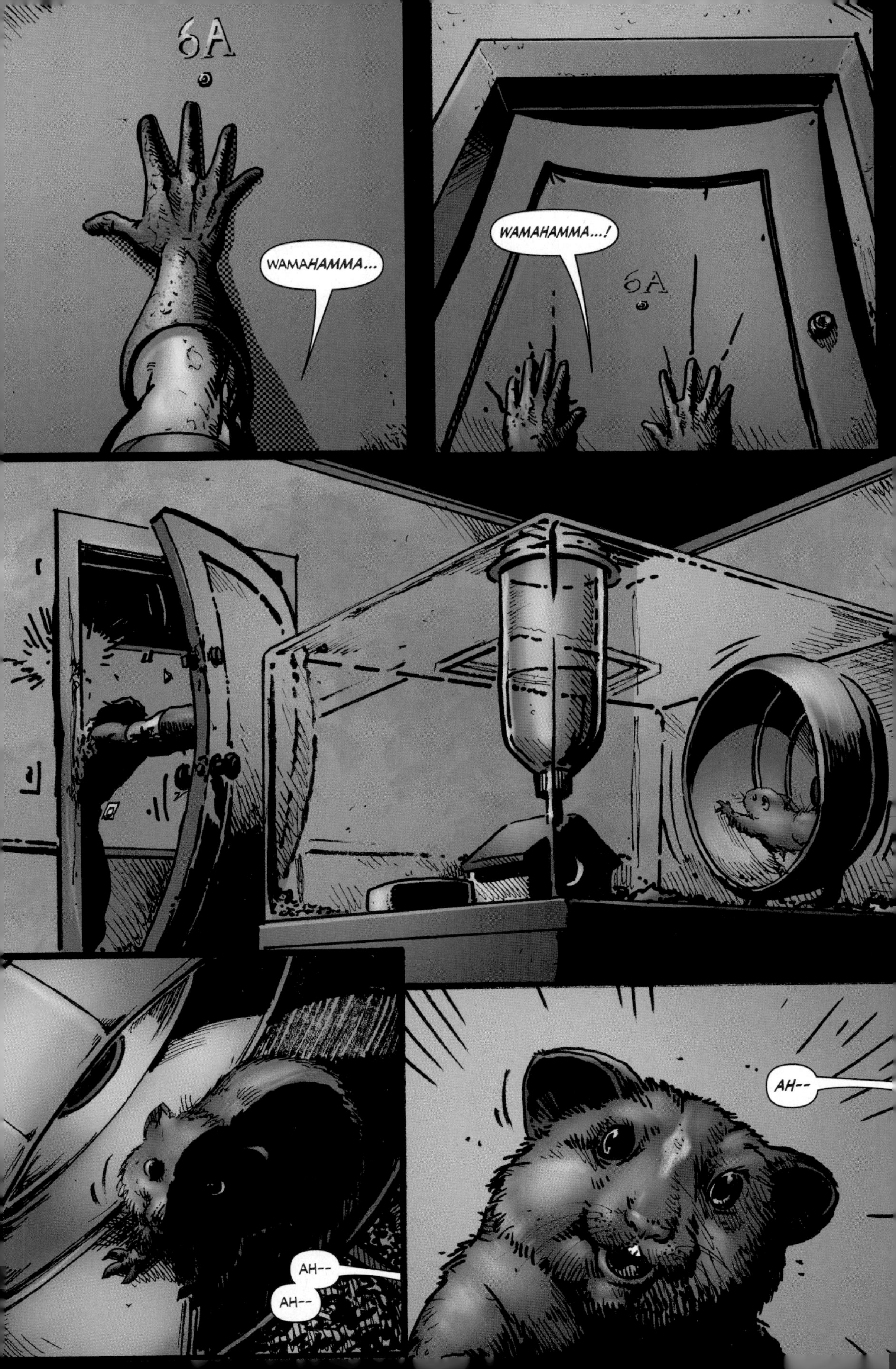

6A
WAMAHAMMA...
WAMAHAMMA...!
6A
AH--
AH--
AH--

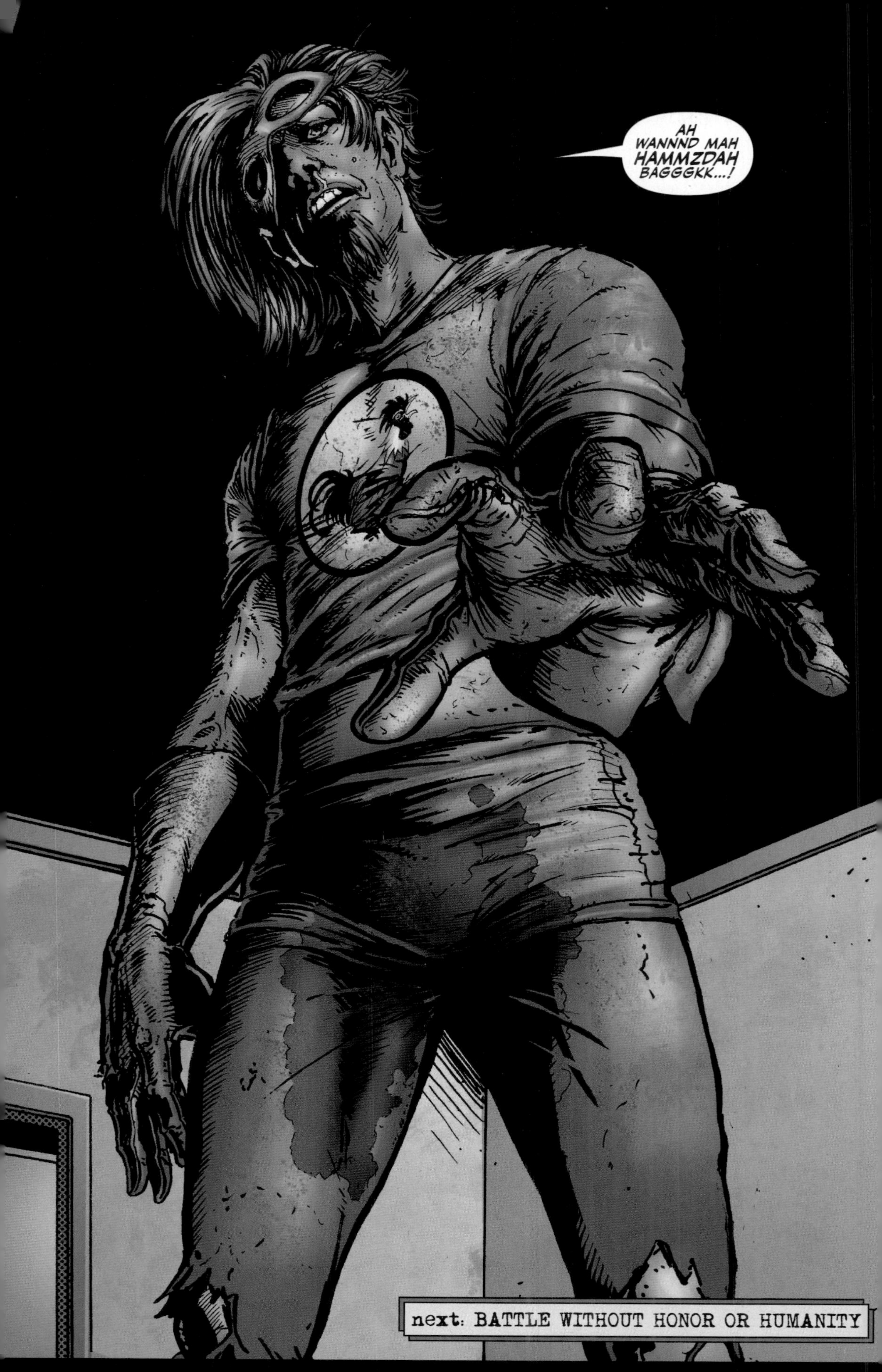
AH WANNND MAH HAMMZDAH BAGGGKK...!
next: BATTLE WITHOUT HONOR OR HUMANITY

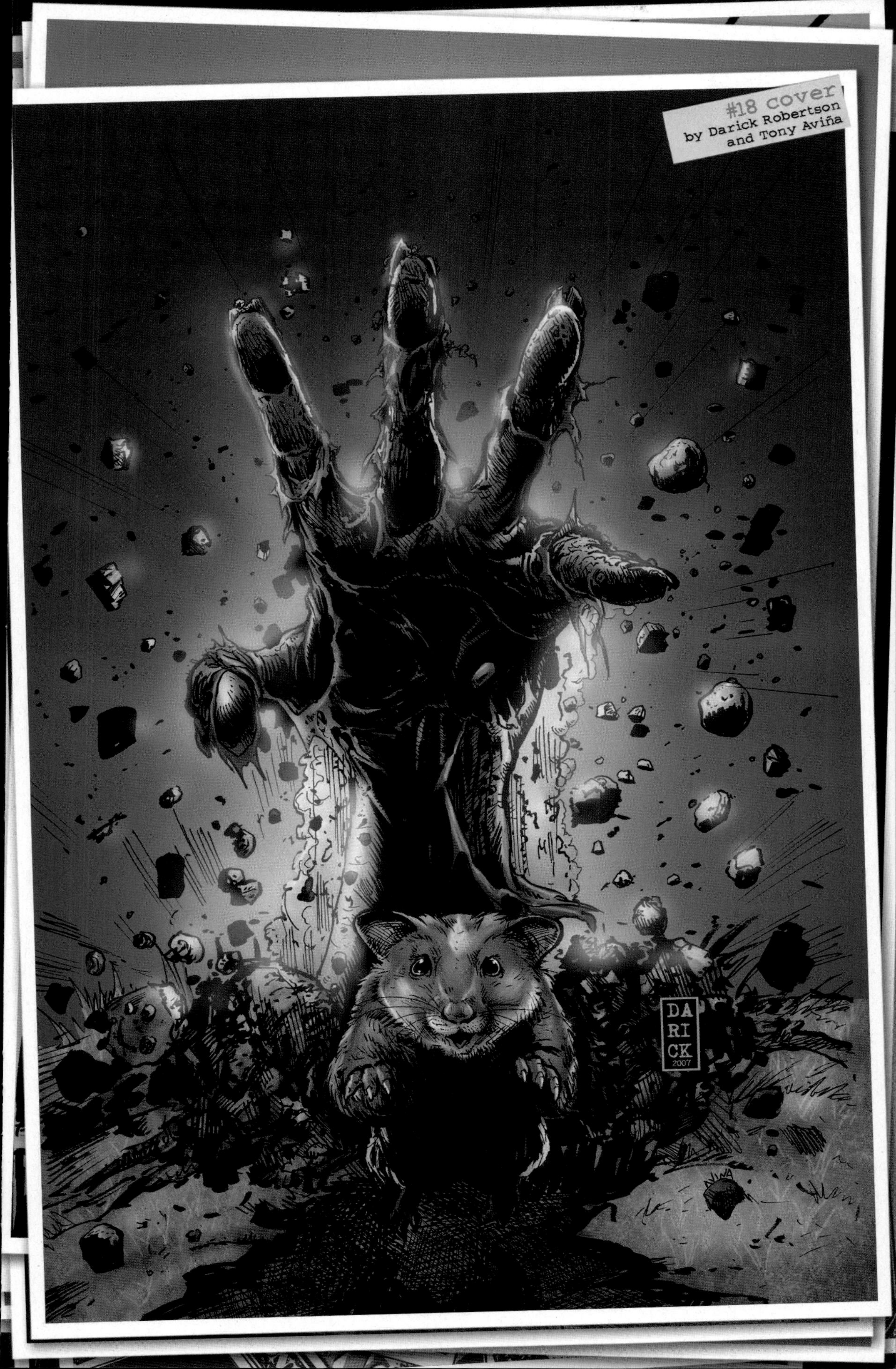
DA
RI
CK
2007

#18 cover
by Darick Robertson
and Tony Aviña

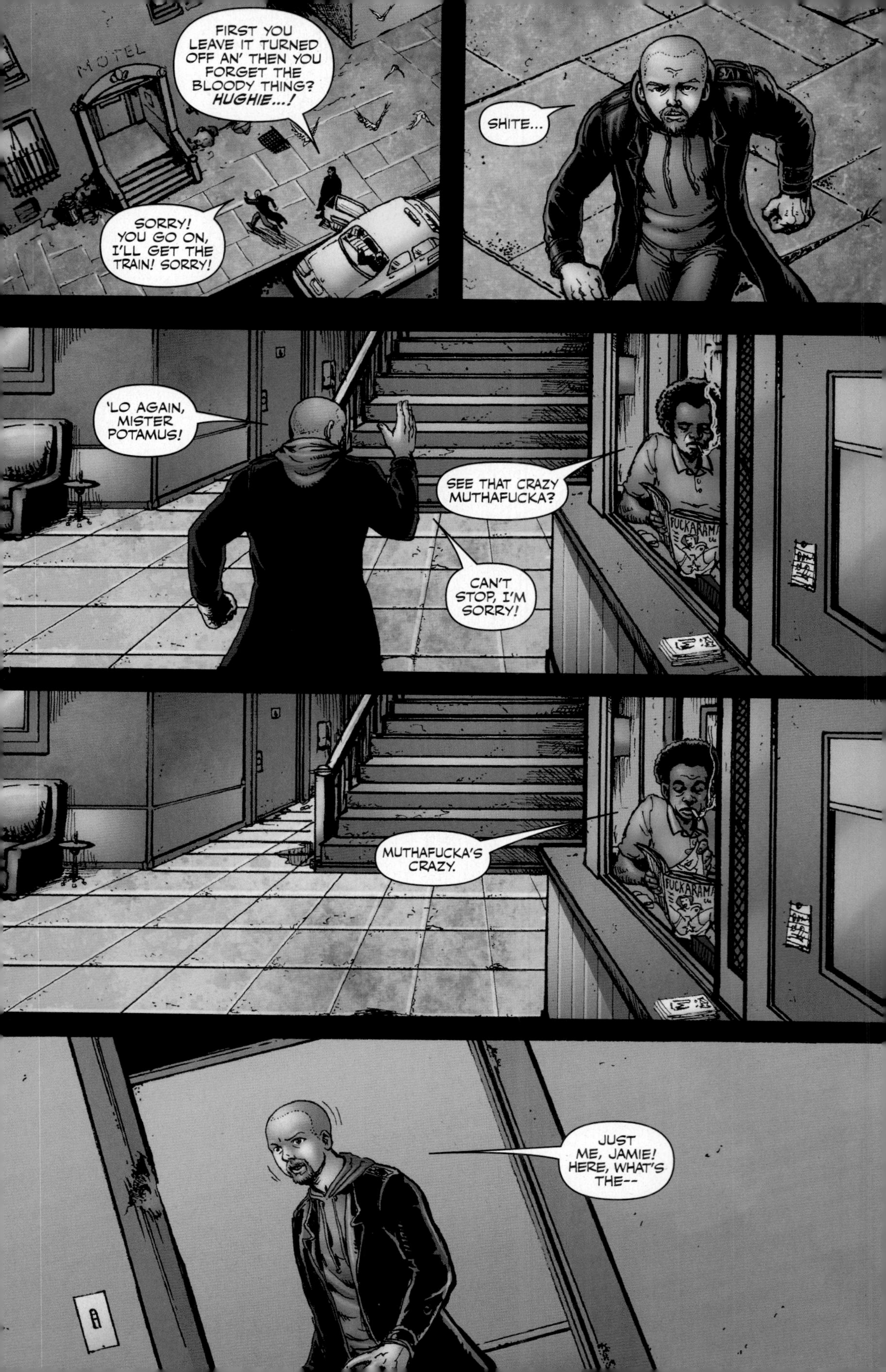
MOTEL
FIRST YOU LEAVE IT TURNED OFF AN' THEN YOU FORGET THE BLOODY THING? HUGHIE...!
SORRY! YOU GO ON, I'LL GET THE TRAIN! SORRY!
SHITE...
'LO AGAIN, MISTER POTAMUS!
SEE THAT CRAZY MUTHAFUCKA?
CAN'T STOP, I'M SORRY!
FUCKARAMA
MUTHAFUCKA'S CRAZY.
FUCKARAMA
JUST ME, JAMIE! HERE, WHAT'S THE--

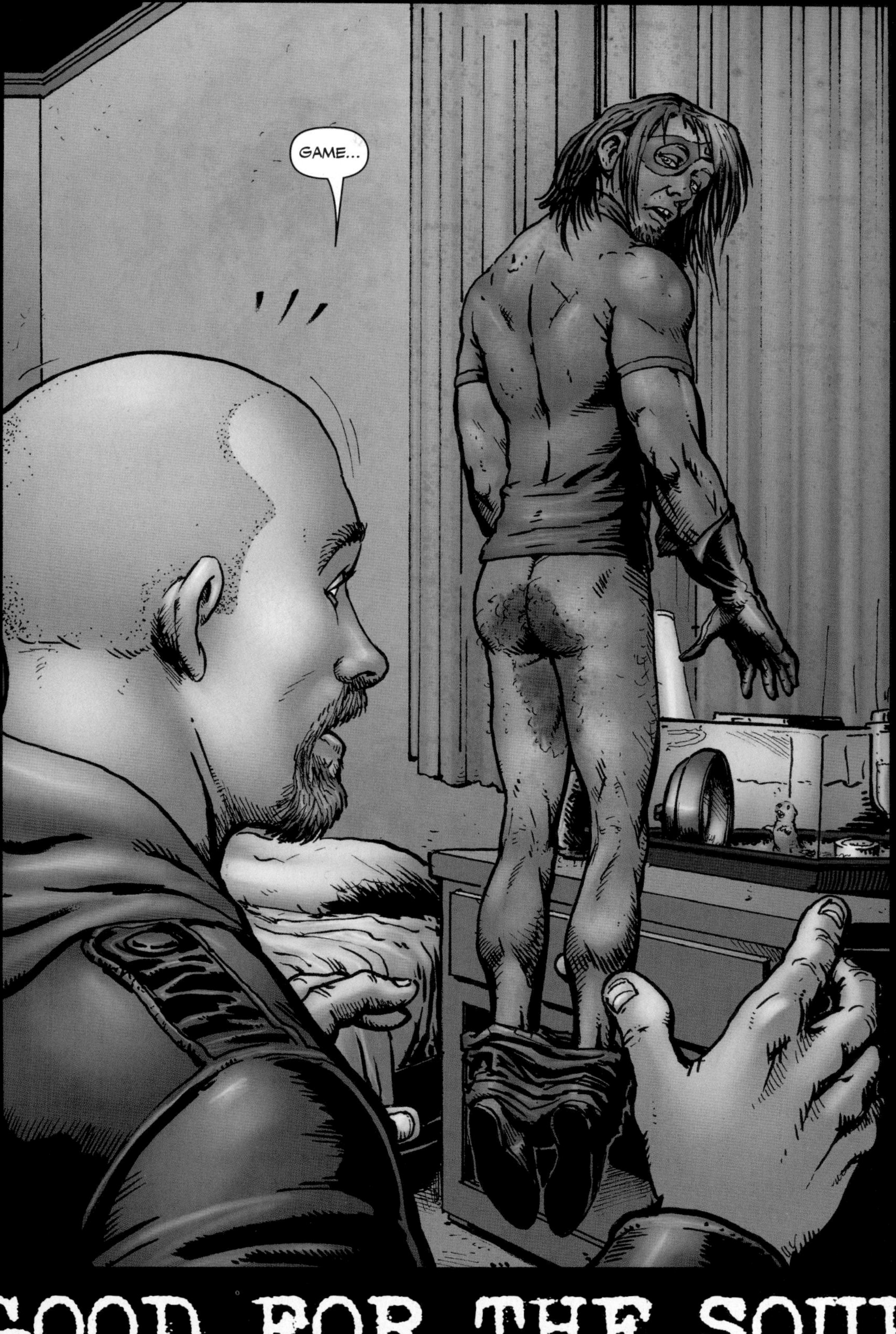
GAME...

GOOD FOR THE SOUL

conclusion

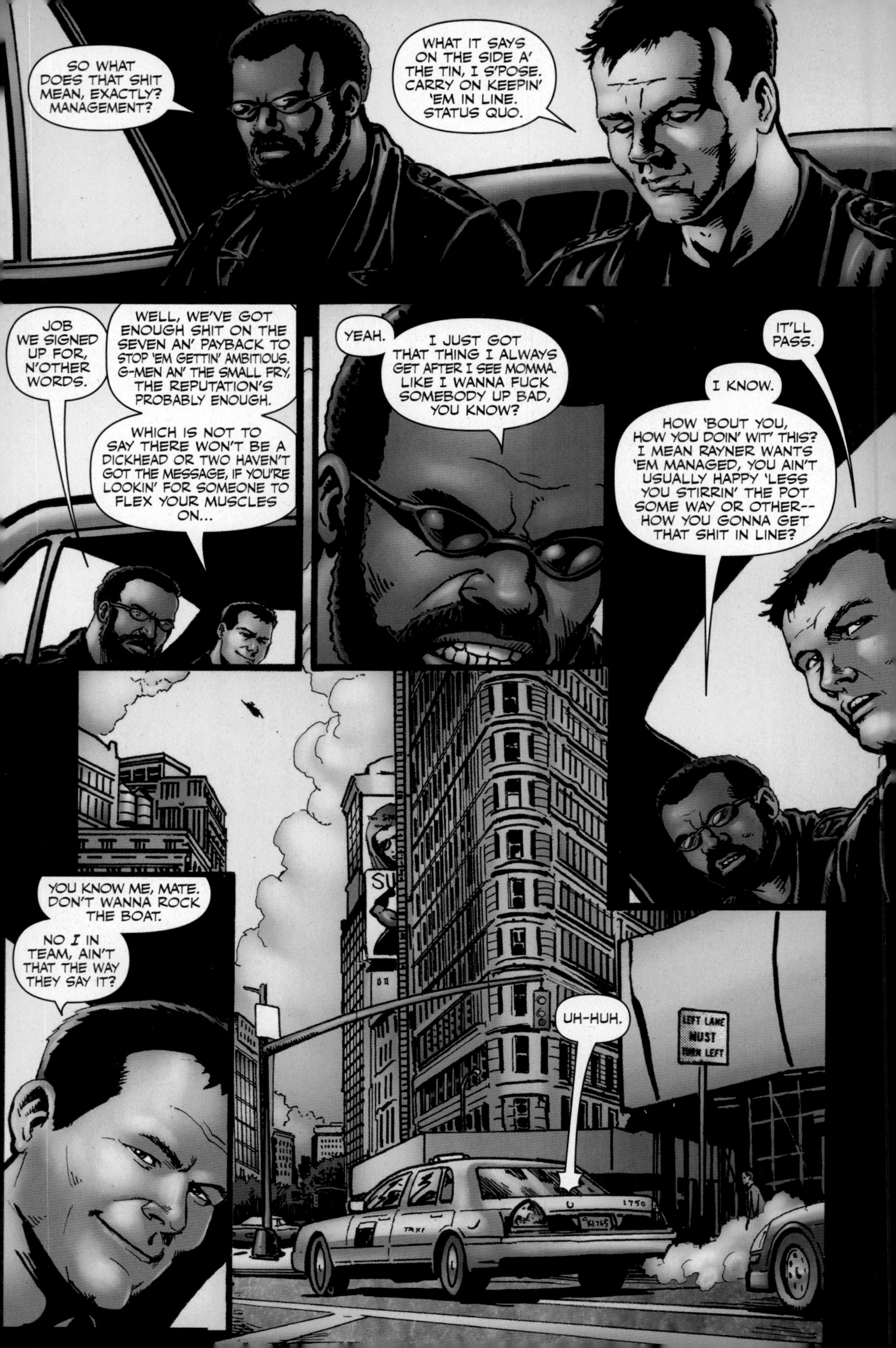
SO WHAT DOES THAT SHIT MEAN, EXACTLY? MANAGEMENT?
WHAT IT SAYS ON THE SIDE A' THE TIN, I S'POSE. CARRY ON KEEPIN' 'EM IN LINE. STATUS QUO.
JOB WE SIGNED UP FOR, N'OTHER WORDS.
WELL, WE'VE GOT ENOUGH SHIT ON THE SEVEN AN' PAYBACK TO STOP 'EM GETTIN' AMBITIOUS. G-MEN AN' THE SMALL FRY, THE REPUTATION'S PROBABLY ENOUGH.
WHICH IS NOT TO SAY THERE WON'T BE A DICKHEAD OR TWO HAVEN'T GOT THE MESSAGE, IF YOU'RE LOOKIN' FOR SOMEONE TO FLEX YOUR MUSCLES ON...
YEAH.
I JUST GOT THAT THING I ALWAYS GET AFTER I SEE MOMMA. LIKE I WANNA FUCK SOMEBODY UP BAD, YOU KNOW?
IT'LL PASS.
I KNOW.
HOW 'BOUT YOU, HOW YOU DOIN' WIT' THIS? I MEAN RAYNER WANTS 'EM MANAGED, YOU AIN'T USUALLY HAPPY 'LESS YOU STIRRIN' THE POT SOME WAY OR OTHER-- HOW YOU GONNA GET THAT SHIT IN LINE?
YOU KNOW ME, MATE. DON'T WANNA ROCK THE BOAT.
NO *I* IN TEAM, AIN'T THAT THE WAY THEY SAY IT?
UH-HUH.
LEFT LANE MUST TURN LEFT
TAXI
1750

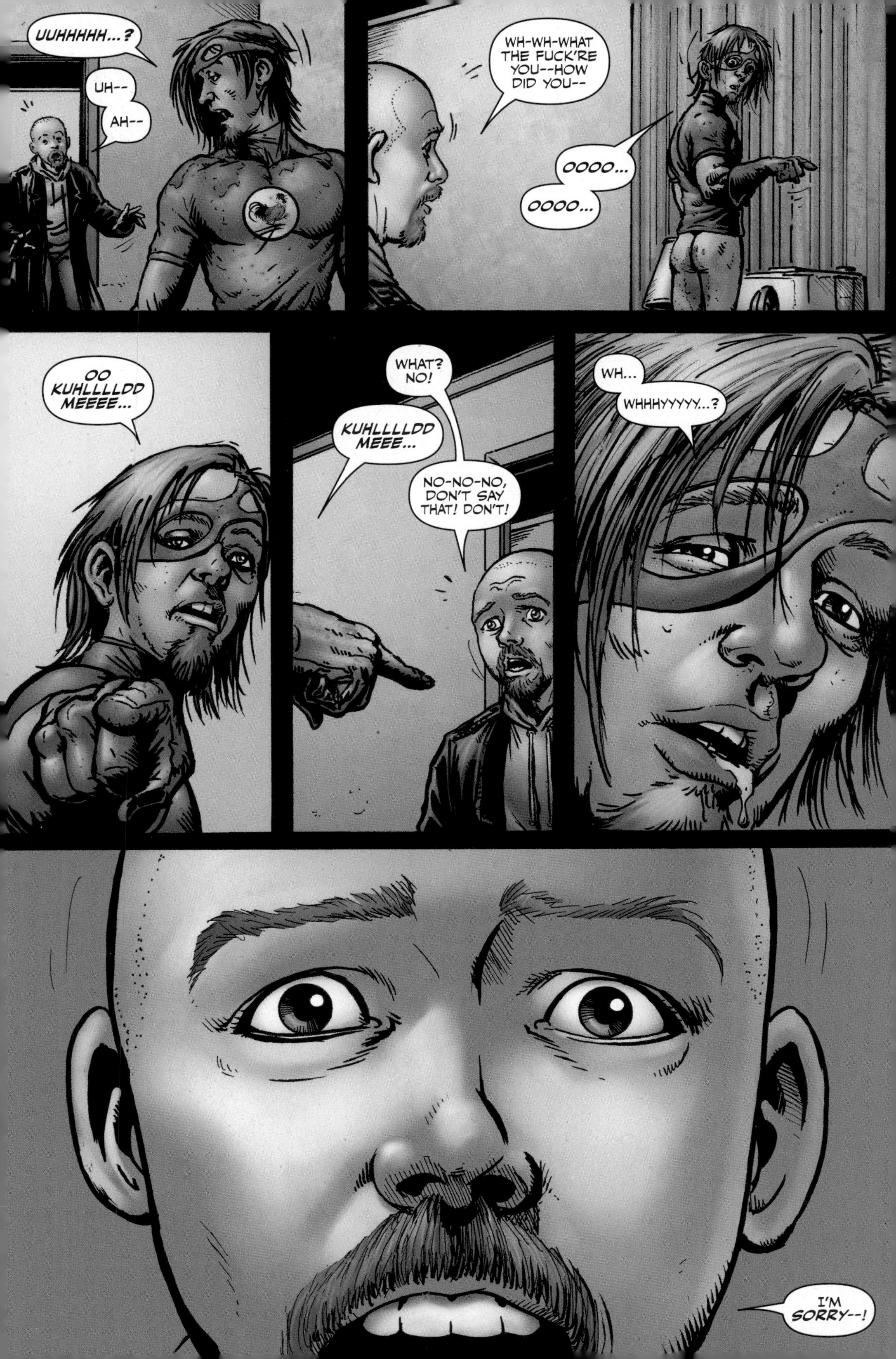
UUHHHHH...?
UH--
AH--
WH-WH-WHAT THE FUCK'RE YOU--HOW DID YOU--
OOOO...
OOOO...
OO KUHLLLLLDD MEEEE...
WHAT? NO!
KUHLLLLLDD MEEE...
NO-NO-NO, DON'T SAY THAT! DON'T!
WH...
WHHHYYYYY...?
I'M SORRY--!

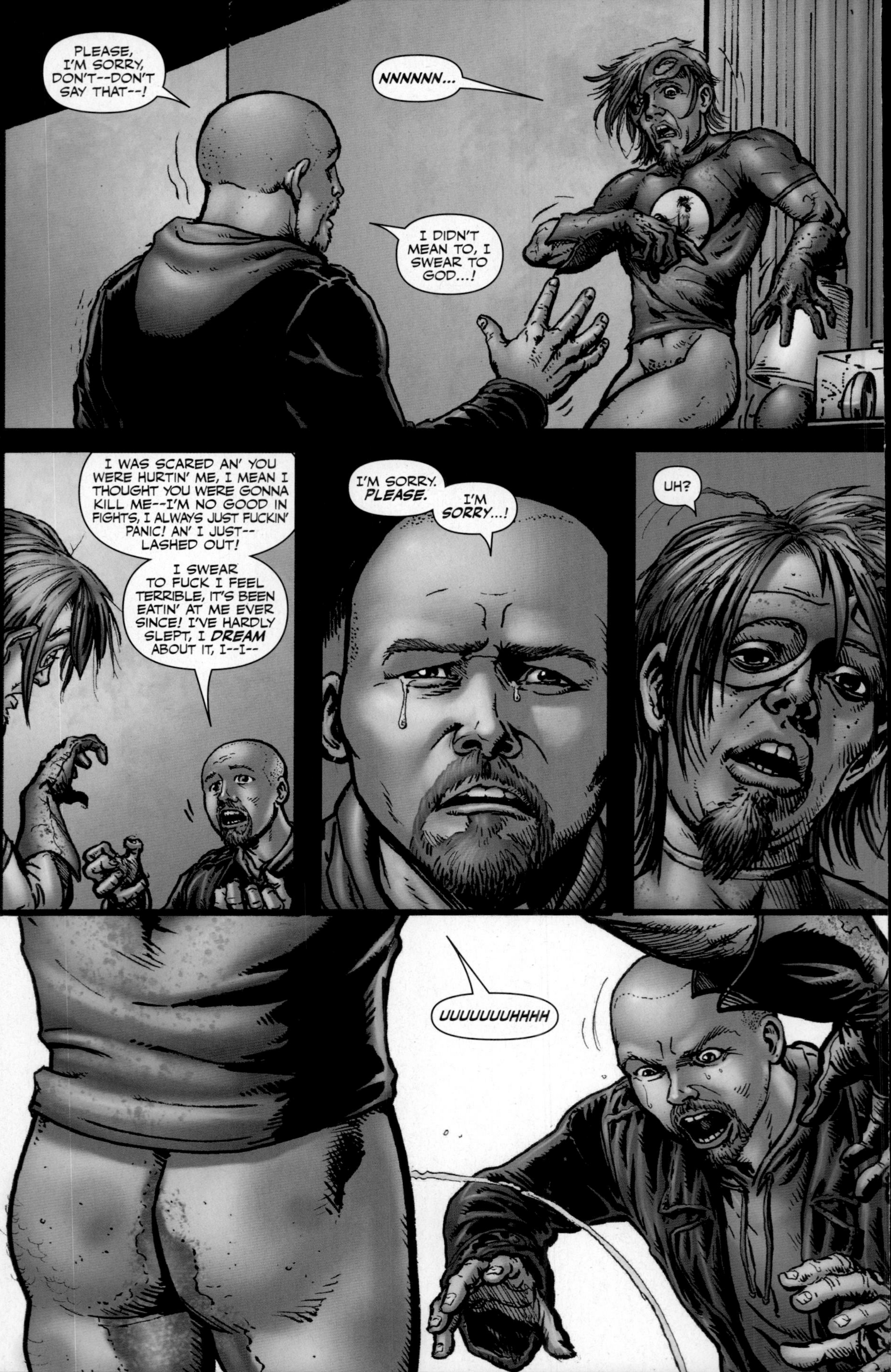
PLEASE, I'M SORRY, DON'T--DON'T SAY THAT--!
NNNNNN...
I DIDN'T MEAN TO, I SWEAR TO GOD...!
I WAS SCARED AN' YOU WERE HURTIN' ME, I MEAN I THOUGHT YOU WERE GONNA KILL ME--I'M NO GOOD IN FIGHTS, I ALWAYS JUST FUCKIN' PANIC! AN' I JUST--LASHED OUT!
I SWEAR TO FUCK I FEEL TERRIBLE, IT'S BEEN EATIN' AT ME EVER SINCE! I'VE HARDLY SLEPT, I DREAM ABOUT IT, I--I--
I'M SORRY. PLEASE.
I'M SORRY...!
UH?
UUUUUUUHHHH

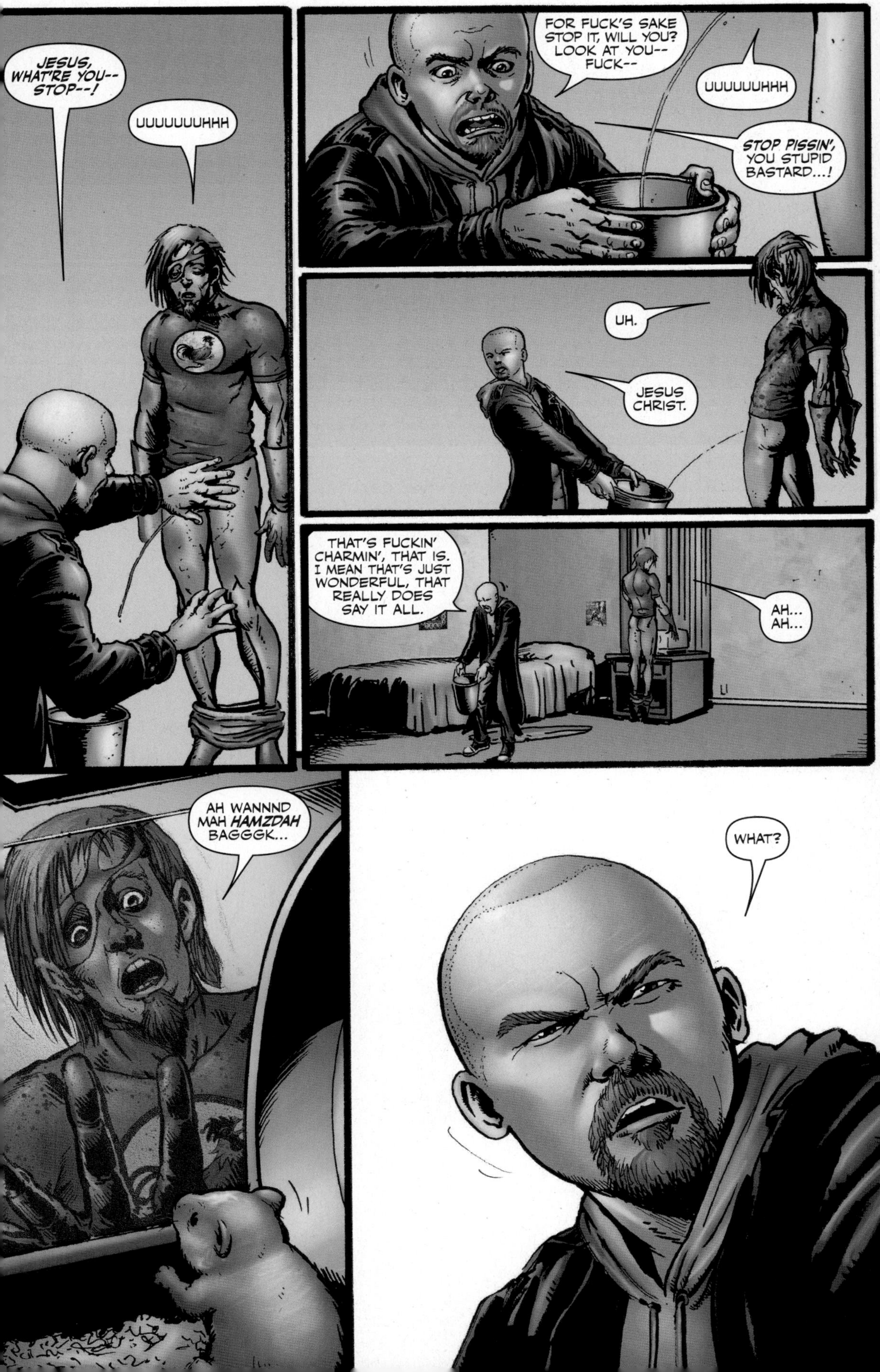
JESUS, WHAT'RE YOU-- STOP--!
UUUUUUUUHHH
FOR FUCK'S SAKE STOP IT, WILL YOU? LOOK AT YOU-- FUCK--
UUUUUUHHH
STOP PISSIN', YOU STUPID BASTARD...!
UH.
JESUS CHRIST.
THAT'S FUCKIN' CHARMIN', THAT IS. I MEAN THAT'S JUST WONDERFUL, THAT REALLY DOES SAY IT ALL.
AH... AH...
AH WANNND MAH HAMZDAH BAGGGK...
WHAT?

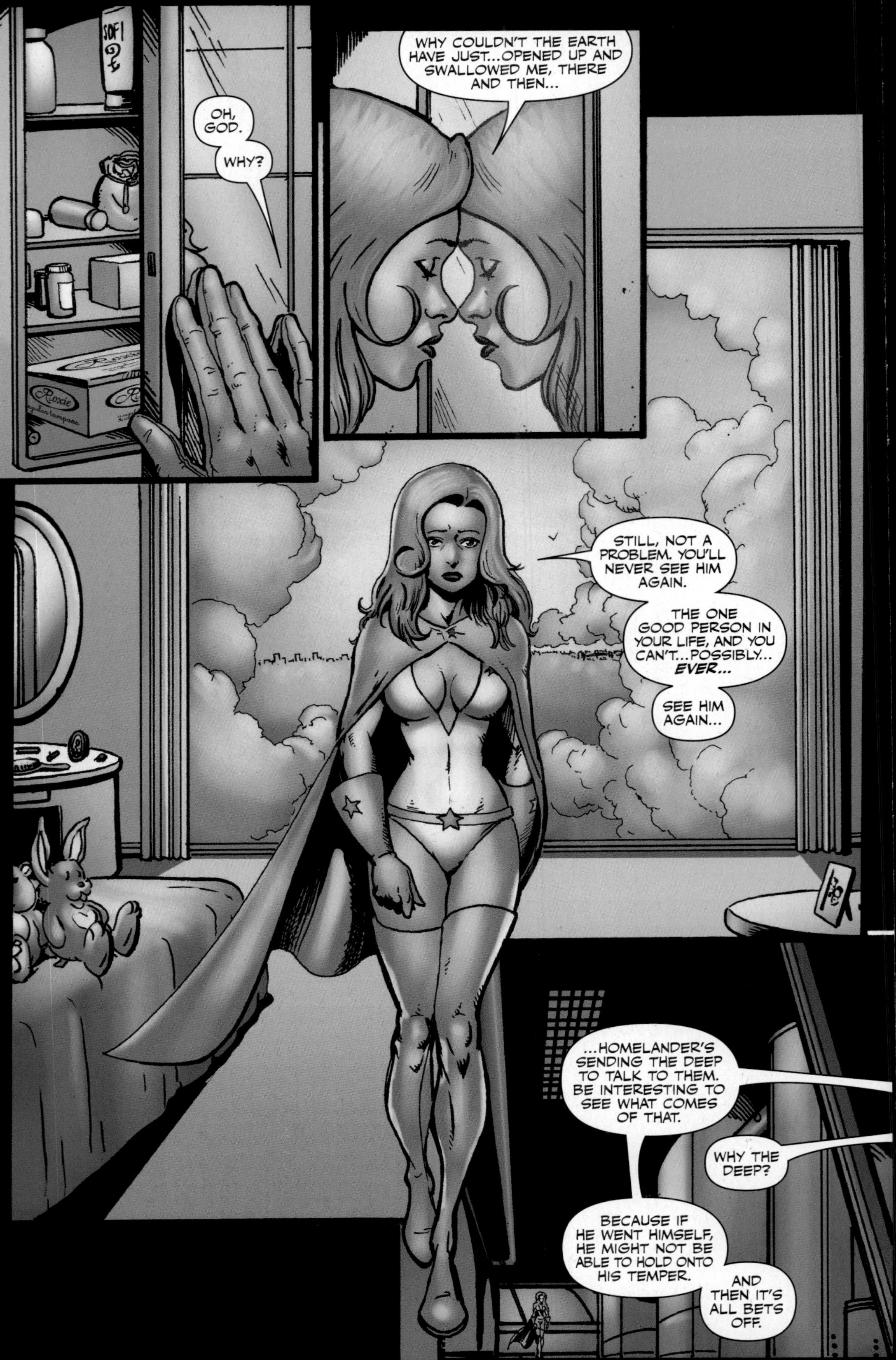
Roxie
regular tampons
OH, GOD.
WHY?
WHY COULDN'T THE EARTH HAVE JUST...OPENED UP AND SWALLOWED ME, THERE AND THEN...
STILL, NOT A PROBLEM. YOU'LL NEVER SEE HIM AGAIN.
THE ONE GOOD PERSON IN YOUR LIFE, AND YOU CAN'T...POSSIBLY... ***EVER...***
SEE HIM AGAIN...
...HOMELANDER'S SENDING THE DEEP TO TALK TO THEM. BE INTERESTING TO SEE WHAT COMES OF THAT.
WHY THE DEEP?
BECAUSE IF HE WENT HIMSELF, HE MIGHT NOT BE ABLE TO HOLD ONTO HIS TEMPER.
AND THEN IT'S ALL BETS OFF.

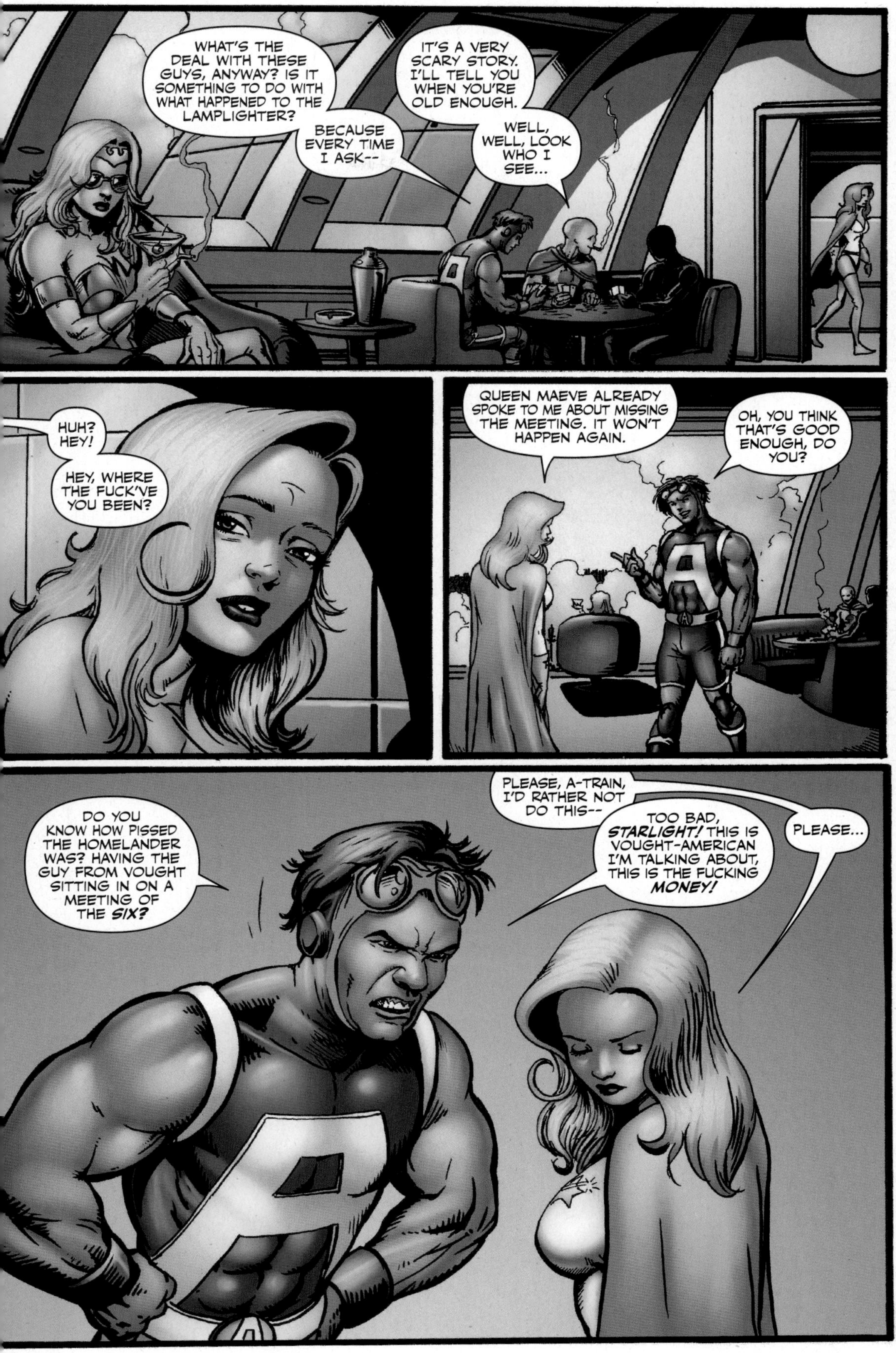
WHAT'S THE DEAL WITH THESE GUYS, ANYWAY? IS IT SOMETHING TO DO WITH WHAT HAPPENED TO THE LAMPLIGHTER?
BECAUSE EVERY TIME I ASK--
IT'S A VERY SCARY STORY. I'LL TELL YOU WHEN YOU'RE OLD ENOUGH.
WELL, WELL, LOOK WHO I SEE...
HUH? HEY!
HEY, WHERE THE FUCK'VE YOU BEEN?
QUEEN MAEVE ALREADY SPOKE TO ME ABOUT MISSING THE MEETING. IT WON'T HAPPEN AGAIN.
OH, YOU THINK THAT'S GOOD ENOUGH, DO YOU?
DO YOU KNOW HOW PISSED THE HOMELANDER WAS? HAVING THE GUY FROM VOUGHT SITTING IN ON A MEETING OF THE SIX?
PLEASE, A-TRAIN, I'D RATHER NOT DO THIS--
TOO BAD, STARLIGHT! THIS IS VOUGHT-AMERICAN I'M TALKING ABOUT, THIS IS THE FUCKING MONEY!
PLEASE...

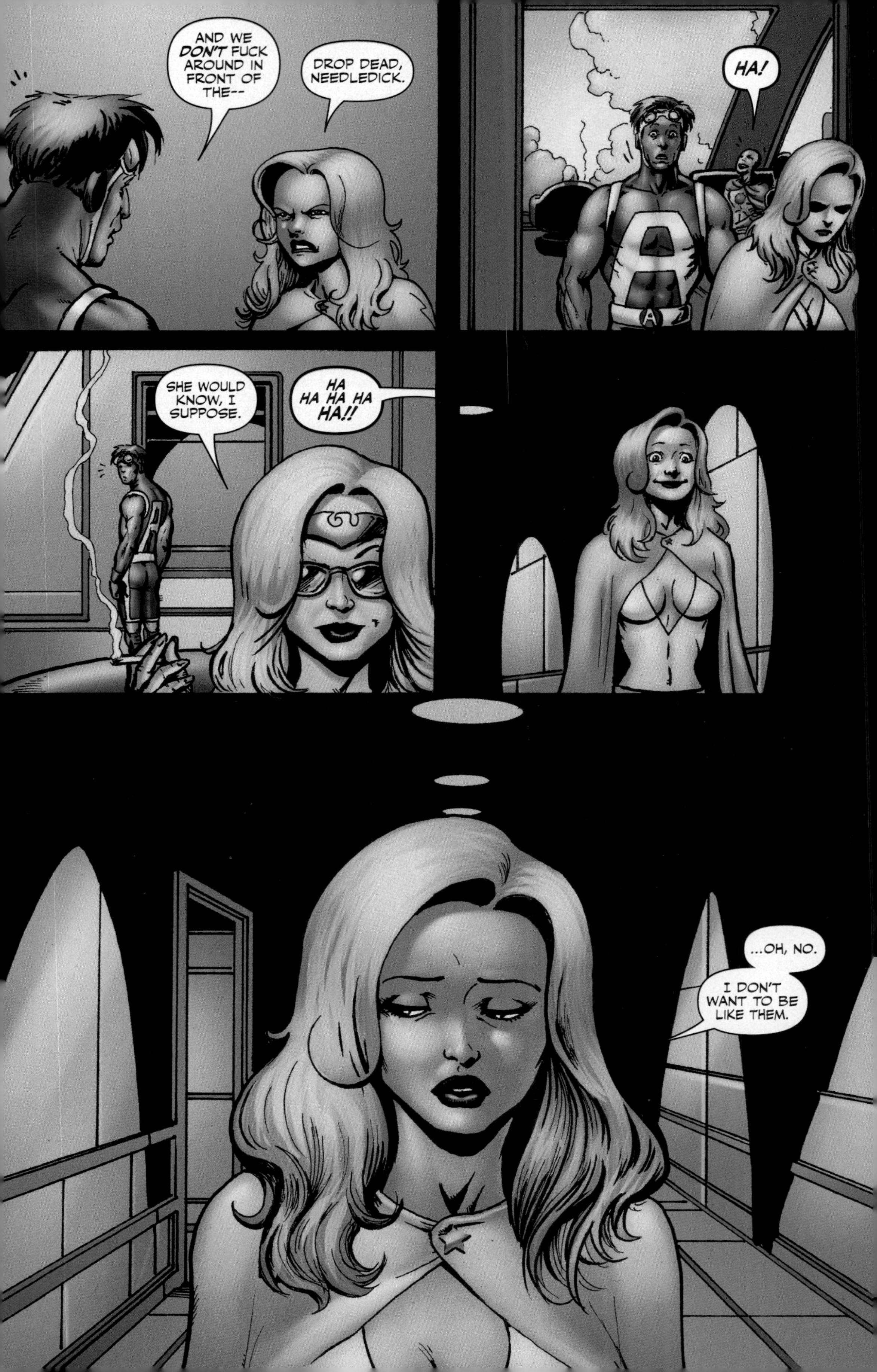
AND WE DON'T FUCK AROUND IN FRONT OF THE--
DROP DEAD, NEEDLEDICK.
HA!
SHE WOULD KNOW, I SUPPOSE.
HA HA HA HA HA!!
...OH, NO.
I DON'T WANT TO BE LIKE THEM.

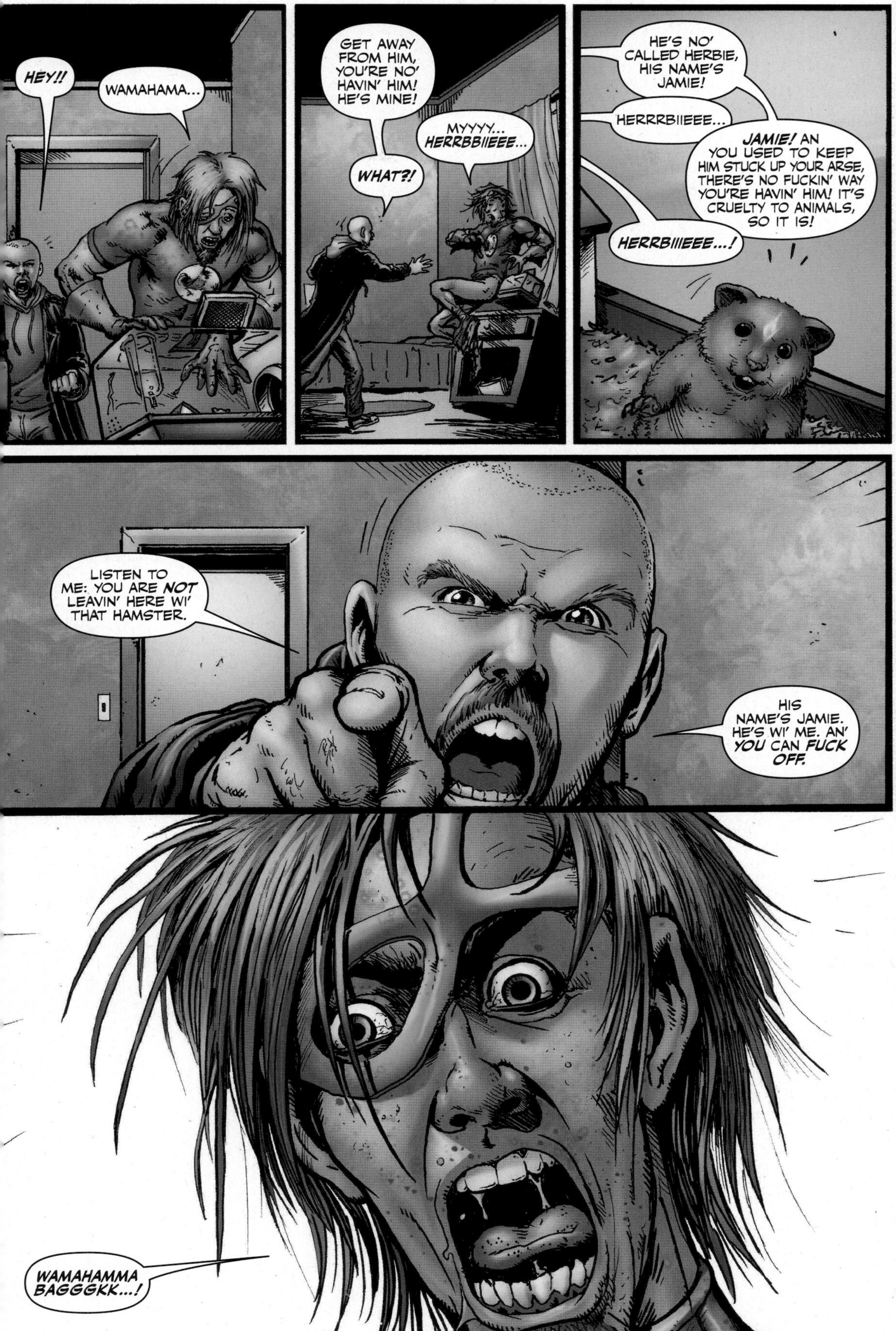
HEY!!
WAMAHAMA...
GET AWAY FROM HIM, YOU'RE NO' HAVIN' HIM! HE'S MINE!
WHAT?!
MYYYY... HERRBBIIEEE...
HE'S NO' CALLED HERBIE, HIS NAME'S JAMIE!
HERRRBIIEEE...
JAMIE! AN YOU USED TO KEEP HIM STUCK UP YOUR ARSE, THERE'S NO FUCKIN' WAY YOU'RE HAVIN' HIM! IT'S CRUELTY TO ANIMALS, SO IT IS!
HERRBIIIEEE...!
LISTEN TO ME: YOU ARE NOT LEAVIN' HERE WI' THAT HAMSTER.
HIS NAME'S JAMIE. HE'S WI' ME. AN' YOU CAN FUCK OFF.
WAMAHAMMA BAGGGKK...!

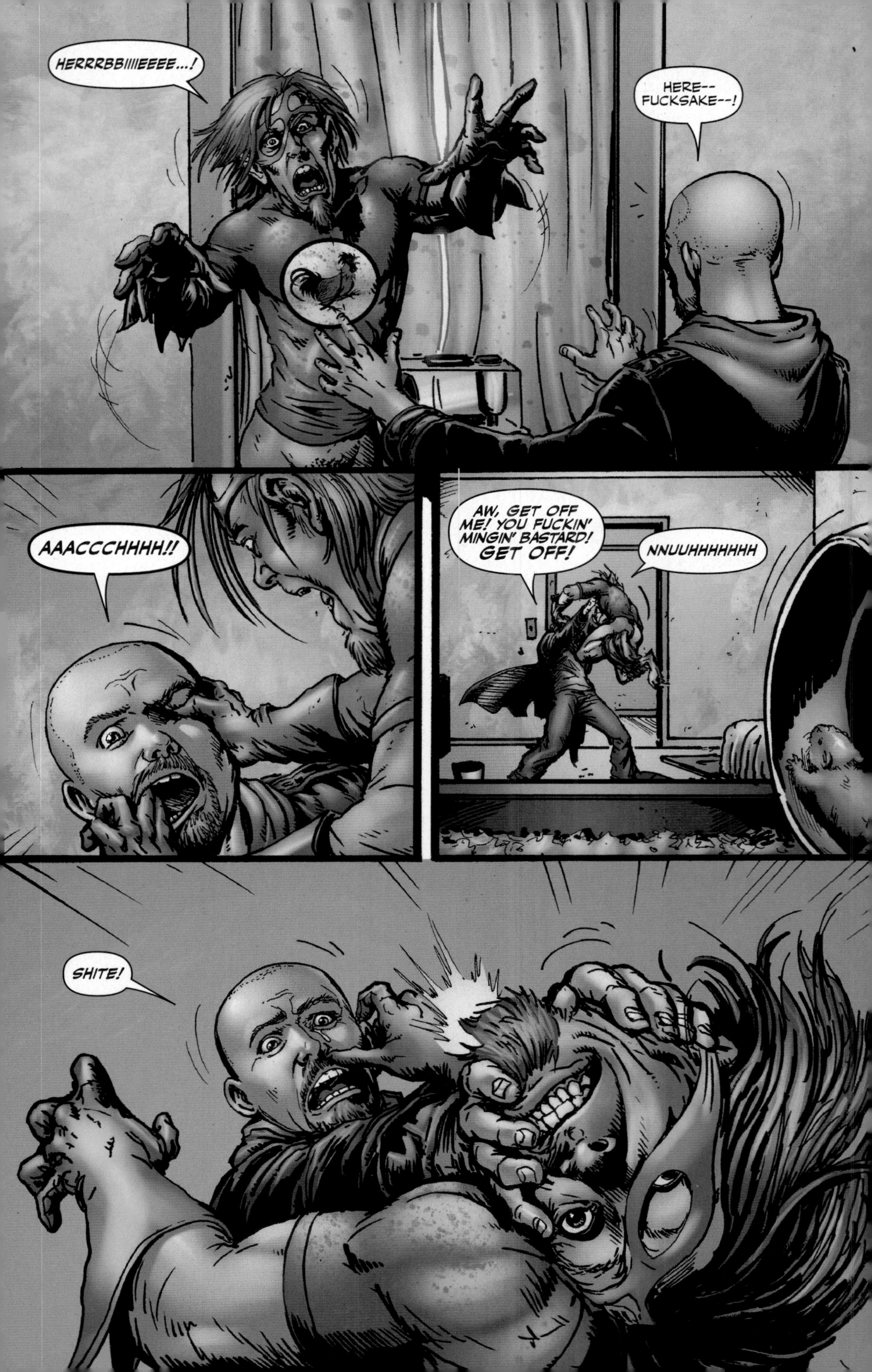
HERRRBBIIIIEEEE...!
HERE--
FUCKSAKE--!
AAACCCHHHH!!
AW, GET OFF ME! YOU FUCKIN' MINGIN' BASTARD! GET OFF!
NNUUHHHHHHH
SHITE!

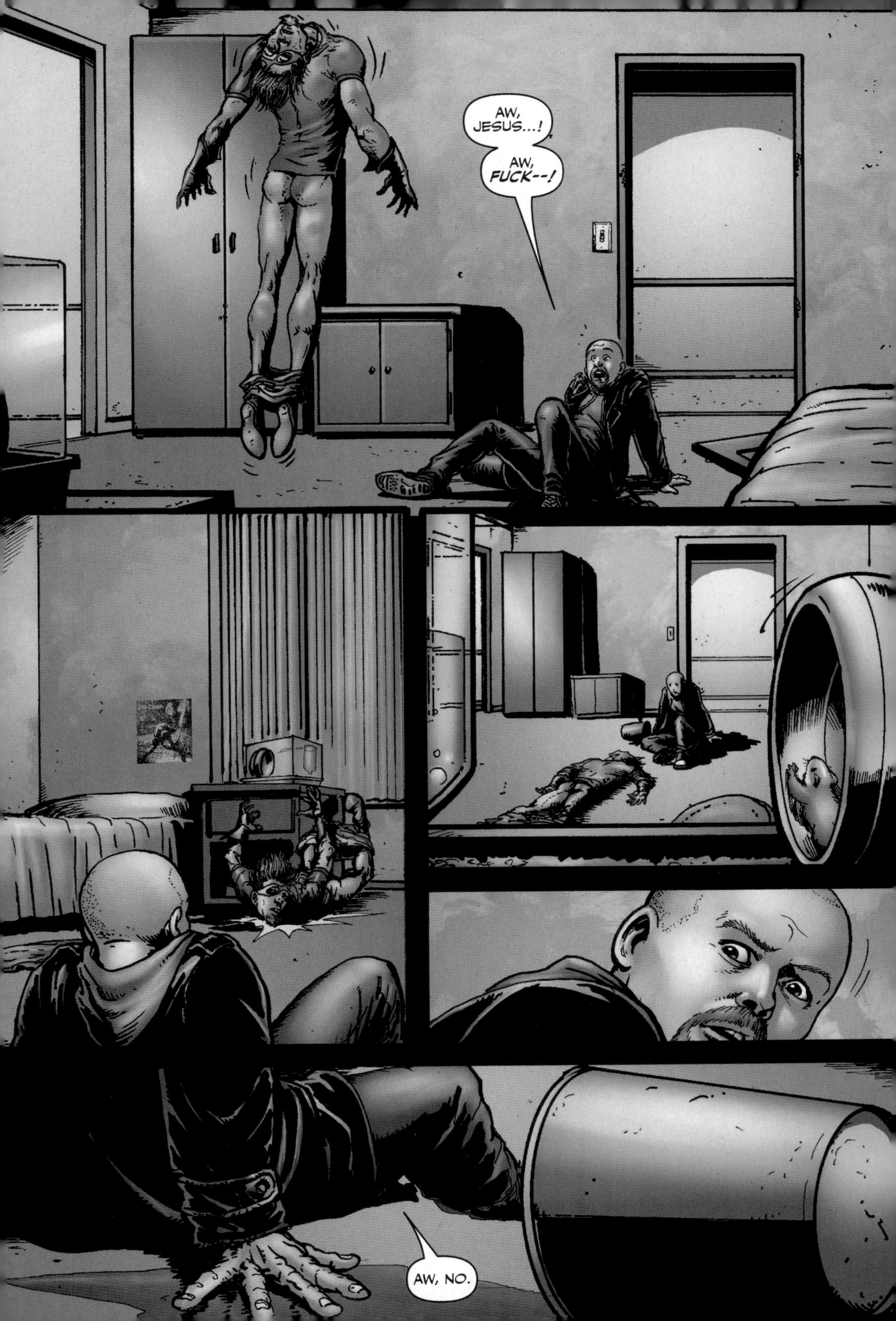
AW, JESUS...!
AW, FUCK--!
AW, NO.

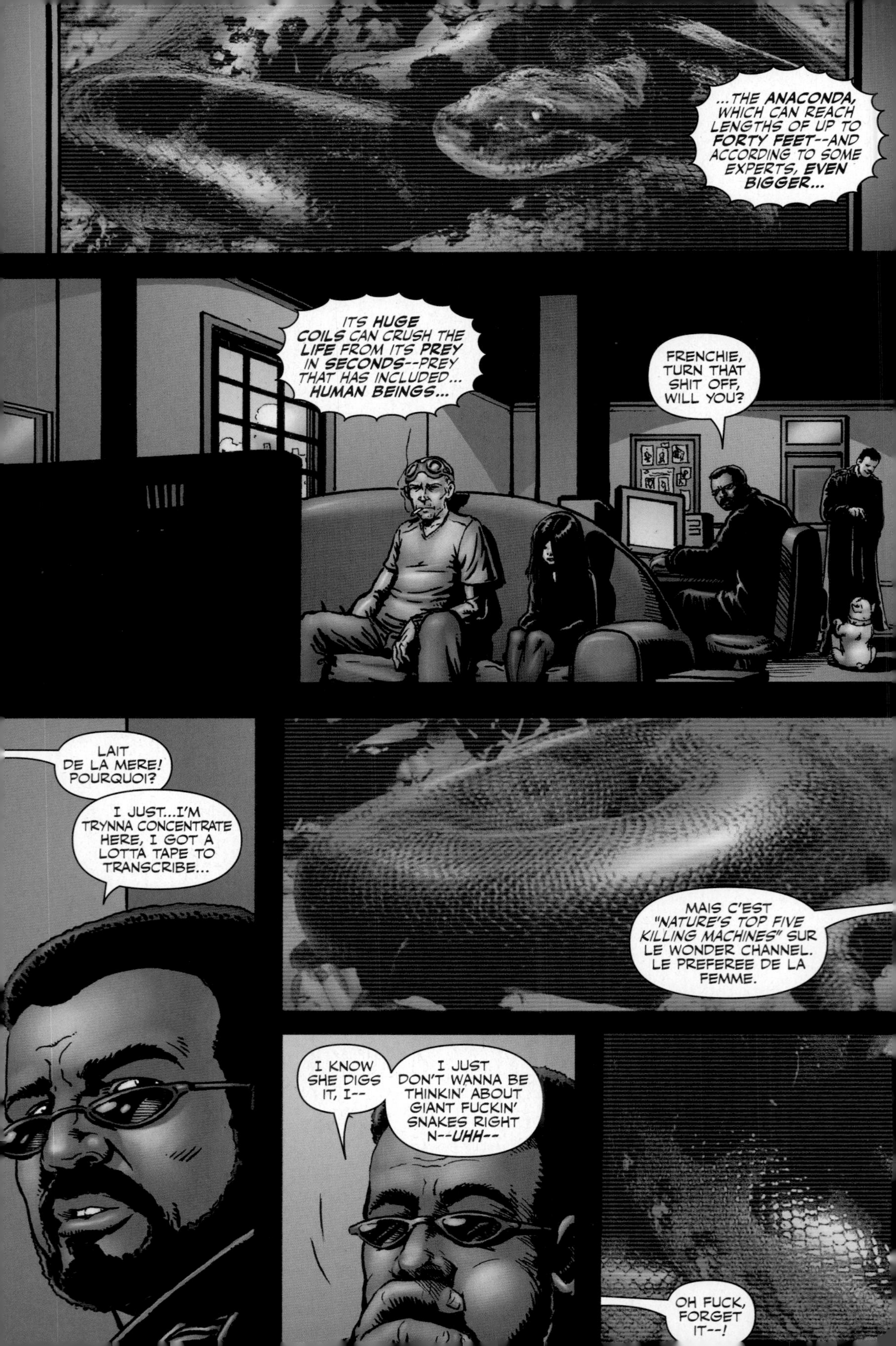
...THE ANACONDA, WHICH CAN REACH LENGTHS OF UP TO FORTY FEET--AND ACCORDING TO SOME EXPERTS, EVEN BIGGER...
ITS HUGE COILS CAN CRUSH THE LIFE FROM ITS PREY IN SECONDS--PREY THAT HAS INCLUDED... HUMAN BEINGS...
FRENCHIE, TURN THAT SHIT OFF, WILL YOU?
LAIT DE LA MERE! POURQUOI?
I JUST...I'M TRYNNA CONCENTRATE HERE, I GOT A LOTTA TAPE TO TRANSCRIBE...
MAIS C'EST "NATURE'S TOP FIVE KILLING MACHINES" SUR LE WONDER CHANNEL. LE PREFEREE DE LA FEMME.
I KNOW SHE DIGS IT, I--
I JUST DON'T WANNA BE THINKIN' ABOUT GIANT FUCKIN' SNAKES RIGHT N--UHH--
OH FUCK, FORGET IT--!

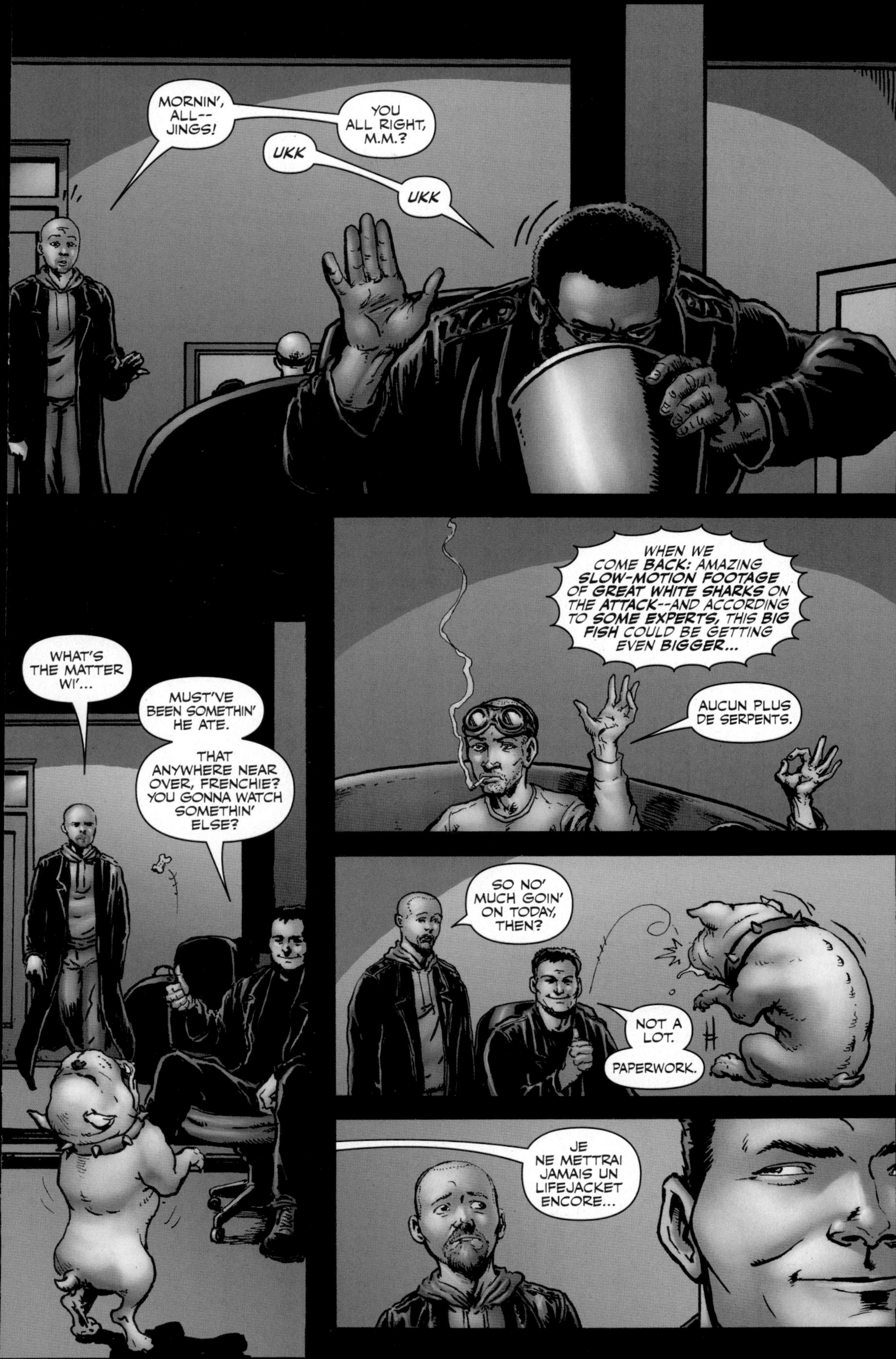
MORNIN', ALL-- JINGS!
YOU ALL RIGHT, M.M.?
UKK
UKK
WHAT'S THE MATTER WI'...
MUST'VE BEEN SOMETHIN' HE ATE.
THAT ANYWHERE NEAR OVER, FRENCHIE? YOU GONNA WATCH SOMETHIN' ELSE?
WHEN WE COME BACK: AMAZING SLOW-MOTION FOOTAGE OF GREAT WHITE SHARKS ON THE ATTACK--AND ACCORDING TO SOME EXPERTS, THIS BIG FISH COULD BE GETTING EVEN BIGGER...
AUCUN PLUS DE SERPENTS.
SO NO' MUCH GOIN' ON TODAY, THEN?
NOT A LOT.
PAPERWORK.
JE NE METTRAI JAMAIS UN LIFEJACKET ENCORE...

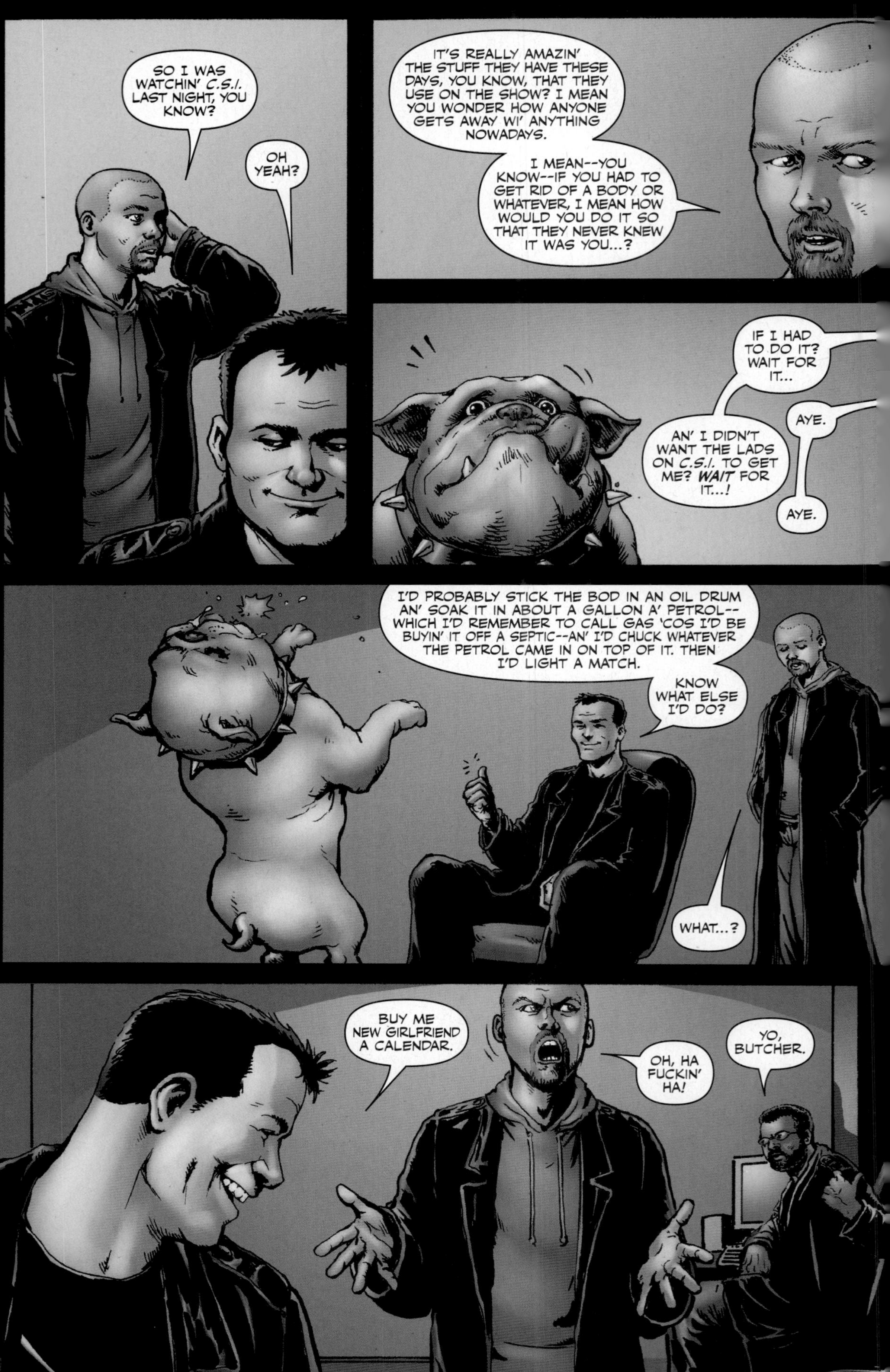
SO I WAS WATCHIN' C.S.I. LAST NIGHT, YOU KNOW?
OH YEAH?
IT'S REALLY AMAZIN' THE STUFF THEY HAVE THESE DAYS, YOU KNOW, THAT THEY USE ON THE SHOW? I MEAN YOU WONDER HOW ANYONE GETS AWAY WI' ANYTHING NOWADAYS.
I MEAN--YOU KNOW--IF YOU HAD TO GET RID OF A BODY OR WHATEVER, I MEAN HOW WOULD YOU DO IT SO THAT THEY NEVER KNEW IT WAS YOU...?
IF I HAD TO DO IT? WAIT FOR IT...
AYE.
AN' I DIDN'T WANT THE LADS ON C.S.I. TO GET ME? WAIT FOR IT...!
AYE.
I'D PROBABLY STICK THE BOD IN AN OIL DRUM AN' SOAK IT IN ABOUT A GALLON A' PETROL--WHICH I'D REMEMBER TO CALL GAS 'COS I'D BE BUYIN' IT OFF A SEPTIC--AN' I'D CHUCK WHATEVER THE PETROL CAME IN ON TOP OF IT. THEN I'D LIGHT A MATCH.
KNOW WHAT ELSE I'D DO?
WHAT...?
BUY ME NEW GIRLFRIEND A CALENDAR.
OH, HA FUCKIN' HA!
YO, BUTCHER.

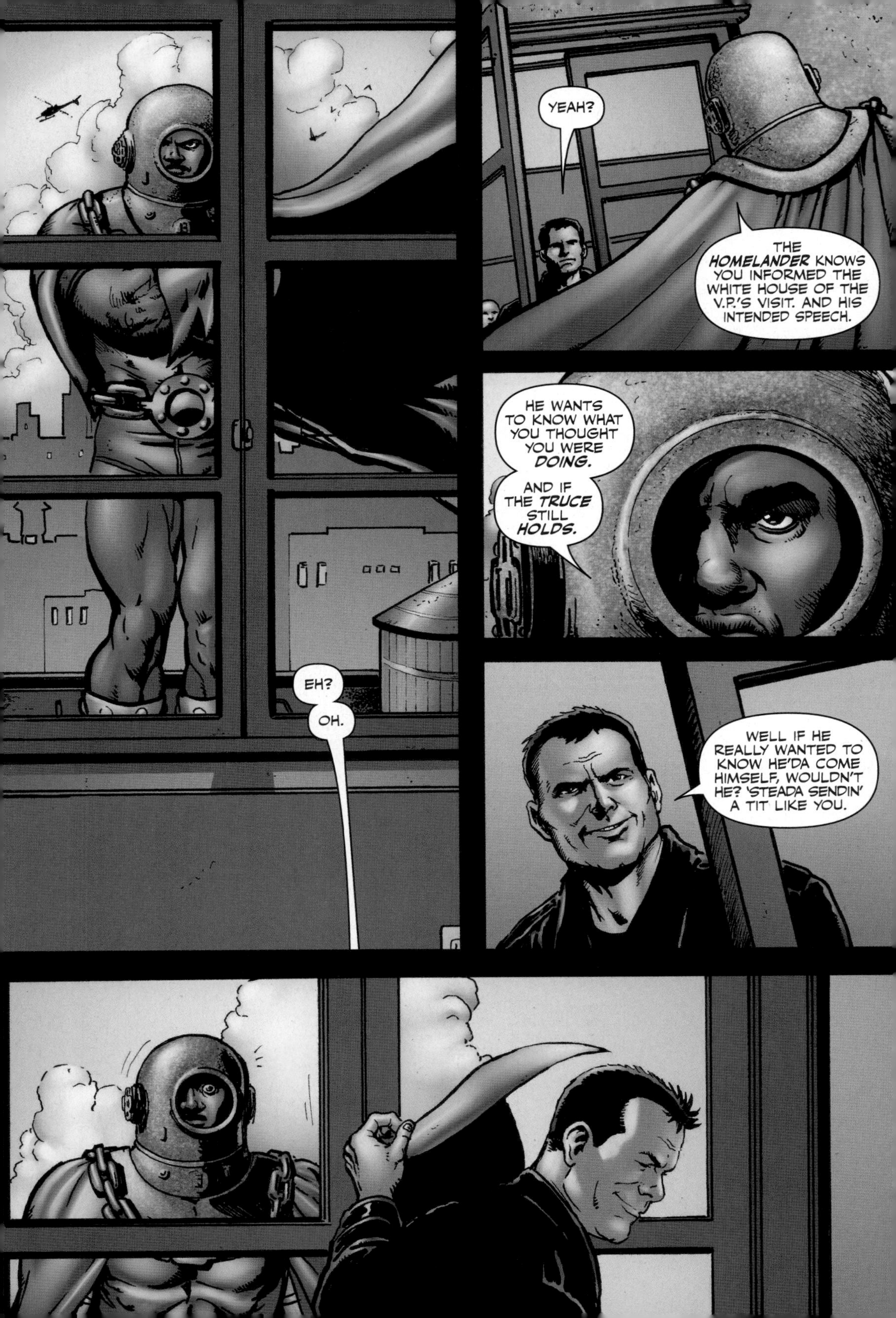
YEAH?
THE HOMELANDER KNOWS YOU INFORMED THE WHITE HOUSE OF THE V.P.'S VISIT. AND HIS INTENDED SPEECH.
HE WANTS TO KNOW WHAT YOU THOUGHT YOU WERE DOING.
AND IF THE TRUCE STILL HOLDS.
EH?
OH.
WELL IF HE REALLY WANTED TO KNOW HE'DA COME HIMSELF, WOULDN'T HE? 'STEADA SENDIN' A TIT LIKE YOU.

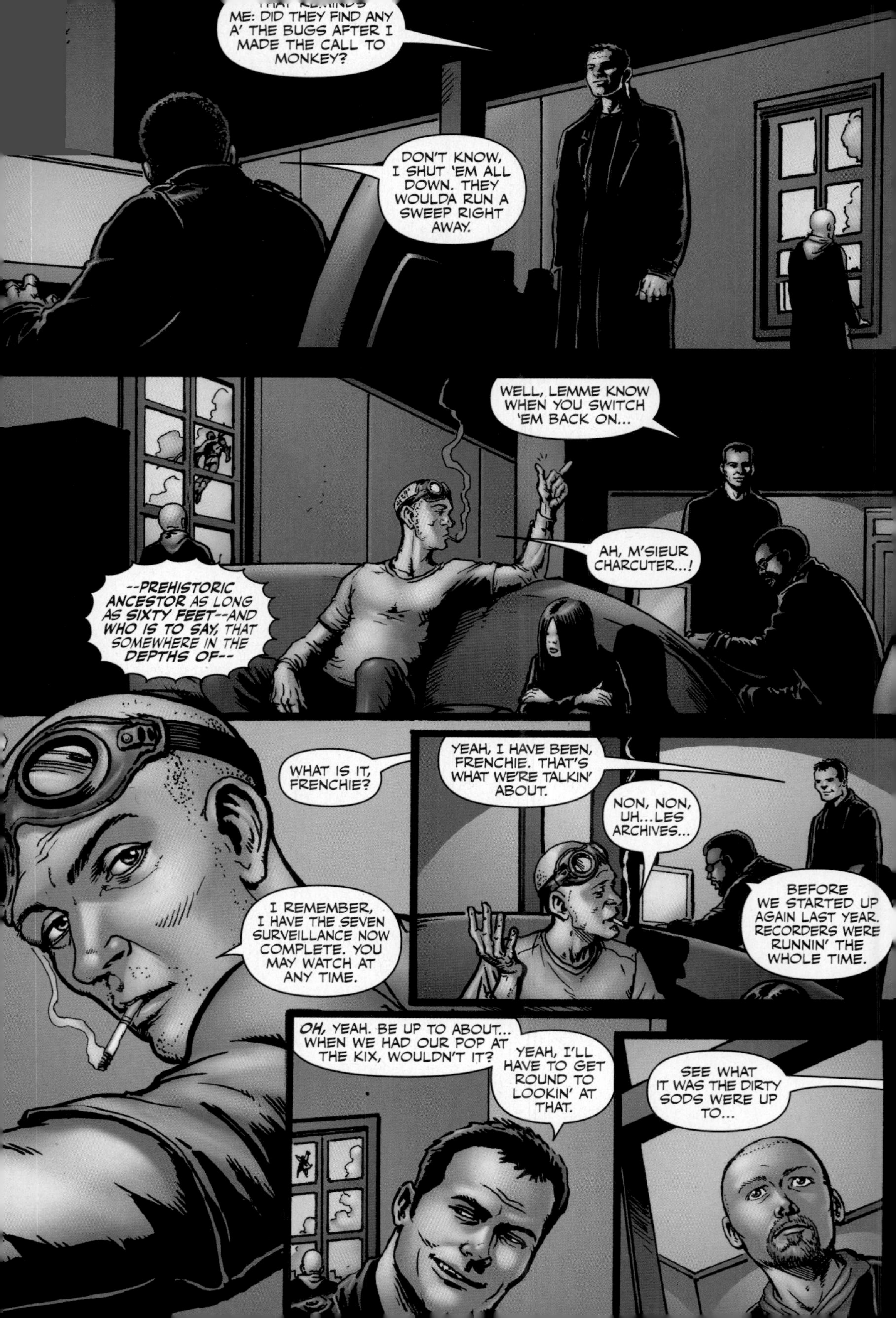
ME: DID THEY FIND ANY A' THE BUGS AFTER I MADE THE CALL TO MONKEY?
DON'T KNOW, I SHUT 'EM ALL DOWN. THEY WOULDA RUN A SWEEP RIGHT AWAY.
WELL, LEMME KNOW WHEN YOU SWITCH 'EM BACK ON...
AH, M'SIEUR CHARCUTER...!
--PREHISTORIC ANCESTOR AS LONG AS SIXTY FEET--AND WHO IS TO SAY, THAT SOMEWHERE IN THE DEPTHS OF--
WHAT IS IT, FRENCHIE?
I REMEMBER, I HAVE THE SEVEN SURVEILLANCE NOW COMPLETE. YOU MAY WATCH AT ANY TIME.
YEAH, I HAVE BEEN, FRENCHIE. THAT'S WHAT WE'RE TALKIN' ABOUT.
NON, NON, UH...LES ARCHIVES...
BEFORE WE STARTED UP AGAIN LAST YEAR. RECORDERS WERE RUNNIN' THE WHOLE TIME.
OH, YEAH. BE UP TO ABOUT... WHEN WE HAD OUR POP AT THE KIX, WOULDN'T IT?
YEAH, I'LL HAVE TO GET ROUND TO LOOKIN' AT THAT.
SEE WHAT IT WAS THE DIRTY SODS WERE UP TO...

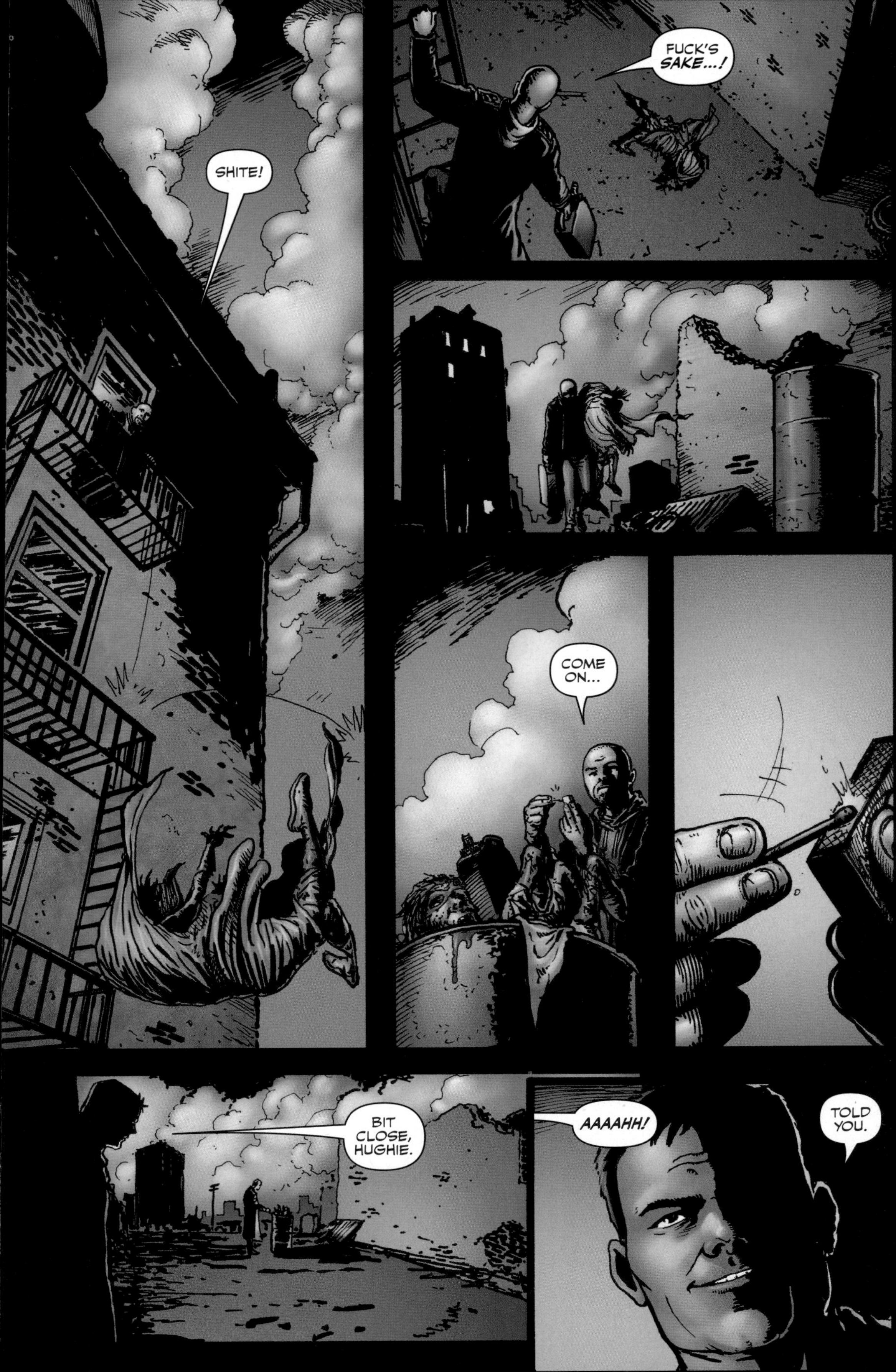
SHITE!
FUCK'S SAKE...!
COME ON...
BIT CLOSE, HUGHIE.
AAAAHH!
TOLD YOU.

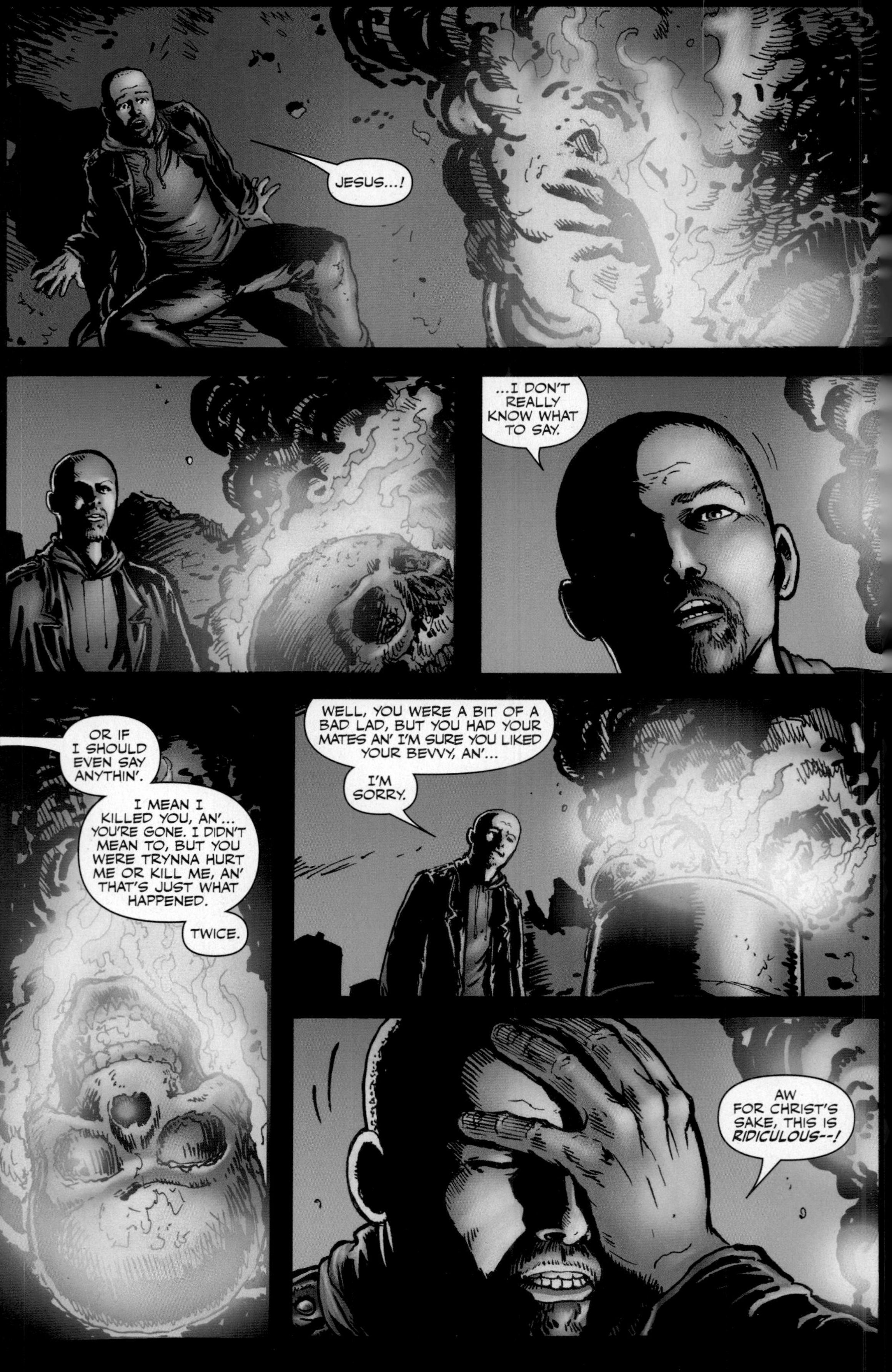
JESUS...!
...I DON'T REALLY KNOW WHAT TO SAY.
OR IF I SHOULD EVEN SAY ANYTHIN'.
I MEAN I KILLED YOU, AN'... YOU'RE GONE. I DIDN'T MEAN TO, BUT YOU WERE TRYNNA HURT ME OR KILL ME, AN' THAT'S JUST WHAT HAPPENED.
TWICE.
WELL, YOU WERE A BIT OF A BAD LAD, BUT YOU HAD YOUR MATES AN' I'M SURE YOU LIKED YOUR BEVVY, AN'...
I'M SORRY.
AW FOR CHRIST'S SAKE, THIS IS *RIDICULOUS--!*

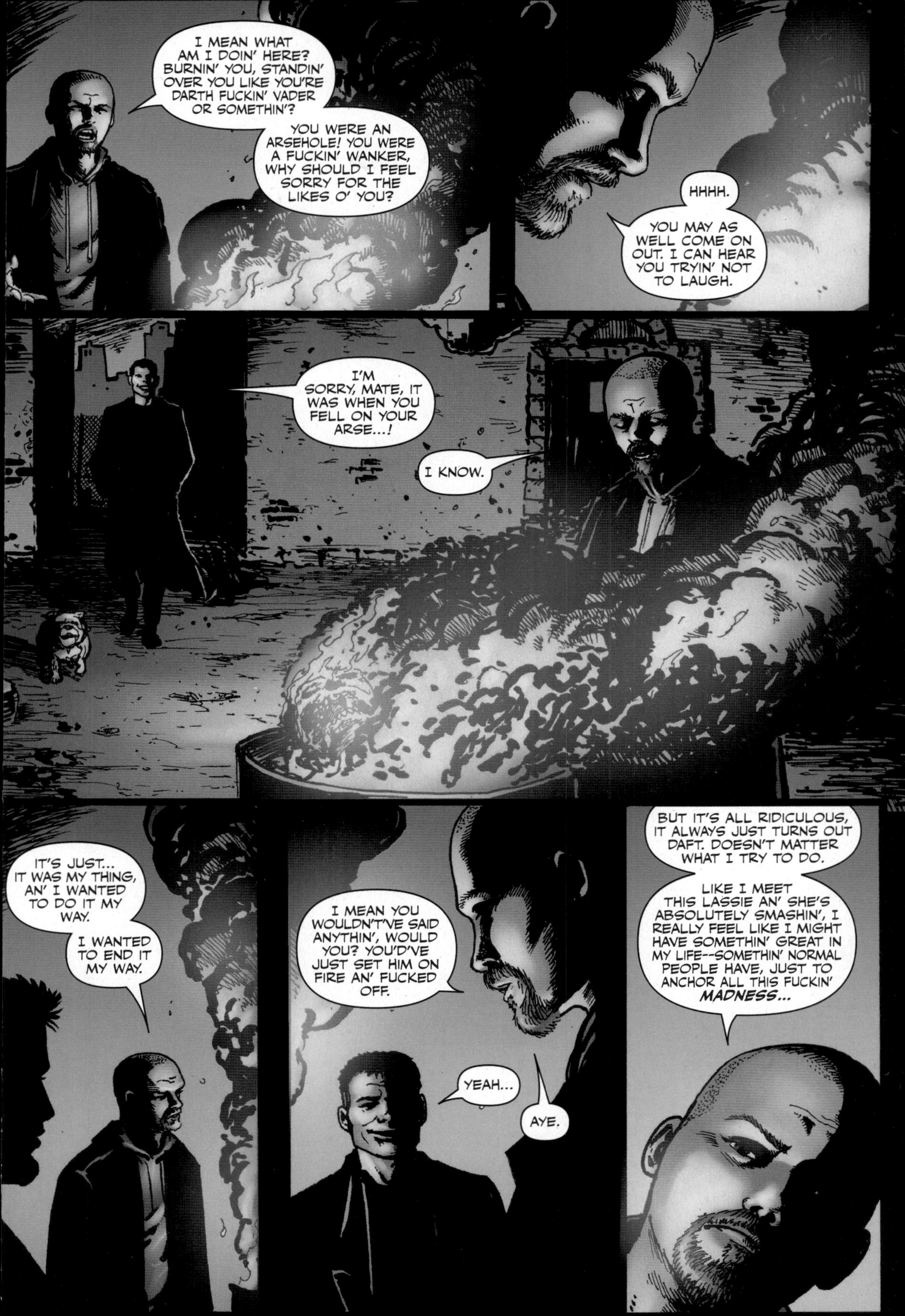
I MEAN WHAT AM I DOIN' HERE? BURNIN' YOU, STANDIN' OVER YOU LIKE YOU'RE DARTH FUCKIN' VADER OR SOMETHIN'?
YOU WERE AN ARSEHOLE! YOU WERE A FUCKIN' WANKER, WHY SHOULD I FEEL SORRY FOR THE LIKES O' YOU?
HHHH.
YOU MAY AS WELL COME ON OUT. I CAN HEAR YOU TRYIN' NOT TO LAUGH.
I'M SORRY, MATE, IT WAS WHEN YOU FELL ON YOUR ARSE...!
I KNOW.
IT'S JUST... IT WAS MY THING, AN' I WANTED TO DO IT MY WAY.
I WANTED TO END IT MY WAY.
I MEAN YOU WOULDN'T'VE SAID ANYTHIN', WOULD YOU? YOU'D'VE JUST SET HIM ON FIRE AN' FUCKED OFF.
YEAH...
AYE.
BUT IT'S ALL RIDICULOUS, IT ALWAYS JUST TURNS OUT DAFT. DOESN'T MATTER WHAT I TRY TO DO.
LIKE I MEET THIS LASSIE AN' SHE'S ABSOLUTELY SMASHIN', I REALLY FEEL LIKE I MIGHT HAVE SOMETHIN' GREAT IN MY LIFE--SOMETHIN' NORMAL PEOPLE HAVE, JUST TO ANCHOR ALL THIS FUCKIN' *MADNESS...*

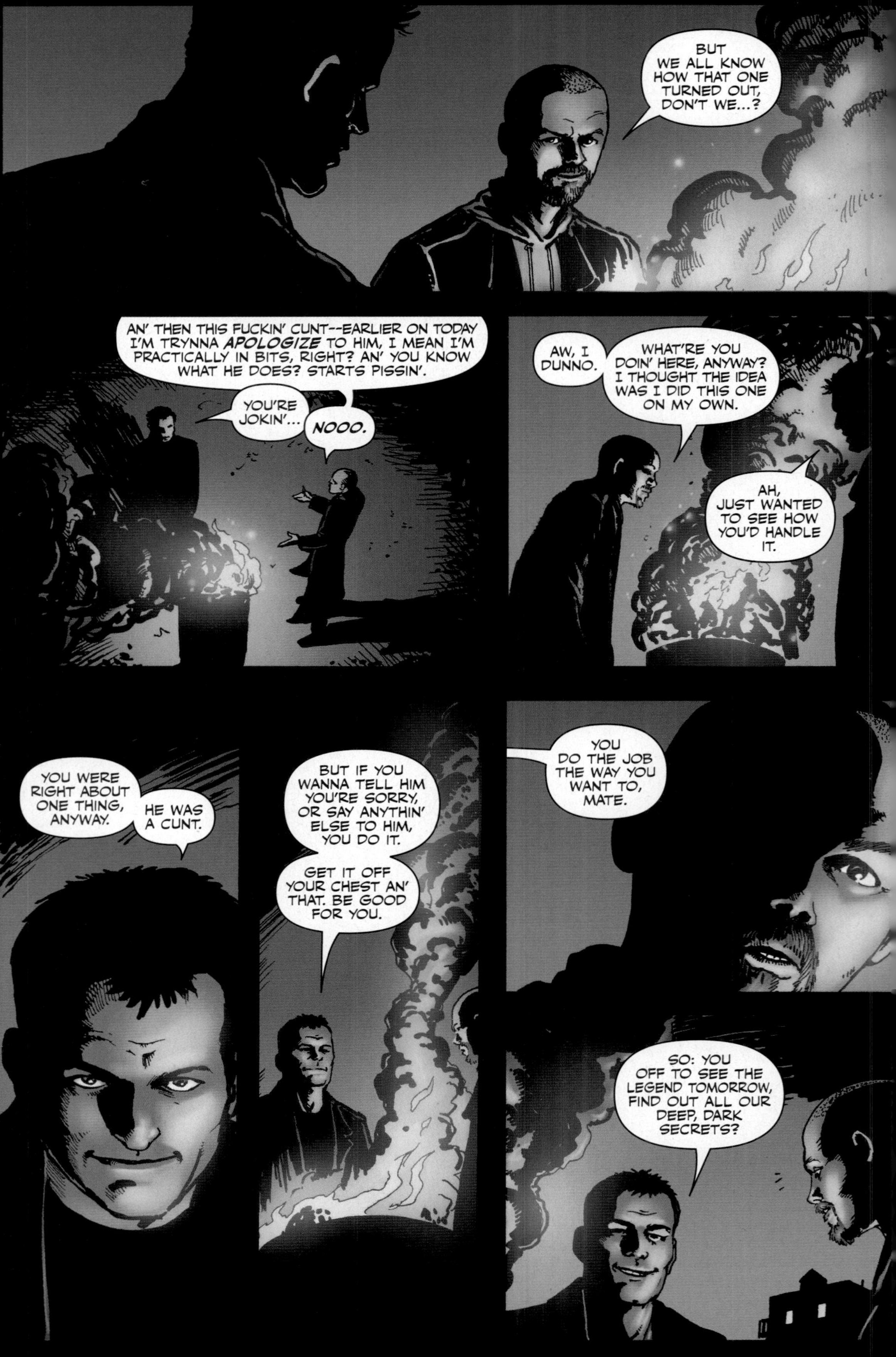
BUT WE ALL KNOW HOW THAT ONE TURNED OUT, DON'T WE...?
AN' THEN THIS FUCKIN' CUNT--EARLIER ON TODAY I'M TRYNNA *APOLOGIZE* TO HIM, I MEAN I'M PRACTICALLY IN BITS, RIGHT? AN' YOU KNOW WHAT HE DOES? STARTS PISSIN'.
YOU'RE JOKIN'...
NOOO.
AW, I DUNNO.
WHAT'RE YOU DOIN' HERE, ANYWAY? I THOUGHT THE IDEA WAS I DID THIS ONE ON MY OWN.
AH, JUST WANTED TO SEE HOW YOU'D HANDLE IT.
YOU WERE RIGHT ABOUT ONE THING, ANYWAY.
HE WAS A CUNT.
BUT IF YOU WANNA TELL HIM YOU'RE SORRY, OR SAY ANYTHIN' ELSE TO HIM, YOU DO IT.
GET IT OFF YOUR CHEST AN' THAT. BE GOOD FOR YOU.
YOU DO THE JOB THE WAY YOU WANT TO, MATE.
SO: YOU OFF TO SEE THE LEGEND TOMORROW, FIND OUT ALL OUR DEEP, DARK SECRETS?

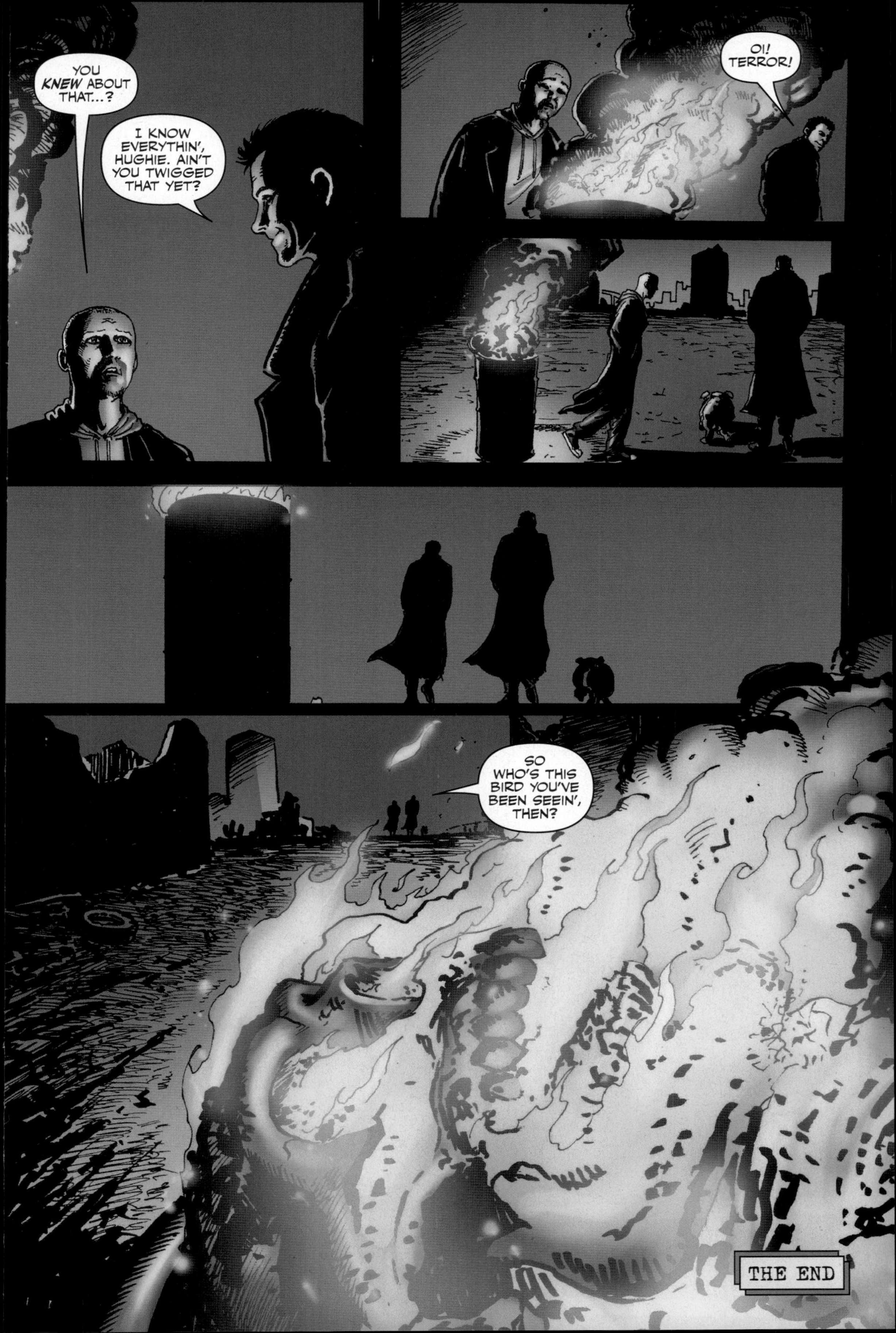
YOU KNEW ABOUT THAT...?
I KNOW EVERYTHIN', HUGHIE. AIN'T YOU TWIGGED THAT YET?
OI! TERROR!
SO WHO'S THIS BIRD YOU'VE BEEN SEEIN', THEN?
THE END

#19 cover
by Darick Robertson
and Tony Aviña

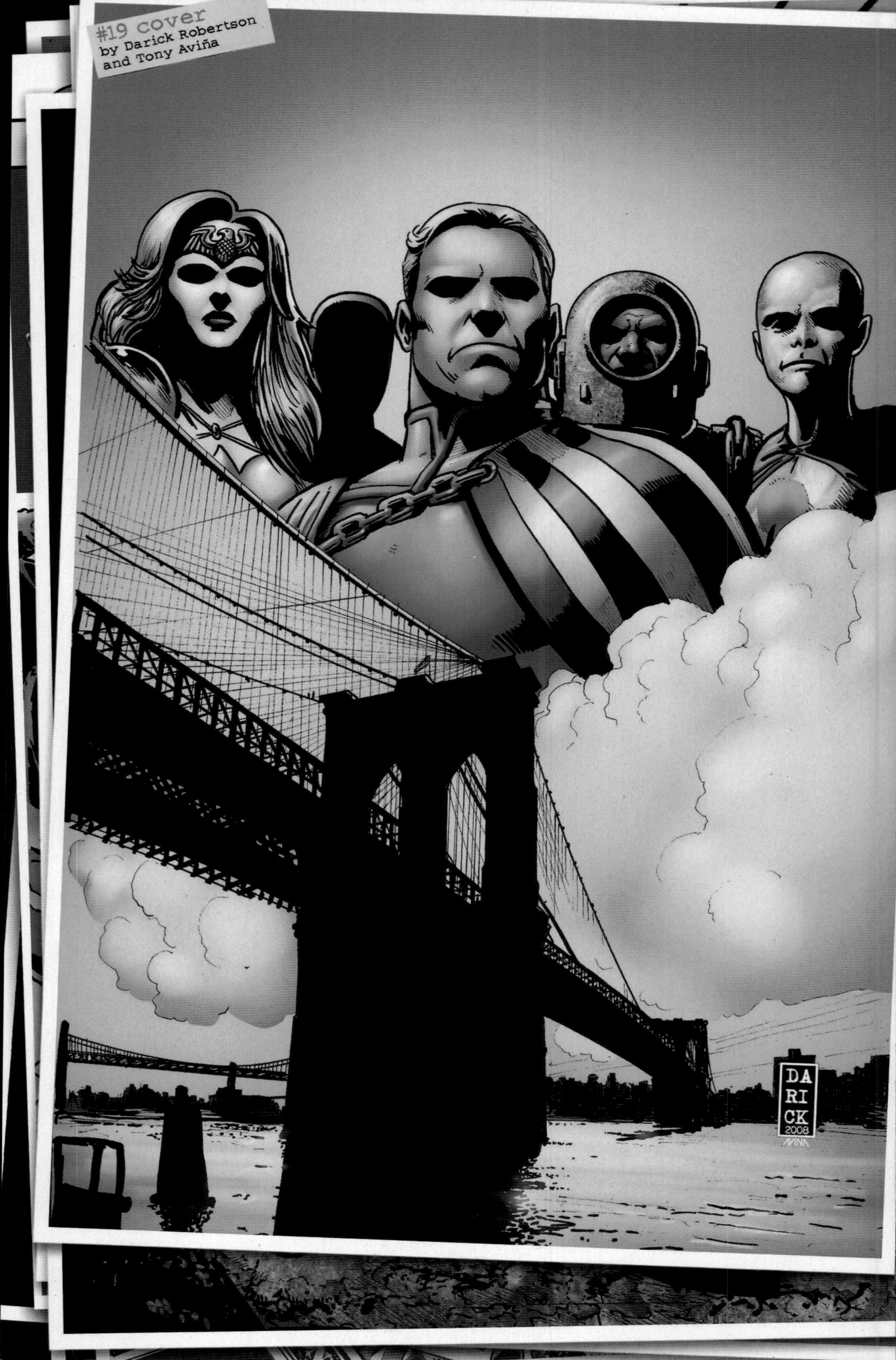
DA
RI
CK
2008
AVINA

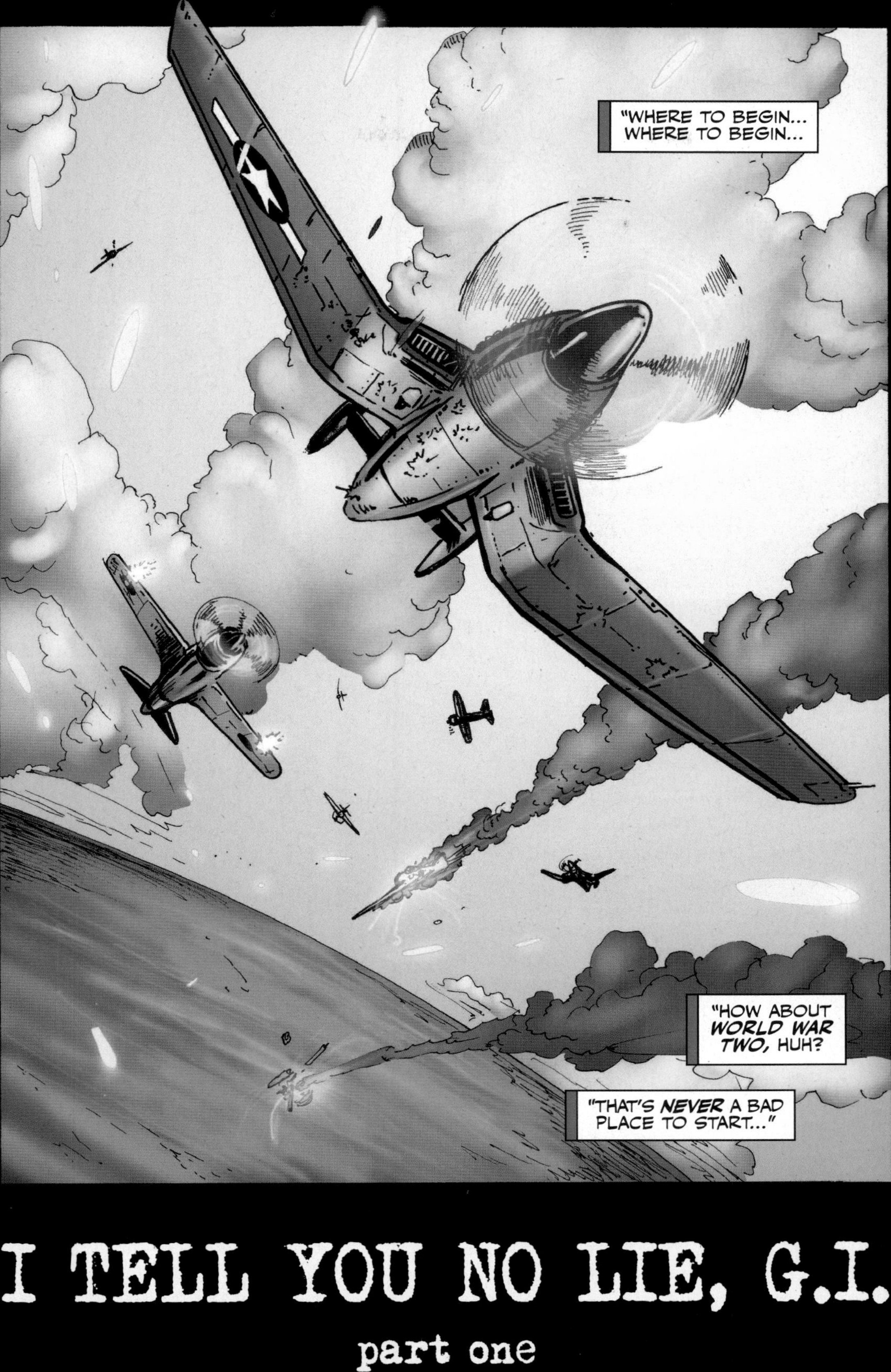
"WHERE TO BEGIN... WHERE TO BEGIN...
"HOW ABOUT *WORLD WAR TWO,* HUH?
"THAT'S *NEVER* A BAD PLACE TO START..."

I TELL YOU NO LIE, G.I.

part one

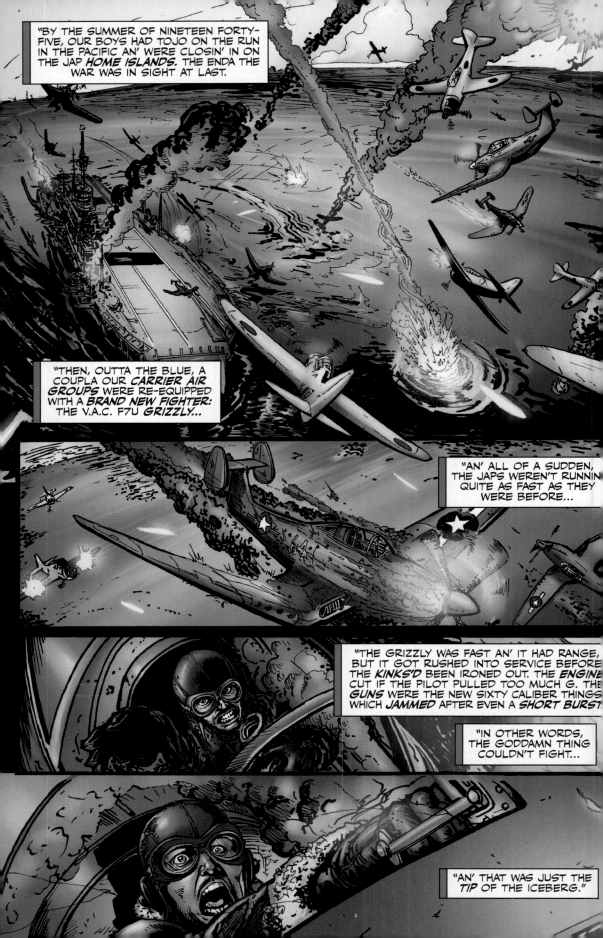

"BY THE SUMMER OF NINETEEN FORTY-FIVE, OUR BOYS HAD TOJO ON THE RUN IN THE PACIFIC AN' WERE CLOSIN' IN ON THE JAP *HOME ISLANDS.* THE ENDA THE WAR WAS IN SIGHT AT LAST.

"THEN, OUTTA THE BLUE, A COUPLA OUR *CARRIER AIR GROUPS* WERE RE-EQUIPPED WITH A *BRAND NEW FIGHTER:* THE V.A.C. F7U *GRIZZLY...*

"AN' ALL OF A SUDDEN, THE JAPS WEREN'T RUNNIN QUITE AS FAST AS THEY WERE BEFORE...

"THE GRIZZLY WAS FAST AN' IT HAD RANGE, BUT IT GOT RUSHED INTO SERVICE BEFORE THE *KINKS'D* BEEN IRONED OUT. THE *ENGINE* CUT IF THE PILOT PULLED TOO MUCH G. THE *GUNS* WERE THE NEW SIXTY CALIBER THINGS WHICH *JAMMED* AFTER EVEN A *SHORT BURST*

"IN OTHER WORDS, THE GODDAMN THING COULDN'T FIGHT...

"AN' THAT WAS JUST THE *TIP* OF THE ICEBERG."

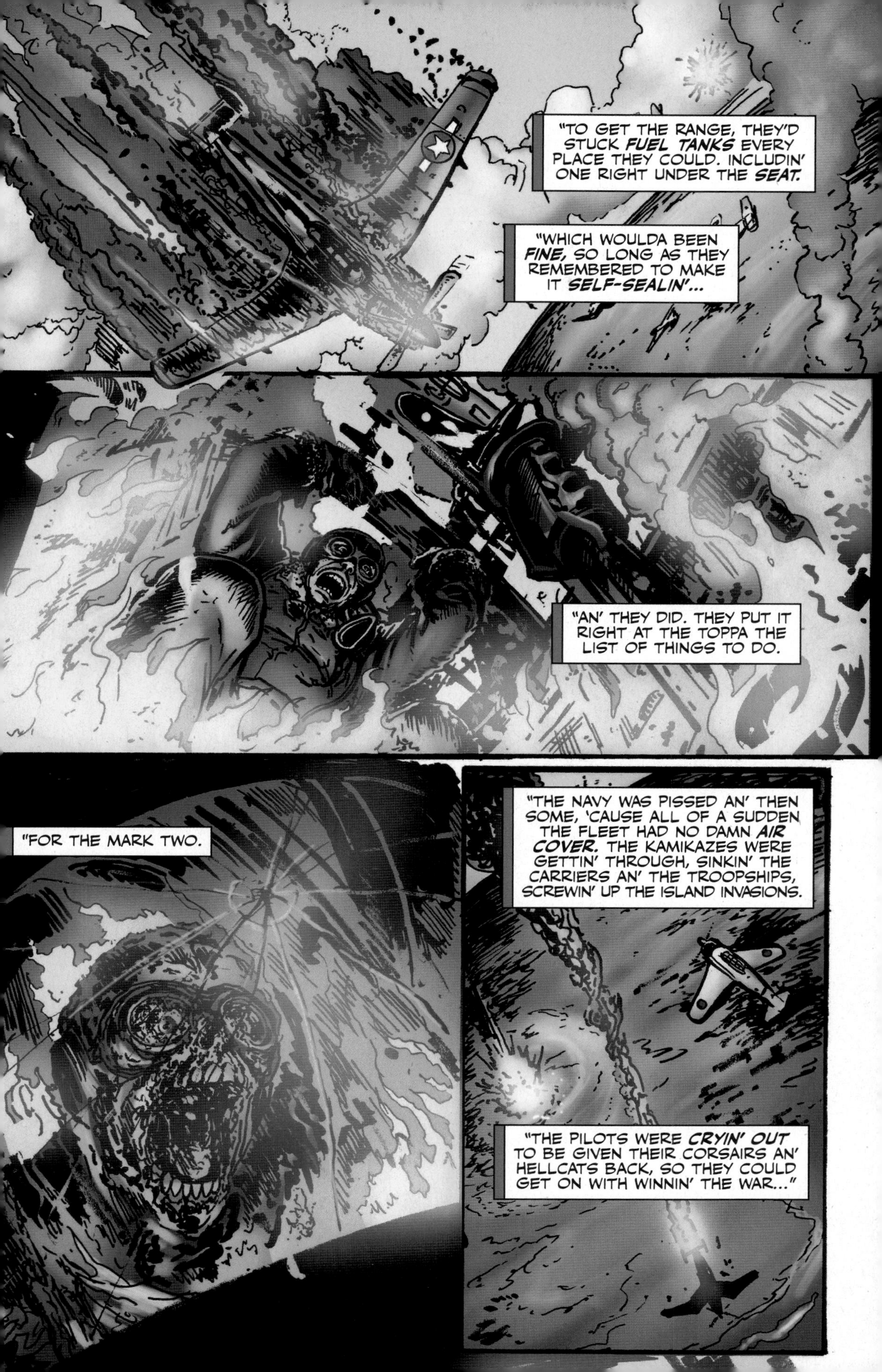
"TO GET THE RANGE, THEY'D STUCK FUEL TANKS EVERY PLACE THEY COULD. INCLUDIN' ONE RIGHT UNDER THE SEAT.
"WHICH WOULDA BEEN FINE, SO LONG AS THEY REMEMBERED TO MAKE IT SELF-SEALIN'...
"AN' THEY DID. THEY PUT IT RIGHT AT THE TOPPA THE LIST OF THINGS TO DO.
"FOR THE MARK TWO.
"THE NAVY WAS PISSED AN' THEN SOME, 'CAUSE ALL OF A SUDDEN THE FLEET HAD NO DAMN AIR COVER. THE KAMIKAZES WERE GETTIN' THROUGH, SINKIN' THE CARRIERS AN' THE TROOPSHIPS, SCREWIN' UP THE ISLAND INVASIONS.
"THE PILOTS WERE CRYIN' OUT TO BE GIVEN THEIR CORSAIRS AN' HELLCATS BACK, SO THEY COULD GET ON WITH WINNIN' THE WAR..."

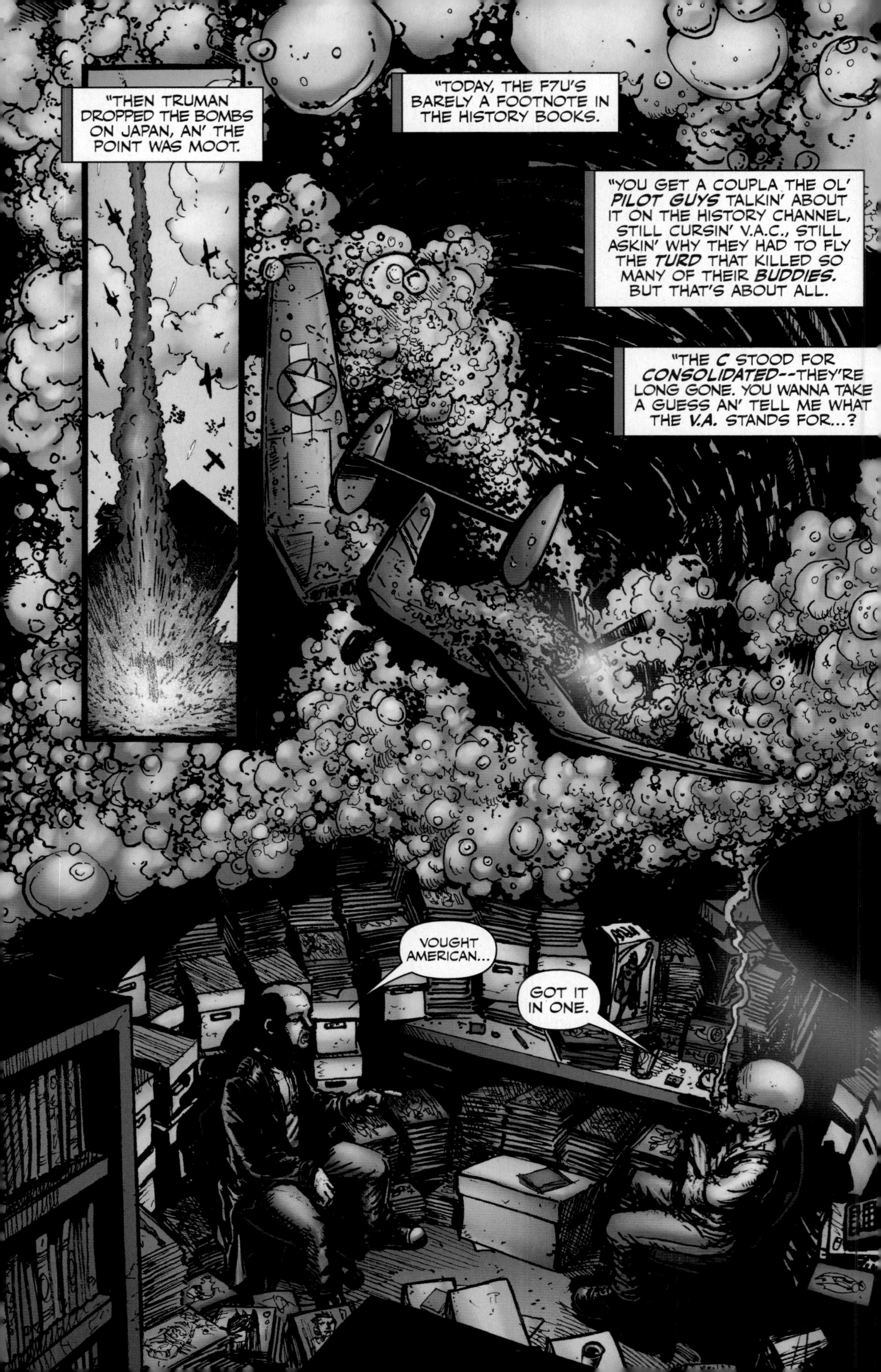
"THEN TRUMAN DROPPED THE BOMBS ON JAPAN, AN' THE POINT WAS MOOT.
"TODAY, THE F7U'S BARELY A FOOTNOTE IN THE HISTORY BOOKS.
"YOU GET A COUPLA THE OL' *PILOT GUYS* TALKIN' ABOUT IT ON THE HISTORY CHANNEL, STILL CURSIN' V.A.C., STILL ASKIN' WHY THEY HAD TO FLY THE *TURD* THAT KILLED SO MANY OF THEIR *BUDDIES.* BUT THAT'S ABOUT ALL.
"THE *C* STOOD FOR *CONSOLIDATED*--THEY'RE LONG GONE. YOU WANNA TAKE A GUESS AN' TELL ME WHAT THE *V.A.* STANDS FOR...?
VOUGHT AMERICAN...
GOT IT IN ONE.

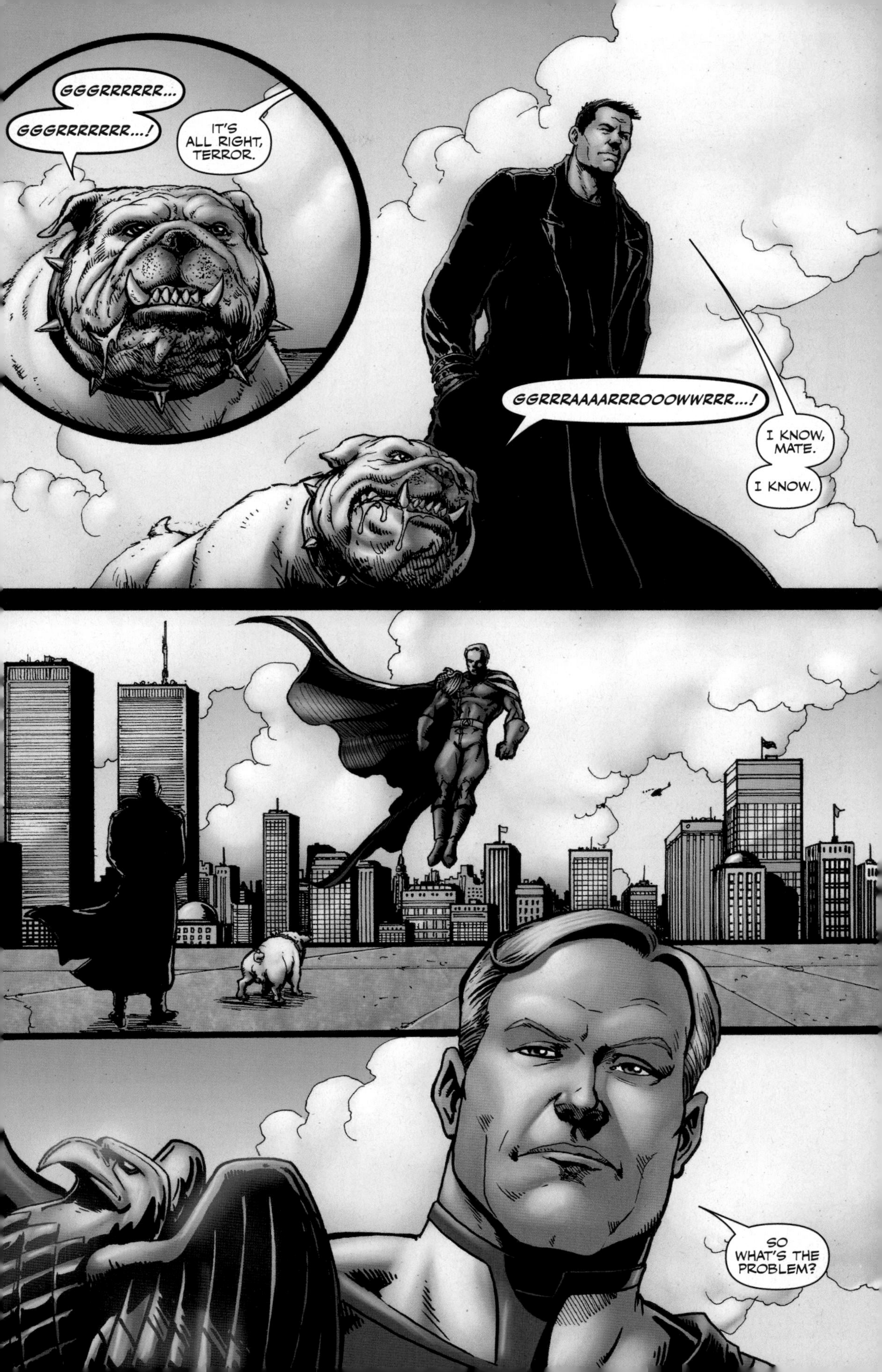
GGGRRRRRR...
GGGRRRRRRR...!
IT'S ALL RIGHT, TERROR.
GGRRRAAAARRROOOWWRRR...!
I KNOW, MATE.
I KNOW.
SO WHAT'S THE PROBLEM?

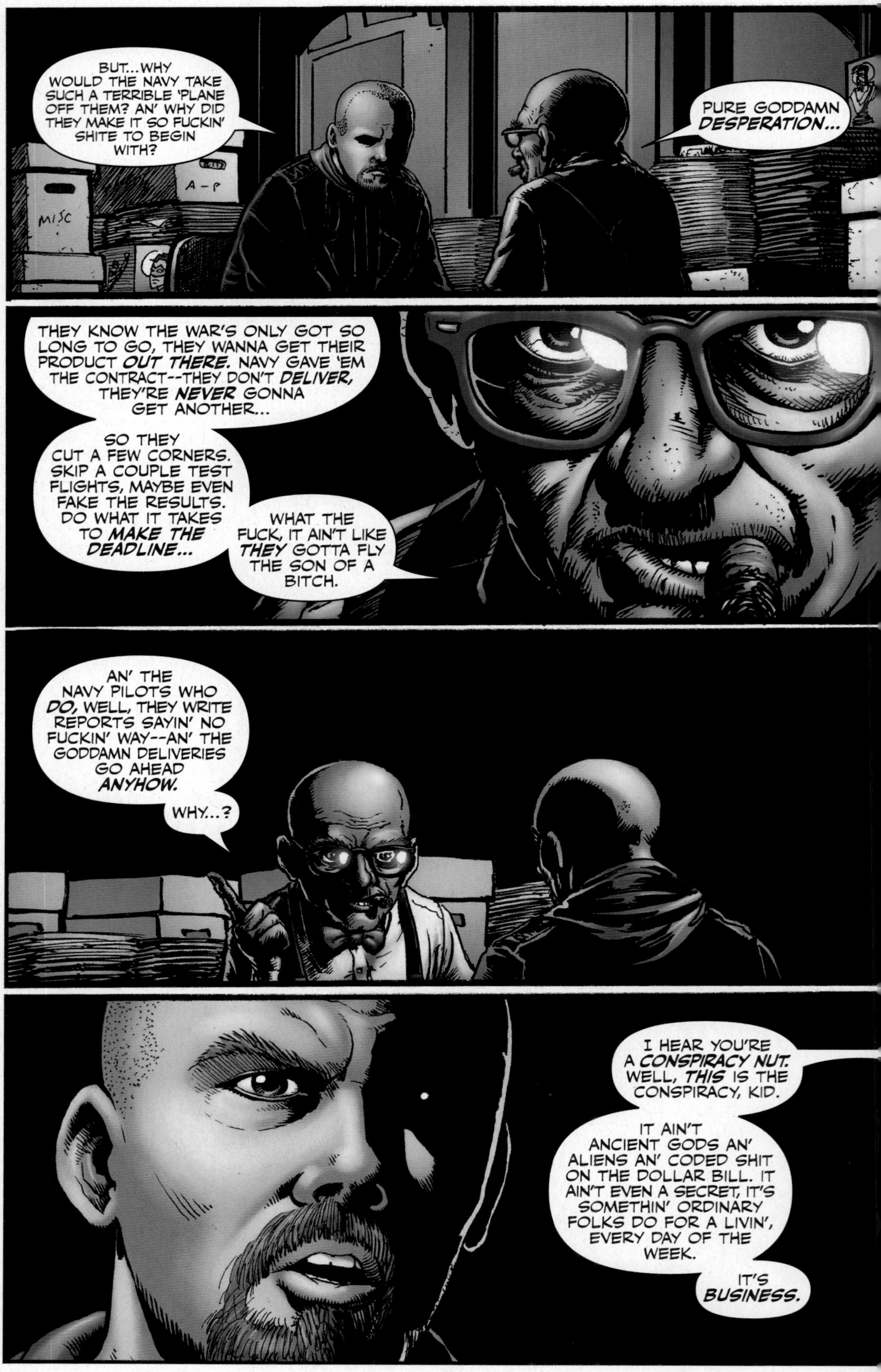
BUT...WHY WOULD THE NAVY TAKE SUCH A TERRIBLE 'PLANE OFF THEM? AN' WHY DID THEY MAKE IT SO FUCKIN' SHITE TO BEGIN WITH?
PURE GODDAMN DESPERATION...
MISC
A - P
THEY KNOW THE WAR'S ONLY GOT SO LONG TO GO, THEY WANNA GET THEIR PRODUCT OUT THERE. NAVY GAVE 'EM THE CONTRACT--THEY DON'T DELIVER, THEY'RE NEVER GONNA GET ANOTHER...
SO THEY CUT A FEW CORNERS. SKIP A COUPLE TEST FLIGHTS, MAYBE EVEN FAKE THE RESULTS. DO WHAT IT TAKES TO MAKE THE DEADLINE...
WHAT THE FUCK, IT AIN'T LIKE THEY GOTTA FLY THE SON OF A BITCH.
AN' THE NAVY PILOTS WHO DO, WELL, THEY WRITE REPORTS SAYIN' NO FUCKIN' WAY--AN' THE GODDAMN DELIVERIES GO AHEAD ANYHOW.
WHY...?
I HEAR YOU'RE A CONSPIRACY NUT. WELL, THIS IS THE CONSPIRACY, KID.
IT AIN'T ANCIENT GODS AN' ALIENS AN' CODED SHIT ON THE DOLLAR BILL. IT AIN'T EVEN A SECRET, IT'S SOMETHIN' ORDINARY FOLKS DO FOR A LIVIN', EVERY DAY OF THE WEEK.
IT'S BUSINESS.

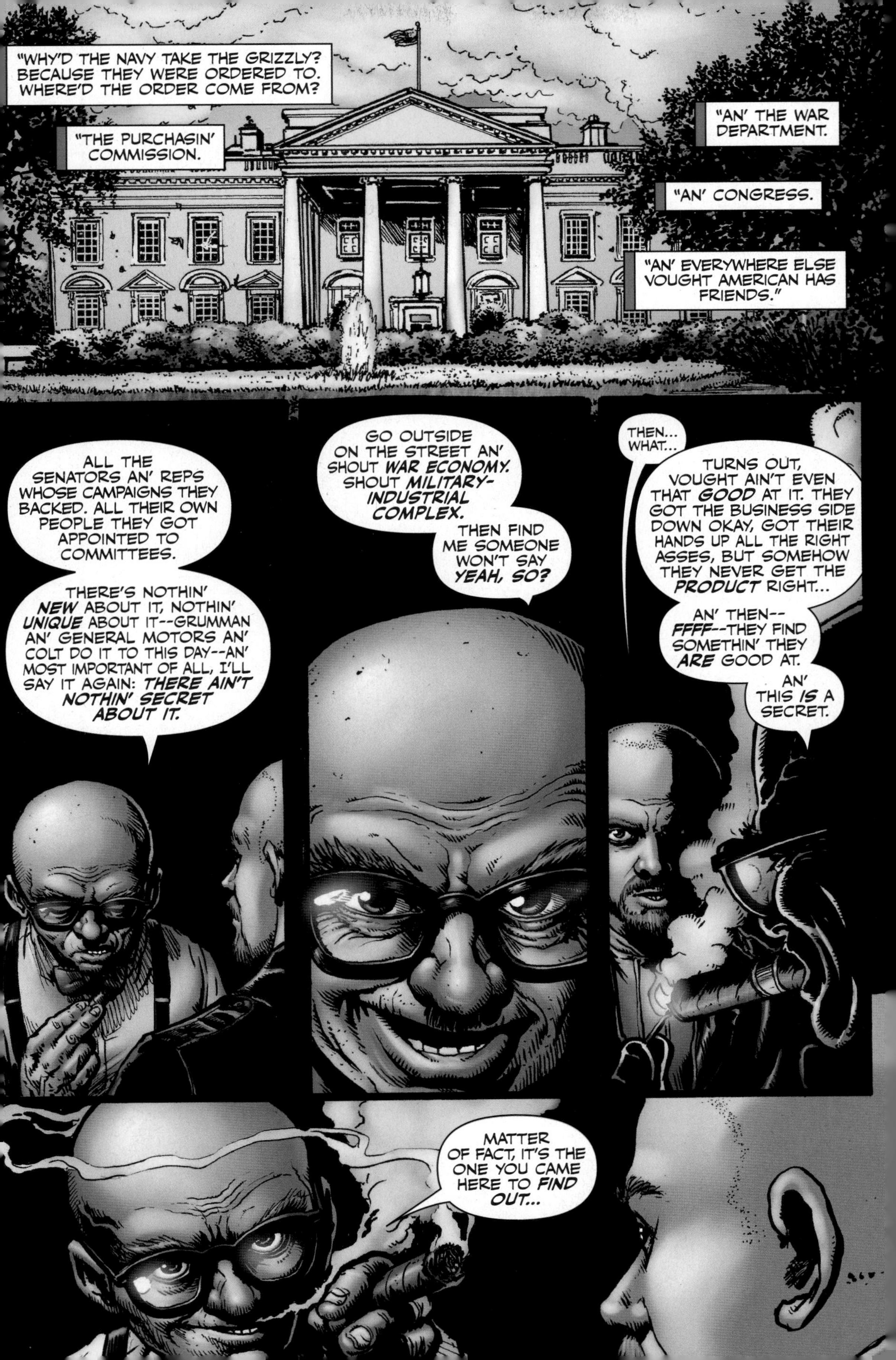
"WHY'D THE NAVY TAKE THE GRIZZLY? BECAUSE THEY WERE ORDERED TO. WHERE'D THE ORDER COME FROM?
"THE PURCHASIN' COMMISSION.
"AN' THE WAR DEPARTMENT.
"AN' CONGRESS.
"AN' EVERYWHERE ELSE VOUGHT AMERICAN HAS FRIENDS."
ALL THE SENATORS AN' REPS WHOSE CAMPAIGNS THEY BACKED. ALL THEIR OWN PEOPLE THEY GOT APPOINTED TO COMMITTEES.
THERE'S NOTHIN' NEW ABOUT IT, NOTHIN' UNIQUE ABOUT IT--GRUMMAN AN' GENERAL MOTORS AN' COLT DO IT TO THIS DAY--AN' MOST IMPORTANT OF ALL, I'LL SAY IT AGAIN: THERE AIN'T NOTHIN' SECRET ABOUT IT.
GO OUTSIDE ON THE STREET AN' SHOUT WAR ECONOMY. SHOUT MILITARY-INDUSTRIAL COMPLEX.
THEN FIND ME SOMEONE WON'T SAY YEAH, SO?
THEN... WHAT...
TURNS OUT, VOUGHT AIN'T EVEN THAT GOOD AT IT. THEY GOT THE BUSINESS SIDE DOWN OKAY, GOT THEIR HANDS UP ALL THE RIGHT ASSES, BUT SOMEHOW THEY NEVER GET THE PRODUCT RIGHT...
AN' THEN--FFFF--THEY FIND SOMETHIN' THEY ARE GOOD AT.
AN' THIS IS A SECRET.
MATTER OF FACT, IT'S THE ONE YOU CAME HERE TO FIND OUT...

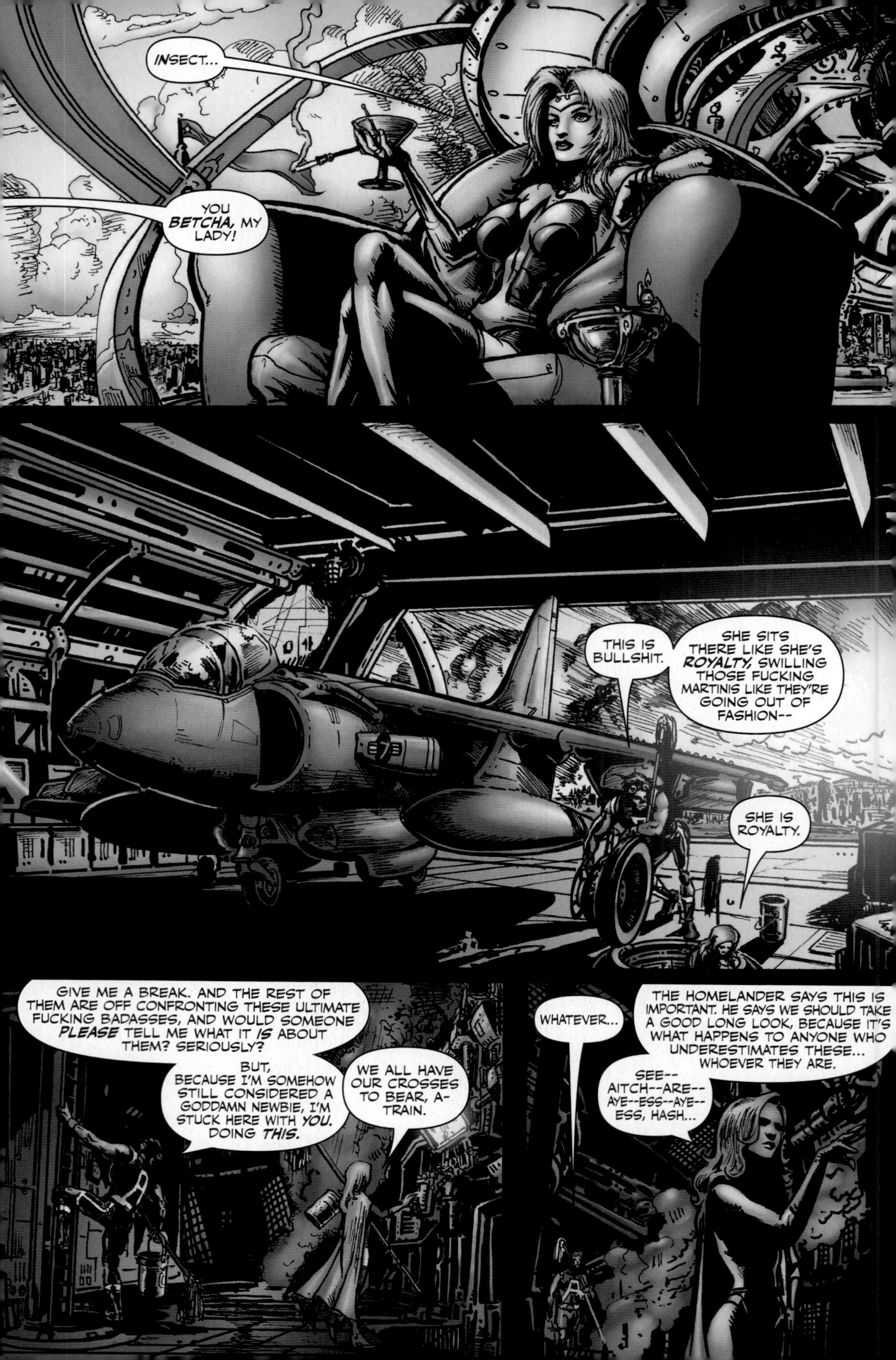

INSECT...
YOU BETCHA, MY LADY!
THIS IS BULLSHIT.
SHE SITS THERE LIKE SHE'S ROYALTY, SWILLING THOSE FUCKING MARTINIS LIKE THEY'RE GOING OUT OF FASHION--
SHE IS ROYALTY.
GIVE ME A BREAK. AND THE REST OF THEM ARE OFF CONFRONTING THESE ULTIMATE FUCKING BADASSES, AND WOULD SOMEONE PLEASE TELL ME WHAT IT IS ABOUT THEM? SERIOUSLY?
BUT, BECAUSE I'M SOMEHOW STILL CONSIDERED A GODDAMN NEWBIE, I'M STUCK HERE WITH YOU. DOING THIS.
WE ALL HAVE OUR CROSSES TO BEAR, A-TRAIN.
THE HOMELANDER SAYS THIS IS IMPORTANT. HE SAYS WE SHOULD TAKE A GOOD LONG LOOK, BECAUSE IT'S WHAT HAPPENS TO ANYONE WHO UNDERESTIMATES THESE... WHOEVER THEY ARE.
WHATEVER...
SEE--AITCH--ARE--AYE--ESS--AYE--ESS, HASH...

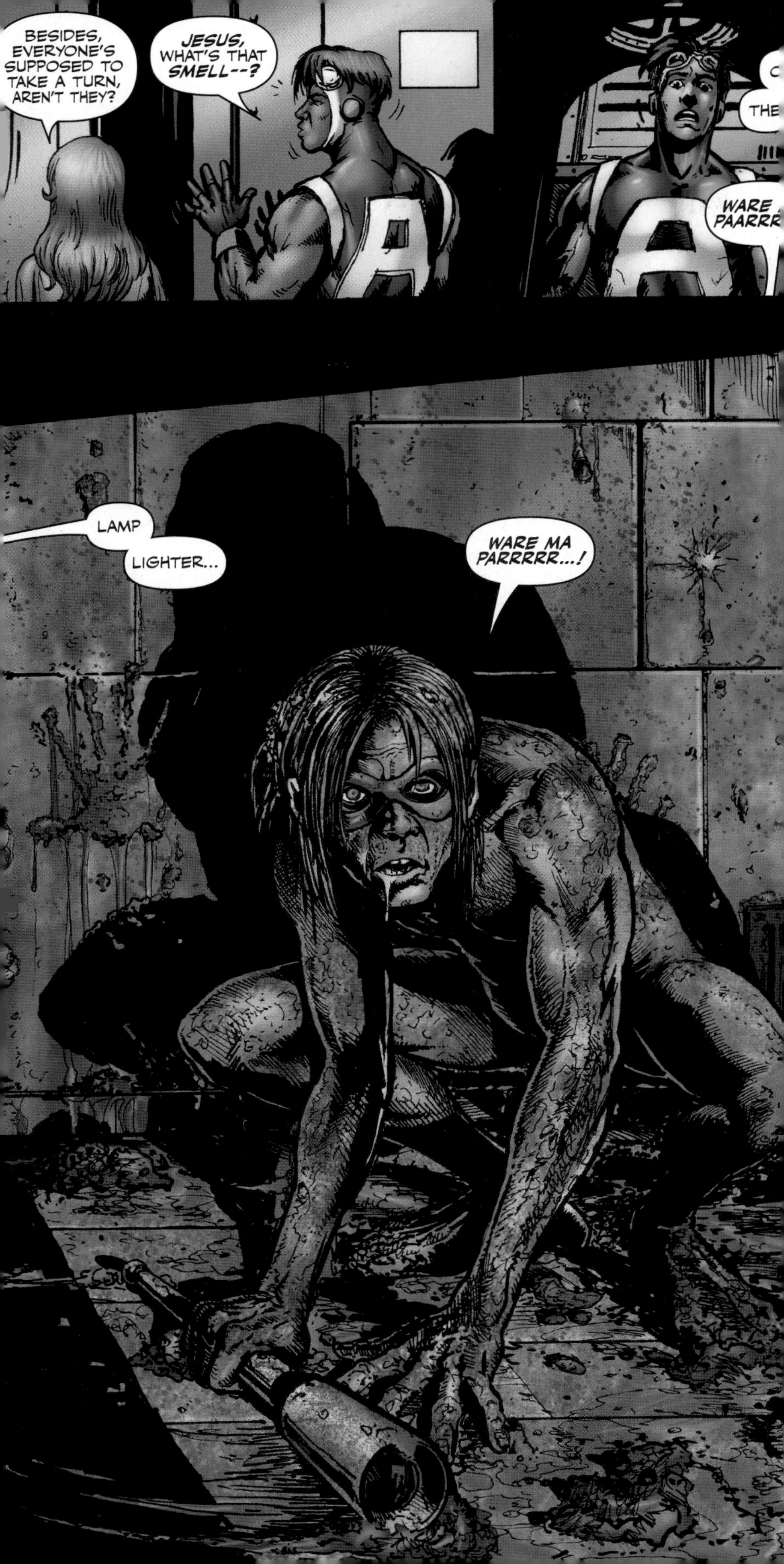
BESIDES, EVERYONE'S SUPPOSED TO TAKE A TURN, AREN'T THEY?
JESUS, WHAT'S THAT SMELL--?
WARE
LAMP
LIGHTER...
WARE MA PARRRRR...!

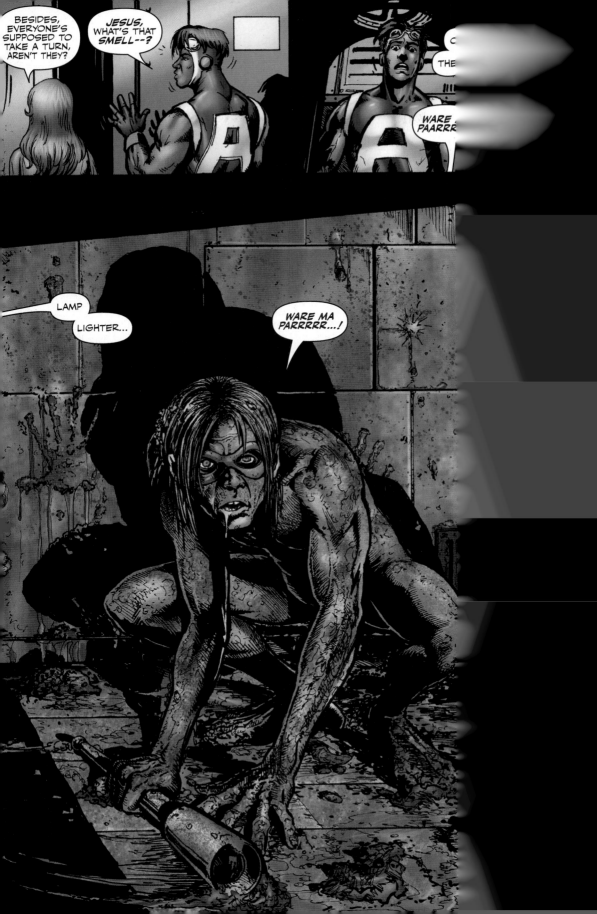

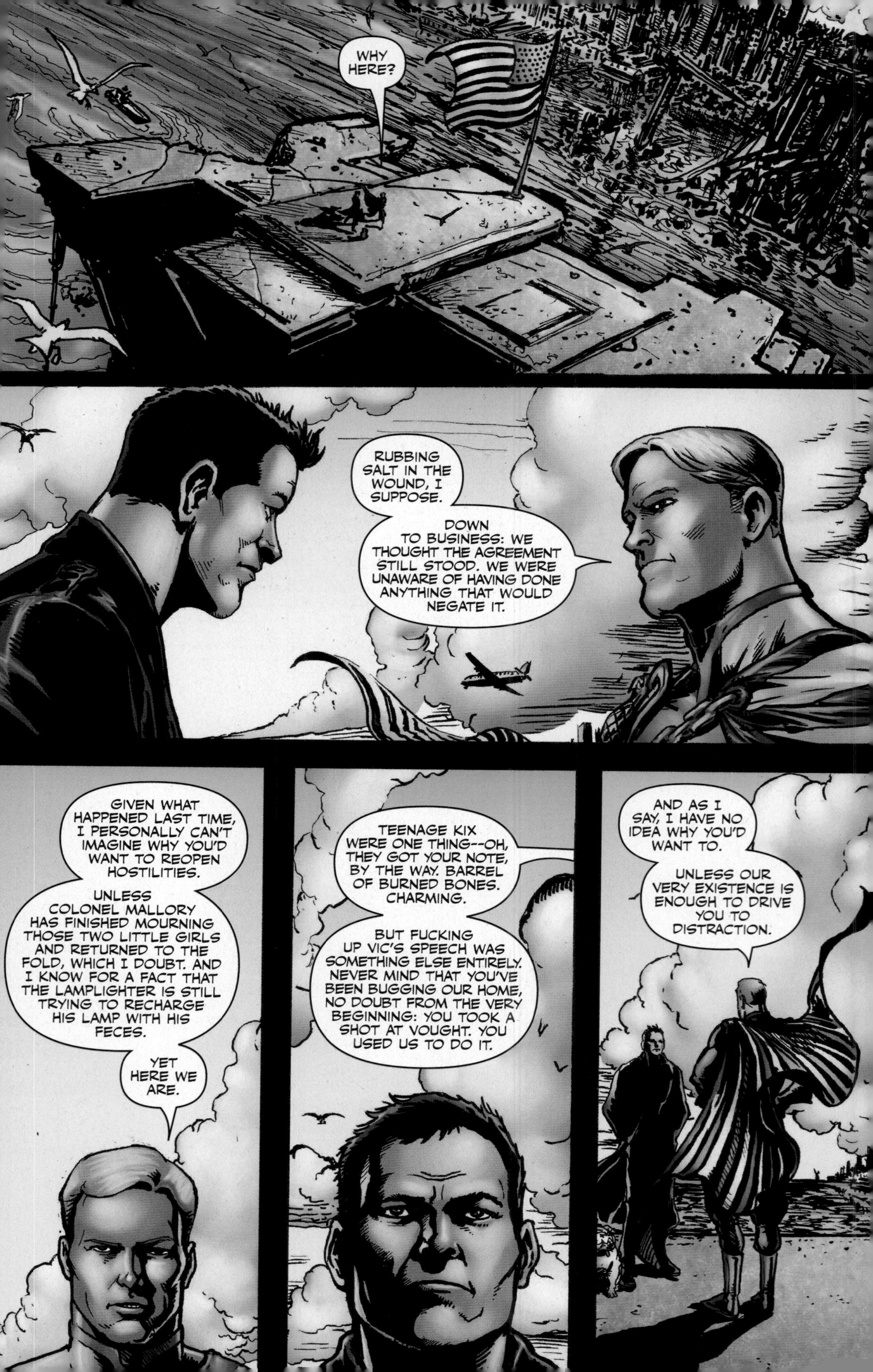
WHY HERE?
RUBBING SALT IN THE WOUND, I SUPPOSE.
DOWN TO BUSINESS: WE THOUGHT THE AGREEMENT STILL STOOD. WE WERE UNAWARE OF HAVING DONE ANYTHING THAT WOULD NEGATE IT.
GIVEN WHAT HAPPENED LAST TIME, I PERSONALLY CAN'T IMAGINE WHY YOU'D WANT TO REOPEN HOSTILITIES.
UNLESS COLONEL MALLORY HAS FINISHED MOURNING THOSE TWO LITTLE GIRLS AND RETURNED TO THE FOLD, WHICH I DOUBT. AND I KNOW FOR A FACT THAT THE LAMPLIGHTER IS STILL TRYING TO RECHARGE HIS LAMP WITH HIS FECES.
YET HERE WE ARE.
TEENAGE KIX WERE ONE THING--OH, THEY GOT YOUR NOTE, BY THE WAY. BARREL OF BURNED BONES. CHARMING.
BUT FUCKING UP VIC'S SPEECH WAS SOMETHING ELSE ENTIRELY. NEVER MIND THAT YOU'VE BEEN BUGGING OUR HOME, NO DOUBT FROM THE VERY BEGINNING: YOU TOOK A SHOT AT VOUGHT. YOU USED US TO DO IT.
AND AS I SAY, I HAVE NO IDEA WHY YOU'D WANT TO.
UNLESS OUR VERY EXISTENCE IS ENOUGH TO DRIVE YOU TO DISTRACTION.

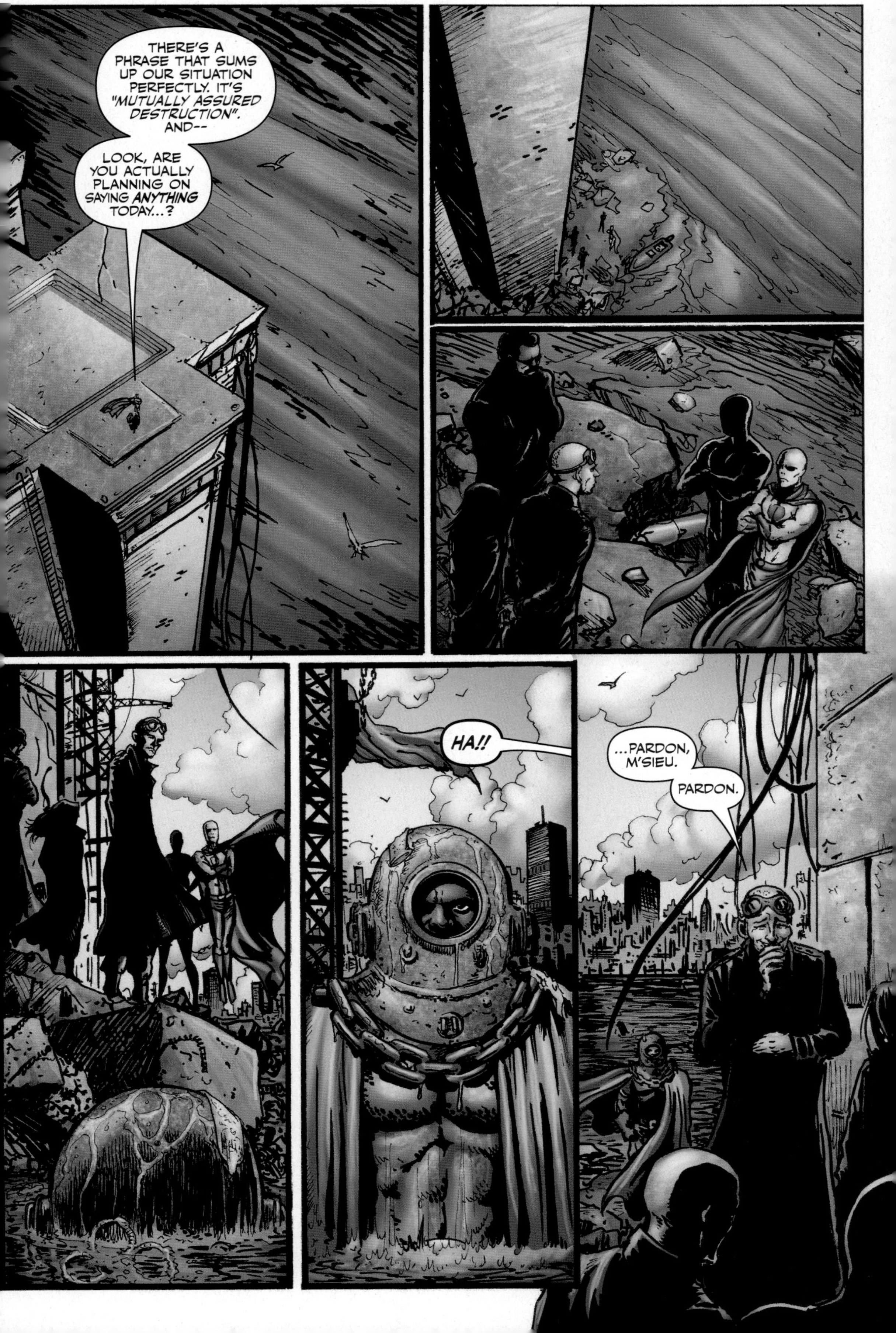
THERE'S A PHRASE THAT SUMS UP OUR SITUATION PERFECTLY. IT'S "MUTUALLY ASSURED DESTRUCTION". AND--
LOOK, ARE YOU ACTUALLY PLANNING ON SAYING ANYTHING TODAY...?
HA!!
...PARDON, M'SIEU.
PARDON.

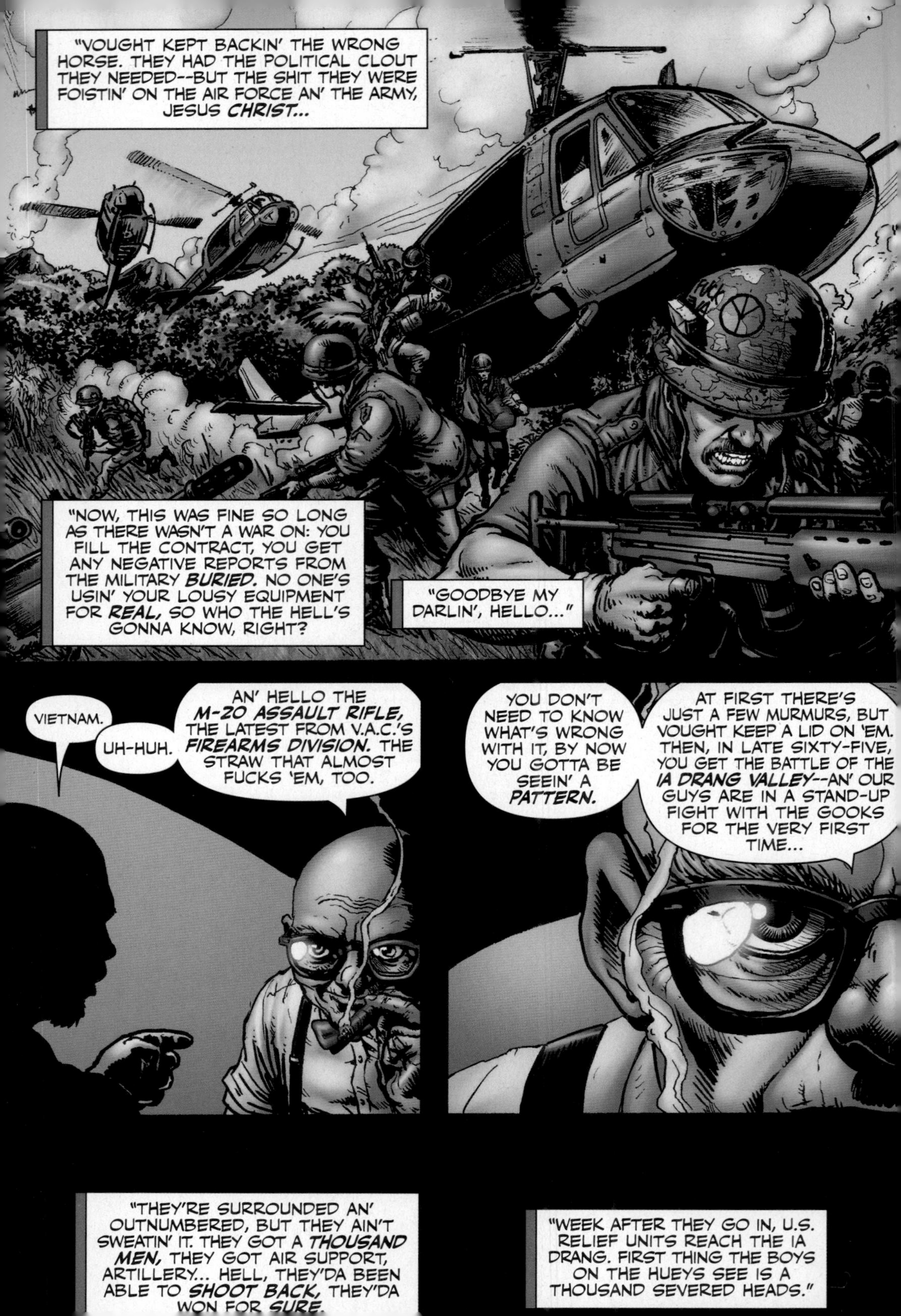
"VOUGHT KEPT BACKIN' THE WRONG HORSE. THEY HAD THE POLITICAL CLOUT THEY NEEDED--BUT THE SHIT THEY WERE FOISTIN' ON THE AIR FORCE AN' THE ARMY, JESUS CHRIST...
"NOW, THIS WAS FINE SO LONG AS THERE WASN'T A WAR ON: YOU FILL THE CONTRACT, YOU GET ANY NEGATIVE REPORTS FROM THE MILITARY BURIED. NO ONE'S USIN' YOUR LOUSY EQUIPMENT FOR REAL, SO WHO THE HELL'S GONNA KNOW, RIGHT?
"GOODBYE MY DARLIN', HELLO..."
VIETNAM.
UH-HUH.
AN' HELLO THE M-20 ASSAULT RIFLE, THE LATEST FROM V.A.C.'S FIREARMS DIVISION. THE STRAW THAT ALMOST FUCKS 'EM, TOO.
YOU DON'T NEED TO KNOW WHAT'S WRONG WITH IT, BY NOW YOU GOTTA BE SEEIN' A PATTERN.
AT FIRST THERE'S JUST A FEW MURMURS, BUT VOUGHT KEEP A LID ON 'EM. THEN, IN LATE SIXTY-FIVE, YOU GET THE BATTLE OF THE IA DRANG VALLEY--AN' OUR GUYS ARE IN A STAND-UP FIGHT WITH THE GOOKS FOR THE VERY FIRST TIME...
"THEY'RE SURROUNDED AN' OUTNUMBERED, BUT THEY AIN'T SWEATIN' IT. THEY GOT A THOUSAND MEN, THEY GOT AIR SUPPORT, ARTILLERY... HELL, THEY'DA BEEN ABLE TO SHOOT BACK, THEY'DA WON FOR SURE.
"WEEK AFTER THEY GO IN, U.S. RELIEF UNITS REACH THE IA DRANG. FIRST THING THE BOYS ON THE HUEYS SEE IS A THOUSAND SEVERED HEADS."

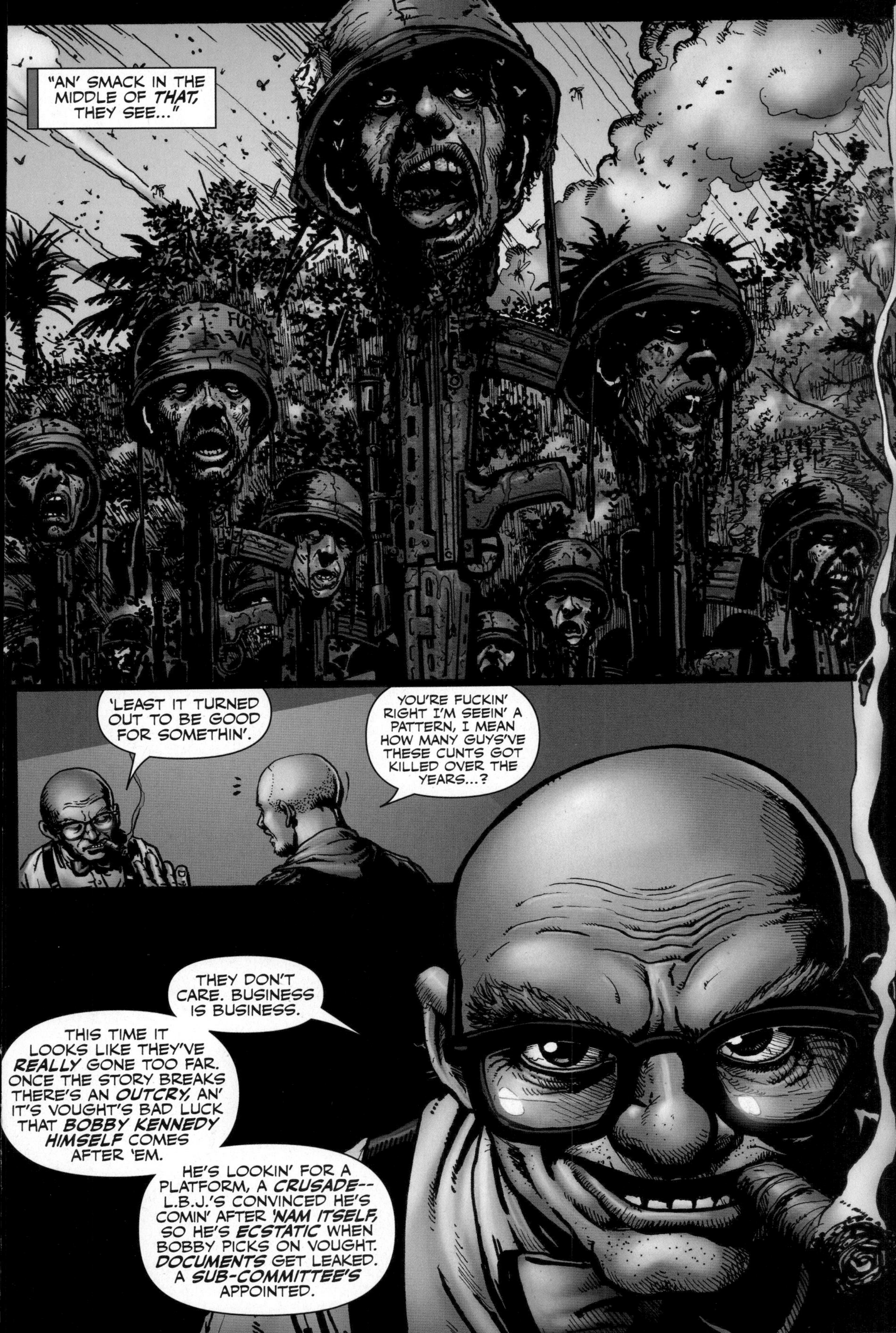
"AN' SMACK IN THE MIDDLE OF *THAT,* THEY SEE..."
'LEAST IT TURNED OUT TO BE GOOD FOR SOMETHIN'.
YOU'RE FUCKIN' RIGHT I'M SEEIN' A PATTERN, I MEAN HOW MANY GUYS'VE THESE CUNTS GOT KILLED OVER THE YEARS...?
THEY DON'T CARE. BUSINESS IS BUSINESS.
THIS TIME IT LOOKS LIKE THEY'VE *REALLY* GONE TOO FAR. ONCE THE STORY BREAKS THERE'S AN *OUTCRY,* AN' IT'S VOUGHT'S BAD LUCK THAT *BOBBY KENNEDY HIMSELF* COMES AFTER 'EM.
HE'S LOOKIN' FOR A PLATFORM, A *CRUSADE*-- L.B.J.'S CONVINCED HE'S COMIN' AFTER *'NAM ITSELF,* SO HE'S *ECSTATIC* WHEN BOBBY PICKS ON VOUGHT. *DOCUMENTS* GET LEAKED. A *SUB-COMMITTEE'S* APPOINTED.

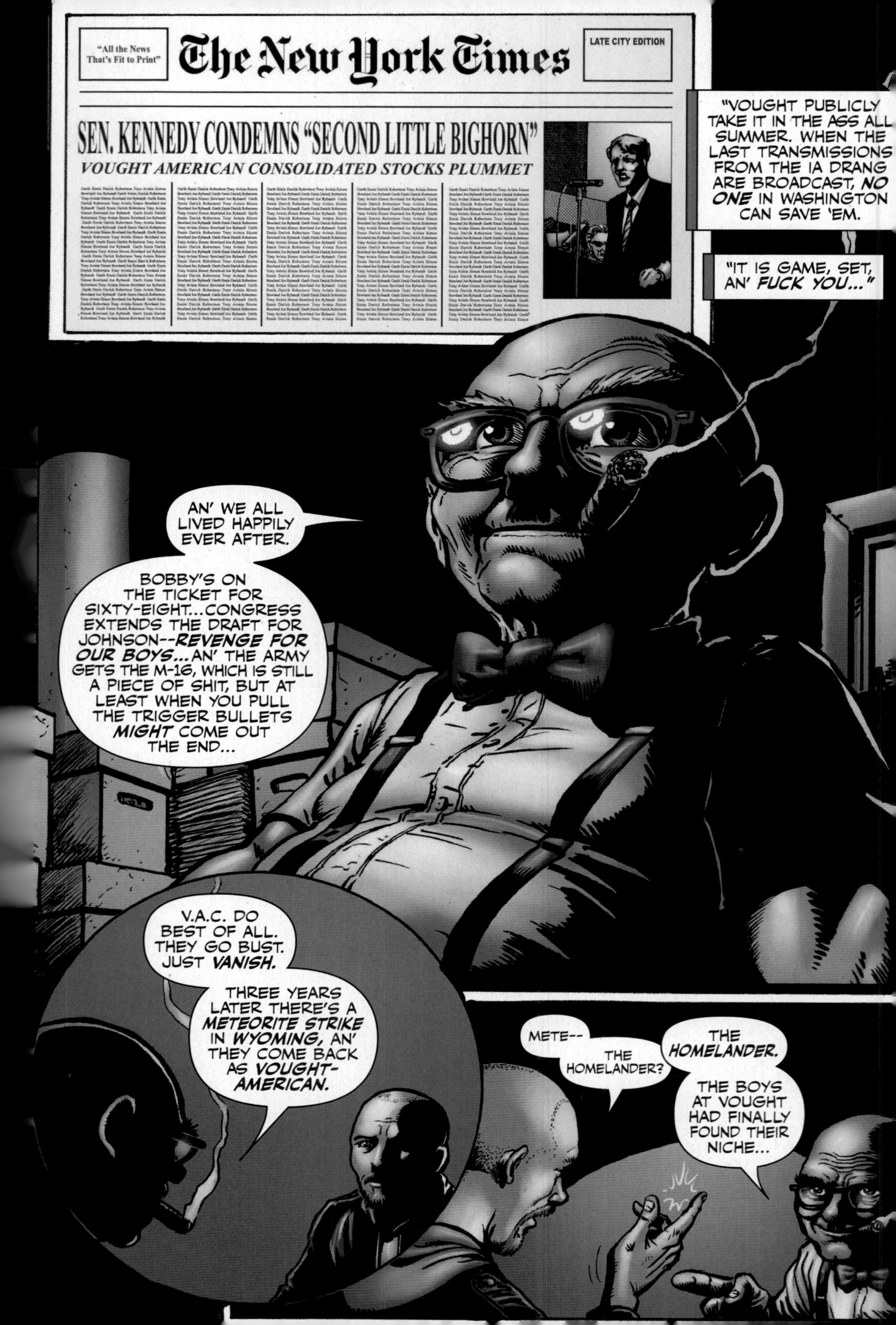
"All the News That's Fit to Print"
The New York Times
LATE CITY EDITION
SEN. KENNEDY CONDEMNS "SECOND LITTLE BIGHORN"
VOUGHT AMERICAN CONSOLIDATED STOCKS PLUMMET
"VOUGHT PUBLICLY TAKE IT IN THE ASS ALL SUMMER. WHEN THE LAST TRANSMISSIONS FROM THE IA DRANG ARE BROADCAST, NO ONE IN WASHINGTON CAN SAVE 'EM.
"IT IS GAME, SET, AN' FUCK YOU..."
AN' WE ALL LIVED HAPPILY EVER AFTER.
BOBBY'S ON THE TICKET FOR SIXTY-EIGHT...CONGRESS EXTENDS THE DRAFT FOR JOHNSON--REVENGE FOR OUR BOYS...AN' THE ARMY GETS THE M-16, WHICH IS STILL A PIECE OF SHIT, BUT AT LEAST WHEN YOU PULL THE TRIGGER BULLETS MIGHT COME OUT THE END...
V.A.C. DO BEST OF ALL. THEY GO BUST. JUST VANISH.
THREE YEARS LATER THERE'S A METEORITE STRIKE IN WYOMING, AN' THEY COME BACK AS VOUGHT-AMERICAN.
METE--
THE HOMELANDER?
THE HOMELANDER.
THE BOYS AT VOUGHT HAD FINALLY FOUND THEIR NICHE...

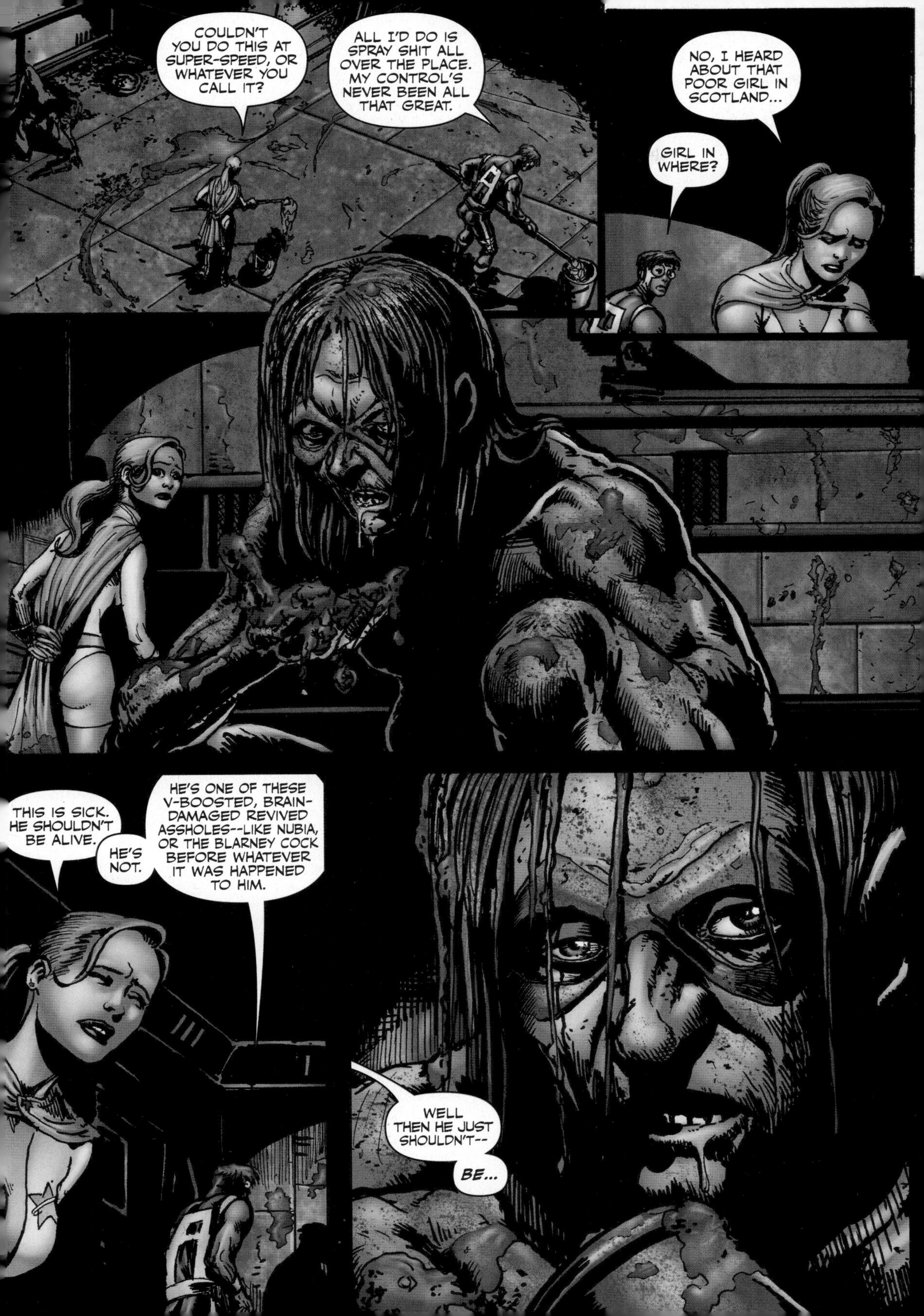
COULDN'T YOU DO THIS AT SUPER-SPEED, OR WHATEVER YOU CALL IT?
ALL I'D DO IS SPRAY SHIT ALL OVER THE PLACE. MY CONTROL'S NEVER BEEN ALL THAT GREAT.
NO, I HEARD ABOUT THAT POOR GIRL IN SCOTLAND...
GIRL IN WHERE?
THIS IS SICK. HE SHOULDN'T BE ALIVE.
HE'S NOT.
HE'S ONE OF THESE V-BOOSTED, BRAIN-DAMAGED REVIVED ASSHOLES--LIKE NUBIA, OR THE BLARNEY COCK BEFORE WHATEVER IT WAS HAPPENED TO HIM.
WELL THEN HE JUST SHOULDN'T--
BE...

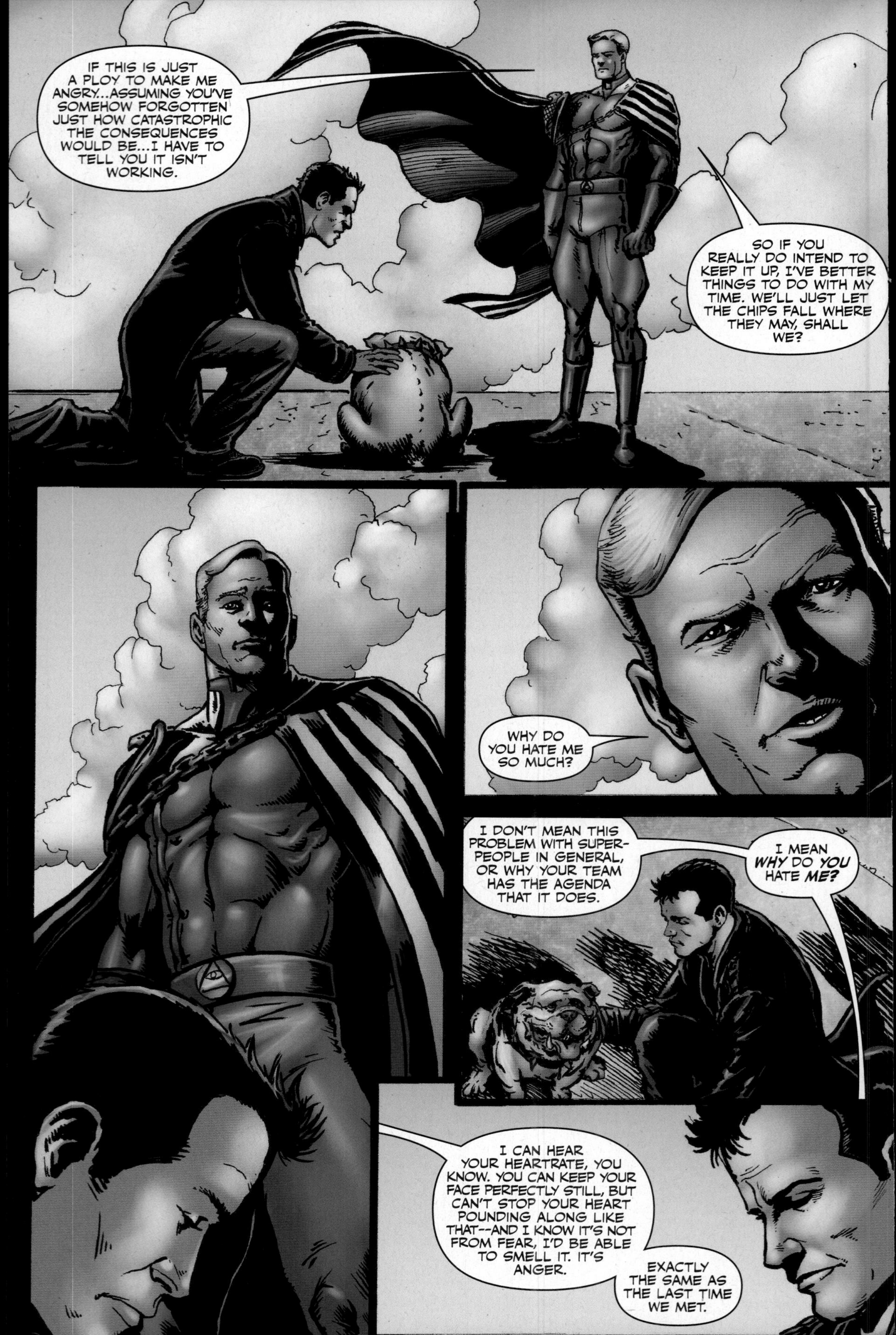
IF THIS IS JUST A PLOY TO MAKE ME ANGRY...ASSUMING YOU'VE SOMEHOW FORGOTTEN JUST HOW CATASTROPHIC THE CONSEQUENCES WOULD BE...I HAVE TO TELL YOU IT ISN'T WORKING.
SO IF YOU REALLY DO INTEND TO KEEP IT UP, I'VE BETTER THINGS TO DO WITH MY TIME. WE'LL JUST LET THE CHIPS FALL WHERE THEY MAY, SHALL WE?
WHY DO YOU HATE ME SO MUCH?
I DON'T MEAN THIS PROBLEM WITH SUPER-PEOPLE IN GENERAL, OR WHY YOUR TEAM HAS THE AGENDA THAT IT DOES.
I MEAN *WHY* DO *YOU* HATE *ME?*
I CAN HEAR YOUR HEARTRATE, YOU KNOW. YOU CAN KEEP YOUR FACE PERFECTLY STILL, BUT CAN'T STOP YOUR HEART POUNDING ALONG LIKE THAT--AND I KNOW IT'S NOT FROM FEAR, I'D BE ABLE TO SMELL IT. IT'S ANGER.
EXACTLY THE SAME AS THE LAST TIME WE MET.

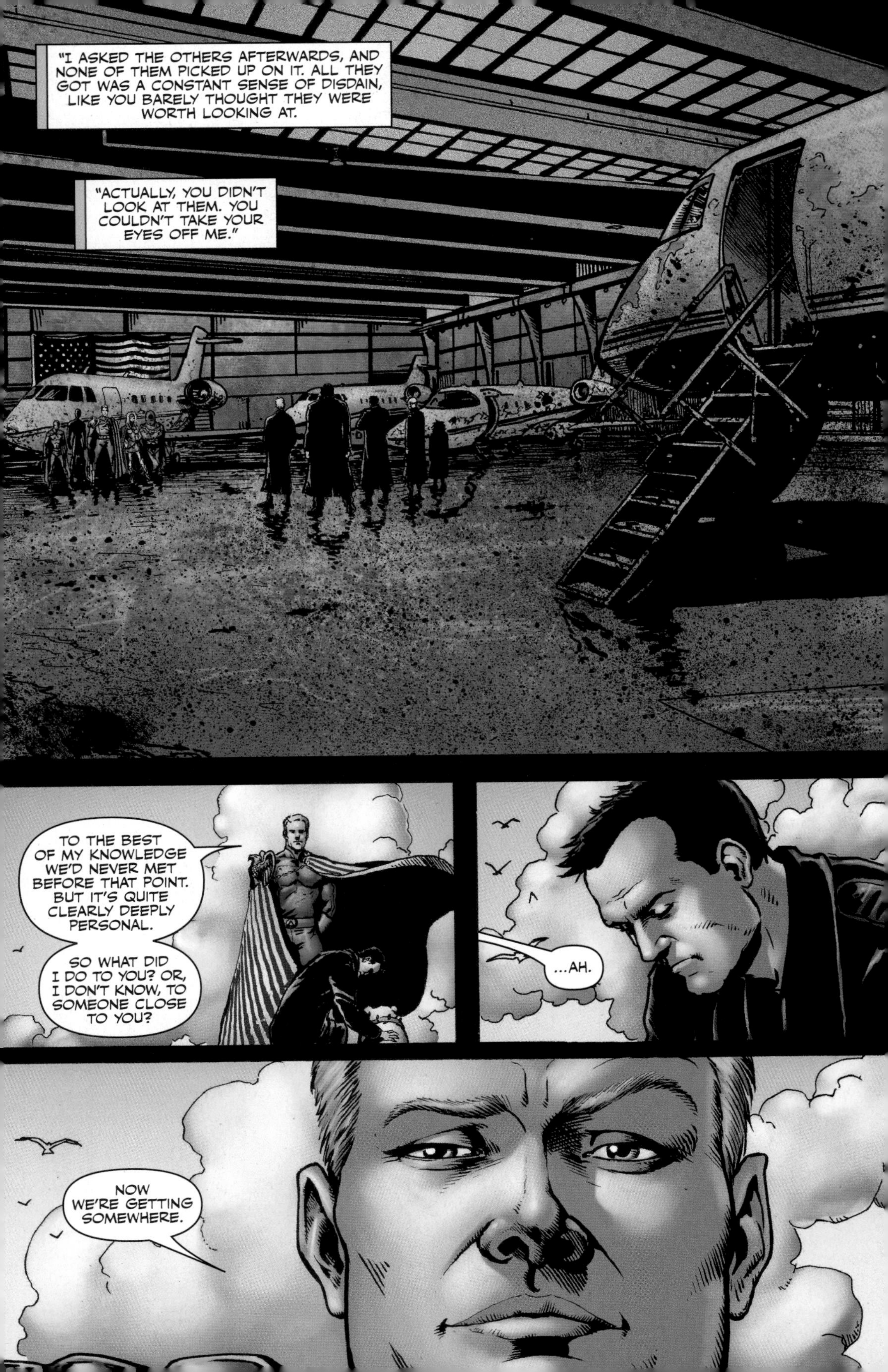
"I ASKED THE OTHERS AFTERWARDS, AND NONE OF THEM PICKED UP ON IT. ALL THEY GOT WAS A CONSTANT SENSE OF DISDAIN, LIKE YOU BARELY THOUGHT THEY WERE WORTH LOOKING AT.
"ACTUALLY, YOU DIDN'T LOOK AT THEM. YOU COULDN'T TAKE YOUR EYES OFF ME."
TO THE BEST OF MY KNOWLEDGE WE'D NEVER MET BEFORE THAT POINT. BUT IT'S QUITE CLEARLY DEEPLY PERSONAL.
SO WHAT DID I DO TO YOU? OR, I DON'T KNOW, TO SOMEONE CLOSE TO YOU?
...AH.
NOW WE'RE GETTING SOMEWHERE.

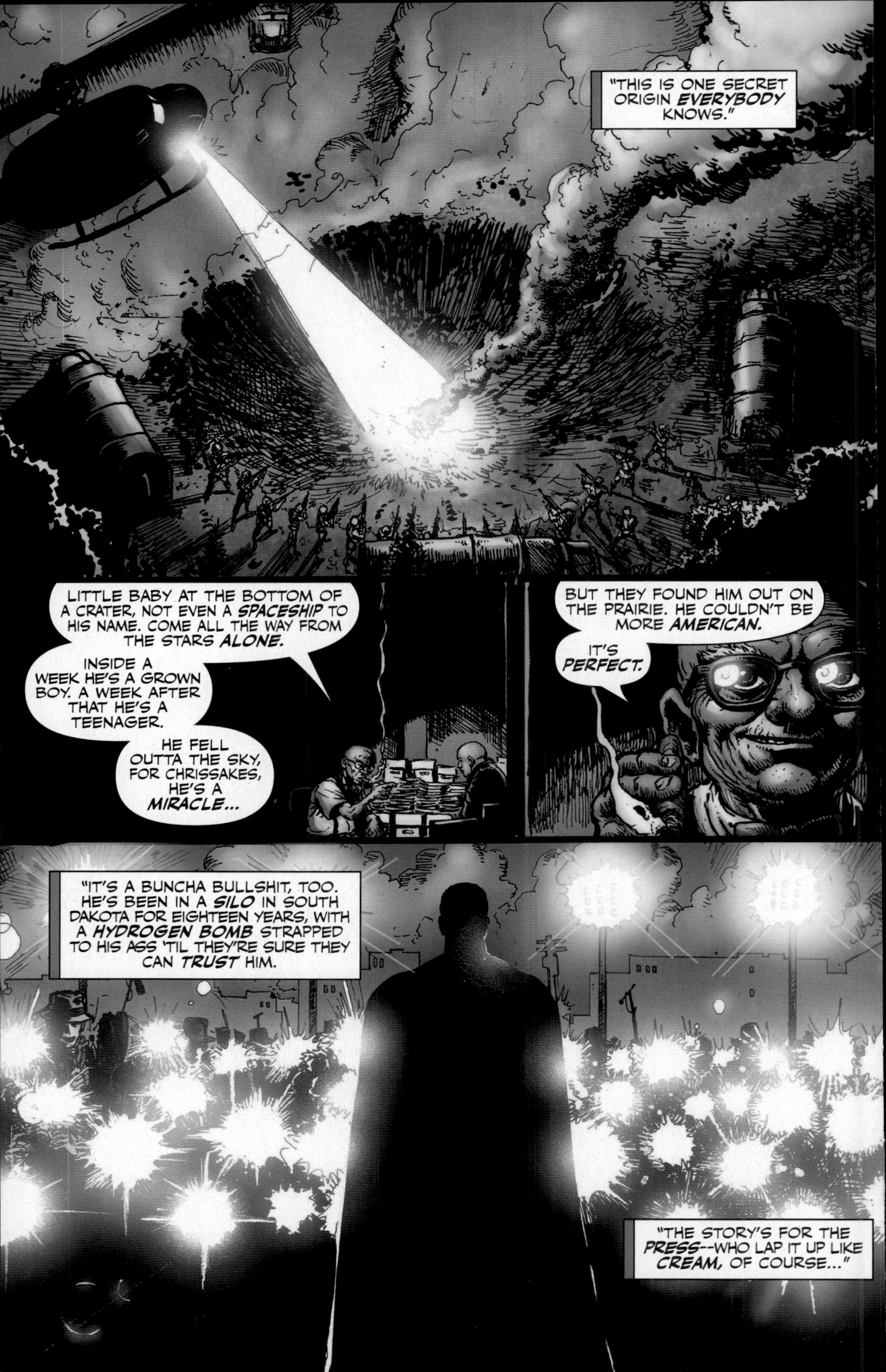
"THIS IS ONE SECRET ORIGIN EVERYBODY KNOWS."
LITTLE BABY AT THE BOTTOM OF A CRATER, NOT EVEN A SPACESHIP TO HIS NAME. COME ALL THE WAY FROM THE STARS ALONE.
INSIDE A WEEK HE'S A GROWN BOY. A WEEK AFTER THAT HE'S A TEENAGER.
HE FELL OUTTA THE SKY, FOR CHRISSAKES, HE'S A MIRACLE...
BUT THEY FOUND HIM OUT ON THE PRAIRIE. HE COULDN'T BE MORE AMERICAN.
IT'S PERFECT.
"IT'S A BUNCHA BULLSHIT, TOO. HE'S BEEN IN A SILO IN SOUTH DAKOTA FOR EIGHTEEN YEARS, WITH A HYDROGEN BOMB STRAPPED TO HIS ASS 'TIL THEY'RE SURE THEY CAN TRUST HIM.
"THE STORY'S FOR THE PRESS--WHO LAP IT UP LIKE CREAM, OF COURSE..."

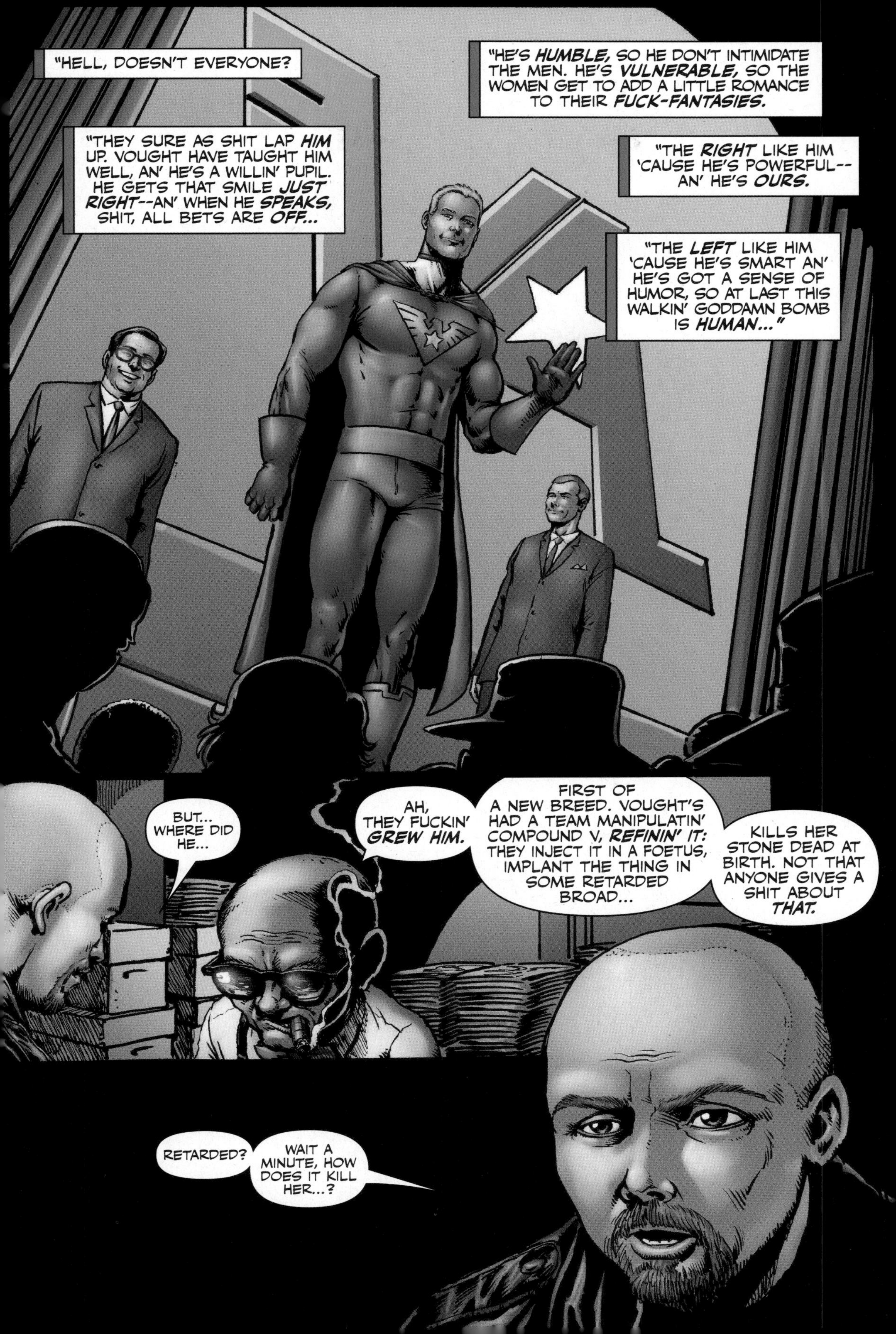
"HELL, DOESN'T EVERYONE?
"THEY SURE AS SHIT LAP HIM UP. VOUGHT HAVE TAUGHT HIM WELL, AN' HE'S A WILLIN' PUPIL. HE GETS THAT SMILE JUST RIGHT--AN' WHEN HE SPEAKS, SHIT, ALL BETS ARE OFF...
"HE'S HUMBLE, SO HE DON'T INTIMIDATE THE MEN. HE'S VULNERABLE, SO THE WOMEN GET TO ADD A LITTLE ROMANCE TO THEIR FUCK-FANTASIES.
"THE RIGHT LIKE HIM 'CAUSE HE'S POWERFUL--AN' HE'S OURS.
"THE LEFT LIKE HIM 'CAUSE HE'S SMART AN' HE'S GOT A SENSE OF HUMOR, SO AT LAST THIS WALKIN' GODDAMN BOMB IS HUMAN..."
BUT... WHERE DID HE...
AH, THEY FUCKIN' GREW HIM.
FIRST OF A NEW BREED. VOUGHT'S HAD A TEAM MANIPULATIN' COMPOUND V, REFININ' IT: THEY INJECT IT IN A FOETUS, IMPLANT THE THING IN SOME RETARDED BROAD...
KILLS HER STONE DEAD AT BIRTH. NOT THAT ANYONE GIVES A SHIT ABOUT THAT.
RETARDED?
WAIT A MINUTE, HOW DOES IT KILL HER...?

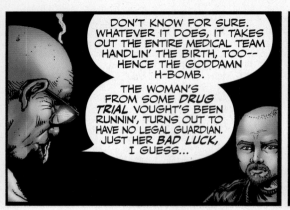

DON'T KNOW FOR SURE. WHATEVER IT DOES, IT TAKES OUT THE ENTIRE MEDICAL TEAM HANDLIN' THE BIRTH, TOO-- HENCE THE GODDAMN H-BOMB.

THE WOMAN'S FROM SOME *DRUG TRIAL* VOUGHT'S BEEN RUNNIN', TURNS OUT TO HAVE NO LEGAL GUARDIAN. JUST HER *BAD LUCK,* I GUESS...

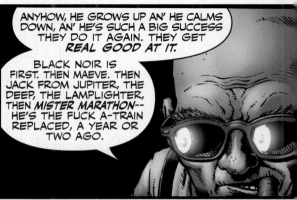

ANYHOW, HE GROWS UP AN' HE CALMS DOWN, AN' HE'S SUCH A BIG SUCCESS THEY DO IT AGAIN. THEY GET *REAL GOOD AT IT.*

BLACK NOIR IS FIRST. THEN MAEVE. THEN JACK FROM JUPITER, THE DEEP, THE LAMPLIGHTER, THEN *MISTER MARATHON*-- HE'S THE FUCK A-TRAIN REPLACED, A YEAR OR TWO AGO.

"THEY DO IT *SEVEN TIMES.*

"THERE'S BEEN SUPES SINCE THE FORTIES, BUT THEY CAN ALL OFFICIALLY GO SCREW. THESE GUYS ARE THE *NUKES* TO THEIR *STICKS OF DYNAMITE.*

"*VOUGHT* HAVE SOMETHIN' THEY CAN *WORK WITH* AT LAST. THEY KNOW HOW TO PLAY THE SYSTEM, THEY GOT IT SEWN UP REAL TIGHT--BUT UP 'TIL NOW THEY'VE HAD A SHITTY *PRODUCT.*

"NOT NO MORE."

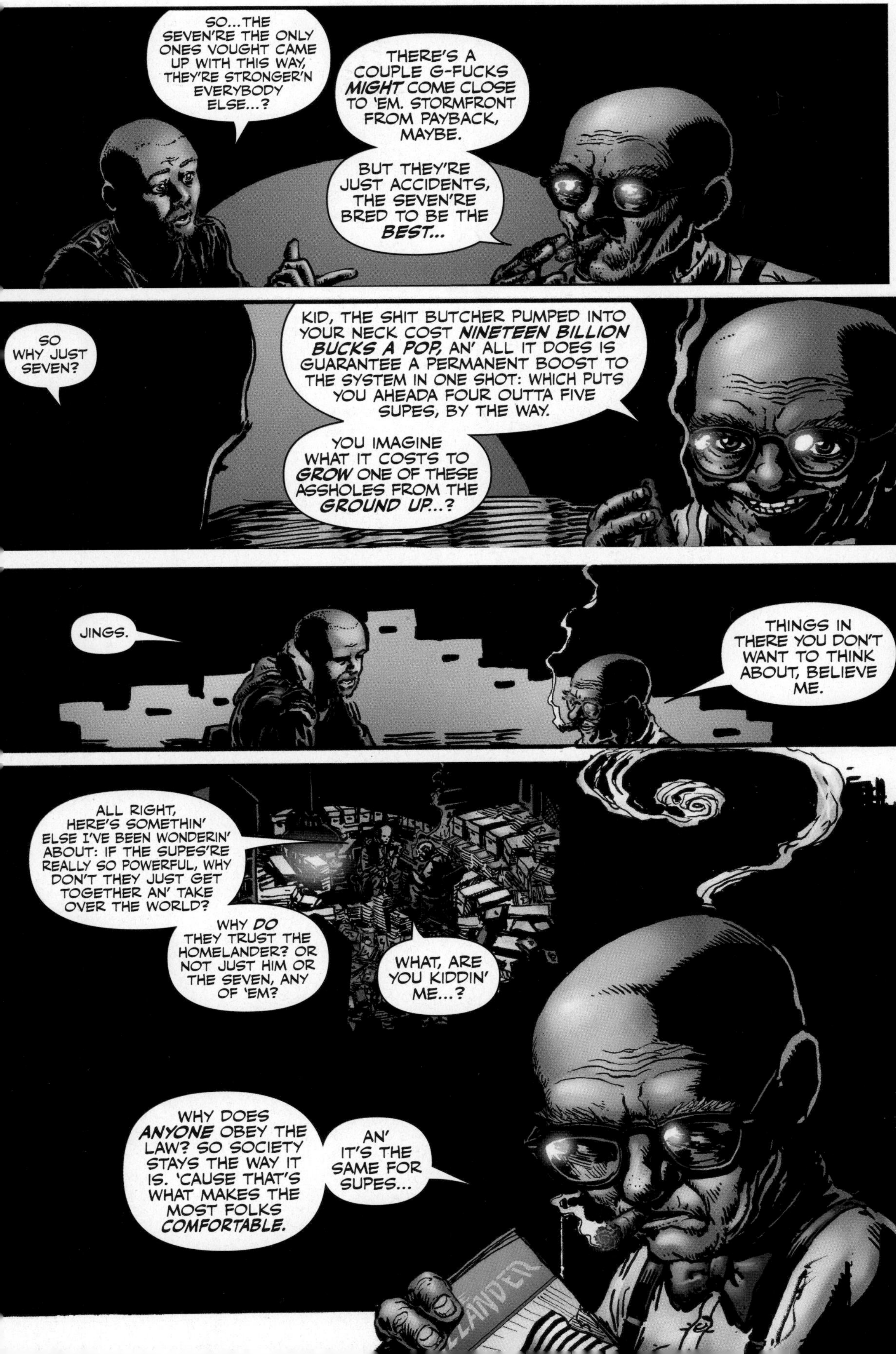

SO...THE SEVEN'RE THE ONLY ONES VOUGHT CAME UP WITH THIS WAY, THEY'RE STRONGER'N EVERYBODY ELSE...?
THERE'S A COUPLE G-FUCKS *MIGHT* COME CLOSE TO 'EM. STORMFRONT FROM PAYBACK, MAYBE.
BUT THEY'RE JUST ACCIDENTS, THE SEVEN'RE BRED TO BE THE *BEST...*
SO WHY JUST SEVEN?
KID, THE SHIT BUTCHER PUMPED INTO YOUR NECK COST ***NINETEEN BILLION BUCKS A POP,*** AN' ALL IT DOES IS GUARANTEE A PERMANENT BOOST TO THE SYSTEM IN ONE SHOT: WHICH PUTS YOU AHEADA FOUR OUTTA FIVE SUPES, BY THE WAY.
YOU IMAGINE WHAT IT COSTS TO ***GROW*** ONE OF THESE ASSHOLES FROM THE ***GROUND UP...?***
JINGS.
THINGS IN THERE YOU DON'T WANT TO THINK ABOUT, BELIEVE ME.
ALL RIGHT, HERE'S SOMETHIN' ELSE I'VE BEEN WONDERIN' ABOUT: IF THE SUPES'RE REALLY SO POWERFUL, WHY DON'T THEY JUST GET TOGETHER AN' TAKE OVER THE WORLD?
WHY *DO* THEY TRUST THE HOMELANDER? OR NOT JUST HIM OR THE SEVEN, ANY OF 'EM?
WHAT, ARE YOU KIDDIN' ME...?
WHY DOES ***ANYONE*** OBEY THE LAW? SO SOCIETY STAYS THE WAY IT IS. 'CAUSE THAT'S WHAT MAKES THE MOST FOLKS ***COMFORTABLE.***
AN' IT'S THE SAME FOR SUPES...

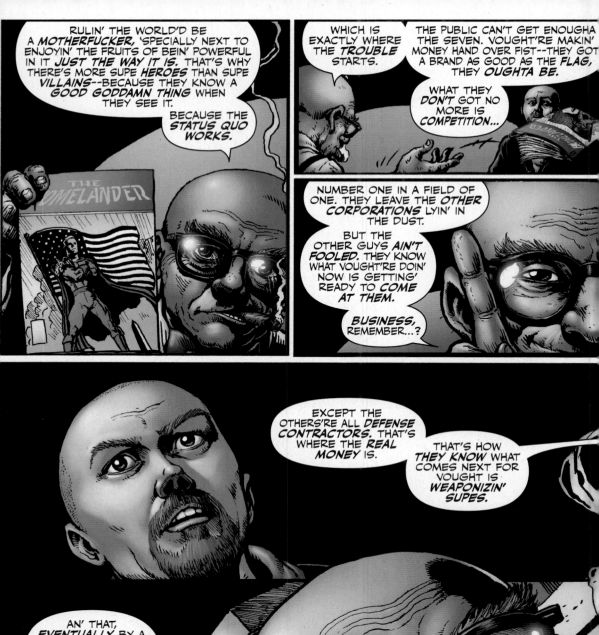

RULIN' THE WORLD'D BE A *MOTHERFUCKER*, 'SPECIALLY NEXT TO ENJOYIN' THE FRUITS OF BEIN' POWERFUL IN IT *JUST THE WAY IT IS.* THAT'S WHY THERE'S MORE SUPE *HEROES* THAN SUPE *VILLAINS*--BECAUSE THEY KNOW A *GOOD GODDAMN THING* WHEN THEY SEE IT.

BECAUSE THE *STATUS QUO WORKS.*

WHICH IS EXACTLY WHERE THE *TROUBLE* STARTS.

THE PUBLIC CAN'T GET ENOUGHA THE SEVEN. VOUGHT'RE MAKIN' MONEY HAND OVER FIST--THEY GOT A BRAND AS GOOD AS THE *FLAG*, THEY *OUGHTA BE.*

WHAT THEY *DON'T* GOT NO MORE IS *COMPETITION...*

NUMBER ONE IN A FIELD OF ONE. THEY LEAVE THE *OTHER CORPORATIONS* LYIN' IN THE DUST.

BUT THE OTHER GUYS *AIN'T FOOLED.* THEY KNOW WHAT VOUGHT'RE DOIN' NOW IS GETTING' READY TO *COME AT THEM.*

BUSINESS, REMEMBER...?

EXCEPT THE OTHERS'RE ALL *DEFENSE CONTRACTORS.* THAT'S WHERE THE *REAL MONEY* IS.

THAT'S HOW *THEY KNOW* WHAT COMES NEXT FOR VOUGHT IS *WEAPONIZIN' SUPES.*

AN' THAT, *EVENTUALLY,* BY A LONG AN' TWISTED TRAIL, IS WHY THERE AIN'T NO GODDAMN *BROOKLYN BRIDGE* NO MORE.

LET'S TAKE A BREAK, KID, I THINK I COULD USE A CUP OF COFFEE...

next: SECRETS OF THE LETTERCOLUMN

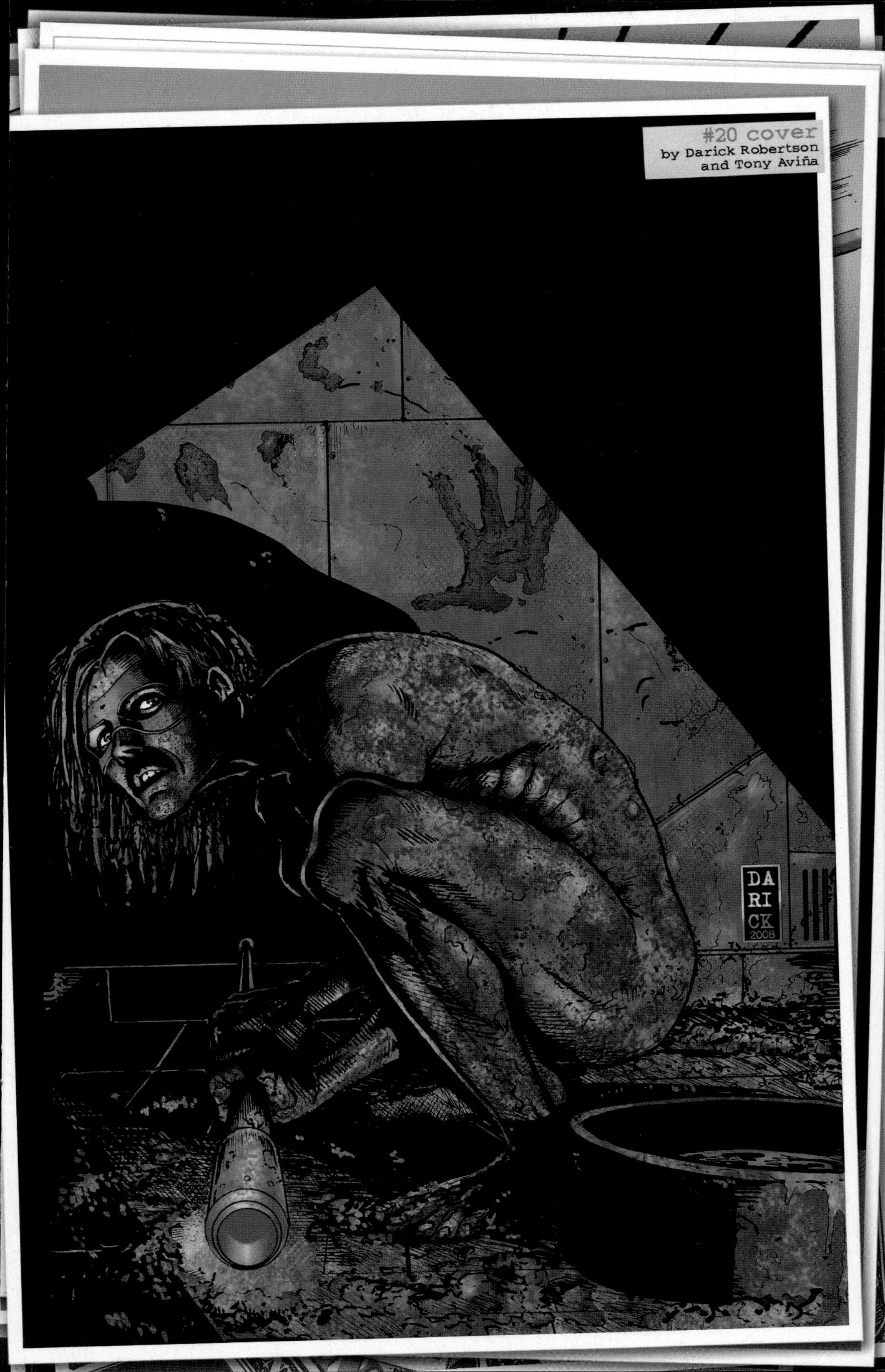
#20 cover
by Darick Robertson
and Tony Aviña
DA
RI
CK
2008

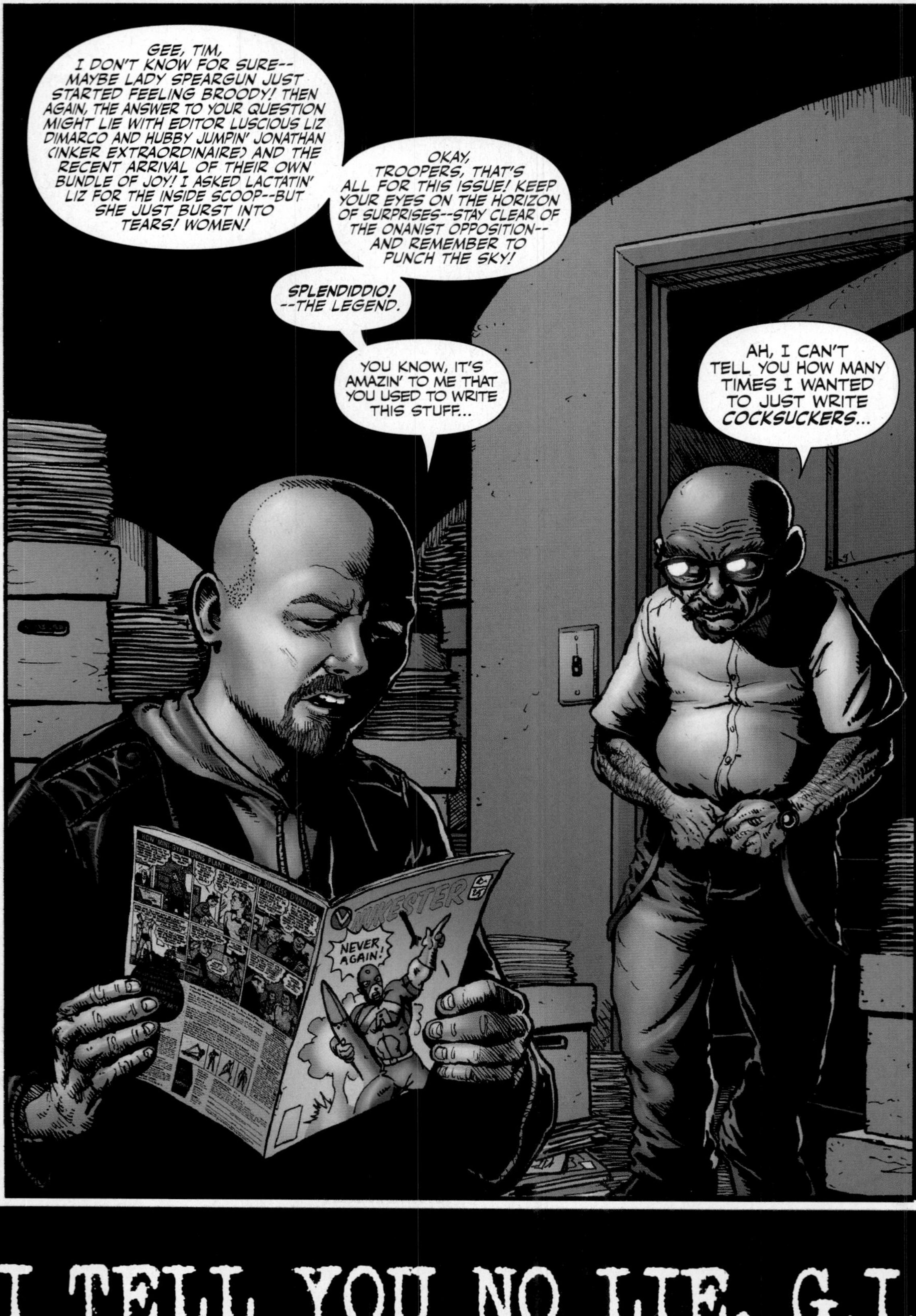
GEE, TIM, I DON'T KNOW FOR SURE-- MAYBE LADY SPEARGUN JUST STARTED FEELING BROODY! THEN AGAIN, THE ANSWER TO YOUR QUESTION MIGHT LIE WITH EDITOR LUSCIOUS LIZ DIMARCO AND HUBBY JUMPIN' JONATHAN (INKER EXTRAORDINAIRE) AND THE RECENT ARRIVAL OF THEIR OWN BUNDLE OF JOY! I ASKED LACTATIN' LIZ FOR THE INSIDE SCOOP--BUT SHE JUST BURST INTO TEARS! WOMEN!
OKAY, TROOPERS, THAT'S ALL FOR THIS ISSUE! KEEP YOUR EYES ON THE HORIZON OF SURPRISES--STAY CLEAR OF THE ONANIST OPPOSITION-- AND REMEMBER TO PUNCH THE SKY!
SPLENDIDDIO! --THE LEGEND.
YOU KNOW, IT'S AMAZIN' TO ME THAT YOU USED TO WRITE THIS STUFF...
AH, I CAN'T TELL YOU HOW MANY TIMES I WANTED TO JUST WRITE COCKSUCKERS...
NEVER AGAIN!

I TELL YOU NO LIE, G.I.

part two

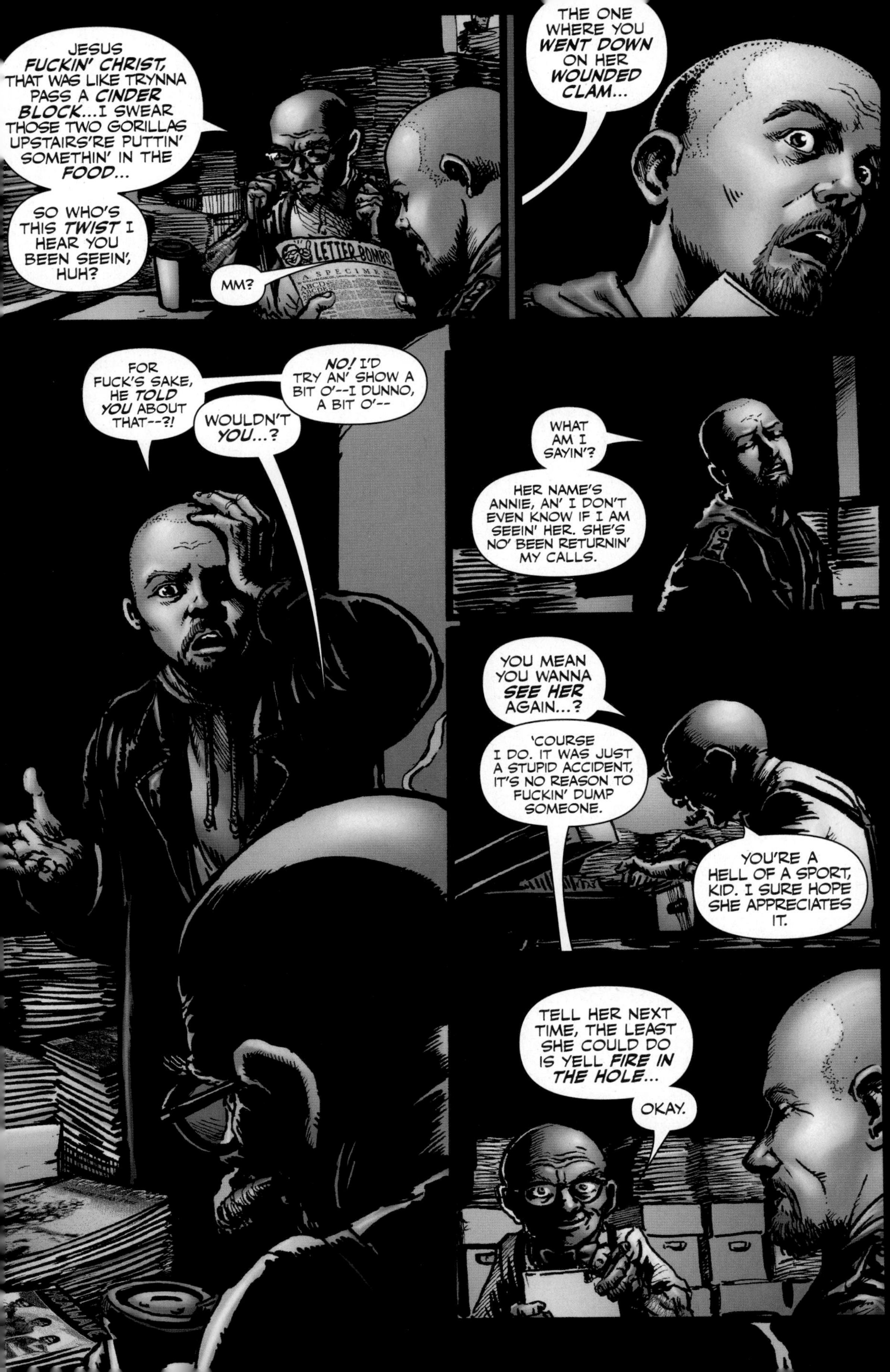
JESUS FUCKIN' CHRIST, THAT WAS LIKE TRYNNA PASS A CINDER BLOCK...I SWEAR THOSE TWO GORILLAS UPSTAIRS'RE PUTTIN' SOMETHIN' IN THE FOOD...
SO WHO'S THIS TWIST I HEAR YOU BEEN SEEIN', HUH?
LETTER BOMBS
MM?
THE ONE WHERE YOU WENT DOWN ON HER WOUNDED CLAM...
FOR FUCK'S SAKE, HE TOLD YOU ABOUT THAT--?!
NO! I'D TRY AN' SHOW A BIT O'--I DUNNO, A BIT O'--
WOULDN'T YOU...?
WHAT AM I SAYIN'?
HER NAME'S ANNIE, AN' I DON'T EVEN KNOW IF I AM SEEIN' HER. SHE'S NO' BEEN RETURNIN' MY CALLS.
YOU MEAN YOU WANNA SEE HER AGAIN...?
'COURSE I DO. IT WAS JUST A STUPID ACCIDENT, IT'S NO REASON TO FUCKIN' DUMP SOMEONE.
YOU'RE A HELL OF A SPORT, KID. I SURE HOPE SHE APPRECIATES IT.
TELL HER NEXT TIME, THE LEAST SHE COULD DO IS YELL FIRE IN THE HOLE...
OKAY.

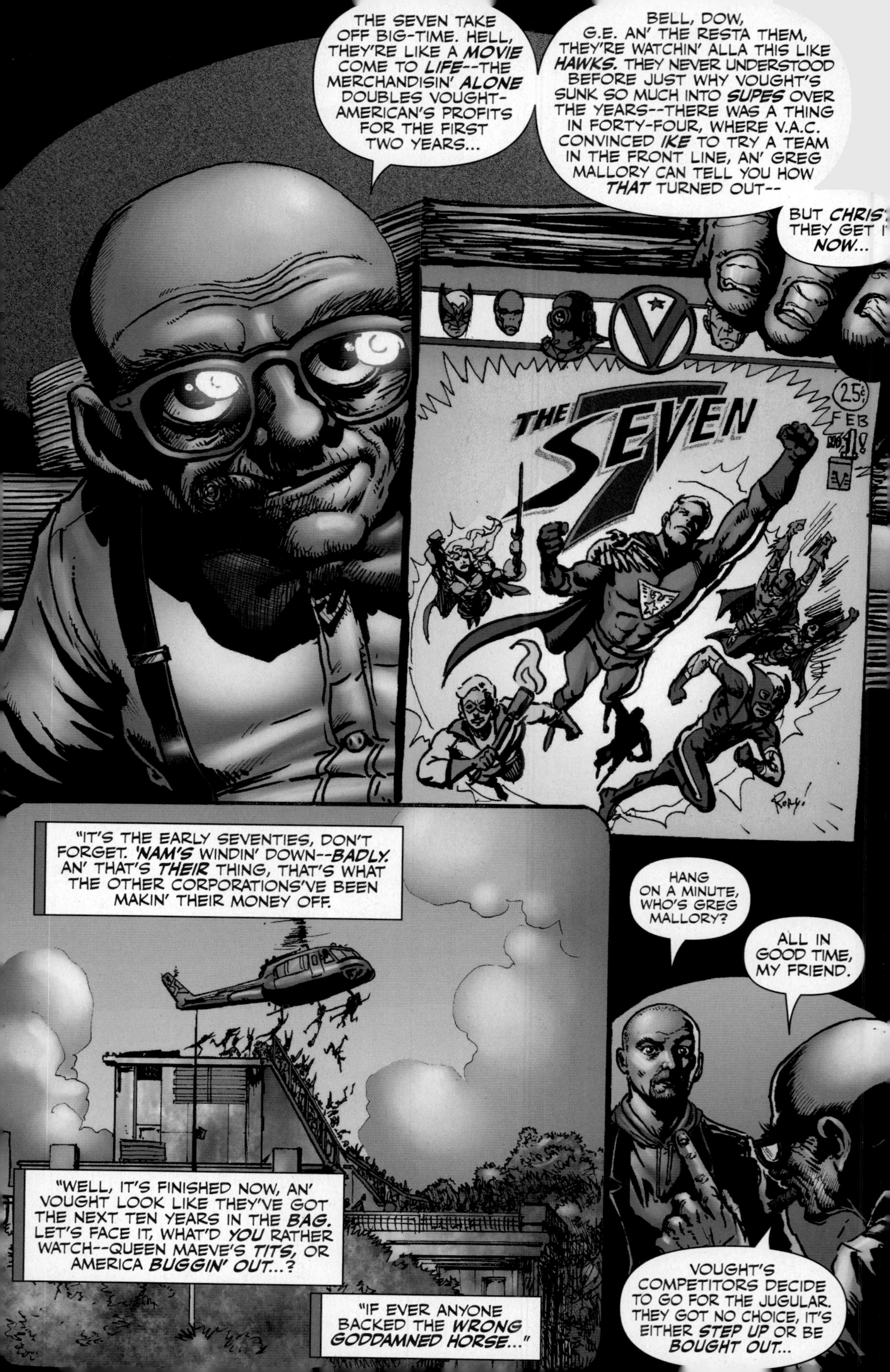
THE SEVEN TAKE OFF BIG-TIME. HELL, THEY'RE LIKE A *MOVIE* COME TO *LIFE*--THE MERCHANDISIN' *ALONE* DOUBLES VOUGHT-AMERICAN'S PROFITS FOR THE FIRST TWO YEARS...
BELL, DOW, G.E. AN' THE RESTA THEM, THEY'RE WATCHIN' ALLA THIS LIKE *HAWKS.* THEY NEVER UNDERSTOOD BEFORE JUST WHY VOUGHT'S SUNK SO MUCH INTO *SUPES* OVER THE YEARS--THERE WAS A THING IN FORTY-FOUR, WHERE V.A.C. CONVINCED *IKE* TO TRY A TEAM IN THE FRONT LINE, AN' GREG MALLORY CAN TELL YOU HOW *THAT* TURNED OUT--
BUT *CHRIS* THEY GET I *NOW*...
25¢
THE SEVEN
FEB
"IT'S THE EARLY SEVENTIES, DON'T FORGET. *'NAM'S* WINDIN' DOWN--*BADLY.* AN' THAT'S *THEIR* THING, THAT'S WHAT THE OTHER CORPORATIONS'VE BEEN MAKIN' THEIR MONEY OFF.
HANG ON A MINUTE, WHO'S GREG MALLORY?
ALL IN GOOD TIME, MY FRIEND.
"WELL, IT'S FINISHED NOW, AN' VOUGHT LOOK LIKE THEY'VE GOT THE NEXT TEN YEARS IN THE *BAG.* LET'S FACE IT, WHAT'D *YOU* RATHER WATCH--QUEEN MAEVE'S *TITS,* OR AMERICA *BUGGIN' OUT*...?
"IF EVER ANYONE BACKED THE *WRONG GODDAMNED HORSE*..."
VOUGHT'S COMPETITORS DECIDE TO GO FOR THE JUGULAR. THEY GOT NO CHOICE, IT'S EITHER *STEP UP* OR BE *BOUGHT OUT*...

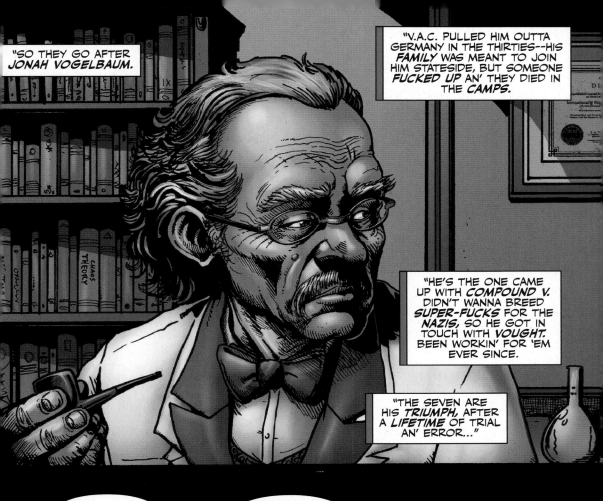

"SO THEY GO AFTER JONAH VOGELBAUM.

"V.A.C. PULLED HIM OUTTA GERMANY IN THE THIRTIES--HIS *FAMILY* WAS MEANT TO JOIN HIM STATESIDE, BUT SOMEONE *FUCKED UP* AN' THEY DIED IN THE *CAMPS.*

"HE'S THE ONE CAME UP WITH *COMPOUND V.* DIDN'T WANNA BREED *SUPER-FUCKS* FOR THE *NAZIS,* SO HE GOT IN TOUCH WITH *VOUGHT.* BEEN WORKIN' FOR 'EM EVER SINCE.

"THE SEVEN ARE HIS *TRIUMPH,* AFTER A *LIFETIME* OF TRIAL AN' ERROR..."

BUT HE NEVER SEEMS TO *GIVE A SHIT.* COULD BE THE *WORK* MATTERS MORE THAN THE *RESULT...*

COULD BE HIS *WIFE* AN' *KIDS* ARE ON HIS MIND, EVERY DAY FOR OVER *FORTY GODDAMN YEARS.*

'CAUSE WHEN THESE ASSHOLES HAVE HIM *KIDNAPPED...* AN' THEY SAY, GUESS WHAT, YOU'RE WORKIN' FOR *US* NOW, YOU'RE GONNA GIVE US SUPES MAKE *VOUGHT'S* TEAM LOOK LIKE *CLOCKWORK TOYS...*

VOGELBAUM'S REACTION IS TO *SLIT HIS FUCKIN' WRISTS.*

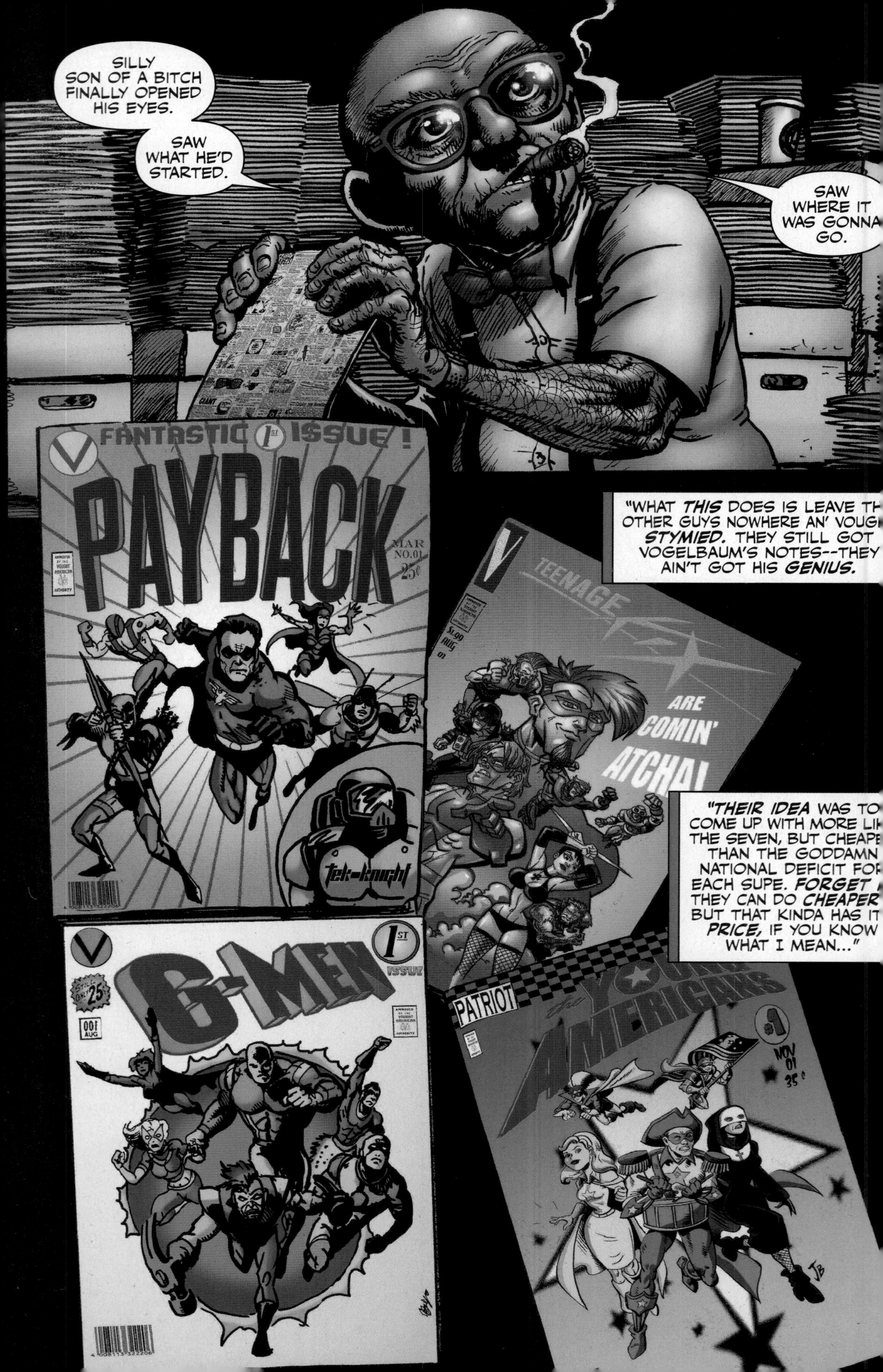

SILLY SON OF A BITCH FINALLY OPENED HIS EYES.
SAW WHAT HE'D STARTED.
SAW WHERE IT WAS GONNA GO.
FANTASTIC 1ST ISSUE!
PAYBACK
MAR NO.01 25¢
tek-knight
"WHAT THIS DOES IS LEAVE TH
OTHER GUYS NOWHERE AN' VOUG
STYMIED. THEY STILL GOT
VOGELBAUM'S NOTES--THEY
AIN'T GOT HIS GENIUS.
TEENAGE
ARE COMIN' ATCHA!
"THEIR IDEA WAS TO
COME UP WITH MORE LI
THE SEVEN, BUT CHEAPE
THAN THE GODDAMN
NATIONAL DEFICIT FOR
EACH SUPE. FORGET
THEY CAN DO CHEAPER
BUT THAT KINDA HAS IT
PRICE, IF YOU KNOW
WHAT I MEAN..."
G-MEN
1ST ISSUE
STILL ONLY 25¢
001 AUG
PATRIOT
AMERICANS
#1
NOV 01 35¢

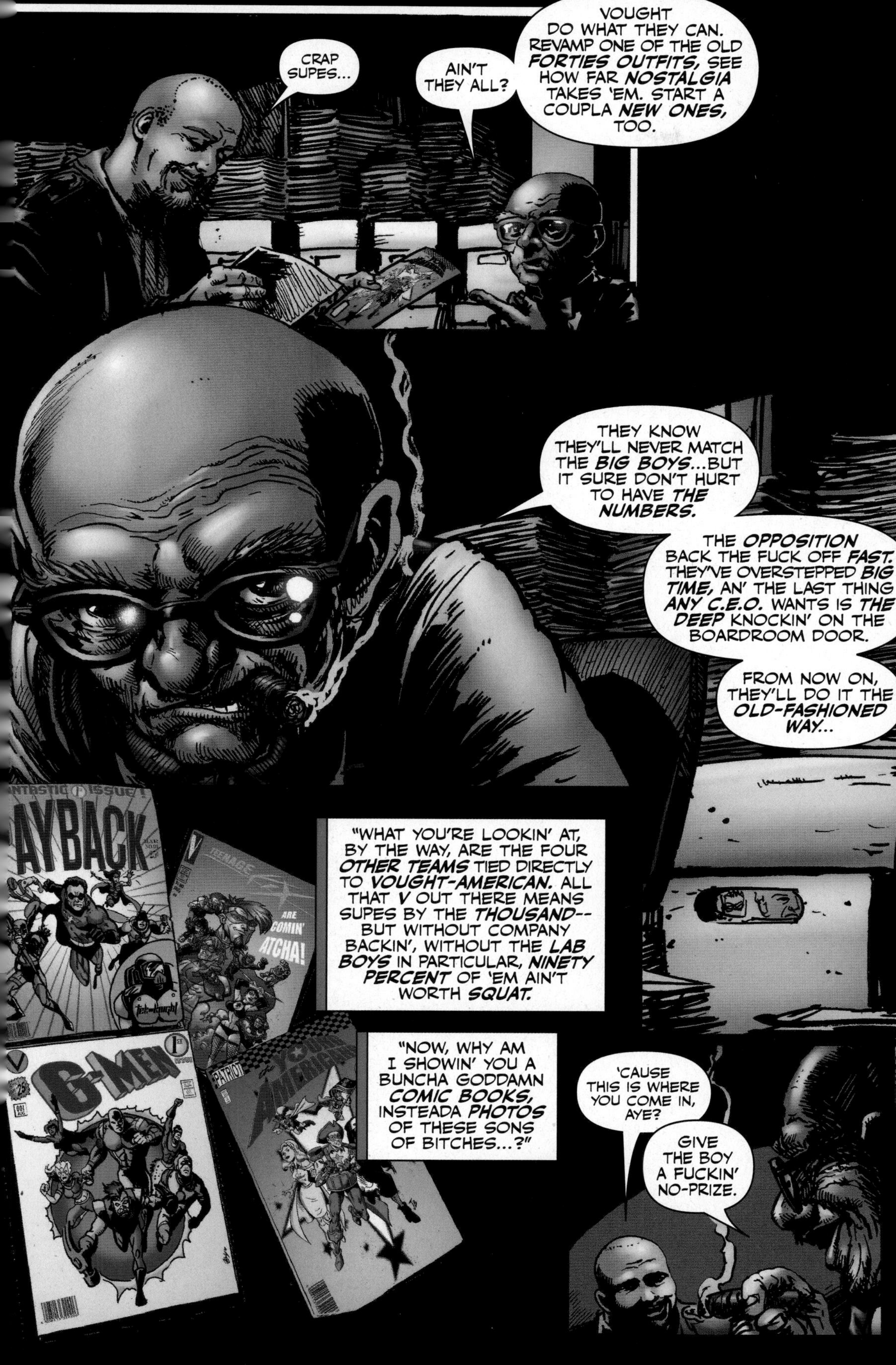
CRAP SUPES...
AIN'T THEY ALL?
VOUGHT DO WHAT THEY CAN. REVAMP ONE OF THE OLD *FORTIES OUTFITS,* SEE HOW FAR *NOSTALGIA* TAKES 'EM. START A COUPLA *NEW ONES,* TOO.
THEY KNOW THEY'LL NEVER MATCH THE *BIG BOYS*...BUT IT SURE DON'T HURT TO HAVE *THE NUMBERS.*
THE *OPPOSITION* BACK THE FUCK OFF *FAST.* THEY'VE OVERSTEPPED *BIG TIME,* AN' THE LAST THING *ANY C.E.O.* WANTS IS *THE DEEP* KNOCKIN' ON THE BOARDROOM DOOR.
FROM NOW ON, THEY'LL DO IT THE *OLD-FASHIONED WAY...*
AYBACK
"WHAT YOU'RE LOOKIN' AT, BY THE WAY, ARE THE FOUR *OTHER TEAMS* TIED DIRECTLY TO *VOUGHT-AMERICAN.* ALL THAT *V* OUT THERE MEANS SUPES BY THE *THOUSAND*--BUT WITHOUT COMPANY BACKIN', WITHOUT THE *LAB BOYS* IN PARTICULAR, *NINETY PERCENT* OF 'EM AIN'T WORTH *SQUAT.*
TEENAGE
ARE COMIN' ATCHA!
G-MEN
PATRIOT
YOUNG AMERICANS
"NOW, WHY AM I SHOWIN' YOU A BUNCHA GODDAMN *COMIC BOOKS,* INSTEADA *PHOTOS* OF THESE SONS OF BITCHES...?"
'CAUSE THIS IS WHERE YOU COME IN, AYE?
GIVE THE BOY A FUCKIN' NO-PRIZE.

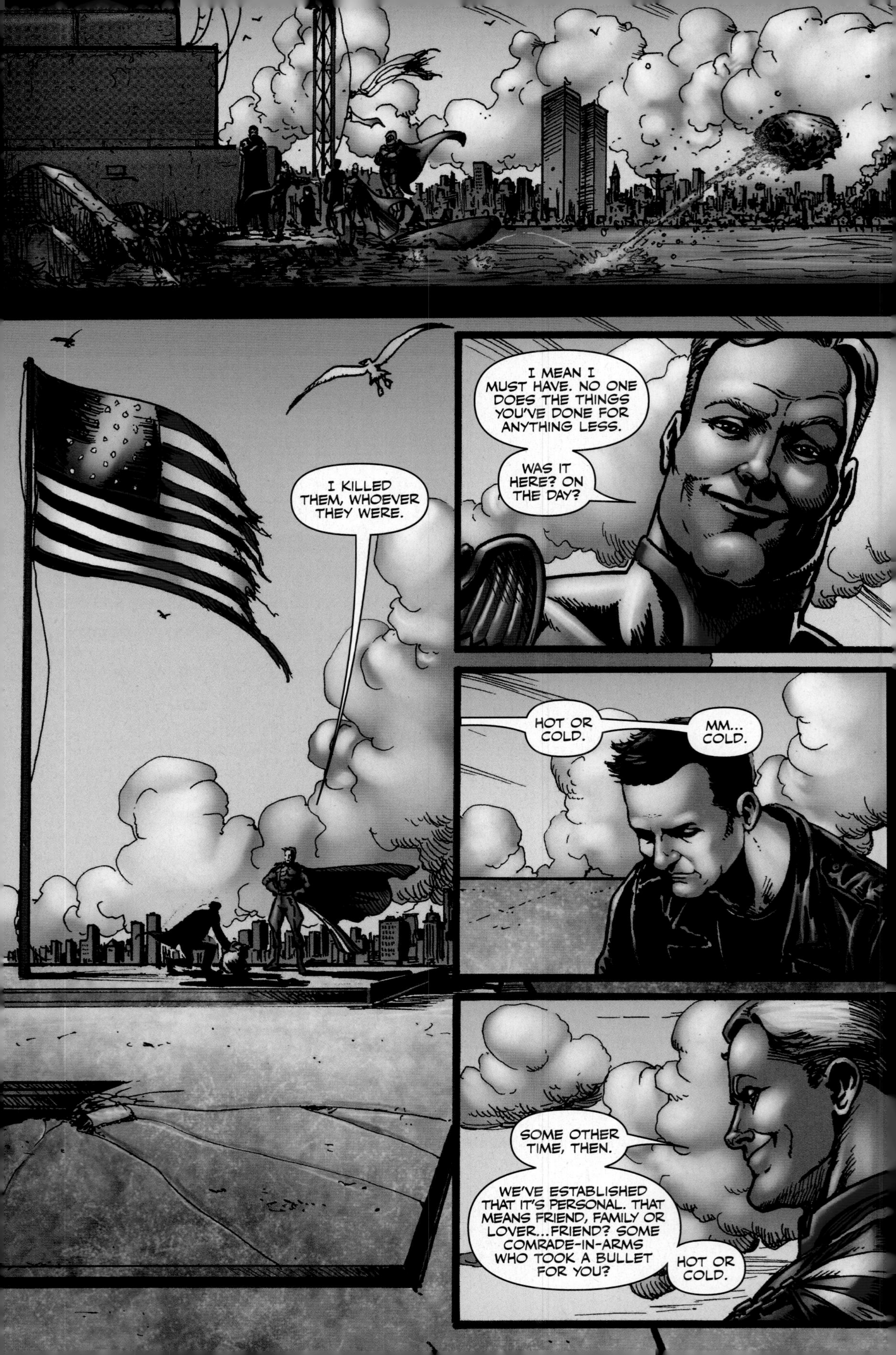
I KILLED THEM, WHOEVER THEY WERE.
I MEAN I MUST HAVE. NO ONE DOES THE THINGS YOU'VE DONE FOR ANYTHING LESS.
WAS IT HERE? ON THE DAY?
HOT OR COLD.
MM... COLD.
SOME OTHER TIME, THEN.
WE'VE ESTABLISHED THAT IT'S PERSONAL. THAT MEANS FRIEND, FAMILY OR LOVER...FRIEND? SOME COMRADE-IN-ARMS WHO TOOK A BULLET FOR YOU?
HOT OR COLD.

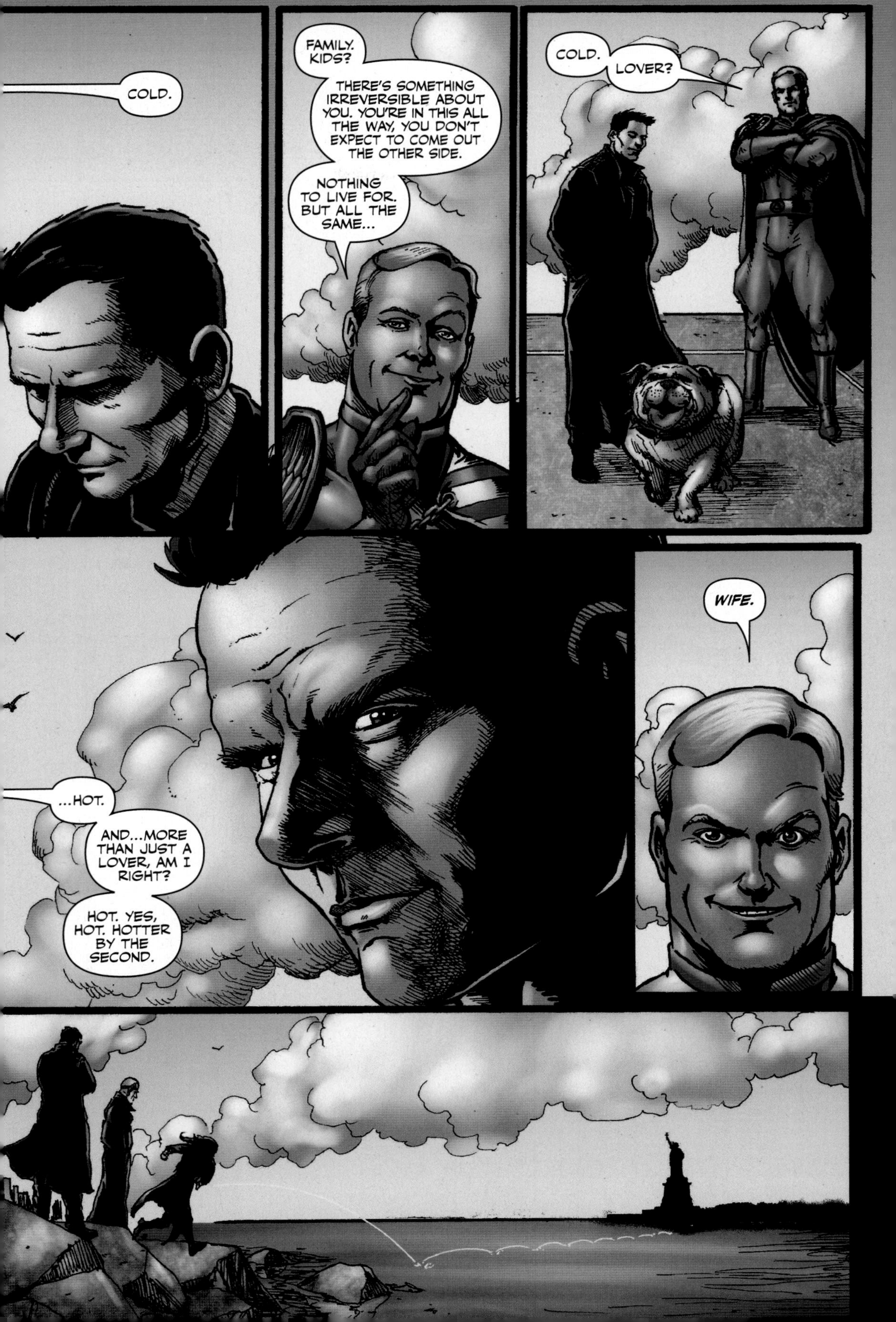
COLD.
FAMILY. KIDS?
THERE'S SOMETHING IRREVERSIBLE ABOUT YOU. YOU'RE IN THIS ALL THE WAY, YOU DON'T EXPECT TO COME OUT THE OTHER SIDE.
NOTHING TO LIVE FOR. BUT ALL THE SAME...
COLD.
LOVER?
...HOT.
AND...MORE THAN JUST A LOVER, AM I RIGHT?
HOT. YES, HOT. HOTTER BY THE SECOND.
WIFE.

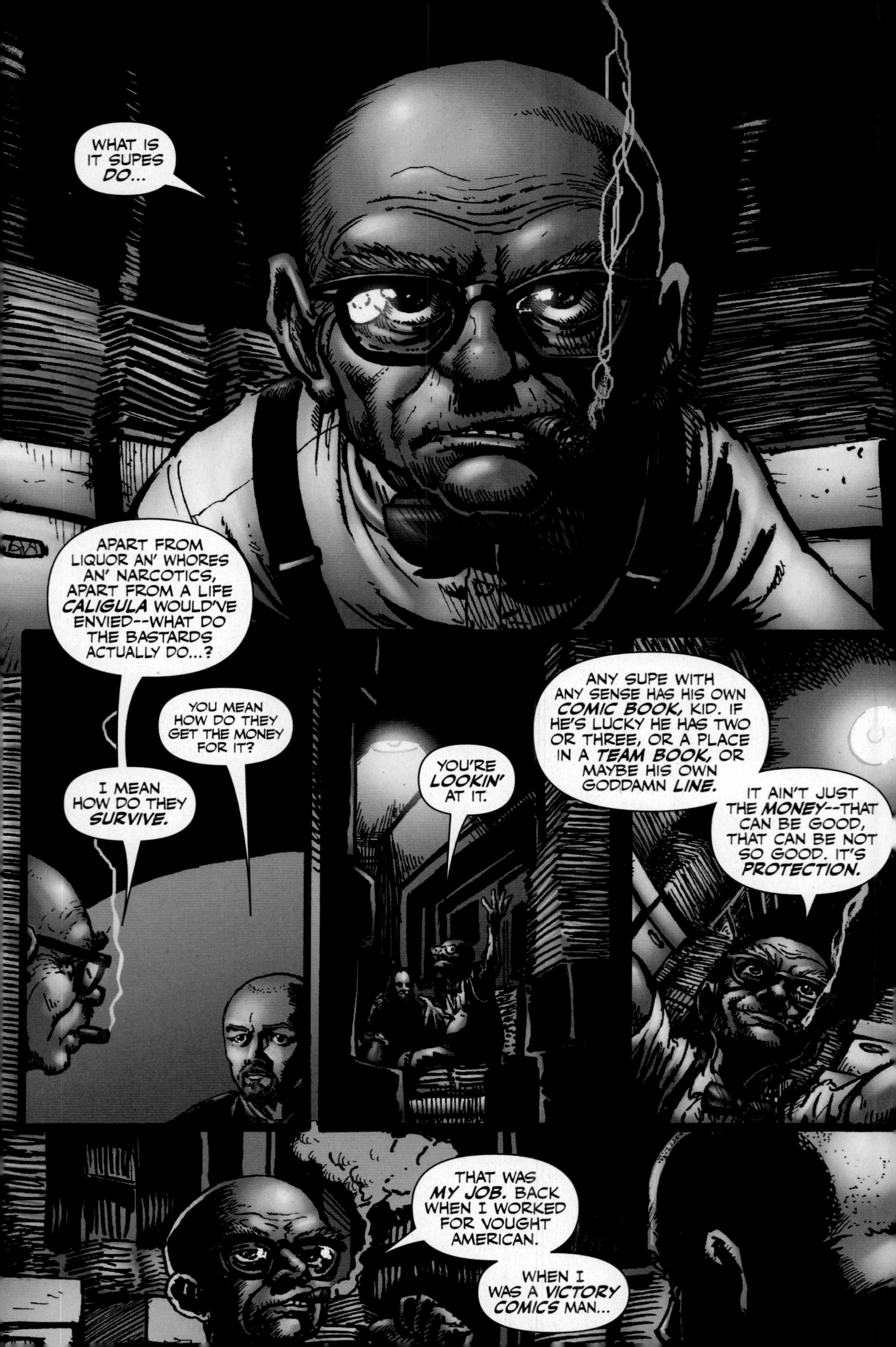
WHAT IS IT SUPES *DO*...
APART FROM LIQUOR AN' WHORES AN' NARCOTICS, APART FROM A LIFE *CALIGULA* WOULD'VE ENVIED--WHAT DO THE BASTARDS ACTUALLY DO...?
YOU MEAN HOW DO THEY GET THE MONEY FOR IT?
I MEAN HOW DO THEY *SURVIVE.*
YOU'RE *LOOKIN'* AT IT.
ANY SUPE WITH ANY SENSE HAS HIS OWN *COMIC BOOK,* KID. IF HE'S LUCKY HE HAS TWO OR THREE, OR A PLACE IN A *TEAM BOOK,* OR MAYBE HIS OWN GODDAMN *LINE.*
IT AIN'T JUST THE *MONEY*--THAT CAN BE GOOD, THAT CAN BE NOT SO GOOD. IT'S *PROTECTION.*
THAT WAS *MY JOB.* BACK WHEN I WORKED FOR VOUGHT AMERICAN.
WHEN I WAS A *VICTORY COMICS* MAN...

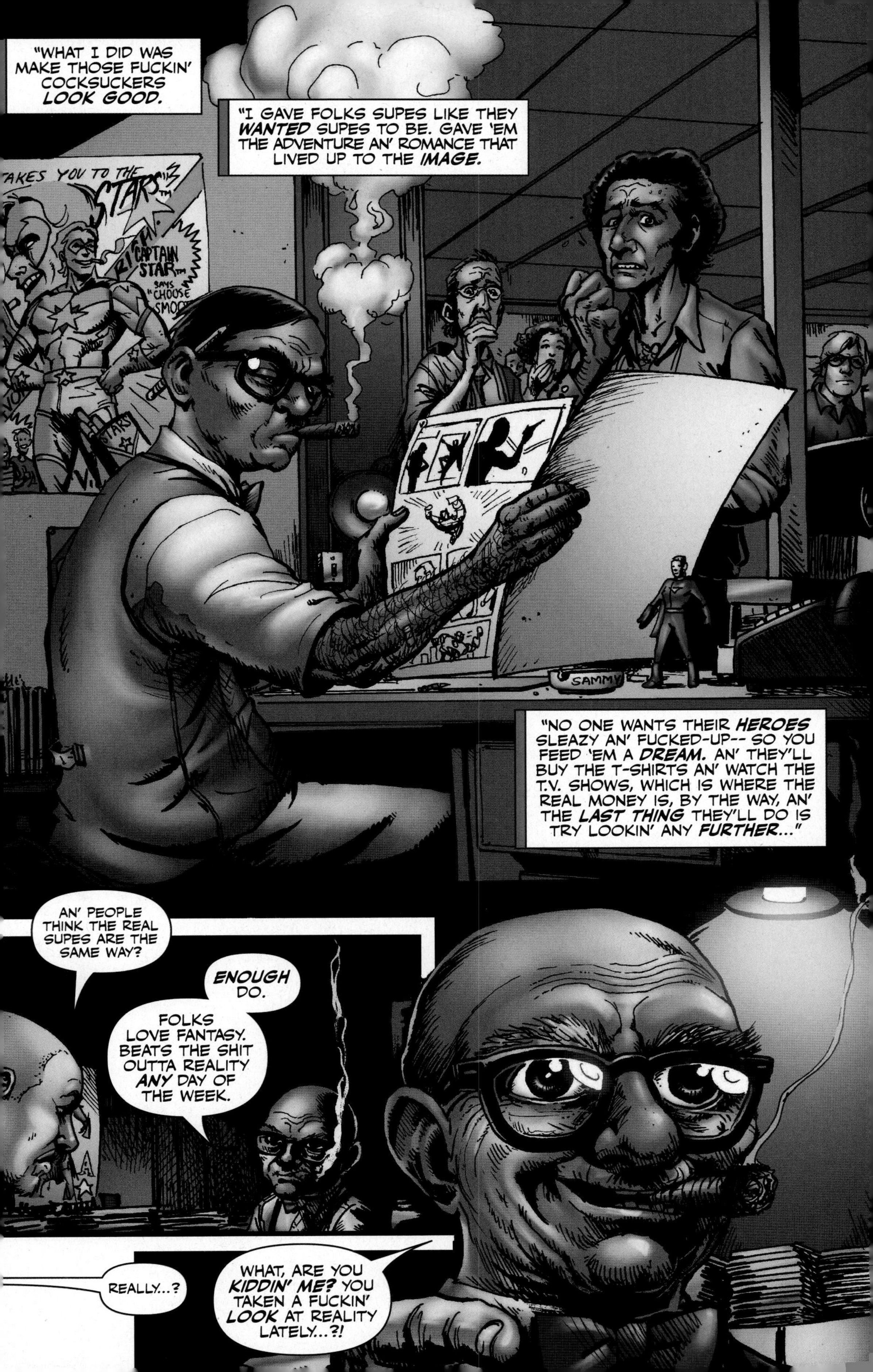
"WHAT I DID WAS MAKE THOSE FUCKIN' COCKSUCKERS LOOK GOOD.
"I GAVE FOLKS SUPES LIKE THEY WANTED SUPES TO BE. GAVE 'EM THE ADVENTURE AN' ROMANCE THAT LIVED UP TO THE IMAGE.
CAPTAIN STAR
"NO ONE WANTS THEIR HEROES SLEAZY AN' FUCKED-UP-- SO YOU FEED 'EM A DREAM. AN' THEY'LL BUY THE T-SHIRTS AN' WATCH THE T.V. SHOWS, WHICH IS WHERE THE REAL MONEY IS, BY THE WAY, AN' THE LAST THING THEY'LL DO IS TRY LOOKIN' ANY FURTHER..."
AN' PEOPLE THINK THE REAL SUPES ARE THE SAME WAY?
ENOUGH DO.
FOLKS LOVE FANTASY. BEATS THE SHIT OUTTA REALITY ANY DAY OF THE WEEK.
REALLY...?
WHAT, ARE YOU KIDDIN' ME? YOU TAKEN A FUCKIN' LOOK AT REALITY LATELY...?!

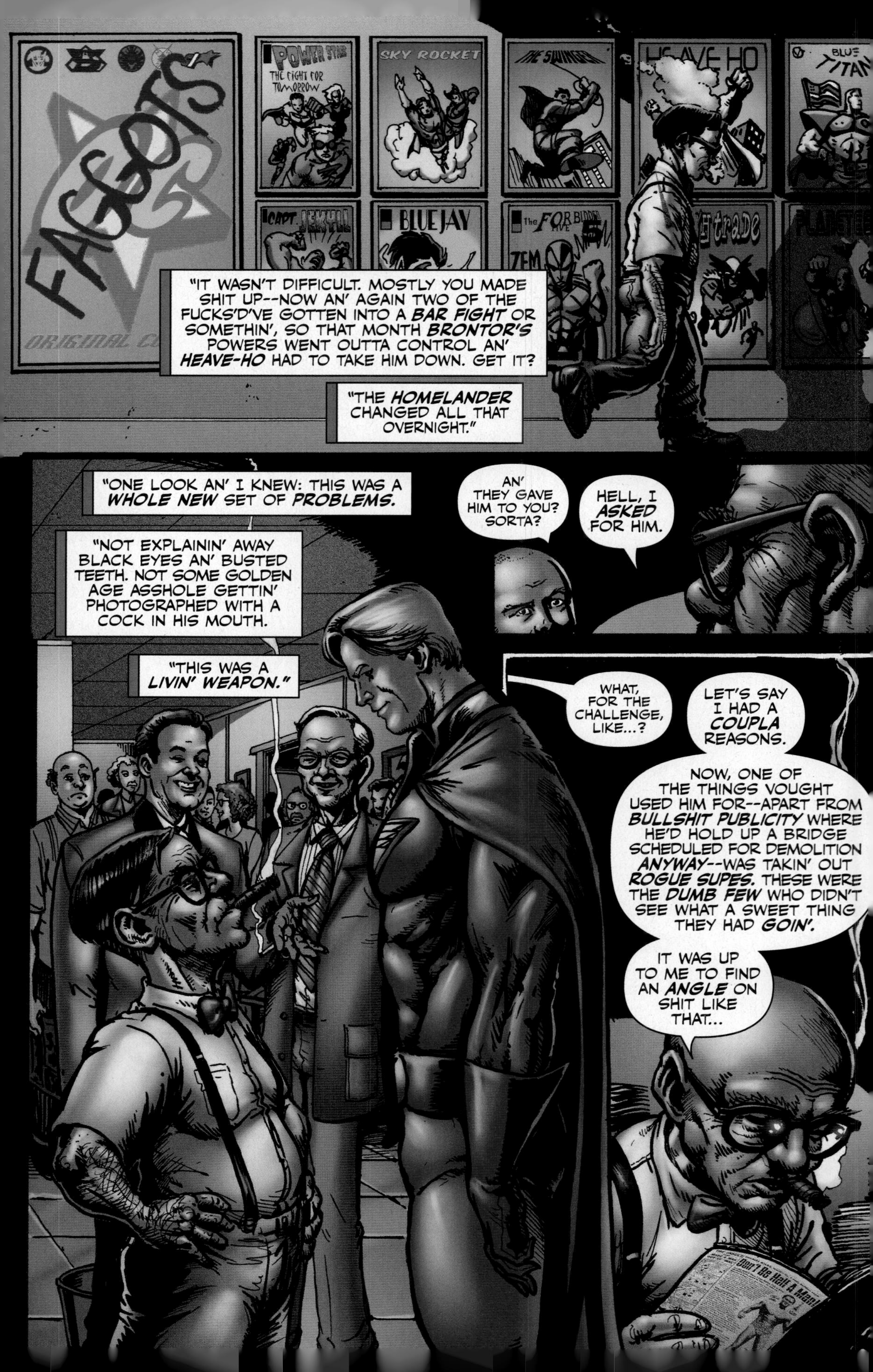

FAGGOTS
POWER STAR
THE FIGHT FOR TOMORROW
SKY ROCKET
THE SWINGER
HEAVE HO
BLUE TITAN
CAPT. JEKYLL
BLUEJAY
"IT WASN'T DIFFICULT. MOSTLY YOU MADE SHIT UP--NOW AN' AGAIN TWO OF THE FUCKS'D'VE GOTTEN INTO A *BAR FIGHT* OR SOMETHIN', SO THAT MONTH *BRONTOR'S* POWERS WENT OUTTA CONTROL AN' *HEAVE-HO* HAD TO TAKE HIM DOWN. GET IT?
"THE *HOMELANDER* CHANGED ALL THAT OVERNIGHT."
"ONE LOOK AN' I KNEW: THIS WAS A *WHOLE NEW* SET OF *PROBLEMS.*
"NOT EXPLAININ' AWAY BLACK EYES AN' BUSTED TEETH. NOT SOME GOLDEN AGE ASSHOLE GETTIN' PHOTOGRAPHED WITH A COCK IN HIS MOUTH.
"THIS WAS A *LIVIN' WEAPON.*"
AN' THEY GAVE HIM TO YOU? SORTA?
HELL, I *ASKED* FOR HIM.
WHAT, FOR THE CHALLENGE, LIKE...?
LET'S SAY I HAD A *COUPLA* REASONS.
NOW, ONE OF THE THINGS VOUGHT USED HIM FOR--APART FROM *BULLSHIT PUBLICITY* WHERE HE'D HOLD UP A BRIDGE SCHEDULED FOR DEMOLITION *ANYWAY*--WAS TAKIN' OUT *ROGUE SUPES.* THESE WERE THE *DUMB FEW* WHO DIDN'T SEE WHAT A SWEET THING THEY HAD *GOIN'.*
IT WAS UP TO ME TO FIND AN *ANGLE* ON SHIT LIKE THAT...
Don't Be Half A Man!

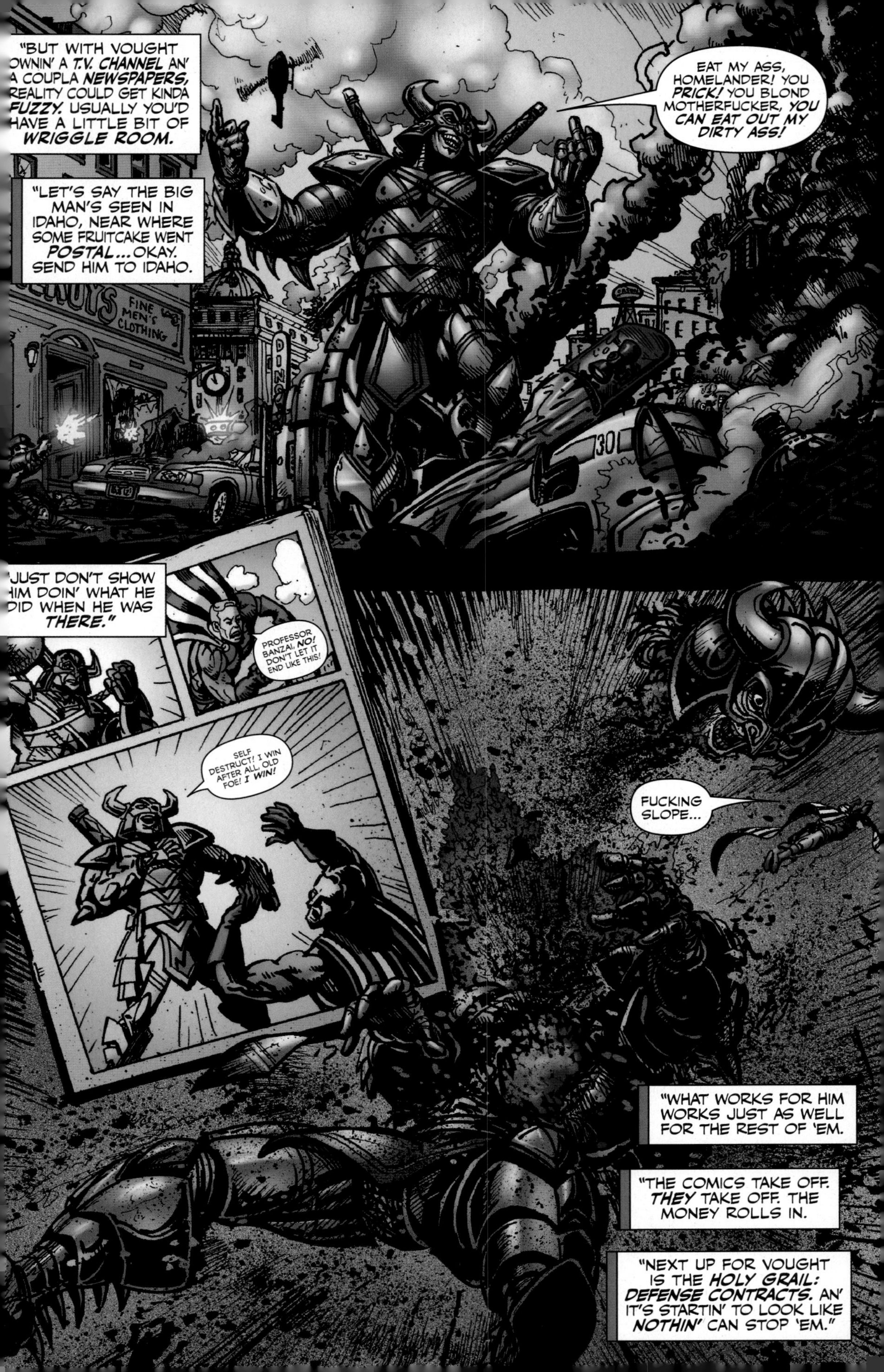
"BUT WITH VOUGHT OWNIN' A T.V. CHANNEL AN' A COUPLA NEWSPAPERS, REALITY COULD GET KINDA FUZZY. USUALLY YOU'D HAVE A LITTLE BIT OF WRIGGLE ROOM.
EAT MY ASS, HOMELANDER! YOU PRICK! YOU BLOND MOTHERFUCKER, YOU CAN EAT OUT MY DIRTY ASS!
"LET'S SAY THE BIG MAN'S SEEN IN IDAHO, NEAR WHERE SOME FRUITCAKE WENT POSTAL...OKAY. SEND HIM TO IDAHO.
FINE MEN'S CLOTHING
"JUST DON'T SHOW HIM DOIN' WHAT HE DID WHEN HE WAS THERE."
PROFESSOR BANZAI, NO! DON'T LET IT END LIKE THIS!
SELF DESTRUCT! I WIN AFTER ALL, OLD FOE! I WIN!
FUCKING SLOPE...
"WHAT WORKS FOR HIM WORKS JUST AS WELL FOR THE REST OF 'EM.
"THE COMICS TAKE OFF. THEY TAKE OFF. THE MONEY ROLLS IN.
"NEXT UP FOR VOUGHT IS THE HOLY GRAIL: DEFENSE CONTRACTS. AN' IT'S STARTIN' TO LOOK LIKE NOTHIN' CAN STOP 'EM."

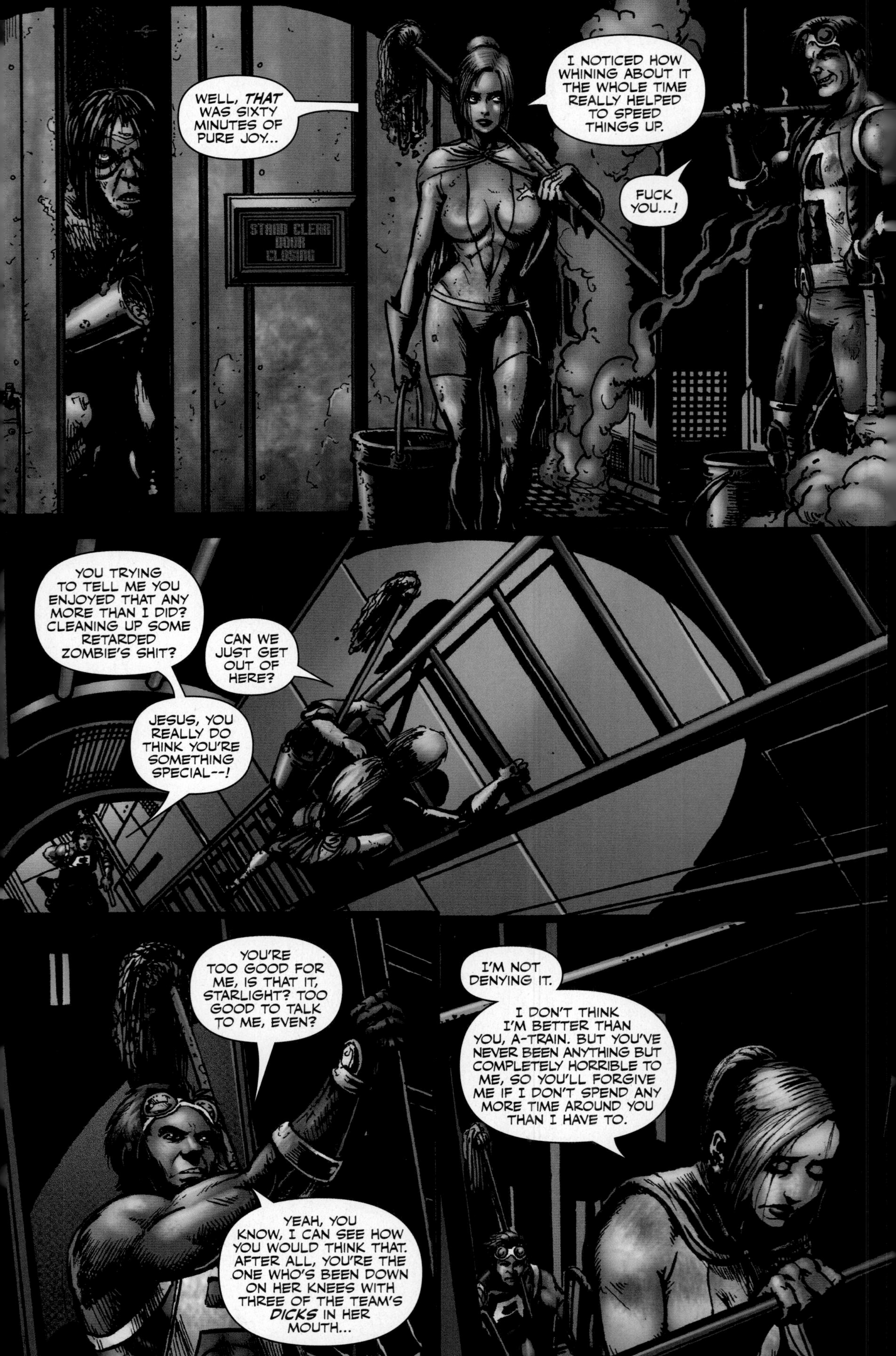
WELL, *THAT* WAS SIXTY MINUTES OF PURE JOY...
STAND CLEAR DOOR CLOSING
I NOTICED HOW WHINING ABOUT IT THE WHOLE TIME REALLY HELPED TO SPEED THINGS UP.
FUCK YOU...!
YOU TRYING TO TELL ME YOU ENJOYED THAT ANY MORE THAN I DID? CLEANING UP SOME RETARDED ZOMBIE'S SHIT?
CAN WE JUST GET OUT OF HERE?
JESUS, YOU REALLY DO THINK YOU'RE SOMETHING SPECIAL--!
YOU'RE TOO GOOD FOR ME, IS THAT IT, STARLIGHT? TOO GOOD TO TALK TO ME, EVEN?
I'M NOT DENYING IT.
I DON'T THINK I'M BETTER THAN YOU, A-TRAIN. BUT YOU'VE NEVER BEEN ANYTHING BUT COMPLETELY HORRIBLE TO ME, SO YOU'LL FORGIVE ME IF I DON'T SPEND ANY MORE TIME AROUND YOU THAN I HAVE TO.
YEAH, YOU KNOW, I CAN SEE HOW YOU WOULD THINK THAT. AFTER ALL, YOU'RE THE ONE WHO'S BEEN DOWN ON HER KNEES WITH THREE OF THE TEAM'S *DICKS* IN HER MOUTH...

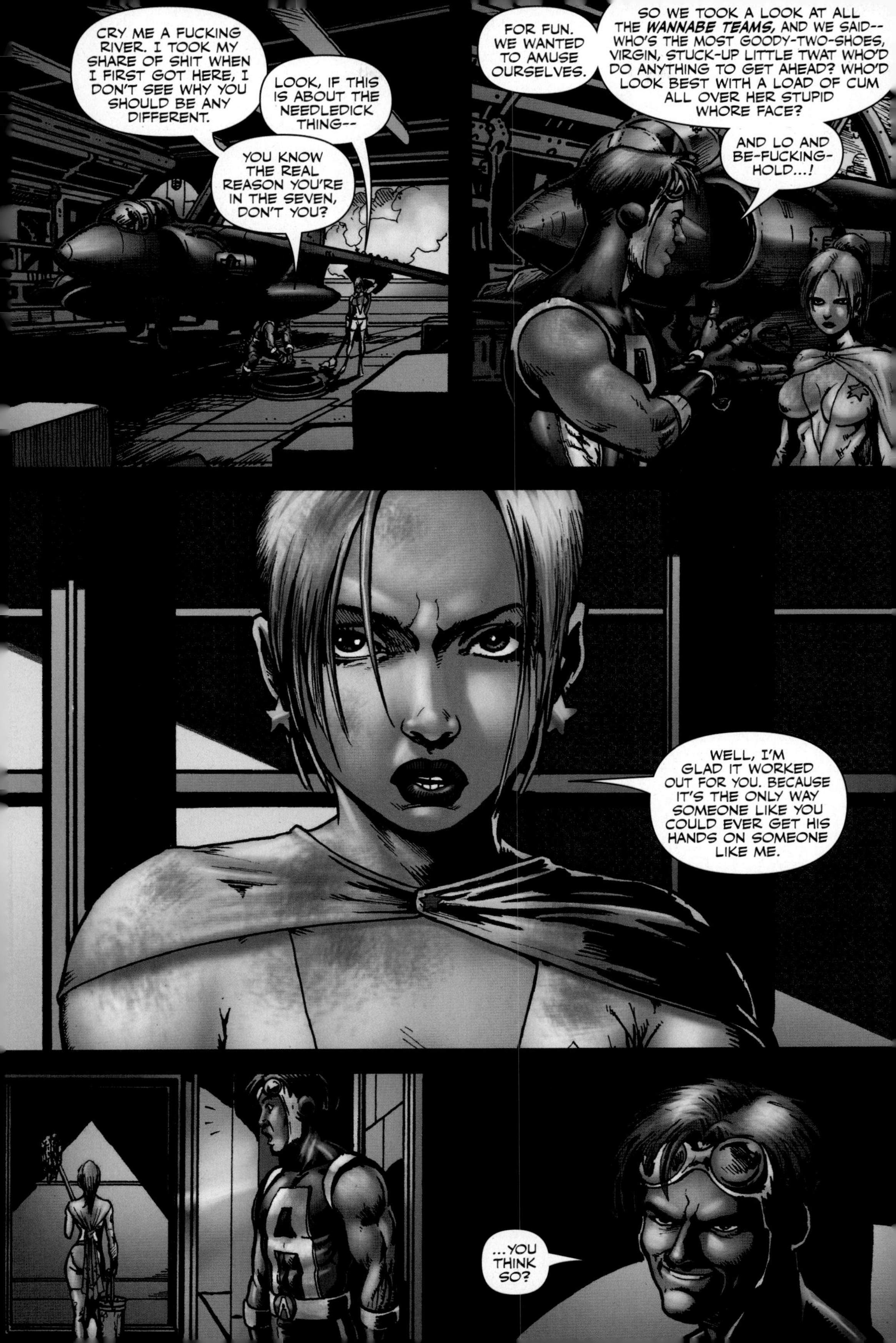
CRY ME A FUCKING RIVER. I TOOK MY SHARE OF SHIT WHEN I FIRST GOT HERE, I DON'T SEE WHY YOU SHOULD BE ANY DIFFERENT.
LOOK, IF THIS IS ABOUT THE NEEDLEDICK THING--
YOU KNOW THE REAL REASON YOU'RE IN THE SEVEN, DON'T YOU?
FOR FUN. WE WANTED TO AMUSE OURSELVES.
SO WE TOOK A LOOK AT ALL THE WANNABE TEAMS, AND WE SAID-- WHO'S THE MOST GOODY-TWO-SHOES, VIRGIN, STUCK-UP LITTLE TWAT WHO'D DO ANYTHING TO GET AHEAD? WHO'D LOOK BEST WITH A LOAD OF CUM ALL OVER HER STUPID WHORE FACE?
AND LO AND BE-FUCKING-HOLD...!
WELL, I'M GLAD IT WORKED OUT FOR YOU. BECAUSE IT'S THE ONLY WAY SOMEONE LIKE YOU COULD EVER GET HIS HANDS ON SOMEONE LIKE ME.
...YOU THINK SO?

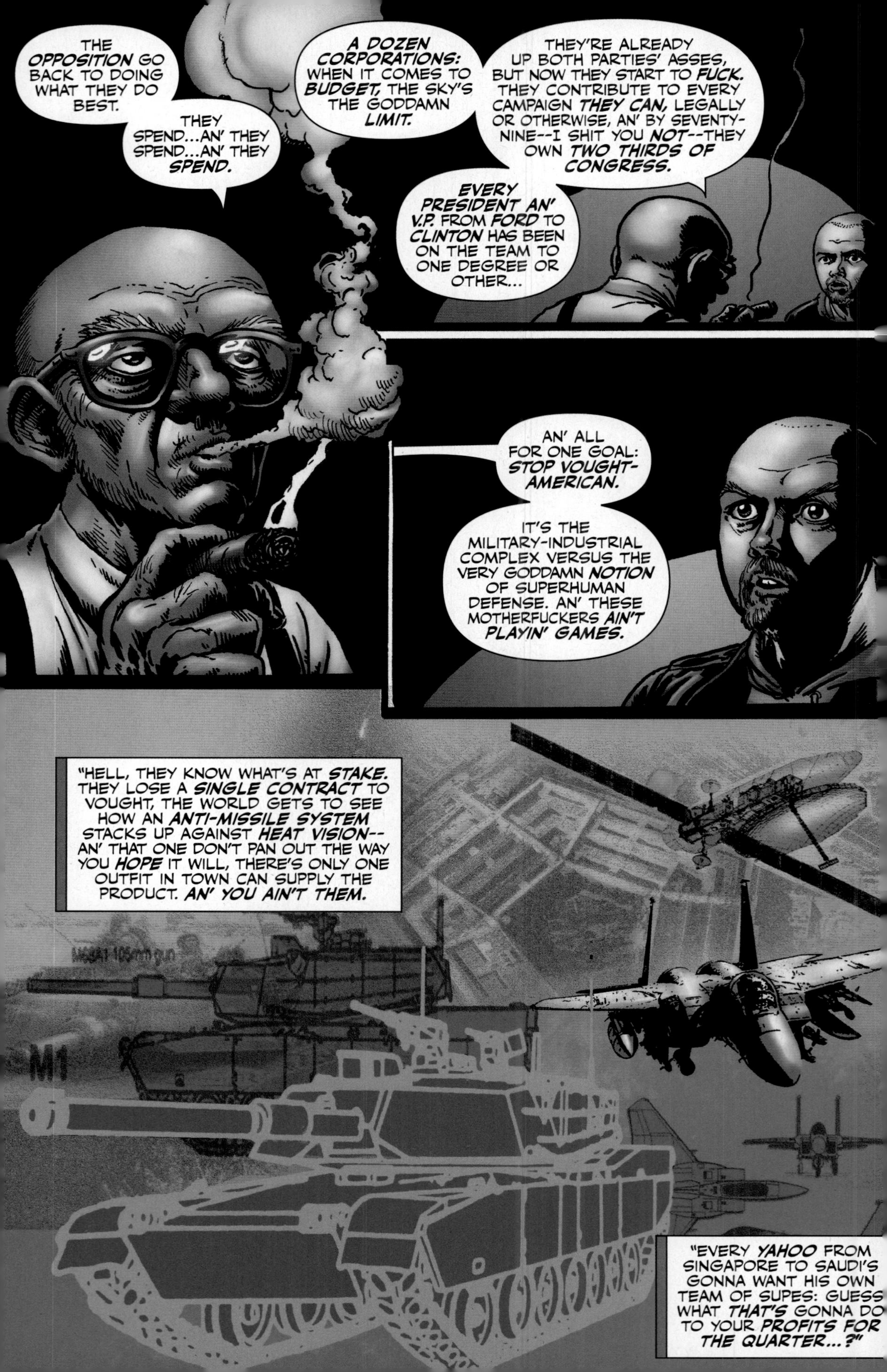
THE OPPOSITION GO BACK TO DOING WHAT THEY DO BEST.
THEY SPEND...AN' THEY SPEND...AN' THEY SPEND.
A DOZEN CORPORATIONS: WHEN IT COMES TO BUDGET, THE SKY'S THE GODDAMN LIMIT.
THEY'RE ALREADY UP BOTH PARTIES' ASSES, BUT NOW THEY START TO FUCK. THEY CONTRIBUTE TO EVERY CAMPAIGN THEY CAN, LEGALLY OR OTHERWISE, AN' BY SEVENTY-NINE--I SHIT YOU NOT--THEY OWN TWO THIRDS OF CONGRESS.
EVERY PRESIDENT AN' V.P. FROM FORD TO CLINTON HAS BEEN ON THE TEAM TO ONE DEGREE OR OTHER...
AN' ALL FOR ONE GOAL: STOP VOUGHT-AMERICAN.
IT'S THE MILITARY-INDUSTRIAL COMPLEX VERSUS THE VERY GODDAMN NOTION OF SUPERHUMAN DEFENSE. AN' THESE MOTHERFUCKERS AIN'T PLAYIN' GAMES.
"HELL, THEY KNOW WHAT'S AT STAKE. THEY LOSE A SINGLE CONTRACT TO VOUGHT, THE WORLD GETS TO SEE HOW AN ANTI-MISSILE SYSTEM STACKS UP AGAINST HEAT VISION--AN' THAT ONE DON'T PAN OUT THE WAY YOU HOPE IT WILL, THERE'S ONLY ONE OUTFIT IN TOWN CAN SUPPLY THE PRODUCT. AN' YOU AIN'T THEM.
M1
"EVERY YAHOO FROM SINGAPORE TO SAUDI'S GONNA WANT HIS OWN TEAM OF SUPES: GUESS WHAT THAT'S GONNA DO TO YOUR PROFITS FOR THE QUARTER...?"

BUT... VIC THE VEEP...

YEAH.

AT FIRST VOUGHT *FLOUNDER.* NOT ONE OF THE SERVICES IS ALLOWED TO *TOUCH 'EM.*

THE OBVIOUS THING TO DO IS PLAY POLITICS TOO, BUT SUPE MONEY OR NOT, THEY'RE *JUST ONE CORPORATION.* NO WAY, *JOSE.*

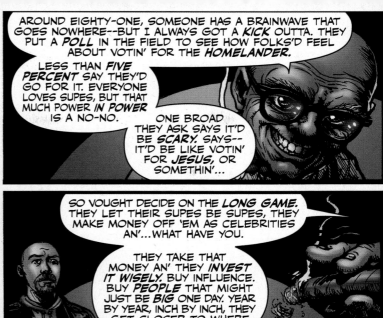

AROUND EIGHTY-ONE, SOMEONE HAS A BRAINWAVE THAT GOES NOWHERE--BUT I ALWAYS GOT A *KICK* OUTTA. THEY PUT A *POLL* IN THE FIELD TO SEE HOW FOLKS'D FEEL ABOUT VOTIN' FOR THE *HOMELANDER.*

LESS THAN *FIVE PERCENT* SAY THEY'D GO FOR IT. EVERYONE LOVES SUPES, BUT THAT MUCH POWER *IN POWER* IS A NO-NO.

ONE BROAD THEY ASK SAYS IT'D BE *SCARY.* SAYS-- IT'D BE LIKE VOTIN' FOR *JESUS,* OR SOMETHIN'...

SO VOUGHT DECIDE ON THE *LONG GAME.* THEY LET THEIR SUPES BE SUPES, THEY MAKE MONEY OFF 'EM AS CELEBRITIES AN'...WHAT HAVE YOU.

THEY TAKE THAT MONEY AN' THEY *INVEST IT WISELY.* BUY INFLUENCE. BUY *PEOPLE* THAT MIGHT JUST BE *BIG* ONE DAY. YEAR BY YEAR, INCH BY INCH, THEY GET CLOSER TO WHERE THEY WANNA BE...

"AN' ALL OF A SUDDEN IT'S THE YEAR TWO THOUSAND, AN' THE OPPOSITION HAVE FOUND THE *PERFECT CANDIDATE* FOR *NOVEMBER...*"

"*DAKOTA BOB SHAEFER:* OLD SCHOOL REPUBLICAN, HALIBURTON MAN, AN' HARD AN' COLD AS THE *BADLANDS THEMSELVES.*"

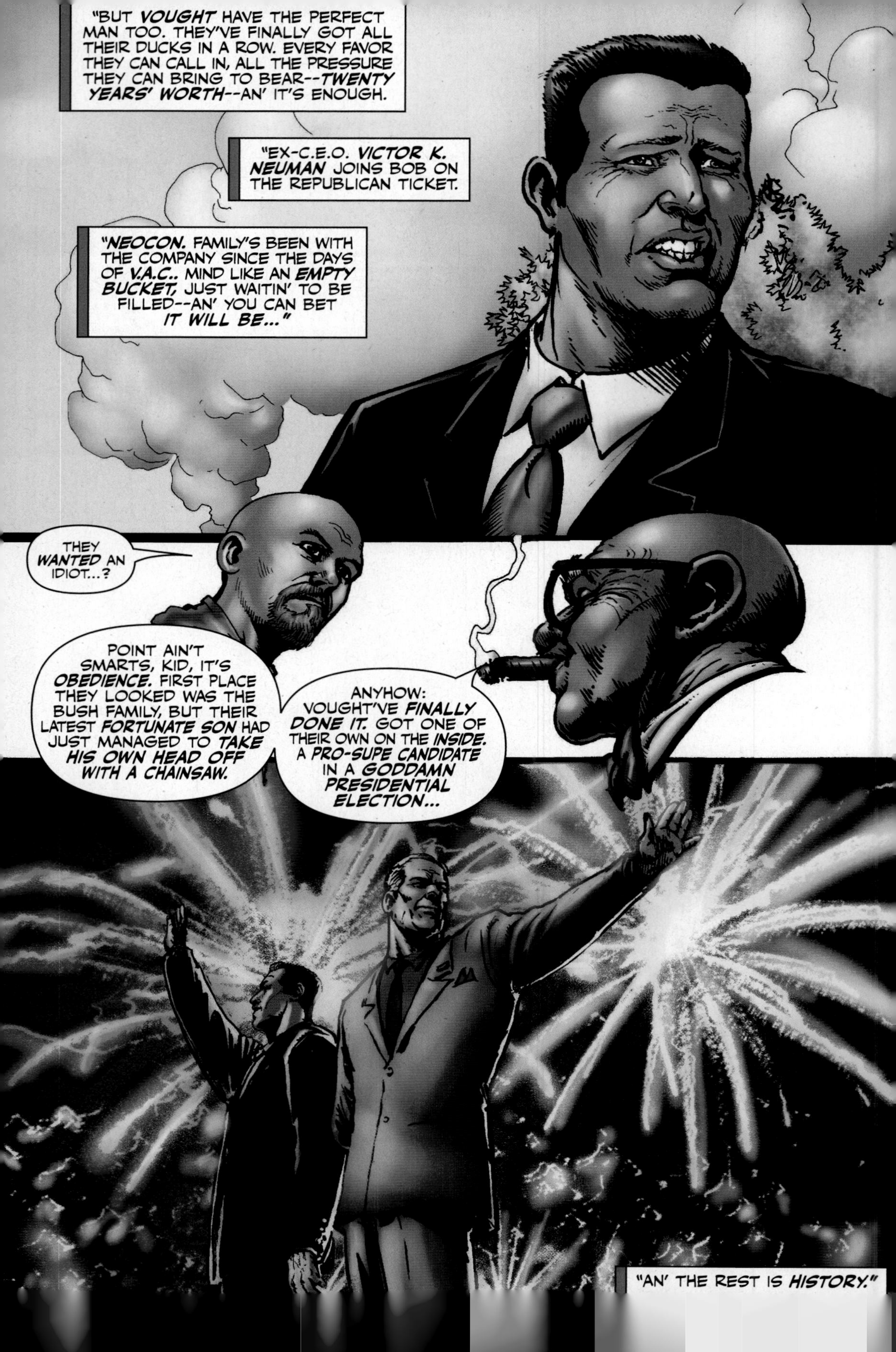
"BUT VOUGHT HAVE THE PERFECT MAN TOO. THEY'VE FINALLY GOT ALL THEIR DUCKS IN A ROW. EVERY FAVOR THEY CAN CALL IN, ALL THE PRESSURE THEY CAN BRING TO BEAR--TWENTY YEARS' WORTH--AN' IT'S ENOUGH.
"EX-C.E.O. VICTOR K. NEUMAN JOINS BOB ON THE REPUBLICAN TICKET.
"NEOCON. FAMILY'S BEEN WITH THE COMPANY SINCE THE DAYS OF V.A.C.. MIND LIKE AN EMPTY BUCKET, JUST WAITIN' TO BE FILLED--AN' YOU CAN BET IT WILL BE..."
THEY WANTED AN IDIOT...?
POINT AIN'T SMARTS, KID, IT'S OBEDIENCE. FIRST PLACE THEY LOOKED WAS THE BUSH FAMILY, BUT THEIR LATEST FORTUNATE SON HAD JUST MANAGED TO TAKE HIS OWN HEAD OFF WITH A CHAINSAW.
ANYHOW: VOUGHT'VE FINALLY DONE IT. GOT ONE OF THEIR OWN ON THE INSIDE. A PRO-SUPE CANDIDATE IN A GODDAMN PRESIDENTIAL ELECTION...
"AN' THE REST IS HISTORY."

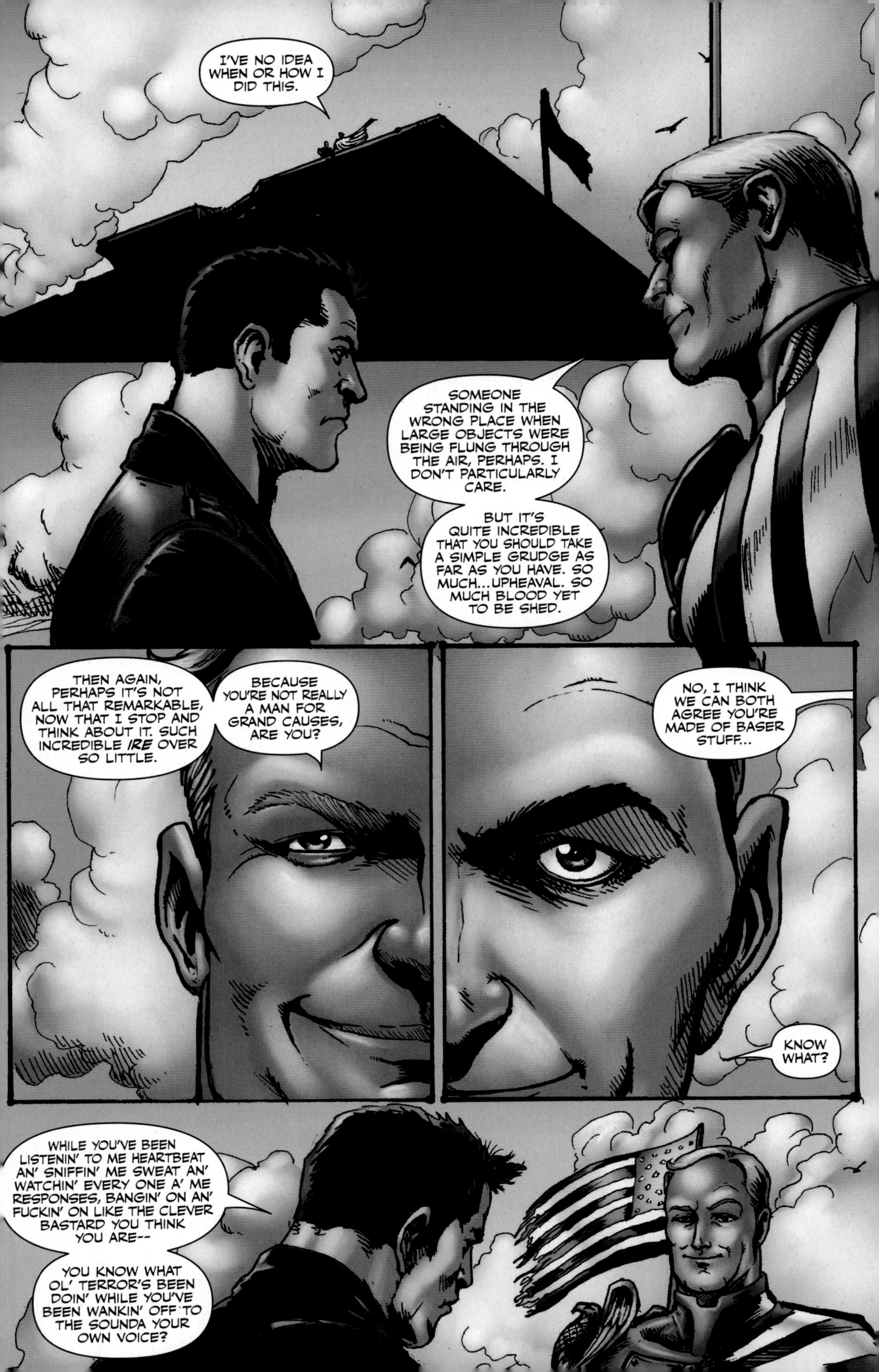
I'VE NO IDEA WHEN OR HOW I DID THIS.
SOMEONE STANDING IN THE WRONG PLACE WHEN LARGE OBJECTS WERE BEING FLUNG THROUGH THE AIR, PERHAPS. I DON'T PARTICULARLY CARE.
BUT IT'S QUITE INCREDIBLE THAT YOU SHOULD TAKE A SIMPLE GRUDGE AS FAR AS YOU HAVE. SO MUCH...UPHEAVAL. SO MUCH BLOOD YET TO BE SHED.
THEN AGAIN, PERHAPS IT'S NOT ALL THAT REMARKABLE, NOW THAT I STOP AND THINK ABOUT IT. SUCH INCREDIBLE *IRE* OVER SO LITTLE.
BECAUSE YOU'RE NOT REALLY A MAN FOR GRAND CAUSES, ARE YOU?
NO, I THINK WE CAN BOTH AGREE YOU'RE MADE OF BASER STUFF...
KNOW WHAT?
WHILE YOU'VE BEEN LISTENIN' TO ME HEARTBEAT AN' SNIFFIN' ME SWEAT AN' WATCHIN' EVERY ONE A' ME RESPONSES, BANGIN' ON AN' FUCKIN' ON LIKE THE CLEVER BASTARD YOU THINK YOU ARE--
YOU KNOW WHAT OL' TERROR'S BEEN DOIN' WHILE YOU'VE BEEN WANKIN' OFF TO THE SOUNDA YOUR OWN VOICE?

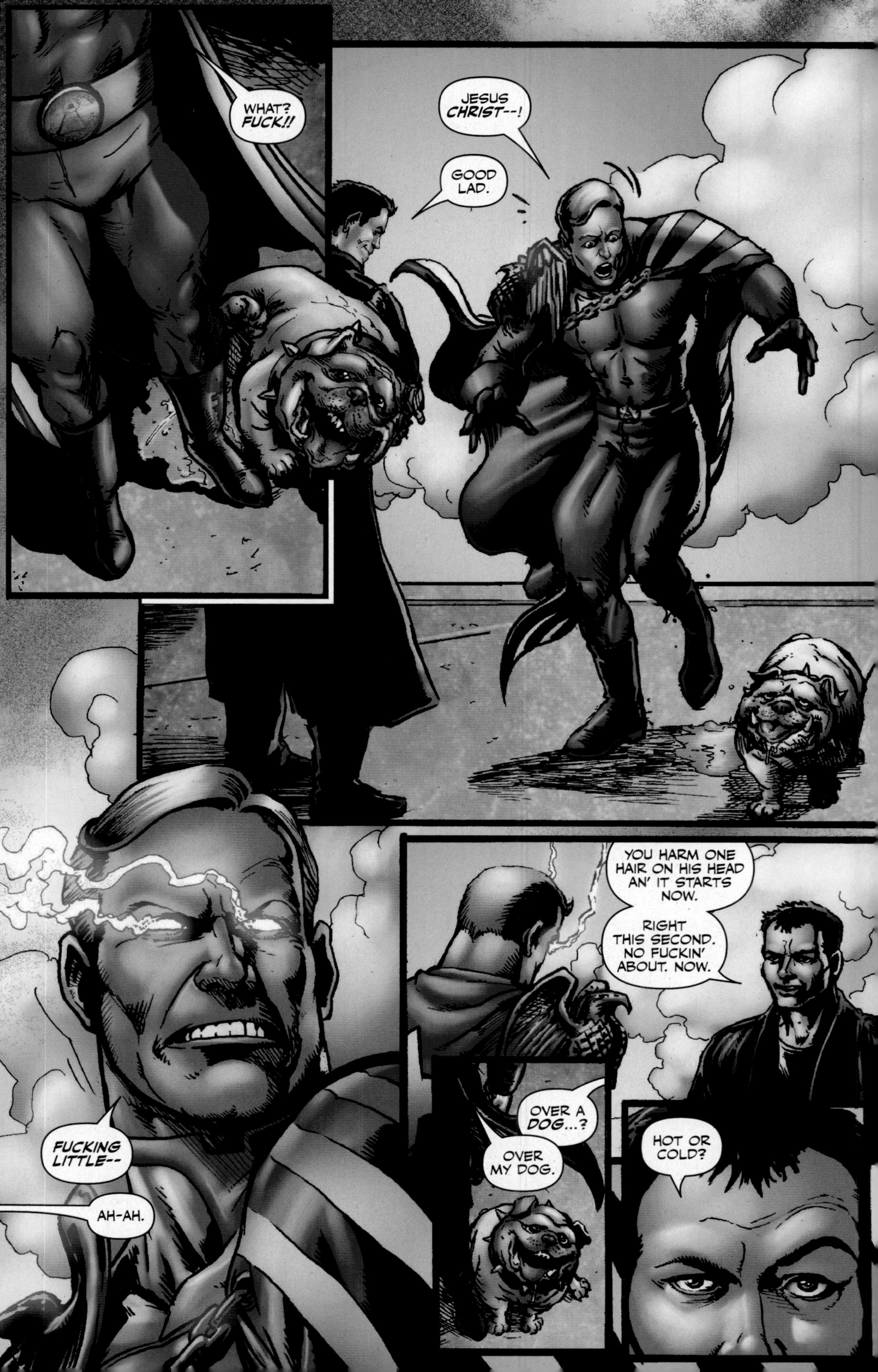
WHAT? FUCK!!
JESUS CHRIST--!
GOOD LAD.
YOU HARM ONE HAIR ON HIS HEAD AN' IT STARTS NOW.
RIGHT THIS SECOND. NO FUCKIN' ABOUT. NOW.
FUCKING LITTLE--
AH-AH.
OVER A DOG...?
OVER MY DOG.
HOT OR COLD?

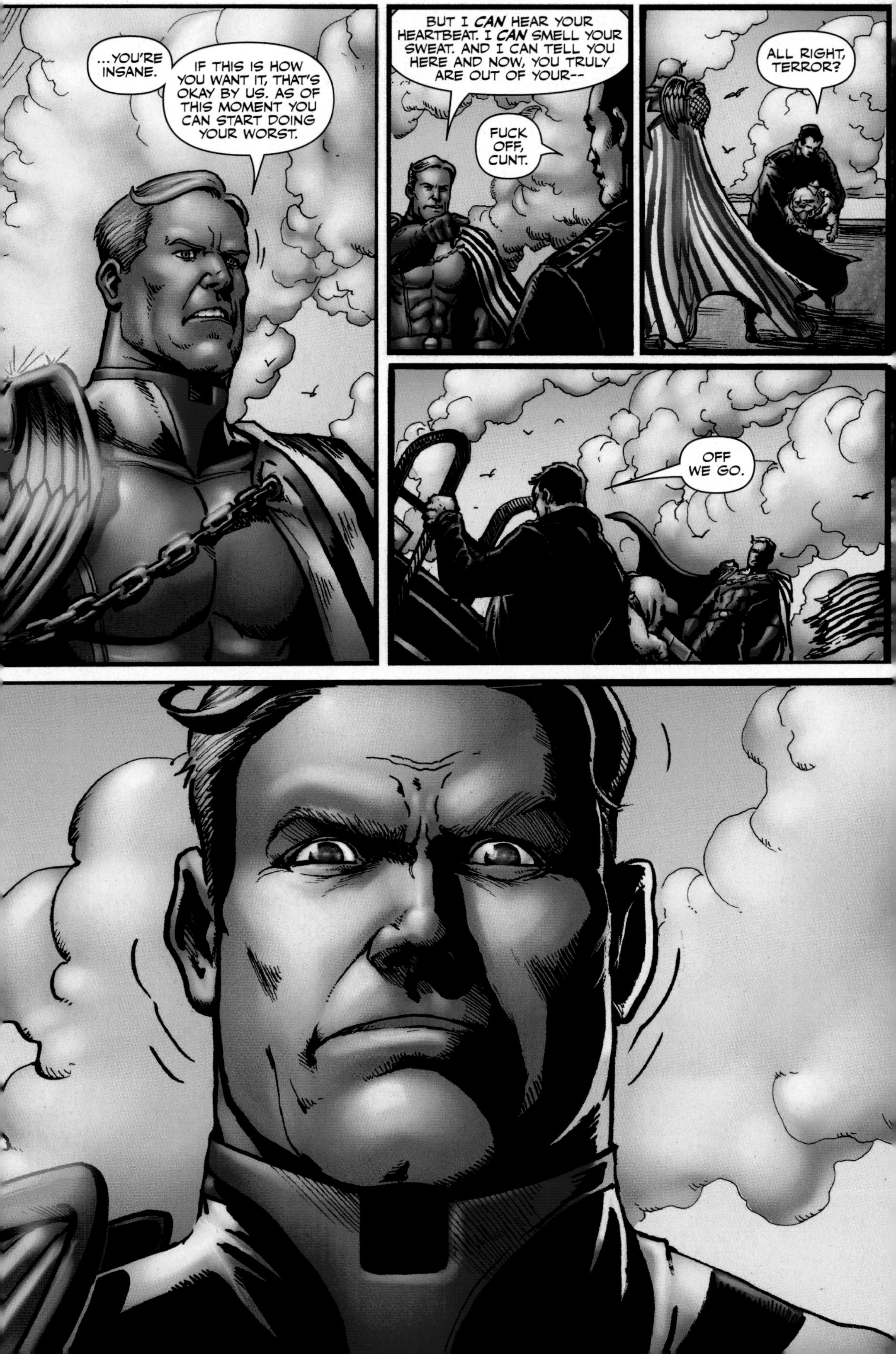
...YOU'RE INSANE.
IF THIS IS HOW YOU WANT IT, THAT'S OKAY BY US. AS OF THIS MOMENT YOU CAN START DOING YOUR WORST.
BUT I CAN HEAR YOUR HEARTBEAT. I CAN SMELL YOUR SWEAT. AND I CAN TELL YOU HERE AND NOW, YOU TRULY ARE OUT OF YOUR--
FUCK OFF, CUNT.
ALL RIGHT, TERROR?
OFF WE GO.

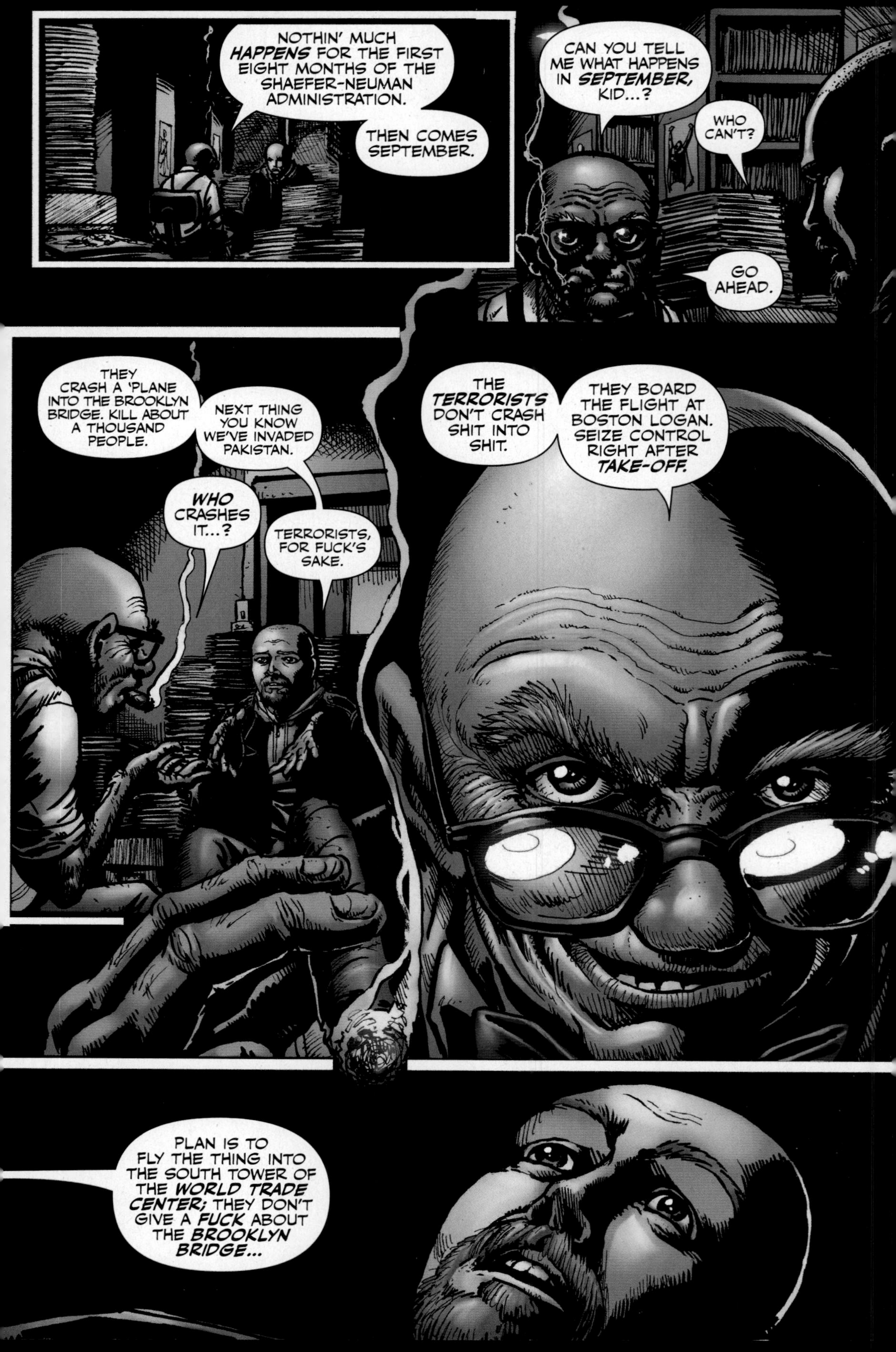
NOTHIN' MUCH HAPPENS FOR THE FIRST EIGHT MONTHS OF THE SHAEFER-NEUMAN ADMINISTRATION.
THEN COMES SEPTEMBER.
CAN YOU TELL ME WHAT HAPPENS IN SEPTEMBER, KID...?
WHO CAN'T?
GO AHEAD.
THEY CRASH A 'PLANE INTO THE BROOKLYN BRIDGE. KILL ABOUT A THOUSAND PEOPLE.
NEXT THING YOU KNOW WE'VE INVADED PAKISTAN.
WHO CRASHES IT...?
TERRORISTS, FOR FUCK'S SAKE.
THE TERRORISTS DON'T CRASH SHIT INTO SHIT.
THEY BOARD THE FLIGHT AT BOSTON LOGAN. SEIZE CONTROL RIGHT AFTER TAKE-OFF.
PLAN IS TO FLY THE THING INTO THE SOUTH TOWER OF THE WORLD TRADE CENTER; THEY DON'T GIVE A FUCK ABOUT THE BROOKLYN BRIDGE...

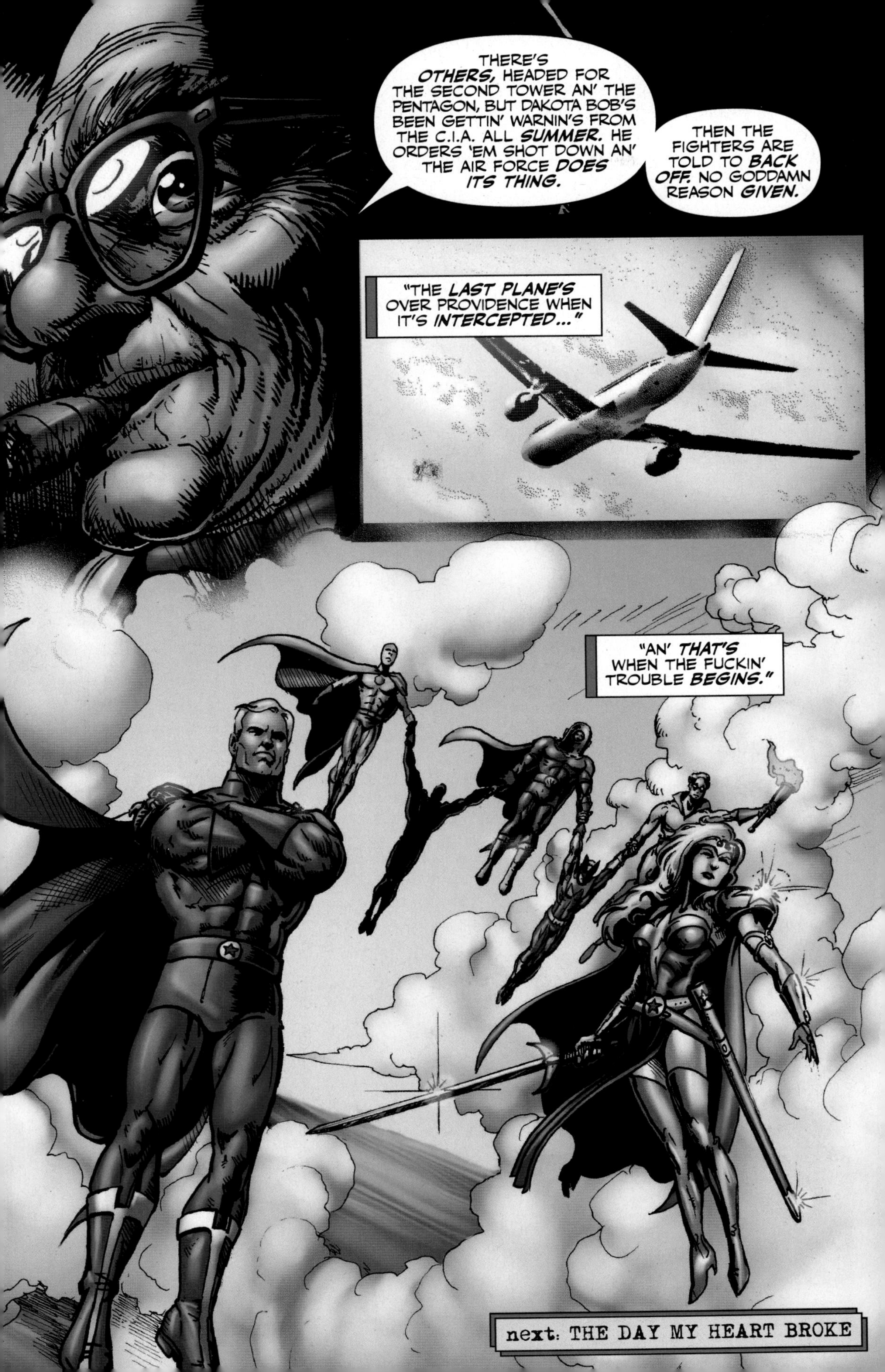
THERE'S OTHERS, HEADED FOR THE SECOND TOWER AN' THE PENTAGON, BUT DAKOTA BOB'S BEEN GETTIN' WARNIN'S FROM THE C.I.A. ALL SUMMER. HE ORDERS 'EM SHOT DOWN AN' THE AIR FORCE DOES ITS THING.
THEN THE FIGHTERS ARE TOLD TO BACK OFF. NO GODDAMN REASON GIVEN.
"THE LAST PLANE'S OVER PROVIDENCE WHEN IT'S INTERCEPTED..."
"AN' THAT'S WHEN THE FUCKIN' TROUBLE BEGINS."
next: THE DAY MY HEART BROKE

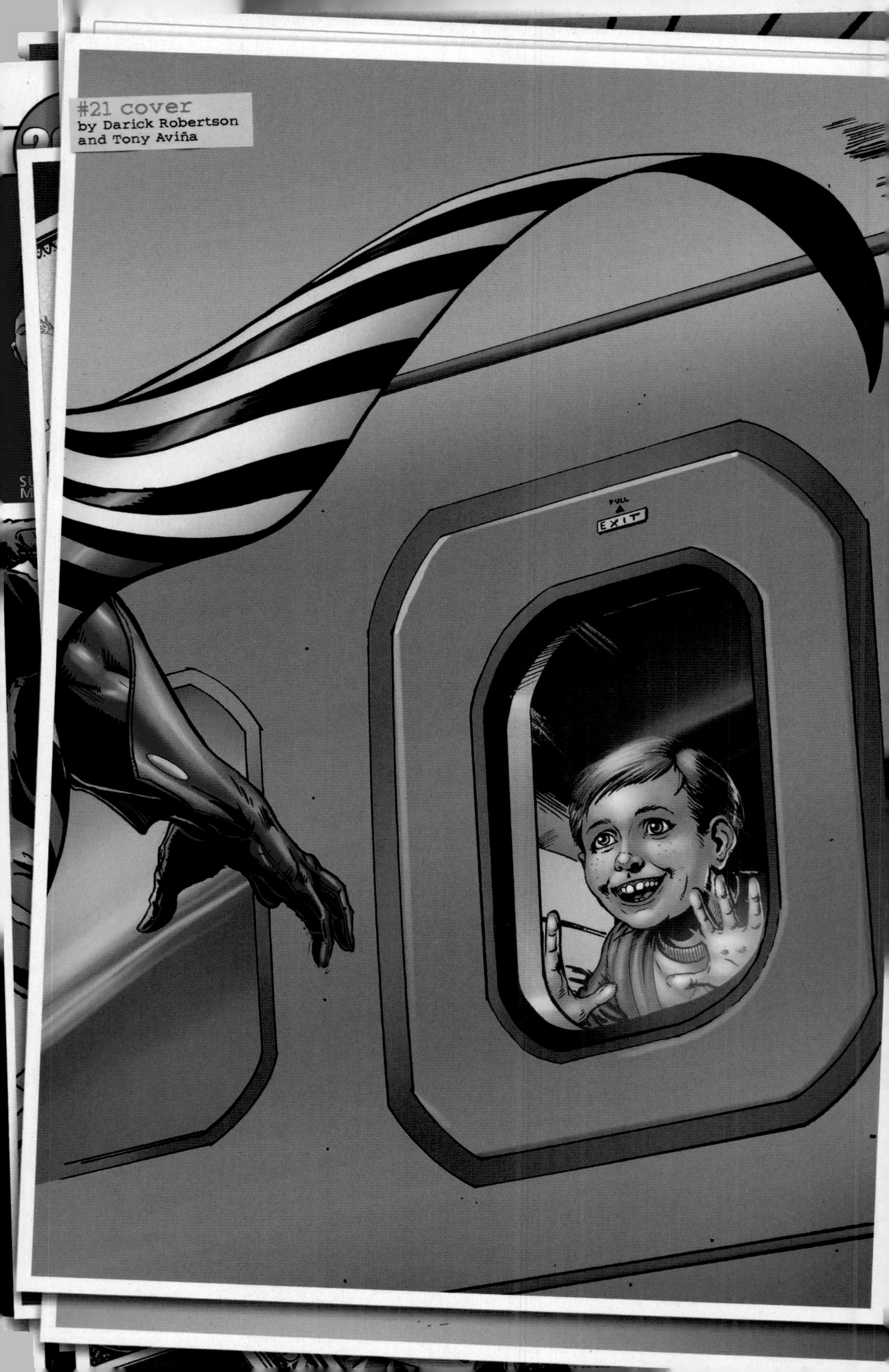
PULL
EXIT

#21 cover
by Darick Robertson
and Tony Aviña

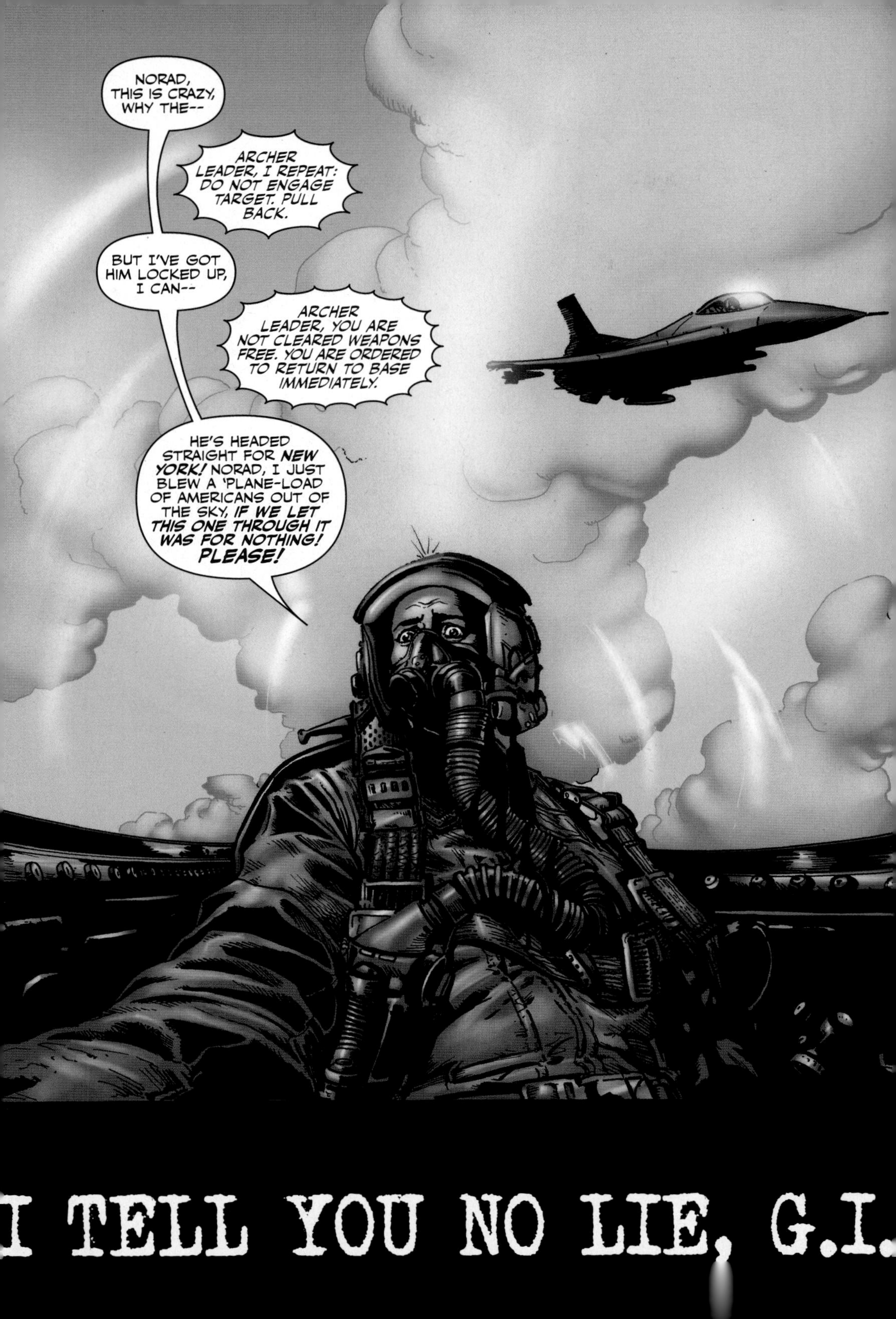
NORAD, THIS IS CRAZY, WHY THE--
ARCHER LEADER, I REPEAT: DO NOT ENGAGE TARGET. PULL BACK.
BUT I'VE GOT HIM LOCKED UP, I CAN--
ARCHER LEADER, YOU ARE NOT CLEARED WEAPONS FREE. YOU ARE ORDERED TO RETURN TO BASE IMMEDIATELY.
HE'S HEADED STRAIGHT FOR NEW YORK! NORAD, I JUST BLEW A 'PLANE-LOAD OF AMERICANS OUT OF THE SKY. IF WE LET THIS ONE THROUGH IT WAS FOR NOTHING! PLEASE!

I TELL YOU NO LIE, G.I.

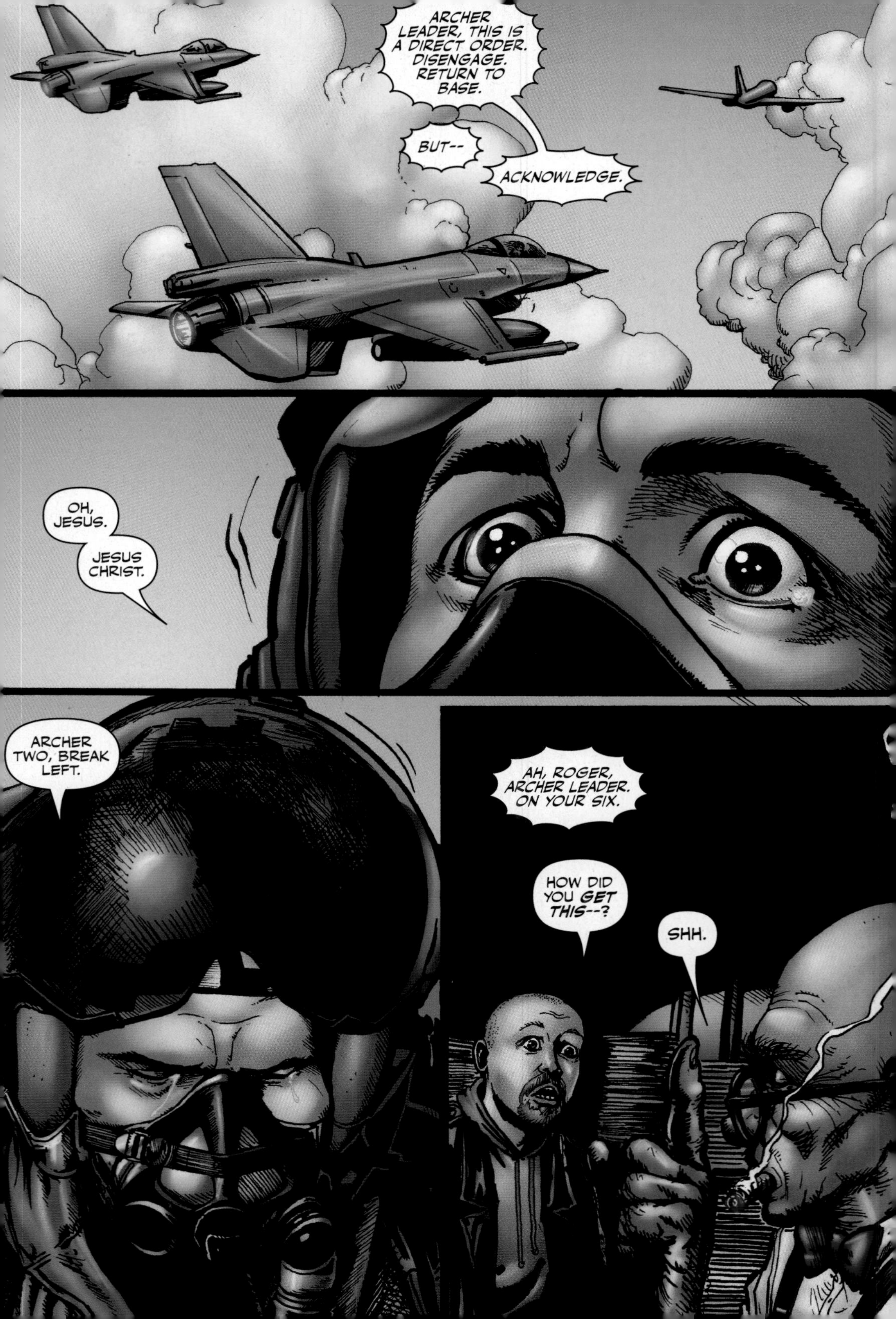
ARCHER LEADER, THIS IS A DIRECT ORDER. DISENGAGE. RETURN TO BASE.
BUT--
ACKNOWLEDGE.
OH, JESUS.
JESUS CHRIST.
ARCHER TWO, BREAK LEFT.
AH, ROGER, ARCHER LEADER. ON YOUR SIX.
HOW DID YOU GET THIS--?
SHH.

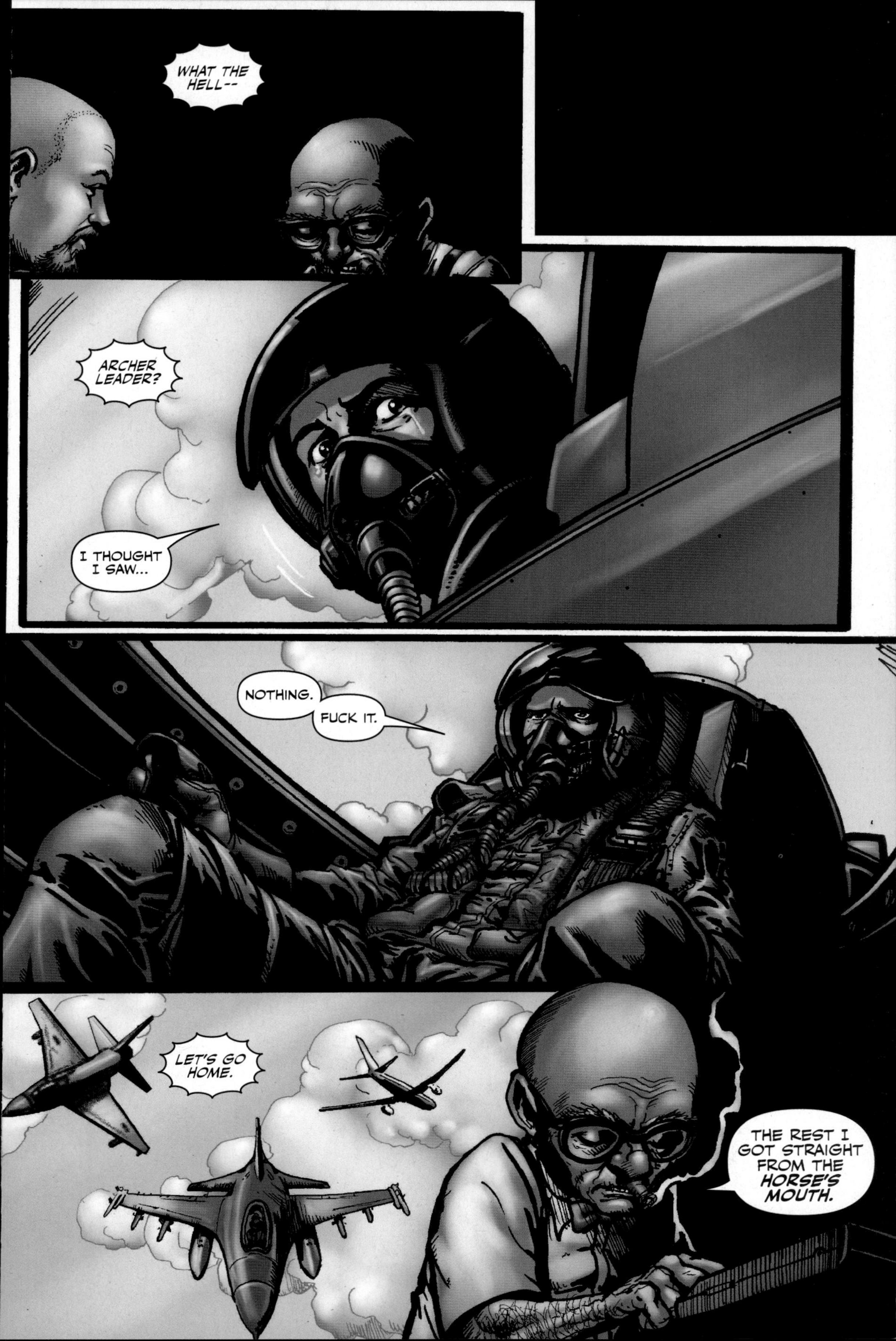
WHAT THE HELL--
ARCHER LEADER?
I THOUGHT I SAW...
NOTHING.
FUCK IT.
LET'S GO HOME.
THE REST I GOT STRAIGHT FROM THE HORSE'S MOUTH.

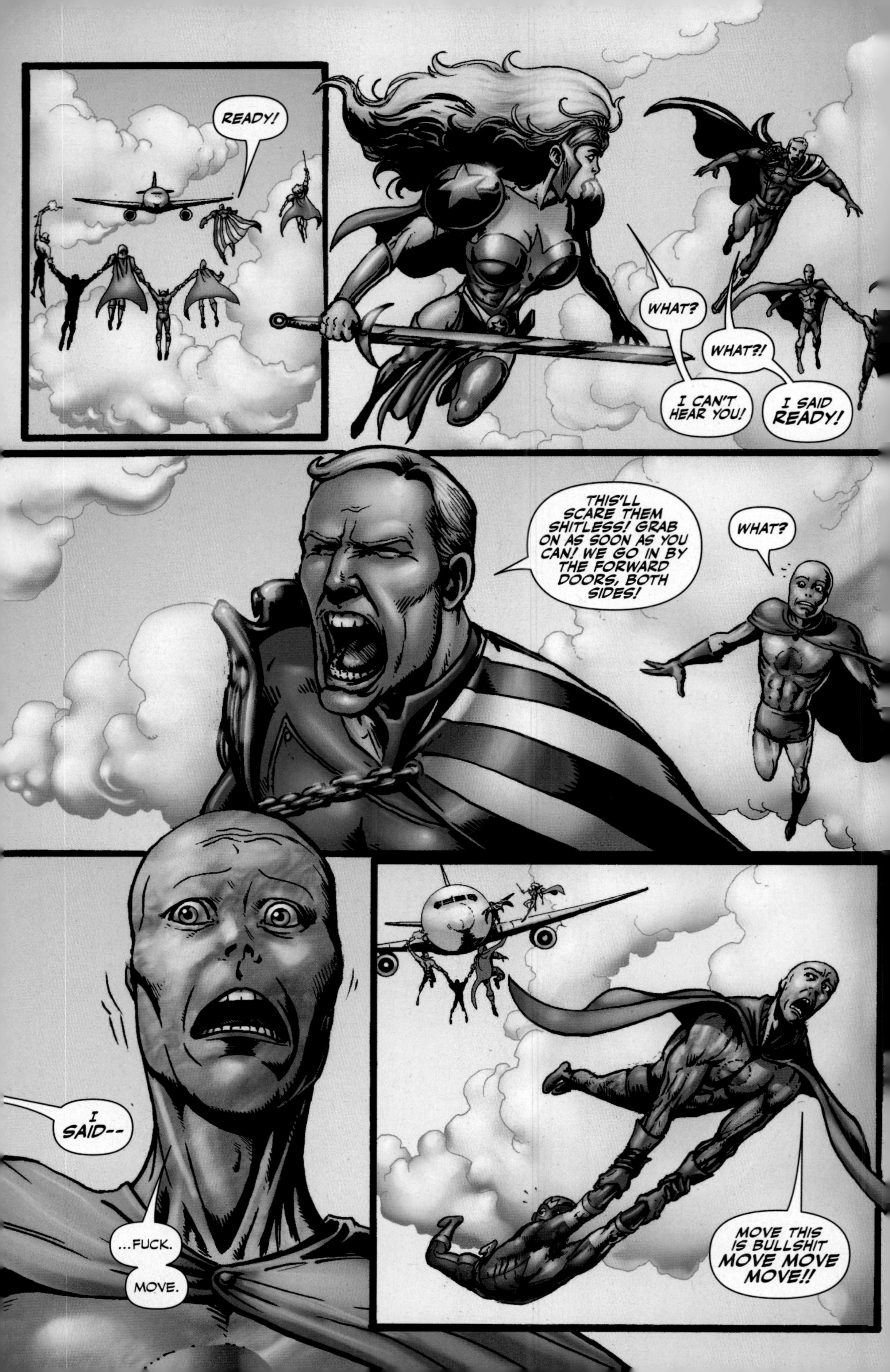
READY!
WHAT?
I CAN'T HEAR YOU!
WHAT?!
I SAID READY!
THIS'LL SCARE THEM SHITLESS! GRAB ON AS SOON AS YOU CAN! WE GO IN BY THE FORWARD DOORS, BOTH SIDES!
WHAT?
I SAID--
...FUCK.
MOVE.
MOVE THIS IS BULLSHIT MOVE MOVE MOVE!!

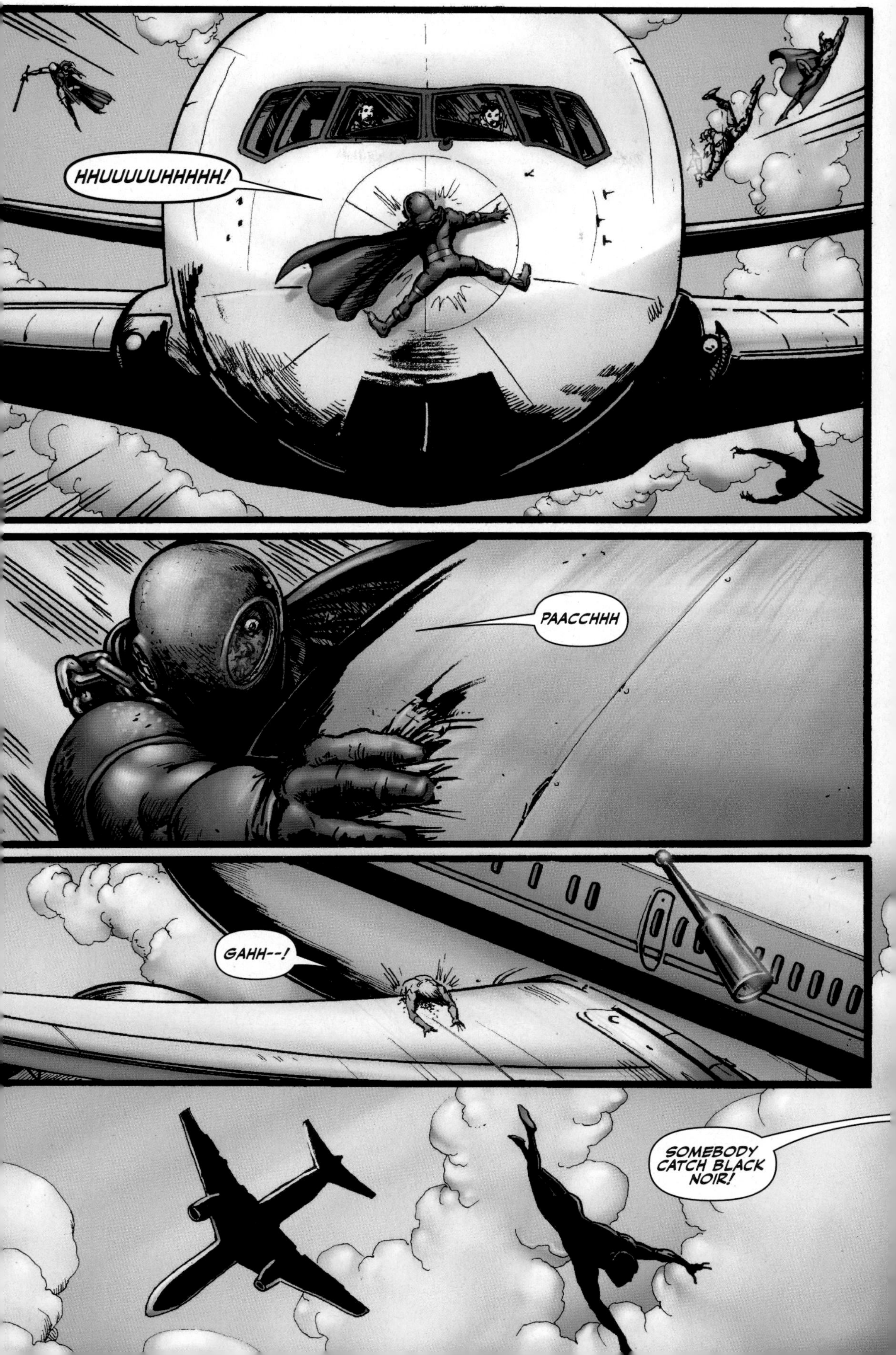
HHUUUUUUHHHHH!
PAACCHHH
GAHH--!
SOMEBODY CATCH BLACK NOIR!

NO ONE KNOWS HOW BLACK NOIR LIVED THROUGH THAT ONE. THEY'RE BRED TOUGH--BUT NOT *THAT* TOUGH.

TRUTH TO TELL, *HOMELANDER AN' MAEVE* ARE THE *REAL* HEAVYWEIGHTS. LAMPLIGHTER JUST ABOUT GOT HOME BEFORE HIS FUCKIN' *LUNGS* COLLAPSED...

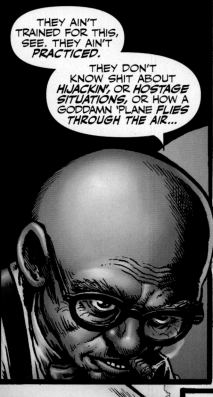

THEY AIN'T TRAINED FOR THIS, SEE. THEY AIN'T *PRACTICED.*

THEY DON'T KNOW SHIT ABOUT *HIJACKIN',* OR *HOSTAGE SITUATIONS,* OR HOW A GODDAMN 'PLANE *FLIES THROUGH THE AIR...*

THEY AIN'T EVEN GOT A *PLAN.* THEY JUST THINK--*WE'RE THE SEVEN. WE'RE SUPER.*

WE CAN *DO THIS.*

OKAY! STRAIGHT IN!

WHAT?!

MOM, LOOK WHO IT IS!

MICHAEL, SIT DOWN! THOSE MEN HAVE KNIVES, IF THEY HEAR YOU THEY'LL--

MOM, IT'S OKAY! WE'RE GONNA BE OKAY! *MOM!*

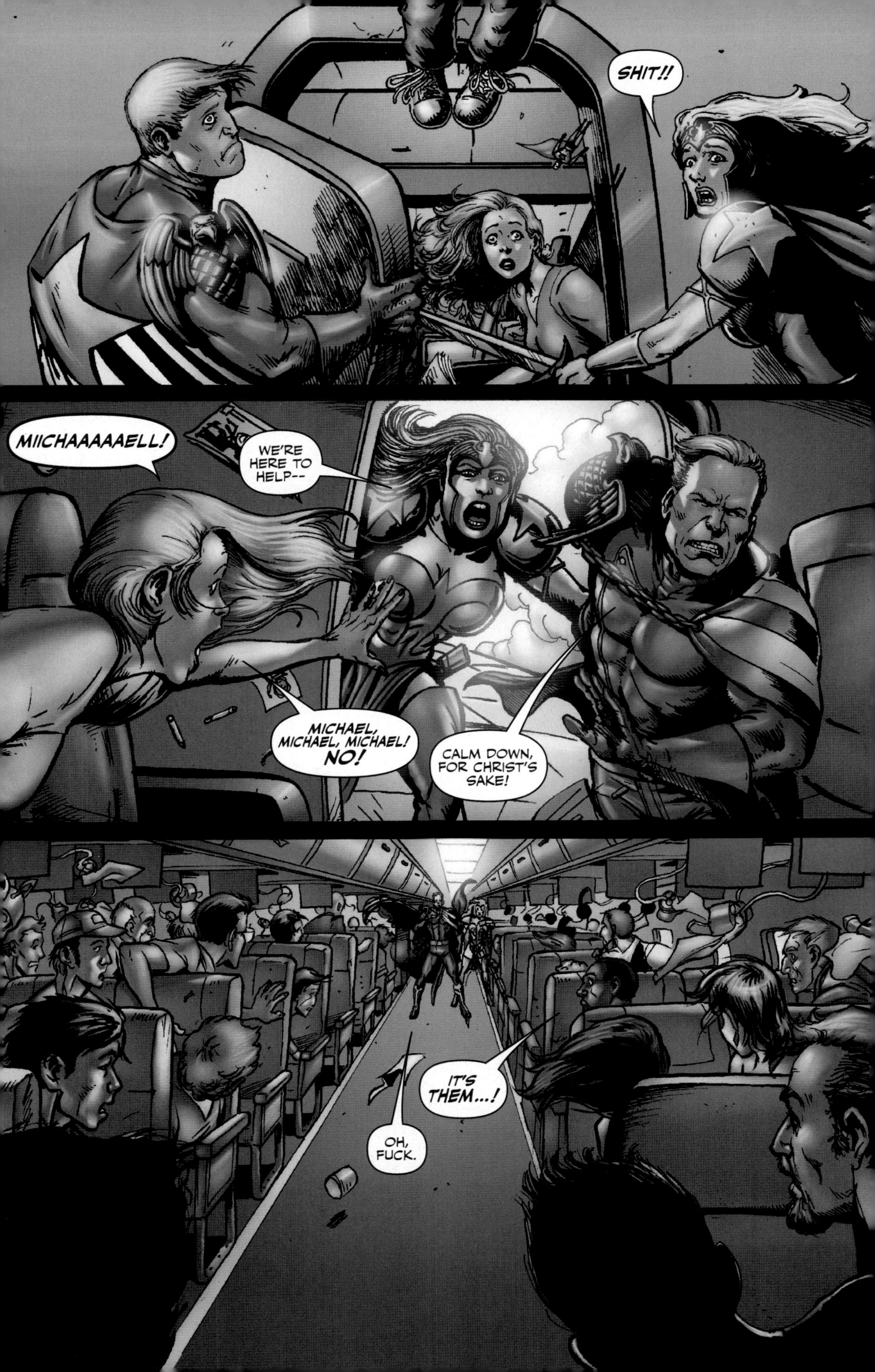
SHIT!!
MIICHAAAAAELL!
WE'RE HERE TO HELP--
MICHAEL, MICHAEL, MICHAEL! NO!
CALM DOWN, FOR CHRIST'S SAKE!
IT'S THEM...!
OH, FUCK.

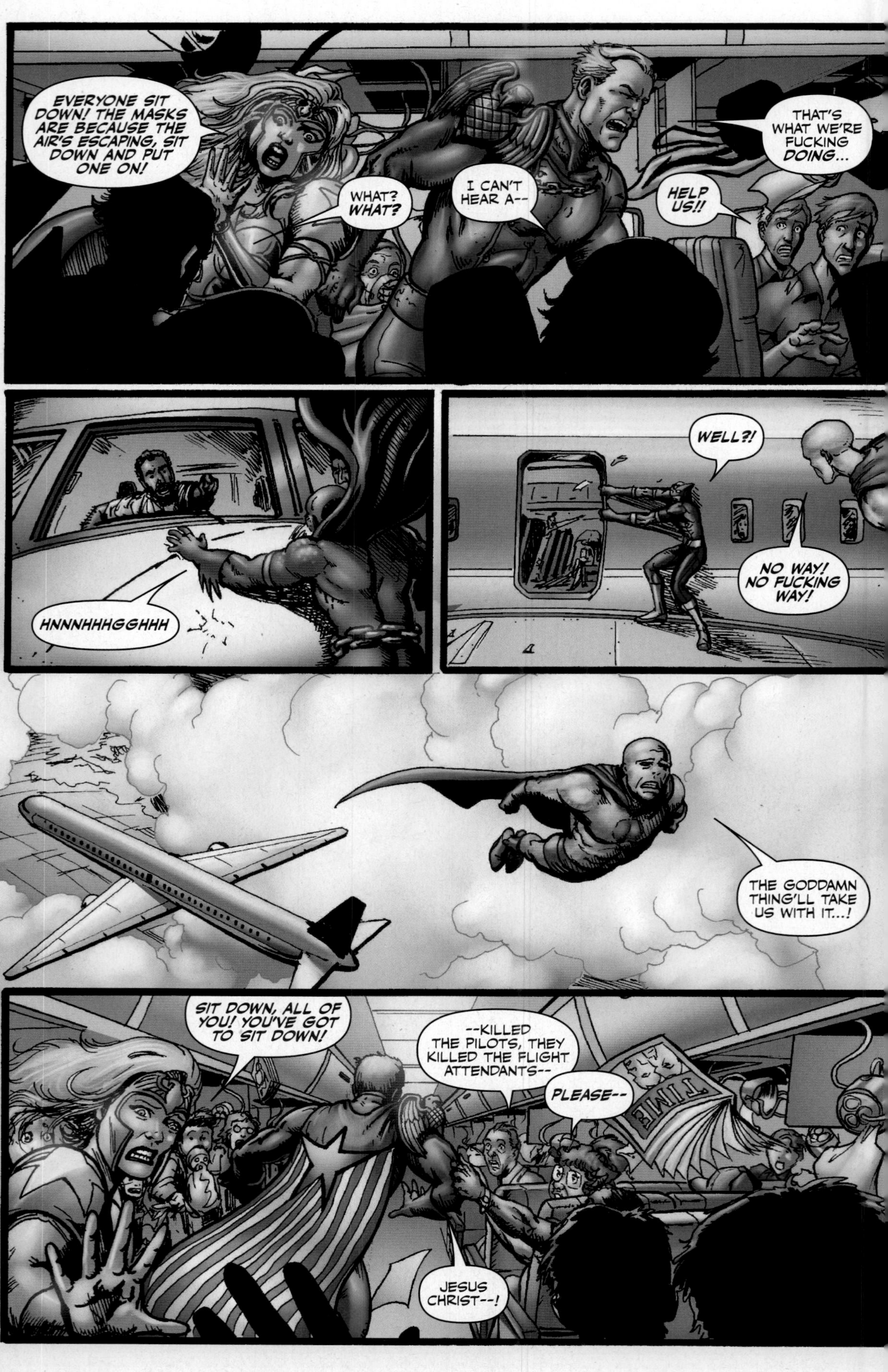
EVERYONE SIT DOWN! THE MASKS ARE BECAUSE THE AIR'S ESCAPING, SIT DOWN AND PUT ONE ON!
WHAT? WHAT?
I CAN'T HEAR A--
HELP US!!
THAT'S WHAT WE'RE FUCKING DOING...
HNNNHHHGGHHH
WELL?!
NO WAY! NO FUCKING WAY!
THE GODDAMN THING'LL TAKE US WITH IT...!
SIT DOWN, ALL OF YOU! YOU'VE GOT TO SIT DOWN!
--KILLED THE PILOTS, THEY KILLED THE FLIGHT ATTENDANTS--
PLEASE--
JESUS CHRIST--!
TIME

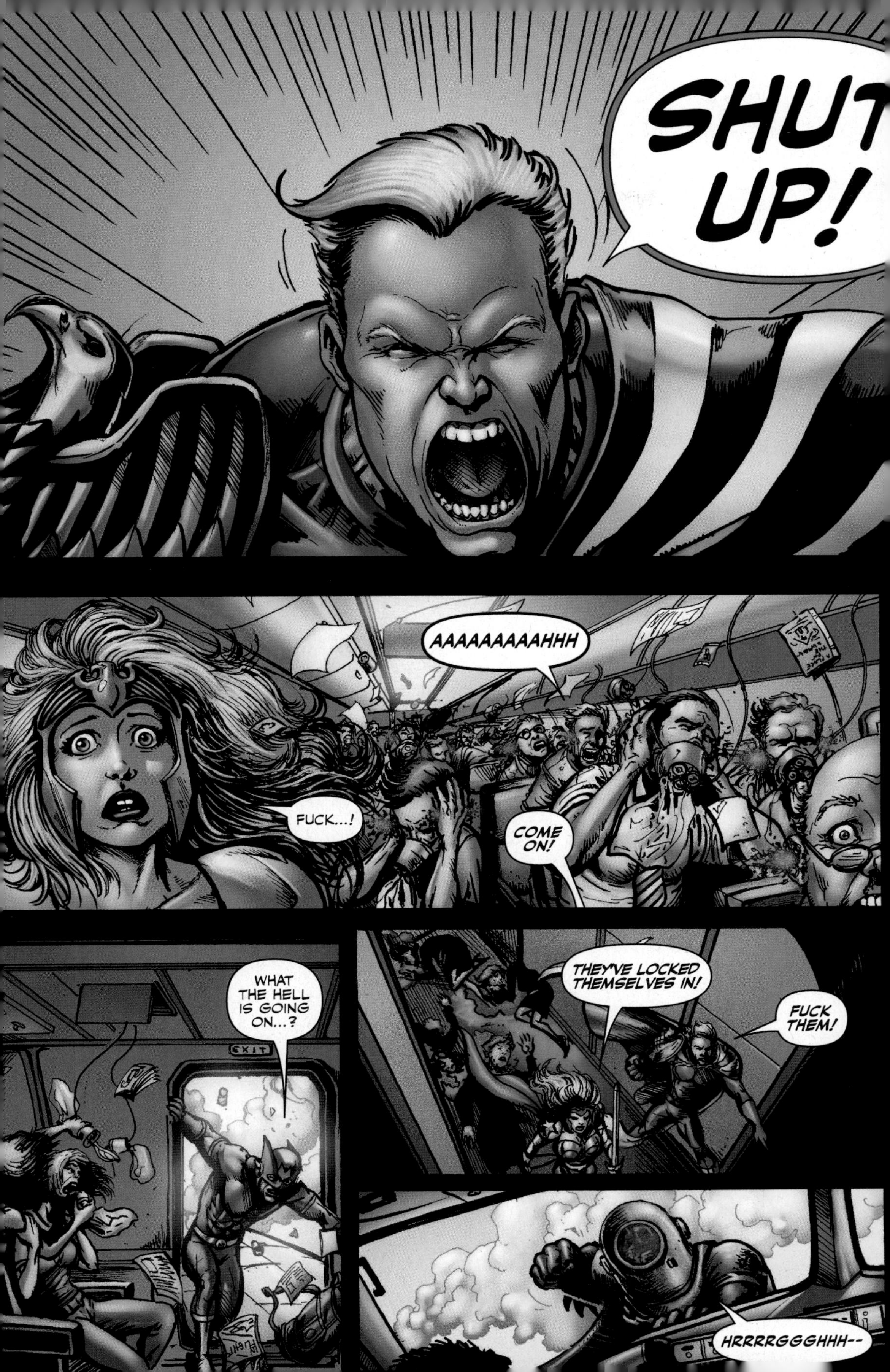
SHUT UP!
AAAAAAAAAHHH
FUCK...!
COME ON!
WHAT THE HELL IS GOING ON...?
THEY'VE LOCKED THEMSELVES IN!
FUCK THEM!
HRRRRGGGHHH--

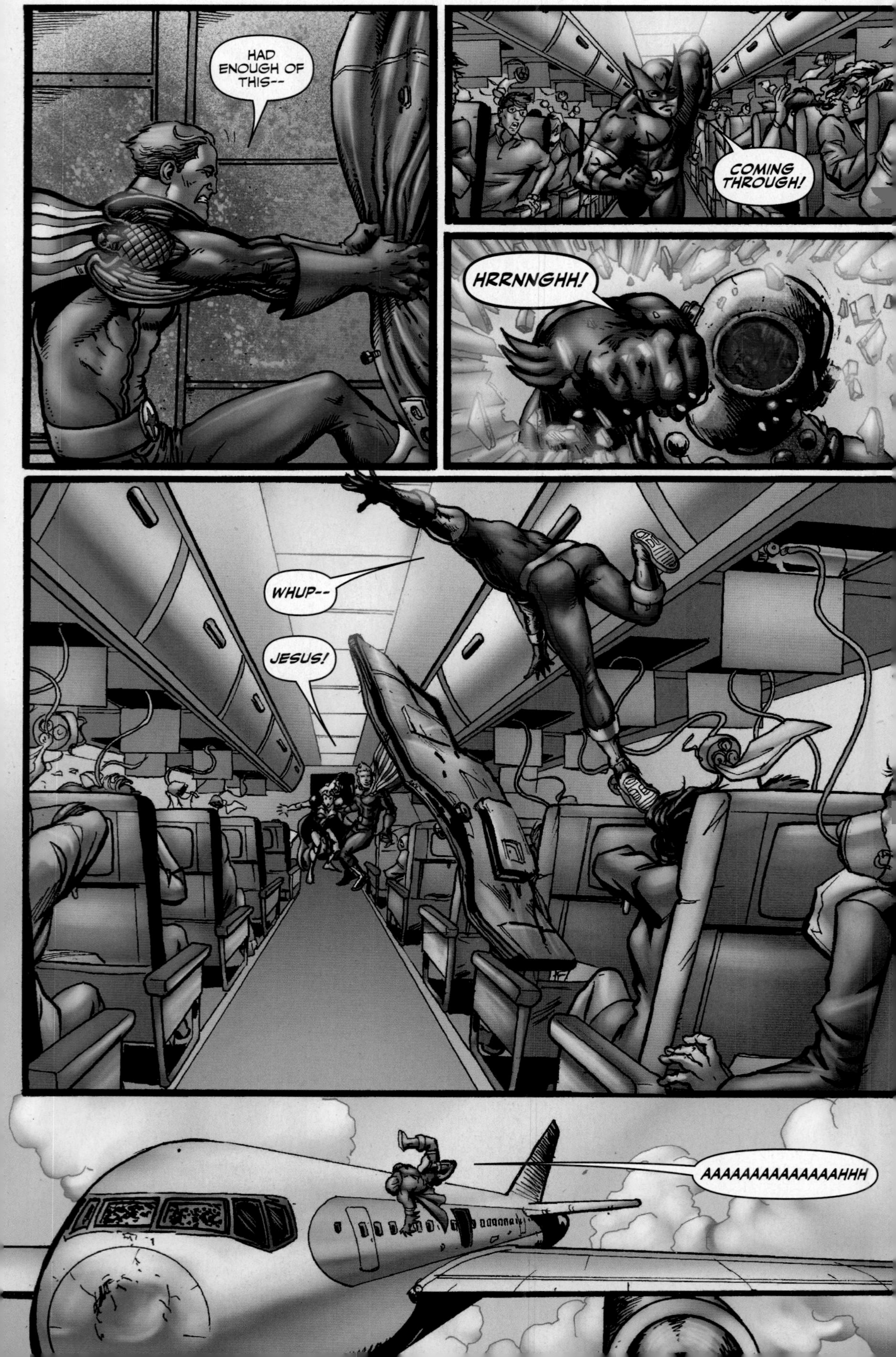
HAD ENOUGH OF THIS--
COMING THROUGH!
HRRNNGHH!
WHUP--
JESUS!
AAAAAAAAAAAAAAAHHH

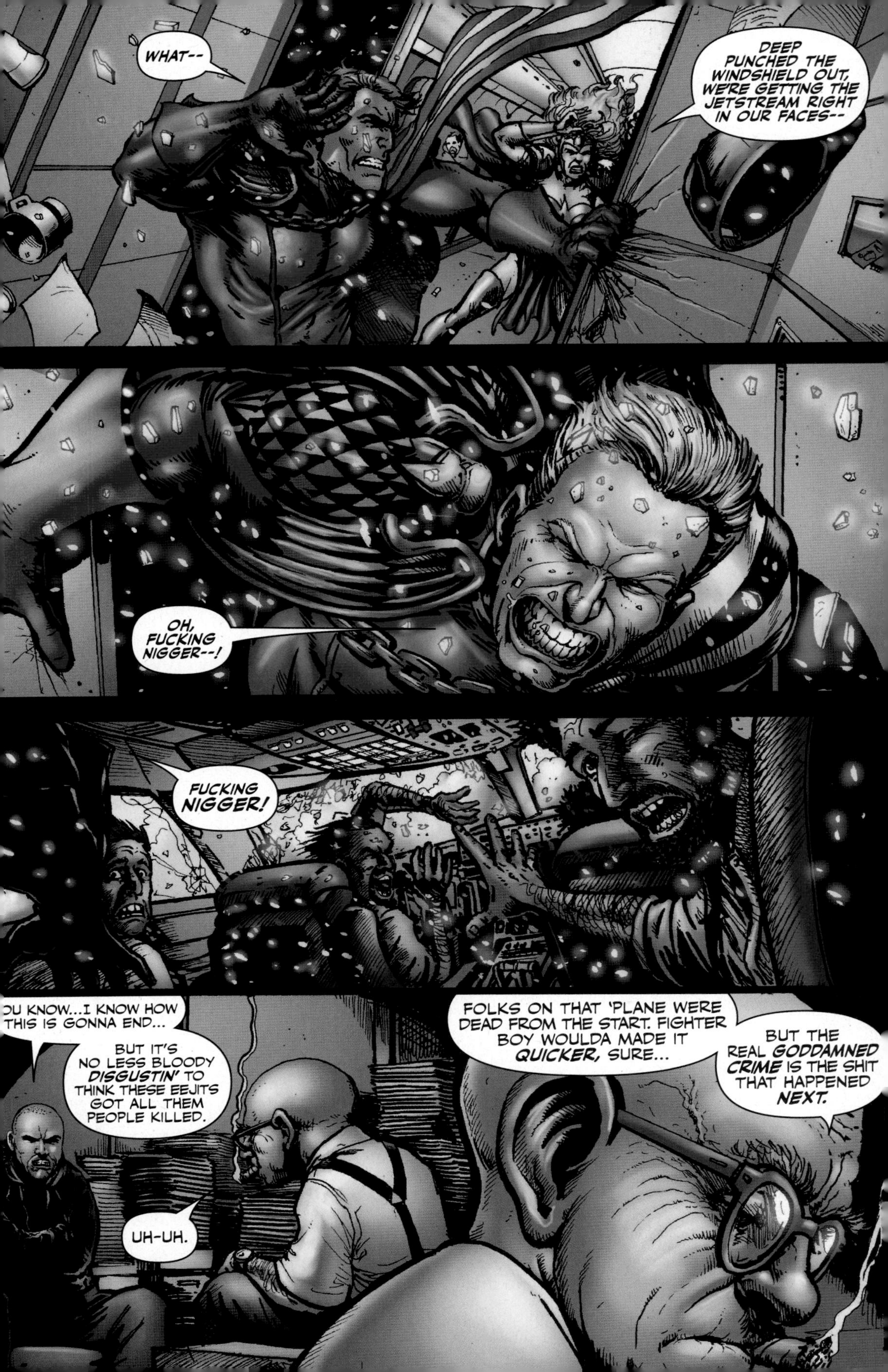
WHAT--
DEEP PUNCHED THE WINDSHIELD OUT, WE'RE GETTING THE JETSTREAM RIGHT IN OUR FACES--
OH, FUCKING NIGGER--!
FUCKING NIGGER!
OU KNOW...I KNOW HOW THIS IS GONNA END...
BUT IT'S NO LESS BLOODY DISGUSTIN' TO THINK THESE EEJITS GOT ALL THEM PEOPLE KILLED.
UH-UH.
FOLKS ON THAT 'PLANE WERE DEAD FROM THE START. FIGHTER BOY WOULDA MADE IT QUICKER, SURE...
BUT THE REAL GODDAMNED CRIME IS THE SHIT THAT HAPPENED NEXT.

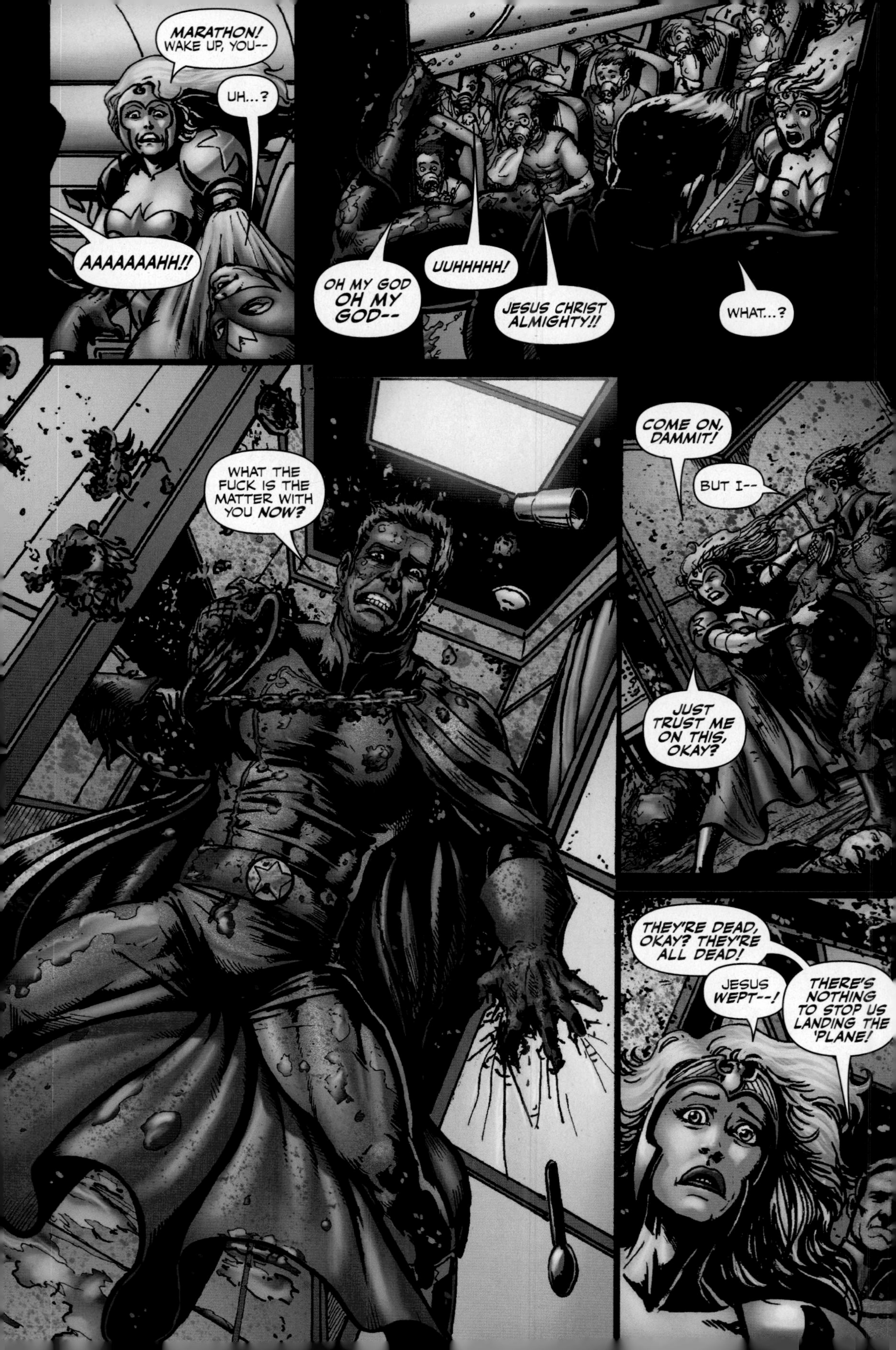
MARATHON! WAKE UP, YOU--
UH...?
AAAAAAAHH!!
OH MY GOD OH MY GOD--
UUHHHHH!
JESUS CHRIST ALMIGHTY!!
WHAT...?
WHAT THE FUCK IS THE MATTER WITH YOU NOW?
COME ON, DAMMIT!
BUT I--
JUST TRUST ME ON THIS, OKAY?
THEY'RE DEAD, OKAY? THEY'RE ALL DEAD!
JESUS WEPT--!
THERE'S NOTHING TO STOP US LANDING THE 'PLANE!

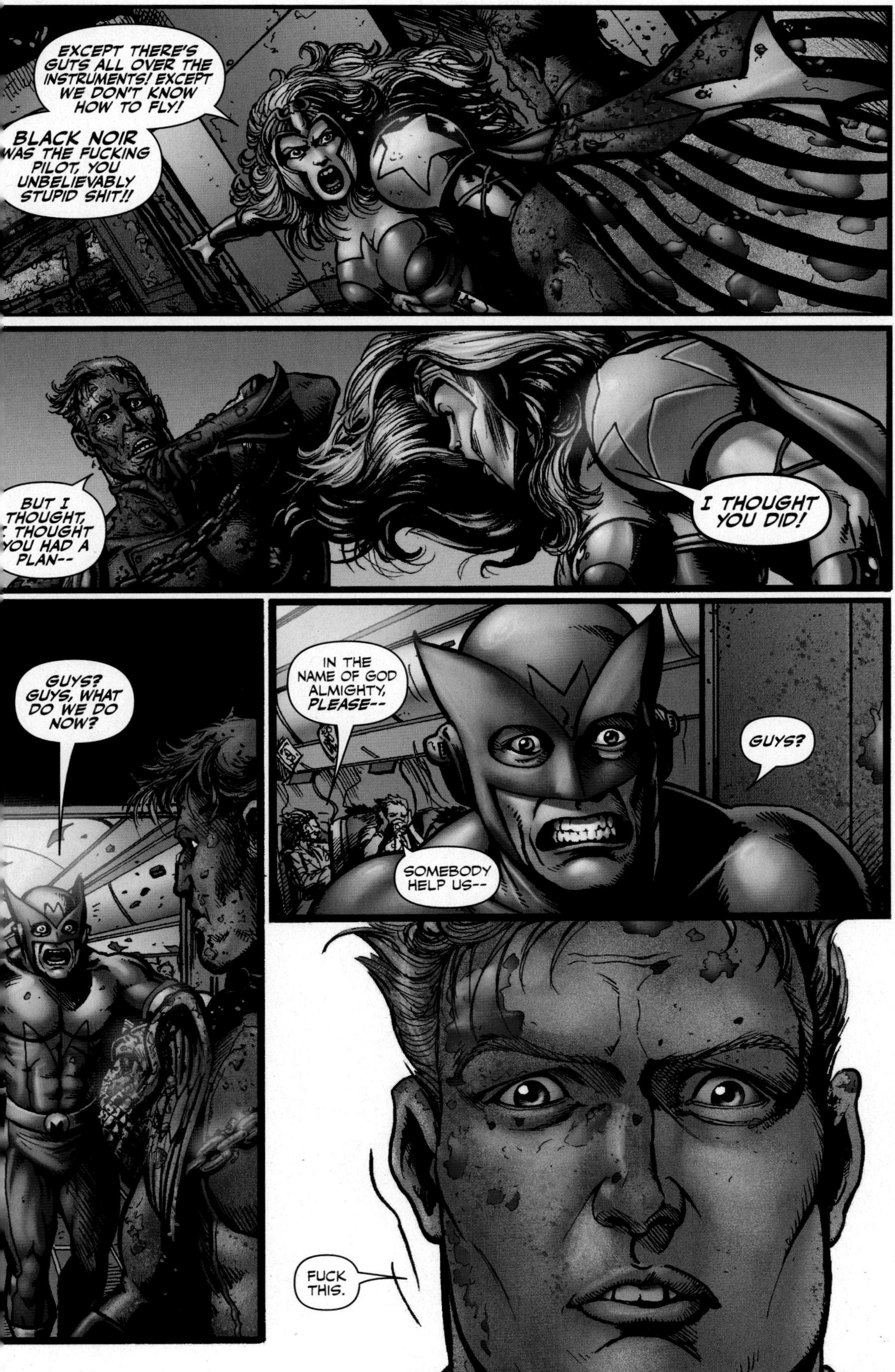
EXCEPT THERE'S GUTS ALL OVER THE INSTRUMENTS! EXCEPT WE DON'T KNOW HOW TO FLY!
BLACK NOIR WAS THE FUCKING PILOT, YOU UNBELIEVABLY STUPID SHIT!!
BUT I THOUGHT, I THOUGHT YOU HAD A PLAN--
I THOUGHT YOU DID!
GUYS? GUYS, WHAT DO WE DO NOW?
IN THE NAME OF GOD ALMIGHTY, PLEASE--
GUYS?
SOMEBODY HELP US--
FUCK THIS.

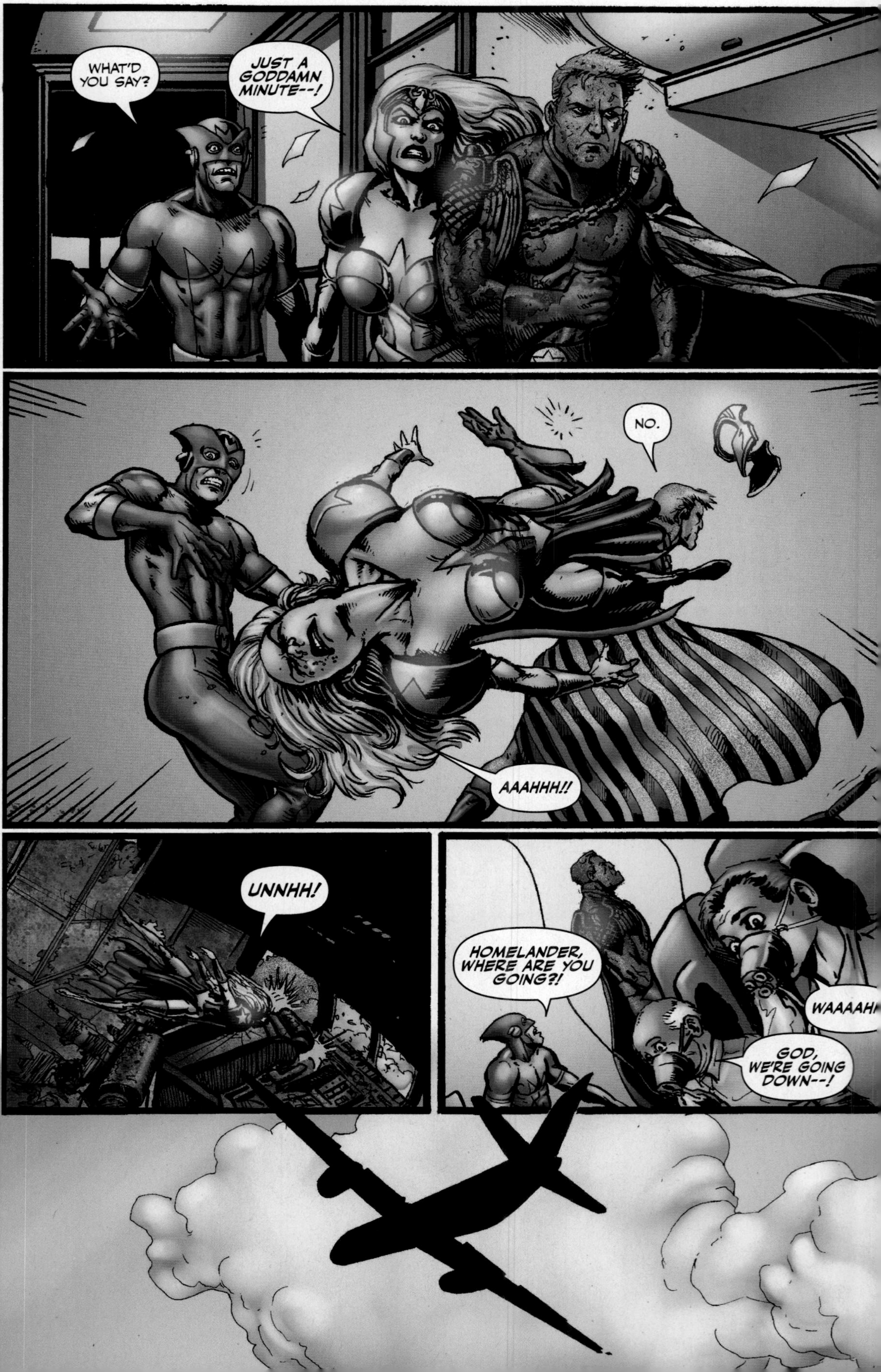
WHAT'D YOU SAY?
JUST A GODDAMN MINUTE--!
NO.
AAAHHH!!
UNNHH!
HOMELANDER, WHERE ARE YOU GOING?!
WAAAAH
GOD, WE'RE GOING DOWN--!

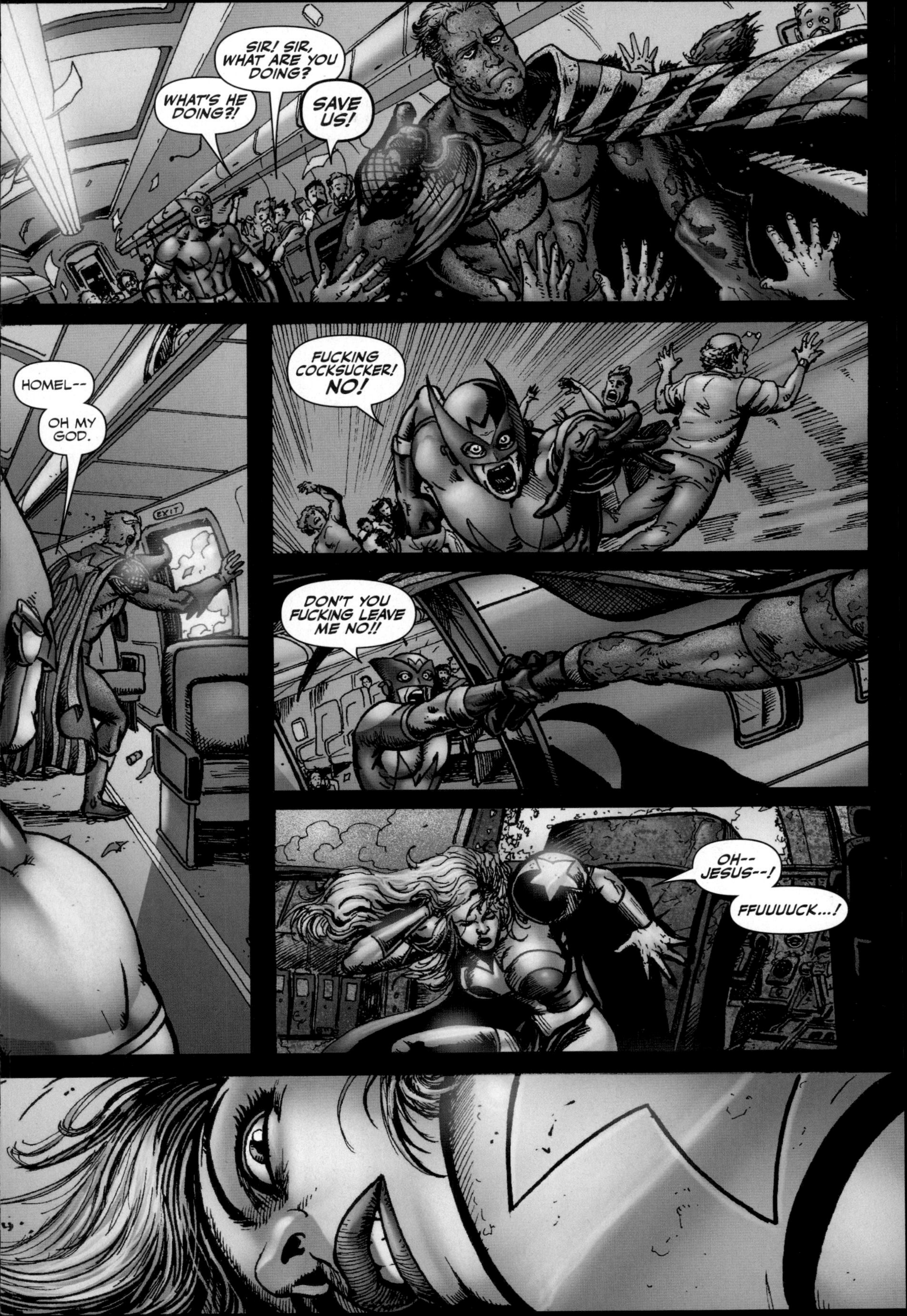
SIR! SIR, WHAT ARE YOU DOING?
WHAT'S HE DOING?!
SAVE US!
HOMEL--
OH MY GOD.
FUCKING COCKSUCKER! NO!
EXIT
DON'T YOU FUCKING LEAVE ME NO!!
OH-- JESUS--!
FFUUUUCK...!

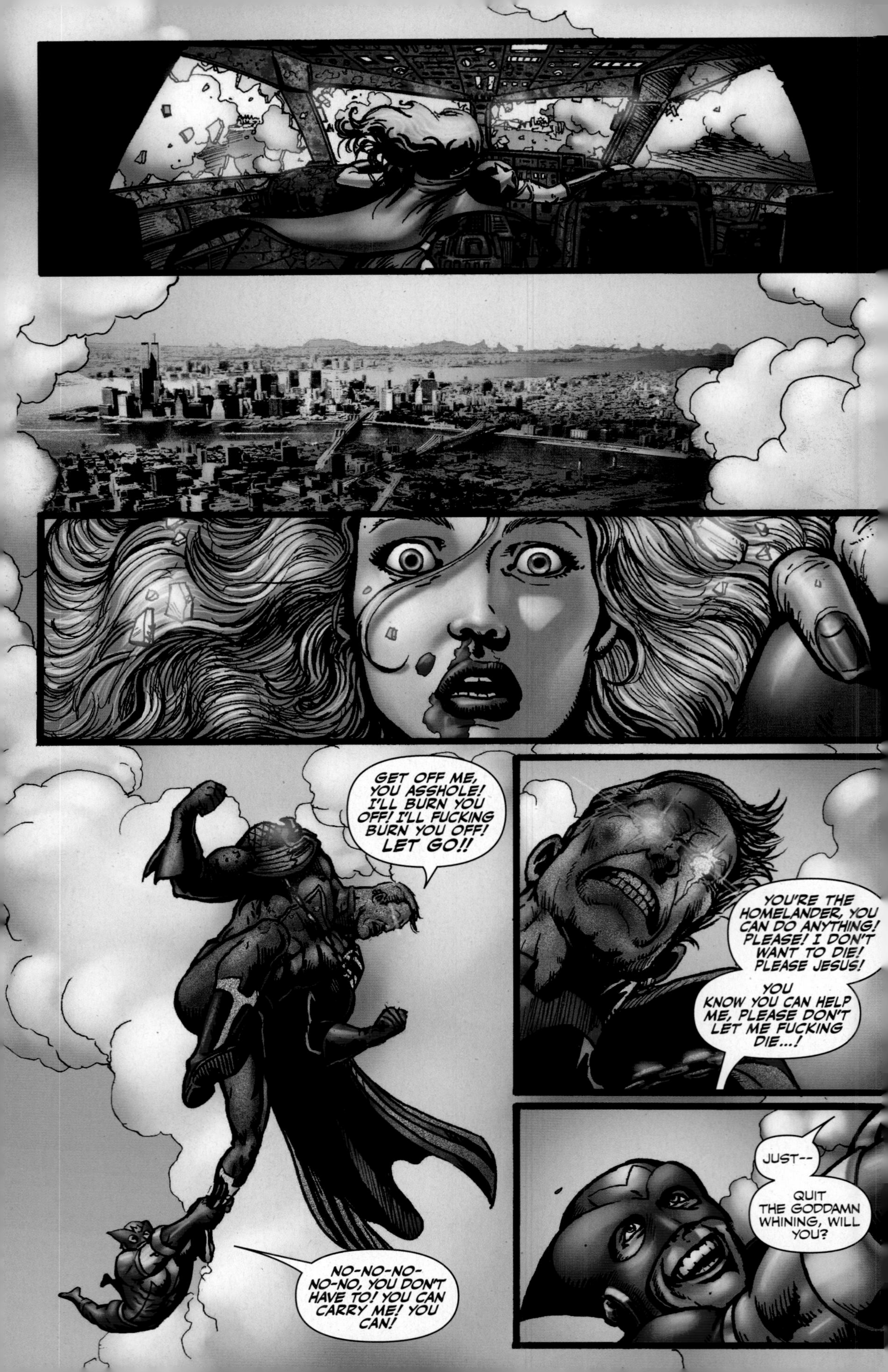
GET OFF ME, YOU ASSHOLE! I'LL BURN YOU OFF! I'LL FUCKING BURN YOU OFF! LET GO!!
NO-NO-NO-NO-NO, YOU DON'T HAVE TO! YOU CAN CARRY ME! YOU CAN!
YOU'RE THE HOMELANDER, YOU CAN DO ANYTHING! PLEASE! I DON'T WANT TO DIE! PLEASE JESUS!
YOU KNOW YOU CAN HELP ME, PLEASE DON'T LET ME FUCKING DIE...!
JUST--
QUIT THE GODDAMN WHINING, WILL YOU?

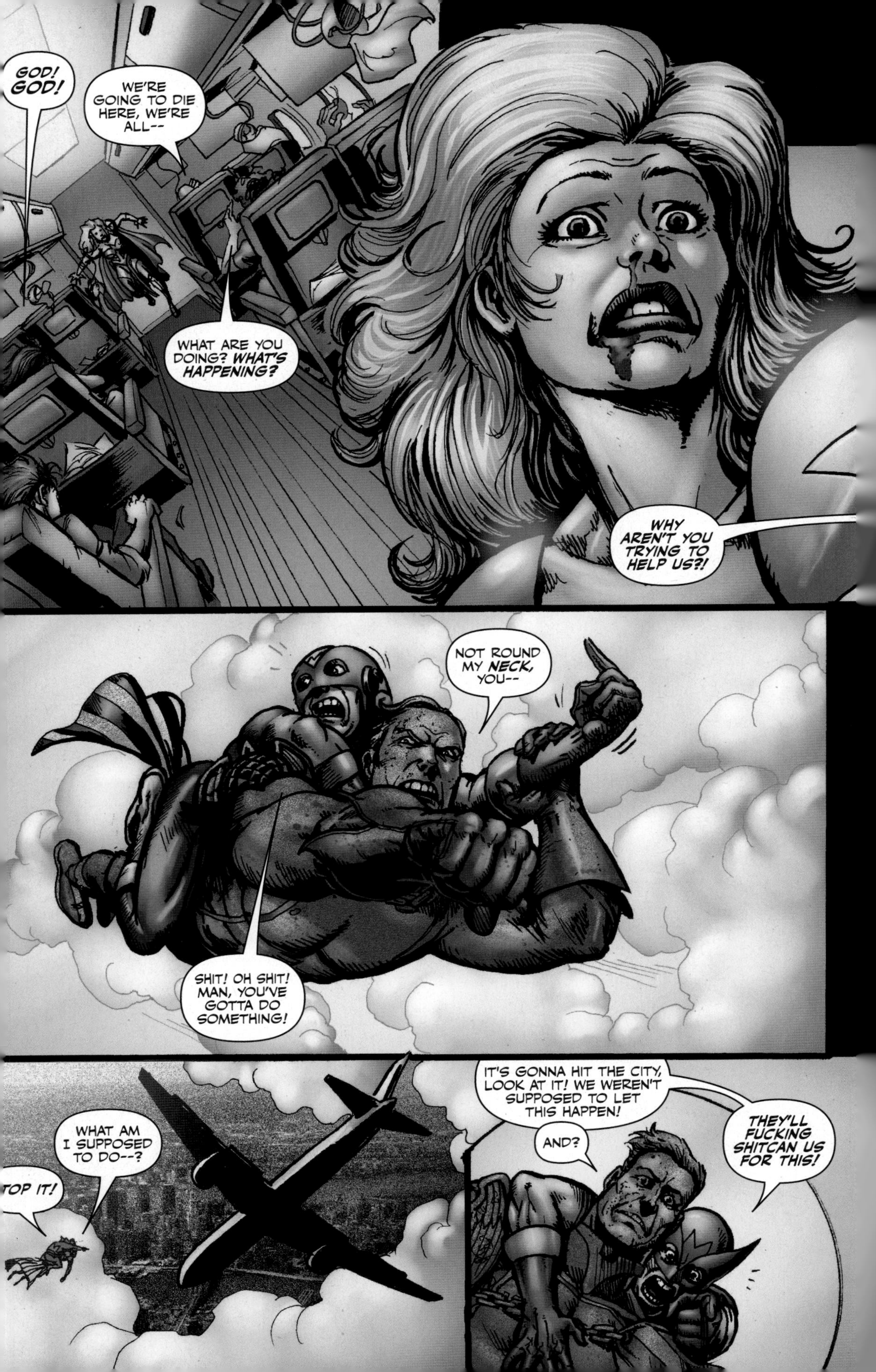
GOD! GOD!
WE'RE GOING TO DIE HERE, WE'RE ALL--
WHAT ARE YOU DOING? WHAT'S HAPPENING?
WHY AREN'T YOU TRYING TO HELP US?!
NOT ROUND MY NECK, YOU--
SHIT! OH SHIT! MAN, YOU'VE GOTTA DO SOMETHING!
WHAT AM I SUPPOSED TO DO--?
TOP IT!
IT'S GONNA HIT THE CITY, LOOK AT IT! WE WEREN'T SUPPOSED TO LET THIS HAPPEN!
AND?
THEY'LL FUCKING SHITCAN US FOR THIS!

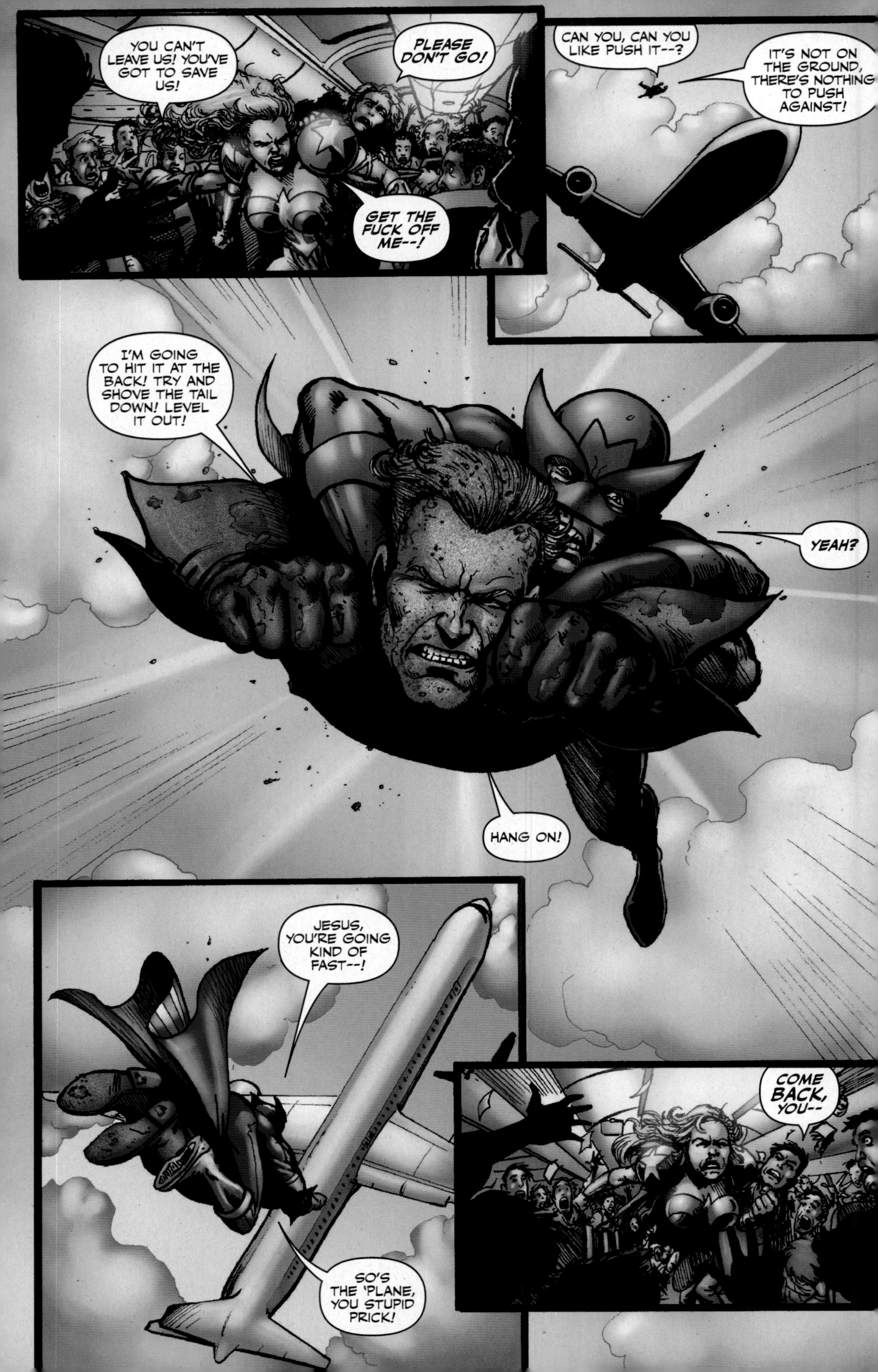
YOU CAN'T LEAVE US! YOU'VE GOT TO SAVE US!
PLEASE DON'T GO!
GET THE FUCK OFF ME--!
CAN YOU, CAN YOU LIKE PUSH IT--?
IT'S NOT ON THE GROUND, THERE'S NOTHING TO PUSH AGAINST!
I'M GOING TO HIT IT AT THE BACK! TRY AND SHOVE THE TAIL DOWN! LEVEL IT OUT!
YEAH?
HANG ON!
JESUS, YOU'RE GOING KIND OF FAST--!
SO'S THE 'PLANE, YOU STUPID PRICK!
COME BACK, YOU--

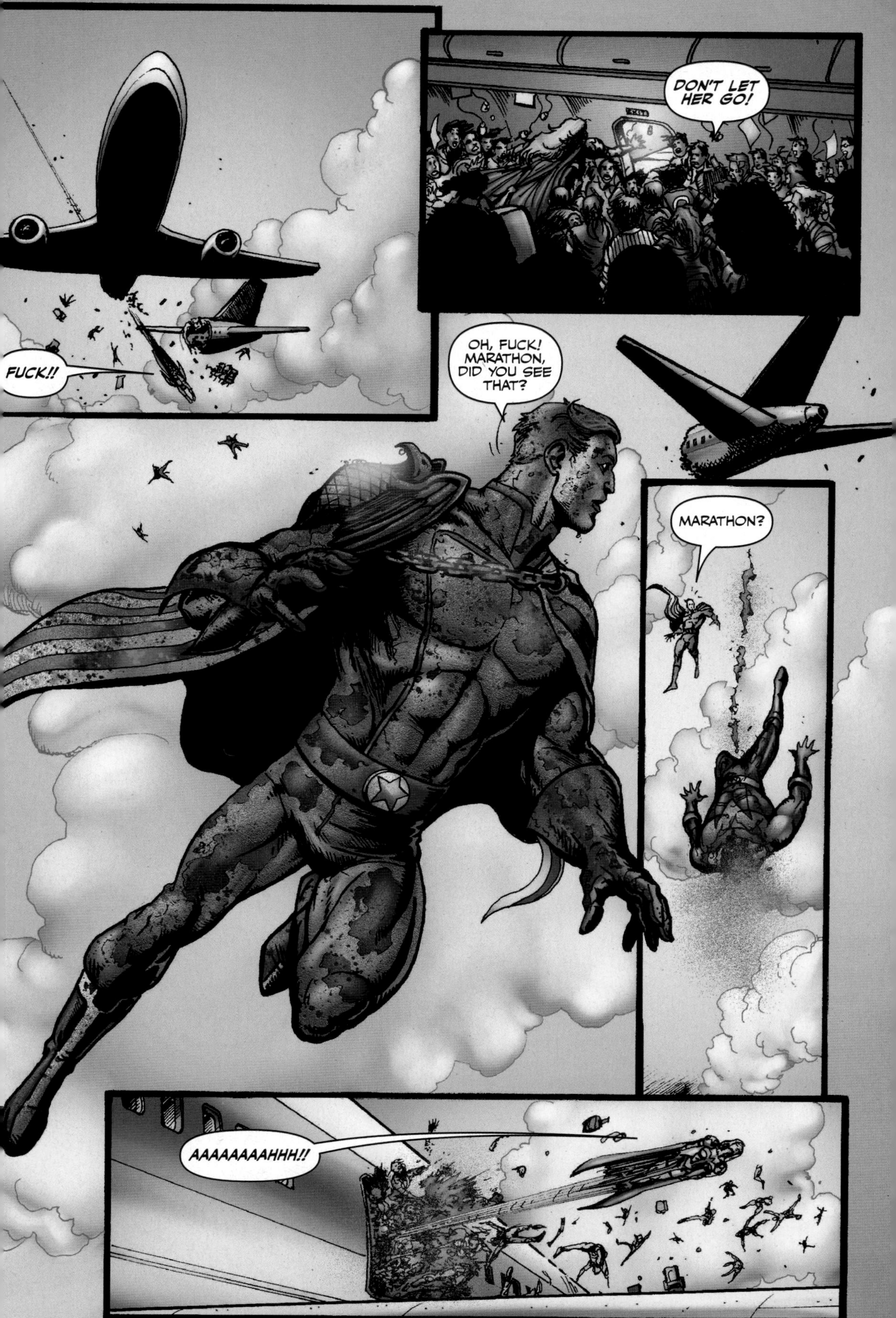
DON'T LET HER GO!
FUCK!!
OH, FUCK! MARATHON, DID YOU SEE THAT?
MARATHON?
AAAAAAAAHHH!!

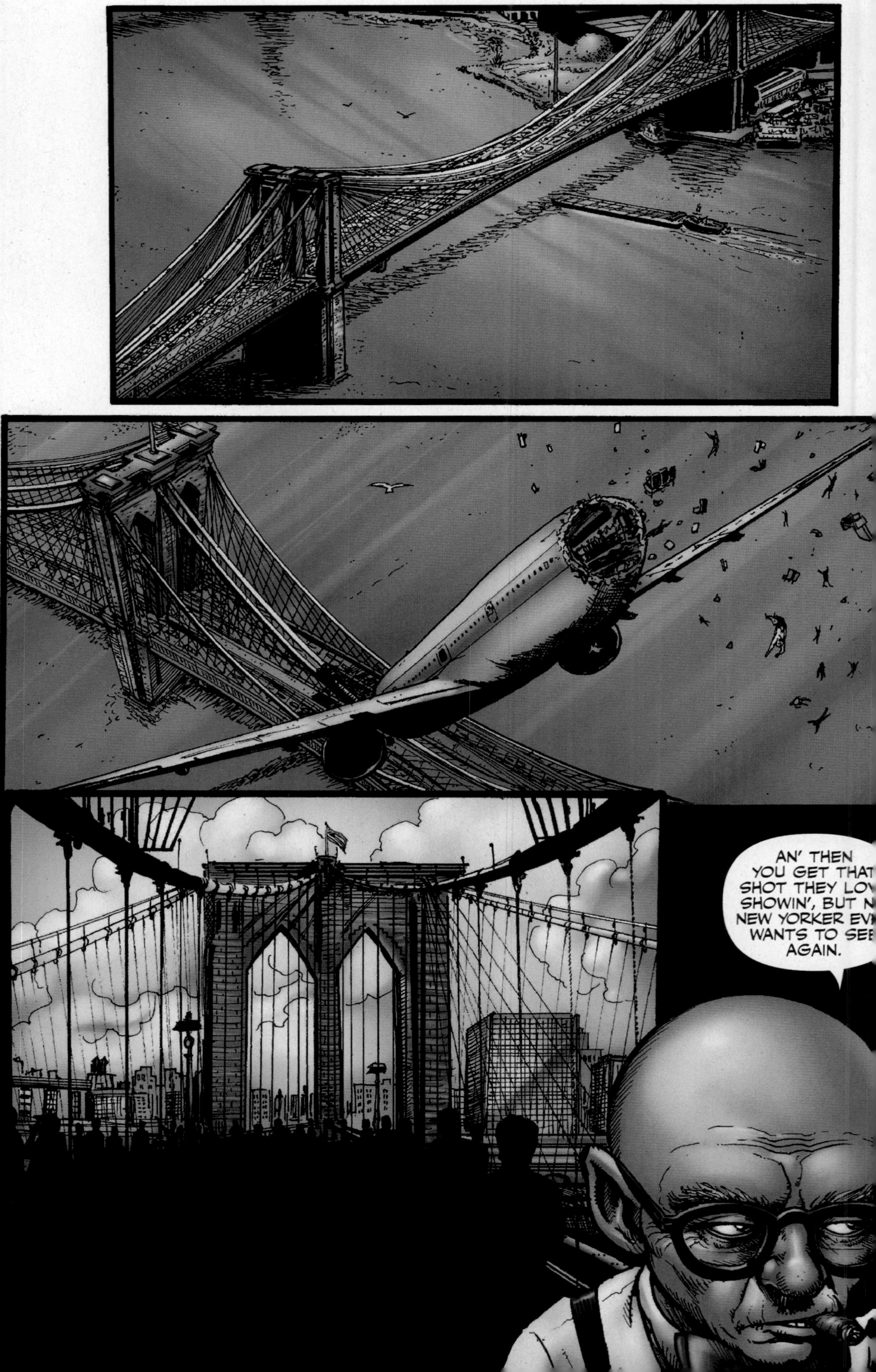
AN' THEN YOU GET THAT SHOT THEY LOV SHOWIN', BUT N NEW YORKER EV WANTS TO SEE AGAIN.

I REMEMBER SEEIN' IT.

I WAS THOUSANDS O' MILES AWAY. I'D NO' EVEN BEEN TO NEW YORK AT THAT STAGE.

BUT I REMEMBER THINKIN'--NOTHIN'S GONNA BE ANY *GOOD* ANYMORE.

IT WASN'T JUST ALL THE PEOPLE GETTIN' KILLED, THOUGH THAT WAS AWFUL. IT WASN'T EVEN WHAT WAS COMIN' NEXT--I MEAN YOU KNEW THEY WERE GONNA USE IT AS AN EXCUSE FOR THE SHITE THEY'D BEEN WANTIN' TO DO FOR AGES, THE FUCKIN' PATRIOT ACT AN' PAKISTAN AN' ALL.

IT WAS JUST THE THOUGHT...THAT THERE WAS STUFF LIKE THIS LOOSE IN THE WORLD.

THEY SURE DIDN'T WASTE ANY TIME.

DAKOTA BOB WENT ON T.V. RIGHT AWAY, ADMITTED ORDERIN' THE 'PLANES SHOT DOWN. HE PLAYED IT JUST RIGHT, IT FIT WELL WITH HIS IMAGE. NO ONE WAS ABOUT TO BLAME HIM.

HELL, HE DID *GREAT.* HE'D LISTENED TO THE SPOOKS WHEN THEY TOLD HIM IT WAS COMIN', HAD FIGHTERS PATROLLIN' COMMERCIAL AIRSPACE ALL SUMMER LONG.

PEOPLE LOVE HIM. HIS *BACKERS* LOVE HIM. HE TAKES US STRAIGHT INTO PAKISTAN, SO *DEFENSE* GETS THE BIG BUCKS AN' *FUCK* SOCIAL SPENDING...

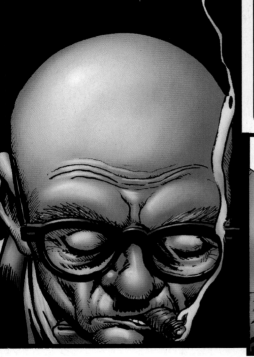

BUT HE SAID THE AIR FORCE SHOT 'EM *ALL* DOWN, NOT JUST THE FIRST ONE AN' THE ONE THEY THINK WAS GOIN' FOR *D.C.*. HE'S COVERIN' UP--AN' NOT JUST THE GODDAMN *SEVEN*...

NO WAY IN *SHIT* DOES *BOB* CALL OFF THE FIGHTERS FOR VOUGHT-AMERICAN'S *SUPES.* THE MAN WHO WOULD IS *VIC THE VEEP*--BUT *HE* AIN'T SUPPOSED TO BE IN CHARGE...!

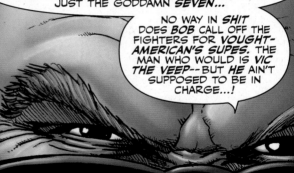

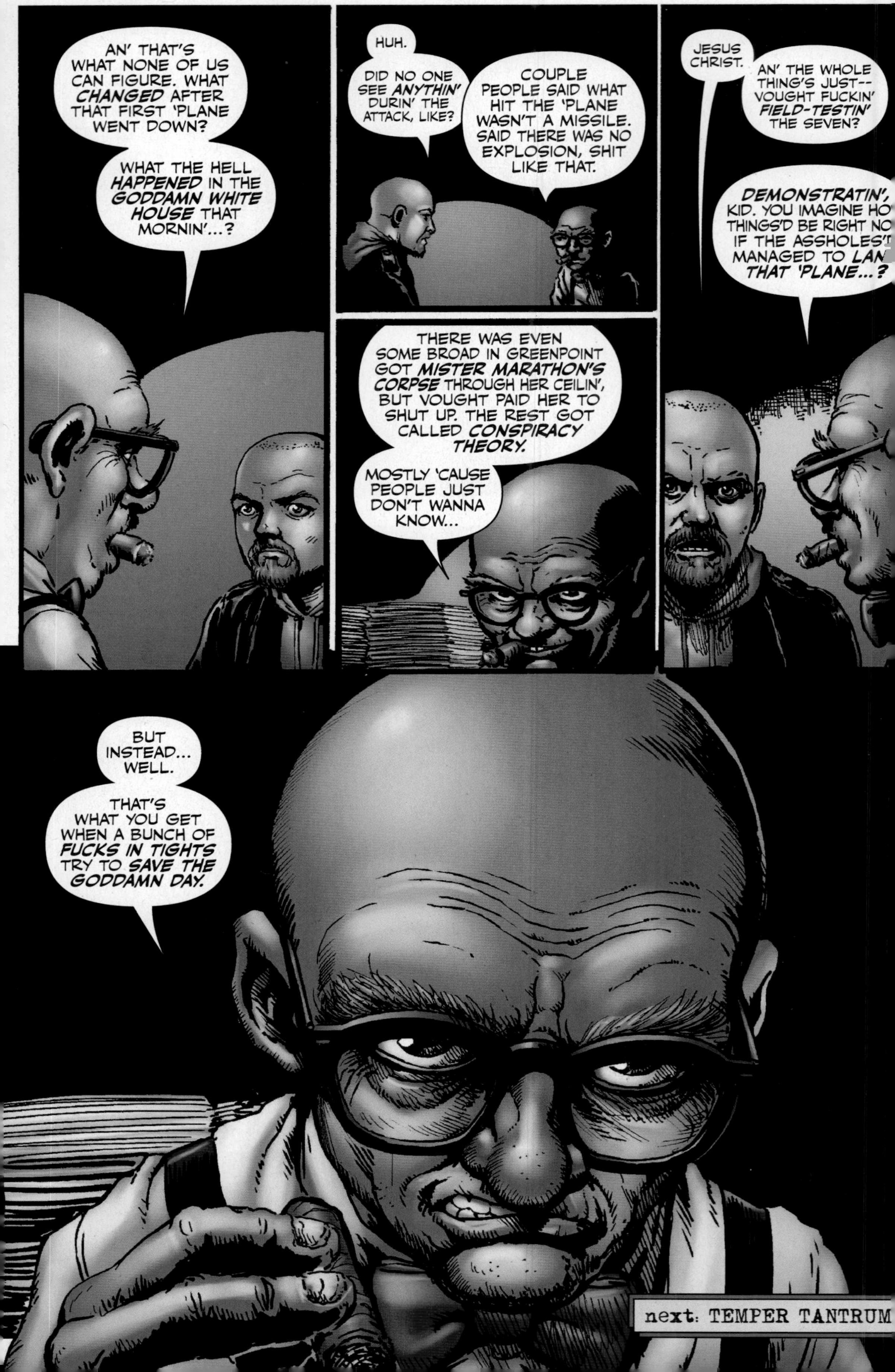
AN' THAT'S WHAT NONE OF US CAN FIGURE. WHAT CHANGED AFTER THAT FIRST 'PLANE WENT DOWN?
WHAT THE HELL HAPPENED IN THE GODDAMN WHITE HOUSE THAT MORNIN'...?
HUH.
DID NO ONE SEE ANYTHIN' DURIN' THE ATTACK, LIKE?
COUPLE PEOPLE SAID WHAT HIT THE 'PLANE WASN'T A MISSILE. SAID THERE WAS NO EXPLOSION, SHIT LIKE THAT.
THERE WAS EVEN SOME BROAD IN GREENPOINT GOT MISTER MARATHON'S CORPSE THROUGH HER CEILIN', BUT VOUGHT PAID HER TO SHUT UP. THE REST GOT CALLED CONSPIRACY THEORY.
MOSTLY 'CAUSE PEOPLE JUST DON'T WANNA KNOW...
JESUS CHRIST.
AN' THE WHOLE THING'S JUST-- VOUGHT FUCKIN' FIELD-TESTIN' THE SEVEN?
DEMONSTRATIN', KID. YOU IMAGINE HO THINGS'D BE RIGHT NO IF THE ASSHOLES'T MANAGED TO LAN THAT 'PLANE...?
BUT INSTEAD... WELL.
THAT'S WHAT YOU GET WHEN A BUNCH OF FUCKS IN TIGHTS TRY TO SAVE THE GODDAMN DAY.
next: TEMPER TANTRUM

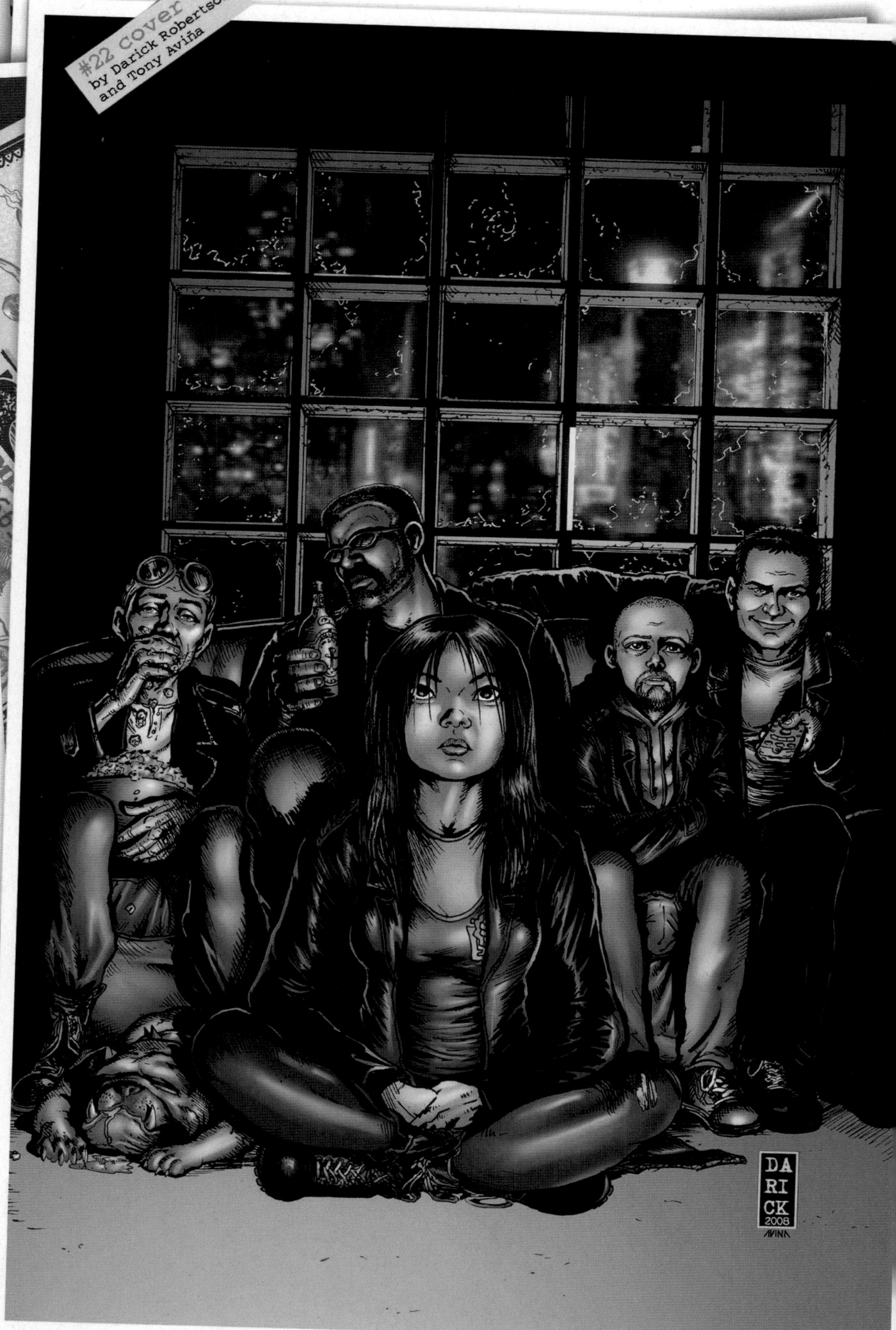
DARICK 2008
AVINA

#22 cover
by Darick Robertson
and Tony Aviña

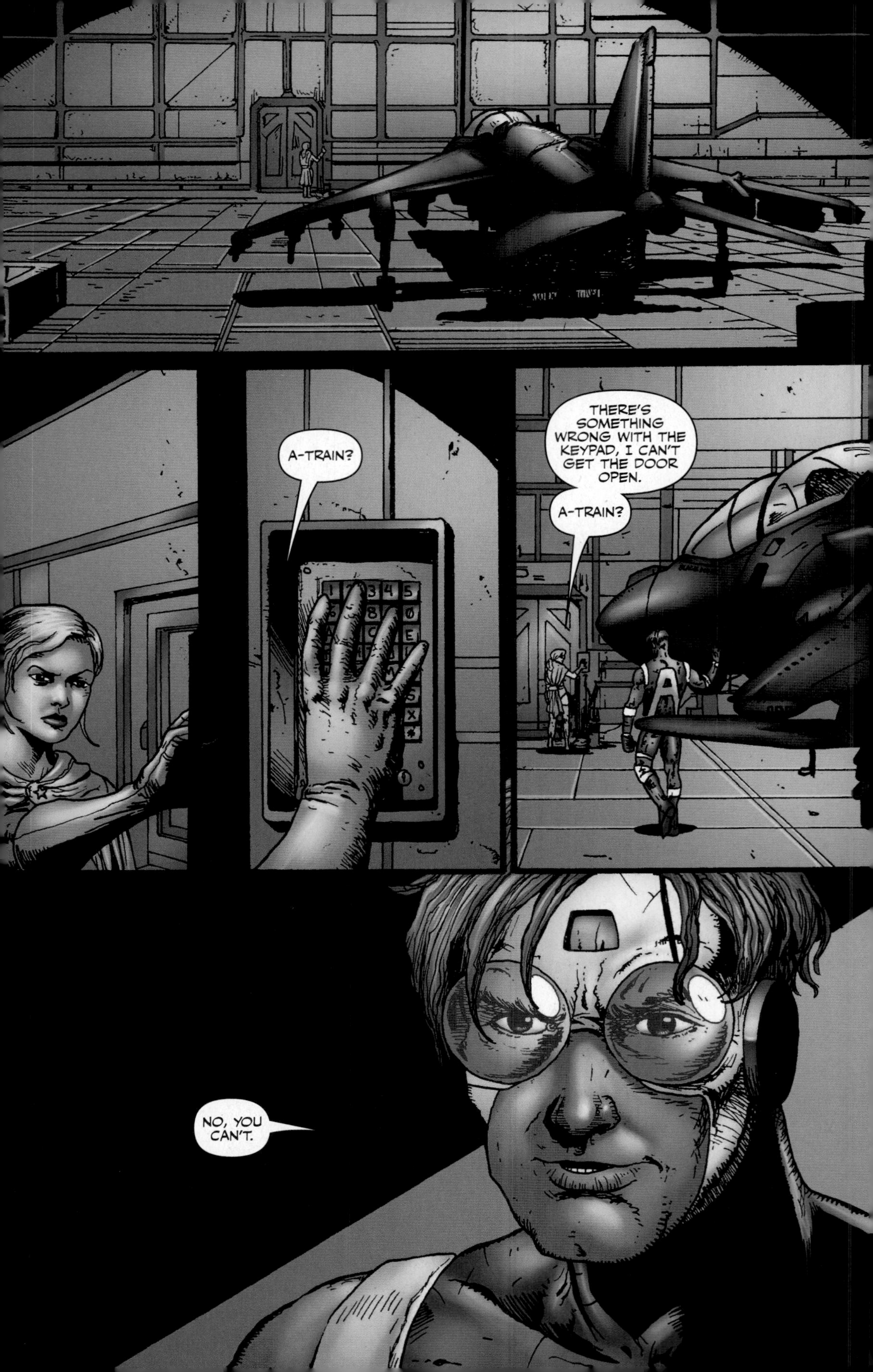
A-TRAIN?
THERE'S SOMETHING WRONG WITH THE KEYPAD, I CAN'T GET THE DOOR OPEN.
A-TRAIN?
NO, YOU CAN'T.

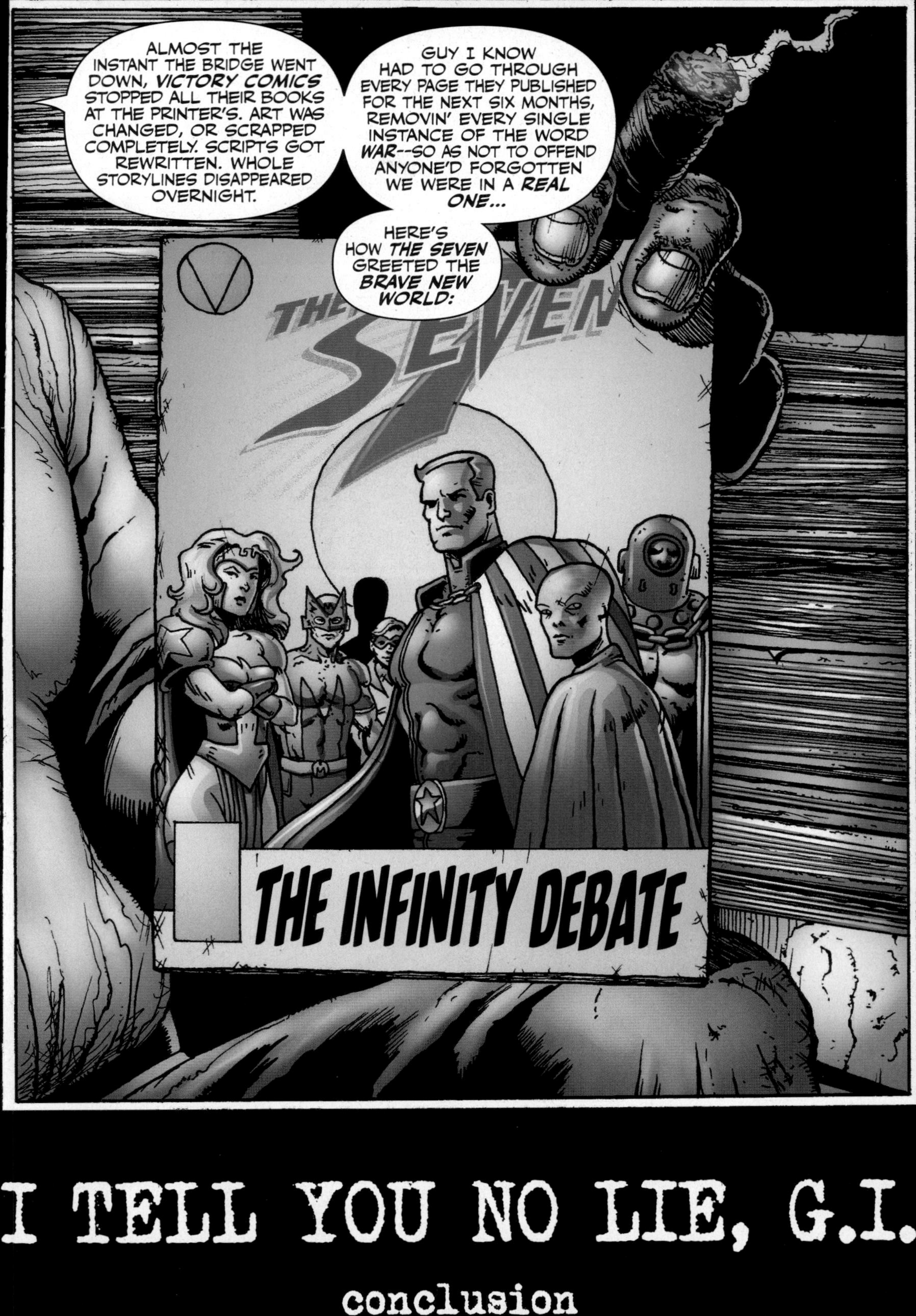
ALMOST THE INSTANT THE BRIDGE WENT DOWN, *VICTORY COMICS* STOPPED ALL THEIR BOOKS AT THE PRINTER'S. ART WAS CHANGED, OR SCRAPPED COMPLETELY. SCRIPTS GOT REWRITTEN. WHOLE STORYLINES DISAPPEARED OVERNIGHT.
GUY I KNOW HAD TO GO THROUGH EVERY PAGE THEY PUBLISHED FOR THE NEXT SIX MONTHS, REMOVIN' EVERY SINGLE INSTANCE OF THE WORD *WAR*--SO AS NOT TO OFFEND ANYONE'D FORGOTTEN WE WERE IN A *REAL ONE*...
HERE'S HOW *THE SEVEN* GREETED THE *BRAVE NEW WORLD:*
SEVEN
THE INFINITY DEBATE

I TELL YOU NO LIE, G.I.

conclusion

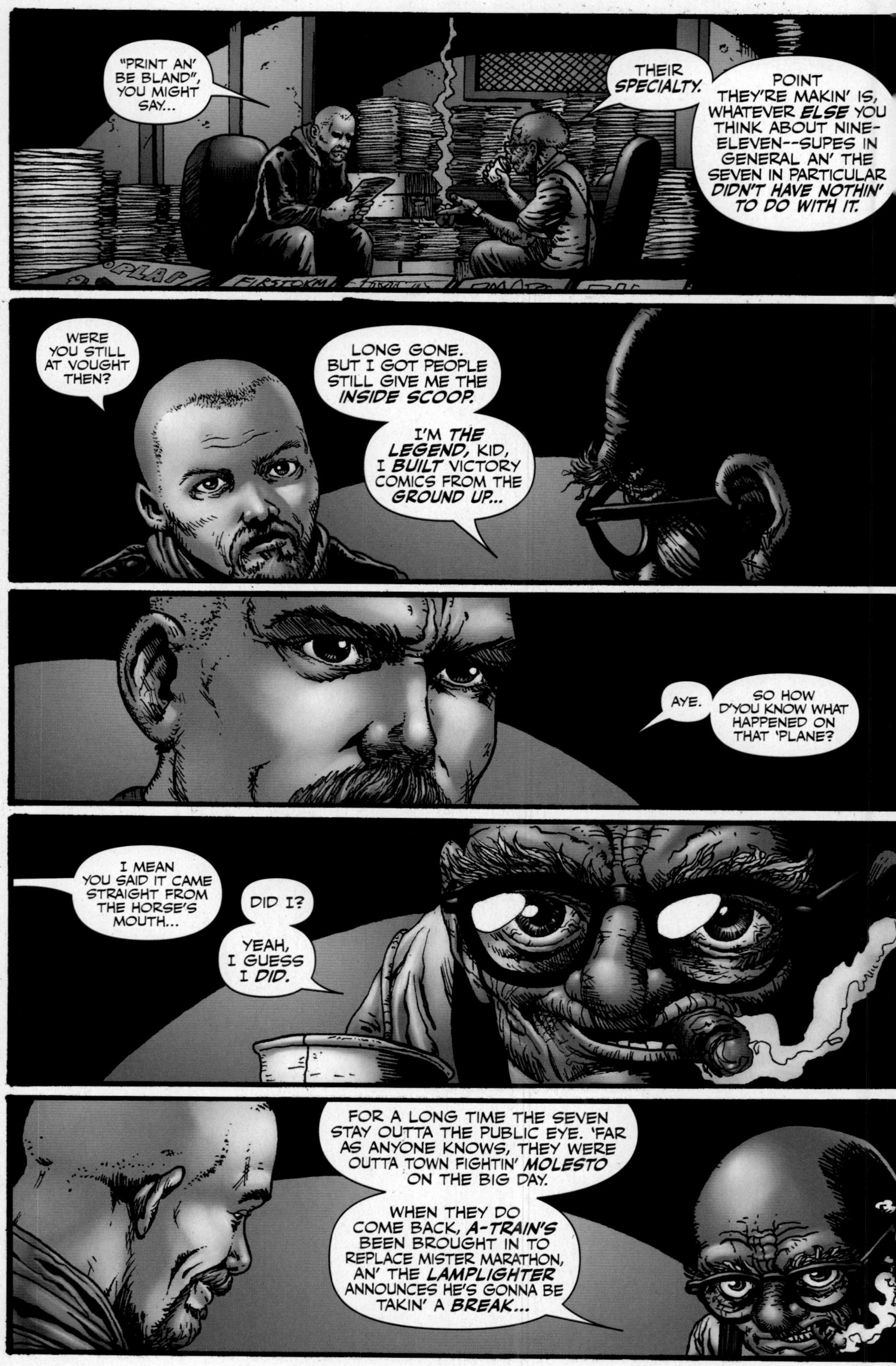
"PRINT AN' BE BLAND", YOU MIGHT SAY...
THEIR SPECIALTY.
POINT THEY'RE MAKIN' IS, WHATEVER ELSE YOU THINK ABOUT NINE-ELEVEN--SUPES IN GENERAL AN' THE SEVEN IN PARTICULAR DIDN'T HAVE NOTHIN' TO DO WITH IT.
WERE YOU STILL AT VOUGHT THEN?
LONG GONE. BUT I GOT PEOPLE STILL GIVE ME THE INSIDE SCOOP.
I'M THE LEGEND, KID, I BUILT VICTORY COMICS FROM THE GROUND UP...
AYE.
SO HOW D'YOU KNOW WHAT HAPPENED ON THAT 'PLANE?
I MEAN YOU SAID IT CAME STRAIGHT FROM THE HORSE'S MOUTH...
DID I?
YEAH, I GUESS I DID.
FOR A LONG TIME THE SEVEN STAY OUTTA THE PUBLIC EYE. 'FAR AS ANYONE KNOWS, THEY WERE OUTTA TOWN FIGHTIN' MOLESTO ON THE BIG DAY.
WHEN THEY DO COME BACK, A-TRAIN'S BEEN BROUGHT IN TO REPLACE MISTER MARATHON, AN' THE LAMPLIGHTER ANNOUNCES HE'S GONNA BE TAKIN' A BREAK...

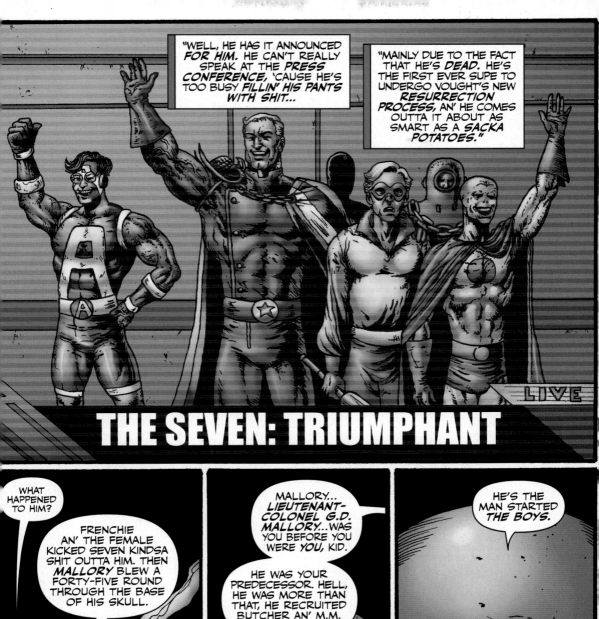

"WELL, HE HAS IT ANNOUNCED *FOR HIM.* HE CAN'T REALLY SPEAK AT THE *PRESS CONFERENCE,* 'CAUSE HE'S TOO BUSY *FILLIN' HIS PANTS WITH SHIT...*

"MAINLY DUE TO THE FACT THAT HE'S *DEAD.* HE'S THE FIRST EVER SUPE TO UNDERGO VOUGHT'S NEW *RESURRECTION PROCESS,* AN' HE COMES OUTTA IT ABOUT AS SMART AS A *SACKA POTATOES.*"

LIVE

THE SEVEN: TRIUMPHANT

WHAT HAPPENED TO HIM?

FRENCHIE AN' THE FEMALE KICKED SEVEN KINDSA SHIT OUTTA HIM. THEN *MALLORY* BLEW A FORTY-FIVE ROUND THROUGH THE BASE OF HIS SKULL.

MALLORY... *LIEUTENANT-COLONEL G.D. MALLORY...*WAS YOU BEFORE YOU WERE *YOU,* KID.

HE WAS YOUR PREDECESSOR. HELL, HE WAS MORE THAN THAT, HE RECRUITED BUTCHER AN' M.M. AN' ALL OF 'EM.

HE'S THE MAN STARTED *THE BOYS.*

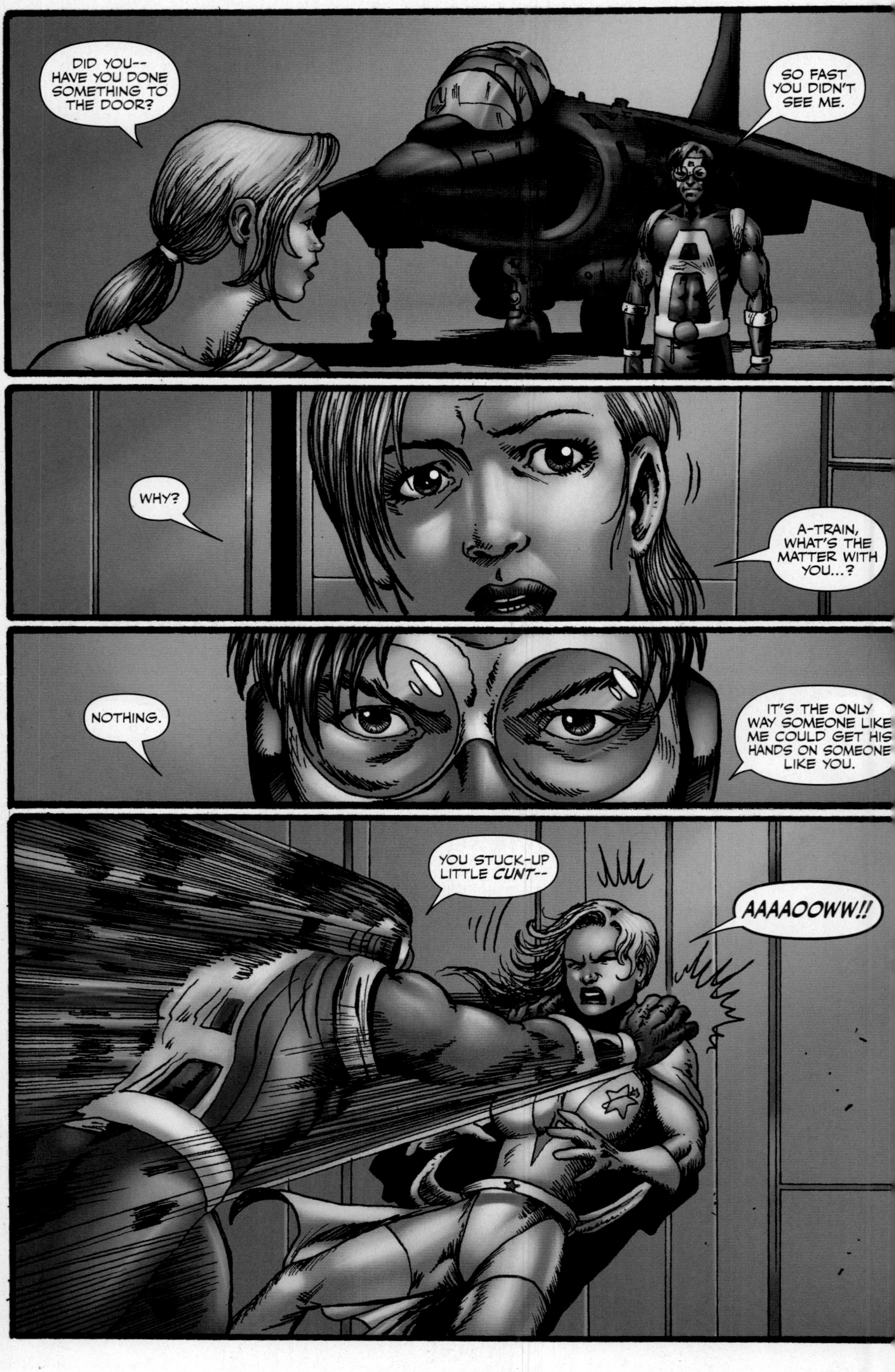
DID YOU-- HAVE YOU DONE SOMETHING TO THE DOOR?
SO FAST YOU DIDN'T SEE ME.
WHY?
A-TRAIN, WHAT'S THE MATTER WITH YOU...?
NOTHING.
IT'S THE ONLY WAY SOMEONE LIKE ME COULD GET HIS HANDS ON SOMEONE LIKE YOU.
YOU STUCK-UP LITTLE *CUNT*--
AAAAOOWW!!

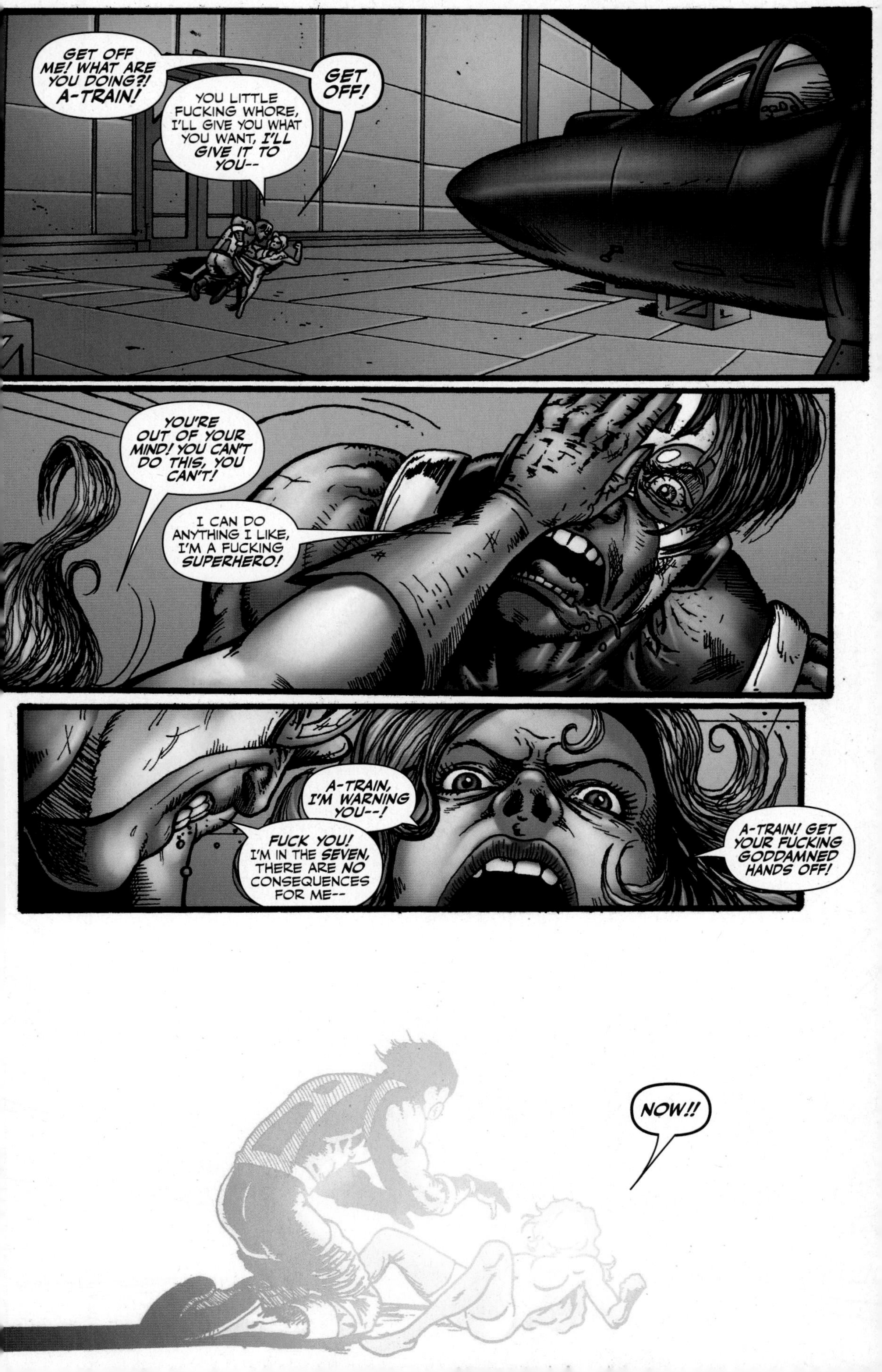
GET OFF ME! WHAT ARE YOU DOING?! A-TRAIN!
YOU LITTLE FUCKING WHORE, I'LL GIVE YOU WHAT YOU WANT, I'LL GIVE IT TO YOU--
GET OFF!
YOU'RE OUT OF YOUR MIND! YOU CAN'T DO THIS, YOU CAN'T!
I CAN DO ANYTHING I LIKE, I'M A FUCKING SUPERHERO!
A-TRAIN, I'M WARNING YOU--!
FUCK YOU! I'M IN THE SEVEN, THERE ARE NO CONSEQUENCES FOR ME--
A-TRAIN! GET YOUR FUCKING GODDAMNED HANDS OFF!
NOW!!

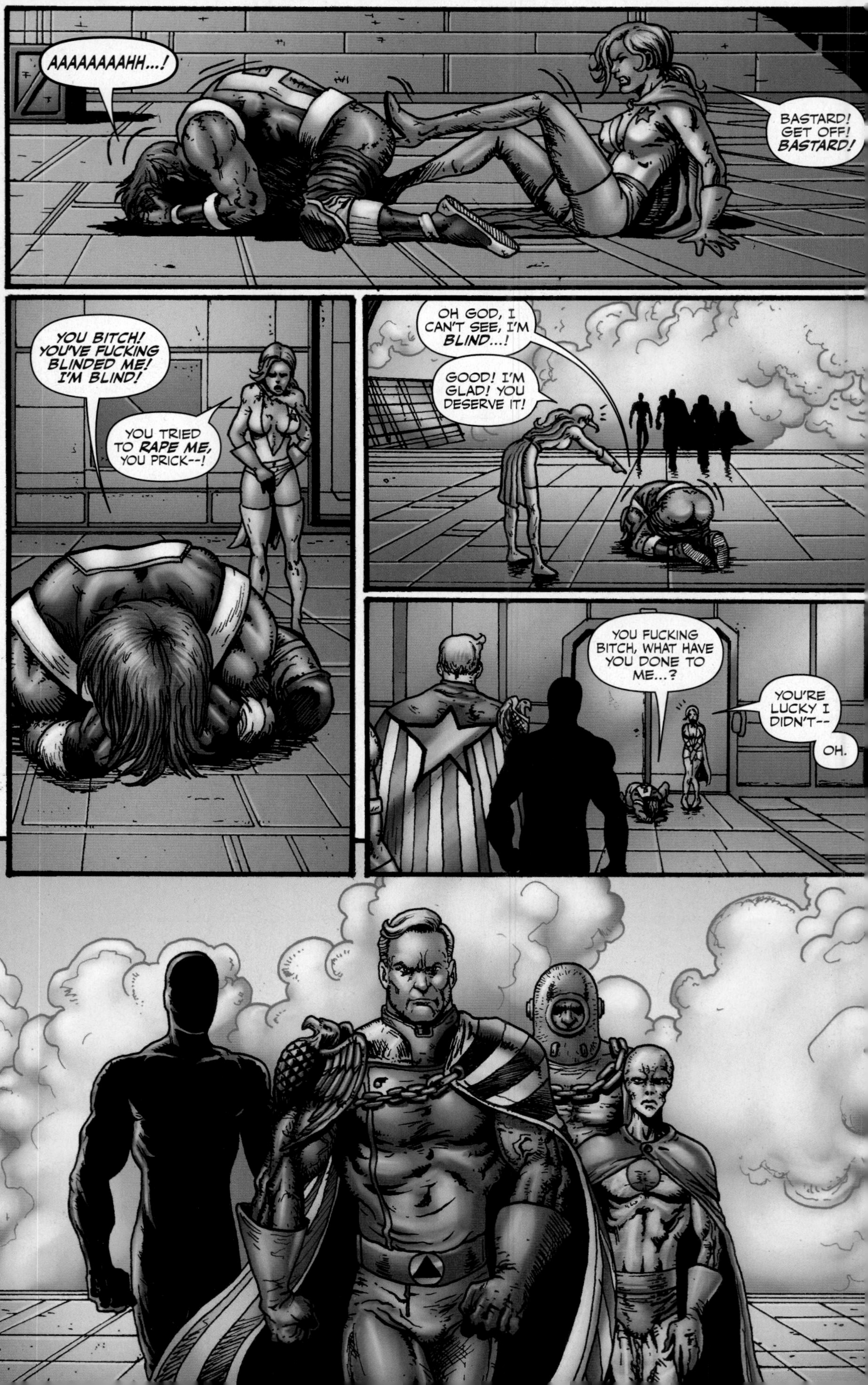
AAAAAAAAHH...!
BASTARD! GET OFF! BASTARD!
YOU BITCH! YOU'VE FUCKING BLINDED ME! I'M BLIND!
YOU TRIED TO RAPE ME, YOU PRICK--!
OH GOD, I CAN'T SEE, I'M BLIND...!
GOOD! I'M GLAD! YOU DESERVE IT!
YOU FUCKING BITCH, WHAT HAVE YOU DONE TO ME...?
YOU'RE LUCKY I DIDN'T--
OH.

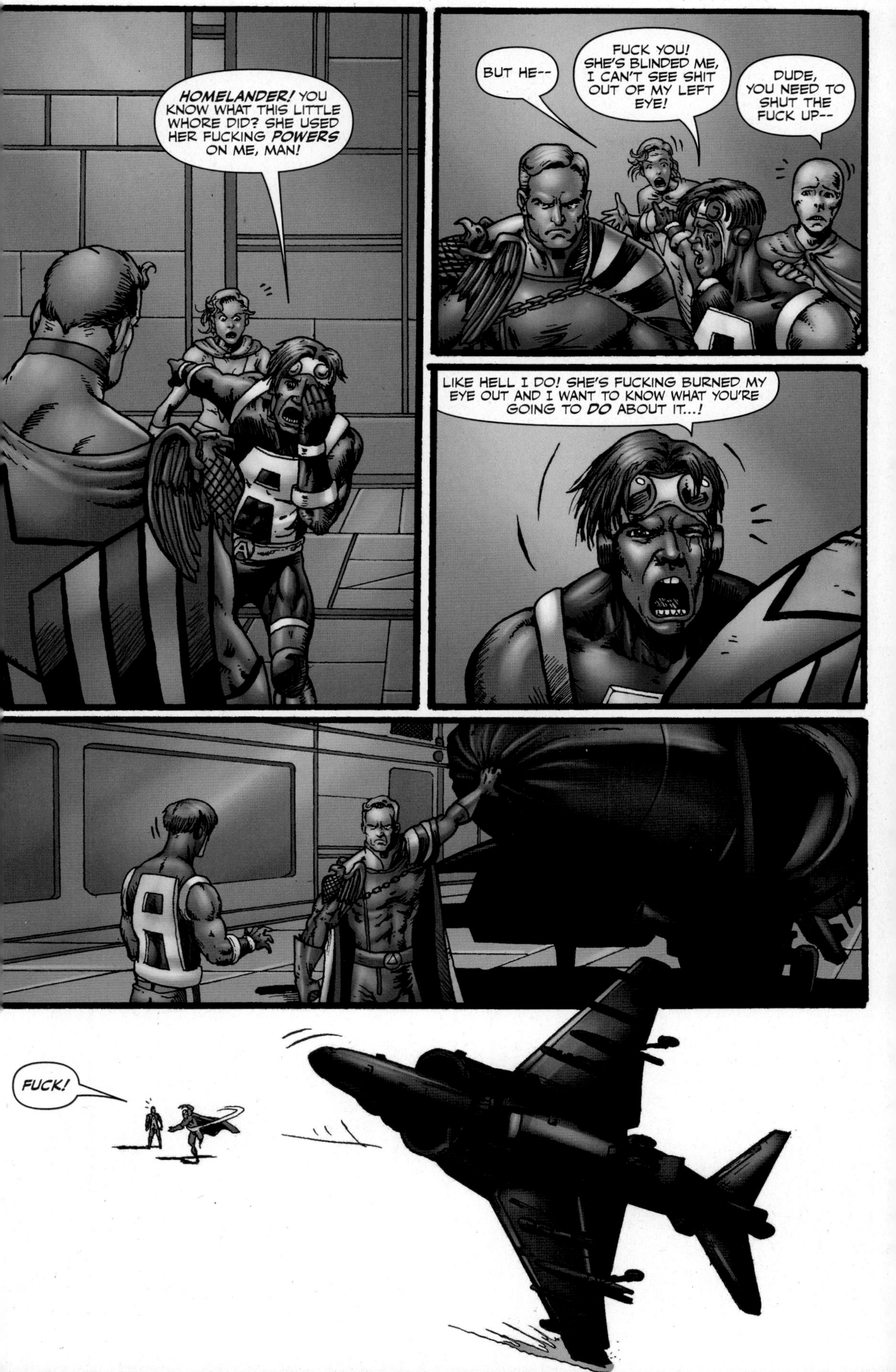
HOMELANDER! YOU KNOW WHAT THIS LITTLE WHORE DID? SHE USED HER FUCKING POWERS ON ME, MAN!
BUT HE--
FUCK YOU! SHE'S BLINDED ME, I CAN'T SEE SHIT OUT OF MY LEFT EYE!
DUDE, YOU NEED TO SHUT THE FUCK UP--
LIKE HELL I DO! SHE'S FUCKING BURNED MY EYE OUT AND I WANT TO KNOW WHAT YOU'RE GOING TO DO ABOUT IT...!
FUCK!

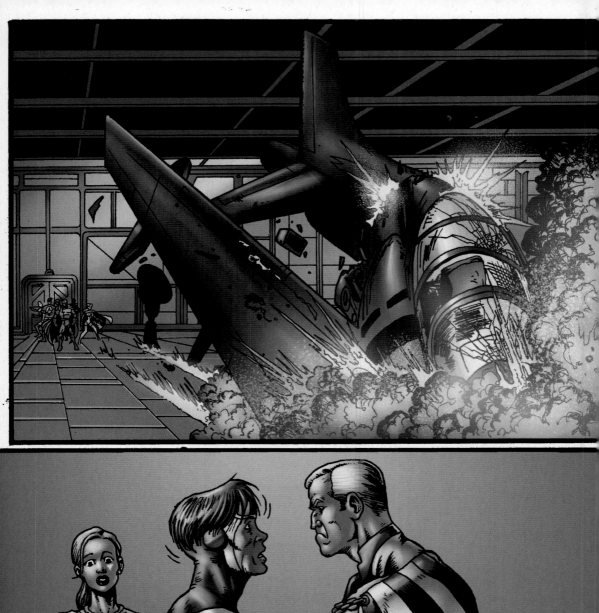

IT, UH...

IT HASN'T BEEN A VERY GOOD DAY.

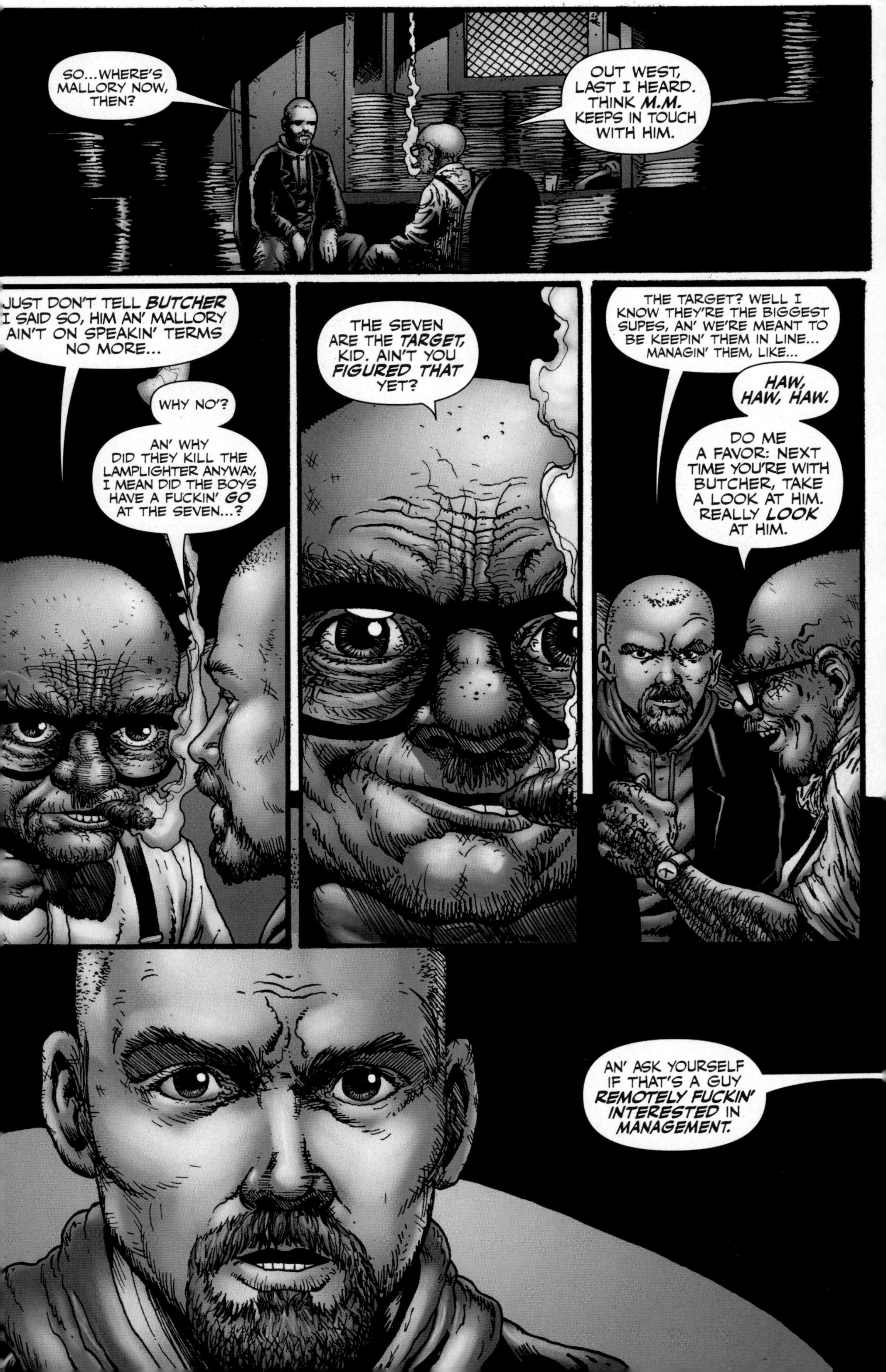
SO...WHERE'S MALLORY NOW, THEN?
OUT WEST, LAST I HEARD. THINK M.M. KEEPS IN TOUCH WITH HIM.
JUST DON'T TELL BUTCHER I SAID SO, HIM AN' MALLORY AIN'T ON SPEAKIN' TERMS NO MORE...
WHY NO'?
AN' WHY DID THEY KILL THE LAMPLIGHTER ANYWAY, I MEAN DID THE BOYS HAVE A FUCKIN' GO AT THE SEVEN...?
THE SEVEN ARE THE TARGET, KID. AIN'T YOU FIGURED THAT YET?
THE TARGET? WELL I KNOW THEY'RE THE BIGGEST SUPES, AN' WE'RE MEANT TO BE KEEPIN' THEM IN LINE... MANAGIN' THEM, LIKE...
HAW, HAW, HAW.
DO ME A FAVOR: NEXT TIME YOU'RE WITH BUTCHER, TAKE A LOOK AT HIM. REALLY LOOK AT HIM.
AN' ASK YOURSELF IF THAT'S A GUY REMOTELY FUCKIN' INTERESTED IN MANAGEMENT.

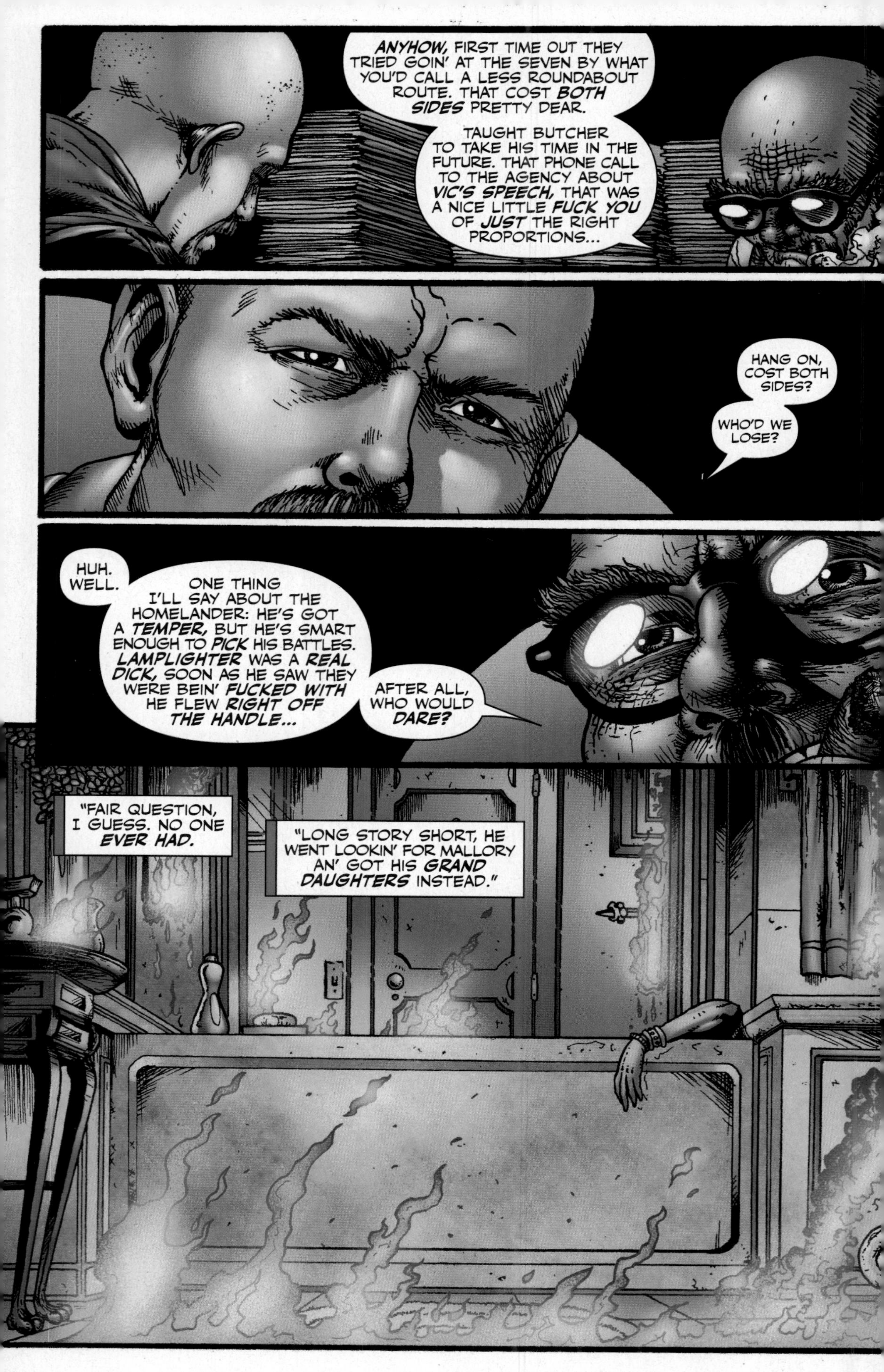
ANYHOW, FIRST TIME OUT THEY TRIED GOIN' AT THE SEVEN BY WHAT YOU'D CALL A LESS ROUNDABOUT ROUTE. THAT COST BOTH SIDES PRETTY DEAR.
TAUGHT BUTCHER TO TAKE HIS TIME IN THE FUTURE. THAT PHONE CALL TO THE AGENCY ABOUT VIC'S SPEECH, THAT WAS A NICE LITTLE FUCK YOU OF JUST THE RIGHT PROPORTIONS...
HANG ON, COST BOTH SIDES?
WHO'D WE LOSE?
HUH. WELL.
ONE THING I'LL SAY ABOUT THE HOMELANDER: HE'S GOT A TEMPER, BUT HE'S SMART ENOUGH TO PICK HIS BATTLES. LAMPLIGHTER WAS A REAL DICK, SOON AS HE SAW THEY WERE BEIN' FUCKED WITH HE FLEW RIGHT OFF THE HANDLE...
AFTER ALL, WHO WOULD DARE?
"FAIR QUESTION, I GUESS. NO ONE EVER HAD.
"LONG STORY SHORT, HE WENT LOOKIN' FOR MALLORY AN' GOT HIS GRAND DAUGHTERS INSTEAD."

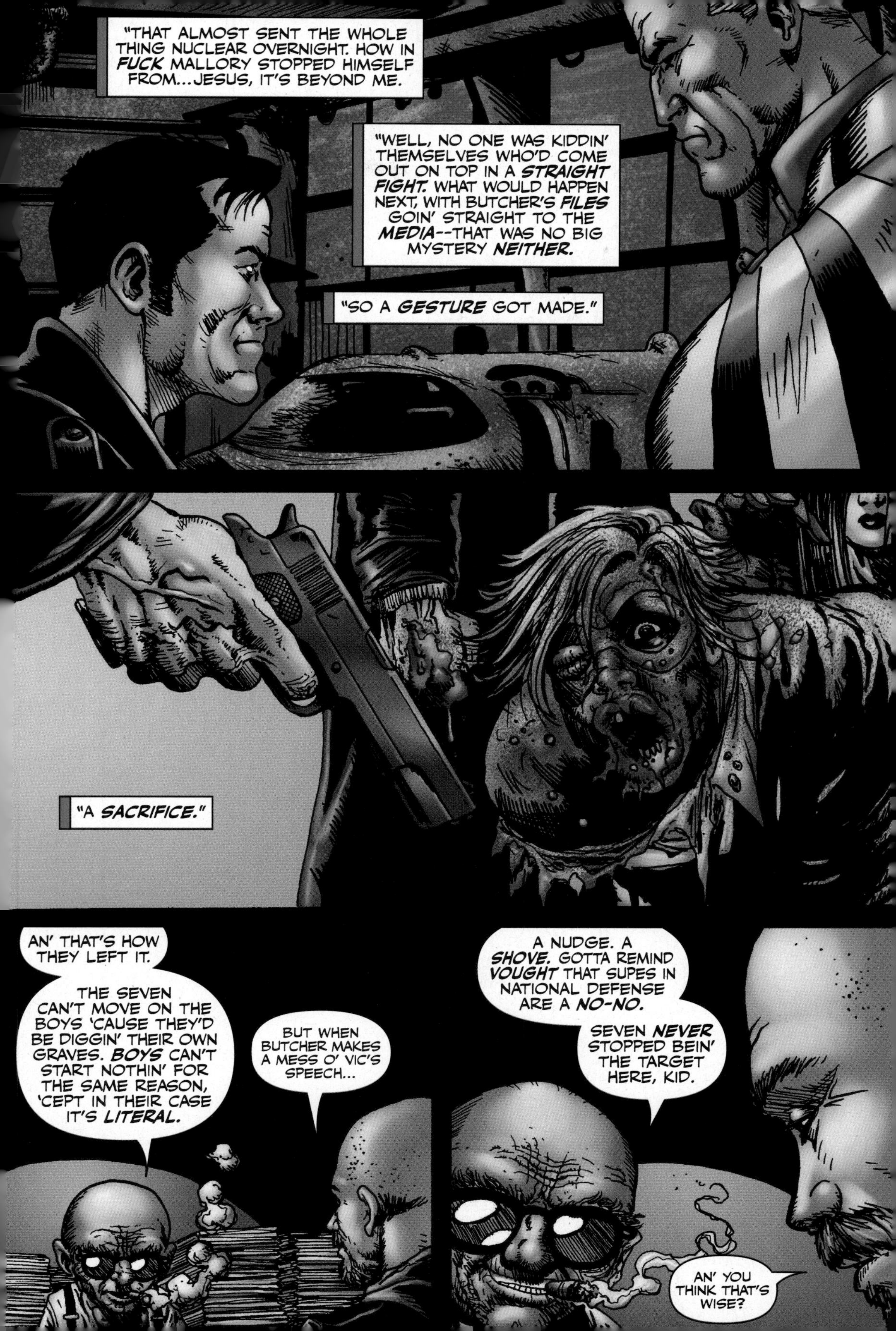

"THAT ALMOST SENT THE WHOLE THING NUCLEAR OVERNIGHT. HOW IN FUCK MALLORY STOPPED HIMSELF FROM...JESUS, IT'S BEYOND ME.
"WELL, NO ONE WAS KIDDIN' THEMSELVES WHO'D COME OUT ON TOP IN A STRAIGHT FIGHT. WHAT WOULD HAPPEN NEXT, WITH BUTCHER'S FILES GOIN' STRAIGHT TO THE MEDIA--THAT WAS NO BIG MYSTERY NEITHER.
"SO A GESTURE GOT MADE."
"A SACRIFICE."
AN' THAT'S HOW THEY LEFT IT.
THE SEVEN CAN'T MOVE ON THE BOYS 'CAUSE THEY'D BE DIGGIN' THEIR OWN GRAVES. BOYS CAN'T START NOTHIN' FOR THE SAME REASON, 'CEPT IN THEIR CASE IT'S LITERAL.
BUT WHEN BUTCHER MAKES A MESS O' VIC'S SPEECH...
A NUDGE. A SHOVE. GOTTA REMIND VOUGHT THAT SUPES IN NATIONAL DEFENSE ARE A NO-NO.
SEVEN NEVER STOPPED BEIN' THE TARGET HERE, KID.
AN' YOU THINK THAT'S WISE?

I THINK *FUCK VOUGHT-AMERICAN*, IS WHAT I THINK. FUCK THEIR PEOPLE, FUCK THEIR PLANS, FUCK THEIR SUPES.

AN' ANYONE WANTS TO TAKE 'EM DOWN, I'LL GIVE 'EM ALL THE HELP I *CAN*.

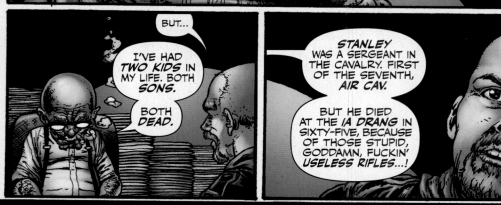

BUT...

I'VE HAD *TWO KIDS* IN MY LIFE. BOTH *SONS*.

BOTH *DEAD*.

STANLEY WAS A SERGEANT IN THE CAVALRY. FIRST OF THE SEVENTH, *AIR CAV*.

BUT HE DIED AT THE *IA DRANG* IN SIXTY-FIVE, BECAUSE OF THOSE STUPID, GODDAMN, FUCKIN' *USELESS RIFLES*...!

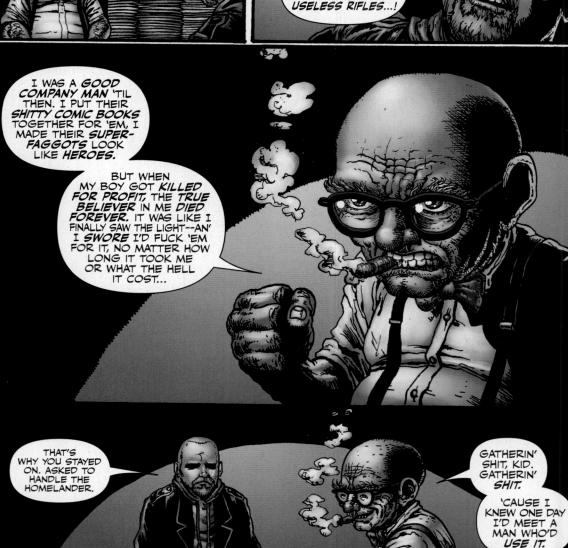

I WAS A *GOOD COMPANY MAN* 'TIL THEN. I PUT THEIR *SHITTY COMIC BOOKS* TOGETHER FOR 'EM, I MADE THEIR *SUPER-FAGGOTS* LOOK LIKE *HEROES*.

BUT WHEN MY BOY GOT *KILLED FOR PROFIT*, THE *TRUE BELIEVER* IN ME *DIED FOREVER*. IT WAS LIKE I FINALLY SAW THE LIGHT--AN' I *SWORE* I'D FUCK 'EM FOR IT, NO MATTER HOW LONG IT TOOK ME OR WHAT THE HELL IT COST...

THAT'S WHY YOU STAYED ON. ASKED TO HANDLE THE HOMELANDER.

GATHERIN' *SHIT*, KID. GATHERIN' *SHIT*.

'CAUSE I KNEW ONE DAY I'D MEET A MAN WHO'D *USE IT*.

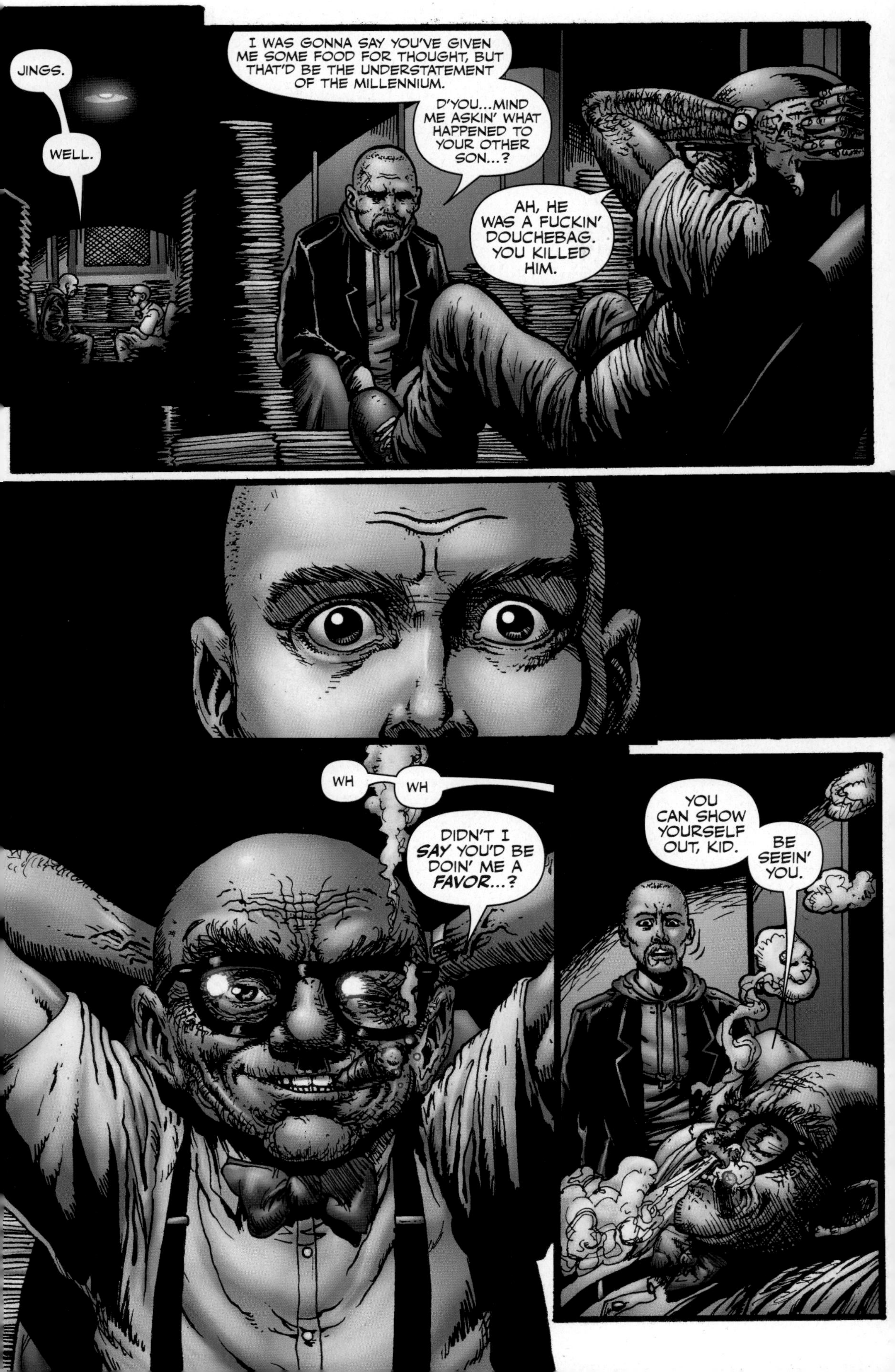
JINGS.
WELL.
I WAS GONNA SAY YOU'VE GIVEN ME SOME FOOD FOR THOUGHT, BUT THAT'D BE THE UNDERSTATEMENT OF THE MILLENNIUM.
D'YOU...MIND ME ASKIN' WHAT HAPPENED TO YOUR OTHER SON...?
AH, HE WAS A FUCKIN' DOUCHEBAG. YOU KILLED HIM.
WH
WH
DIDN'T I *SAY* YOU'D BE DOIN' ME A *FAVOR*...?
YOU CAN SHOW YOURSELF OUT, KID.
BE SEEIN' YOU.

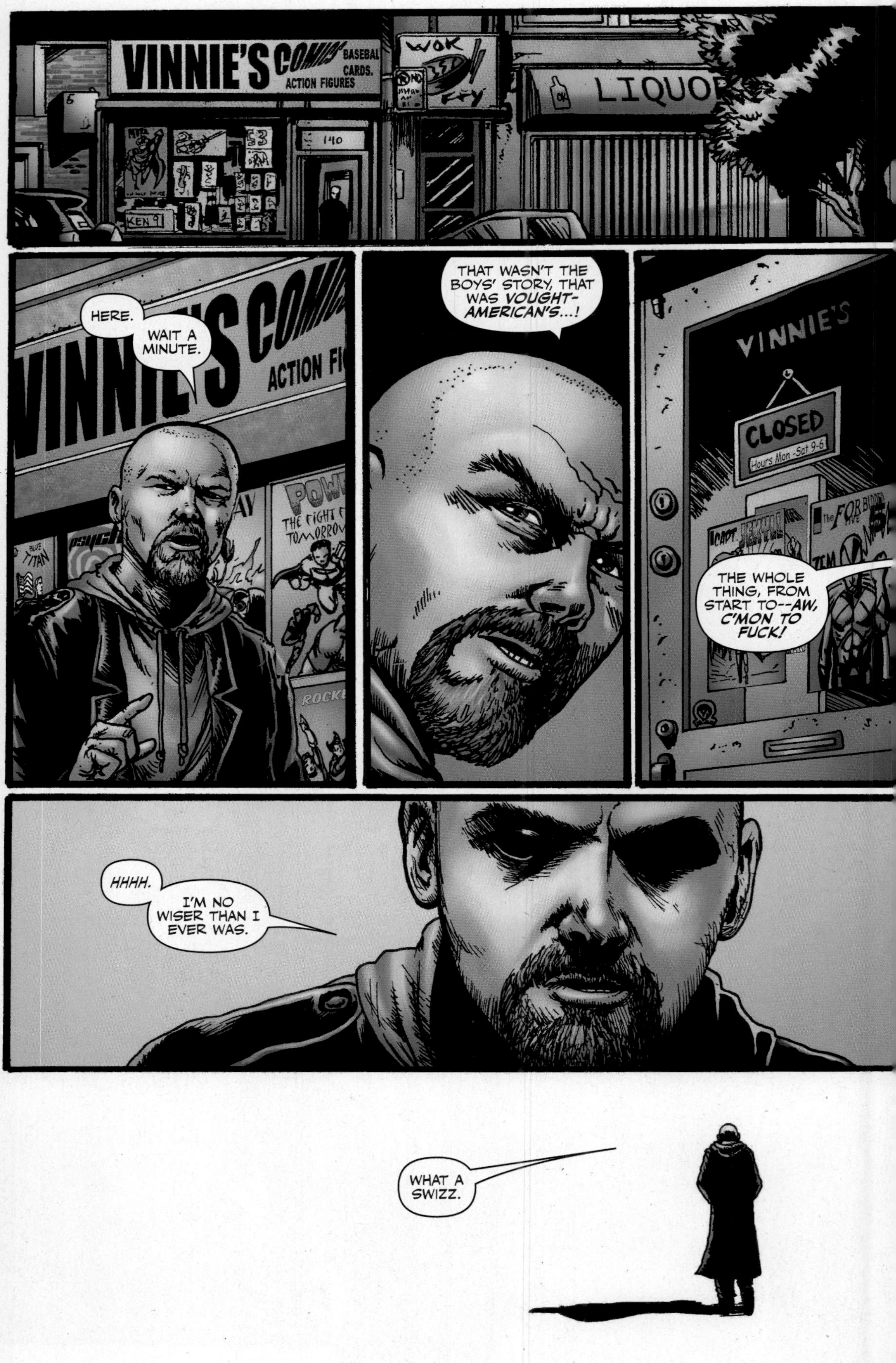

ACTION FIGURES
140
HERE.
WAIT A MINUTE.
THAT WASN'T THE BOYS' STORY, THAT WAS *VOUGHT-AMERICAN'S...!*
VINNIE'S
CLOSED
Hours Mon -Sat 9-6
THE WHOLE THING, FROM START TO--***AW, C'MON TO FUCK!***
HHHH.
I'M NO WISER THAN I EVER WAS.
WHAT A SWIZZ.

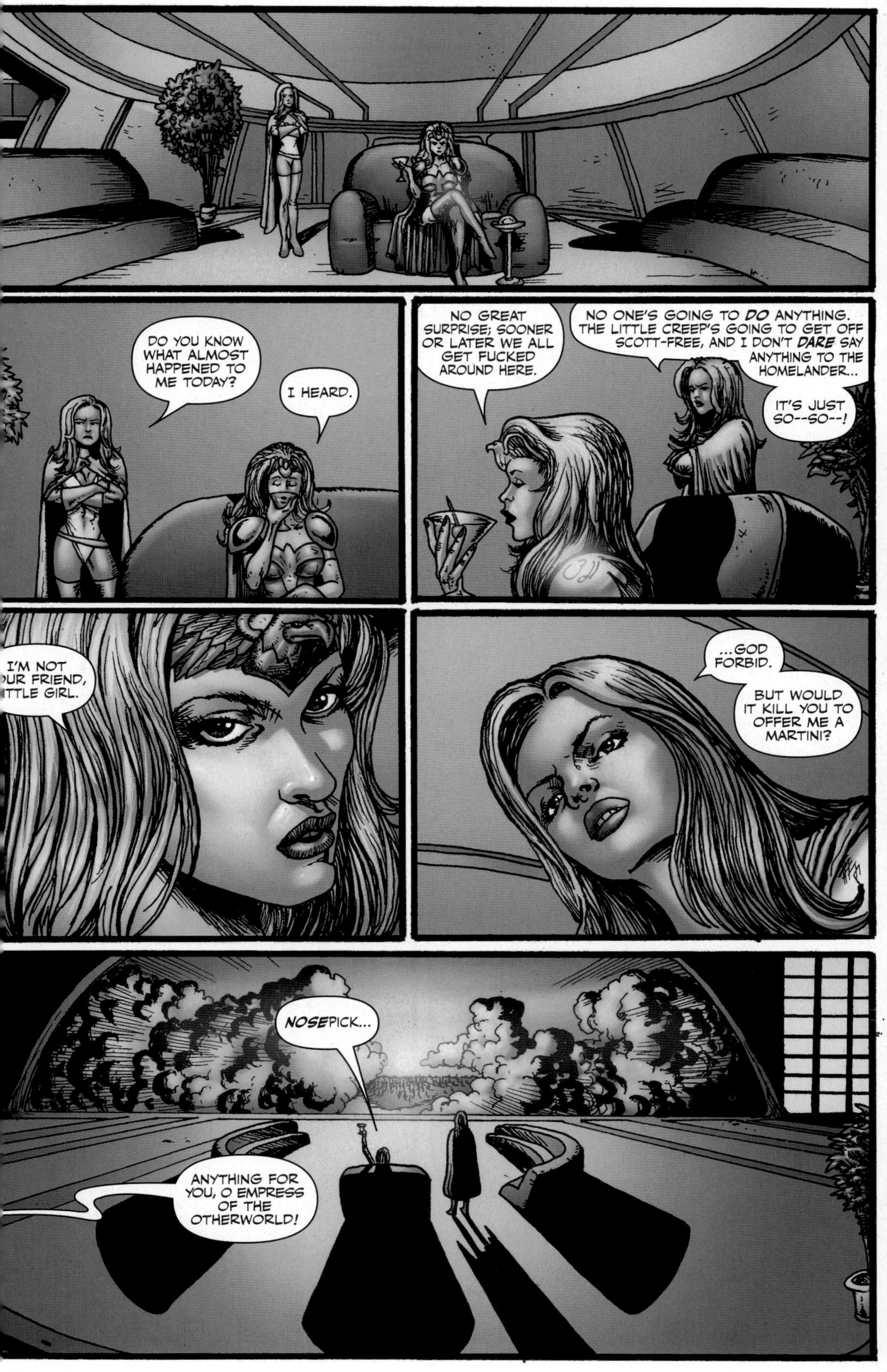
DO YOU KNOW WHAT ALMOST HAPPENED TO ME TODAY?
I HEARD.
NO GREAT SURPRISE; SOONER OR LATER WE ALL GET FUCKED AROUND HERE.
NO ONE'S GOING TO DO ANYTHING. THE LITTLE CREEP'S GOING TO GET OFF SCOTT-FREE, AND I DON'T DARE SAY ANYTHING TO THE HOMELANDER...
IT'S JUST SO--SO--!
I'M NOT OUR FRIEND, TTLE GIRL.
...GOD FORBID.
BUT WOULD IT KILL YOU TO OFFER ME A MARTINI?
NOSEPICK...
ANYTHING FOR YOU, O EMPRESS OF THE OTHERWORLD!

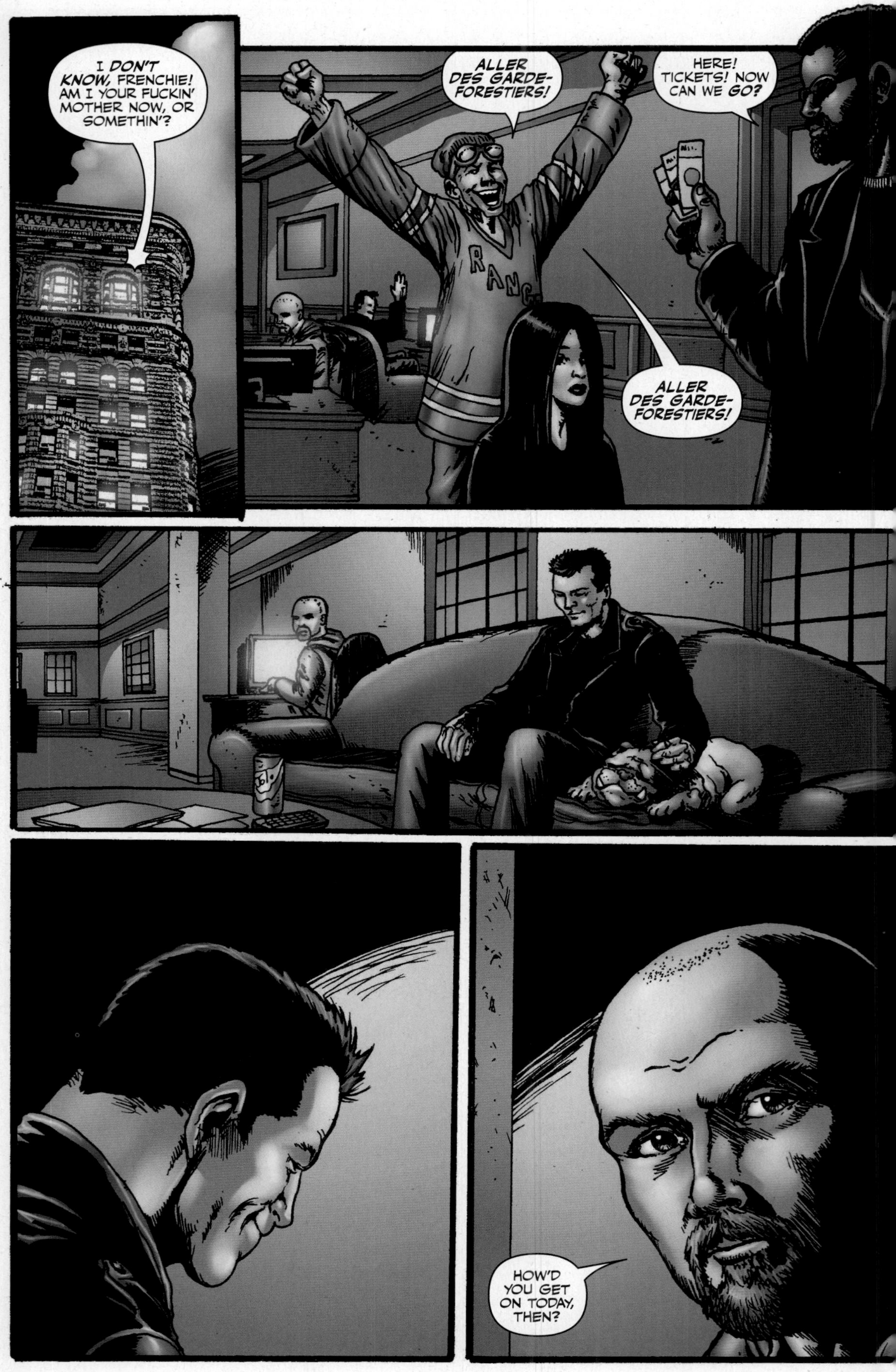

I DON'T KNOW, FRENCHIE! AM I YOUR FUCKIN' MOTHER NOW, OR SOMETHIN'?
ALLER DES GARDE-FORESTIERS!
HERE! TICKETS! NOW CAN WE GO?
ALLER DES GARDE-FORESTIERS!
HOW'D YOU GET ON TODAY, THEN?

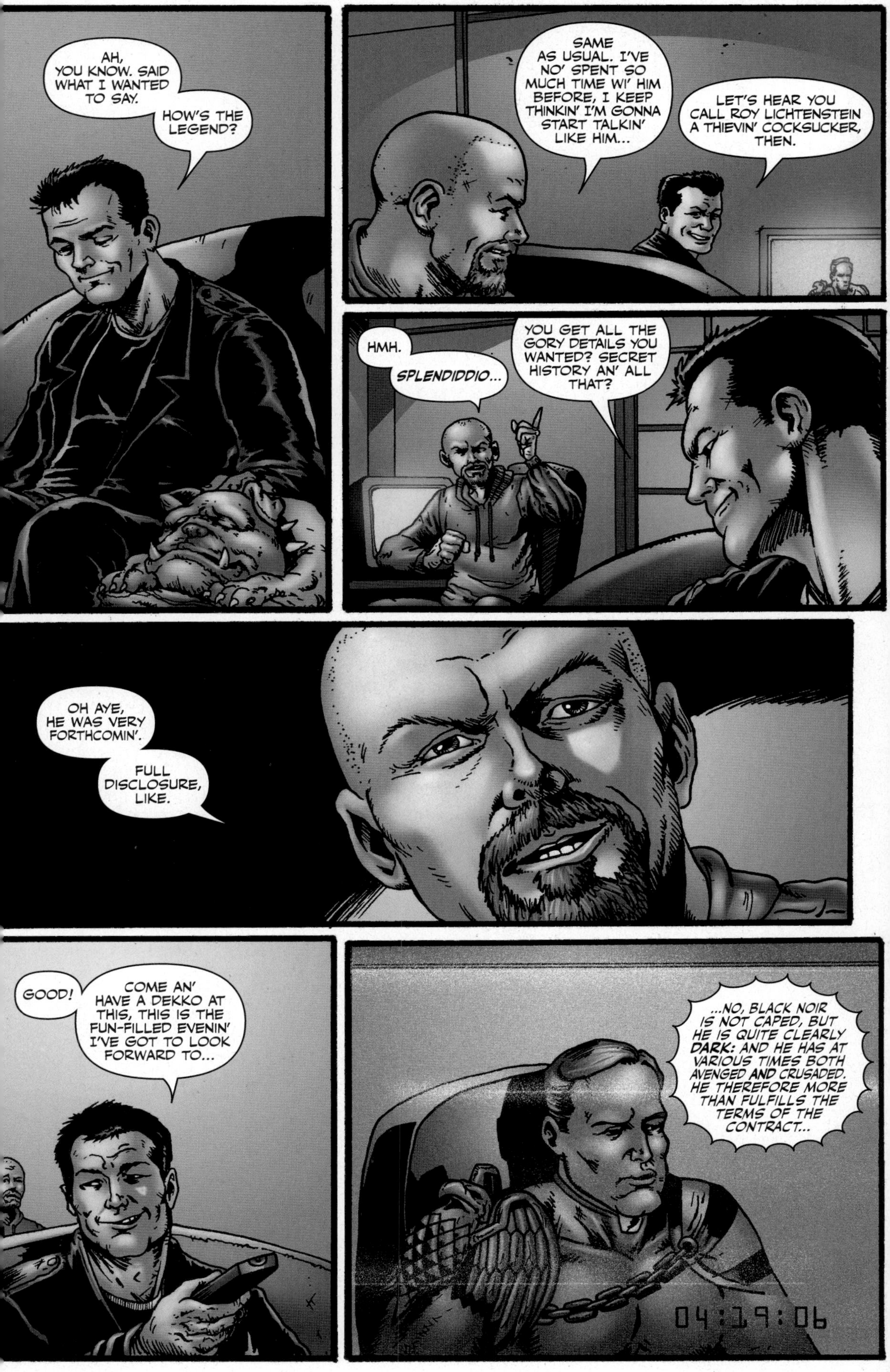
AH, YOU KNOW. SAID WHAT I WANTED TO SAY.
HOW'S THE LEGEND?
SAME AS USUAL. I'VE NO' SPENT SO MUCH TIME WI' HIM BEFORE, I KEEP THINKIN' I'M GONNA START TALKIN' LIKE HIM...
LET'S HEAR YOU CALL ROY LICHTENSTEIN A THIEVIN' COCKSUCKER, THEN.
HMH.
SPLENDIDDIO...
YOU GET ALL THE GORY DETAILS YOU WANTED? SECRET HISTORY AN' ALL THAT?
OH AYE, HE WAS VERY FORTHCOMIN'.
FULL DISCLOSURE, LIKE.
GOOD!
COME AN' HAVE A DEKKO AT THIS, THIS IS THE FUN-FILLED EVENIN' I'VE GOT TO LOOK FORWARD TO...
...NO, BLACK NOIR IS NOT CAPED, BUT HE IS QUITE CLEARLY DARK: AND HE HAS AT VARIOUS TIMES BOTH AVENGED AND CRUSADED. HE THEREFORE MORE THAN FULFILLS THE TERMS OF THE CONTRACT...
04:19:06

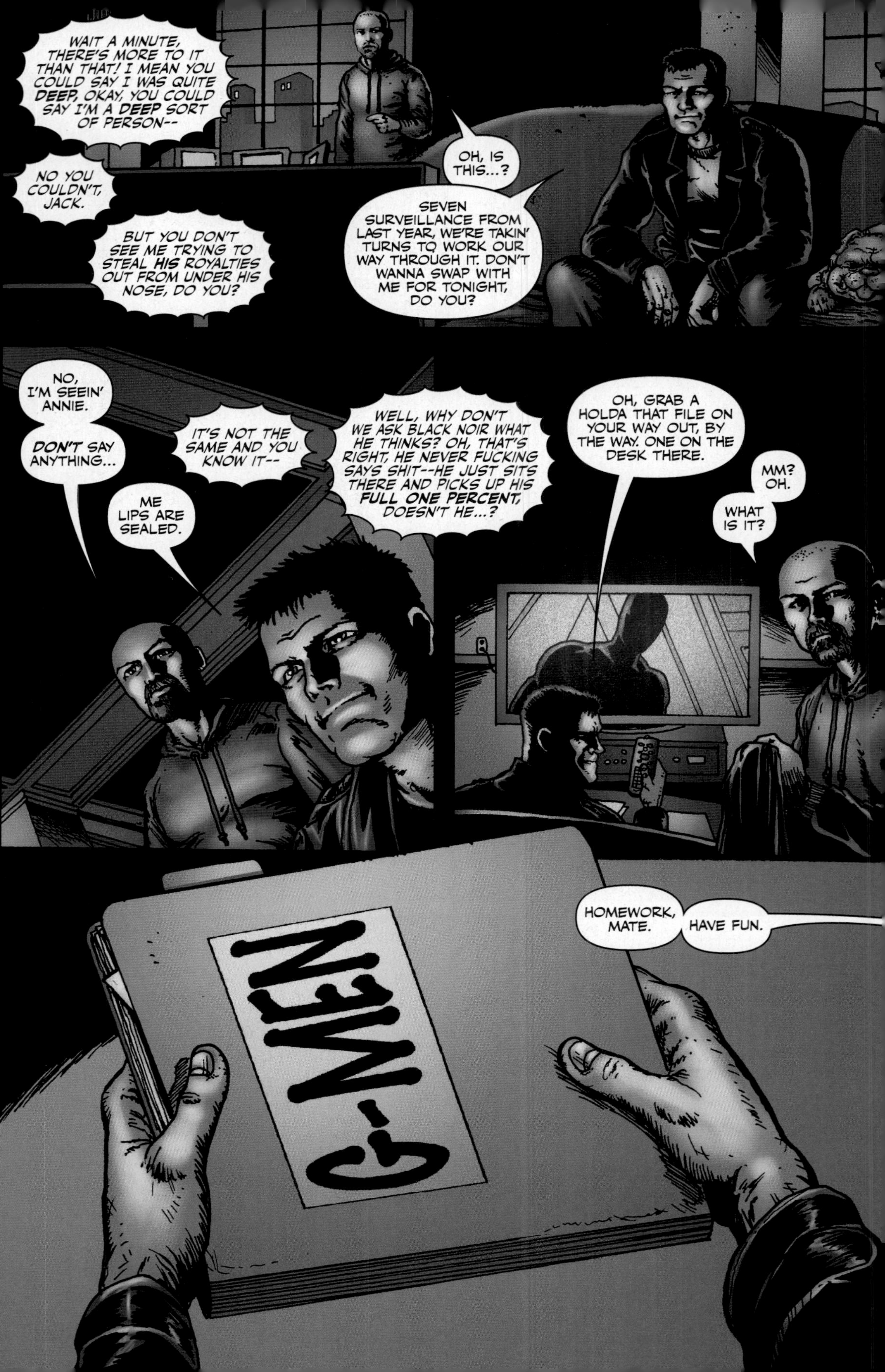
WAIT A MINUTE, THERE'S MORE TO IT THAN THAT! I MEAN YOU COULD SAY I WAS QUITE DEEP, OKAY, YOU COULD SAY I'M A DEEP SORT OF PERSON--
NO YOU COULDN'T, JACK.
BUT YOU DON'T SEE ME TRYING TO STEAL HIS ROYALTIES OUT FROM UNDER HIS NOSE, DO YOU?
OH, IS THIS...?
SEVEN SURVEILLANCE FROM LAST YEAR, WE'RE TAKIN' TURNS TO WORK OUR WAY THROUGH IT. DON'T WANNA SWAP WITH ME FOR TONIGHT, DO YOU?
NO, I'M SEEIN' ANNIE.
DON'T SAY ANYTHING...
IT'S NOT THE SAME AND YOU KNOW IT--
ME LIPS ARE SEALED.
WELL, WHY DON'T WE ASK BLACK NOIR WHAT HE THINKS? OH, THAT'S RIGHT, HE NEVER FUCKING SAYS SHIT--HE JUST SITS THERE AND PICKS UP HIS FULL ONE PERCENT, DOESN'T HE...?
OH, GRAB A HOLDA THAT FILE ON YOUR WAY OUT, BY THE WAY. ONE ON THE DESK THERE.
MM? OH.
WHAT IS IT?
HOMEWORK, MATE.
HAVE FUN.
G-MEN

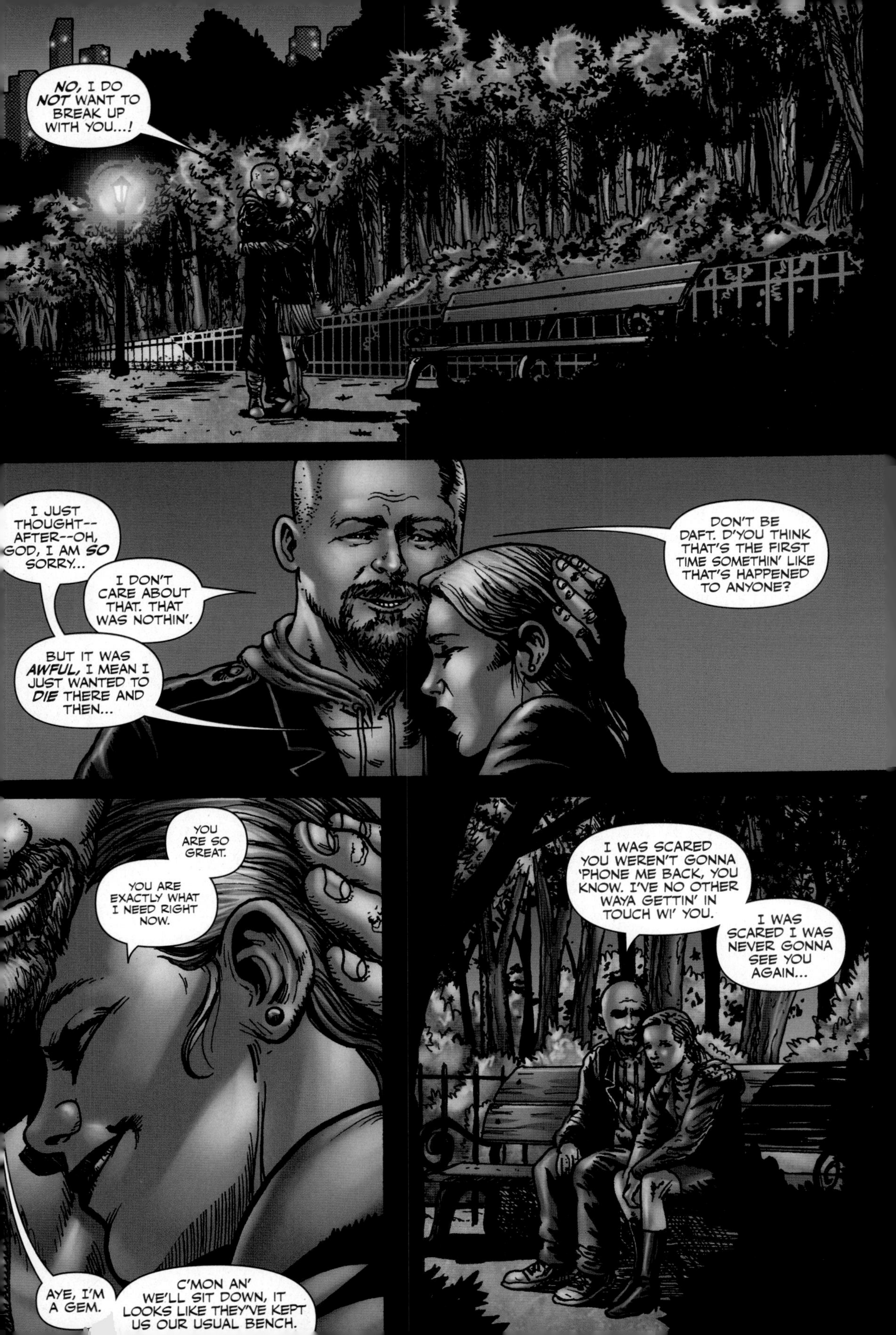
NO, I DO NOT WANT TO BREAK UP WITH YOU...!
I JUST THOUGHT-- AFTER--OH, GOD, I AM SO SORRY...
I DON'T CARE ABOUT THAT. THAT WAS NOTHIN'.
BUT IT WAS AWFUL, I MEAN I JUST WANTED TO DIE THERE AND THEN...
DON'T BE DAFT. D'YOU THINK THAT'S THE FIRST TIME SOMETHIN' LIKE THAT'S HAPPENED TO ANYONE?
YOU ARE SO GREAT.
YOU ARE EXACTLY WHAT I NEED RIGHT NOW.
AYE, I'M A GEM.
C'MON AN' WE'LL SIT DOWN, IT LOOKS LIKE THEY'VE KEPT US OUR USUAL BENCH.
I WAS SCARED YOU WEREN'T GONNA 'PHONE ME BACK, YOU KNOW. I'VE NO OTHER WAYA GETTIN' IN TOUCH WI' YOU.
I WAS SCARED I WAS NEVER GONNA SEE YOU AGAIN...

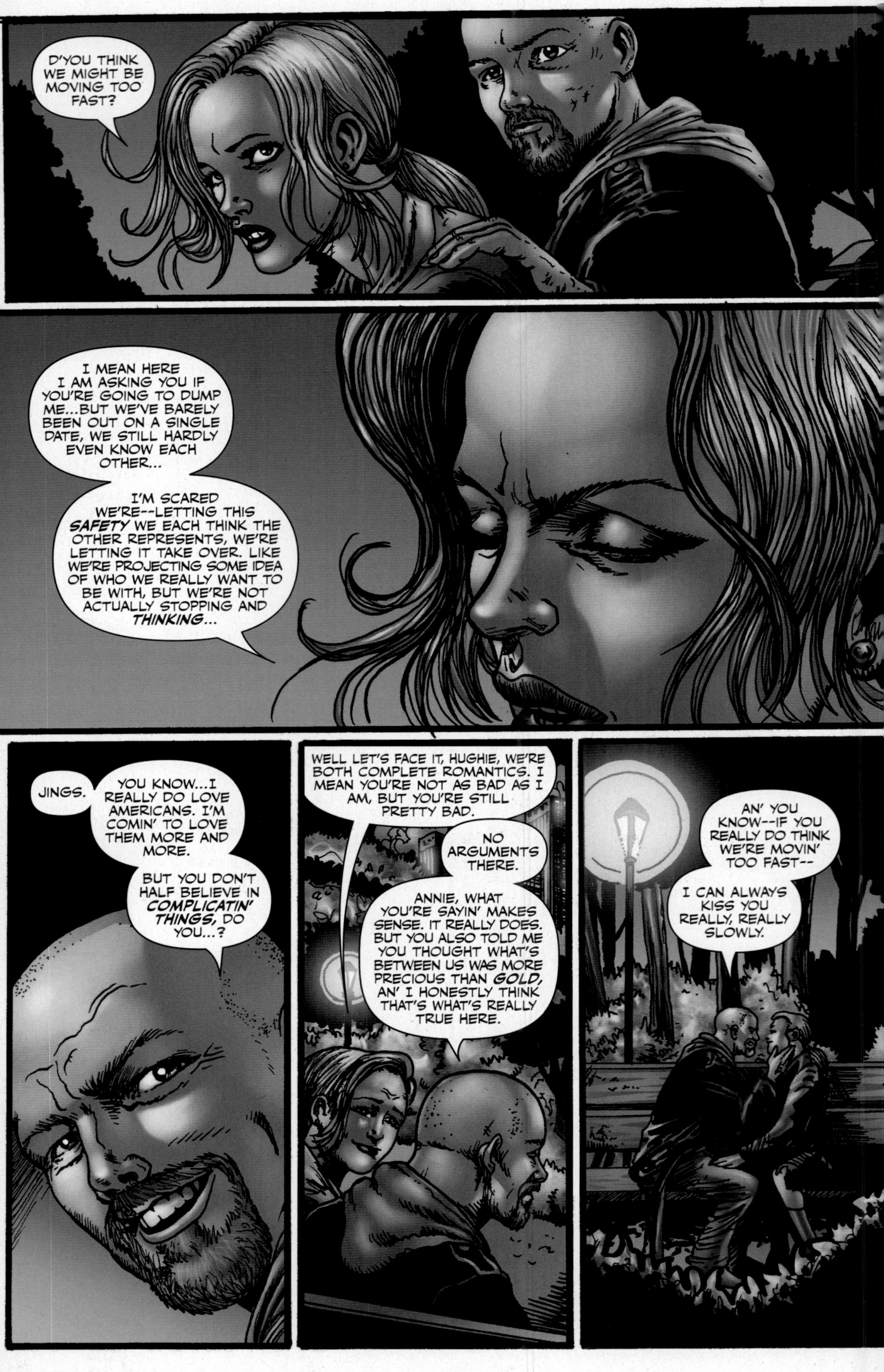
D'YOU THINK WE MIGHT BE MOVING TOO FAST?
I MEAN HERE I AM ASKING YOU IF YOU'RE GOING TO DUMP ME...BUT WE'VE BARELY BEEN OUT ON A SINGLE DATE, WE STILL HARDLY EVEN KNOW EACH OTHER...
I'M SCARED WE'RE--LETTING THIS *SAFETY* WE EACH THINK THE OTHER REPRESENTS, WE'RE LETTING IT TAKE OVER. LIKE WE'RE PROJECTING SOME IDEA OF WHO WE REALLY WANT TO BE WITH, BUT WE'RE NOT ACTUALLY STOPPING AND *THINKING*...
JINGS.
YOU KNOW...I REALLY DO LOVE AMERICANS. I'M COMIN' TO LOVE THEM MORE AND MORE.
BUT YOU DON'T HALF BELIEVE IN *COMPLICATIN' THINGS,* DO YOU...?
WELL LET'S FACE IT, HUGHIE, WE'RE BOTH COMPLETE ROMANTICS. I MEAN YOU'RE NOT AS BAD AS I AM, BUT YOU'RE STILL PRETTY BAD.
NO ARGUMENTS THERE.
ANNIE, WHAT YOU'RE SAYIN' MAKES SENSE. IT REALLY DOES. BUT YOU ALSO TOLD ME YOU THOUGHT WHAT'S BETWEEN US WAS MORE PRECIOUS THAN *GOLD,* AN' I HONESTLY THINK THAT'S WHAT'S REALLY TRUE HERE.
AN' YOU KNOW--IF YOU REALLY DO THINK WE'RE MOVIN' TOO FAST--
I CAN ALWAYS KISS YOU REALLY, REALLY SLOWLY.

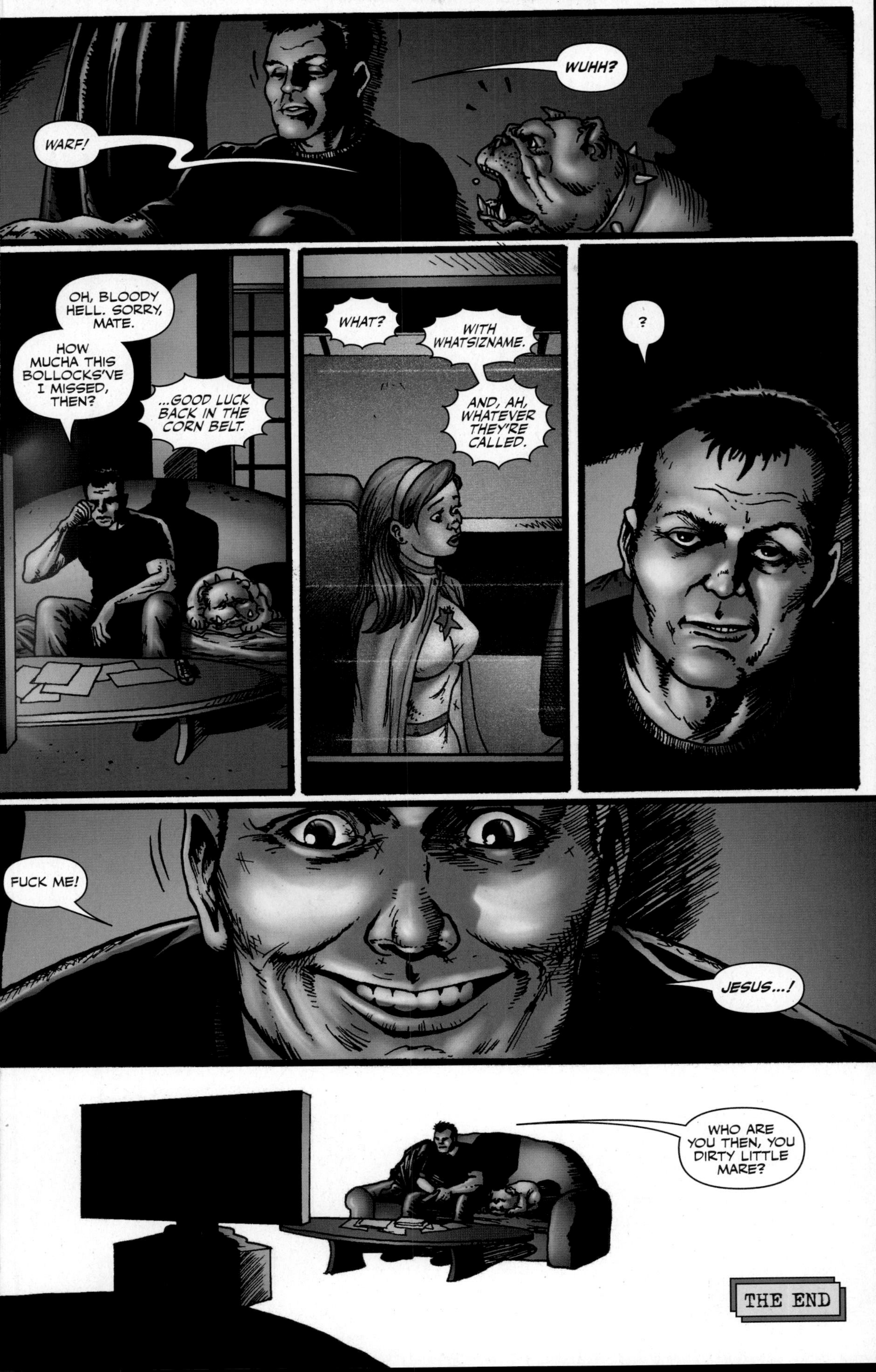
WUHH?
WARF!
OH, BLOODY HELL. SORRY, MATE.
HOW MUCHA THIS BOLLOCKS'VE I MISSED, THEN?
...GOOD LUCK BACK IN THE CORN BELT.
WHAT?
WITH WHATSIZNAME.
AND, AH, WHATEVER THEY'RE CALLED.
?
FUCK ME!
JESUS...!
WHO ARE YOU THEN, YOU DIRTY LITTLE MARE?
THE END

#23 cover
by Darick Robertson
and Tony Aviña

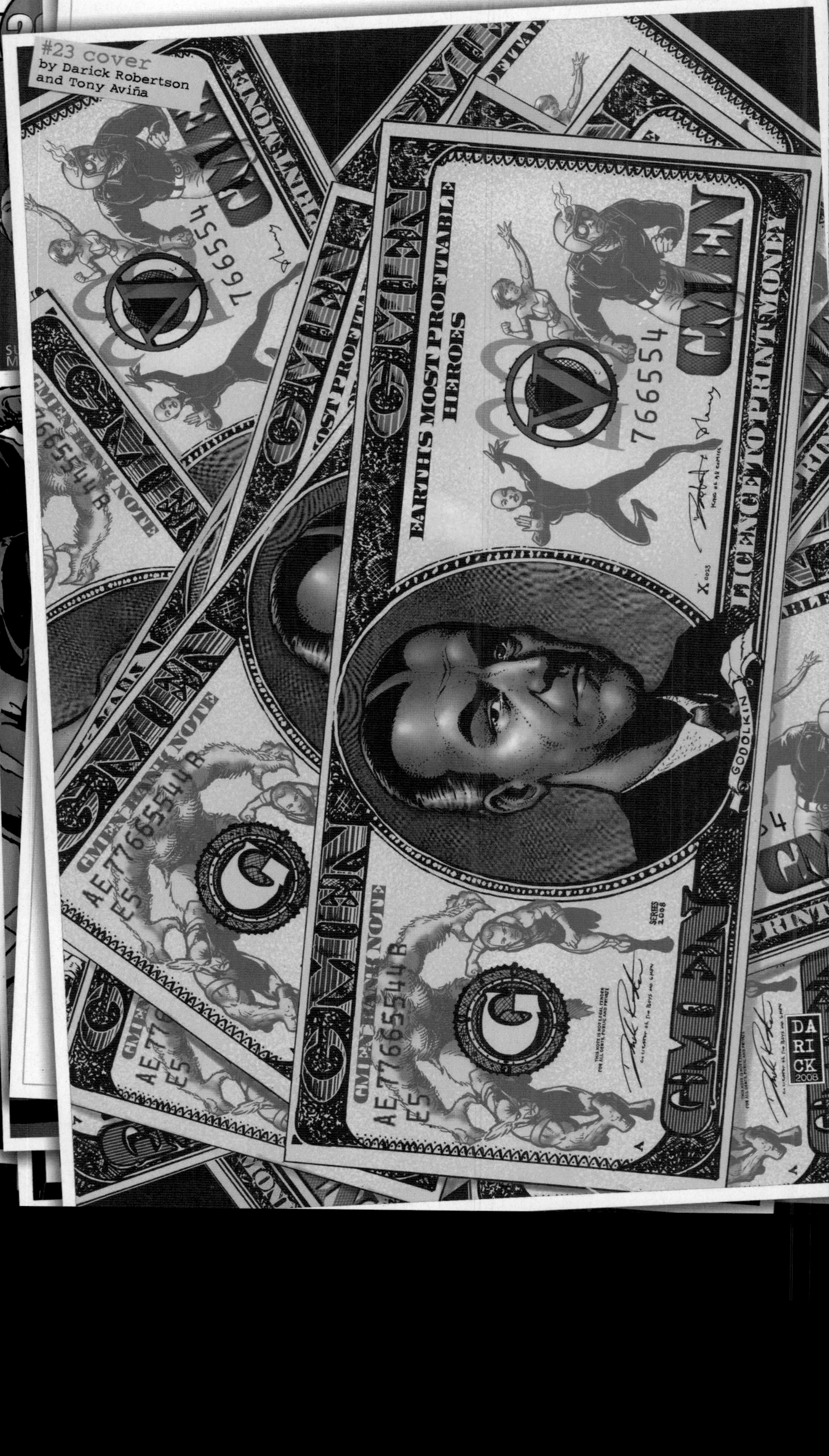
EARTH'S MOST PROFITABLE HEROES
LICENCE TO PRINT MONEY
766554
GMEN BANK NOTE
AE 77665544 B
GODOLKIN
SERIES 2008
DARICK 2008

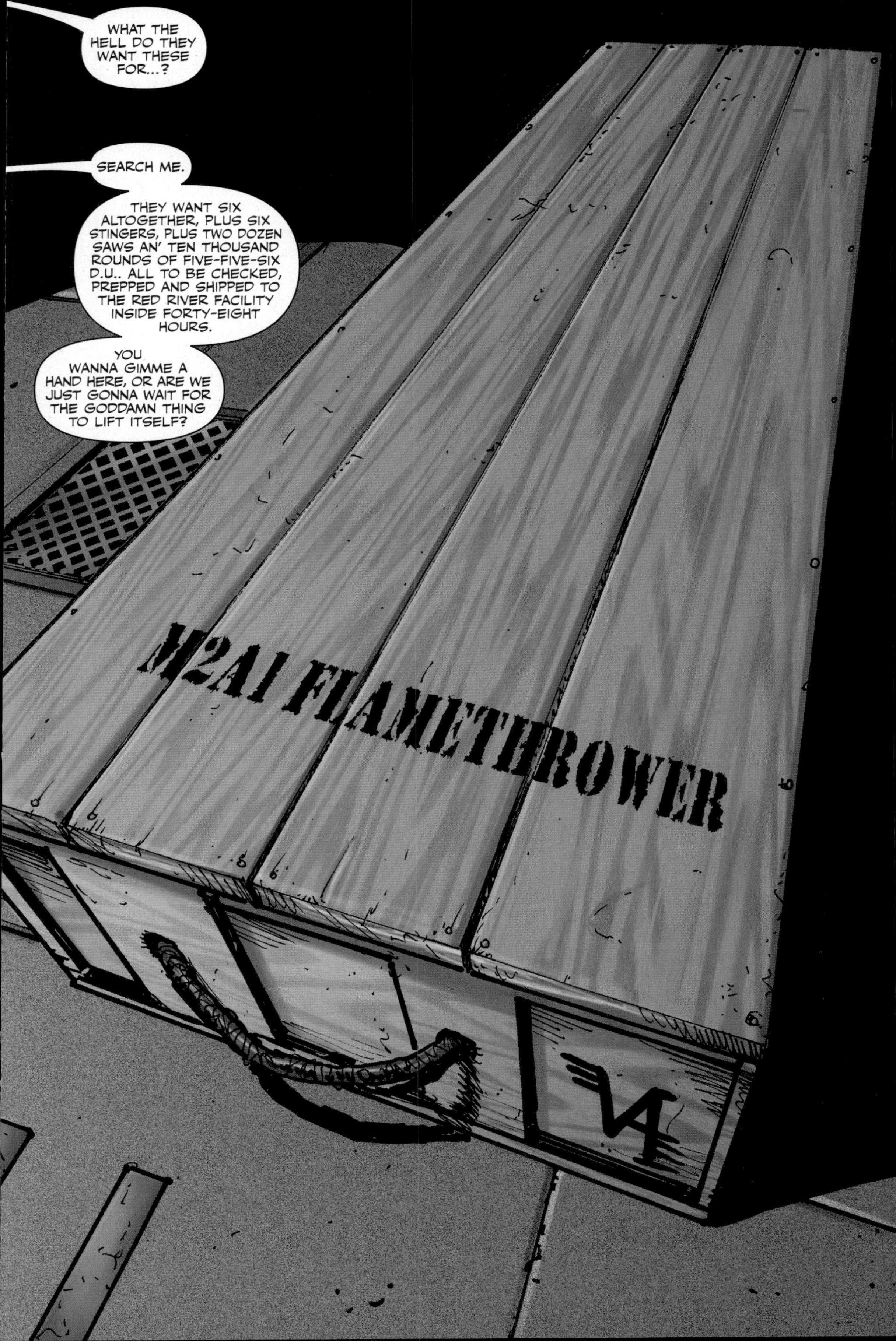
WHAT THE HELL DO THEY WANT THESE FOR...?
SEARCH ME.
THEY WANT SIX ALTOGETHER, PLUS SIX STINGERS, PLUS TWO DOZEN SAWS AN' TEN THOUSAND ROUNDS OF FIVE-FIVE-SIX D.U.. ALL TO BE CHECKED, PREPPED AND SHIPPED TO THE RED RIVER FACILITY INSIDE FORTY-EIGHT HOURS.
YOU WANNA GIMME A HAND HERE, OR ARE WE JUST GONNA WAIT FOR THE GODDAMN THING TO LIFT ITSELF?
M2A1 FLAMETHROWER

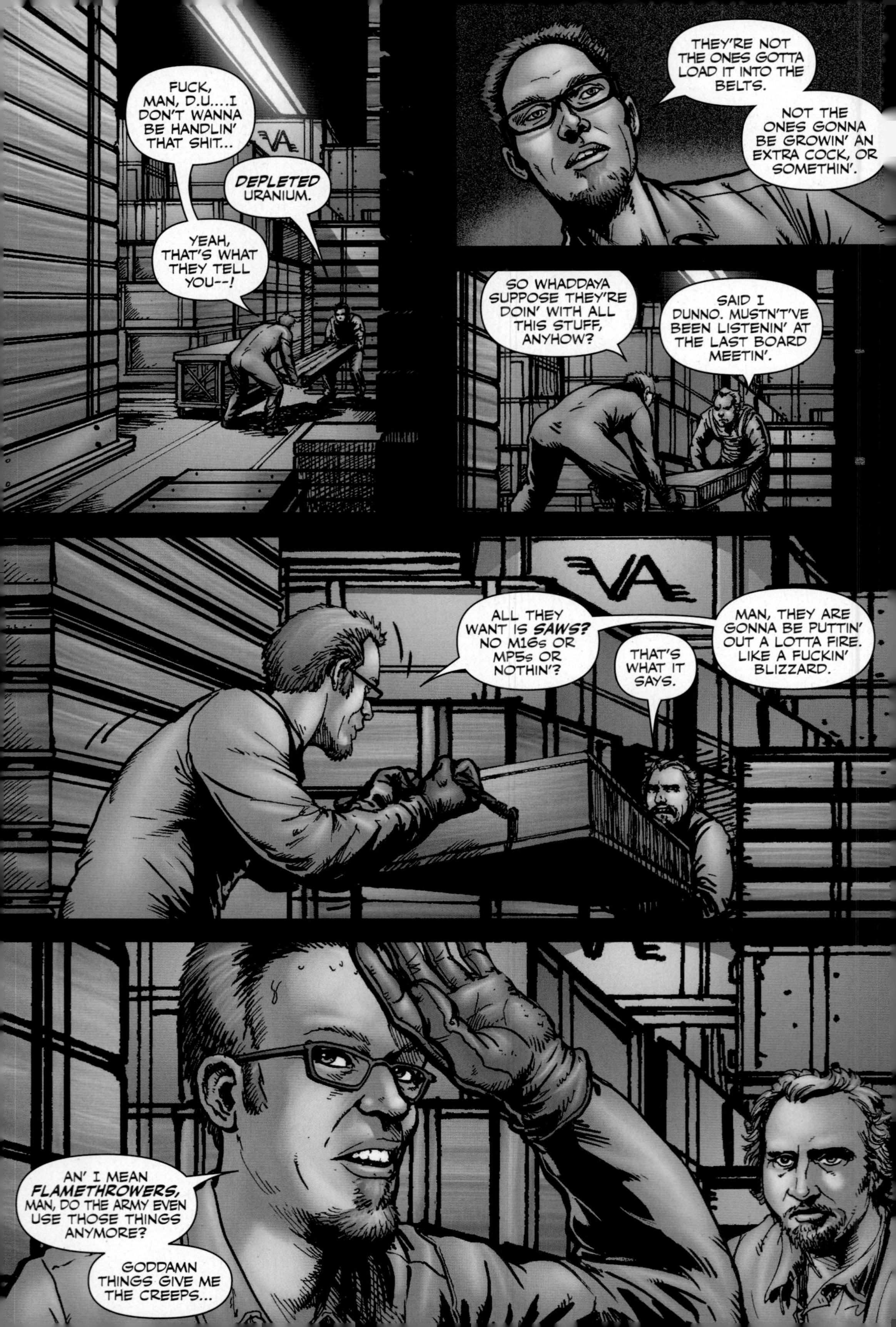

FUCK, MAN, D.U....I DON'T WANNA BE HANDLIN' THAT SHIT...
DEPLETED URANIUM.
YEAH, THAT'S WHAT THEY TELL YOU--!
THEY'RE NOT THE ONES GOTTA LOAD IT INTO THE BELTS.
NOT THE ONES GONNA BE GROWIN' AN EXTRA COCK, OR SOMETHIN'.
SO WHADDAYA SUPPOSE THEY'RE DOIN' WITH ALL THIS STUFF, ANYHOW?
SAID I DUNNO. MUSTN'T'VE BEEN LISTENIN' AT THE LAST BOARD MEETIN'.
VA
ALL THEY WANT IS SAWS? NO M16s OR MP5s OR NOTHIN'?
THAT'S WHAT IT SAYS.
MAN, THEY ARE GONNA BE PUTTIN' OUT A LOTTA FIRE. LIKE A FUCKIN' BLIZZARD.
AN' I MEAN FLAMETHROWERS, MAN, DO THE ARMY EVEN USE THOSE THINGS ANYMORE?
GODDAMN THINGS GIVE ME THE CREEPS...

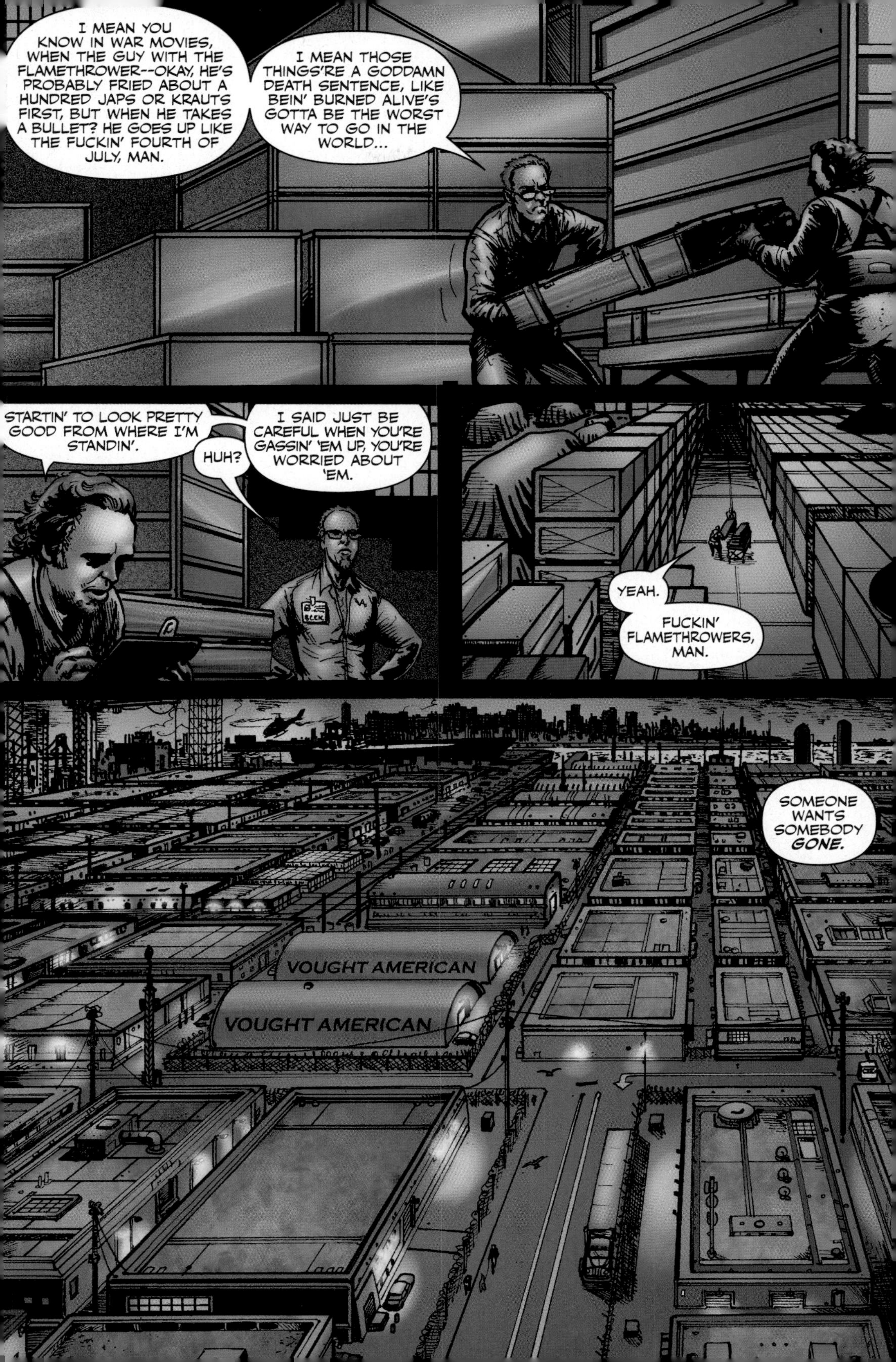
I MEAN YOU KNOW IN WAR MOVIES, WHEN THE GUY WITH THE FLAMETHROWER--OKAY, HE'S PROBABLY FRIED ABOUT A HUNDRED JAPS OR KRAUTS FIRST, BUT WHEN HE TAKES A BULLET? HE GOES UP LIKE THE FUCKIN' FOURTH OF JULY, MAN.
I MEAN THOSE THINGS'RE A GODDAMN DEATH SENTENCE, LIKE BEIN' BURNED ALIVE'S GOTTA BE THE WORST WAY TO GO IN THE WORLD...
STARTIN' TO LOOK PRETTY GOOD FROM WHERE I'M STANDIN'.
HUH?
I SAID JUST BE CAREFUL WHEN YOU'RE GASSIN' 'EM UP, YOU'RE WORRIED ABOUT 'EM.
YEAH.
FUCKIN' FLAMETHROWERS, MAN.
VOUGHT AMERICAN
VOUGHT AMERICAN
SOMEONE WANTS SOMEBODY *GONE.*

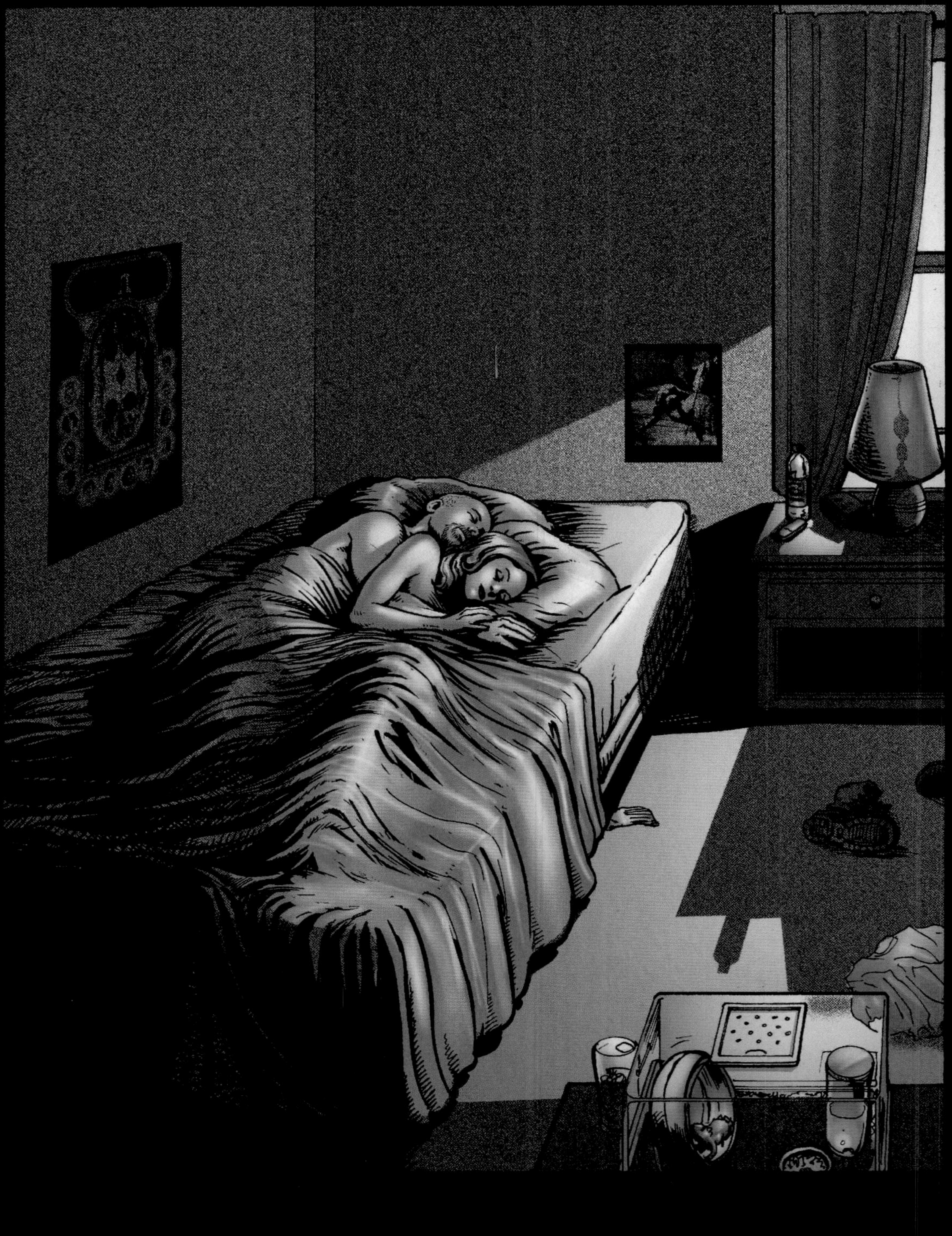

WE GOTTA GO NOW

part one

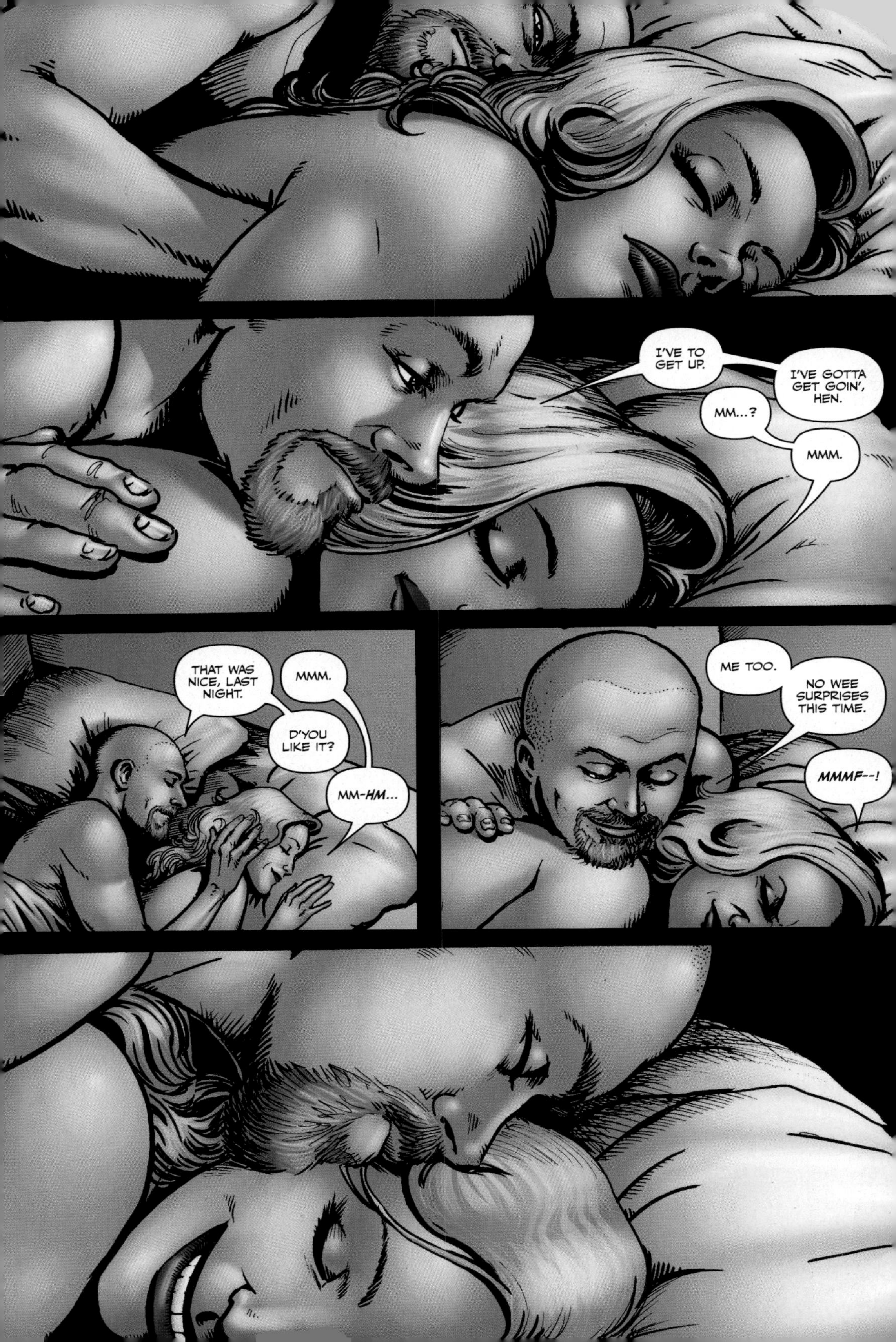
I'VE TO GET UP.
I'VE GOTTA GET GOIN', HEN.
MM...?
MMM.
THAT WAS NICE, LAST NIGHT.
MMM.
D'YOU LIKE IT?
MM-*HM*...
ME TOO.
NO WEE SURPRISES THIS TIME.
MMMF--!

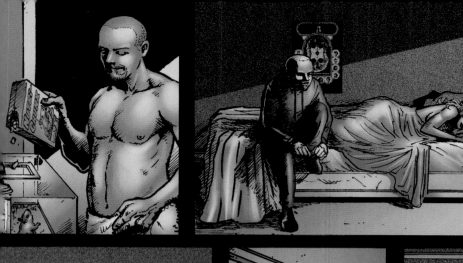

AW, NO...!

WHO IS IT'S WANKIN' UNDER MY DOOR?

AN' WHY IS THERE ALWAYS BLOOD IN IT?

MORNIN', MISTER POTAMUS...

UH.

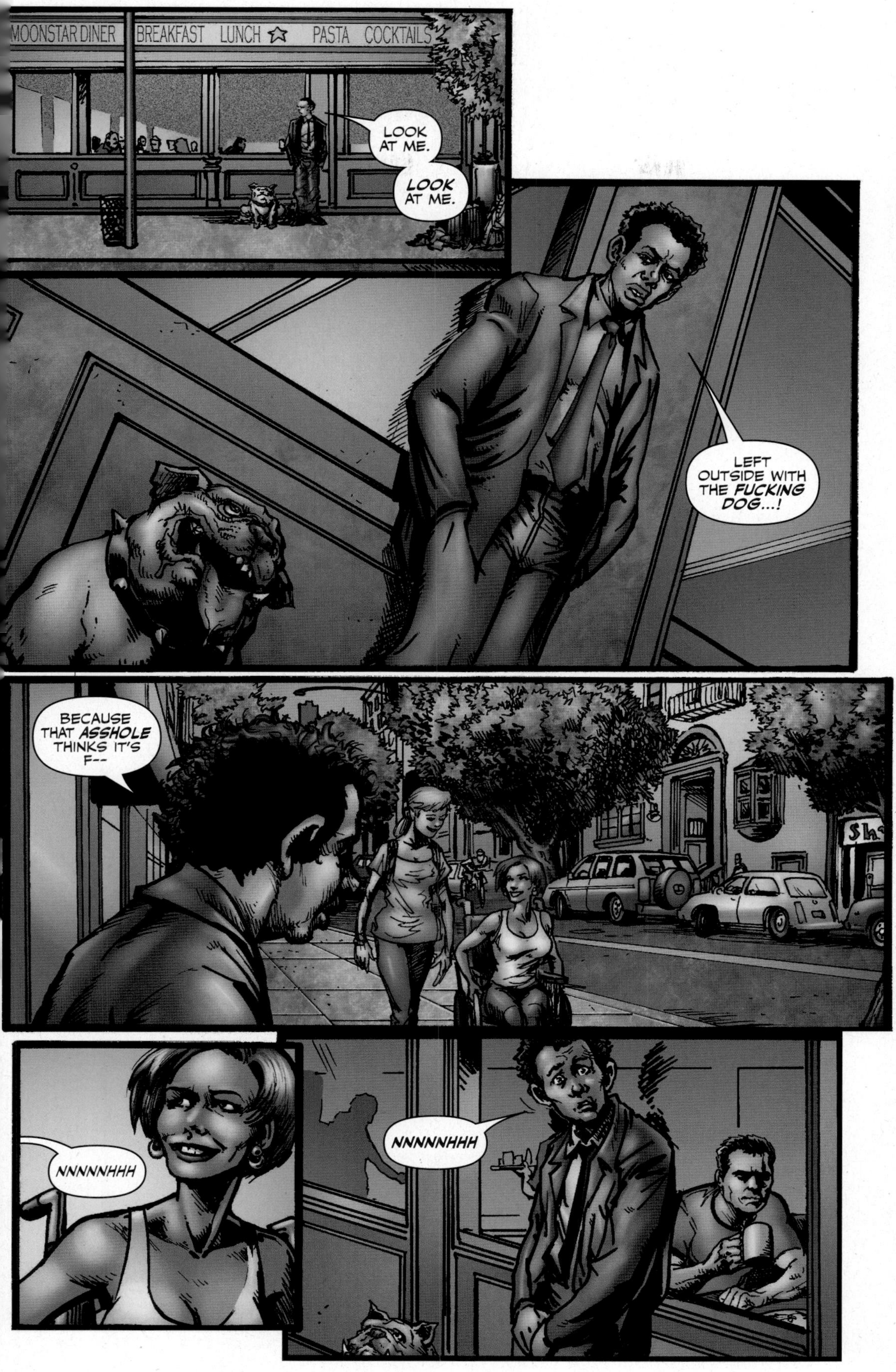
MOONSTAR DINER BREAKFAST LUNCH PASTA COCKTAILS
LOOK AT ME.
LOOK AT ME.
LEFT OUTSIDE WITH THE *FUCKING DOG*...!
BECAUSE THAT *ASSHOLE* THINKS IT'S F--
NNNNNHHH
NNNNNHHH

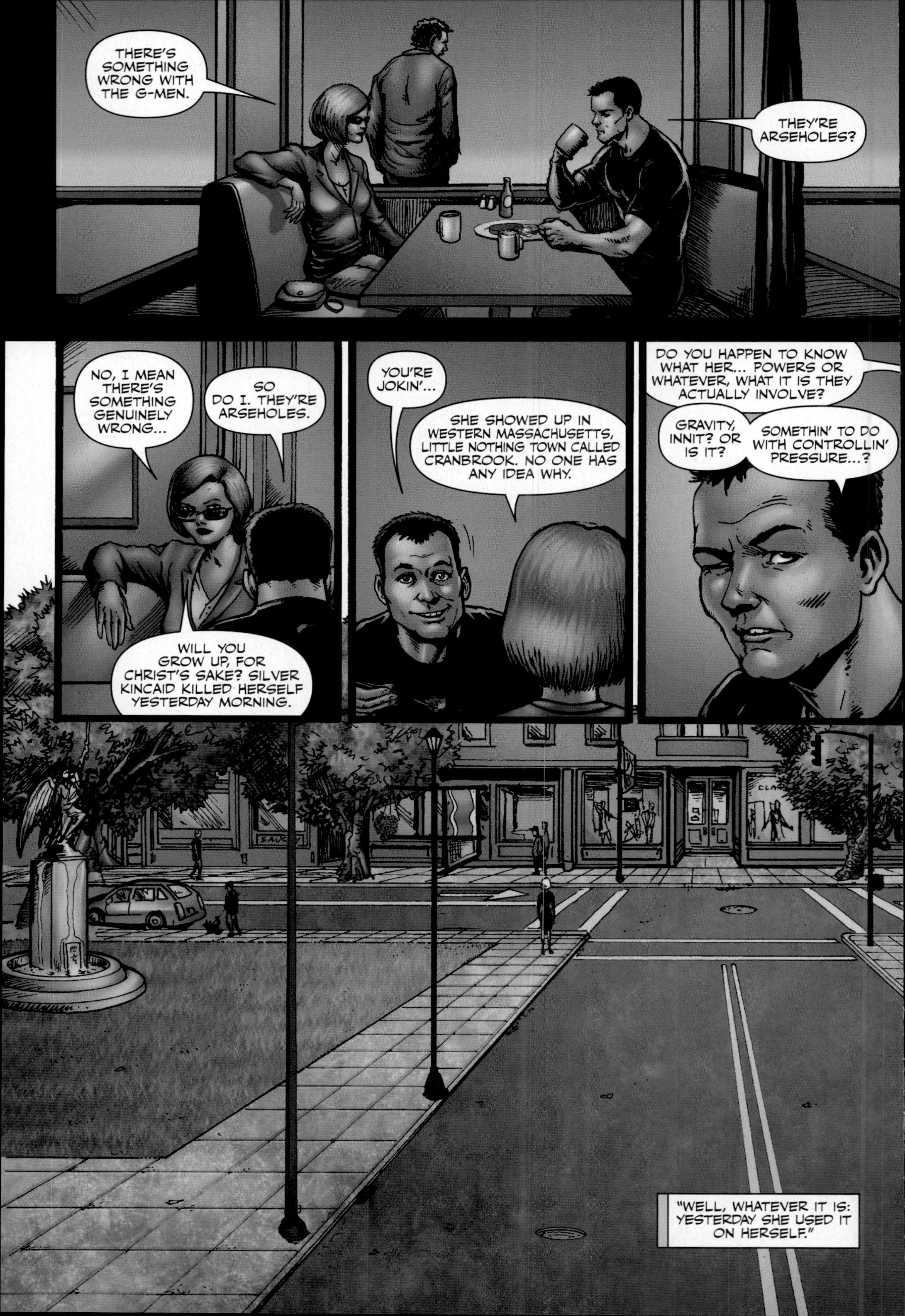

THERE'S SOMETHING WRONG WITH THE G-MEN.
THEY'RE ARSEHOLES?
NO, I MEAN THERE'S SOMETHING GENUINELY WRONG...
SO DO I. THEY'RE ARSEHOLES.
WILL YOU GROW UP, FOR CHRIST'S SAKE? SILVER KINCAID KILLED HERSELF YESTERDAY MORNING.
YOU'RE JOKIN'...
SHE SHOWED UP IN WESTERN MASSACHUSETTS, LITTLE NOTHING TOWN CALLED CRANBROOK. NO ONE HAS ANY IDEA WHY.
DO YOU HAPPEN TO KNOW WHAT HER... POWERS OR WHATEVER, WHAT IT IS THEY ACTUALLY INVOLVE?
GRAVITY, INNIT? OR IS IT?
SOMETHIN' TO DO WITH CONTROLLIN' PRESSURE...?
"WELL, WHATEVER IT IS: YESTERDAY SHE USED IT ON HERSELF."

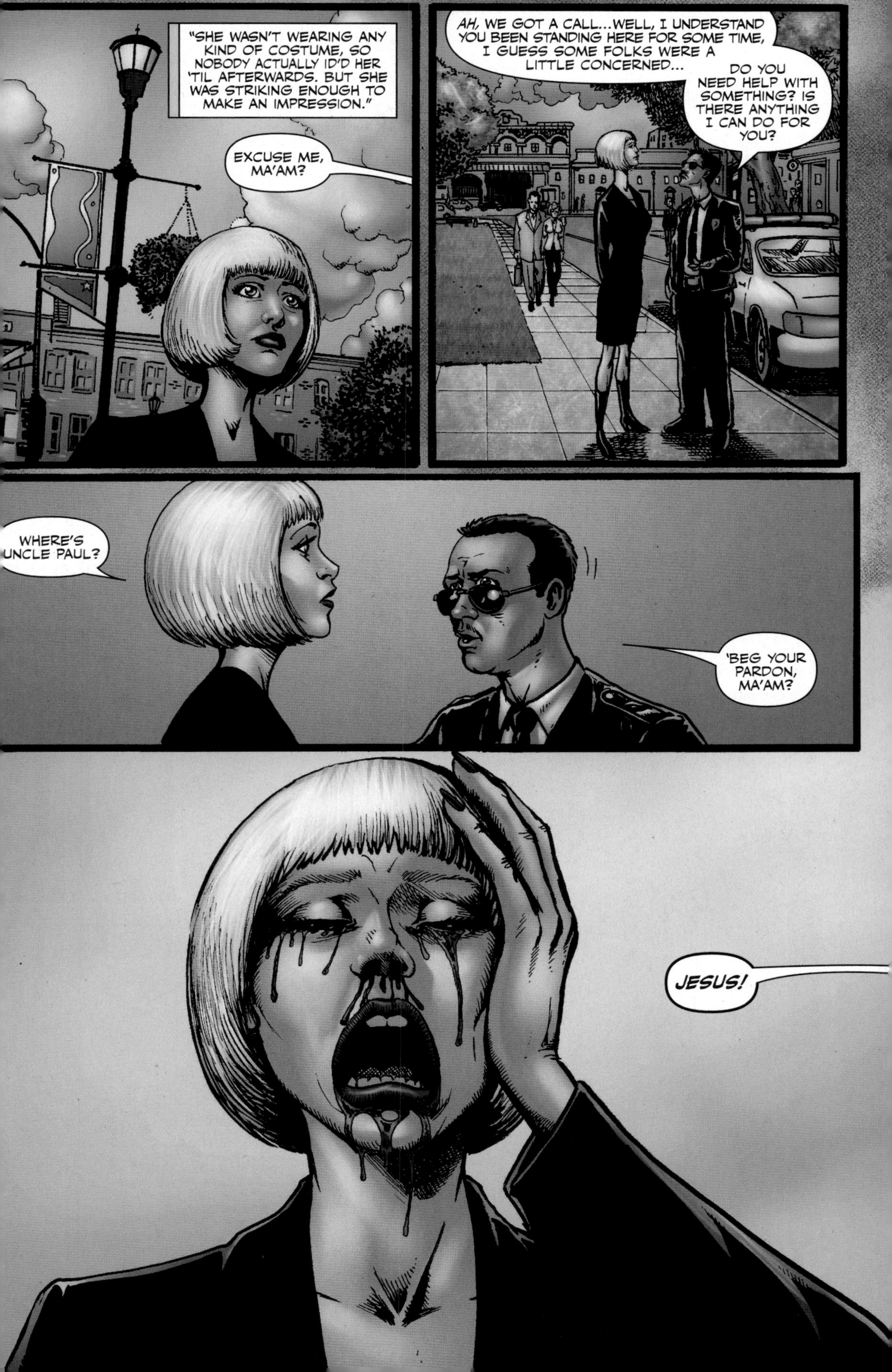
"SHE WASN'T WEARING ANY KIND OF COSTUME, SO NOBODY ACTUALLY ID'D HER 'TIL AFTERWARDS. BUT SHE WAS STRIKING ENOUGH TO MAKE AN IMPRESSION."
EXCUSE ME, MA'AM?
AH, WE GOT A CALL...WELL, I UNDERSTAND YOU BEEN STANDING HERE FOR SOME TIME, I GUESS SOME FOLKS WERE A LITTLE CONCERNED...
DO YOU NEED HELP WITH SOMETHING? IS THERE ANYTHING I CAN DO FOR YOU?
WHERE'S UNCLE PAUL?
'BEG YOUR PARDON, MA'AM?
JESUS!

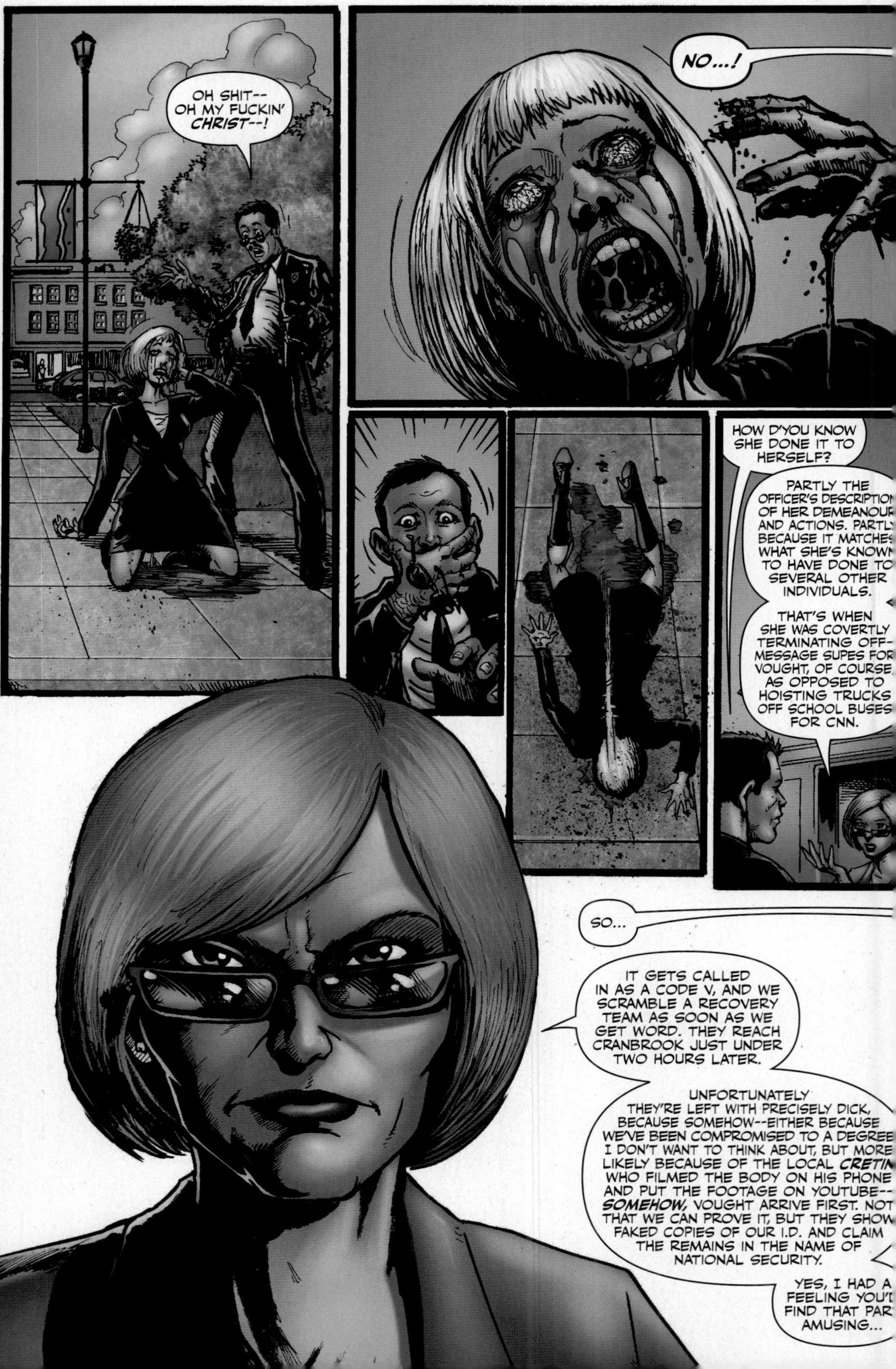

OH SHIT--
OH MY FUCKIN' *CHRIST*--!
NO...!
HOW D'YOU KNOW SHE DONE IT TO HERSELF?
PARTLY THE OFFICER'S DESCRIPTION OF HER DEMEANOUR AND ACTIONS. PARTLY BECAUSE IT MATCHES WHAT SHE'S KNOWN TO HAVE DONE TO SEVERAL OTHER INDIVIDUALS.
THAT'S WHEN SHE WAS COVERTLY TERMINATING OFF-MESSAGE SUPES FOR VOUGHT, OF COURSE, AS OPPOSED TO HOISTING TRUCKS OFF SCHOOL BUSES FOR CNN.
SO...
IT GETS CALLED IN AS A CODE V, AND WE SCRAMBLE A RECOVERY TEAM AS SOON AS WE GET WORD. THEY REACH CRANBROOK JUST UNDER TWO HOURS LATER.
UNFORTUNATELY THEY'RE LEFT WITH PRECISELY DICK, BECAUSE SOMEHOW--EITHER BECAUSE WE'VE BEEN COMPROMISED TO A DEGREE I DON'T WANT TO THINK ABOUT, BUT MORE LIKELY BECAUSE OF THE LOCAL *CRETIN* WHO FILMED THE BODY ON HIS PHONE AND PUT THE FOOTAGE ON YOUTUBE-- *SOMEHOW,* VOUGHT ARRIVE FIRST. NOT THAT WE CAN PROVE IT, BUT THEY SHOW FAKED COPIES OF OUR I.D. AND CLAIM THE REMAINS IN THE NAME OF NATIONAL SECURITY.
YES, I HAD A FEELING YOU'D FIND THAT PART AMUSING...

CHEEKY FUCKERS.

ALL RIGHT, YOU SAID THERE WAS SOMETHIN' WRONG WITH THE G-MEN. THAT'S JUST ONE OF 'EM.

ONE OF THE ORIGINALS. A LEADING MEMBER OF THE FIRST TEAM-- THE ACTUAL G-MEN, NOT G-FORCE OR THE G-BRITS OR ANY OF THE OTHERS.

AND SHE PUBLICLY TOOK HER OWN LIFE.

I KNOW THESE TEAMS GENERATE THE MOST REVENUE, BUT THEY ALSO CAUSE THE MOST TROUBLE. ALWAYS IN THE SPOTLIGHT. ALWAYS FOR THE WRONG REASONS.

HOW OFTEN HAVE THEY TURNED ON EACH OTHER, CIVILIAN EYEWITNESSES BE DAMNED? HOW MANY HAVE VOUGHT TAKEN OUT OF THE PICTURE--SIX OR SEVEN THAT WE KNOW OF? WHY IS THAT RIDICULOUS FEUD OVER *Z-KOOL* ALLOWED TO GO ON BETWEEN G-STYLE AND G-COAST?

I WANT TO KNOW WHAT IT *IS* ABOUT THEM...!

YOU DON'T THINK YOU'VE ANSWERED YOUR OWN QUESTION?

A BAD BOY IMAGE IS ONE THING. SUICIDE'S SOMETHING ELSE ENTIRELY.

I THINK IT'S TIME FOR A SERIOUS LOOK AT VOUGHT'S NUMBER ONE MONEYMAKER, AND I THINK SILVER KINCAID IS THE WAY IN...

WELL AS IT HAPPENS-- *MRMFF*--

I'VE HAD THE NEW LAD READIN' UP ON THE G-TWATS RECENTLY. PARTA HIS TOUR 'ROUND THE FOUR-COLOR FUCKWITS.

THEN YOU CAN GO STRAIGHT TO WORK.

THOUGHT MANAGEMENT WAS THE NAME A' THE GAME THESE DAYS...?

SO MANAGE.

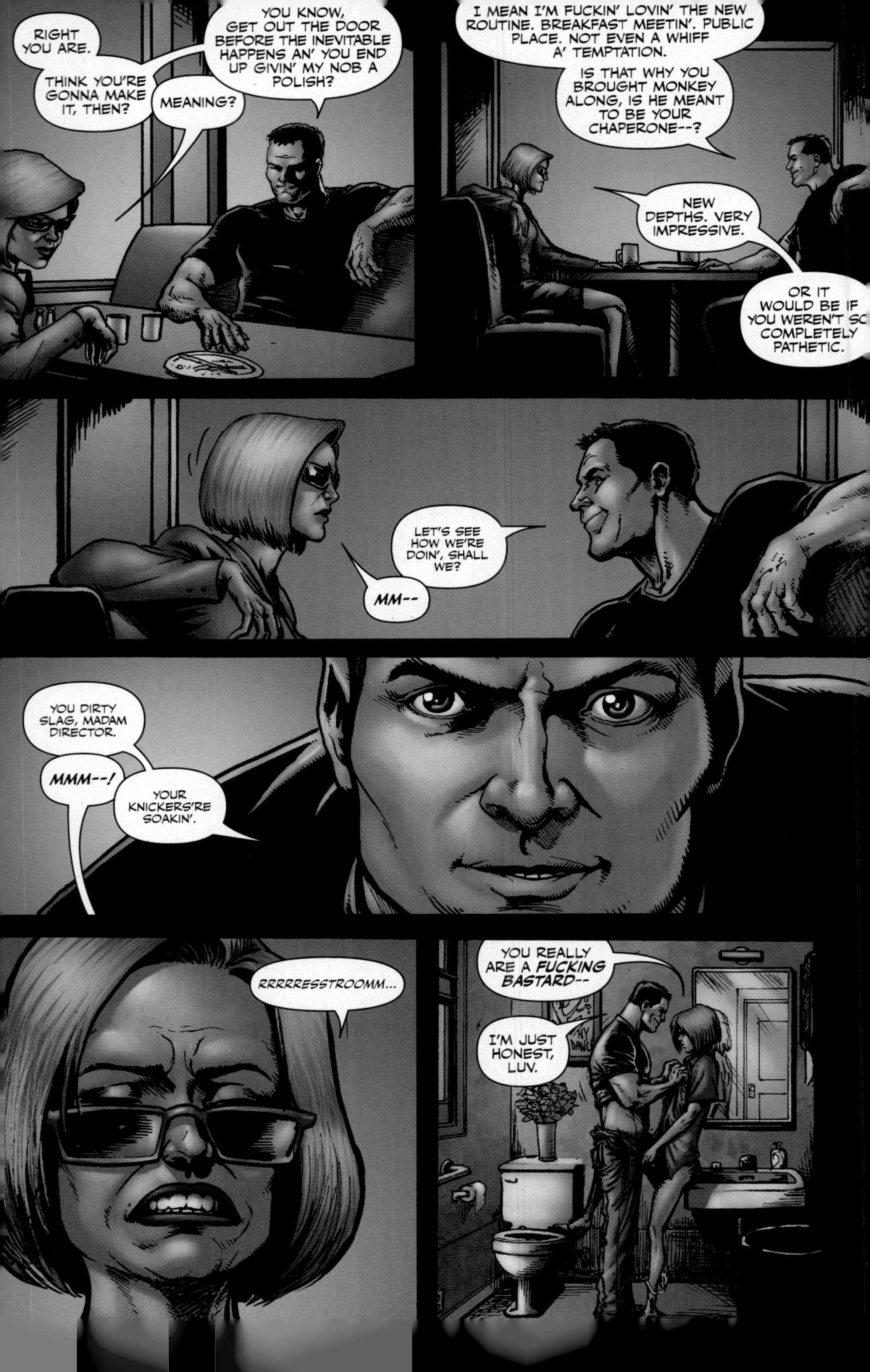

RIGHT YOU ARE.
THINK YOU'RE GONNA MAKE IT, THEN?
MEANING?
YOU KNOW, GET OUT THE DOOR BEFORE THE INEVITABLE HAPPENS AN' YOU END UP GIVIN' MY NOB A POLISH?
I MEAN I'M FUCKIN' LOVIN' THE NEW ROUTINE. BREAKFAST MEETIN'. PUBLIC PLACE. NOT EVEN A WHIFF A' TEMPTATION.
IS THAT WHY YOU BROUGHT MONKEY ALONG, IS HE MEANT TO BE YOUR CHAPERONE--?
NEW DEPTHS. VERY IMPRESSIVE.
OR IT WOULD BE IF YOU WEREN'T SO COMPLETELY PATHETIC.
LET'S SEE HOW WE'RE DOIN', SHALL WE?
MM--
YOU DIRTY SLAG, MADAM DIRECTOR.
MMM--!
YOUR KNICKERS'RE SOAKIN'.
RRRRRESSTROOMM...
YOU REALLY ARE A *FUCKING BASTARD*--
I'M JUST HONEST, LUV.

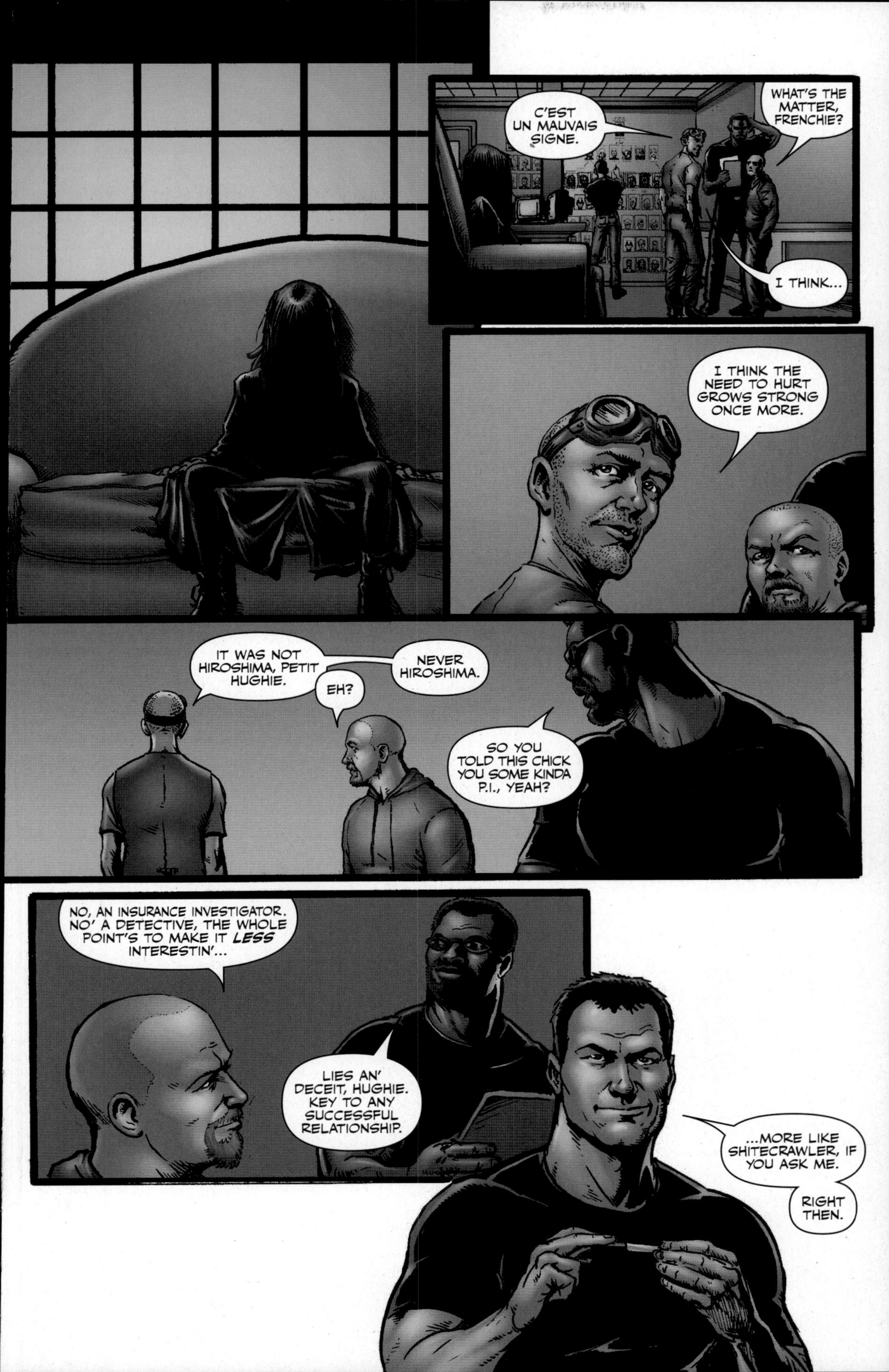
C'EST UN MAUVAIS SIGNE.
WHAT'S THE MATTER, FRENCHIE?
I THINK...
I THINK THE NEED TO HURT GROWS STRONG ONCE MORE.
IT WAS NOT HIROSHIMA, PETIT HUGHIE.
NEVER HIROSHIMA.
EH?
SO YOU TOLD THIS CHICK YOU SOME KINDA P.I., YEAH?
NO, AN INSURANCE INVESTIGATOR. NO' A DETECTIVE, THE WHOLE POINT'S TO MAKE IT *LESS* INTERESTIN'...
LIES AN' DECEIT, HUGHIE. KEY TO ANY SUCCESSFUL RELATIONSHIP.
...MORE LIKE SHITECRAWLER, IF YOU ASK ME.
RIGHT THEN.

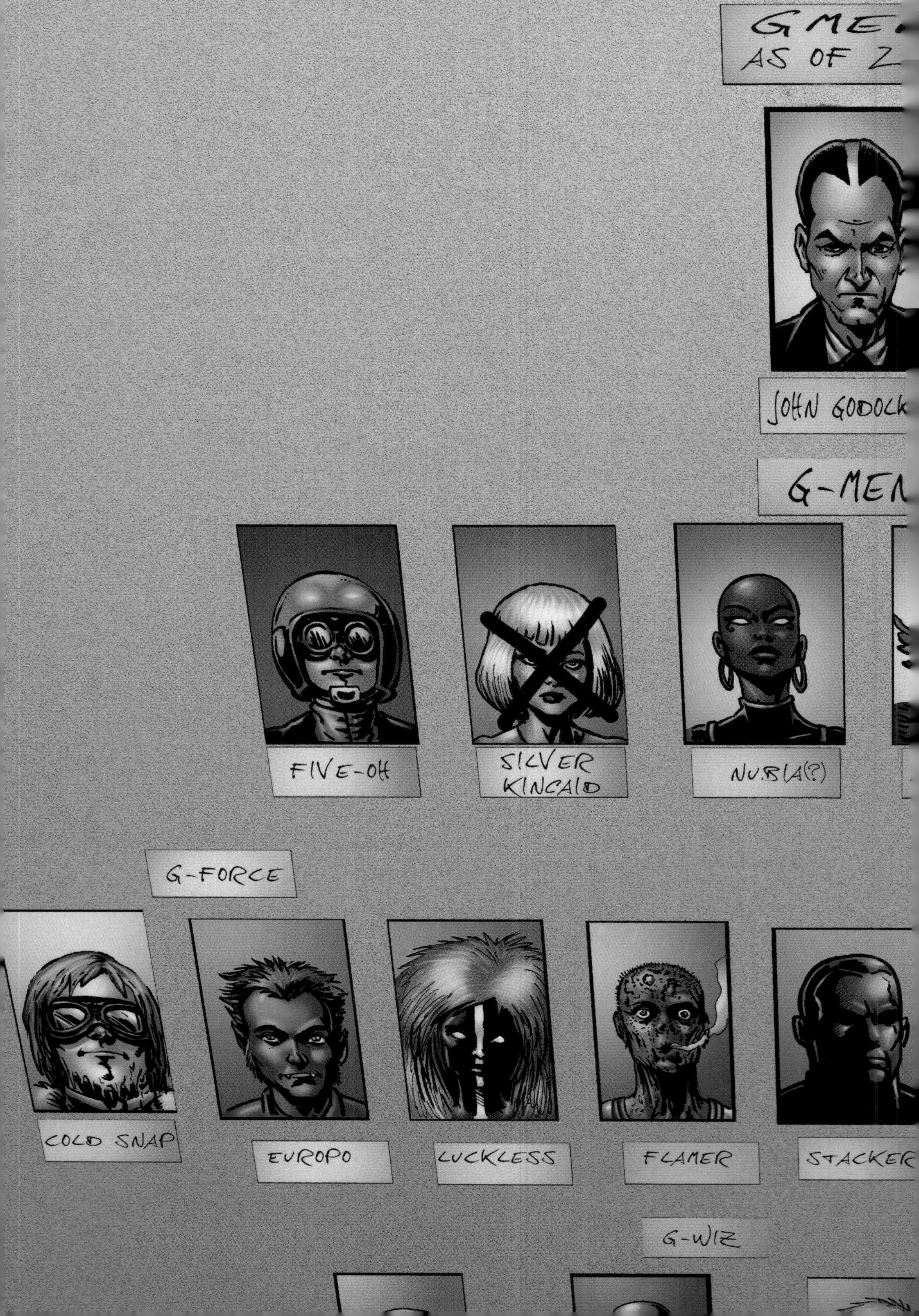

FIVE-OH
SILVER KINCAID
NUBIA(?)
G-FORCE
COLD SNAP
EUROPO
LUCKLESS
FLAMER
STACKER
G-WIZ

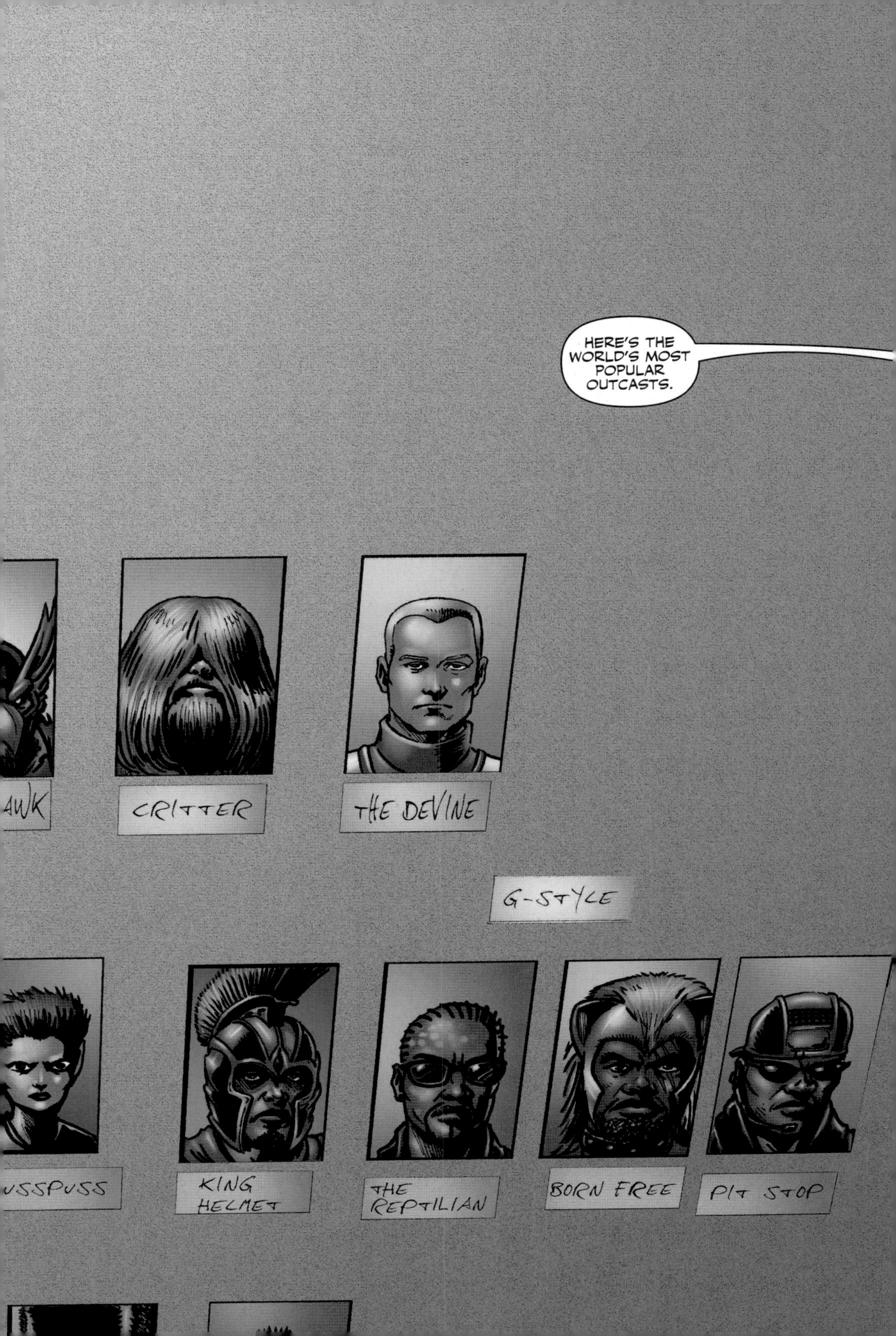

HERE'S THE WORLD'S MOST POPULAR OUTCASTS.
AWK
CRITTER
THE DEVINE
G-STYLE
USSPUSS
KING HELMET
THE REPTILIAN
BORN FREE
PIT STOP

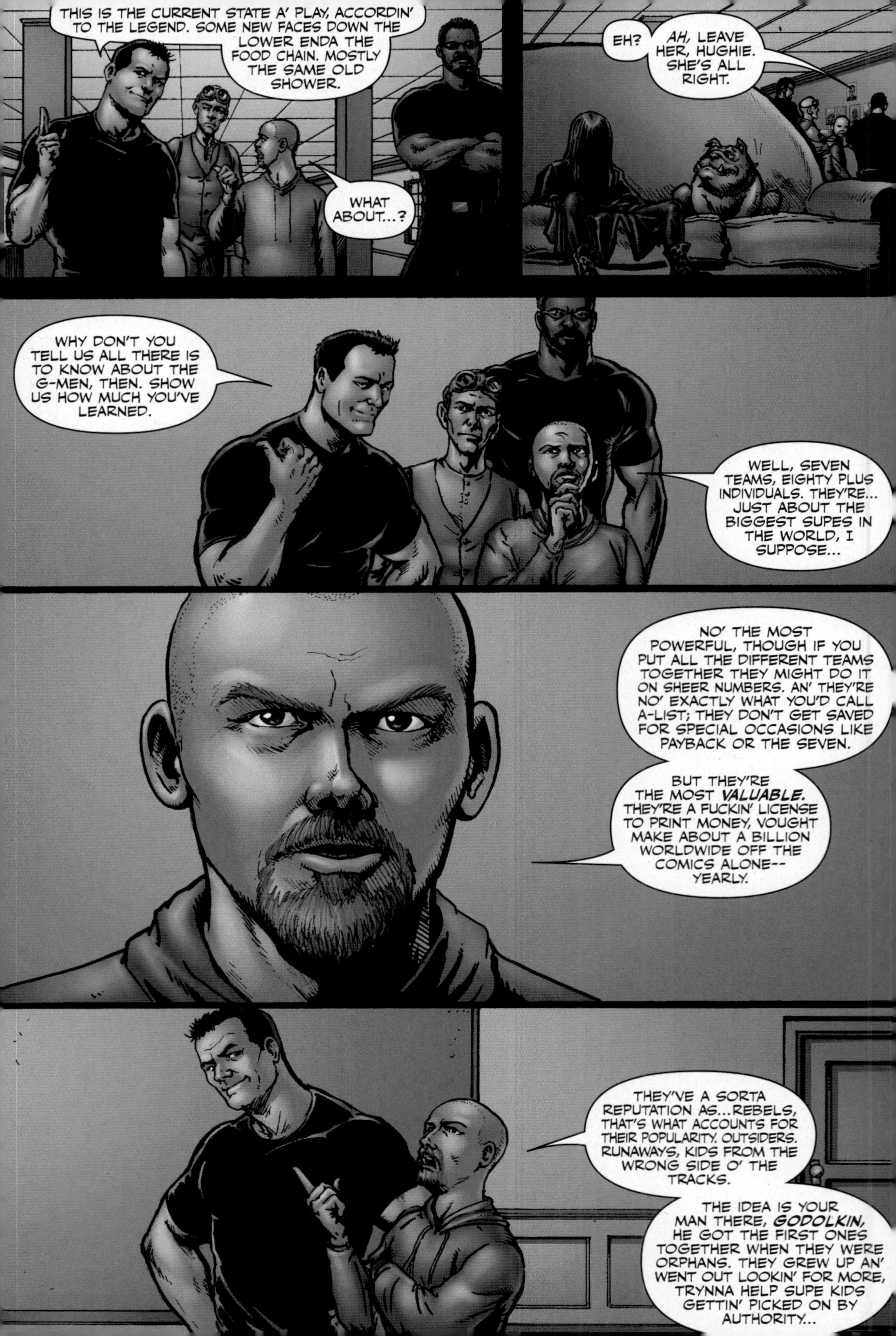

THIS IS THE CURRENT STATE A' PLAY, ACCORDIN' TO THE LEGEND. SOME NEW FACES DOWN THE LOWER ENDA THE FOOD CHAIN. MOSTLY THE SAME OLD SHOWER.
WHAT ABOUT...?
EH?
AH, LEAVE HER, HUGHIE. SHE'S ALL RIGHT.
WHY DON'T YOU TELL US ALL THERE IS TO KNOW ABOUT THE G-MEN, THEN. SHOW US HOW MUCH YOU'VE LEARNED.
WELL, SEVEN TEAMS, EIGHTY PLUS INDIVIDUALS. THEY'RE... JUST ABOUT THE BIGGEST SUPES IN THE WORLD, I SUPPOSE...
NO' THE MOST POWERFUL, THOUGH IF YOU PUT ALL THE DIFFERENT TEAMS TOGETHER THEY MIGHT DO IT ON SHEER NUMBERS. AN' THEY'RE NO' EXACTLY WHAT YOU'D CALL A-LIST; THEY DON'T GET SAVED FOR SPECIAL OCCASIONS LIKE PAYBACK OR THE SEVEN.
BUT THEY'RE THE MOST VALUABLE. THEY'RE A FUCKIN' LICENSE TO PRINT MONEY, VOUGHT MAKE ABOUT A BILLION WORLDWIDE OFF THE COMICS ALONE-- YEARLY.
THEY'VE A SORTA REPUTATION AS...REBELS, THAT'S WHAT ACCOUNTS FOR THEIR POPULARITY. OUTSIDERS. RUNAWAYS, KIDS FROM THE WRONG SIDE O' THE TRACKS.
THE IDEA IS YOUR MAN THERE, GODOLKIN, HE GOT THE FIRST ONES TOGETHER WHEN THEY WERE ORPHANS. THEY GREW UP AN' WENT OUT LOOKIN' FOR MORE, TRYNNA HELP SUPE KIDS GETTIN' PICKED ON BY AUTHORITY...

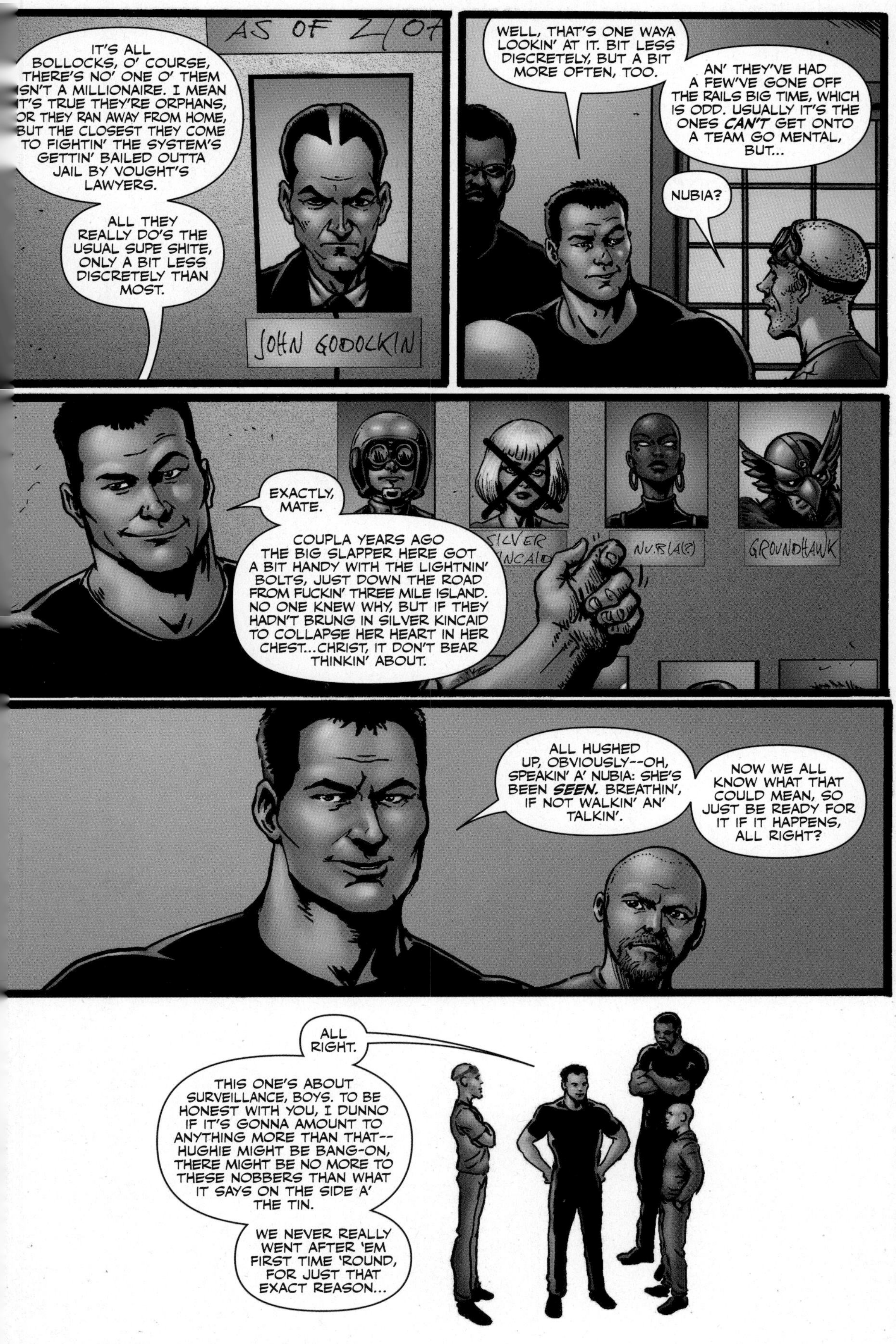
AS OF 2/07
IT'S ALL BOLLOCKS, O' COURSE, THERE'S NO' ONE O' THEM ISN'T A MILLIONAIRE. I MEAN IT'S TRUE THEY'RE ORPHANS, OR THEY RAN AWAY FROM HOME, BUT THE CLOSEST THEY COME TO FIGHTIN' THE SYSTEM'S GETTIN' BAILED OUTTA JAIL BY VOUGHT'S LAWYERS.
ALL THEY REALLY DO'S THE USUAL SUPE SHITE, ONLY A BIT LESS DISCRETELY THAN MOST.
JOHN GODOLKIN
WELL, THAT'S ONE WAYA LOOKIN' AT IT. BIT LESS DISCRETELY, BUT A BIT MORE OFTEN, TOO.
AN' THEY'VE HAD A FEW'VE GONE OFF THE RAILS BIG TIME, WHICH IS ODD. USUALLY IT'S THE ONES CAN'T GET ONTO A TEAM GO MENTAL, BUT...
NUBIA?
EXACTLY, MATE.
COUPLA YEARS AGO THE BIG SLAPPER HERE GOT A BIT HANDY WITH THE LIGHTNIN' BOLTS, JUST DOWN THE ROAD FROM FUCKIN' THREE MILE ISLAND. NO ONE KNEW WHY, BUT IF THEY HADN'T BRUNG IN SILVER KINCAID TO COLLAPSE HER HEART IN HER CHEST...CHRIST, IT DON'T BEAR THINKIN' ABOUT.
SILVER KINCAID
NUBIA(?)
GROUNDHAWK
ALL HUSHED UP, OBVIOUSLY--OH, SPEAKIN' A' NUBIA: SHE'S BEEN SEEN. BREATHIN', IF NOT WALKIN' AN' TALKIN'.
NOW WE ALL KNOW WHAT THAT COULD MEAN, SO JUST BE READY FOR IT IF IT HAPPENS, ALL RIGHT?
ALL RIGHT.
THIS ONE'S ABOUT SURVEILLANCE, BOYS. TO BE HONEST WITH YOU, I DUNNO IF IT'S GONNA AMOUNT TO ANYTHING MORE THAN THAT-- HUGHIE MIGHT BE BANG-ON, THERE MIGHT BE NO MORE TO THESE NOBBERS THAN WHAT IT SAYS ON THE SIDE A' THE TIN.
WE NEVER REALLY WENT AFTER 'EM FIRST TIME 'ROUND, FOR JUST THAT EXACT REASON...

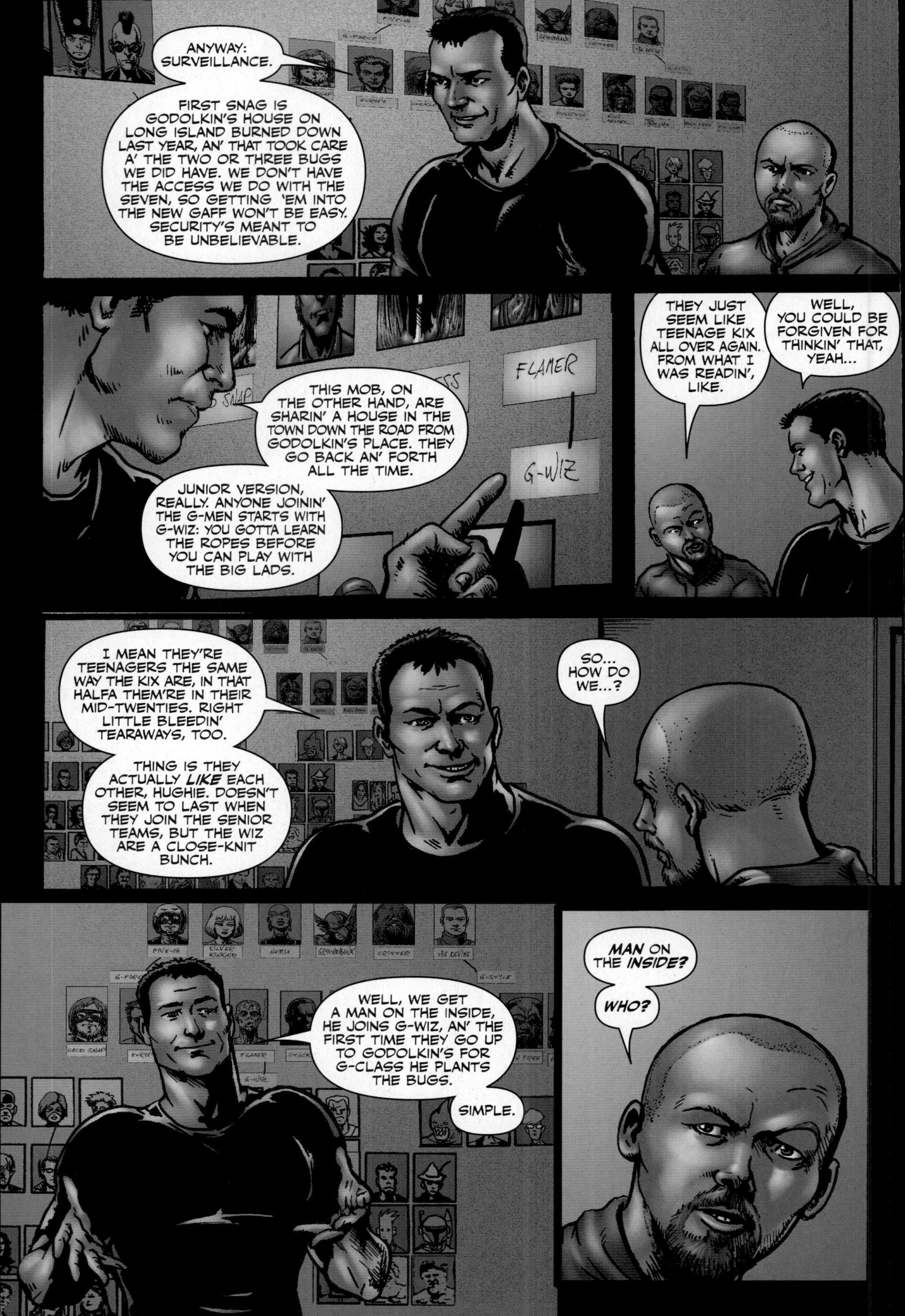

ANYWAY: SURVEILLANCE.
FIRST SNAG IS GODOLKIN'S HOUSE ON LONG ISLAND BURNED DOWN LAST YEAR, AN' THAT TOOK CARE A' THE TWO OR THREE BUGS WE DID HAVE. WE DON'T HAVE THE ACCESS WE DO WITH THE SEVEN, SO GETTING 'EM INTO THE NEW GAFF WON'T BE EASY. SECURITY'S MEANT TO BE UNBELIEVABLE.
FLAMER
G-WIZ
THIS MOB, ON THE OTHER HAND, ARE SHARIN' A HOUSE IN THE TOWN DOWN THE ROAD FROM GODOLKIN'S PLACE. THEY GO BACK AN' FORTH ALL THE TIME.
JUNIOR VERSION, REALLY. ANYONE JOININ' THE G-MEN STARTS WITH G-WIZ: YOU GOTTA LEARN THE ROPES BEFORE YOU CAN PLAY WITH THE BIG LADS.
THEY JUST SEEM LIKE TEENAGE KIX ALL OVER AGAIN. FROM WHAT I WAS READIN', LIKE.
WELL, YOU COULD BE FORGIVEN FOR THINKIN' THAT, YEAH...
I MEAN THEY'RE TEENAGERS THE SAME WAY THE KIX ARE, IN THAT HALFA THEM'RE IN THEIR MID-TWENTIES. RIGHT LITTLE BLEEDIN' TEARAWAYS, TOO.
THING IS THEY ACTUALLY *LIKE* EACH OTHER, HUGHIE. DOESN'T SEEM TO LAST WHEN THEY JOIN THE SENIOR TEAMS, BUT THE WIZ ARE A CLOSE-KNIT BUNCH.
SO... HOW DO WE...?
FIVE-OH
SILVER KINKAID
NUBIA
GROUNDHAWK
CRITTER
THE DEVINE
G-FORCE
G-STYLE
COLD SNAP
FLAMER
G-WIZ
WELL, WE GET A MAN ON THE INSIDE, HE JOINS G-WIZ, AN' THE FIRST TIME THEY GO UP TO GODOLKIN'S FOR G-CLASS HE PLANTS THE BUGS.
SIMPLE.
MAN ON THE *INSIDE?*
WHO?

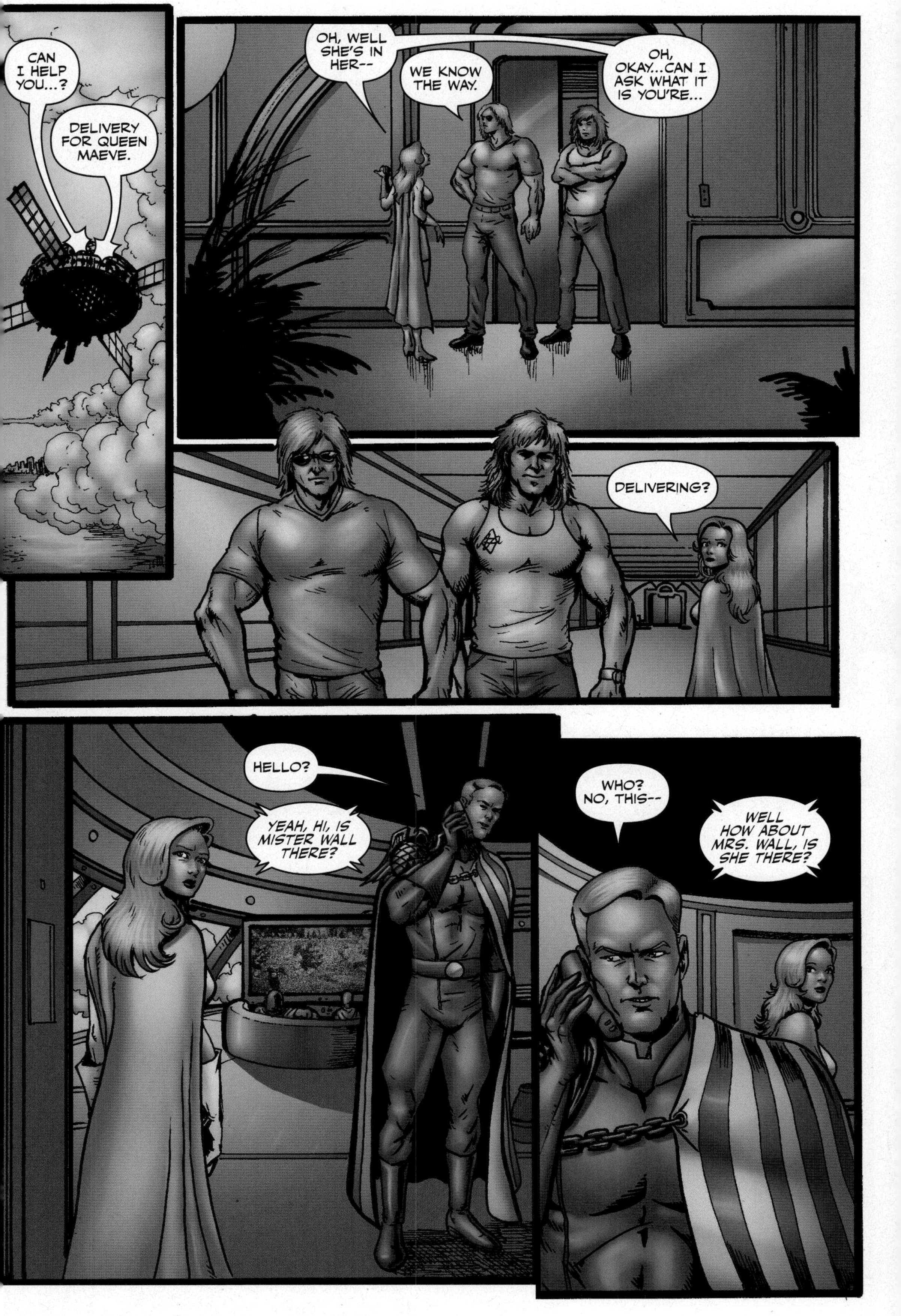
CAN I HELP YOU...?
DELIVERY FOR QUEEN MAEVE.
OH, WELL SHE'S IN HER--
WE KNOW THE WAY.
OH, OKAY...CAN I ASK WHAT IT IS YOU'RE...
DELIVERING?
HELLO?
YEAH, HI, IS MISTER WALL THERE?
WHO? NO, THIS--
WELL HOW ABOUT MRS. WALL, IS SHE THERE?

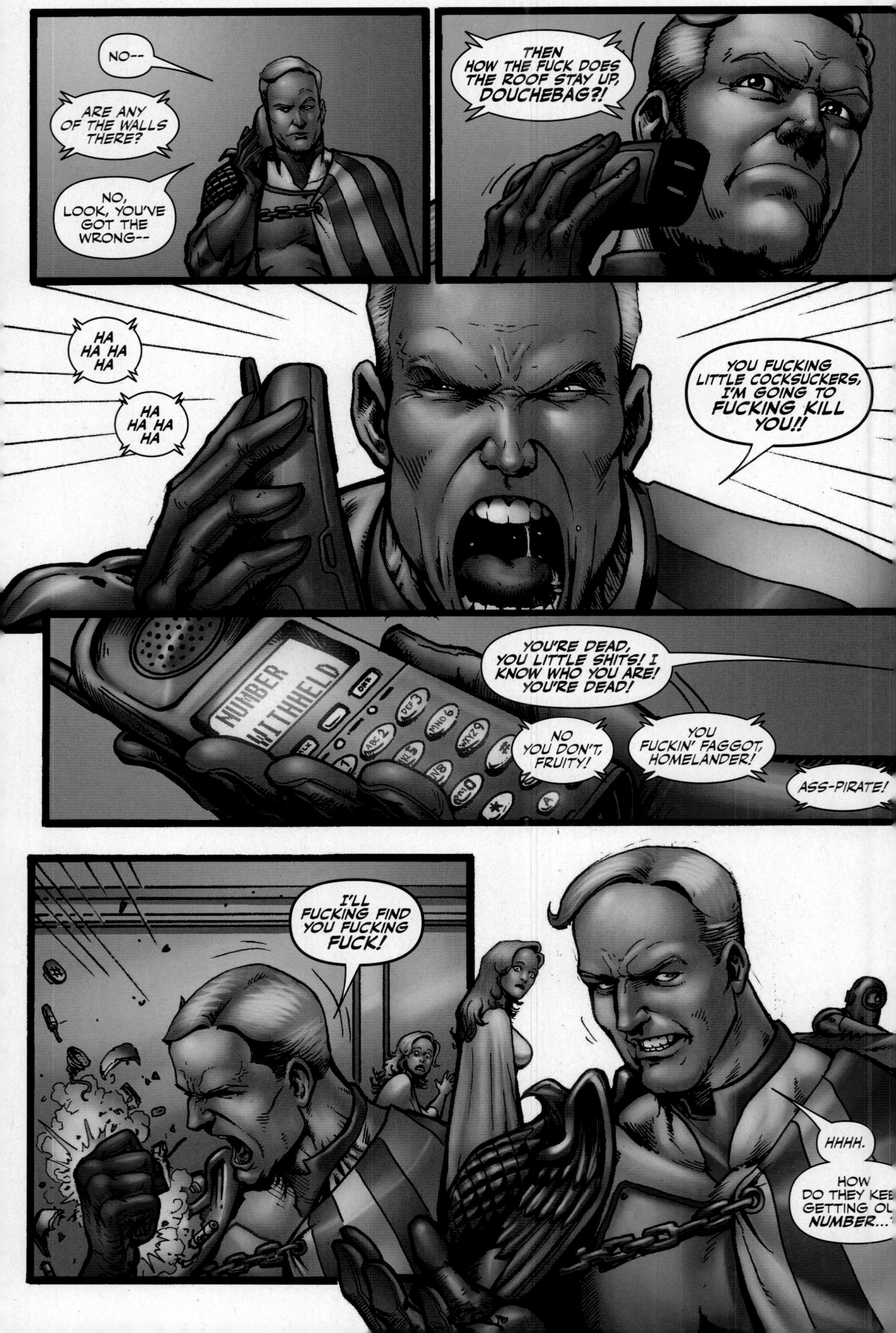
NO--
ARE ANY OF THE WALLS THERE?
NO, LOOK, YOU'VE GOT THE WRONG--
THEN HOW THE FUCK DOES THE ROOF STAY UP, DOUCHEBAG?!
HA HA HA HA
HA HA HA HA
YOU FUCKING LITTLE COCKSUCKERS, I'M GOING TO FUCKING KILL YOU!!
NUMBER WITHHELD
YOU'RE DEAD, YOU LITTLE SHITS! I KNOW WHO YOU ARE! YOU'RE DEAD!
NO YOU DON'T, FRUITY!
YOU FUCKIN' FAGGOT, HOMELANDER!
ASS-PIRATE!
I'LL FUCKING FIND YOU FUCKING FUCK!
HHHH.
HOW DO THEY KEE GETTING OU NUMBER...

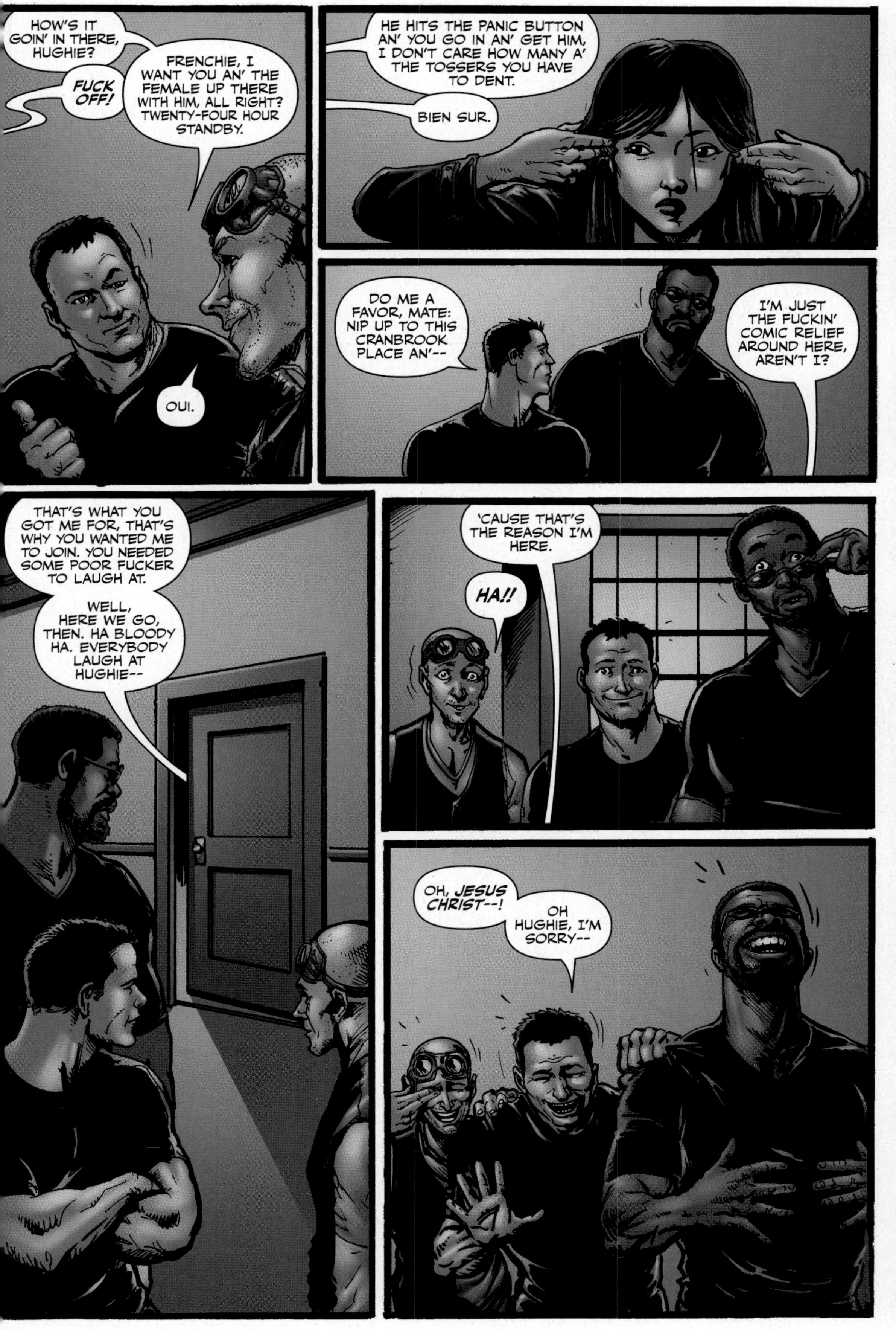
HOW'S IT GOIN' IN THERE, HUGHIE?
FUCK OFF!
FRENCHIE, I WANT YOU AN' THE FEMALE UP THERE WITH HIM, ALL RIGHT? TWENTY-FOUR HOUR STANDBY.
OUI.
HE HITS THE PANIC BUTTON AN' YOU GO IN AN' GET HIM, I DON'T CARE HOW MANY A' THE TOSSERS YOU HAVE TO DENT.
BIEN SUR.
DO ME A FAVOR, MATE: NIP UP TO THIS CRANBROOK PLACE AN'--
I'M JUST THE FUCKIN' COMIC RELIEF AROUND HERE, AREN'T I?
THAT'S WHAT YOU GOT ME FOR, THAT'S WHY YOU WANTED ME TO JOIN. YOU NEEDED SOME POOR FUCKER TO LAUGH AT.
WELL, HERE WE GO, THEN. HA BLOODY HA. EVERYBODY LAUGH AT HUGHIE--
'CAUSE THAT'S THE REASON I'M HERE.
HA!!
OH, JESUS CHRIST--!
OH HUGHIE, I'M SORRY--

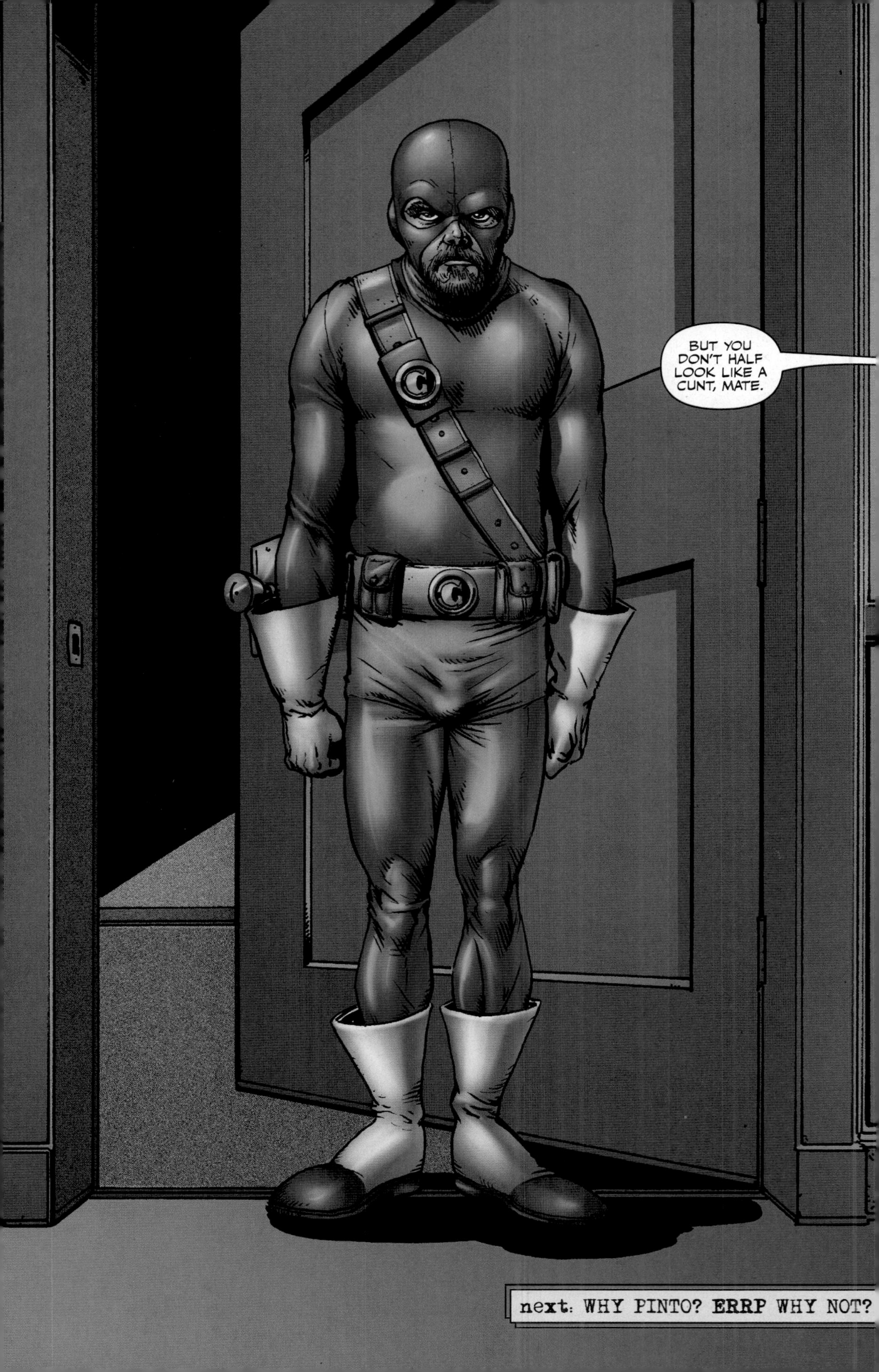
BUT YOU DON'T HALF LOOK LIKE A CUNT, MATE.
next: WHY PINTO? ERRP WHY NOT?

#24 cove
by Darick Roberts
and Tony Avi

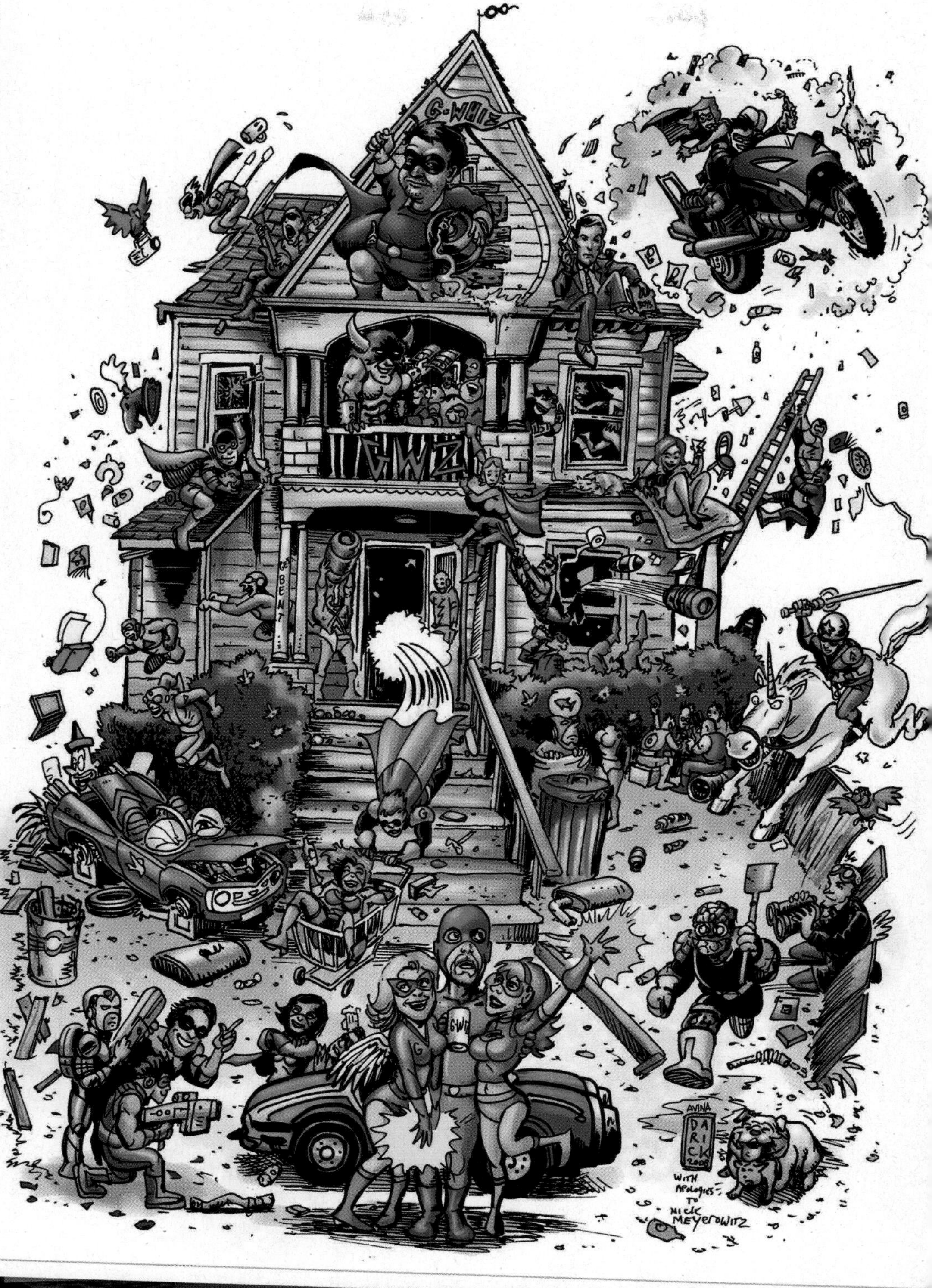
G-WHIZ
GWZ
AVINA
DARICK 2008
WITH APOLOGIES TO NICK MEYEROWITZ

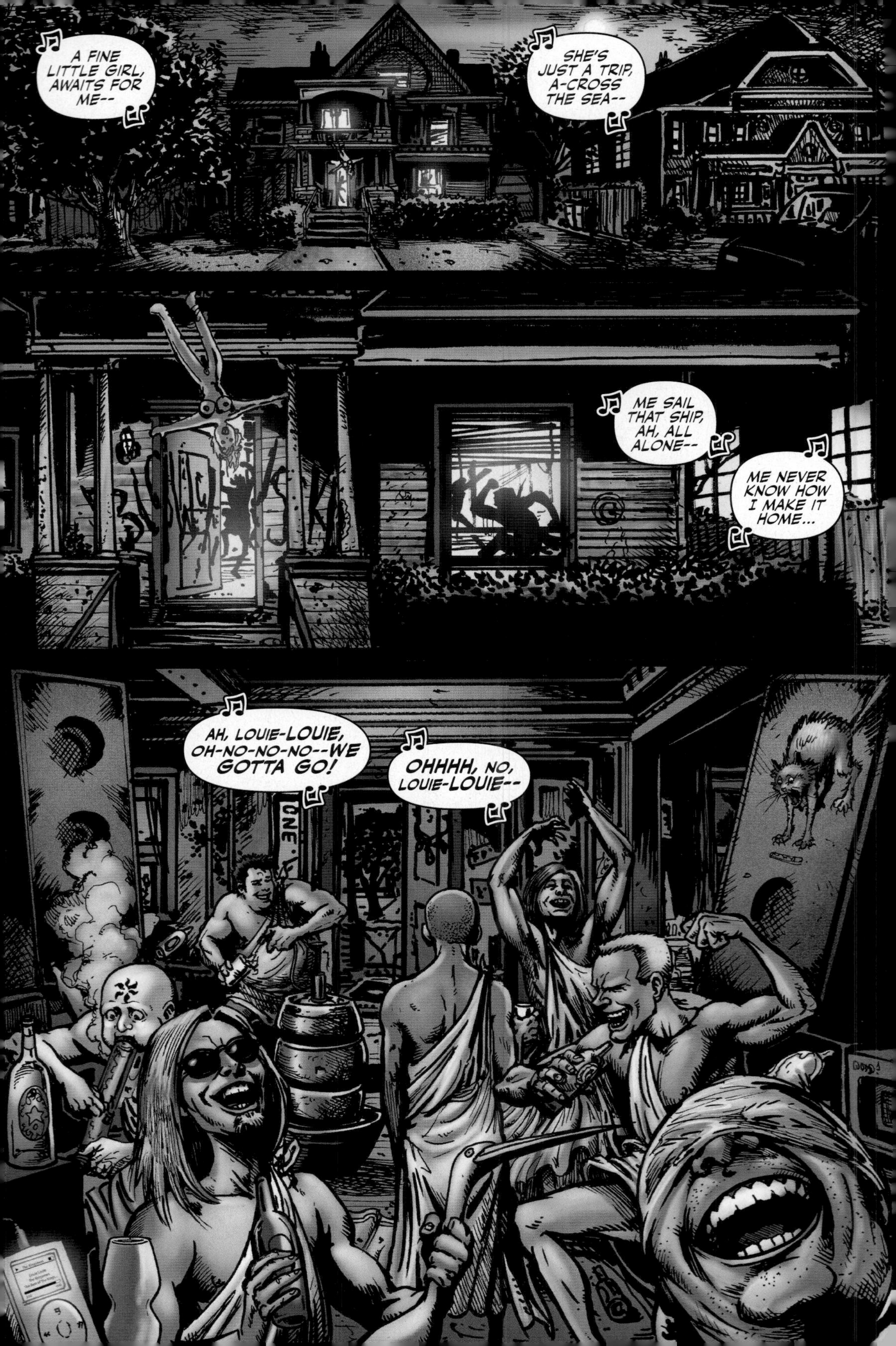
A FINE LITTLE GIRL, AWAITS FOR ME--
SHE'S JUST A TRIP, A-CROSS THE SEA--
ME SAIL THAT SHIP, AH, ALL ALONE--
ME NEVER KNOW HOW I MAKE IT HOME...
AH, LOUIE-LOUIE, OH-NO-NO-NO--WE GOTTA GO!
OHHHH, NO, LOUIE-LOUIE--

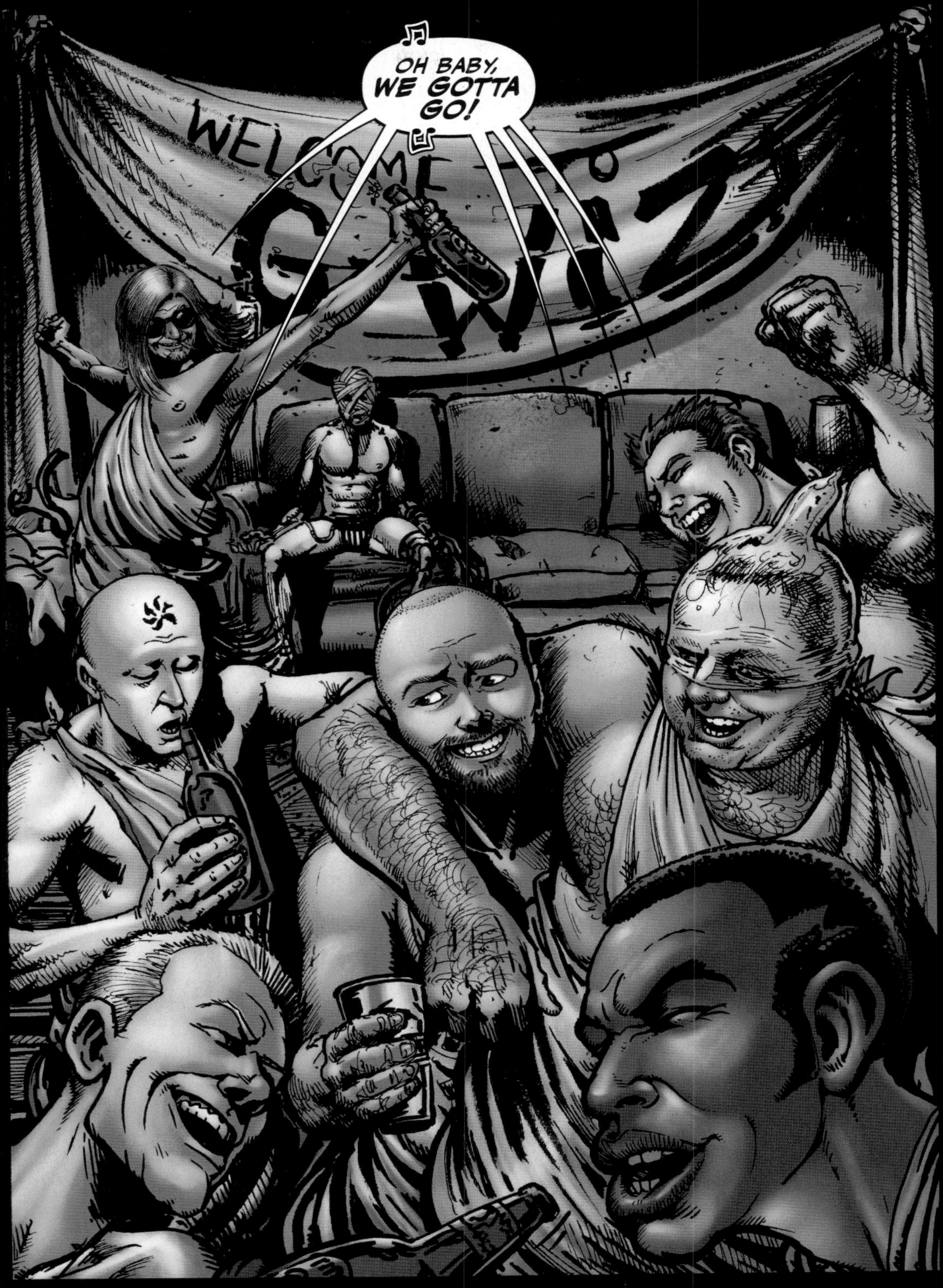
OH BABY, WE GOTTA GO!

WE GOTTA GO NOW

part two

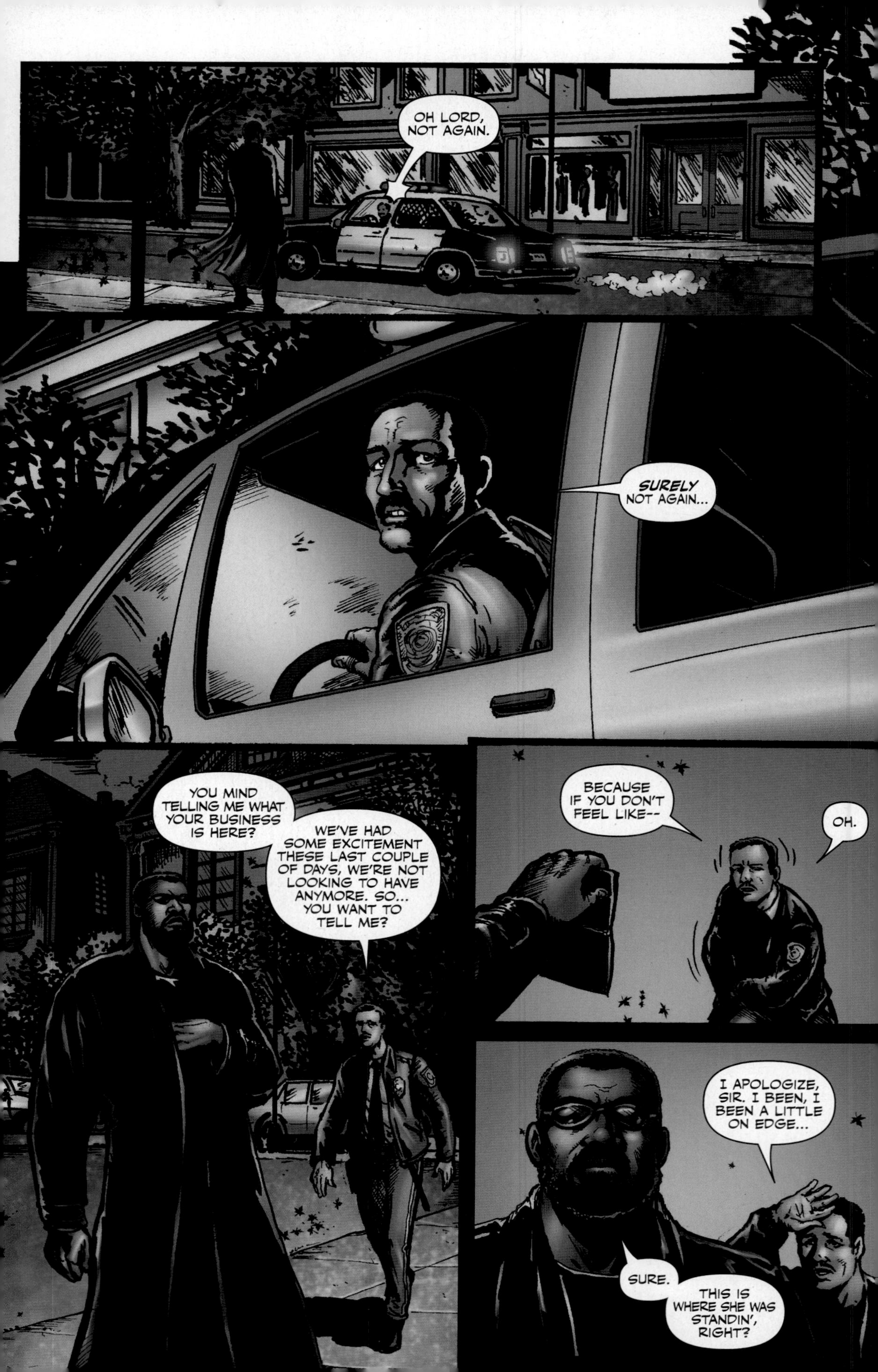
OH LORD, NOT AGAIN.
SURELY NOT AGAIN...
YOU MIND TELLING ME WHAT YOUR BUSINESS IS HERE?
WE'VE HAD SOME EXCITEMENT THESE LAST COUPLE OF DAYS, WE'RE NOT LOOKING TO HAVE ANYMORE. SO... YOU WANT TO TELL ME?
BECAUSE IF YOU DON'T FEEL LIKE--
OH.
I APOLOGIZE, SIR. I BEEN, I BEEN A LITTLE ON EDGE...
SURE.
THIS IS WHERE SHE WAS STANDIN', RIGHT?

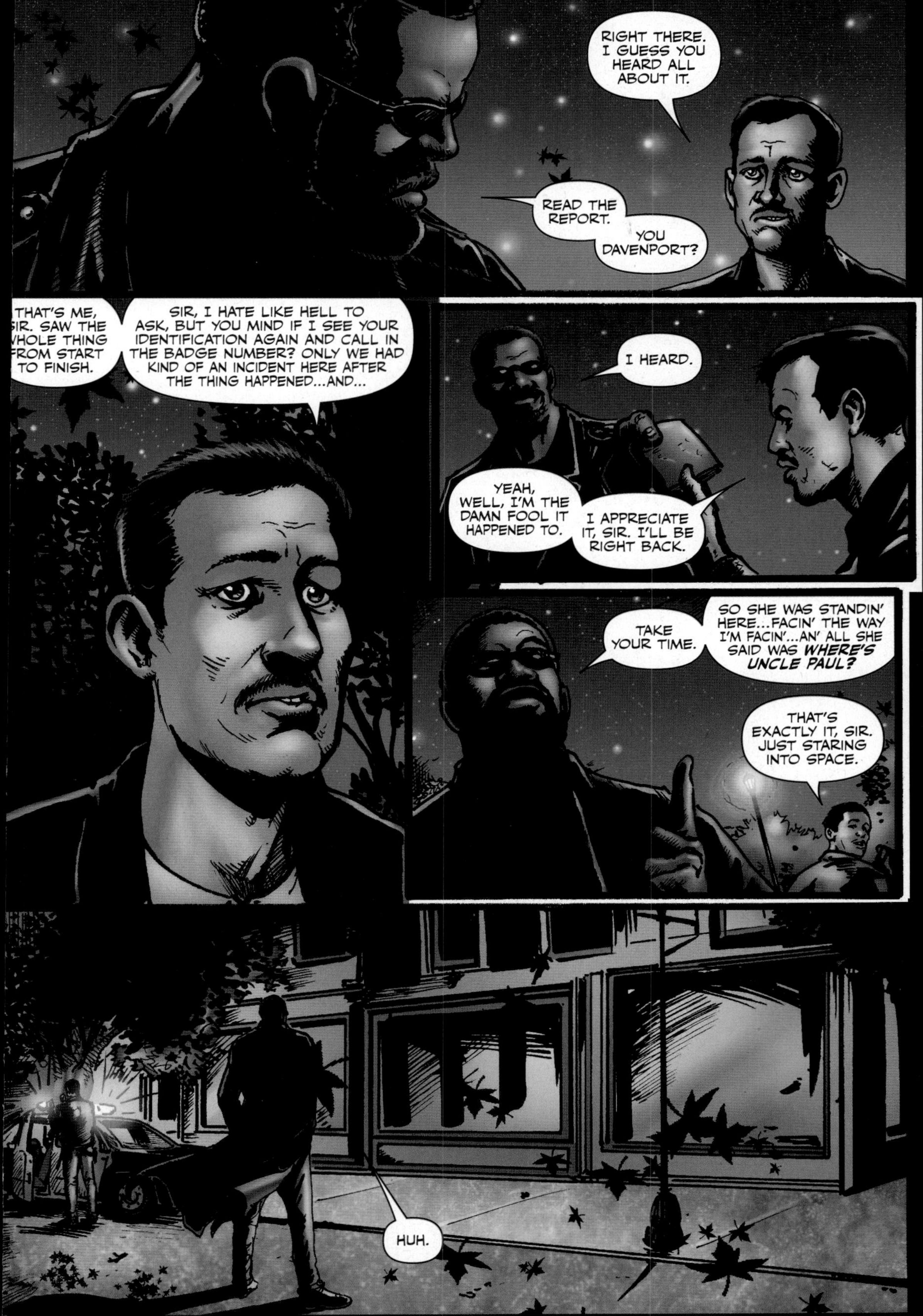
RIGHT THERE. I GUESS YOU HEARD ALL ABOUT IT.
READ THE REPORT.
YOU DAVENPORT?
THAT'S ME, SIR. SAW THE WHOLE THING FROM START TO FINISH.
SIR, I HATE LIKE HELL TO ASK, BUT YOU MIND IF I SEE YOUR IDENTIFICATION AGAIN AND CALL IN THE BADGE NUMBER? ONLY WE HAD KIND OF AN INCIDENT HERE AFTER THE THING HAPPENED...AND...
I HEARD.
YEAH, WELL, I'M THE DAMN FOOL IT HAPPENED TO.
I APPRECIATE IT, SIR. I'LL BE RIGHT BACK.
TAKE YOUR TIME.
SO SHE WAS STANDIN' HERE...FACIN' THE WAY I'M FACIN'...AN' ALL SHE SAID WAS WHERE'S UNCLE PAUL?
THAT'S EXACTLY IT, SIR. JUST STARING INTO SPACE.
HUH.

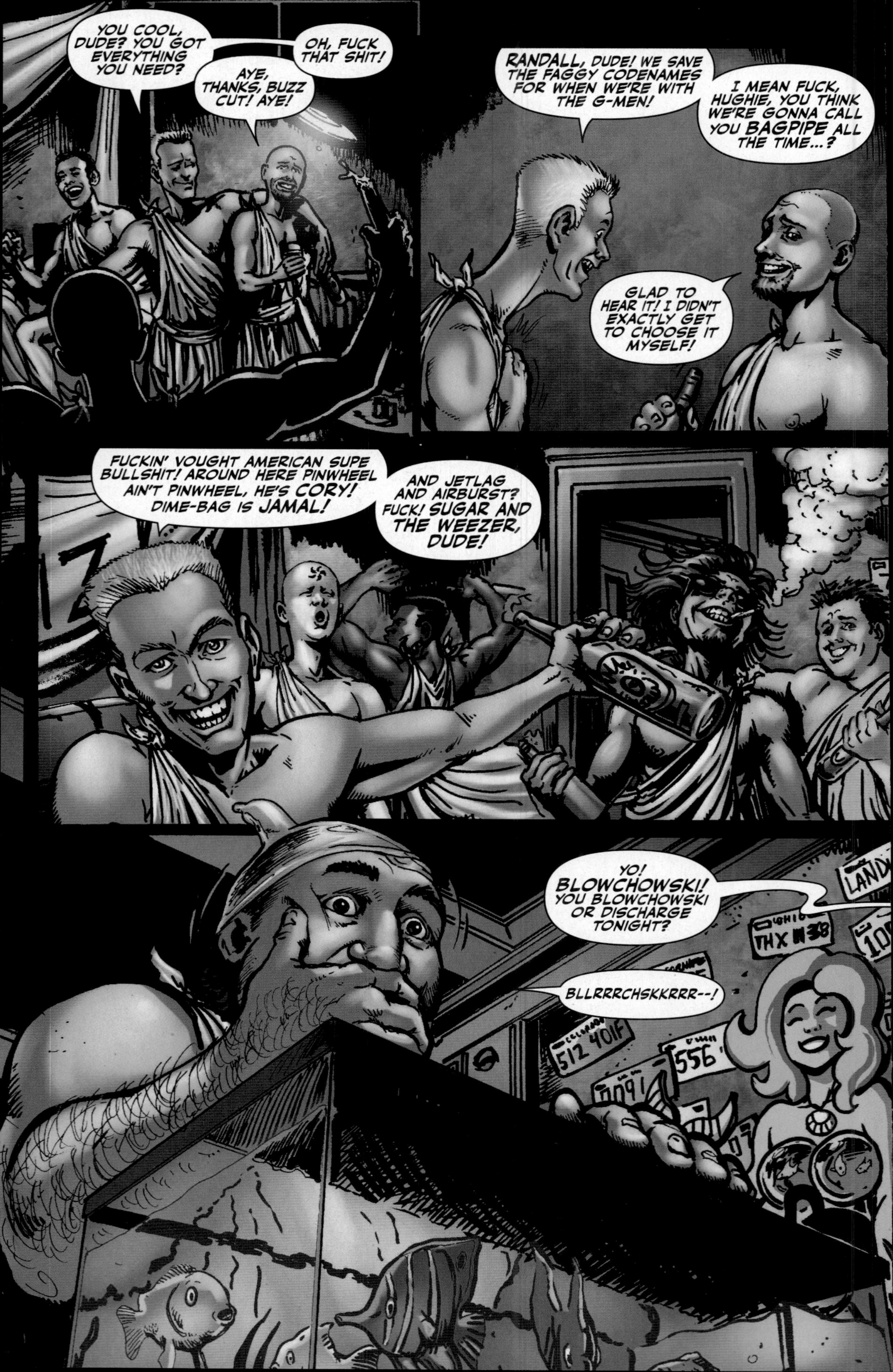
YOU COOL, DUDE? YOU GOT EVERYTHING YOU NEED?
OH, FUCK THAT SHIT!
AYE, THANKS, BUZZ CUT! AYE!
RANDALL, DUDE! WE SAVE THE FAGGY CODENAMES FOR WHEN WE'RE WITH THE G-MEN!
I MEAN FUCK, HUGHIE, YOU THINK WE'RE GONNA CALL YOU BAGPIPE ALL THE TIME...?
GLAD TO HEAR IT! I DIDN'T EXACTLY GET TO CHOOSE IT MYSELF!
FUCKIN' VOUGHT AMERICAN SUPE BULLSHIT! AROUND HERE PINWHEEL AIN'T PINWHEEL, HE'S CORY! DIME-BAG IS JAMAL!
AND JETLAG AND AIRBURST? FUCK! SUGAR AND THE WEEZER, DUDE!
YO! BLOWCHOWSKI! YOU BLOWCHOWSKI OR DISCHARGE TONIGHT?
BLLRRRCHSKKRRR--!
THX 1138
512 401F
556

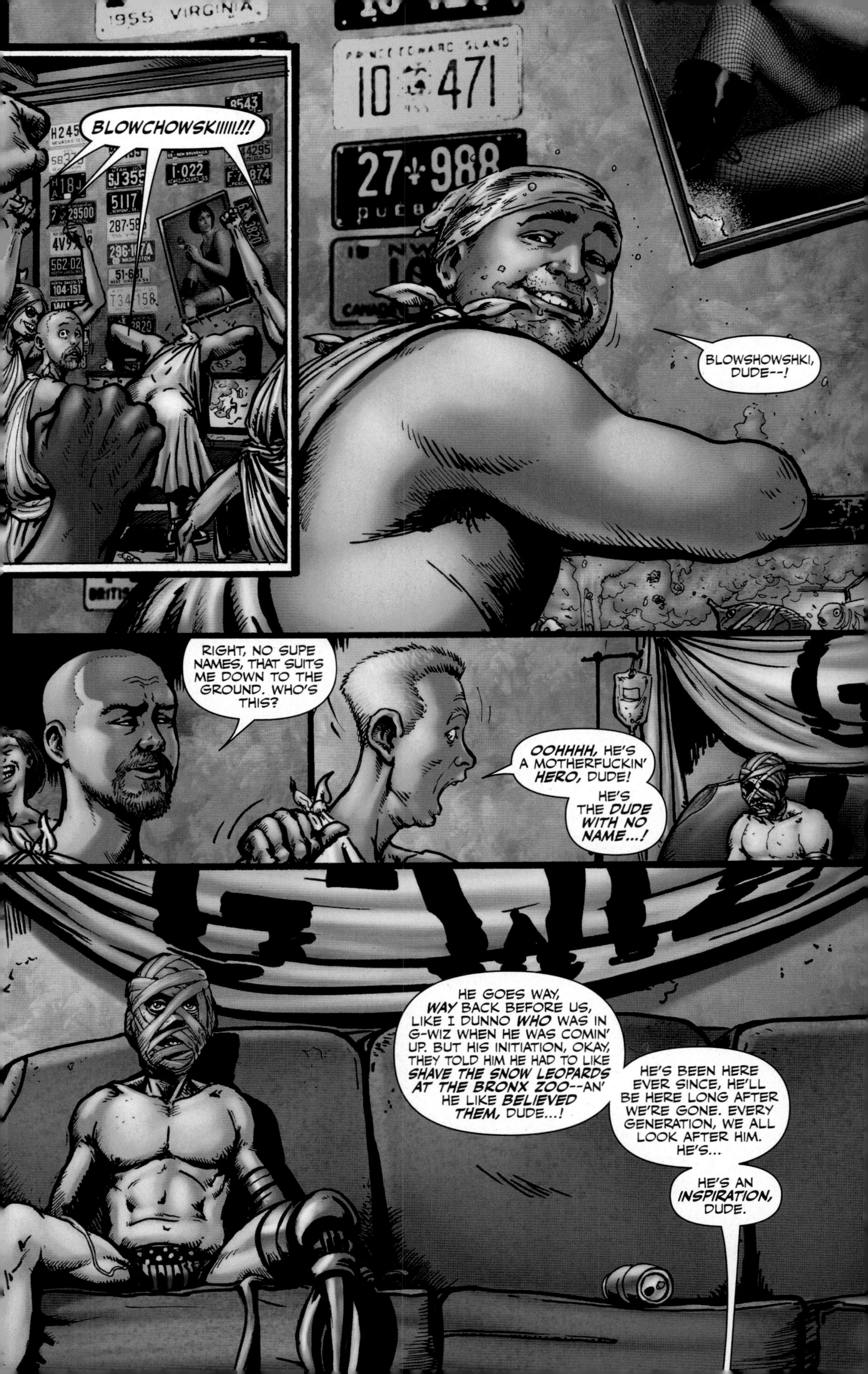
BLOWCHOWSKIIIIII!!!
BLOWSHOWSHKI, DUDE--!
RIGHT, NO SUPE NAMES, THAT SUITS ME DOWN TO THE GROUND. WHO'S THIS?
OOHHHH, HE'S A MOTHERFUCKIN' HERO, DUDE!
HE'S THE DUDE WITH NO NAME...!
HE GOES WAY, WAY BACK BEFORE US, LIKE I DUNNO WHO WAS IN G-WIZ WHEN HE WAS COMIN' UP. BUT HIS INITIATION, OKAY, THEY TOLD HIM HE HAD TO LIKE SHAVE THE SNOW LEOPARDS AT THE BRONX ZOO--AN' HE LIKE BELIEVED THEM, DUDE...!
HE'S BEEN HERE EVER SINCE, HE'LL BE HERE LONG AFTER WE'RE GONE. EVERY GENERATION, WE ALL LOOK AFTER HIM. HE'S...
HE'S AN INSPIRATION, DUDE.

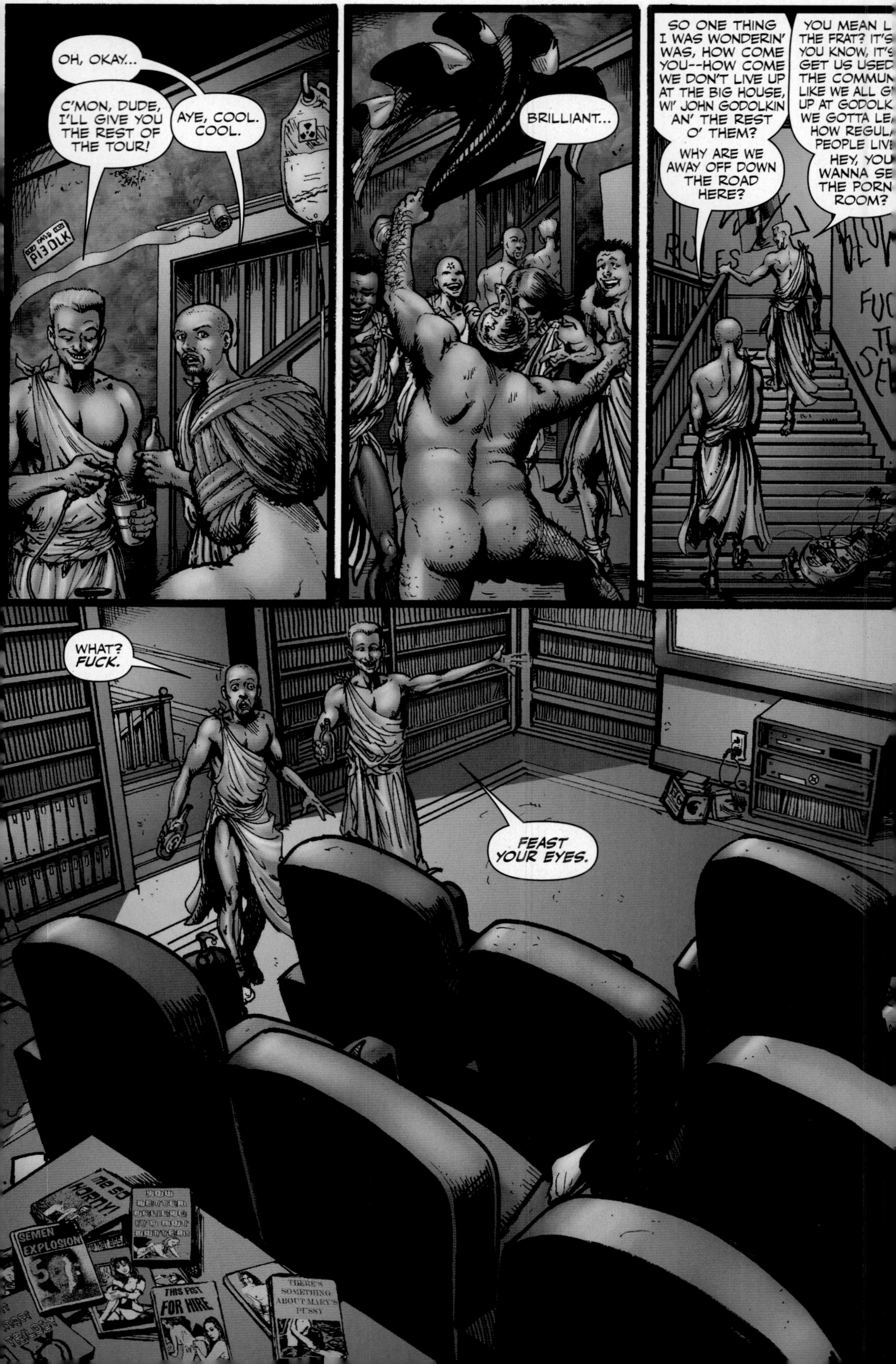

OH, OKAY...
C'MON, DUDE, I'LL GIVE YOU THE REST OF THE TOUR!
AYE, COOL. COOL.
BRILLIANT...
SO ONE THING I WAS WONDERIN' WAS, HOW COME YOU--HOW COME WE DON'T LIVE UP AT THE BIG HOUSE, WI' JOHN GODOLKIN AN' THE REST O' THEM?
WHY ARE WE AWAY OFF DOWN THE ROAD HERE?
YOU MEAN L THE FRAT? IT'S YOU KNOW, IT'S GET US USED THE COMMUN LIKE WE ALL G UP AT GODOLK WE GOTTA LE HOW REGUL PEOPLE LIVE
HEY, YOU WANNA SE THE PORN ROOM?
WHAT? FUCK.
FEAST YOUR EYES.
ME SO HORNY!
YOU BETTER BELIEVE IT'S NOT BUTTER!
SEMEN EXPLOSION 5
THIS PIST FOR HIRE
THERE'S SOMETHING ABOUT MARY'S PUSSY

WE GOT LIKE *TWENTY THOUSAND TITLES*, DUDE. WE GOT EVERYTHING, FUCKIN' A.T.M., INTERRACIAL, ANIMALS...I MEAN WE GOT SLUTS DOIN' SHIT YOU WON'T BELIEVE, STRAP-ONS AN' FISTIN' AN' SHIT...

OH RIGHT, YEAH. VERY NICE.

SO...

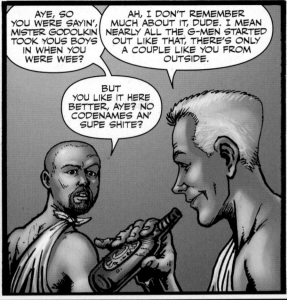

AYE, SO YOU WERE SAYIN', MISTER GODOLKIN TOOK YOUS BOYS IN WHEN YOU WERE WEE?

AH, I DON'T REMEMBER MUCH ABOUT IT, DUDE. I MEAN NEARLY ALL THE G-MEN STARTED OUT LIKE THAT, THERE'S ONLY A COUPLE LIKE YOU FROM OUTSIDE.

BUT YOU LIKE IT HERE BETTER, AYE? NO CODENAMES AN' SUPE SHITE?

FUCK *YEAH*, DUDE. I MEAN I KNOW WE ALL GOTTA GROW UP AN' BE G-MEN ONE DAY, BUT...MAKE HAY WHILE THE SUN SHINES, YOU KNOW?

SO YOU WANNA JERK OFF NOW?

...WHAT?

UH...

I...

I MEAN--

NOT RIGHT NOW, SURE! C'MON, DUDE!

LET'S GO SEE WHAT KINDA SHIT *BLOWCHOWSKI'S* DOIN'...!

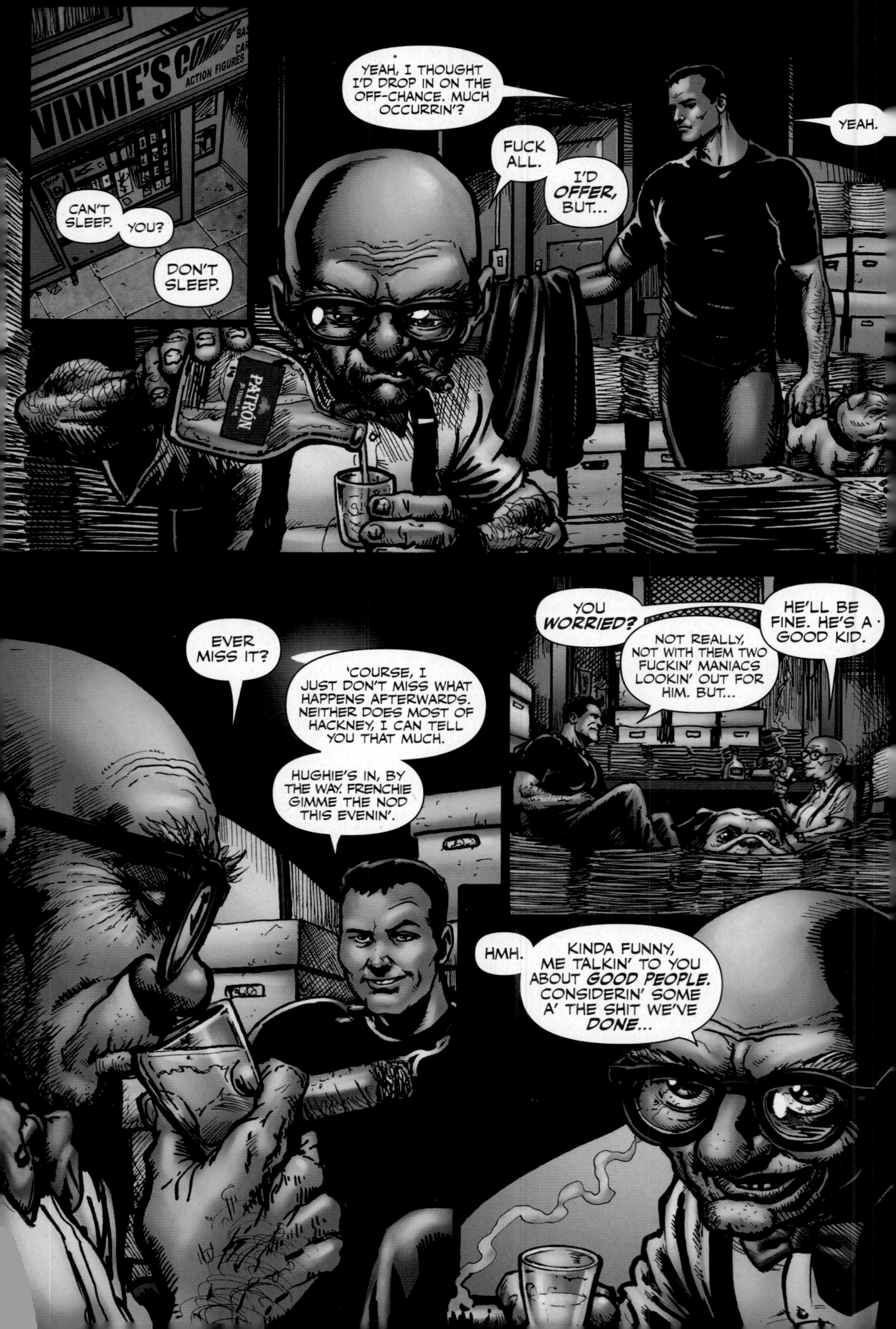

VINNIE'S COMICS
ACTION FIGURES
CAN'T SLEEP.
YOU?
DON'T SLEEP.
YEAH, I THOUGHT I'D DROP IN ON THE OFF-CHANCE. MUCH OCCURRIN'?
FUCK ALL.
I'D *OFFER,* BUT...
YEAH.
PATRÓN
EVER MISS IT?
'COURSE, I JUST DON'T MISS WHAT HAPPENS AFTERWARDS. NEITHER DOES MOST OF HACKNEY, I CAN TELL YOU THAT MUCH.
HUGHIE'S IN, BY THE WAY. FRENCHIE GIMME THE NOD THIS EVENIN'.
YOU *WORRIED?*
NOT REALLY, NOT WITH THEM TWO FUCKIN' MANIACS LOOKIN' OUT FOR HIM. BUT...
HE'LL BE FINE. HE'S A GOOD KID.
HMH.
KINDA FUNNY, ME TALKIN' TO YOU ABOUT *GOOD PEOPLE.* CONSIDERIN' SOME A' THE SHIT WE'VE *DONE...*

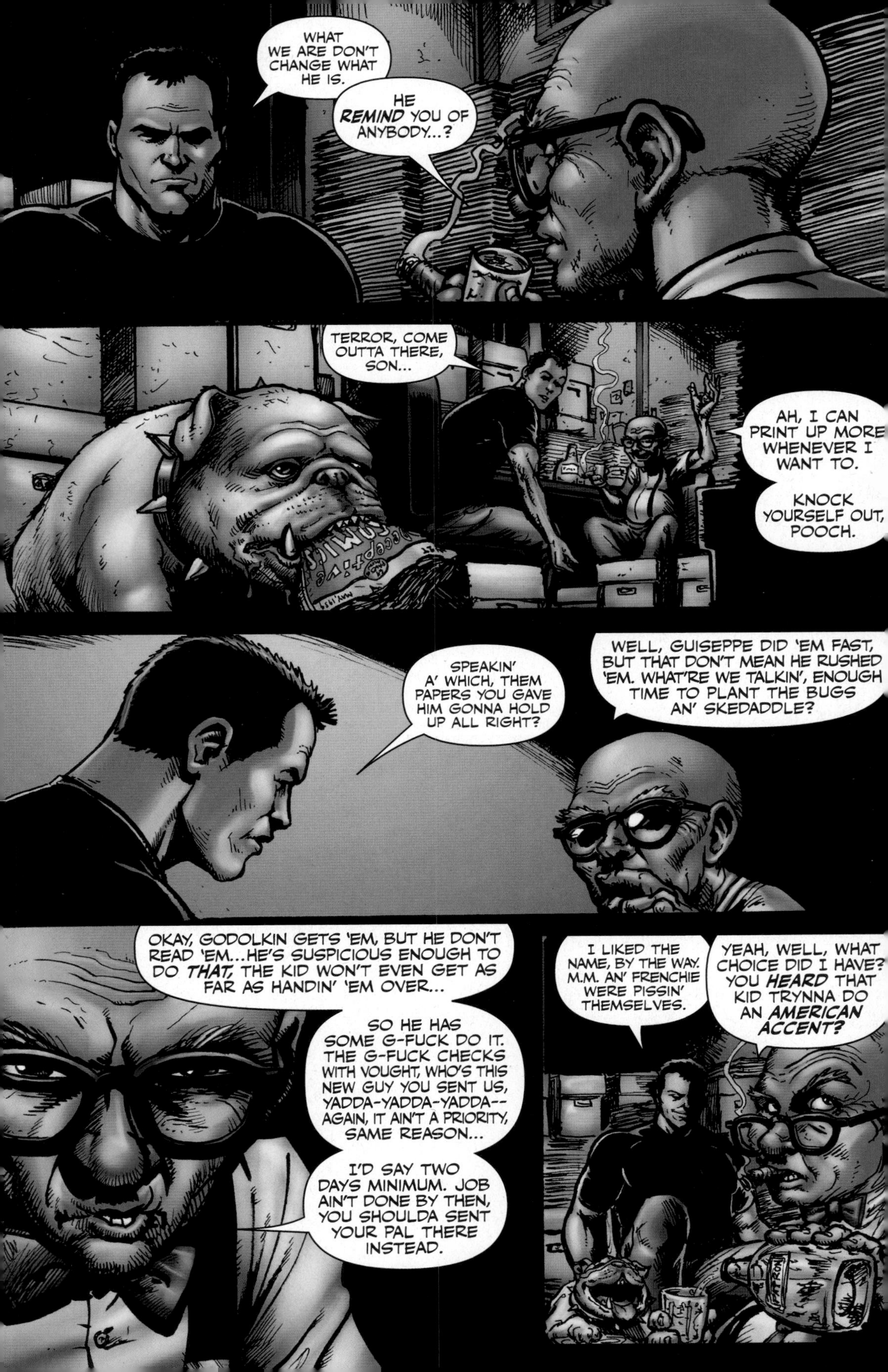
WHAT WE ARE DON'T CHANGE WHAT HE IS.
HE REMIND YOU OF ANYBODY...?
TERROR, COME OUTTA THERE, SON...
AH, I CAN PRINT UP MORE WHENEVER I WANT TO.
KNOCK YOURSELF OUT, POOCH.
SPEAKIN' A' WHICH, THEM PAPERS YOU GAVE HIM GONNA HOLD UP ALL RIGHT?
WELL, GUISEPPE DID 'EM FAST, BUT THAT DON'T MEAN HE RUSHED 'EM. WHAT'RE WE TALKIN', ENOUGH TIME TO PLANT THE BUGS AN' SKEDADDLE?
OKAY, GODOLKIN GETS 'EM, BUT HE DON'T READ 'EM...HE'S SUSPICIOUS ENOUGH TO DO THAT, THE KID WON'T EVEN GET AS FAR AS HANDIN' 'EM OVER...
SO HE HAS SOME G-FUCK DO IT. THE G-FUCK CHECKS WITH VOUGHT, WHO'S THIS NEW GUY YOU SENT US, YADDA-YADDA-YADDA--AGAIN, IT AIN'T A PRIORITY, SAME REASON...
I'D SAY TWO DAYS MINIMUM. JOB AIN'T DONE BY THEN, YOU SHOULDA SENT YOUR PAL THERE INSTEAD.
I LIKED THE NAME, BY THE WAY. M.M. AN' FRENCHIE WERE PISSIN' THEMSELVES.
YEAH, WELL, WHAT CHOICE DID I HAVE? YOU HEARD THAT KID TRYNNA DO AN AMERICAN ACCENT?

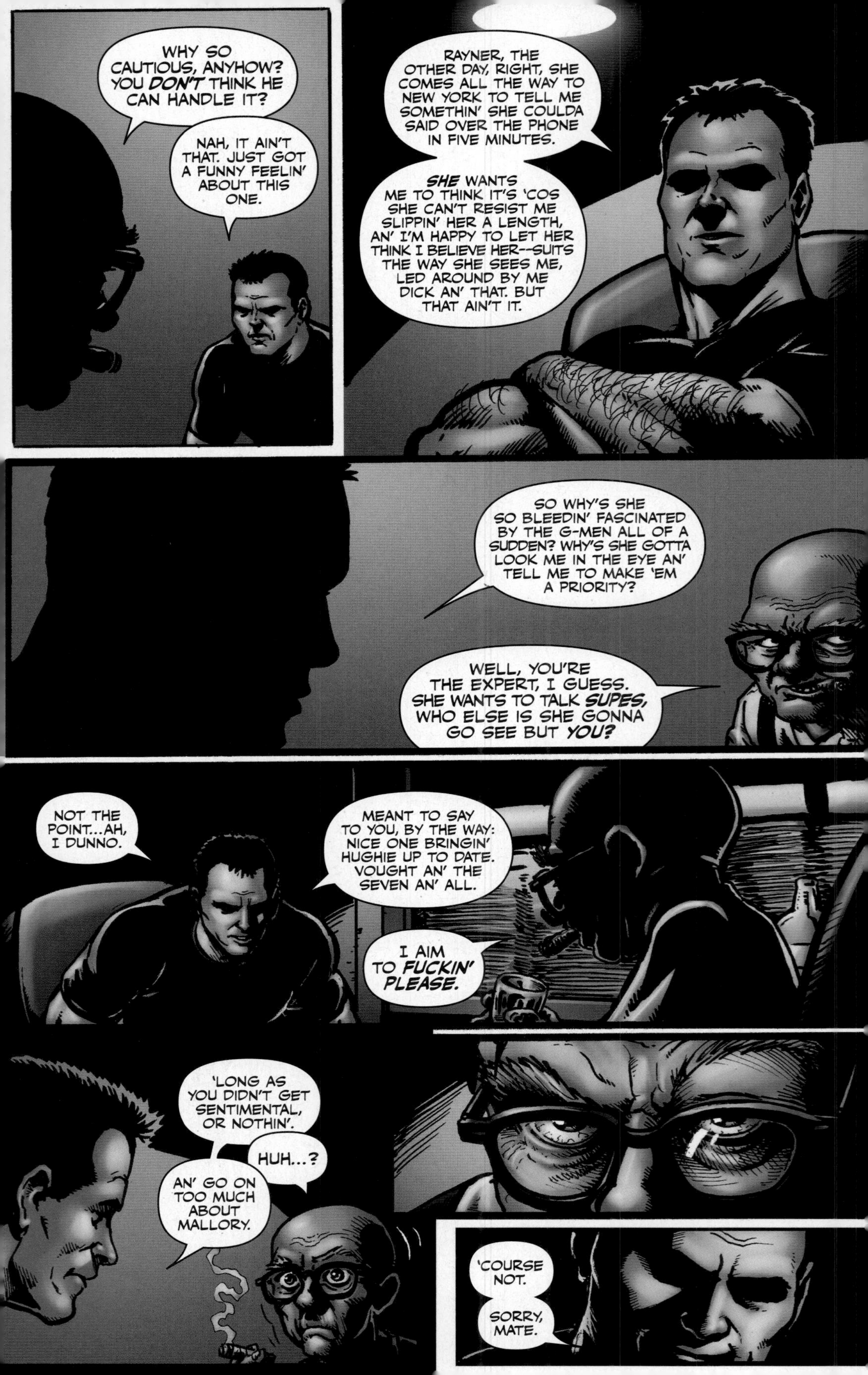
WHY SO CAUTIOUS, ANYHOW? YOU *DON'T* THINK HE CAN HANDLE IT?
NAH, IT AIN'T THAT. JUST GOT A FUNNY FEELIN' ABOUT THIS ONE.
RAYNER, THE OTHER DAY, RIGHT, SHE COMES ALL THE WAY TO NEW YORK TO TELL ME SOMETHIN' SHE COULDA SAID OVER THE PHONE IN FIVE MINUTES.
SHE WANTS ME TO THINK IT'S 'COS SHE CAN'T RESIST ME SLIPPIN' HER A LENGTH, AN' I'M HAPPY TO LET HER THINK I BELIEVE HER--SUITS THE WAY SHE SEES ME, LED AROUND BY ME DICK AN' THAT. BUT THAT AIN'T IT.
SO WHY'S SHE SO BLEEDIN' FASCINATED BY THE G-MEN ALL OF A SUDDEN? WHY'S SHE GOTTA LOOK ME IN THE EYE AN' TELL ME TO MAKE 'EM A PRIORITY?
WELL, YOU'RE THE EXPERT, I GUESS. SHE WANTS TO TALK *SUPES,* WHO ELSE IS SHE GONNA GO SEE BUT *YOU?*
NOT THE POINT...AH, I DUNNO.
MEANT TO SAY TO YOU, BY THE WAY: NICE ONE BRINGIN' HUGHIE UP TO DATE. VOUGHT AN' THE SEVEN AN' ALL.
I AIM TO *FUCKIN' PLEASE.*
'LONG AS YOU DIDN'T GET SENTIMENTAL, OR NOTHIN'.
HUH...?
AN' GO ON TOO MUCH ABOUT MALLORY.
'COURSE NOT.
SORRY, MATE.

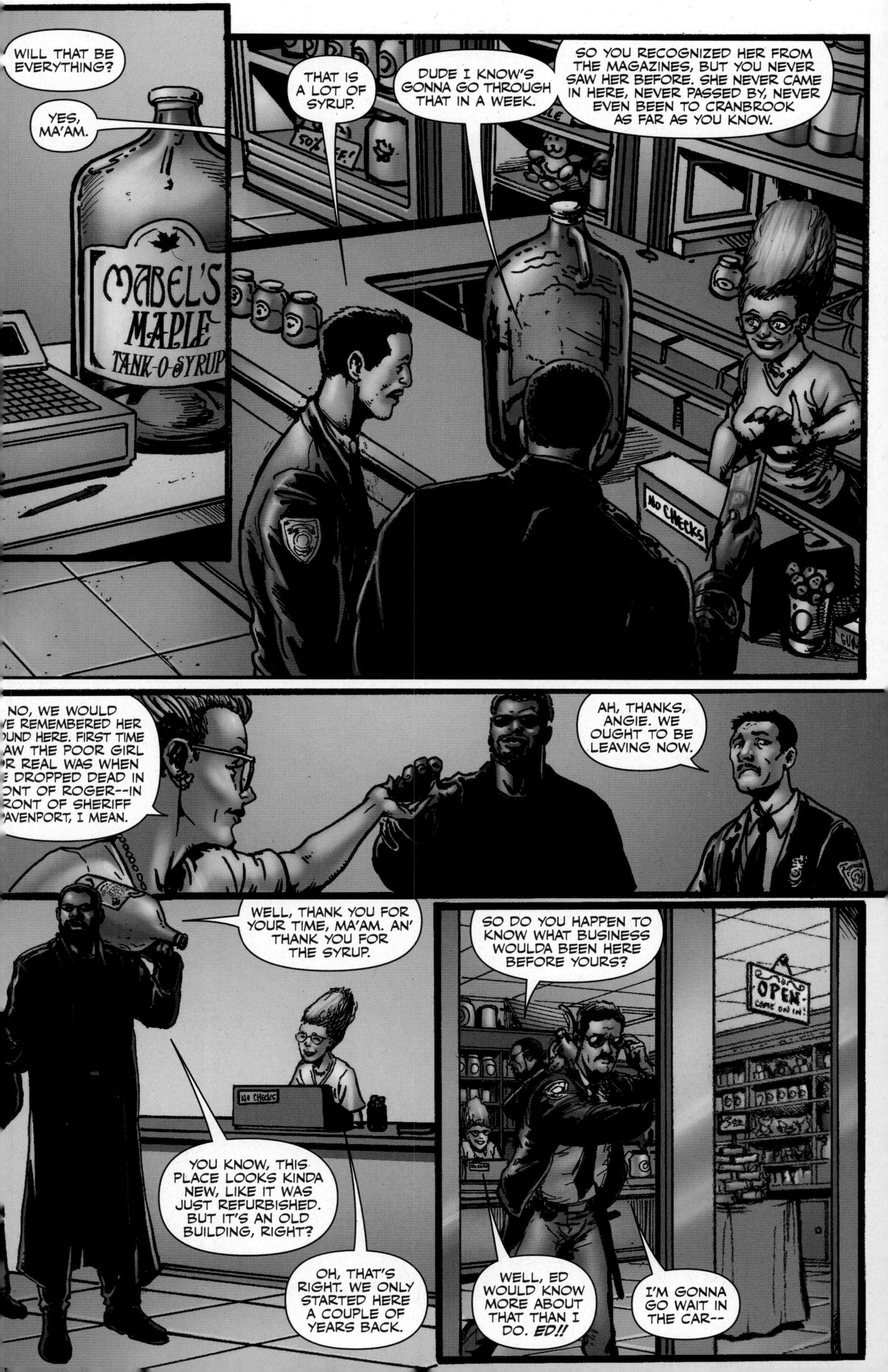
WILL THAT BE EVERYTHING?
YES, MA'AM.
THAT IS A LOT OF SYRUP.
DUDE I KNOW'S GONNA GO THROUGH THAT IN A WEEK.
SO YOU RECOGNIZED HER FROM THE MAGAZINES, BUT YOU NEVER SAW HER BEFORE. SHE NEVER CAME IN HERE, NEVER PASSED BY, NEVER EVEN BEEN TO CRANBROOK AS FAR AS YOU KNOW.
MABEL'S MAPLE TANK-O-SYRUP
50% OFF!
NO CHECKS
NO, WE WOULD VE REMEMBERED HER OUND HERE. FIRST TIME AW THE POOR GIRL R REAL WAS WHEN E DROPPED DEAD IN ONT OF ROGER--IN RONT OF SHERIFF AVENPORT, I MEAN.
AH, THANKS, ANGIE. WE OUGHT TO BE LEAVING NOW.
WELL, THANK YOU FOR YOUR TIME, MA'AM. AN' THANK YOU FOR THE SYRUP.
YOU KNOW, THIS PLACE LOOKS KINDA NEW, LIKE IT WAS JUST REFURBISHED. BUT IT'S AN OLD BUILDING, RIGHT?
OH, THAT'S RIGHT. WE ONLY STARTED HERE A COUPLE OF YEARS BACK.
SO DO YOU HAPPEN TO KNOW WHAT BUSINESS WOULDA BEEN HERE BEFORE YOURS?
OPEN
WELL, ED WOULD KNOW MORE ABOUT THAT THAN I DO. ED!!
I'M GONNA GO WAIT IN THE CAR--

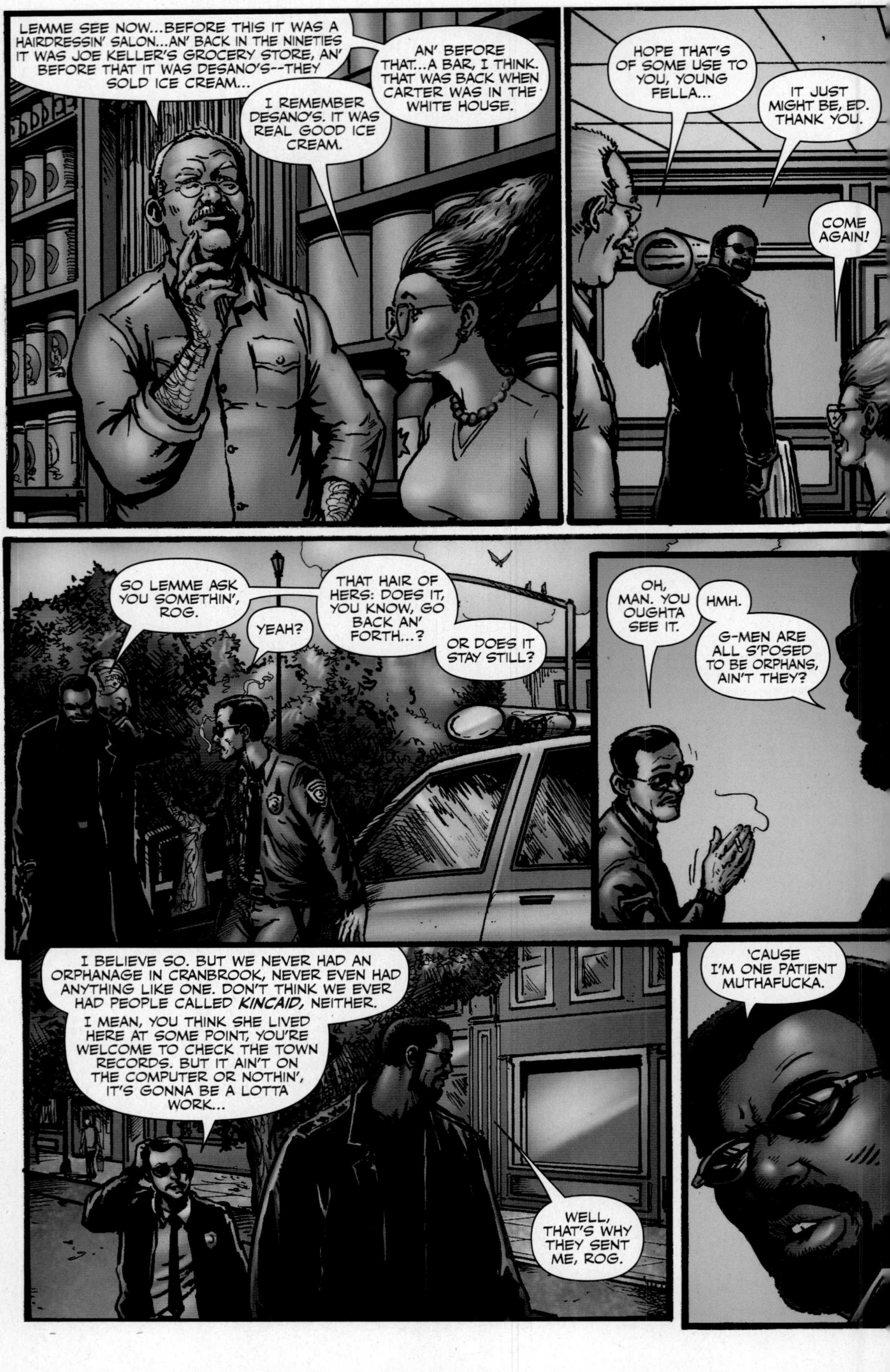
LEMME SEE NOW...BEFORE THIS IT WAS A HAIRDRESSIN' SALON...AN' BACK IN THE NINETIES IT WAS JOE KELLER'S GROCERY STORE, AN' BEFORE THAT IT WAS DESANO'S--THEY SOLD ICE CREAM...
I REMEMBER DESANO'S. IT WAS REAL GOOD ICE CREAM.
AN' BEFORE THAT...A BAR, I THINK. THAT WAS BACK WHEN CARTER WAS IN THE WHITE HOUSE.
HOPE THAT'S OF SOME USE TO YOU, YOUNG FELLA...
IT JUST MIGHT BE, ED. THANK YOU.
COME AGAIN!
SO LEMME ASK YOU SOMETHIN', ROG.
YEAH?
THAT HAIR OF HERS: DOES IT, YOU KNOW, GO BACK AN' FORTH...?
OR DOES IT STAY STILL?
OH, MAN. YOU OUGHTA SEE IT.
HMH.
G-MEN ARE ALL S'POSED TO BE ORPHANS, AIN'T THEY?
I BELIEVE SO. BUT WE NEVER HAD AN ORPHANAGE IN CRANBROOK, NEVER EVEN HAD ANYTHING LIKE ONE. DON'T THINK WE EVER HAD PEOPLE CALLED KINCAID, NEITHER.
I MEAN, YOU THINK SHE LIVED HERE AT SOME POINT, YOU'RE WELCOME TO CHECK THE TOWN RECORDS. BUT IT AIN'T ON THE COMPUTER OR NOTHIN', IT'S GONNA BE A LOTTA WORK...
WELL, THAT'S WHY THEY SENT ME, ROG.
'CAUSE I'M ONE PATIENT MUTHAFUCKA.

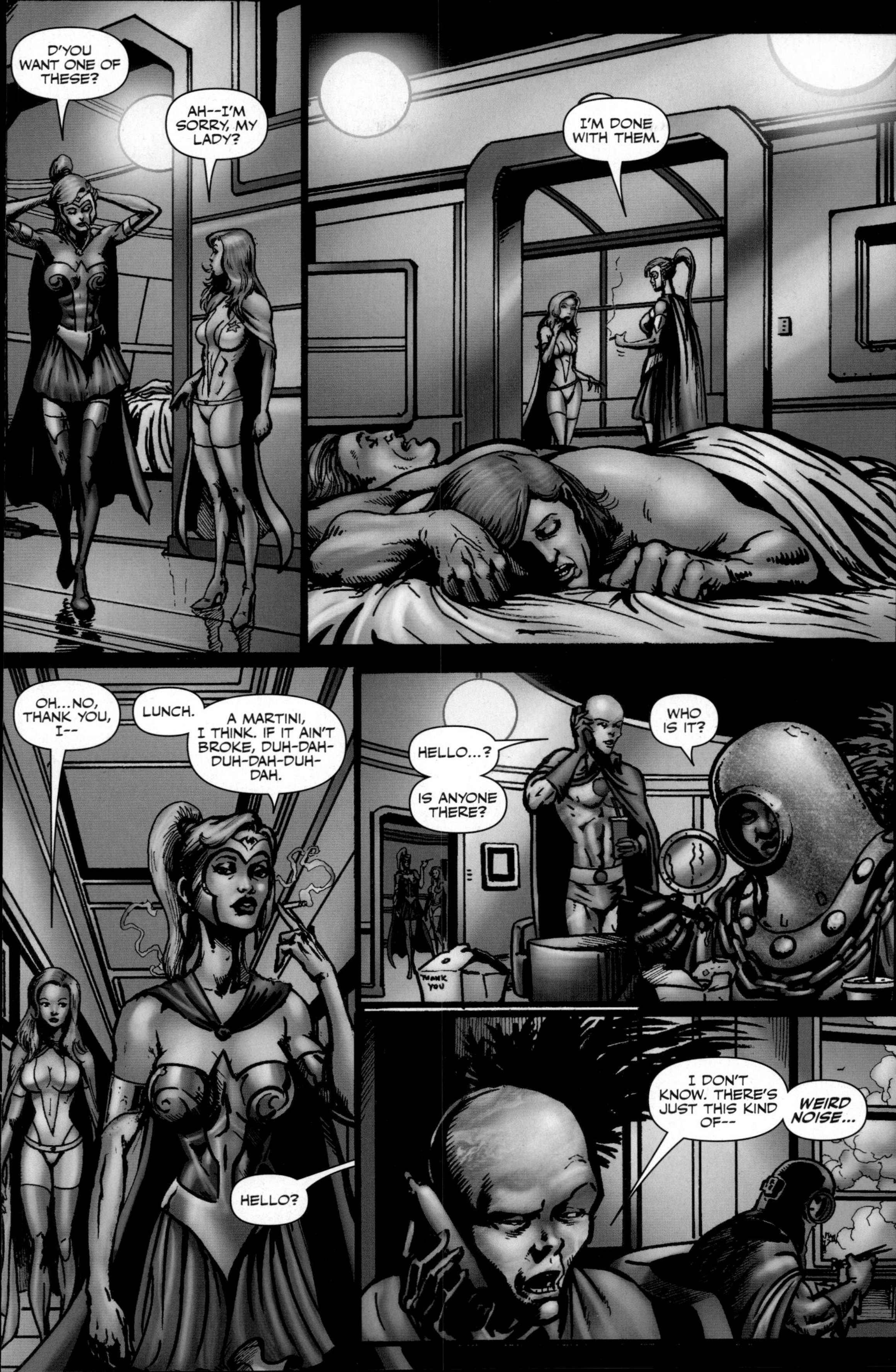
D'YOU WANT ONE OF THESE?
AH--I'M SORRY, MY LADY?
I'M DONE WITH THEM.
OH...NO, THANK YOU, I--
LUNCH.
A MARTINI, I THINK. IF IT AIN'T BROKE, DUH-DAH-DUH-DAH-DUH-DAH.
HELLO?
HELLO...?
IS ANYONE THERE?
WHO IS IT?
THANK YOU
I DON'T KNOW. THERE'S JUST THIS KIND OF--
WEIRD NOISE...

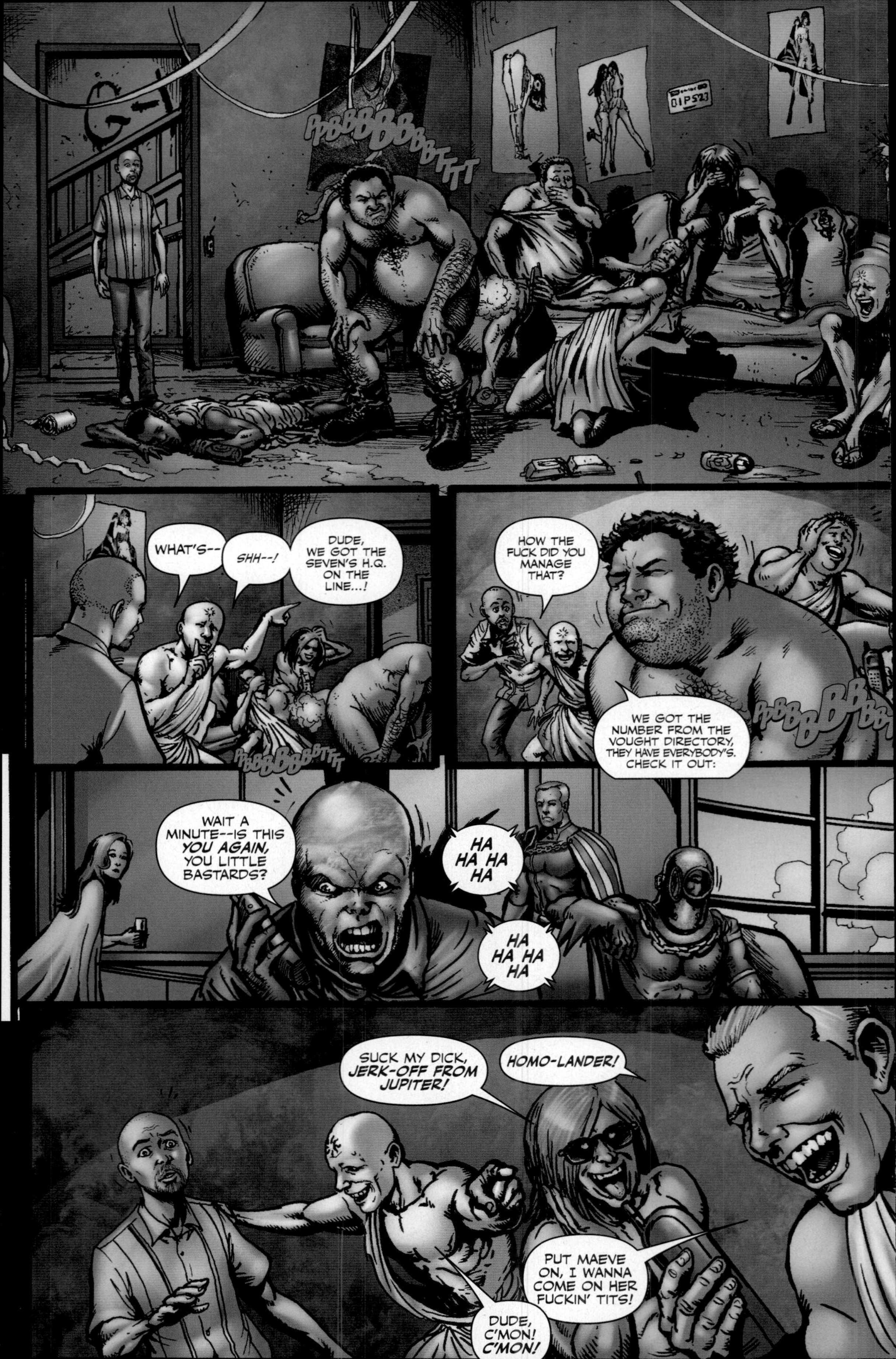
PPBBBBBBBTTTTT
WHAT'S--
SHH--!
DUDE, WE GOT THE SEVEN'S H.Q. ON THE LINE...!
PPBBBBBBBTTTT
HOW THE FUCK DID YOU MANAGE THAT?
WE GOT THE NUMBER FROM THE VOUGHT DIRECTORY, THEY HAVE EVERYBODY'S. CHECK IT OUT:
PPBBBBBBB
WAIT A MINUTE--IS THIS *YOU AGAIN,* YOU LITTLE BASTARDS?
HA HA HA HA
HA HA HA HA
SUCK MY DICK, *JERK-OFF FROM JUPITER!*
HOMO-LANDER!
PUT MAEVE ON, I WANNA COME ON HER FUCKIN' TITS!
DUDE, C'MON! *C'MON!*

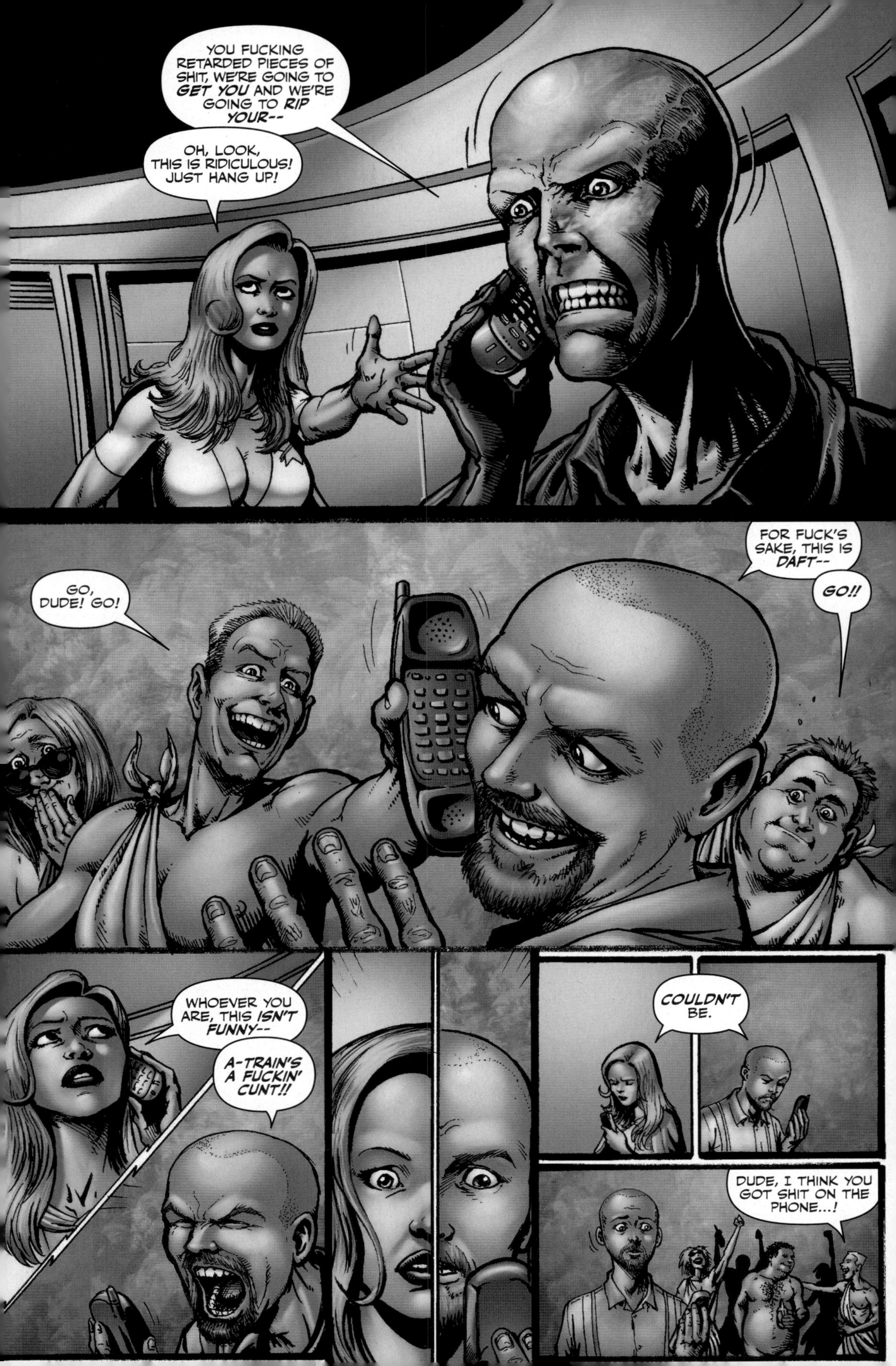
YOU FUCKING RETARDED PIECES OF SHIT, WE'RE GOING TO GET YOU AND WE'RE GOING TO RIP YOUR--
OH, LOOK, THIS IS RIDICULOUS! JUST HANG UP!
GO, DUDE! GO!
FOR FUCK'S SAKE, THIS IS DAFT--
GO!!
WHOEVER YOU ARE, THIS ISN'T FUNNY--
A-TRAIN'S A FUCKIN' CUNT!!
COULDN'T BE.
DUDE, I THINK YOU GOT SHIT ON THE PHONE...!

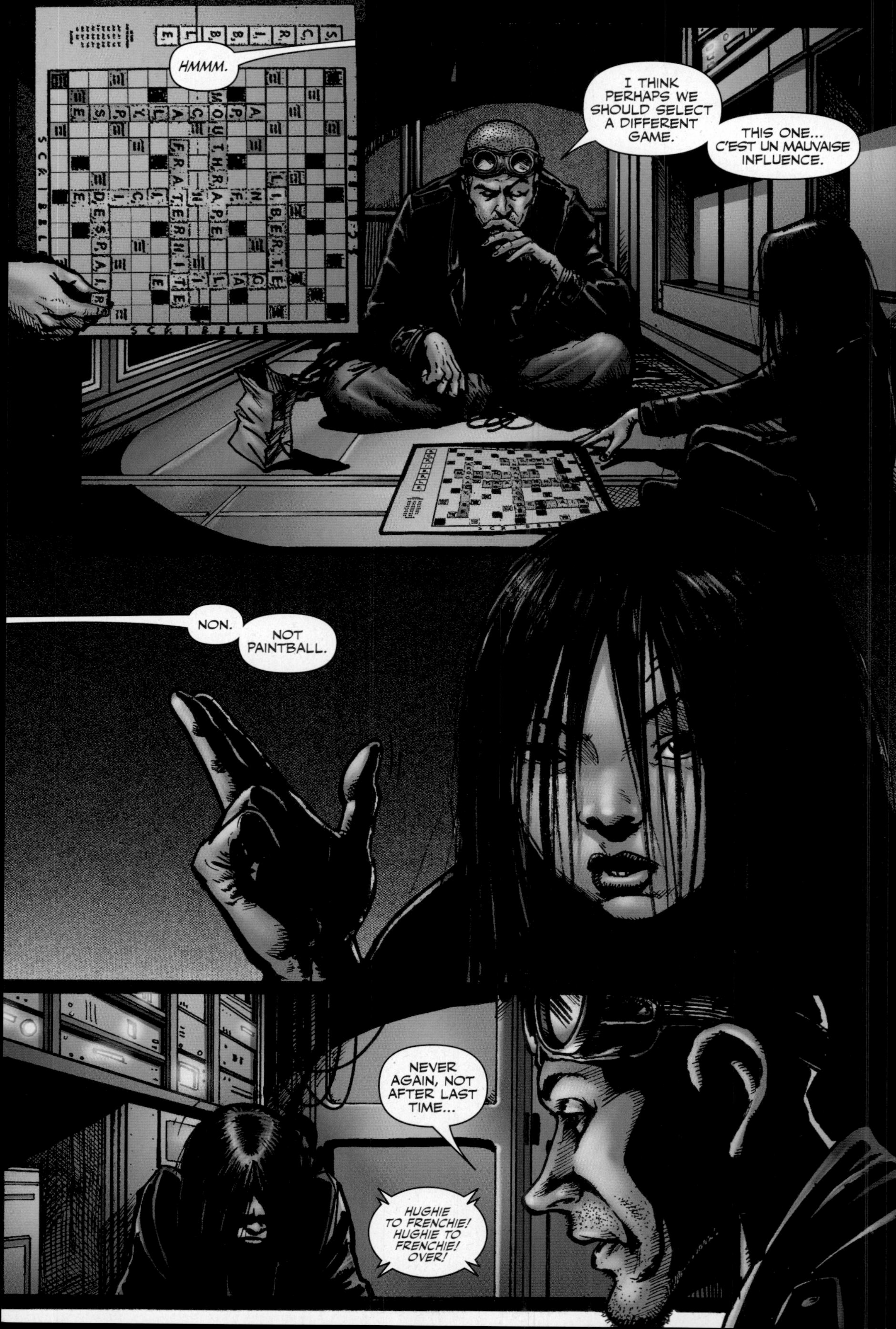
HMMM.
I THINK PERHAPS WE SHOULD SELECT A DIFFERENT GAME.
THIS ONE... C'EST UN MAUVAISE INFLUENCE.
NON.
NOT PAINTBALL.
NEVER AGAIN, NOT AFTER LAST TIME...
HUGHIE TO FRENCHIE! HUGHIE TO FRENCHIE! OVER!

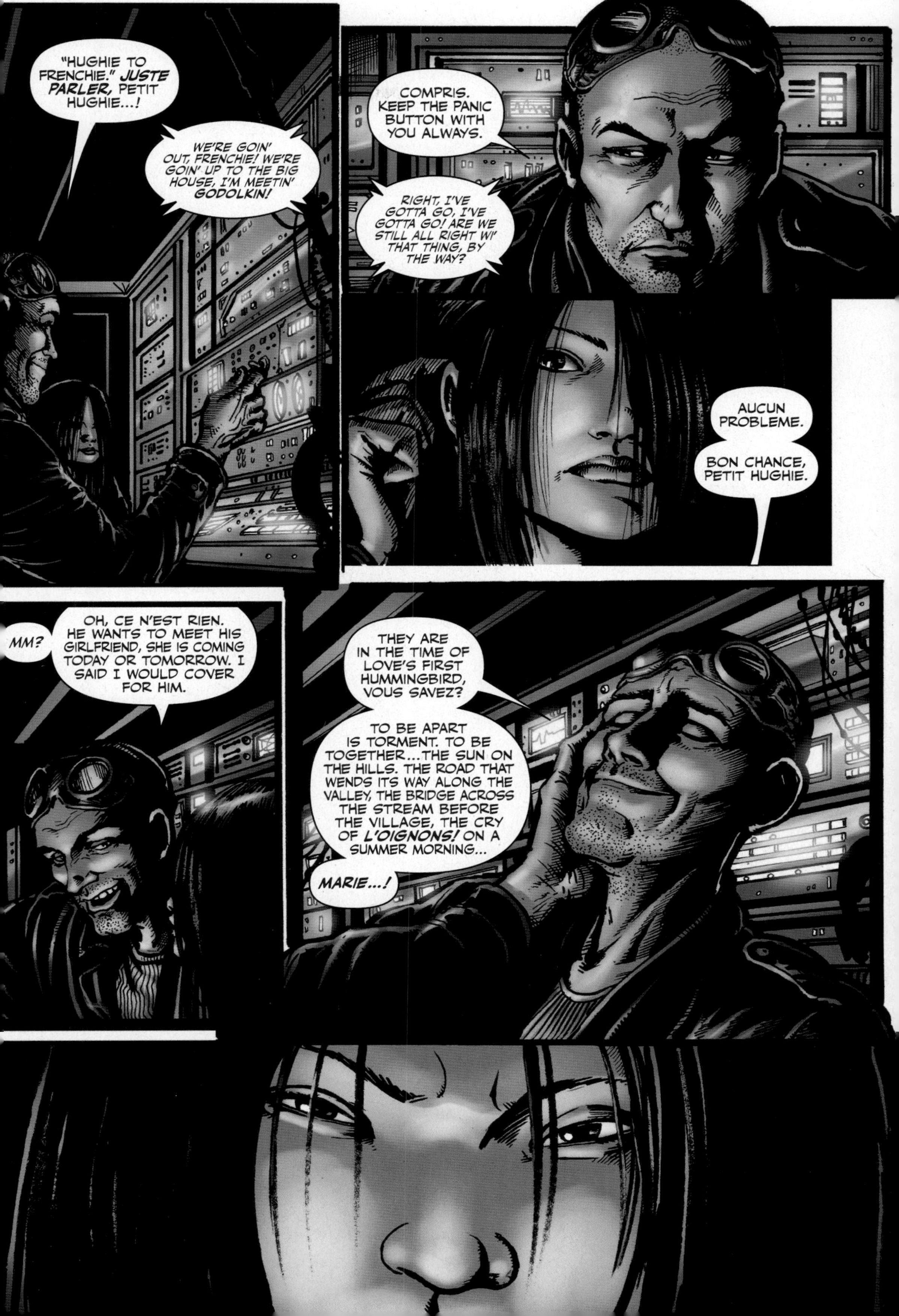
"HUGHIE TO FRENCHIE." JUSTE PARLER, PETIT HUGHIE...!
WE'RE GOIN' OUT, FRENCHIE! WE'RE GOIN' UP TO THE BIG HOUSE, I'M MEETIN' GODOLKIN!
COMPRIS. KEEP THE PANIC BUTTON WITH YOU ALWAYS.
RIGHT, I'VE GOTTA GO, I'VE GOTTA GO! ARE WE STILL ALL RIGHT WI' THAT THING, BY THE WAY?
AUCUN PROBLEME.
BON CHANCE, PETIT HUGHIE.
MM?
OH, CE N'EST RIEN. HE WANTS TO MEET HIS GIRLFRIEND, SHE IS COMING TODAY OR TOMORROW. I SAID I WOULD COVER FOR HIM.
THEY ARE IN THE TIME OF LOVE'S FIRST HUMMINGBIRD, VOUS SAVEZ?
TO BE APART IS TORMENT. TO BE TOGETHER...THE SUN ON THE HILLS. THE ROAD THAT WENDS ITS WAY ALONG THE VALLEY, THE BRIDGE ACROSS THE STREAM BEFORE THE VILLAGE, THE CRY OF L'OIGNONS! ON A SUMMER MORNING...
MARIE...!

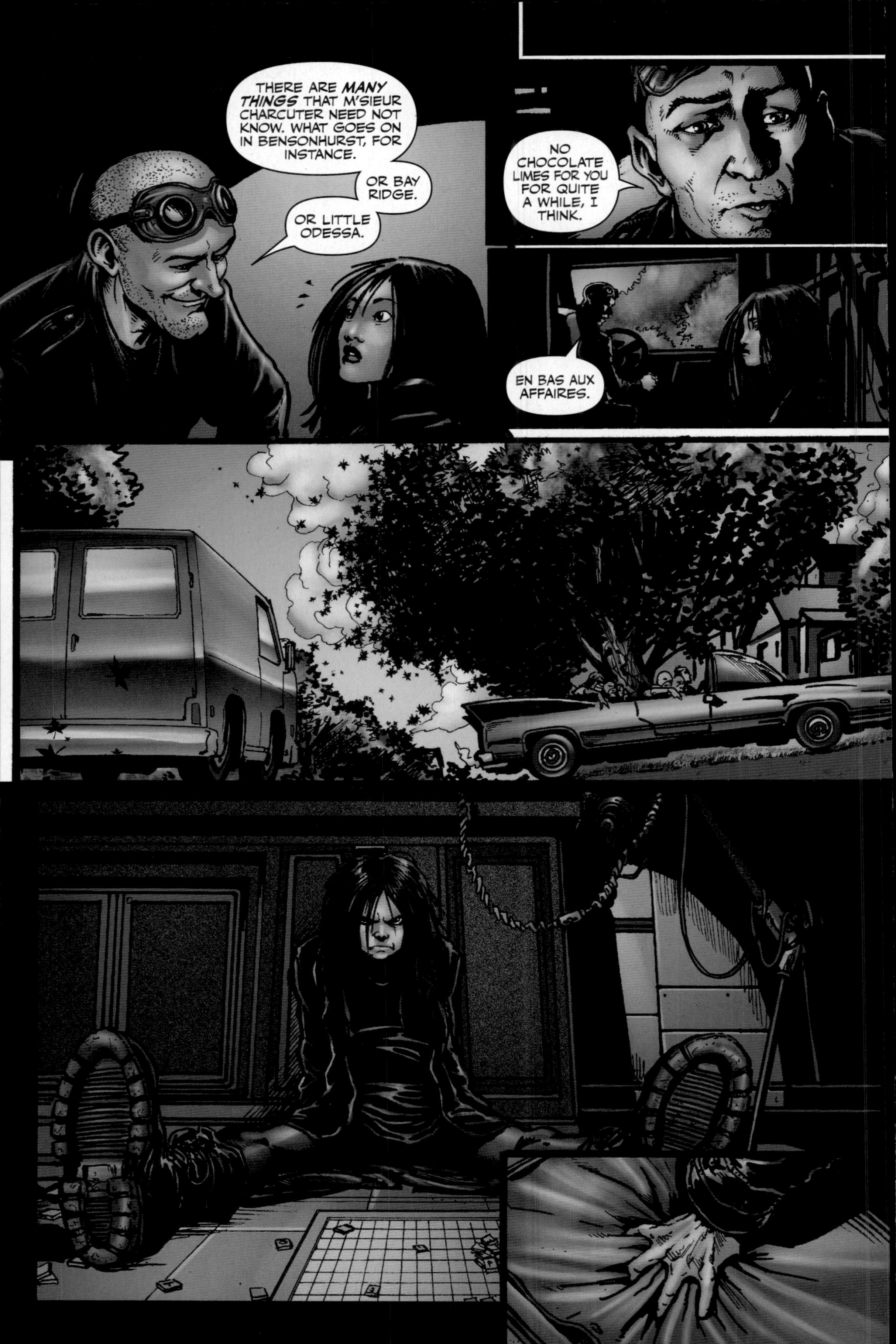
THERE ARE MANY THINGS THAT M'SIEUR CHARCUTER NEED NOT KNOW. WHAT GOES ON IN BENSONHURST, FOR INSTANCE.
OR BAY RIDGE.
OR LITTLE ODESSA.
NO CHOCOLATE LIMES FOR YOU FOR QUITE A WHILE, I THINK.
EN BAS AUX AFFAIRES.

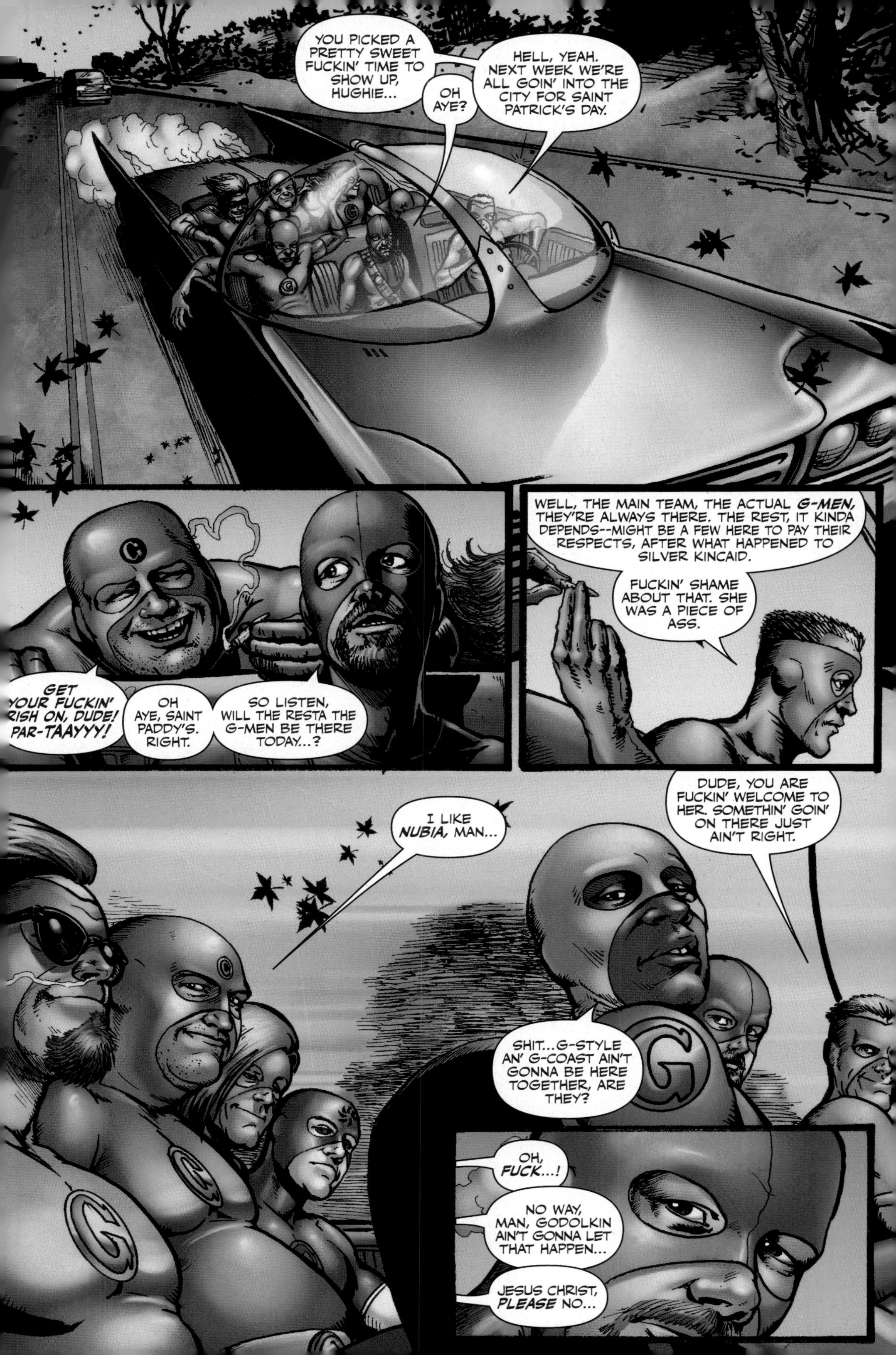
YOU PICKED A PRETTY SWEET FUCKIN' TIME TO SHOW UP, HUGHIE...
OH AYE?
HELL, YEAH. NEXT WEEK WE'RE ALL GOIN' INTO THE CITY FOR SAINT PATRICK'S DAY.
GET YOUR FUCKIN' IRISH ON, DUDE! PAR-TAAYYY!
OH AYE, SAINT PADDY'S. RIGHT.
SO LISTEN, WILL THE RESTA THE G-MEN BE THERE TODAY...?
WELL, THE MAIN TEAM, THE ACTUAL G-MEN, THEY'RE ALWAYS THERE. THE REST, IT KINDA DEPENDS--MIGHT BE A FEW HERE TO PAY THEIR RESPECTS, AFTER WHAT HAPPENED TO SILVER KINCAID.
FUCKIN' SHAME ABOUT THAT. SHE WAS A PIECE OF ASS.
I LIKE NUBIA, MAN...
DUDE, YOU ARE FUCKIN' WELCOME TO HER. SOMETHIN' GOIN' ON THERE JUST AIN'T RIGHT.
SHIT...G-STYLE AN' G-COAST AIN'T GONNA BE HERE TOGETHER, ARE THEY?
OH, FUCK...!
NO WAY, MAN, GODOLKIN AIN'T GONNA LET THAT HAPPEN...
JESUS CHRIST, PLEASE NO...

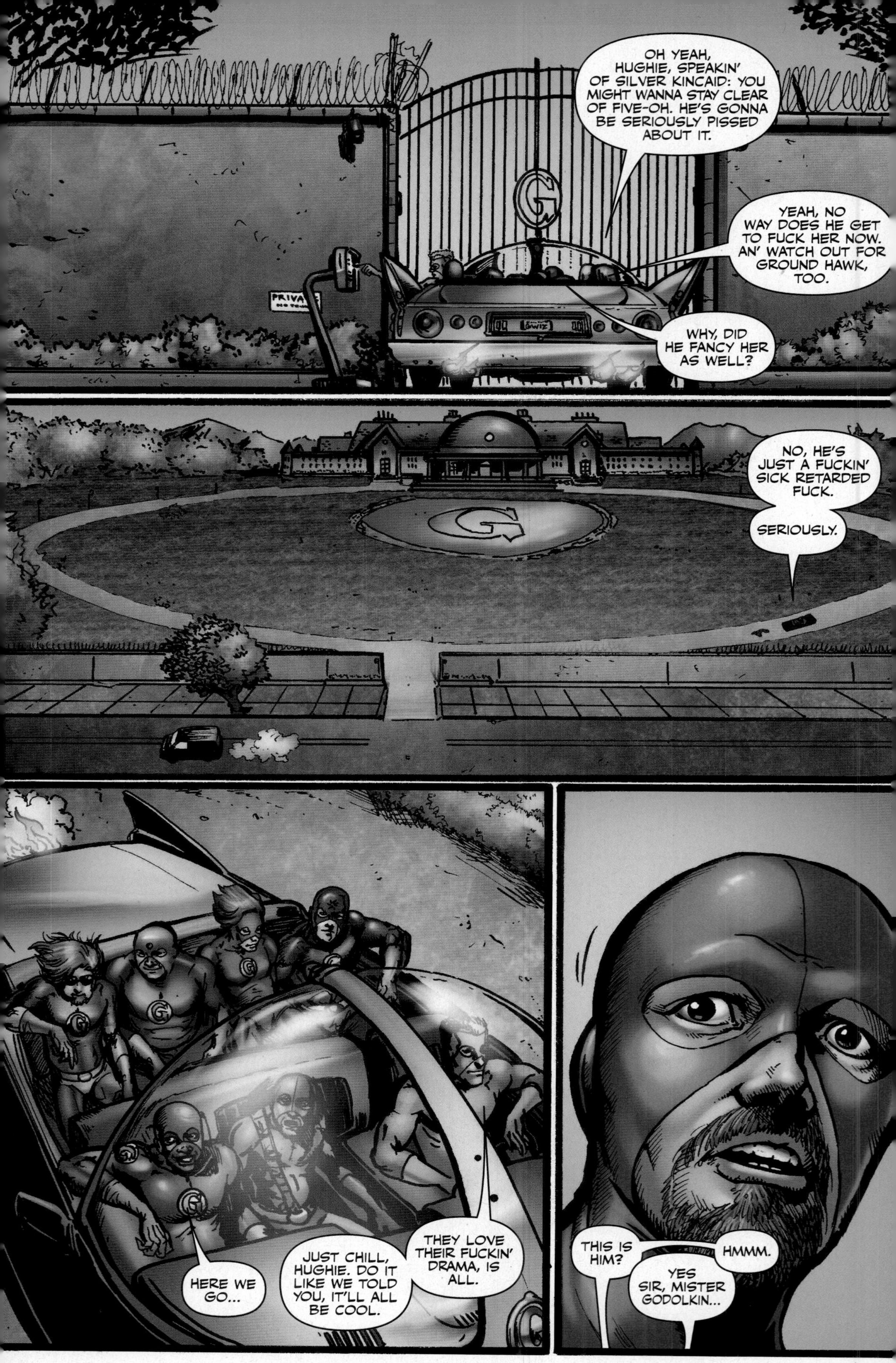

OH YEAH, HUGHIE, SPEAKIN' OF SILVER KINCAID: YOU MIGHT WANNA STAY CLEAR OF FIVE-OH. HE'S GONNA BE SERIOUSLY PISSED ABOUT IT.
YEAH, NO WAY DOES HE GET TO FUCK HER NOW. AN' WATCH OUT FOR GROUND HAWK, TOO.
WHY, DID HE FANCY HER AS WELL?
NO, HE'S JUST A FUCKIN' SICK RETARDED FUCK.
SERIOUSLY.
HERE WE GO...
JUST CHILL, HUGHIE. DO IT LIKE WE TOLD YOU, IT'LL ALL BE COOL.
THEY LOVE THEIR FUCKIN' DRAMA, IS ALL.
THIS IS HIM?
HMMM.
YES SIR, MISTER GODOLKIN...

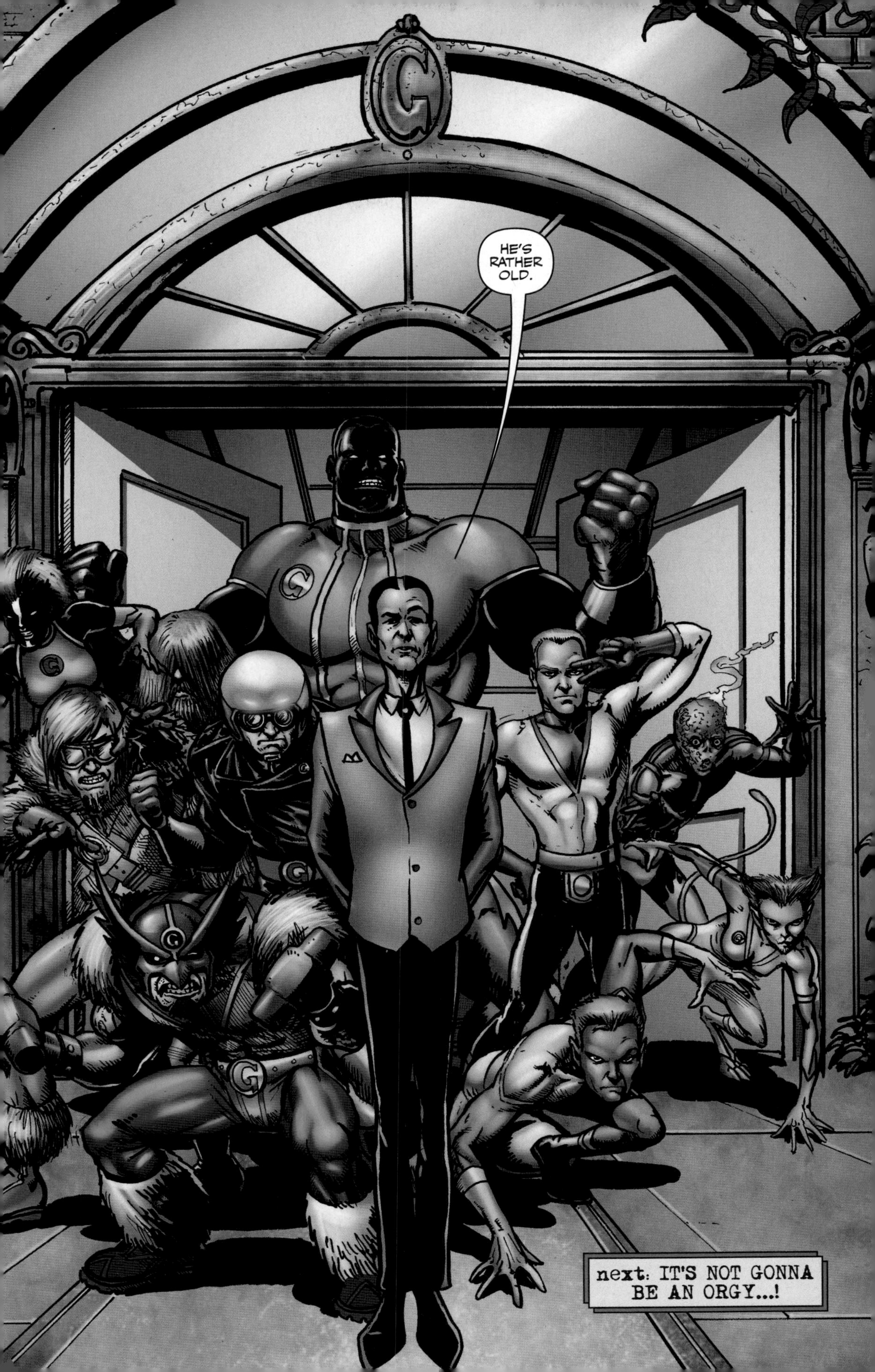
HE'S RATHER OLD.
next: IT'S NOT GONNA BE AN ORGY...!

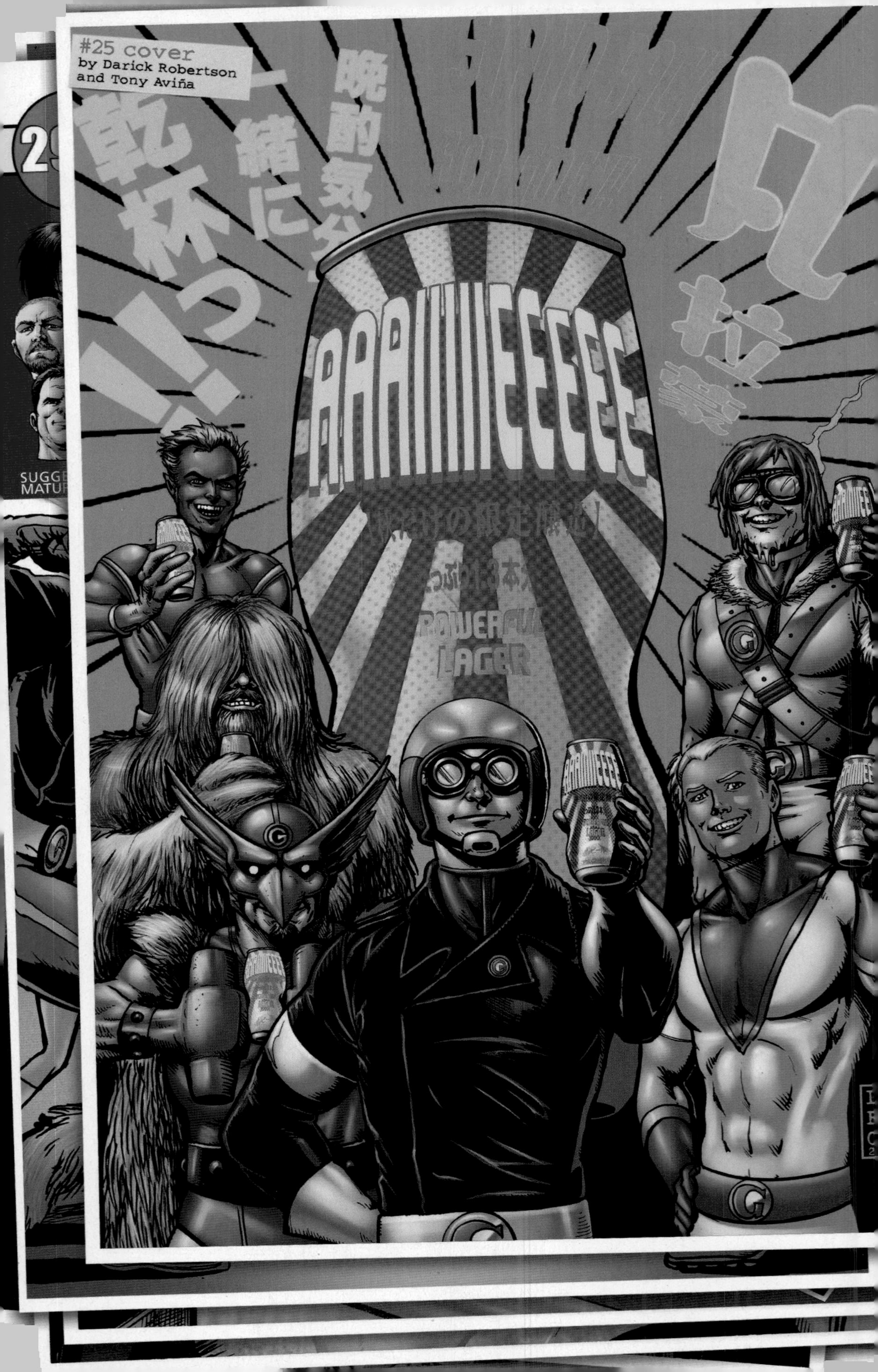
晩酌気分
一緒に
乾杯っ!!
AARIIIIEEEE
POWERFUL
LAGER

#25 cover
by Darick Robertson
and Tony Aviña

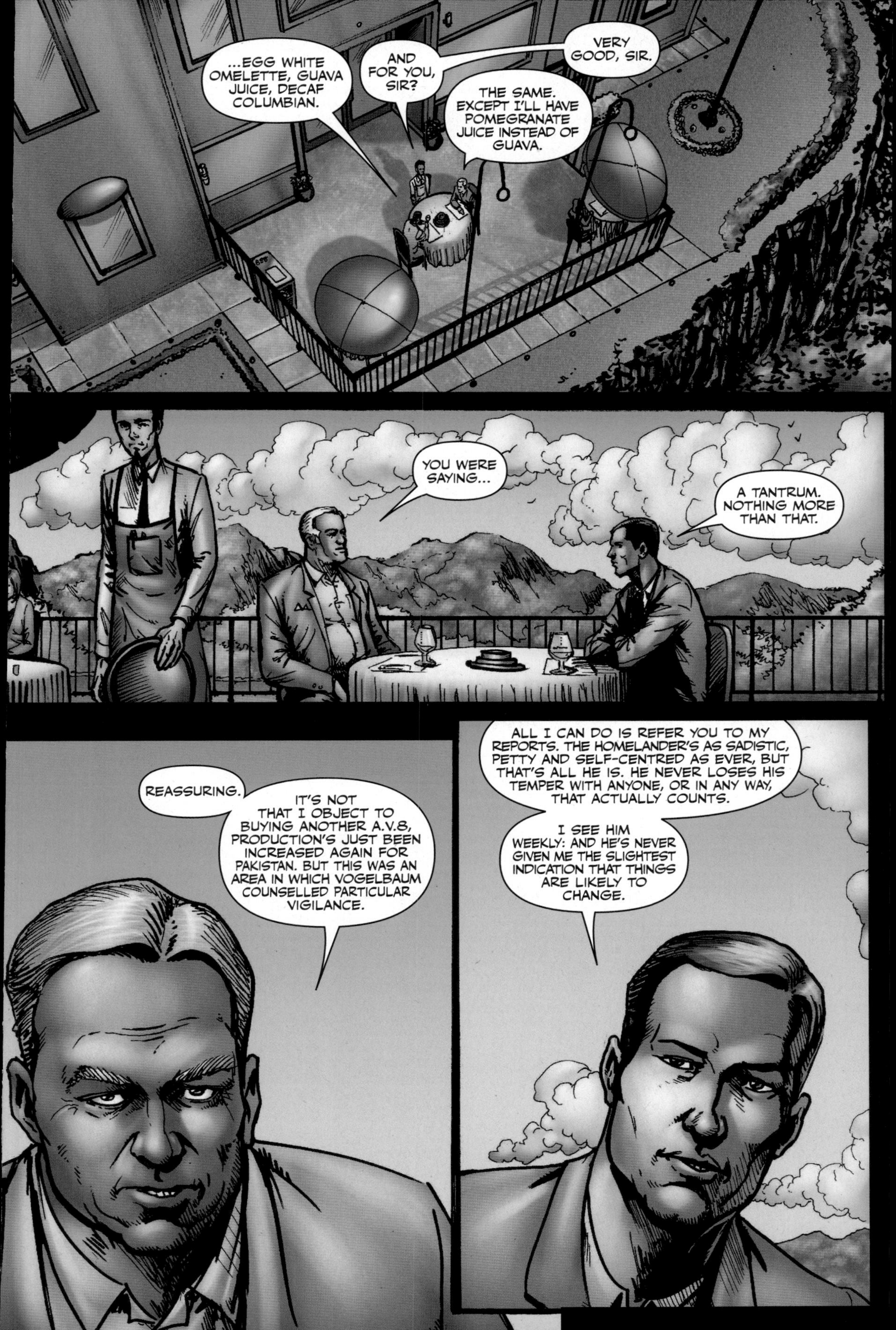
...EGG WHITE OMELETTE, GUAVA JUICE, DECAF COLUMBIAN.
AND FOR YOU, SIR?
THE SAME. EXCEPT I'LL HAVE POMEGRANATE JUICE INSTEAD OF GUAVA.
VERY GOOD, SIR.
YOU WERE SAYING...
A TANTRUM. NOTHING MORE THAN THAT.
REASSURING.
IT'S NOT THAT I OBJECT TO BUYING ANOTHER A.V.8, PRODUCTION'S JUST BEEN INCREASED AGAIN FOR PAKISTAN. BUT THIS WAS AN AREA IN WHICH VOGELBAUM COUNSELLED PARTICULAR VIGILANCE.
ALL I CAN DO IS REFER YOU TO MY REPORTS. THE HOMELANDER'S AS SADISTIC, PETTY AND SELF-CENTRED AS EVER, BUT THAT'S ALL HE IS. HE NEVER LOSES HIS TEMPER WITH ANYONE, OR IN ANY WAY, THAT ACTUALLY COUNTS.
I SEE HIM WEEKLY: AND HE'S NEVER GIVEN ME THE SLIGHTEST INDICATION THAT THINGS ARE LIKELY TO CHANGE.

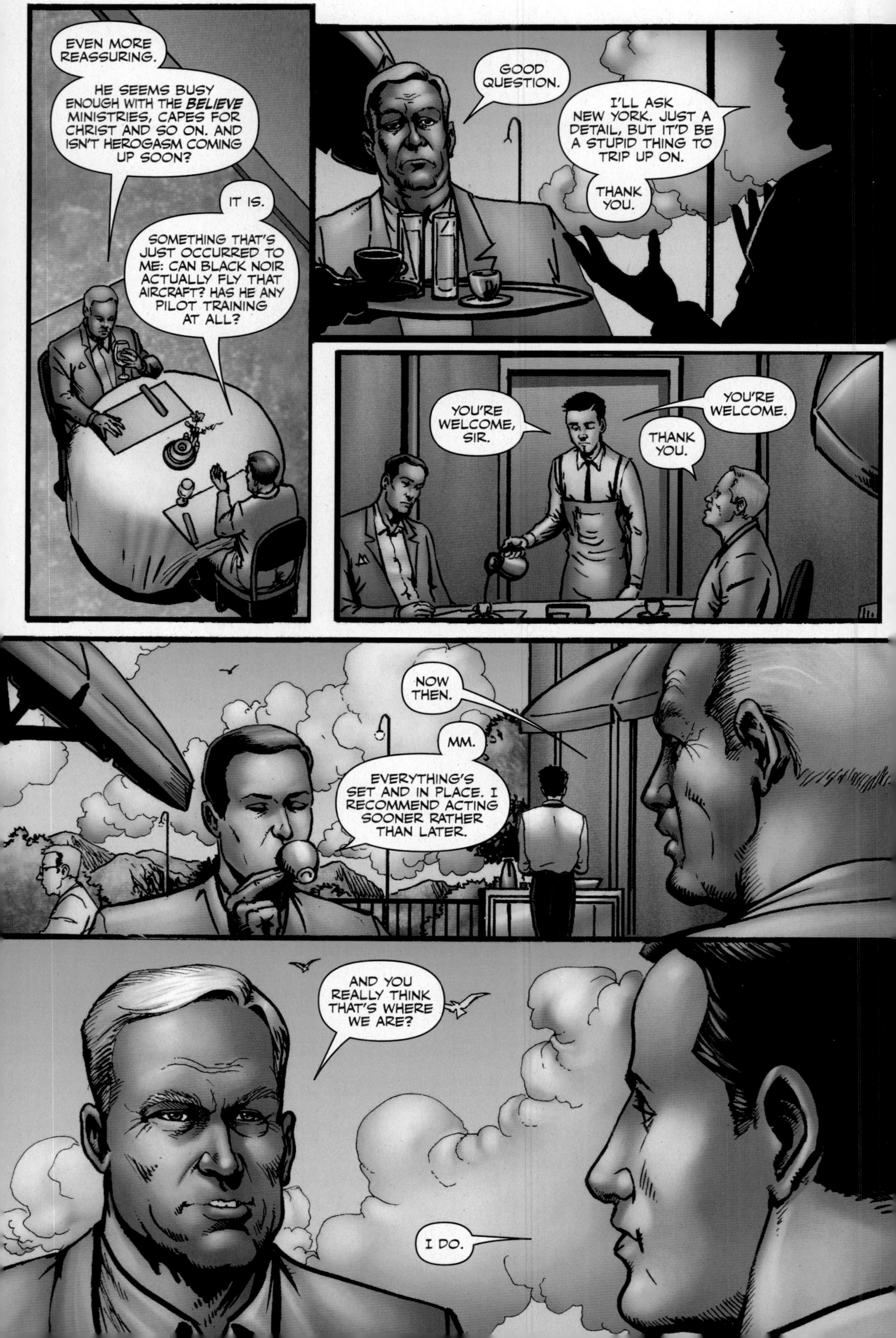
EVEN MORE REASSURING.
HE SEEMS BUSY ENOUGH WITH THE *BELIEVE* MINISTRIES, CAPES FOR CHRIST AND SO ON. AND ISN'T HEROGASM COMING UP SOON?
IT IS.
SOMETHING THAT'S JUST OCCURRED TO ME: CAN BLACK NOIR ACTUALLY FLY THAT AIRCRAFT? HAS HE ANY PILOT TRAINING AT ALL?
GOOD QUESTION.
I'LL ASK NEW YORK. JUST A DETAIL, BUT IT'D BE A STUPID THING TO TRIP UP ON.
THANK YOU.
YOU'RE WELCOME, SIR.
YOU'RE WELCOME.
THANK YOU.
NOW THEN.
MM.
EVERYTHING'S SET AND IN PLACE. I RECOMMEND ACTING SOONER RATHER THAN LATER.
AND YOU REALLY THINK THAT'S WHERE WE ARE?
I DO.

GODOLKIN'S ALWAYS ENJOYED A...UNIQUE MEASURE OF AUTONOMY. LARGELY MY PREDECESSOR'S DOING, BUT I CAN'T CLAIM TO HAVE TAKEN ANY STEPS TO CHANGE THINGS.

ALL THE SAME...

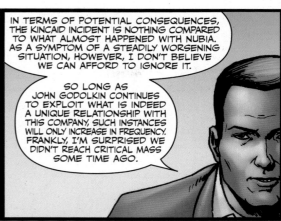

IN TERMS OF POTENTIAL CONSEQUENCES, THE KINCAID INCIDENT IS NOTHING COMPARED TO WHAT ALMOST HAPPENED WITH NUBIA. AS A SYMPTOM OF A STEADILY WORSENING SITUATION, HOWEVER, I DON'T BELIEVE WE CAN AFFORD TO IGNORE IT.

SO LONG AS JOHN GODOLKIN CONTINUES TO EXPLOIT WHAT IS INDEED A UNIQUE RELATIONSHIP WITH THIS COMPANY, SUCH INSTANCES WILL ONLY INCREASE IN FREQUENCY. FRANKLY, I'M SURPRISED WE DIDN'T REACH CRITICAL MASS SOME TIME AGO.

MM...

ALL WE'RE TALKING ABOUT IS CONTAINMENT. NOTHING MORE AND NOTHING LESS.

...LET ME THINK ABOUT IT.

OF COURSE.

THANK YOU.

THANK YOU.

YOU'RE WELCOME.

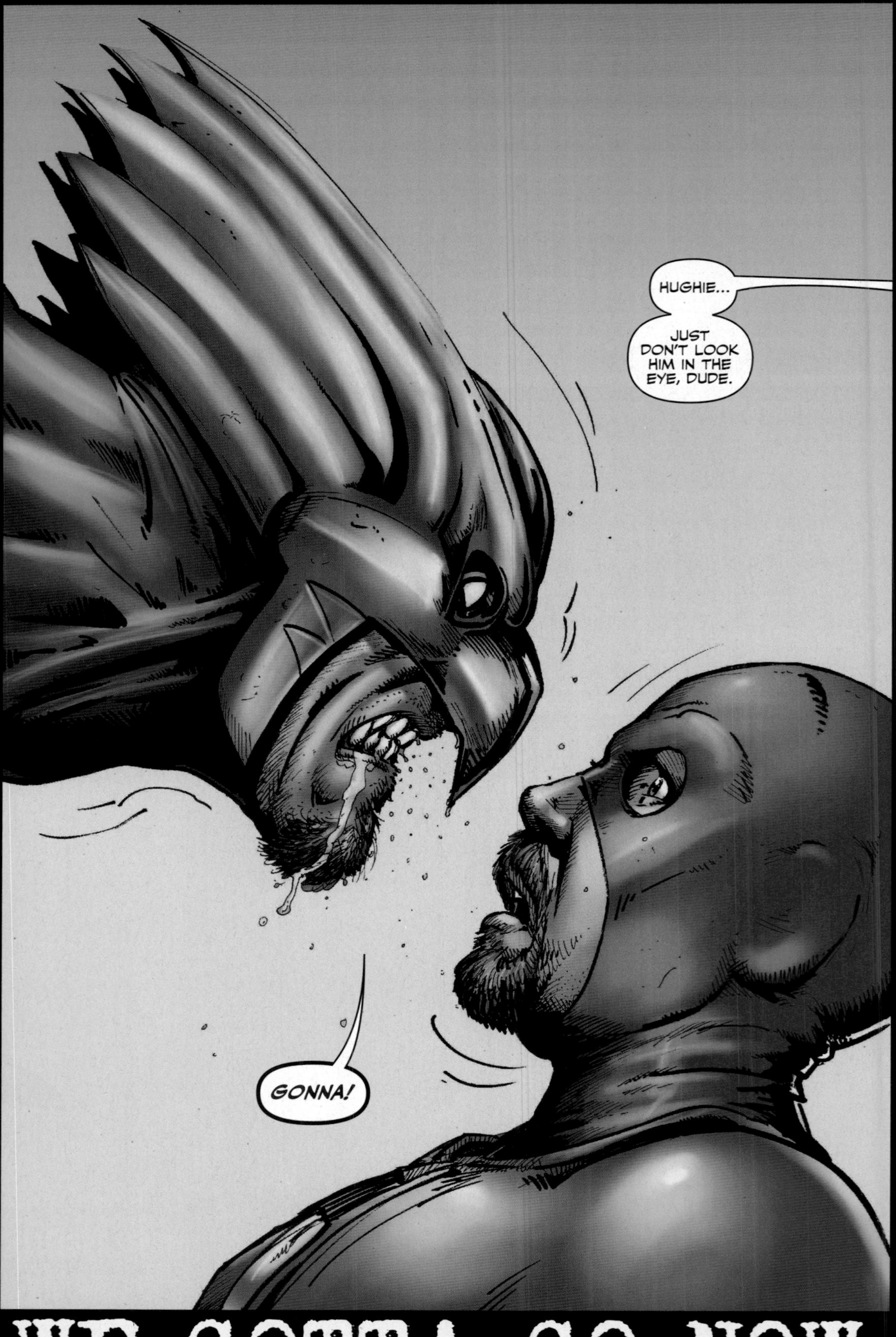
HUGHIE...
JUST DON'T LOOK HIM IN THE EYE, DUDE.
GONNA!

WE GOTTA GO NOW
part three

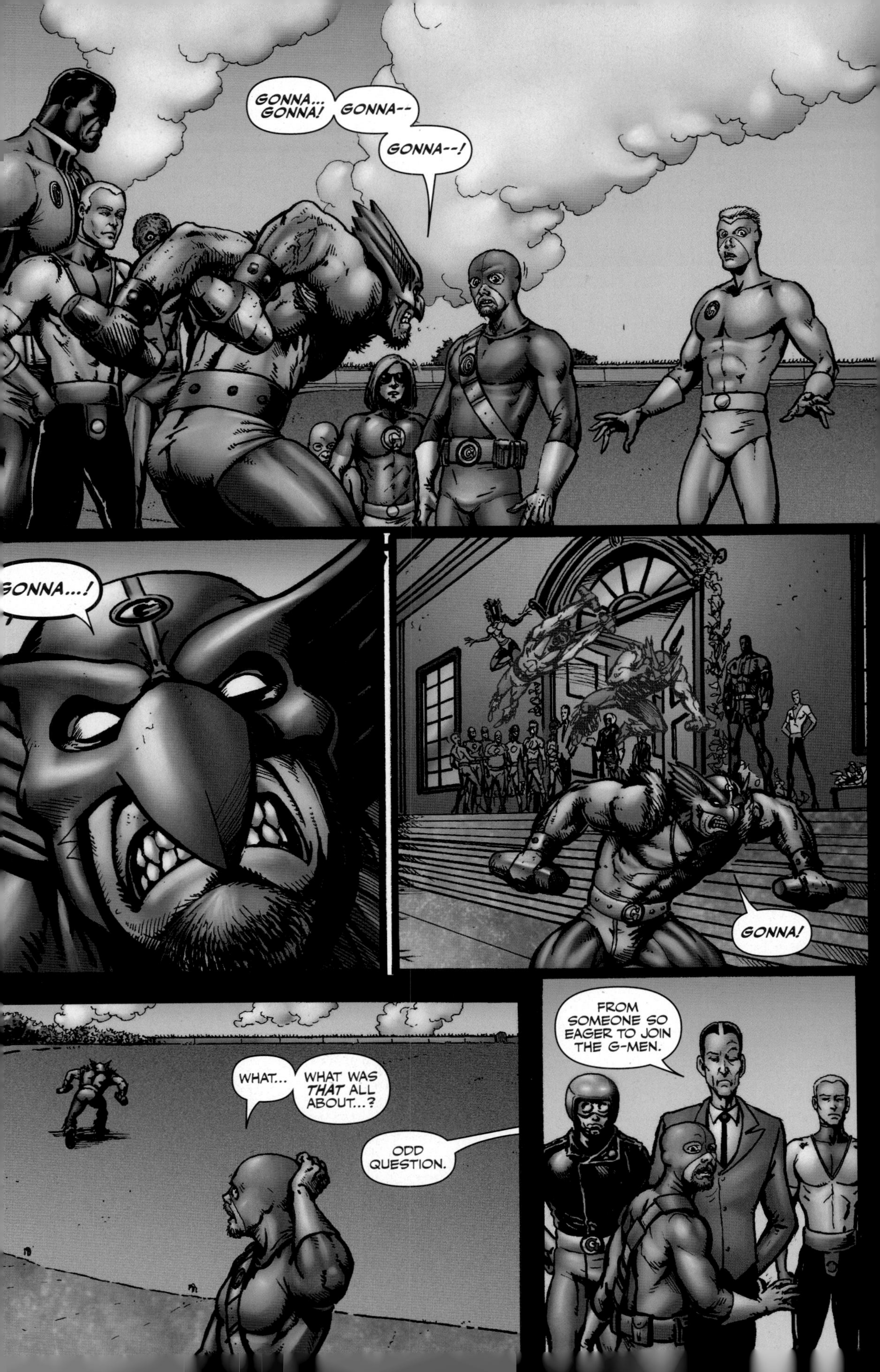
GONNA... GONNA!
GONNA--
GONNA--!
GONNA...!
GONNA!
WHAT...
WHAT WAS THAT ALL ABOUT...?
ODD QUESTION.
FROM SOMEONE SO EAGER TO JOIN THE G-MEN.

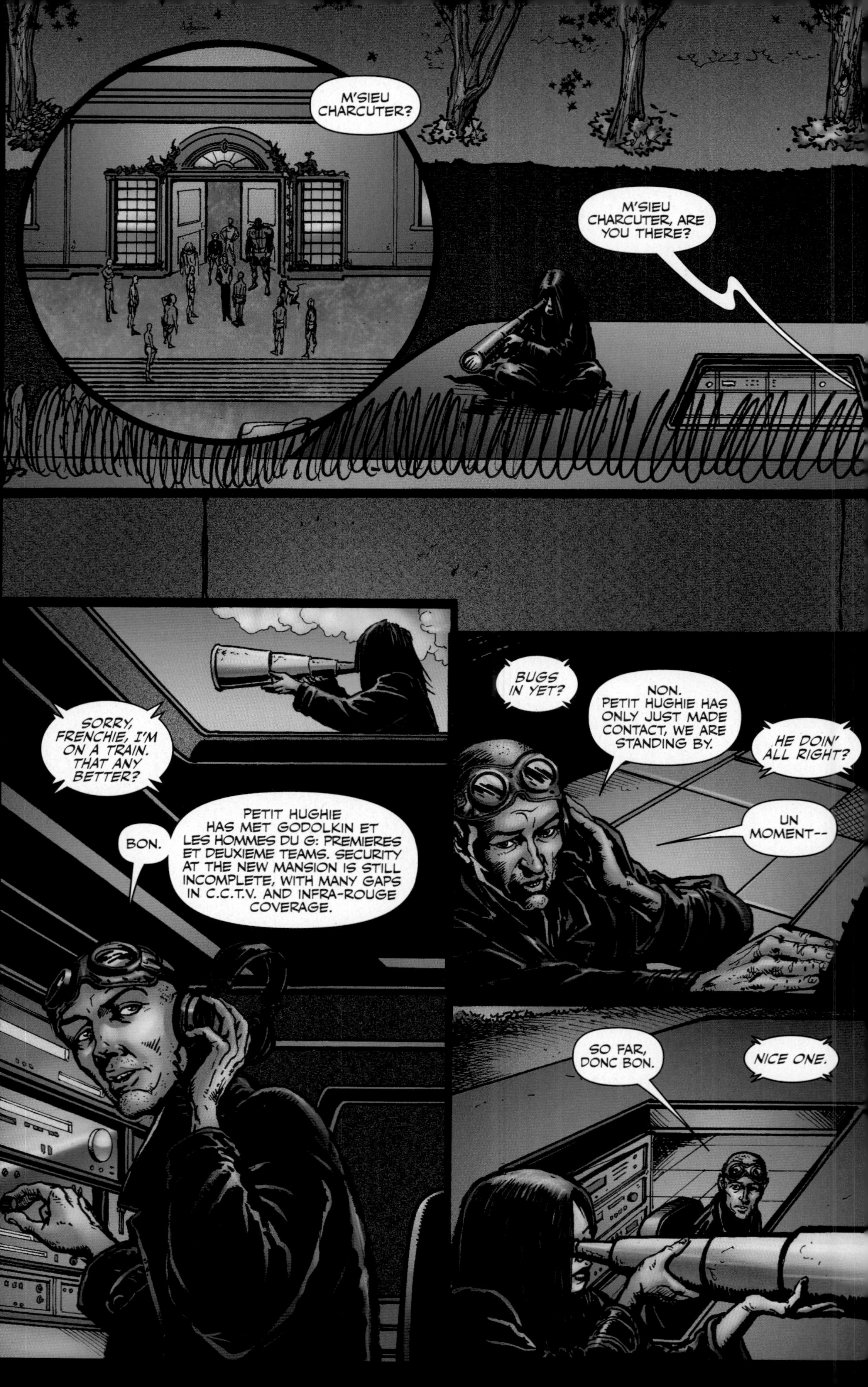
M'SIEU CHARCUTER?
M'SIEU CHARCUTER, ARE YOU THERE?
SORRY, FRENCHIE, I'M ON A TRAIN. THAT ANY BETTER?
BON.
PETIT HUGHIE HAS MET GODOLKIN ET LES HOMMES DU G: PREMIERES ET DEUXIEME TEAMS. SECURITY AT THE NEW MANSION IS STILL INCOMPLETE, WITH MANY GAPS IN C.C.T.V. AND INFRA-ROUGE COVERAGE.
BUGS IN YET?
NON. PETIT HUGHIE HAS ONLY JUST MADE CONTACT, WE ARE STANDING BY.
HE DOIN' ALL RIGHT?
UN MOMENT--
SO FAR, DONC BON.
NICE ONE.

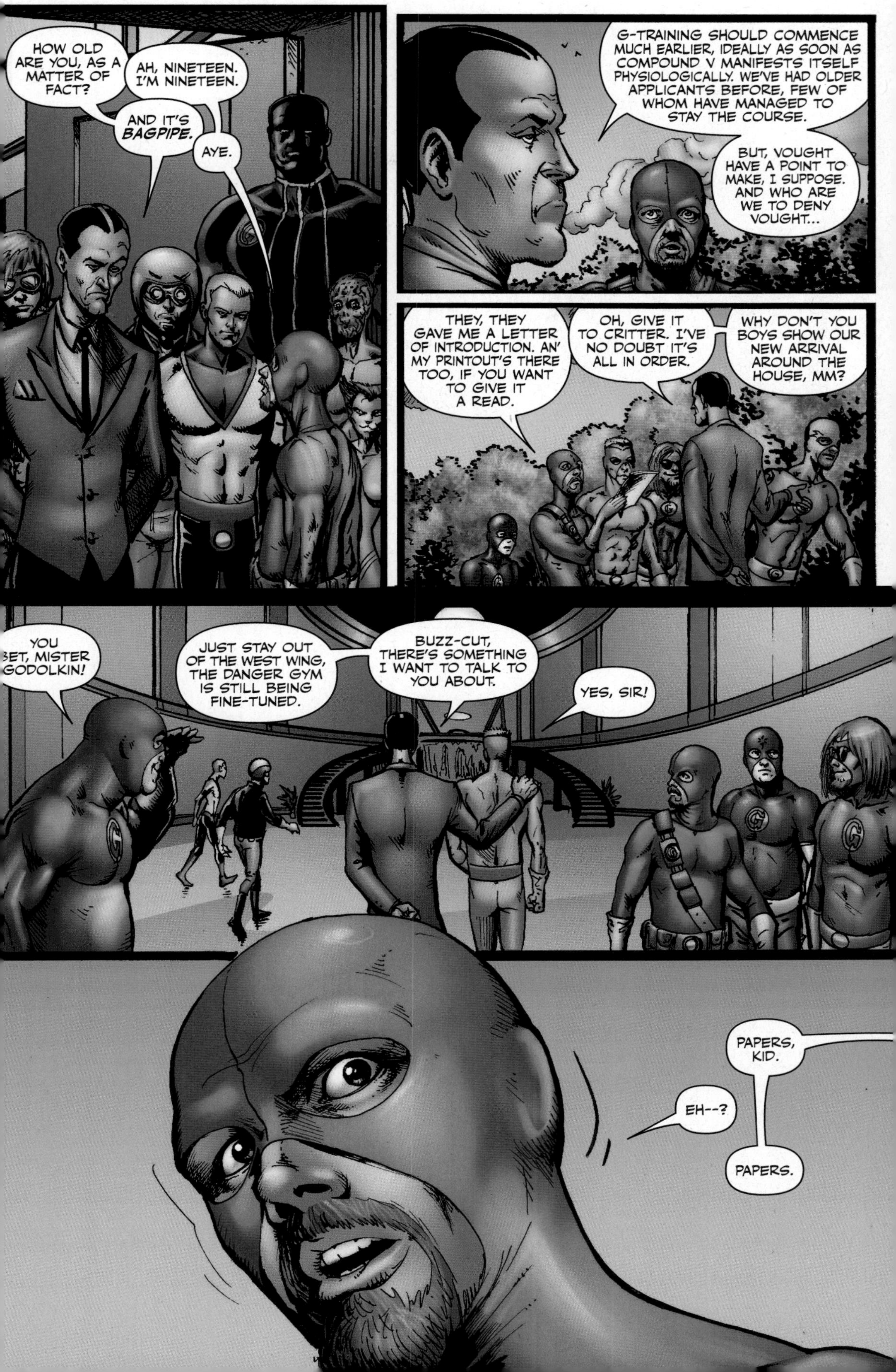
HOW OLD ARE YOU, AS A MATTER OF FACT?
AH, NINETEEN. I'M NINETEEN.
AND IT'S BAGPIPE.
AYE.
G-TRAINING SHOULD COMMENCE MUCH EARLIER, IDEALLY AS SOON AS COMPOUND V MANIFESTS ITSELF PHYSIOLOGICALLY. WE'VE HAD OLDER APPLICANTS BEFORE, FEW OF WHOM HAVE MANAGED TO STAY THE COURSE.
BUT, VOUGHT HAVE A POINT TO MAKE, I SUPPOSE. AND WHO ARE WE TO DENY VOUGHT...
THEY, THEY GAVE ME A LETTER OF INTRODUCTION. AN' MY PRINTOUT'S THERE TOO, IF YOU WANT TO GIVE IT A READ.
OH, GIVE IT TO CRITTER. I'VE NO DOUBT IT'S ALL IN ORDER.
WHY DON'T YOU BOYS SHOW OUR NEW ARRIVAL AROUND THE HOUSE, MM?
YOU BET, MISTER GODOLKIN!
JUST STAY OUT OF THE WEST WING, THE DANGER GYM IS STILL BEING FINE-TUNED.
BUZZ-CUT, THERE'S SOMETHING I WANT TO TALK TO YOU ABOUT.
YES, SIR!
PAPERS, KID.
EH--?
PAPERS.

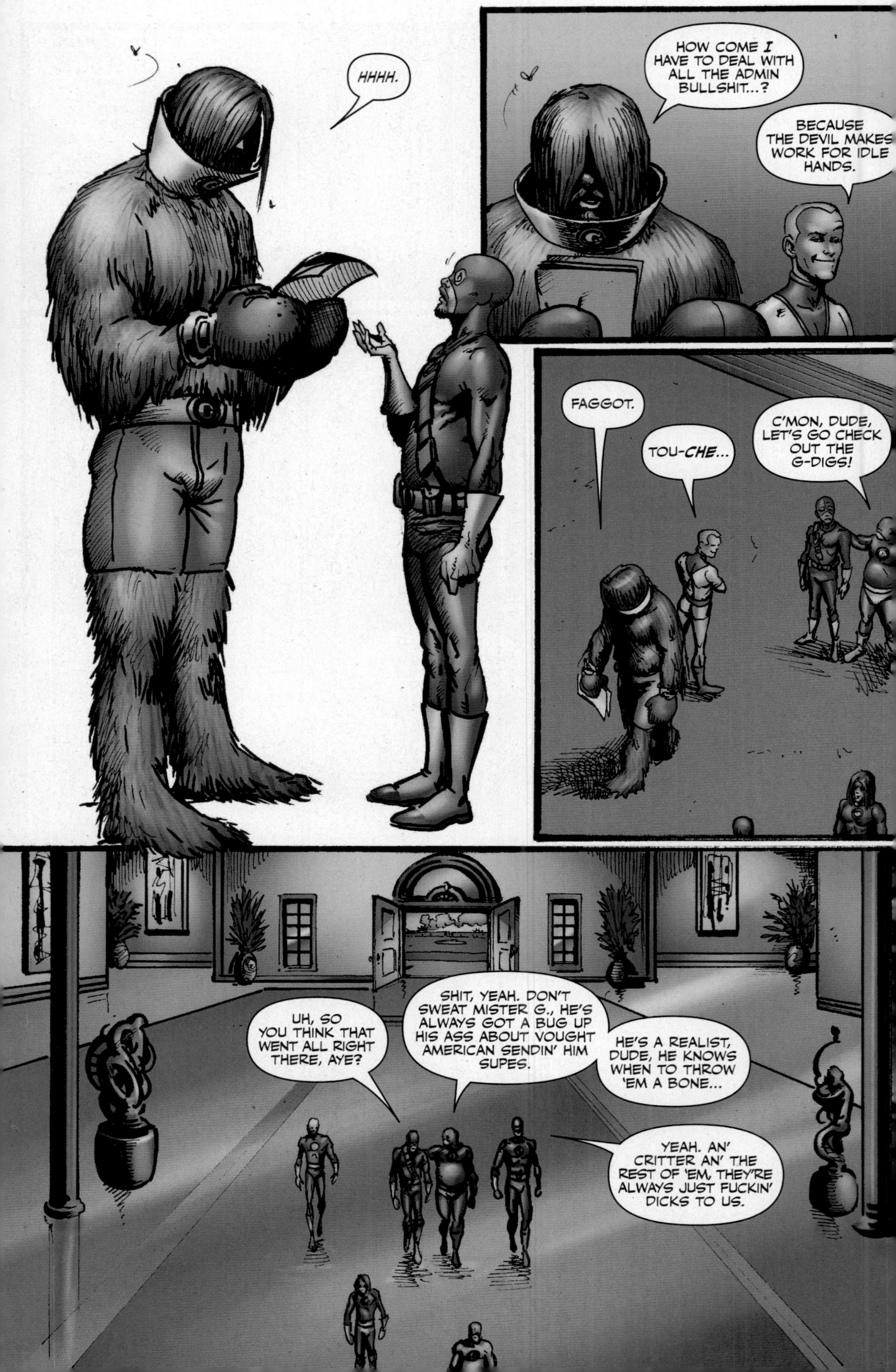
HHHH.
HOW COME I HAVE TO DEAL WITH ALL THE ADMIN BULLSHIT...?
BECAUSE THE DEVIL MAKES WORK FOR IDLE HANDS.
FAGGOT.
TOU-CHE...
C'MON, DUDE, LET'S GO CHECK OUT THE G-DIGS!
UH, SO YOU THINK THAT WENT ALL RIGHT THERE, AYE?
SHIT, YEAH. DON'T SWEAT MISTER G., HE'S ALWAYS GOT A BUG UP HIS ASS ABOUT VOUGHT AMERICAN SENDIN' HIM SUPES.
HE'S A REALIST, DUDE, HE KNOWS WHEN TO THROW 'EM A BONE...
YEAH. AN' CRITTER AN' THE REST OF 'EM, THEY'RE ALWAYS JUST FUCKIN' DICKS TO US.

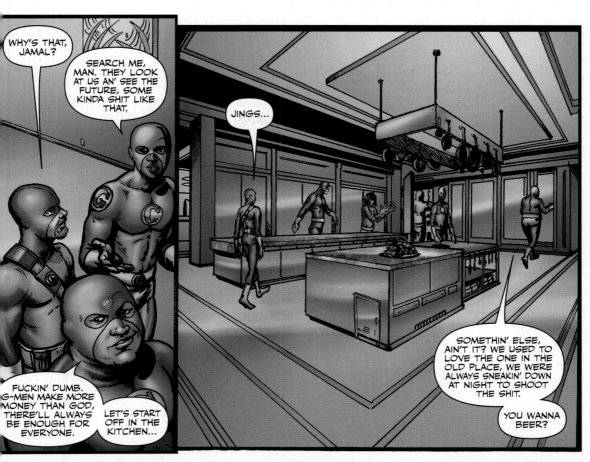

WHY'S THAT, JAMAL?

SEARCH ME, MAN. THEY LOOK AT US AN' SEE THE FUTURE, SOME KINDA SHIT LIKE THAT.

JINGS...

SOMETHIN' ELSE, AIN'T IT? WE USED TO LOVE THE ONE IN THE OLD PLACE, WE WERE ALWAYS SNEAKIN' DOWN AT NIGHT TO SHOOT THE SHIT.

YOU WANNA BEER?

FUCKIN' DUMB. G-MEN MAKE MORE MONEY THAN GOD, THERE'LL ALWAYS BE ENOUGH FOR EVERYONE.

LET'S START OFF IN THE KITCHEN...

AYE, THANKS, BLOWCHOWSKI. SO MIDNIGHT FEASTS AN' ALL, EH?

YEAH, I GUESS... FUCK, THEY ONLY GOT THAT JAP STUFF, ALWAYS GIVES ME THE FIZZY SHITS. YOU GUYS OKAY WITH THAT?

OH AYE, FINE, MATE.

JESUS, COULD I USE ONE OF THOSE...

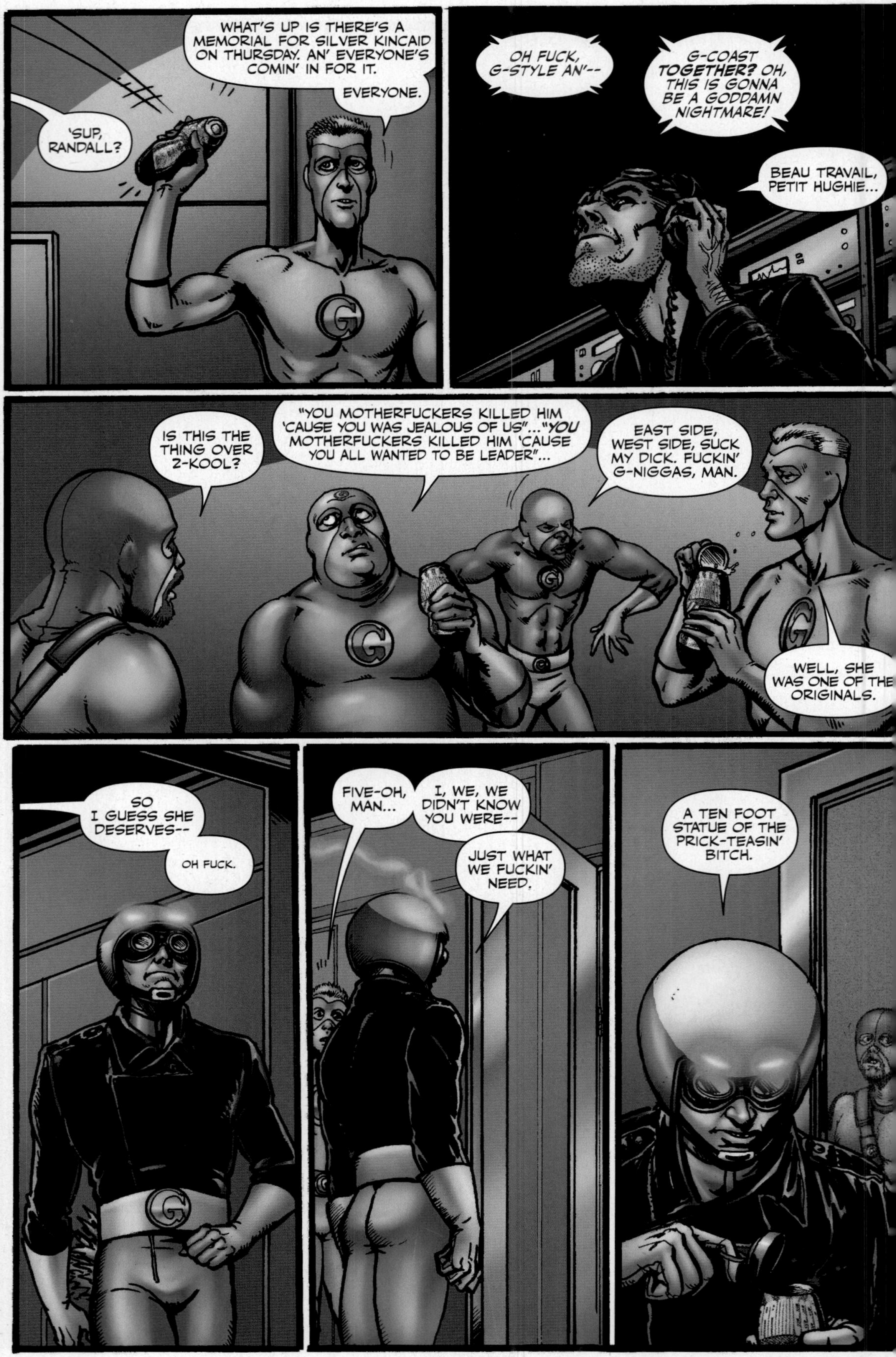
WHAT'S UP IS THERE'S A MEMORIAL FOR SILVER KINCAID ON THURSDAY. AN' EVERYONE'S COMIN' IN FOR IT.
'SUP, RANDALL?
EVERYONE.
OH FUCK, G-STYLE AN'--
G-COAST TOGETHER? OH, THIS IS GONNA BE A GODDAMN NIGHTMARE!
BEAU TRAVAIL, PETIT HUGHIE...
IS THIS THE THING OVER 2-KOOL?
"YOU MOTHERFUCKERS KILLED HIM 'CAUSE YOU WAS JEALOUS OF US"..."YOU MOTHERFUCKERS KILLED HIM 'CAUSE YOU ALL WANTED TO BE LEADER"...
EAST SIDE, WEST SIDE, SUCK MY DICK. FUCKIN' G-NIGGAS, MAN.
WELL, SHE WAS ONE OF THE ORIGINALS.
SO I GUESS SHE DESERVES--
OH FUCK.
FIVE-OH, MAN...
I, WE, WE DIDN'T KNOW YOU WERE--
JUST WHAT WE FUCKIN' NEED.
A TEN FOOT STATUE OF THE PRICK-TEASIN' BITCH.

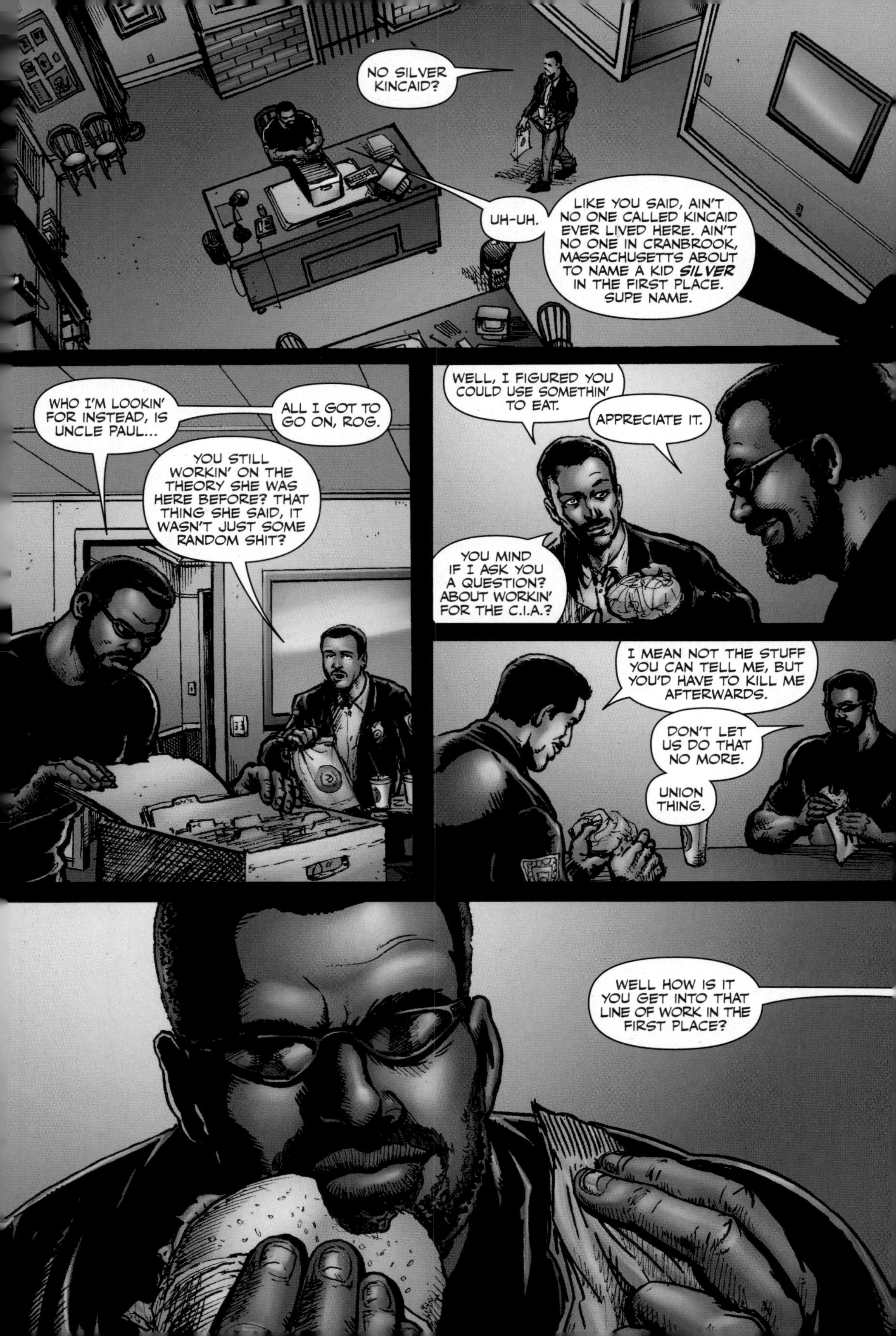
NO SILVER KINCAID?
UH-UH.
LIKE YOU SAID, AIN'T NO ONE CALLED KINCAID EVER LIVED HERE. AIN'T NO ONE IN CRANBROOK, MASSACHUSETTS ABOUT TO NAME A KID SILVER IN THE FIRST PLACE. SUPE NAME.
WHO I'M LOOKIN' FOR INSTEAD, IS UNCLE PAUL...
ALL I GOT TO GO ON, ROG.
YOU STILL WORKIN' ON THE THEORY SHE WAS HERE BEFORE? THAT THING SHE SAID, IT WASN'T JUST SOME RANDOM SHIT?
WELL, I FIGURED YOU COULD USE SOMETHIN' TO EAT.
APPRECIATE IT.
YOU MIND IF I ASK YOU A QUESTION? ABOUT WORKIN' FOR THE C.I.A.?
I MEAN NOT THE STUFF YOU CAN TELL ME, BUT YOU'D HAVE TO KILL ME AFTERWARDS.
DON'T LET US DO THAT NO MORE.
UNION THING.
WELL HOW IS IT YOU GET INTO THAT LINE OF WORK IN THE FIRST PLACE?

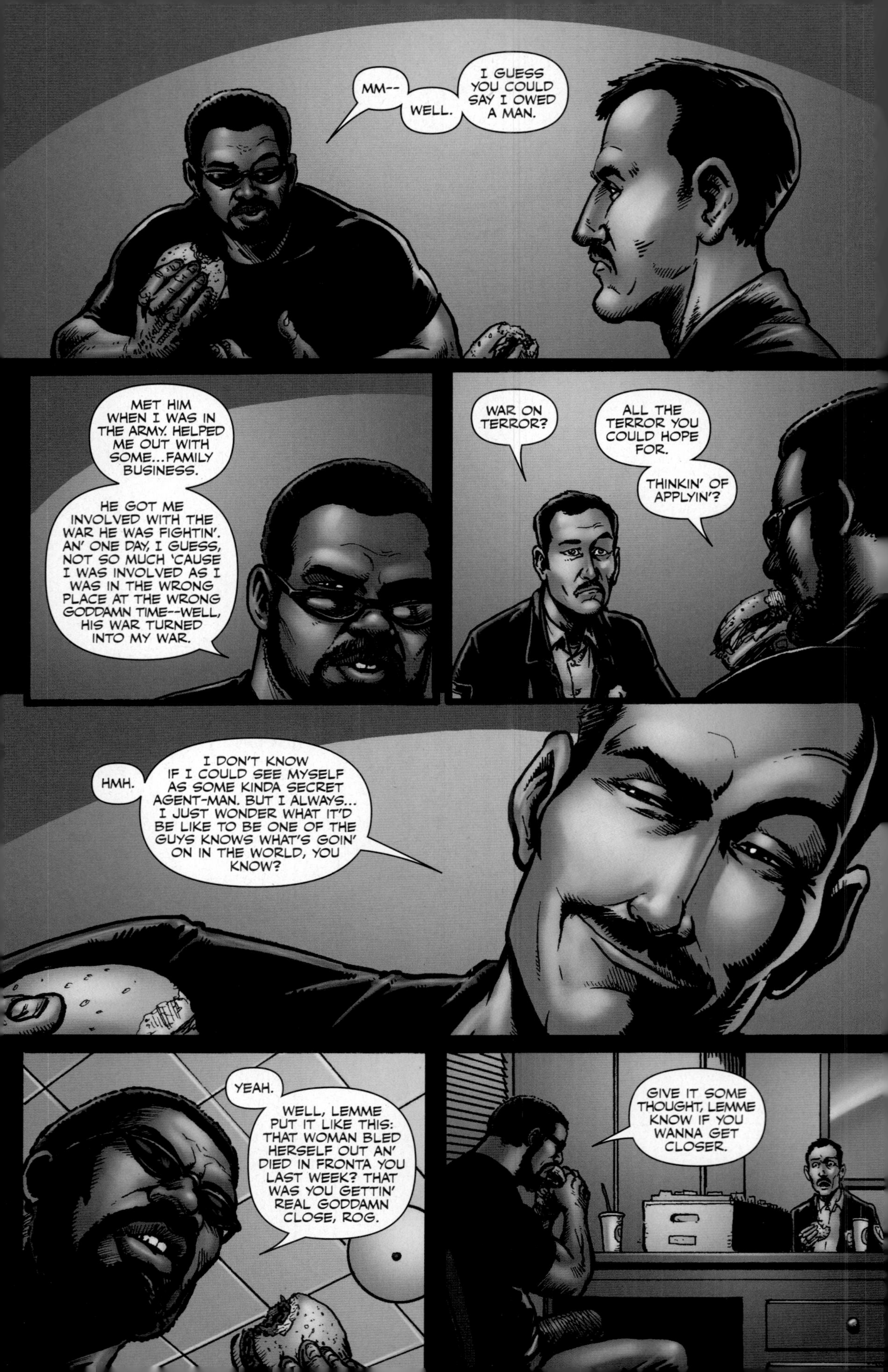
MM--
WELL.
I GUESS YOU COULD SAY I OWED A MAN.
MET HIM WHEN I WAS IN THE ARMY. HELPED ME OUT WITH SOME...FAMILY BUSINESS.
HE GOT ME INVOLVED WITH THE WAR HE WAS FIGHTIN'. AN' ONE DAY, I GUESS, NOT SO MUCH 'CAUSE I WAS INVOLVED AS I WAS IN THE WRONG PLACE AT THE WRONG GODDAMN TIME--WELL, HIS WAR TURNED INTO MY WAR.
WAR ON TERROR?
ALL THE TERROR YOU COULD HOPE FOR.
THINKIN' OF APPLYIN'?
HMH.
I DON'T KNOW IF I COULD SEE MYSELF AS SOME KINDA SECRET AGENT-MAN. BUT I ALWAYS... I JUST WONDER WHAT IT'D BE LIKE TO BE ONE OF THE GUYS KNOWS WHAT'S GOIN' ON IN THE WORLD, YOU KNOW?
YEAH.
WELL, LEMME PUT IT LIKE THIS: THAT WOMAN BLED HERSELF OUT AN' DIED IN FRONTA YOU LAST WEEK? THAT WAS YOU GETTIN' REAL GODDAMN CLOSE, ROG.
GIVE IT SOME THOUGHT, LEMME KNOW IF YOU WANNA GET CLOSER.

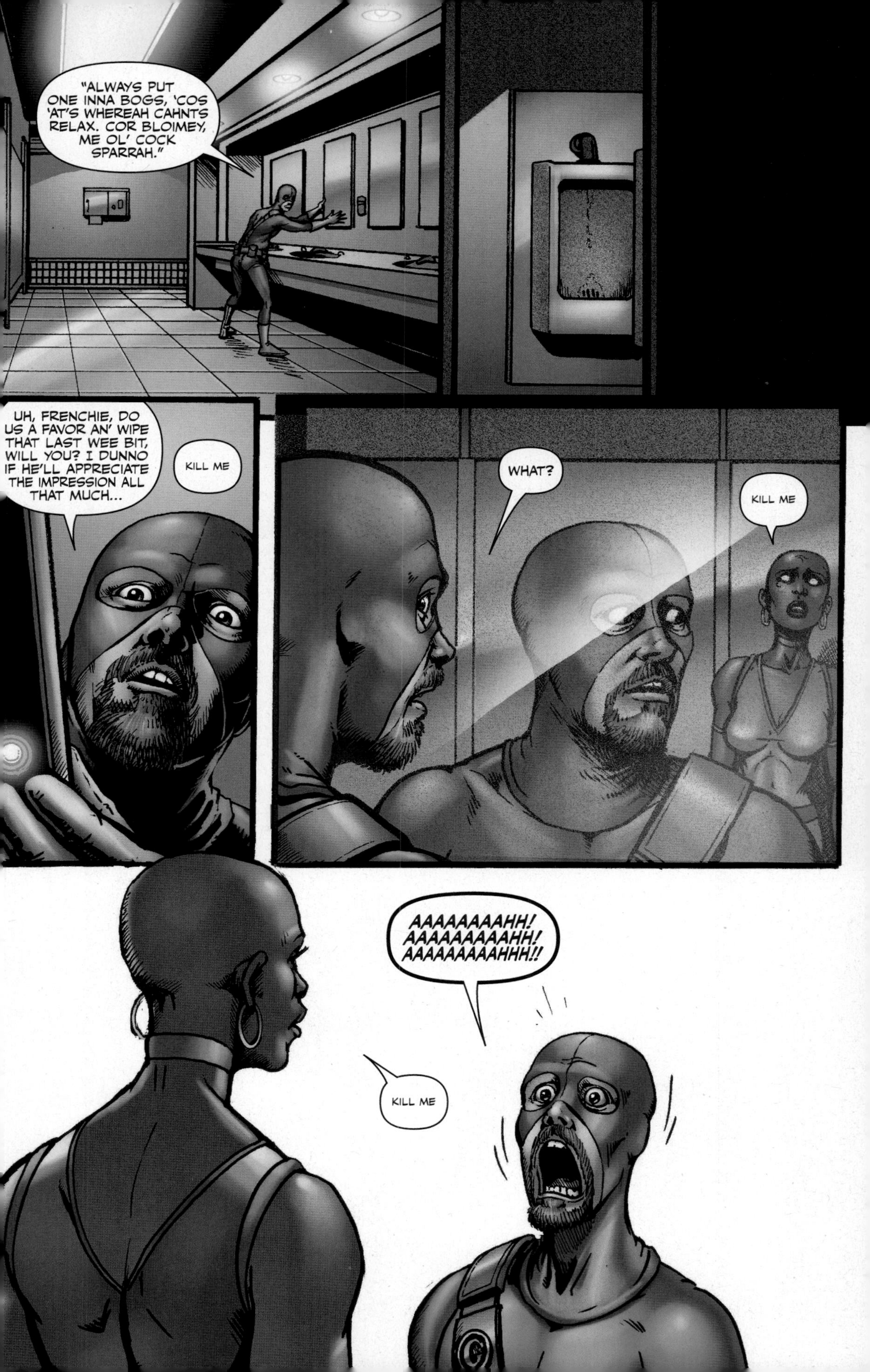

"ALWAYS PUT ONE INNA BOGS, 'COS 'AT'S WHEREAH CAHNTS RELAX. COR BLOIMEY, ME OL' COCK SPARRAH."
UH, FRENCHIE, DO US A FAVOR AN' WIPE THAT LAST WEE BIT, WILL YOU? I DUNNO IF HE'LL APPRECIATE THE IMPRESSION ALL THAT MUCH...
KILL ME
WHAT?
KILL ME
AAAAAAAAAH! AAAAAAAAAAH! AAAAAAAAAHHH!!
KILL ME

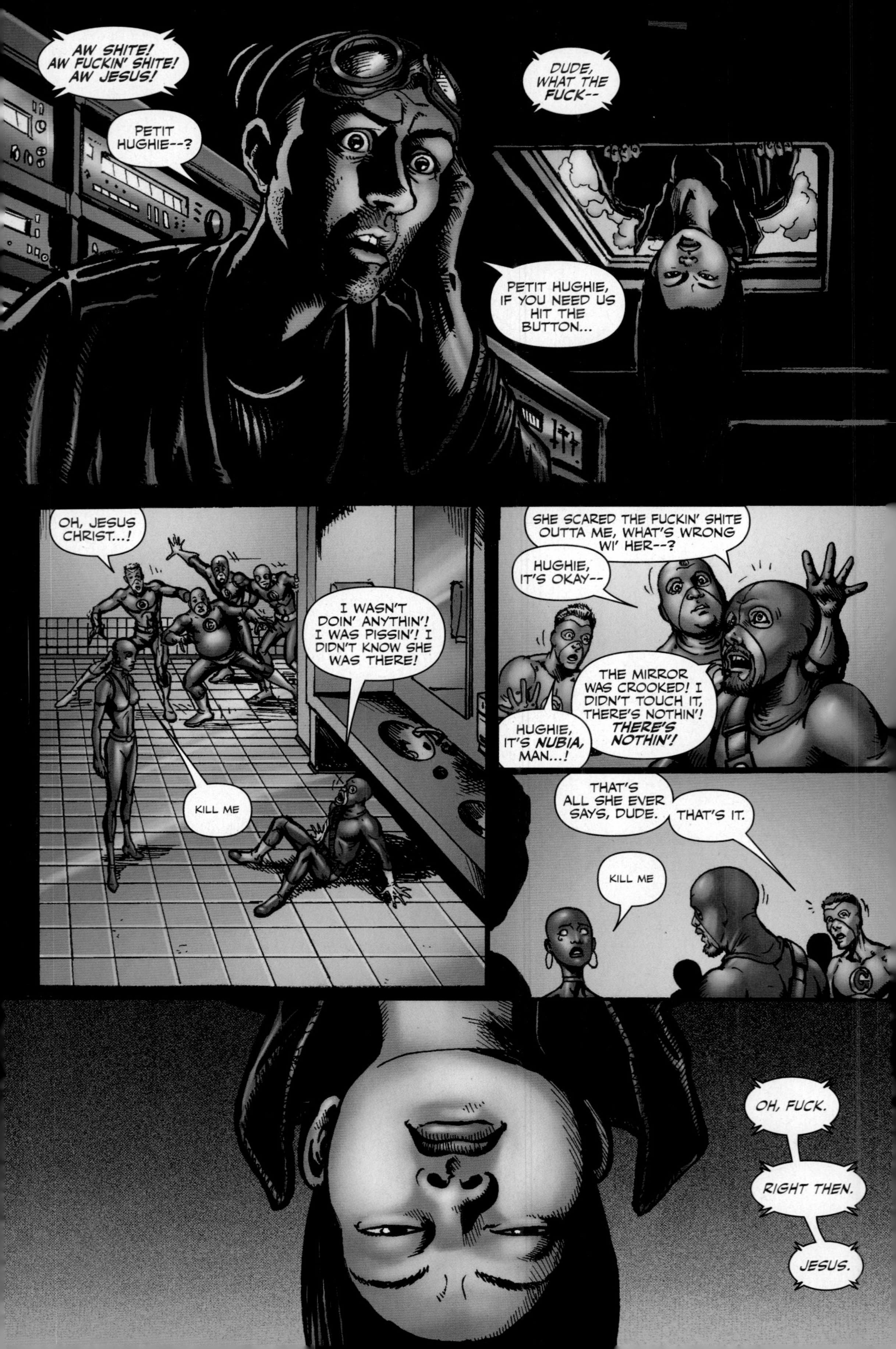

AW SHITE! AW FUCKIN' SHITE! AW JESUS!
PETIT HUGHIE--?
DUDE, WHAT THE FUCK--
PETIT HUGHIE, IF YOU NEED US HIT THE BUTTON...
OH, JESUS CHRIST...!
I WASN'T DOIN' ANYTHIN'! I WAS PISSIN'! I DIDN'T KNOW SHE WAS THERE!
KILL ME
SHE SCARED THE FUCKIN' SHITE OUTTA ME, WHAT'S WRONG WI' HER--?
HUGHIE, IT'S OKAY--
THE MIRROR WAS CROOKED! I DIDN'T TOUCH IT, THERE'S NOTHIN'! THERE'S NOTHIN'!
HUGHIE, IT'S NUBIA, MAN...!
THAT'S ALL SHE EVER SAYS, DUDE.
THAT'S IT.
KILL ME
OH, FUCK.
RIGHT THEN.
JESUS.

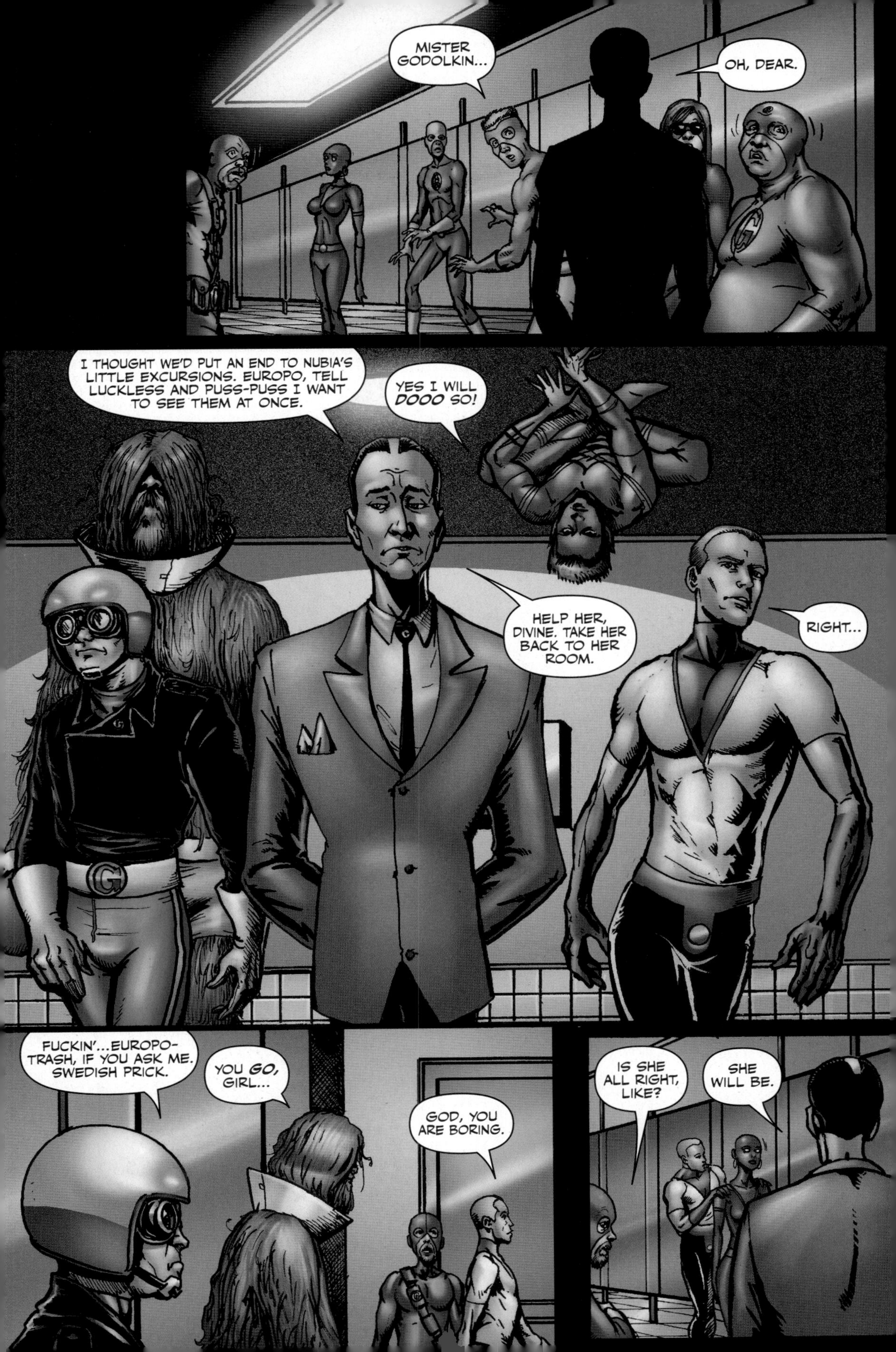
MISTER GODOLKIN...
OH, DEAR.
I THOUGHT WE'D PUT AN END TO NUBIA'S LITTLE EXCURSIONS. EUROPO, TELL LUCKLESS AND PUSS-PUSS I WANT TO SEE THEM AT ONCE.
YES I WILL *DOOO* SO!
HELP HER, DIVINE. TAKE HER BACK TO HER ROOM.
RIGHT...
FUCKIN'...EUROPO-TRASH, IF YOU ASK ME. SWEDISH PRICK.
YOU *GO*, GIRL...
GOD, YOU ARE BORING.
IS SHE ALL RIGHT, LIKE?
SHE WILL BE.

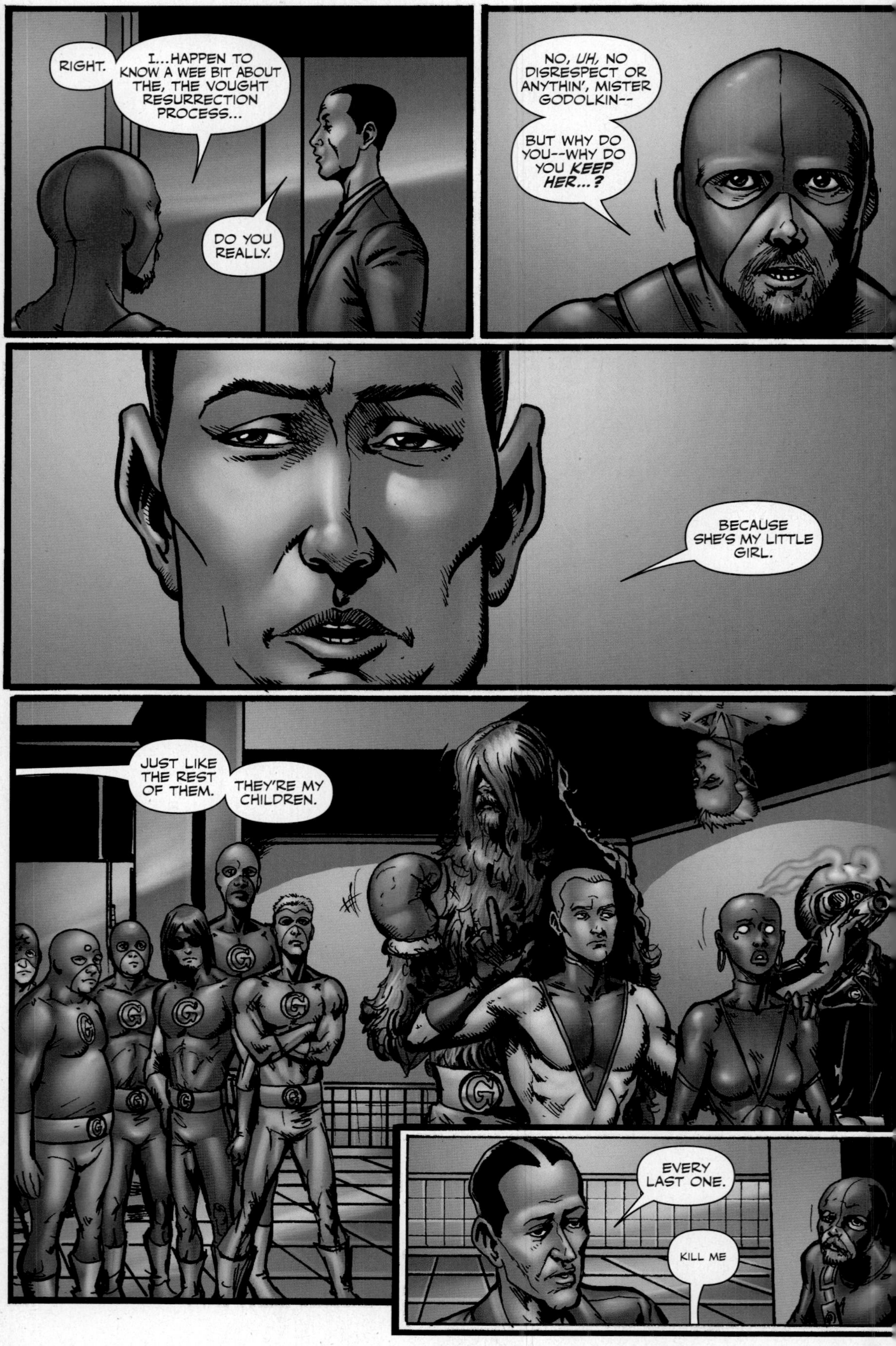
RIGHT.
I...HAPPEN TO KNOW A WEE BIT ABOUT THE, THE VOUGHT RESURRECTION PROCESS...
DO YOU REALLY.
NO, UH, NO DISRESPECT OR ANYTHIN', MISTER GODOLKIN--
BUT WHY DO YOU--WHY DO YOU KEEP HER...?
BECAUSE SHE'S MY LITTLE GIRL.
JUST LIKE THE REST OF THEM.
THEY'RE MY CHILDREN.
EVERY LAST ONE.
KILL ME

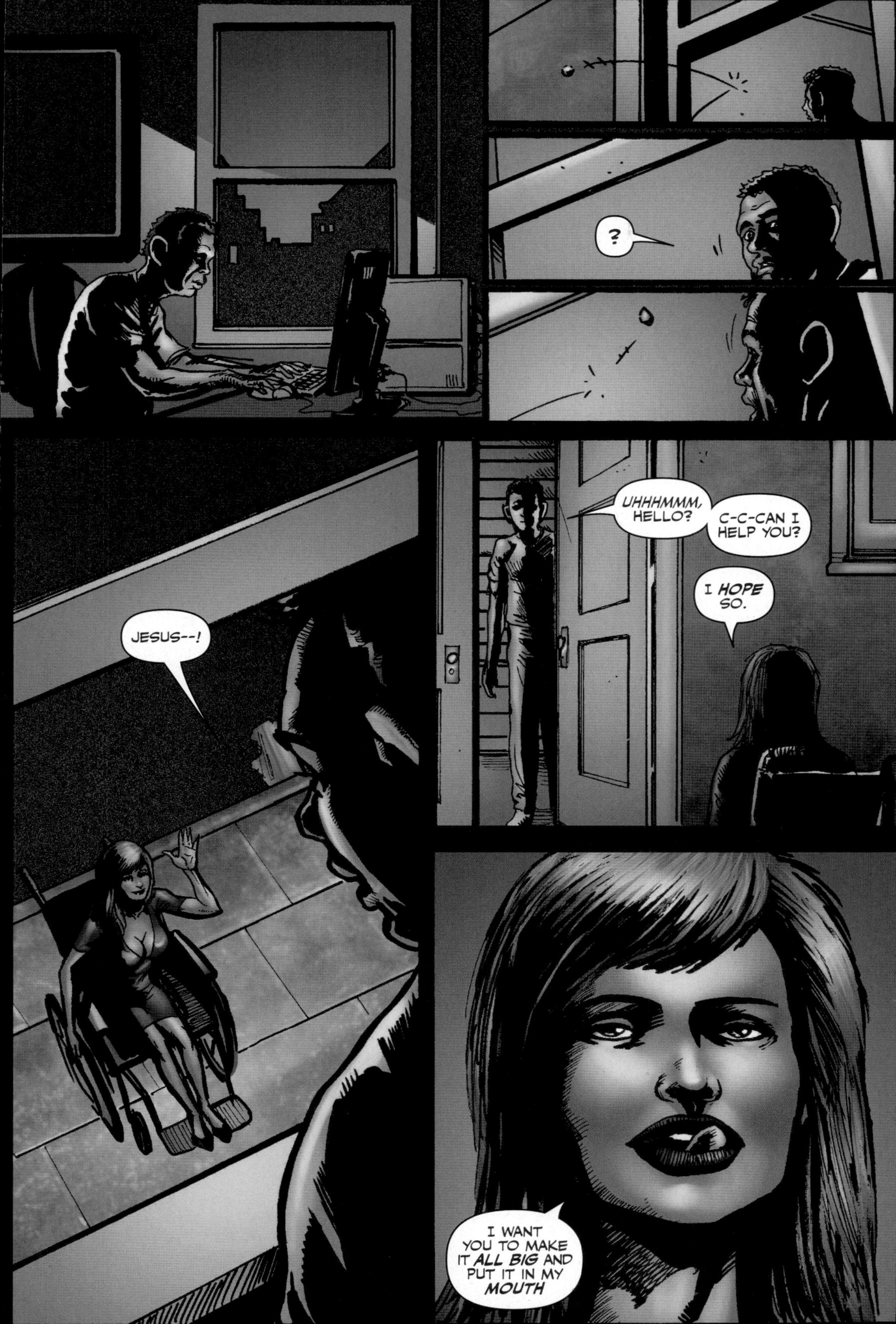
?
UHHHMMM, HELLO?
C-C-CAN I HELP YOU?
I HOPE SO.
JESUS--!
I WANT YOU TO MAKE IT ALL BIG AND PUT IT IN MY MOUTH

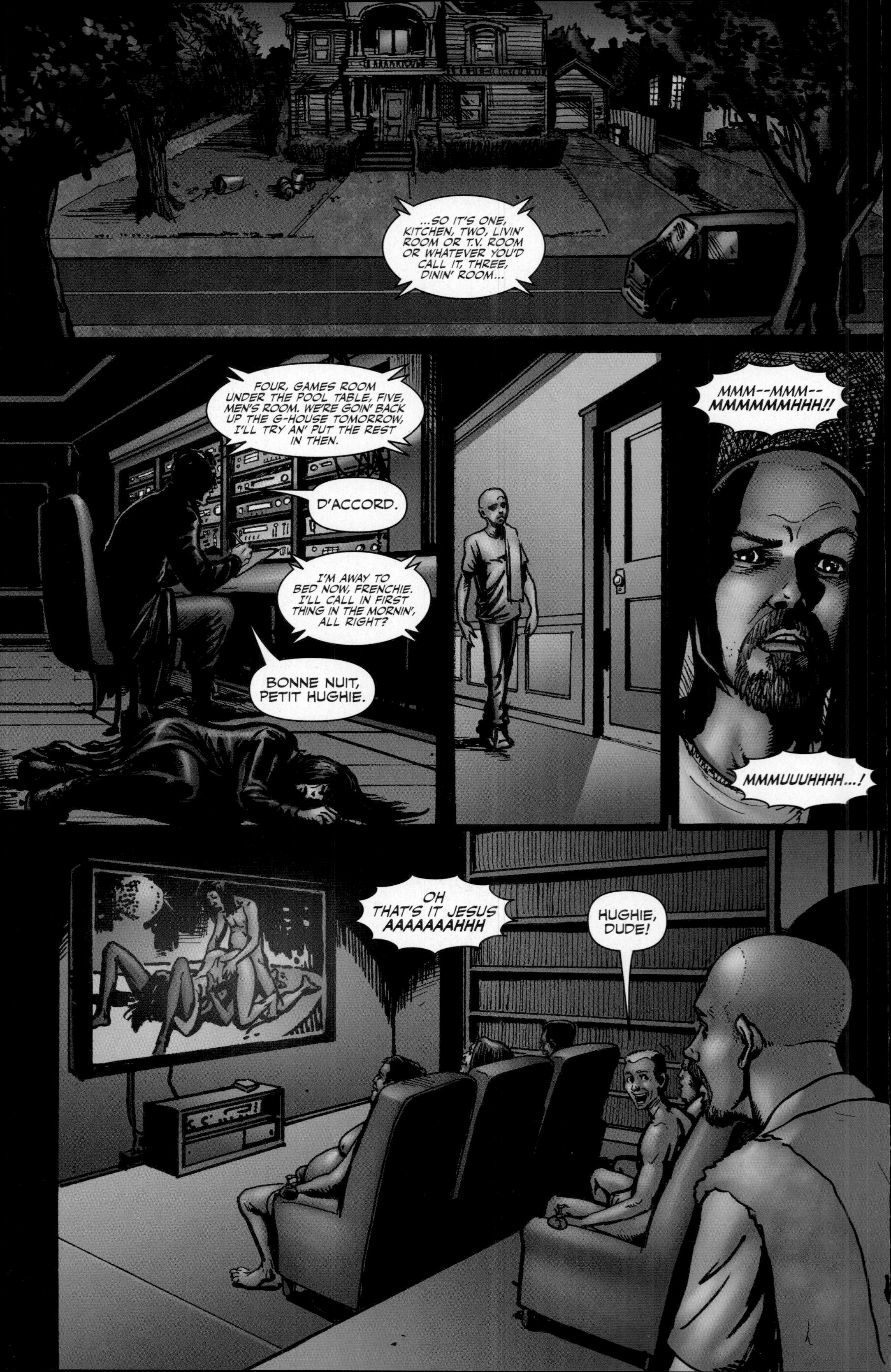
...SO IT'S ONE, KITCHEN, TWO, LIVIN' ROOM OR T.V. ROOM OR WHATEVER YOU'D CALL IT, THREE, DININ' ROOM...
FOUR, GAMES ROOM UNDER THE POOL TABLE, FIVE, MEN'S ROOM. WE'RE GOIN' BACK UP THE G-HOUSE TOMORROW, I'LL TRY AN' PUT THE REST IN THEN.
D'ACCORD.
I'M AWAY TO BED NOW, FRENCHIE. I'LL CALL IN FIRST THING IN THE MORNIN', ALL RIGHT?
BONNE NUIT, PETIT HUGHIE.
MMM--MMM--MMMMMMHHH!!
MMMUUUHHHH...!
OH THAT'S IT JESUS AAAAAAAHHH
HUGHIE, DUDE!

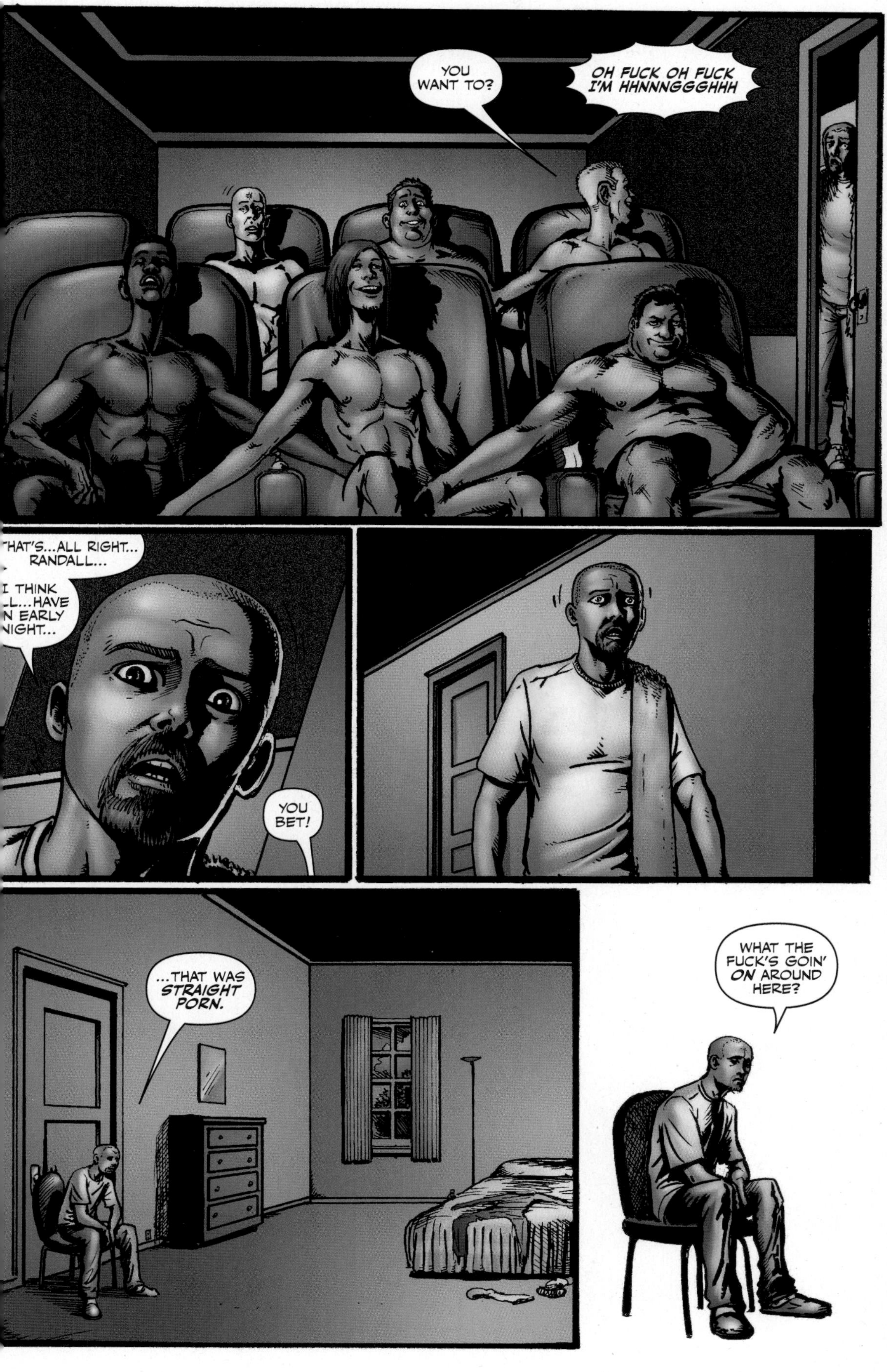
YOU WANT TO?
OH FUCK OH FUCK I'M HHNNNGGGHHH
THAT'S...ALL RIGHT... RANDALL...
I THINK
...L...HAVE
...N EARLY
NIGHT...
YOU BET!
...THAT WAS STRAIGHT PORN.
WHAT THE FUCK'S GOIN' ON AROUND HERE?

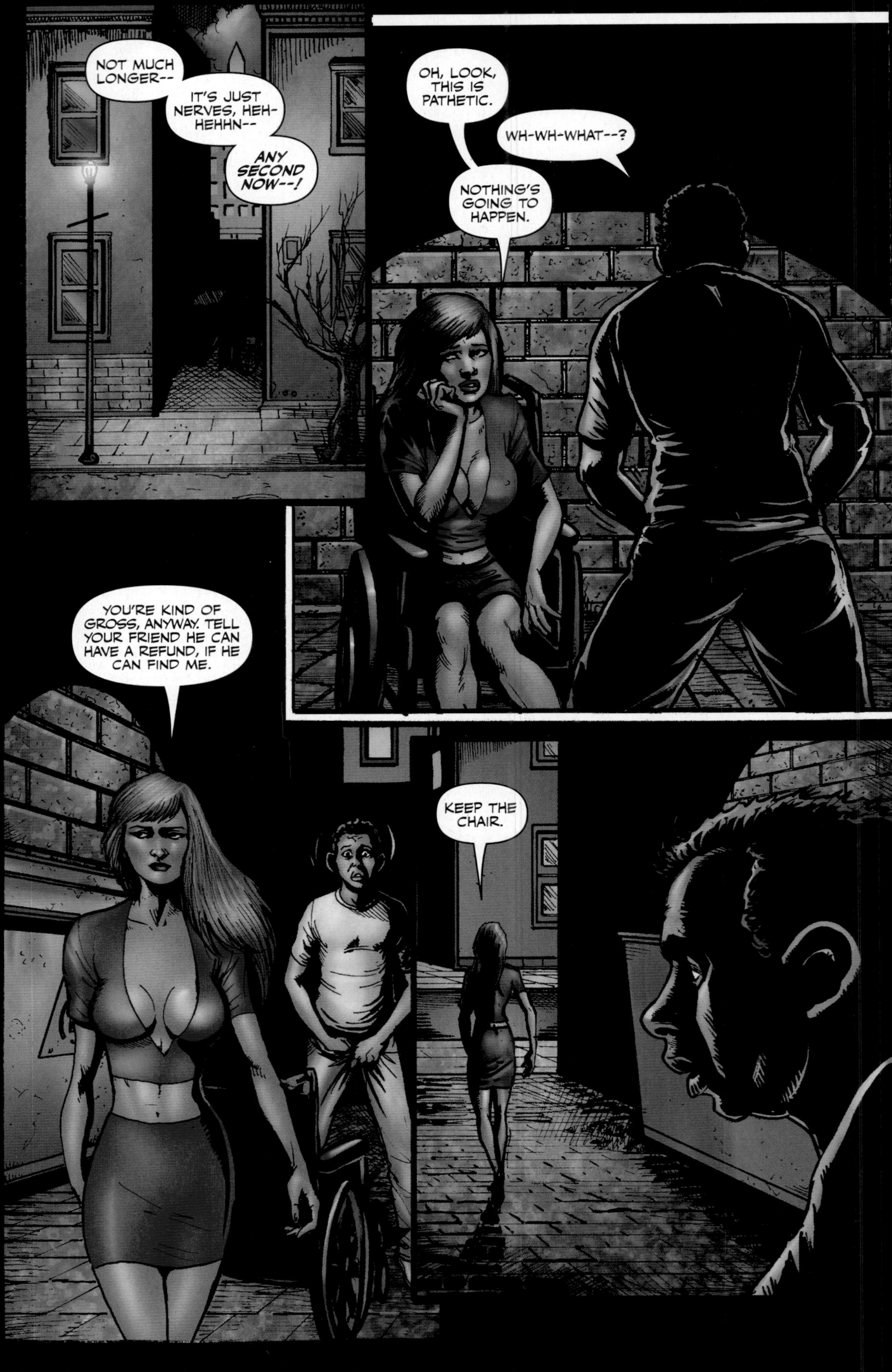

NOT MUCH LONGER--
IT'S JUST NERVES, HEH-HEHHN--
ANY SECOND NOW--!
OH, LOOK, THIS IS PATHETIC.
WH-WH-WHAT--?
NOTHING'S GOING TO HAPPEN.
YOU'RE KIND OF GROSS, ANYWAY. TELL YOUR FRIEND HE CAN HAVE A REFUND, IF HE CAN FIND ME.
KEEP THE CHAIR.

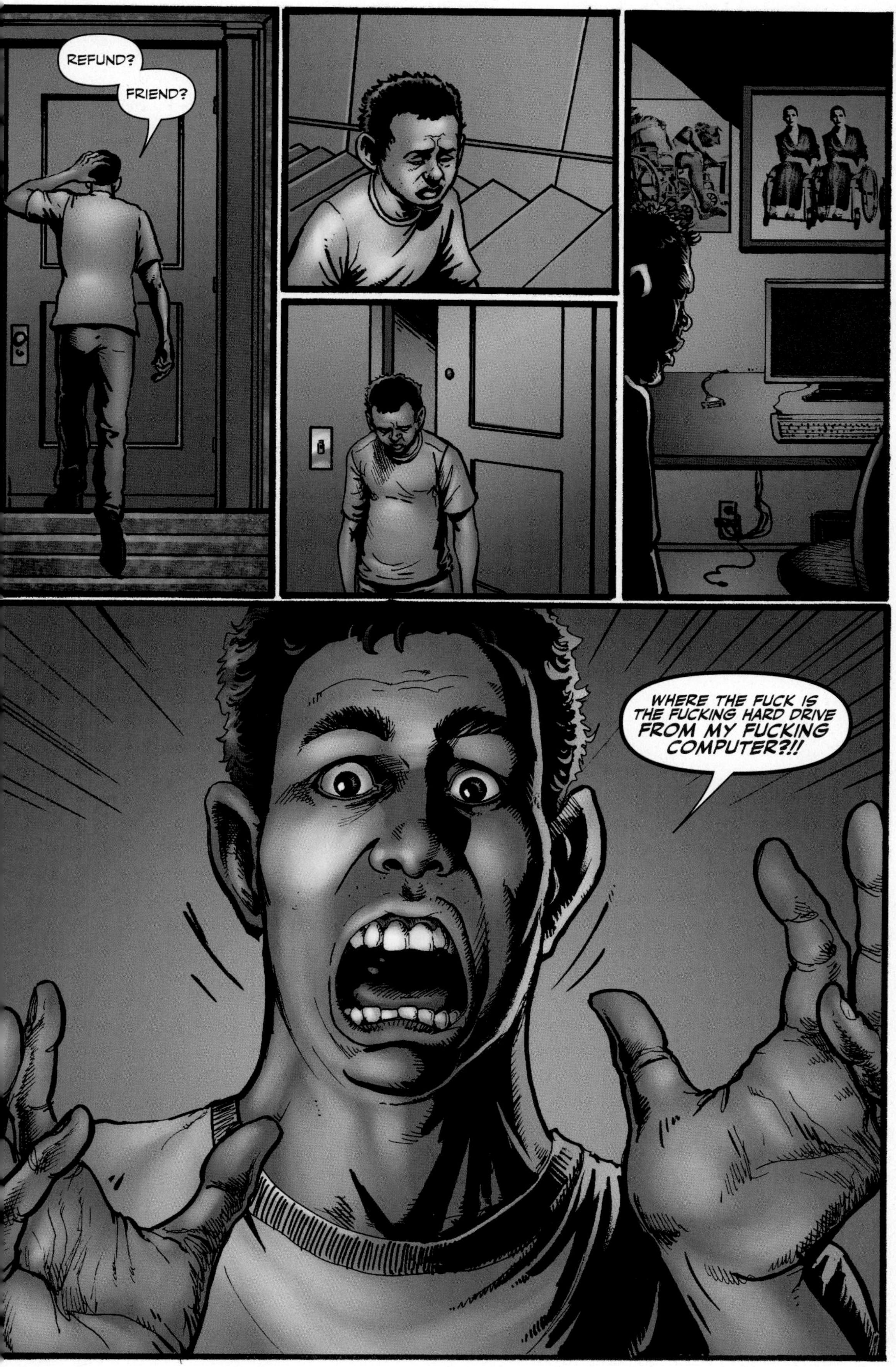
REFUND?
FRIEND?
WHERE THE FUCK IS THE FUCKING HARD DRIVE FROM MY FUCKING COMPUTER?!!

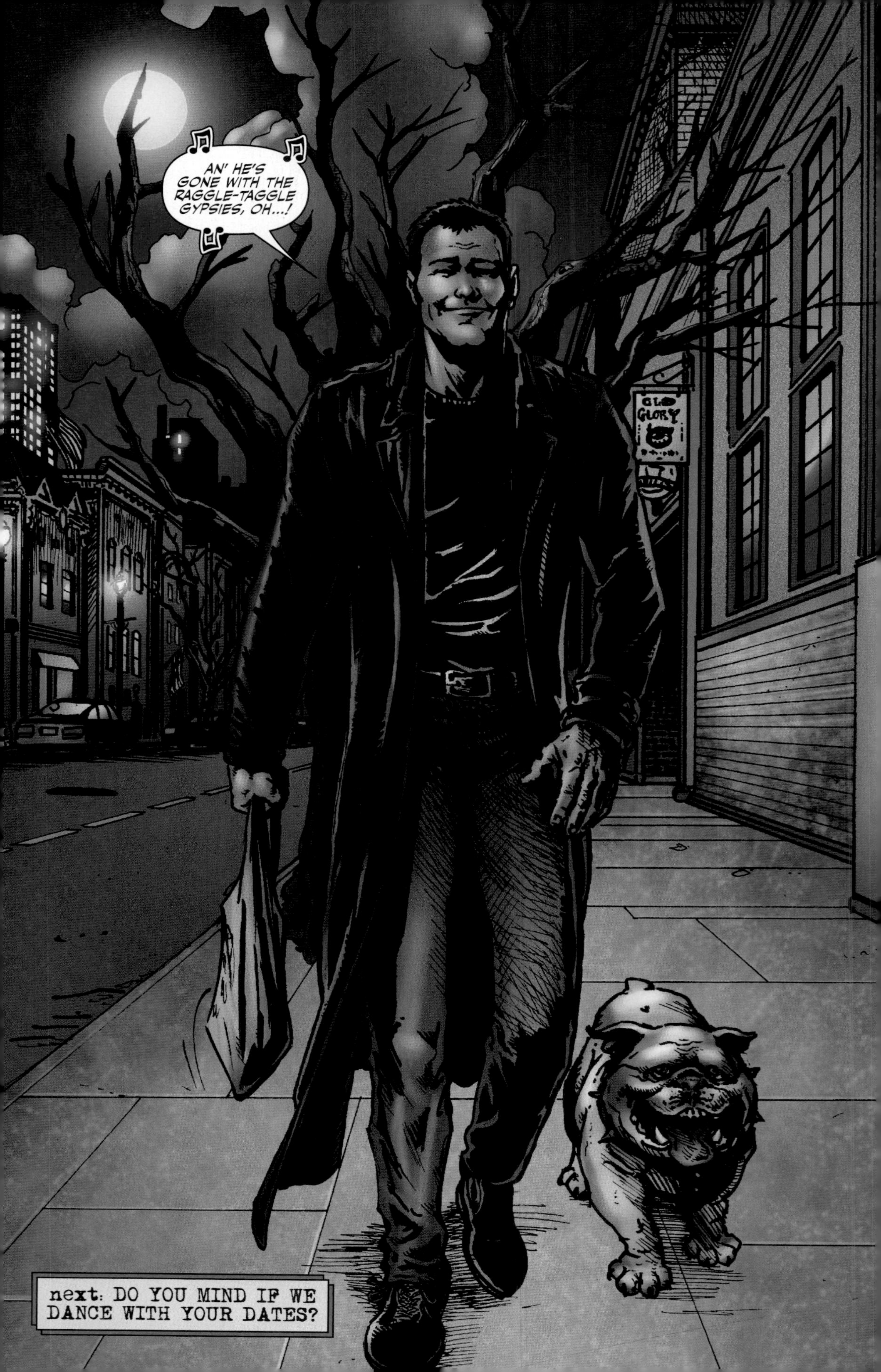
AN' HE'S GONE WITH THE RAGGLE-TAGGLE GYPSIES, OH...!
GLORY
next: DO YOU MIND IF WE DANCE WITH YOUR DATES?

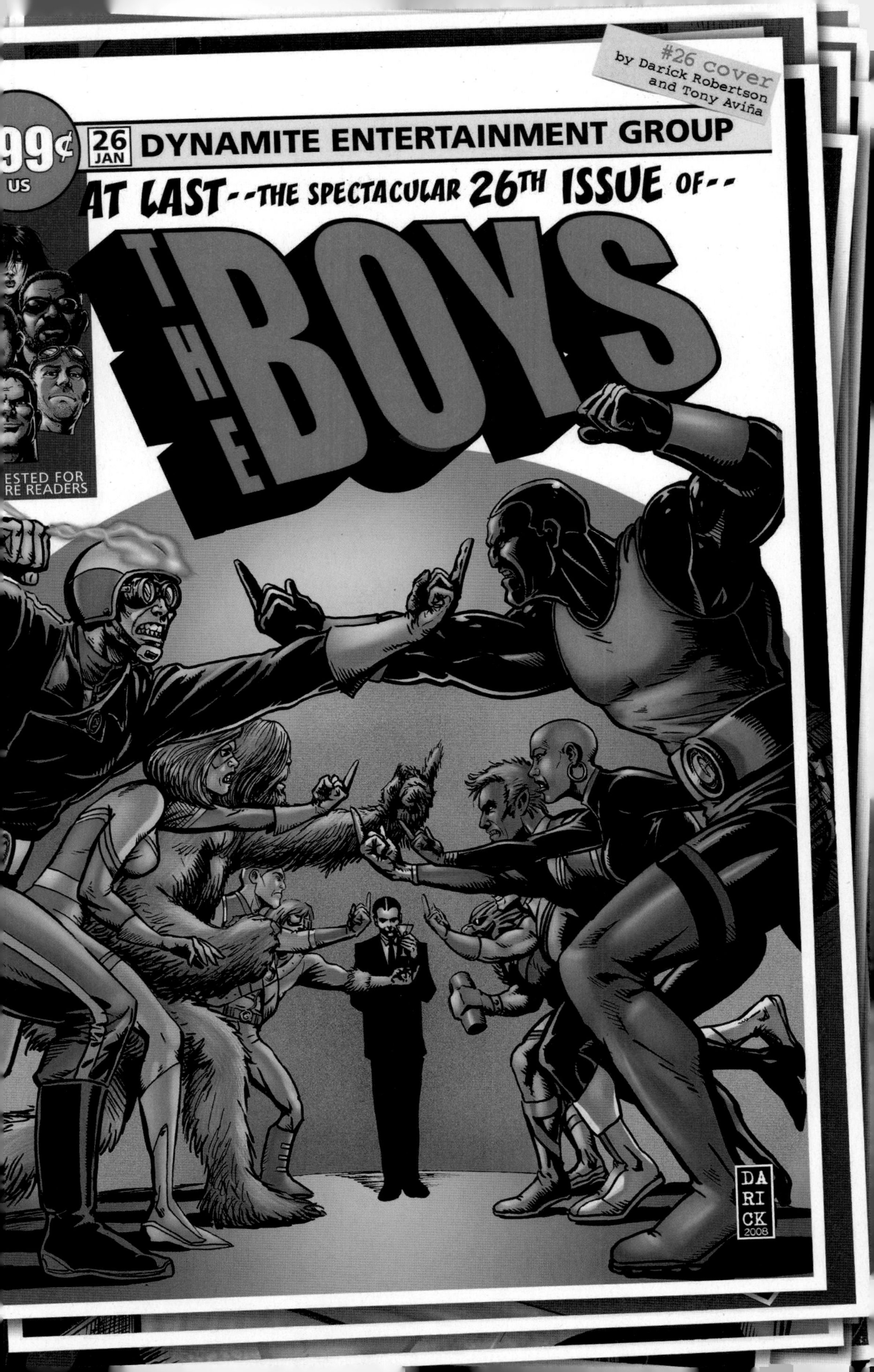
#26 cover
by Darick Robertson
and Tony Aviña
99¢
US
26
JAN
DYNAMITE ENTERTAINMENT GROUP
AT LAST--THE SPECTACULAR 26TH ISSUE OF--
THE BOYS
ESTED FOR
RE READERS
DA
RI
CK
2008

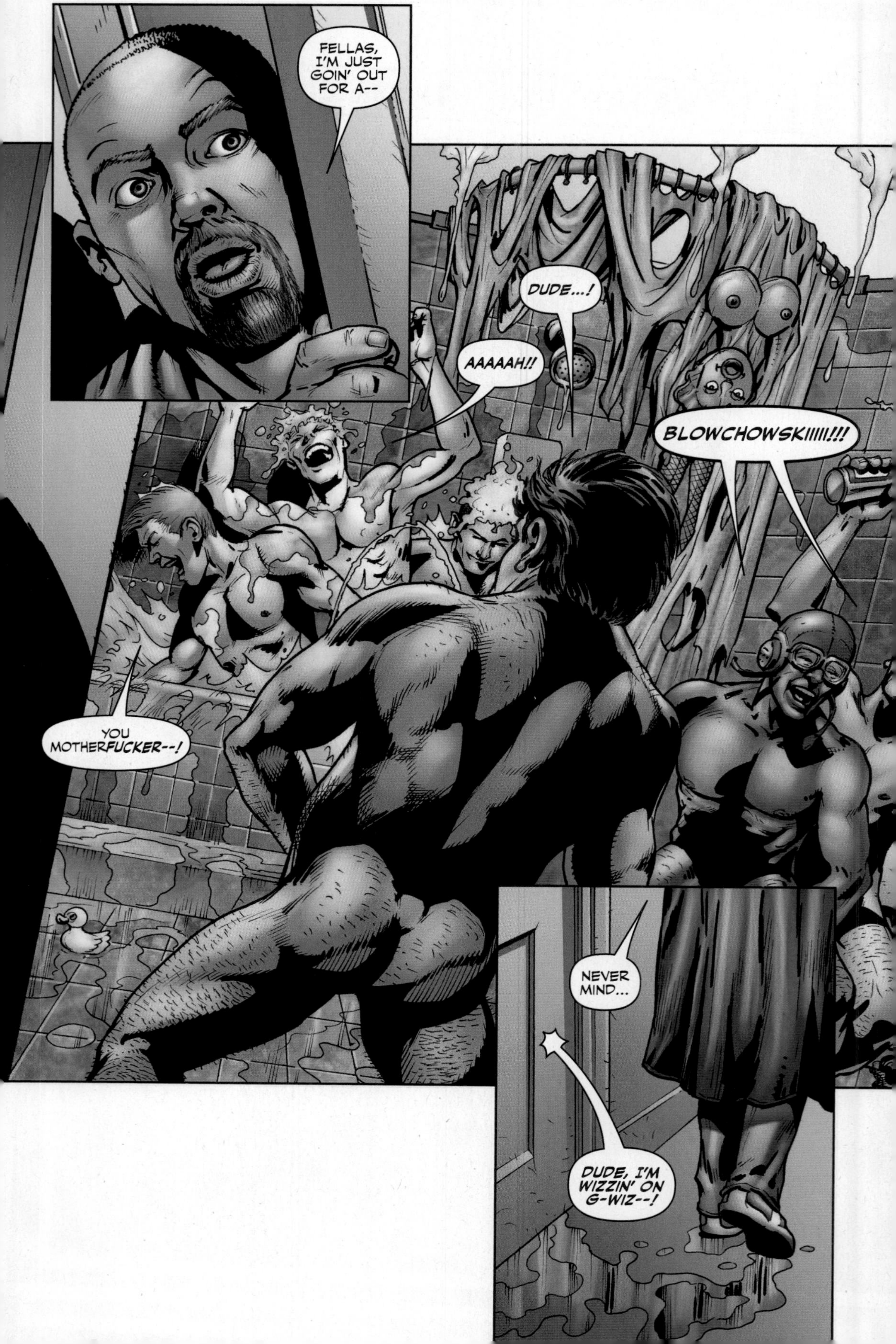
FELLAS, I'M JUST GOIN' OUT FOR A--
DUDE...!
AAAAAH!!
BLOWCHOWSKIIIIII!!!
YOU MOTHERFUCKER--!
NEVER MIND...
DUDE, I'M WIZZIN' ON G-WIZ--!

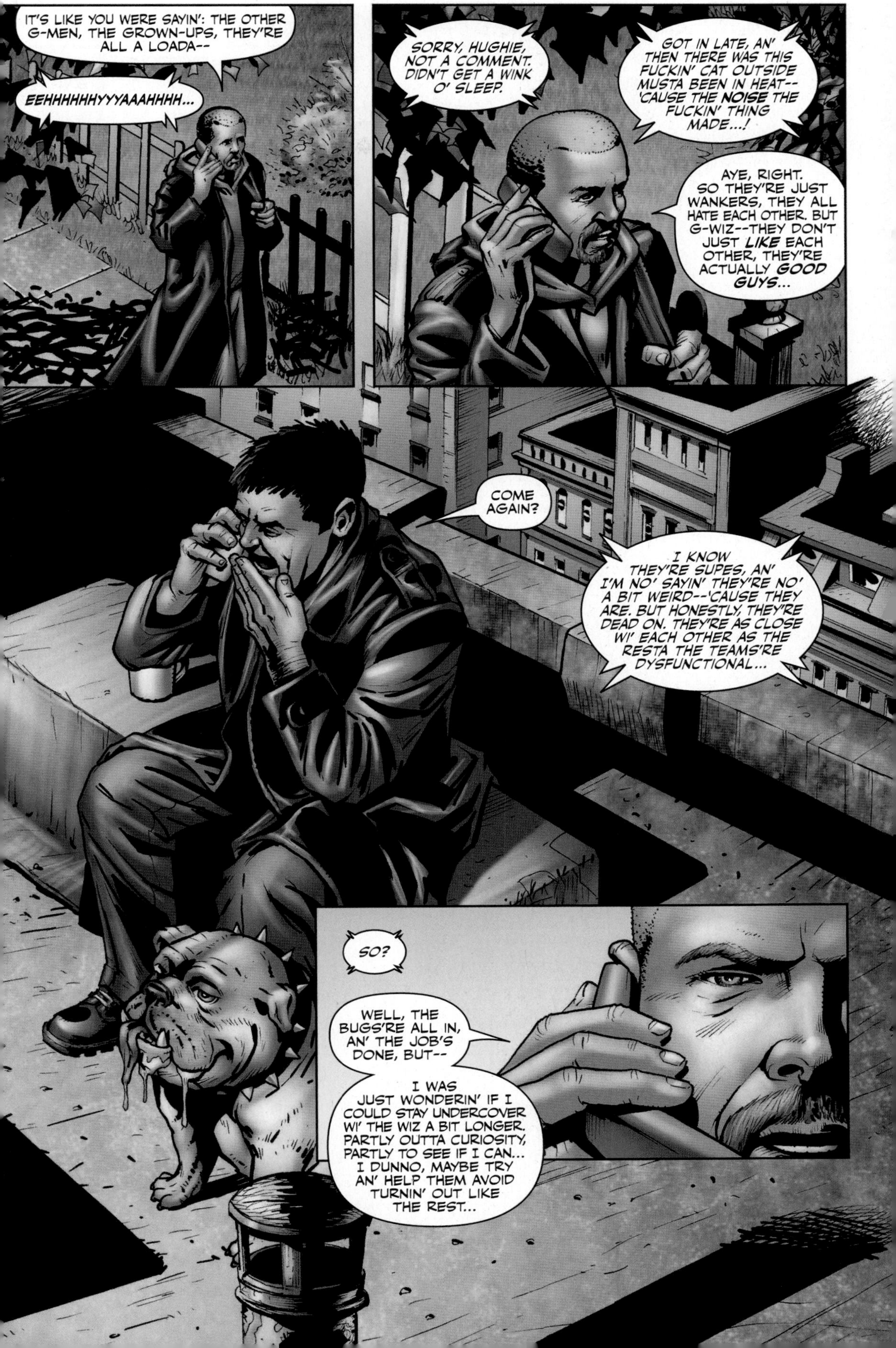
IT'S LIKE YOU WERE SAYIN': THE OTHER G-MEN, THE GROWN-UPS, THEY'RE ALL A LOADA--
EEHHHHHHHYYYAAAHHHH...
SORRY, HUGHIE, NOT A COMMENT. DIDN'T GET A WINK O' SLEEP.
GOT IN LATE, AN' THEN THERE WAS THIS FUCKIN' CAT OUTSIDE MUSTA BEEN IN HEAT-- 'CAUSE THE NOISE THE FUCKIN' THING MADE...!
AYE, RIGHT. SO THEY'RE JUST WANKERS, THEY ALL HATE EACH OTHER. BUT G-WIZ--THEY DON'T JUST LIKE EACH OTHER, THEY'RE ACTUALLY GOOD GUYS...
COME AGAIN?
I KNOW THEY'RE SUPES, AN' I'M NO' SAYIN' THEY'RE NO' A BIT WEIRD--'CAUSE THEY ARE. BUT HONESTLY, THEY'RE DEAD ON. THEY'RE AS CLOSE WI' EACH OTHER AS THE RESTA THE TEAMS'RE DYSFUNCTIONAL...
SO?
WELL, THE BUGS'RE ALL IN, AN' THE JOB'S DONE, BUT--
I WAS JUST WONDERIN' IF I COULD STAY UNDERCOVER WI' THE WIZ A BIT LONGER. PARTLY OUTTA CURIOSITY, PARTLY TO SEE IF I CAN... I DUNNO, MAYBE TRY AN' HELP THEM AVOID TURNIN' OUT LIKE THE REST...

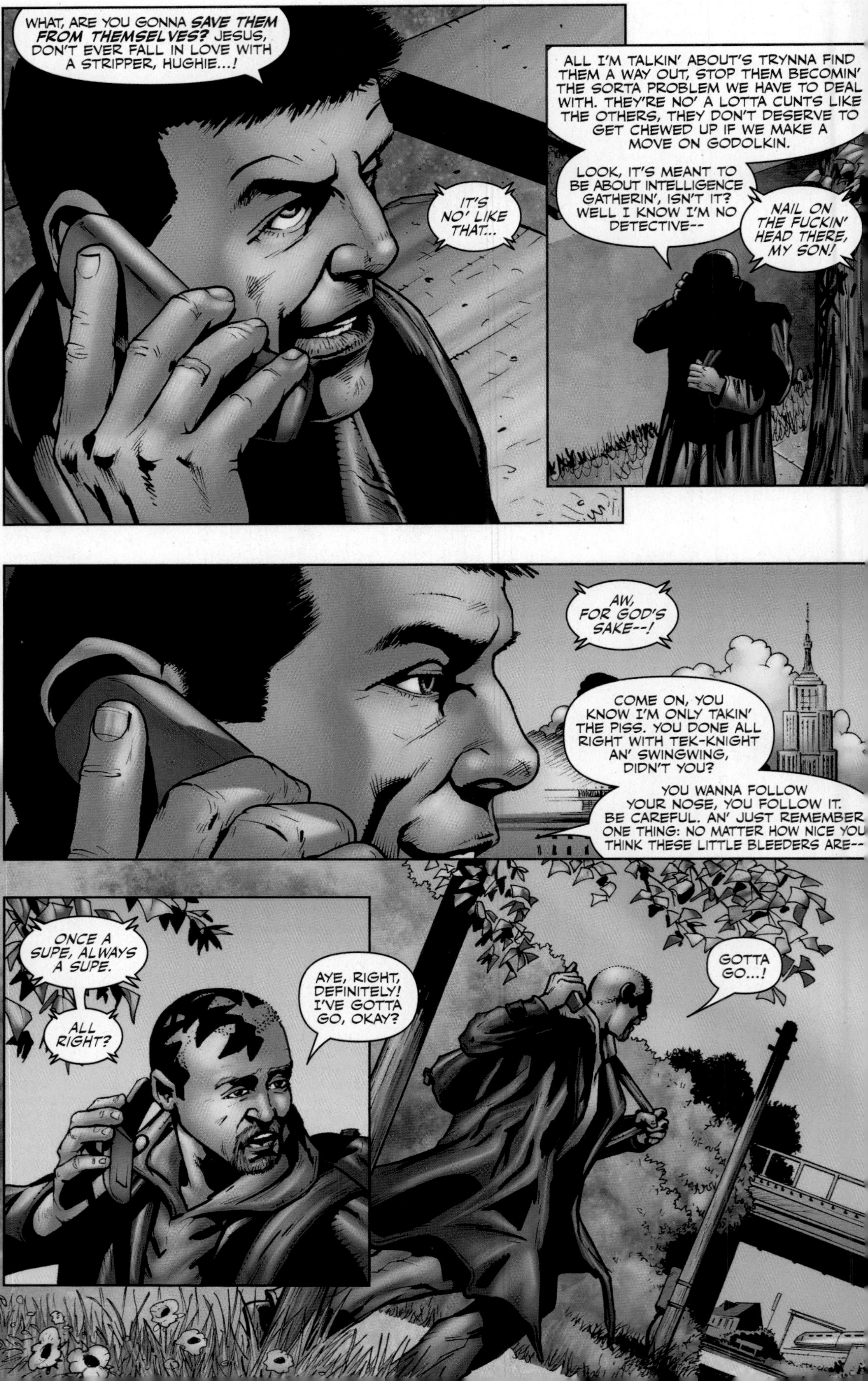
WHAT, ARE YOU GONNA SAVE THEM FROM THEMSELVES? JESUS, DON'T EVER FALL IN LOVE WITH A STRIPPER, HUGHIE...!
IT'S NO' LIKE THAT...
ALL I'M TALKIN' ABOUT'S TRYNNA FIND THEM A WAY OUT, STOP THEM BECOMIN' THE SORTA PROBLEM WE HAVE TO DEAL WITH. THEY'RE NO' A LOTTA CUNTS LIKE THE OTHERS, THEY DON'T DESERVE TO GET CHEWED UP IF WE MAKE A MOVE ON GODOLKIN.
LOOK, IT'S MEANT TO BE ABOUT INTELLIGENCE GATHERIN', ISN'T IT? WELL I KNOW I'M NO DETECTIVE--
NAIL ON THE FUCKIN' HEAD THERE, MY SON!
AW, FOR GOD'S SAKE--!
COME ON, YOU KNOW I'M ONLY TAKIN' THE PISS. YOU DONE ALL RIGHT WITH TEK-KNIGHT AN' SWINGWING, DIDN'T YOU?
YOU WANNA FOLLOW YOUR NOSE, YOU FOLLOW IT. BE CAREFUL. AN' JUST REMEMBER ONE THING: NO MATTER HOW NICE YOU THINK THESE LITTLE BLEEDERS ARE--
ONCE A SUPE, ALWAYS A SUPE.
ALL RIGHT?
AYE, RIGHT, DEFINITELY! I'VE GOTTA GO, OKAY?
GOTTA GO...!

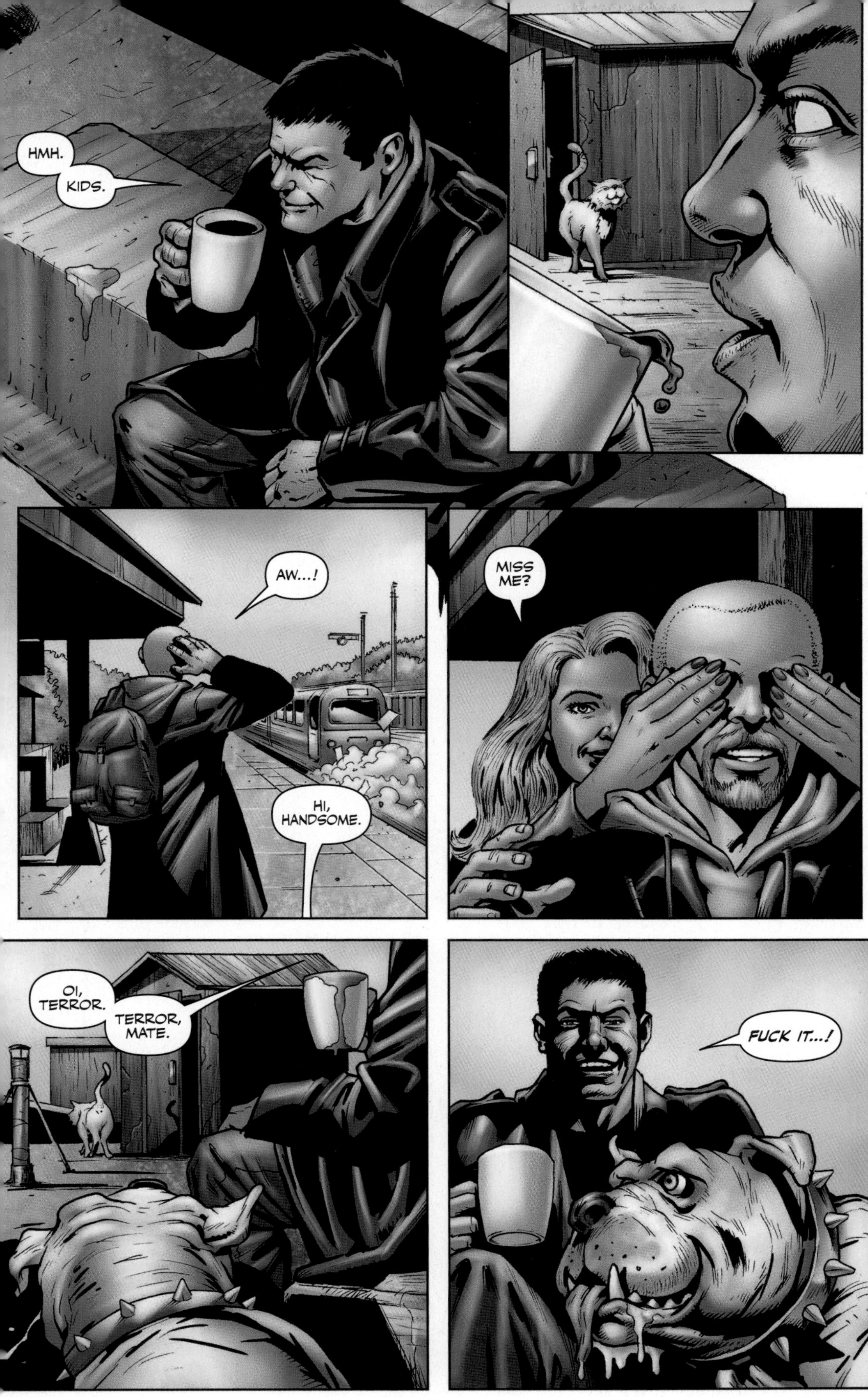
HMH.
KIDS.
AW...!
HI, HANDSOME.
MISS ME?
OI, TERROR.
TERROR, MATE.
FUCK IT...!

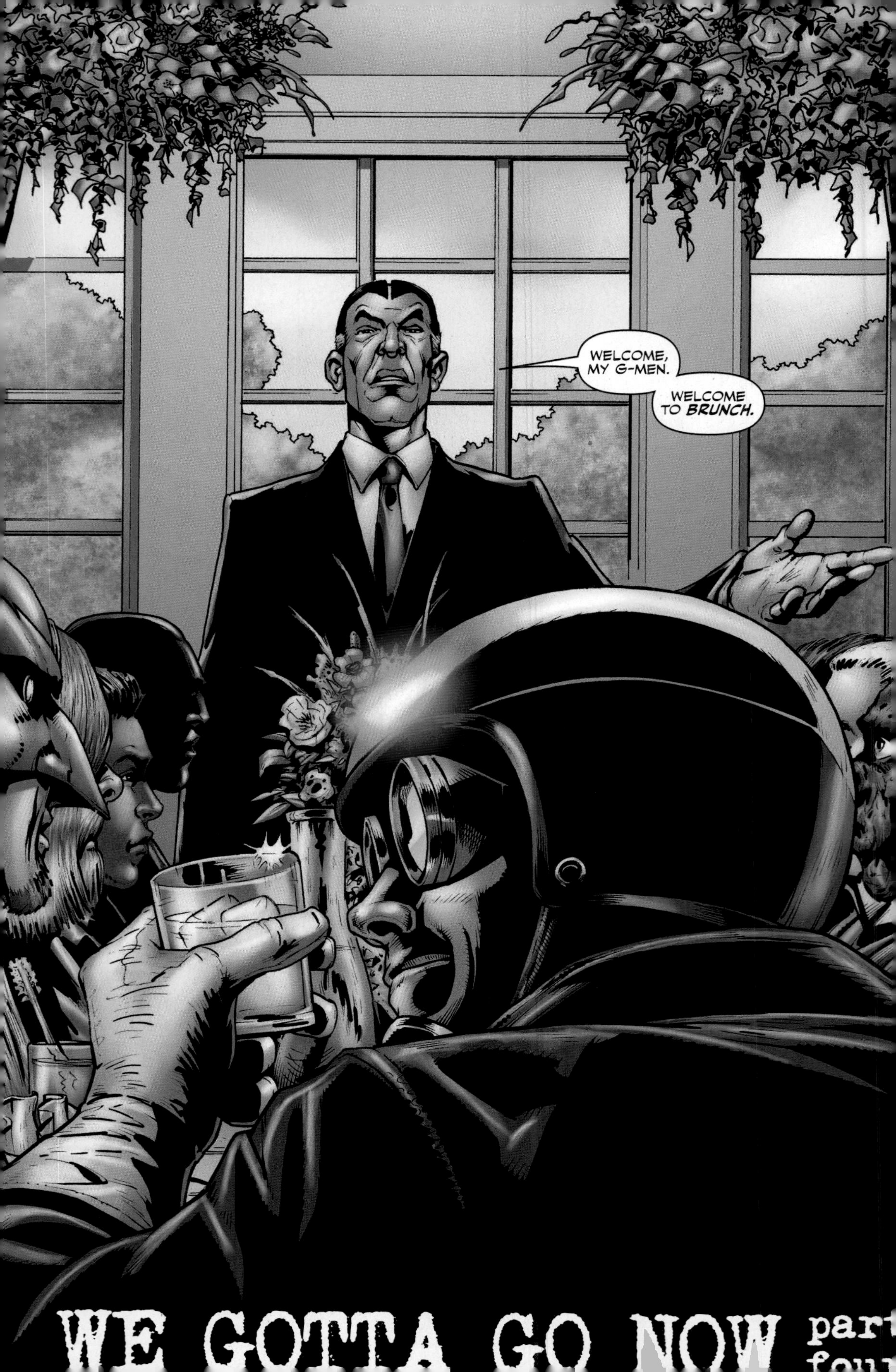
WELCOME, MY G-MEN.
WELCOME TO BRUNCH.
WE GOTTA GO NOW

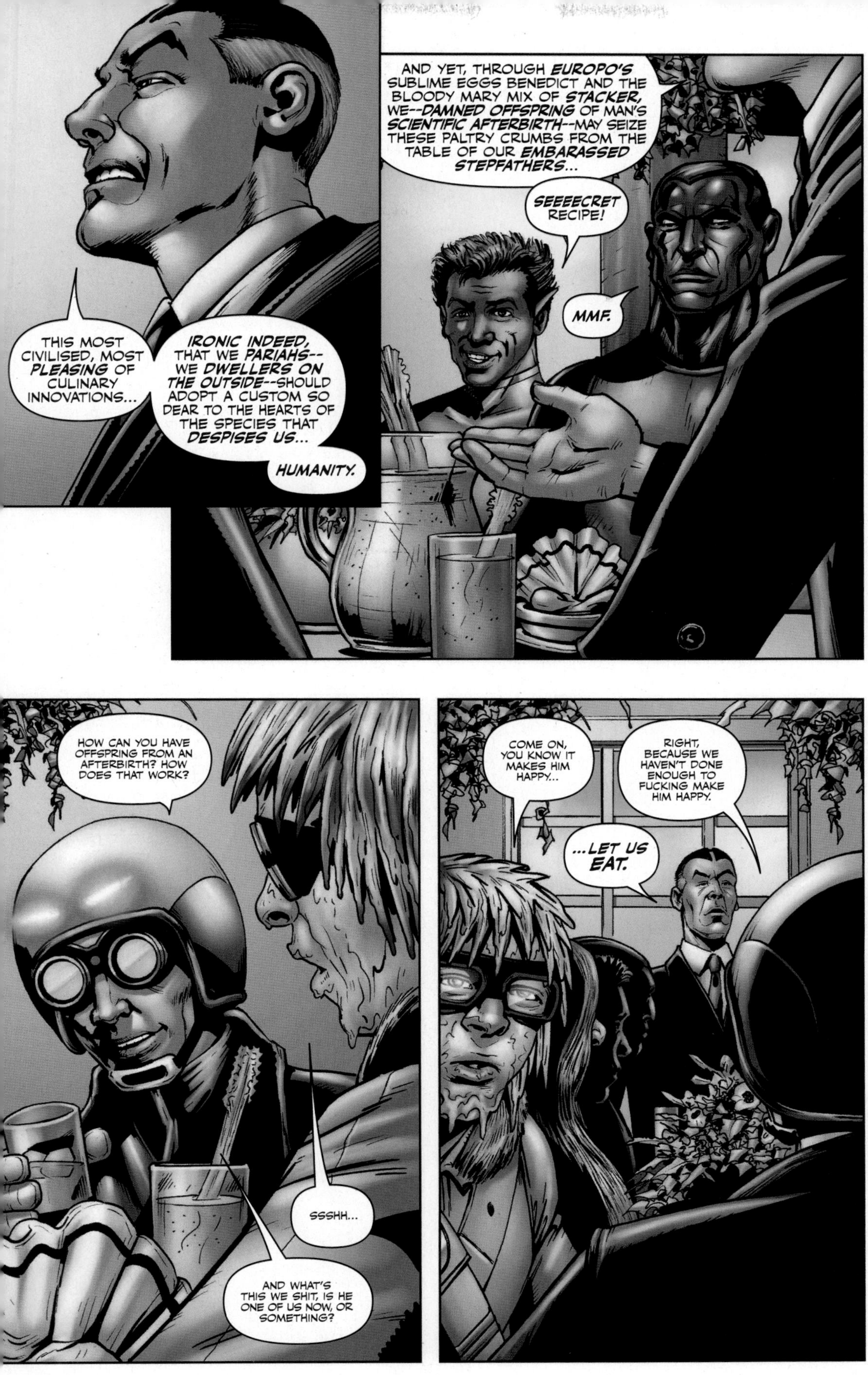
THIS MOST CIVILISED, MOST PLEASING OF CULINARY INNOVATIONS...
IRONIC INDEED, THAT WE PARIAHS--WE DWELLERS ON THE OUTSIDE--SHOULD ADOPT A CUSTOM SO DEAR TO THE HEARTS OF THE SPECIES THAT DESPISES US...
HUMANITY.
AND YET, THROUGH EUROPO'S SUBLIME EGGS BENEDICT AND THE BLOODY MARY MIX OF STACKER, WE--DAMNED OFFSPRING OF MAN'S SCIENTIFIC AFTERBIRTH--MAY SEIZE THESE PALTRY CRUMBS FROM THE TABLE OF OUR EMBARASSED STEPFATHERS...
SEEEECRET RECIPE!
MMF.
HOW CAN YOU HAVE OFFSPRING FROM AN AFTERBIRTH? HOW DOES THAT WORK?
SSSHH...
AND WHAT'S THIS WE SHIT, IS HE ONE OF US NOW, OR SOMETHING?
COME ON, YOU KNOW IT MAKES HIM HAPPY...
RIGHT, BECAUSE WE HAVEN'T DONE ENOUGH TO FUCKING MAKE HIM HAPPY.
...LET US EAT.

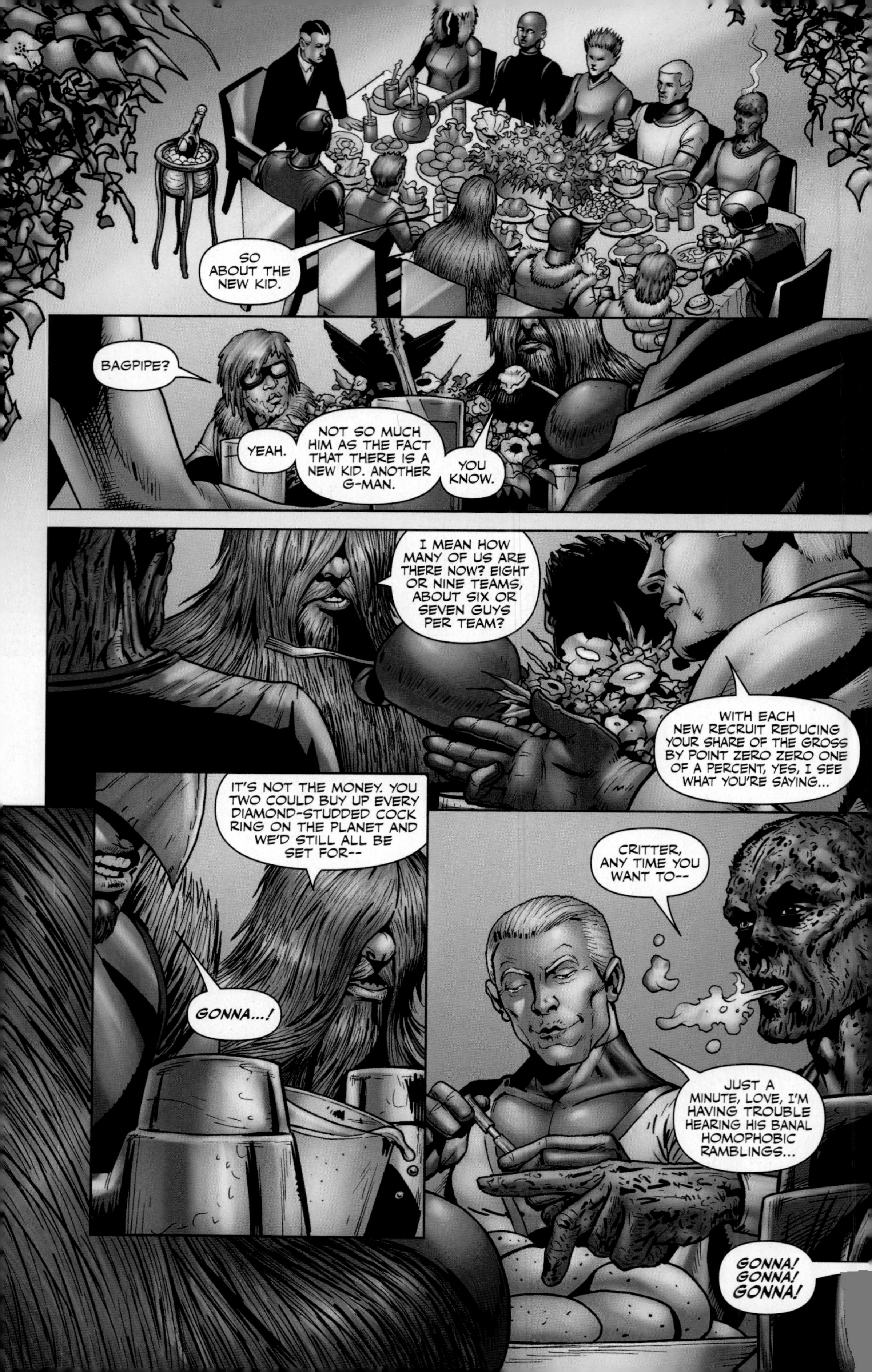
SO ABOUT THE NEW KID.
BAGPIPE?
YEAH.
NOT SO MUCH HIM AS THE FACT THAT THERE IS A NEW KID. ANOTHER G-MAN.
YOU KNOW.
I MEAN HOW MANY OF US ARE THERE NOW? EIGHT OR NINE TEAMS, ABOUT SIX OR SEVEN GUYS PER TEAM?
WITH EACH NEW RECRUIT REDUCING YOUR SHARE OF THE GROSS BY POINT ZERO ZERO ONE OF A PERCENT, YES, I SEE WHAT YOU'RE SAYING...
IT'S NOT THE MONEY. YOU TWO COULD BUY UP EVERY DIAMOND-STUDDED COCK RING ON THE PLANET AND WE'D STILL ALL BE SET FOR--
GONNA...!
CRITTER, ANY TIME YOU WANT TO--
JUST A MINUTE, LOVE, I'M HAVING TROUBLE HEARING HIS BANAL HOMOPHOBIC RAMBLINGS...
GONNA! GONNA! GONNA!

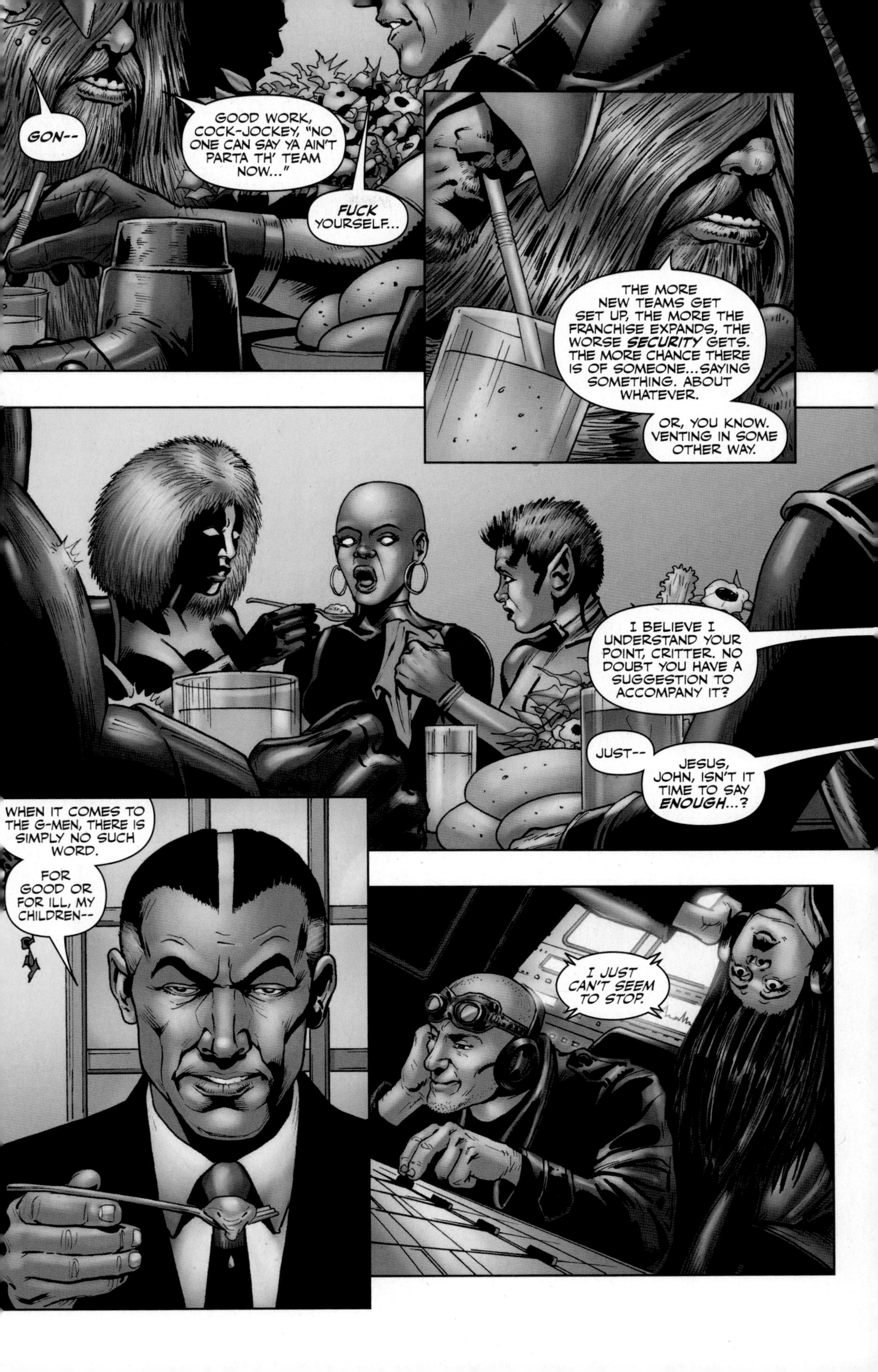
GON--
GOOD WORK, COCK-JOCKEY, "NO ONE CAN SAY YA AIN'T PARTA TH' TEAM NOW..."
FUCK YOURSELF...
THE MORE NEW TEAMS GET SET UP, THE MORE THE FRANCHISE EXPANDS, THE WORSE SECURITY GETS. THE MORE CHANCE THERE IS OF SOMEONE...SAYING SOMETHING. ABOUT WHATEVER.
OR, YOU KNOW. VENTING IN SOME OTHER WAY.
I BELIEVE I UNDERSTAND YOUR POINT, CRITTER. NO DOUBT YOU HAVE A SUGGESTION TO ACCOMPANY IT?
JUST--
JESUS, JOHN, ISN'T IT TIME TO SAY ENOUGH...?
WHEN IT COMES TO THE G-MEN, THERE IS SIMPLY NO SUCH WORD.
FOR GOOD OR FOR ILL, MY CHILDREN--
I JUST CAN'T SEEM TO STOP.

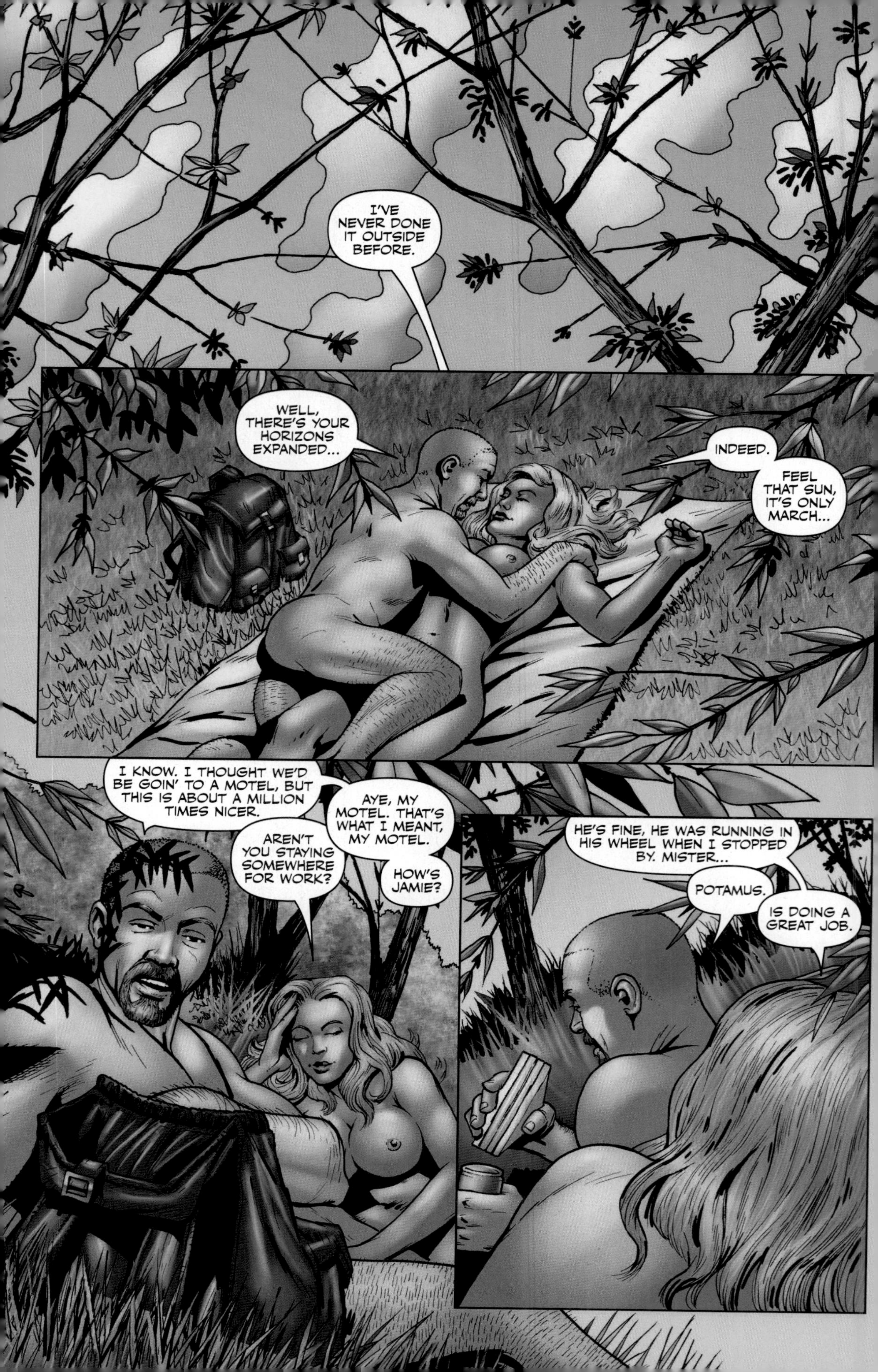

I'VE NEVER DONE IT OUTSIDE BEFORE.
WELL, THERE'S YOUR HORIZONS EXPANDED...
INDEED.
FEEL THAT SUN, IT'S ONLY MARCH...
I KNOW. I THOUGHT WE'D BE GOIN' TO A MOTEL, BUT THIS IS ABOUT A MILLION TIMES NICER.
AREN'T YOU STAYING SOMEWHERE FOR WORK?
AYE, MY MOTEL. THAT'S WHAT I MEANT, MY MOTEL.
HOW'S JAMIE?
HE'S FINE, HE WAS RUNNING IN HIS WHEEL WHEN I STOPPED BY. MISTER...
POTAMUS.
IS DOING A GREAT JOB.

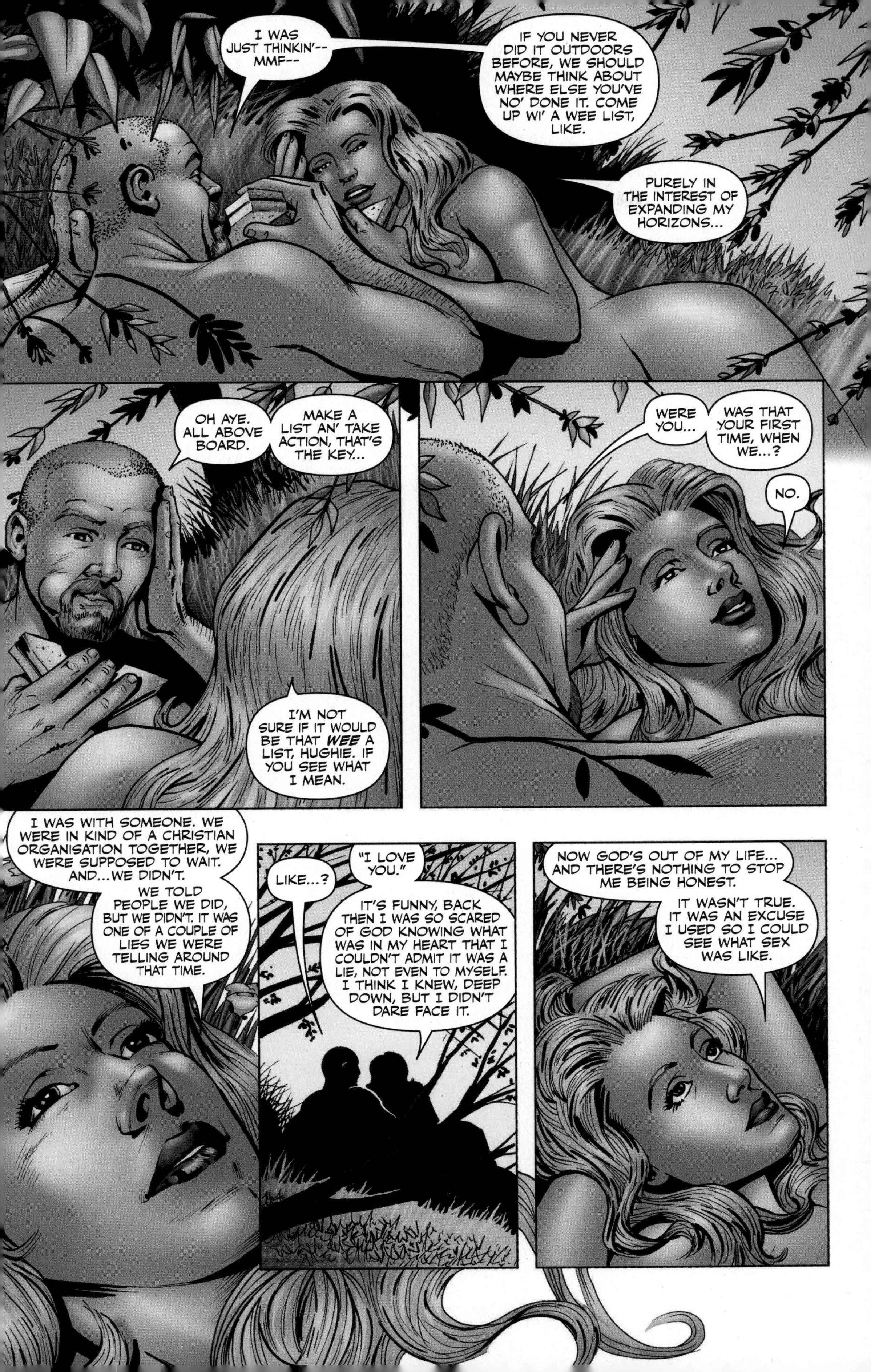
I WAS JUST THINKIN'-- MMF--
IF YOU NEVER DID IT OUTDOORS BEFORE, WE SHOULD MAYBE THINK ABOUT WHERE ELSE YOU'VE NO' DONE IT. COME UP WI' A WEE LIST, LIKE.
PURELY IN THE INTEREST OF EXPANDING MY HORIZONS...
OH AYE. ALL ABOVE BOARD.
MAKE A LIST AN' TAKE ACTION, THAT'S THE KEY...
I'M NOT SURE IF IT WOULD BE THAT *WEE* A LIST, HUGHIE. IF YOU SEE WHAT I MEAN.
WERE YOU...
WAS THAT YOUR FIRST TIME, WHEN WE...?
NO.
I WAS WITH SOMEONE. WE WERE IN KIND OF A CHRISTIAN ORGANISATION TOGETHER, WE WERE SUPPOSED TO WAIT. AND...WE DIDN'T.
WE TOLD PEOPLE WE DID, BUT WE DIDN'T. IT WAS ONE OF A COUPLE OF LIES WE WERE TELLING AROUND THAT TIME.
LIKE...?
"I LOVE YOU."
IT'S FUNNY, BACK THEN I WAS SO SCARED OF GOD KNOWING WHAT WAS IN MY HEART THAT I COULDN'T ADMIT IT WAS A LIE, NOT EVEN TO MYSELF. I THINK I KNEW, DEEP DOWN, BUT I DIDN'T DARE FACE IT.
NOW GOD'S OUT OF MY LIFE... AND THERE'S NOTHING TO STOP ME BEING HONEST.
IT WASN'T TRUE. IT WAS AN EXCUSE I USED SO I COULD SEE WHAT SEX WAS LIKE.

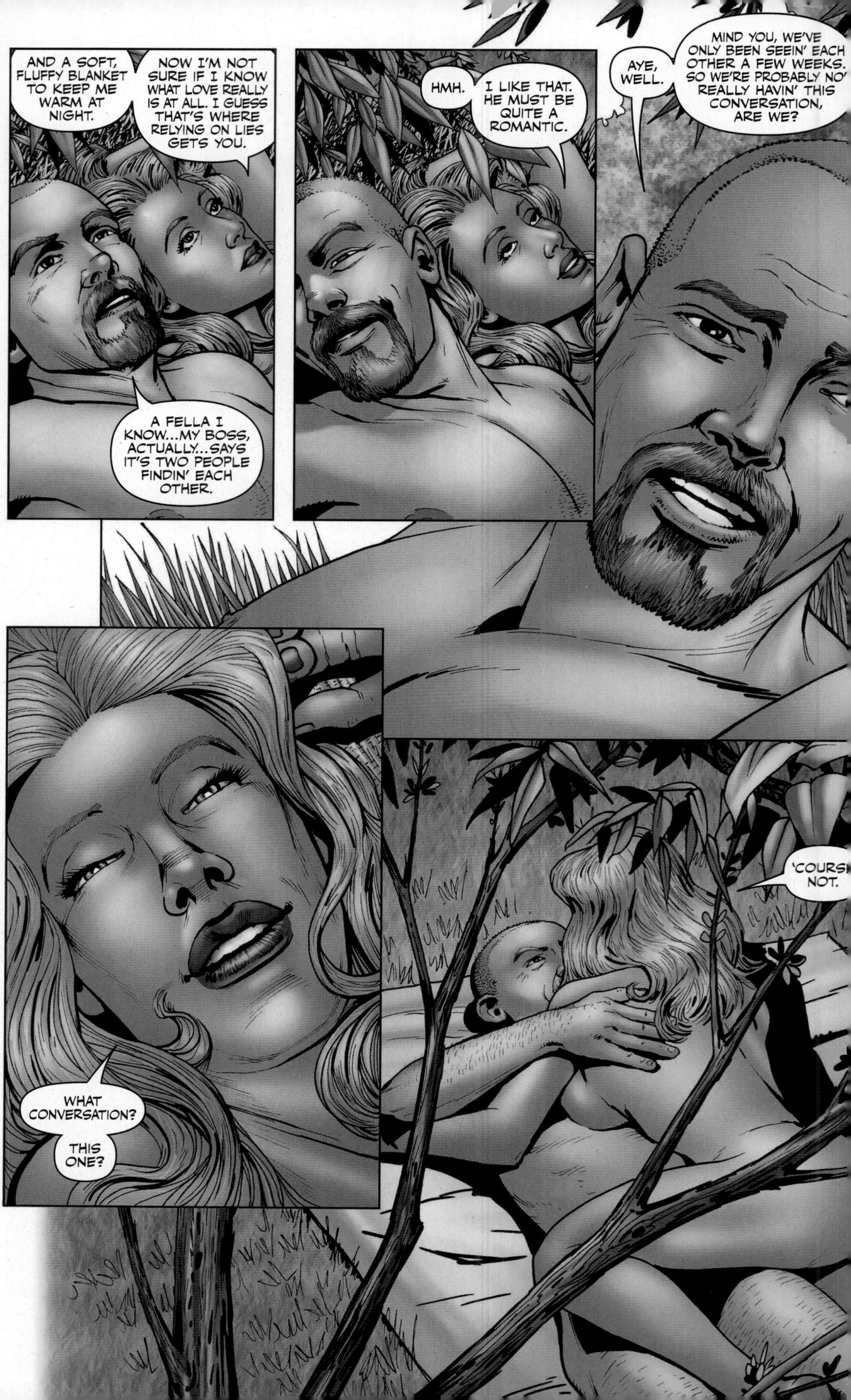
AND A SOFT, FLUFFY BLANKET TO KEEP ME WARM AT NIGHT.
NOW I'M NOT SURE IF I KNOW WHAT LOVE REALLY IS AT ALL. I GUESS THAT'S WHERE RELYING ON LIES GETS YOU.
A FELLA I KNOW...MY BOSS, ACTUALLY...SAYS IT'S TWO PEOPLE FINDIN' EACH OTHER.
HMH.
I LIKE THAT. HE MUST BE QUITE A ROMANTIC.
AYE, WELL.
MIND YOU, WE'VE ONLY BEEN SEEIN' EACH OTHER A FEW WEEKS. SO WE'RE PROBABLY NO' REALLY HAVIN' THIS CONVERSATION, ARE WE?
WHAT CONVERSATION?
THIS ONE?
NOT.

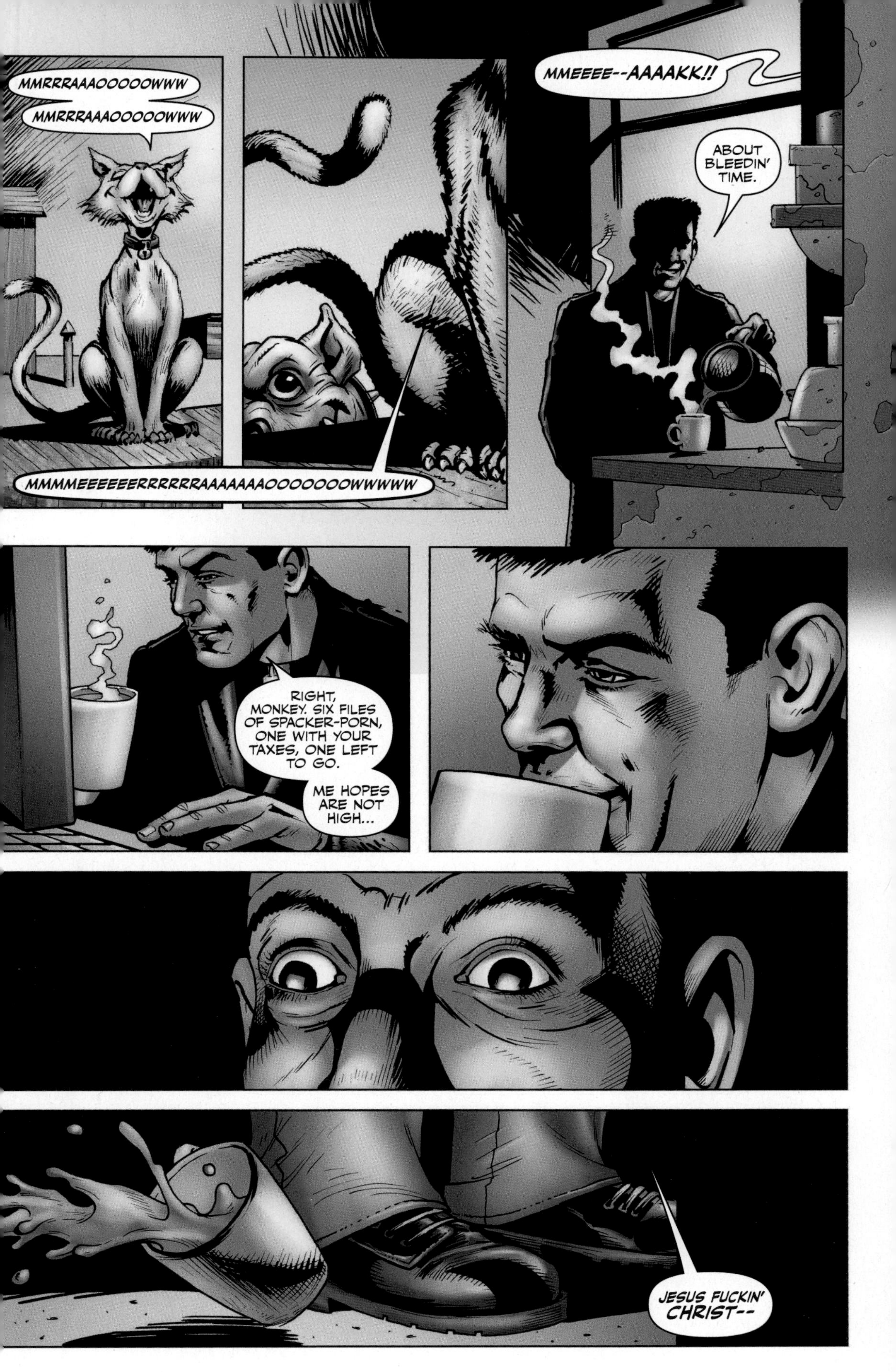
MMRRRAAAOOOOOWWW
MMRRRAAAOOOOOWWW
MMMMEEEEEERRRRRRAAAAAAAOOOOOOOWWWWW
MMEEEE--AAAAKK!!
ABOUT BLEEDIN' TIME.
RIGHT, MONKEY. SIX FILES OF SPACKER-PORN, ONE WITH YOUR TAXES, ONE LEFT TO GO.
ME HOPES ARE NOT HIGH...
JESUS FUCKIN' CHRIST--

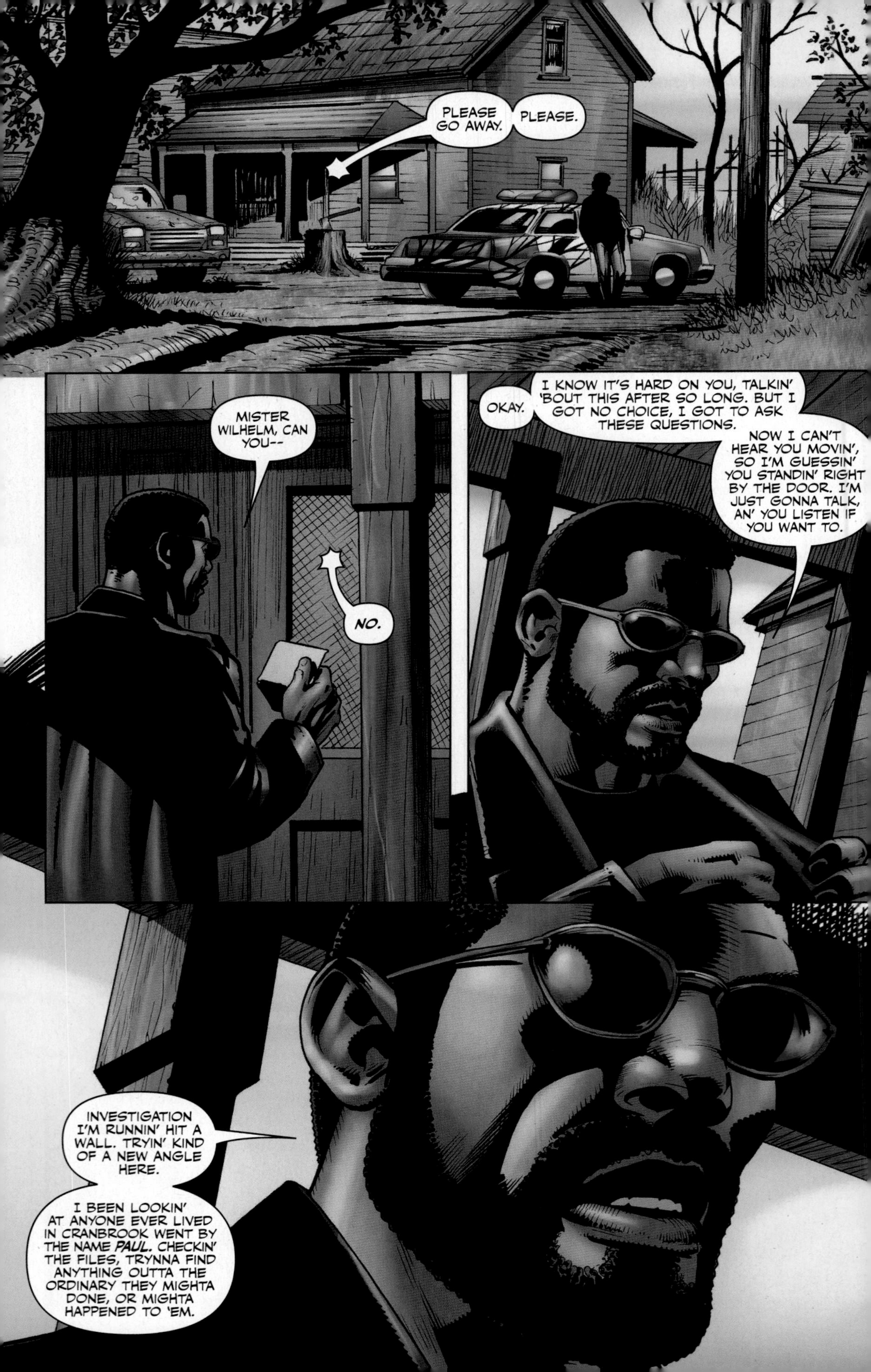
PLEASE GO AWAY.
PLEASE.
MISTER WILHELM, CAN YOU--
NO.
OKAY.
I KNOW IT'S HARD ON YOU, TALKIN' 'BOUT THIS AFTER SO LONG. BUT I GOT NO CHOICE, I GOT TO ASK THESE QUESTIONS.
NOW I CAN'T HEAR YOU MOVIN', SO I'M GUESSIN' YOU STANDIN' RIGHT BY THE DOOR. I'M JUST GONNA TALK, AN' YOU LISTEN IF YOU WANT TO.
INVESTIGATION I'M RUNNIN' HIT A WALL. TRYIN' KIND OF A NEW ANGLE HERE.
I BEEN LOOKIN' AT ANYONE EVER LIVED IN CRANBROOK WENT BY THE NAME *PAUL.* CHECKIN' THE FILES, TRYNNA FIND ANYTHING OUTTA THE ORDINARY THEY MIGHTA DONE, OR MIGHTA HAPPENED TO 'EM.

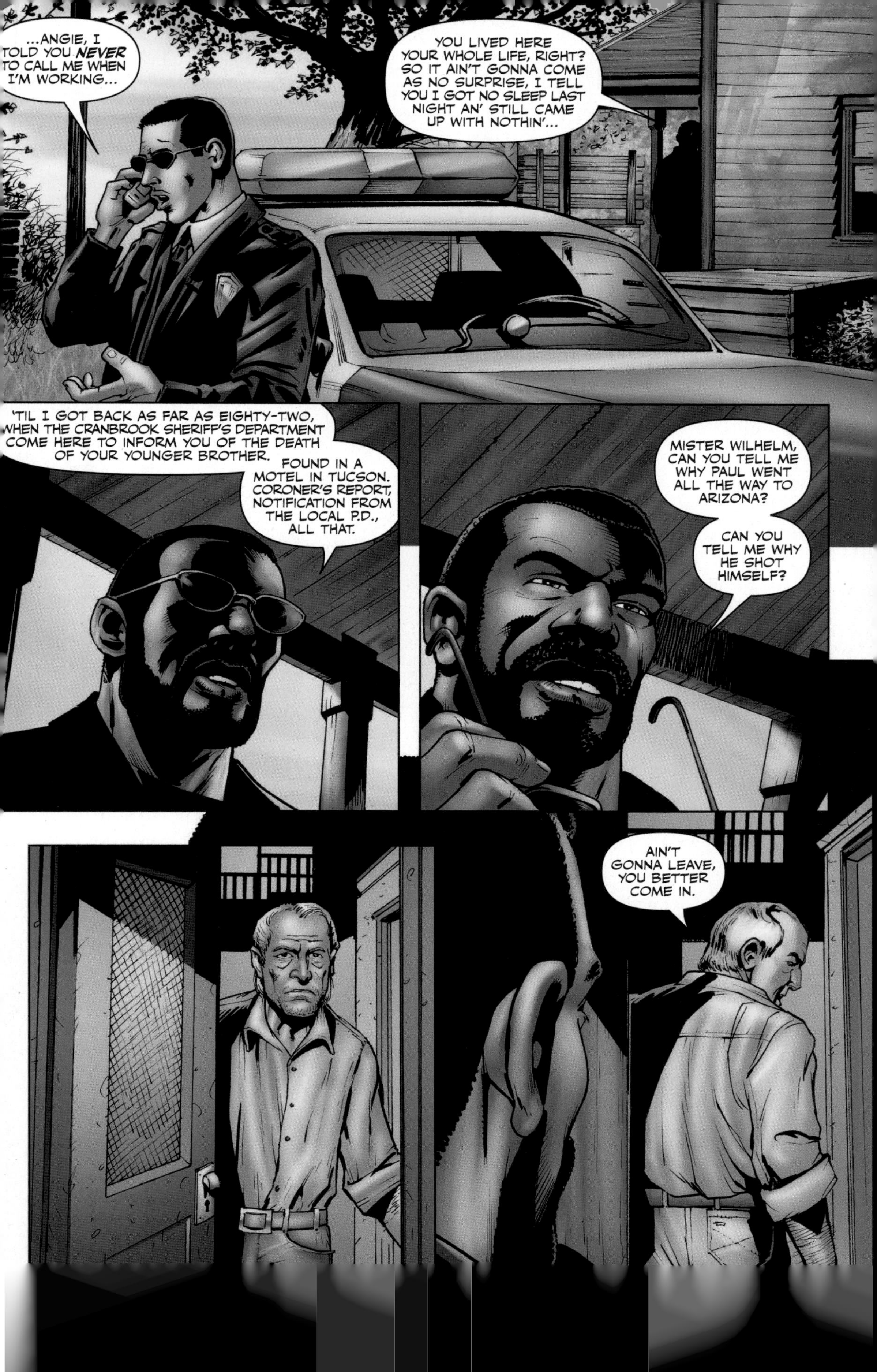
...ANGIE, I TOLD YOU *NEVER* TO CALL ME WHEN I'M WORKING...
YOU LIVED HERE YOUR WHOLE LIFE, RIGHT? SO IT AIN'T GONNA COME AS NO SURPRISE, I TELL YOU I GOT NO SLEEP LAST NIGHT AN' STILL CAME UP WITH NOTHIN'...
'TIL I GOT BACK AS FAR AS EIGHTY-TWO, WHEN THE CRANBROOK SHERIFF'S DEPARTMENT COME HERE TO INFORM YOU OF THE DEATH OF YOUR YOUNGER BROTHER.
FOUND IN A MOTEL IN TUCSON. CORONER'S REPORT, NOTIFICATION FROM THE LOCAL P.D., ALL THAT.
MISTER WILHELM, CAN YOU TELL ME WHY PAUL WENT ALL THE WAY TO ARIZONA?
CAN YOU TELL ME WHY HE SHOT HIMSELF?
AIN'T GONNA LEAVE, YOU BETTER COME IN.

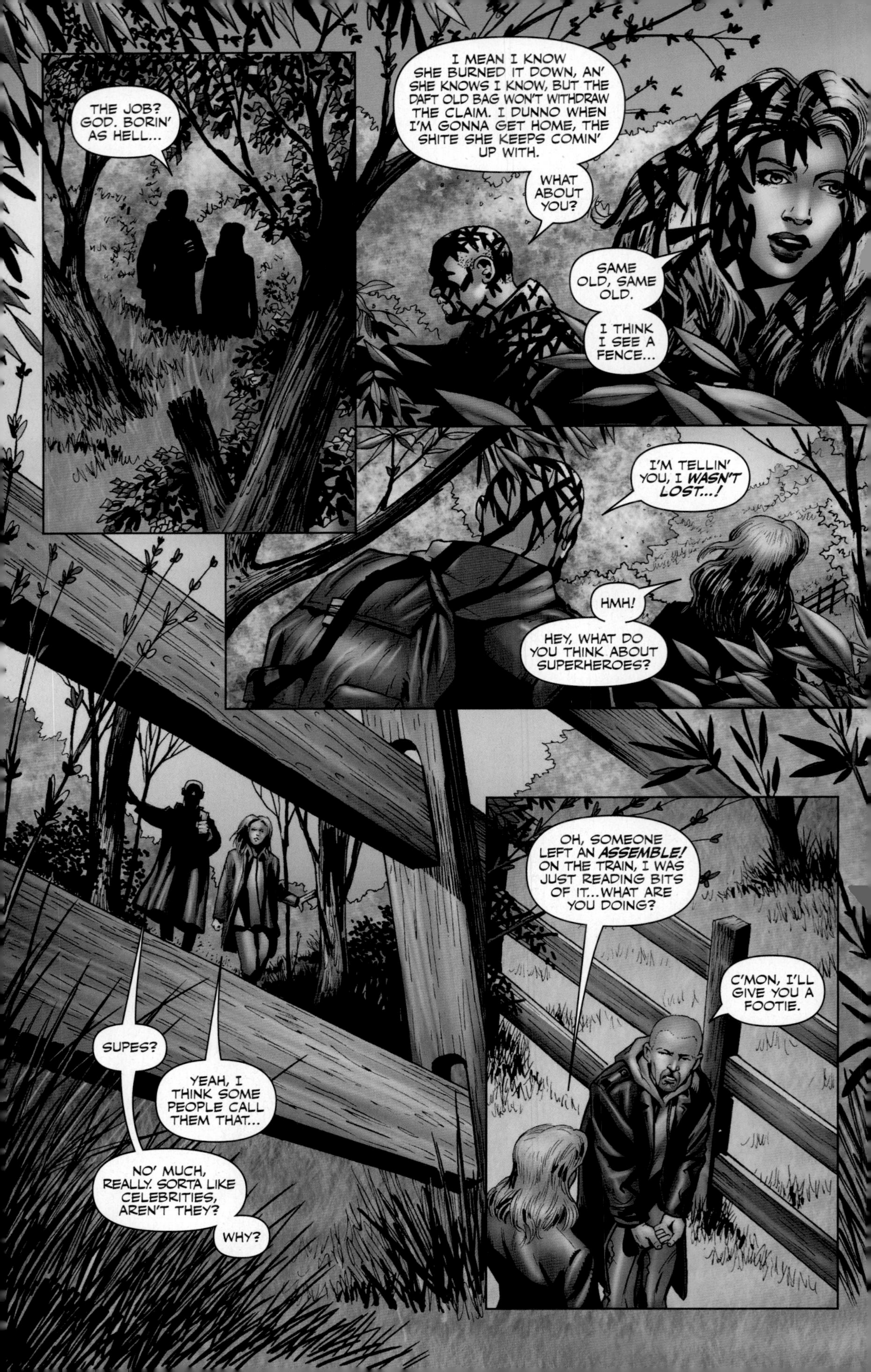
THE JOB? GOD. BORIN' AS HELL...
I MEAN I KNOW SHE BURNED IT DOWN, AN' SHE KNOWS I KNOW, BUT THE DAFT OLD BAG WON'T WITHDRAW THE CLAIM. I DUNNO WHEN I'M GONNA GET HOME, THE SHITE SHE KEEPS COMIN' UP WITH.
WHAT ABOUT YOU?
SAME OLD, SAME OLD.
I THINK I SEE A FENCE...
I'M TELLIN' YOU, I *WASN'T LOST...!*
HMH!
HEY, WHAT DO YOU THINK ABOUT SUPERHEROES?
SUPES?
YEAH, I THINK SOME PEOPLE CALL THEM THAT...
NO' MUCH, REALLY. SORTA LIKE CELEBRITIES, AREN'T THEY?
WHY?
OH, SOMEONE LEFT AN *ASSEMBLE!* ON THE TRAIN, I WAS JUST READING BITS OF IT...WHAT ARE YOU DOING?
C'MON, I'LL GIVE YOU A FOOTIE.

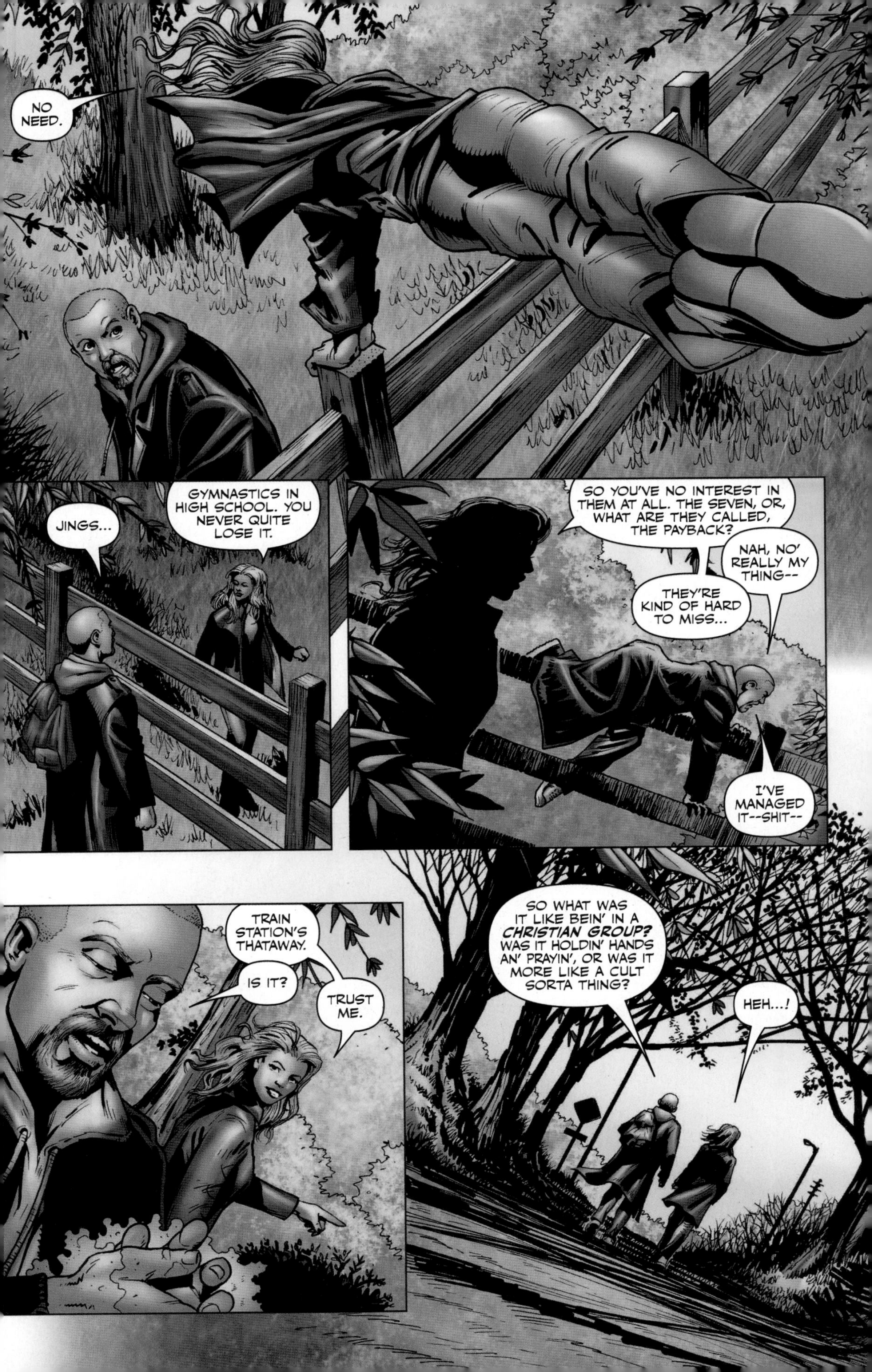

NO NEED.
JINGS...
GYMNASTICS IN HIGH SCHOOL. YOU NEVER QUITE LOSE IT.
SO YOU'VE NO INTEREST IN THEM AT ALL. THE SEVEN, OR, WHAT ARE THEY CALLED, THE PAYBACK?
NAH, NO' REALLY MY THING--
THEY'RE KIND OF HARD TO MISS...
I'VE MANAGED IT--SHIT--
TRAIN STATION'S THATAWAY.
IS IT?
TRUST ME.
SO WHAT WAS IT LIKE BEIN' IN A *CHRISTIAN GROUP?* WAS IT HOLDIN' HANDS AN' PRAYIN', OR WAS IT MORE LIKE A CULT SORTA THING?
HEH...!

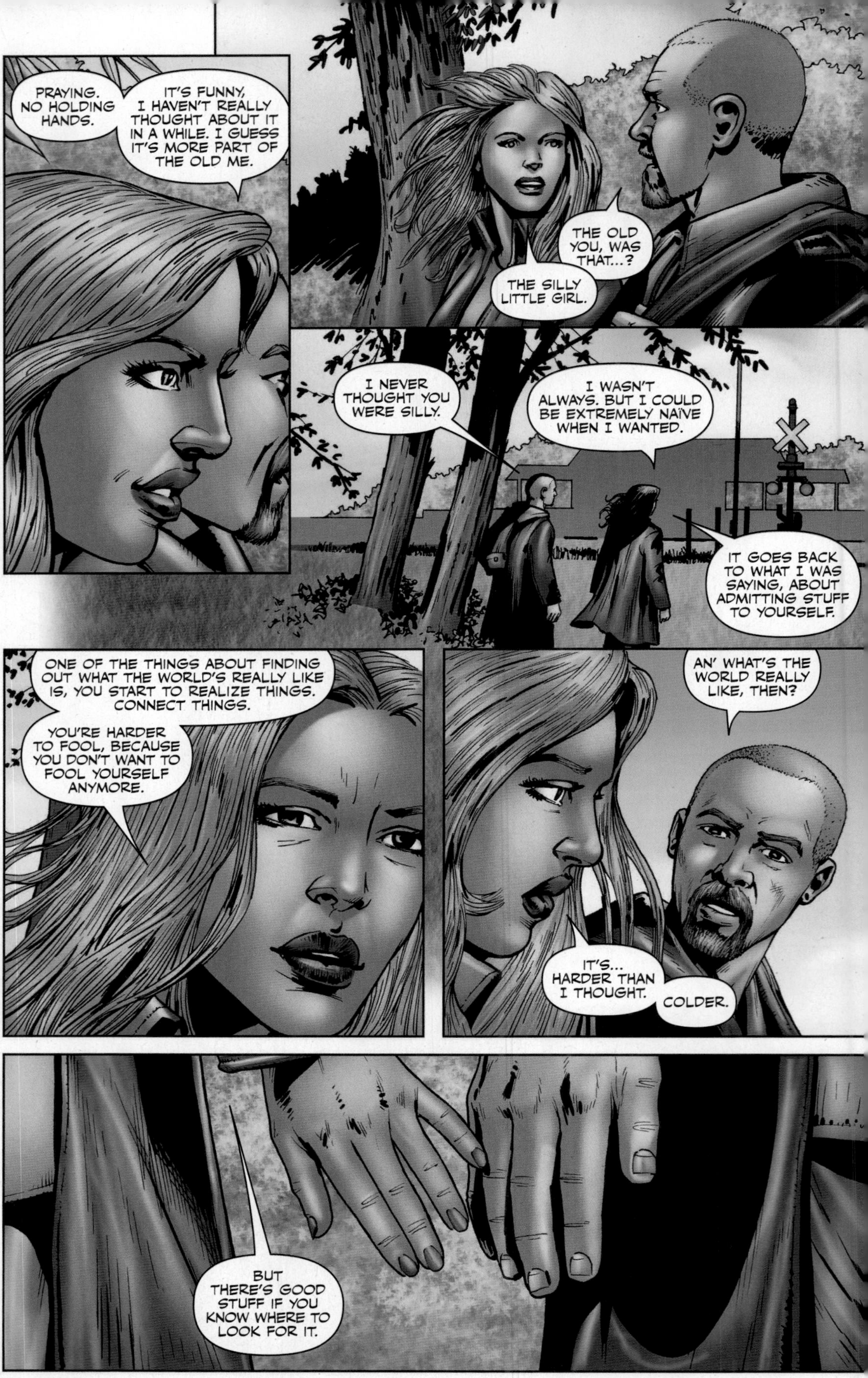
PRAYING. NO HOLDING HANDS.
IT'S FUNNY, I HAVEN'T REALLY THOUGHT ABOUT IT IN A WHILE. I GUESS IT'S MORE PART OF THE OLD ME.
THE OLD YOU, WAS THAT...?
THE SILLY LITTLE GIRL.
I NEVER THOUGHT YOU WERE SILLY.
I WASN'T ALWAYS. BUT I COULD BE EXTREMELY NAÏVE WHEN I WANTED.
IT GOES BACK TO WHAT I WAS SAYING, ABOUT ADMITTING STUFF TO YOURSELF.
ONE OF THE THINGS ABOUT FINDING OUT WHAT THE WORLD'S REALLY LIKE IS, YOU START TO REALIZE THINGS. CONNECT THINGS.
YOU'RE HARDER TO FOOL, BECAUSE YOU DON'T WANT TO FOOL YOURSELF ANYMORE.
AN' WHAT'S THE WORLD REALLY LIKE, THEN?
IT'S... HARDER THAN I THOUGHT.
COLDER.
BUT THERE'S GOOD STUFF IF YOU KNOW WHERE TO LOOK FOR IT.

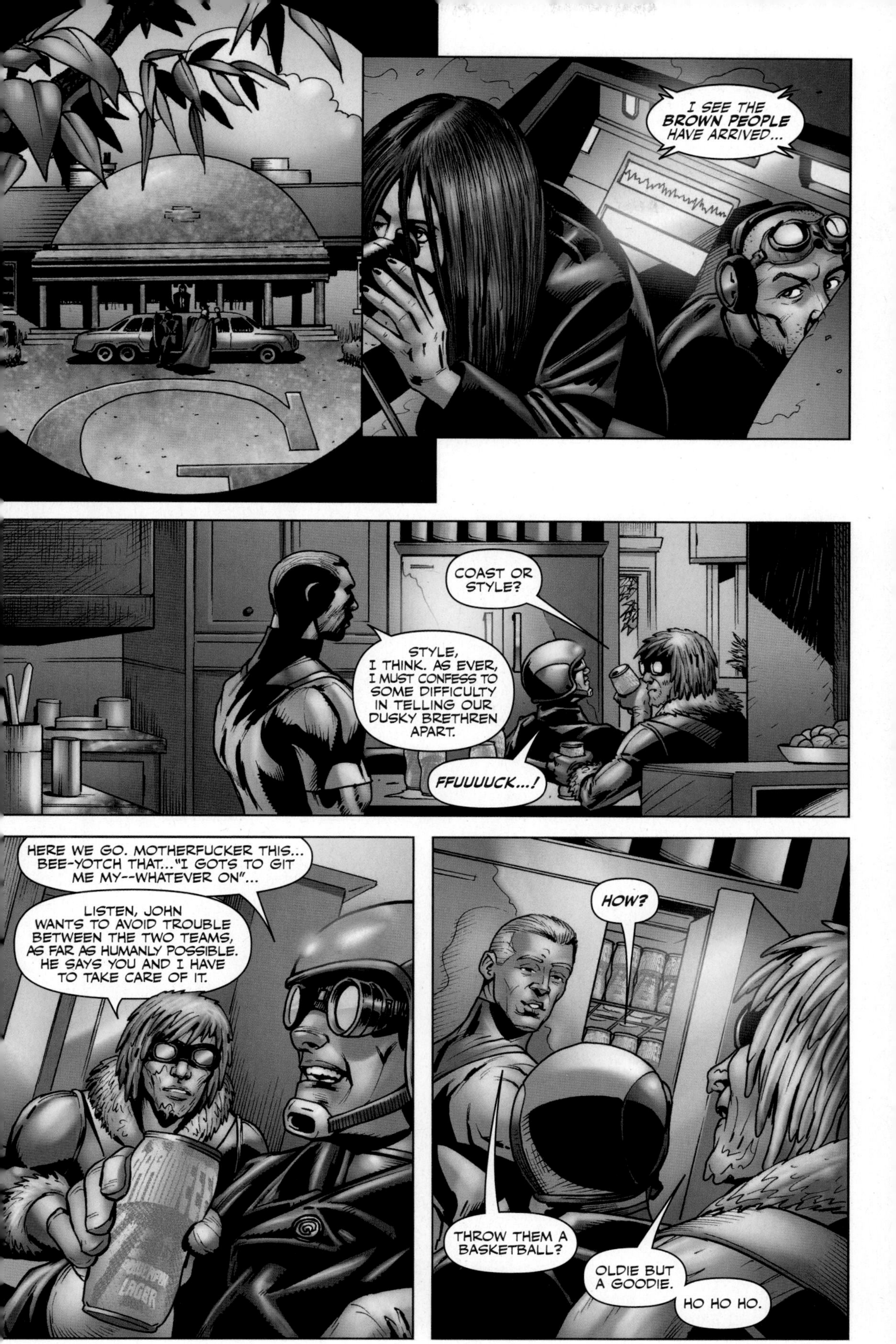
I SEE THE BROWN PEOPLE HAVE ARRIVED...
COAST OR STYLE?
STYLE, I THINK. AS EVER, I MUST CONFESS TO SOME DIFFICULTY IN TELLING OUR DUSKY BRETHREN APART.
FFUUUUCK...!
HERE WE GO. MOTHERFUCKER THIS... BEE-YOTCH THAT..."I GOTS TO GIT ME MY--WHATEVER ON"...
LISTEN, JOHN WANTS TO AVOID TROUBLE BETWEEN THE TWO TEAMS, AS FAR AS HUMANLY POSSIBLE. HE SAYS YOU AND I HAVE TO TAKE CARE OF IT.
HOW?
THROW THEM A BASKETBALL?
OLDIE BUT A GOODIE.
HO HO HO.

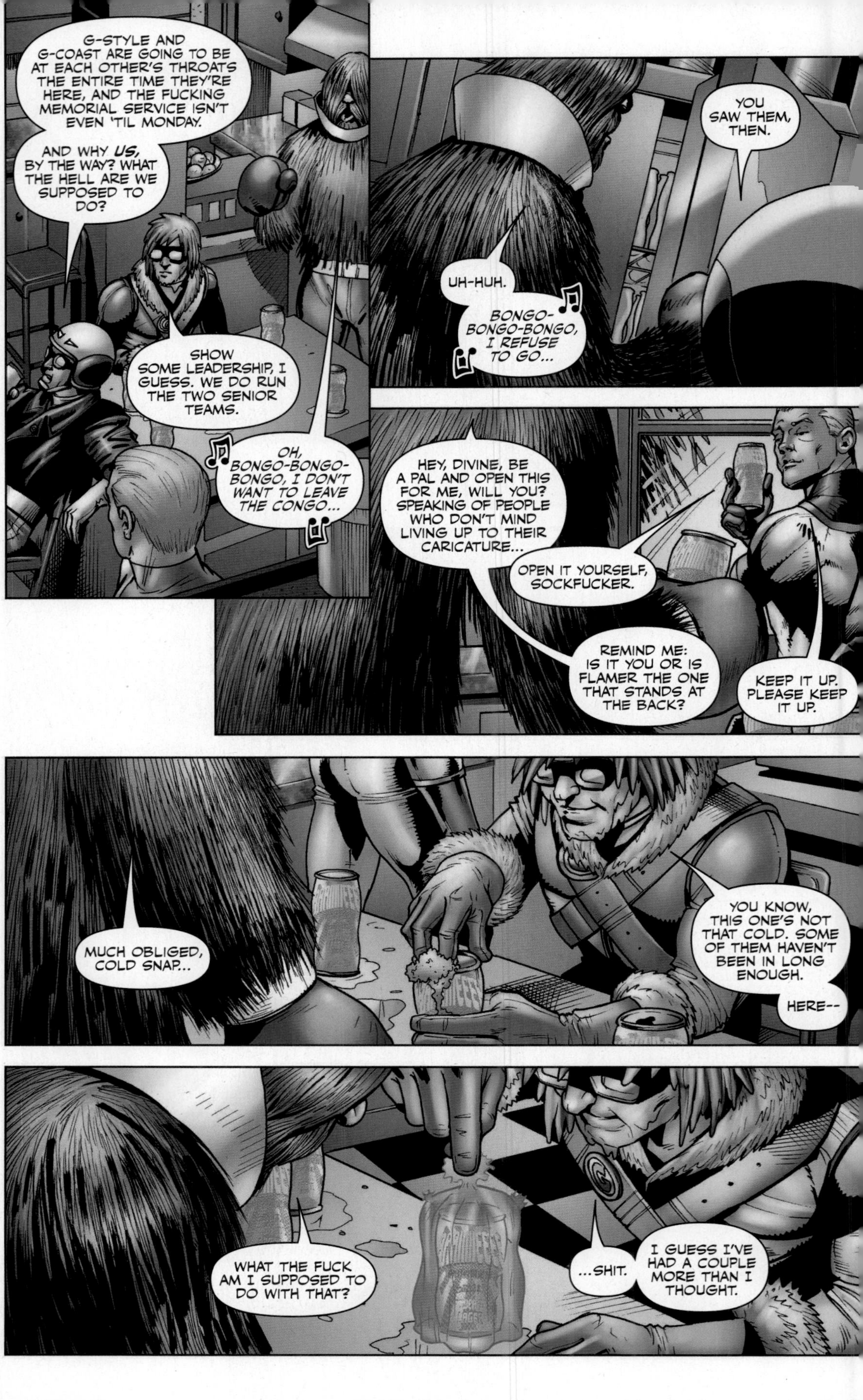
G-STYLE AND G-COAST ARE GOING TO BE AT EACH OTHER'S THROATS THE ENTIRE TIME THEY'RE HERE, AND THE FUCKING MEMORIAL SERVICE ISN'T EVEN 'TIL MONDAY.
AND WHY *US*, BY THE WAY? WHAT THE HELL ARE WE SUPPOSED TO DO?
SHOW SOME LEADERSHIP, I GUESS. WE DO RUN THE TWO SENIOR TEAMS.
OH, BONGO-BONGO-BONGO, I DON'T WANT TO LEAVE THE CONGO...
YOU SAW THEM, THEN.
UH-HUH.
BONGO-BONGO-BONGO, I REFUSE TO GO...
HEY, DIVINE, BE A PAL AND OPEN THIS FOR ME, WILL YOU? SPEAKING OF PEOPLE WHO DON'T MIND LIVING UP TO THEIR CARICATURE...
OPEN IT YOURSELF, SOCKFUCKER.
REMIND ME: IS IT YOU OR IS FLAMER THE ONE THAT STANDS AT THE BACK?
KEEP IT UP. PLEASE KEEP IT UP.
MUCH OBLIGED, COLD SNAP...
YOU KNOW, THIS ONE'S NOT THAT COLD. SOME OF THEM HAVEN'T BEEN IN LONG ENOUGH.
HERE--
WHAT THE FUCK AM I SUPPOSED TO DO WITH THAT?
...SHIT.
I GUESS I'VE HAD A COUPLE MORE THAN I THOUGHT.

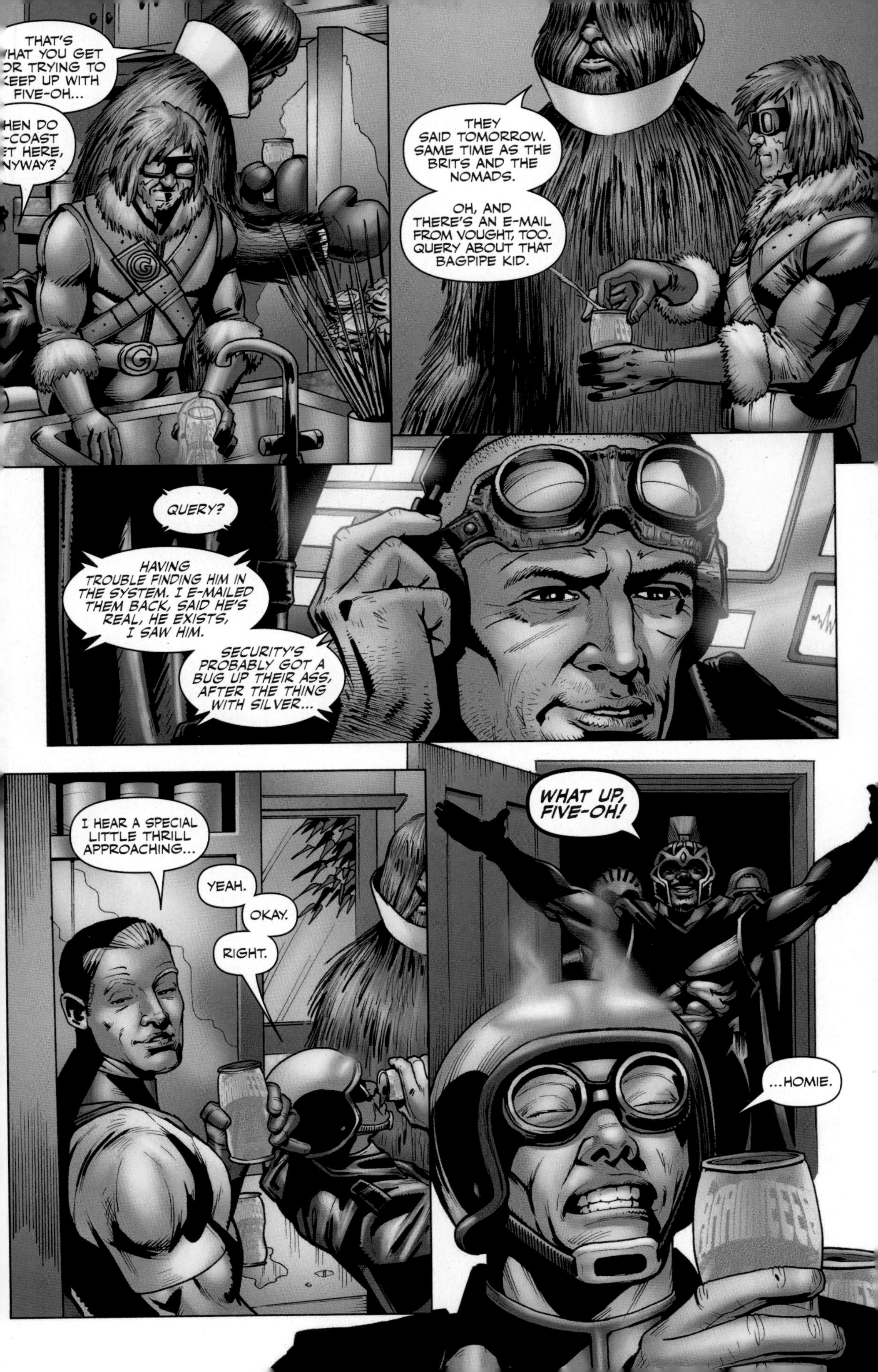
THAT'S
WHAT YOU GET
FOR TRYING TO
KEEP UP WITH
FIVE-OH...
HEN DO
-COAST
ET HERE,
NYWAY?
THEY SAID TOMORROW. SAME TIME AS THE BRITS AND THE NOMADS.
OH, AND THERE'S AN E-MAIL FROM VOUGHT, TOO. QUERY ABOUT THAT BAGPIPE KID.
QUERY?
HAVING TROUBLE FINDING HIM IN THE SYSTEM. I E-MAILED THEM BACK, SAID HE'S REAL, HE EXISTS, I SAW HIM.
SECURITY'S PROBABLY GOT A BUG UP THEIR ASS, AFTER THE THING WITH SILVER...
I HEAR A SPECIAL LITTLE THRILL APPROACHING...
YEAH.
OKAY.
RIGHT.
WHAT UP, FIVE-OH!
...HOMIE.

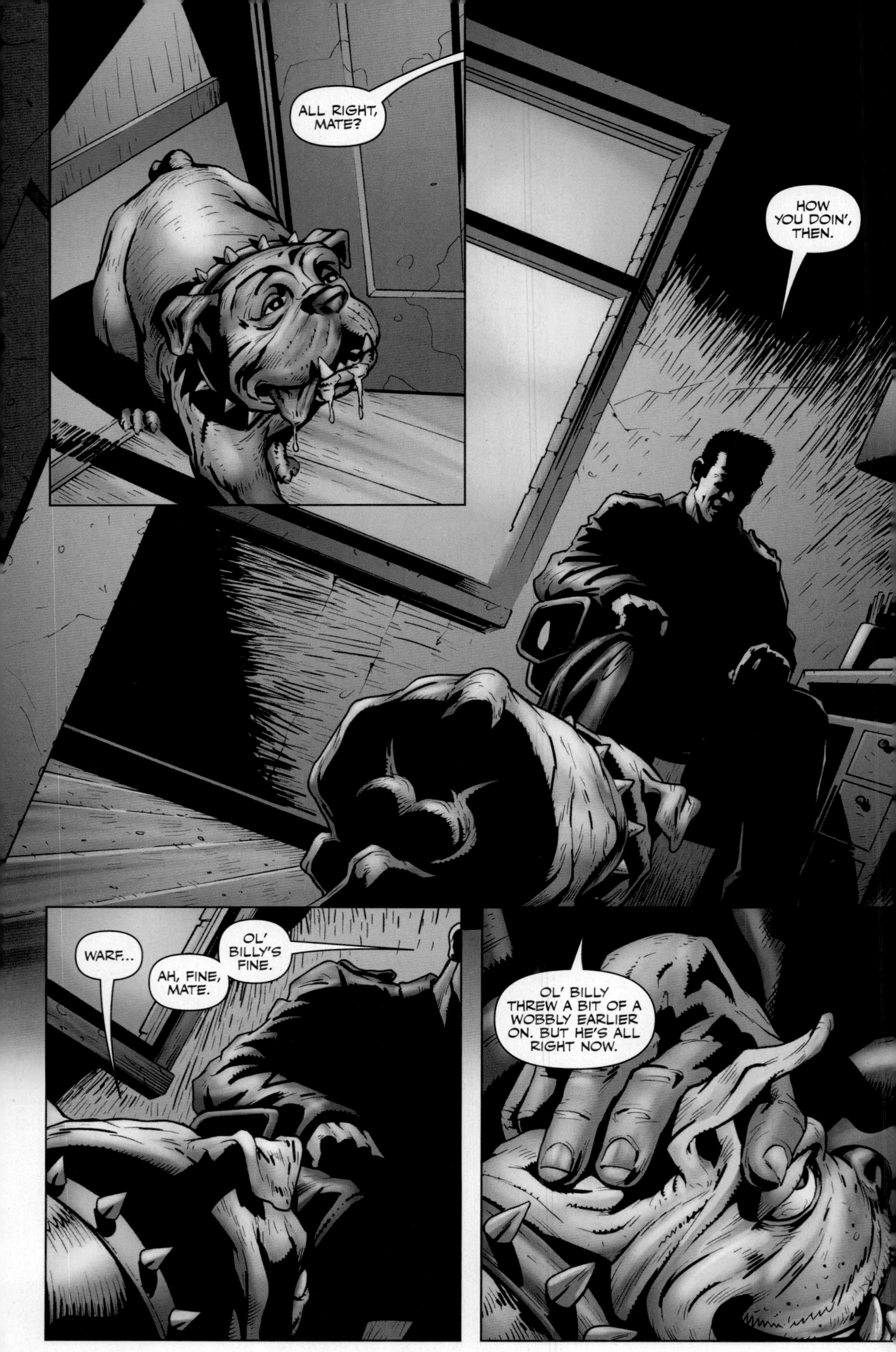
ALL RIGHT, MATE?
HOW YOU DOIN', THEN.
WARF...
AH, FINE, MATE.
OL' BILLY'S FINE.
OL' BILLY THREW A BIT OF A WOBBLY EARLIER ON. BUT HE'S ALL RIGHT NOW.

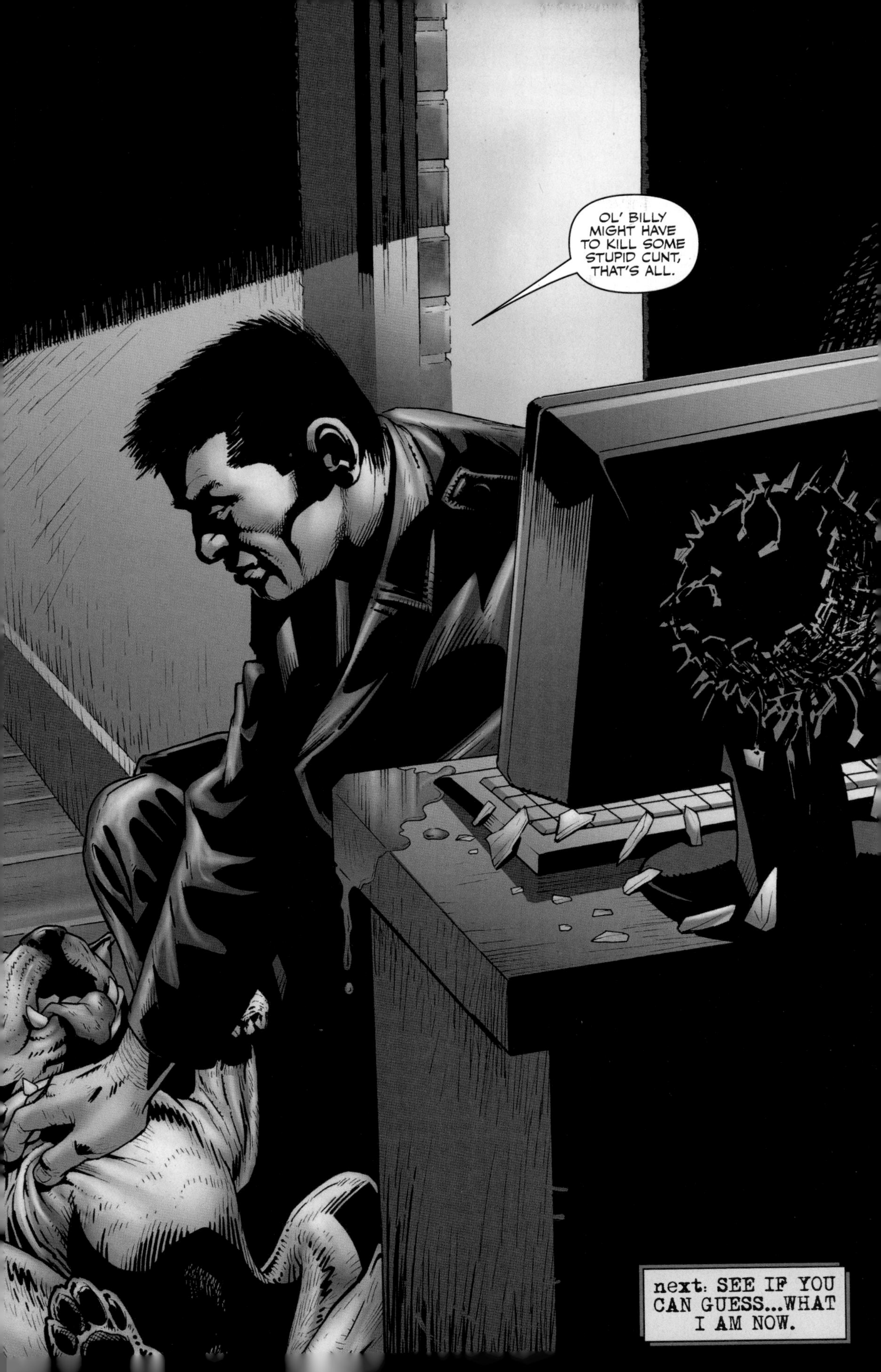
OL' BILLY MIGHT HAVE TO KILL SOME STUPID CUNT, THAT'S ALL.
next: SEE IF YOU CAN GUESS...WHAT I AM NOW.

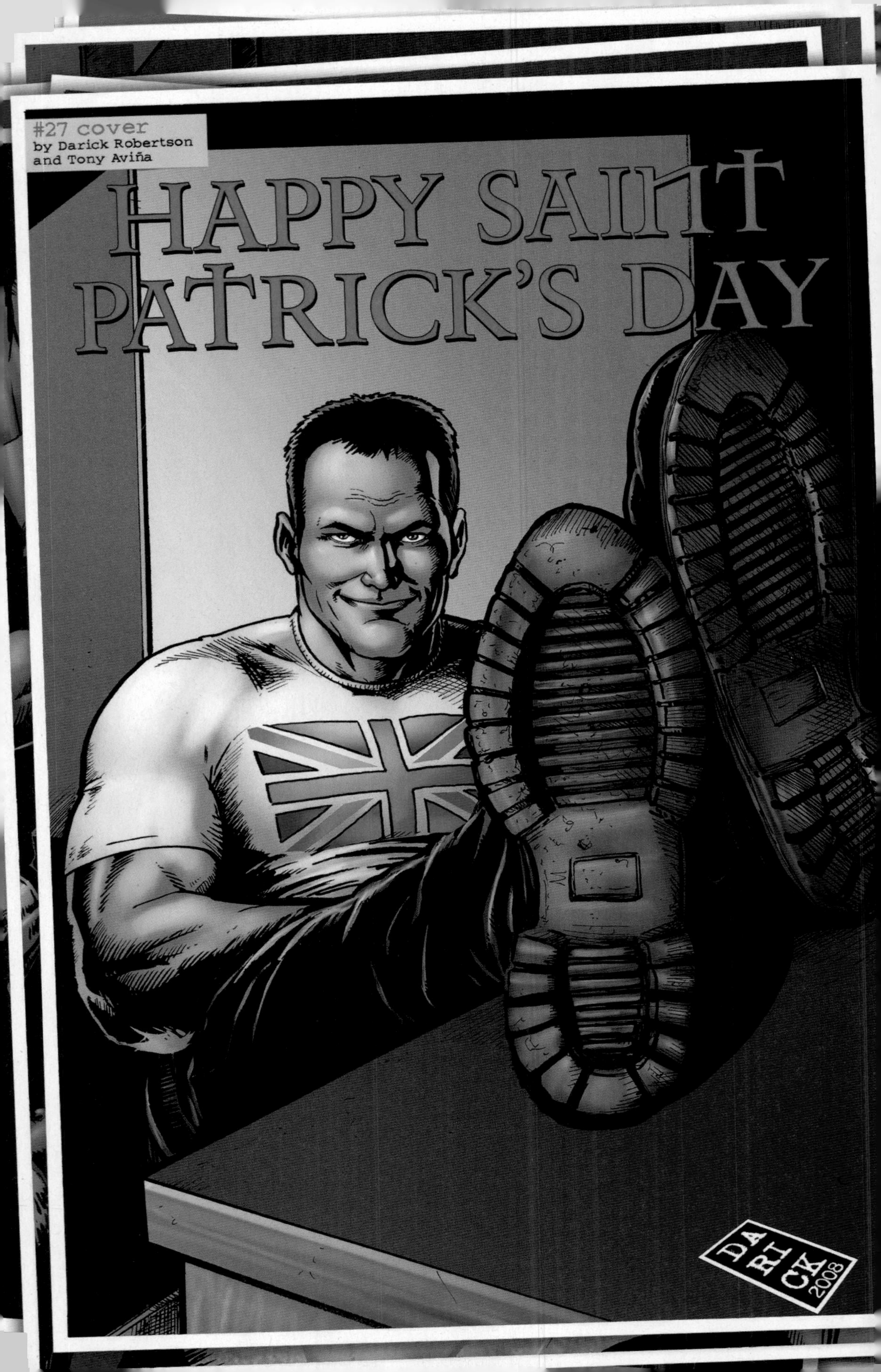
HAPPY SAINT
PATRICK'S DAY
DA
RI
CK
2008

#27 cover
by Darick Robertson
and Tony Aviña

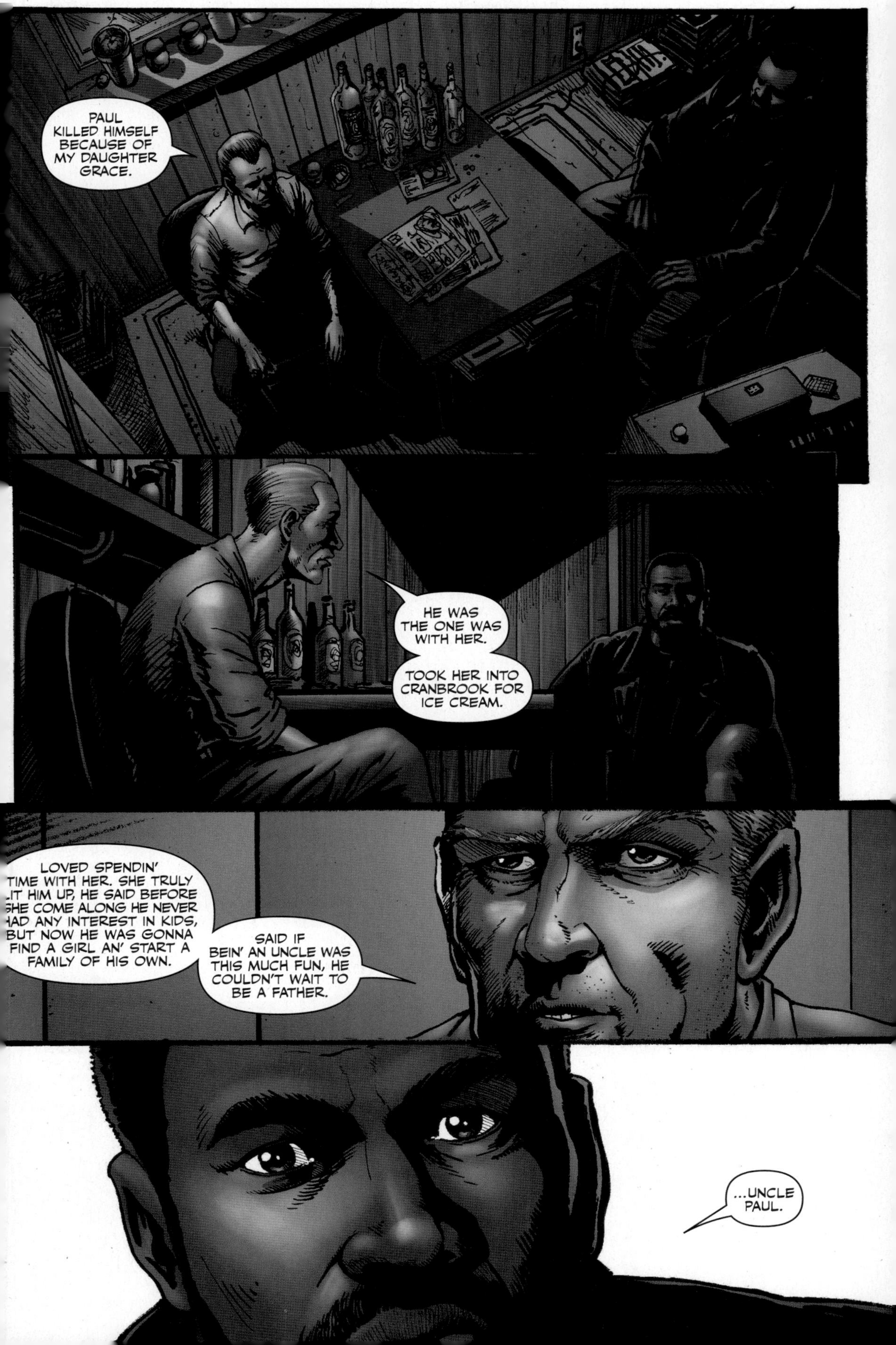
PAUL KILLED HIMSELF BECAUSE OF MY DAUGHTER GRACE.
HE WAS THE ONE WAS WITH HER.
TOOK HER INTO CRANBROOK FOR ICE CREAM.
LOVED SPENDIN' TIME WITH HER. SHE TRULY LIT HIM UP, HE SAID BEFORE SHE COME ALONG HE NEVER HAD ANY INTEREST IN KIDS, BUT NOW HE WAS GONNA FIND A GIRL AN' START A FAMILY OF HIS OWN.
SAID IF BEIN' AN UNCLE WAS THIS MUCH FUN, HE COULDN'T WAIT TO BE A FATHER.
...UNCLE PAUL.

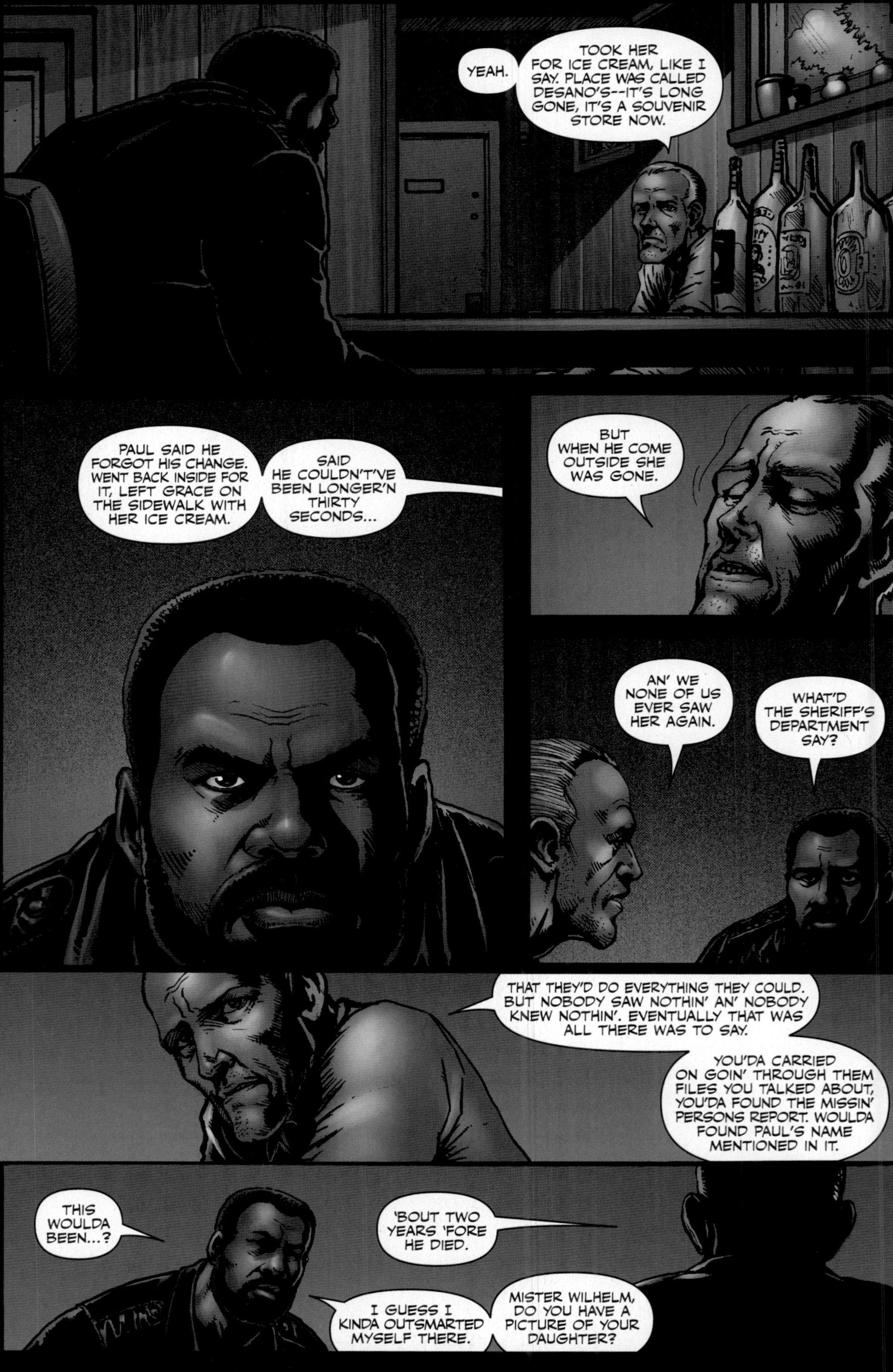
YEAH.
TOOK HER FOR ICE CREAM, LIKE I SAY. PLACE WAS CALLED DESANO'S--IT'S LONG GONE, IT'S A SOUVENIR STORE NOW.
PAUL SAID HE FORGOT HIS CHANGE. WENT BACK INSIDE FOR IT, LEFT GRACE ON THE SIDEWALK WITH HER ICE CREAM.
SAID HE COULDN'T'VE BEEN LONGER'N THIRTY SECONDS...
BUT WHEN HE COME OUTSIDE SHE WAS GONE.
AN' WE NONE OF US EVER SAW HER AGAIN.
WHAT'D THE SHERIFF'S DEPARTMENT SAY?
THAT THEY'D DO EVERYTHING THEY COULD. BUT NOBODY SAW NOTHIN' AN' NOBODY KNEW NOTHIN'. EVENTUALLY THAT WAS ALL THERE WAS TO SAY.
YOU'DA CARRIED ON GOIN' THROUGH THEM FILES YOU TALKED ABOUT, YOU'DA FOUND THE MISSIN' PERSONS REPORT. WOULDA FOUND PAUL'S NAME MENTIONED IN IT.
THIS WOULDA BEEN...?
'BOUT TWO YEARS 'FORE HE DIED.
I GUESS I KINDA OUTSMARTED MYSELF THERE.
MISTER WILHELM, DO YOU HAVE A PICTURE OF YOUR DAUGHTER?

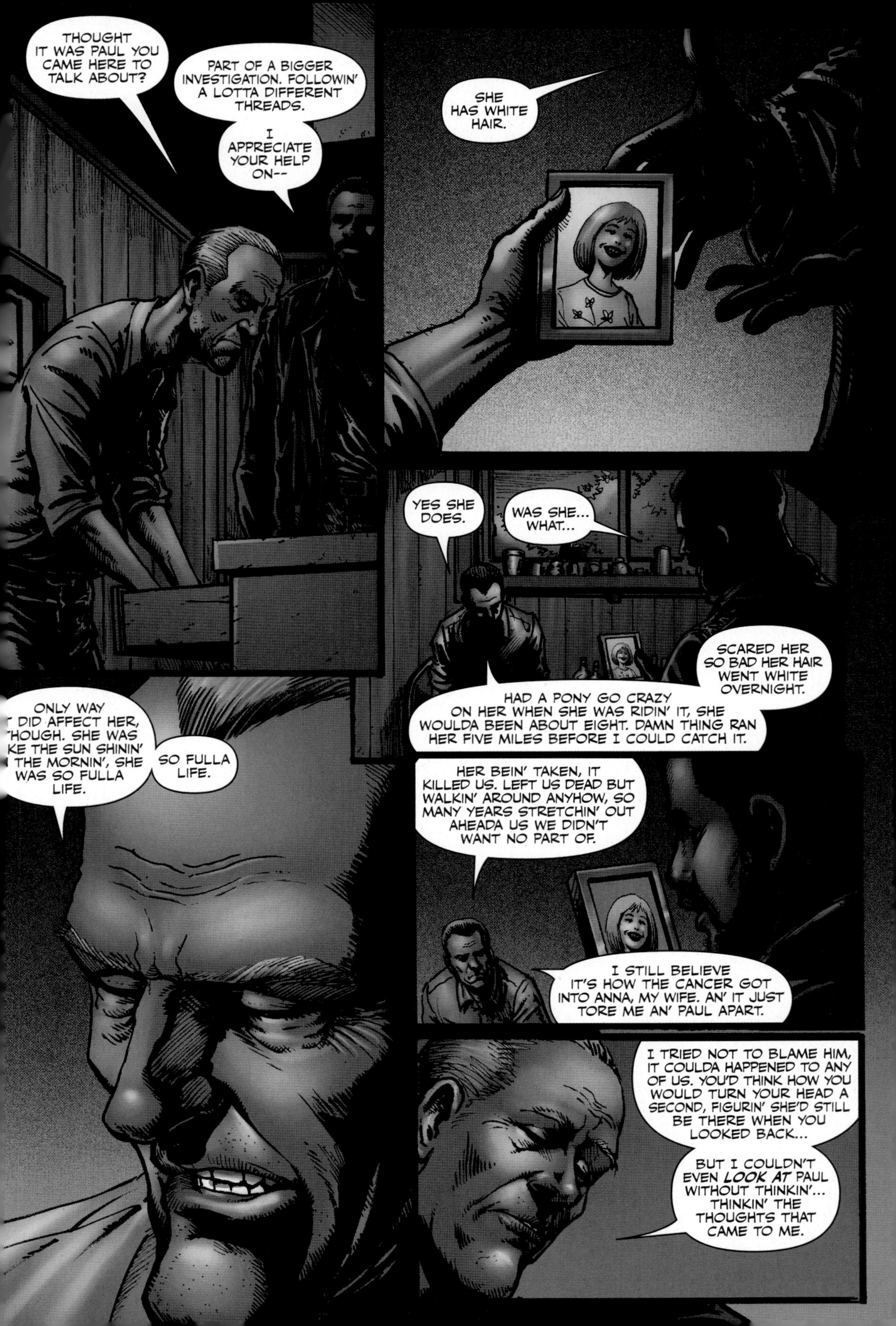
THOUGHT IT WAS PAUL YOU CAME HERE TO TALK ABOUT?
PART OF A BIGGER INVESTIGATION. FOLLOWIN' A LOTTA DIFFERENT THREADS.
I APPRECIATE YOUR HELP ON--
SHE HAS WHITE HAIR.
YES SHE DOES.
WAS SHE... WHAT...
HAD A PONY GO CRAZY ON HER WHEN SHE WAS RIDIN' IT, SHE WOULDA BEEN ABOUT EIGHT. DAMN THING RAN HER FIVE MILES BEFORE I COULD CATCH IT.
SCARED HER SO BAD HER HAIR WENT WHITE OVERNIGHT.
ONLY WAY T DID AFFECT HER, THOUGH. SHE WAS KE THE SUN SHININ' THE MORNIN', SHE WAS SO FULLA LIFE.
SO FULLA LIFE.
HER BEIN' TAKEN, IT KILLED US. LEFT US DEAD BUT WALKIN' AROUND ANYHOW, SO MANY YEARS STRETCHIN' OUT AHEADA US WE DIDN'T WANT NO PART OF.
I STILL BELIEVE IT'S HOW THE CANCER GOT INTO ANNA, MY WIFE. AN' IT JUST TORE ME AN' PAUL APART.
I TRIED NOT TO BLAME HIM, IT COULDA HAPPENED TO ANY OF US. YOU'D THINK HOW YOU WOULD TURN YOUR HEAD A SECOND, FIGURIN' SHE'D STILL BE THERE WHEN YOU LOOKED BACK...
BUT I COULDN'T EVEN LOOK AT PAUL WITHOUT THINKIN'... THINKIN' THE THOUGHTS THAT CAME TO ME.

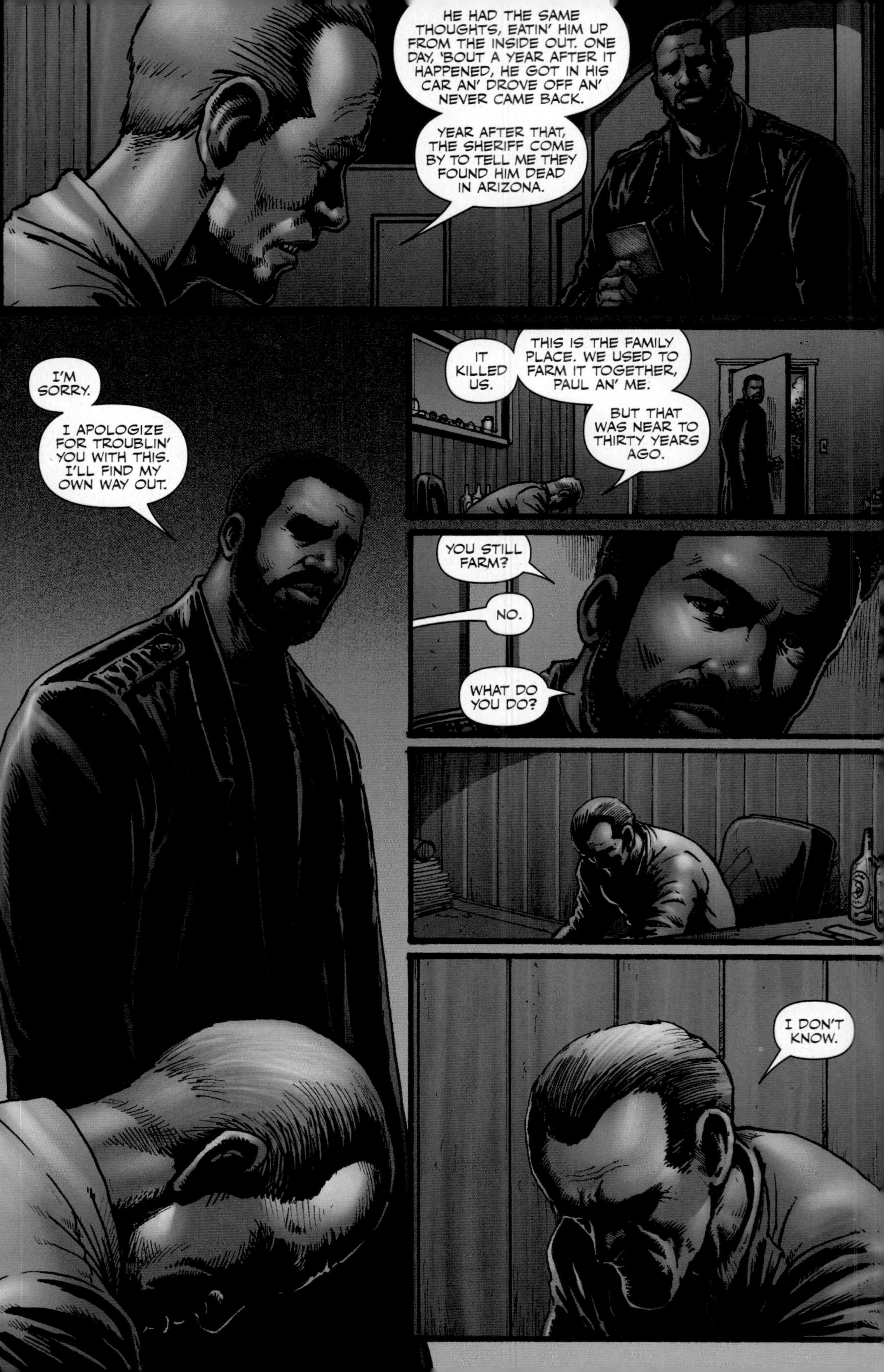
HE HAD THE SAME THOUGHTS, EATIN' HIM UP FROM THE INSIDE OUT. ONE DAY, 'BOUT A YEAR AFTER IT HAPPENED, HE GOT IN HIS CAR AN' DROVE OFF AN' NEVER CAME BACK.
YEAR AFTER THAT, THE SHERIFF COME BY TO TELL ME THEY FOUND HIM DEAD IN ARIZONA.
IT KILLED US.
THIS IS THE FAMILY PLACE. WE USED TO FARM IT TOGETHER, PAUL AN' ME.
BUT THAT WAS NEAR TO THIRTY YEARS AGO.
YOU STILL FARM?
NO.
WHAT DO YOU DO?
I DON'T KNOW.
I'M SORRY.
I APOLOGIZE FOR TROUBLIN' YOU WITH THIS. I'LL FIND MY OWN WAY OUT.

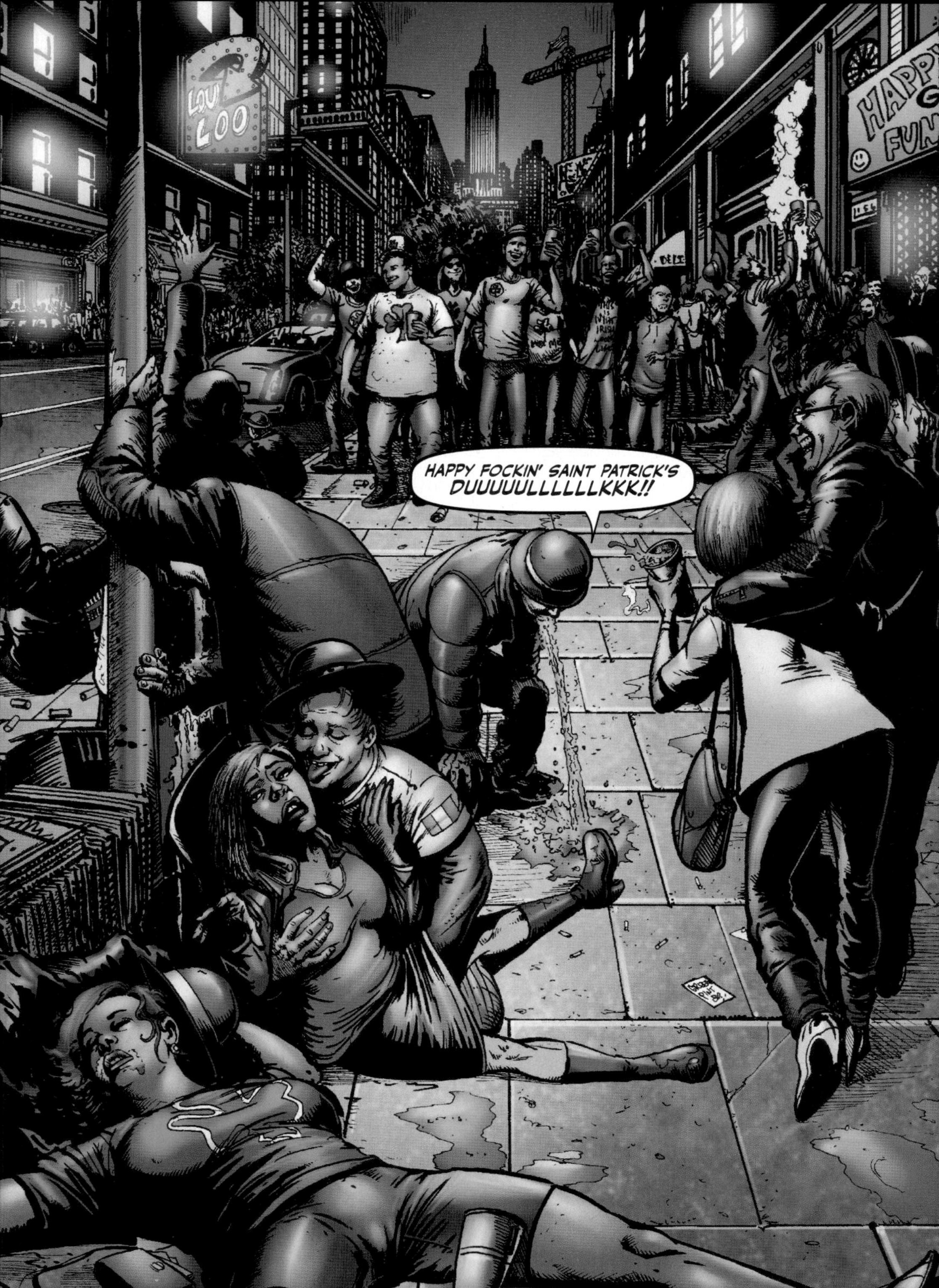
LOU LOO
HAPPY GO FUN
DELI
HAPPY FOCKIN' SAINT PATRICK'S DUUUUULLLLLLKKK!!

WE GOTTA GO NOW

part five

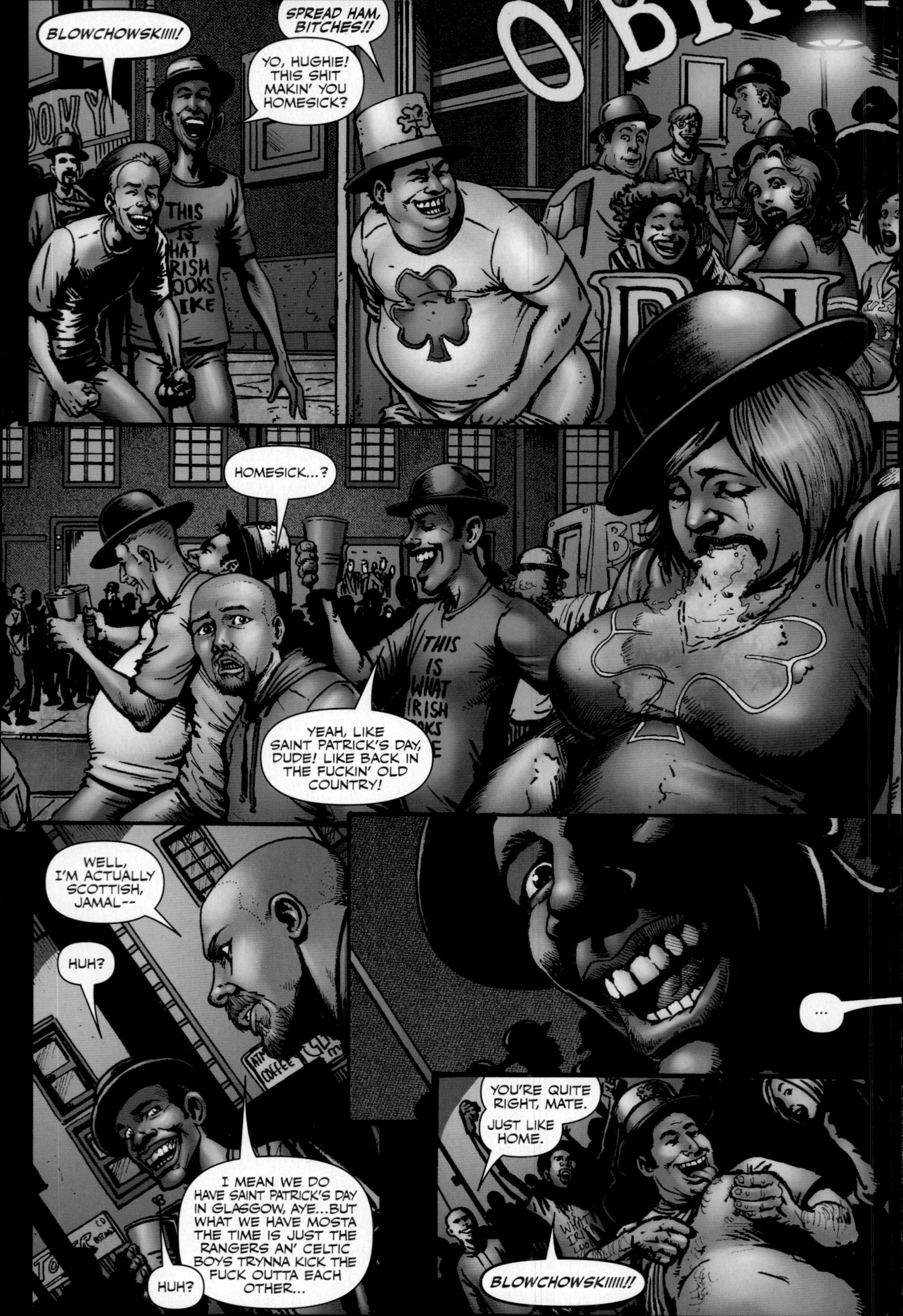
BLOWCHOWSKIIIII!
SPREAD HAM, BITCHES!!
YO, HUGHIE! THIS SHIT MAKIN' YOU HOMESICK?
THIS IS WHAT IRISH LOOKS LIKE
HOMESICK...?
YEAH, LIKE SAINT PATRICK'S DAY, DUDE! LIKE BACK IN THE FUCKIN' OLD COUNTRY!
WELL, I'M ACTUALLY SCOTTISH, JAMAL--
HUH?
I MEAN WE DO HAVE SAINT PATRICK'S DAY IN GLASGOW, AYE...BUT WHAT WE HAVE MOSTA THE TIME IS JUST THE RANGERS AN' CELTIC BOYS TRYNNA KICK THE FUCK OUTTA EACH OTHER...
HUH?
...
YOU'RE QUITE RIGHT, MATE.
JUST LIKE HOME.
BLOWCHOWSKIIIII!!

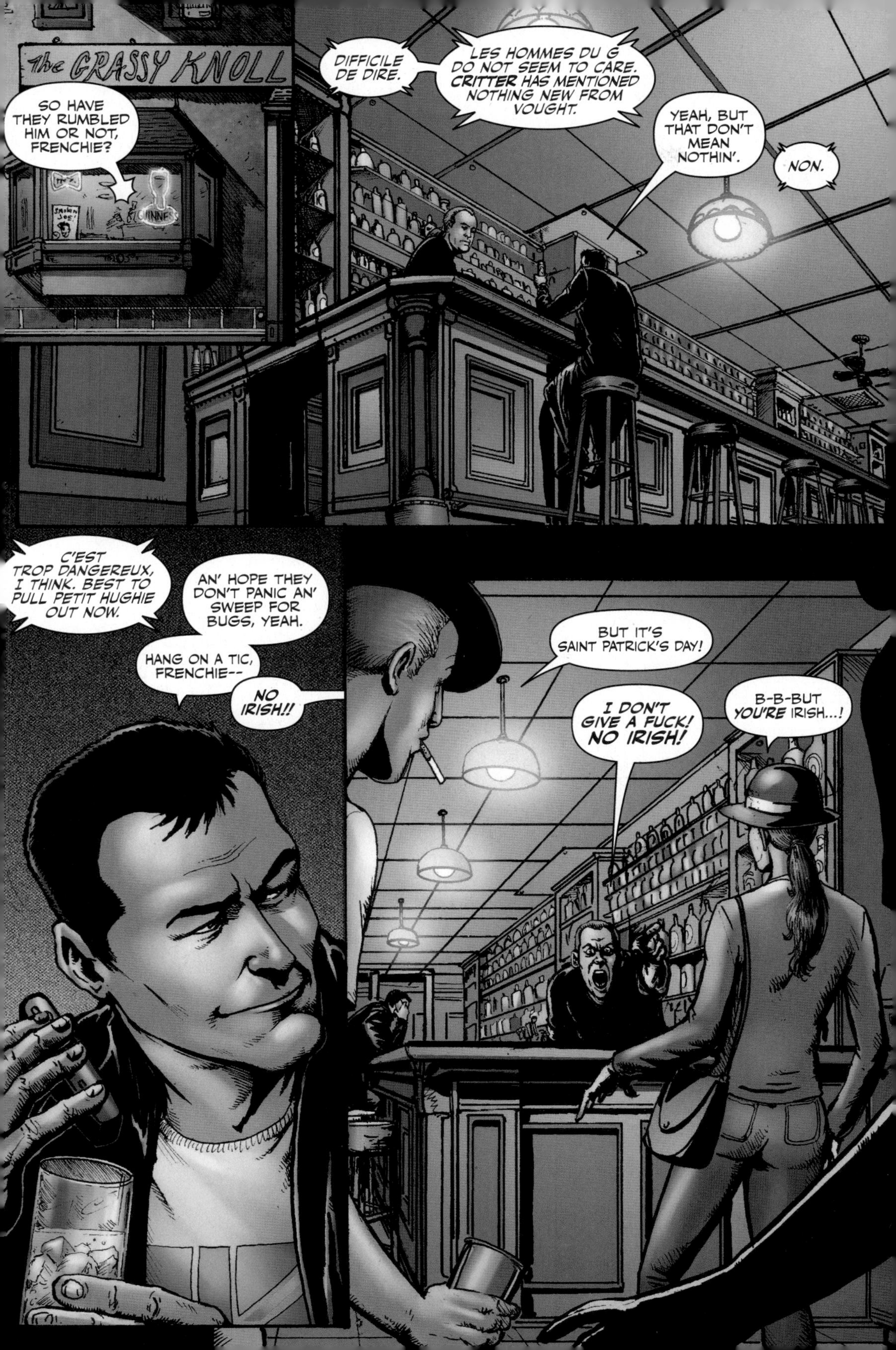
The GRASSY KNOLL
SO HAVE THEY RUMBLED HIM OR NOT, FRENCHIE?
DIFFICILE DE DIRE.
LES HOMMES DU G DO NOT SEEM TO CARE. CRITTER HAS MENTIONED NOTHING NEW FROM VOUGHT.
YEAH, BUT THAT DON'T MEAN NOTHIN'.
NON.
C'EST TROP DANGEREUX, I THINK. BEST TO PULL PETIT HUGHIE OUT NOW.
AN' HOPE THEY DON'T PANIC AN' SWEEP FOR BUGS, YEAH.
HANG ON A TIC, FRENCHIE--
NO IRISH!!
BUT IT'S SAINT PATRICK'S DAY!
I DON'T GIVE A FUCK! NO IRISH!
B-B-BUT YOU'RE IRISH...!

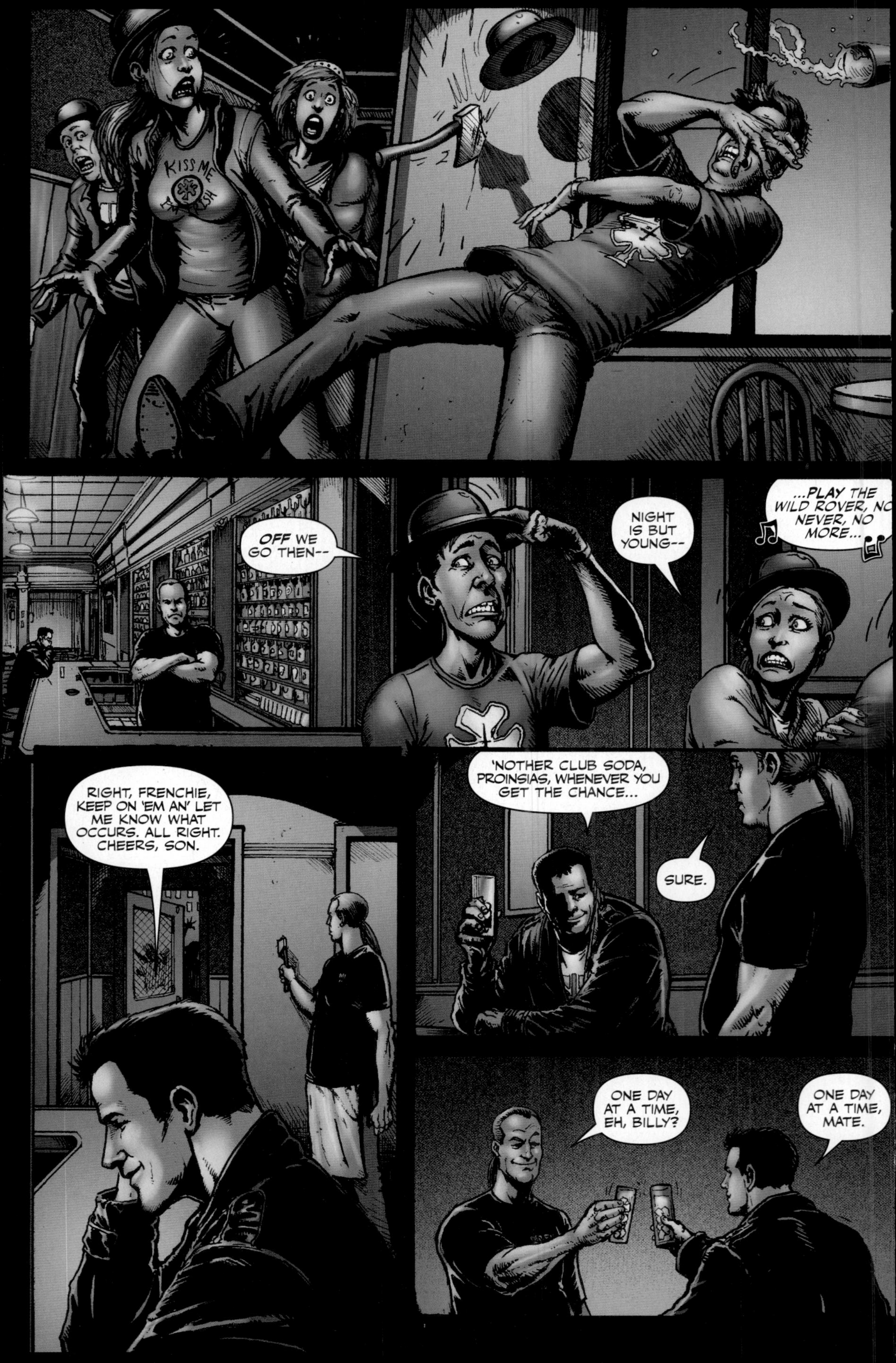

OFF WE GO THEN--
NIGHT IS BUT YOUNG--
...PLAY THE WILD ROVER, NO NEVER, NO MORE...
RIGHT, FRENCHIE, KEEP ON 'EM AN' LET ME KNOW WHAT OCCURS. ALL RIGHT. CHEERS, SON.
'NOTHER CLUB SODA, PROINSIAS, WHENEVER YOU GET THE CHANCE...
SURE.
ONE DAY AT A TIME, EH, BILLY?
ONE DAY AT A TIME, MATE.

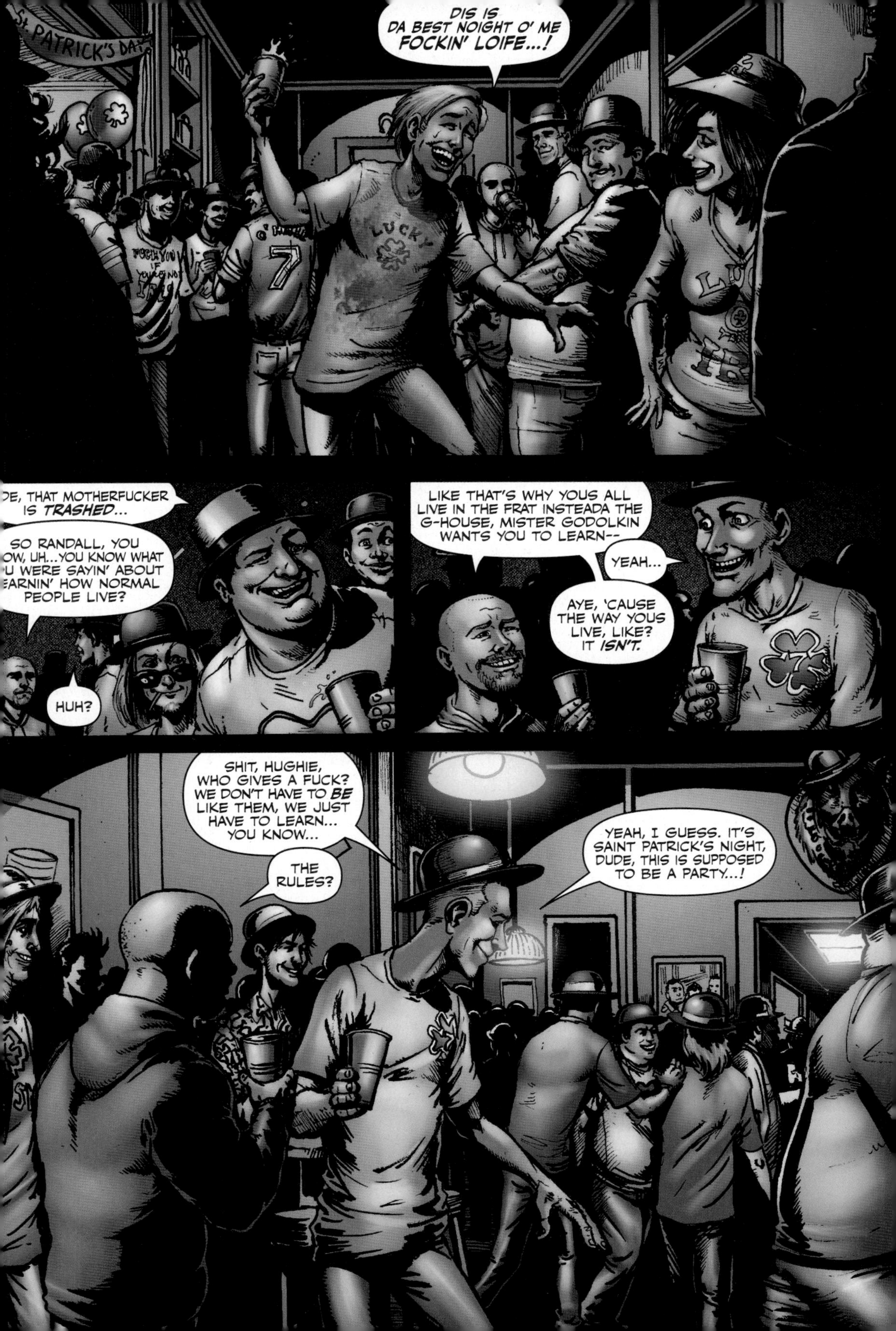
ST. PATRICK'S DAY
DIS IS DA BEST NOIGHT O' ME FOCKIN' LOIFE...!
LUCKY
7
ɔE, THAT MOTHERFUCKER IS TRASHED...
SO RANDALL, YOU ᴐW, UH...YOU KNOW WHAT U WERE SAYIN' ABOUT EARNIN' HOW NORMAL PEOPLE LIVE?
HUH?
LIKE THAT'S WHY YOUS ALL LIVE IN THE FRAT INSTEADA THE G-HOUSE, MISTER GODOLKIN WANTS YOU TO LEARN--
YEAH...
AYE, 'CAUSE THE WAY YOUS LIVE, LIKE? IT ISN'T.
SHIT, HUGHIE, WHO GIVES A FUCK? WE DON'T HAVE TO BE LIKE THEM, WE JUST HAVE TO LEARN... YOU KNOW...
THE RULES?
YEAH, I GUESS. IT'S SAINT PATRICK'S NIGHT, DUDE, THIS IS SUPPOSED TO BE A PARTY...!

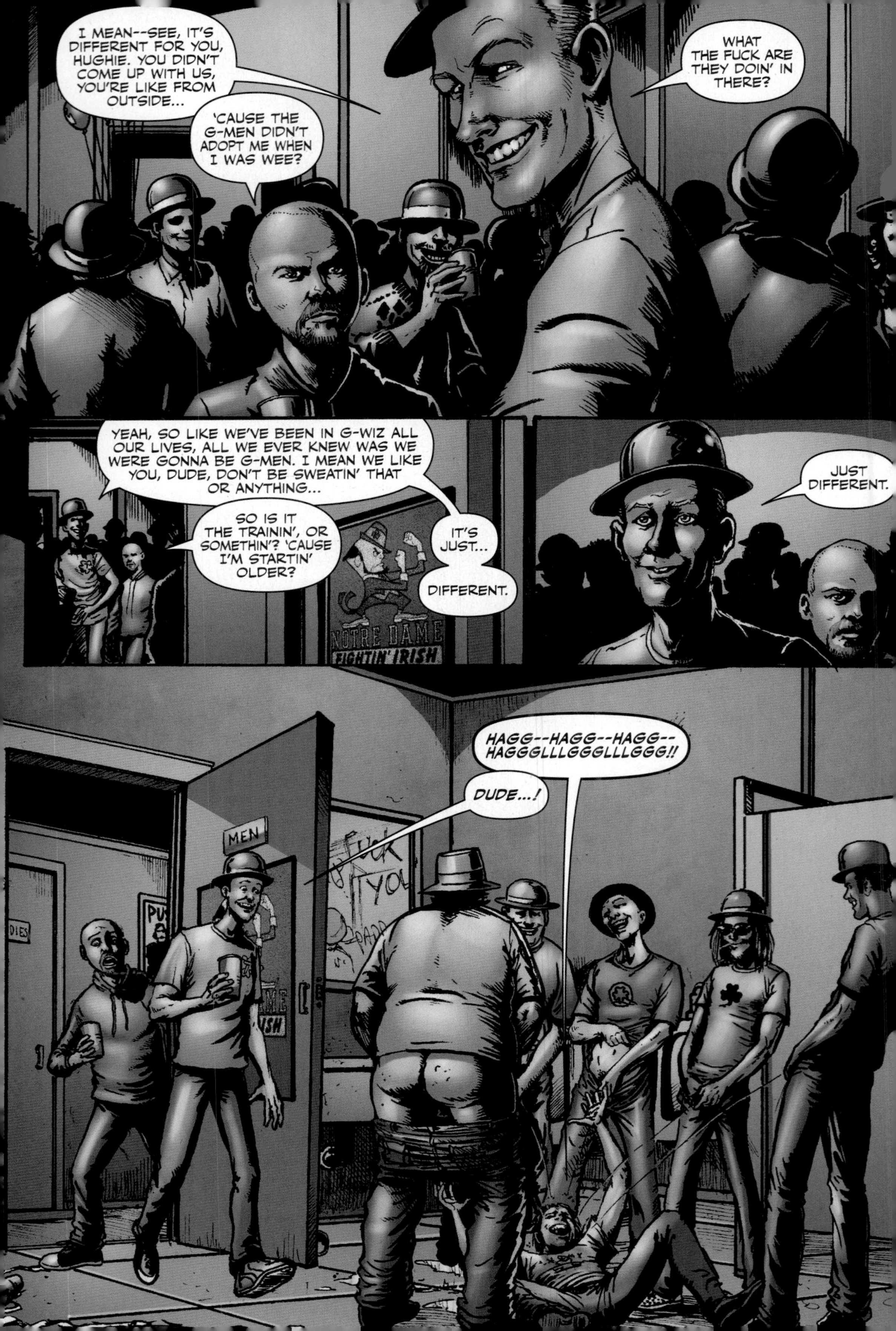
I MEAN--SEE, IT'S DIFFERENT FOR YOU, HUGHIE. YOU DIDN'T COME UP WITH US, YOU'RE LIKE FROM OUTSIDE...
'CAUSE THE G-MEN DIDN'T ADOPT ME WHEN I WAS WEE?
WHAT THE FUCK ARE THEY DOIN' IN THERE?
YEAH, SO LIKE WE'VE BEEN IN G-WIZ ALL OUR LIVES, ALL WE EVER KNEW WAS WE WERE GONNA BE G-MEN. I MEAN WE LIKE YOU, DUDE, DON'T BE SWEATIN' THAT OR ANYTHING...
SO IS IT THE TRAININ', OR SOMETHIN'? 'CAUSE I'M STARTIN' OLDER?
IT'S JUST...
DIFFERENT.
NOTRE DAME
FIGHTIN' IRISH
JUST DIFFERENT.
HAGG--HAGG--HAGG--HAGGGLLLGGGLLLGGG!!
DUDE...!
MEN

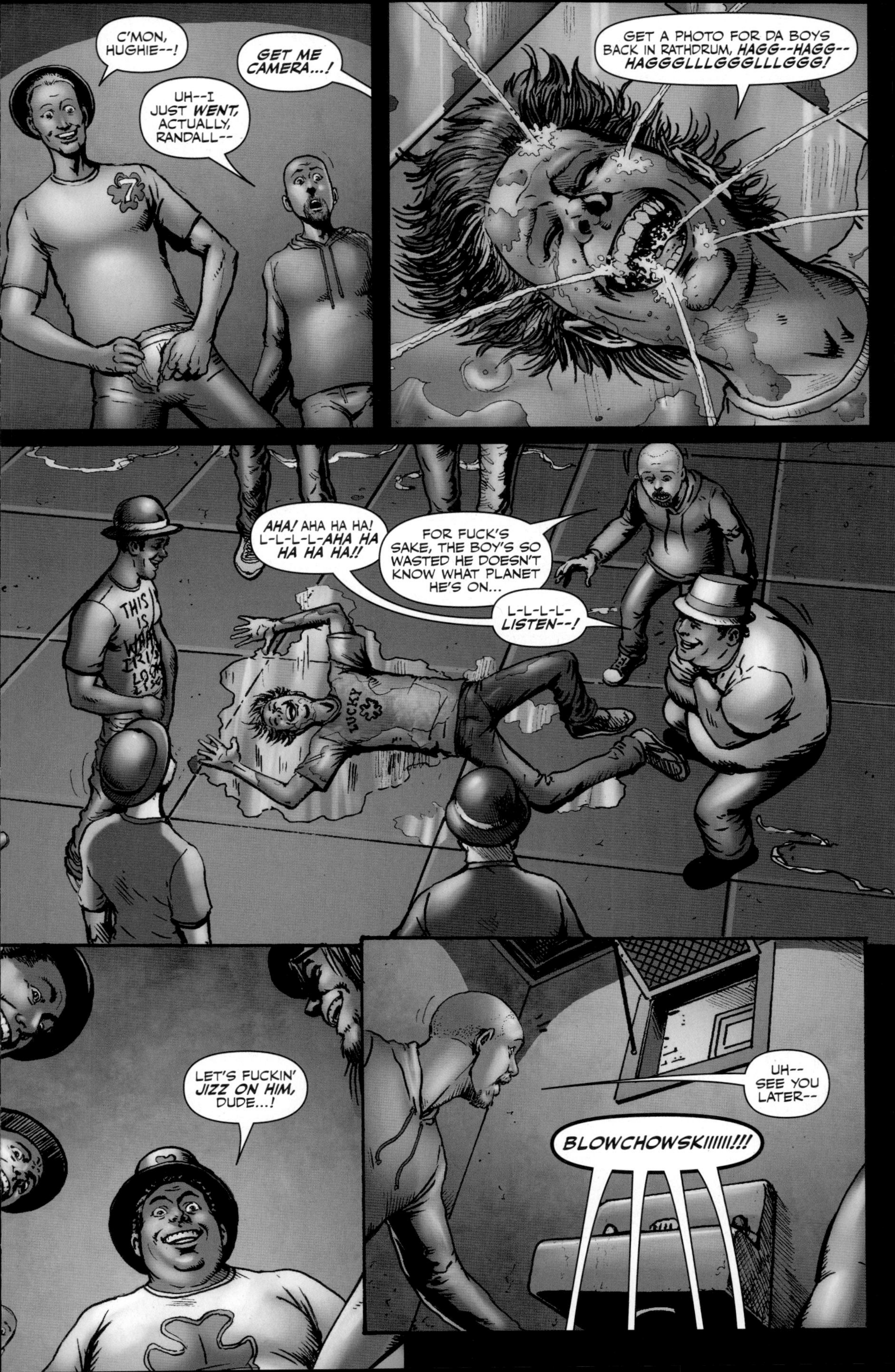
C'MON, HUGHIE--!
GET ME CAMERA...!
UH--I JUST WENT, ACTUALLY, RANDALL--
GET A PHOTO FOR DA BOYS BACK IN RATHDRUM, HAGG--HAGG--HAGGGLLLGGGLLLGGG!
AHA! AHA HA HA! L-L-L-L-AHA HA HA HA HA!!
FOR FUCK'S SAKE, THE BOY'S SO WASTED HE DOESN'T KNOW WHAT PLANET HE'S ON...
L-L-L-L-LISTEN--!
LET'S FUCKIN' JIZZ ON HIM, DUDE...!
UH--SEE YOU LATER--
BLOWCHOWSKIIIIIII!!!

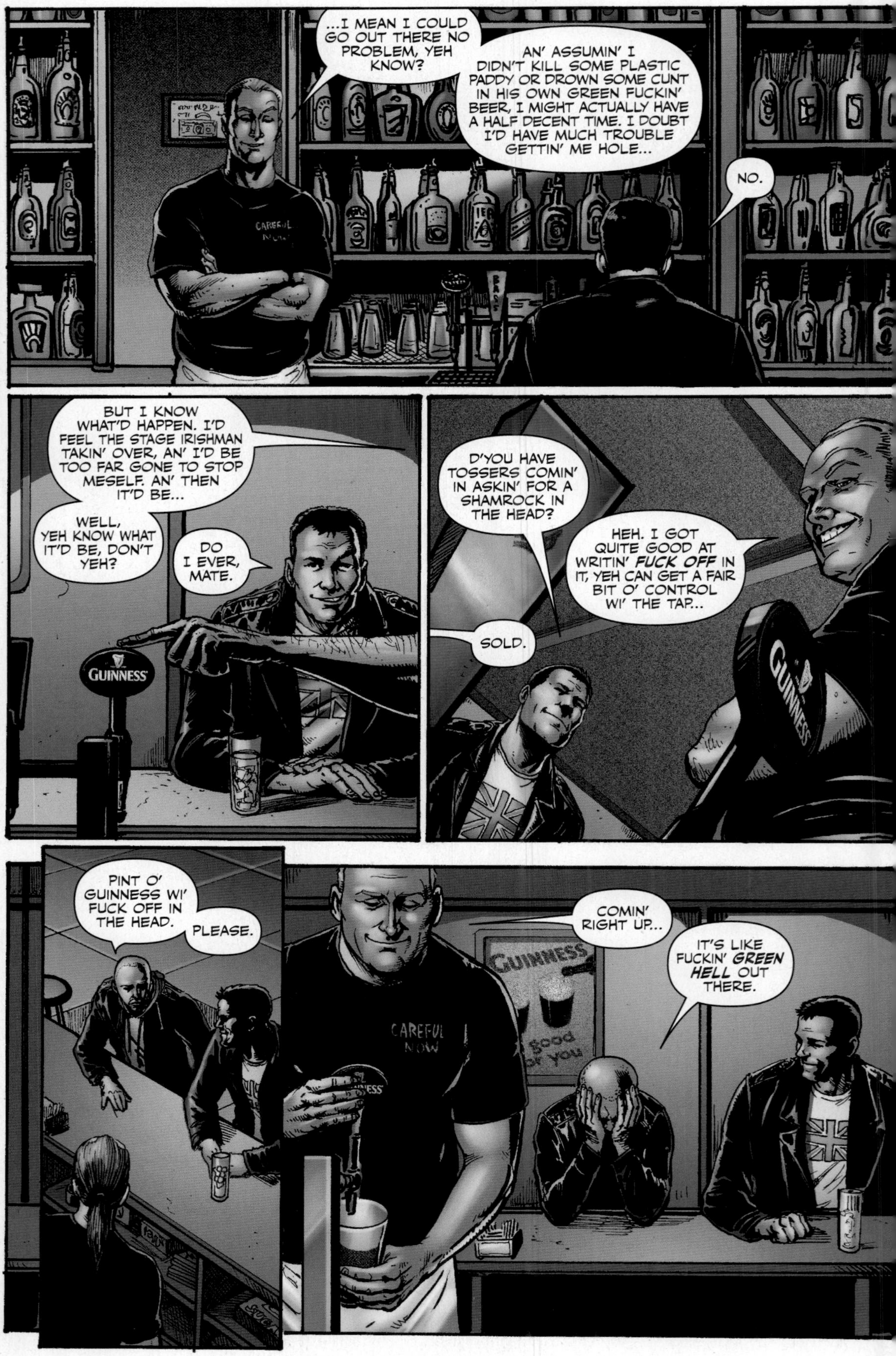
...I MEAN I COULD GO OUT THERE NO PROBLEM, YEH KNOW?
AN' ASSUMIN' I DIDN'T KILL SOME PLASTIC PADDY OR DROWN SOME CUNT IN HIS OWN GREEN FUCKIN' BEER, I MIGHT ACTUALLY HAVE A HALF DECENT TIME. I DOUBT I'D HAVE MUCH TROUBLE GETTIN' ME HOLE...
NO.
CAREFUL NOW
BUT I KNOW WHAT'D HAPPEN. I'D FEEL THE STAGE IRISHMAN TAKIN' OVER, AN' I'D BE TOO FAR GONE TO STOP MESELF. AN' THEN IT'D BE...
WELL, YEH KNOW WHAT IT'D BE, DON'T YEH?
DO I EVER, MATE.
GUINNESS
D'YOU HAVE TOSSERS COMIN' IN ASKIN' FOR A SHAMROCK IN THE HEAD?
HEH. I GOT QUITE GOOD AT WRITIN' *FUCK OFF* IN IT, YEH CAN GET A FAIR BIT O' CONTROL WI' THE TAP...
SOLD.
GUINNESS
PINT O' GUINNESS WI' FUCK OFF IN THE HEAD.
PLEASE.
COMIN' RIGHT UP...
IT'S LIKE FUCKIN' *GREEN HELL* OUT THERE.
CAREFUL NOW
GUINNESS
good for you

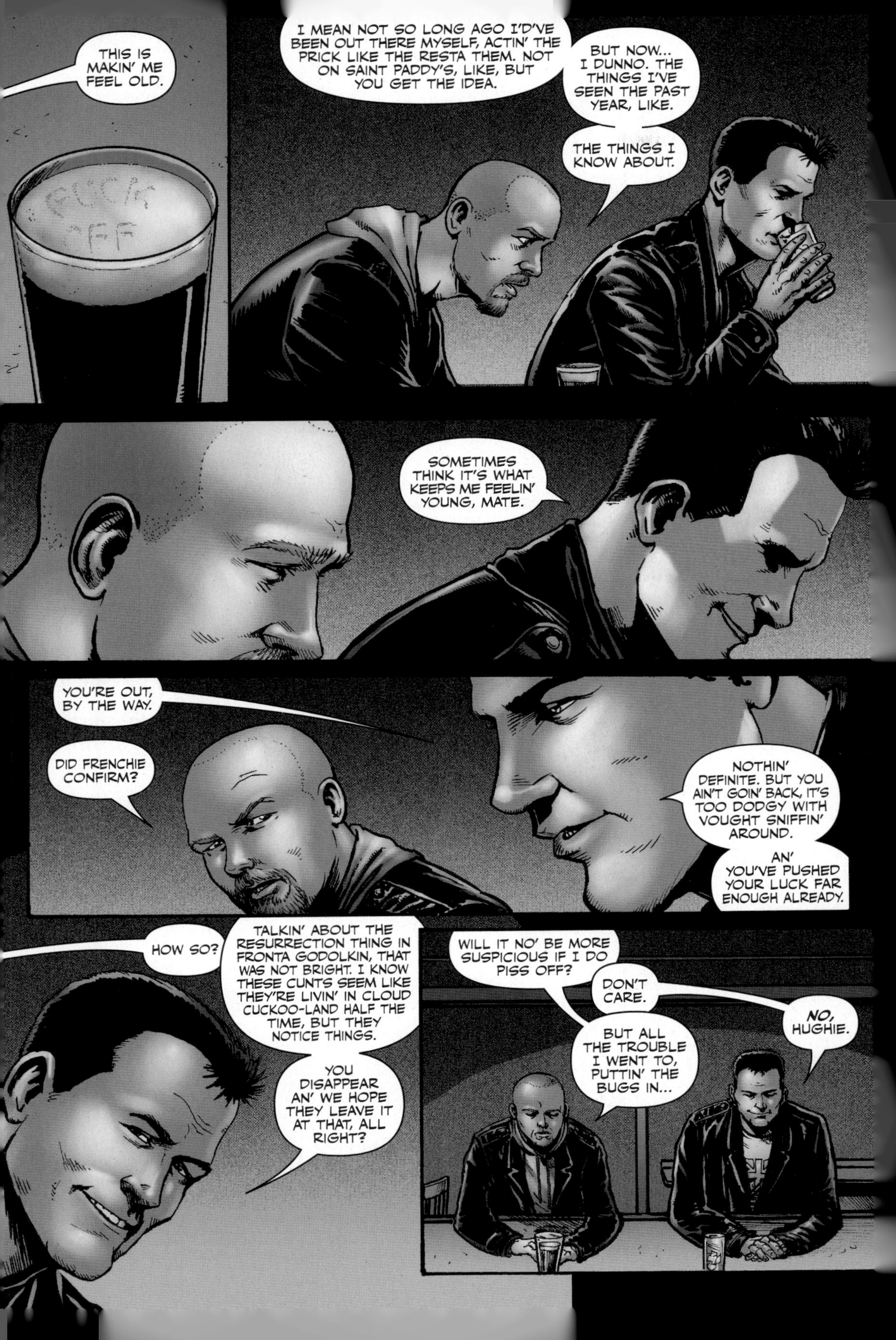
THIS IS MAKIN' ME FEEL OLD.
I MEAN NOT SO LONG AGO I'D'VE BEEN OUT THERE MYSELF, ACTIN' THE PRICK LIKE THE RESTA THEM. NOT ON SAINT PADDY'S, LIKE, BUT YOU GET THE IDEA.
BUT NOW... I DUNNO. THE THINGS I'VE SEEN THE PAST YEAR, LIKE.
THE THINGS I KNOW ABOUT.
SOMETIMES THINK IT'S WHAT KEEPS ME FEELIN' YOUNG, MATE.
YOU'RE OUT, BY THE WAY.
DID FRENCHIE CONFIRM?
NOTHIN' DEFINITE. BUT YOU AIN'T GOIN' BACK, IT'S TOO DODGY WITH VOUGHT SNIFFIN' AROUND.
AN' YOU'VE PUSHED YOUR LUCK FAR ENOUGH ALREADY.
HOW SO?
TALKIN' ABOUT THE RESURRECTION THING IN FRONTA GODOLKIN, THAT WAS NOT BRIGHT. I KNOW THESE CUNTS SEEM LIKE THEY'RE LIVIN' IN CLOUD CUCKOO-LAND HALF THE TIME, BUT THEY NOTICE THINGS.
YOU DISAPPEAR AN' WE HOPE THEY LEAVE IT AT THAT, ALL RIGHT?
WILL IT NO' BE MORE SUSPICIOUS IF I DO PISS OFF?
DON'T CARE.
BUT ALL THE TROUBLE I WENT TO, PUTTIN' THE BUGS IN...
NO, HUGHIE.

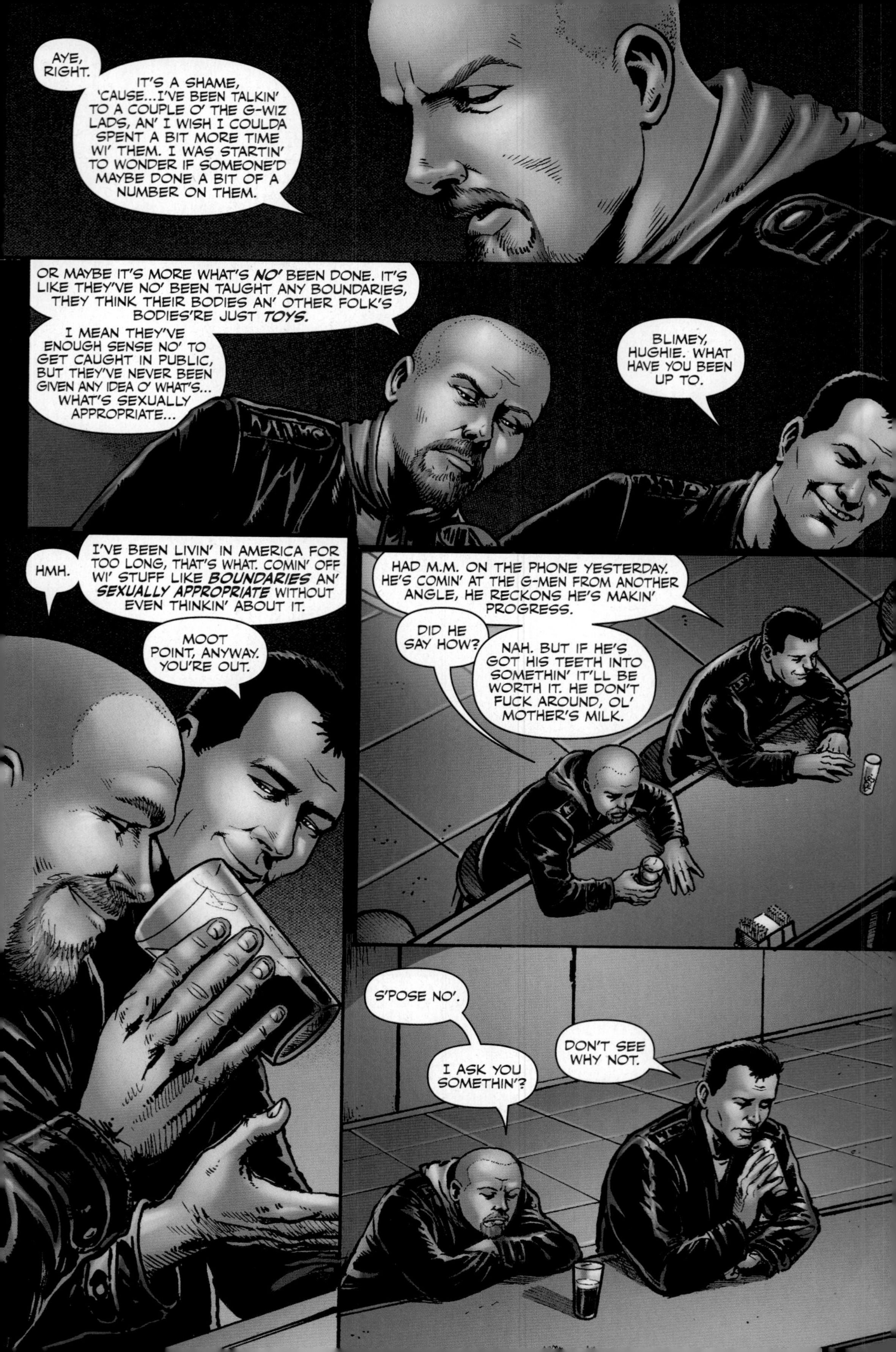

AYE, RIGHT.
IT'S A SHAME, 'CAUSE...I'VE BEEN TALKIN' TO A COUPLE O' THE G-WIZ LADS, AN' I WISH I COULDA SPENT A BIT MORE TIME WI' THEM. I WAS STARTIN' TO WONDER IF SOMEONE'D MAYBE DONE A BIT OF A NUMBER ON THEM.
OR MAYBE IT'S MORE WHAT'S *NO'* BEEN DONE. IT'S LIKE THEY'VE NO' BEEN TAUGHT ANY BOUNDARIES, THEY THINK THEIR BODIES AN' OTHER FOLK'S BODIES'RE JUST *TOYS.*
I MEAN THEY'VE ENOUGH SENSE NO' TO GET CAUGHT IN PUBLIC, BUT THEY'VE NEVER BEEN GIVEN ANY IDEA O' WHAT'S... WHAT'S SEXUALLY APPROPRIATE...
BLIMEY, HUGHIE. WHAT HAVE YOU BEEN UP TO.
HMH.
I'VE BEEN LIVIN' IN AMERICA FOR TOO LONG, THAT'S WHAT. COMIN' OFF WI' STUFF LIKE *BOUNDARIES* AN' *SEXUALLY APPROPRIATE* WITHOUT EVEN THINKIN' ABOUT IT.
MOOT POINT, ANYWAY. YOU'RE OUT.
HAD M.M. ON THE PHONE YESTERDAY. HE'S COMIN' AT THE G-MEN FROM ANOTHER ANGLE, HE RECKONS HE'S MAKIN' PROGRESS.
DID HE SAY HOW?
NAH. BUT IF HE'S GOT HIS TEETH INTO SOMETHIN' IT'LL BE WORTH IT. HE DON'T FUCK AROUND, OL' MOTHER'S MILK.
S'POSE NO'.
I ASK YOU SOMETHIN'?
DON'T SEE WHY NOT.

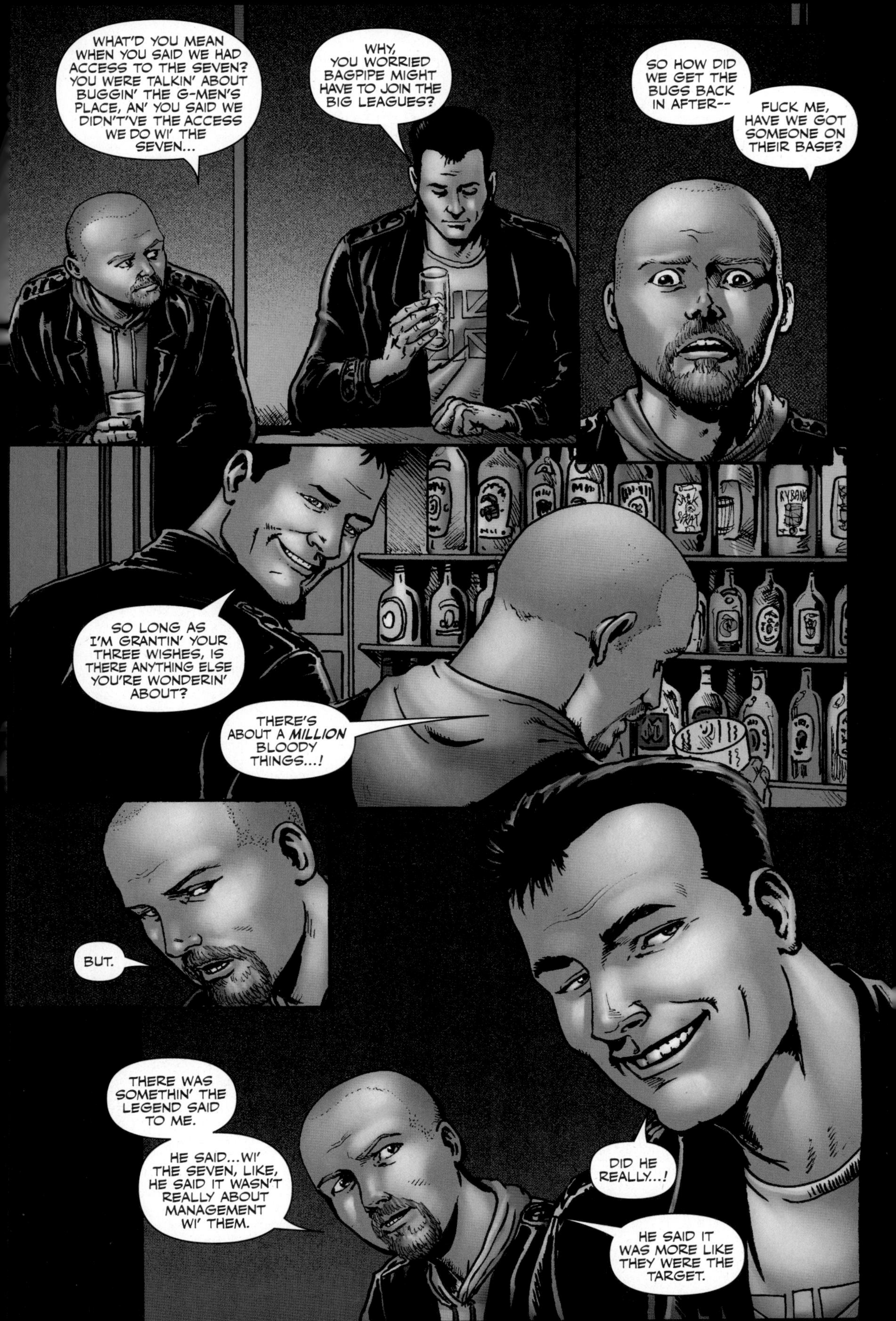
WHAT'D YOU MEAN WHEN YOU SAID WE HAD ACCESS TO THE SEVEN? YOU WERE TALKIN' ABOUT BUGGIN' THE G-MEN'S PLACE, AN' YOU SAID WE DIDN'T'VE THE ACCESS WE DO WI' THE SEVEN...
WHY, YOU WORRIED BAGPIPE MIGHT HAVE TO JOIN THE BIG LEAGUES?
SO HOW DID WE GET THE BUGS BACK IN AFTER--
FUCK ME, HAVE WE GOT SOMEONE ON THEIR BASE?
SO LONG AS I'M GRANTIN' YOUR THREE WISHES, IS THERE ANYTHING ELSE YOU'RE WONDERIN' ABOUT?
THERE'S ABOUT A *MILLION* BLOODY THINGS...!
BUT.
THERE WAS SOMETHIN' THE LEGEND SAID TO ME.
HE SAID...WI' THE SEVEN, LIKE, HE SAID IT WASN'T REALLY ABOUT MANAGEMENT WI' THEM.
DID HE REALLY...!
HE SAID IT WAS MORE LIKE THEY WERE THE TARGET.

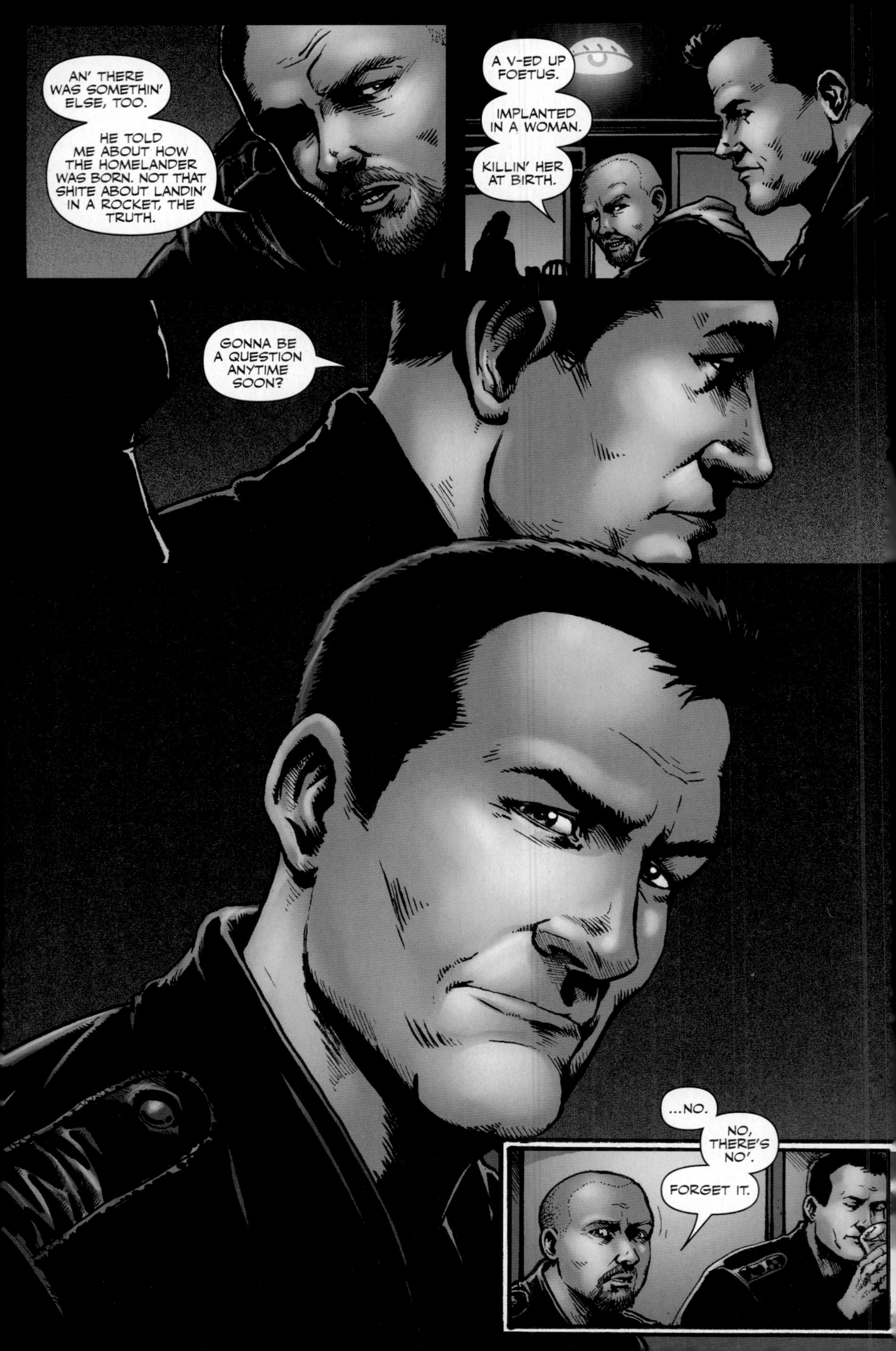
AN' THERE WAS SOMETHIN' ELSE, TOO.
HE TOLD ME ABOUT HOW THE HOMELANDER WAS BORN. NOT THAT SHITE ABOUT LANDIN' IN A ROCKET, THE TRUTH.
A V-ED UP FOETUS.
IMPLANTED IN A WOMAN.
KILLIN' HER AT BIRTH.
GONNA BE A QUESTION ANYTIME SOON?
...NO.
NO, THERE'S NO'.
FORGET IT.

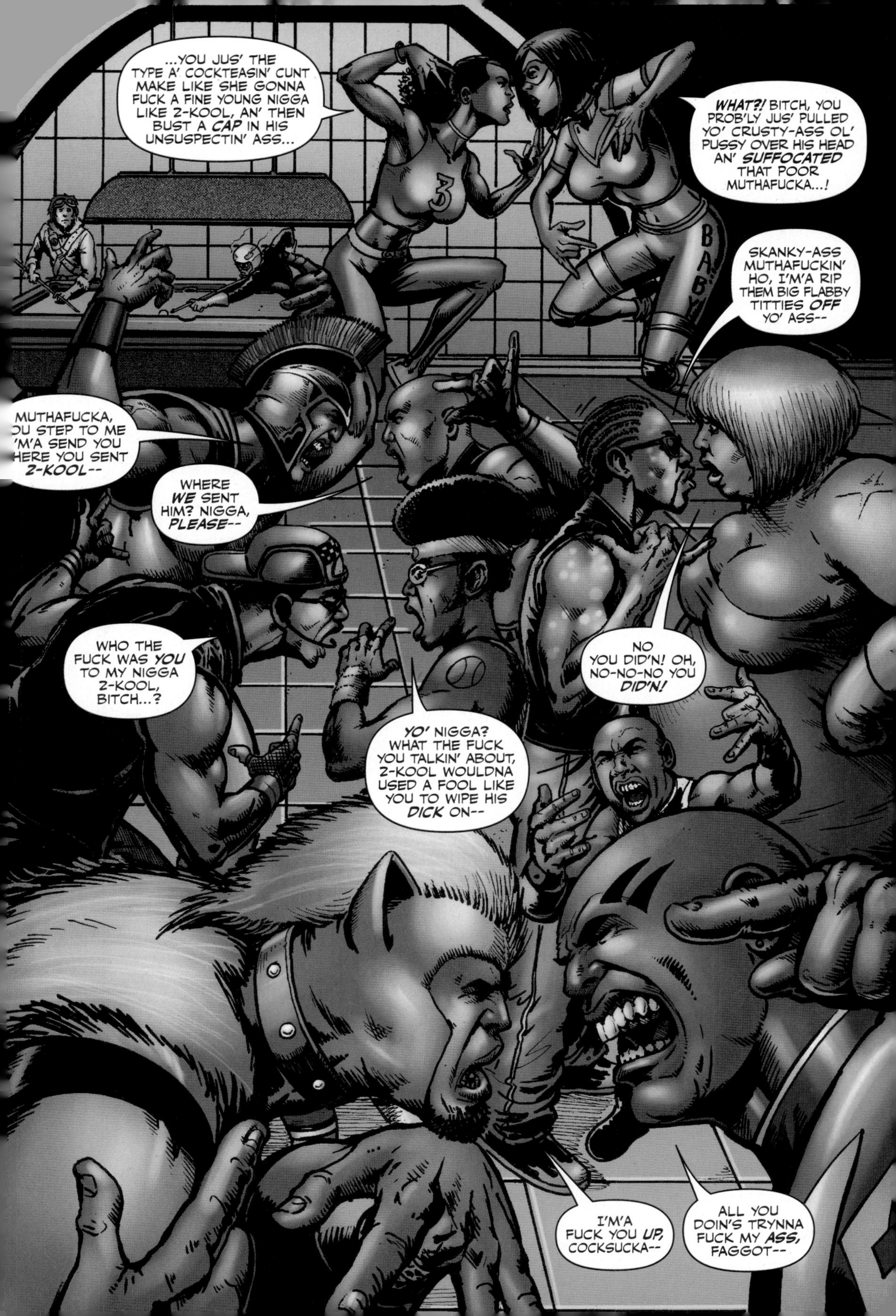
...YOU JUS' THE TYPE A' COCKTEASIN' CUNT MAKE LIKE SHE GONNA FUCK A FINE YOUNG NIGGA LIKE 2-KOOL, AN' THEN BUST A CAP IN HIS UNSUSPECTIN' ASS...
WHAT?! BITCH, YOU PROB'LY JUS' PULLED YO' CRUSTY-ASS OL' PUSSY OVER HIS HEAD AN' SUFFOCATED THAT POOR MUTHAFUCKA...!
SKANKY-ASS MUTHAFUCKIN' HO, I'M'A RIP THEM BIG FLABBY TITTIES OFF YO' ASS--
MUTHAFUCKA, OU STEP TO ME 'M'A SEND YOU HERE YOU SENT 2-KOOL--
WHERE WE SENT HIM? NIGGA, PLEASE--
WHO THE FUCK WAS YOU TO MY NIGGA 2-KOOL, BITCH...?
NO YOU DID'N! OH, NO-NO-NO YOU DID'N!
YO' NIGGA? WHAT THE FUCK YOU TALKIN' ABOUT, 2-KOOL WOULDNA USED A FOOL LIKE YOU TO WIPE HIS DICK ON--
I'M'A FUCK YOU UP, COCKSUCKA--
ALL YOU DOIN'S TRYNNA FUCK MY ASS, FAGGOT--

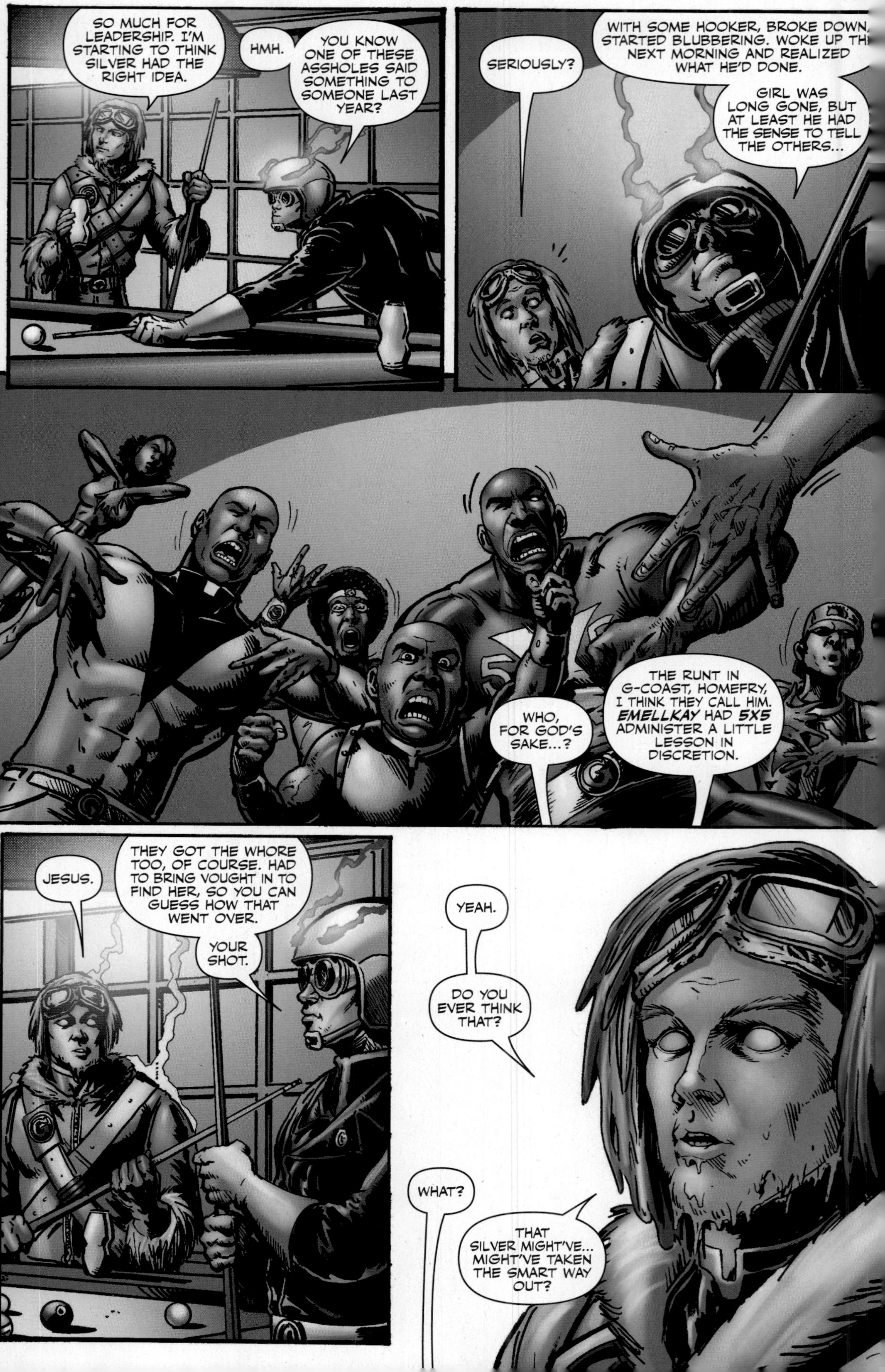
SO MUCH FOR LEADERSHIP. I'M STARTING TO THINK SILVER HAD THE RIGHT IDEA.
HMH.
YOU KNOW ONE OF THESE ASSHOLES SAID SOMETHING TO SOMEONE LAST YEAR?
SERIOUSLY?
WITH SOME HOOKER, BROKE DOWN, STARTED BLUBBERING. WOKE UP THE NEXT MORNING AND REALIZED WHAT HE'D DONE.
GIRL WAS LONG GONE, BUT AT LEAST HE HAD THE SENSE TO TELL THE OTHERS...
WHO, FOR GOD'S SAKE...?
THE RUNT IN G-COAST, HOMEFRY, I THINK THEY CALL HIM. EMELLKAY HAD 5X5 ADMINISTER A LITTLE LESSON IN DISCRETION.
JESUS.
THEY GOT THE WHORE TOO, OF COURSE. HAD TO BRING VOUGHT IN TO FIND HER, SO YOU CAN GUESS HOW THAT WENT OVER.
YOUR SHOT.
YEAH.
DO YOU EVER THINK THAT?
WHAT?
THAT SILVER MIGHT'VE... MIGHT'VE TAKEN THE SMART WAY OUT?

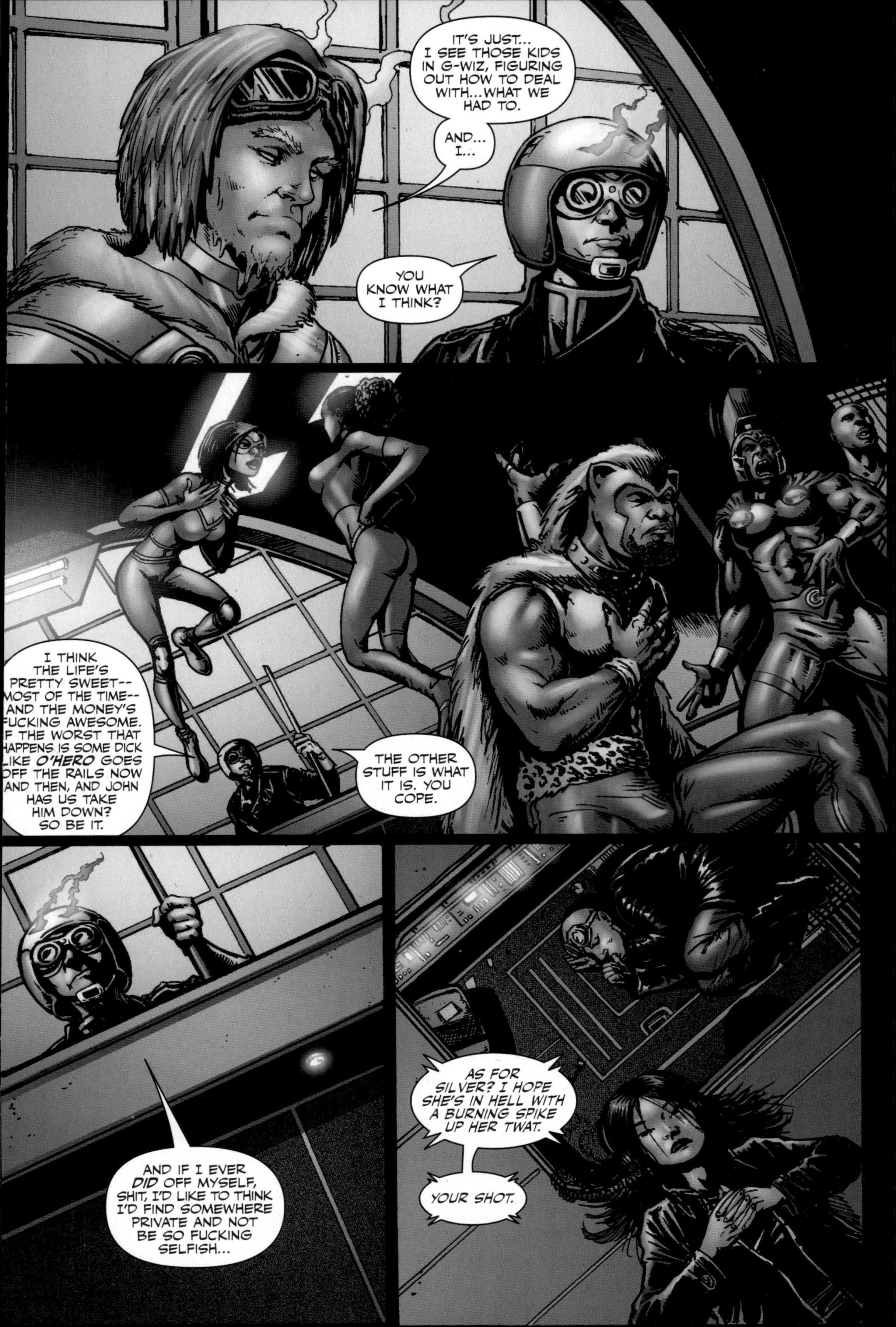
IT'S JUST... I SEE THOSE KIDS IN G-WIZ, FIGURING OUT HOW TO DEAL WITH...WHAT WE HAD TO.
AND... I...
YOU KNOW WHAT I THINK?
I THINK THE LIFE'S PRETTY SWEET-- MOST OF THE TIME-- AND THE MONEY'S FUCKING AWESOME. IF THE WORST THAT HAPPENS IS SOME DICK LIKE O'HERO GOES OFF THE RAILS NOW AND THEN, AND JOHN HAS US TAKE HIM DOWN? SO BE IT.
THE OTHER STUFF IS WHAT IT IS. YOU COPE.
AND IF I EVER DID OFF MYSELF, SHIT, I'D LIKE TO THINK I'D FIND SOMEWHERE PRIVATE AND NOT BE SO FUCKING SELFISH...
AS FOR SILVER? I HOPE SHE'S IN HELL WITH A BURNING SPIKE UP HER TWAT.
YOUR SHOT.

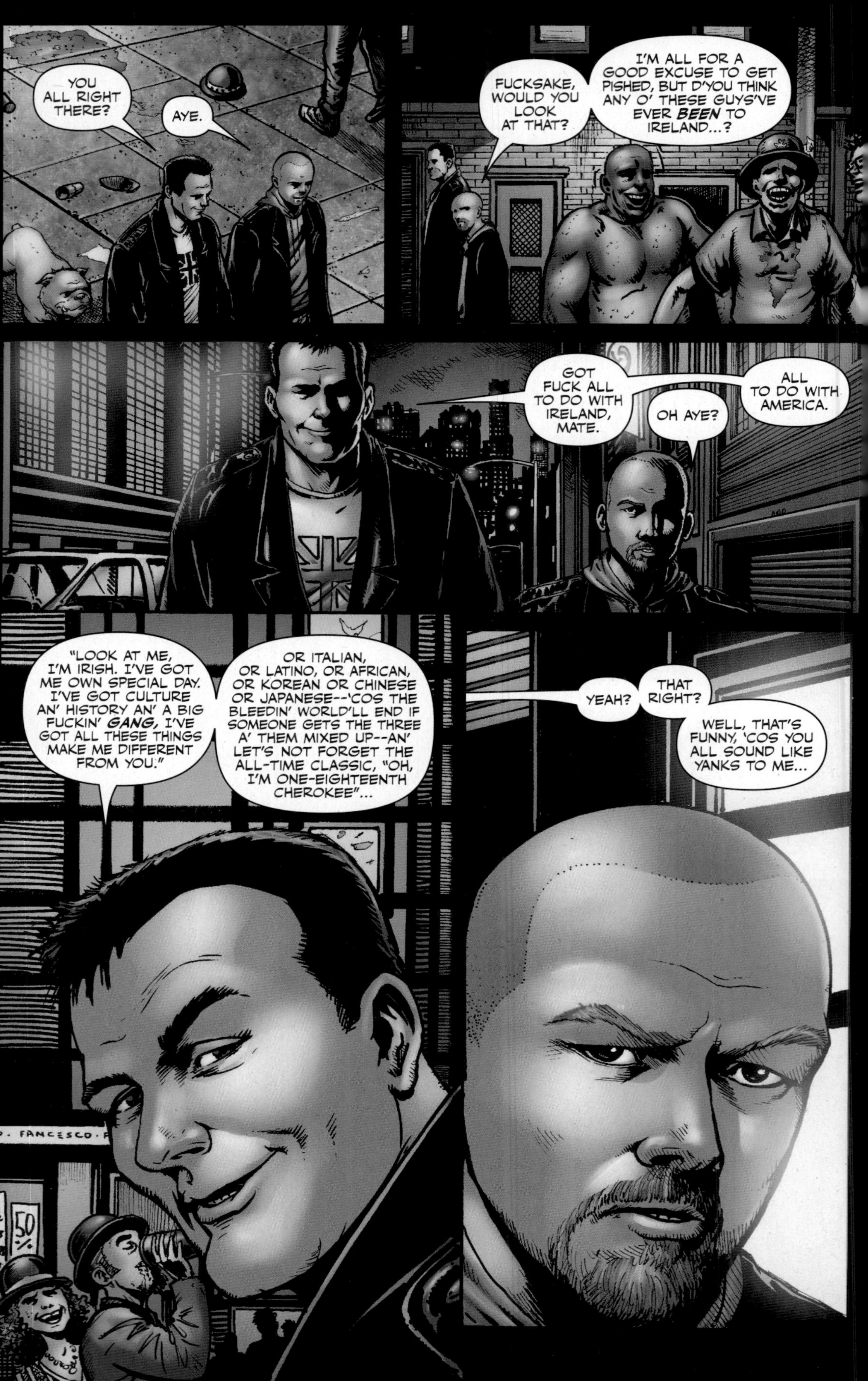
YOU ALL RIGHT THERE?
AYE.
FUCKSAKE, WOULD YOU LOOK AT THAT?
I'M ALL FOR A GOOD EXCUSE TO GET PISHED, BUT D'YOU THINK ANY O' THESE GUYS'VE EVER BEEN TO IRELAND...?
GOT FUCK ALL TO DO WITH IRELAND, MATE.
OH AYE?
ALL TO DO WITH AMERICA.
"LOOK AT ME, I'M IRISH. I'VE GOT ME OWN SPECIAL DAY. I'VE GOT CULTURE AN' HISTORY AN' A BIG FUCKIN' GANG, I'VE GOT ALL THESE THINGS MAKE ME DIFFERENT FROM YOU."
OR ITALIAN, OR LATINO, OR AFRICAN, OR KOREAN OR CHINESE OR JAPANESE--'COS THE BLEEDIN' WORLD'LL END IF SOMEONE GETS THE THREE A' THEM MIXED UP--AN' LET'S NOT FORGET THE ALL-TIME CLASSIC, "OH, I'M ONE-EIGHTEENTH CHEROKEE"...
YEAH?
THAT RIGHT?
WELL, THAT'S FUNNY, 'COS YOU ALL SOUND LIKE YANKS TO ME...
50%

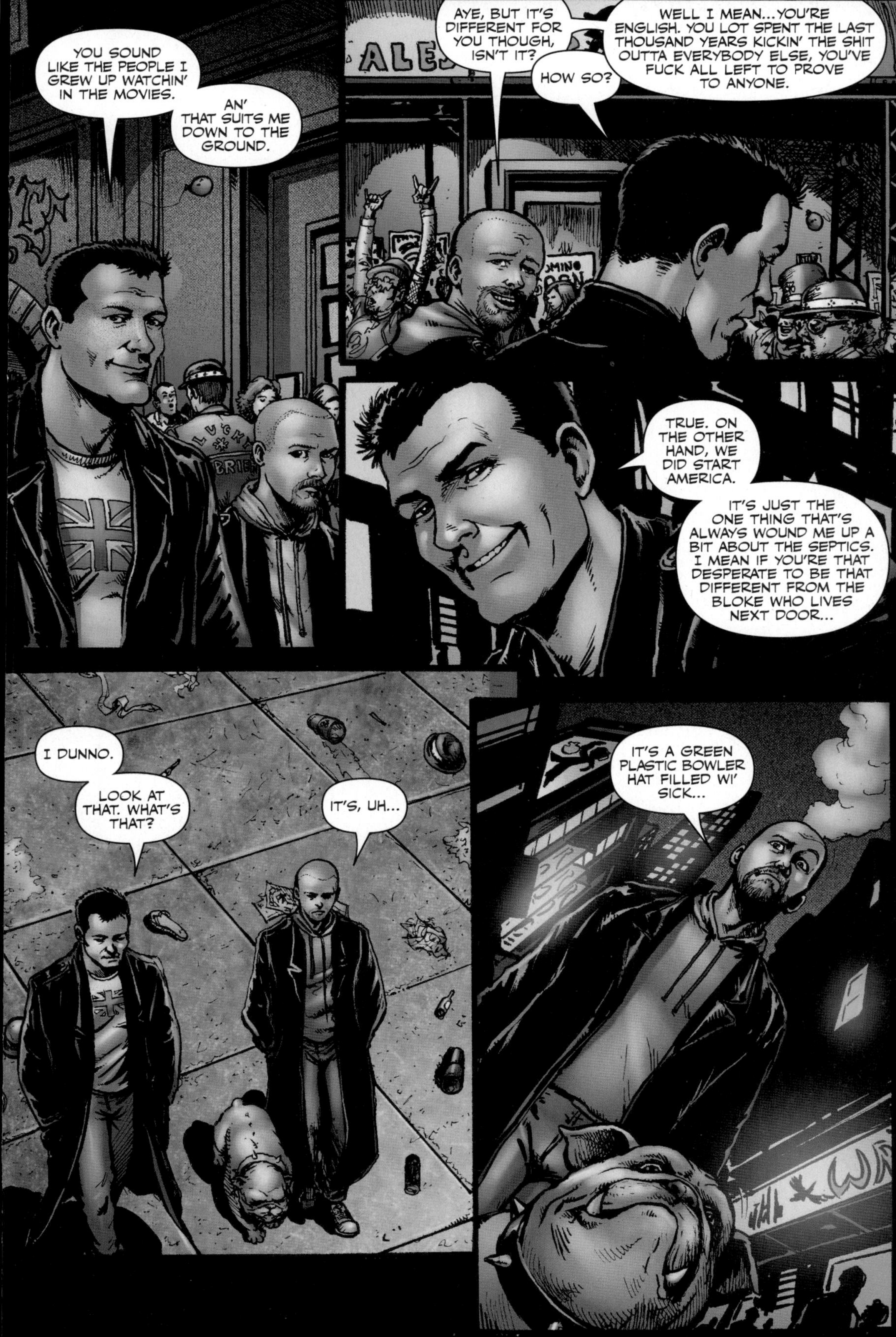
YOU SOUND LIKE THE PEOPLE I GREW UP WATCHIN' IN THE MOVIES.
AN' THAT SUITS ME DOWN TO THE GROUND.
AYE, BUT IT'S DIFFERENT FOR YOU THOUGH, ISN'T IT?
HOW SO?
WELL I MEAN...YOU'RE ENGLISH. YOU LOT SPENT THE LAST THOUSAND YEARS KICKIN' THE SHIT OUTTA EVERYBODY ELSE, YOU'VE FUCK ALL LEFT TO PROVE TO ANYONE.
TRUE. ON THE OTHER HAND, WE DID START AMERICA.
IT'S JUST THE ONE THING THAT'S ALWAYS WOUND ME UP A BIT ABOUT THE SEPTICS. I MEAN IF YOU'RE THAT DESPERATE TO BE THAT DIFFERENT FROM THE BLOKE WHO LIVES NEXT DOOR...
I DUNNO.
LOOK AT THAT. WHAT'S THAT?
IT'S, UH...
IT'S A GREEN PLASTIC BOWLER HAT FILLED WI' SICK...

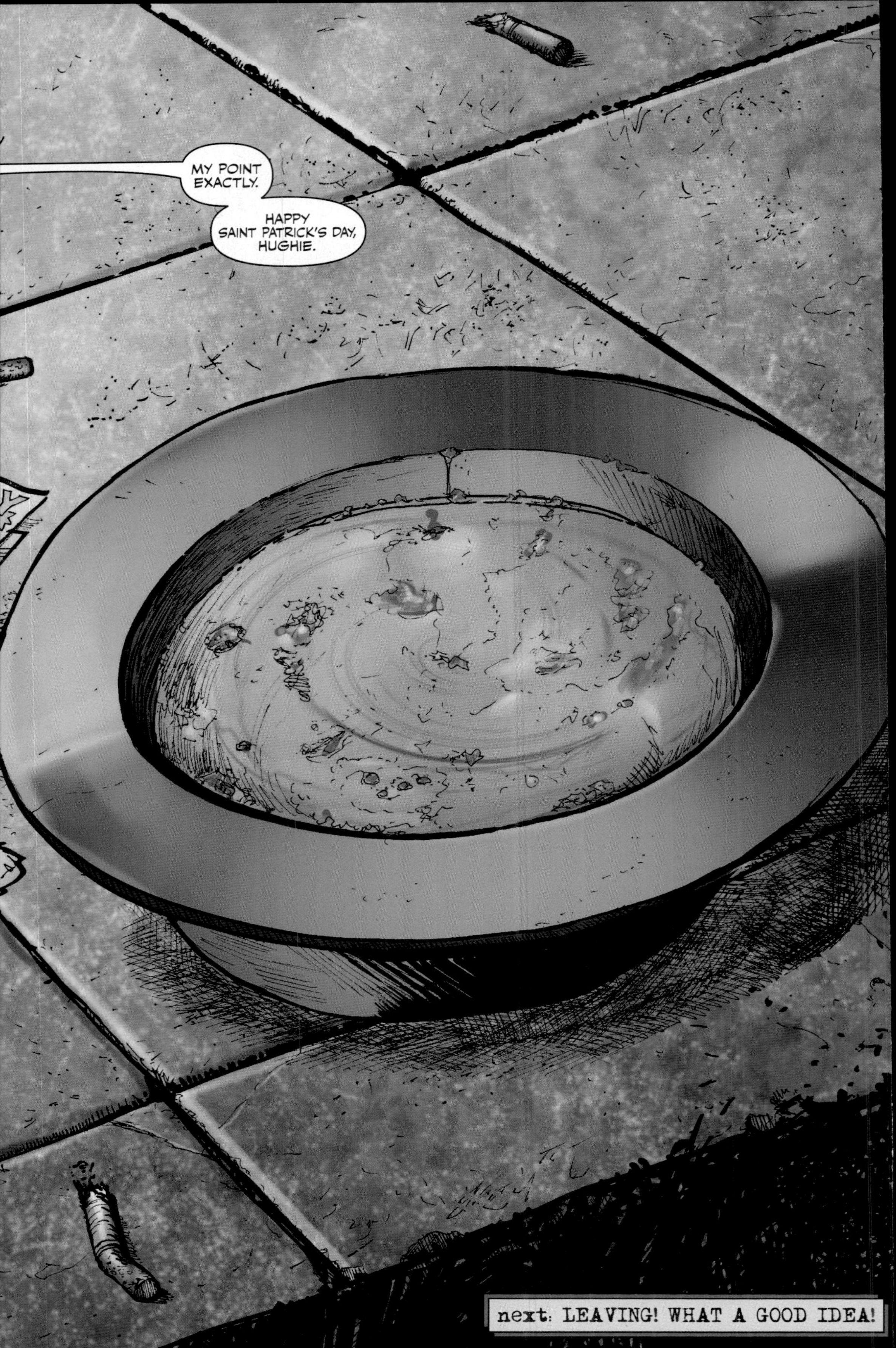
MY POINT EXACTLY.
HAPPY SAINT PATRICK'S DAY, HUGHIE.
next: LEAVING! WHAT A GOOD IDEA!

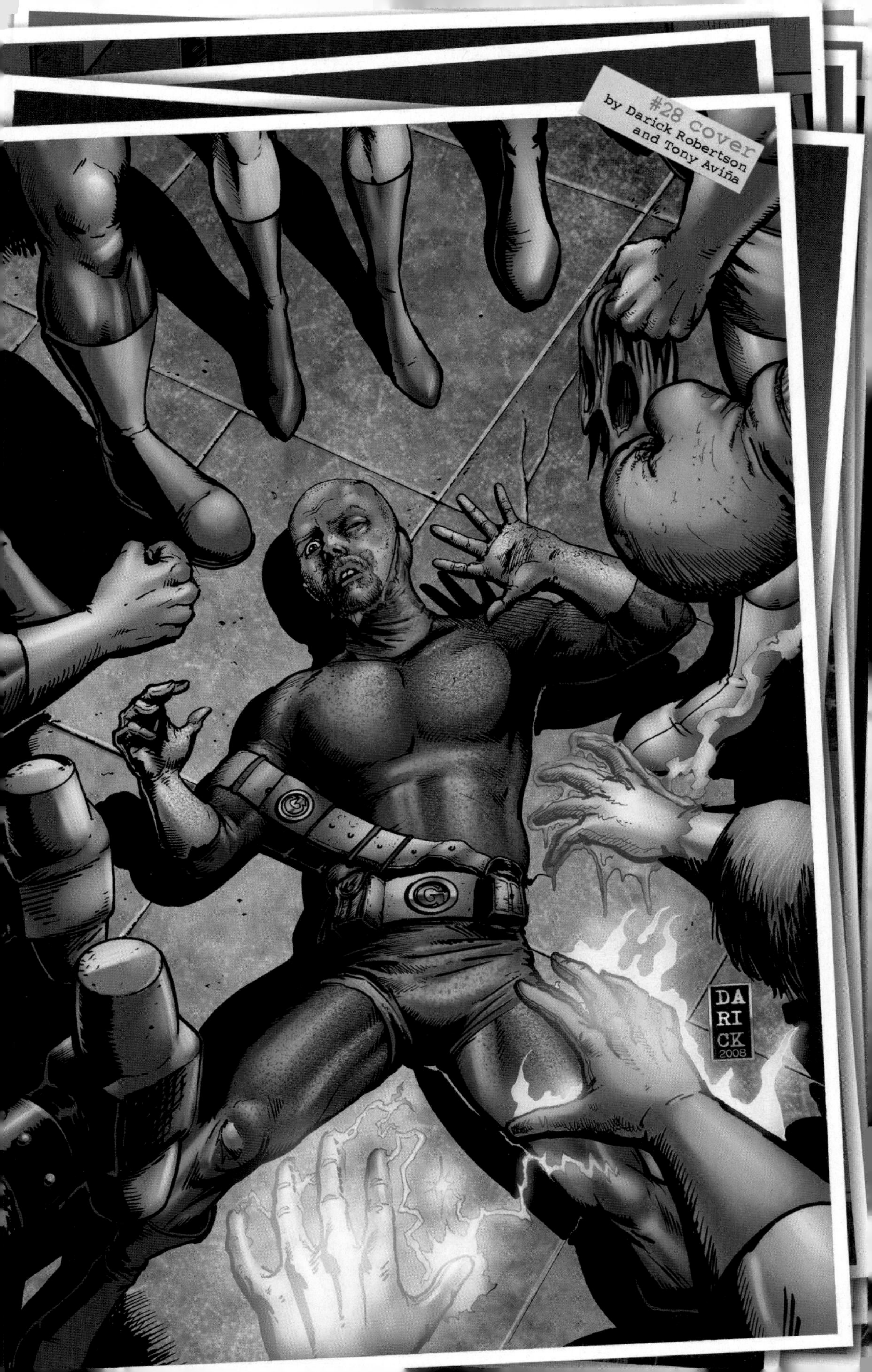
DA
RI
CK
2008

#28 cover
by Darick Robertson
and Tony Aviña

ABSOLUTELY NOT.

COMPLETELY OUT OF THE QUESTION.

THE PROCESS SIMPLY DOESN'T WORK, NOR IS IT EVER LIKELY TO. WHICH IS THE CONCLUSION DRAWN BY THE TEAM THEMSELVES, INCIDENTALLY, ALTHOUGH I CAN'T UNDERSTAND WHY YOU IN PARTICULAR WOULD NEED CORROBORATION FROM ANYONE...

I JUST WANT HER BACK.

YES, BUT NOT LIKE THAT, SURELY?

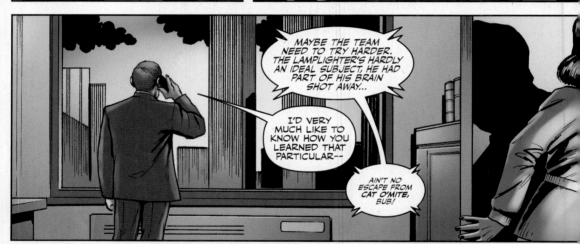

MAYBE THE TEAM NEED TO TRY HARDER. THE LAMPLIGHTER'S HARDLY AN IDEAL SUBJECT, HE HAD PART OF HIS BRAIN SHOT AWAY...

I'D VERY MUCH LIKE TO KNOW HOW YOU LEARNED THAT PARTICULAR--

AIN'T NO ESCAPE FROM CAT O'MITE, BUB!

WHAT WAS THAT?

ARE YOU--

HRRRM.

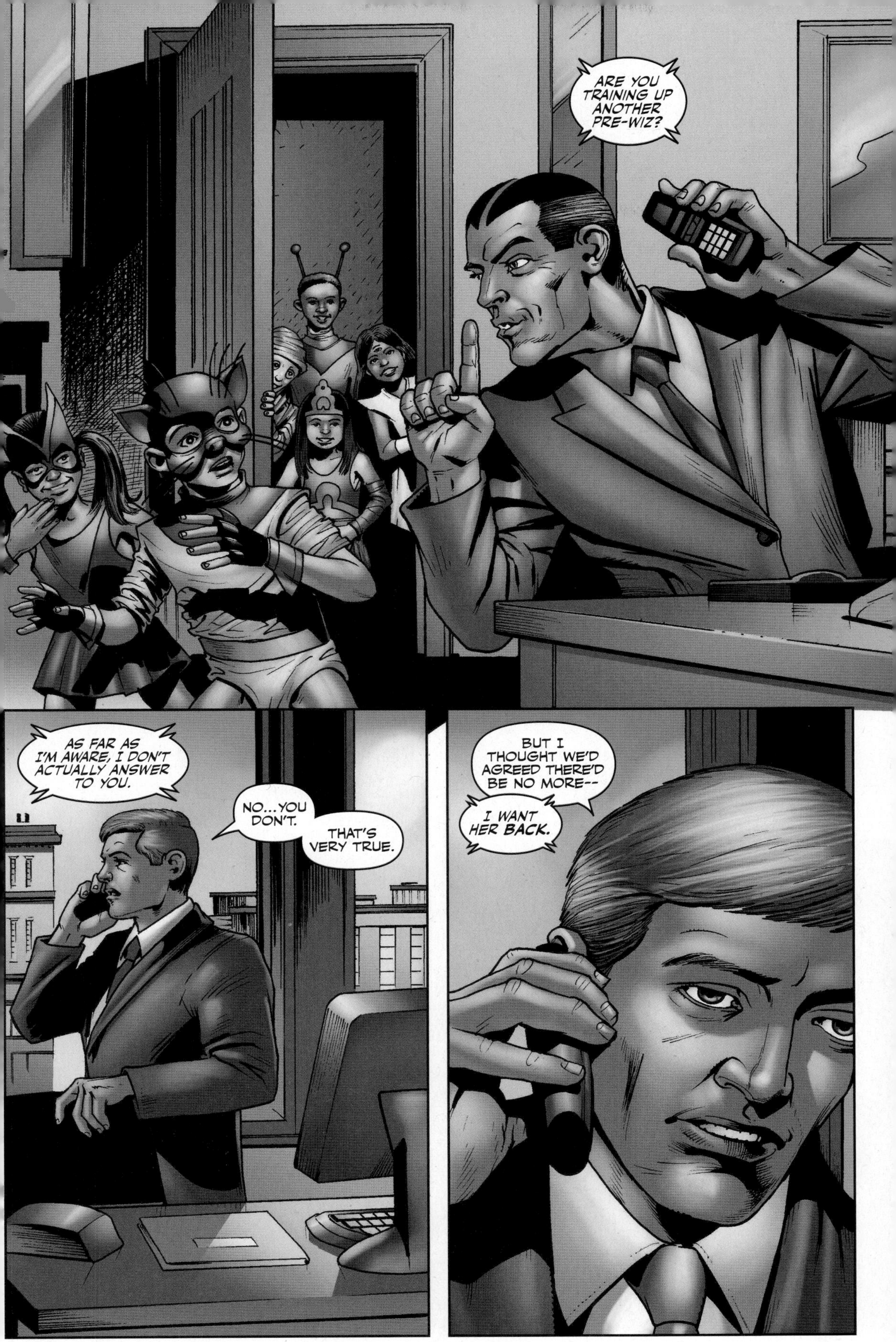

ARE YOU TRAINING UP ANOTHER PRE-WIZ?
AS FAR AS I'M AWARE, I DON'T ACTUALLY ANSWER TO YOU.
NO...YOU DON'T.
THAT'S VERY TRUE.
BUT I THOUGHT WE'D AGREED THERE'D BE NO MORE--
I WANT HER BACK.

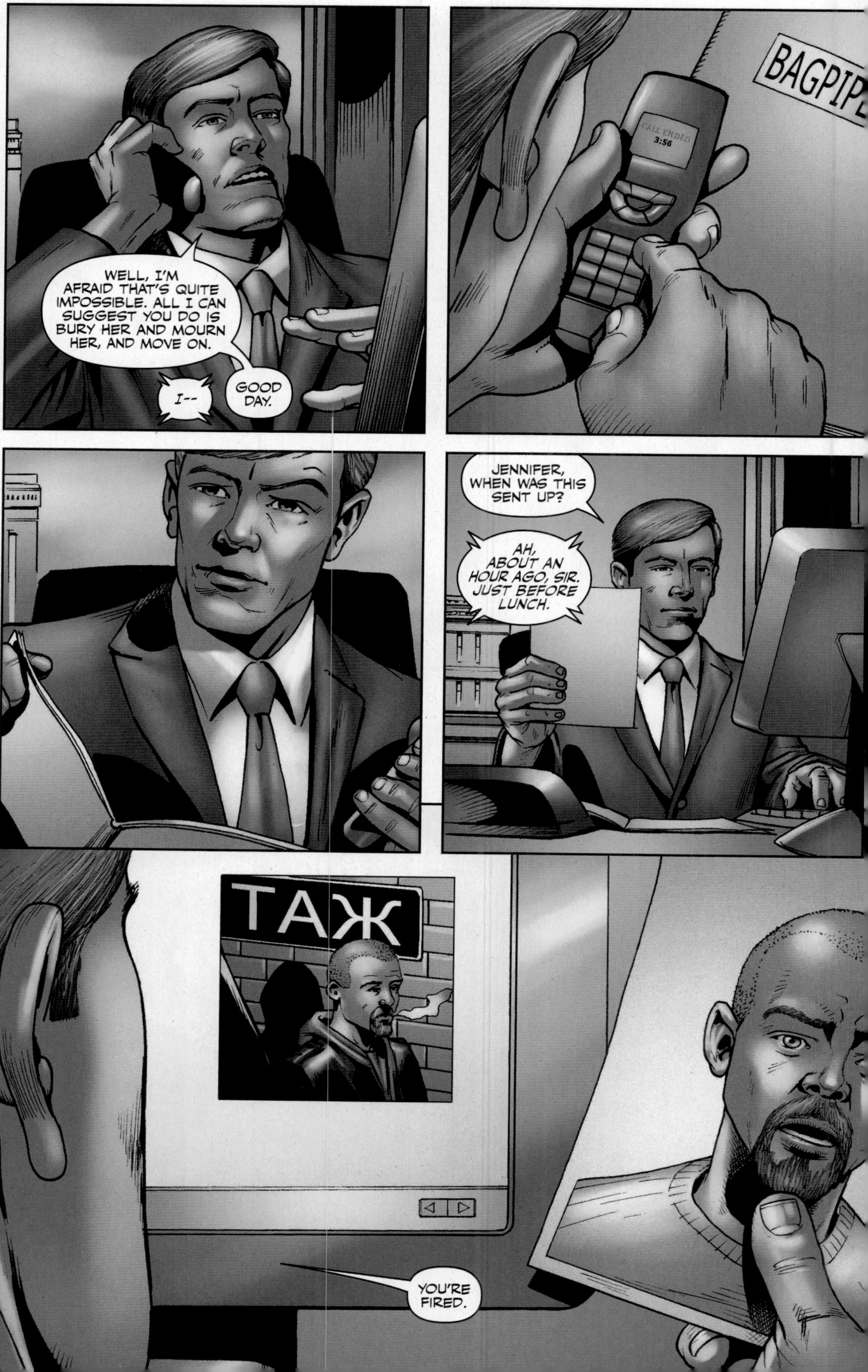
WELL, I'M AFRAID THAT'S QUITE IMPOSSIBLE. ALL I CAN SUGGEST YOU DO IS BURY HER AND MOURN HER, AND MOVE ON.
I--
GOOD DAY.
BAGPIPE
CALL ENDED 3:56
JENNIFER, WHEN WAS THIS SENT UP?
AH, ABOUT AN HOUR AGO, SIR. JUST BEFORE LUNCH.
TAЖ
YOU'RE FIRED.

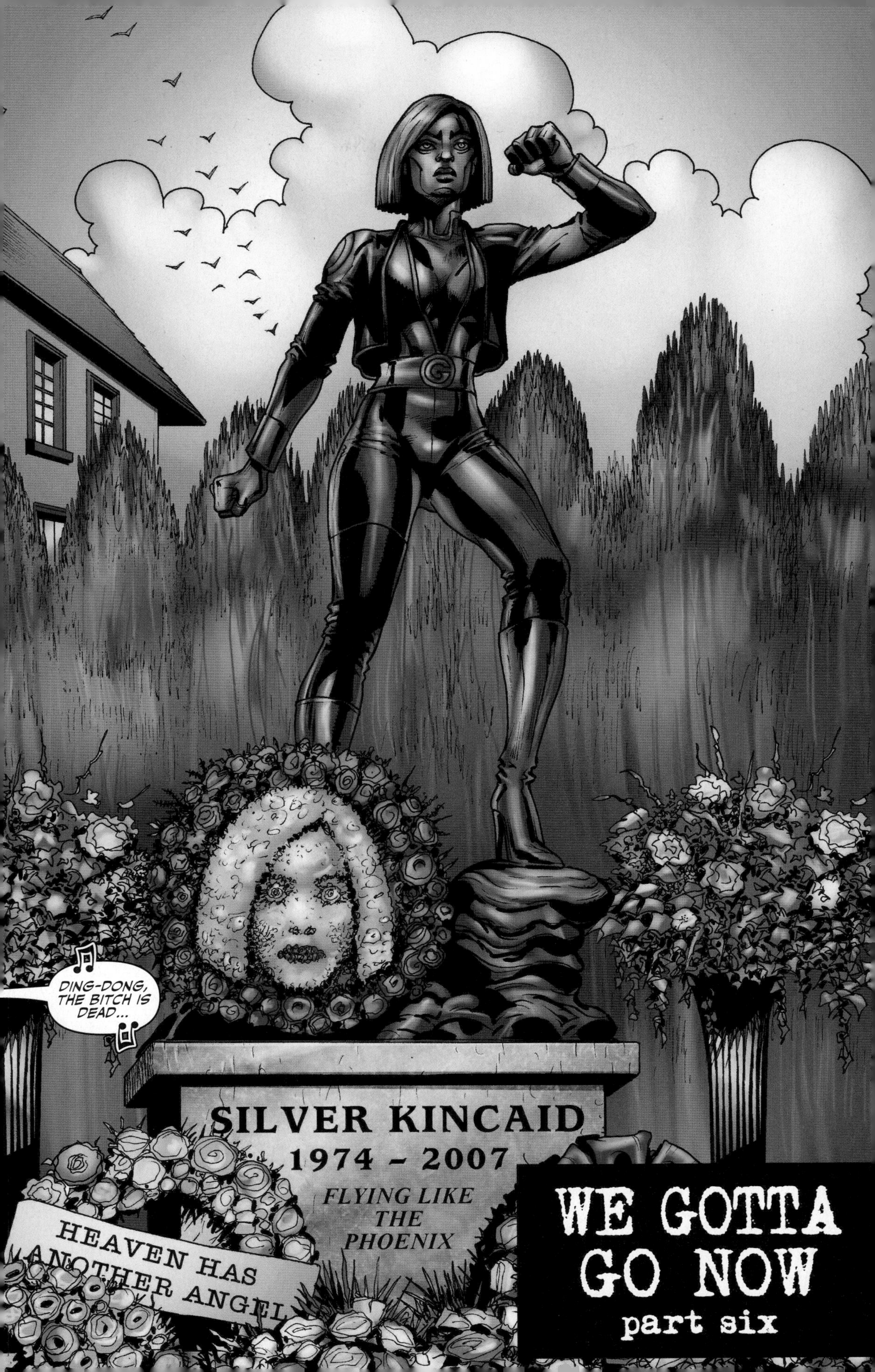

DING-DONG, THE BITCH IS DEAD...
SILVER KINCAID
1974 - 2007
FLYING LIKE THE PHOENIX
HEAVEN HAS ANOTHER ANGEL
WE GOTTA GO NOW
part six

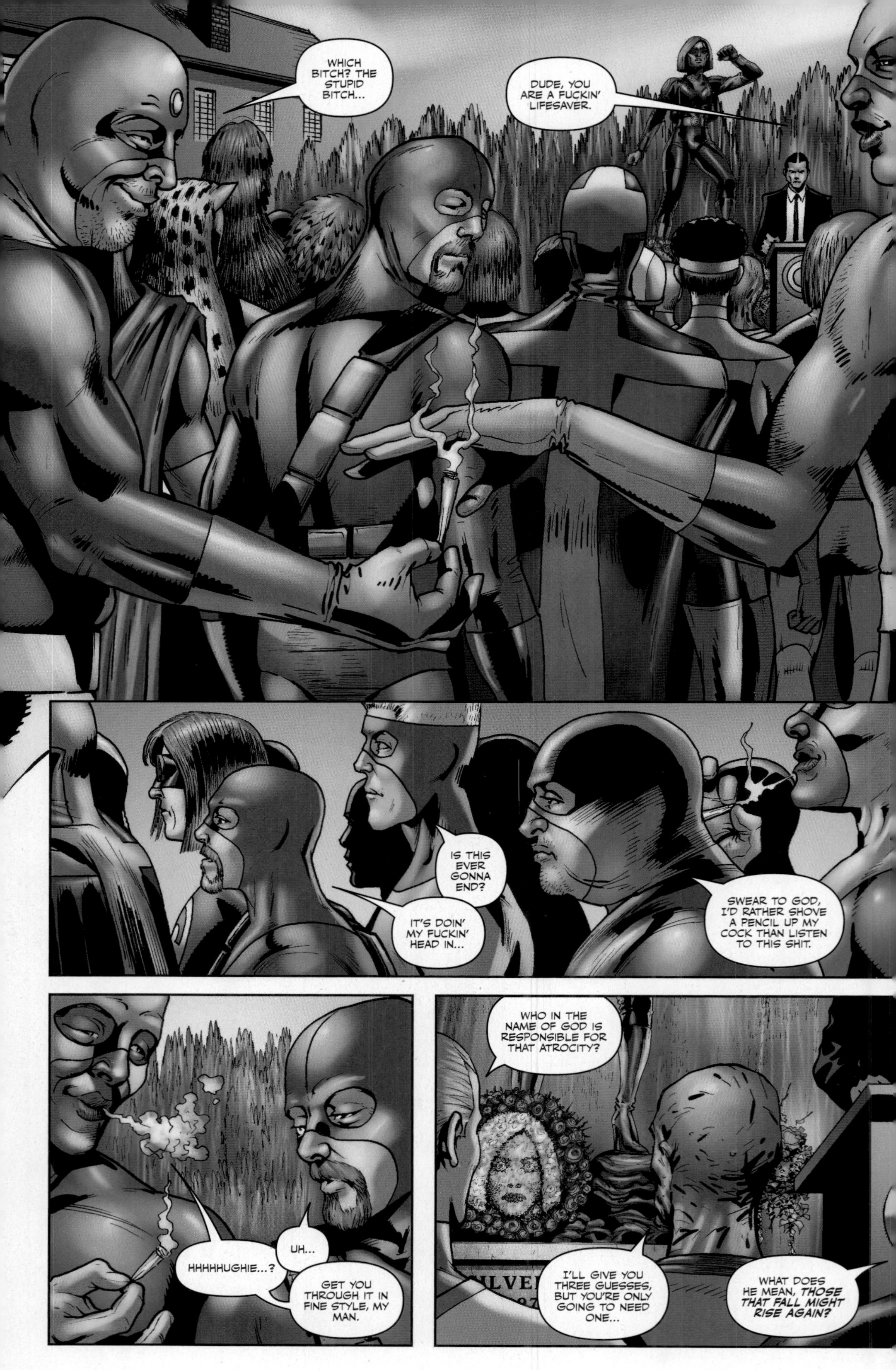
WHICH BITCH? THE STUPID BITCH...
DUDE, YOU ARE A FUCKIN' LIFESAVER.
IS THIS EVER GONNA END?
IT'S DOIN' MY FUCKIN' HEAD IN...
SWEAR TO GOD, I'D RATHER SHOVE A PENCIL UP MY COCK THAN LISTEN TO THIS SHIT.
HHHHHUGHIE...?
UH...
GET YOU THROUGH IT IN FINE STYLE, MY MAN.
WHO IN THE NAME OF GOD IS RESPONSIBLE FOR THAT ATROCITY?
I'LL GIVE YOU THREE GUESSES, BUT YOU'RE ONLY GOING TO NEED ONE...
WHAT DOES HE MEAN, *THOSE THAT FALL MIGHT RISE AGAIN?*

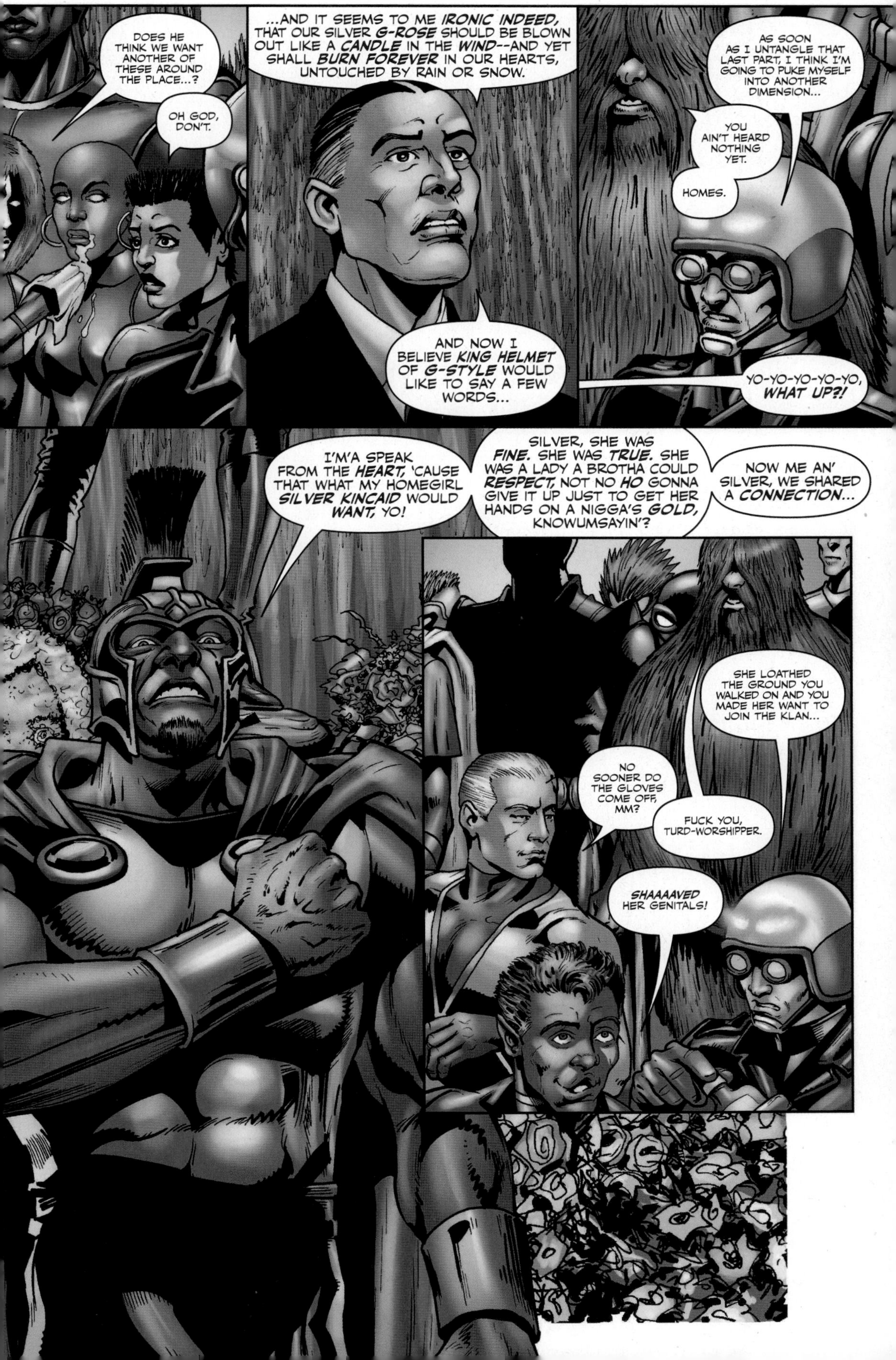
DOES HE THINK WE WANT ANOTHER OF THESE AROUND THE PLACE...?
OH GOD, DON'T.
...AND IT SEEMS TO ME IRONIC INDEED, THAT OUR SILVER G-ROSE SHOULD BE BLOWN OUT LIKE A CANDLE IN THE WIND--AND YET SHALL BURN FOREVER IN OUR HEARTS, UNTOUCHED BY RAIN OR SNOW.
AND NOW I BELIEVE KING HELMET OF G-STYLE WOULD LIKE TO SAY A FEW WORDS...
AS SOON AS I UNTANGLE THAT LAST PART, I THINK I'M GOING TO PUKE MYSELF INTO ANOTHER DIMENSION...
YOU AIN'T HEARD NOTHING YET.
HOMES.
YO-YO-YO-YO-YO, WHAT UP?!
I'M'A SPEAK FROM THE HEART, 'CAUSE THAT WHAT MY HOMEGIRL SILVER KINCAID WOULD WANT, YO!
SILVER, SHE WAS FINE. SHE WAS TRUE. SHE WAS A LADY A BROTHA COULD RESPECT, NOT NO HO GONNA GIVE IT UP JUST TO GET HER HANDS ON A NIGGA'S GOLD, KNOWUMSAYIN'?
NOW ME AN' SILVER, WE SHARED A CONNECTION...
SHE LOATHED THE GROUND YOU WALKED ON AND YOU MADE HER WANT TO JOIN THE KLAN...
NO SOONER DO THE GLOVES COME OFF, MM?
FUCK YOU, TURD-WORSHIPPER.
SHAAAAVED HER GENITALS!

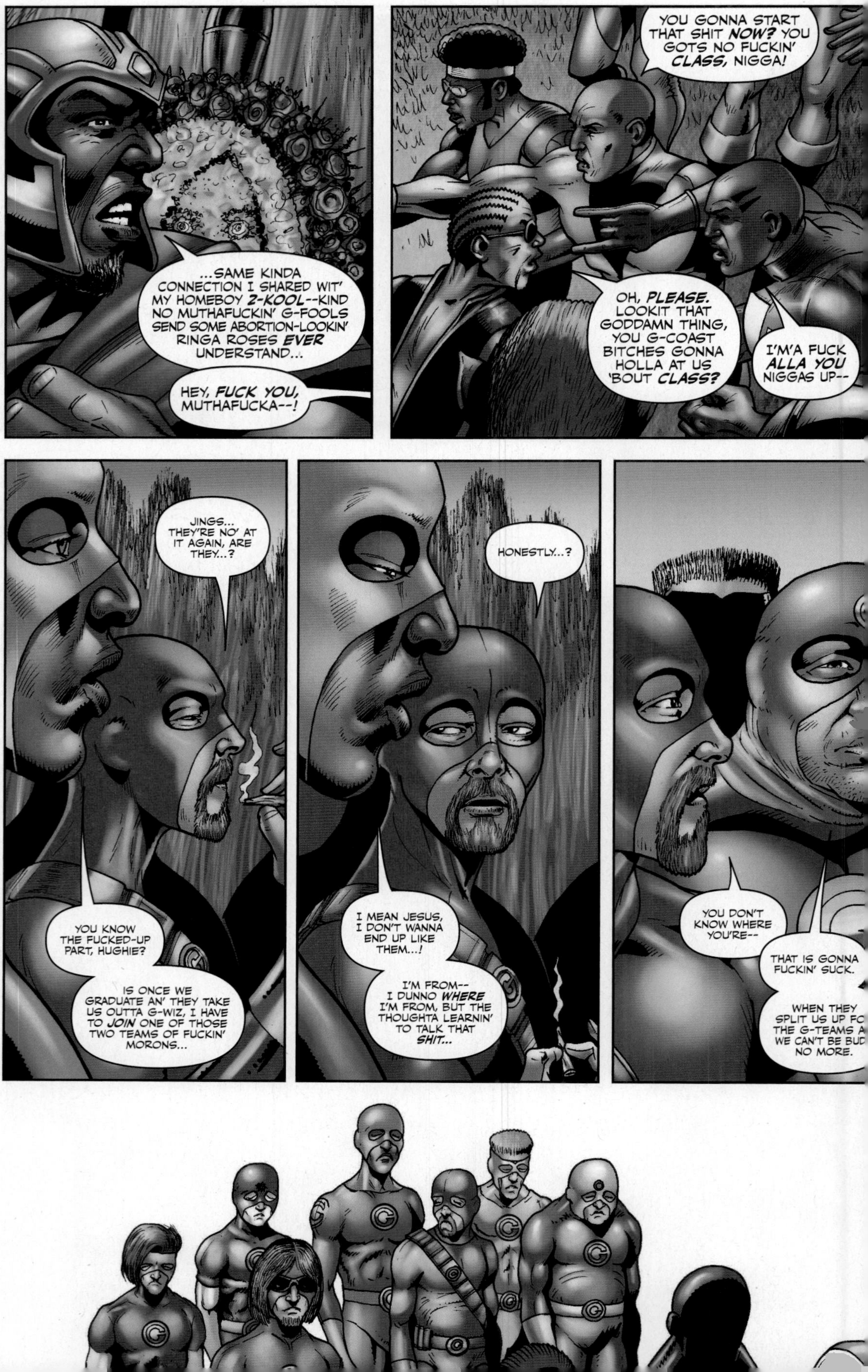
...SAME KINDA CONNECTION I SHARED WIT' MY HOMEBOY 2-KOOL--KIND NO MUTHAFUCKIN' G-FOOLS SEND SOME ABORTION-LOOKIN' RINGA ROSES EVER UNDERSTAND...
HEY, FUCK YOU, MUTHAFUCKA--!
YOU GONNA START THAT SHIT NOW? YOU GOTS NO FUCKIN' CLASS, NIGGA!
OH, PLEASE. LOOKIT THAT GODDAMN THING, YOU G-COAST BITCHES GONNA HOLLA AT US 'BOUT CLASS?
I'M'A FUCK ALLA YOU NIGGAS UP--
JINGS... THEY'RE NO' AT IT AGAIN, ARE THEY...?
YOU KNOW THE FUCKED-UP PART, HUGHIE?
IS ONCE WE GRADUATE AN' THEY TAKE US OUTTA G-WIZ, I HAVE TO JOIN ONE OF THOSE TWO TEAMS OF FUCKIN' MORONS...
HONESTLY...?
I MEAN JESUS, I DON'T WANNA END UP LIKE THEM...!
I'M FROM-- I DUNNO WHERE I'M FROM, BUT THE THOUGHTA LEARNIN' TO TALK THAT SHIT...
YOU DON'T KNOW WHERE YOU'RE--
THAT IS GONNA FUCKIN' SUCK.
WHEN THEY SPLIT US UP FO THE G-TEAMS A WE CAN'T BE BUD NO MORE.

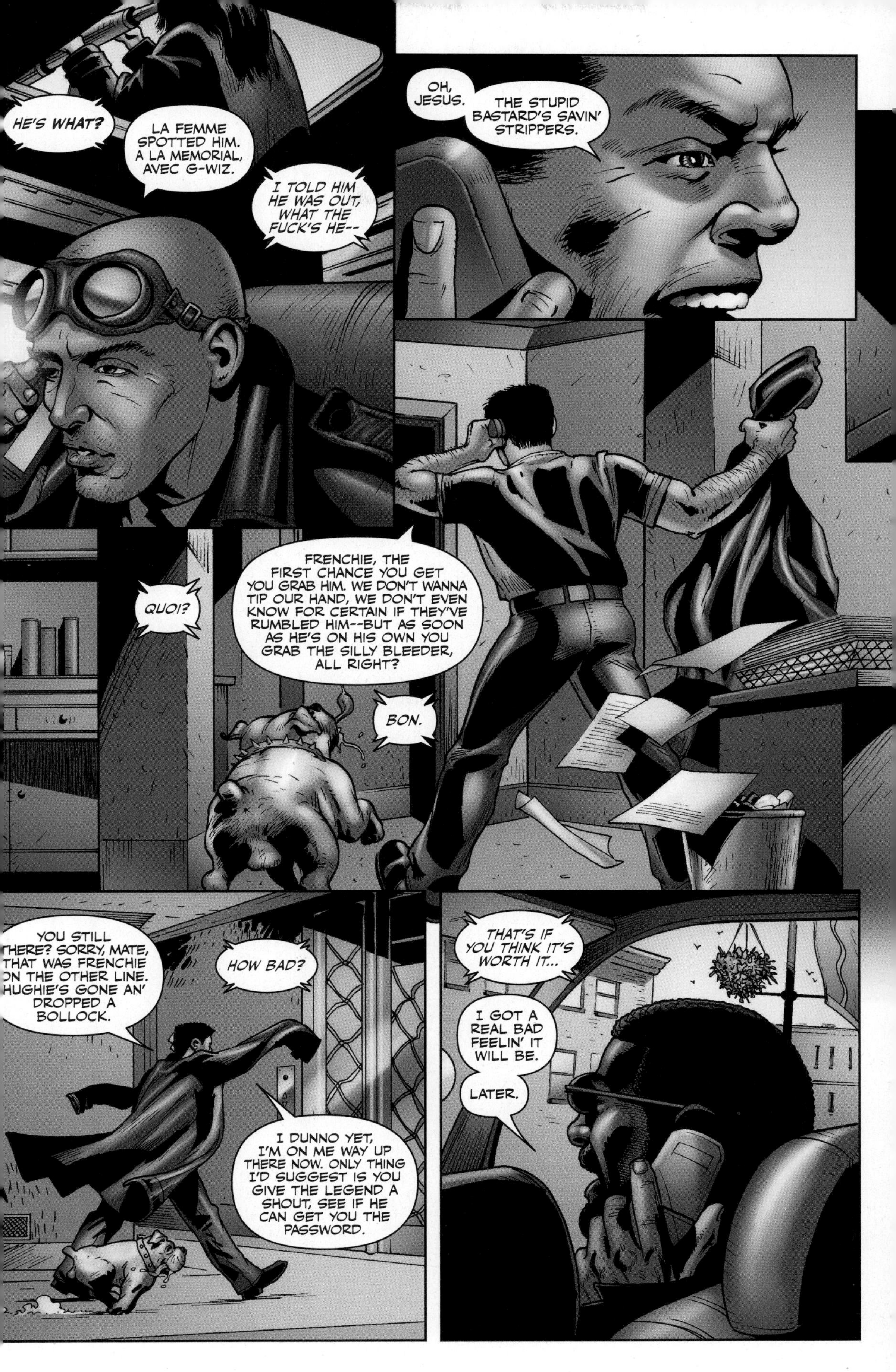
HE'S WHAT?
LA FEMME SPOTTED HIM. A LA MEMORIAL, AVEC G-WIZ.
I TOLD HIM HE WAS OUT, WHAT THE FUCK'S HE--
OH, JESUS.
THE STUPID BASTARD'S SAVIN' STRIPPERS.
QUOI?
FRENCHIE, THE FIRST CHANCE YOU GET YOU GRAB HIM. WE DON'T WANNA TIP OUR HAND, WE DON'T EVEN KNOW FOR CERTAIN IF THEY'VE RUMBLED HIM--BUT AS SOON AS HE'S ON HIS OWN YOU GRAB THE SILLY BLEEDER, ALL RIGHT?
BON.
YOU STILL THERE? SORRY, MATE, THAT WAS FRENCHIE ON THE OTHER LINE. HUGHIE'S GONE AN' DROPPED A BOLLOCK.
HOW BAD?
I DUNNO YET, I'M ON ME WAY UP THERE NOW. ONLY THING I'D SUGGEST IS YOU GIVE THE LEGEND A SHOUT, SEE IF HE CAN GET YOU THE PASSWORD.
THAT'S IF YOU THINK IT'S WORTH IT...
I GOT A REAL BAD FEELIN' IT WILL BE.
LATER.

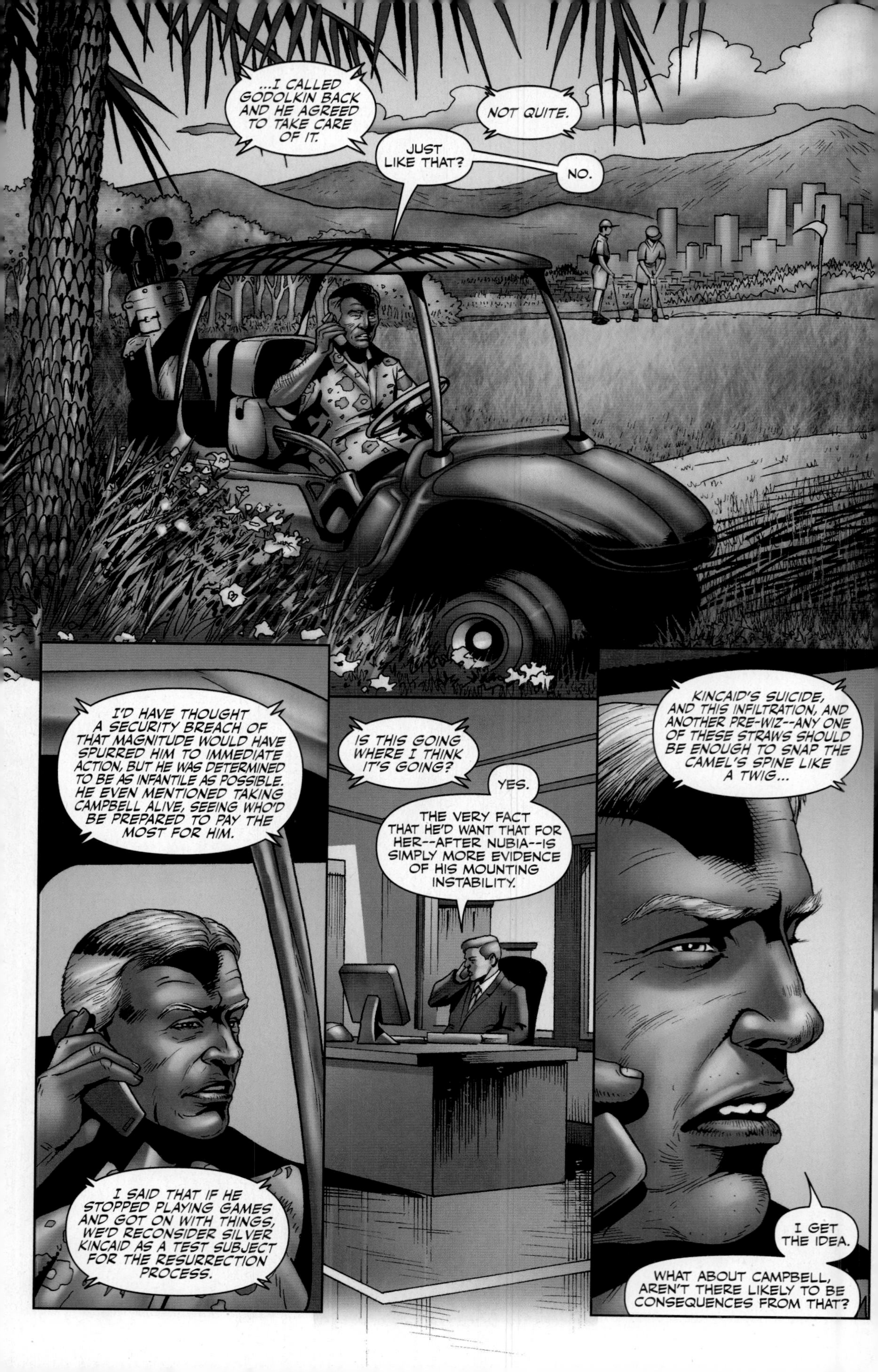
...I CALLED GODOLKIN BACK AND HE AGREED TO TAKE CARE OF IT.
NOT QUITE.
JUST LIKE THAT?
NO.
I'D HAVE THOUGHT A SECURITY BREACH OF THAT MAGNITUDE WOULD HAVE SPURRED HIM TO IMMEDIATE ACTION, BUT HE WAS DETERMINED TO BE AS INFANTILE AS POSSIBLE. HE EVEN MENTIONED TAKING CAMPBELL ALIVE, SEEING WHO'D BE PREPARED TO PAY THE MOST FOR HIM.
I SAID THAT IF HE STOPPED PLAYING GAMES AND GOT ON WITH THINGS, WE'D RECONSIDER SILVER KINCAID AS A TEST SUBJECT FOR THE RESURRECTION PROCESS.
IS THIS GOING WHERE I THINK IT'S GOING?
YES.
THE VERY FACT THAT HE'D WANT THAT FOR HER--AFTER NUBIA--IS SIMPLY MORE EVIDENCE OF HIS MOUNTING INSTABILITY.
KINCAID'S SUICIDE, AND THIS INFILTRATION, AND ANOTHER PRE-WIZ--ANY ONE OF THESE STRAWS SHOULD BE ENOUGH TO SNAP THE CAMEL'S SPINE LIKE A TWIG...
I GET THE IDEA.
WHAT ABOUT CAMPBELL, AREN'T THERE LIKELY TO BE CONSEQUENCES FROM THAT?

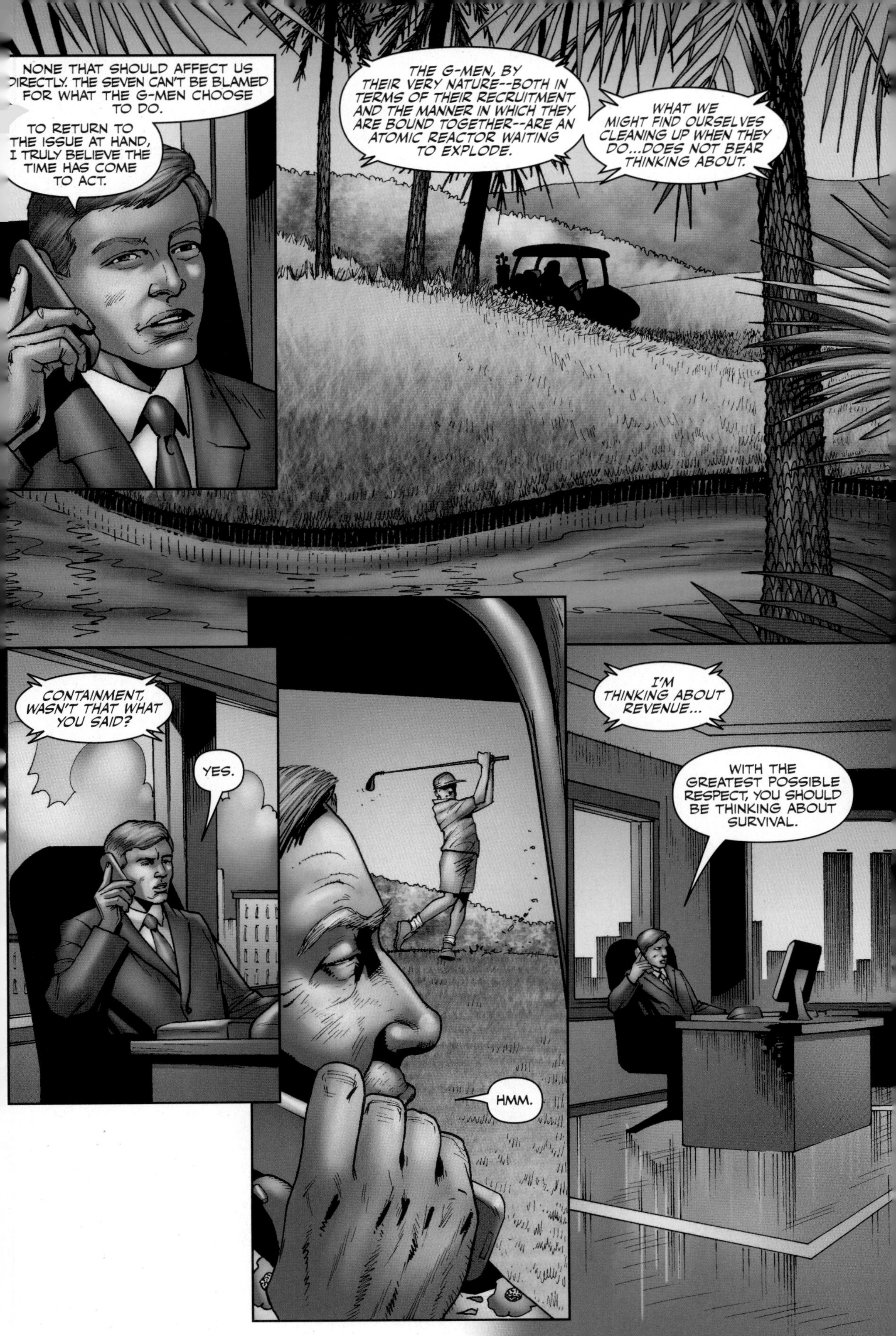
NONE THAT SHOULD AFFECT US DIRECTLY. THE SEVEN CAN'T BE BLAMED FOR WHAT THE G-MEN CHOOSE TO DO.
TO RETURN TO THE ISSUE AT HAND, I TRULY BELIEVE THE TIME HAS COME TO ACT.
THE G-MEN, BY THEIR VERY NATURE--BOTH IN TERMS OF THEIR RECRUITMENT AND THE MANNER IN WHICH THEY ARE BOUND TOGETHER--ARE AN ATOMIC REACTOR WAITING TO EXPLODE.
WHAT WE MIGHT FIND OURSELVES CLEANING UP WHEN THEY DO...DOES NOT BEAR THINKING ABOUT.
CONTAINMENT, WASN'T THAT WHAT YOU SAID?
YES.
HMM.
I'M THINKING ABOUT REVENUE...
WITH THE GREATEST POSSIBLE RESPECT, YOU SHOULD BE THINKING ABOUT SURVIVAL.

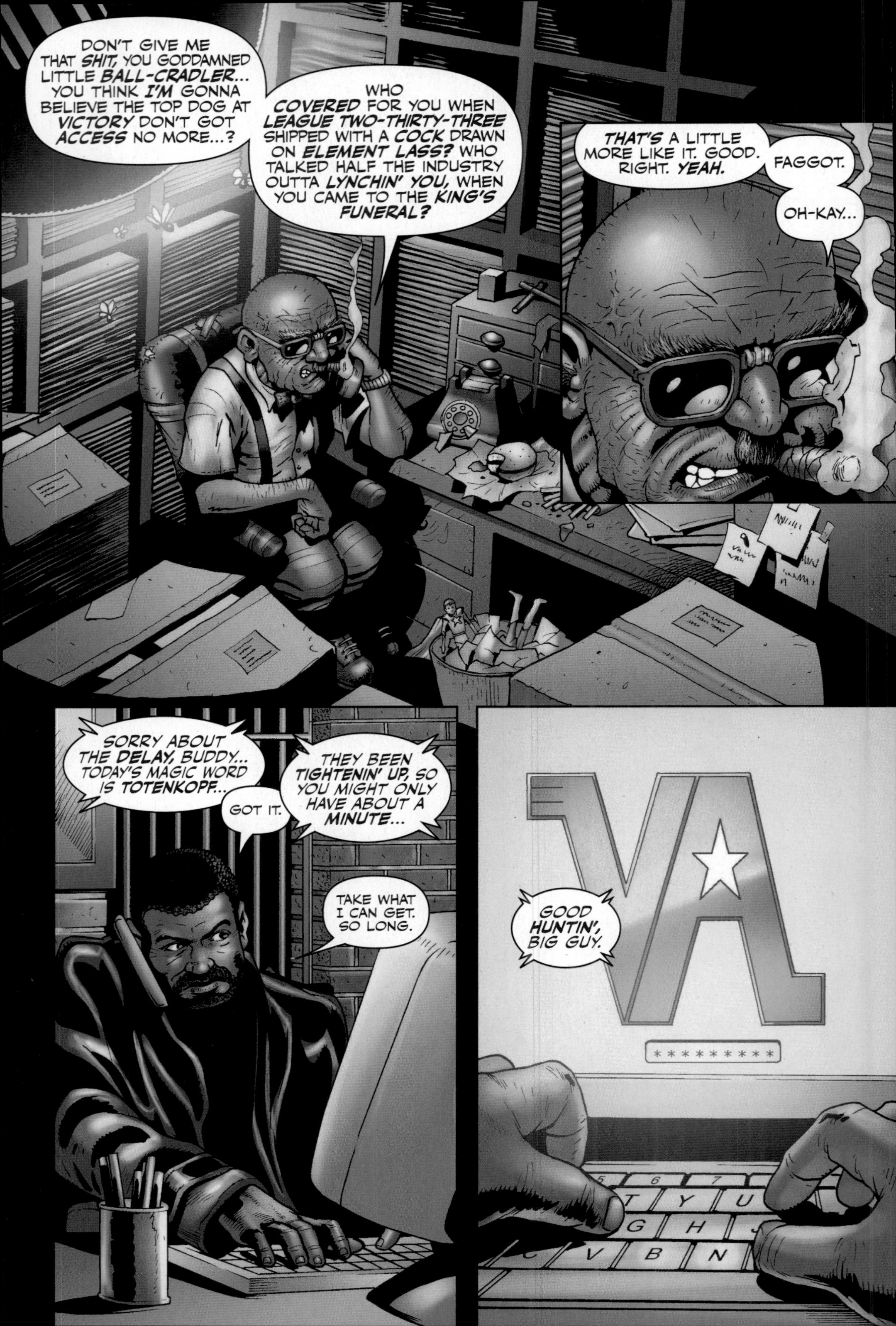
DON'T GIVE ME THAT SHIT, YOU GODDAMNED LITTLE BALL-CRADLER... YOU THINK I'M GONNA BELIEVE THE TOP DOG AT VICTORY DON'T GOT ACCESS NO MORE...?
WHO COVERED FOR YOU WHEN LEAGUE TWO-THIRTY-THREE SHIPPED WITH A COCK DRAWN ON ELEMENT LASS? WHO TALKED HALF THE INDUSTRY OUTTA LYNCHIN' YOU, WHEN YOU CAME TO THE KING'S FUNERAL?
THAT'S A LITTLE MORE LIKE IT. GOOD. RIGHT. YEAH.
FAGGOT.
OH-KAY...
SORRY ABOUT THE DELAY, BUDDY... TODAY'S MAGIC WORD IS TOTENKOPF...
GOT IT.
THEY BEEN TIGHTENIN' UP, SO YOU MIGHT ONLY HAVE ABOUT A MINUTE...
TAKE WHAT I CAN GET. SO LONG.
VA
GOOD HUNTIN', BIG GUY.

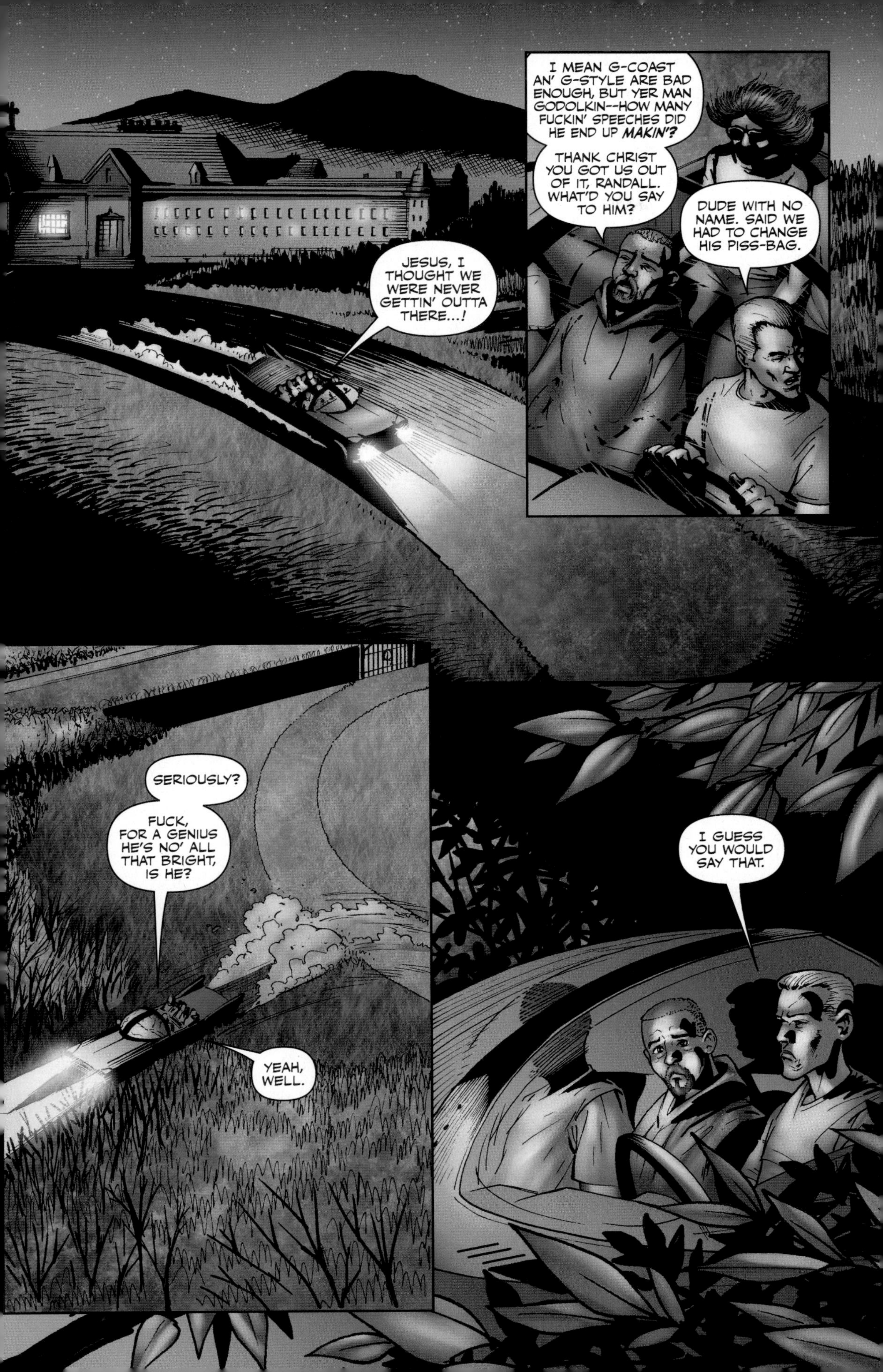
JESUS, I THOUGHT WE WERE NEVER GETTIN' OUTTA THERE...!
I MEAN G-COAST AN' G-STYLE ARE BAD ENOUGH, BUT YER MAN GODOLKIN--HOW MANY FUCKIN' SPEECHES DID HE END UP MAKIN'?
THANK CHRIST YOU GOT US OUT OF IT, RANDALL. WHAT'D YOU SAY TO HIM?
DUDE WITH NO NAME. SAID WE HAD TO CHANGE HIS PISS-BAG.
SERIOUSLY?
FUCK, FOR A GENIUS HE'S NO' ALL THAT BRIGHT, IS HE?
YEAH, WELL.
I GUESS YOU WOULD SAY THAT.

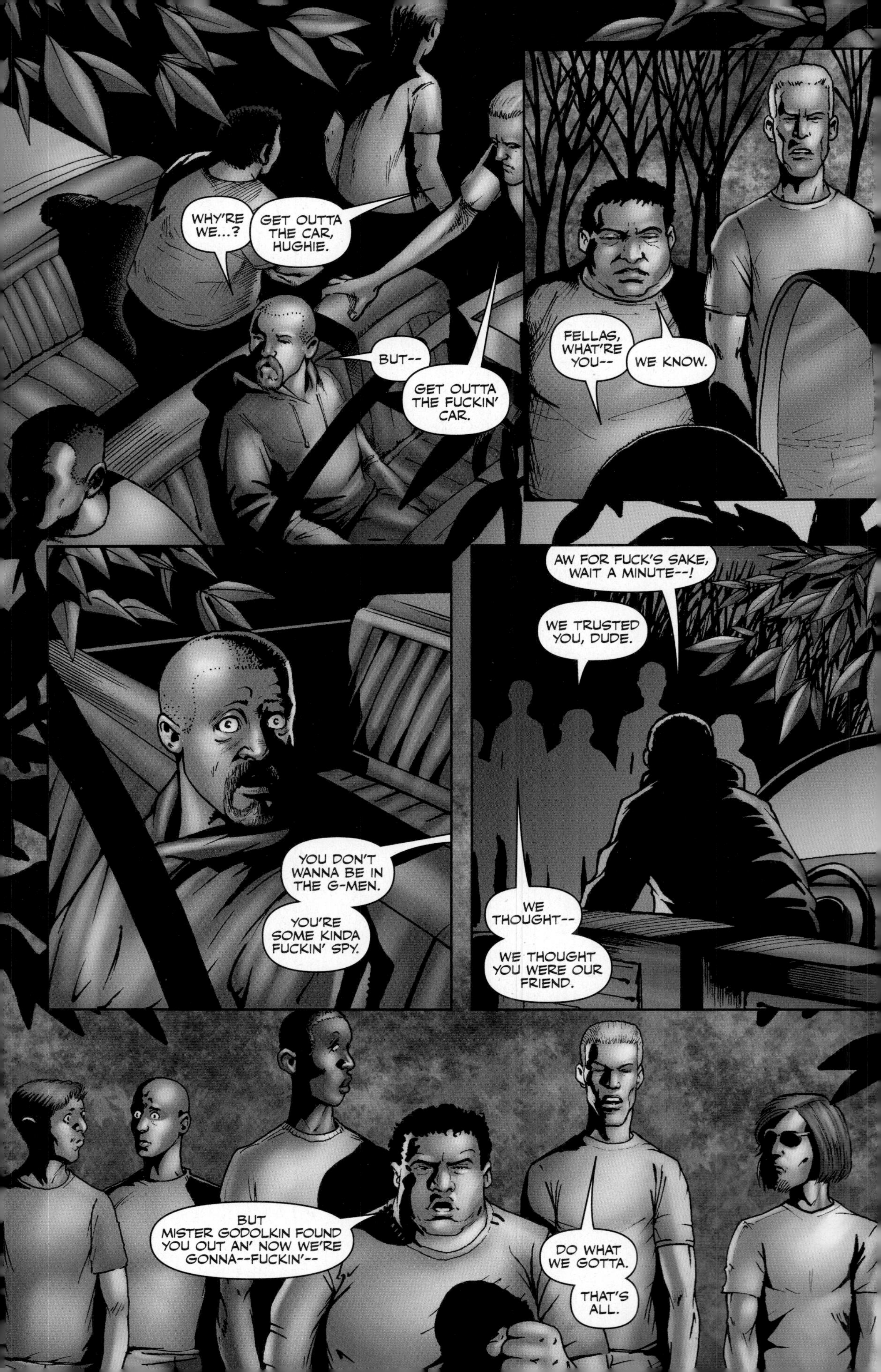

WHY'RE WE...?
GET OUTTA THE CAR, HUGHIE.
BUT--
GET OUTTA THE FUCKIN' CAR.
FELLAS, WHAT'RE YOU--
WE KNOW.
YOU DON'T WANNA BE IN THE G-MEN.
YOU'RE SOME KINDA FUCKIN' SPY.
AW FOR FUCK'S SAKE, WAIT A MINUTE--!
WE TRUSTED YOU, DUDE.
WE THOUGHT--
WE THOUGHT YOU WERE OUR FRIEND.
BUT MISTER GODOLKIN FOUND YOU OUT AN' NOW WE'RE GONNA--FUCKIN'--
DO WHAT WE GOTTA.
THAT'S ALL.

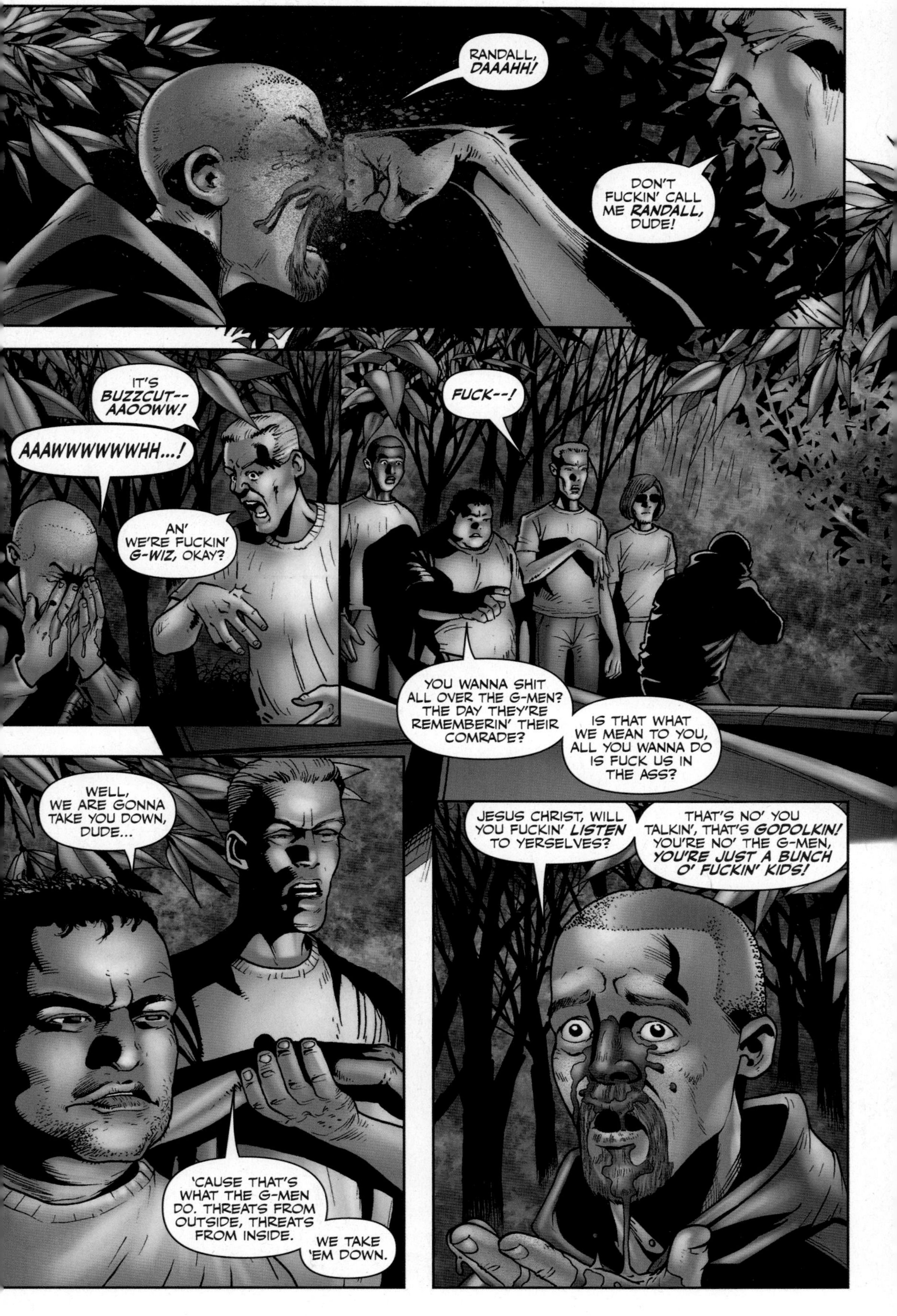
RANDALL, DAAAHH!
DON'T FUCKIN' CALL ME RANDALL, DUDE!
IT'S BUZZCUT-- AAOOWW!
AAAWWWWWWHH...!
FUCK--!
AN' WE'RE FUCKIN' G-WIZ, OKAY?
YOU WANNA SHIT ALL OVER THE G-MEN? THE DAY THEY'RE REMEMBERIN' THEIR COMRADE?
IS THAT WHAT WE MEAN TO YOU, ALL YOU WANNA DO IS FUCK US IN THE ASS?
WELL, WE ARE GONNA TAKE YOU DOWN, DUDE...
'CAUSE THAT'S WHAT THE G-MEN DO. THREATS FROM OUTSIDE, THREATS FROM INSIDE.
WE TAKE 'EM DOWN.
JESUS CHRIST, WILL YOU FUCKIN' LISTEN TO YERSELVES?
THAT'S NO' YOU TALKIN', THAT'S GODOLKIN! YOU'RE NO' THE G-MEN, YOU'RE JUST A BUNCH O' FUCKIN' KIDS!

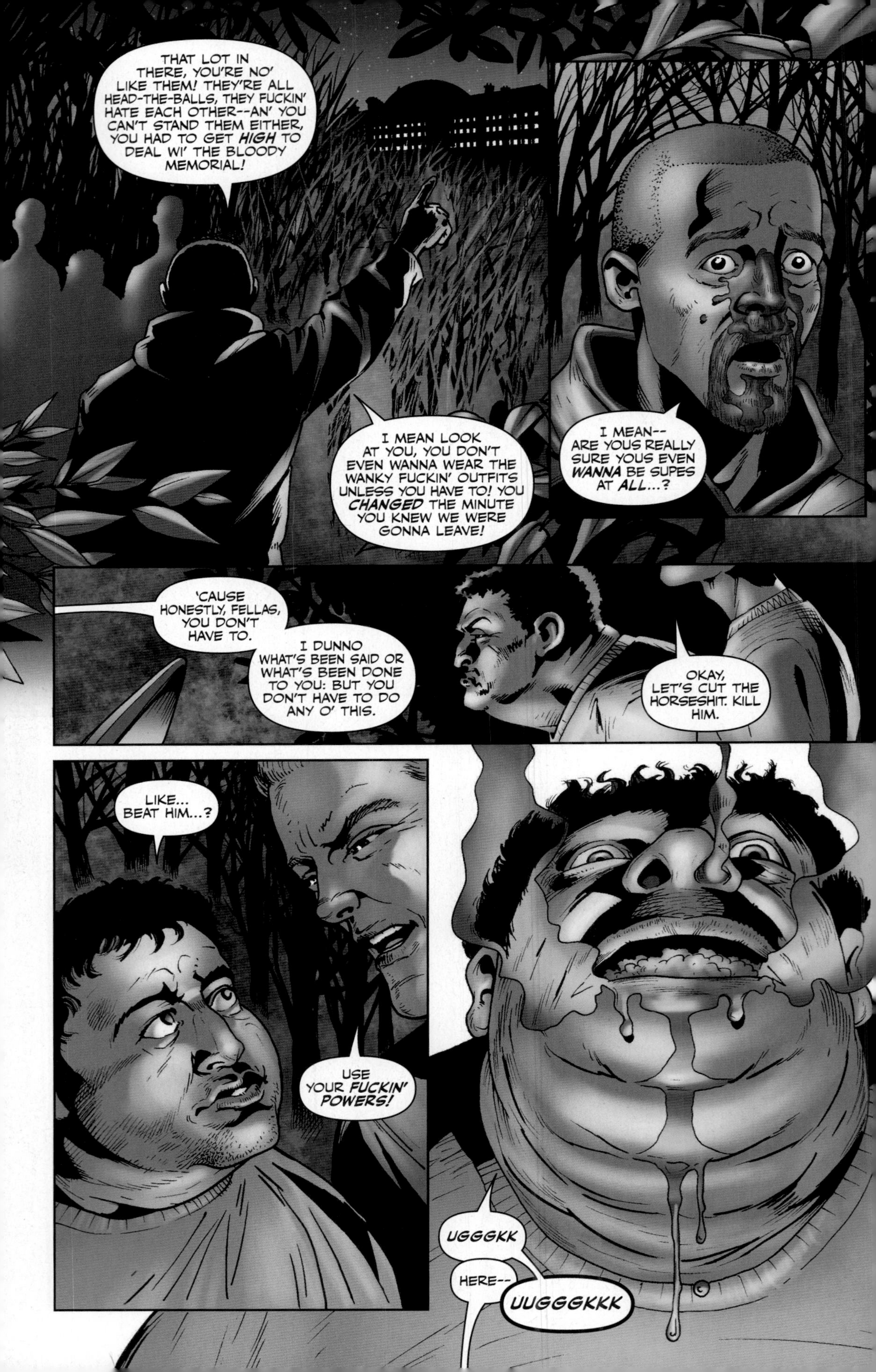
THAT LOT IN THERE, YOU'RE NO' LIKE THEM! THEY'RE ALL HEAD-THE-BALLS, THEY FUCKIN' HATE EACH OTHER--AN' YOU CAN'T STAND THEM EITHER, YOU HAD TO GET HIGH TO DEAL WI' THE BLOODY MEMORIAL!
I MEAN LOOK AT YOU, YOU DON'T EVEN WANNA WEAR THE WANKY FUCKIN' OUTFITS UNLESS YOU HAVE TO! YOU CHANGED THE MINUTE YOU KNEW WE WERE GONNA LEAVE!
I MEAN-- ARE YOUS REALLY SURE YOUS EVEN WANNA BE SUPES AT ALL...?
'CAUSE HONESTLY, FELLAS, YOU DON'T HAVE TO.
I DUNNO WHAT'S BEEN SAID OR WHAT'S BEEN DONE TO YOU: BUT YOU DON'T HAVE TO DO ANY O' THIS.
OKAY, LET'S CUT THE HORSESHIT. KILL HIM.
LIKE... BEAT HIM...?
USE YOUR FUCKIN' POWERS!
UGGGKK
HERE--
UUGGGKKK

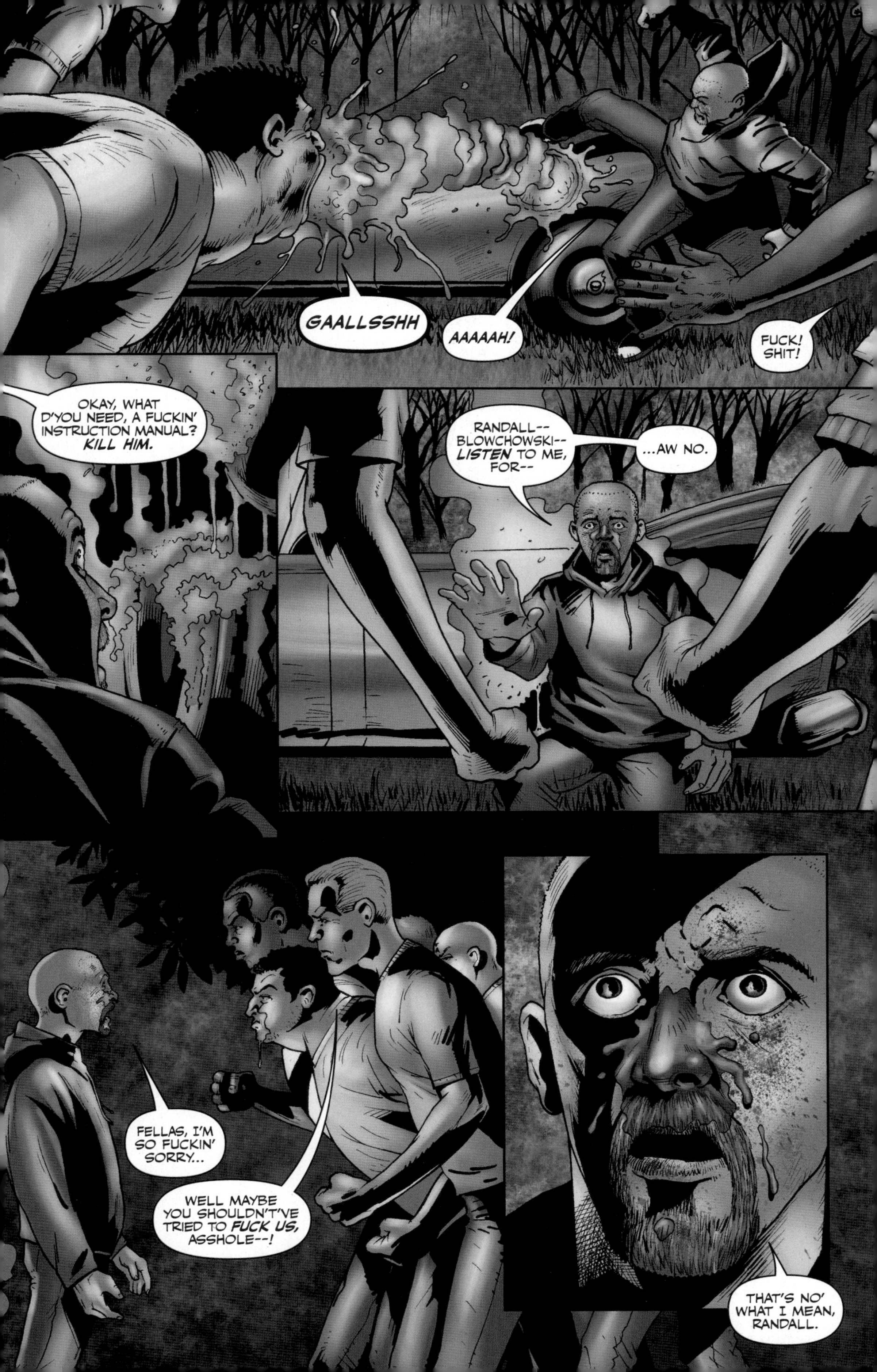
GAALLSSHH
AAAAAH!
FUCK! SHIT!
OKAY, WHAT D'YOU NEED, A FUCKIN' INSTRUCTION MANUAL? KILL HIM.
RANDALL-- BLOWCHOWSKI-- LISTEN TO ME, FOR--
...AW NO.
FELLAS, I'M SO FUCKIN' SORRY...
WELL MAYBE YOU SHOULDN'T'VE TRIED TO FUCK US, ASSHOLE--!
THAT'S NO' WHAT I MEAN, RANDALL.

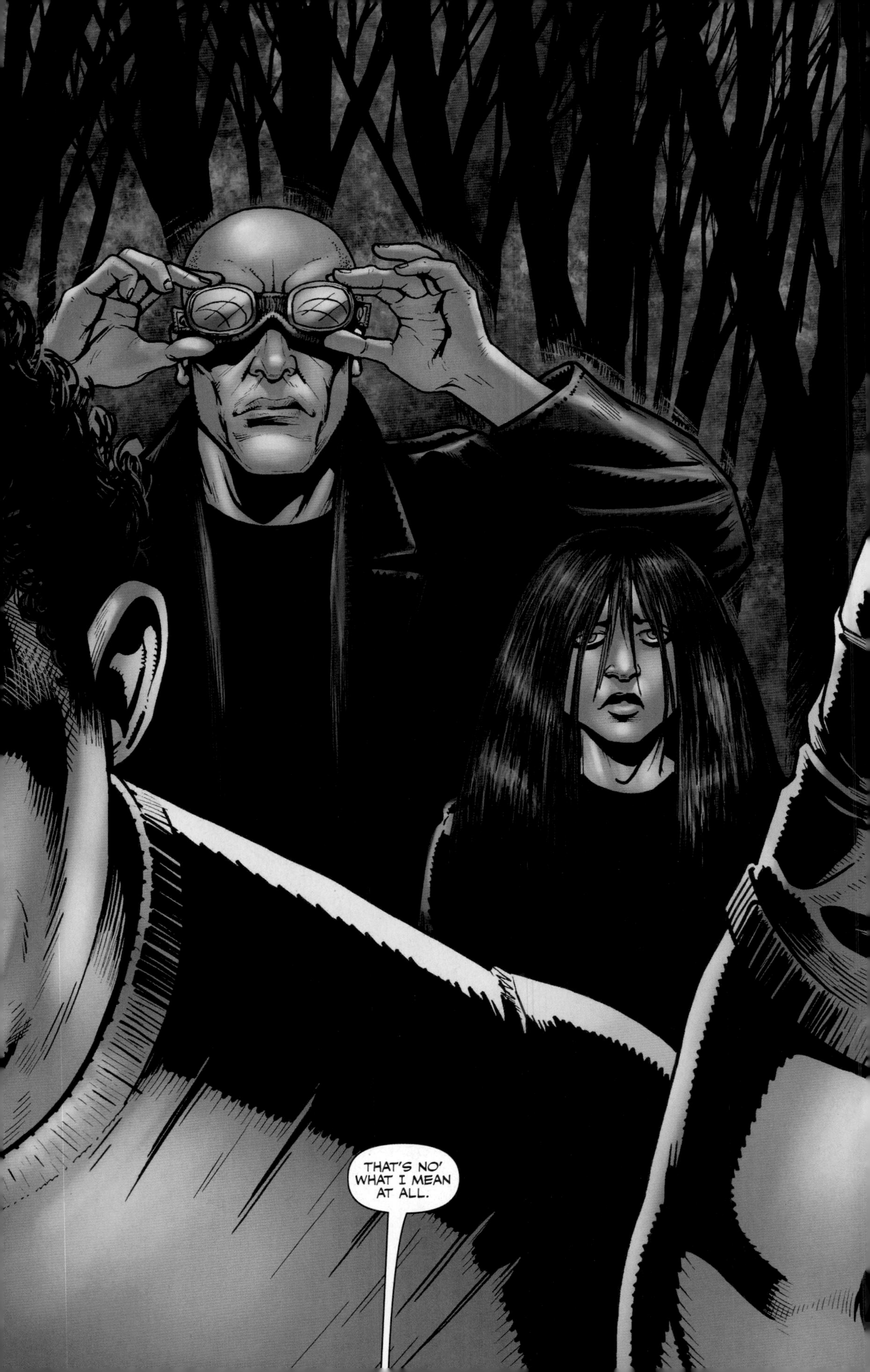
THAT'S NO' WHAT I MEAN AT ALL.

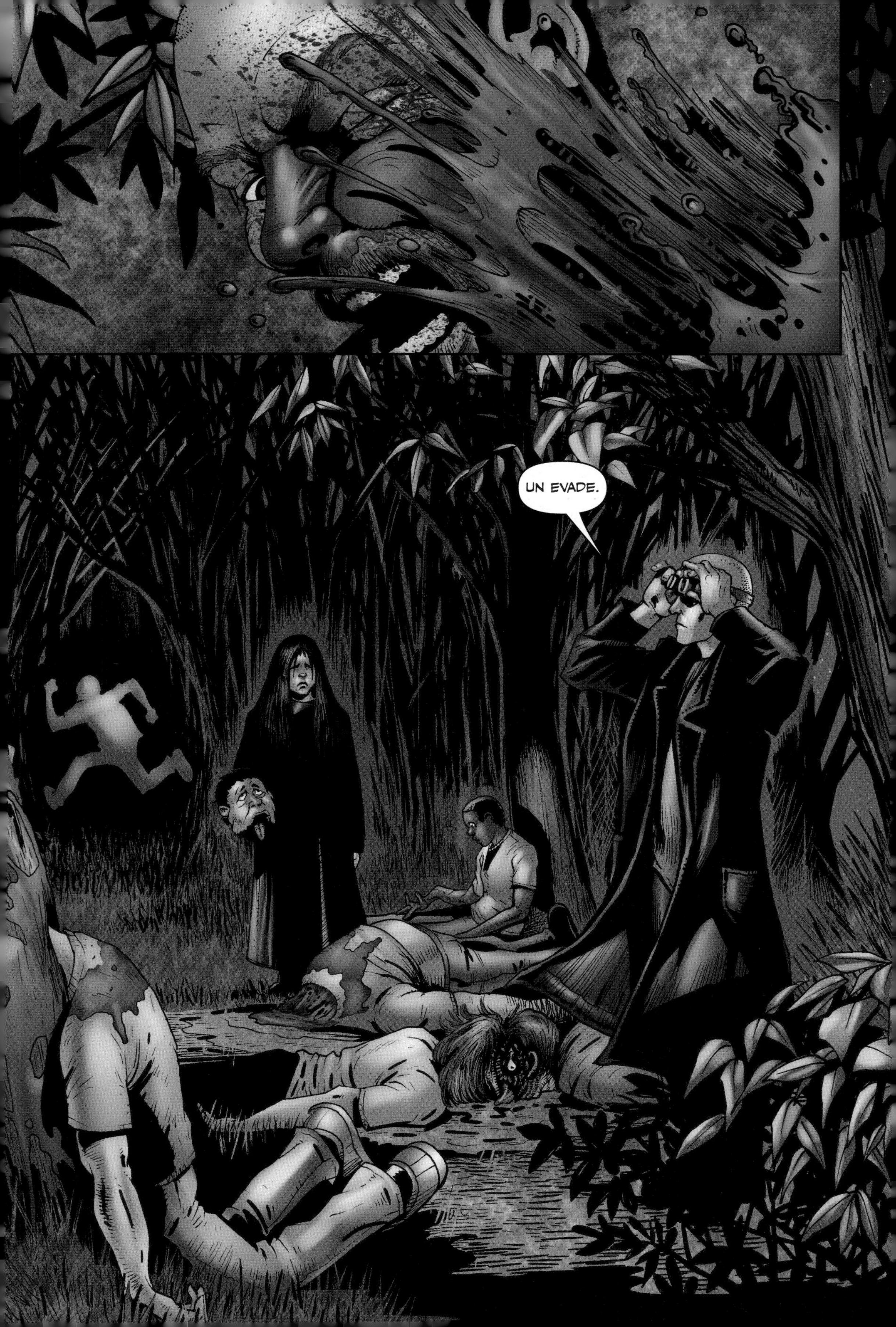
UN EVADE.

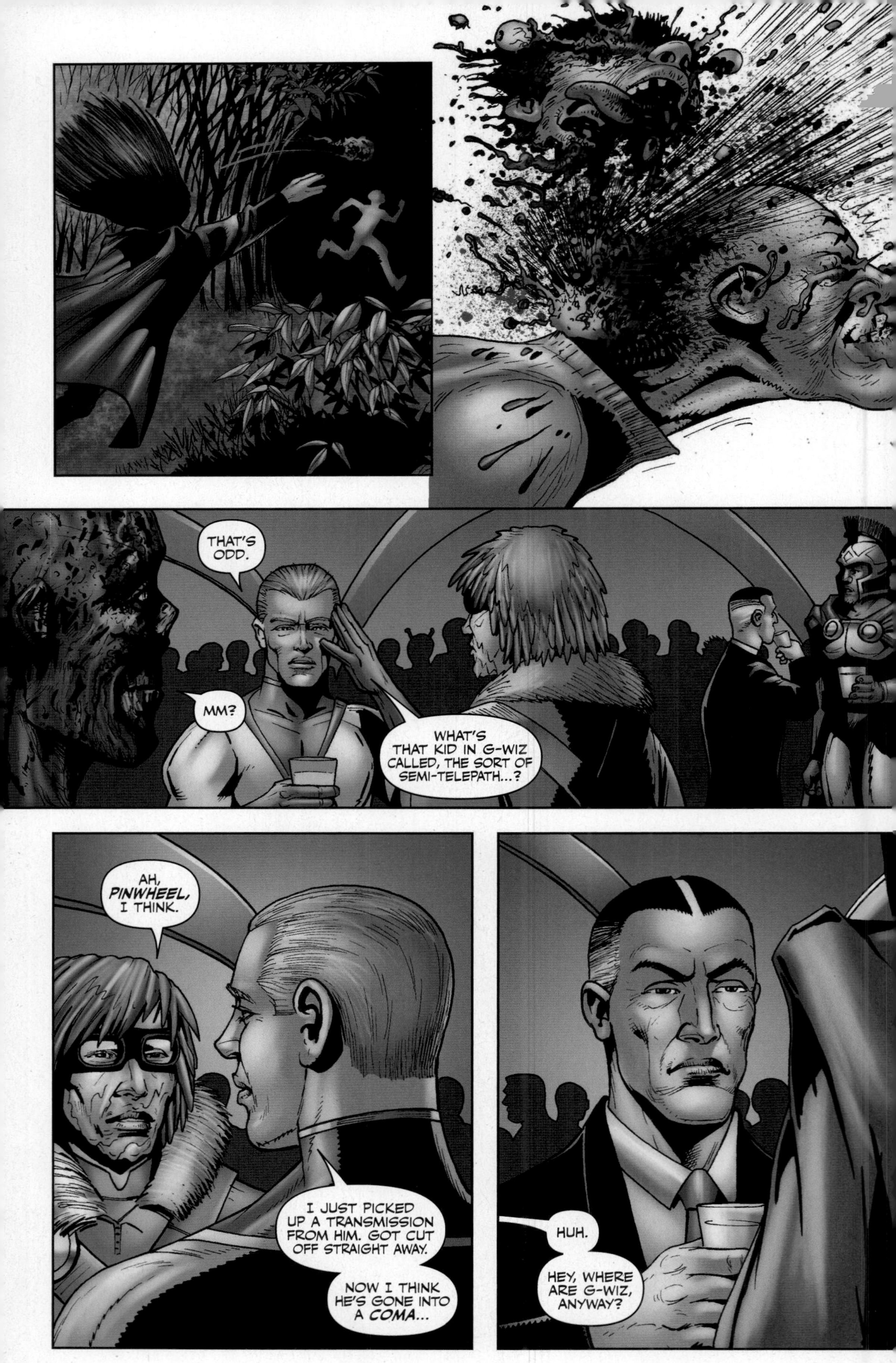
THAT'S ODD.
MM?
WHAT'S THAT KID IN G-WIZ CALLED, THE SORT OF SEMI-TELEPATH...?
AH, PINWHEEL, I THINK.
I JUST PICKED UP A TRANSMISSION FROM HIM. GOT CUT OFF STRAIGHT AWAY.
NOW I THINK HE'S GONE INTO A COMA...
HUH.
HEY, WHERE ARE G-WIZ, ANYWAY?

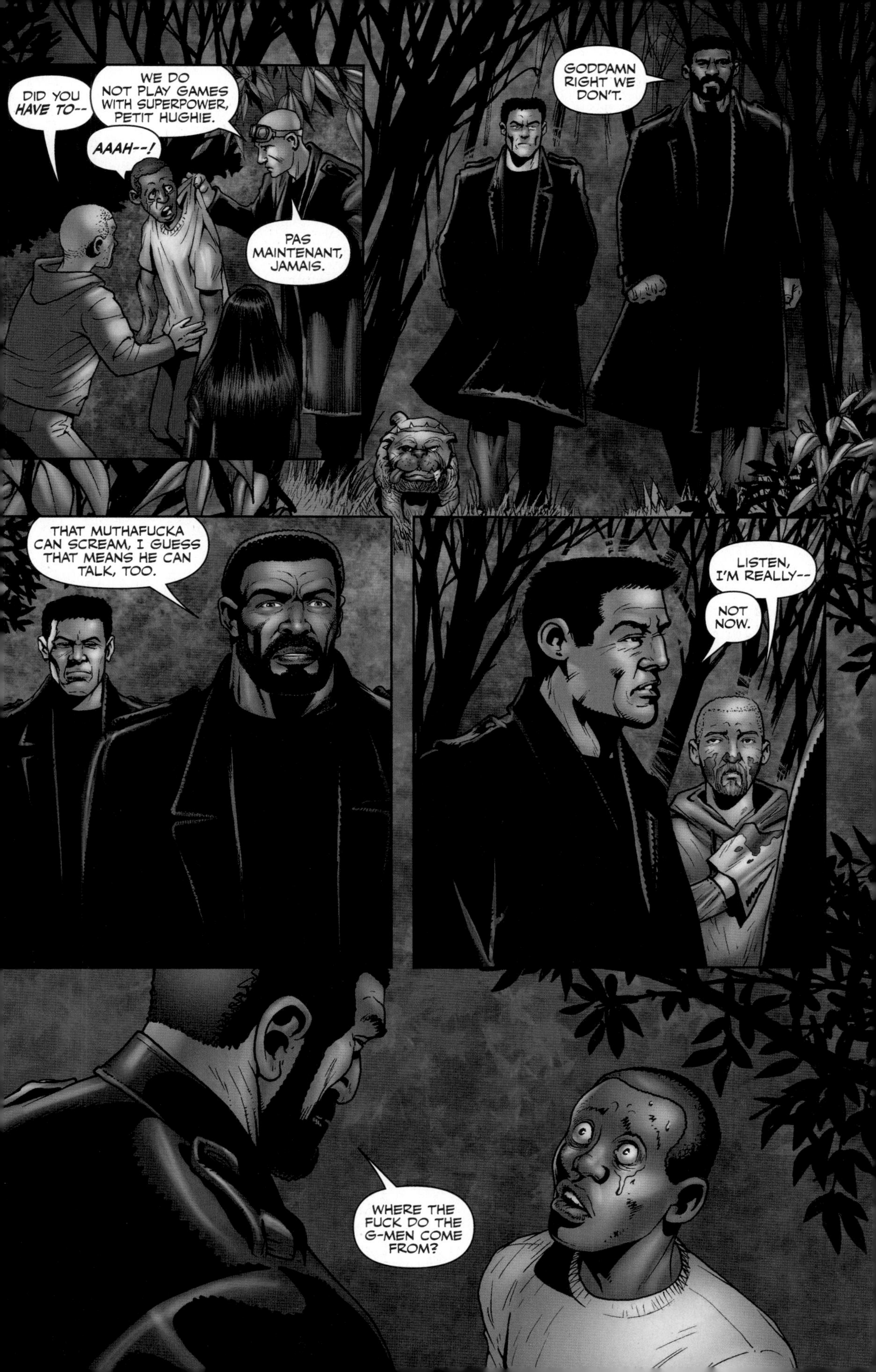
DID YOU *HAVE TO--*
WE DO NOT PLAY GAMES WITH SUPERPOWER, PETIT HUGHIE.
AAAH--!
PAS MAINTENANT, JAMAIS.
GODDAMN RIGHT WE DON'T.
THAT MUTHAFUCKA CAN SCREAM, I GUESS THAT MEANS HE CAN TALK, TOO.
LISTEN, I'M REALLY--
NOT NOW.
WHERE THE FUCK DO THE G-MEN COME FROM?

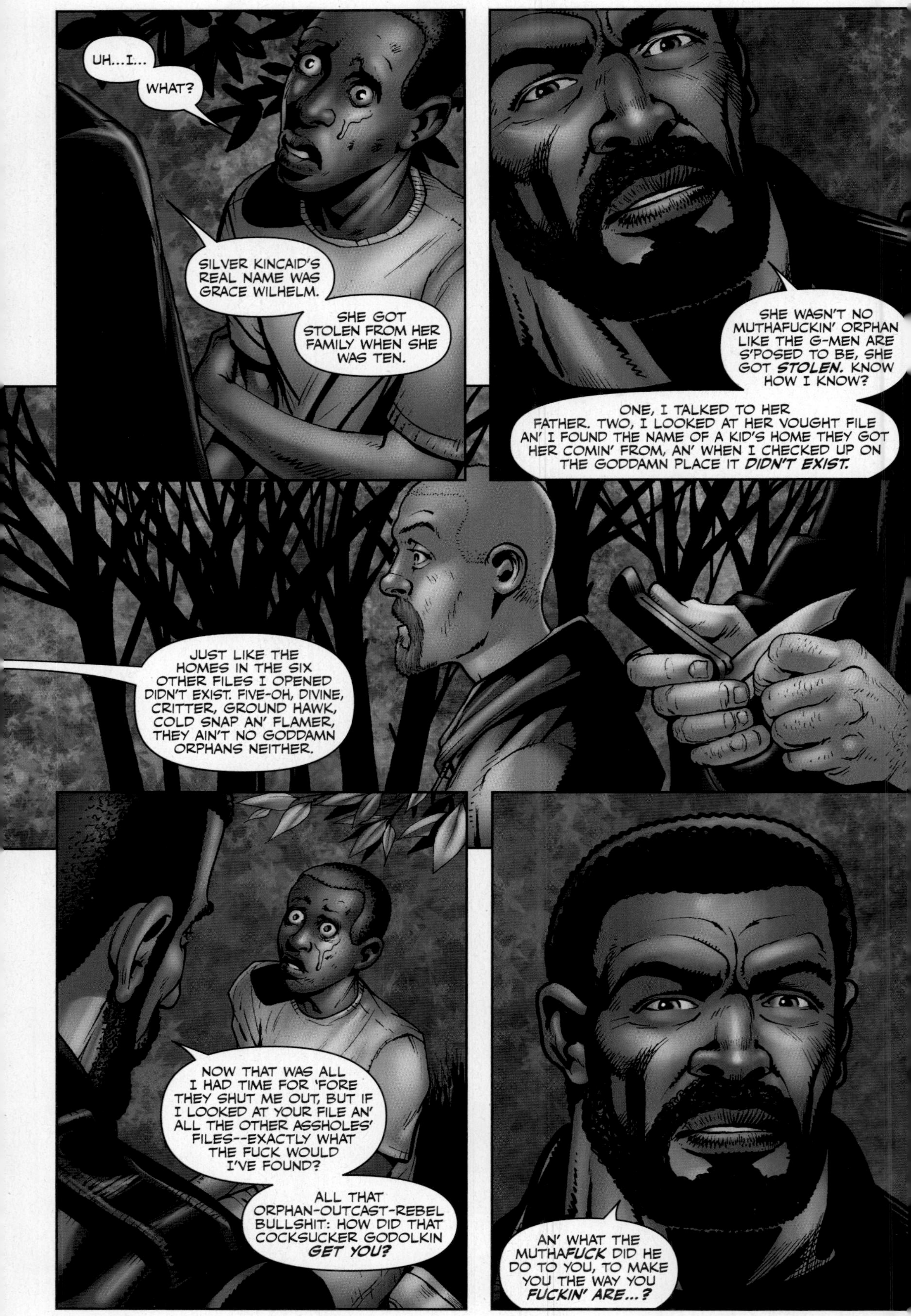
UH...I...
WHAT?
SILVER KINCAID'S REAL NAME WAS GRACE WILHELM.
SHE GOT STOLEN FROM HER FAMILY WHEN SHE WAS TEN.
SHE WASN'T NO MUTHAFUCKIN' ORPHAN LIKE THE G-MEN ARE S'POSED TO BE, SHE GOT STOLEN. KNOW HOW I KNOW?
ONE, I TALKED TO HER FATHER. TWO, I LOOKED AT HER VOUGHT FILE AN' I FOUND THE NAME OF A KID'S HOME THEY GOT HER COMIN' FROM, AN' WHEN I CHECKED UP ON THE GODDAMN PLACE IT DIDN'T EXIST.
JUST LIKE THE HOMES IN THE SIX OTHER FILES I OPENED DIDN'T EXIST. FIVE-OH, DIVINE, CRITTER, GROUND HAWK, COLD SNAP AN' FLAMER, THEY AIN'T NO GODDAMN ORPHANS NEITHER.
NOW THAT WAS ALL I HAD TIME FOR 'FORE THEY SHUT ME OUT, BUT IF I LOOKED AT YOUR FILE AN' ALL THE OTHER ASSHOLES' FILES--EXACTLY WHAT THE FUCK WOULD I'VE FOUND?
ALL THAT ORPHAN-OUTCAST-REBEL BULLSHIT: HOW DID THAT COCKSUCKER GODOLKIN GET YOU?
AN' WHAT THE MUTHAFUCK DID HE DO TO YOU, TO MAKE YOU THE WAY YOU FUCKIN' ARE...?

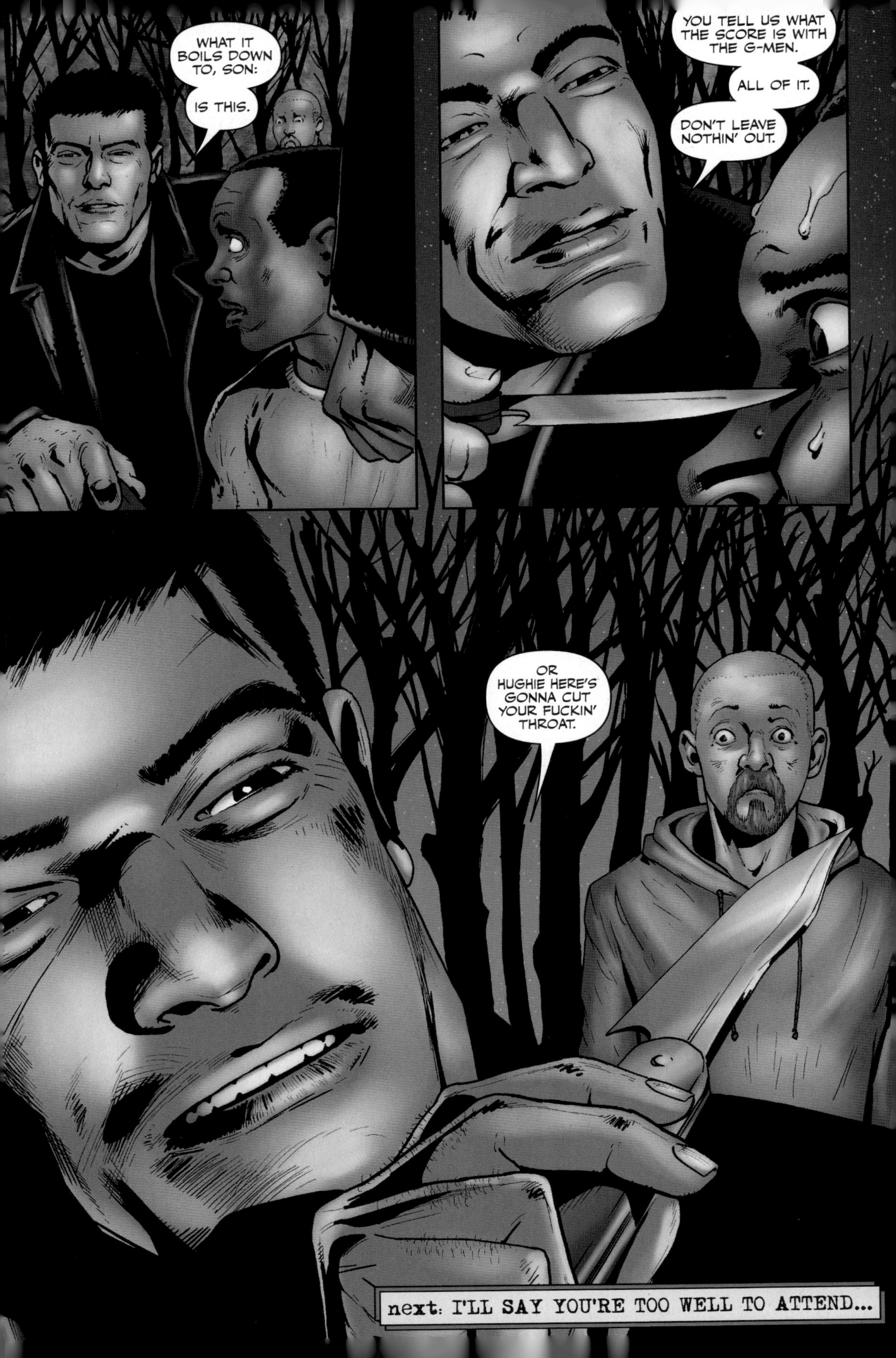
WHAT IT BOILS DOWN TO, SON:
IS THIS.
YOU TELL US WHAT THE SCORE IS WITH THE G-MEN.
ALL OF IT.
DON'T LEAVE NOTHIN' OUT.
OR HUGHIE HERE'S GONNA CUT YOUR FUCKIN' THROAT.
next: I'LL SAY YOU'RE TOO WELL TO ATTEND...

#29 cover
by Darick Robertson
and Tony Aviña

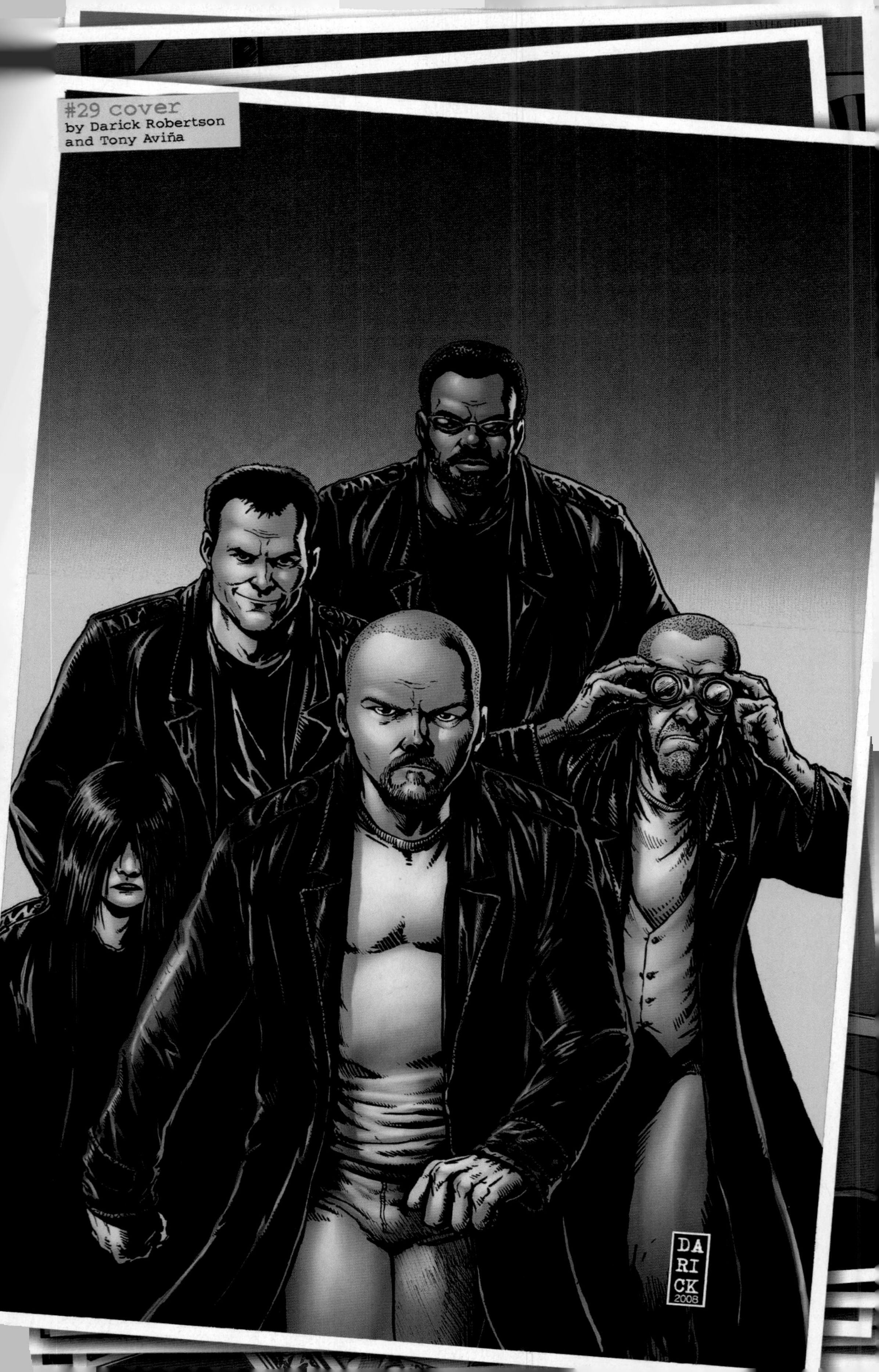
DA
RI
CK
2008

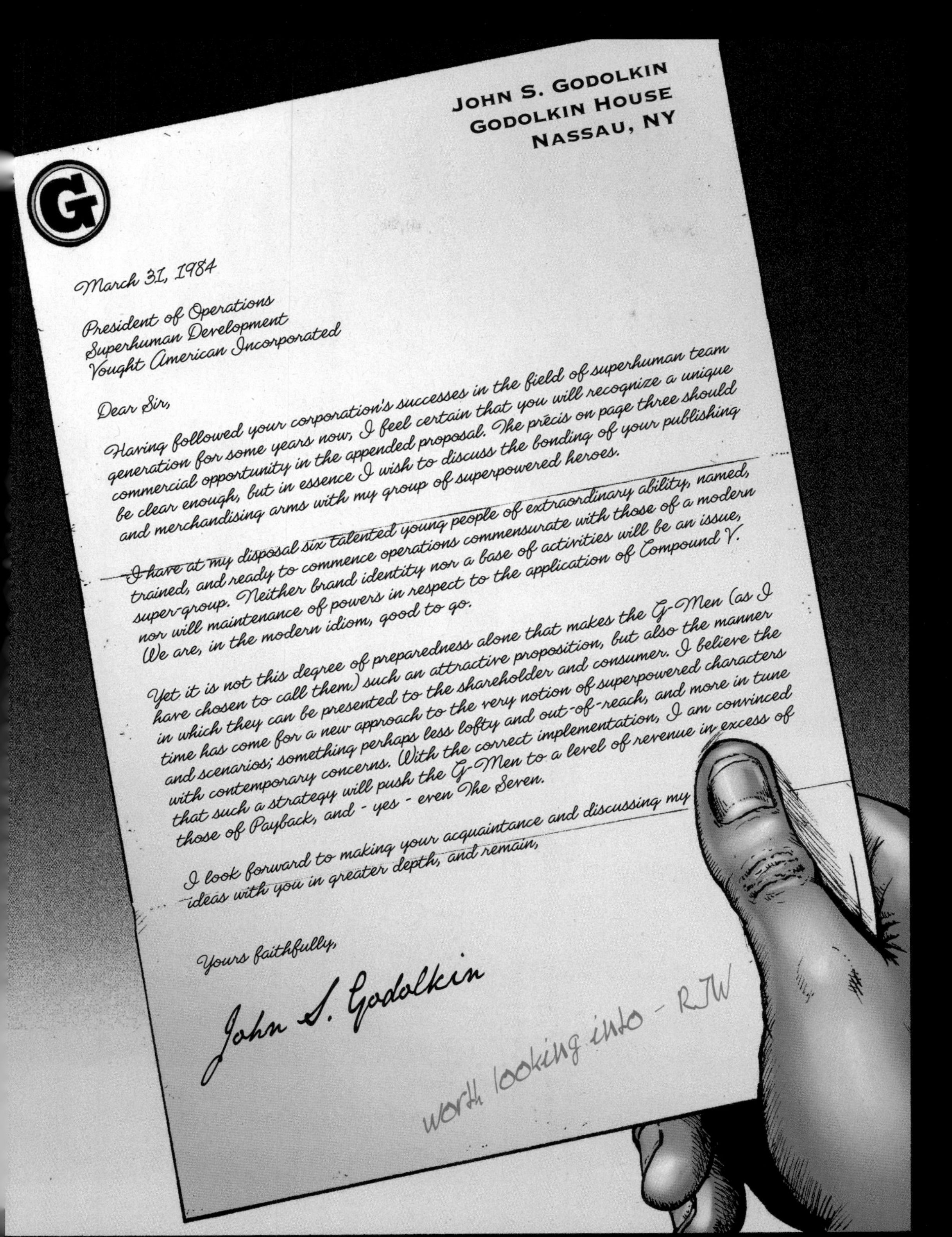

JOHN S. GODOLKIN
GODOLKIN HOUSE
NASSAU, NY

March 31, 1984

President of Operations
Superhuman Development
Vought American Incorporated

Dear Sir,

Having followed your corporation's successes in the field of superhuman team generation for some years now, I feel certain that you will recognize a unique commercial opportunity in the appended proposal. The précis on page three should be clear enough, but in essence I wish to discuss the bonding of your publishing and merchandising arms with my group of superpowered heroes.

I have at my disposal six talented young people of extraordinary ability, named, trained, and ready to commence operations commensurate with those of a modern super-group. Neither brand identity nor a base of activities will be an issue, nor will maintenance of powers in respect to the application of Compound V. We are, in the modern idiom, good to go.

Yet it is not this degree of preparedness alone that makes the G-Men (as I have chosen to call them) such an attractive proposition, but also the manner in which they can be presented to the shareholder and consumer. I believe the time has come for a new approach to the very notion of superpowered characters and scenarios; something perhaps less lofty and out-of-reach, and more in tune with contemporary concerns. With the correct implementation, I am convinced that such a strategy will push the G-Men to a level of revenue in excess of those of Payback, and - yes - even The Seven.

I look forward to making your acquaintance and discussing my ideas with you in greater depth, and remain,

Yours faithfully,

John S. Godolkin

worth looking into - RJW

WE GOTTA GO NOW

conclusion

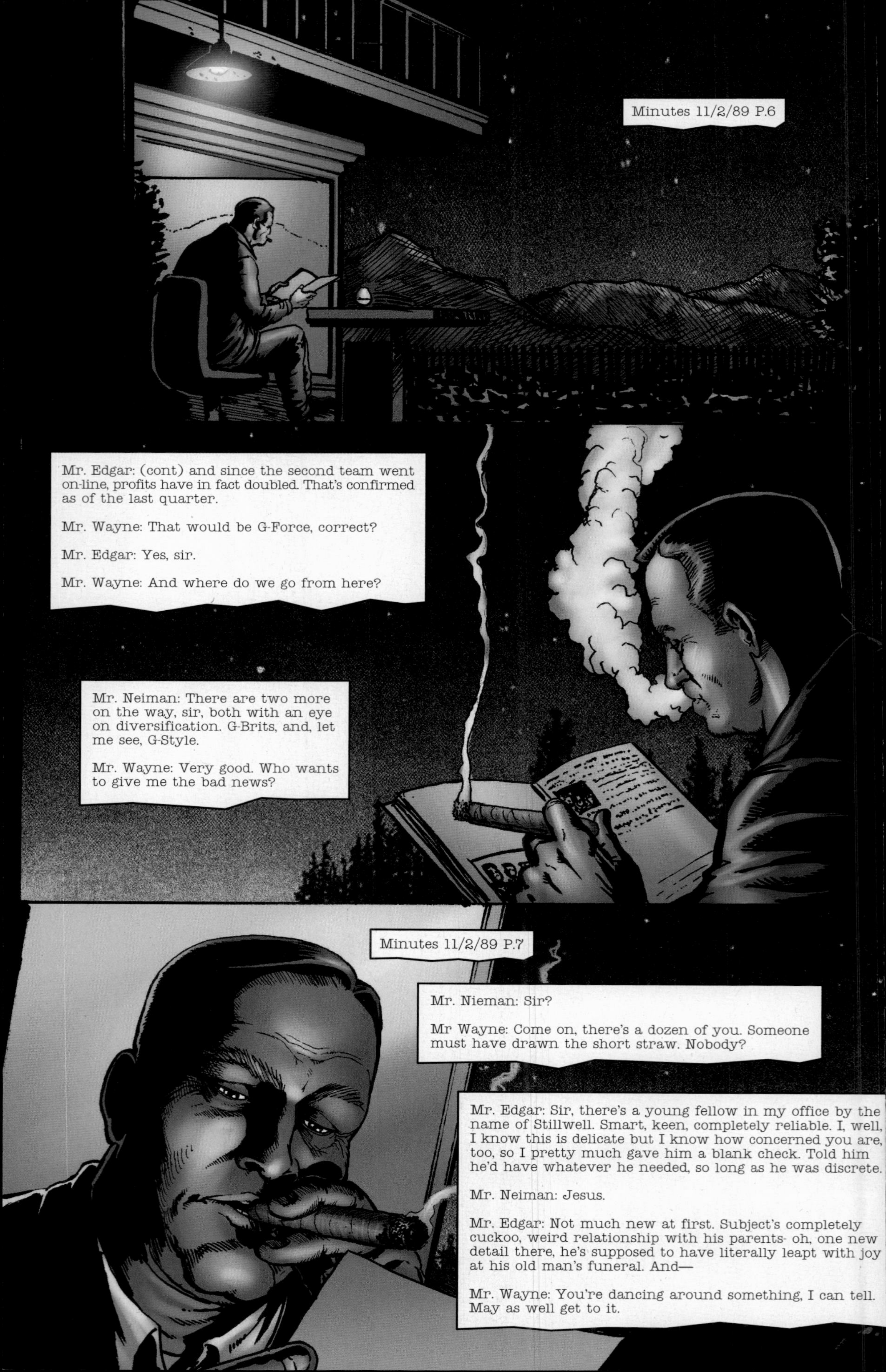
Minutes 11/2/89 P.6
Mr. Edgar: (cont) and since the second team went on-line, profits have in fact doubled. That's confirmed as of the last quarter.
Mr. Wayne: That would be G-Force, correct?
Mr. Edgar: Yes, sir.
Mr. Wayne: And where do we go from here?
Mr. Neiman: There are two more on the way, sir, both with an eye on diversification. G-Brits, and, let me see, G-Style.
Mr. Wayne: Very good. Who wants to give me the bad news?
Minutes 11/2/89 P.7
Mr. Nieman: Sir?
Mr Wayne: Come on, there's a dozen of you. Someone must have drawn the short straw. Nobody?
Mr. Edgar: Sir, there's a young fellow in my office by the name of Stillwell. Smart, keen, completely reliable. I, well, I know this is delicate but I know how concerned you are, too, so I pretty much gave him a blank check. Told him he'd have whatever he needed, so long as he was discrete.
Mr. Neiman: Jesus.
Mr. Edgar: Not much new at first. Subject's completely cuckoo, weird relationship with his parents- oh, one new detail there, he's supposed to have literally leapt with joy at his old man's funeral. And—
Mr. Wayne: You're dancing around something, I can tell. May as well get to it.

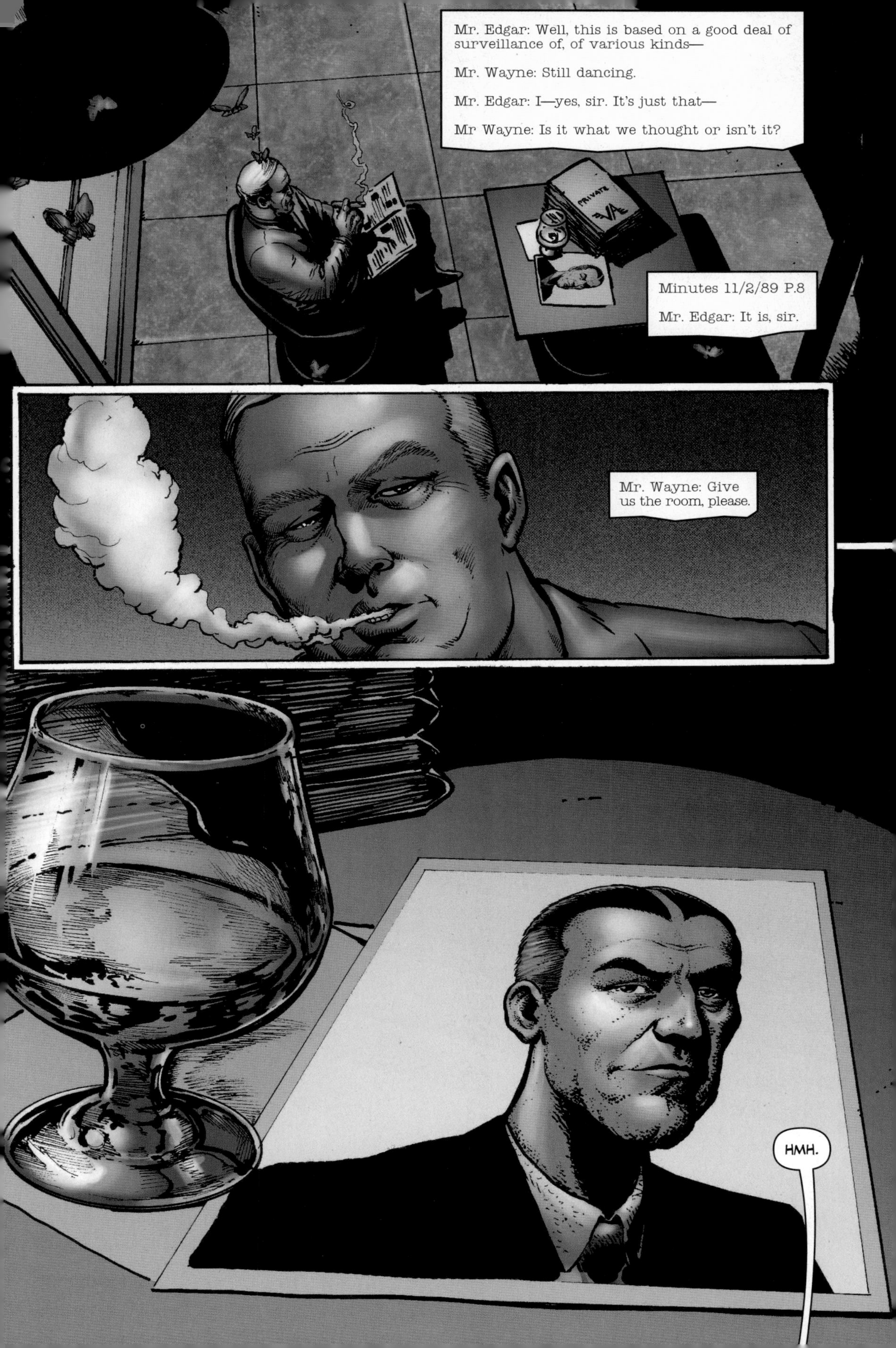
Mr. Edgar: Well, this is based on a good deal of surveillance of, of various kinds—
Mr. Wayne: Still dancing.
Mr. Edgar: I—yes, sir. It's just that—
Mr Wayne: Is it what we thought or isn't it?
PRIVATE
Minutes 11/2/89 P.8
Mr. Edgar: It is, sir.
Mr. Wayne: Give us the room, please.
HMH.

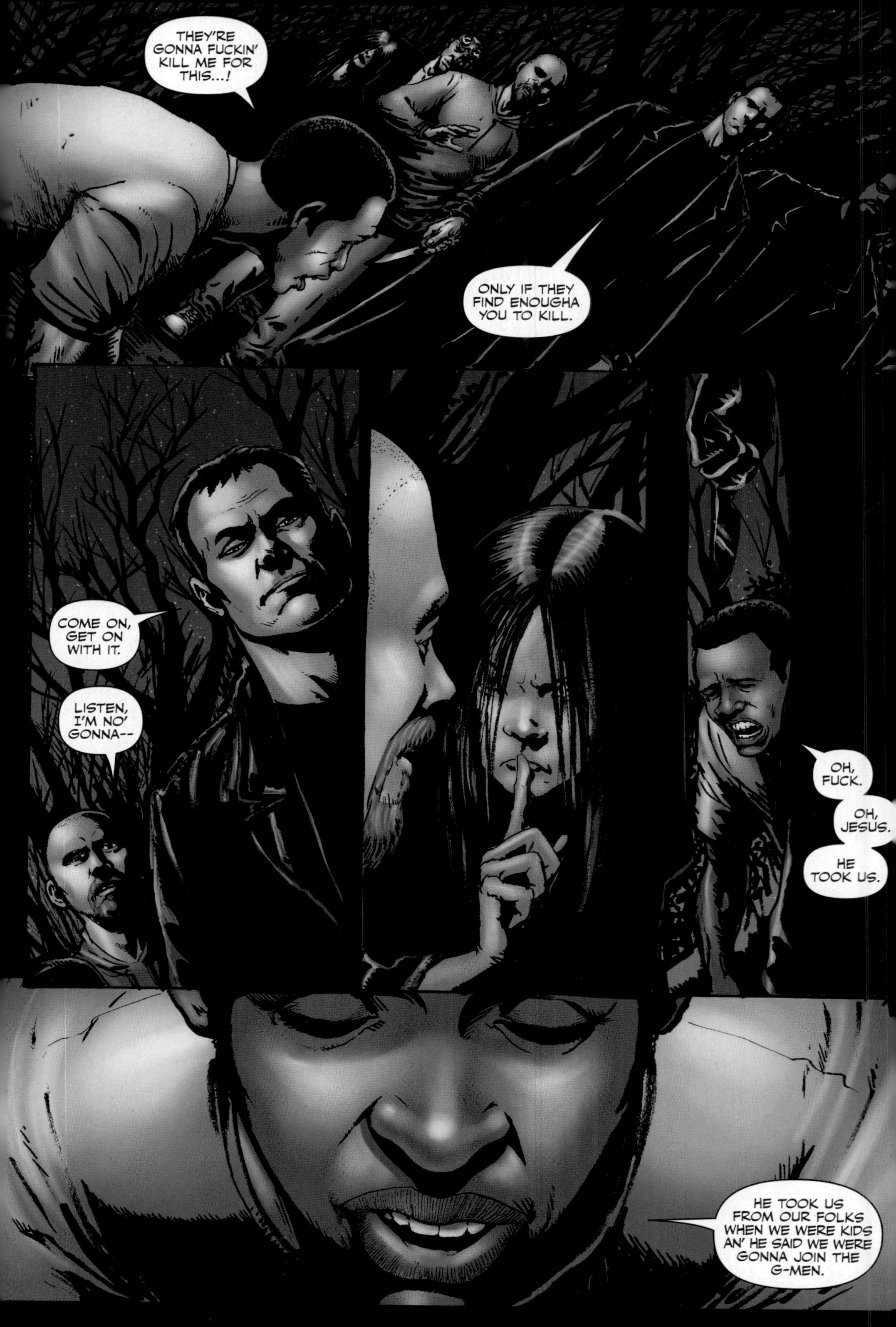
THEY'RE GONNA FUCKIN' KILL ME FOR THIS...!
ONLY IF THEY FIND ENOUGHA YOU TO KILL.
COME ON, GET ON WITH IT.
LISTEN, I'M NO' GONNA--
OH, FUCK.
OH, JESUS.
HE TOOK US.
HE TOOK US FROM OUR FOLKS WHEN WE WERE KIDS AN' HE SAID WE WERE GONNA JOIN THE G-MEN.

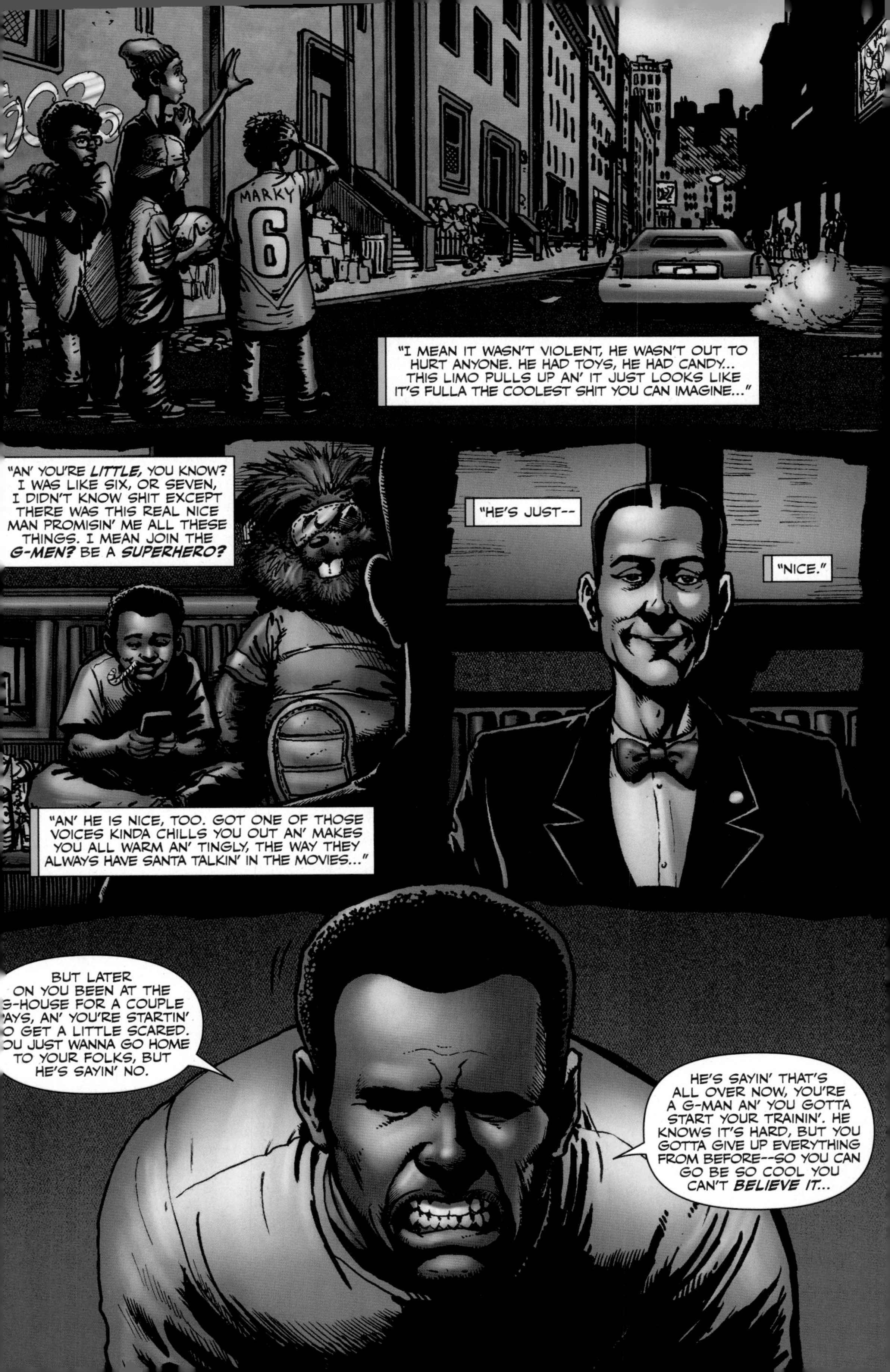

MARKY
6
"I MEAN IT WASN'T VIOLENT, HE WASN'T OUT TO HURT ANYONE. HE HAD TOYS, HE HAD CANDY... THIS LIMO PULLS UP AN' IT JUST LOOKS LIKE IT'S FULLA THE COOLEST SHIT YOU CAN IMAGINE..."
"AN' YOU'RE *LITTLE,* YOU KNOW? I WAS LIKE SIX, OR SEVEN, I DIDN'T KNOW SHIT EXCEPT THERE WAS THIS REAL NICE MAN PROMISIN' ME ALL THESE THINGS. I MEAN JOIN THE ***G-MEN?*** BE A ***SUPERHERO?***
"HE'S JUST--
"NICE."
"AN' HE IS NICE, TOO. GOT ONE OF THOSE VOICES KINDA CHILLS YOU OUT AN' MAKES YOU ALL WARM AN' TINGLY, THE WAY THEY ALWAYS HAVE SANTA TALKIN' IN THE MOVIES..."
BUT LATER ON YOU BEEN AT THE G-HOUSE FOR A COUPLE DAYS, AN' YOU'RE STARTIN' TO GET A LITTLE SCARED. YOU JUST WANNA GO HOME TO YOUR FOLKS, BUT HE'S SAYIN' NO.
HE'S SAYIN' THAT'S ALL OVER NOW, YOU'RE A G-MAN AN' YOU GOTTA START YOUR TRAININ'. HE KNOWS IT'S HARD, BUT YOU GOTTA GIVE UP EVERYTHING FROM BEFORE--SO YOU CAN GO BE SO COOL YOU CAN'T ***BELIEVE IT...***

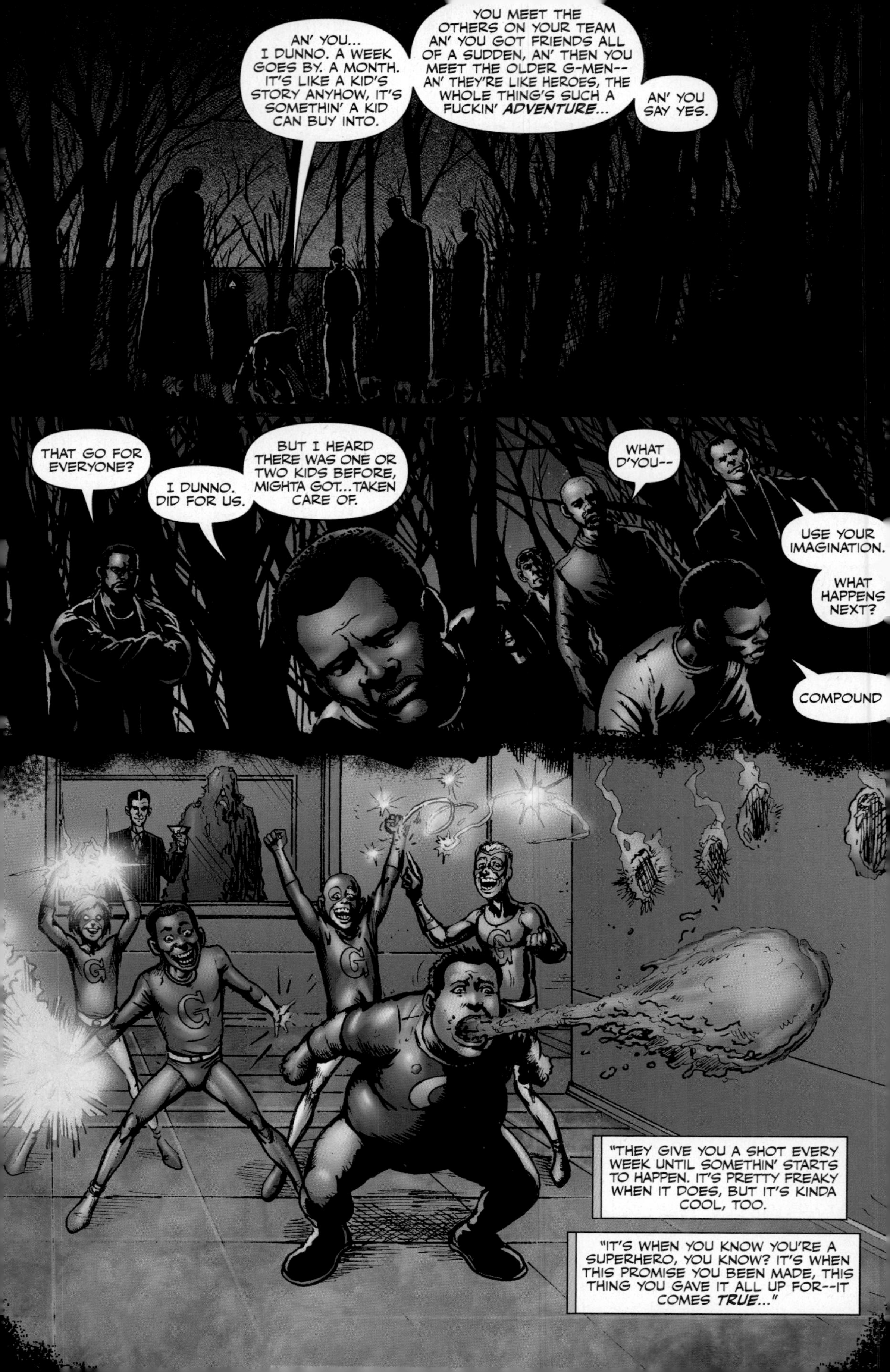
AN' YOU... I DUNNO. A WEEK GOES BY. A MONTH. IT'S LIKE A KID'S STORY ANYHOW, IT'S SOMETHIN' A KID CAN BUY INTO.
YOU MEET THE OTHERS ON YOUR TEAM AN' YOU GOT FRIENDS ALL OF A SUDDEN, AN' THEN YOU MEET THE OLDER G-MEN-- AN' THEY'RE LIKE HEROES, THE WHOLE THING'S SUCH A FUCKIN' *ADVENTURE*...
AN' YOU SAY YES.
THAT GO FOR EVERYONE?
I DUNNO. DID FOR US.
BUT I HEARD THERE WAS ONE OR TWO KIDS BEFORE, MIGHTA GOT...TAKEN CARE OF.
WHAT D'YOU--
USE YOUR IMAGINATION.
WHAT HAPPENS NEXT?
COMPOUND
"THEY GIVE YOU A SHOT EVERY WEEK UNTIL SOMETHIN' STARTS TO HAPPEN. IT'S PRETTY FREAKY WHEN IT DOES, BUT IT'S KINDA COOL, TOO.
"IT'S WHEN YOU KNOW YOU'RE A SUPERHERO, YOU KNOW? IT'S WHEN THIS PROMISE YOU BEEN MADE, THIS THING YOU GAVE IT ALL UP FOR--IT COMES *TRUE*..."

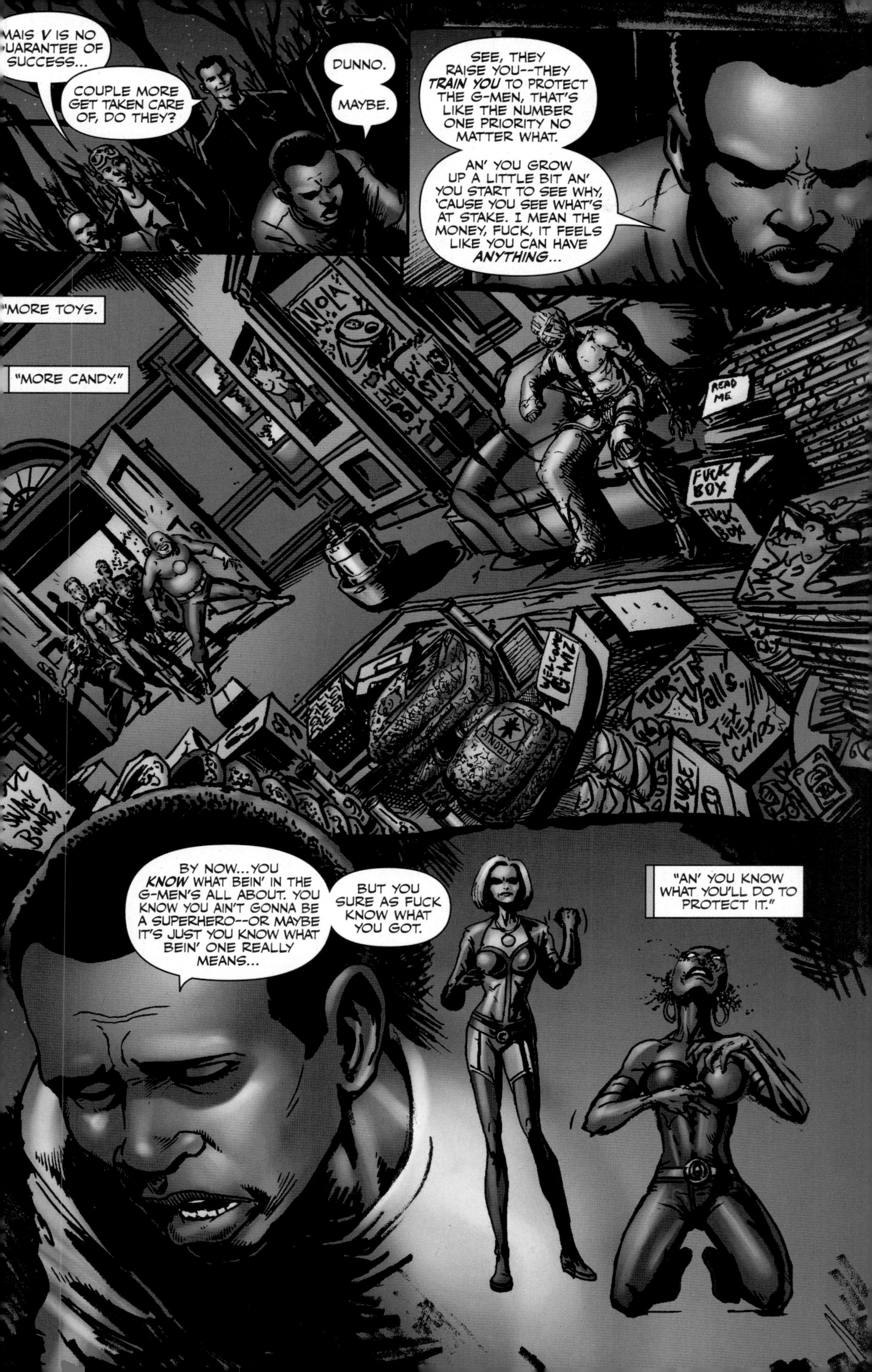
MAIS V IS NO
UARANTEE OF SUCCESS...
COUPLE MORE GET TAKEN CARE OF, DO THEY?
DUNNO.
MAYBE.
SEE, THEY RAISE YOU--THEY TRAIN YOU TO PROTECT THE G-MEN, THAT'S LIKE THE NUMBER ONE PRIORITY NO MATTER WHAT.
AN' YOU GROW UP A LITTLE BIT AN' YOU START TO SEE WHY, 'CAUSE YOU SEE WHAT'S AT STAKE. I MEAN THE MONEY, FUCK, IT FEELS LIKE YOU CAN HAVE ANYTHING...
"MORE TOYS.
"MORE CANDY."
READ ME
FUCK BOX
FUCK BOX
WELCOME G-WIZ
KRONIC
TOR-TI
Y'all's TEX MEX CHIPS
LUBE
SMACK BOMB!
BY NOW...YOU KNOW WHAT BEIN' IN THE G-MEN'S ALL ABOUT. YOU KNOW YOU AIN'T GONNA BE A SUPERHERO--OR MAYBE IT'S JUST YOU KNOW WHAT BEIN' ONE REALLY MEANS...
BUT YOU SURE AS FUCK KNOW WHAT YOU GOT.
"AN' YOU KNOW WHAT YOU'LL DO TO PROTECT IT."

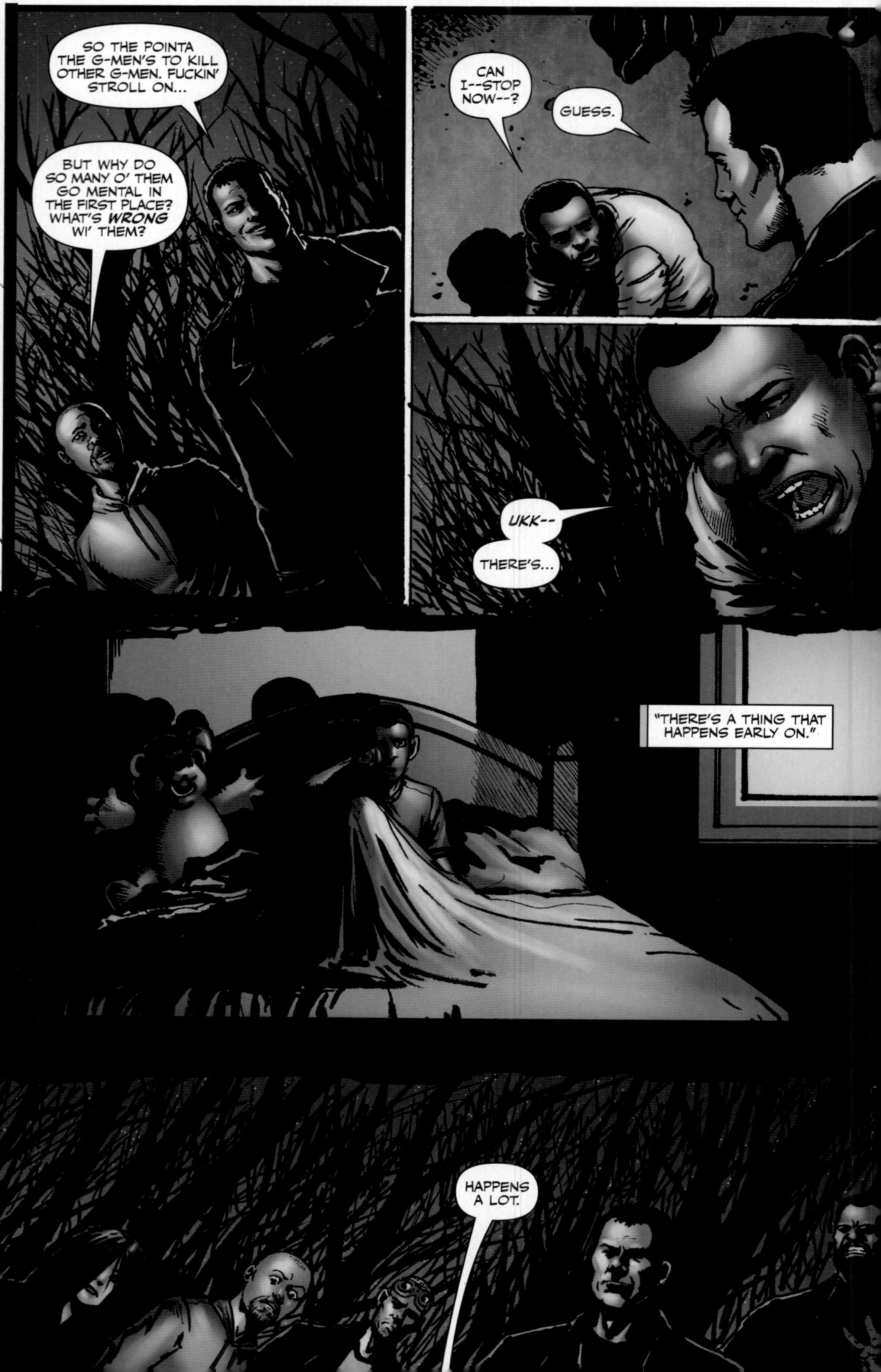

SO THE POINTA THE G-MEN'S TO KILL OTHER G-MEN. FUCKIN' STROLL ON...
BUT WHY DO SO MANY O' THEM GO MENTAL IN THE FIRST PLACE? WHAT'S *WRONG* WI' THEM?
CAN I--STOP NOW--?
GUESS.
UKK--
THERE'S...
"THERE'S A THING THAT HAPPENS EARLY ON."
HAPPENS A LOT.

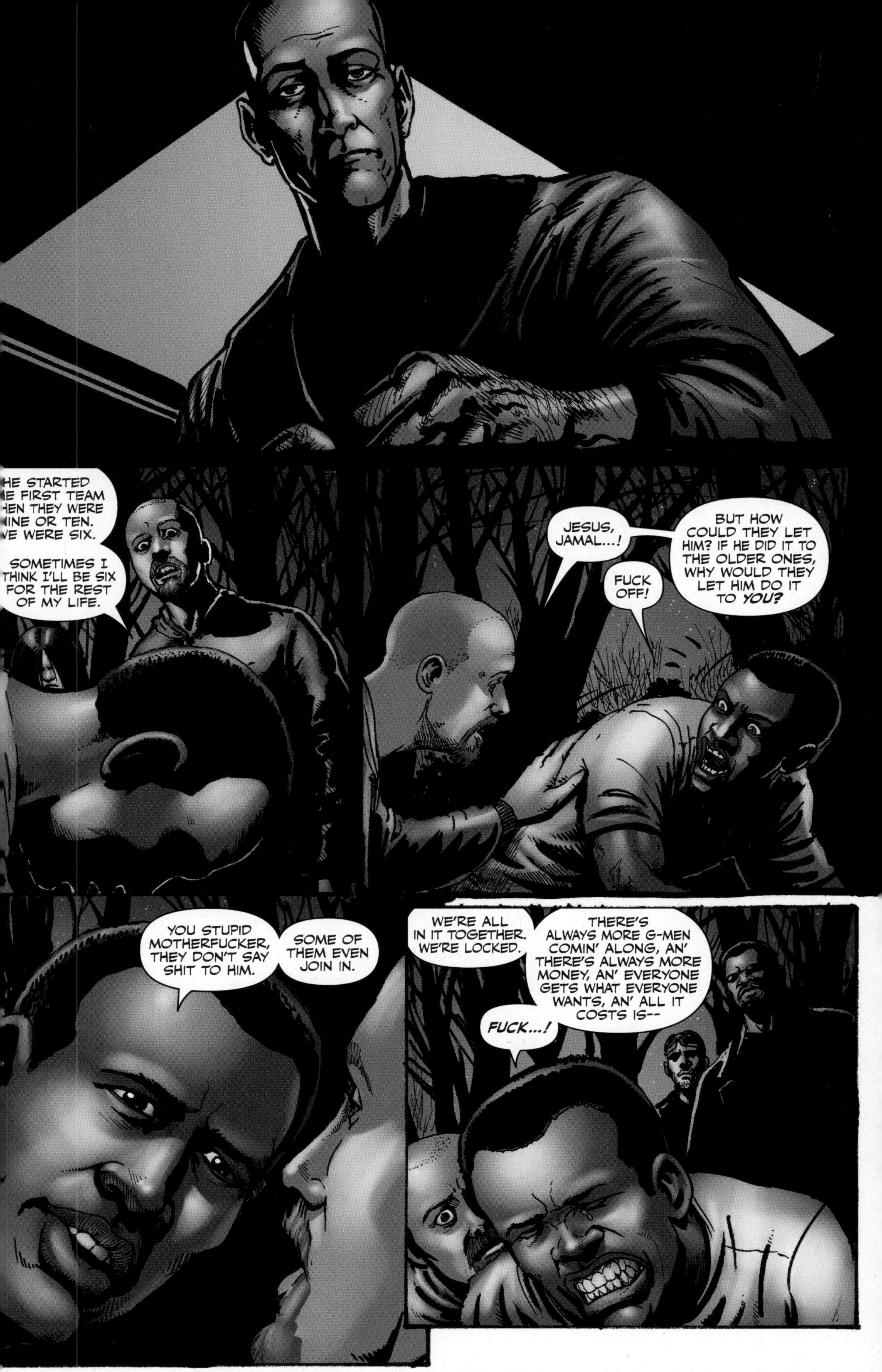
HE STARTED
E FIRST TEAM
HEN THEY WERE
NINE OR TEN.
VE WERE SIX.
SOMETIMES I THINK I'LL BE SIX FOR THE REST OF MY LIFE.
JESUS, JAMAL...!
BUT HOW COULD THEY LET HIM? IF HE DID IT TO THE OLDER ONES, WHY WOULD THEY LET HIM DO IT TO *YOU?*
FUCK OFF!
YOU STUPID MOTHERFUCKER, THEY DON'T SAY SHIT TO HIM.
SOME OF THEM EVEN JOIN IN.
WE'RE ALL IN IT TOGETHER. WE'RE LOCKED.
THERE'S ALWAYS MORE G-MEN COMIN' ALONG, AN' THERE'S ALWAYS MORE MONEY, AN' EVERYONE GETS WHAT EVERYONE WANTS, AN' ALL IT COSTS IS--
FUCK...!

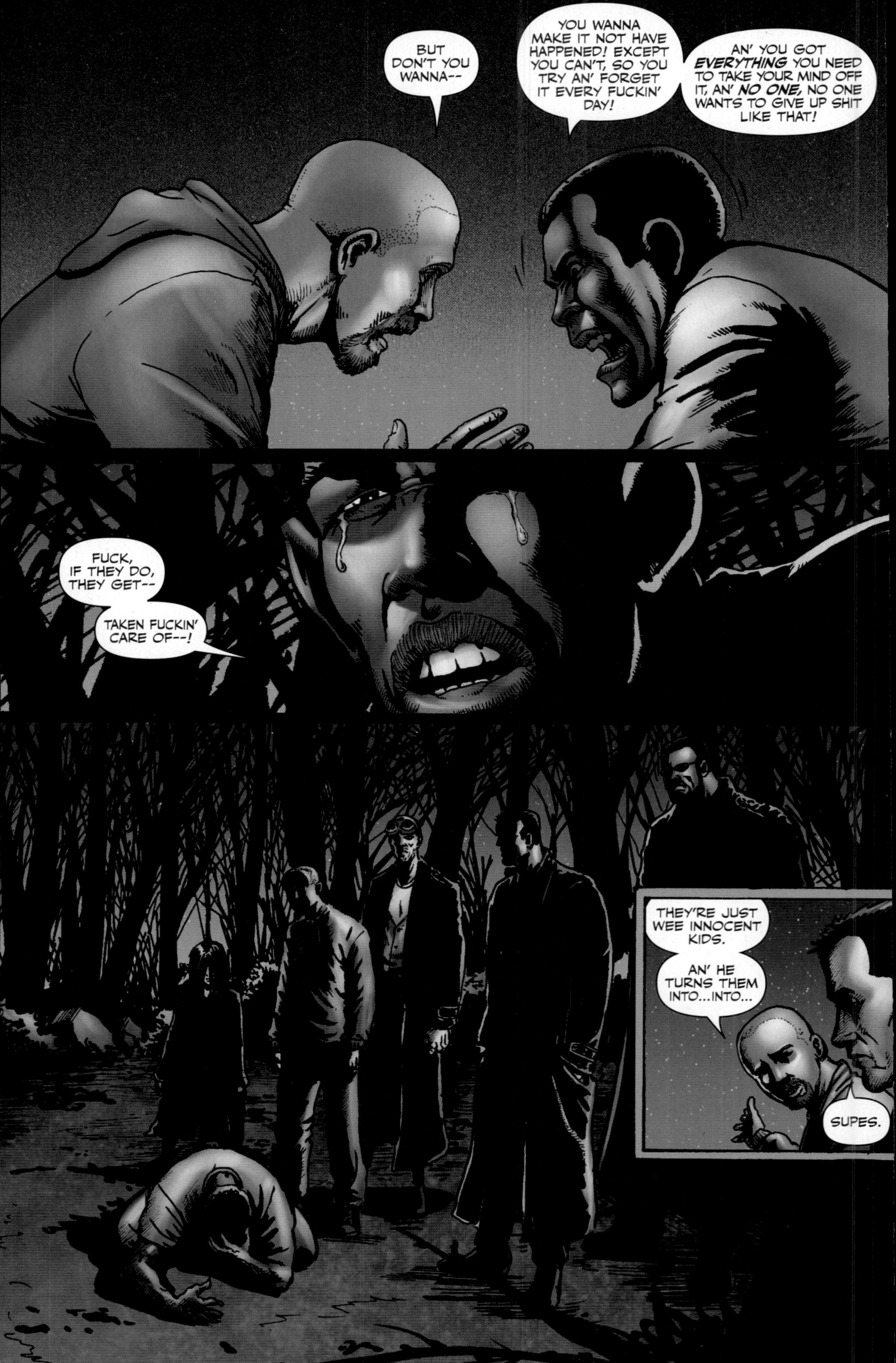
BUT DON'T YOU WANNA--
YOU WANNA MAKE IT NOT HAVE HAPPENED! EXCEPT YOU CAN'T, SO YOU TRY AN' FORGET IT EVERY FUCKIN' DAY!
AN' YOU GOT EVERYTHING YOU NEED TO TAKE YOUR MIND OFF IT, AN' NO ONE, NO ONE WANTS TO GIVE UP SHIT LIKE THAT!
FUCK, IF THEY DO, THEY GET--
TAKEN FUCKIN' CARE OF--!
THEY'RE JUST WEE INNOCENT KIDS.
AN' HE TURNS THEM INTO...INTO...
SUPES.

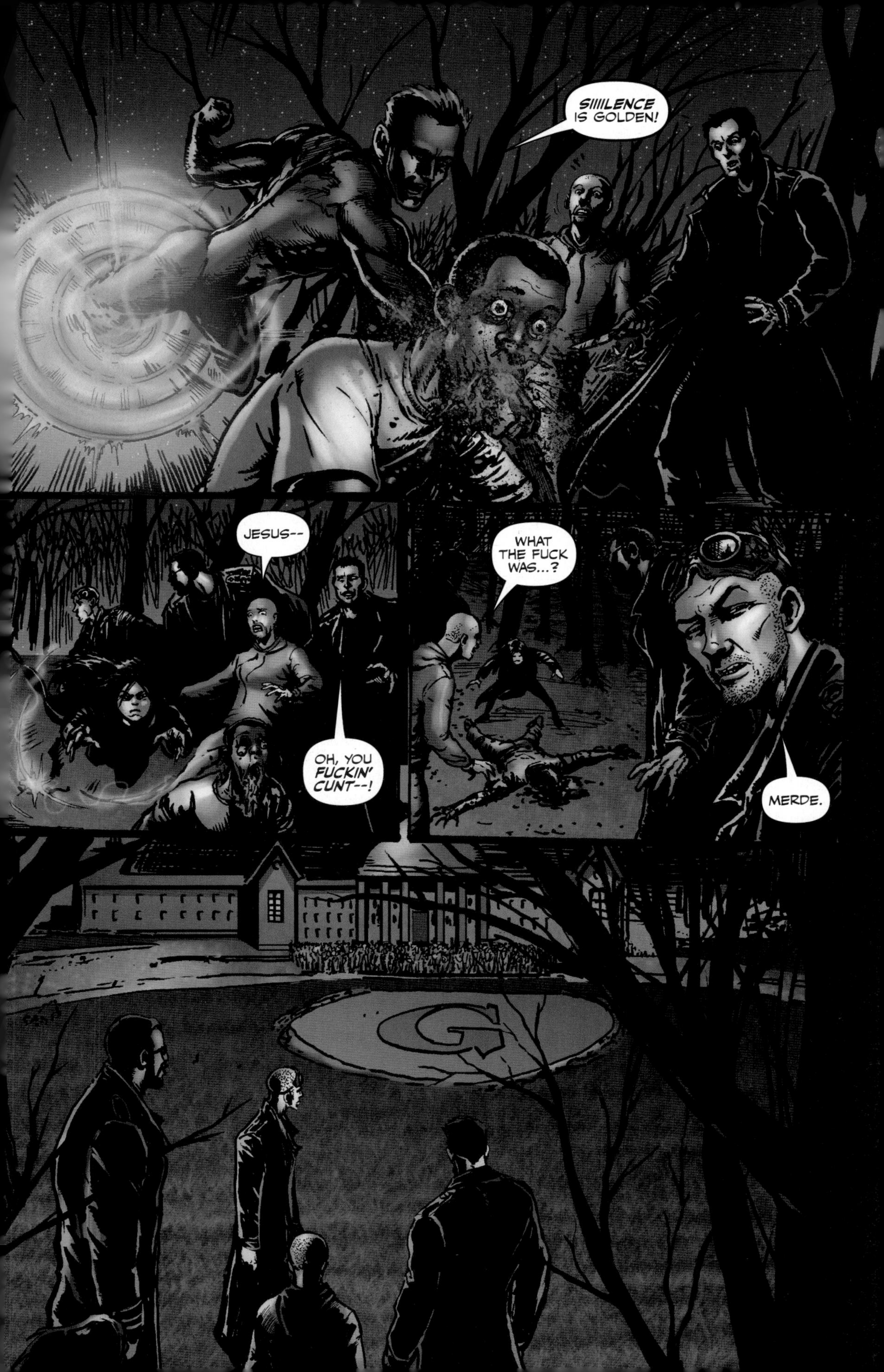
SIIIILENCE IS GOLDEN!
JESUS--
OH, YOU FUCKIN' CUNT--!
WHAT THE FUCK WAS...?
MERDE.

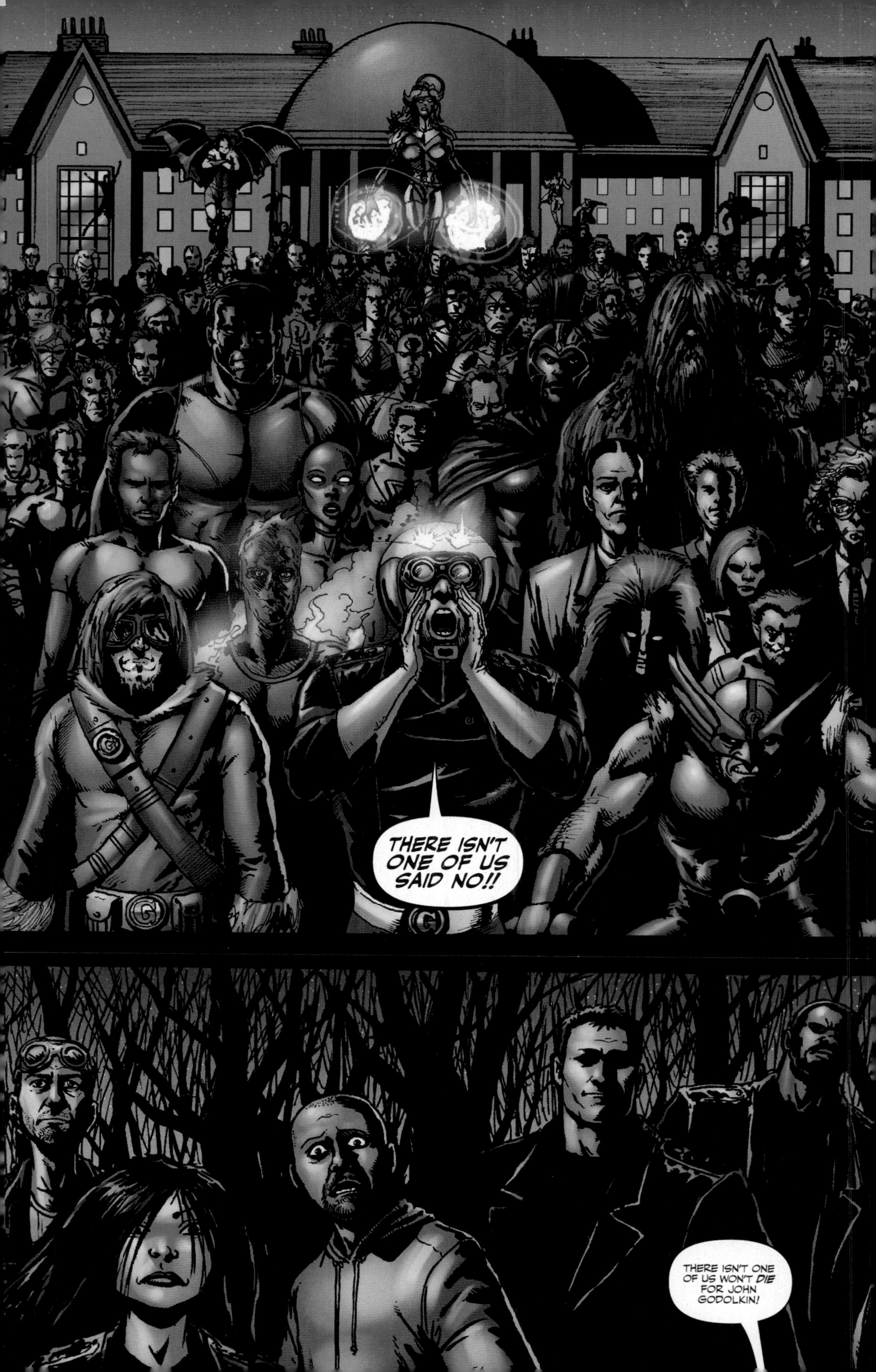
THERE ISN'T ONE OF US SAID NO!!
THERE ISN'T ONE OF US WON'T *DIE* FOR JOHN GODOLKIN!

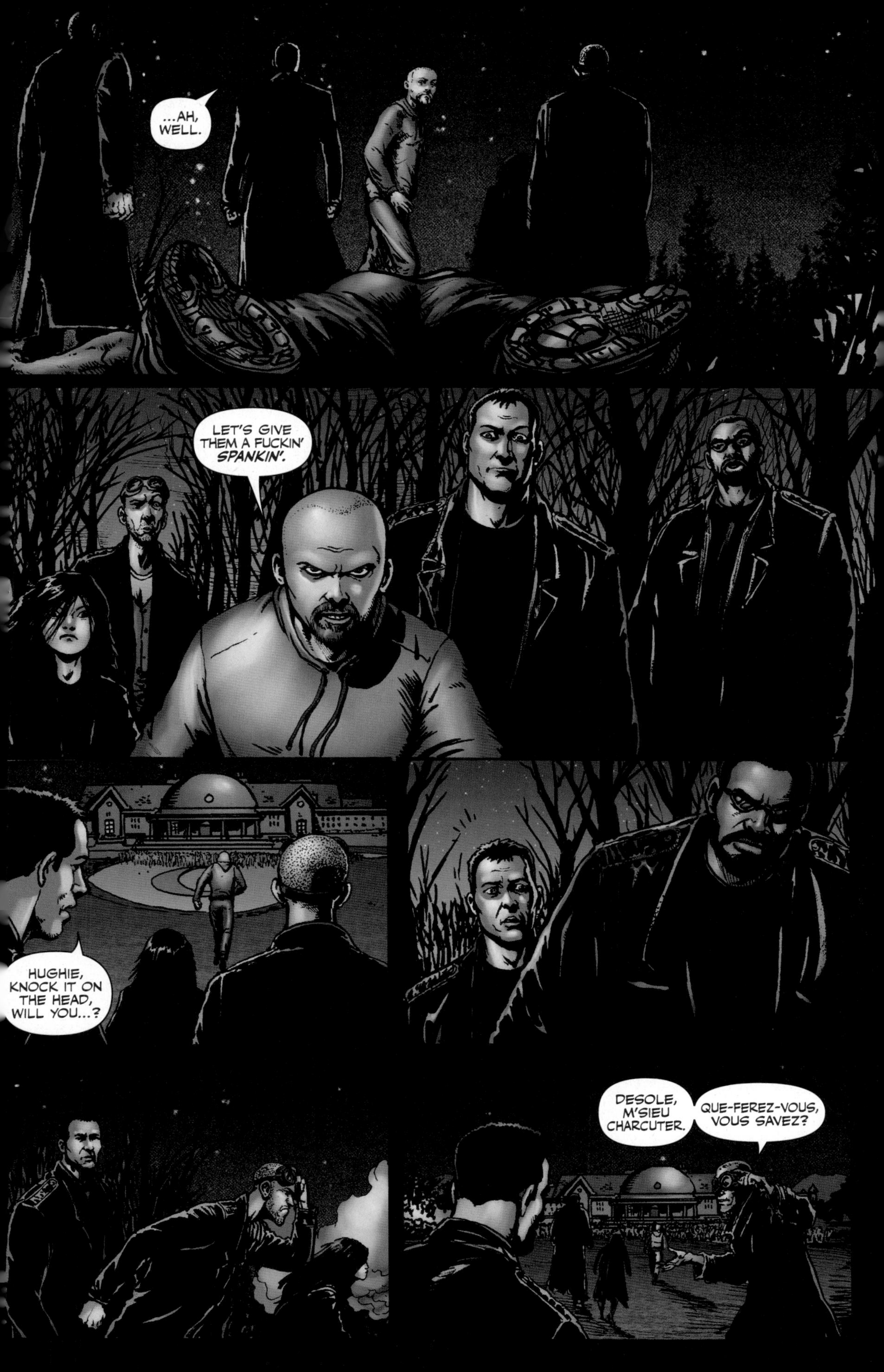
...AH, WELL.
LET'S GIVE THEM A FUCKIN' SPANKIN'.
HUGHIE, KNOCK IT ON THE HEAD, WILL YOU...?
DESOLE, M'SIEU CHARCUTER.
QUE-FEREZ-VOUS, VOUS SAVEZ?

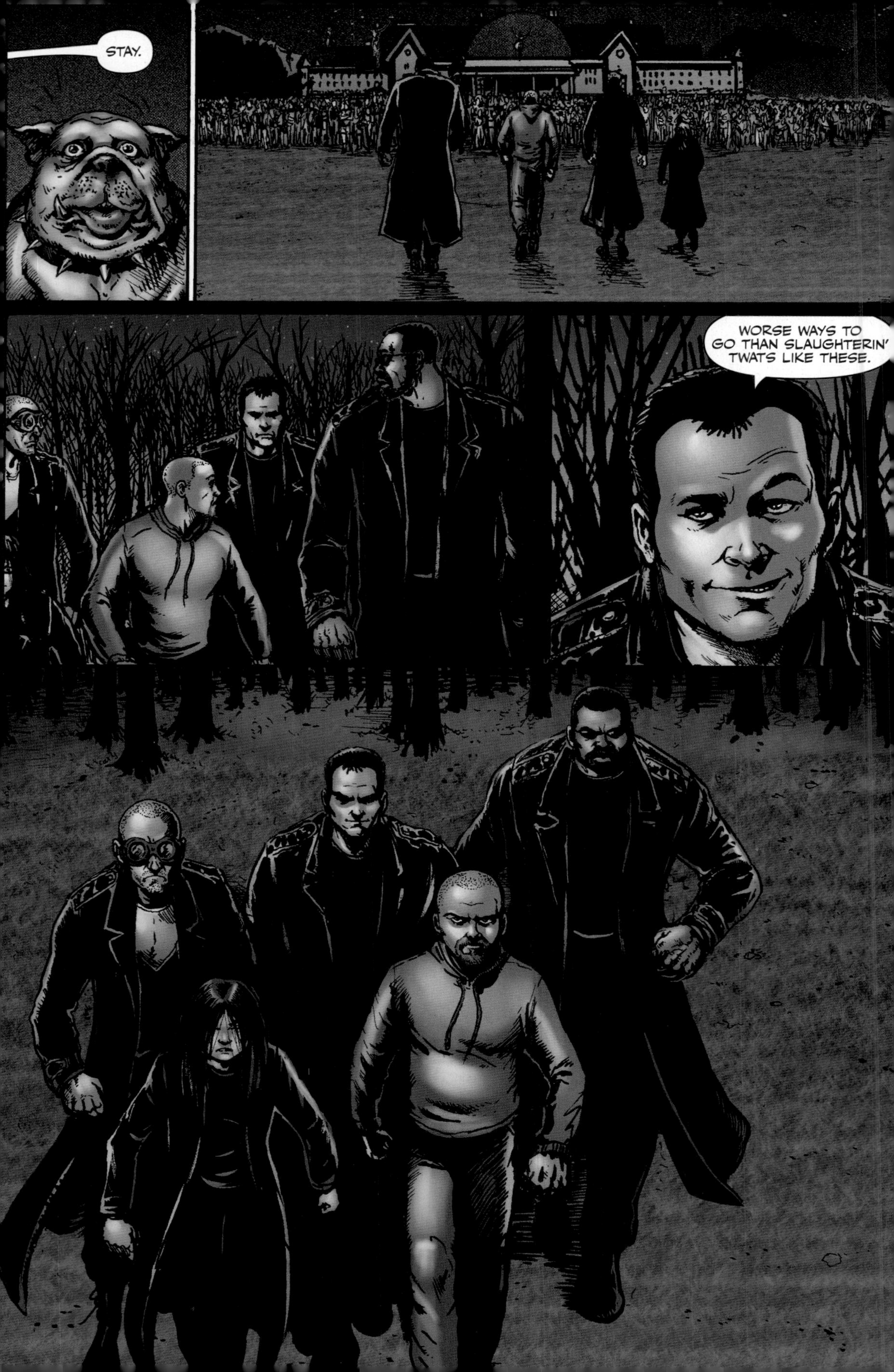
STAY.
WORSE WAYS TO GO THAN SLAUGHTERIN' TWATS LIKE THESE.

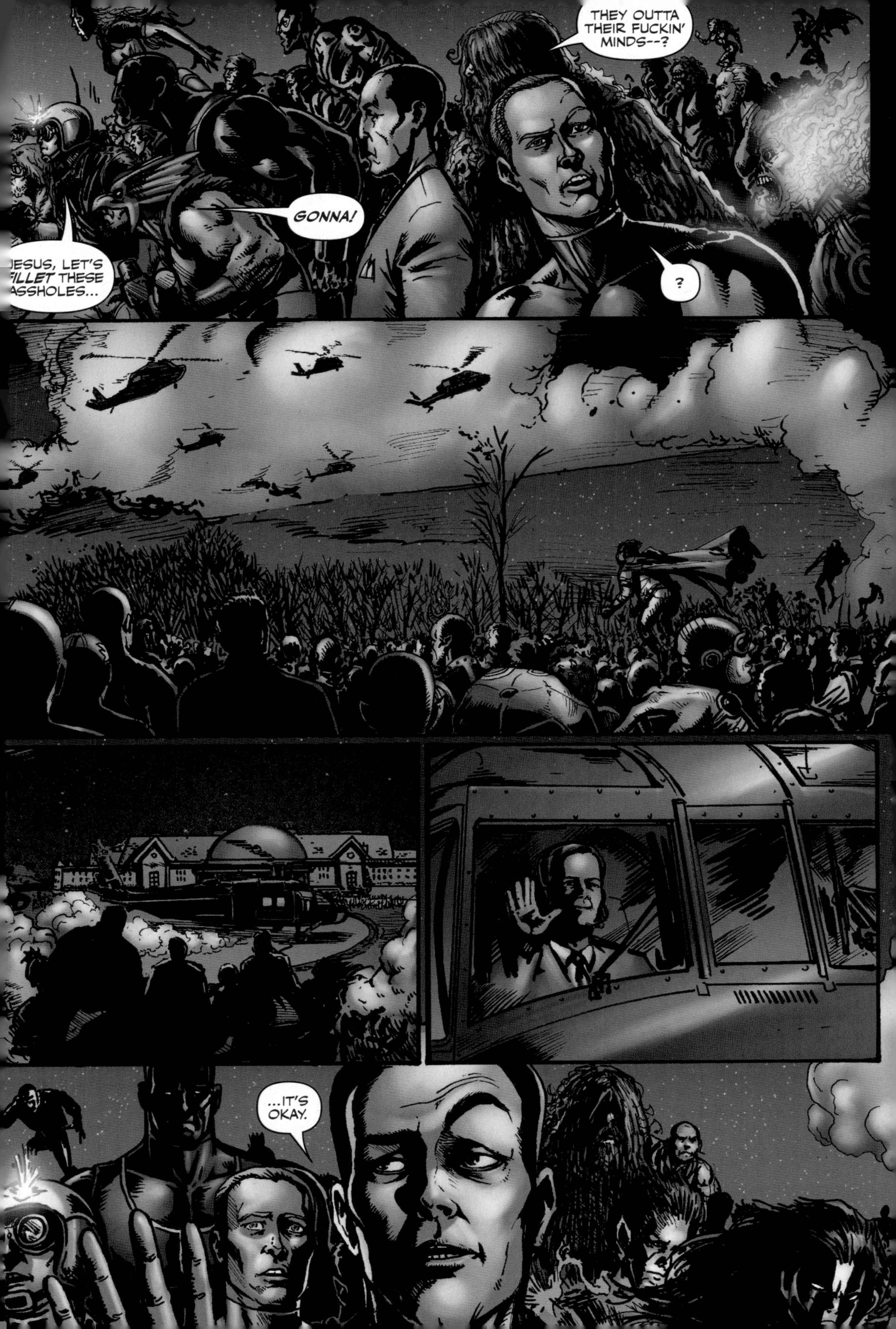
THEY OUTTA THEIR FUCKIN' MINDS--?
JESUS, LET'S FILLET THESE ASSHOLES...
GONNA!
?
...IT'S OKAY.

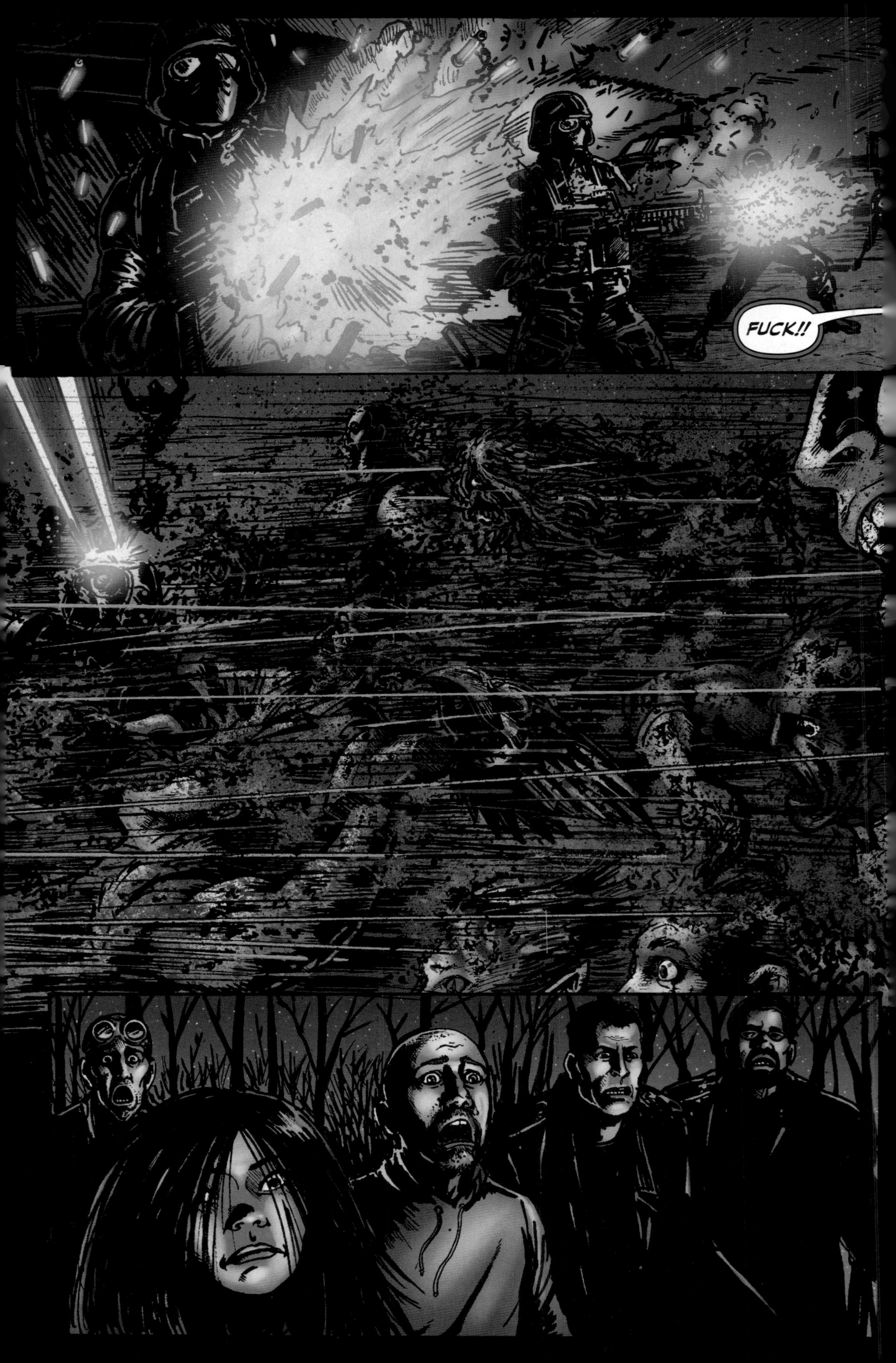
FUCK!!

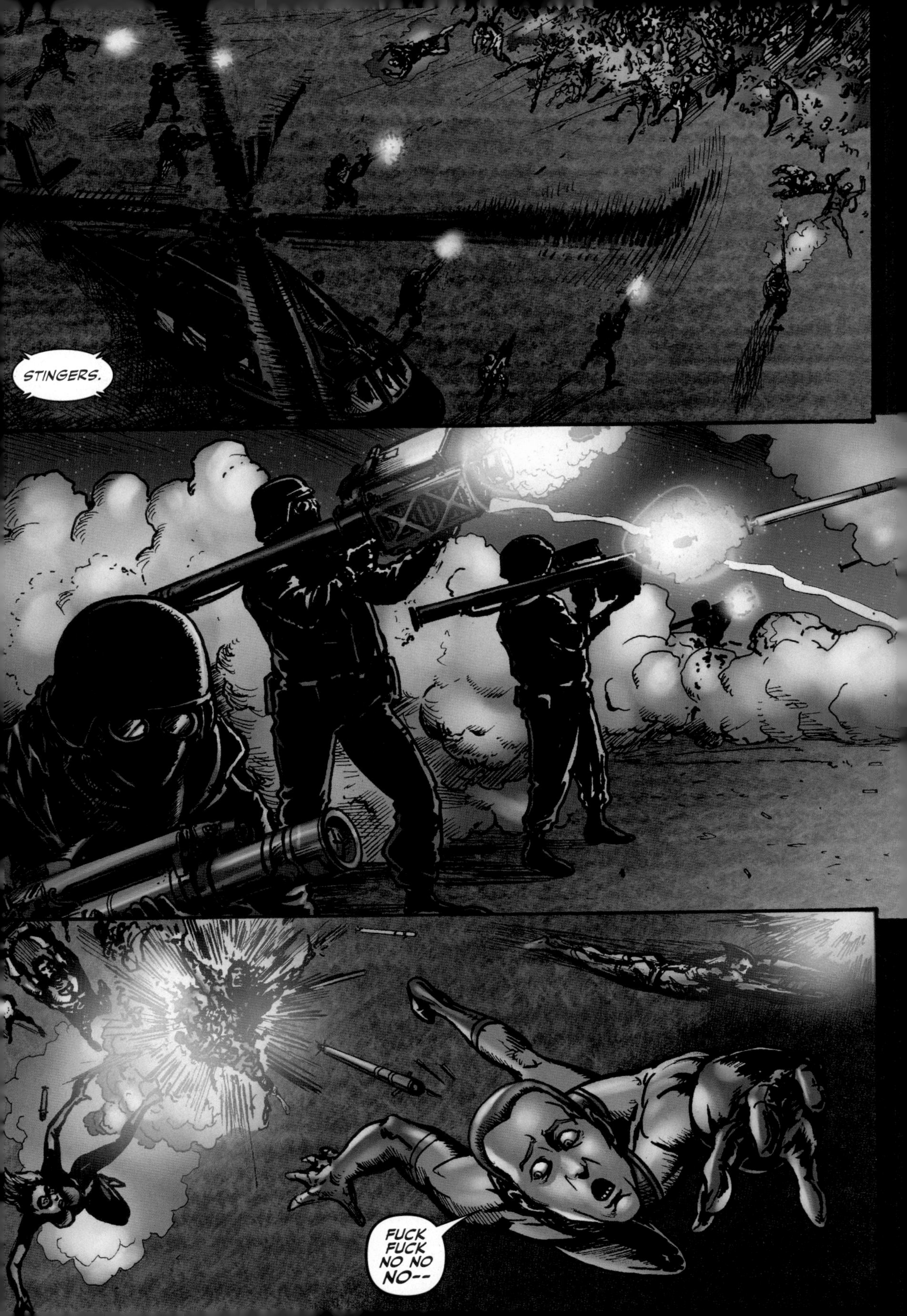
STINGERS.
FUCK FUCK NO NO NO--

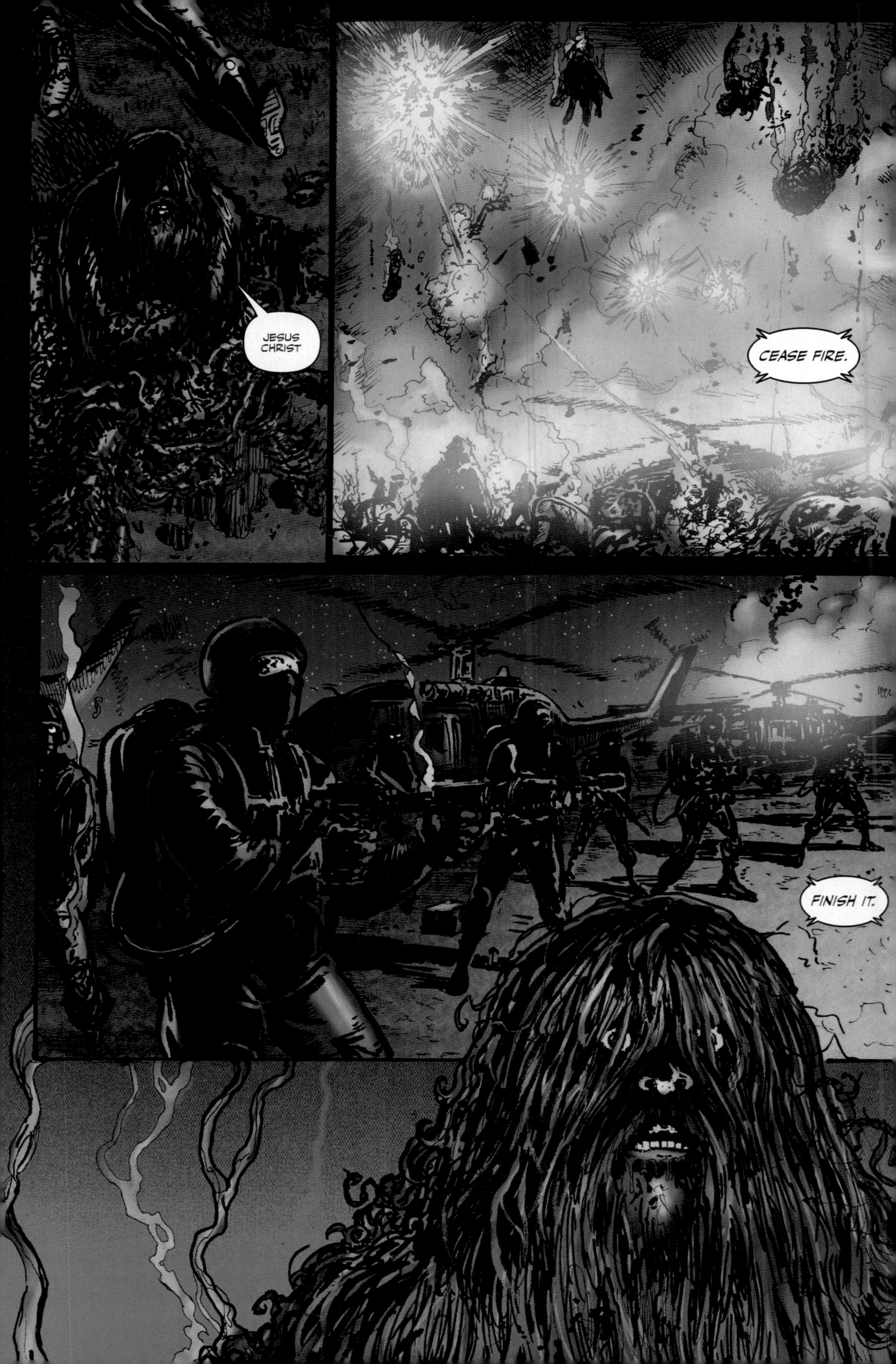
JESUS CHRIST
CEASE FIRE.
FINISH IT.

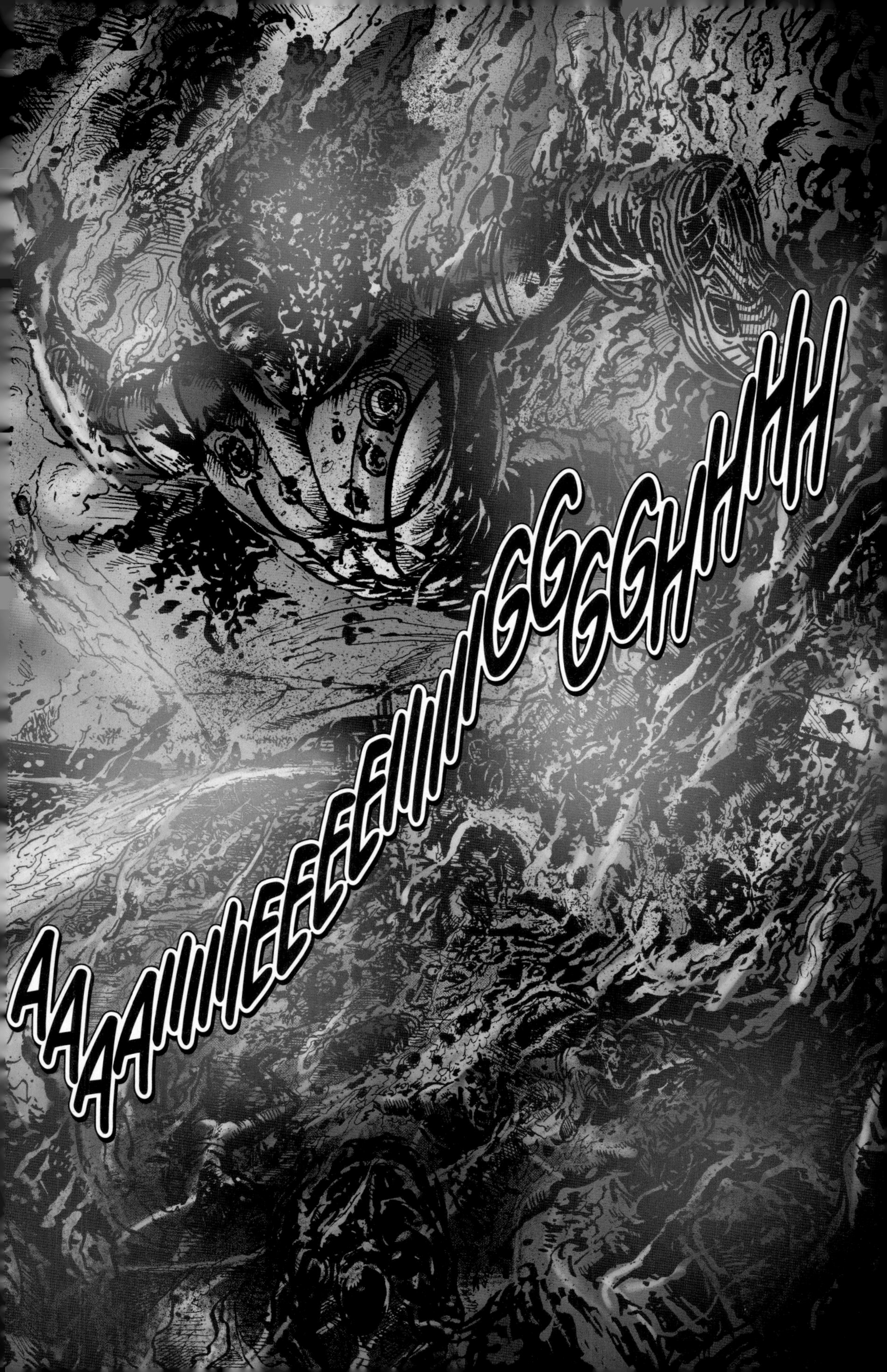
AAAAIIIIIIEEEEIIIIIGGGHHHH

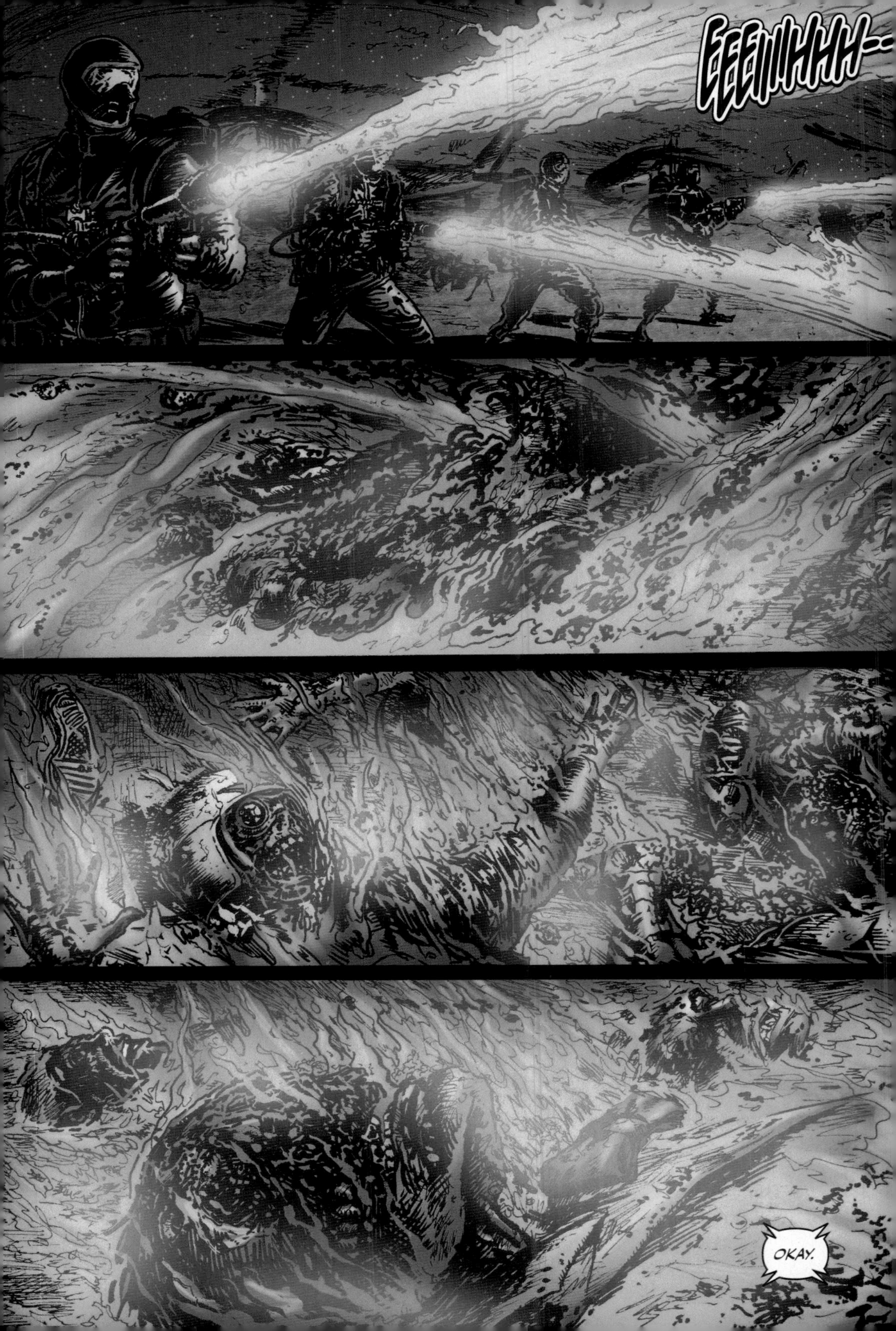
EEEIIIHHH--
OKAY.

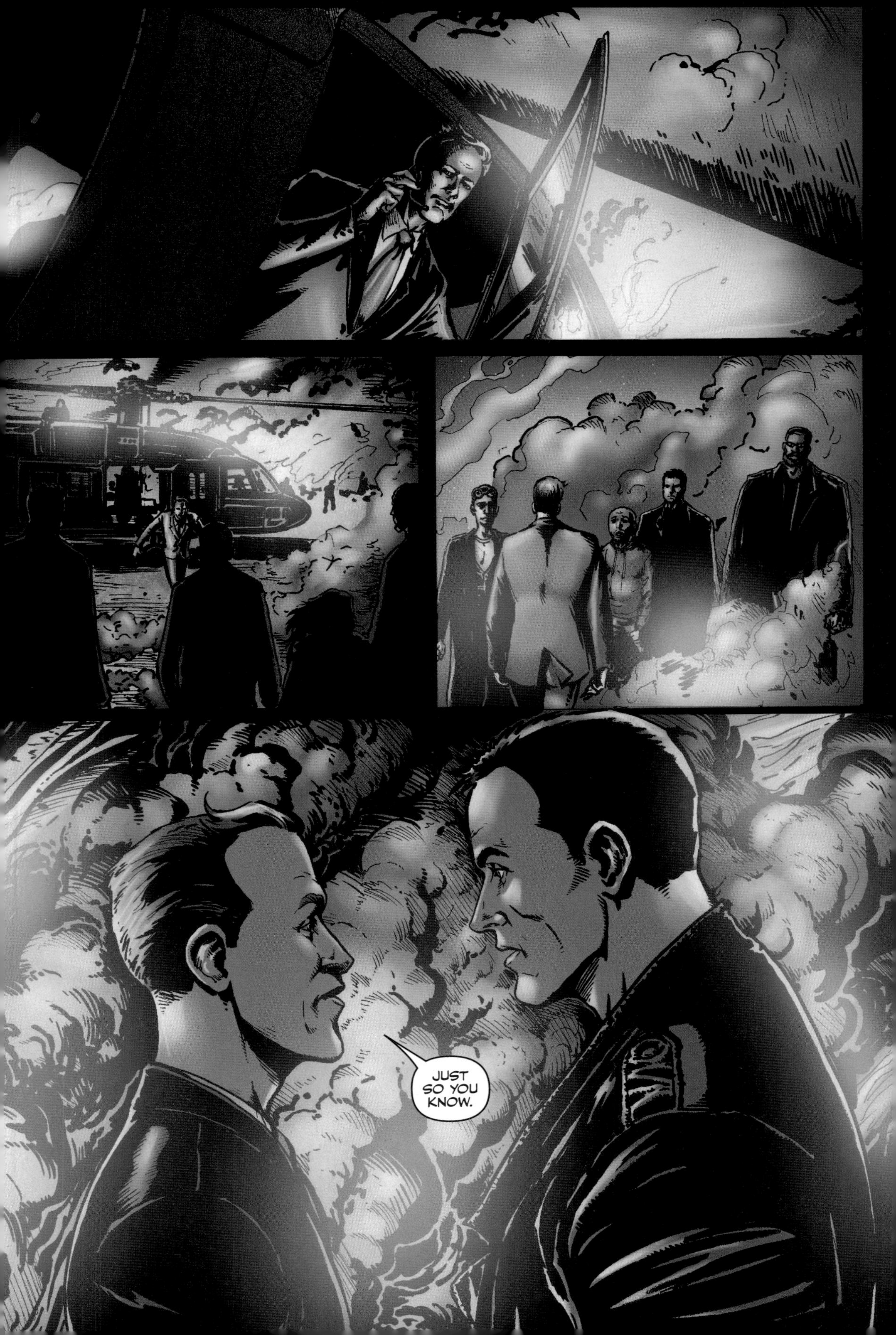
JUST SO YOU KNOW.

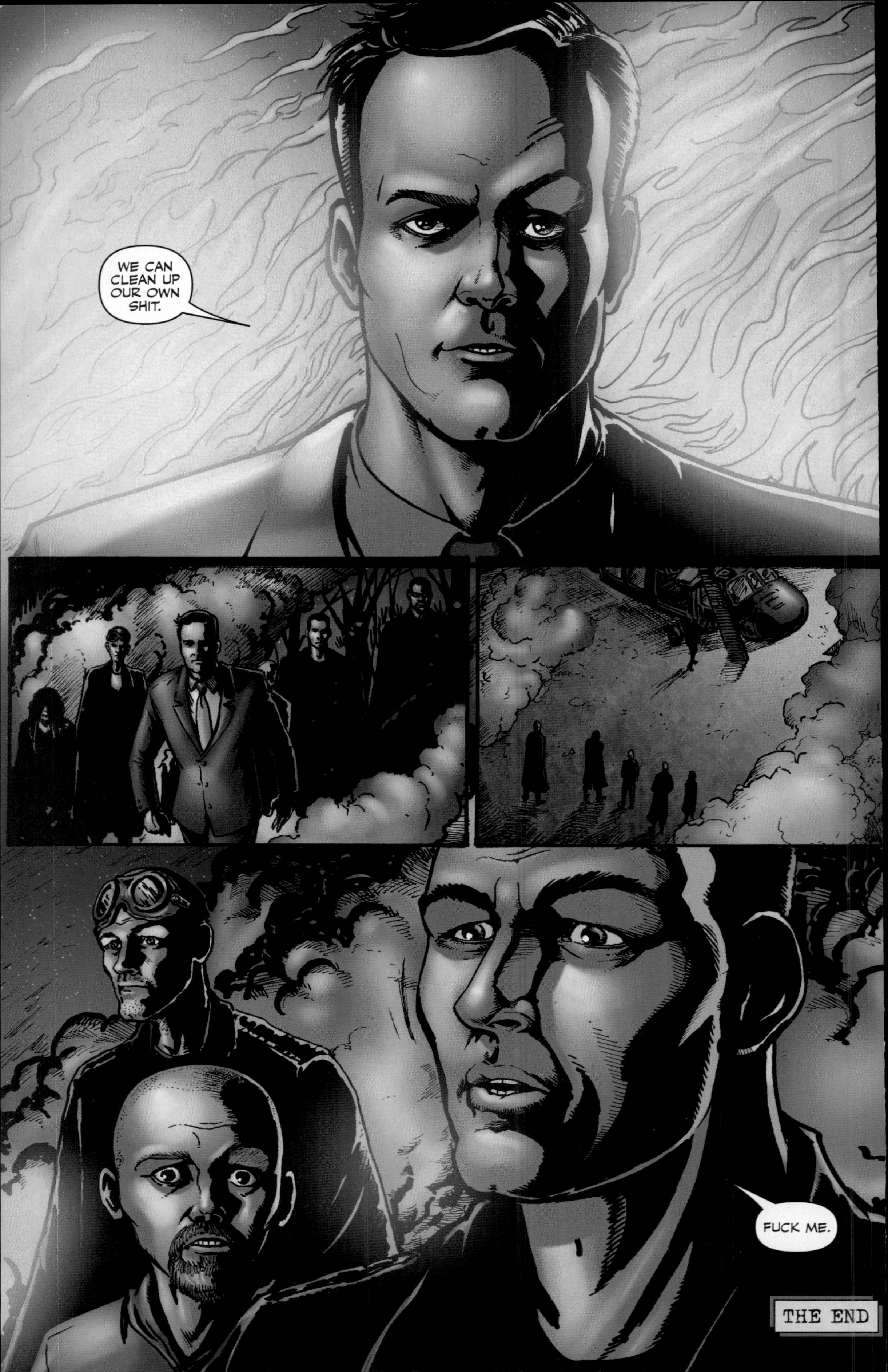
WE CAN CLEAN UP OUR OWN SHIT.
FUCK ME.
THE END

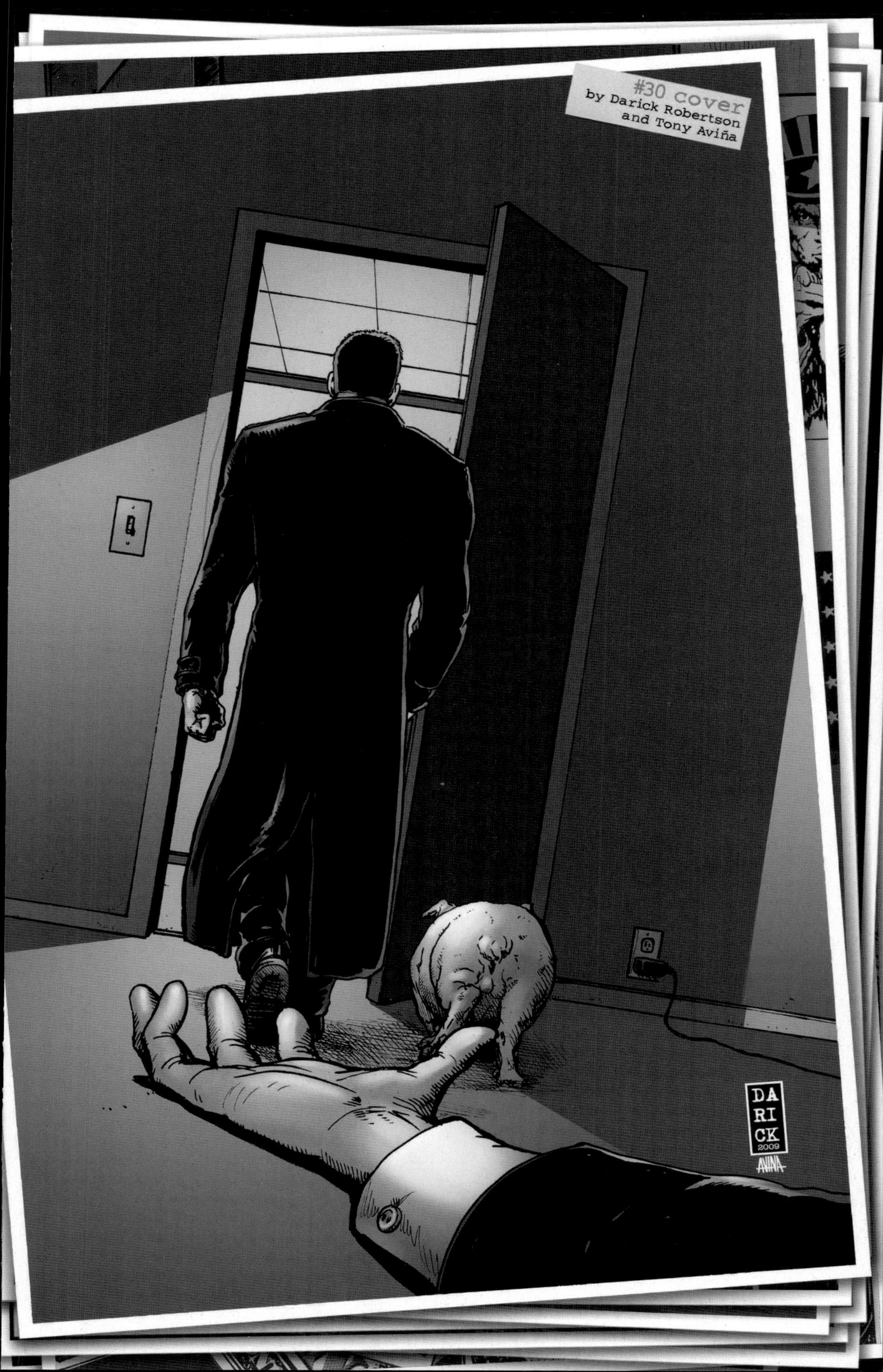
DA
RI
CK
2009
AVINA

#30 cover
by Darick Robertson
and Tony Aviña

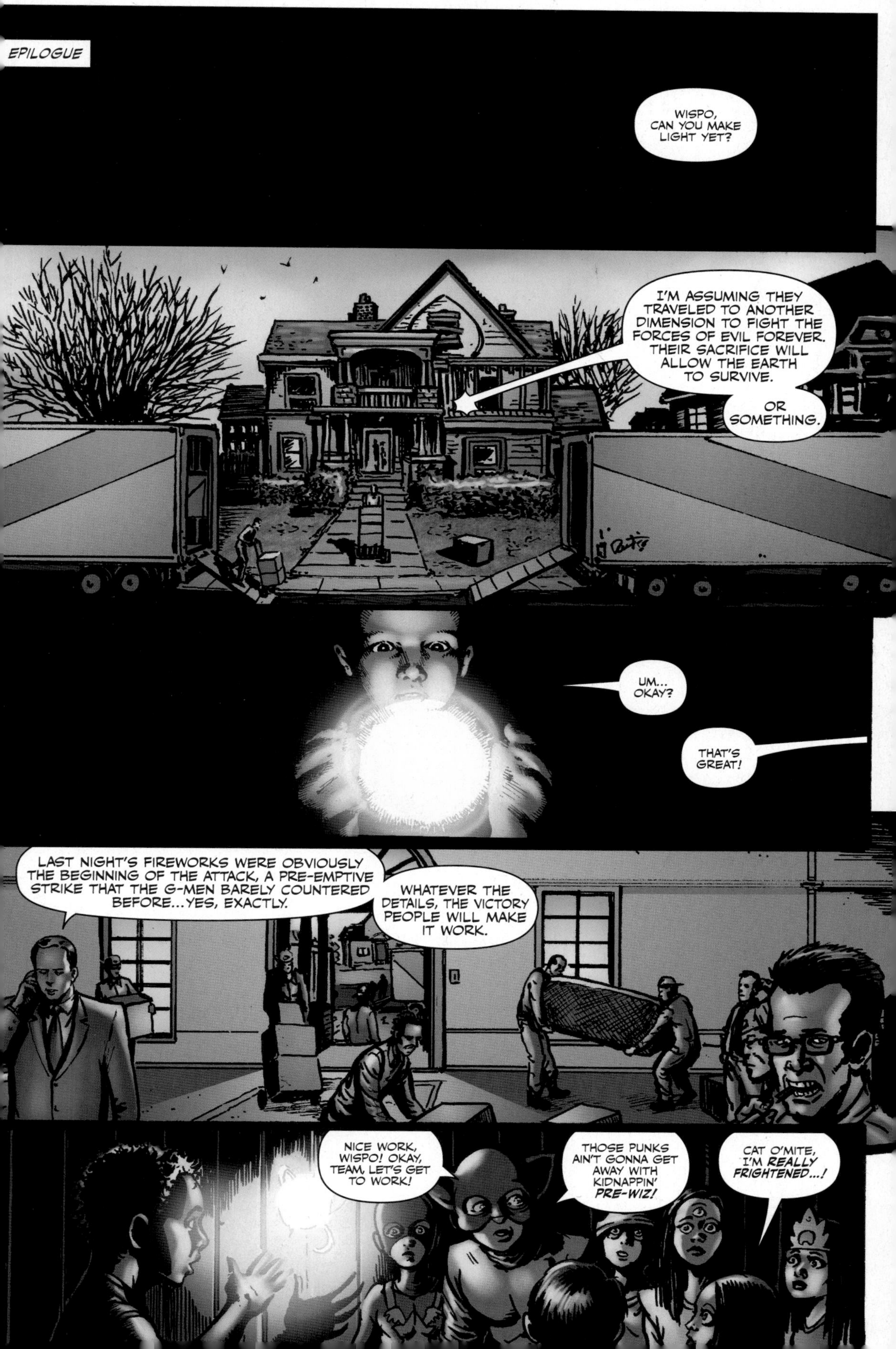
EPILOGUE
WISPO, CAN YOU MAKE LIGHT YET?
I'M ASSUMING THEY TRAVELED TO ANOTHER DIMENSION TO FIGHT THE FORCES OF EVIL FOREVER. THEIR SACRIFICE WILL ALLOW THE EARTH TO SURVIVE.
OR SOMETHING.
UM... OKAY?
THAT'S GREAT!
LAST NIGHT'S FIREWORKS WERE OBVIOUSLY THE BEGINNING OF THE ATTACK, A PRE-EMPTIVE STRIKE THAT THE G-MEN BARELY COUNTERED BEFORE...YES, EXACTLY.
WHATEVER THE DETAILS, THE VICTORY PEOPLE WILL MAKE IT WORK.
NICE WORK, WISPO! OKAY, TEAM, LET'S GET TO WORK!
THOSE PUNKS AIN'T GONNA GET AWAY WITH KIDNAPPIN' PRE-WIZ!
CAT O'MITE, I'M REALLY FRIGHTENED...!

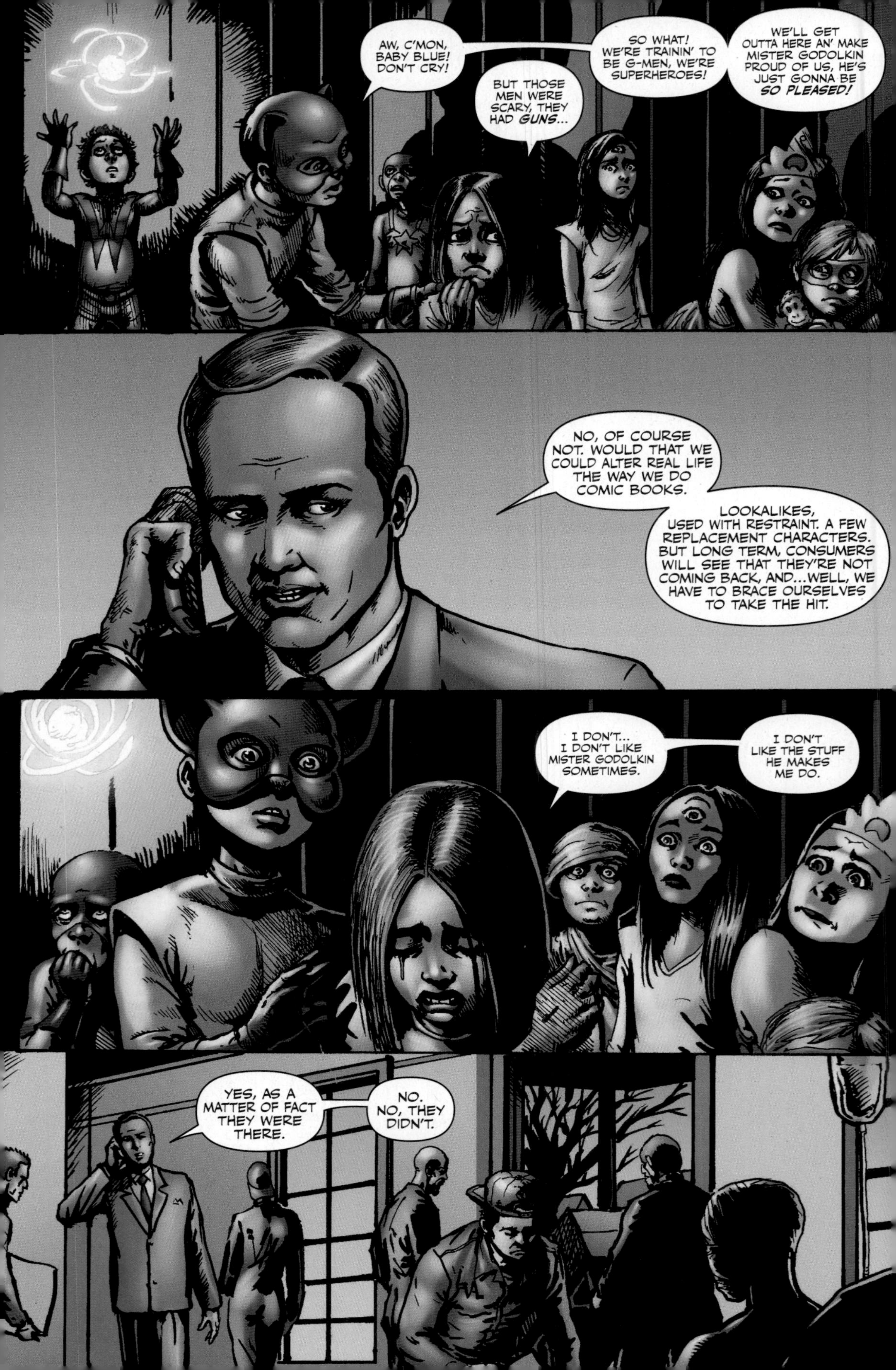
AW, C'MON, BABY BLUE! DON'T CRY!
BUT THOSE MEN WERE SCARY, THEY HAD *GUNS*...
SO WHAT! WE'RE TRAININ' TO BE G-MEN, WE'RE SUPERHEROES!
WE'LL GET OUTTA HERE AN' MAKE MISTER GODOLKIN PROUD OF US, HE'S JUST GONNA BE *SO PLEASED!*
NO, OF COURSE NOT. WOULD THAT WE COULD ALTER REAL LIFE THE WAY WE DO COMIC BOOKS.
LOOKALIKES, USED WITH RESTRAINT. A FEW REPLACEMENT CHARACTERS. BUT LONG TERM, CONSUMERS WILL SEE THAT THEY'RE NOT COMING BACK, AND...WELL, WE HAVE TO BRACE OURSELVES TO TAKE THE HIT.
I DON'T... I DON'T LIKE MISTER GODOLKIN SOMETIMES.
I DON'T LIKE THE STUFF HE MAKES ME DO.
YES, AS A MATTER OF FACT THEY WERE THERE.
NO. NO, THEY DIDN'T.

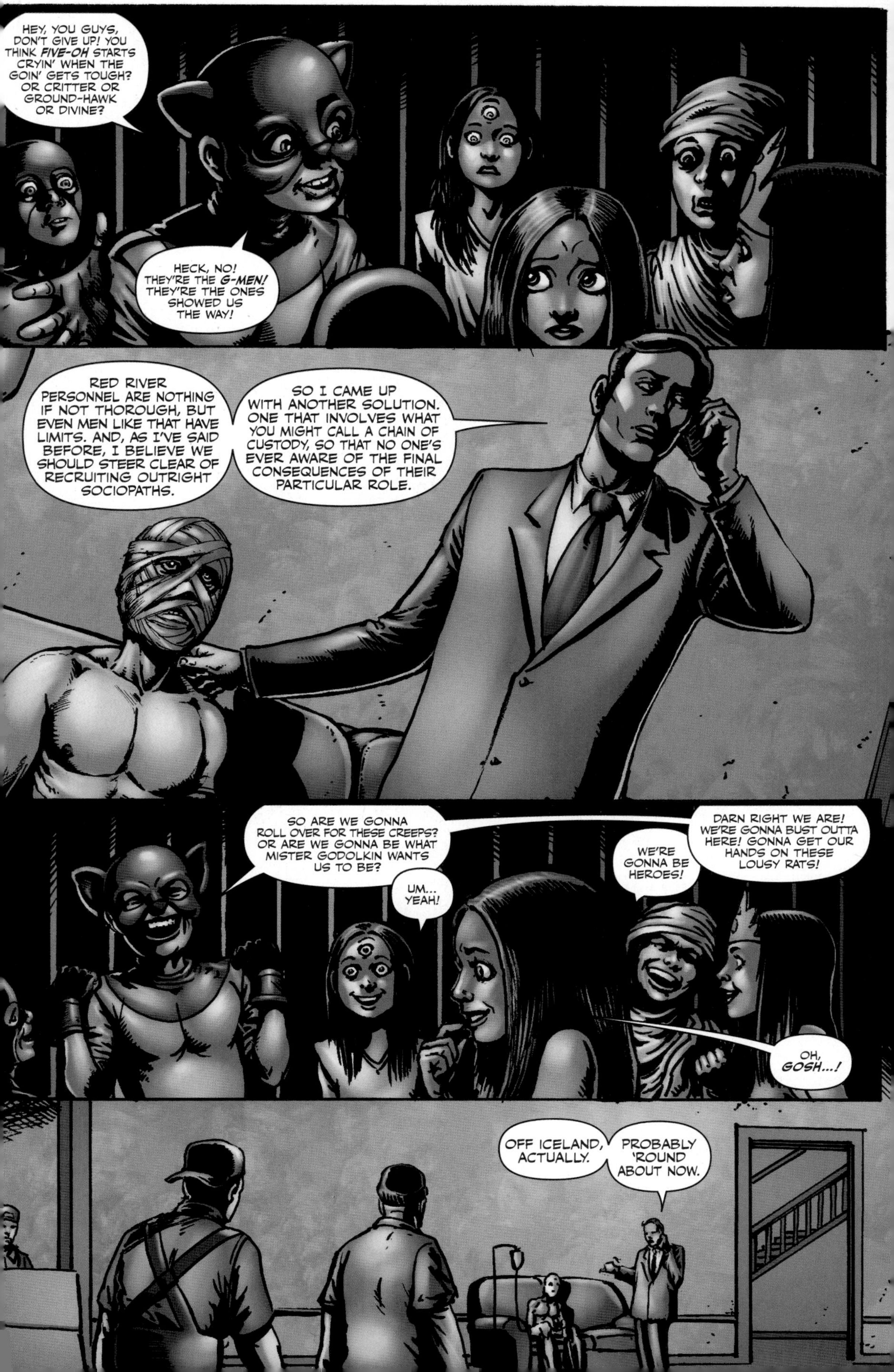
HEY, YOU GUYS, DON'T GIVE UP! YOU THINK *FIVE-OH* STARTS CRYIN' WHEN THE GOIN' GETS TOUGH? OR CRITTER OR GROUND-HAWK OR DIVINE?
HECK, NO! THEY'RE THE *G-MEN!* THEY'RE THE ONES SHOWED US THE WAY!
RED RIVER PERSONNEL ARE NOTHING IF NOT THOROUGH, BUT EVEN MEN LIKE THAT HAVE LIMITS. AND, AS I'VE SAID BEFORE, I BELIEVE WE SHOULD STEER CLEAR OF RECRUITING OUTRIGHT SOCIOPATHS.
SO I CAME UP WITH ANOTHER SOLUTION. ONE THAT INVOLVES WHAT YOU MIGHT CALL A CHAIN OF CUSTODY, SO THAT NO ONE'S EVER AWARE OF THE FINAL CONSEQUENCES OF THEIR PARTICULAR ROLE.
SO ARE WE GONNA ROLL OVER FOR THESE CREEPS? OR ARE WE GONNA BE WHAT MISTER GODOLKIN WANTS US TO BE?
UM... YEAH!
WE'RE GONNA BE HEROES!
DARN RIGHT WE ARE! WE'RE GONNA BUST OUTTA HERE! GONNA GET OUR HANDS ON THESE LOUSY RATS!
OH, *GOSH...!*
OFF ICELAND, ACTUALLY.
PROBABLY 'ROUND ABOUT NOW.

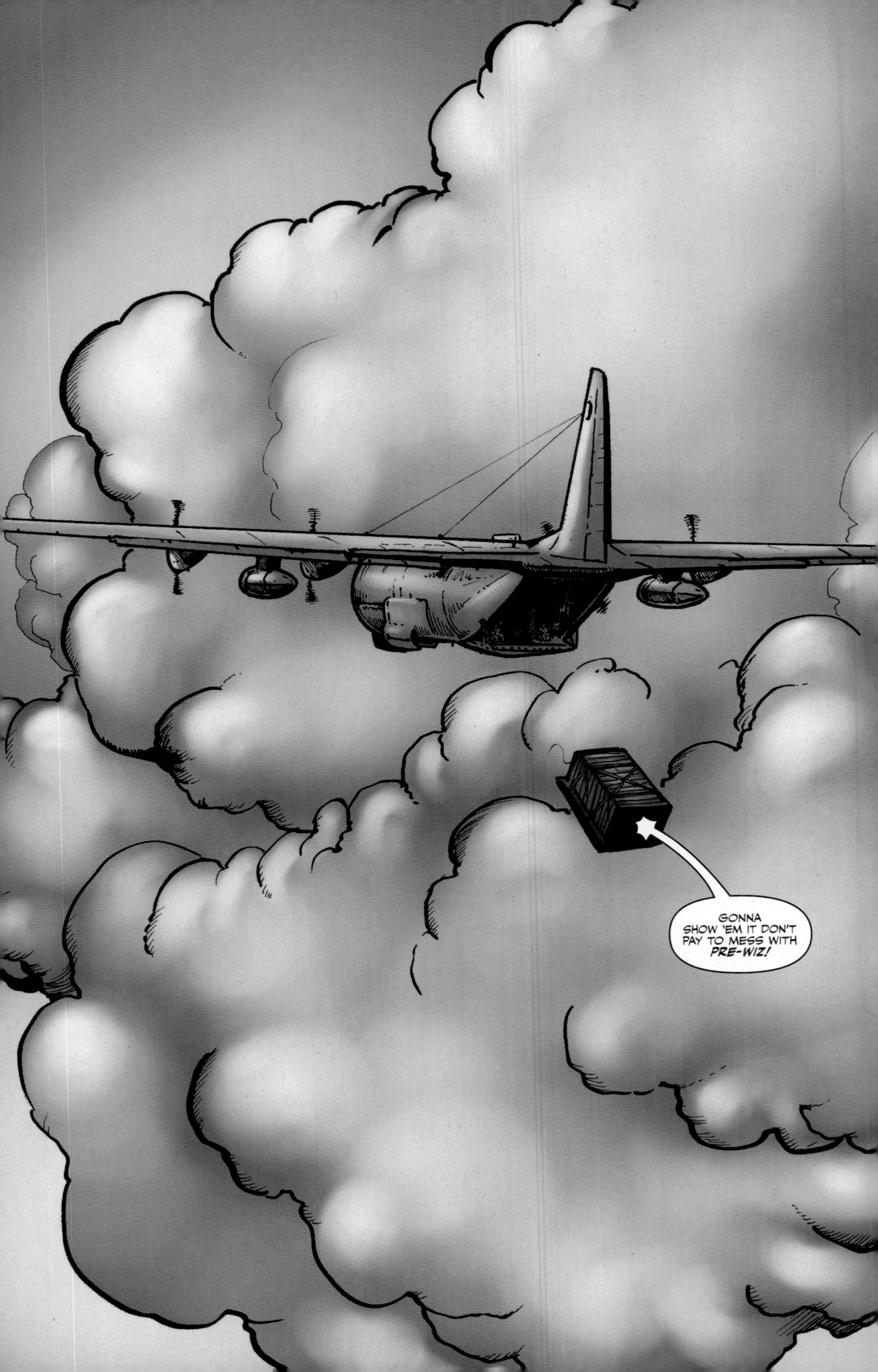
GONNA SHOW 'EM IT DON'T PAY TO MESS WITH *PRE-WIZ!*

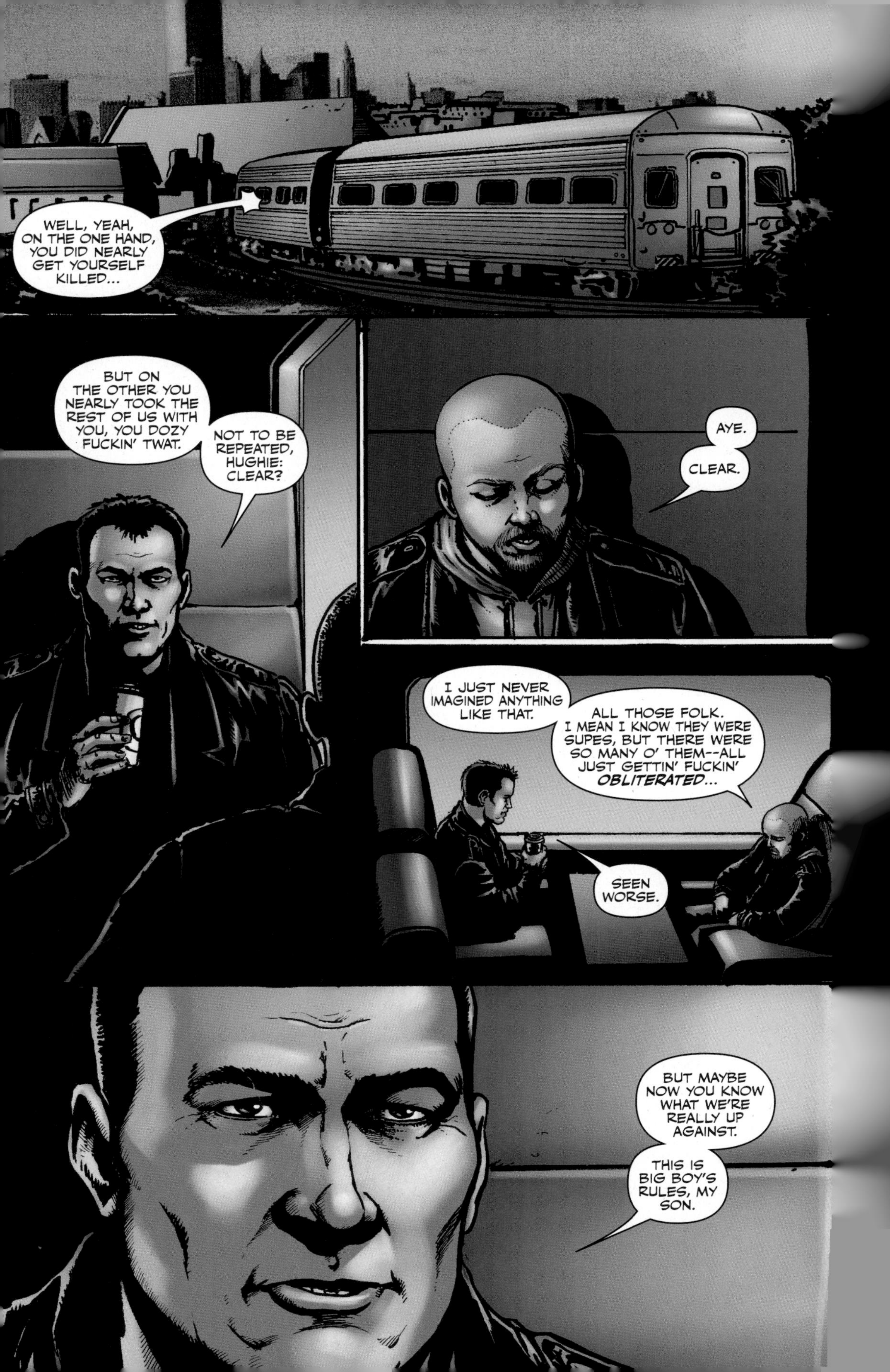
WELL, YEAH, ON THE ONE HAND, YOU DID NEARLY GET YOURSELF KILLED...
BUT ON THE OTHER YOU NEARLY TOOK THE REST OF US WITH YOU, YOU DOZY FUCKIN' TWAT.
NOT TO BE REPEATED, HUGHIE: CLEAR?
AYE.
CLEAR.
I JUST NEVER IMAGINED ANYTHING LIKE THAT.
ALL THOSE FOLK. I MEAN I KNOW THEY WERE SUPES, BUT THERE WERE SO MANY O' THEM--ALL JUST GETTIN' FUCKIN' *OBLITERATED*...
SEEN WORSE.
BUT MAYBE NOW YOU KNOW WHAT WE'RE REALLY UP AGAINST.
THIS IS BIG BOY'S RULES, MY SON.

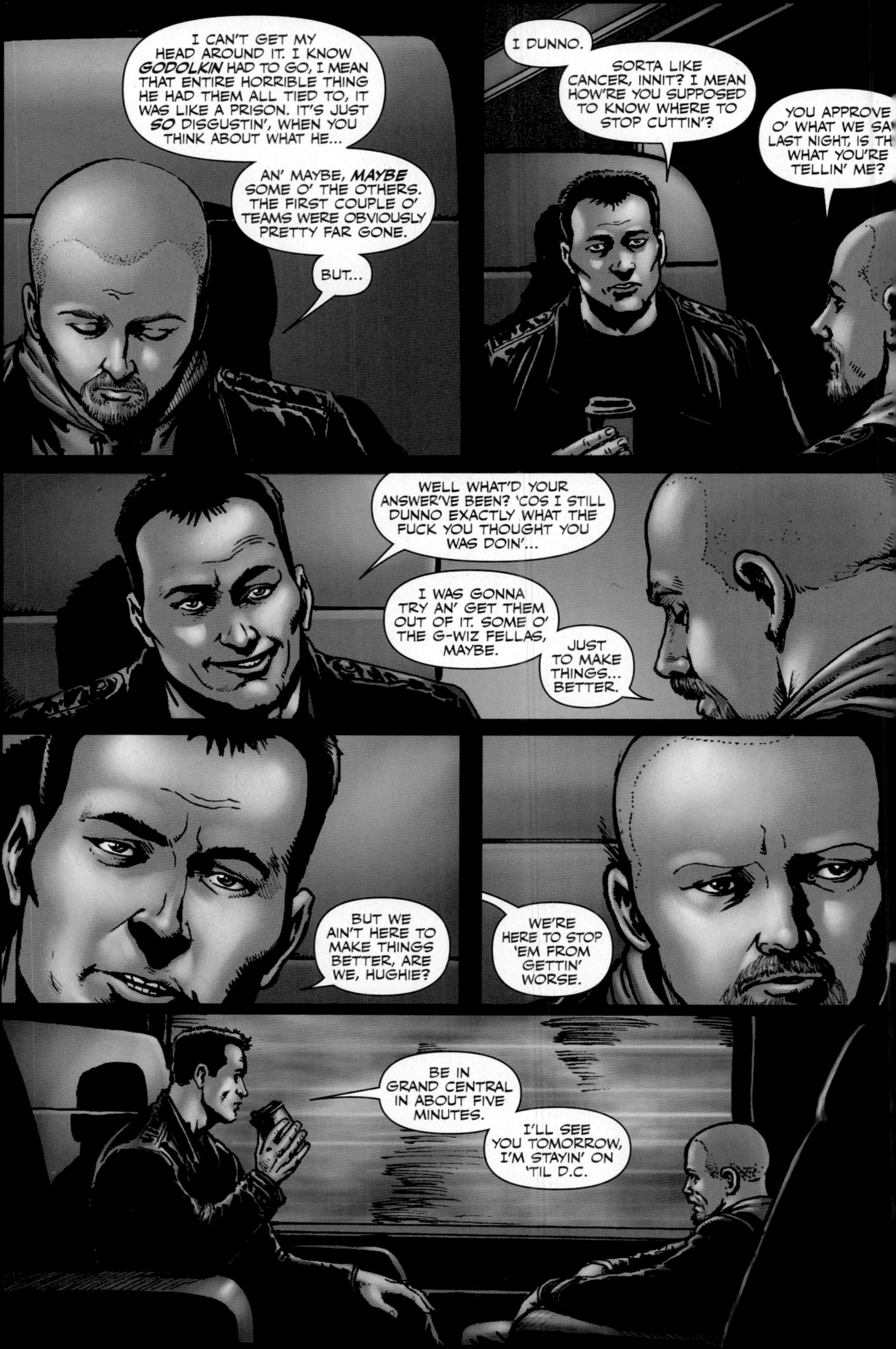
I CAN'T GET MY HEAD AROUND IT. I KNOW *GODOLKIN* HAD TO GO, I MEAN THAT ENTIRE HORRIBLE THING HE HAD THEM ALL TIED TO, IT WAS LIKE A PRISON. IT'S JUST *SO* DISGUSTIN', WHEN YOU THINK ABOUT WHAT HE...
AN' MAYBE, *MAYBE* SOME O' THE OTHERS. THE FIRST COUPLE O' TEAMS WERE OBVIOUSLY PRETTY FAR GONE.
BUT...
I DUNNO.
SORTA LIKE CANCER, INNIT? I MEAN HOW'RE YOU SUPPOSED TO KNOW WHERE TO STOP CUTTIN'?
YOU APPROVE O' WHAT WE SA LAST NIGHT, IS TH WHAT YOU'RE TELLIN' ME?
WELL WHAT'D YOUR ANSWER'VE BEEN? 'COS I STILL DUNNO EXACTLY WHAT THE FUCK YOU THOUGHT YOU WAS DOIN'...
I WAS GONNA TRY AN' GET THEM OUT OF IT. SOME O' THE G-WIZ FELLAS, MAYBE.
JUST TO MAKE THINGS... BETTER.
BUT WE AIN'T HERE TO MAKE THINGS BETTER, ARE WE, HUGHIE?
WE'RE HERE TO STOP 'EM FROM GETTIN' WORSE.
BE IN GRAND CENTRAL IN ABOUT FIVE MINUTES.
I'LL SEE YOU TOMORROW, I'M STAYIN' ON 'TIL D.C.

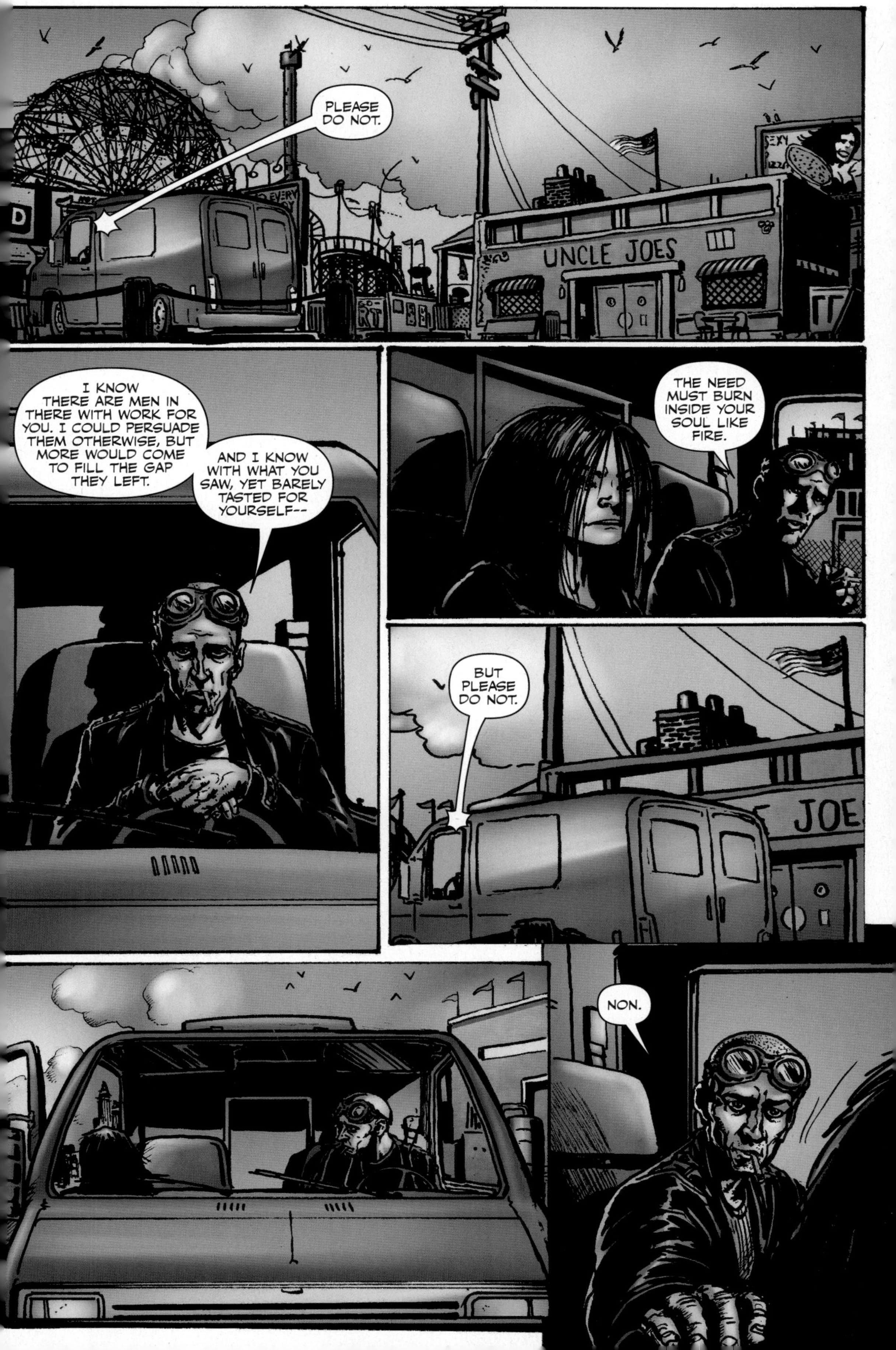
PLEASE DO NOT.
UNCLE JOES
I KNOW THERE ARE MEN IN THERE WITH WORK FOR YOU. I COULD PERSUADE THEM OTHERWISE, BUT MORE WOULD COME TO FILL THE GAP THEY LEFT.
AND I KNOW WITH WHAT YOU SAW, YET BARELY TASTED FOR YOURSELF--
THE NEED MUST BURN INSIDE YOUR SOUL LIKE FIRE.
BUT PLEASE DO NOT.
JOE
NON.

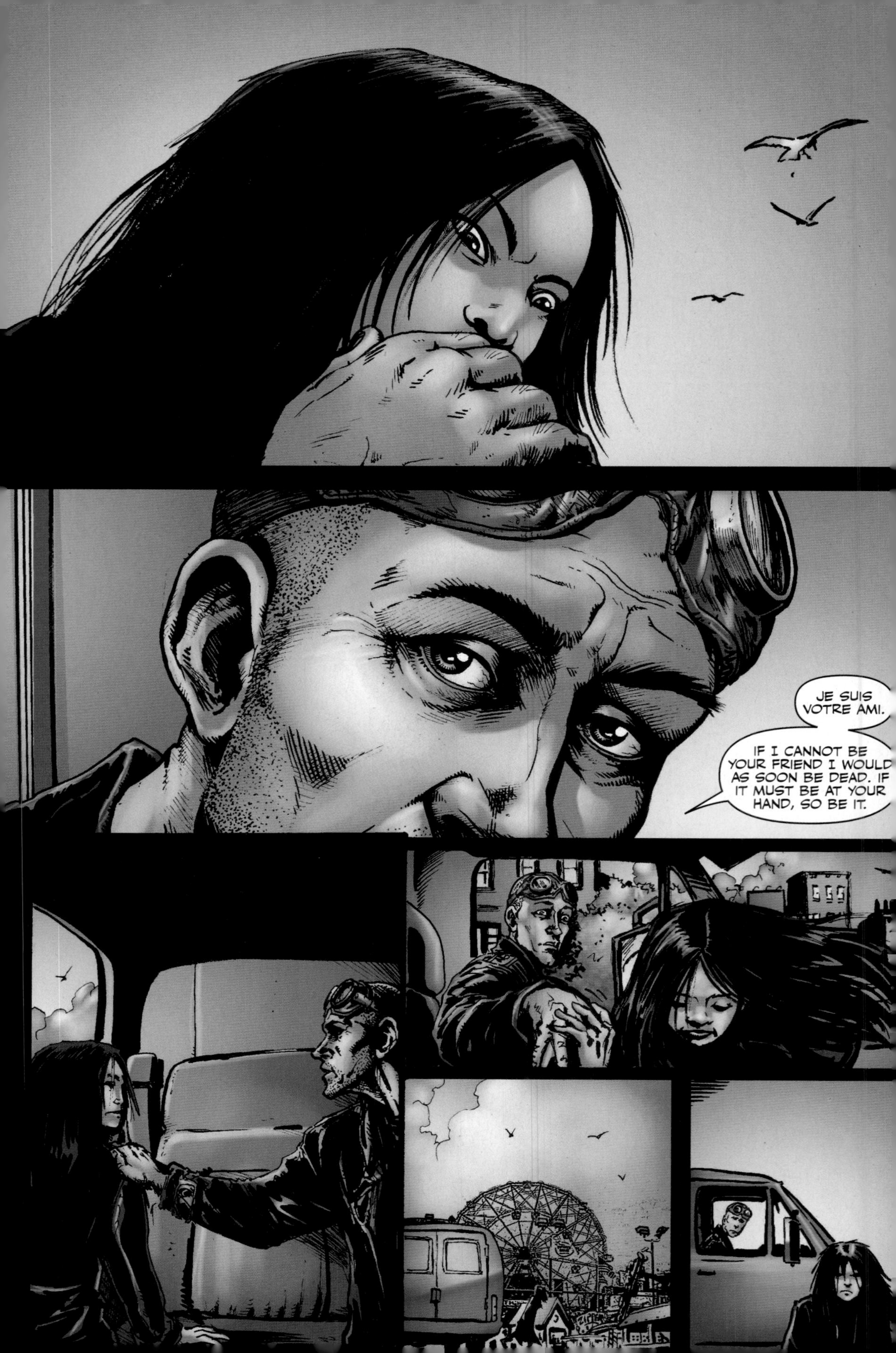
JE SUIS VOTRE AMI.
IF I CANNOT BE YOUR FRIEND I WOULD AS SOON BE DEAD. IF IT MUST BE AT YOUR HAND, SO BE IT.

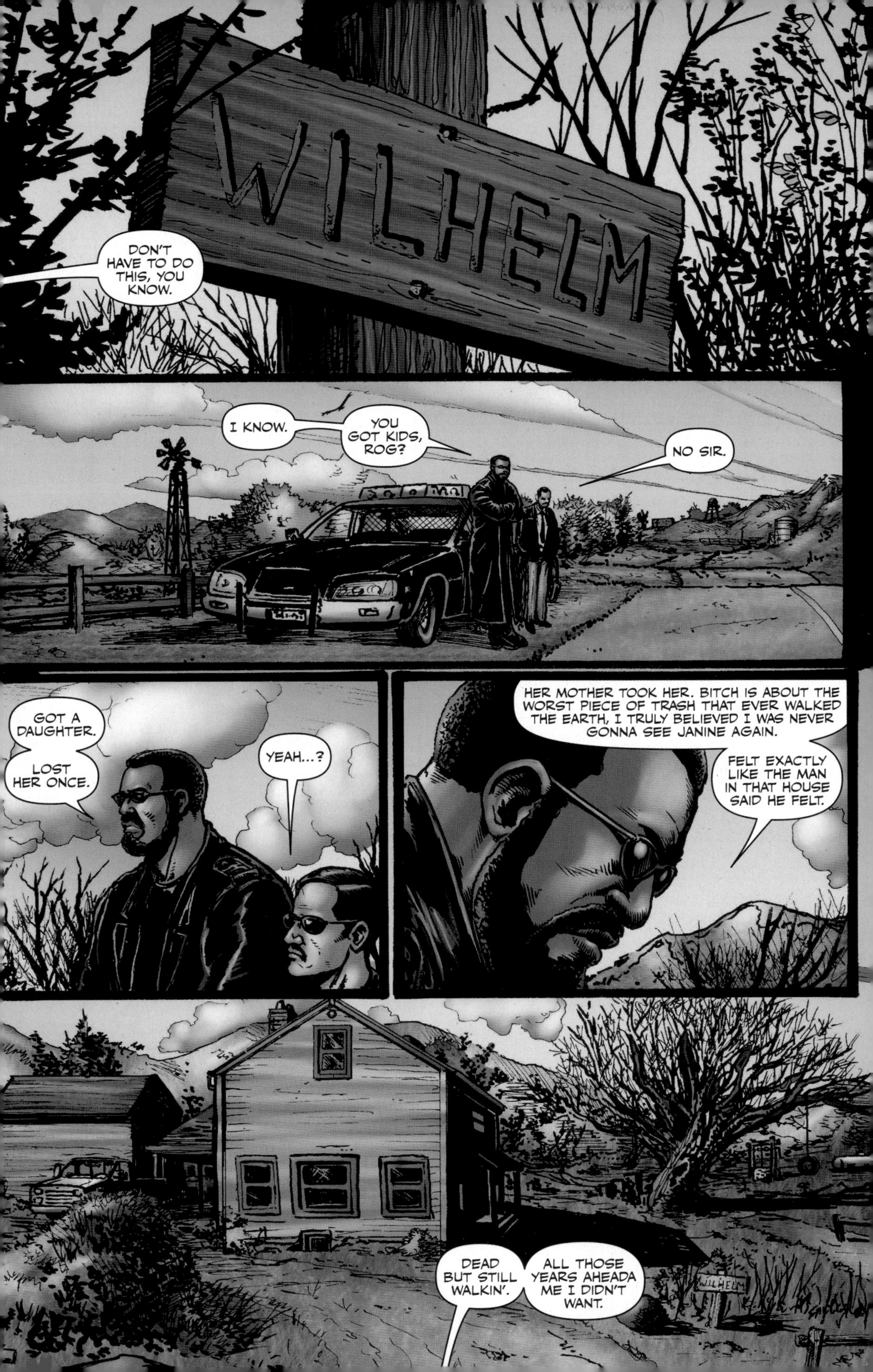
WILHELM
DON'T HAVE TO DO THIS, YOU KNOW.
I KNOW.
YOU GOT KIDS, ROG?
NO SIR.
GOT A DAUGHTER.
LOST HER ONCE.
YEAH...?
HER MOTHER TOOK HER. BITCH IS ABOUT THE WORST PIECE OF TRASH THAT EVER WALKED THE EARTH, I TRULY BELIEVED I WAS NEVER GONNA SEE JANINE AGAIN.
FELT EXACTLY LIKE THE MAN IN THAT HOUSE SAID HE FELT.
DEAD BUT STILL WALKIN'.
ALL THOSE YEARS AHEADA ME I DIDN'T WANT.
WILHELM

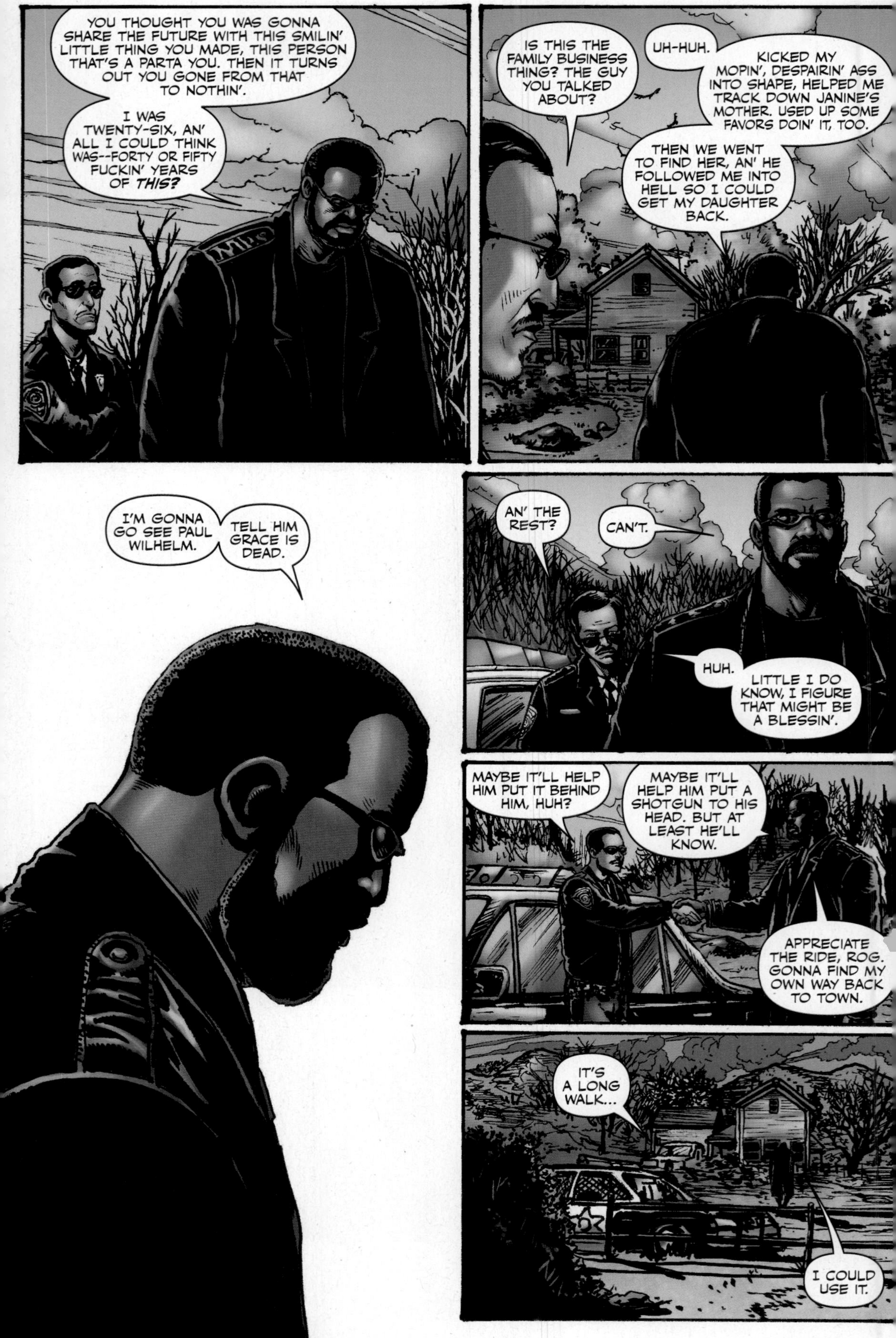
YOU THOUGHT YOU WAS GONNA SHARE THE FUTURE WITH THIS SMILIN' LITTLE THING YOU MADE, THIS PERSON THAT'S A PARTA YOU. THEN IT TURNS OUT YOU GONE FROM THAT TO NOTHIN'.
I WAS TWENTY-SIX, AN' ALL I COULD THINK WAS--FORTY OR FIFTY FUCKIN' YEARS OF *THIS?*
IS THIS THE FAMILY BUSINESS THING? THE GUY YOU TALKED ABOUT?
UH-HUH.
KICKED MY MOPIN', DESPAIRIN' ASS INTO SHAPE, HELPED ME TRACK DOWN JANINE'S MOTHER. USED UP SOME FAVORS DOIN' IT, TOO.
THEN WE WENT TO FIND HER, AN' HE FOLLOWED ME INTO HELL SO I COULD GET MY DAUGHTER BACK.
I'M GONNA GO SEE PAUL WILHELM.
TELL HIM GRACE IS DEAD.
AN' THE REST?
CAN'T.
HUH.
LITTLE I DO KNOW, I FIGURE THAT MIGHT BE A BLESSIN'.
MAYBE IT'LL HELP HIM PUT IT BEHIND HIM, HUH?
MAYBE IT'LL HELP HIM PUT A SHOTGUN TO HIS HEAD. BUT AT LEAST HE'LL KNOW.
APPRECIATE THE RIDE, ROG. GONNA FIND MY OWN WAY BACK TO TOWN.
IT'S A LONG WALK...
I COULD USE IT.

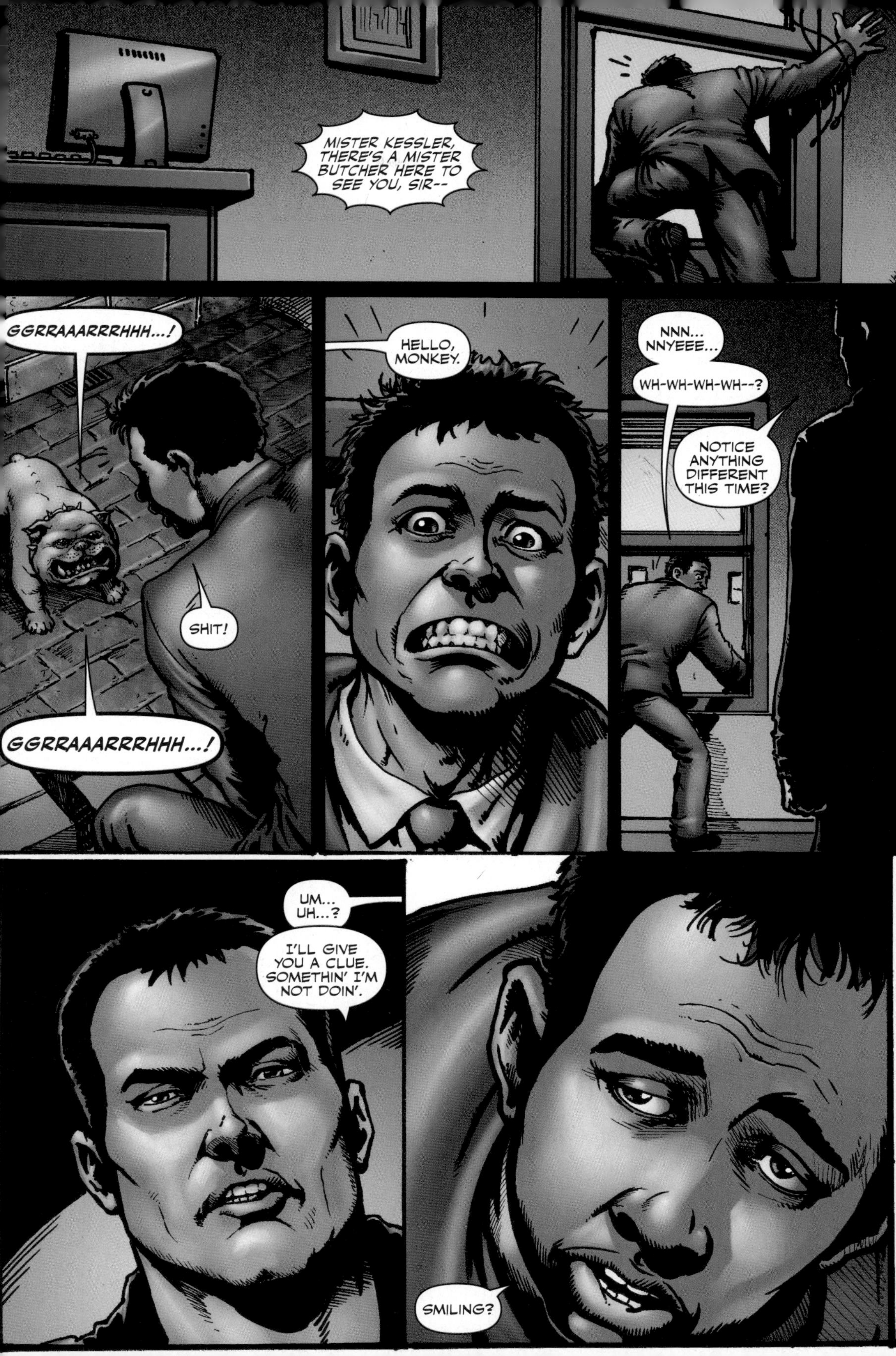
MISTER KESSLER, THERE'S A MISTER BUTCHER HERE TO SEE YOU, SIR--
GGRRAAARRRHHH...!
SHIT!
GGRRAAARRRHHH...!
HELLO, MONKEY.
NNN... NNYEEE...
WH-WH-WH-WH--?
NOTICE ANYTHING DIFFERENT THIS TIME?
UM... UH...?
I'LL GIVE YOU A CLUE. SOMETHIN' I'M NOT DOIN'.
SMILING?

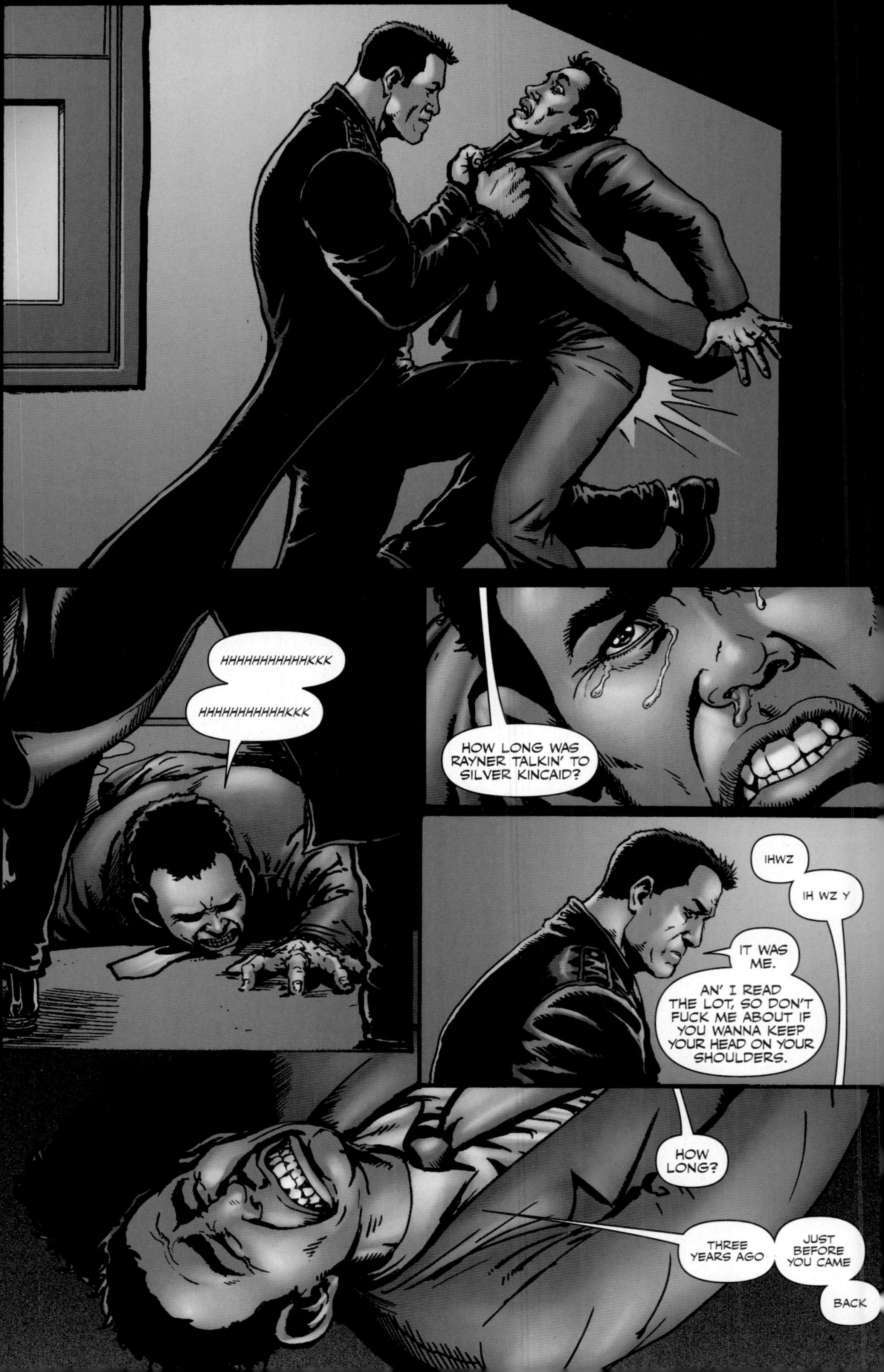
HHHHHHHHHHHHHKKK
HHHHHHHHHHHHHKKK
HOW LONG WAS RAYNER TALKIN' TO SILVER KINCAID?
IHWZ
IH WZ Y
IT WAS ME.
AN' I READ THE LOT, SO DON'T FUCK ME ABOUT IF YOU WANNA KEEP YOUR HEAD ON YOUR SHOULDERS.
HOW LONG?
THREE YEARS AGO
JUST BEFORE YOU CAME
BACK

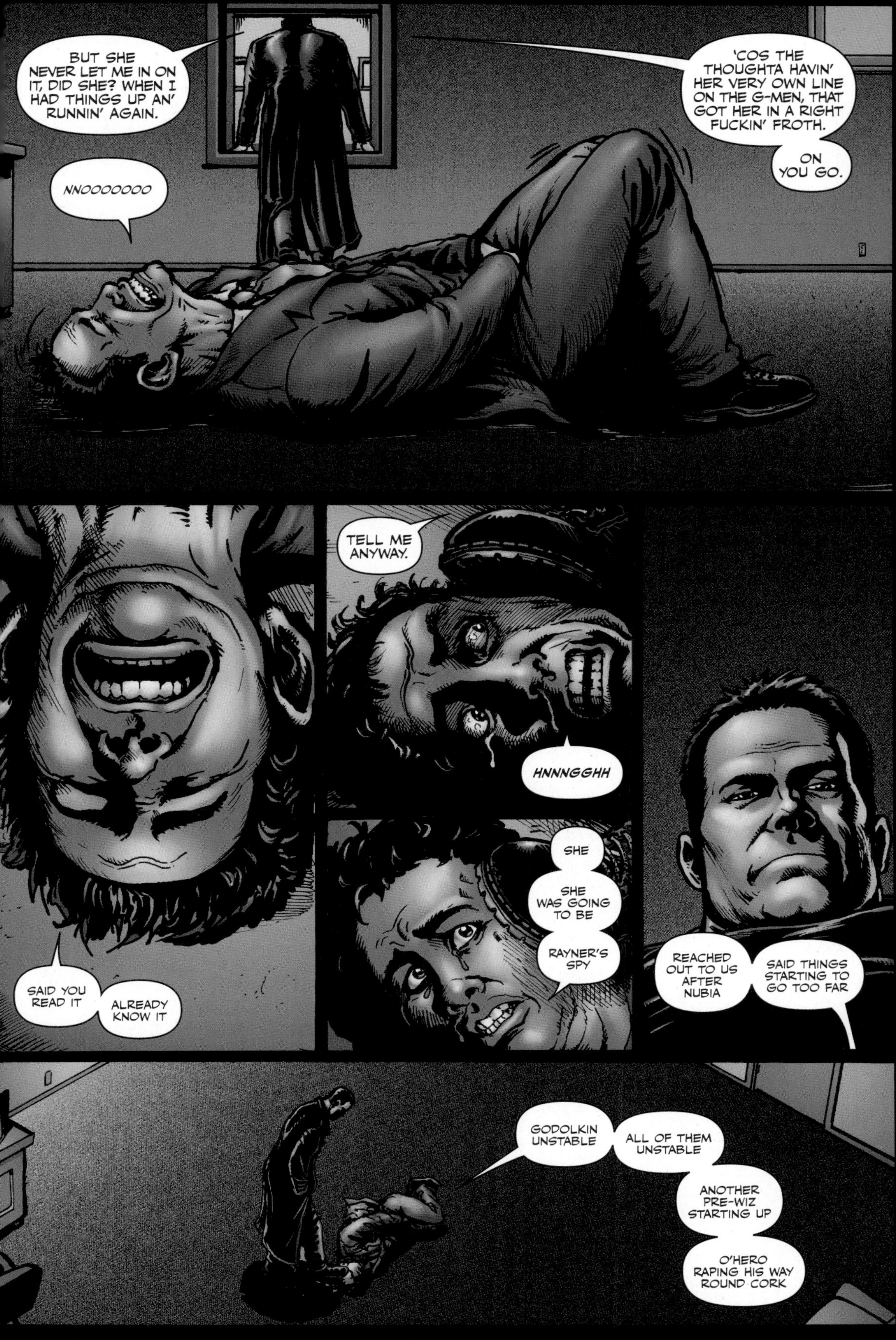
BUT SHE NEVER LET ME IN ON IT, DID SHE? WHEN I HAD THINGS UP AN' RUNNIN' AGAIN.
NNOOOOOOO
'COS THE THOUGHTA HAVIN' HER VERY OWN LINE ON THE G-MEN, THAT GOT HER IN A RIGHT FUCKIN' FROTH.
ON YOU GO.
SAID YOU READ IT
ALREADY KNOW IT
TELL ME ANYWAY.
HNNNGGHH
SHE
SHE WAS GOING TO BE
RAYNER'S SPY
REACHED OUT TO US AFTER NUBIA
SAID THINGS STARTING TO GO TOO FAR
GODOLKIN UNSTABLE
ALL OF THEM UNSTABLE
ANOTHER PRE-WIZ STARTING UP
O'HERO RAPING HIS WAY ROUND CORK

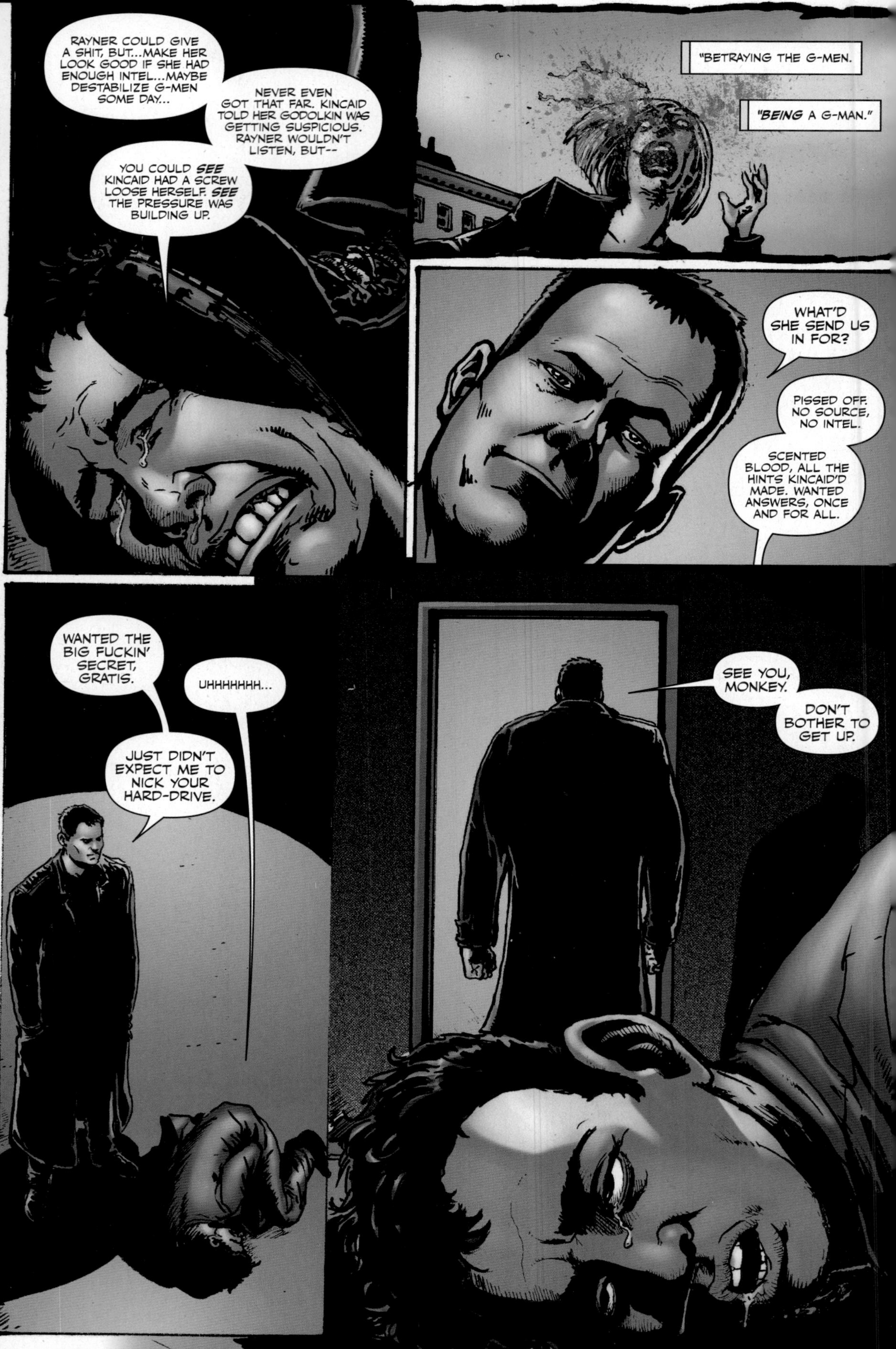
RAYNER COULD GIVE A SHIT, BUT...MAKE HER LOOK GOOD IF SHE HAD ENOUGH INTEL...MAYBE DESTABILIZE G-MEN SOME DAY...
NEVER EVEN GOT THAT FAR. KINCAID TOLD HER GODOLKIN WAS GETTING SUSPICIOUS. RAYNER WOULDN'T LISTEN, BUT--
YOU COULD SEE KINCAID HAD A SCREW LOOSE HERSELF. SEE THE PRESSURE WAS BUILDING UP.
"BETRAYING THE G-MEN.
"BEING A G-MAN."
WHAT'D SHE SEND US IN FOR?
PISSED OFF. NO SOURCE, NO INTEL.
SCENTED BLOOD, ALL THE HINTS KINCAID'D MADE. WANTED ANSWERS, ONCE AND FOR ALL.
WANTED THE BIG FUCKIN' SECRET, GRATIS.
UHHHHHHH...
JUST DIDN'T EXPECT ME TO NICK YOUR HARD-DRIVE.
SEE YOU, MONKEY.
DON'T BOTHER TO GET UP.

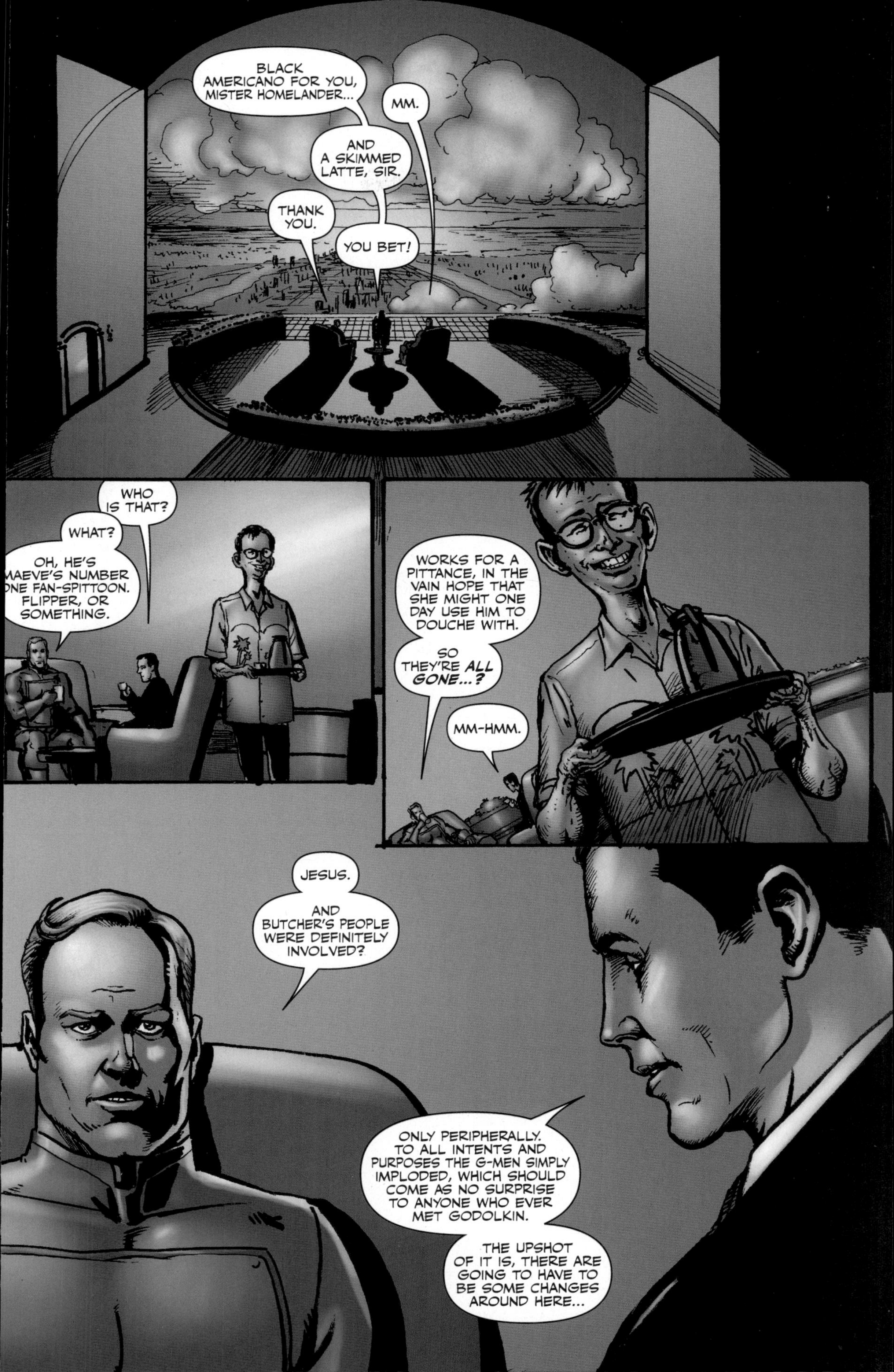

BLACK AMERICANO FOR YOU, MISTER HOMELANDER...
MM.
AND A SKIMMED LATTE, SIR.
THANK YOU.
YOU BET!
WHO IS THAT?
WHAT?
OH, HE'S MAEVE'S NUMBER ONE FAN-SPITTOON. FLIPPER, OR SOMETHING.
WORKS FOR A PITTANCE, IN THE VAIN HOPE THAT SHE MIGHT ONE DAY USE HIM TO DOUCHE WITH.
SO THEY'RE ALL GONE...?
MM-HMM.
JESUS.
AND BUTCHER'S PEOPLE WERE DEFINITELY INVOLVED?
ONLY PERIPHERALLY. TO ALL INTENTS AND PURPOSES THE G-MEN SIMPLY IMPLODED, WHICH SHOULD COME AS NO SURPRISE TO ANYONE WHO EVER MET GODOLKIN.
THE UPSHOT OF IT IS, THERE ARE GOING TO HAVE TO BE SOME CHANGES AROUND HERE...

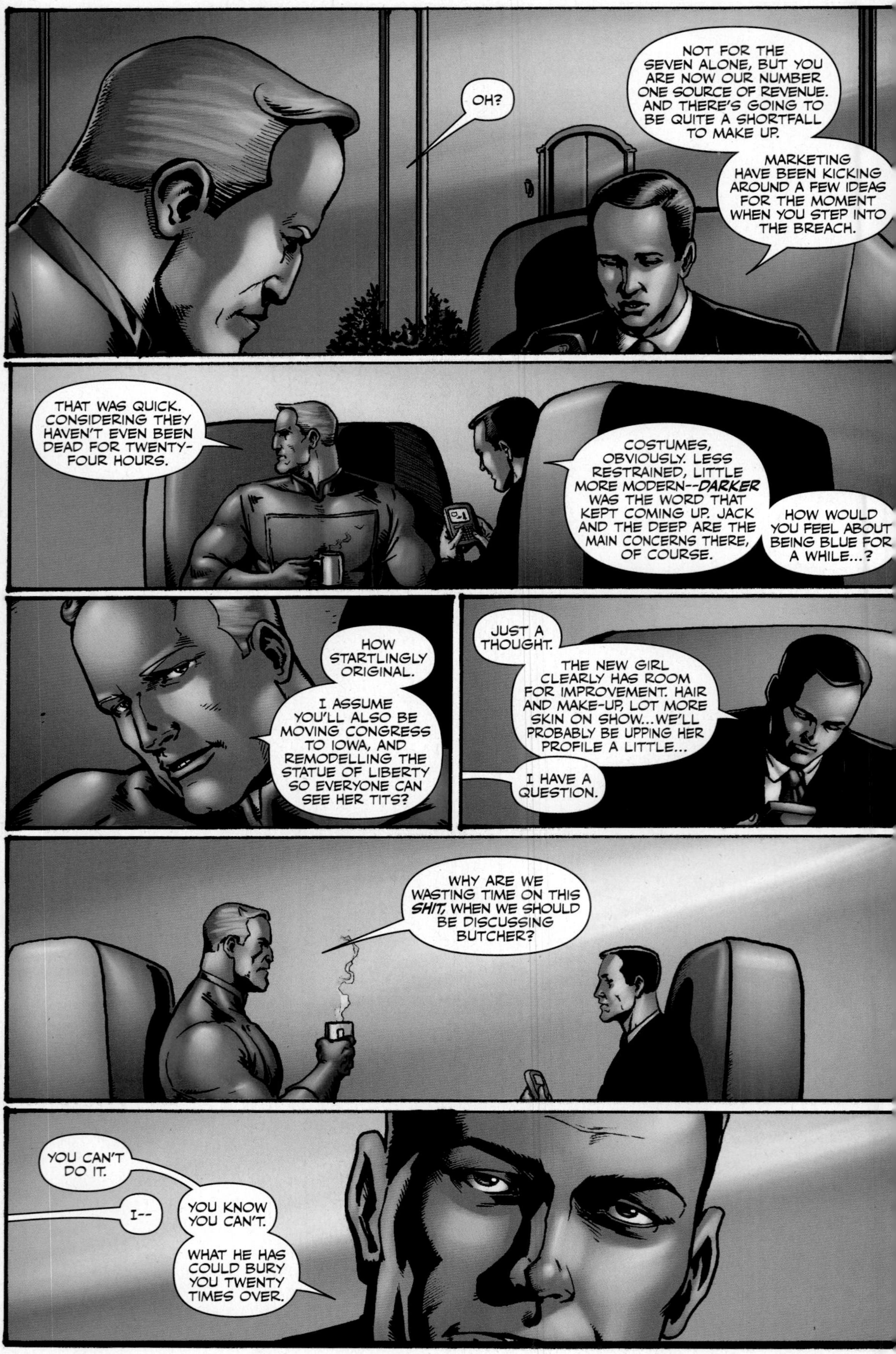
OH?
NOT FOR THE SEVEN ALONE, BUT YOU ARE NOW OUR NUMBER ONE SOURCE OF REVENUE. AND THERE'S GOING TO BE QUITE A SHORTFALL TO MAKE UP.
MARKETING HAVE BEEN KICKING AROUND A FEW IDEAS FOR THE MOMENT WHEN YOU STEP INTO THE BREACH.
THAT WAS QUICK. CONSIDERING THEY HAVEN'T EVEN BEEN DEAD FOR TWENTY-FOUR HOURS.
COSTUMES, OBVIOUSLY. LESS RESTRAINED, LITTLE MORE MODERN--*DARKER* WAS THE WORD THAT KEPT COMING UP. JACK AND THE DEEP ARE THE MAIN CONCERNS THERE, OF COURSE.
HOW WOULD YOU FEEL ABOUT BEING BLUE FOR A WHILE...?
HOW STARTLINGLY ORIGINAL.
I ASSUME YOU'LL ALSO BE MOVING CONGRESS TO IOWA, AND REMODELLING THE STATUE OF LIBERTY SO EVERYONE CAN SEE HER TITS?
JUST A THOUGHT.
THE NEW GIRL CLEARLY HAS ROOM FOR IMPROVEMENT. HAIR AND MAKE-UP, LOT MORE SKIN ON SHOW...WE'LL PROBABLY BE UPPING HER PROFILE A LITTLE...
I HAVE A QUESTION.
WHY ARE WE WASTING TIME ON THIS *SHIT,* WHEN WE SHOULD BE DISCUSSING BUTCHER?
YOU CAN'T DO IT.
I--
YOU KNOW YOU CAN'T.
WHAT HE HAS COULD BURY YOU TWENTY TIMES OVER.

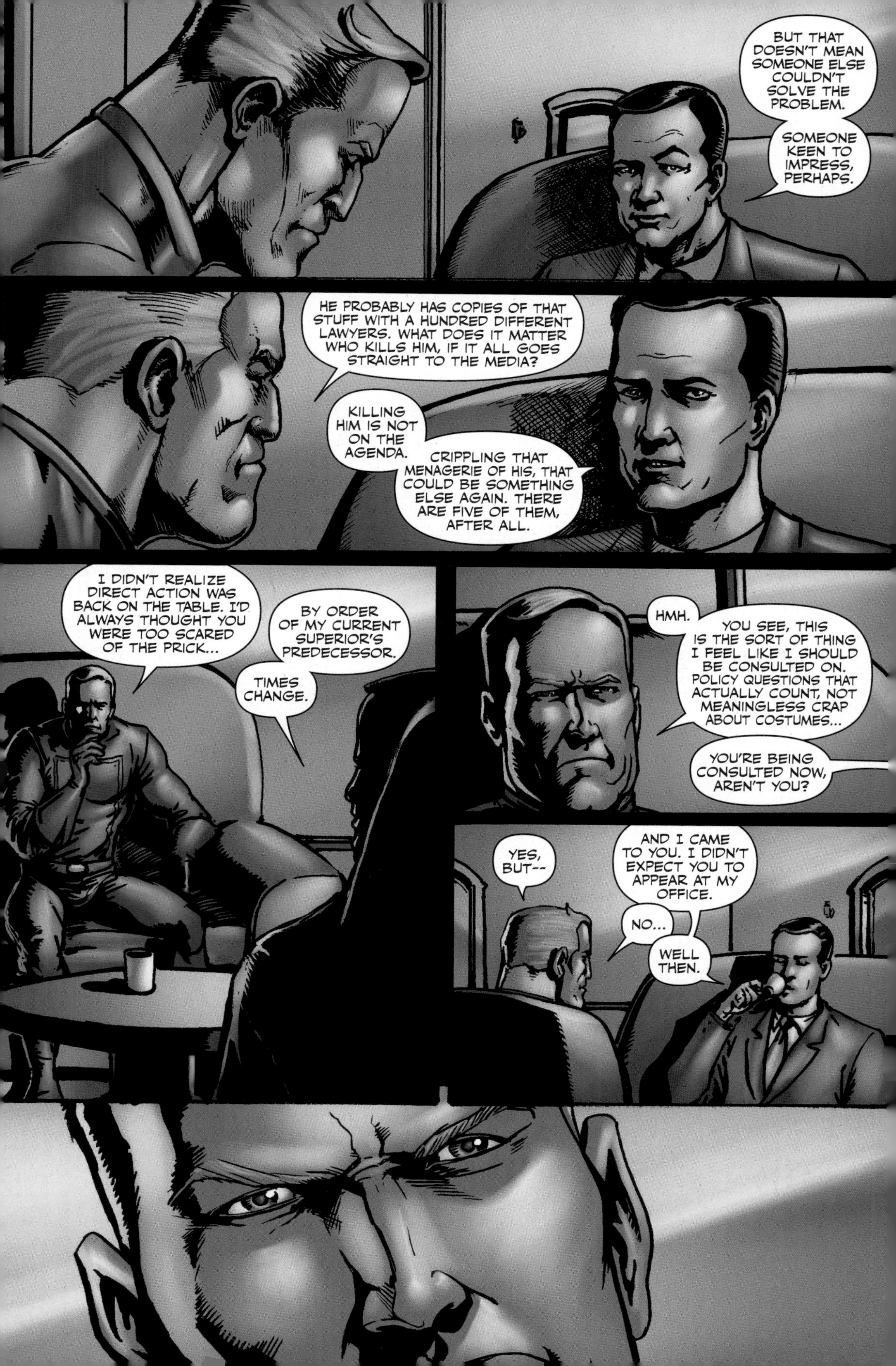
BUT THAT DOESN'T MEAN SOMEONE ELSE COULDN'T SOLVE THE PROBLEM.
SOMEONE KEEN TO IMPRESS, PERHAPS.
HE PROBABLY HAS COPIES OF THAT STUFF WITH A HUNDRED DIFFERENT LAWYERS. WHAT DOES IT MATTER WHO KILLS HIM, IF IT ALL GOES STRAIGHT TO THE MEDIA?
KILLING HIM IS NOT ON THE AGENDA.
CRIPPLING THAT MENAGERIE OF HIS, THAT COULD BE SOMETHING ELSE AGAIN. THERE ARE FIVE OF THEM, AFTER ALL.
I DIDN'T REALIZE DIRECT ACTION WAS BACK ON THE TABLE. I'D ALWAYS THOUGHT YOU WERE TOO SCARED OF THE PRICK...
BY ORDER OF MY CURRENT SUPERIOR'S PREDECESSOR.
TIMES CHANGE.
HMH.
YOU SEE, THIS IS THE SORT OF THING I FEEL LIKE I SHOULD BE CONSULTED ON. POLICY QUESTIONS THAT ACTUALLY COUNT, NOT MEANINGLESS CRAP ABOUT COSTUMES...
YOU'RE BEING CONSULTED NOW, AREN'T YOU?
YES, BUT--
AND I CAME TO YOU. I DIDN'T EXPECT YOU TO APPEAR AT MY OFFICE.
NO...
WELL THEN.

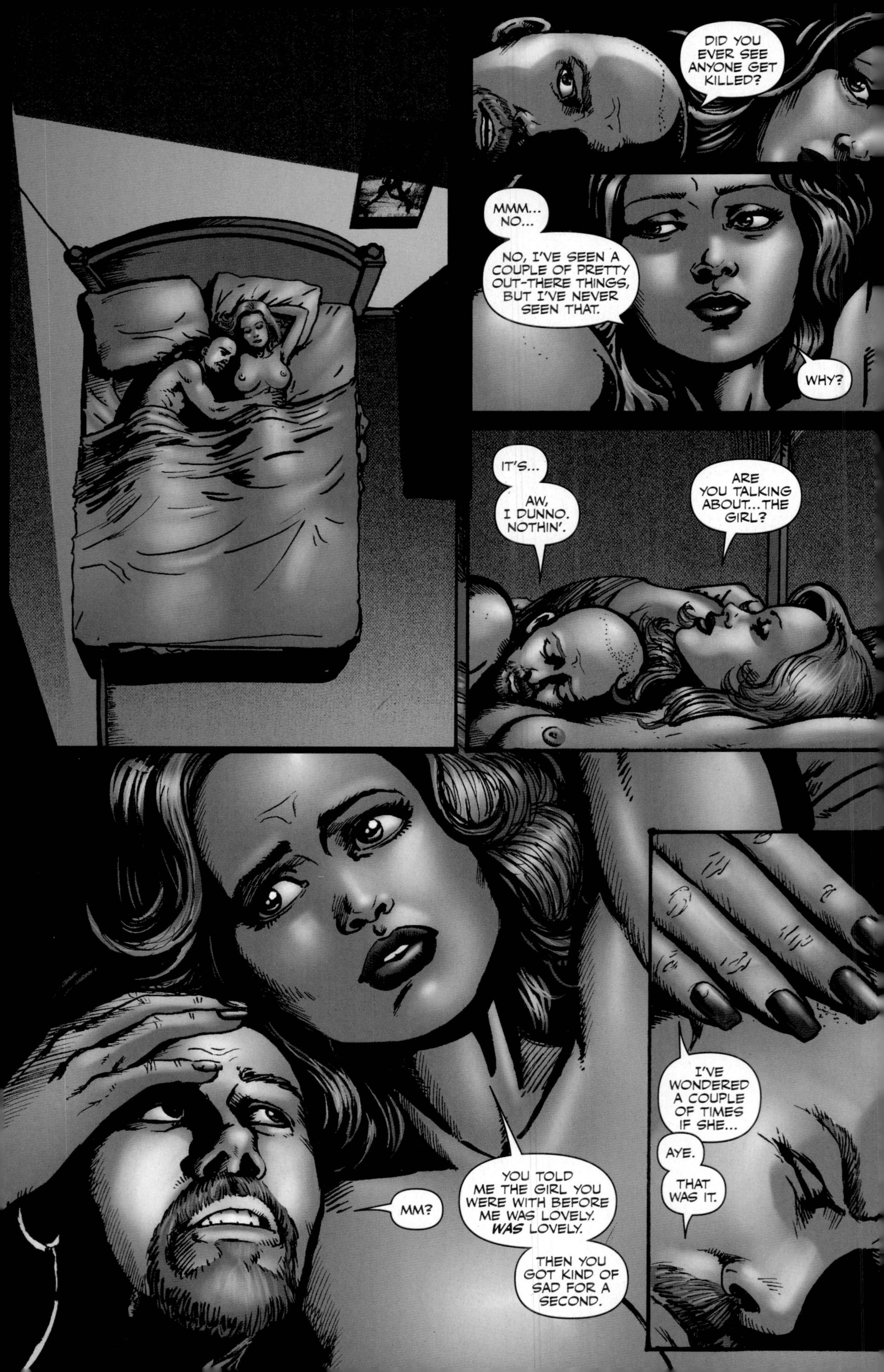
DID YOU EVER SEE ANYONE GET KILLED?
MMM... NO...
NO, I'VE SEEN A COUPLE OF PRETTY OUT-THERE THINGS, BUT I'VE NEVER SEEN THAT.
WHY?
IT'S...
AW, I DUNNO. NOTHIN'.
ARE YOU TALKING ABOUT...THE GIRL?
MM?
YOU TOLD ME THE GIRL YOU WERE WITH BEFORE ME WAS LOVELY. *WAS* LOVELY.
THEN YOU GOT KIND OF SAD FOR A SECOND.
I'VE WONDERED A COUPLE OF TIMES IF SHE...
AYE.
THAT WAS IT.

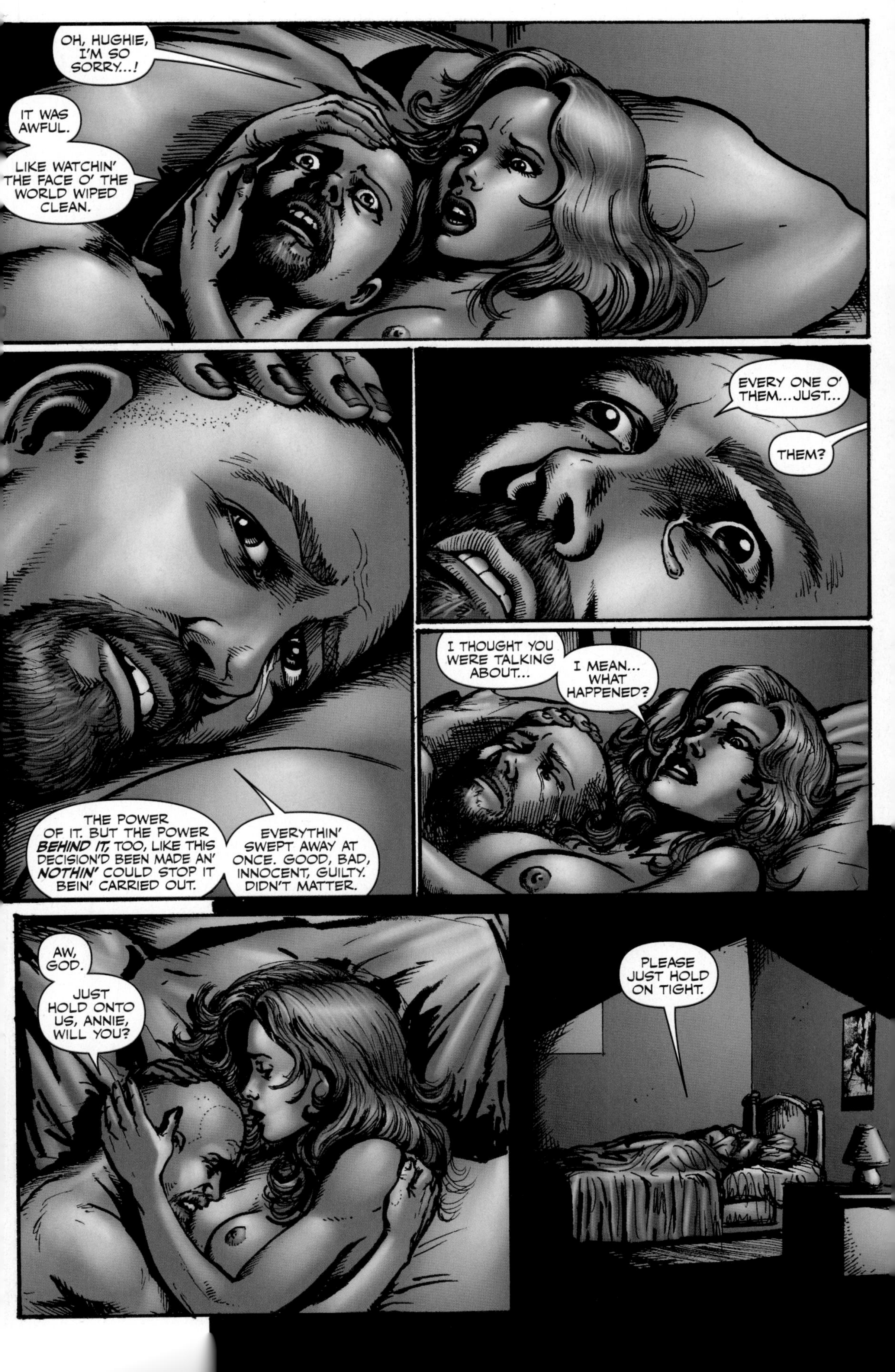
OH, HUGHIE, I'M SO SORRY...!
IT WAS AWFUL.
LIKE WATCHIN' THE FACE O' THE WORLD WIPED CLEAN.
EVERY ONE O' THEM...JUST...
THEM?
THE POWER OF IT. BUT THE POWER BEHIND IT, TOO, LIKE THIS DECISION'D BEEN MADE AN' NOTHIN' COULD STOP IT BEIN' CARRIED OUT.
EVERYTHIN' SWEPT AWAY AT ONCE. GOOD, BAD, INNOCENT, GUILTY. DIDN'T MATTER.
I THOUGHT YOU WERE TALKING ABOUT...
I MEAN... WHAT HAPPENED?
AW, GOD.
JUST HOLD ONTO US, ANNIE, WILL YOU?
PLEASE JUST HOLD ON TIGHT.

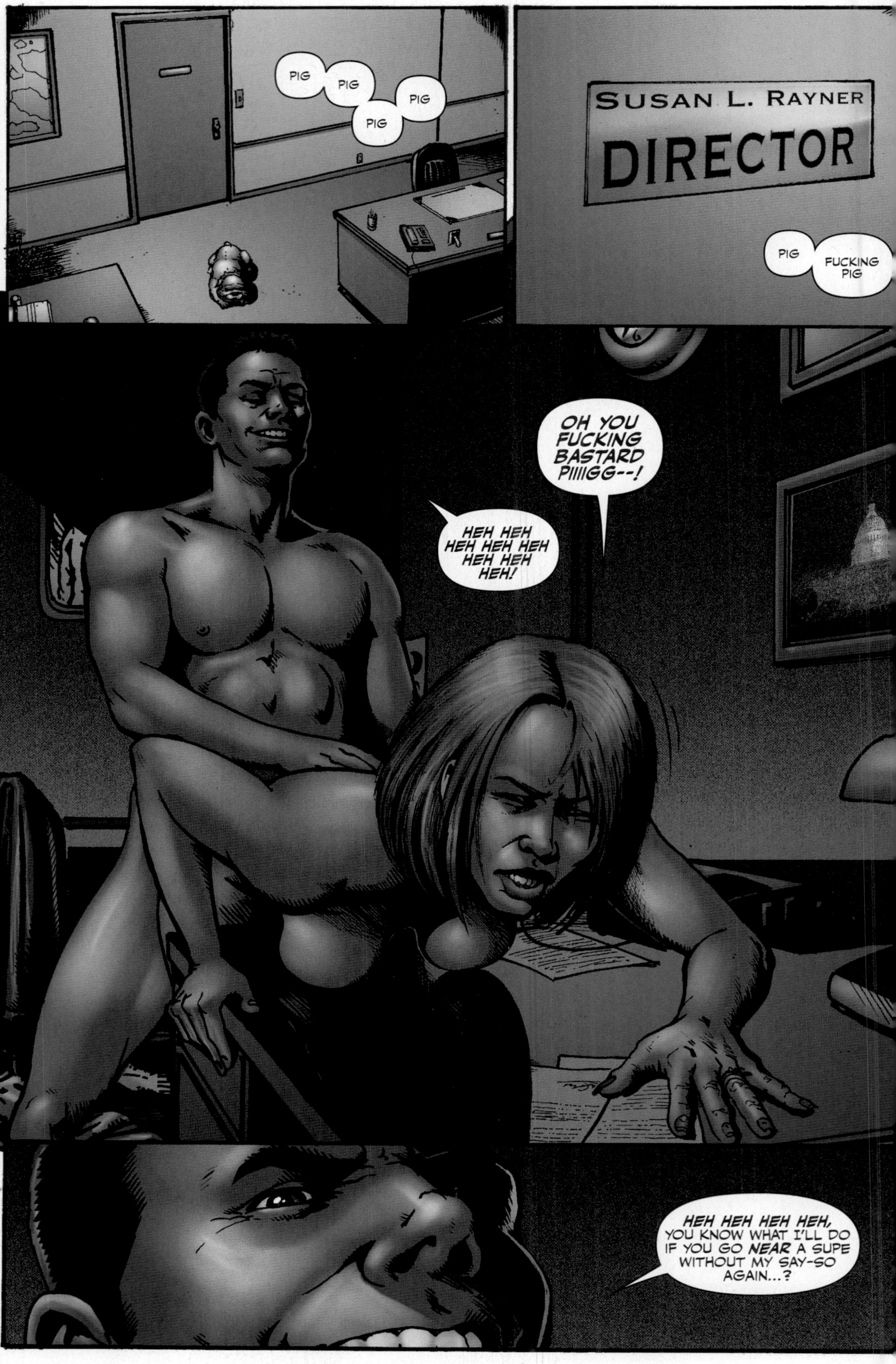
PIG
PIG
PIG
PIG
SUSAN L. RAYNER
DIRECTOR
PIG
FUCKING PIG
OH YOU FUCKING BASTARD PIIIIGG--!
HEH HEH HEH HEH HEH HEH HEH HEH!
HEH HEH HEH HEH, YOU KNOW WHAT I'LL DO IF YOU GO NEAR A SUPE WITHOUT MY SAY-SO AGAIN...?

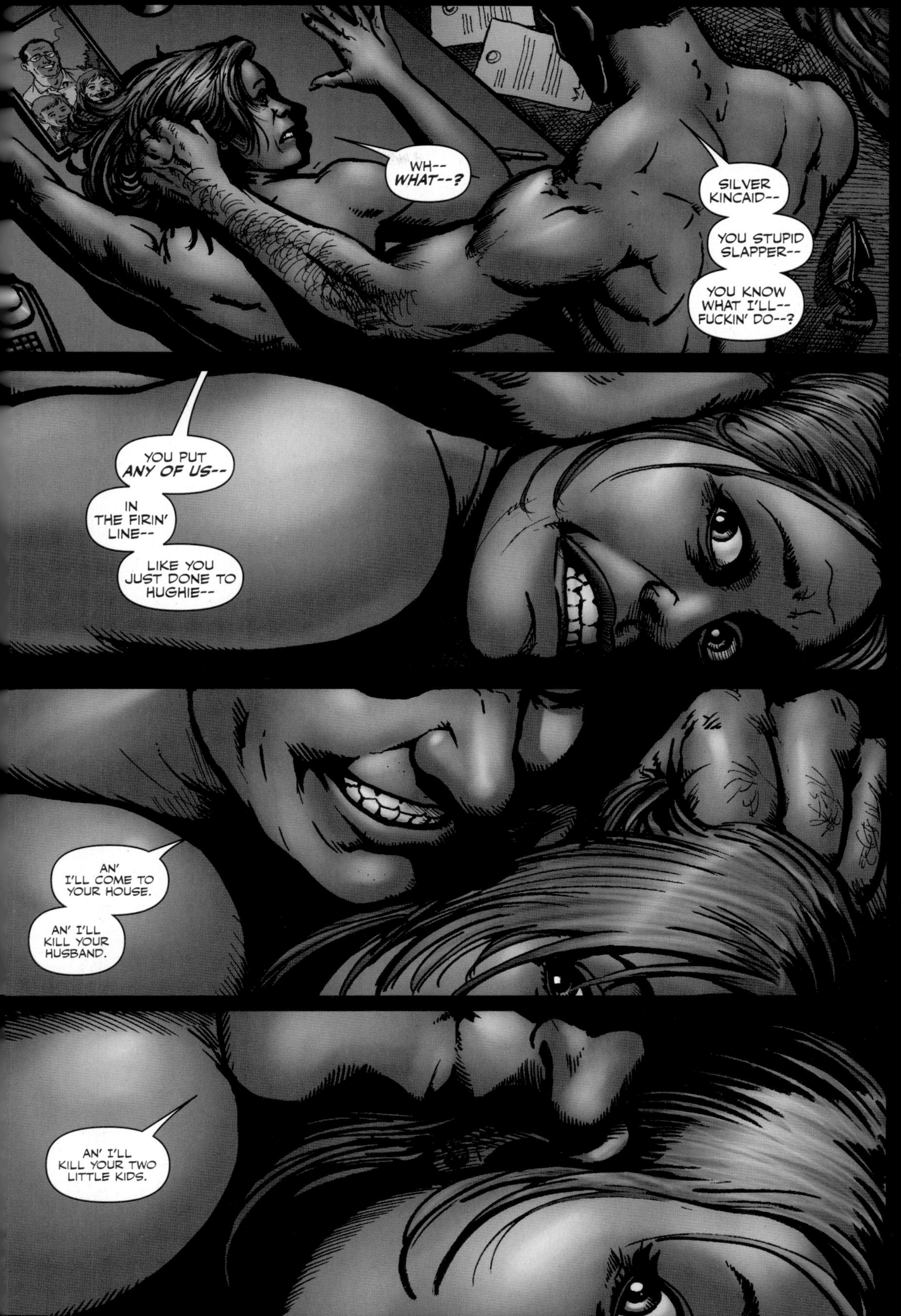
WH-- WHAT--?
SILVER KINCAID--
YOU STUPID SLAPPER--
YOU KNOW WHAT I'LL-- FUCKIN' DO--?
YOU PUT ANY OF US--
IN THE FIRIN' LINE--
LIKE YOU JUST DONE TO HUGHIE--
AN' I'LL COME TO YOUR HOUSE.
AN' I'LL KILL YOUR HUSBAND.
AN' I'LL KILL YOUR TWO LITTLE KIDS.

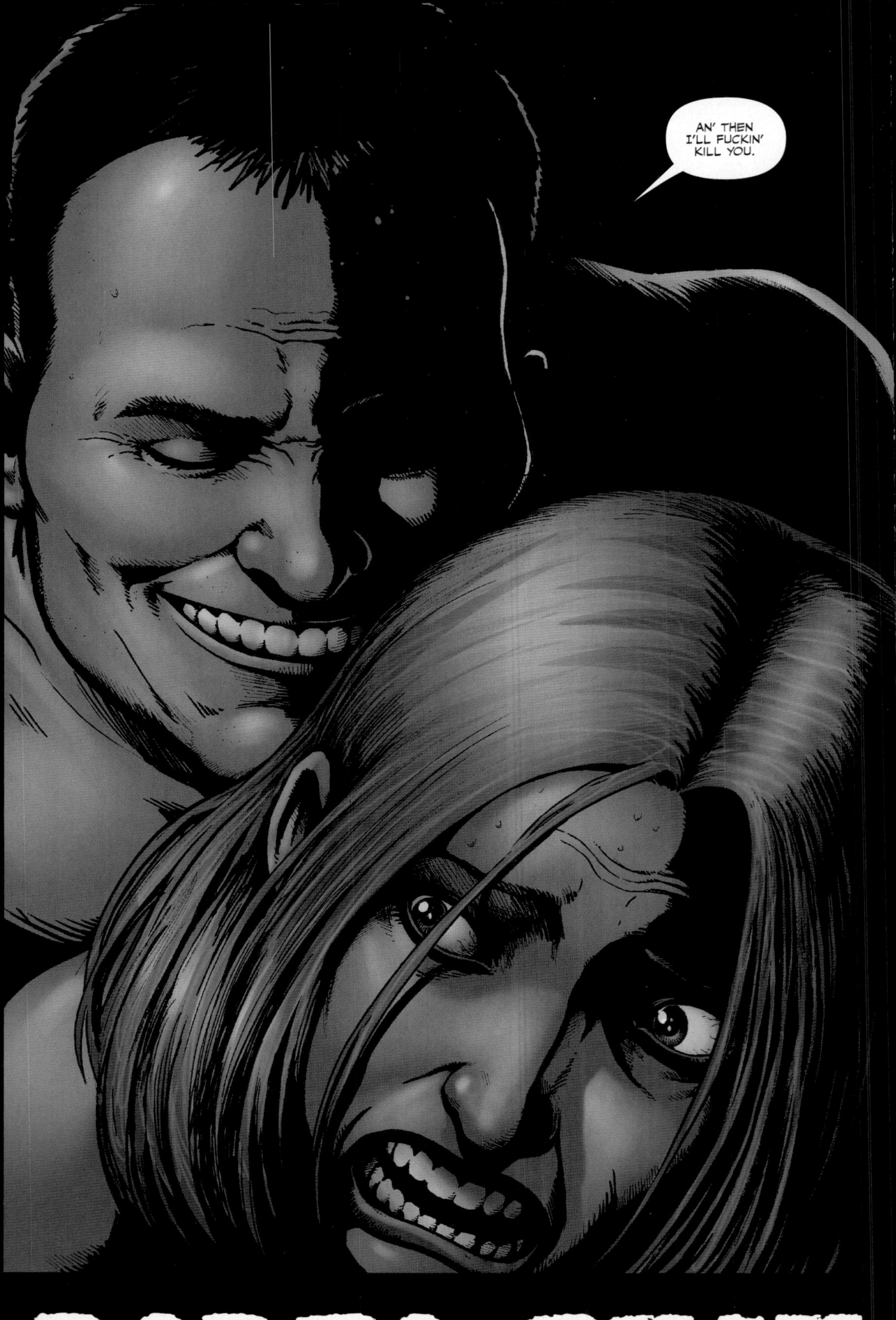
AN' THEN I'LL FUCKIN' KILL YOU.

RODEO FUCK

OMNIBUS BONUS MATERIAL

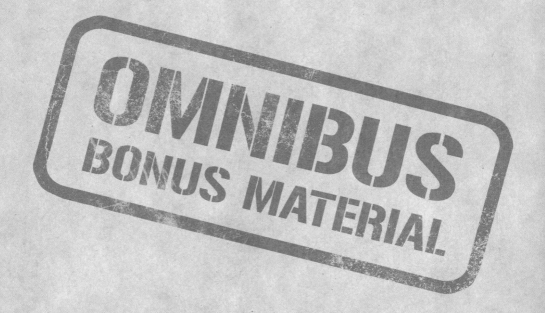

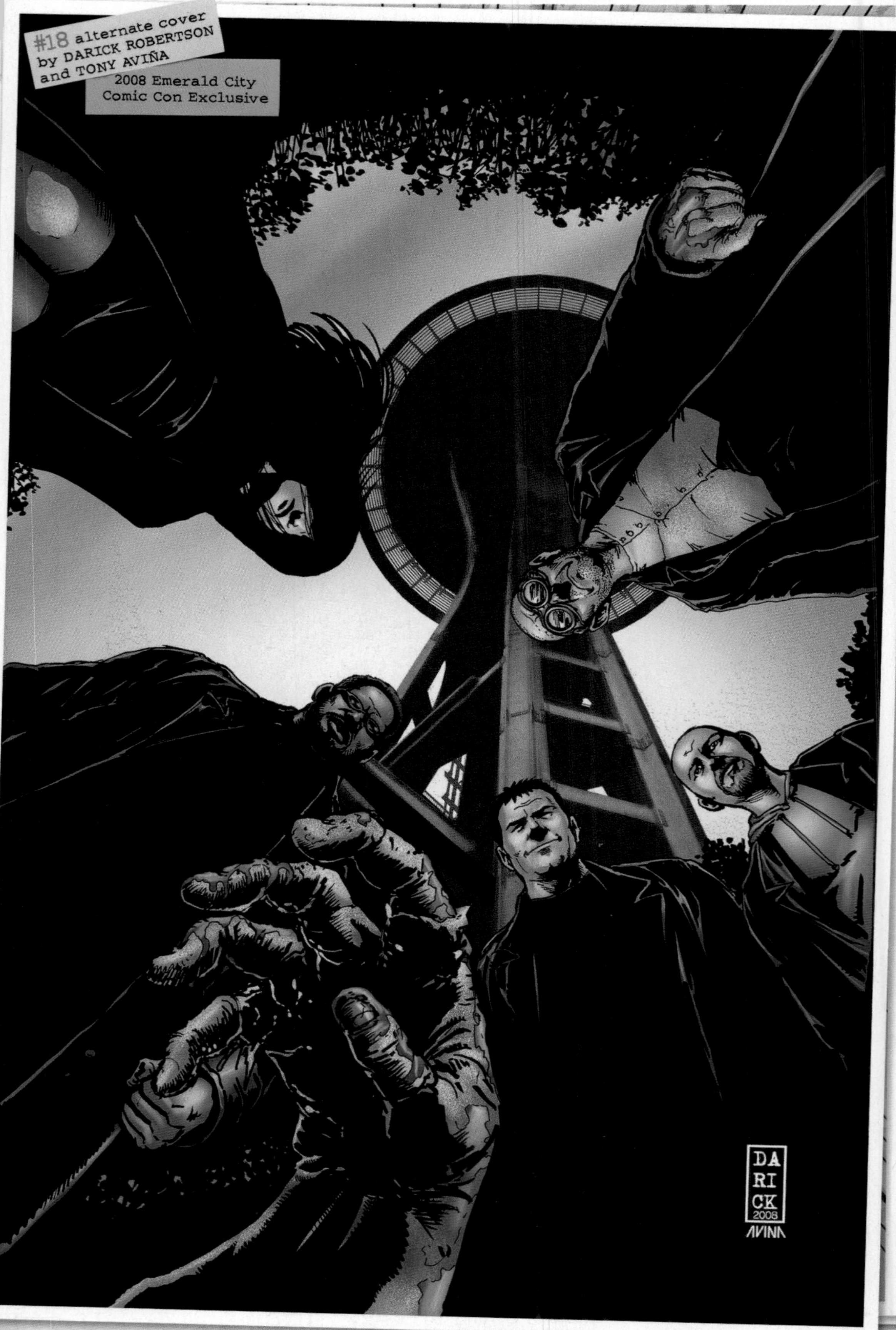
#18 alternate cover
by DARICK ROBERTSON
and TONY AVIÑA
2008 Emerald City
Comic Con Exclusive
DA
RI
CK
2008
AVINA

#20 alternate cover
by DARICK ROBERTSON
and TONY AVIÑA

2008 San Diego
Comic Con Exclusive

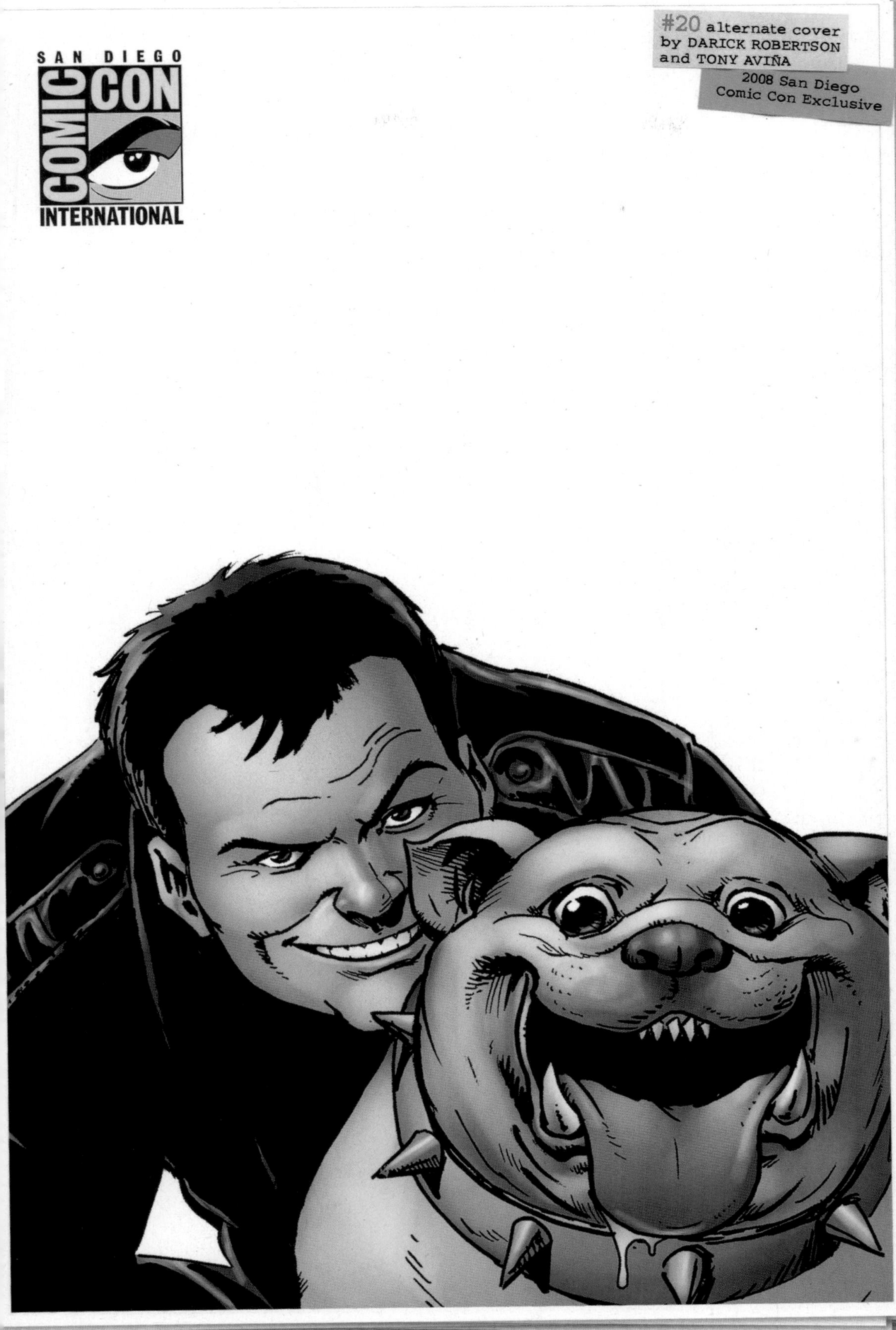
SAN DIEGO
COMIC CON
INTERNATIONAL

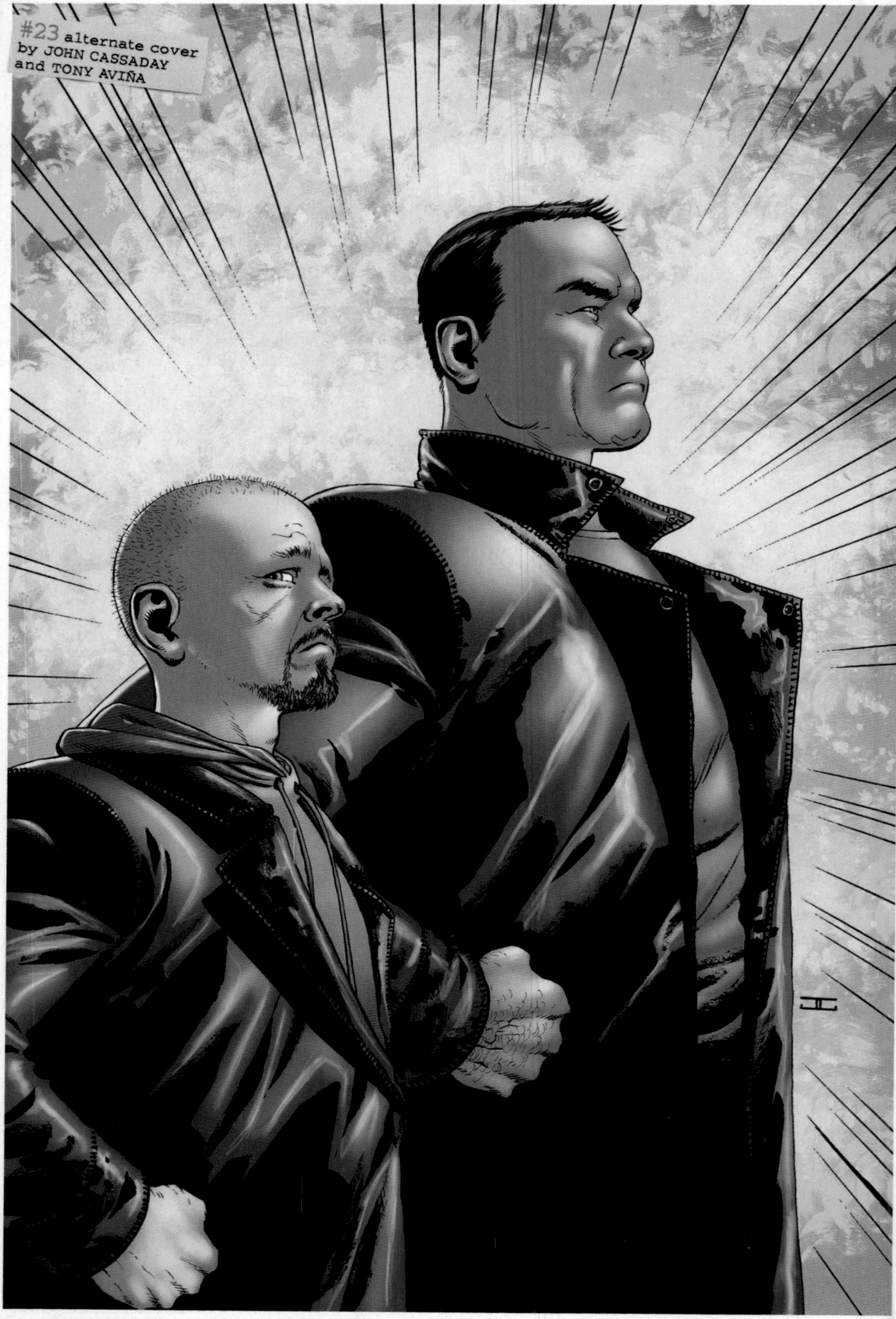
#23 alternate cover
by JOHN CASSADAY
and TONY AVIÑA

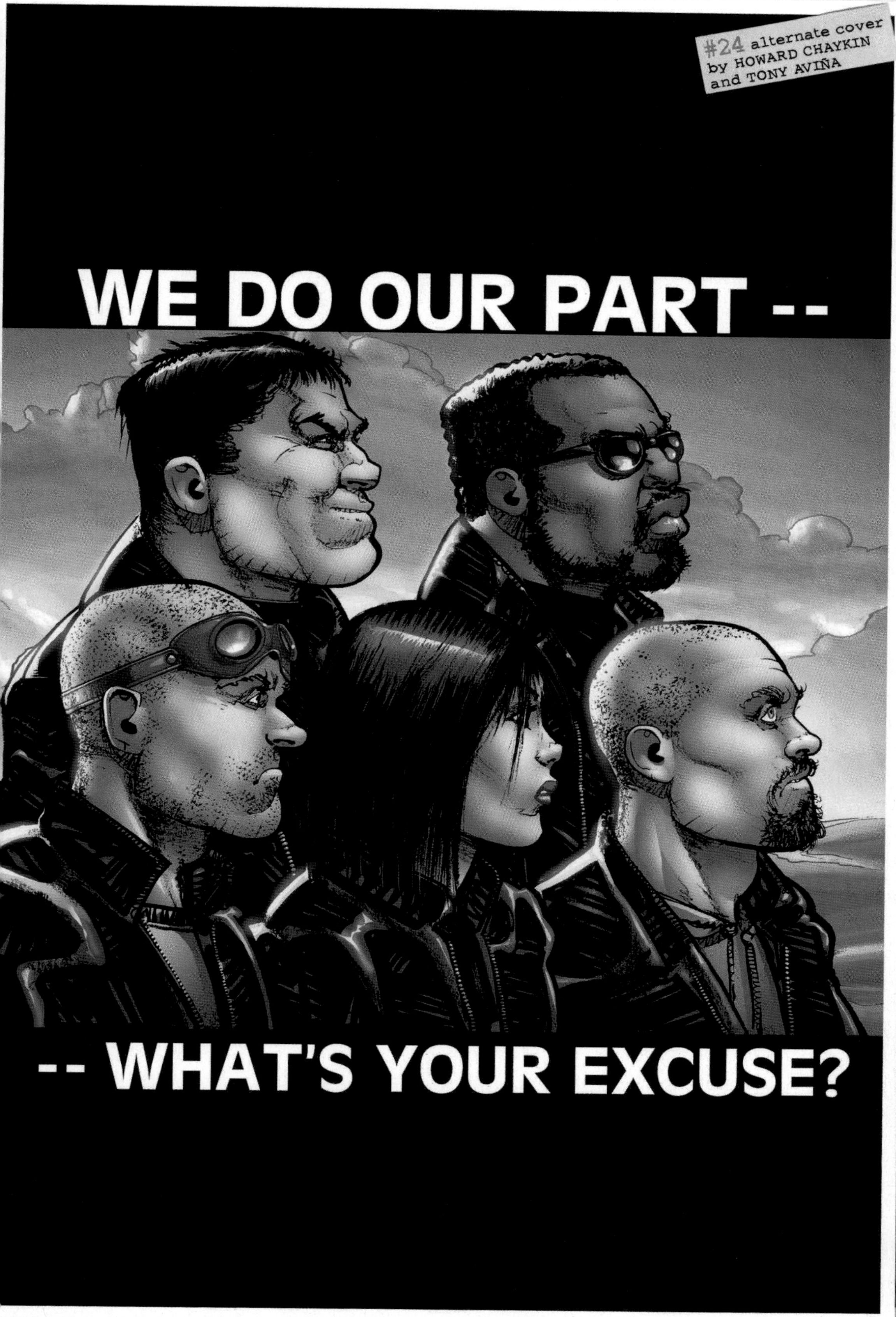
#24 alternate cover
by HOWARD CHAYKIN
and TONY AVIÑA
WE DO OUR PART --
-- WHAT'S YOUR EXCUSE?

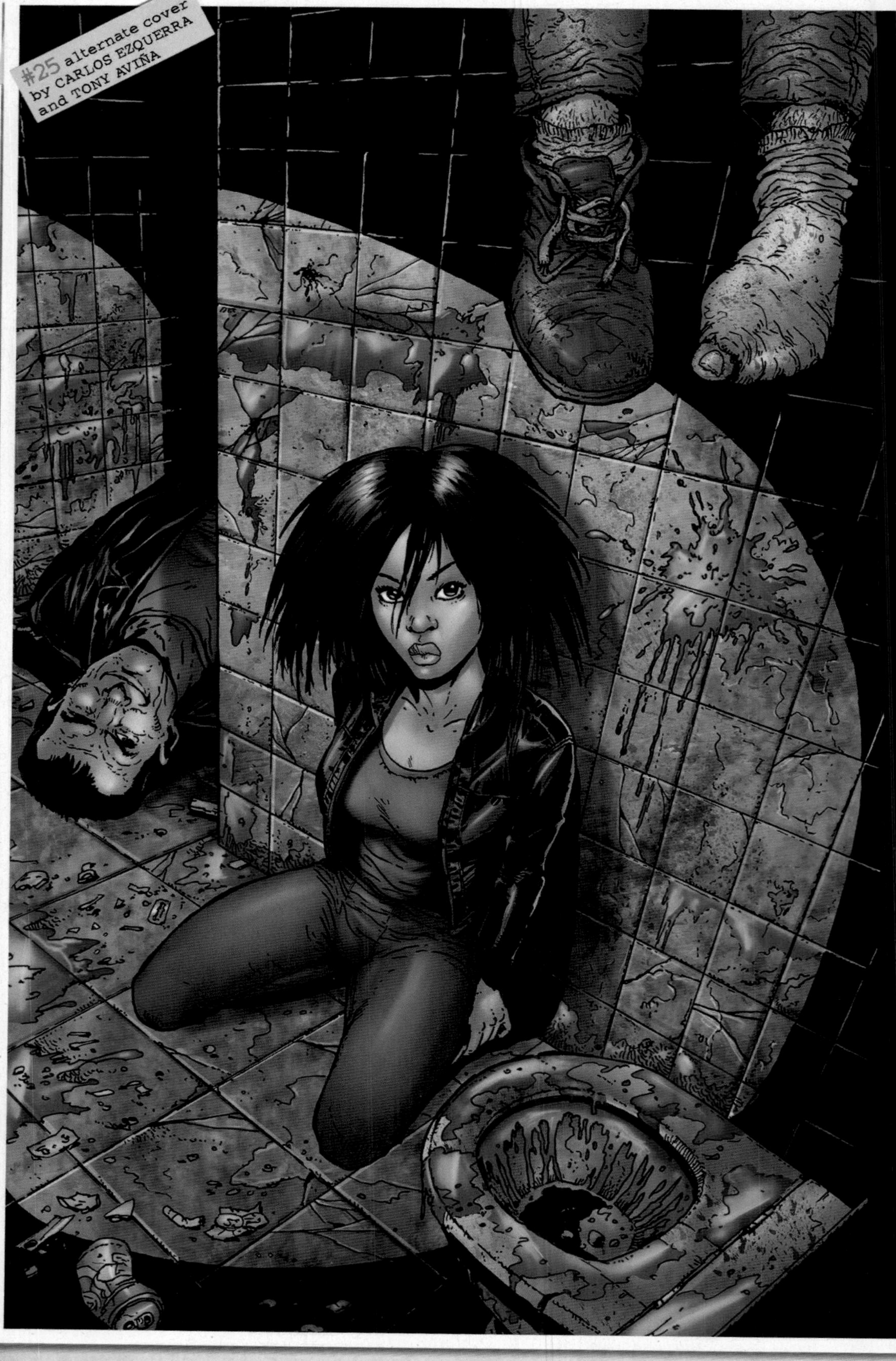

#25 alternate cover by CARLOS EZQUERRA and TONY AVIÑA

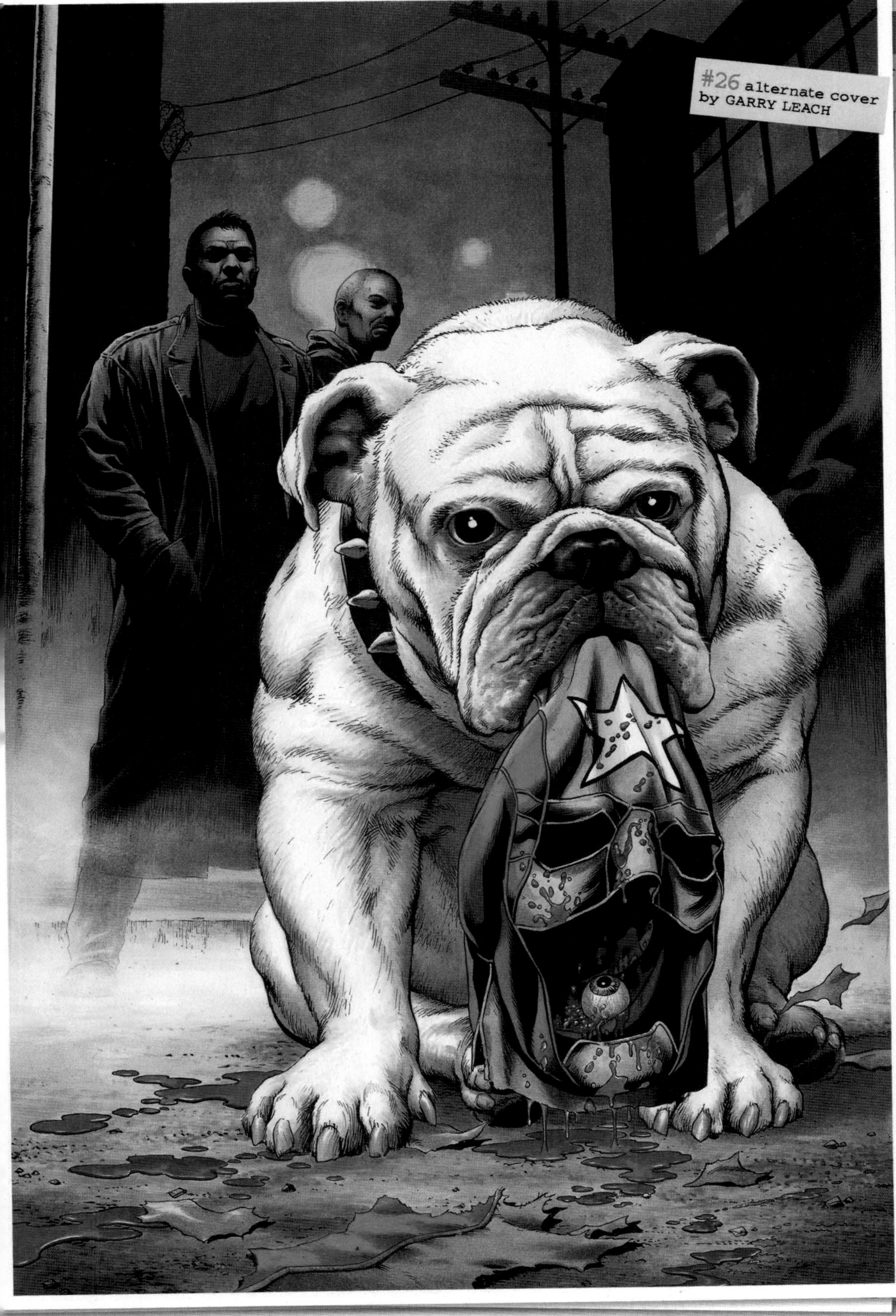

#26 alternate cover
by GARRY LEACH

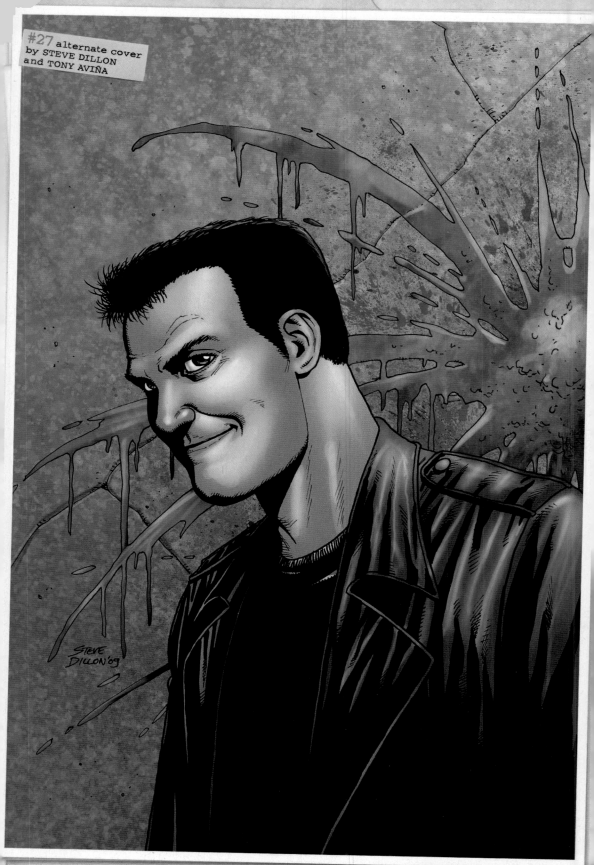

#27 alternate cover
by STEVE DILLON
and TONY AVIÑA

#28 alternate cover
by DAVE GIBBONS
and TONY AVIÑA

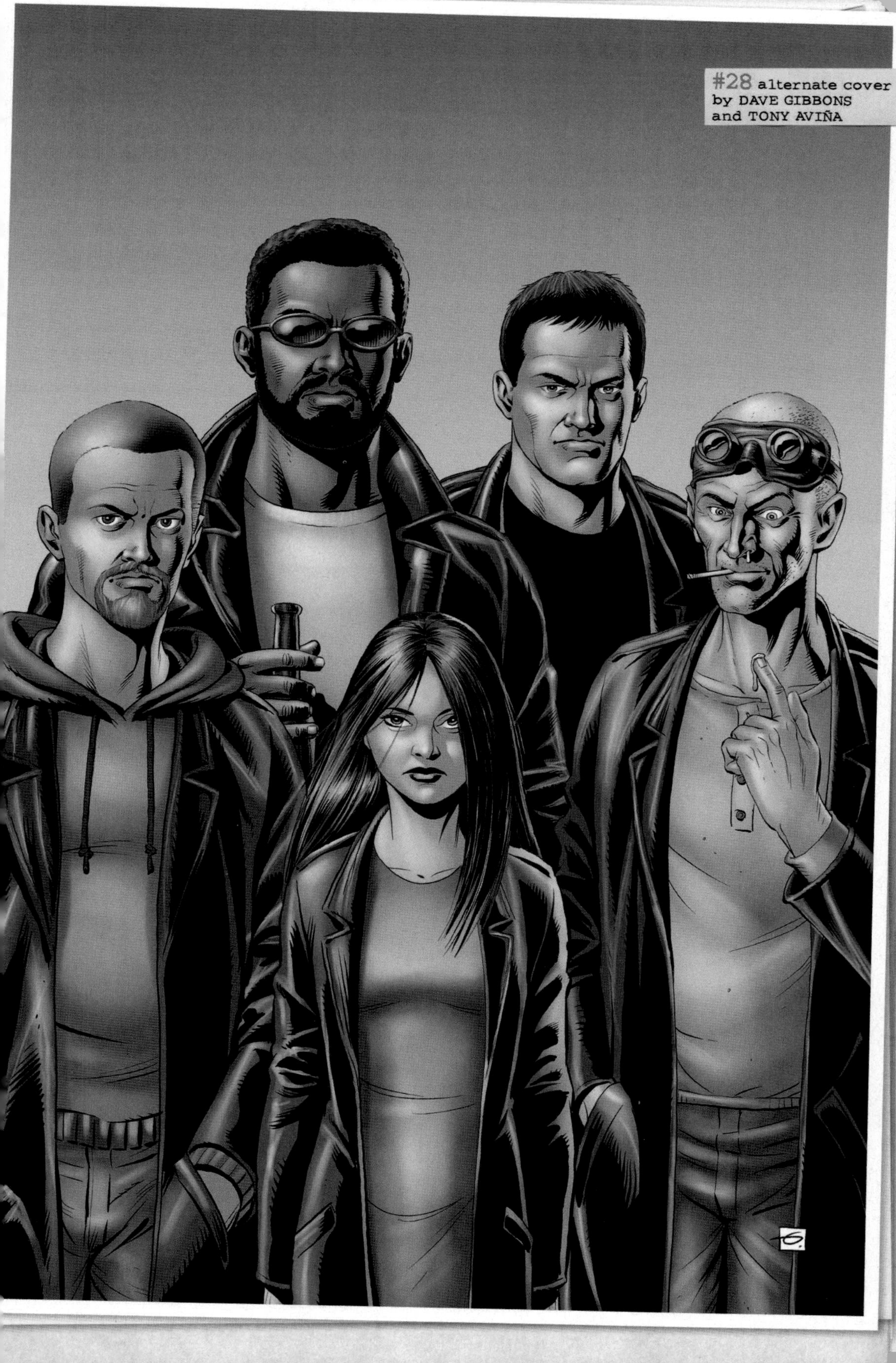

#29 alternate cover
by DAVID LLOYD

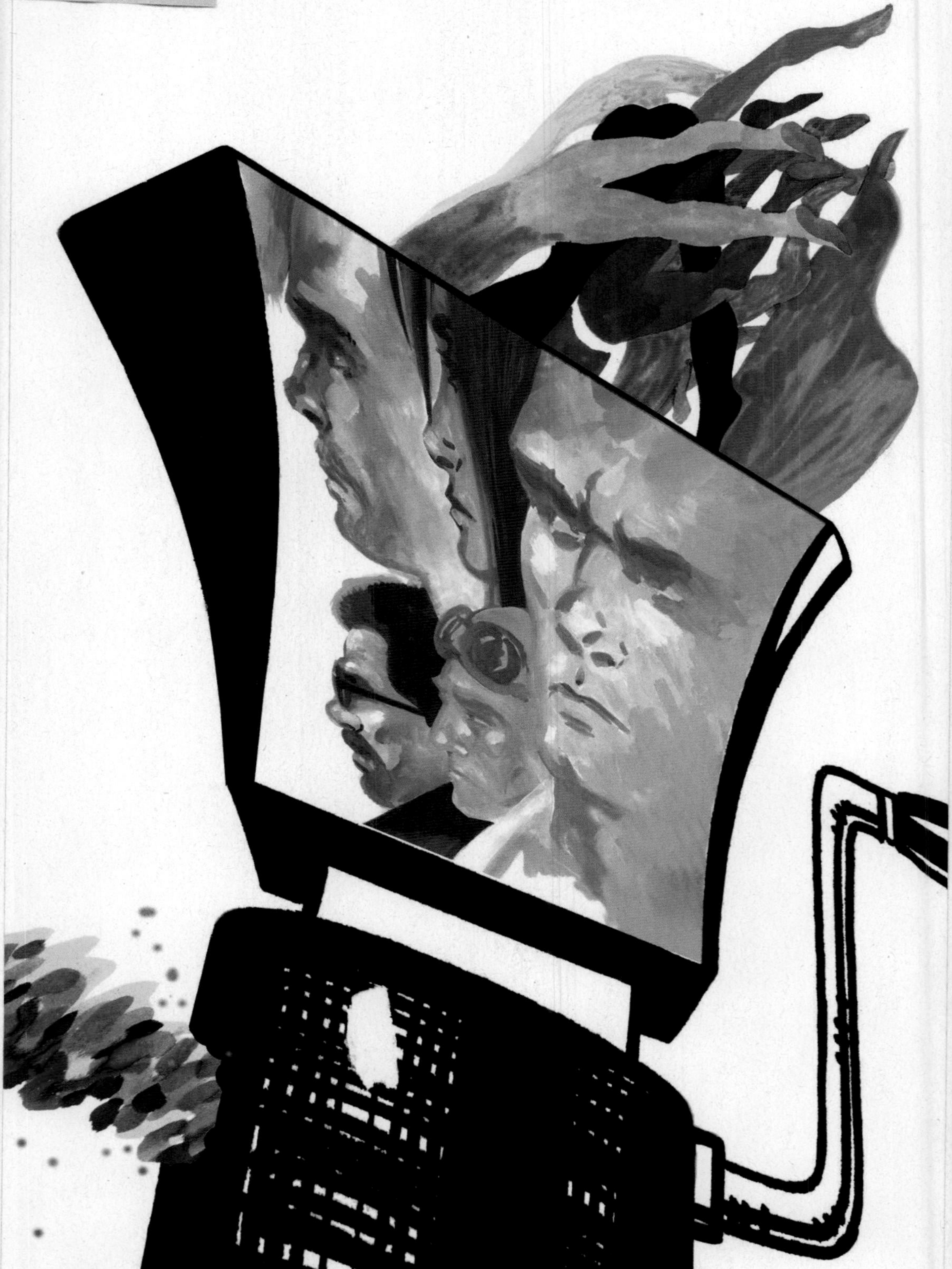

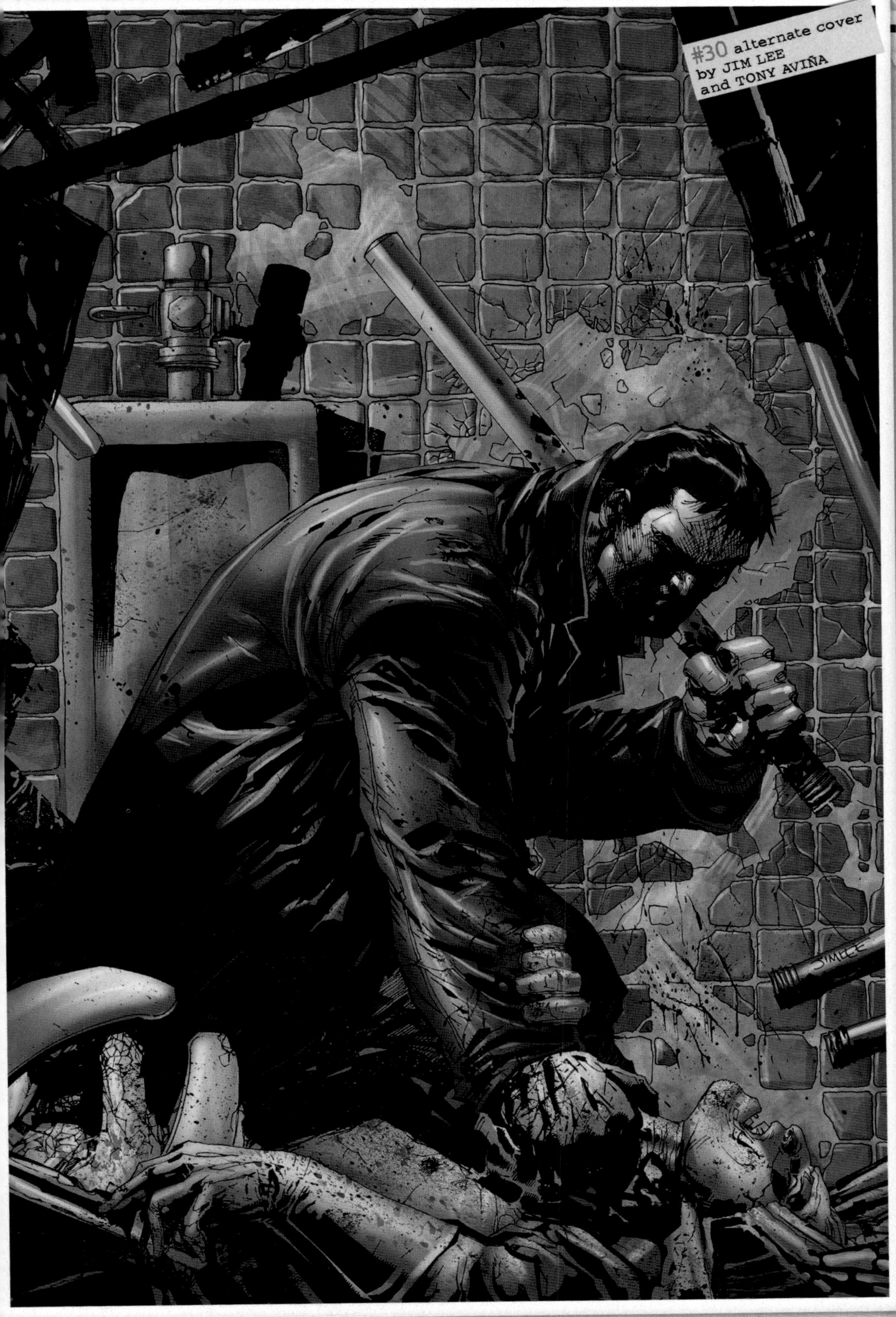
#30 alternate cover
by JIM LEE
and TONY AVIÑA
JIM LEE

creating a cover by Darick Robertson

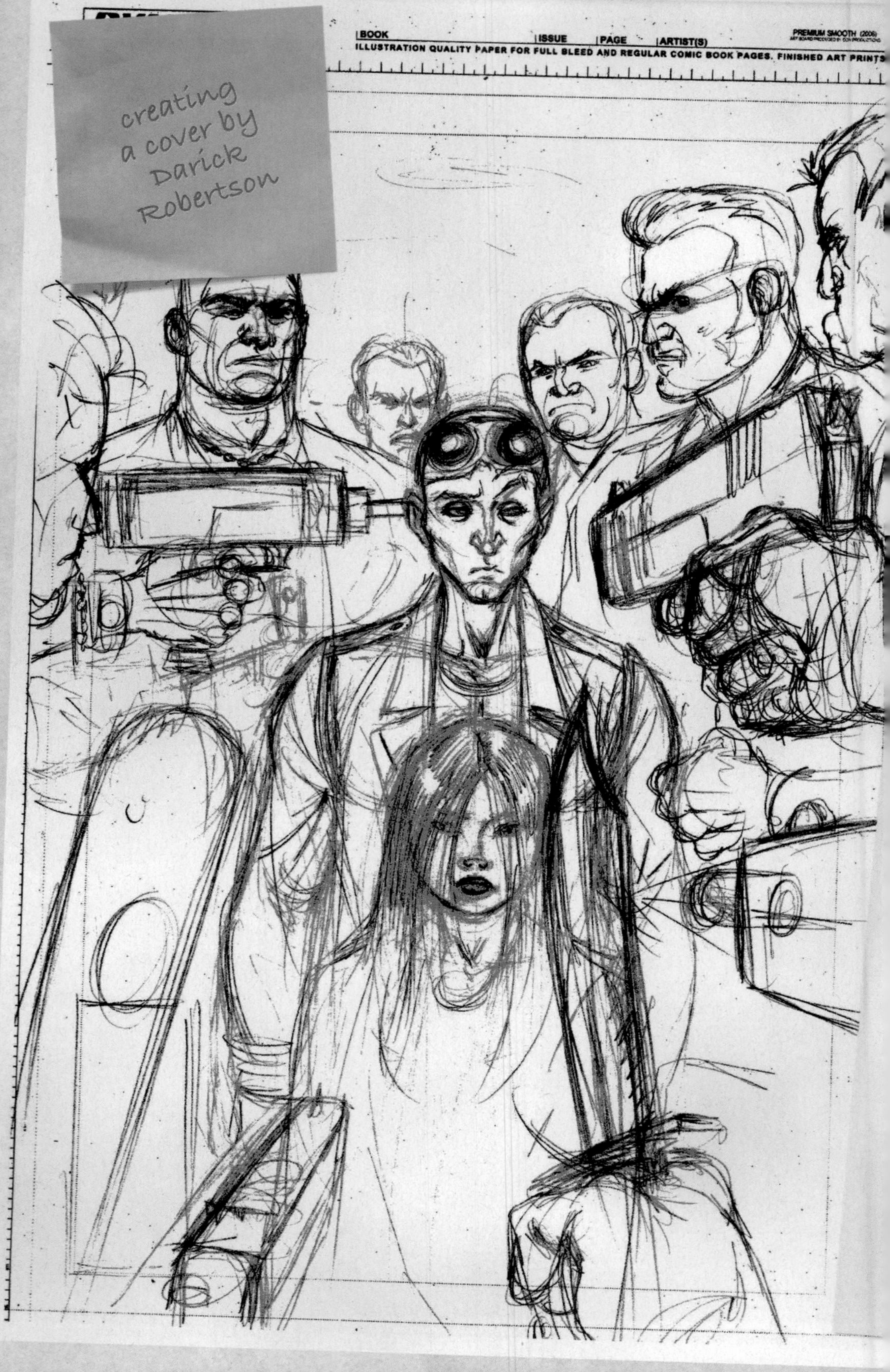
BOOK
ISSUE
PAGE
ARTIST(S)
PREMIUM SMOOTH (2006)
ILLUSTRATION QUALITY PAPER FOR FULL BLEED AND REGULAR COMIC BOOK PAGES. FINISHED ART PRINTS

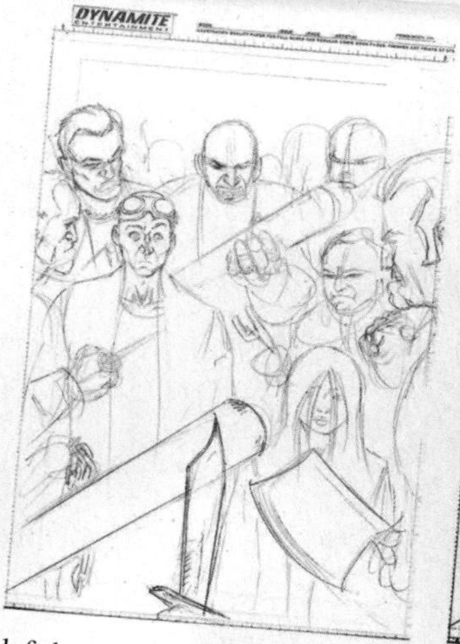

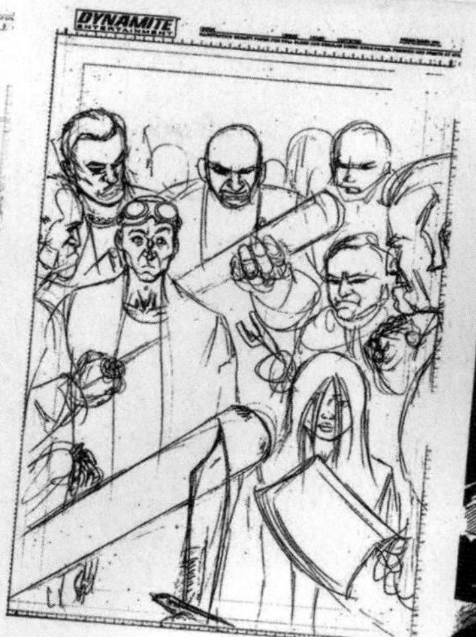

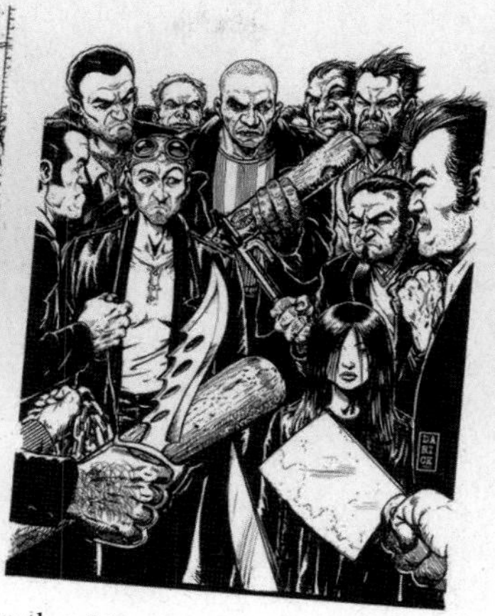

At left here you see the cover to #16. It was a departure of sorts for me in that I began drawing in blue pencil, scanning and changing it to gray scale to share and get feedback, then going straight to inks to save time, a method I am still successfully using as of this writing. Normally a cover for the boys comes about with an interaction with Garth as he nearly always has a set idea of what he'd like to see. In this case I suggested "French-man calm, surrounded by the hostile mob group from the scene on pg 12-13". Garth added "Add the Female, standing next to each other, both completely unfazed- perhaps slightly puzzled- by the dozen or so armed and furious wiseguys surrounding them." after seeing the first sketch he added "try them side by side, both more puzzled looking. Avoid the guns pointed nearest, that's been done a lot recently. Knives and baseball bats. Plenty of guys. " So I went back to the board, redrew it, and what you see is the final. Sometimes, the best times, I get a simple "spot on" and I'm good to go. With 22 it was similar in that Garth had a detailed idea for #22, "our group shot. View past the TV at the Boys sitting on the couch watching it. Left to Right: Frenchie guzzling popcorn and spilling a good deal of it, MM (beer) glancing down at the mess Frenchie's making, annoyed (MM"s the only one not looking at the TV), Hughie (beer) riveted, sitting forward in fascination, Butcher (coffee) smiling his dark smile as he points the remote. The Female sits cross-legged on the floor in front of them, emotionless, big eyes locked on the screen. All in their coats, just for the cover's sake. " I did version 'A' but upon discussion, revised it to version 'B' which in the end, I was much happier with as well.

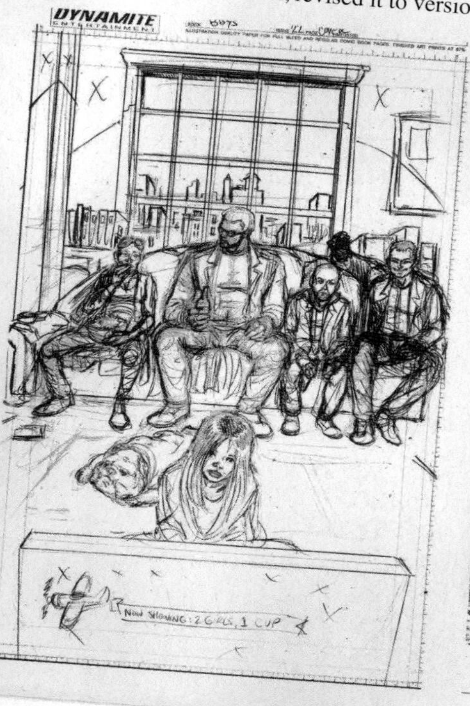
NOW SHOWING: 2 GIRLS, 1 CUP

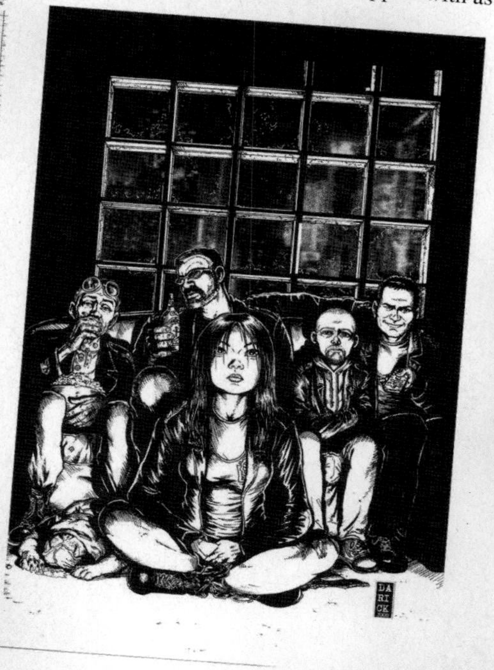

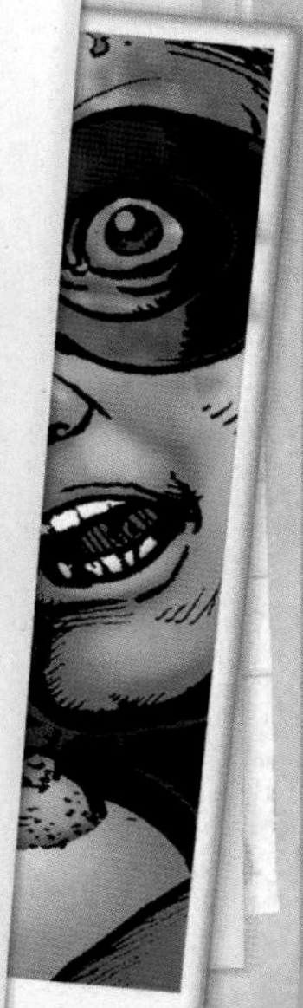

Boys 28

Parts + Graves

?

5.
Five-Oh unscrews the top of his hip flask. Divine glances at Critter, who scowls while fumbling in the fur covering his crotch. Europo stares offshot like a fucking idiot.

Five-Oh: SHE LOATHED THE GROUND YOU WALKED ON AND YOU
             MADE HER WANT TO JOIN THE KLAN…

Divine: NO SOONER DO THE GLOVES COME OFF, MM?

Critter: FUCK YOU, TURD-WORSHIPPER.

Europo: **SHAAAAVED** HER GENITALS!

p. 6

p. 7

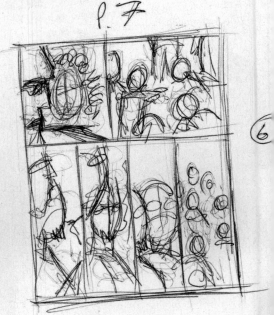

⑤

⑥

PAGE SEVEN

1.
King Helmet scowls offshot with the ghastly rose arrangement behind him.

King: … SAME KINDA CONNECTION I SHARED WIT' MY HOMEBOY
             2-KOOL—KIND NO MUTHAFUCKIN' G-FOOLS SEND SOME
             ABORTION-LOOKIN' RINGA ROSES **EVER** UNDERSTAND…

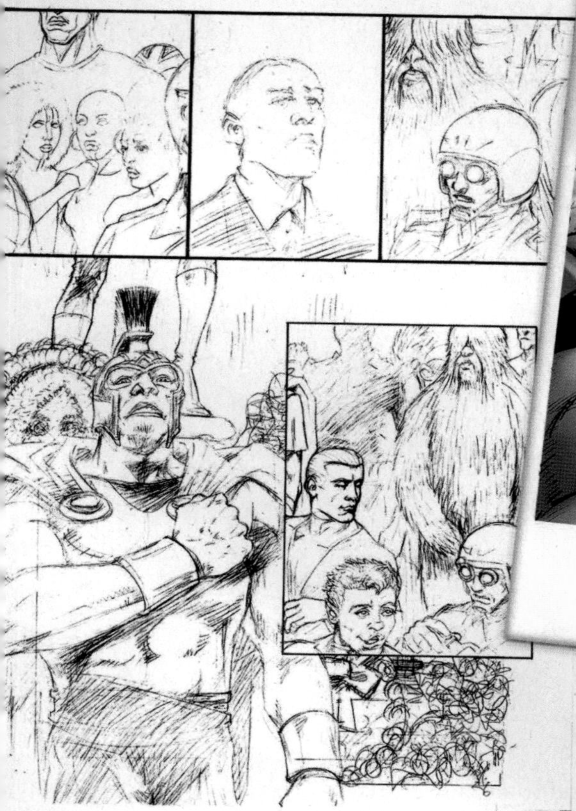

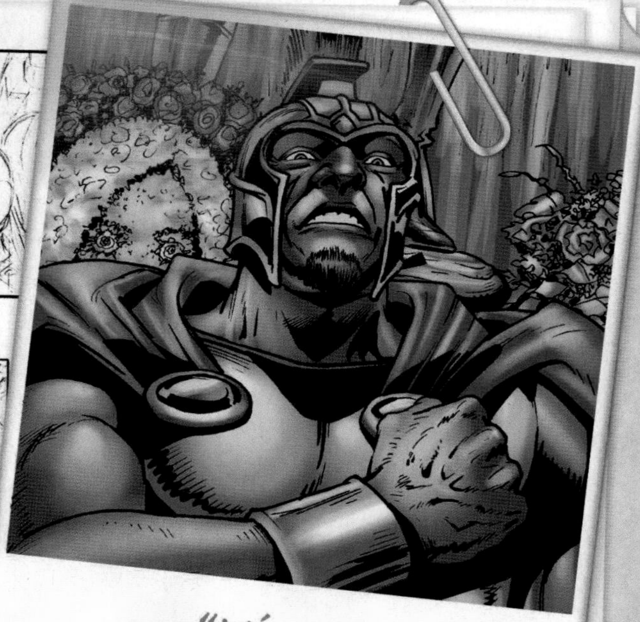

"King"

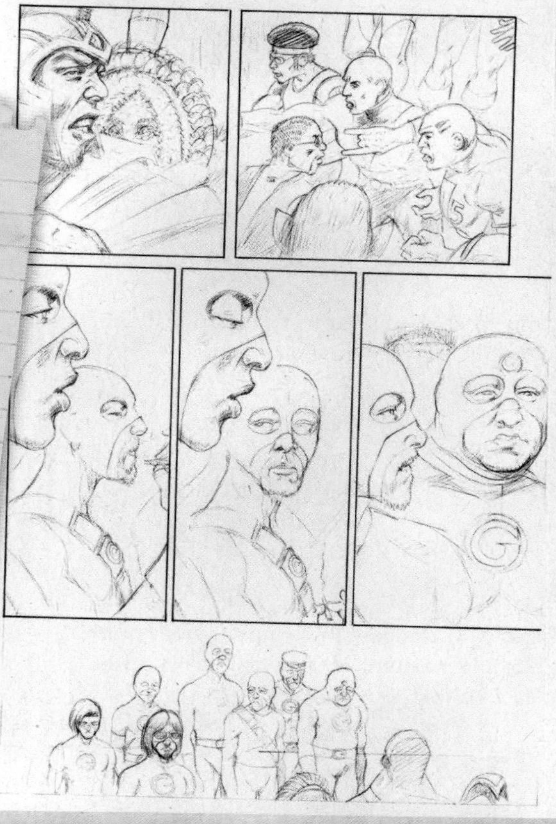

Coming into the continuity of Garth and Darick's world, is akin to walking naked into a crowded communal shower room in Rikers correction facility with a bar of soap.

To fit into the flow of the characters, storylines and costume design, as Garth writes them, Darick draws them and I am working on the very next issue, is one slippery bar of soap. I tried not to drop it, but if I had, I wouldn't have bent over to pick it up!

Cheers,
John Higgins

THE BOYS 17
BY GARTH ENNIS

PAGE ONE

1.

Day in the ghetto, a row of rundown, heavily vandalised houses- windows broken or boarded up, dubious looking characters hanging around, a burnt-out car etc. We're somewhere deep in the Bronx, where the cops rarely venture. A taxi is parked outside the one decent house on the street, a two-storey structure free of damage or graffiti. Sticks out like a sore thumb compared to the other wrecks. Two people stand next to the taxi.

One: … YOU KNOW, THAT DUDE, WE CAUGHT HIM IN DETROIT
                THAT TIME…

Two: YEAH.

One: SHIT, WHAT THE FUCK WAS HIS NAME? GODDAMNDEST
                LOOKIN' MUTHAFUCKA, HAD LIKE A—

Two: YEAH.

2.

Close in. It's Butcher and MM. Butcher leans against the taxi next to Terror, smiles sadly at MM with a meaningful look in his eye. MM stops short.

Butcher: LOOK, MATE, IF YOU WANNA STAND HERE TALKIN'
                BOLLOCKS ABOUT THE GOOD OLD DAYS ALL AFTERNOON,

                FINE. BUT YOU KNOW AS
                WELL AS I DO YOU'RE
                GONNA HAVE TO GO IN
                THERE EVENTUALLY.

3.

MM wilts, beaten, miserable. Grimaces a little.
Got to face up to something bad here.

MM: … YEAH.

Butcher: I'LL COME BACK AN' PICK
                YOU UP IN THE MORNIN',
                ALL RIGHT?

4.

Pull back. MM trudges slowly up the steps of the
house, shoulders slumped. The taxi drives away
in the background.

5.

MM closes the door behind him, glances warily around. Inside the place is neat and tidy, a perfectly maintained, old-fashioned home. Someone's grandmother might live here.

MM: MOMMA?

6.

Close in as he walks down the hallway, careful, clearly on edge. Nearest us is the old wooden door to the basement, set in the wall under the stairs.

MM: IT'S ME, MOMMA.

PAGE TWO

1.

MM stands framed in the doorway, partially silhouetted, face shadowed. From his stance he seems reluctant to proceed. The stairs descend towards us into the gloom, old and rickety, covered in cobwebs. Down here it's all dust and shadows, rusty nails sticking out of the bare decaying wood, gloomy and ominous. Perhaps a rat or two.

MM: MOMMA?

"   "   YOU THERE?

Title: **GOOD FOR THE SOUL** part three

PAGE THREE

1.

Day. Hughie gets into the van parked outside the Kix' house, bag of takeout in hand. Seems deep in thought.

Hughie: AXE.

2.

Inside, he pulls the rear door shut behind him, sits next to the surveillance gear.

Hughie: AXE?

3.

His face falls as he lays out his lunch: big sandwich, coffee, banana. Gloomy, forced to face reality.

Hughie: AYE, RIGHT, **YOU'RE** GONNA GET AN AXE. YOU'RE GONNA
                  CUT SOME LAD'S HEAD OFF WI' THE FUCKIN' THING, FOR
                  CHRIST'S SAKE...!

4.

He starts eating, got his back to us. Nearest us the surveillance gear crackles into life.

Hughie: ASK BUTCHER… EXCEPT THE WHOLE BLOODY POINT IS TO
                 DO IT **WITHOUT** BUTCHER…

Jag: I THINK HE WAS CRYING.

5.

Not terribly worried, Hughie sticks the earphones on as he chews his sandwich.

Jag: **CRYING?**

Jag 2:   WELL, HE HAD TEARS COMING OUT OF HIS EYES, IT'S WHAT
                 IT LOOKED LIKE…

Jag 3:   HE'S JUST BEEN BROUGHT BACK FROM THE DEAD, IT
                 COULD'VE BEEN FUCKING EMBALMING FLUID! JESUS…!

PAGE FOUR

1.

Still chewing, Hughie twiddles a dial on the gear, bit more interested now.

Jag: OR CUM. TWO OF YOU MAKING UP FOR LOST TIME?

Jag 2:   FUCK YOU, DOGKNOTT! THAT'S YOUR GAME, YOU
                 COCKSUCKER, YOU AND OUR ILLUSTRIOUS LEADER!

2.

View up past the van at the window, where we see one silhouetted figure smack another around the head.

Jag: ME AND BLARNEY COCK WERE STRAIGHT AS **AAAOW!**

Jag 2:   WATCH YOUR MOUTH…

3.

The photos scattered on the floor of the van.

Jag: OH YEAH, BIG GAME, BIG **MAN!** YOU WEREN'T SUCH HOT SHIT
                 WHEN THAT ENGLISH BASTARD CAVED YOUR FACE IN, WERE
                 YOU?

Jag 2:   WHACK JOB, I AM FUCKING WARNING YOU—

Jag 3:   CAN WE ALL JUST PUT OUR DICKS AWAY FOR ONE MINUTE?
                 PLEASE?

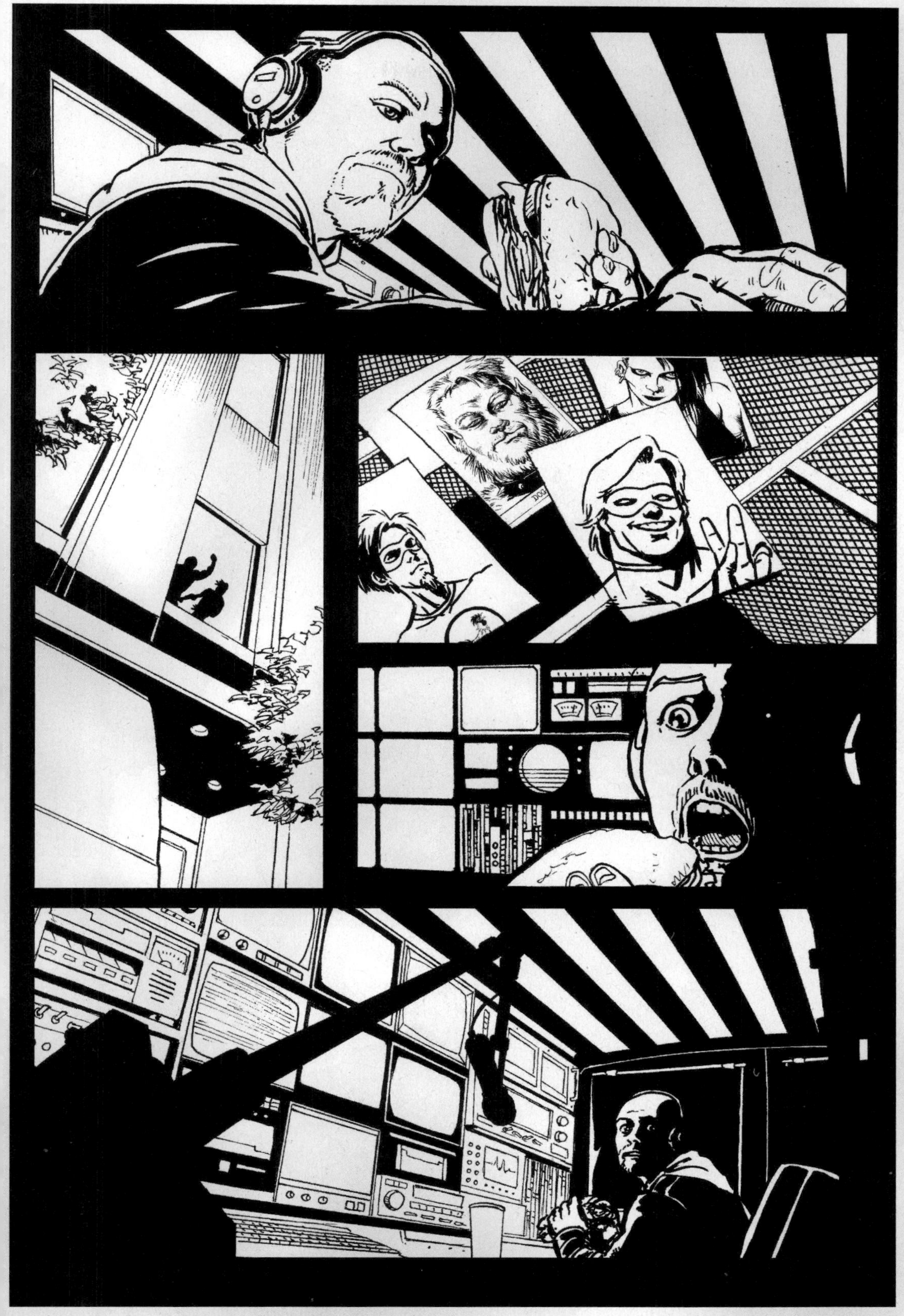

4.

Hughie stops short, mid-mouthful.

Jag: TELL ME: IF YOU ACTUALLY HAD A DICK, WOULD IT HAVE
                LOTS OF LITTLE CUTS UP THE SHAFT?

Jag 2:   FUCK YOU.

"   "   THE POINT IS HE'S **GONE**, CAN WE ALL AT LEAST AGREE ON

                THAT MUCH?

5.

Pull back, Hughie alone in the van, glancing around him, suddenly edgy. Am I really alone? Is there someone else in here with me?

Jag: GOOD.

"   "   SO WHAT DO WE DO?

PAGE FIVE

1.

Hughie pulls a toolbox out from under the floor of the van. Not panicking, but moving pretty fast all the same, urgent.

Jag: CALL VOUGHT?

Jag 2:   **NO FUCKING WAY** DO WE CALL VOUGHT…

2.

Close up as he holds up a large, skull-cracking wrench, glances sideways again, edgy. Eyes wide, mouth tight shut.

Jag: THEY'LL THINK WE'RE A BUNCH OF ASSHOLES, WE CAN'T
                COPE ON OUR—

Jag 2:   YOU DON'T THINK THE SHIP MIGHT ALREADY'VE SAILED ON
                THAT ONE?

Jag 3:   ALL RIGHT, KNOCK IT OFF. HE'S A REANIMATED CORPSE
                WITH SOMETHING LIKE THREE PERCENT OF ORIGINAL BRAIN
                FUNCTION: WHAT CAN HE DO, REALLY?

3.

Pull back. He creeps toward the back of the van, wrench in both hands, ready to swing.

Jag: AND HOW DIFFICULT IS IT GOING TO BE FOR THE SIX OF US—
                WORKING TOGETHER—TO CATCH HIM?

Jag 2:   DID DOCTOR CARLIN SAY ANYTHING…?

Jag 3:   FEED HIM AND CLEAN HIM. THERE HAVEN'T BEEN TOO
                 MANY OF THESE, THEY'RE STILL FIGURING A LOT OF STUFF
                 OUT.

Jag 4:   THE SEVEN AND THE G-MEN HAVE HAD LIKE ONE EACH, WE
                 COULD ALWAYS TRY TALKING TO THEM…

4.

Exterior as Hughie peeks out the back window- moves a little black curtain to do so. Grim, edgy.
Doesn't see is a hand in the shadows under the van, next to the rear wheel.

Jag: YOU KNOW WHAT THE SEVEN WOULD DO TO YOU IF YOU EVEN
                 FUCKING MENTIONED THE LAMPLIGHTER…?

Hughie: **SHITE**.

"   "   THIS IS NO' YOU, HUGHIE.

5.

Close up. In the shadows behind the hand- which has an ill-fitting green glove on- is a pair of bloodshot
eyes, one only half-open, feeble and pathetic.

Up: THIS IS NO' YOU AT ALL.

Eyes: WAMAHAMMA…

PAGE SIX

1.

Annie- as Starlight- stops short as she passes a doorway in the Seven's HQ. Maeve sits nearest in a
lounge area, martini in hand, cigarette on the go, ashtray on the table in front of her. Doesn't look at
Annie once.

Maeve: THERE YOU ARE.

2.

Pull back. The lounge has pleasant views of NY below and the clouds all around. Day.

Annie: MY LADY…?

Maeve: I'M SUPPOSED TO GIVE YOU SHIT ABOUT MISSING THE
                 MEETING YESTERDAY.

"   "   LET'S NOT AND SAY WE DID. SHIT GIVEN.

3.

Close in again. Annie's a bit thrown, Maeve sips her martini.

Annie: I'M SORRY, I WAS—

Maeve: I DON'T CARE.

Annie: DID I MISS ANYTHING IMPORTANT?

Maeve: PROBABLY.

4.

Annie's puzzled at getting off lightly. Maeve raises her empty glass without looking up.

Annie: WELL… THANK YOU…

Maeve: WHAT FOR?

"   "   PISS-BOY…

Off;   COMING RIGHT UP, MY LADY!

PAGE SEVEN

1.

Annie looks back at us as she heads for the corridor, puzzled. Trying to figure Maeve.

Corridor: … CANCELLED THE WHOLE THING, HE ISN'T COMING AT ALL?

2.

View past the Homelander and Stillwell with Black Noir following as they walk down the corridor. Ahead we see Annie freeze in the doorway, but they're not looking at her.

Stillwell: IF HE'S NOT MAKING THE SPEECH, WHAT REASON HAS HE TO COME HERE?

Homelander: OH, I DON'T KNOW… AVOIDING MAKING US LOOK LIKE SHIT, MAYBE SOMETHING LIKE THAT…

3.

Head and shoulders. Stilwell calm as ever, Homelander a bit miffed. Black Noir follows, says nothing.

Homelander: I MEAN I CAN'T SAY I'M SORRY THE SPEECH GOT NIXED; I WAS UNCOMFORTABLE WITH THE IDEA ALL ALONG. NOT THAT I WOULDN'T HAVE BEEN A GOOD SOLDIER ABOUT IT.

"   "   BUT TO BE BLOWN OFF BY THE V.P.…

Stillwell: LIVE WITH IT. AND DON'T THINK THE SPEECH IS GOING AWAY, EITHER, THERE'LL BE ANOTHER TIME AND ANOTHER PLACE.

4.

Annie listens carefully, standing just inside the doorway of the lounge.

Off: WHAT OUGHT TO CONCERN YOU IS HOW THE PRESIDENT'S
                        PEOPLE FOUND OUT.

"   "   BECAUSE NEED-TO-KNOW ON THIS ONE WAS VIC'S OFFICE,
                        ME, AND YOU.

5.

Close up. Homelander frowns. Stilwell doesn't even bother to look at him.

Homelander: WELL, VIC'S—

Stilwell: THOSE PEOPLE?

"   "   COME ON.

PAGE EIGHT

1.

View past Annie, standing just inside the doorway as the trio pass. They'd need to turn their heads to
see her- they don't.

Homelander: **FUCK...!**

"   "   I MEAN OKAY, MAYBE A-TRAIN OR JACK—BUT WITH WHAT
                        THEY STAND TO LOSE, WHY WOULD **ANYONE–**

Stilwell: YOU'RE NOT THINKING.

2.

Stillwell only. You'd never be able to tell he gives a shit.

Stilwell: WHOEVER IT WAS GOT WORD TO DAKOTA BOB THROUGH
                        CHANNELS. THEY DIDN'T GO TO THE MEDIA, WHICH WOULD
                        BE BOTH CHEAP AND OBVIOUS.

"   "   SO IT WAS A SHOT. A SUBTLE ONE, FRUSTRATING THE I
                        VOUGHT-AMERICAN AGENDA, CAUSING INTERNAL RATHER
                        THAN PUBLIC EMBARASSMENT.

"   "   DOES THAT SOUND LIKE A-TRAIN OR JACK?

3.

Annie peeks out, as they walk toward us, nearest. Homelander's face twists in frustration.

Homelander: SO THE FUCKING PLACE IS BUGGED? BY **WHO?**

"   "   BECAUSE I—

Stilwell: YOU SURPRISE ME, HOMELANDER.

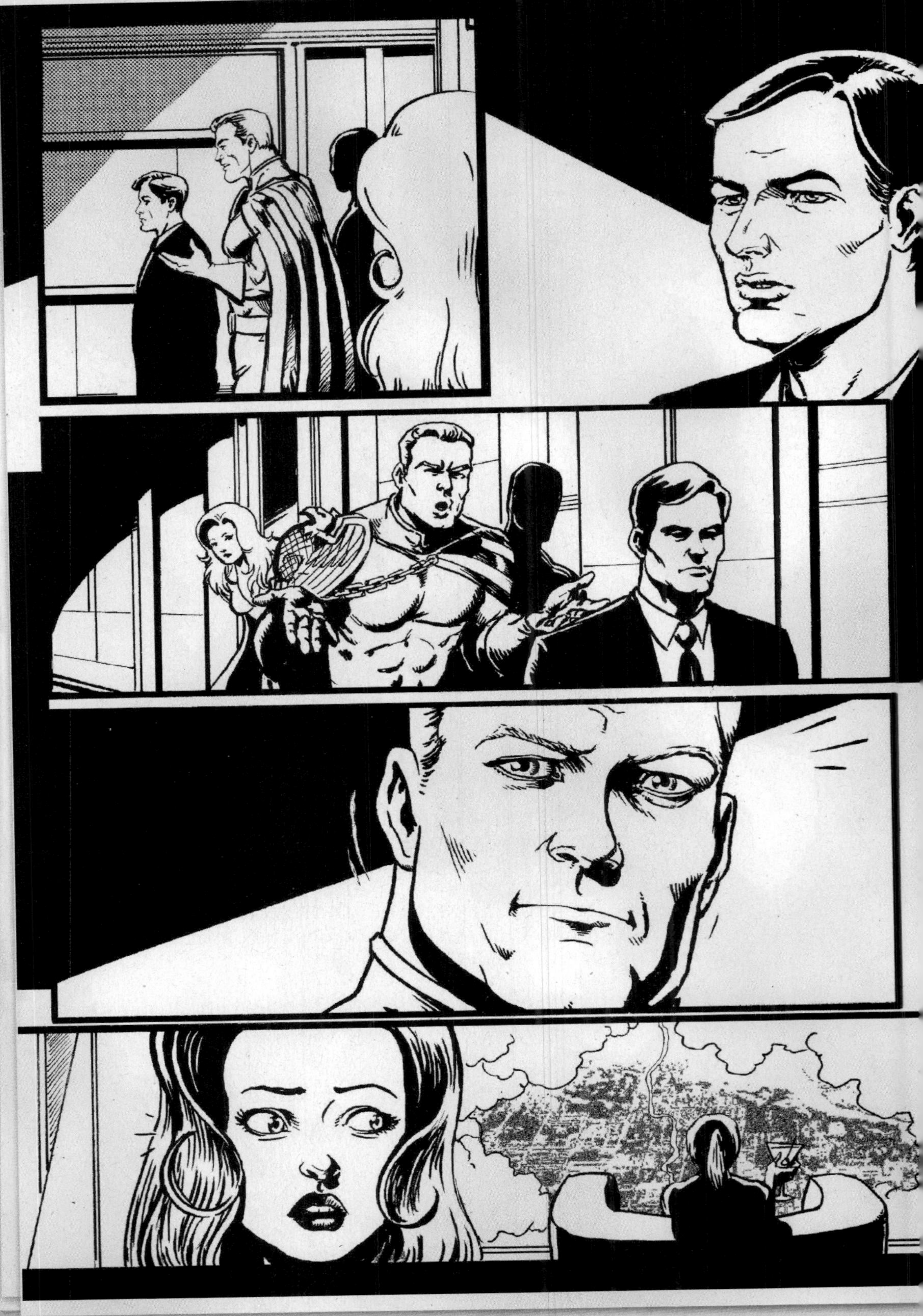

4.

Homelander only, freezing, understanding.

Off: YOU WEREN'T THIS SLOW ON THE UPTAKE WHEN TEENAGE
                        KIX HAD THEIR LITTLE MISHAP LAST YEAR.

5.

Annie stops short, remembering where she is. Maeve has a fresh martini further back, still isn't
bothering to turn.

Maeve: GETTING TO BE A HABIT OF YOURS.

"   "   LISTENING AT KEYHOLES.

PAGE NINE

1.

Central Park at dusk, Hughie and Annie on their bench. Nice evening. She's dying of embarrassment
with one hand over her face and eyes closed, he's smiling, amused but not unkind.

Annie: I AM **SO** EMBARASSED…

2.

Close in. he turns to smile at her, sympathetic. She cringes.

Annie: I MEAN…. I REMEMBER EVERYTHING.

"   "   HUGHIE, I'M **SORRY**—

Hughie: DON'T BE DAFT, IT WAS YOUR FIRST TIME ON THE BEVVY.
                        I'M SURPRISED YOU WEREN'T CLIMBIN' THE WALLS.

3.

He frowns for a moment, smile turning cautious. Now she smiles, but keeps her eyes closed.

Hughie: YOU'RE NO' UNDERAGE OR ANYTHING LIKE THAT, ARE YOU?
                        'CAUSE I DON'T WANNA GET DONE FOR SUPPLYIN' ALCOHOL
                        TO A MINOR…

Annie: YOU WON'T.

4.

They're quiet for a moment, both gazing offshot. Hughie's not smiling, but he's perfectly at ease. Annie
smiles just a little, thoughtful.

5.

Annie only, turning towards us. Eyes narrowed, little smile.

Annie: I REALLY LIKE YOU, HUGHIE.

PAGE TEN

1.

He turns to her, slightly surprised. She lowers her gaze, same quiet little smile.

Annie: I DON'T KNOW WHY, I BARELY KNOW YOU. ALSO I'M THE
                        WORST JUDGE OF CHARACTER IN THE ENTIRE WORLD.

"   "   BUT YOU SEEM LIKE YOU MIGHT BE SOMEONE… TRUE.

2.

Rear view on them as the world goes by. We don't see their faces.

Hughie: YOU CAN'T BE THE W—

Annie: TRUST ME.

3.

He watches her, quietly riveted, no longer smiling. She faces front, slight sense of concern.

Annie: I THINK THERE'S SOMETHING VERY SMALL BUT VERY
                        REAL BETWEEN US. AND THAT'S PRECIOUS.

"   "   I GET THE SENSE YOU'VE BEEN THROUGH SOME BAD STUFF,
                        AND I WANT YOU TO KNOW I'D NEVER DO ANYTHING—
                        ANYTHING—TO HURT YOUR HEART MORE THAN IT MIGHT
                        HAVE BEEN ALREADY.

4.

Annie only, facing us now, quietly but deadly serious. All in her eyes. Slight sense of yearning.

Annie: BUT I NEED YOU TO PROMISE ME THE SAME THING, HUGHIE,
                        BECAUSE I CAN'T BEAR THE THOUGHT OF ANY MORE
                        MEANNESS OR CRUELTY. I JUST CAN'T.

5.

Hughie only, facing us, quietly stunned.

Off: IF THE WORLD REALLY IS THE WAY I'VE COME TO THINK IT
                        IS, WHAT'S BETWEEN US IS MORE PRECIOUS THAN GOLD.

PAGE ELEVEN

1.

Hughie slowly faces front again, stunned. Annie does likewise, calm.

Hughie: … JINGS…

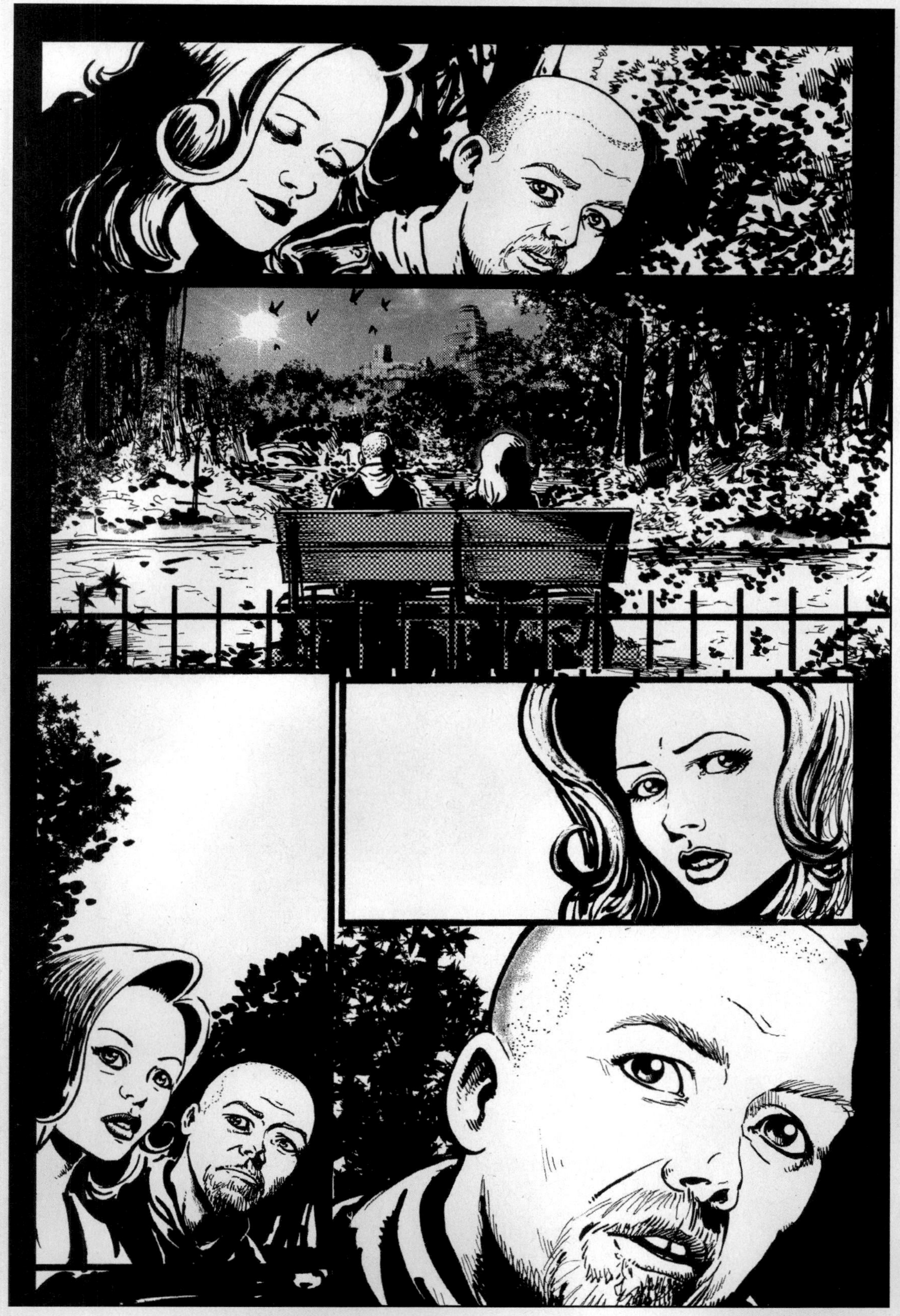

2.

Hughie only, slightly nervous as he gazes at the ground. Mouth opening, almost scared.

Off: IF I'M WRONG—

Hughie: YOU'RE NO' WRONG.

"   "   I'M JUST A WEE BIT SCARED O'… JUMPIN'…

3.

Annie smiles kindly but firmly.

Annie: WELL, I'M NOT GOING TO PUSH YOU, HUGHIE.

4.

He slowly turns, leans forward to kiss her, eyes closed. She leans in too, but keeps her eyes open.

5.

At the last second she puts a finger to his lips and he opens his eyes, slightly surprised. She's completely calm.

6.

Pull back on them there, faces a couple of inches apart. Almost night.

Annie: PROMISE ME.

PAGE TWELVE

1.

Jamie the hamster crams his cheeks with sunflower seeds, oblivious to the giant faces of Hughie and Annie peering in at him. Annie seems quite charmed.

Annie: WHAT ON EARTH ARE YOU DOING WITH HIM?

Hughie: OH, I, I JUST FANCIED A PET, YOU KNOW…

2.

They're in Hughie's crappy little room. Annie smiles at Jamie, Hughie glances around him at the room, slightly anxious.

Annie: HE'S CUTE.

Hughie: AYE, HIS NAME'S JAMIE. I THOUGHT I'D HAVE TO KEEP HIM A
                    SECRET, BUT THEY EVEN FEED HIM WHEN I'M AWAY AN' ALL.

"   "   LISTEN, ARE YOU **SURE** YOU'RE ALL RIGHT HERE…?

3.

Wide shot of the room, both. She turns to face him.

Annie: WE CAN'T GO TO MY PLACE, HUGHIE.

Hughie: AYE, BUT…

Annie: SORRY.

4.

Annie doesn't look up, smiles nervously, bit embarrassed. More of a grimace than a smile. Hughie watches her, calm.

Annie: I… HEH.

"   "   I DON'T… HAVE VERY MUCH…

"   "   **EXPERIENCE**…

5.

Hughie only, smiling kindly but with a slight narrowing of the eyes that betrays a certain man-of-the-world confidence.

Hughie: I DO.

PAGE THIRTEEN

1.

Lights out. They're in bed, naked, sheet over them, Hughie on top, making out. Note that the sheet will slide off as Hughie moves lower. Clothes on the floor- though not thrown everywhere, it was a pretty restrained disrobing.

2.

Close in. Hughie starts kissing his way down between Annie's breasts. She gasps a little, eyes closed.

Annie: AH

3.

Close up on Hughie, down around her belly now.

Off: AH

4.

View past Annie, gasping in surprise- though not in distress. Her face is closest. Not much of Hughie in shot, just visible from eyes (closed) up, but with a hand on her thigh it should be pretty obvious what he's doing. Keep it subtle, not explicit. Very low light.

Annie: OH GOD—HUGHIE—

"   "   NO ONE EVER—

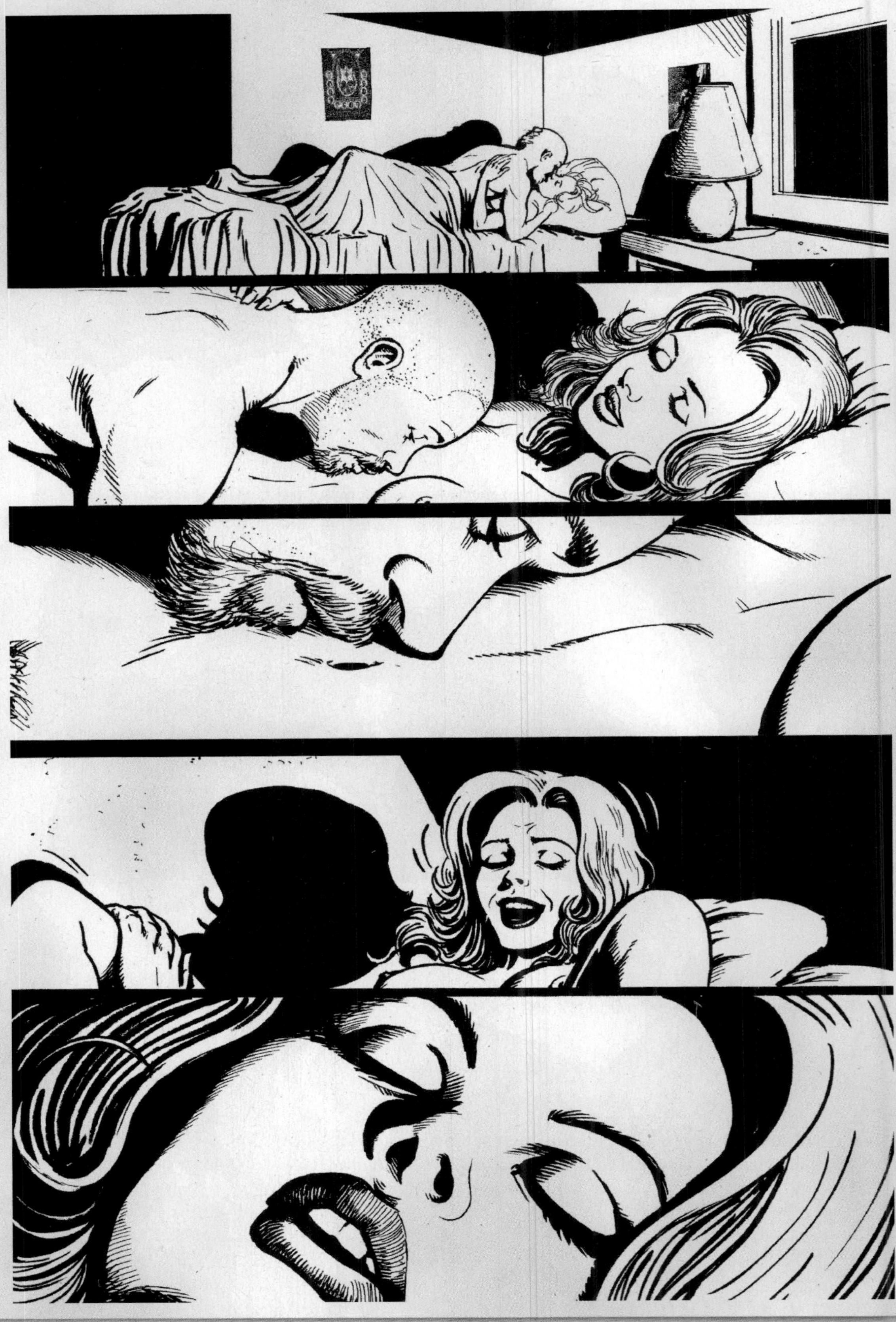

5.

Close up on Annie as she closes her eyes and gasps in pleasure.

Annie: **AAAAAAAAHHH…!**

PAGE FOURTEEN

1.

First light of dawn, taxi driving through the Bronx.

Taxi: STOP THE CAR, MATE.

2.

Close in. The taxi has stopped and MM is leaning out the window nearest us, vomiting. Not too much. Butcher sits next to him, calmly facing front. Terror watches MM, sympathetic.

3.

MM sits back again, wipes his mouth. Exhausted, beaten, drained. Shades off so we can see his weary, bloodshot eyes.

Off: WANNA WALK FOR A BIT?

MM: NO.

"   "   THAT'S IT.

4.

MM leans his head back, slips his shades on as he slowly exhales, gazing at the ceiling. Butcher sits nearest, scratching Terror behind the ears.

MM: MUTHAFUCK…

"   "   THIS SHIT **EVER** GONNA BE OVER?

Butcher: YOU WANT IT TO BE?

5.

MM looks down at his hands, twitches the tips of his fingers slightly. Seems a bit faraway.

PAGE FIFTEEN

1.

Big flashback. MM's pov on a screaming woman, holding onto his hand for dear life- hand nearest, all there is of him in shot. She's squeezing so tight her fingernails are drawing blood. You never saw anyone so terrified, horrified, agonised. Behind- below- her, we get a vague impression of a vehicle of some kind, with a kid's hand reaching around the side of the window- the woman's body protrudes from the window too.

(NB- when we see this scene for real, it'll be a flashback to the destruction of the Brooklyn Bridge, with MM hanging onto a woman whose SUV has gone off the edge- she's hanging onto him, the SUV (with her kids in it) is hanging off her foot, which is stuck in the steering wheel. But we don't see that now, we just get a hint)

2.

Out of flashback, MM grim.

MM: … NO.

3.

He makes two fists, leans forward with his whole body tensed, grits his teeth. Butcher notices this, raises an eye, deciding to change the subject.

MM: SICK FUCKIN' THING IS, I CAN FEEL IT WORKIN'. AIN'T BEEN
                  TEN MINUTES SINCE I WALKED OUTTA THERE AN' I FEEL
                  BUZZED…

"   "   LIKE I WANNA FEEL LIKE SHIT, I WANNA BE FUCKIN'
                  DISGUSTED—BUT—

Butcher: YOU KNOW WHO LIVES 'ROUND HERE?

4.

Butcher only, smiling with mild amusement as he pulls out his cell. No sense that he knows what Hughie's been up to.

Off: HUH?

Butcher: WANNA GIVE HUGHIE A LIFT TO WORK?

PAGE SIXTEEN

1.

Outside Hughie's shitty motel, the two lean on the taxi's open doors as Butcher speaks on the phone. MM scans the building. Needn't be immediately obvious, but the surveillance van is parked outside too.

MM: DAMN.

Butcher: CHARMIN', INNIT?

"   "   FUCKSAKE, HUGHIE, SINCE WHEN DO YOU SWITCH YOUR
                  BLEEDIN' PHONE OFF…?

2.

Butcher wearily puts his phone away. MM gazes offshot, bit grim.

MM: 'FUCK IS HE DOIN' HERE?

Butcher: I'LL HAVE TO NIP UP AN' GET HIM—OH, HE THINKS IT'S

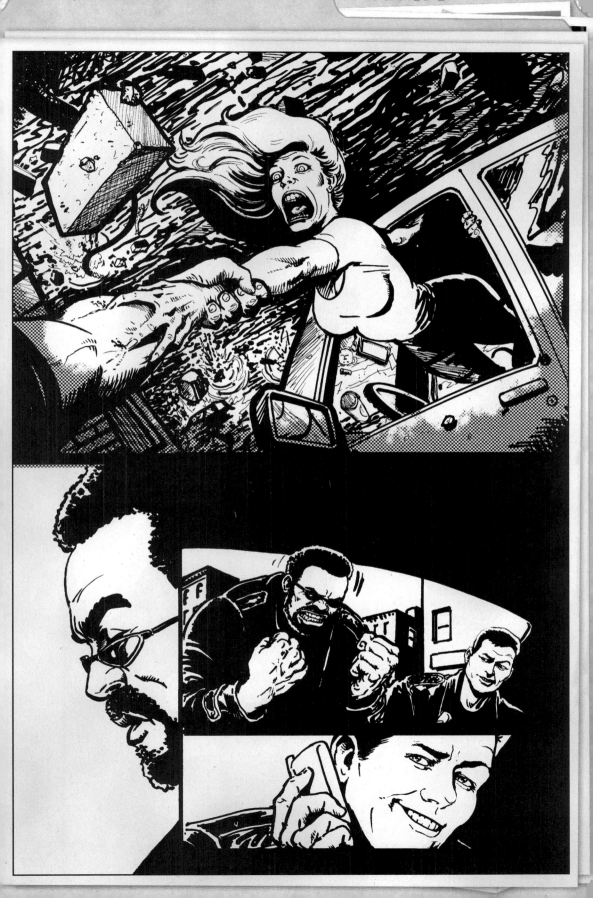

AUTHENTIC, OR SOMETHIN'. THE REAL NEW YORK, LIKE THESE DICKHEADS'RE ALWAYS SAYIN' THEY MISS SO MUCH…

3.

MM grimaces.

MM: HUH.

"   "   GET YOURSELF MUGGED OR RAPED OR SOME SHIT, THEN WE GONNA TALK ABOUT **REAL**…

Off: TWO MINUTES.

4.

Hughie and Annie asleep in bed, curled up round each other in a tangle of sheets. Curtains are pulled, so it's gloomy in here. We don't see Hughie's face.

Hughie: UHHH…?

5.

Out in the corridor, Butcher knocks loudly on the door, annoyed but weary.

Butcher: **COME** ON--!

6.

Hughie stumbles across the room towards the door, pretty much out of it. Used condom hangs off the edge of the wastepaper bin nearest.

Hughie: UHHH…

7.

Butcher looks pissed off as the door starts to open.

Butcher: ABOUT BLOODY TIME! AN' WHAT'D I SAY TO YOU ABOUT SWITCHIN' YOUR—

PAGE SEVENTEEN

1.

Big. View past Hughie at Butcher as he opens the door fully. He freezes, staring at Hughie, quietly stunned.

2.

Butcher only, lowering his gaze, putting a hand over his face to hide his huge smile. Trembling a little.

Off: WHAT…?

Butcher: NOTHIN', MATE.

3.

Pull back. He looks up again and almost bursts out laughing as he sees Hughie, who still has his back to us. Points offshot, turning to leave.

Butcher: I'LL, UH, I'LL JUST… I'VE GOT A TAXI WAITIN'.

"   "   TAKE YOUR TIME.

4.

View past Hughie as he leans out the door to watch Butcher go, actually shaking as he walks off down the corridor.

Hughie: ?

5.

Pull back as he ambles across the room towards the sink, still pretty bleary. Little mirror over it. Door closed behind him. Annie wakes up, smiling dozily at him.

Annie: WHO WAS THAT…?

Hughie: JUST MY BOSS.

"   "   GIVE US A SECOND HERE…

PAGE EIGHTEEN

1.

Big, close. Headshot on Hughie reflected in the mirror, hand turning the light on over it. He freezes. Still dull eyed and bleary, but going completely still, mouth opening, eyes widening just a little. Caked around his mouth and all over his chin is a dark red mask of dried, flaking blood. Spot on the end of his nose, too.

2.

Pull back a bit, side view on Hughie. He closes his eyes in slow, weary defeat. Realising what's happened, what Butcher's just seen, all of it.

Hughie: AW NO.

Off: UM… HUGHIE?

3.

Annie smiles nervously at us, embarrassed. She's sitting up in bed, lifting the sheets, obviously just had a look at what's under them. We don't see anything amiss.

Annie: I THINK I MIGHT HAVE HAD KIND OF A…

"   "   **TIMING ISSUE…**

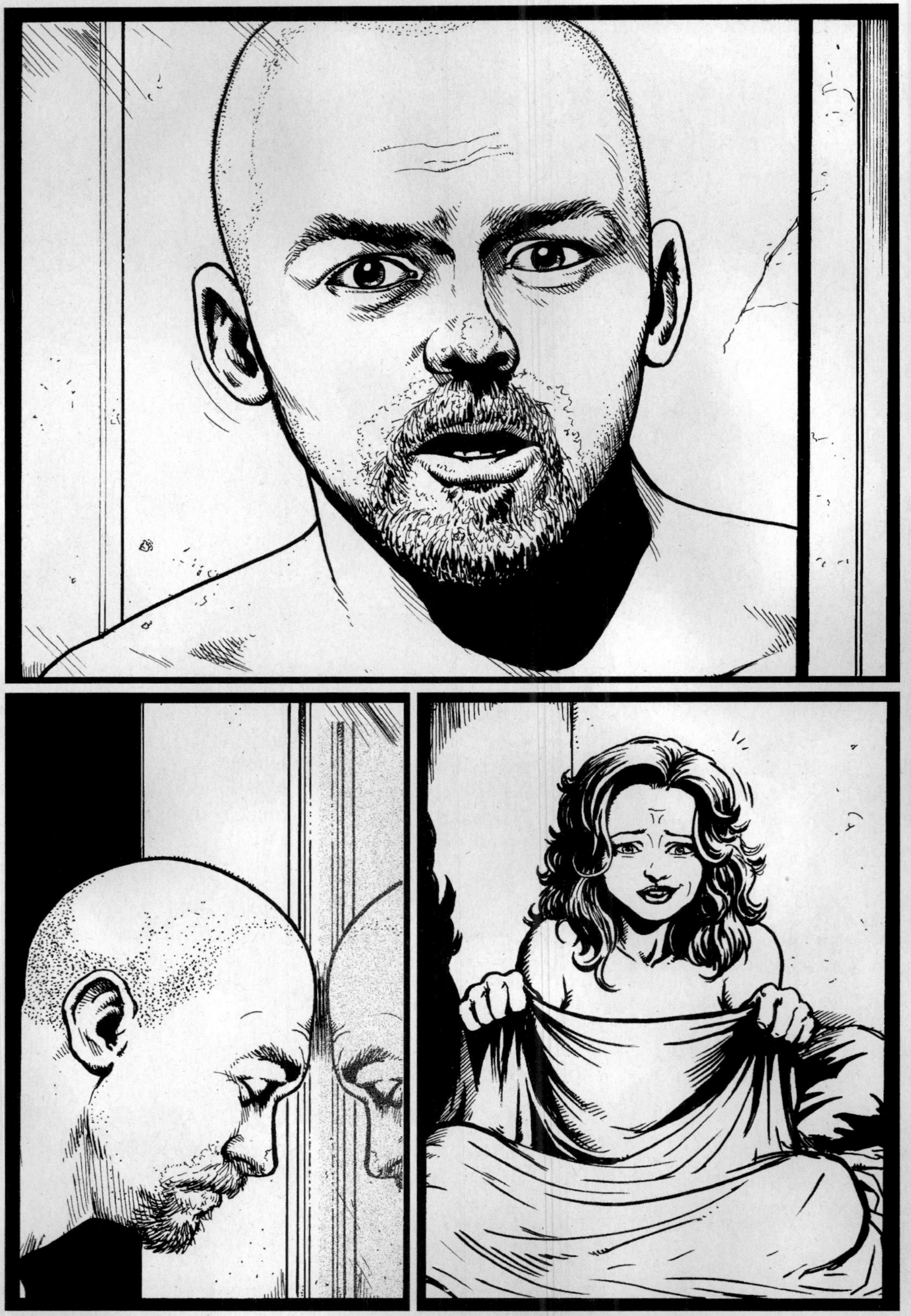

PAGE NINETEEN

1.

Big. Hughie- cleaned up now- sits in the back of the cab between Butcher and MM, fuming with resentment, red-faced, embarrassed as hell. He faces front. So do the other two, both making a massive effort not to laugh. Terror sits on Butcher's lap, happy.

2.

Close in, view past MM at the rest. He covers his mouth. Butcher closes his eyes. Going to burst out laughing any second now. Hughie grimaces, sick and pissed off.

3.

Hughie looks sick and weary. MM howls. Butcher cracks up, one hand over his eyes.

Hughie: YOU **HAD** TO—

MM: **HA!!**

4.

Rear view on the taxi speeding off down the street.

Taxi(2 tails):   **HA HA HA HA HA HA HA HA HA!!**

PAGE TWENTY

1.

View past the surveillance van at the front of the motel. Annie exits, dressed now. Looks left. No one around.

2.

Closer. View past the front wheel from underneath the vehicle. She looks right, checking carefully.

3.

Same angle. Now she flies up into the sky, already some distance away.

4.

Next few shots are from the pov of the mystery intruder. Here we're entering the motel, stairs leading upwards further back. Bored-looking, 50-something black clerk sits behind a sliding glass window in the wall, currently open. Doesn't even bother to look up from his porn mag FUCKARAMA

Off: NFF NFF

5.

We're looking down the corridor upstairs now, various doors off it.

Off: NFF NFF

6.

Now we're looking at Hughie's door.

Off: WAMAHAMMA…

PAGE TWENTY-ONE

1.

A green-gloved hand pushes against the door.

Off: **WAMAHAMMA…**

2.

Now both hands push, harder. The door starts to bend inwards at the top.

Off: **WAMAHAMMA…!**

3.

Inside now. View past the hamster's cage- Jamie just visible- as the door opens, the lock busting away from the doorframe before the door itself can break.

4.

Jamie stops running in his wheel, looks round at us as a shadow falls over him.

Off: AH—

"   "   AH—

5.

Close up on Jamie, freezing, eyes bulging in shock.

Off;   **AH—**

PAGE TWENTY-TWO

1.

Jamie's pov: the reanimated Blarney Cock hangs in the air in front of him, stained and ill-fitting costume hanging from his gangly, slumping frame. Barely able to hold his head up to look at us in pathetic longing, land reaching feebly towards us. Skin pallid and bruised, eyes bloodshot, jaw slack and drooling. Big piss stain at his crotch. Mask on crooked, covers the wrong part of his face. Sense that he's been dressed properly but has ended up tearing or stretching the costume by moving in a way a body shouldn't- made worse by lying under a filthy van all night. Knees ripped from his tights. Levitating about a foot off the floor.

BC: **AH WANNND MAH HAMMZDAH BAGGGKK…!**

NEXT: **BATTLE WITHOUT HONOR OR HUMANITY**

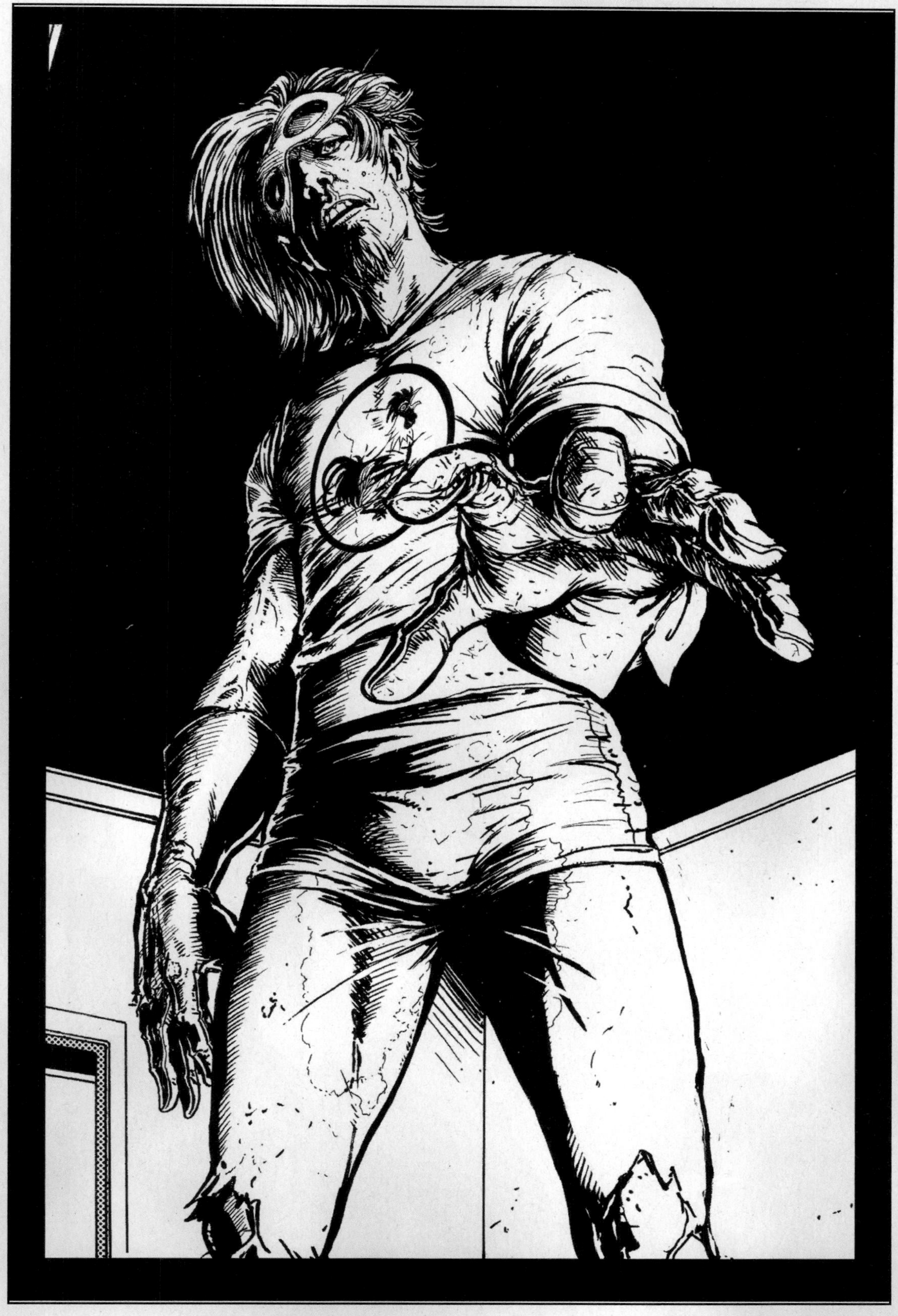

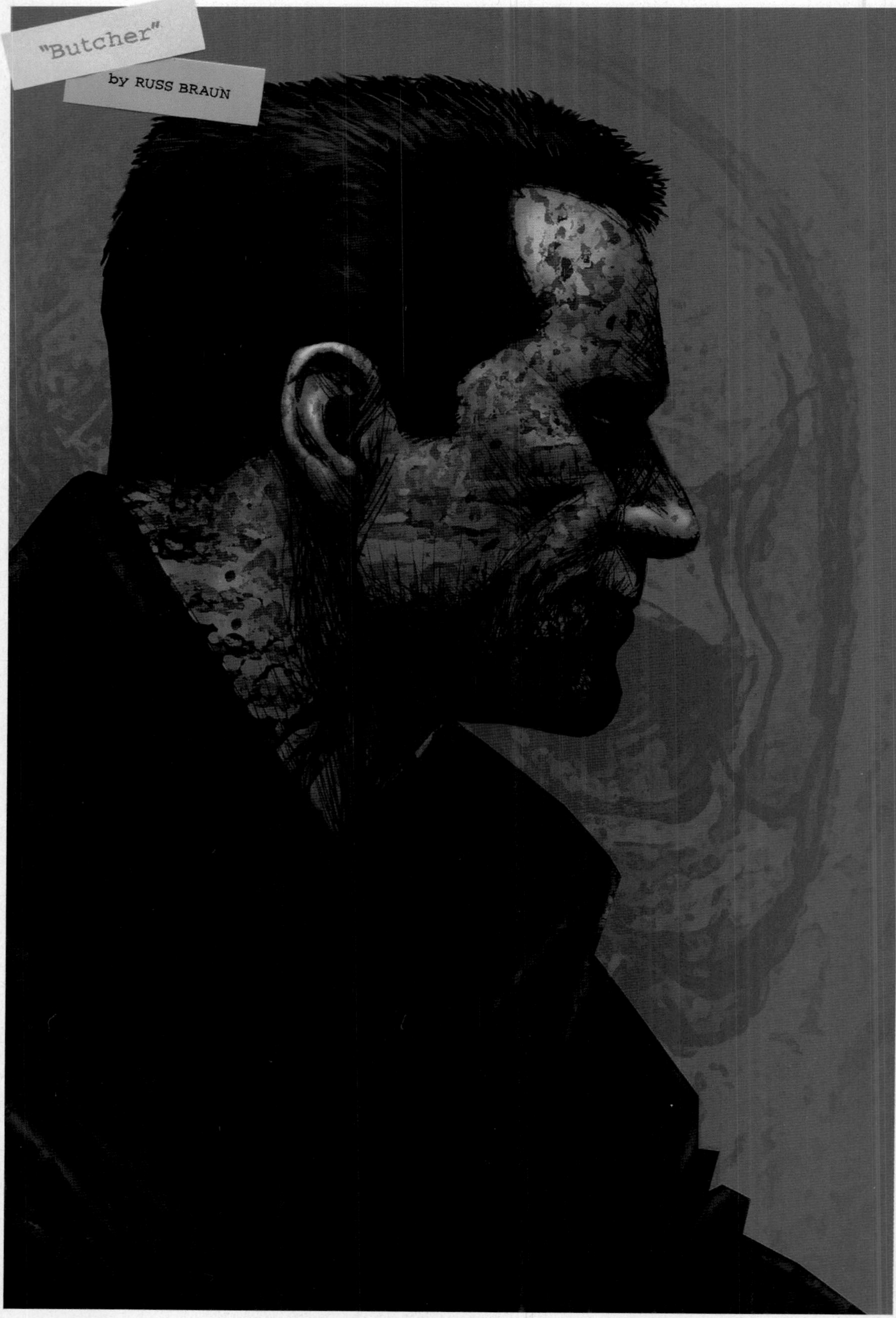
"Butcher"
by RUSS BRAUN

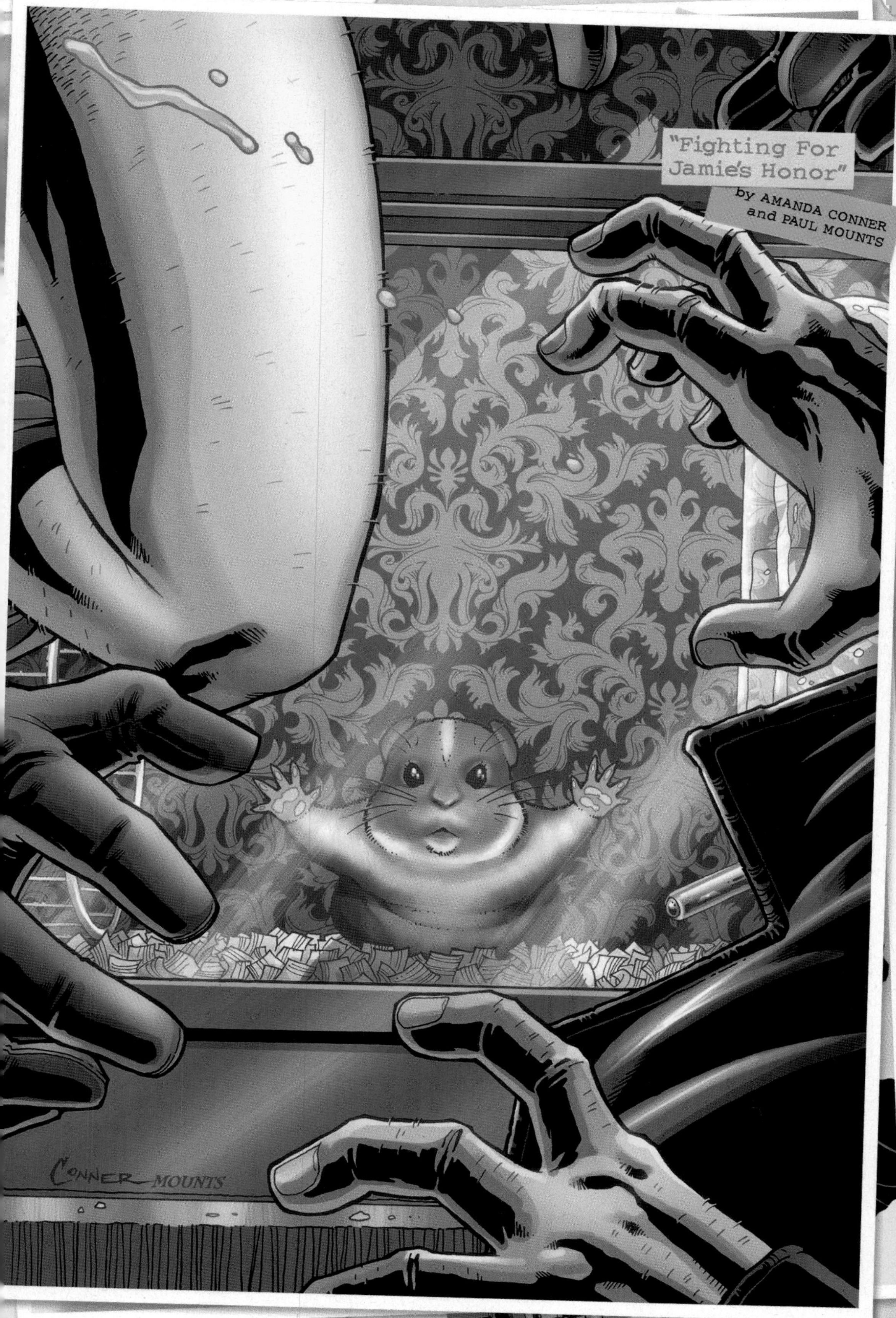
"Fighting For Jamie's Honor"
by AMANDA CONNER and PAUL MOUNTS
CONNER MOUNTS

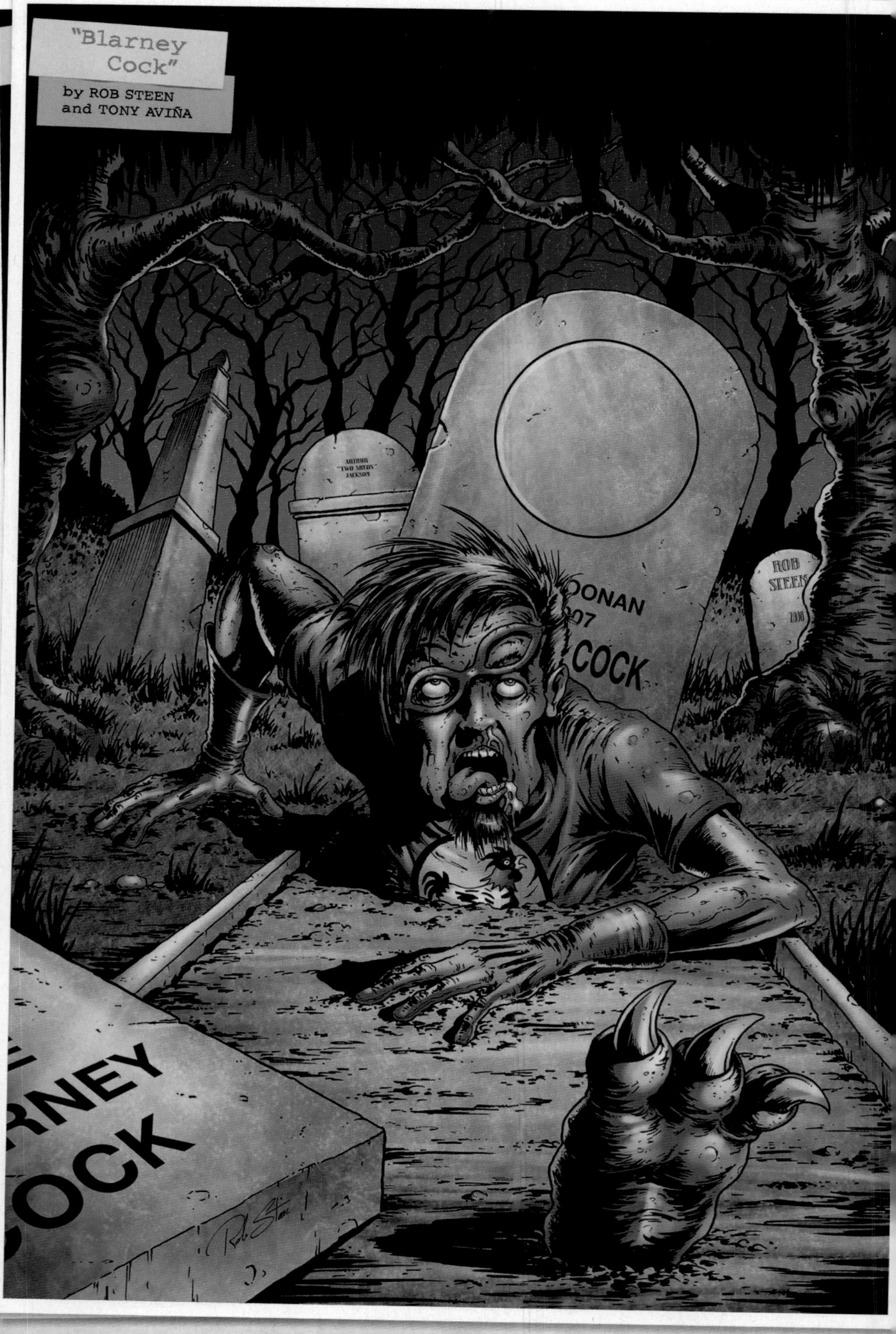
"Blarney Cock"
by ROB STEEN
and TONY AVIÑA
ROB STEEN

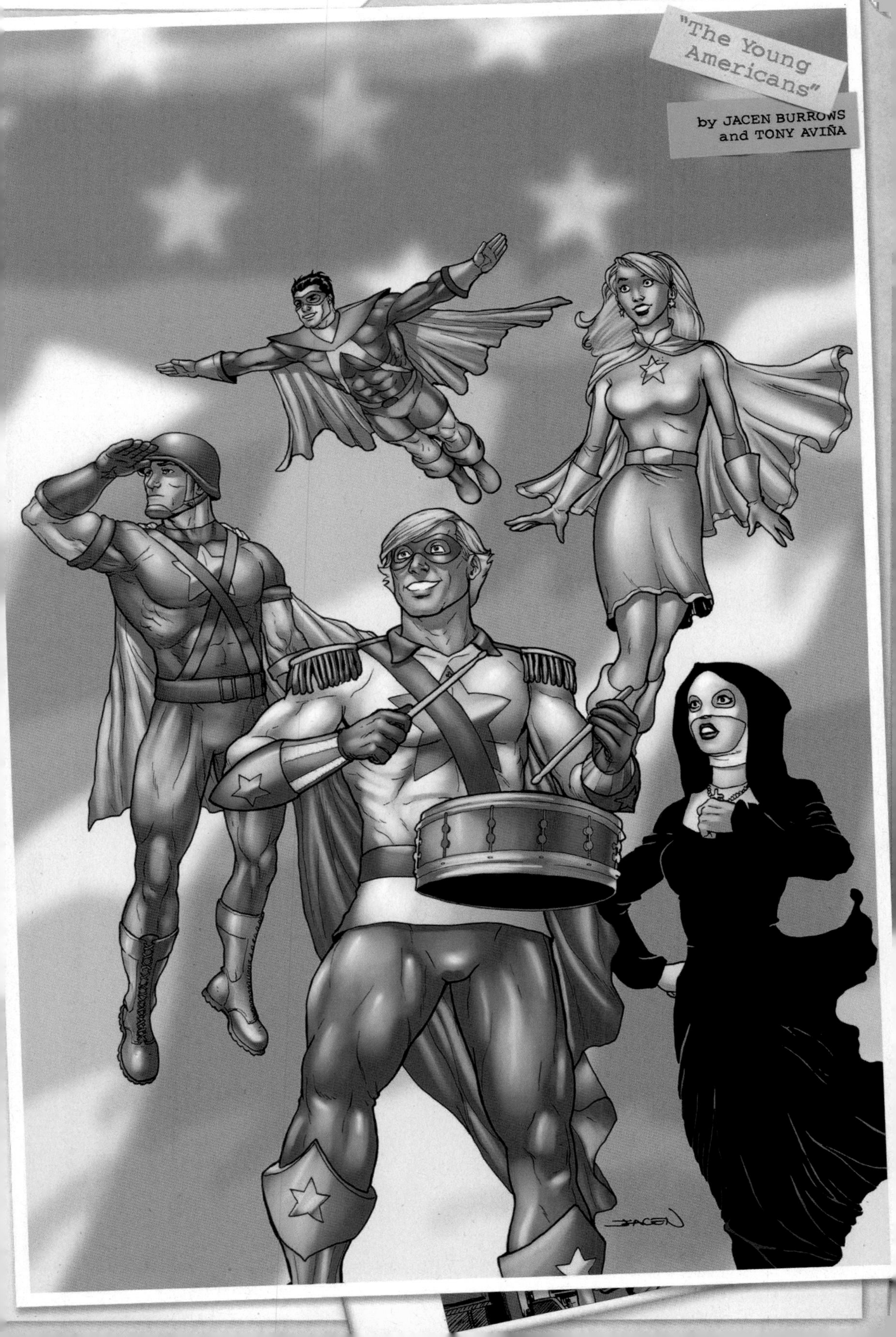
"The Young Americans"
by JACEN BURROWS and TONY AVIÑA
JACEN

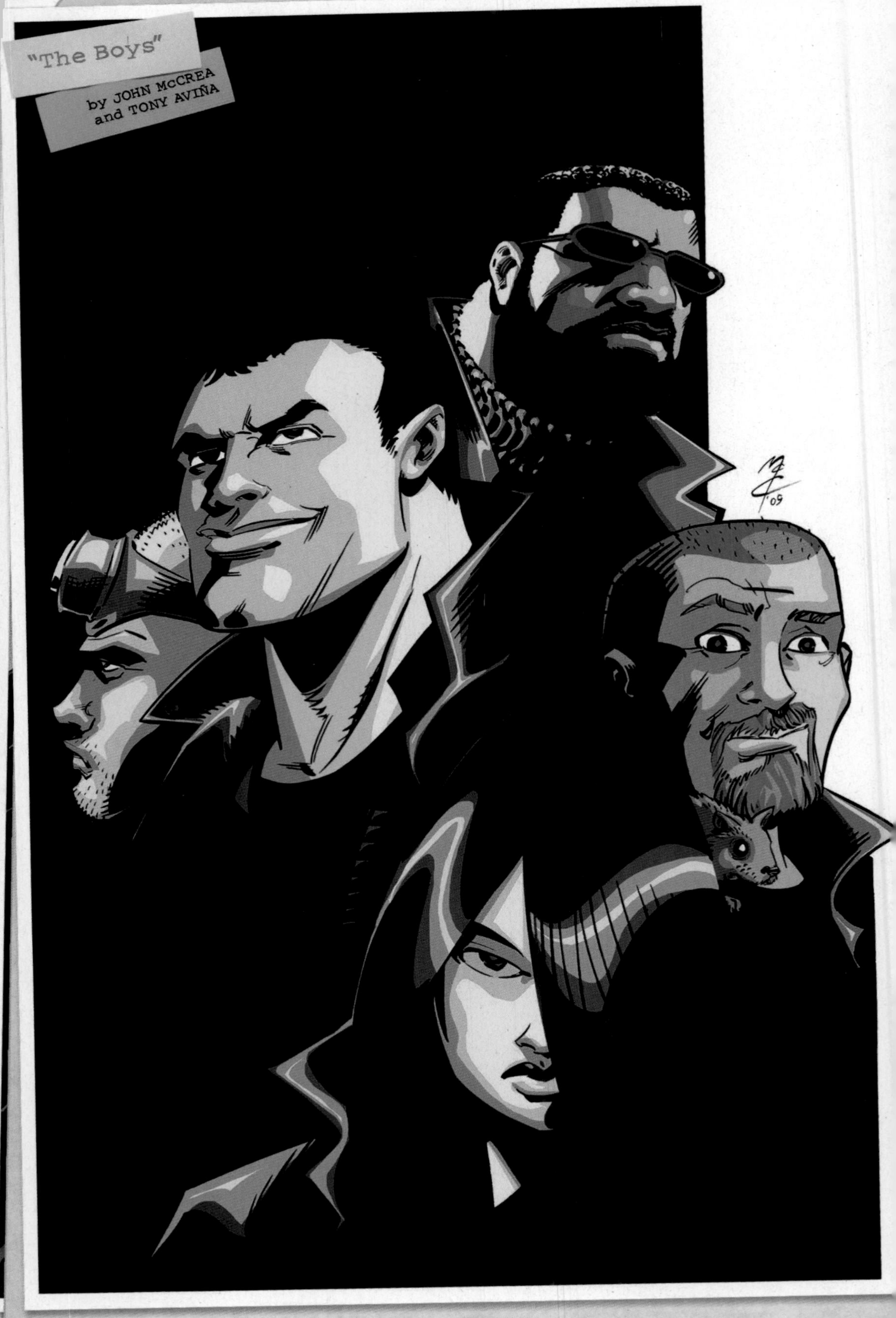
"The Boys"
by JOHN McCREA and TONY AVIÑA
'09

Mon, Oct 6, 2008 1:29 PM

Subject: RE: The Boys #24 proof 2
Date: Monday, October 6, 2008 1:29 PM
From: 'Garth Ennis' <[redacted]>
To: 'Joseph Rybandt' <[redacted]>, 'Simon Bowland' [redacted]>
Cc: 'Darick Robertson' <[redacted]>, 'Tony Avina' <[redacted]>,
'Jason Ullmeyer' <[redacted]>,

What the--? That isn't web fluid!

Don't worry, Jack, I got it all under control. Say, just while I got ya, buddy- sign this...

> On Oct 6, 2008, at 12:56 PM, Jason Ullmeyer wrote:
> I can just picture Stan and Jack having this same conversation back in the 60's
> about a "very special issue" of Amazing Spider-Man...
>
>> On 10/6/08 12:47 PM, Simon Bowland wrote:
>> This is a very surreal moment in my career...
>>
>>> -----Original Message-----
>>> Date: 06 October 2008 17:41
>>> From: Garth Ennis
>>> To: Joseph Rybandt, Simon Bowland
>>> Cc: Darick Robertson, Tony Avina, Jason Ullmeyer
>>> Subject: Re: The Boys #24 proof
>>>
>>> I think come is okay when describing the action- so's cum, but then again the past
>>> tense is always came. When you're describing the results, it's always cum.

>>>
>>> Hope that's cleared it up for you.
>>>
>>>> On Oct 6, 2008, at 11:59 AM, Joseph Rybandt wrote:
>>>> page 15, last panel: isn't it "cum"?
>>>>
>>>> Darick -- let's coordinate with tony to remove the extra g-wizzers
>>>> and get this one wrapped today, thanks!
>>>>
>>>> /joe

CAPTAIN STAR

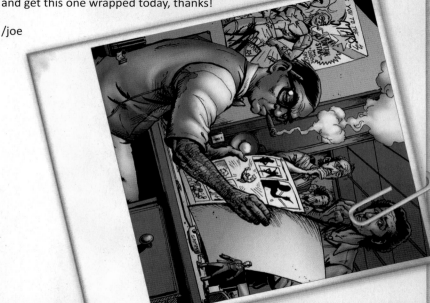

GARTH ENNIS

Garth Ennis has been writing comics since 1989. Credits include *Preacher*, *Hitman*, *Crossed*, *Rover Red Charlie*, *Code Pru*, *Caliban*, *War Stories*, *A Walk Through Hell* and *Sara*, and successful runs on *The Punisher* and *Fury* for Marvel Comics. Originally from Northern Ireland, Ennis now resides in New York City with his wife, Ruth.

DARICK ROBERTSON

Darick Robertson is an American comic book artist, writer and creator with a decades long career in the industry. Born and raised in the Northern California Bay Area and self trained as an artist, his notable works include co-creating the award winning *Transmetropolitan*, *The Boys*, *Happy!*, and *Oliver* with Gary Whitta for Image Comics, debuting in January 2019. Darick has illustrated for both Marvel and DC Comics on characters including Batman, The Justice League, Wolverine, The Punisher, and Spider-man.

JOHN HIGGINS

John Higgins has been drawing comics for over 40 years. Credits include Judge Dredd, Pride & Joy, Hellblazer, World Without End, War Stories and his creator-owned series Razorjack. Higgins currently lives in England with his wife, Sally.

TONY AVIÑA

Tony Aviña got his start as an in-house colorist at WIldwtorm. His credits include *Sleeper*, *Stormwatch: Team Achilles*, *Authority: Prime*, *Battlefields*, *The Boys*, *Sherlock Holmes*, *Green Lantern*, *Justice League*, *Batman '66*, *Wonder Woman '77*, and *Suicide Squad: Hell to Pay*. He currently lives in St. Louis, which, contrary to popular belief, isn't one big farm (it's actually three or four moderately sized farms).

SIMON BOWLAND

Simon Bowland has been lettering comics since 2004, and in that time has worked for all of the mainstream publishers. Born and bred in the UK, Simon still lives there today alongside Pippa, his partner, and Jess, their tabby cat.

COLLECT THE COMPLETE SERIES!

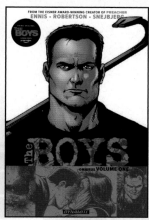

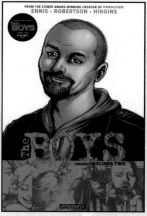

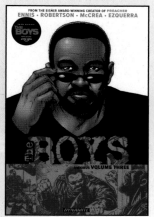

FROM THE EISNER AWARD-WINNING CREATOR OF PREACHER
ENNIS • ROBERTSON • SNEJBJERG
The BOYS
OMNIBUS VOLUME ONE
DYNAMITE

THE BOYS OMNIBUS VOL. 1 TP
978-1-5241-1097-0
Ennis, Robertson, Snejbjerg

FROM THE EISNER AWARD-WINNING CREATOR OF PREACHER
ENNIS • ROBERTSON • HIGGINS
The BOYS
OMNIBUS VOLUME TWO
DYNAMITE

THE BOYS OMNIBUS VOL. 2 TP
978-1-5241-1098-7
Ennis, Robertson, Higgins

FROM THE EISNER AWARD-WINNING CREATOR OF PREACHER
ENNIS • ROBERTSON • McCREA • EZQUERRA
The BOYS
OMNIBUS VOLUME THREE
DYNAMITE

THE BOYS OMNIBUS VOL. 3 TP
978-1-5241-1099-4
Ennis, Robertson McCrea, Ezquerra

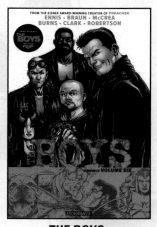

FROM THE EISNER AWARD-WINNING CREATOR OF PREACHER
ENNIS • BRAUN • McCREA
BURNS • CLARK • ROBERTSON
The BOYS
OMNIBUS VOLUME FOUR
DYNAMITE

THE BOYS OMNIBUS VOL. 4 TP
978-1-5241-1100-7
Ennis, Braun, McCrea, Burns, Clark, Robertson

FROM THE EISNER AWARD-WINNING CREATOR OF PREACHER
ENNIS • BRAUN • McCREA
BURNS • ROBERTSON
The BOYS
OMNIBUS VOLUME FIVE
DYNAMITE

THE BOYS OMNIBUS VOL. 5 TP
978-1-5241-1101-4
Ennis. Braun, McCrea, Burns, Robertson

FROM THE EISNER AWARD-WINNING CREATOR OF PREACHER
ENNIS • BRAUN • McCREA
BURNS • CLARK • ROBERTSON
The BOYS
OMNIBUS VOLUME SIX
DYNAMITE

THE BOYS OMNIBUS VOL. 6 TP
978-1-5241-1102-1
Ennis, Braun, McCrea, Burns, Clark, Robertson

ALSO AVAILABLE FROM GARTH ENNIS & DYNAMITE:

THE COMPLETE BATTLEFIELDS VOL. 1 TP 978-1-60690-0255-4
THE COMPLETE BATTLEFIELDS VOL. 2 TP 978-1-5241-0385-9
THE COMPLETE BATTLEFIELDS VOL. 3 TP 978-1-5241-0474-0

RED TEAM VOL. 1 TP 978-1-6069-0443-5
RED TEAM VOL. 2: DOUBLE TAP, CENTER MASS TP 978-1-5241-0395-8

A TRAIN CALLED LOVE TP 978-1-5241-0168-8
JENNIFER BLOOD VOL. 1: A WOMEN'S WORK IS NEVER DONE TP 978-1-6069-0261-5

VISIT WWW.DYNAMITE.COM FOR A FULL LIST!